No industry provides more household names than brewing; none retains a firmer place in British culture; and at the height of the temperance movement none was more controversial. Yet this volume provides the first extended account of brewing in the modern period. Thoroughly based upon research in brewing archives, it surveys the industry from 1830 to 1980, tracing its development from one in which there were thousands of firms producing beer to one now dominated by half a dozen large companies. It is an account which carries the reader from the porters, ales and stouts, the vast vats, drays and myriad beer houses of early Victorian England, to the draught lagers, giant fermenters, beer tankers and theme pubs of the late twentieth century.

In this wide-ranging book the authors discuss free trade in beer, the impact of temperance, and the emergence of the great Victorian breweries together with their acquisition of public houses and company status. In the twentieth century, they examine the impact of two World Wars, the movement for improved public houses, the sobriety of the 1920s, and the revolution sweeping the industry since the 1950s. New material is introduced; the different experiences of hundreds of breweries, large and small, are traced across a century and a half. The book will fascinate all those interested in the history of a great traditional industry – beer enthusiasts and professional historians alike.

THE BRITISH BREWING INDUSTRY
1830–1980

THE BRITISH BREWING INDUSTRY 1830–1980

T. R. GOURVISH
Director, Business History Unit,
London School of Economics and Political Science

and

R. G. WILSON
Director, Centre of East Anglian Studies,
University of East Anglia

Research by

FIONA WOOD

CAMBRIDGE
UNIVERSITY PRESS

Published by the Press Syndicate of the University of Cambridge
The Pitt Building, Trumpington Street, Cambridge CB2 1RP
40 West 20th Street, New York, NY 10011–4211, USA
10 Stamford Road, Oakleigh, Melbourne 3166, Australia

First published 1994

Printed in Great Britain at the University Press, Cambridge

A catalogue record for this book is available from the British Library

Library of Congress cataloguing in publication data

Gourvish, T. R. (Terence Richard)
The British brewing industry, 1830–1980 / T. R. Gourvish and R. G. Wilson.
p. cm.
Includes bibliographical references and index.
ISBN 0 521 45232 5
I. Brewing industry – Great Britain – History.
I. Wilson, R. G. (Richard George) II. Title.
TP573.G7G68 1994
338.4'7663'30941–dc20 93–4313 CIP

ISBN 0 521 45232 5 hardback

CE

For D.C.C.

Contents

List of illustrations — *page* x
List of tables — xiv
Plate acknowledgements — xviii
Preface — xix
List of abbreviations — xxiii

PART 1 THE BREWING INDUSTRY, 1830–1914

1 The Beer Act, 1830–1870 — 3
2 Consumption and production — 23
3 Changes in structure and location, 1830–1880 — 64
4 Markets and distribution — 127
5 Costs, prices and profits — 179
6 Partnerships, companies and capital, 1830–1885 — 226
7 The scramble for property and its aftermath, 1885–1914 — 267

PART 2 THE BREWING INDUSTRY, 1914–1980

8 Production and consumption, 1914–1955 — 317
9 Organisation and management – a 'picturesque dinosaur'? — 373
10 The sale of beer, 1914–1955 — 408
11 Merger mania, 1955–1980 — 447
12 Profits, productivity and prices — 498
13 Technology and retailing — 534
14 Postscript — 581

Appendix — 600
Glossary — 638
Bibliography — 644
Index — 664

Illustrations

PLATES

(between pages 102 and 103)

1 Cartoon of the Beer Act (1830)
2 Cross-section of J. W. Astley's brewery (1900) illustrating the brewing process
3 Truman's union room, Burton upon Trent (1889)
4 Worthington's laboratory (1889)
5 The laboratory of Robert Deuchar Ltd, Duddingston brewery (*c.* 1945)
6 Porter vats of Barclay Perkins (*c.* 1850)
7 The partners of Truman Hanbury Buxton (1886)
8 The proprietors and employees of H. Newton and Co. (*c.* 1890)
9 Bass's steam cooperage (1889)
10 A general view of Burton upon Trent (1873)
11 Nine smaller Burton upon Trent breweries (1888)
12 Lacon's Great Yarmouth Brewery (1894)
13 The first Earl of Iveagh (1847–1927)
14 John Smith (1823–79)
15 Sir Andrew Walker Bt. (1824–93)
16 Railway sidings, Truman's brewery, Burton upon Trent (*c.* 1885)
17 Guinness's stables (*c.* 1910)
18 Guinness's loading wharf (*c.* 1910)
19 Steam-wagon, W. H. Brakspear and Sons, (*c.* 1905)
20 Drays and vans, Mitchells & Butlers (*c.* 1910)
21 Lorries, Mitchells & Butlers (*c.* 1928)

(between pages 230 and 231)

22 W. H. Bailey, Bass's London manager
23 John Shorthose, Bass's Newcastle agent
24 Some of Bass's agencies (*c.* 1900)

25 Eldridge Pope's Dorchester brewery (1881)
26 Bass's Sleaford Maltings, built 1903–6
27 Bass's trip to Blackpool (1911)
28 The train arrangements for Bass's 1911 trip
29 Barrel bank, Burton upon Trent (*c.* 1885)
30 The King's Ale at Bass (1902)
31 Sir Walter Greene Bt. (1842–1920)
32 Sir James Agg-Gardner (1846–1927)
33 'Poor Old Allsopp' (1890)
34 The 'Crown', Cricklewood, before refurbishment (1898)
35 The 'Crown', Cricklewood (*c.* 1930)
36 The 'Queen's Arms', Peckham (*c.* 1890)
37 The bar at the 'Dover Castle', Westminster Bridge Road (1895)
38 The 'Crooked Billet', Newcastle upon Tyne (*c.* 1898)
39 The Portland Beer Stores, Sheffield (*c.* 1910)
40 Bottling plant, Brakspear's Brewery (*c.* 1900)
41 Demonstration against the 1908 Licensing Bill

(between pages 358 and 359)

42 Brewing in the First World War: the use of female labour
43 Sir William Waters Butler (1866–1939)
44 Sir Sydney Oswald Nevile (1873–1969)
45 Beer duty protest: William Younger's advertisement, 1932
46 Samuel Allsopp's board, 1929
47 'A Guinness a Day': advertisement, *c.* 1930
48 Whitbread advertising, 1935
49 Brewing managers and offices: Bristol Brewery Georges, *c.* 1945
50 F. A. Simonds and secretary, 1951
51 The Whitbread 'umbrella', 1956
52 'Perpendicular drinking': the 'Nag's Head', Covent Garden (1951)
53 The 'Improved Public House': the 'Traveller's Rest', before refurbishment
54 The 'Traveller's Rest' in 1929
55 The 'Improved Public House': the 'Holly Bush' (1937): view from the bowling green
56 The 'Holly Bush': view from the Gentlemen's Smoke Room
57 The 'Improved Public House': the 'Downham Tavern' (1930)
58 The 'Terminus Hotel', Bristol (*c.* 1927).
59 Skol lager advertisement (1960)
60 Harp lager and the 'Cool Blonde' (1964)

61 Andy Capp: 'There must be summat good on't Telly tonight' (1958)

(between pages 486 and 487)

62 Charles Clore (1904–79)
63 Simon Harvey Combe (1903–65)
64 Watney Mann's property development: the 'Crown', Edgware Road (1959)
65 E. P. Taylor (1901–89)
66 Allied Breweries' companies (1963)
67 Col. Bill Whitbread, in 1957
68 'Time Gentlemen Please': the Allied/Boddingtons' takeover battle (1970)
69 Courage's Berkshire Brewery, Reading (1980)
70 Bottling line, John Jeffrey's brewery (1950s)
71 Modern bottling line, Carlsberg's Northampton Brewery (1974)
72 The copper room, J. W. Green (1935)
73 Modern fermentation: Bass Charrington's Runcorn Brewery (1974)
74 Watneys' 'Red Revolution' advertisement (1970s)
75 Whitbread board, 1978
76 Sir Alan Walker (1911–1978)
77 The brewing process (*c*. 1880)
78 Modern brewing process (*c*. 1970)
79 Continuous fermentation (1970)
80 Truman's dray (1940s)
81 Brewery yard of Joshua Tetley & Sons (1940s)
82 Brewers' Society advertising campaign: 'Look in at the Local' (1966)
83 The 'Packaged Pint': the 'Welcome Inn', Eltham (1969)

FIGURES

4.1 The location of Barclay Perkins's 'country customers' *c*. 1905 — *page* 145
8.1 Convictions for drunkenness in England and Wales, 1919–38 — 336
8.2 UK beer production (excluding Eire), 1919–38 — 338
8.3 UK beer consumption (excluding Eire), 1919–38 — 340
8.4 UK beer production (excluding Eire), 1919–55 — 366
8.5 UK beer consumption, 1938–55 — 369
11.1 UK beer production and consumption, 1955–79 — 452

11.2 UK alcohol consumption by product, 1955–79 453
12.1 Beer price and retail price indices, 1939–80 520
13.1 The modern brewing process 535

Tables

1.1	Annual output of common brewers and brewing victuallers, 1818–30	*page* 9
1.2	The number of beer houses licensed in England and Wales, 1831–1914	18
2.1	UK beer production, 1831–1914	24
2.2	Percentage expenditure upon alcoholic beverages in the United Kingdom, 1870–1914	28
2.3	Per capita consumption of beer for the United Kingdom and England and Wales, 1800–1913	30
2.4	Drunkenness proceedings in classified districts, 1891–1931	32
2.5	Per capita expenditure upon alcohol in the United Kingdom, 1820–1913	34
3.1	Malt brewed in England and Wales, and Scotland, 1831–1900	68
3.2	Beer brewed in selected excise districts, 1832–1900	70
3.3	Brewing in the London excise collection district, 1831–80	76
3.4	Estimated output of the eleven leading London brewers, 1830–80	79
3.5	The London porter and ale sales of Whitbread, Reid's and Truman, 1833–80	81
3.6	Brewing in Burton upon Trent, 1831–1900	91
3.7	Sales of Guinness, 1830–1914	99
3.8	Beer production in Scotland, 1831–1914	104
3.9	Number of common brewers paying for licences in the UK, 1834–1914	111
3.10	Sir Edmund Lacon & Co., sales of strong beer, 1838–57	117
3.11	Sir Edmund Lacon & Co., sales of strong beer, 1858–74	118
3.12	Bristol Brewery Georges, beer sales, 1830–94	120

4.1	The London tied trade of Barclay Perkins, Reid's and Whitbread, 1830–75	131
4.2	Loans made to publicans by four leading London breweries, 1830–85	132
4.3	Worthington's free and tied trade, 1910	155
4.4	Tetley's beer sales from its four major stores, 1859–1905	160
4.5	Net profit calculation of the Tadcaster Tower Brewery's ten Castleford houses, 1885	167
5.1	The gross profit of Lacon & Sons, year ending 30 Sept. 1891	181
5.2	Lacon's Brewing Costs, 1890–1	182
5.3	Bass, Ratcliff & Gretton, summary of malting, 1889–1914	191
5.4	Main changes in the excise duties on beer and materials used in its production, 1801–1914	195
5.5	The distribution costs of Lacon & Sons for the year ending 30 Sept. 1891	201
5.6	Wholesale and retail price of beer after 1830	206
5.7	Whitbread: percentage return on partners' capital, 1818–67	213
6.1	Capital and loan capital of Truman Hanbury Buxton, 1830–76	230
6.2	Number of victuallers, beer house sellers and on-licences per head of population in England and Wales, 1831–1911	252
7.1	Barrels of beer bottled by Whitbread, 1870–1910	300
7.2	Brewing profits, 1897–1914	308
8.1	UK beer production, 1913–20	320
8.2	Company profitability (ordinary dividends), 1910–20	333
8.3	The retail price of draught beer, 1920–38	341
8.4	Company profitability (ordinary dividends), 1921–38	344
8.5	UK wholesale brewers, 1914	350
8.6	Brands and market preferences for beer, 1933 and 1938	355
8.7	UK beer production, 1938–45	360
8.8	UK beer production, 1945–55	367
8.9	Company profitability (ordinary dividends), 1939–55	369
9.1	Structure of the brewing industry, *c.* 1919, 1955	379
10.1	UK beer production (excluding Eire), 1913–55	410
10.2	Liquor licences and clubs, 1913–55	412

10.3 Clubs and on-licensed premises in selected counties and county boroughs, 1938 and 1955 416
10.4 Estimates of expenditure on public house improvement in England and Wales, 1922–55 428
10.5 Beer sales in selected Whitbread public houses, 1930s and 1955 431
10.6 Brewers' tied estates and free-trade distribution, 1948/9 436
10.7 Tied house rents and imputed costs (England and Wales), 1949 443
11.1 Brewing industry concentration, 1952–80 448
11.2 Alcohol and beer consumption, 1955–79 454
11.3 Licensed premises in the United Kingdom, 1951–89 456
11.4 Supermarkets, superstores, and off-licence provision, 1958–79 456
11.5 Beer sales volumes, 1960–89 458
11.6 The emergence of the 'Big Six', 1955–72 461
11.7 Leading brewing companies, ranked by tied estate (on-licences), 1963–70 472
12.1 Average output/capacity per plant of the largest brewing companies, 1966–85 504
12.2 UK brewery investments, acquisitions and closures by the largest companies, 1966–85 506
12.3 Composition of UK brewing costs, 1964–5 510
12.4 Labour productivity in brewing and malting, 1958–80 513
13.1 Technological economies in brewing, 1950–80 542
13.2 Brewery motor vehicles and horse deliveries, 1945 550
13.3 Bass/Worthington beer consignments, 1927–69 553
13.4 The beer market, 1960–80 558
13.5 Brewers' Society collective advertising campaigns, 1948–70 560
13.6 Indices of beer and total UK advertising expenditure, 1955–79 561
13.7 Selected beer advertisers (press and TV), 1955–79 562
13.8 Average public house barrelages, rents and margins, 1967–79 575
14.1 Beer production and consumption, 1979–90 582
14.2 Beer duty and prices, 1978–90 583
14.3 Composition of the beer market, 1979–90 585
14.4 Corporate structure of brewing, 1985–6 588
14.5 Brewing bids and mergers, 1982–6 592

APPENDIX

I Beer consumption and expenditure in England and Wales, 1831–1913 600

II Bass's costs and profit per barrel, 1908 604

III UK beer imports and exports, 1830–1914 607

IV Barrels of beer brewed by five leading London breweries, 1830–1914 610

V Truman Hanbury Buxton: average price of malt purchased, 1830–1914 613

VI Hop prices, 1830–1912 614

VII Drunkenness convictions/charges proved in England and Wales, 1910–55 617

VIII UK beer statistics (excluding Eire), 1919–55 618

IX Ordinary dividends of twenty-five 'representative' companies, 1910–55 620

X Chronology of brewery mergers, 1955–80 623

XI UK beer statistics, 1955–90 630

XII UK beer imports and exports, 1955–90 631

XIII Excise duty and VAT on beer, 1950–80 632

XIV Labour productivity in brewing and malting, 1954–80 633

XV Brewers' Society collective advertising campaigns, 1948–70 634

XVI Beer advertising expenditure, 1955–79 635

XVII Selected beer advertisers (press and TV), 1955–79 636

XVIII Consumers' expenditure, beer duty and prices, 1978–90 637

Plate acknowledgements

The authors and publishers wish to thank the following for kind permission to reproduce illustrations.

Bass Museum, Bass Brewers for Plates 9, 20–1, 22–4, 26–30, 33, 53–6, 65 and 73; Whitbread Brewing Archive, Whitbread plc for Plates 8, 12, 32, 44, 48, 51–2, 67, 72 and 75; Courage Ltd Archives for Plates 7, 49–50, 58, 69 and 80; Scottish Brewing Archive, Glasgow University for Plates 5, 42 and 70; Allied Archive, Allied Breweries for Plates 34–5, 39, 46, 59 and 78; Guinness Brewing Worldwide Ltd for Plates 13, 17–18, 47 and 60; Royal Commission on the Historical Monuments of England for Plates 36–7; Hulton Deutsch Collection Ltd for Plates 1, 6, 41, 62 and 83; The British Library for Plates 45 and 68; Robin Combe, Derek Hill and the Castle Museum, Norwich for Plate 63; Eldridge Pope & Co. for Plate 25; The Brewers' Society for Plates 43, 57, 71, 76 and 82; The Centre for the Study of Cartoons and Caricature, University of Kent at Canterbury, and Mirror Group Newspapers for Plate 61; The Board of Trustees of the National Museums and Galleries on Merseyside (Walker Art Gallery) for Plate 15; Nicholas Trevor and *Country Life* Magazine for Plate 31; Brewing Research Foundation International for Plates 19 and 40; Institute of Brewing for Plate 79; John Smith's Tadcaster Brewery Ltd for Plate 14; Joshua Tetley & Son Ltd for Plate 81; Grand Met for Plate 64; *Investors' Chronicle* for Plate 66; Tresises (Printers), Burton upon Trent for Plate 11; *Campaign* for Plate 74.

Preface

In November 1989 the Brewers' Society invited us to write a history of the British brewing industry in the century and a half after 1830. Exactly thirty years earlier, Peter Mathias had produced a widely acclaimed survey of the 1700–1830 period, concentrating particularly upon the great London breweries. Yet no comparable account of the modern (post-1830) industry followed. This remains true despite the general surveys by J. E. Vaizey (1960) and by K. H. Hawkins and C. L. Pass (1979); the industry in Scotland has received fuller treatment from Ian Donnachie (1979).

It was clear from the outset, however, that our volume could not match the detail of Mathias especially in his delineation of the excise and the malt and hops trades. For after 1830 the evidence itself begins to overwhelm. Firms grew in size; the industry generated a mass of statistical material, and company law insisted that those firms which came within its purview in the late nineteenth century kept proper records. And after the 1870s, the specialist brewing journals and financial press provide a wealth of detail, covering every aspect of the trade, to daunt the stoutest researcher. Moreover, the industry itself is difficult to confine since it runs in so many directions. The problem is not simply that until recently it encompassed hundreds of firms of various sizes across Britain, nor that the retailing of beer through scores of thousands of outlets is unusually complex. The industry is pervasive in other respects. In its raw material supplies it possesses close links with agriculture; it has always been conspicuously taxed; and the sale of beer is enmeshed in licensing laws. In all these areas, especially when the temperance storm raged, the industry was forced into the forefront of national politics.

We have tried to keep a balance between these many themes by sticking to the essential developments, economic and social, within the brewing industry itself. It means that some aspects, for example the intricacies of the malt trade, receive short shrift. Inevitably, there are some differences of emphasis between Parts I and II, reflecting variations in both the sorts of evidence which have survived and the problems which the industry encountered. Part I, which was written by Richard Wilson, covers the years up to 1914. During that time a wide-ranging industry of many, various-sized breweries had at its head a small number of great brewing partnerships and their successor companies. In contrast, the period of Part II, the responsibility of Terry Gourvish, witnessed remarkable changes in the structure and output of the industry, especially after the Second World War, as numerous businesses disappeared and giant combines emerged.

At the outset, one brewer assured us that in his view there were two difficult things in life which at first sight seemed simple – running a pub and writing a book. The latter task for us was made easier by the vast network of help running across the industry, though this support was never as liquid as our colleagues imagined. The list of names which follows is long and gratifying. We must single out for special thanks the members of our Steering Committee: Sam Whitbread (Chairman), Edward Guinness, Ewart Boddington, Ron Matthews, Donald Coleman and the chief press officer of the Society (Mike Ripley) and its statistician (Chris Thurman). Edward Guinness shared with us his knowledge of the industry and enthusiasm for the project. Donald Coleman combined, with rare skill, sharp criticism and warm friendship. To him, we dedicate our efforts. For two years we had admirable research assistance from Fiona Wood, appropriately a post-graduate student of Peter Mathias. She made the transition from historian of Fenland transport systems to brewing specialist, from vodka-and-tonic drinker to consumer of 'Young's *Ordinary*' with remarkable ease.

The following kindly agreed to be interviewed on their experience in the modern brewing industry: Anthony Avis and Philip Bradfer-Lawrence (Bass Charrington); Charles Bartholomew (Wadworth); Dr Anthony Button (Grand Met); Martin Corke (Greene King); Anthony Fuller (Fuller, Smith & Turner); Trevor Kerslake (Guinness); George King and Charles Ritchie (Maclay); Evadne Lloyd (Flowers, Whitbread); Frank Pike (Hall & Woodhouse); Philip Pope (Eldridge Pope); and John Young (Young's).

A key group of archivists, dedicated to the history of the industry, gave us unstinted help in our search for material and illustrations: Diana Lay and J. D. Burkett (Bass); Reg Carrington-Porter (Allied); Sue

Garland (Guinness); Harriet Kineally (Greater London Record Office); Charles McMaster (formerly Scottish Brewing Archive, Edinburgh); Lesley Norris and George Tattershall-Walker (John Smith's); Nicholas Redman (Whitbread); and Ken Thomas (Courage).

Several companies provided access to modern records, principally board minutes, reports and accounts, covering the period *c.* 1955–80: Allied-Lyons plc; Boddington Group plc; Eldridge Pope & Co. plc (to 1963); Fosters Brewing Group Ltd; Guinness plc; Scottish & Newcastle Breweries plc; Wadworth & Co. Ltd; and Whitbread plc. Our thanks to the following for facilitating this access: D. S. Mitchell and Henry Fearn (Allied-Lyons); Edward Englefield (Boddington); Michael Clarke (Eldridge Pope); Graham Griffin and Bernard Ryan (FBG); G. W. King and Brian Beanland (Guinness); Michael Pearey and Rex Homer (Scottish & Newcastle); Ian Gordon-Finlayson (Wadworth); Michael Hampton and Pat Jardine (Whitbread).

Dr W. M. Mathew read with exemplary care chapters 1–7, making many helpful comments. Similarly, Dr Tony Portno (Bass), Peter Jarvis (Whitbread), Alan Leach and David Long (Brewers' Society) read portions of Part II in draft and offered valuable advice. Christine Clark, a research student of Richard Wilson, discussed the malting sections with us; Dr Nick Tiratsoo and Dr Steve Fielding provided excellent research help; and Dr Christopher Napier gave advice on the calculation of brewing profits. Judith Sparks typed chapters 1–7 with the skill and patience economic historians at the University of East Anglia have enjoyed for many years; Sonia Copeland and Bella White performed similar services in the production of Part II; Mavis Wesley put in many of the finishing touches to the manuscript on her word processor.

The following gave help at many points: Christopher and Jeremy Pope and Douglas Pratt (Eldridge Pope); Fred West, W. Gordon Bertwistle and Rachel Multon (Wadworth); Richard P. Kershaw (Joseph Holt plc); C. A. Sandland and Helen Osborne (Young's Brewery); R. G. Anderson, R. E. Bell and Brian Renwick (Allied); J. E. Chambers, Jim Dickson and Jim Merrington (Scottish & Newcastle); Robin Evans, Sarah Elsom and Alan Bentley (Bass); Chris Butchers and Don Brown (Bass, Cape Hill); Brian Hanks and Liz Gill (Grand Met); Paul Smith and Peter Walsh (Guinness); Patricia Oliver (J. Walter Thompson); John Williams (Bristol Record Office); Colin Waite (Joshua Tetley); Dorothy Sheridan (Tom Harrisson Mass-Observation Archive, Sussex University); Louise Wright, Joanna Haskins and Alan Cary (Department of Transport); Joanna Irvin (Walker Art Gallery, Liverpool);

Helen Lewis (Institute of Brewing); Sue Henderson (Brewing Research Foundation International); M. J. Swarbrick (Westminster City Archive); Isabel Tucker (English Hop Products Ltd); Judy Simpson (editor, *The Brewer*); Alma Topen (Scottish Brewing Archive, Glasgow); Alain Jeunemaître (LSE); C. J. Marchbanks (Institute of Brewing); Jennifer Sunderland (Advertising Association Library); Susan Wilkie (Centre for Information on Beverage Alcohol); John Rae (Portman Group); Judy Slinn (Oxford Polytechnic); Jean Wilson (Scottish Office); Jan le Cluse (*The Grocer*); Shirley Braithwaite (Bryant Jackson); Keith Vernon (Lancashire Polytechnic); Tom Corran; John Seekings; T. A. B. Corley (University of Reading); Katherine Watson (University of York); Mikulas Teich (University of Cambridge); and Tom and Joyce of the 'British Flag', Macclesfield.

Generosity was only to be expected in an industry noted for its hospitality and traditions. Nevertheless, we have found it a wonderful source of strength together with the support provided by our families and colleagues. We hope, in spite of errors and omissions, that the result of all this trust will encourage others to appreciate and to research further this great industry. For none is more revealing about British culture, history and attitudes.

T.R.G.
R.G.W.

Abbreviations

AAS	Annual Abstract of Statistics
Abv	Alcohol by volume
APV	Aluminium Plant and Vessel Co. Ltd
AWP	Amusement with Prizes
blls	barrels
BLPES	British Library of Political and Economic Science, London School of Economics
BM&B	Bass Mitchells & Butlers
BMRB	British Market Research Bureau
Bodd	Boddington Group plc
BRF	Brewing Research Foundation
BS	Brewers' Society
BSWG	Brewing Sector Working Group
B(THB)	Breweries (Truman Hanbury Buxton)
BWTE	Brewers' without Tied Estate
CAMRA	Campaign for Real Ale
CBI	Confederation of British Industry
CIU	Working Men's Clubs and Institute Union
Cd, Cm, Cmd, Cmnd	Command
COBC	Cheltenham Original Brewery Company
Cos. House	Companies House
CSO	Central Statistical Office
DBB	Dictionary of Business Biography
DOR	Defence of the Realm
DTI	Department of Trade and Industry
EC	European Commission
EEC	European Economic Community
EP	Eldridge Pope & Co. plc
FBG	Fosters Brewing Group Ltd

FBI	Federation of British Industries
GABBA	Guinness, Allied and Bush Boake Allen
GLC	Greater London Council
GLRO	Greater London Record Office
G Met, Grand Met	Grand Metropolitan
GPR	Guinness Archive, Park Royal, London
GDP	Gross Domestic Product
HGV	Heavy Goods Vehicle
IDV	International Distillers & Vintners Ltd
ICI	Imperial Chemical Industries
ics	in-can system
ICTA	Ind Coope Tetley Ansell
JIB	Journal of the Institute of Brewing
LAB	Low Alcohol Beer
LCC	London County Council
MAFF	Ministry of Agriculture, Fisheries and Food
MC	Monopolies Commission
MMC	Monopolies and Mergers Commission
MO	Tom Harrisson Mass-Observation Archive, Sussex University
MORI	Market Opinion and Research International Ltd
MRC	Modern Records Centre, University of Warwick
n.a.	not available
NAB	No Alcohol Beer
NBPI	National Board for Prices and Incomes
NEDO	National Economic Development Office
NTDA	National Trade Defence (Development) Association
Parl. Deb.	*Parliamentary Debates*
PC	Price Commission
PP	*Parliamentary Papers*
PRD	Park Royal Department (Guinness)
PRO	Public Record Office
R & D	Research and Development
SBA	Scottish Brewing Archive
SCHC	Select Committee of the House of Commons
SCHL	Select Committee of the House of Lords
S&N	Scottish & Newcastle
SD	Standard Deviation
TFP	Total Factor Productivity

TGWU	Transport and General Workers' Union
VAT	Value Added Tax
W&Co.	Whitbread & Co. Archive, London
WMTB	Watney Mann & Truman Brewers

PART 1

THE BREWING INDUSTRY 1830–1914

1

The Beer Act, 1830–1870

The year 1830 is a good date to begin a history of the modern brewing industry. Although it marks, as precise dates so seldom do in industry, no dramatic watershed in terms of technology, output or organisation, the Beer Act of that year did effectively 'free' the trade in the sale of beer. Licences of all retail outlets had hitherto been entirely and jealously controlled by magistrates, and were increasingly becoming the valuable possession of brewers eager to exploit their custom. Regulation, giving arbitrary powers to magistrates and monopolistic ones to brewers, was anathema to the first, full-blooded generation of free traders. In effect the Act created a fourth type of public house, the beer house. Inns, taverns and alehouses (which possessed no spirit licence) still came within the surveillance of magistrates, but any householder who paid rates might apply for a two guinea excise license to sell beer – and brew it where he could manage to – on his premises. Within a mere eight years almost 46,000 of these beer houses were added to the stock of some 51,000 licensed premises existing in 1830. Clearly the centuries-old industry was dramatically shaken up. This chapter will examine the origins of the Act and assess its impact upon the brewing industry between 1830 and 1870.

The Beer Act of 1830 is one of the most extraordinary pieces of all nineteenth-century legislation. 'How the deuce this Beer Act ever passed we cannot very well comprehend' is a fair summary of the bewilderment of contemporaries and historians alike.[1] In fact the majority of the latter manage almost totally to ignore it. Yet the Act is an important piece of legislation. The late W. L. Burn reckoned 'it is quite arguable that this Act was more revolutionary in its immediate social

[1] *The Chartist*, 31 March 1839, quoted in B. Harrison, *Drink and the Victorians* (1971), p. 74.

consequences than any other of the reform age'.[2] It is also significant in helping make more comprehensible 'the sheer crazy diversity of solutions' canvassed by a troubled generation of politicians and thinkers between 1810 and 1830.[3] This is not the place to provide an extended survey of the background to the Act itself. That would take a deal of space, its origins stretching back over fifteen years and encompassing a number of parliamentary enquiries and pieces – albeit pretty ineffective – of legislation. The Beer Act was not devised in the summer of 1830 by the desperate Wellington government converted to free trade on its death bed.

Fortunately, there is one sound account of the origins of the Act which makes sense of the enquiries and legislation after 1816 and interprets them as a solution, by Whigs and Liberal Tories alike, to achieve 'free licensing' in the trade.[4] Of course events in 1829–30 did bring matters, mulled over inconclusively in the years after 1815, rapidly to a head. The Wellington government did make its mind up quickly, but the thinking behind the Act has longer roots than the crisis of 1830 itself. It is clearly more accurate to view it as part of that hectic reassessment undertaken after 1815 by a varied clique of Members of Parliament, Justices of the Peace, clergymen (often of an evangelical tinge), businessmen and bankers, and above all economic theorists and popularists who were forced to think out a whole range of new policies, social and economic, which would reconcile the prevailing political economy of Smith and Ricardo with the profound changes which almost twenty-five years of European War (1793–1815), population explosion, and rapid economic growth and fluctuation had brought about.[5]

In relation to this wider context it is necessary to stress briefly three points to provide a readily comprehensible introduction to the 1830 Act. The first is the mechanism of licensing public houses, the second the question of the brewers' monopoly of retail outlets in London, and the

2 W. L. Burn, *The Age of Equipoise* (1964), p. 281 footnote.

3 P. Mandler, 'Tories and Paupers: Christian Political Economy and the Making of the New Poor Law', *The Historical Journal*, 33 (1990), p. 83.

4 Harrison, *Drink and the Victorians*, pp. 64–86 provides the only full account of the Act and its origins. See also P. Mathias, *The Brewing Industry in England, 1700–1830* (1959), pp. 228–43 and S. and B. Webb, *The History of Liquor Licensing Principally from 1700 to 1830* (1903), pp. 93–134. But there is a need for an essay which explores the full political and economic dimensions of the debate between 1815 and 1830 about 'free licensing'.

5 B. Hilton, *Corn, Cash and Commerce: The Economic Policies of the Tory Governments, 1815–1830* (1977) which inexplicably ignores the Beer Act. See also his *The Age of Atonement* (1988) and Mandler 'Tories and Paupers' and 'The Making of the New Poor Law Redivivus', *Past and Present*, 117 (1987), pp. 131–57.

third, the profitability of brewing and farming ventures between 1815 and 1830.

Since the 1550s, the licensing of inns, taverns and alehouses had been controlled by magistrates, informally at first, and then in annual brewster sessions after 1729. In certain periods their creation of licences was lax and in none ungenerous (even after the 1780s when a new generation of 'moral' magistrates tightened procedures).[6] What reformers, after 1815, increasingly drew attention to, however, was the conspicuous way justices arbitrarily exercised their powers to create and withhold licences. Any two magistrates granting a licence conferred a substantial additional or 'monopoly' value on the newly licensed property. In the provinces by the 1820s this might be little more than £100; in London it was often nearer £1,000. To most Whigs and some Liberal Tories the system was one more instance of the corruption and restriction that was all too evident in government and economy alike. Chapter and verse for these allegations were revealed by the *Select Committee on the Police of the Metropolis* (1816–17) which devoted much of its evidence to the licensing question.[7] Instances of collusion between magistrates and brewers were paraded, and one zealous witness sought a wider audience for his views by organising a series of public meetings and petitions in London in 1818.[8] In fact the report of the Committee was moderate in its tone, and the Liverpool government, with plenty on its plate, took no action. One independent MP, Henry Bennet, however, did attempt to put some of its recommendations into operation by introducing in 1817 and 1819 the Bills which took the first, barely identifiable 'free licensing' steps. Without government support, and opposed by those great London brewers who were members of parliament, they got nowhere. But Bennet was not rebuffed by his failure and in 1822 introduced a third Bill. This was a more notable departure because it introduced the principle of any householder rated in excess of £20 per annum being able to obtain a licence to sell beer without the consent of magistrates. It

[6] Webbs, *Liquor Licensing*, pp. 15–84; P. Clark, *The English Alehouse: A Social History, 1200–1830* (1983), pp. 250–72.

[7] SCHC on State of the Police of the Metropolis, first report: *PP* (1817) VII.

[8] Mathias, *Brewing Industry*, pp. 238–40. J. T. B. Beaumont, a Middlesex magistrate and speculative builder, had complained that he was unable to obtain licences for 'superior public house[s]' on estates he had built in Stepney and Shepherd's Bush. His petition, carrying 14,000 signatures, resulted in the SCHC on Public Breweries, report, *PP* (1818) III, p. 295. For the evidence see the 'Minutes taken before the Committee to whom the Petition of Several Inhabitants of London and its Vicinity, complaining of the high price and inferior quality of Beer was referred', published in *PP* (1819) V, pp. 453–557.

was also significant because it so raised the alarm of provincial brewers that they formed the Country Brewers' Society (see p. 13) to oppose the Bill. Even without their intervention it would have failed, but the campaign for free licensing began to attract prominent political champions in Huskisson and Brougham. The interesting point is that the debate about free trade had been fully rehearsed by 1822, eight years before the 'revolutionary' Act.

The second strand, the question of monopoly, was, like that of licensing, basically a London issue. Indeed much of the criticism launched against the big London brewers had already been aired in the enquiry into the Police of the Metropolis in 1816, but it was given a fuller statement in the Committee on Public Breweries in 1818.[9] Basically, the complaint was that the big London brewers controlled at least half of their retail outlets by direct ownership, lease or, most frequently, loan, and that not only did market leaders meet regularly at Brewers' Hall to fix retail prices but they sold an inferior product at too high a price in their tied public houses.

As so often in nineteenth-century parliamentary enquiries, several hares were raised. Although the London brewers maintained that control of public houses was even more widespread in the country, little evidence was produced to support their claim. By a careful selection it might easily have been sustained, at least in South-East England. After a welter of figures about prices and profits had been aired, the great porter houses, represented by Barclay and Calvert, maintained it was impossible to brew a better beer from consistently high-quality materials more cheaply, and that wherever else adulterated beer might be found it was not in their breweries. Theirs was a position the Committee generally accepted. On the other hand the charge of price fixing stuck, and the evidence about the adulteration of beer in the previous decade – upon which the Committee increasingly concentrated – was highly injurious to the brewing interest.

Even to a less fastidious generation the revelations were alarming. High prices of materials and duties after 1803 had encouraged less reputable brewers and publicans alike to use an increasingly wide battery of adulterants. Not all were harmful, but the supposedly widespread use amongst small brewers and victuallers of vitriol and copperas, liquorice, quassia and wormwood, coculus indicus and opium,

[9] See previous note. The next two paragraphs are based upon this evidence. See also F. Accum, *Treatise on Adulterations of Food and Culinary Poisoning* (1820) and R. G. Wilson, *Greene King: A Business and Family History* (1983), pp. 23–5.

and the more occasional and exotic resort to grains of paradise to bring beer into condition, to increase its strength and to impart the flavour of hops, gave the entire industry, in spite of Barclay's and Calvert's protestations, a bad name (see Plate 1). An entry in Reid's accounts (1809–89) reveals that the firm spent no less than £6,913 on average per annum on caramel 'colouring' between 1810 and 1818. In the latter year, the practice was suddenly discontinued. The hand that compiled the Abstract around 1880 added: 'The use of Malt colouring (extracted from sugar?) discontinued; and "Roasted Malt" substituted in lieu thereof.'[10] The Excise officers, listing the number of convictions, suggested that adulteration was a natural consequence of the tied trade because publicans were under much pressure to pay off their debts to the brewers.[11] Professor Andrew Ure, the well-known Scottish political economist and chemist, and far too serious to tell a tall Glaswegian story, recalled that the amount of opium added to the beer sold on one early Clyde paddle steamer was so excessive that he could have carried out post-mortems on its victims without their realising what was happening.[12] Even if the Committee's report was vague in its appeal to the vigilance of magistrates and its recommendations about steps to erode the brewers' monopoly of public house ownership, the evidence itself was manna to the 'free licensing' camp.

But the measures which the Chancellor of the Exchequer took in 1823 and 1824 to implement action against the common brewers and to ease beer prices were quite unequal to the task. The 'Intermediate Beer' Act of 1823 and the 'Retail Brewing' Act of 1824, both clearly pursuing free-trade objectives, were two very curious experiments in the industry underlining the hesitancy of the government and the strength of the brewing interest. The first created a separate class of brewery, fixing a new level of duty and price for a beer of 'intermediate' strength, which could only be sold 'off' their premises or to a specially designated category of publican; the second, rather more popular, lowered licence duties for those small brewers who sold only by retail. Neither made any mark on the industry. Too restrictive to disturb the larger brewers, the first was a total flop; the second, by which 3 per cent of output was produced in 1829, defeated its object because retail breweries were most numerous in Cornwall and the West Midlands where breweries with

10 GLRO, Acc. 75.108, Reid Abstract of Rests (1809–89).

11 Fifteen smaller brewers (only Meux amongst the big porter brewers in 1812) had been prosecuted between 1815 and 1818 and seventeen publicans for adulteration. SCHC, *PP* (1819) V, pp. 18–19.

12 Quoted in Wilson, *Greene King*, p. 25.

tied house estates were almost non-existent.[13] The newly formed Country Brewers' Society believed these retail brewers to be a low lot of adulterators. And ineffective as this legislation was in reforming the serious shortcomings of the industry revealed between 1816 and 1819, the government believed it had done enough for the moment to meet the critics of the trade. It is significant that the Country Brewers held no meetings between 1825 and 1829, except for their boozy annual banquets, whereas previously they had complained about the press of business (and lack of subscriptions) surrounding Bennet and Brougham's abortive Bills and the 'Intermediate Brewers' and 'Retail Brewing' Acts in 1822–4.[14] No special meeting was called when in 1828 Estcourt's Licensing Act was passed. Badly drafted, it nevertheless consolidated existing law until 1872. It embraced some of the free traders' ideas by limiting magistrates' discretion and it was thought to have finally settled the licensing question.

In fact the whole climate of licensing appeared to be changing in the 1820s. The Webbs, when they wrote their 'free trade' chapter in *The History of Liquor Licensing*, asserted with their usual vigour,

> we have to take account of what seems, between 1820 and 1830, to have become almost an obsession of the mind of every enlightened legislator, Tory and Radical alike, that every person ought to be left free to invest his capital and employ his talents in whatever way he thought best; that cheapness and good quality could only be secured by an absolutely unrestricted competition; and that there was no reason why the number and position of public houses should not be left as free as those of bakers' shops.

There is some truth in their depiction of this proto-Thatcherite vision. Certainly Justices do seem to have imbibed some of these sentiments: the number of ale house licences increased by 7.4 per cent and those enjoying a spirit licence by 22.8 per cent between 1824 and 1830.[15] These are not the actions of a restrictive magistracy.

But the question of high beer prices, the third strand of the 1830 Act, had not been resolved. Ever since the early 1800s there had been complaints that the price of beer was too high. The allegations dogged the enquiries of 1816 and 1818; they were still being made in the 1820s. Free traders and agriculturalists desperately seeking to stimulate cereal prices after their collapse in 1813 blamed the large brewers; the latter in

[13] The clearest accounts are in Mathias, *Brewing Industry*, pp. 241–2 and Harrison, *Drink and the Victorians*, pp. 72–3.

[14] Brewers' Society Library, Country Brewers' Society Minute Book No. 1.

[15] Webbs, *Liquor Licensing*, pp. 95, 115–16.

Table 1.1. *Annual output of common brewers and brewing victuallers 'in the whole Kingdom', 1818–30 (figures in thousands of barrels)*

	Common brewers		Brewing victuallers	
	Strong beer	Small or table beer	Strong beer	Small or table beer
1818	3833	1073	1740	431
1819	4015	1114	1881	455
1820	3764	1073	1887	451
1821	3807	1056	2005	474
1822	3858	1051	2161	479
1823	4143	1067	2310	485
1824	3744	895	2346	560
1825	3920	922	2580	564
1826	4124	1011	2562	574
1827	–	–	–	–
1828	3897	1000	2334	488
1829	3942	978	2402	497
1830	3569	880	2166	450

Source: Mathias, *Brewing Industry*, p. 543

turn shifted responsibility to the government. The arguments are instructive partly because they almost exactly mirror the situation a century later when beer consumption collapsed in 1921 after duties had notably advanced shortly before a general easing of retail prices. Certainly, after 1815 the brewers could argue that their output was stagnant, and in many years declining, and that per capita consumption had been falling sharply since 1800 (Table 1.1). And they also could point to the fact that strong beer and hop duties remained unchanged after 1813 when retail prices began to fall rapidly. Malt duty rates, which had advanced sharply in 1802–4, were reduced after 1816 by over 40 per cent to relieve, like the Corn Laws of the previous year, the agricultural interest.[16] On the other hand, the government pointed to the high profits made by brewers – variously revealed in the enquiries of 1818

[16] The strong beer duty was 10s per barrel; malt duty per bushel was reduced to 2s 5d (12.1p) from 4s 5¾d (22.4p) in 1816 (it rose to 3s 7¼d (18.0p) in 1819–22 and then fell to 2s 7d (12.9p) where it remained until 1830). After 1816 the exaction of the beer duty was roughly double that of the malt duty since on an approximate average a barrel of beer could be brewed from two bushels of malt. Hop duty remained unchanged at 2d (0.8p) per lb. See Mathias, *Brewing Industry*, pp. 546–7.

and 1830 to be in the region of 10–12.5 per cent – and the fact that in many years after 1815, when malting barley was cheaper than it had been for more than thirty years, brewers, hesitant to adjust the price of beer, made substantial windfall profits. Yet on balance, since the beer duty remained high, the brewers had the edge of the argument.

The discussion about duties and prices which raged throughout the 1820s at every meeting where landowners and farmers came together was extended in two ways. First, it is evident that although the standard of living of the working class, at least of those in full employment and not engaged in agriculture, might not have fallen as much as historians once thought (especially between 1815 and 1830), the double duties on malt and beer, adding as much as 160 per cent to the cost of brewing materials, fell particularly hard upon it.[17] The price of beer, amidst generally falling prices after 1813, remained too high. Moreover, the well-to-do, who owned their own brewing utensils, were able to avoid the beer duties on the payment of a minimal licence fee. Secondly, the situation was given a new and important twist after 1825 (1823 in Scotland and Ireland) when spirit duties were substantially reduced – supposedly to abate illicit trading – from 11s 9d (58.75p) to 7s (35p) per gallon. Sales doubled in the following year. The ruling classes were shocked by the excesses of spirit drinking by working men and women, especially in the capital, and began to equate it with the marked increase in criminal convictions. They became anxious, therefore, to revive beer drinking – held to be more wholesome, more temperate and more beneficial to the economy. Similar views to those on spirits were advanced about tea drinking, although until the 1840s, when per capita consumption increased sharply, it was a growing, but not a serious, alternative to the national drink. In effect, in days long before advertising, a beer-is-best, best-for-health, best-for-Britain campaign was gaining momentum in the late 1820s.

In 1829–30 these views became entangled with two events which were to give the whole issue of 'free trade' in beer a quick, final push after fifteen years of gestation. The first was the general depression in agriculture which gathered momentum in the late 1820s. Prices of cereals had hit depths in the 1820s which had not been experienced since the early 1790s, whereas poor rates, tithes and rents – all of which had been driven to unprecedented levels in the war years – hardly budged for the beleaguered cereal farmers of the South and East. Vastly oversupplied

[17] M. W. Flinn, 'Trends in Real Wages, 1750–1850', *Economic History Review*, 2nd ser. 25 (1972), pp. 395–413.

with labour in the winter months, the countryside became rife with unrest. In late 1829 and early 1830 Parliament was inundated with a great series of petitions and addresses from county meetings. In all 174 were presented. The Suffolk meeting in February 1830 which considered 'the unparalleled distress of all classes dependent on Agriculture' was typical.[18] Invariably they sought relief through the reduction of taxation on necessities, and many specifically demanded the repeal or lowering of taxes on malt and beer. Secondly, the Wellington government, apart from the distress of the cereal growing areas of Britain, was in the direst straits. In a perpetual state of jitters because George IV's deteriorating health threatened an automatic general election on his death (26 June 1830), the Tory party had been torn apart by the passage of the Catholic Emancipation Act and major amendments to the Corn Laws in 1828. It was desperately looking for a piece of legislation to revive its flagging popularity. Early in the spring of 1830 it hit upon an apparently ideal solution: free trade in beer. It was a measure, well-rehearsed in argument, which would revive the agrarian interest, assuage the Canningite free traders, offer considerable relief to the working classes, and run into little Whig opposition. Its mind already made up about the outcome, the government appointed a committee on the Sale of Beer by Retail on 4 March 1830.

Announcing the financial implications of the repeal of the beer duties in the budget of 15 March, the government published its Bill three weeks later. It did not even bother to wait for the publication of the Committee's report.[19] To the Webbs, uninterested in, even hostile to the brewing industry, it was 'a perfunctory select committee, appointed to endorse a foregone conclusion, [which] gave formal audience to the exaggerated estimates of ruin apprehended by existing licence-holders'.[20] To historians of brewing, however, the Committee's findings are not without interest because, though hasty and predictable, they do provide insight into an industry which was at this period long on statistics but short on internally generated comment. As in 1816–18, evidence was drawn chiefly from the metropolis. Of the twenty-nine witnesses, no fewer than twenty-two came from the London area. They were headed by three London porter brewers, Charles Barclay, Thomas Fowell Buxton and Charles Calvert – all MPs and men of vast

[18] *Bury and Norwich Post*, 10 Feb. 1830. Sir R. Heron, *Notes* (1851, 2nd edn), pp. 182–3 provides an account of the Lincolnshire meeting on 8 January.

[19] SCHC, Report from the Select Committee on the Sale of Beer by Retail, report and evidence: *PP* (1830) X, upon which this paragraph is based.

[20] Webbs, *Liquor Licensing*, p. 122.

substance. The rest were a more motley bunch: three provincial brewers representing, not very persuasively, the views of the Country Brewers' Society; a couple of excisemen and public house auctioneers and brokers; a handful of victuallers, some with a significant trade in wines and spirits; two retail brewers from Staffordshire, and a City gin-palace proprietor.

The Webbs were right in contending that what witnesses had to do was reconcile themselves to a line of questioning whose basic premise was that the beer duty would be repealed to compensate the industry for the imposition of free licensing. Much of the evidence was familiar: about adulteration; about the effects of high duties on beer prices; about the decline in beer consumption (about 11 per cent between 1827 and 1830) in the face of cheap spirits. But the key brewers' witness, Charles Barclay, gave confident evidence. Of course beer was badly treated; of course the retail trade would be revolutionised and not for the better; but if duties were repealed, prices could, he reckoned, be reduced by 15 to 18 shillings (75p–90p) a barrel. And in an oft-quoted question-and-answer he concluded: 'Who are to supply these beer shops? The persons who can sell the cheapest and the best, and we say we can sell cheaper and better than others. We are power-loom brewers, if I may so speak.'[21] In comparison, the evidence of the three country brewers was tame. Two of these, Alfred Head from Stratford-near-Bow in Essex and William Steward from Great Yarmouth, were essentially public house proprietors with little active brewing interests, selected by the Country Brewers' Society because they could represent the threat of the Bill to all those country brewers who owned tied houses. They underlined the way the Bill would affect their considerable capital, and they reckoned bad debts would increase appreciably (Steward declaring an interest in 140–150 houses valued at £65,000). But either they were hesitant to be drawn out generally about the prospects for country brewers or they were not invited to do so. Robert Wheeler, from High Wycombe, made assertions similar to Barclay's. Free trade would have a most deleterious effect on the capital of brewers and publicans, but, in his opinion, 'the intelligence and capital of the brewers will do the business on a scale that must beat the competition of most of those small concerns if they are left fairly to work'.[22] The Licensed Victuallers, who would be the great losers by free trade, were given shorter shrift. Although the brewers were obliged to acknowledge their fears, there was a considerable gap

[21] SCHC on Sale of Beer, *PP* (1830) X, p. 16.
[22] *Ibid.*, p. 22.

between their economic interests and social outlook which Committee members implicitly endorsed.

The passage of the Act between April and mid-July was far from untroubled. It was not helped by George IV's death on 26 June, two thirds of the way through proceedings. But the government stuck to its guns, aided by the Whigs and either the support or abstention of Irish members in key divisions. It was the one substantial piece of legislation in the barren parliamentary session of 1830. Although the contents of the Bill were now fought out principally between the various sections of the Tory party, some supporting Wellington, others, principally the ultra or far right Tories, wanted to press the repeal of the malt tax rather than the beer duty in order to aid landlords and farmers rather than brewers. They were also opposed to a further diminution of magistrates' powers and to the threat the Act posed to law and order in the countryside. The brewers themselves were similarly divided. The great London brewers broadly accepted that the government's scheme must pass. Although they supported (in part pressed into this position by the victuallers) no fewer than three unsuccessful amendments of Monck (21 May), Knatchbull (21 June) and Maberly (1 July), all basically seeking to prevent consumption on the premises of the new beer houses (and which would in effect have wrecked the Act), their private thoughts were set out in a letter from Thomas Fowell Buxton to J. J. Gurney:

> I am far from dissatisfied with the free trade, when the interests of others were concerned, and it would be awkward to change when my own are in jeopardy. Secondly, I believe in the principles of free trade, and expect that they will do us good in the long run, though the immediate loss may be large. Thirdly I have long expected the change. And, lastly, I am pleased to have an opportunity of proving that our real monopoly is one of skill and capital.[23]

Few country brewers, however, achieved this sense of detachment.[24]

It is the actions of the Country Brewers' Society which reveal the qualms of the average brewer about the government's legislation.[25] Formed eight years previously, the infant Society represented the views of perhaps no more than fifty big brewers in the South-East of England. They were, like one of their chief spokesmen, William Steward, invariably large tied house owners and, since they were not inured to the hurly-burly of fierce competition like Buxton and Barclay in London,

23 C. Buxton, *Memorials of Sir Thomas Fowell Buxton, Bart.* (1848), p. 234.

24 One brewer who was pro-Beer Act was the ultra-Tory, Benjamin Greene of Bury St Edmunds. See Wilson, *Greene King*, pp. 28–30.

25 This paragraph is based upon the brief entries recorded in the First Minute Book of the Society in the Brewers' Society Library.

they could not envisage that they would emerge unscathed from the effects of the new legislation. Their campaign in the early summer of 1830 reveals both their apprehension and their naïvety. Throughout April, May and June their committee met daily to monitor progress and make representations to Members of Parliament when the three main amendments to the Bill were introduced. They co-operated quite amicably with the Victuallers' Committee, they appointed a parliamentary agent, they arranged for the presentation of numerous petitions, they sought meetings with the Chancellor of the Exchequer. But his ear was not to be bent to their wrecking schemes, and without the flexibility of the London brewers (with whom they appear to have held virtually no communication) they were driven further and further into a corner by a ruggedly determined government. Receiving 228 petitions against the Bill, and only ten in favour, it punched steadily on. By late June, the minutes of the Society (albeit very thin at this stage in its history) revealed their total lack of direction. The entry for 23–25 June recorded, 'Much discussion on this and the two following days as to what course ought to be pursued. No particular Measure determined.' The King's death did not bring the respite they prayed for because the Government made the final passage of their Bill its first priority in the rest of the session. By 1 July the Society's strategy was in tatters. Its weary Secretary summed up a long discussion tersely. To the question from the Chair, 'whether to oppose the Bill under *all* or any circumstance', the decision recorded was, 'to let the several clauses be proposed, but not to give any specific directions for an Opposition to the Bill itself. Agreed nem. con.' The Act passed quickly through the Lords and was given its final reading on 12 July. All that was left was for the Society to pass its votes of thanks and, as was customary in the nineteenth century, to spend generously (200 gns) on inscribed plate for its two most assiduous members, Benjamin Wood and John Farnell. Its thanks, conveyed to Sir Edward Knatchbull, a leading Tory ultra, the Duke of Richmond, Lord Malmesbury and Lord Falmouth, revealed the narrow alley it had got itself into. No wonder it wrote as the epitaph of its campaign on 2 July: 'to persevere in a vexatious and a useless opposition would tend only to increase the general persecution against Brewers'.

The Act itself was very straightforward. The duties on strong beer (10s per barrel) and cider were repealed. After 11 October 1830 any rate payer could apply for a two-guineas-per-annum excise licence to sell beer on or off the premises. Opening hours (a generous 5 a.m. to 10 p.m.

except on Sundays during the hours of divine service) were tighter than those of other public houses, otherwise the conditions of tenure, specified in the licence, were similar.

The Act has always had an appalling press. The Mayor of Arundel, William Holmes, told a Parliamentary select committee: 'I was obliged to get out of my gig three times from people coming along, waggoners drunk, when I was returning from shooting on the very day of the operation of the bill.'[26] The celebrations continued. A fortnight later Sydney Smith reckoned: 'Everyone is drunk. Those who are not singing are sprawling. The sovereign people are in a beastly state.'[27] And other literary references were deeply hostile for decades. Historians have taken their cue from the Webbs:

> it is hard to find a redeeming feature of this debauch ... The decision to allow Free Trade in beer, [they thundered from their collectivist pulpit in 1903] momentous ... in its consequences, may indeed be cited as the leading case of legislation based on abstract theory ... without investigation of previous experiments, without inquiry into the existing facts, and even without any clear conception of the state of society which it was desired to bring about.[28]

Brian Harrison, dismissing most of the Webbs' moralising, thought 'the beershop system was a way of controlling houses which might otherwise have sold beer illegally'.[29] Both views, given the context of debate in the 1820s, seem rather wide of the mark. For the Act was clearly the logical outcome of all those discussions about duties, prices and consumption, about the agrarian and industrial interests, about the threat of cheap spirits, about the venality of magistrates and brewers magnified from evidence presented in 1816–18. Then in 1829–30 the Wellington government ran into an acute political and economic crisis. Having selected a quick escape route to popularity, it could not stimulate the sale of a basic commodity – native and nutritious in comparison with wines, some spirits, tea and coffee – without removing its retail monopoly. Only then would prices fall, agriculture revive, and the working classes be reconciled. Drunkenness might increase in the short term, but market forces must triumph. These policies were no more abstract than most political solutions, and concern about the number of unlicensed premises was not a prime consideration in the hectic summer of 1830.

If the context of the Act is wide ranging and its content brief, its

[26] SCHC, State and Management of Beershops, *PP* (1833) XV, p. 46.
[27] Lady Holland, *Memoir of the Revd. Sydney Smith* (1855), II, p. 310.
[28] Webbs, *Liquor Licensing*, p. 114.
[29] Harrison, *Drink and the Victorians*, p. 81.

impact was dramatic. Within six months, 24,324 licences had been taken out, and within eight years the number had almost doubled to 45,717. In town and countryside alike they proliferated. In Liverpool 800 were opened within the first three weeks of the Act; Merthyr Tydfil had 200 in 1839. In largely rural Wales the number of people licensed to sell beer increased from 1,242 to 2,809 within three years; in Suffolk in 1840 there were 577 beer houses in comparison with 700 fully licensed houses.[30] Whether in Wales, the South-East or the North (the Act did not extend to Ireland and Scotland) the situation was similar. But, as Harrison points out, the 'debauch' view does not extend much beyond the literary disclosures, for the evidence of consumption, derived with no great exactitude from the malt tax figures (revealing a dramatic 1829–31 increase of 40 per cent), had levelled off by the late 1830s. Indeed, John Wood, chairman of the Board of Excise, thought that the increase in coffee, tea and cocoa revenues, and the 'falling off in the malt consumption' between 1836 and 1850, might 'be attributed, in a considerable degree, to the altered habits of the population'.[31]

Yet in the eyes of the magistracy and clergy the beer houses never lost their seedy reputation. Usually located in unsuitable premises, they were identified from the outset – like the alehouses had been two or three centuries earlier – as centres of disaffection and crime. The ruling classes, especially in country areas, deplored their influence; and opposition to them became so orchestrated that the government set up a select committee in 1833 to scrutinise their working and examine claims that they were closely linked with the outburst of rural unrest in 1830–1.[32] In effect, the inquiry provided an opportunity for the magistracy to let off steam. It also revealed, when some of them were questioned more closely, how out of touch they were becoming with their localities and the recreations of the labouring classes. Assertions far outstripped hard evidence. Beer house keepers were represented as a

30 *Ibid.*, p. 124; W. R. Lambert, *Drink and Sobriety in Victorian Wales c. 1820–c. 1895* (1983), p. 21; Wilson, *Green King*, pp. 29–30.

31 Harrison, *Drink and the Victorians*, p. 70.

32 See note 26 above. This paragraph is based upon the minutes of evidence, pp. 7–257. Many of the allegations made about the beer houses in 1833 were repeated in SCHL, Operation of the Acts for the Sale of Beer, *PP* (1849 and 1850) IV and VI. The evidence is partly in the form of replies to a set of vague questions sent to chairmen of Quarter Sessions, chaplains of county gaols, chief constables and, where there were no rural police, clerks of Petty Sessions. The reply of the chaplain of Reading gaol (p. 86) is typical. He has 'ascertained by investigation that about four-fifths of the offences committed by the agricultural population are traceable to beer houses, the keepers of which tempt to profligacy and vice, encouraging drinking and gambling, and keeping prostitutes under the name of servants'.

feckless, 'slippery' set of people, and the beer shops as the cause of 'a very great deal of drunkenness; a very great increase of idleness; a very great deal of extravagance'. They encouraged poaching, gambling, whoring and, although nowhere was this conclusively proved, they were said to provide a direct link with the outbreak of incendiarism aimed at the Justices, clergy and farmers of the South-East of England. One Berkshire magistrate memorably portrayed the labouring classes emerging 'pot-valiant' from the beer houses to 'go about and do considerable mischief'. And a picture is drawn from the evidence taken by the committee, of the male working class, rural and urban alike, being paid in the beer houses on Saturday evening, drinking themselves comatose in the following thirty hours, wrecking family life, increasing the poor rates, and undermining work attitudes. The churchwarden of Brede in Sussex saw the rising generation 'sinking into moral depravity which I fear will ultimately be productive of insubordinate principles'. Only the chief constable of Leeds provided closer statistical analysis. And it made gloomy reading, for he calculated that drunkenness charges had increased over three times from the 639 in the three years preceding the Act to the thirty months period following it.

The magistrates in 1833 wanted the rateable value of beer houses fixed at a £15 minimum (around three times that of the majority licensed since 1830), and brewing licences suppressed for beer house keepers producing under 200 barrels a year. By these moves they believed the 'lowest', most disreputable, houses would be closed. But the Whig government, believing such restriction would grossly undermine the free-trade aspects of the Act, thereby offending the nascent temperance movement and a Tory magistracy, did very little. The Act of 1834 made a distinction between the excise duty paid on 'on' and 'off' licensed premises, and laid down that 'on' beer house licences would in future only be granted on the production of certificates of good character signed by six ratepayers in the parish. The Act of 1840 contained clauses about minimum rateable values, of £8, £11 or £15, related to the number of inhabitants in a district, and extended opening hours to conform more with those of their public house competitors.[33] Certainly, the boom in beer houses was over by the later 1830s. The total of 40,102 on-licences issued in 1837 was only exceeded twice in 1853 and 1856

[33] Webbs, *Liquor Licensing*, p. 129; Pratt, *The Licensed Trade*, pp. 87–8. According to S. R. Bosanquet, Chairman of the Monmouthshire Quarter Sessions, 'the certificates ... are wholly inoperative; for they [the beer houses] are mostly brothels of the worst description'. SCHL, Operation of the Acts for the Sale of Beer, IV and V, p. 105.

Table 1.2. *The number of beer houses licensed in England and Wales, 1831–1914*

	'On' licences	'Off' licences		'On' licences	'Off' licences
1831	30,978		1875	39,267	4,211
1836	39,104	5,030	1880	37,639	11,765
1840	36,871	5,742	1885	32,960	12,609
1845	32,624	3,687	1890	31,766	12,497
1850	36,080	3,343	1895	30,496	12,376
1855	39,877	2,911	1900	29,394	12,331
1860	41,094	2,947	1905	28,522	12,082
1865	42,637	2,853	1910	24,891	11,653
1870	44,501	3,078	1914	26,517	17,929

Source: Wilson, *Alcohol and the Nation*, pp. 395–8.

before a further brief resurgence in the 1860s to an all-time record of 49,120 in 1869, the year in which effective restrictive legislation about their control was finally passed (Table 1.2).

Yet it is unlikely that the effects of the 1830 Act upon the lives of labouring families in the generation following its passage were as deleterious as the rural ruling classes claimed in 1833. In Cornwall, Devon, Northumberland and Nottingham the reputation of the beer houses was nothing like as bad as the authorities represented it in Lancashire, Suffolk and Sussex.[34] But the proliferation of beer shops allowed magistrates everywhere to maintain that there were many features in working-class culture, which they either disliked or failed to comprehend, which were seriously undermined by the Act. The chief constable of Lancashire in 1849 thought the beer houses were 'the most serious social evil of the day'; and the chaplain of Abingdon gaol wrote that, 'by the testimony of the prisoners generally, these houses may be considered as the first stage of "The Felon's Progress"'.[35] Therefore the beer houses, especially since total beer consumption rose sharply from the 1850s to the 1870s (see pp. 29–37), became the focus for apprehension about social changes both in the countryside and in the rapidly expanding towns. And in terms of the free-trade rationale behind the Beer Act there were occurrences, already predicted in 1830, which

[34] *Ibid.*, pp. 87–100.
[35] *Ibid.*, p. 100.

seriously limited its aim to transform the production and sale of beer. For the beer houses failed to make any inroads into the growing proportion of beer produced by commercial brewers, the latter controlling from the outset, by a variety of tying arrangements, the sale of beer through many beer houses.

Certainly, the promised revolution never took off. Those beer house producers who were meant to open up competition and lower beer prices did not produce more than 13.4 per cent of output at their peak in 1836 (see pp. 67–72). The reason was clear from the outset. They were incapable of producing a reliable beer. Frequently, they had difficulty in finding even the minimal cost of a brewer's licence, still more in raising an adequate capital (£25–£100 in the early 1830s) to buy a decent set of brewing utensils. Often they had insufficient credit to pay their rents and rates and obtain regular supplies of malt, or, in summer, when demand was brisk, additional supplies of beer from a common brewer. Partly because they had little room to store beer, partly because their credit credentials were poor, they therefore brewed minimal amounts – often no more than a hogshead at a time. Brewing without saccharometers, and using inferior malts, their extraction rates fell far below those of commercial brewers who made their own quality malts more cheaply. John Pritchard, a Hampshire excise officer, believed they produced 'a very bad beverage'. A Lancashire overseer of the poor thought the beer house brewers sold 'a very thick and very new brew'.[36] With a price advantage of no more than 1d (0.42p) a quart in comparison with beer supplied by common brewers to their own pubs, most observers believed the badness of the beer far outweighed its relative cheapness.

With all these disadvantages the beer house 'revolution', calculated to shake up the industry, quickly fizzled out. By 1860 beer house keepers were producing less than 10 per cent of output. Only in the Birmingham area, where they produced an astonishing 49 per cent of beer as late as 1880, was the beer house keeper a force in making beer. Elsewhere the beer houses became an easy prey for the common brewer. Linked closely with him from the outset for supplies, they seldom owned their own property. When common brewers became more acquisitive for public houses after 1860 they easily picked off those beer houses they wanted, their proprietors, attracted by a good price, having no particular vested interest in keeping unreliable tenants afloat. And the hope

[36] *PP* (1833) XV, SCHC on the Sale of Beer, pp. 82, 235.

that the beer houses would deal a mortal blow in terms of price competition to those large brewers, who were believed to be keeping up beer prices by their ownership of extensive tied house holdings, was quickly dashed. A magistrate who gave evidence to the 1833 committee illustrated this graphically. He recalled that two country brewers had predicted that the Act would curtail their hunting activities and probably ruin them. Now, two seasons later, their sales were up by more than a third and they appeared 'with new coats and better horses'.[37]

The output of the great London brewers also increased. Barclay Perkins's production, for example, rose from 262,252 barrels in 1830 to 405,819 in 1839, and Truman's from 170,809 to 314,860 in the same period (see pp. 77–81). Some of this increase must have gone to supplying the 1,684 beer houses that flourished in the London excise collection district by 1840. Whitbread's ledgers at this date indicate that they were providing for seventy-nine London beer houses in comparison with 643 licensed victuallers.[38] And some London brewers, brewing ale rather than porter, pushed their sales much harder in the beer houses. This allowed Mann, Crossman & Paulin, the fastest growing of all mid-Victorian breweries in the capital, their entry into the trade. In 1850 they supplied about 500 beer houses and boasted the largest share of the beer house market.[39] In the country a similar picture of immediate dependency by the beer house keeper upon the common brewer emerges. Indeed, since the example comes from Leeds, a renowned centre of publican brewing, it is compelling. Henry Bentley, who had recently moved from Huddersfield to begin commercial brewing at Woodlesford, just outside Leeds, produced over 3,000 barrels for around 140 customers in the year the Beer Act came into force.[40] These – and many of them were private accounts – were located along the River Aire, especially in Leeds, and along the London turnpike road. No fewer than forty-six of these 140 accounts were acquired between 11 October (the day the Mayor of Arundel had to get out of his gig so repeatedly) and the end of the year. In the first heady fortnight, thirty-one new accounts were opened, no fewer than seventeen of them in the industrial area of Leeds and Hunslet. Indeed, so many deliveries were made and in such small quantities that it appears

37 *Ibid.*, p. 78.
38 Whitbread Archives, Rest Books W/22/42.
39 SCHL into Acts for the Sale of Beer, *PP* (1850) XVIII, Qs. 139, 145. Evidence of Robert Crossman.
40 The section on Bentley's is based upon a reconstruction of their trading account for 1830 taken from their Sales Ledger (1828–32), Whitbread Archives, 288/72.

that Bentley's beer was briefly rationed. And the evidence from Bristol Brewery Georges underlines the point that the 1830s were a far less gloomy decade for country brewers than the calamity their leaders had forecast in the summer of 1830. Georges' expenditure on malt increased from an average of £14,297 in 1829–30 to £28,052 in 1839–40.[41] Of course, the prospects facing Bentley's in the autumn of 1830 soon settled down as some of the accounts were closed when they went unpaid, and prices crept back up in 1831. But because so many beer houses were supplied by common brewers from the outset, their impact in the retailing of beer was no more than in its production. In most areas, with hand-to-mouth finances, beer house keepers were seldom in a strong enough position to resist the blandishments of common brewers. Indeed many, especially in the South and East, were set up with the latters' support. Independence for them, built upon the rock of 'free trade', was a chimera because so few possessed adequate capital and credit resources.

The Beer Act of 1830 is an extraordinarily controversial piece of legislation – in its concept, in its attack upon vested interests, and in its creation (so nonchalantly uncalculated) of over 45,000 additional, uncontrolled retail outlets. For forty years, justices, parsons and police could lay the blame for most of the evils of the new industrial society at its door. Yet its impact in terms of the brewing industry should not be overstated. In no decade after 1830 was the proportion of beer produced by common brewers diminished. Indeed it grew healthily. Nor was the price of beer slashed beyond the winter of debauch in 1830–1; at least not beyond that which the removal of the beer duty itself allowed. Thus the attempt to create new outlets to supply cheaper beer was abortive – except in the Midlands and some northern areas where the beer houses fitted easily into the existing system of publican brewing. Moreover, evidence from the South-East and London suggests that brewers went on buying, leasing, and making loans to publicans much as they had in the past. The new outlets did not remain outside this network, and commercial decisions were taken about them by brewers based upon the usual criteria. Some beer houses never enjoyed a decent turnover. Others in the larger cities commanded a large barrelage. Yet all retained a third-class status, inferior to the established inns and taverns whose locations and whose serving of food and spirits allowed them to retain and attract a more affluent, socially mobile clientele. In spite of the beer

[41] Courage's Archive (Bristol), Georges Private Ledger 1827–46, 35740/GR/3(a).

houses' failure to halt the advance of the larger brewers after 1830, the trade did remain sufficiently free for almost half a century to allow new entrants into the industry. Whether, had there been no Beer Act, a much less dramatic growth of retail outlets would have led brewers into acquiring public houses and curtailing the free trade much earlier than the 1880s depends upon how readily justices would have issued licences in the areas of fastest population growth. Both are unanswerable questions. Certainly the Beer Act – a curious mixture of up-to-date political economy and old-fashioned Georgian indifference to the social consequences of legislation – acknowledged the universal belief that the consumption of beer (as opposed to spirits) was not harmful. Indeed, in its wholesomeness, and the benefits it brought to British agriculture, beer production was to be encouraged. The temperance movement, barely under way in 1830, was not opposed at this stage to beer consumption. Teetotalism was a product of the 1840s. But whatever the debate surrounding the Act and its impact upon the industry, the 45,000 beer houses which were its principal legacy were not in themselves responsible for the rapid growth in beer output and consumption in the fifty years after 1830.

2

Consumption and production

This chapter begins by looking at the output of the beer industry for the whole period covered by Part I of this book, 1830–1914. Fortunately, it presents less of a task for its historian than would a similar exercise in the other great Victorian industries since beer production has historically generated a mass of statistics for excise purposes. Like most economic data, however, they have their shortcomings, but these are few in comparison with the chapter's second task – the reconstruction of shifts in demand and taste of drinkers more than a hundred years ago. The third and fourth parts of the chapter deal with the art of brewing beer and the impact of notable scientific discoveries in the nineteenth century.

I

G. B. Wilson, in his invaluable collection of statistics about the production and consumption of alcohol, wrote in his chapter on beer: 'the records of Beer Production in the United Kingdom prior to 1880 are very unsatisfactory'. His strictures arose from the fact that between 1830 and 1880 excise duties were levied upon bushels of malt used, not barrels of beer produced for sale (they had been raised upon both before 1830); that increasing amounts of sugar were used in making beer after the 1850s; and that evasion of the malt tax was widespread.[1] He then went on to make a series of calculations which converted the quantities of malt and sugar declared for excise by common, publican and beer house brewers into standard barrels (i.e. of an average original gravity of 1055°) of beer produced (Table 2.1). Like all exercises in the manipulation of historical data his figures have come to assume a veracity they

[1] G. B. Wilson, *Alcohol and the Nation* (1940), pp. 48–60. Private brewing was excluded from his calculations. He made the contemporary assumption that it required two bushels of malt to produce a 36 gallon barrel of standard gravity (1055°) beer.

Table 2.1. *UK beer production, 1831–1914 (annual averages)*

Year	England and Wales	Scotland	Ireland	UK
1831–4	13,486	518	846	14,850
1835–9	14,908	574	941	16,423
1840–4	13,824	449	540	14,813
1845–9	14,059	469	647	15,175
1850–4	15,222	560	633	16,416
1855–9	16,150	612	932	17,694
1860–4	18,382	852	1,176	20,411
1865–9	22,154	1,166	1,485	24,805
1870–4	25,087	1,284	1,736	28,107
1875–9	28,217	1,149	2,061	31,427
1880–4	25,002	1,138	2,083	28,223
1885–9	25,532	1,453	2,355	29,340
1890–4	27,735	1,749	2,609	32,093
1895–9	30,290	2,052	2,864	35,206
1900–4	30,577	1,981	3,244	35,802
1905–9	28,692	1,778	3,382	33,852
1910–14	28,863	1,856	4,022	34,741

Figures in thousands of standard (1055° gravity) barrels

Note:

'The figures from 1831–80 are based on the quantities of malt (and sugar) used in brewing. From 1881 to 1889 the "standard" barrel had an original gravity of 1057°, not 1055°; the quantities have been calculated on the basis of 1055° to preserve "uniformity".' See also A. R. Prest, *Consumers' Expenditure in the United Kingdom, 1900–1919* (1954), pp. 76, 85, where Wilson's standard barrelages after 1870 are converted into bulk barrels.

Source and note: Wilson, *Alcohol and the Nation*, pp. 369–70.

do not inherently possess. Certainly, when Wilson estimates output based upon the new beer tax introduced by Gladstone in his 1880 budget, the seam does show. The year 1881 was not an easy one in the industry, yet it is doubtful if production declined by 11.4 per cent in England and Wales. More probably, it represents in part the 6 per cent waste allowance that the authorities introduced with the new duty.

Two features of Table 2.1 need to be stressed. First, in the half century after 1830 (ignoring a hiccup in 'the hungry forties') growth was pronounced. At its peak, in 1876, it was, in England and Wales, some 121 per cent above its 1830 level. Thereafter expansion was hesitant – although not in Ireland. Output in England and Wales of some 29,032,000 standard barrels in 1876 was not exceeded for another twenty years. At the pit of the recession in 1883 production was 17.8 per cent below its peak seven years earlier. Then recovery from 1896 to 1899 was marked, taking output to a United Kingdom record of 37,404,000 barrels in the latter year. After 1900 there was renewed stagnation – although the depression in the industry, at least in terms of output, was not as marked as in the early 1880s. Brewers had always paid careful attention to the malt tax figures released annually. After 1880 their study of the beer output statistics, enormously encouraged by comment in the brewing trade journals flourishing from the 1870s, became an obsession. And each brewer, paranoid about keeping his own barrelage figures to himself, made careful calculations about these in relation to national output trends and to statistics that revealed the increasing size of common brewers.

Secondly, growth at an annual average rate of 1.74 per cent per annum between 1831 and 1876 was less than that achieved in other major industries in Victorian Britain. Because it was large, beer consumption had limits. Especially from the 1880s there were other leisure preferences for consumers; and the industry, for a variety of reasons, never developed a strong export trade. After the late 1870s growth almost ceased. Therefore, judged solely in terms of output, no other important industry, not even agriculture, the worst casualty of the Great Depression (1873–96), fared as badly in the forty years before the First World War as brewing. In 1910–14 production was a mere 2–3 per cent above the level for 1875–9. Yet, even during the difficult years after 1900, many contemporaries identified brewing as amongst the most profitable of industrial undertakings. This interesting paradox, of sluggish output and rising prosperity, is explicable in terms of two developments hidden behind the columns of figures recorded in Table 2.1.

Private brewing, producing around one-fifth of beer consumed in 1830, collapsed almost entirely in the next forty years. Small-scale *publican* brewers, selling beer solely from single retail outlets, were similarly if more slowly eliminated by their bigger rivals. They produced an estimated 45 per cent of beer for sale in 1830. By the end of the century this had declined, albeit at very different rates in different areas, to around 5 per cent. By the outbreak of the Great War it was negligible. Consequently, the output figures of the industry understate the growth potential for *common* or *commercial* brewers since their total market increased from rather less than 8 million barrels in 1830 to almost 30 million by 1900. It is this growth which explains the outstanding opportunities for those Victorian brewers who possessed the right entrepreneurial qualities to grasp them.

The aggregate output figures derived from the malt and, after 1880, the beer duties can be broken down further. Excise districts, which frequently shifted their boundaries, were seldom coterminous with county borders. Officers collected the raw data about the numbers of brewers, victuallers and beer house keepers and the amount of malt each brewed. From these the national returns were constructed.[2] These compilations provide an invaluable tool for historians of the industry, allowing them to determine the growth of commercial brewing and the pace at which publican brewing was eliminated in approximately sixty collection areas – their total varied slightly from decade to decade. An under-utilised source, they form part of the statistical basis of Chapter 3 which surveys the development of brewing in the various regions. From an additional statistical source, the duty paid upon brewers' licences (a fee which varied with the number of barrels brewed), it is also possible to trace nationally the numbers of breweries within broad production bands (see p. 111) between 1830 and 1914.[3] All these data together with the numerous barrelage figures of individual brewers allow an unrivalled statistical view of the transformation of a great Victorian industry. They reveal in 1830 a scene in which, except in London and a few dozen provincial breweries producing more than 20,000 barrels each, the scale of production was small. In many areas it was purely domestic in dimension. By 1914, although there were still around 1,100 breweries, the industry was dominated by fifty-four, turning out more than a hundred times the minimum threshold qualification for a commercial brewery, 1,000 barrels. In 1920, around 5 per cent of the breweries in the United Kingdom were reckoned to brew over 65 per cent of the beer produced.[4] This transformation in scope across three-quarters of a century was initiated by the marked growth in output between 1830 and 1880. When the rate fell away after 1880, a contrary set of forces, activated by licensing restrictions and company flotations, pushed many breweries into expansion by merger and accelerated acquisition of tied retail outlets.

2 Examples of the returns will be found for Suffolk in Wilson, *Greene King*, p. 267 and for Yorkshire in E. Sigsworth, 'The Brewing Trade during the Industrial Revolution: The Case of Yorkshire', *Borthwick Papers*, 31 (1967).

3 See also Wilson, *Alcohol and the Nation*, pp. 48–9.

4 *Ibid.*

II

When we turn from the output of beer to the consumption in Victorian Britain the issues become more complex, and this for two principal reasons. First, there are no official statistics of drink expenditure. Of course, there were numerous *estimates* which not surprisingly often reveal considerable gaps between the calculations made by temperance advocates and those by the brewers' lobby. Whether they relate to total spending or per capita consumption data, they are best used to indicate broad trends rather than fine tuning between individual years. Secondly, the consumption of alcohol was one of the great nineteenth-century social questions. On few other issues was more ink spilt. The historian of the industry needs therefore to tread an over-hung path with great care. Most contemporaries agreed that consumption was high and increasing, at least before the 1880s. But there agreement stopped, for the causes and consequences of what made men drink were hotly debated. The more extreme temperance advocates believed that the issue was primarily one of temptation. Only when public houses (whose numbers had increased so rapidly after the 1830 Act) were closed, and prohibition of production was enforced by the state, could the evils of drink – poverty, crime, prostitution, lunacy, disease and death – be abolished. Lord Chief Justice Coleridge put the association of drink and crime most eloquently: 'I can keep no terms with a vice that fills our gaols, that destroys the comfort of homes and the peace of families, and debases and brutalises the people of these islands.'[5] On the other hand there were those who believed that the causes of poverty and crime – indeed of drunkenness – were related to more profound social changes, and that abstinence and prohibition were no realistic way forward.

The brewers, of course, did not see the drink question in these terms – certainly not from the perspective of temperance reformers and not necessarily from the viewpoint of those who saw drinkers being gradually weaned from intemperate consumption by what Rowntree and Sherwell called the 'counter-attractions', of leisure and education.[6] Brewers normally explained shifts in consumption in terms of employment and wages, and defended their overall position in terms of supplying the working man with a first-rate pint of beer in a comfortable pub, while distancing themselves from allegations about growing drunkenness.

[5] Quoted in P. Snowden, *Socialism and the Drink Question* (1908), p. 7.
[6] J. Rowntree and A. Sherwell, *The Temperance Problem and Social Reform* (9th edn, 1901).

Table 2.2. *Percentage expenditure upon alcoholic beverages in the United Kingdom, 1870–1914*

	Total expenditure (£m.)	Beer %	Spirits %	Wine %	Cider %
1870	158.7	56.7	31.9	10.6	0.7
1890	131.0	59.1	32.0	8.1	0.6
1914	187.9	68.7	26.1	4.6	0.6

Source: Prest, *Consumers' Expenditure*, pp. 75, 85.

It was a difficult tightrope to walk. Inevitably, they were drawn into the centre of the great debate about drink in the nineteenth century. We must, therefore, consider the evidence about beer consumption, the discussions surrounding the figures, and ways in which shifts in its levels affected the fortunes and strategies of Victorian brewers.

Social historians of nineteenth-century Britain, examining the central question of living standards in a rapidly expanding urban industrial society, have relied a good deal upon the evidence of drink consumption. In this the statistics about beer are central (Table 2.2). In England and Wales, although not in Ireland and Scotland, beer was the national drink. Consumed at all levels in society, often before the 1860s as a more temperate substitute for spirits, it was above all a mainstay of working-class diets. Professor Leone Levi, who produced a survey of the brewing industry for M. T. Bass in 1871, believed three-quarters of all beer produced was drunk by them; and it troubled many a Victorian reformer that their great demand so evidently eroded their meagre wages. More recently, historians have taken their evidence from G. B. Wilson's accessible battery of alcohol statistics, above all borrowing his consumption of beer per capita figures.[7] The accepted account is that consumption, as a consequence of high taxation and pressure upon working-class living standards, fell sharply between 1800 and 1830; that it did not improve markedly before the mid-1850s; and that for the next twenty years an increasingly urban population celebrated its newly won prosperity in mid-Victorian Britain by consuming amounts of beer at a level more than 50 per cent higher per head than in the 1830s. After

[7] Wilson, *Alcohol and the Nation*, pp. 331–2.; for the calculations by Leone Levi (who was Professor of Commerce and Commercial Law at King's College, London) see below, p. 183.

1880, although real wages were increasing appreciably as a consequence of falling prices in the last quarter of the nineteenth century, drink consumption eased, possibly as a consequence of temperance propaganda but more probably because the working-class male began to look beyond the pub for his leisure. The railways, sports, music hall and a whole range of cheap mass-manufactured goods opened up new horizons. But at least before 1914, beer was not toppled from its place in working-class lives.

This account, which fits so neatly two of the great fixed points of nineteenth-century social history – declining (or scarcely advancing) working-class living standards before the late 1840s, and the growth of recreational opportunities for the majority of workers after the 1870s – has one central weakness. The fall in consumption between 1800 and 1830 is well understood. But how could per capita levels have increased by over half between the 1830s and 1870s unless Sydney Smith and all those magistrates so horrified by the Beer Act were talking through their hats in the 1830s? Was the new industrial society, dedicated to hard work and an increasing precision in its labours, being launched on a torrent of beer? The answers seem to lie in a loose interpretation of G. B. Wilson's consumption-per-head figures. For the period 1800–29 he calculated these for *England and Wales* only. Then in 1830 he switched his series to the *United Kingdom* (including Ireland) as a whole. The effect is pronounced, as Table 2.3. shows. In *England and Wales* he reckoned consumption was around 34 gallons per head in 1800–4; by 1825–9 it had fallen to 28.4 gallons. His post-1830 *United Kingdom* series suggests it declined catastrophically to 21.7 gallons in 1830–4, and did not recover before mid-century. A leading historian of the standard of living could therefore conclude: 'This method [calculations from the malt tax], carefully employed by Dr. George Wilson, indicates a fall in beer consumption from the beginning of the century down to 1851.'[8] What Wilson did was calculate consumption for the United Kingdom as a whole *after* 1830, ignoring the fact that Scotland and Ireland were not essentially beer-drinking countries. In 1840 they together produced a mere 7.7 per cent of United Kingdom beer – for populations representing 40.6 per cent of the total. Even by 1913 the Customs and Excise reckoned that both countries only consumed 10.7 per cent of the total standard barrelage of the United Kingdom.[9] And

[8] J. Burnett, *Plenty and Want* (1966), p. 11.
[9] Wilson, *Alcohol and the Nation*, p. 226.

Table 2.3. *Per capita consumption of beer in gallons for the United Kingdom and England and Wales, 1800–1913 (annual averages)*

	United Kingdom	England and Wales
1800–04	–	33.9
1805–09	–	32.8
1810–14	–	30.2
1815–19	–	28.0
1820–24	–	29.0
1825–29	–	28.4
1830–34	21.7	33.8
1835–39	22.9	35.4
1840–44	19.5	30.5
1845–49	19.4	29.2
1850–54	21.1	29.5
1855–59	22.0	29.3
1860–64	24.7	31.6
1865–69	28.8	35.9
1870–74	31.1	38.2
1875–79	33.2	40.5
1880–84	29.1	33.6
1885–89	28.3	32.5
1890–94	29.7	33.4
1895–99	31.2	34.5
1900–04	30.2	34.3
1905–09	27.3	30.9
1910–13	26.9	29.4

Source: Wilson, *Alcohol and the Nation*, pp. 331–3, 369–70; Mitchell and Deane, *Abstract of British Historical Statistics* (1962), pp. 8–10.

English beer was not pouring into either: there was, after 1830, a net outflow from both sources. It is possible to argue that evasion of the malt duties after 1830 was more rampant in the farthest flung corners of both countries, but in reality *United Kingdom* consumption per capita figures severely depress those for *England and Wales*, the great beer-drinking centres of the United Kingdom.[10]

If, instead, calculations are made solely for *England and Wales* (the second column of Table 2.3.) between 1800 and 1914 a series is obtained that makes a good deal more sense than those historians have relied

[10] For a discussion of the significance of malt tax evasion in Ireland, see P. Lynch and J. Vaizey, *Guinness's Brewery in the Irish Economy, 1759–1876* (1960), pp. 81–3.

upon to date.[11] Essentially, it shows that levels of consumption in the 1830s were far higher than indicated in Wilson's *United Kingdom* averages – so heavily weighted by Ireland's large pre-famine population. A massive 33.8 gallons per head – more than the peak United Kingdom level for the late 1870s – is much more consistent with the reality of the Beer Act and its creation of 40,000 new retail outlets opened solely for the sale of beer in the 1830s. And advances between the late-1840s and the late-1870s are still marked, not in terms of an implausible 71 per cent increase but of one of under 40 per cent. Reduced per capita consumption in the 1840s and 1850s, and again after 1880, complies with what we know about pressures upon living standards in the former period and the impact of 'counter-attractions' in the latter – when it was reduced by rather more than a quarter from its late 1870s peak to the outbreak of the First World War. The table raises two key questions. Why, when levels of consumption were already high, did they increase sharply between the late 1850s and the late 1870s? Why did they not recover thereafter when living standards continued to rise appreciably at least to 1900?

The first question closely relates to a broader issue many Victorians pondered. What made men drink so much alcohol in the first place? The temperance reformers knew. It was the easy availability of drink in over 100,000 public houses and beer shops and an all-pervasive drink culture. Joseph Livesey, the Preston teetotal leader, believed in 1828 there was no escape from its treadmill. 'The fashion of drinking begins with us at our birth and follows us till we are laid in the grave.'[12] He was right in maintaining that high levels of consumption were traditional in Britain, but there were other causes besides the handiness of pubs and the force of custom and celebration. Contemporaries always mentioned the climate and the way the seasons affected consumption levels. And

11 Of course, these are minimum estimates. Private brewing was important before *c.* 1860, although by no means all its output evaded excise payments since private brewers frequently bought their materials from public maltsters. After 1830 there was a growing 'import' of beers from Ireland and Scotland. It should not be exaggerated before 1850. Guinness were selling 250,000 barrels a year in England by 1875; the Scottish brewers considerably less according to Donnachie's observations about their English trade in the late nineteenth century (Lynch and Vaizey, *Guinness's Brewery*, p. 230; I. Donnachie, *A History of the Brewing Industry in Scotland* (1979), pp. 214–21). And it was not a one-way trade: the Burton brewers especially had considerable sales in both countries.

12 Quoted in Wilson, *Alcohol and the Nation*, p. 230. This sentiment and phraseology makes a nice parallel with Adam Smith: 'desire of bettering our condition ... comes with us from the womb, and never leaves us till we go into the grave'. A. Smith, *Wealth of Nations*, Glasgow edn by R. H. Campbell and A. S. Skinner, Oxford, 1976, II.iii. p. 28.

Table 2.4. *Drunkenness proceedings in classified districts, 1891–1931 (rate per 10,000 population)*

	1891	1911	1931
Seaports	157.1	99.1	22.2
Mining counties	108.4	61.6	8.4
Metropolis	57.2	85.5	23.9
Manufacturing towns	72.0	61.7	13.5
Spas and resorts	30.0	27.1	9.2
Agricultural counties	22.2	15.9	4.4
Home Counties	24.2	15.8	2.9

Source: Wilson, *Alcohol and the Nation*, pp. 437–8.

water supplies, remaining hazardous to health before public health measures made an impact in the 1870s, especially encouraged the drinking of weaker small or 'table' beers. Work practices were frequently laborious and beer was widely believed to aid the heaviest labour. Moreover, it provided nutrition, albeit in expensive form. The medical profession almost universally prescribed alcohol for the relief of various conditions before the 1870s. It believed beer, especially stouts and the Burton ales, constituted an excellent tonic. These were all causes sustaining high levels of consumption, and dating back to the previous century and beyond.[13] But what the sharper observer began to pick out in the discussion about drink levels was the impact of the growth of towns upon working-class lives.

The United Kingdom in 1830, although urbanising more rapidly than any other European country, was still predominantly rural. Besides London there were a mere seven towns with populations of more than 100,000, and only nineteen above 50,000. But as Britain industrialised quickly after the 1830s its rate of urbanisation increased appreciably. Fifty years later, by 1881, there were no fewer than fifty cities boasting populations of more than 100,000. Including Greater London, 38 per cent of Britain's population was congregated in them. By the end of the century four-fifths of it could be designated urban – almost a complete reversal of the balance a century earlier. This most profound of all Victorian social changes therefore provided a crucial opening for the

[13] For a fuller discussion of these issues, see Harrison, *Drink and the Victorians*, chapters 2 and 14.

brewing industry: a shifting, rapidly increasing population which created an unprecedented market for common brewers. Philip Snowden, the Labour politician, writing in 1908, thought 'the drink question in our country resolves itself into grappling with the traffic as a town problem'. Indeed he believed, 'the temperance agitation arose with the growth of modern towns'.[14] Those, like Snowden, who identified the Victorian drink question as fundamentally urban in its roots, based their opinions upon three observations. First, when prohibition was attempted in half a dozen states in America after the 1850s, it patently only worked in remote rural areas, leaving untouched the far greater urban problem. Secondly, when the statistics of drunkenness proceedings in Britain (favourites with temperance reformers) were surveyed they revealed a pronounced urban and industrial dimension. Indeed, as Table 2.4. shows, there was a predictable hierarchy of prosecutions. Clear-cut as they might appear, these statistics must, as Harrison insists, be treated with great caution. Commenting upon a dramatic, threefold surge in proceedings between 1857 and 1876, he wrote: 'it is doubtful whether they reliably indicate changing levels of drunkenness, still less of drink consumption', because they fluctuated wildly from year to year in London. Moreover, the great differences revealed between Durham and Lancashire on the one hand and the Home Counties on the other seemed implausible.[15] Why should prosecutions in Liverpool in 1870 be almost ten times those in Birmingham? Clearly a good deal depended upon the varying reactions of police and magistrates to the surge in consumption in the 1860s and 1870s and to the drink question generally. Nevertheless, for contemporaries, they underlined the marked urban dimension of alcohol consumption. Thirdly, there was a growing acknowledgement that urbanisation created the conditions that encouraged heavy drinking. In the vast new towns of early and mid-Victorian Britain, housing conditions were frequently grim for the working classes. Overcrowded with children and, often, lodgers, the menfolk, subject to long hours of work often of a casual nature, found the bars and club rooms of public houses havens of comparative warmth and companionship. Even *The Times* acknowledged this line of argument: 'a man drinks, not only because his brute nature is strong and craves the stimulus, but because he has no other interests, and must do something; or because his home is uncomfortable

[14] Snowden, *Socialism and the Drink Question*, pp. 123–4.
[15] Harrison, *Drink and the Victorians*, p. 315.

Table 2.5. *Per capita expenditure upon alcohol in the United Kingdom, 1820–1913 (in £s)*

	Hoyle	Burns	Prest		Hoyle	Burns	Prest
1820	2.43	–	–	1875	4.36	4.36	4.00
1825	2.97	–	–	1880	3.55	3.61	4.37
1830	2.82	–	–	1884	3.54	3.51	4.24
1835	3.15	–	–	1890	–	3.65	4.23
1840	2.94	3.02	–	1895	–	3.64	4.12
1845	2.65	2.65	–	1899	–	4.00	4.54
1850	2.94	2.98	–	1905	–	–	4.00
1855	2.73	2.53	–	1910	–	–	3.63
1860	2.93	2.90	–	1913	–	–	3.82
1865	3.56	3.56	–				
1870	3.80	3.80	4.19				

Source: Hoyle's figures from Wilson, *Alcohol and the Nation*, p. 223; Burns's from *Alliance News*, 1 March 1900; Prest, *Consumers' Expenditure*, pp. 75, 85; population statistics from Mitchell and Deane, *Abstract*, p. 8–10.

and his life dull, and he needs some real enjoyment; or because he is fond of Company, and only wishes to be like the rest'.[16]

These observations about beer drinking as a time-honoured thirst quencher, a panacea of physical and psychological pressures in a harsh new urban and industrial world, now require relating more precisely to the figures of real wages and overall consumption patterns in the half-century after 1830. The data about expenditure upon alcohol are far from perfect. There are at least two series that temperance advocates relied upon; both include spending upon wine and spirits. Prest's calculations for 1870–1914 are also given, although they seem too high, especially in the light of Leone Levi's comment in 1872 that Hoyle's well-known contemporary estimates were liberal (Table 2.5).[17]

What do these average-per-head figures mean? Certainly all those interested in the drink question wanted to manipulate them to tackle the issues of working-class spending on alcohol and the relationship between drink and poverty.[18] The difficulty is, of course, that they

[16] *The Times*, 10 Oct. 1873.
[17] Wilson, *Alcohol and the Nation*, p. 223–5.
[18] Good discussions of the Victorian drink question will be found in Harrison, *Drink and the Victorians*, especially chapters 2, 14, 15; Wilson, *Alcohol and the Nation*, pp. 223–70; R. B. Weir, 'The Drink Trades', in R. Church (ed.), *The Dynamics of Victorian Business* (1980), pp. 212–35; Rowntree and Sherwell, *Temperance Problem*,

indicate *average* spending upon all forms of alcohol. Baxter, Levi, Jevons, Rowntree and Sherwell made a number of assumptions of variable plausibility to unravel Hoyle's figures – which, though commanding widespread acceptance at the time, were only informed guesses. The working class, three-quarters of the population, consumed two-thirds of all forms of alcohol – which meant, according to a British Association Committee in 1882, three-quarters of all beer and spirits (explaining why the output series for both were in such close unison between 1870 and 1914) and a mere 10 per cent of wines.[19] Even if these parameters were roughly accurate, it left open the question of abstainers, children and women. Rowntree and Sherwell reckoned the abstainers to be at least 3 million in 1899. Children under 15 (35 per cent of the population) were considered not to drink any form of alcohol; and women, more improbably, were assumed to consume half the quantity of men. On the basis of these calculations Rowntree and Sherwell reckoned that in 1899 the average adult male consumption was 76 gallons of beer, 2.57 gallons of spirits and 0.96 of wine.[20] If the assumptions made by Rowntree and Sherwell are projected backwards, the figures are 72 gallons for 1844 (an average year of the 1840s) and 103 gallons (a hefty 16 pints a week) in the peak year of 1876, or in terms of expenditure £5.4 and £7.6 a year per head respectively on beer alone.

Again, all these figures are approximate averages that should not be pressed too far. Moreover, there was clearly a great difference in consumption between regions and occupations, whatever the shortcomings of the drunkenness proceedings figures (Table 2.4). Rowntree produced a survey of the alcohol consumption of 9,613 workers in 1899. On the one hand, workers in cocoa factories – presumably under the eagle eyes of his own Quaker family and friends – spent 1s 6d (7.5p) a week, whilst, on the other, dockers at the Albert docks – only eight were inveigled into completing the questionnaire – spent a massive 8s 4½d (41.9p). The sample average was 3s 8½d (18.3p).[21] Dudley Baxter thirty years earlier believed a 'temperate town workman' (i.e. labourer), earning £50–£60 a year, would spend, with his wife, 2s to 2s 6d a week on 75 gallons of beer a year and a modest amount (1–2 gallons) of spirits,

especially chapters 1 and 9; Snowden, *Socialism and the Drink Question*; E. A. Pratt, *The Licensed Trade: An Independent Survey* (1907); A. E. Dingle, 'Drink and Working Class Living Standards in Britain, 1870–1914', *Economic History Review*, 2nd ser. 25 (1972), pp. 608–22.

19 Rowntree and Sherwell, *Temperance Problem*, p. 10.

20 *Ibid.*, p. 6.

21 *Ibid.*, pp. 14–20, 616.

whilst the family of 'a temperate artisan', with £90–£100 a year, would spend 4s 6d to 5s (22.5p–25p) a week, equivalent to 150 gallons of beer and 2.4 gallons of spirits a year.[22] Both estimates reveal high intakes of beer around 1870 (which all contemporaries acknowledged) and underline the fact that beer was the largest item of working-class expenditure, ranking well above amounts spent upon meat or bread. Late Victorian observers believed that somewhere between 14 and 25 per cent of working-class incomes was spent on drink. Although the figure declined appreciably – from around 15 per cent in 1876 to about 9 per cent by 1908 according to A. E. Dingle – it was the expenditure of the poorest, accounting perhaps for as much as a quarter of their incomes, that was alarming and led to the more extreme calculations.[23] In fact, Charles Booth's survey of labouring life in East London and Seebohm Rowntree's in York effectively quashed the charge that drink was the prime cause of poverty. Surveying some 4,000 cases, Booth demonstrated that drink and thriftlessness accounted for only 14 per cent of the poverty in the East End. Rowntree's 1899 analysis of primary poverty among 7,230 inhabitants in York did not cite drink at all – although of the 13,072 persons in secondary poverty the 'immediate causes' were 'Drink, betting and gambling, ignorant or careless housekeeping, and other improvident expenditure, the latter often induced by irregularity of income.'[24] As Snowden concluded in his comments on these figures, the real cause of heavy drinking was not poverty itself but 'poverty of leisure, poverty of knowledge ... those who maintain that drink is the main cause of poverty know little of the extent of poverty'.[25]

However heated the debate became it was universally agreed that levels of consumption had advanced appreciably in the 1860s and 1870s. The figures (Table 2.3) for England and Wales suggest a growth in per capita beer consumption from around 29 gallons in the 1840s and 1850s to over 40 in the late 1870s. This is explained by two phenomena. First, there was after the early 1850s a marked advance in money wages, especially pronounced between 1860 and 1874, which outstripped rises in real wages.[26] Secondly, the working classes spent a good deal of their increased earnings upon alcohol. Again the contemporary explanation is

[22] R. D. Baxter, *The Taxation of the United Kingdom* (1869), pp. 112–13, 169–70.
[23] Dingle, 'Drink and Living Standards', p. 611. Rowntree and Sherwell were convinced 'every working class family spent on an average in 1899 ... on alcoholic liquor a sum [six shillings] ... equal to nearly one-fifth of the entire family income' (*Temperance Problem*, p. 10).
[24] Quoted in Snowden, *Socialism and the Drink Question*, p. 89.
[25] *Ibid.*, p. 51.
[26] Dingle, 'Drink and Living Standards', p. 616.

partial. There were those like Charles Roberts, an MP and leading temperance advocate, who believed that 'in fat years the first thought of John Bull is to take the spare cash he finds in his pocket and spend it in the public house'.[27] The President of the Liverpool Chamber of Commerce in 1879, explaining the increase in consumption of the 1870s, thought 'the rise of wages coming upon a class of men ill-prepared for it, was a positive evil of the highest degree'.[28] The facts were that levels did advance because the average workmen at this stage had few other leisure opportunities in the new towns, and that in Dingle's word's, 'it is likely that the peak of drink consumption in the 1870s was a response to a situation in which purchasing power had temporarily outstripped the supply of consumer goods available, once basic needs had been satisfied'.[29] In other words, at least for the skilled, higher-income, wage earners, the pub provided opportunities both for leisure and for a less restrictive and dreary diet. In these circumstances, the 1860s and 1870s were wonderful years for those commercial brewers beginning to improve their range of beers and extend their tied house holdings.

After the late 1870s the equation was reversed. Real wages, except in six sticky years from 1876 to 1882 (when beer production fell by some 18.3 per cent in terms of standard barrels), advanced to 1900: not because money wages outdistanced prices as between 1850 and 1875, but for the reason that prices generally fell very sharply during the depression of the 1880s and 1890s. As Hobsbawm showed, although money wages in many years did not advance at all, living standards of the *entire* working classes rose.[30] But for the first time they did not expend this increase upon alcohol. And after 1900, when the advance in real wages lost its momentum as prices exceeded wage rises, the trend intensified. What were its causes?

First a warning: the movement should not be exaggerated. In England and Wales consumption fell back from its all-time high of 42.1 gallons per head in 1876 to an average of 29.4 in the years 1910–13. This lower level was simply a return to those of the 1840s and 1850s which have never been represented as ones of modest consumption. Drinkers had not turned away from the national beverage in 1914. Nevertheless,

[27] Quoted in K. Hawkins, 'The Conduct and Development of the Brewing Industry in England and Wales, 1880–1938' (unpublished University of Bradford PhD thesis, 1981), p. 6.

[28] Quoted in Dingle, 'Drink and Living Standards', p. 615.

[29] *Ibid.*, p. 618.

[30] E. J. Hobsbawm, *Labouring Men* (1968 edn), pp. 293–4; and his *Industry and Empire* (1969), p. 162.

this decline in per capita consumption and the inappreciable rise after 1876 in production, even in peak years in the late 1890s and 1913–14, worried brewers. Company chairmen after 1900 frequently lamented the trend. The managing director of Greene King was typical, thinking in 1904 there was 'a tendency amongst the public not to use the Public Houses as formerly'; and in 1908 putting the firm's declining barrelage down to 'the decreased consumption of drink amongst all classes'.[31]

Historians have offered a whole raft of explanations for the decrease. Most are generally agreed that the role of temperance propaganda, and the way the drink question was constantly kept before the public after 1870 – by a series of discussions about local veto, by Royal Commissions and by legislation after 1900 – was not central.[32] As late as 1909 the *Brewers' Manual* roundly opined: 'Beer consumption is the readiest index available of the prosperity or penury of the working classes.'[33] This suggests that shifts in consumption are to be explained primarily in terms of the fluctuating fortunes of the predominant industry in any locality. Yet clearly after the 1880s important breaks with the past were occurring in people's spending decisions. Some of the background factors to these are difficult to locate with any precision. The changing perception of beer, away from the old view that it induced strength and was medically beneficial, was important. The decline in the consumption of alcohol amongst the upper and middle classes appears to have set in during the 1870s, primarily as a result of changing social habits, then, by a demonstration effect (exactly as in matters of family limitation), the habit slowly percolating through the skilled working class. Certainly, most commentators were agreed that the periodic heavy drinking binges, which had been such a feature of labourers' lives, were diminishing. There was greater sobriety at work; 'Saint Monday' retreating as the Saturday half-day became more common.[34] All this fits Dingle's argument that the timing of the shift in drink consumption patterns was determined in the main by changes in the supply of consumer goods. A whole range of cheaper articles, often imported, was made available by improved retailing and distribution methods. Even a cursory glance at the popular and provincial press around the turn of the century makes this explanation convincing. Suddenly from the late 1880s newspapers come alive with the line drawings and bold print of advertisements for

[31] Wilson, *Greene King*, pp. 131, 135.
[32] Harrison, *Drink and the Victorians*, pp. 317–18.
[33] Quoted in Wilson, *Alcohol and the Nation*, p. 234.
[34] Harrison, *Drink and the Victorians*, chapter 14.

mass-produced clothing and shoes, machine-produced furniture, and packaged foodstuffs. Chairs and brass bedsteads, boots and corsets were the spearhead of this consumer revolution.

Of course there were other origins of the shift away from drink consumption. A significant factor was that the price of beer remained unchanged. In comparison with foodstuffs – whose prices sharply declined in the 1880s and 1890s – it became relatively expensive (see pp. 207–11). This was crucially important in a period when money wages were not increasing. Large discounts to publicans and the 'long pull' did not disguise the fact that beer prices remained essentially the same. And little advertising, except by the great bottling brewers – Bass, Allsopp and Whitbread – was undertaken before 1914. Therefore, not surprisingly in these conditions, especially given the temperance context, the consumption of its main competitors in family budgets both made more headway after 1870. Tea imports increased by 160 per cent between 1870 and 1913. Spending upon tobacco grew from £13.5 to £40.3 million in the same period.[35] These statistics gladdened the hearts of temperance activists who also pointed to the impact of increased leisure opportunities. Hours of work began slowly to decrease, especially with Saturday half-days becoming usual by the 1890s. The working classes were increasingly able to enjoy the benefits of cheap travel, by rail, tram and bicycle, as well as a variety of sporting and open-air activities. Parks proliferated in the improving cities. Thrift and self-education – middle-class-propelled movements – became realisable goals, at least for those skilled workers in full employment. Austen Chamberlain, Chancellor of the Exchequer, summarised the whole movement when he explained the effects of declining liquor consumption in his Budget speech of 1905:

> I think the mass of our people are beginning to find other ways of expending some portion of the time and money which used previously to be spent in the public house. No change has been more remarkable in the habits of the people than the growing attendance in the last fifteen years at outdoor games and sports, and large places of public entertainment like theatres, music-halls and so forth, which, though not conducted on strictly temperance lines, do not lend themselves to the consumption of drink or offer it as their chief attraction. Again, the extension of cheap railway fares and the enormous growth in cheap excursions absorb a further portion of the money which used formerly to be spent on drink.[36]

[35] A. R. Prest, *Consumers' Expenditure in the United Kingdom, 1900–1919* (1954), pp. 69–72, 89–91.

[36] Quoted in Wilson, *Alcohol and the Nation*, pp. 241–2.

Chamberlain was commenting upon the origins of a profound social revolution. But its effects, at least before 1914, should not be exaggerated. Until then, sport and the active pursuit of leisure remained substantially middle-class quests.[37] Changes in the pattern of consumption – by a better fed, better clothed and better housed working class – are more persuasive in explaining the per capita contraction in beer drinking in the forty years after 1875. With adaptation to changing technology, especially the radio and cinema, Chamberlain's analysis best expounds the much faster down-turn which came in the forty years after the Great War. Whatever the precise causes of the origins of this secular decline in beer consumption between 1880 and 1960 – and these will always be debatable – its effects were sufficiently pronounced before 1914 to convince many brewers after the 1880s that the only way forward was by the wholesale acquisition of tied outlets and the absorption of smaller rivals.

III

No aspect of the history of brewing is more difficult to reconstruct than changes in taste of more than a century ago. In no other area is exactitude a more elusive goal. Yet contemporaries were adamant that significant shifts did take place in the types of beer consumed in Victorian Britain. But the precise timing, the degree of change in strength, colour and flavour of the main beers – porter and stout, strong, mild and pale ales – is impossible to reconstruct with precision. And the questions surrounding how these tastes were created and shifted are also indefinite. Clearly, changes in social habits and work practices, and the impact of temperance reforms, of alterations in taxation, of imports of lighter beers (tiny as these were) from the Continent after 1870, of fashions for a particular beer, influenced brewers in their decisions about the beers they produced. They were adamant, however, that the real force in determining taste was the consumer not the brewer. Thomas Fowell Buxton, pondering in 1811 on what determined the success of a particular porter brewery in London, believed 'it is the customer who ultimately decides'.[38] W. L. Tizard, self-styled 'Pro-

[37] H. Meller, *Leisure and the Changing City, 1870–1914* (1976), p. 206–36.

[38] GLRO, Acc. 73.36, B/THB, 'T. F. Buxton's Book of Observations' (1811–16); W. L. Tizard, *The Theory and Practice of Brewing* (2nd edn, 1846), pp. 133–4. But Tizard continued 'it is, however, in the power of the skilful brewer to improve the quality of such beer by gradual means, which he may do almost imperceptibly until the public and himself will be equally gratified'.

fessor of Brewing' thought in 1845, 'the brewer is in great measure bound to conform to the will and taste of his customers . . . as the market is, so must be the commodity'. Buxton was convinced that the consumer would always seek out the best beer. Producers are fond of ascribing sovereignty to the consumer, but many a brewer realised to his cost that preference could and did change.[39]

It is an oversimplification to represent beer production in 1830 as consisting of porter (essentially a weak stout) in London and old, vatted, 'stock' or winter-brewed beers in the provinces. Certainly any meaningful difference in nomenclature between beer and ale had disappeared more than a century earlier, but considerable variations between beers in the various regions had not.

> How different, for instance, is the ale brewed in Scotland from that produced in the South and West of England! Who is there in Britain that cannot discover a difference of flavour and gust between the London and Dublin porter? Who that has travelled would expect to find the London taste in Newcastle ale, or either of these in the ales prepared at Liverpool, Lincoln, Nottingham, Sheffield, Birmingham, Derby, the Staffordshire potteries, Maidstone, Dorchester, Devonport, Alton or North or South Wales? The eighty seven brewers of Manchester supply as many varieties of flavour and excellence, but still it is all Manchester ale. Each respective article in any of these places if of good quality, is preferred by the local consumers 'of the cheer' generally, to every other that in their opinion can be brewed.[40]

Yet, like wine writers today, brewers and drinkers alike found it difficult to describe the distinctive qualities of their regional beers. Moreover, the ledgers of contemporary common brewers show that most produced a variety of beers even if they were aimed at the particular taste of their locality. Bentley's of Woodlesford for instance, only two years in business by 1830, produced in that year five beers: three ales of varying strength, a porter and a 'best stout porter'.[41] Georges, primarily porter-brewers in Bristol at this stage, also produced ales at various prices, and indicated, at least to their foreign customers, that they were prepared to experiment with brewing a strong mild Taunton ale and a lighter-coloured, heavily hopped Burton ale.[42] No doubt publican brewers, restricted both in their capital and their facilities for storage, produced only the ale of their region. But whatever the variety – whether pale and bitter as in the celebrated Burton ales, mature and sharp as in East

[39] H. A. Monckton, *A History of English Ale and Beer* (1966), p. 144.
[40] Tizard, *Theory and Practice*, p. 133. See also *Brewers' Journal*, 15 Nov. 1900.
[41] Whitbread Archives, 288/72, Bentley's Sales Ledger, 1828–32.
[42] Courage Archives (Bristol), 35740/GR/5, Georges' Foreign Letter Book, 1818–35.

Anglia, or sweet and mild as in the North-East – all these beers were strong. They were the product of traditional tastes, themselves the results of centuries of combinations of local malts, water, yeast and brewing practices; they met the demand for the heavy, irregular bouts of drinking in the pre-industrial calendar; they kept out the cold before the railways made coal fires usual. Lacking in quality what they made up for in strength, they were not ideal for either regular or, especially, summer consumption. Only porter and the cheapest milds (both frequently diluted by indigent publicans) and, of course, the light table or small beers were weaker.

This beer map of the 1830s, porter in the capital and some of the bigger cities and an infinite variety of strong ales in the regions, appears to have changed in two ways in the next half century. The first was an increasing demand for mild, sweet ales. Again London, partly since its water was ideally suited to its production, appears to have taken the lead in this. A witness to the 1833 Committee on the Sale of Beer thought that the London beer drinker now

> will have nothing but what is mild, and that has caused a considerable revolution in the trade, so much so that Barclay and Perkins, and other great houses, finding that there is a decrease in the consumption of porter, and an increase in the consumption of ale, have gone into the ale trade; nearly all the new trade is composed of mild ale.[43]

To the 1870s at least, the two beers, porter (itself now vatted for shorter periods) and mild, vied with each other as the most popular tipple in the metropolis. Around the turn of the century they still remained the two bulk beers produced by Truman. 'It is strange', wrote a visitor to Cobb's Margate brewery in 1875, 'how the taste of these days [the French Wars, 1793–1815] for old stale beer has turned to the opposite extreme in the liking for new and sweet by the present generation.'[44] Barnard, the chief chronicler of the British beer industry in the early 1890s, accounting for the success of Mann, Crossman & Paulin as the fastest-growing London ale brewers of the mid-Victorian period, thought 'the fickle public has got tired of the vinous flavoured vatted porter and transferred its affections to the new and luscious mild ale'.[45] Like porter, retailing at 4d or 5d a quart pot, it was cheap beer much in

[43] SCHC on the Sale of Beer, p. 230, Q3906.
[44] *Licensed Victuallers' Gazette*, 4 Dec. 1875.
[45] A. Barnard, *Noted Breweries of Great Britain and Ireland*, I (1889), p. 378. For Barnard's survey of the industry see Chapter 3, n. 97.

demand by the first two generations of unsophisticated drinkers in the big industrial towns.

The second shift in beer tastes was the demand for Burton ales. After the 1840s the railways made Burton India export bitter (an innovation of the post-1815 years) available in rapidly increasing quantities (see pp. 89–98). But Burton beer was never a cheap drink, selling at 7d or 8d a quart. Quality and cost, however, made it a status drink for the expanding lower middle class of clerks and shopkeepers, the armies of rail travellers, and those 'aristocrats of labour' whose standards of living rose appreciably after 1850. The other factor in its impact on beer tastes was the ease with which a generation of country brewers succeeded in imitating, usually more cheaply, its light, sparkling, bitter qualities. Making a good Burton-type ale was the *sine qua non* for that generation of brewers who reaped the rewards of the great increase of consumption in the 1860s and 1870s. When Edward Greene, a celebrated East Anglian brewer and MP, died in 1891 after fifty-five years in the business, the *London Star* commented: 'He was one of the first country brewers to discover that beer need not be vile, black, turgid stuff, but brewed a bright amber-coloured liquid of Burton type which he sold at a shilling per gallon, and made a fortune.'[46]

Neither the milds (which were usually lighter in colour and less easy to adulterate than the cloudy black London porter) nor the pale ales were weak beers, although they were less strong than the old vatted ales which went increasingly out of favour in the 1860s and 1870s – except in rural pockets like South-West England and Suffolk. Strength was not seriously impaired, because the malt tax between 1830 and 1880 was levied uniformly on all qualities of malt; brewers therefore having no incentive to use anything but the best malts which gave them the finest extracts.[47] Moreover, although the mild and bitter ales were not vatted, they remained heavily hopped. British beer was unusual both in its

[46] Quoted in his obituary both in the *Brewers' Journal* and the *Bury and Norwich Post*, 21 April 1891. A visitor to Greene's brewery in 1875 commented that his real pride was his best bitter, 'For without flattery this ale is equal to any of the kind we have tasted, and though, of course, not possessing the exact flavour of the Burton beers, which is just now fashionable, is full of character and flavour of its own, which to many palates would be even preferable' (*Bury and Norwich Post*, 17 April 1875).

[47] A Mr Lawrence who addressed a Brewing Congress on 'The Beer of the Future' (*Brewing Trade Review*, 1 Dec. 1886) believed, however, reductions in the strength of beer began as early as the mid-1850s, 'At the time of the Crimean War the Malt Duty was increased by 4s per quarter ... and the running beers were reduced from 24½ lbs gravity to 22 lb ... From that time to the present the tendency has been towards a decrease in the strength of beer, and an increase in the demand for the light bitter beers and beers of the kind as mentioned by Dr. Graham as the conversational beers.'

strength and, contemporaries maintained, its narcotic effect – encouraging drowsiness or stupefaction as the temperance reformers preferred – which generous hopping produced. Such beer, best suited to winter celebration and sustenance, met with increasing strictures both from the temperance lobby and from importers of British beer in America and the Colonies. The latter demanded star-bright, lager beers which spread everywhere in the United States and on the Continent after the 1850s and in Australia forty years later. Our export beers, a critic averred in 1890, contained 'too much alcohol, too much sediment, too much hops and too little gas'. In Britain the effects of export demand were indirect, but nevertheless important. 'Lager beer in this country', wrote the editor of the *Brewers' Journal* in 1890, 'has certainly not realised the future prophesied for it some years back. That this is so is in great measure attributable to the competition it at once met with at the hands of English brewers, who altered the character of their beers to meet the demands of the times.'[48]

After the 1880s this demand for weaker, brighter beers was by and large met by brewers. A Birmingham brewer writing in 1907 is worth quoting at length:

> I have known Birmingham intimately during a period extending over fifty five years . . . At the commencement of the time mentioned there was scarcely a 'tied' house in the town; nearly every licensee brewed his own malt liquors. At that period 90 per cent of the working men got drunk on Saturday night; drunkenness was common all the week through, and there was no interference with a drunken man by the police unless he became violent. With the imperfect system of brewing in the public-houses, the insanitary condition of the brew-houses, and the unsuitable appliances, the beers brewed were mostly of inferior quality and more alcoholic than is the case now, strong ales being specially demanded by the customers. Since the brewers have had more control over the houses, beers have undergone a great improvement, for with the aid of scientific knowledge, hygienic breweries and suitable appliances, they have succeeded in producing beers containing 25 per cent less of alcohol than the beers formerly retailed in Birmingham public-houses. Those now produced are more wholesome, less intoxicating, lighter in character, more palatable, more nutritious, of lighter and better condition, and more suitable for general consumption. Such beers have gradually won the public taste, and are produced and sold at a much lower cost than the heavy and intoxicating ales of the past.[49]

Making an obvious plea for the benefits of tied trade in the West Midlands, he was correct in identifying nationwide trends. Improved brewing techniques allowed brewers to produce a purer, lighter beer,

[48] *Brewers' Journal*, 15 Feb. 1890.
[49] Quoted in Pratt, *Licensed Trade*, pp. 297–8.

whereas before 1880 they had found it difficult to brew a weaker and yet stable beer. Now, by using first-rate malts, and experimenting with sugar and (after 1880) a proportion of maize and rice substitutes to attain stability and brilliance, they produced good 'running' or 'summer' ales. Never stored, brewed throughout the year – although in summer this could still cause serious problems to 1914 – they remained cheap, partly because the brewers, often receiving payment within a month of mashing his brew, improved his turnover. E. R. Moritz, Consulting Chemist to the Country Brewers' Society, in an article in 1895 on 'The Rush to Running Ales', maintained:

> It is, however, essentially within the last ten years that these lighter ales, both of pale and mild character, have come especially to the front. The public in this period has come to insist more and more strongly upon extreme freshness of palate with a degree of brilliancy and sparkle that our fathers never dreamt of.[50]

Barnard, who was thoroughly up to date in his lack of enthusiasm for the old strong beers, wrote on his visit to Joule's brewery at Stone: 'The growing trade for pale ale is one of the most practical reforms ever wrought, as the spirit contained in it is diluted to a point which makes this pleasant beverage comparatively harmless to both the stomach and the head.'[51] An increasing number of brewers and drinkers were beginning to concur with his views. Another factor in the popularity of light beer was the growing taste for bottled beers after the 1880s. Again, the brewer had to adapt his practices to produce a special light, bright beer – eventually filtered and carbonated – which threw no sediment and retained no cloudiness. Bottled beer was, in comparison with draught, expensive, but excessive competition from the 1890s forced brewers and bottlers into offering massive discounts; and the tendency for people to drink less meant that they could shift their preferences away from the cheapest milds and porters.

Therefore what occurred from around 1880 was a growing demand for lighter beers which were much more uniform in character than those of the 1830s. Again, the trend to uniformity should not be overstated. Many a turn-of-the-century country brewer would have claimed his beers possessed readily identifiable regional characteristics, but in reality these had had to be adapted to the competition of beers with a national distribution: Bass, Allsopp and Worthington from Burton, Guinness from Dublin, Younger's and McEwan's Edinburgh ales, and

[50] *Brewers' Almanack* (1895), p. 153.
[51] Barnard, *Noted Breweries*, III, p. 84.

Whitbread's bottled ales and stouts by 1914. Barnard noted for instance that the two principal Welsh brewers, Brain of Cardiff and Soames of Wrexham, were giving up the spiced, heady Welsh ales in favour of Burton-type beers; and, similarly, Newcastle upon Tyne brewers were switching from sweet milds brewed universally in the 1860s to pale ales of the Burton-Edinburgh varieties.[52] Moreover the widespread practice of bottling by leading brewers and contract bottlers from the 1890s encouraged uniformity of taste. In fact, by the 1880s, most brewers of any scale were producing eight to ten beers. These invariably included a stout and a variety of mild, bitter and pale 'running' ales to meet competitors whether national, regional or local. But by 1900 the brewing press was concentrating its comments upon the growing fashion of running ales, often of a light, 'family' character. Julian Baker, writing in 1905, states the variety and classification of beers in Edwardian Britain succinctly:

> Roughly speaking, they may be divided into strong, medium, and light. In the strong, we may include stock or old ales, and the heavier stouts. The medium, comprises the lighter stouts, superior bitter beers, mild or four-[pence] ale, which latter is still the beverage of the working classes, and porter. The light beers, of which increasing quantities are being brewed every year, are more or less the outcome of the demand of the middle classes for a palatable and easily consumable beverage. A good example of this type of beer is the so-called 'family-ale', and the cheap kinds of bottled bitter beers and porters.[53]

The trend, then, from heavier, sweeter beers to those of a pale, lighter and less heavily hopped nature was clearly identifiable, if somewhat imprecise, by the last decade of the nineteenth century. Once more, however, the reduction in strength should not be pressed too far. The real break comes during and after the Great War as a consequence of raw material controls and undreamt of advances in duties. But the origins of the trend can be traced to the 1880s. In 1880 Gladstone reckoned the *average* original gravity of mild worts, on which beer duty was levied, to be 1057°; in 1889 this standard or average was reduced to 1055° (the basis of taxation to the abolition of the hypothetical standard barrel in 1933). By 1907 E. A. Pratt believed 'that the bulk of the mild ale now produced in this country ... is much nearer 1048° than 1055°'. This was such a marked decline – Pratt reckoned of around 15 to 20 per cent between the early 1880s and 1907 – that he concluded: 'we have the

[52] Barnard, *Noted Brewers*, III, pp. 168–80, 466–81, 524–43. Although in his notice of Barras the Newcastle brewers he noted that the taste for pale ale was primarily urban. Miners in the Durham/Northumberland pit villages still drank strong mild (p. 179).

[53] J. L. Baker, *The Brewing Industry* (1905), pp. 11–12.

important fact that the British working-man's beer of to-day is already practically a temperance beverage'.[54]

Nowhere is the average more meaningless. When Truman in 1902 tested the original and final gravities of the mild ales and porters of their nine chief competitors against their own the results were revealing. The cheap milds varied from 1038° to 1059° (the average, very close to Pratt's, was 1047.6°); for porter from 1044° to Meux's 1077° (1055° average). Their records show that the original gravity of their mild – much the most popular beer they sold – was reduced by some 5.3 per cent between 1897 and 1906.[55] But it is their reaction which is interesting. If Truman had trouble with their beers, or felt that they failed to stand comparison with their chief rivals, they increased their gravities slightly, although they reckoned it cost them £10,000 for each extra degree of original gravity for the 300,000 barrels of their best-selling line.[56] This was the time-honoured practice of good brewers. In general, however, gravities were gently easing downwards, receiving modest fillips when duties increased during the Boer War or materials advanced in price. But they had not crashed, as Pratt suggested. Those days, which old Edwardian brewers recalled, of very variable strong beers brewed without much control, had passed by the 1880s. More 'scientific', lighter beers had taken their place. It was a change that both the consumer and the brewer applauded.

IV

It is difficult to describe the manufacture of beer in the mid-nineteenth century because practices amongst the thousands of brewers varied. Of course, whatever the scale of the brewing, the transformation of malt into beer had to pass through the same three key stages, mashing, boiling and fermentation (see Plate 2). But each stage, for which there was a precise scientific underpinning, enshrined practices that had evolved long before the science of brewing was formulated. Therefore, every brewer jealously guarded inherited secrets which he applied at every point of manufacture. In 1835 Black, in his *Practical Treatise on Brewing*, thought that as a result chemistry – in comparison with its progress in transforming dyeing, calico printing, linen and glass making

[54] Pratt, *Licensed Trade*, pp. 229–30, 241.
[55] GLRO, Acc. 77.94, B/THB, Truman's Monthly Reports, May 1902, March 1906.
[56] *Ibid.* Although in 1902 they reckoned raising gravity 1 lb on 400,000 barrels of ale and porter would cost them £5,000. In 1901 they brewed 337,255 barrels of x ale (mild) and 89,243 of porter.

– had made little progress. A decade later Tizard wrote, 'many operative brewers ... even now ridicule and despise the idea of chemistry being in any way connected with the art of brewing'.[57] Some as a consequence, in the provinces at least, were completely in the dark about even the essential use of the thermometer and saccharometer introduced into leading breweries more than half a century previously. Yet, as these two authors of the most widely used brewing manuals of the mid-Victorian period argued, real progress in producing uniformly good beers for mass consumption would be achieved only if brewers paid scrupulous attention to cleanliness and the elaborate analysis of materials and measurements of heats. What occurred after the 1830s was the evolution of a much greater uniformity of practice based upon an unfolding of scientific explanations. Every Georgian brewer – the London porter brewers very successfully – had retailed a thick, heavy, winter-brewed beer suited to local tastes. The art of brewing by the 1870s was to produce regularly throughout the year a wider range of quick-maturing beers, including light, bright ales – technically a much more difficult feat.

> Improved systems of brewing [wrote a visitor to the Northampton Brewery Company in 1875] cause beers to mature in a period that would have astonished our grandfathers, and old ales are now drunk that have been brewed in less time than was of old required to make the sweetest and mildest ales even moderately drinkable, and men of the time of the Whitbreads, the Meux's and the Calverts who wasted fortunes in building vats each larger than the other would almost turn in their graves could they learn that their successors have their beers fit for consumption in less time than it took to fill their gigantic tuns.[58]

It is the bases of these changes, increasingly bringing together a closer observation of brewing science with modest mechanical advances and unspectacular pieces of engineering, that we must now trace in this account of the three stages of making beer.

It might seem best to begin this section with a discourse on malt. But malt and malting are subjects in themselves. Indeed, the trade was a distinct one, although since most brewers were also maltsters and malt was a prime cost of brewing, this is discussed below in Chapter 5. Here, the assumption is that brewers made or bought varieties of those malts best suited to the different beers they made. This was the foundation of their success. As J. M. Hanbury explained to his fellow Truman directors in 1902, with more truth than eloquence: 'Better barley means more

[57] William Black, *A Practical Treatise on Brewing* (4th edn, 1849), pp. 1–2; Tizard, *Theory and Practice*, pp. vi–vii, 137, 210.

[58] *Licensed Victuallers' Gazette*, 9 Oct. 1875.

weight, better extract, better quality of extract, better beer, increase in trade, decrease in returns, and better reputation.'[59] It is essential at the outset, however, to say something about the brewers' supplies of water.

All breweries had to possess a good water supply in terms of both quantity and quality. For every barrel of beer produced, some fifteen or sixteen barrels of water were necessary by 1900 to carry out the various brewing processes. This could be expensive if the brewery had to draw appreciable amounts from water companies to supplement its own supplies. One large London firm reckoned it cost £7 16s per thousand barrels of beer produced, presenting them with an annual bill of almost £4,000. Guinness's expenditure was rather less, but then they appear to have drawn their water successively from the Poddle and Dodder rivers, the Grand Canal, and, after 1870, the River Vartry.[60] But most brewers relied upon their own wells, at least for their brewing water, and took additional supplies for cooling and washing from rivers and water companies. Technology allowed them to drive wells deeper and deeper in the course of the nineteenth century. Some were surface affairs: Bentley & Shaw of Huddersfield exceptionally used nothing but spring water; Tizard noted that the celebrated wells at Bass's Burton Brewery were no deeper than 24 feet in the early 1840s.[61] Half a century later, their complex of wells ranged from 30 to 190 feet.[62] But in other regions depths were far in excess of this; Truman bored 850 feet deep to tap a purer water beneath the London clay.[63] Requirements everywhere were for waters containing as few organic traces as possible. Consequences could be serious, for such traces tended to produce hasty secondary fermentations which caused running beers to 'kick up' in summer. When in August 1884 Truman's light beers became thoroughly unsound, their Burton brewer who came across to give advice thought both their 'street' and well water was too polluted for ale brewing. He concluded that their mains, which had not been cleaned for years, should be replaced.[64] The problems of organic matter were being successfully tackled by the use of charcoal filters by the 1870s. Southby boldly claimed in 1885 that by the use of Rawling's patent filters he had

59 GLRO, Acc. 77.94, B/THB, Monthly Reports, October 1902.

60 Guinness spent £2,300 in 1876 on their water. Lynch and Vaizey (p. 240) state they were then consuming 750,000 gallons a *day* which seems very high in comparison with the 4,000,000 gallons a *year* Truman used to produce around 500,000 barrels early this century, even though high water costs made them careful.

61 Barnard, *Noted Breweries*, IV, pp. 66–7; Tizard, *Theory and Practice*, p. 116.

62 Barnard, *Noted Breweries*, I, pp. 69–70.

63 *Ibid.*, I, p. 189.

64 GLRO, Acc. 77.94, B/THB, Monthly Reports, August–September 1884.

'succeeded in purifying water containing large amounts of sewage and in brewing excellent beers with the purified waters'.[65] Presumably readership of his tome was restricted to brewers rather than drinkers.

Of course, waters varied considerably; and by the mid-nineteenth century chemical analysis of them was usual. Every brewing manual included obligatory chapters on water and, though they tended to blind their readers with long lists of the different trace minerals found in the waters in various brewing centres, the essential division remained between hard and soft.[66] Burton and London were usually taken to represent the polarities. The former's fame was dependent upon its extremely hard water, filtered through beds of gypsum to give a high content of calcium and magnesium sulphates, allowing high hopping rates, and achieving a good fermentation, to provide unequalled pale ales. In contrast, London well waters, taken deep from beneath the clay bed, had quite different properties. They brought out more fully the saccharine matter from malt to produce full-flavoured stouts and porters. Similarly, Great Yarmouth's waters naturally produced a first-rate mild beer.[67] In few other areas – Tadcaster, Alton and Wrexham were exceptional in almost equalling Burton water – could excellent pale ales be easily produced, but by the 1870s breweries were treating their waters to make tolerable imitations of Burton beers and good running pales and milds. For example, Whitbread began brewing pale ale in 1866 by adding gypsum to their water, a practice rapidly emulated by other London and provincial brewers.[68] Fox's of Farnborough – 'the brewery in the fields' as Barnard labelled it in 1891 – possessed a 'Burtonising tank' with which to treat its water with gypsum taken from the banks of the River Trent.[69] Indeed Barnard conveys the impression that by 1890, given a good deep well, brewers could easily produce the regular range of eight or ten beers, even if it was difficult to produce the exact quality of the best Burton ales. Only in London does Truman's record suggest (hinting that its competitors encountered similar problems) that it was, without perpetual care, more difficult to manufacture, at least in summer, sound running ales. On at least two occasions their water supplies were a principal cause of the problem.

65 E. R. Southby, *A Systematic Handbook of Practical Brewing* (2nd edn, 1885), p. 187.

66 F. Faulkner, *The Art of Brewing* (1875), pp. 3–6.

67 Because they contained 'an extraordinary quantity of chlorides'. Southby, *Practical Brewing*, p. 165.

68 D. M. Knox, 'The Development of the London Brewing Industry, 1830–1914, with Special Reference to Whitbread and Company' (unpublished B.Litt. thesis, University of Oxford, 1956), p. 143.

69 Barnard, *Noted Breweries*, IV, p. 77.

Mashing was the key process in the first stage of the brewing process.[70] In it diastase, a substance carefully cultivated in the malting of barley, was released in water at temperatures below 170°F. This rapidly acted upon the high starch content of the malt to produce 'wort' – essentially a solution of malt sugar. What was required was to obtain the fullest possible extract of this maltose. Quality of malt was all-important, but there was a practical problem in effectively removing all the extract when large quantities of malt were brewed. In London porter breweries, already by 1800, several of the laborious hand processes had been mechanised upon the introduction of the steam engine.[71] After 1830 there were a number of refinements as power mashing became usual in all commercial breweries. Yet the stages whereby they were transformed to become largely mechanised in production is uncertain, for the detailed catalogue of innovation, available after the 1880s through combing company minutes books, has only rarely survived for the key transition phase of the 1830s to 1870s period.[72]

Malt was screened, lightly ground by stones (later by rollers) and conveyed to the grist case by 'archimedean' screws – preparatory processes in which steam power increasingly replaced horse wheels after the 1830s. It was then mixed in the mash tun with liquor (as water is known in breweries), already heated to the required temperature. Mashing still posed several problems for the Victorian brewer. First, there was a choice of materials for the construction of the two mash tuns found in most breweries.[73] Here, as with every type of brewing vessel, there was endless debate about cost, easy cleaning, durability and chemical reaction. Traditionalists swore by best oak. The Scots, dis-

70 This section on the Victorian processes is taken from five widely used contemporary accounts: Black, *Practical Treatise*; Tizard, *Theory and Practice*; Faulkner, *Art of Brewing* (2nd edn 1876); Southby, *Practical Brewing*; E. R. Moritz and G. H. Morris, *A Text Book of the Science of Brewing* (1891). Together they provide a good view of best-practice brewing in Victorian Britain. H. S. Corran, *A History of Brewing* (1975) provides a useful modern survey.

71 Mathias, *Brewing Industry*, pp. 78–98.

72 A study of mechanisation in the industry between the 1810s and 1870s which examined the way horse wheels were replaced by steam engines and the speed with which various mechanical aids were introduced would be useful. The provincial press carried numerous, detailed notices of the sale of brewery plant.

73 The mash tun measured the size of a brewery, sale notices indicating the capacity of the tun in quarters mashed. For example Steward, Head & Co. were selling their 20 quarter plant at St Margaret's Brewery, Ipswich in 1826 (*Bury and Norwich Post*, 15 March 1826). Some were as small as 10 and 15 quarters. At the other end of the scale Truman in 1889 possessed six iron tuns with a total capacity of 700 quarters (Barnard, *Noted Breweries*, I, pp. 187–95).

carding economy, lined theirs with thick copper sheeting. The porter brewers advocated cast iron after 1830. Whatever the material, since the spent grains (dried and fed to cattle) had to be removed by men wielding shovels and a metal false bottom fixed to allow easy drainage, mash tuns had to be of the soundest construction. The second area of discussion was the temperature at which malt was best mashed. The old test had been that water in the tun should be boiled and then cooled to the temperature at which the brewer could first see his reflection in the liquor once the clouds of steam had cleared. Thermometers had come into general use in brewing in the 1780s, but there was no strict agreement about the precise temperature or duration of the mash seventy years later. The Scots brewed at 178°–190°F around 1840 and let their mash 'stand' for as long as four hours.[74] Admittedly, different beers required different temperatures, and in England mashing heats tended to be reduced from the 168°–170°F Black recommended (diastase began to be destroyed above 170°F) in the 1830s to the 144°–154°F Southby advocated half a century later. And by the 1880s tuns tended to be fitted with steam-heated jackets so that temperatures could be exactly maintained during the two hours of the mash.

But the major advance was in the effective mechanisation of washing the extract from the ground malt. Previously this had been achieved by two or three successive mashes – exceptionally five – of the same grains, each, subsequent to the first, producing a weaker second or third wort. This was a laborious process, especially when carried out with the traditional mashing oars. First, mechanical mashing rakes, steam driven in the great London breweries after the 1790s and powered by horse wheels in the provinces, became common in all the bigger breweries after the 1800s.[75] Indeed it was impossible to brew large quantities without them. Then after the 1830s sparging machines, first used widely in Scotland, that sprinkled heated liquor over the mash were introduced. They did not speed up mashing times and it was easy to over-saturate the mash, but they obviated the need for second and third mashes. Both machines saved labour. A further innovation was the use

[74] Donnachie, *Brewing Industry in Scotland*, p. 108.

[75] Mathias, *Brewing Industry*, pp. 93–6. The East Anglian evidence (*Bury and Norwich Post*, 15 March and 4 Oct. 1826; 11 Oct. 1837; 15 Oct. 1845) suggests that mashing machines, invariably driven by horse wheel, were widespread by the 1820s. Sparging, however, appears to have made no progress by 1845. This was not surprising since it met with opposition south of the border. Black decried it, although Tizard, typically, brought out a variant of his own, the 'hystericon'. Black, *Practical Treatise*, p. 64; Tizard, *Theory and Practice*, pp. 181–209; Donnachie, *Brewing Industry in Scotland*, pp. 108–10.

of patent mashing machines to mix the malt and liquor thoroughly – always a problem at the beginning of the first mash when no more than two barrels of liquor were run over each quarter of malt. 'Balling', akin to lumpy porridge on a vast scale, had to be avoided. After 1853 Steel's mashing machine, a simple device based upon earlier prototypes, mixing liquor and malt in a cylinder outside the mash tun, was widely and quickly adopted. Therefore mashing, a somewhat hit-and-miss affair except in the largest breweries, had become 'improved' and completely mechanised by the 1860s. Extract rates were raised; exactitude was more easily attained. The introduction of sugar and unmalted grains into the grist caused only minor adjustments. Other systems of brewing – the more elaborate, expensive German decoction system (which achieved even higher extract rates) and the American Pidgeon system (which was an advance when large quantities of maize and rice were used) – never caught on in Britain in the last quarter of the nineteenth century. For British beers, in which malt was still the major ingredient, our 'improved' system was believed best.

Boiling was the least problematic major stage in the brewing process. Nevertheless there were varieties of practice and equipment. The Scottish brewers advocated a 'short' boil of not much more than an hour for their worts. Elsewhere brewers boiled longer, some up to three hours, especially the second wort. Tizard eccentrically advocated none in winter, arguing that it was unnecessary in making cider or spirit.[76] By the late nineteenth century, at least in large steam-heated breweries, the worts were drained straight from the mash tuns to the copper. Traditional practice, however, was for at least the second wort to be collected in underbacks (simply large wooden vessels) to await boiling. Southby maintained these must be heated by copper piping so that the temperature of the wort did not fall whilst awaiting transfer to the copper, otherwise 'injurious fermentation action, of an acid, or putrid character is likely to be set up'.[77] Coppers varied greatly in size from some 20 to 220 barrels; and it was usual practice by 1850 for breweries to possess two, ideally of around 80–100 barrel capacity each. In Burton they were open; elsewhere they tended to be fitted with domed lids, escape valves and pans. The aim in boiling was to obtain a strong ebullition, and extract the flavour from the hops which were added at this stage to give the resulting beer its bitterness and prevent it souring quickly. Again, there were variations in practice. At Burton large quantities of hops

[76] Tizard, *Theory and Practice*, pp. 282–6.
[77] Southby, *Practical Brewing*, p. 305.

(17 lb per quarter of malt for the finest export ales) were added before the wort came to the boil. Imitative country bitters were brewed with around 7–10 lb, and London porters and milds with between 4 lb and 6 lb; and the best hops were added last, just before the boil finished so that a good aromatic flavour was imparted.

After the wort had been somewhat reduced by vigorous boiling, and their flavour released, the hops were removed in the hop back and the excess wort squeezed from them. Often they would be re-used in the boiling of the second wort for weaker running ales – although this gave them a bitter flavour and was discouraged by the better brewers. The wort was then pumped as rapidly as possible to big, open coolers, no deeper than six inches, on the top floor of the brewery. Louvred windows and fans created draughts, for it was essential that the wort was aerated at this stage, that sediment deposited, and that it cooled quickly to around 60°F so that fermentation with the yeast could begin. The process of cooling varied from four to nine hours, but ideally it would have been accomplished within five or six, for at this stage, in summer at least, the brewers' problems began. Constructed in wood, coolers, however well cleaned, were prone to infection. Tizard thought, in advocating slate or tile squares, that 'the best cure for a wooden cooler is to burn it'.[78] But the problem went deeper than this. Steam, slow to clear in hazy, hot weather, condensed on dust laden beams and fell back into the squares, causing the worts to become acidic and setting up irregular fermentations. 'It is therefore', wrote Black, 'the difficulty of preserving worts in summer so as to go sound into the gyle (fermenting) tun, on which the uncertainty in fermentation during that season depends; and not the interference of the atmosphere with the process of fermentation.'[79]

The way round the problem was the introduction of 'refrigerators'. Again, these were first used in London breweries in the 1800s. Simple heat-exchange mechanisms, they were initially extremely expensive pieces of equipment to install.[80] Perhaps in no other area of brewing engineering was more ingenuity displayed. Three systems were tried. First, horizontal ones in which cold water passed through pipes over which flowed the hot wort in the opposite direction. Moreton's refrigerator was the best model of this type and was widely used. Secondly,

[78] Tizard, *Theory and Practice*, p. 316.
[79] Black, *Practical Treatise*, p. 23.
[80] Mathias, *Brewing Industry*, p. 75. Barclay Perkins paid £1,900 for a refrigerator in 1817.

there were those in which the wort flowed in a film over the outside of pipes placed vertically – much as in a milk cooler – and, thirdly, those in which the wort flowed inside the pipes and the water outside. There were acute cleaning problems with the first and third types, and by the late 1880s, the second type, with either flat or corrugated pipes on Baudelot's or Lawrence's patent, were most generally advocated.[81] Vertical, economic of space and water, they gave the wort an excellent aeration. Yet brewers, still perplexed by second fermentations, clung to their cooling squares. Barnard noted in 1891: 'a great many brewers we have visited during the last twelve months have gone back to their coolers, and have thereby secured sounder beer'.[82] Undoubtedly some brewers were sceptical of the new ways of working, but in reality 'refrigerators' were an important factor in making summer brewing possible by the 1830s. And when the change came for fresher, running ales they were essential. For although acidity and secondary fermentations were much less of a problem with vatted stouts and porters, 'foxing' spelt disaster in running ales. This difficulty was not solved quickly, but without 'refrigeration' all-year-round brewing, which made such sound economic sense for brewers, would have been impossible.

The next stage in beer production, fermentation, was even more critical than cooling. The difficulty of its intricacies and permutations puzzled scientists and brewers alike throughout the nineteenth century. As late as 1891, after Pasteur's and Hansen's important findings on yeast were known, Moritz and Morris wrote that it was 'a series of phenomena, the complexities of which is hardly to be equalled in technical processes'.[83] Fifty or sixty years earlier Black and Tizard had simply scratched their heads. Both could characterise good and bad fermentations, both lament the lack of scientific understanding. 'It is impossible', wrote Black, however, 'to describe by writing, the different anomalous appearance which takes place in fermentation, and therefore equally impossible to say what should be done under certain circumstances, unless by present inspection and examination.' Basically, brewers were advised to use their smell and taste and, if either were defective, litmus paper.[84]

In fermentation, the addition of fresh yeast converted maltose into alcohol and carbon dioxide (most of which escaped). During the

[81] Southby, *Practical Brewing*, pp. 104–6.
[82] Barnard, *Noted Breweries*, IV, p. 202.
[83] Moritz and Morris, *Science of Brewing*, p. 281.
[84] Black, *Practical Treatise*, pp. 92–100; Tizard, *Theory and Practice*, pp. 307–9.

process, which within different temperature ranges could vary from three days in England to three weeks in Bavaria, the yeast reproduced itself. Yet since alcohol is an antiseptic there is a limit to its production before the yeast is affected. With beer yeasts this is about 6 per cent by weight. And as the wort was converted into alcohol it became less dense or, in scientific terms, its specific gravity fell. This is called attenuation. The art of the brewer, armed with two eighteenth-century innovations, the thermometer and the saccharometer, to test these specific gravities, was to attenuate his beer at the correct gravity. If he stopped fermentation too high, the beer went into a vigorous secondary fermentation in the cask producing a cloudy, acidic drink. On the other hand, if he attenuated the brew at too low a point, the beer was flat and lifeless. Best pale ales with an original gravity of 22–6 lb were attenuated at around 6–7 lb. Trumans brewed their porter and cheap running ales to about 19 lb, i.e. they ran more liquor over each quarter of malt to produce a weaker wort than for best ale, and then attenuated their ales to about 4.7 lb and porters to about 5.5 lb. The general rule was to attenuate strong ales and stout at around one-third of their original gravity; and light ales by as much as one-fifth in warmer weather, to prevent their 'kicking up'.

Since the process was not understood scientifically before the 1880s a number of fermenting systems had evolved in the nineteenth century, each with its own advocates. All of them involved top fermentation; all made some attempt to control heats by 'attemperators' during the process; all 'roused' the beer in some degree to allow the yeast to imbibe oxygen; all, except in Scotland, pitched the wort and yeast at quite high temperatures. By the 1880s the process had been made safer by the use of microscopes to examine yeasts and the earlier introduction of attemperators to restrain heating and cooling in the fermentation cycle.[85] But long before, brewers had rules of thumb about yeast quantities and age,

[85] Attemperators in the fermenting tuns were simply copper pipes to convey hot or cold water to control temperatures during fermentation. Introduced in London in the 1800s, they seem to be in widespread use by the 1840s. Certainly, summer brewing was becoming general. Both the Scottish system of fermenting at much lower heats (45°–58°F) and the Yorkshire square system (controlled to 60°–62°F) were important in this respect. But elsewhere beers were being produced throughout the year. Robert Brakspear brewed at Henley throughout the year on average twice a week between 1795 and 1811 (F. Sheppard, *Brakspear's Brewery, Henley-on-Thames, 1779–1979* (1979), p. 17; a stray ale account in Courage's Archive (Tadcaster), JA/B/75, shows that an unnamed brewery, producing 8,000 barrels in 1835, brewed 11–14 times a month throughout the year – porter and vatted beers in winter, milds in summer. It also makes clear from comments about the state of different fermentations that these were much easier to control in winter. Nevertheless, these two random references from small breweries suggest that historians (especially Sigsworth, 'Science and the Brewing Industry', p. 536) have exaggerated the stop in summer brewing before the 1870s.

and the ways in which it was more effective if changed from making one type of beer to another. Most were aware of the need for absolute cleanliness.

At the turn of the eighteenth century, when the brewer had stopped his fermentation and separated his beer from the yeast (often with the aid of a flour and salt 'dressing'), it was then run straight into vats or trade casks. For it was desirable to encourage a secondary fermentation with strong ales, porter and stout to give them a creamy head, full palate and briskness. Pale and running ales, however, required different treatment. Therefore three different systems of fermentation evolved. At Burton in the 1840s, and elsewhere later, beers were 'cleansed' after about 36–40 hours into fermentation in union casks which allowed the carbon dioxide to expel the yeast through swan-necked pipes into yeast troughs (see Plate 3). Thought to be unparalleled for producing bright, pale ales, it was expensive in terms of casks, buildings and cooling equipment. For in summer, temperatures in the union rooms were kept below 50°F. Nevertheless it was widespread by the 1880s, and many large breweries produced at least their best ales on the union system. The second was known as the 'skimming' system. In its early stages identical to practices in Burton, after 36 hours the beer was roused in the fermenting vessels at three-hourly intervals, and the yeast cleared by parachutes or yeast waggons before each rousing. In Scotland and Ireland brewers often practised a variant of the skimming system and elsewhere brewers were not unknown to devise their own distinctive modifications.[86] After attenuation the yeast was separated and the beer run off into pontos or racking squares. But for bright, running beers settling backs were necessary where the beer stayed for several days before being racked into the casks and fined, just before dispatch, with an isinglass solution. Barnard noted that in several London breweries the demand for light ales meant the replacement of vats by settling squares. The third system was confined to Yorkshire and contiguous counties along the Pennines. Known as the Yorkshire square system, it was achieved by a well-aerated fermentation by pumping and running beers from two sets of stone squares one above the other. Again, attemperators allowed temperatures to be controlled. Finally, although there were experiments in Britain in the 1880s to produce lager (see

[86] Donnachie, *Brewing Industry in Scotland*, pp. 110–11; Southby, *Practical Brewing*, p. 351 for a description of practices in Scotland and the Irish breweries. Alfred Leney's Phoenix Brewery, Dover, had devised a complex system all its own (Barnard, *Noted Breweries*, IV pp. 184–94.

pp. 177), the German system of bottom fermentation at very low temperatures (40°F–45°F), with a long period of secondary fermentation during cold storage, never caught on.

These English systems of fermentation, in comparison with practices in south Germany and the other lager-producing centres, were undoubtedly somewhat idiosyncratic. Often carried out at temperatures near the safety margin, they nevertheless produced the type of beer the British consumer demanded – full flavoured, strong and quite bright. But it was often at the cost of acidity and a narcoticising effect. Extreme care had to be taken about cleanliness, and although the production of strong ales, porters and stouts caused few problems except in the hottest two months of the year, making consistent light ales throughout the year, even after the pure yeast discovery of Hansen in the 1880s, was a constant headache for brewers. Refrigerators and attemperators, neither of them very sophisticated pieces of engineering, made the production of these increasingly popular beers possible.[87] And although breweries had to extend greatly the size and complexity of their fermenting capacity, especially with the Burton unions, the English system was much cheaper than bottom fermentation which required large quantities of ice in summer and a vast cellarage, and entailed a much slower turnover of capital.

V

When the *Brewers' Journal* celebrated its golden jubilee in 1915 its editors wrote: 'Perhaps the most phenomenal growth of *The Journal* has been on the side of the science of brewing ... Is there, we may ask, another industry – possibly there is none in this country – in which so much scientific activity has taken place as in brewing during the period under review?'[88] Yet twenty-five years ago, Eric Sigsworth in a pioneering article, 'Science and the Brewing Industry, 1850–1900', questioned the impact of the post-Pasteurian revolution in brewing *chemistry* upon brewing *practice*. 'It would appear', he concluded, 'no comparable revolution in practice occurred.'[89] His argument centred upon two points: that the practical implication of Pasteur's and Hansen's findings about bacteria and pure yeast had already been absorbed empirically by

87 *Brewing Trade Review*, 1 July 1887 viewed the switch from cask fermented beers to bright running beers, artificially fined and without secondary fermentation, somewhat critically.

88 *Brewers' Journal*, 15 July 1915.

89 *Economic History Review*, 17 (1965), p. 541.

brewers not necessarily understanding the scientific reasons for their actions; and that Pasteur's work related principally to 'bottom' fermentation, and was therefore of limited applicability in Britain where drinkers demanded a cask beer in which a secondary fermentation had taken place. This second point, given the taste for bright running beers in which a secondary fret was anathema, is highly questionable. Indeed the whole argument, that science had little impact on practice, that brewers were hostile to its impetus, and that here, as leaders elsewhere in British industry, they buried their heads in the sand at the approach of science into their domain, is at least a questionable one.

There is no doubt about the importance of the revolution in brewing science following from the publication of Pasteur's *Etudes sur la bière* (1876), translated into English three years later. The dark ages of empiricism were at an end. After decades of false and incomplete trails, Pasteur explained the fermentation process precisely in terms of the life-cycle of yeast. He showed how secondary and tertiary fermentations arose from bacteriological infections and harmful strains within the yeast itself. But it was E. C. Hansen's experiments at the Carlsberg brewery in the early 1880s which demonstrated that yeasts themselves could be infected, that there were different species of yeasts, and that pure types of these could be isolated. In fact his work initially had limited impact in England, since it was not translated until 1896.[90] And both Pasteur's and Hansen's findings on bacteria and yeast, as in the parable, fell upon ground of variable fertility. Undoubtedly much the most friable patch was in Burton upon Trent. For here the great Burton brewers, partly to offset serious charges of adulteration (the French going so far as to suggest they used strychnine in 1852), had employed a series of chemists since 1845. Böttinger, Griess, Cornelius O'Sullivan, Horace and Adrian Brown (Burtonians and half-brothers) and G. H. Morris were scientists of national distinction, as well as being head-brewers. O'Sullivan and the two Browns were awarded Fellowships of the Royal Society and a string of medals. Together they did important work on barley, starches, brewing sugars and maltose.[91] Horace Brown, at Worthington and later director of Guinness's Research Laboratory in Dublin, was a brilliant practical chemist whose contributions were significant in almost every branch of brewing science and technology

[90] Horace Brown remained unconvinced about pure yeasts for English Beers. H. T. Brown, 'Reminiscences of Fifty Years Experience of the Application of Scientific Method to Brewing Practice', *Journal of the Institute of Brewing*, 22 (1916), pp. 317–27.

[91] A brief summary appears in C. C. Owen, *The Development of Industry in Burton upon Trent* (1978), pp. 89–95.

(see Plate 4).[92] From the 1860s to the 1880s – Burton's golden age – brewing chemists there, especially after the foundation of the Bacterium Club in 1876, made Pasteur's and Hansen's findings intelligible. They adapted them to English beers, extended them in notable ways by their own experimentation, and made them known more generally to brewers. 'Burton on Trent', stated Professor H. E. Armstrong 'probably was the most active and stimulating centre in the country, the home of real bio-chemistry.'[93]

Elsewhere, except at Guinness where Forbes Watson did important work on yeast and fermentation processes in the 1900s, the ground was stonier. The Royal Commission on Technical Instruction was informed by Professor Graham in 1882, 'scarcely a laboratory [exists] anywhere else in England except at Burton'.[94] This situation appears to have been rapidly transformed in the mid and late 1880s. Barnard noted the presence of laboratories in almost every large brewery, although sometimes, when they were recorded in smaller ones, there is a distinct impression that they were limited to little more than a microscope and a forcing-tray. Some brewers in London, backward in science because wedded to porter and stout, made dramatic late conversions. J. M. Hanbury, a director of Truman and President of the Institute of Brewing in 1899–1900, told those present at the Annual Dinner in 1900, 'we had no chemist in our brewery a short time ago, and now we have seven or eight'.[95] A good deal of the proselytising of brewers to the significance of science in their affairs was carried out by the Institute of Brewers, and its forerunner the Laboratory Club, founded in London in 1886 by E. R. Moritz, the Consulting Chemist to the Country Brewers' Society. Certainly, the march of brewing science, measured in terms of the general employment of chemists in the leading breweries and growing membership of the Institute of Brewing from 290 in 1892 to almost 1,000 ten years later, is impressive.[96] And the lively discussions about both the theory and practice of every stage of production, filling the early volumes of the *Laboratory Club Transactions* and the *Journal of*

[92] Brown, 'Reminiscences' provides an excellent autobiographical account. See also H. Lloyd-Hind, 'Pasteur to 1936 – An Account of the Development of Science in Brewing', *Journal of the Institute of Brewing*, 43 (1937), pp. 222–33 and the 50th Jubilee issue, 42 (1936), pp. 479–95.

[93] *Journal of the Institute of Brewing*, 22 (1916), p. 349.

[94] Quoted in Sigsworth, 'Science and Brewing', p. 539.

[95] *Brewers' Journal*, 15 Feb. 1900. In fact they employed their first chemist in 1888. 'We find him a very useful person, in fact I don't think we could do without him now' (Acc. 77.94 B/THB, Monthly Reports, Nov. 1888.

[96] *Journal of the Institute of Brewing*, 8 (1902), p. 232; 20 (1914), p. 146.

the Institute of Brewing, are testimony to the increasing role of science in brewing. Charles Babington underlined its place at the Annual Banquet of the Institute in 1904: 'To succeed now the brewer must turn to the laboratory. He cannot afford to neglect the teaching of science, as in the darkest days of twenty-five years ago . . . Those days and methods are as dead and gone as King John and sheet armour.'[97] And besides developments in practice, research and training were discussed within an international context. Indeed the title Institute of Brewing had deliberate continental overtones.[98] Yet the reality behind the façade, once the excitement of the lecture and the heady fumes of the annual banquet had cleared, was rather different.

Founded in 1890, the Institute had three satellites: in the North (1891), Yorkshire and the North-East (1893), and the Midlands (1894), centred upon Manchester, Leeds and Birmingham respectively.[99] Although these were important in attracting the membership of country brewers and the four bodies were federated in 1895 and amalgamated in 1904, regional rivalries, the lack of overall direction, and shoe-string budgets effectively put a stop, at least before 1920, to Moritz's original aim of a programme of planned research and examinations for brewers, validated by the Institute. On the one hand, the Institute was content to allow the Burton laboratories and those of Guinness to provide the research lead, and on the other, whilst desirous of closing the gap between the patent inadequacies of the British pupillage system of training brewers and the state-aided scheme in Germany, it failed to win round most brewers to its examination proposals. 'We are strongly of the opinion', wrote the editor of the influential *Brewing Trade Review* in 1913, 'that in the first place the selection and training of the brewery pupil is of far more importance than the examination of the finished article.'[100] There are other instances of the Institute's toothlessness. In 1900 an attempt to raise £30,000 to fund central offices and a laboratory in London met with a dismal response.[101] Even the Boer War could not carry all the blame for the brewers' divisions about their role and purpose. As so often in Britain, exasperated individual effort came to the rescue. In Birmingham, at Mason's University College, the British School of Brewing and Malting was established in 1900, with Adrian Brown as its distinguished founding professor. The Midland Brewers,

97 *Brewing Trade Review*, 1 April 1904.
98 *Brewing Trade Review*, 1 Feb. 1891.
99 W. H. Bird, *A History of the Institute of Brewing* (1955), pp. 1–21, 113–15.
100 *Brewing Trade Review*, 1 Nov. 1913.
101 Bird, *Institute of Brewing*, pp. 5–6.

led by William Waters Butler, a powerful man of foresight both in brewing and in the foundation of Birmingham University, raised over £25,000 to establish the department. As early as 1902 it was 'overwhelmed with students'.[102] Its success saved the Institute's face. There were other less prestigious courses for brewers, both at Sir John Cass's Technical Institute and at Manchester School of Technology in the 1890s.[103] Horace Brown, doyen of brewing scientists, thought in 1916 that the means of training were in place, but that the failure to implement them in most breweries should be laid fairly and squarely at the doors of their directors.[104]

Undoubtedly there was hostility and ignorance in the industry in the face of the march of brewing science. When J. M. Hanbury addressed the Institute of Brewing in 1900 he illustrated this point by recalling that 'one very large London brewer had told him the other day that he has never heard of this Institution'; another, when asked by Hanbury about comparisons in the diastase of his malt – a term in general use for sixty years – between this year and last, blankly replied 'What the devil are you talking about?'[105] Brewers believed there was no room for the trainees from Birmingham and Manchester. Admittedly there was change from the days Frank Lott recalled in 1894 of 'a brewery as the last resource for a young man . . . failed for the Army, the Church, or one of the learned professions'.[106] But Brown's outburst in 1916 about the 'total ignorance of principles . . . a mere smattering of so-called scientific knowledge picked up anyhow' of young brewers suggest that change in Britain came slowly. The gap between British and German training systems remained wide since brewers here clung to their pupillage system. Science came a poor second.

Nevertheless, it is possible to close the apparent gap between the progress of science and the lack of serious training. The feat lies principally in the nature of the brewing industry. Two great steps forward were made after 1880: the production of low-cost, consistent, running beers and of a good, mass-produced bottled beer by chilling, filtering and carbonating. At their basis were the findings of Pasteur,

[102] *Brewers' Journal*, 15 Feb. 1900; *Journal of the Institute of Brewing*, 8 (1902), pp. 220–40; *Brewing Trade Review*, 1 March 1913.

[103] But the *Brewing Trade Review*, 1 Nov. 1913 'pointed out that the City Guilds have for some years held technological examinations (at Cass's Institute) in brewing . . . and that they have hopelessly failed to attain any popularity or seriously attract the notice of the brewery proprietor, brewer, or pupil'.

[104] Brown 'Reminiscences', pp. 344–5.

[105] *Brewers' Journal*, 15 Feb. 1900.

[106] *Journal of the Institute of Brewing* (1894–5), p. 178.

Hansen and the Burton chemists. W. T. Rothwell, president of the North of England Institute of Brewing in 1902, summarised the changes succinctly:

> Nowadays, by expert knowledge, by general intellectual advancement, by improved appliances, and the employment of brewers' engineers and chemists, they were enabled to brew the very best beers every day in the year. It made very little difference in the brewing of ales whether it was on the hottest day in summer or the coldest day in winter. That desirable state of affairs had been brought about by scientific knowledge.[107]

In other words, providing a brewer absorbed scientific findings about absolute cleanliness, good materials and up-to-date cooling plant; kept his yeasts in condition; and consulted a laboratory if things appeared to be going wrong: then he could provide first-rate beers without possessing a sound understanding of the latest scientific advances. And the latter were increasingly complex. But by reading the brewing journals (which discussed these in the context of brewing practice and related them to the latest equipment), by membership of the Institute of Brewing, and by modernising his brewery, he could keep abreast of developments. The industry was unusual in that although science improved the means of production, the end-product was a question of taste rather than precise measurement. There were, therefore, different routes to perfection. A Twickenham brewer stated this viewpoint, common amongst brewers before 1914, at an early discussion of the Laboratory Club. 'Perhaps Dr. Moritz can explain how it is that there were many brewers who, although utterly ignorant of science, are successful, while many scientific brewers are quite the reverse.'[108] Moritz gently pointed out in his reply the place for experience as well as science. Thus, although science made great advances to allow the transformation of production after 1880 it was grudgingly accepted by many brewers (Plate 5). Overstressing their adherence to tradition, sceptical about the place of scientific training, they were allowed to protect themselves from its march in some measure by their acquisition of tied houses. Nevertheless, most brewers turned out better beers in 1900 than they had fifty years earlier. In this, science played a large part.

107 *Journal of the Institute of Brewing*, 8 (1902), p. 221.

108 *Brewing Trade Review*, 1 Dec. 1886. See the similar comment of George Mumford of Liverpool.

3

Changes in structure and location, 1830–1880

This third chapter provides a general view of the brewing industry in Victorian Britain. It first examines the decline of private and publican brewing which *together* accounted for rather more than half of beer production in 1830, before looking at the opposite end of the brewing spectrum – the great focus of commercial brewing, London. Then the rise of the industry in Burton upon Trent, the most spectacular aspect of nineteenth-century brewing, is discussed along with similar advances in Dublin and Edinburgh. Finally, the broad changes in the scale of country brewing, as production outside London and Burton was always called, are outlined.

I

In Georgian Britain most gentlemen and farmers who employed much labour, as well as such institutions as colleges, hospitals and poor houses, brewed their own ale. All of them possessed sets of brewing utensils, and their servants brewed beer, often under the supervision of an itinerant brewer, of variable strength and goodness. The scale of output varied from the big institutions and households of the great, mashing sizeable quantities of malt regularly, at least between October and March, to farm labourers producing the odd barrel against harvest. Certainly knowledge and practice of brewing at the beginning of the nineteenth century was universal in the countryside and market town. In Norfolk, Parson Woodforde brewed more barrels himself than he bought from Bircham, the common brewer in nearby Reepham.[1] Even labouring families, disadvantaged by poor equipment and inadequate storage space, occasionally brewed, so that when William Cobbett wrote

[1] R. L. Winstanley (ed.), *James Woodforde: Diary of the First Six Norfolk Years, 1776–1781* (Parson Woodforde Society, 1981–4), I, pp. 52, 61, 78, 97, 104, 120, 161; II, pp. 15, 73, 92; III, p. 92.

his *Cottage Economy* in 1823 he devoted no less than a quarter of its contents to the subject of beer making. And as late as the mid-1860s, admittedly in an area where commercial brewing had a weak hold, John Fielden of Todmorden revealed that a survey of 9,822 families in the Halifax, Huddersfield, Leeds and Bradford district disclosed that no fewer than 7,465 of them brewed their own beer.[2] Twenty years later cottage brewing was still strong in Suffolk, around Bradford and Halifax, and in Wales. When Sir William Harcourt in 1886 abolished the 30p licence fee for cottage brewing levied on houses below an annual value of £8 (a sliding-scale duty for private brewers, related to rateable values, had been introduced in 1880 when the reinstated Beer Duty replaced the malt tax) there were 95,300 licences in existence. But a free licence enabled a cottager to brew no more than 4 bushels of malt (producing around two barrels) and 4 lb of hops. Total quantities brewed privately therefore were miniscule in relation to national output. And by 1900 the number of licences issued had fallen to 12,607. Except perhaps in Suffolk, where there were still farmer-maltsters small enough to deal in odd bushels of malt, private brewing was a dying art.[3]

Unfortunately, it is not easy to estimate how much beer was produced by the 'private' brewer in the nineteenth century since evasion of duties in this area was evidently rife. G. B. Wilson calculated that it fell from around 22.5 per cent of total beer output in 1830–4 to 2.7 per cent of total output in England and Wales in 1866–70.[4] Thereafter, private brewing was insignificant in the industry. In outline the trend is clear. The proportion had already declined appreciably in the years between 1700 and 1830. Reckoned to have been half total output around 1700, it had fallen, probably most quickly during the high-price, high-duty period of the French Wars (1793–1815), to around one-fifth by the 1830s.[5] This is the figure contemporaries bandied about; and it did decline sharply after 1830, as opponents of the Beer Act had forecast, when the beer duty (never paid on home brewed beer) was abolished. The chief economic incentive in domestic brewing disappeared overnight. With the sole tax now on malt, private brewers, unable to produce extraction rates comparable to those achieved by commercial brewers, were at a clear disadvantage.

After 1830, those who had at one time made their own beer turned

2 Sigsworth, 'Brewing Trade during the Industrial Revolution' p. 7, n. 15, tables 1–3.
3 *Brewing Trade Review* (1887), pp. 290, 328–9; *Suffolk Review*, 1 (1956–8), pp. 156–60.
4 Wilson, *Alcohol and the Nation*, pp. 55–6; *PP* (1867) XI Select Committee on the Malt Tax. Appendix No. 3 'Estimated Quantity of Malt used Annually by Private Brewers'.
5 W. Ford, *An Historical Account of the Malt Trade and Laws* (1849), p. 50.

increasingly to the common brewer to provide their households with a more consistent, less troublesome and probably cheaper source of supply. For example, in 1883 Lord Wenlock sold his brewing plant at Escrick Hall, valued at £147.50 for its fifty-one casks, two sets of unions and some vats, to the Tadcaster Tower Brewery. Thereafter, he obtained his beer from them, even having some sent to his London house. Quality was an important consideration, for practical as the concept might have seemed to contemporaries, and romantic to us now, household brewing must often have produced fitful beer. The 'private' trade, therefore, became an increasingly important item in the accounts of many common brewers after 1830. The largest began to employ travellers, supplying the servant-keeping classes, many of whom would never have dreamt of entering a public house themselves, with a variety and quality of beer their forebears had not enjoyed when they produced their own. Barnard noted that many of his country brewers relied upon a substantial private trade, sometimes for as much as half their business.[6] Their ledgers contained columns of private orders for barrels, firkins, jars and dozen bottles of every kind of beer and stout. Ind Coope in 1899 rejoiced that they were the largest family-trade brewers in the world.[7]

The shift from home production to 'private' orders from common brewers is a notable feature of the Victorian brewing industry. For in spite of the temperance band-waggon, there was still an almost universal belief that a daily glass of good beer or stout was an aid to good health and convalescence. It was this view, encouraged by the brewers marketing purer, lighter beers and attested by scientists and doctors, that largely sustained the private trade.

In one aspect we know much more about the publican than the private brewer in the nineteenth century. Statistics, based upon the brewers' licence duty and their malt entry books, have survived which allow the measurement of activity and geographical concentration in a way that is impossible for the home brewer. From another standpoint, however, our knowledge of publican brewers is incomplete. Very little of their written records appears to have survived. Often their accounts, jotted down in the flimsiest, beer-stained notebooks, must have been

[6] Bass North (Leeds), Tadcaster Tower Brewery, Partners' Diaries, Dec. 1882, Feb. 1883; in volume IV, Barnard noted several breweries who relied upon a good private trade: Bentley & Shaw, Huddersfield; Hepworth, Ripon; Hardy's Kimberley Brewery (Notts); Robin, Brighton; Pike, Spicer & Co., Portsmouth; Phoenix Brewery, Dover; Lion Brewery, Ashford. 'The principal trade of the Lion Brewery is with private families, and the nobility and gentry of the district' (p. 204).

[7] *Ind Coope and Co. Ltd. Souvenir 1799–1899* (1899), p. 11.

cursory and their correspondence non-existent. Plentiful head counts, detailed census returns after 1851, trade directories and the architectural record provide an overall view. But the details of how they operated, both as brewers themselves and in their relations with maltsters and commercial brewers, in their employment of itinerant brewers, of their proneness to bankruptcy are, at the moment, defective. It is an interesting and unmarked byway of Victorian economic and social history.[8]

Table 3.1 sets out the proportions of malt made into beer by common brewers, licensed victuallers and beer house keepers in England and Wales and Scotland between 1830 and 1900. The figures give a unique statistical view of an industry in a crucial stage of its transition, from a point where commercial and domestic production were roughly equal, to one in which large-scale output overwhelmingly predominated. The shift can be pin-pointed with a chronological and geographical precision rare in industrial studies. Yet, as always in history, the reasons for some of the movements, especially those of pronounced regional differences, are less easy to explain satisfactorily. And the statistics themselves, complete as they might appear, are inevitably imperfect. Many excise districts shifted their boundaries – some more than once – in the course of these seventy years. Occasionally figures look inherently implausible (see Table 3.2); and evasion and persistent under-declaration means that calculations to two decimal places should not have sacrosanct status. After 1860 perhaps their biggest flaw is that commercial brewers, for two decades before the malt tax was repealed in 1880, were using increasing amounts of sugar in their mash tuns. But the nub of the problem for the brewing historian in surveying them is to provide a convincing explanation of their movement.

The broad trend is clear enough. Discounting private brewing, common or commercial brewers in England and Wales produced around 55 per cent of beer output on Queen Victoria's accession, the licensed victualler just under 33 per cent, and the beer house keeper – the new entrant to the industry in 1830 – around 12.5 per cent. At the

[8] The retail drink trade produced a variety of journals, of which the best, the *Licensed Victuallers' Gazette*, goes back to 1872. These have never been systematically used by historians of the industry. Good guides of a general nature are provided by Mark Girouard, *Victorian Pubs* (1975); B. Harrison, 'Pubs' in H. J. Dyos and M. Wolff (eds.), *The Victorian City: Images and Realities*, I (1973), pp. 161–90; A. Crawford, M. Dunn and R. Thorne, *Birmingham Pubs 1880–1914* (1986); Clark, *English Alehouses* stops at 1830. All, however, are weak on the actual brewing activities of the licensed victualler. A good plan of a Victorian pub brewhouse, *The Golden Lion* at Southwick (Hampshire) appears in M. F. Tighe, 'A Gazetteer of Hampshire Breweries', *Proceedings of the Hampshire Field Club*, 27 (1972), pp. 92, 103–4.

Table 3.1. *Numbers of and quantities of malt brewed by common brewers, victuallers and beer house keepers in England and Wales, and Scotland, 1831–1900*

Year ending		[1] Common brewers		[2] Licensed victuallers				[3] Persons licensed to sell beer[a]				Per cent brewed by		
		No.	Bushels brewed by (in mills)	[4] Total	[5] No. brewing	[5] as percentage of [4]	Bushels brewed by (in mills)	[6] Total	[7] No. brewing	[7] as percentage of [6]	Bushels brewed by (in mills)	[1]	[2]	[3]
5. 1.1832	England and Wales	1,654	14.26	50,547	23,889	47.3	9.01	31,937	13,446	42.1	2.99	54	34	11
	Scotland	221	0.83	17,861	318	1.8	0.09	–	–	–	–	90	10	–
5. 1.1841	England and Wales	2,258	17.69	57,379	26,880	46.8	8.55	42,613	16,376	38.9	3.37	60	29	11
	Scotland	197	0.89	16,015	245	1.5	0.10	–	–	–	–	90	10	–
10.10.1850	England and Wales	2,281	17.80	59,676	25,851	43.4	7.15	39,158	13,448	34.3	3.23	63	25	11
	Scotland	151	0.83	14,971	178	1.2	0.12	–	–	–	–	88	12	–
10.10.1860	England and Wales	2,326	26.02	64,455	24,578	38.1	7.33	44,504	12,283	27.6	3.34	71	20	9
	Scotland	105	1.41	12,040	126	1.0	0.22	–	–	–	–	87	13	–
30. 9.1870	England and Wales	2,512	33.94	69,903	20,093	28.7	7.03	47,568	9,735	20.5	3.27	77	16	7
	Scotland	79	1.73	12,644	123	1.0	0.30	–	–	–	–	85	15	–
30. 9.1880	England and Wales	2,507	41.93	69,761	12,336	17.7	5.00	49,404	6,157	12.5	2.71	84	10	5
	Scotland	88	1.87	12,259	81	0.7	0.38	–	–	–	–	83	17	–
30. 9.1890	England and Wales	2,175	42.70	73,016	6,312	8.6	2.92	44,296	3,319	7.5	1.70	90	6	4
	Scotland	115	3.90	11,767	37	0.3	0.25	–	–	–	–	92	8	–
30. 9.1900	England and Wales	1,711	45.45	73,271	2,884	3.9	1.50	41,579	1,582	3.8	0.88	95	3	2
	Scotland	125	3.65	11,208	3	0.03	0.01	–	–	–	–	100	–	–

[a] These are almost all beer house keepers, although from 1841 the figures do distinguish between those brewing 'to be drunk on premises' and 'not to be drunk on premises'. Columns 6 and 7 present the total of both categories.

Source: PP (1831–2) XXXIV Parts 1 and 2; (1841) XXVI Parts 1 and 2; (1851) LIII Parts 1 and 2; (1861) LVIII Parts 1 and 2; (1870) LXII Parts 1 and 2; (1881) LXXX Parts 1 and 2; (1890–1) LXXVII; (1901) LXIX.

end of her reign, the first produced 95 per cent, the other two categories together a diminutive 5 per cent (in Scotland this pattern of concentration had been already achieved by 1830). Yet until the mid-1860s, as Table 3.1 reveals, membership of the publican brewing fraternity did not fall sharply, despite the declining proportion of output. Then, as common brewers began to acquire public houses on an unprecedented scale, and invariably closed down the brewing activities of those where brewing had taken place on the premises, their numbers contracted quickly. The key decades are the 1870s and 1880s. In the year ending September 1870, 20,095 victuallers and 9,735 beer house keepers still produced some 23 per cent of total output. By 1890 their numbers had fallen by more than two-thirds. Ten years later they were on the endangered species list of Victorian domestic producers.

It would be too simple, however, to argue that publican brewers were extinguished by a race of increasingly rapacious common brewers after 1865. As the range of beers was extended in the nineteenth century, the publican brewer, often with no more than a shallow well in his yard and an indifferent set of brewing utensils, could not match the common brewer in producing the new types of beers. For generations they had made, and sometimes acquired an excellent local reputation for, dark mild or vatted 'old' beers of the region. Now, however, they had to compete with and buy in pale and bitter ales. Their traditional trade contracted. Inevitably, their affairs became inextricably intertwined with those of their chief creditors, the maltster and common brewer. Many publican brewers simply folded because their burden of debt became too great, forcing them into some arrangement, either in the supply of beer or outright ownership with the common brewer, which gave the latter control. Again, this was no new feature, but, possibly because of the increasing scale of operations and accelerating ferocity of the industrial business cycle, the proclivity grew. Of course, some brewing publicans (or often, in practice, the owners of their premises) willingly sold out to the brewers when pub prices rose sharply after 1870; but all faced, year in year out, the problem of quality, lower extraction rates and therefore little or no price advantage. The triumph of 'power-loom' brewing, which Charles Barclay had proclaimed in London in 1830, spread everywhere in Victorian Britain.

We have already seen that the great changes in brewing heralded by the Beer Act of 1830 never came about. Beer house brewing in almost all areas was a predictable flop (see pp. 19–21). The situation of the licensed victuallers was in some respects different. Always reckoned to

Table 3.2. *Beer brewed by common brewers, victuallers and beer house keepers in selected excise districts, 1832–1900*

Year	Excise collection district	[1] Common brewers No.	[2] Licensed victuallers No.	Percentage brewing [2]	[3] Persons licensed to sell beer No.	Percentage brewing [3]	Per cent of beer brewed by [1]	[2]	[3]
1832	Lichfield[a]	5	871	94.4	582	84.4	10	68	23
	Dorset	30	349	39.5	329	31.0	60	27	12
	Liverpool	56	1,264	2.9	595	4.4	90	6	4
	Manchester	29	619	86.1	820	86.6	24	50	25
	Norwich	22	1,057	3.8	346	12.4	89	7	5
	Edinburgh	31	1,858	0.1	–	–	100	–	–
1841	Lichfield	14	1,031	97.2	948	85.1	9	60	31
	Dorset	46	402	58.2	690	21.6	62	32	7
	Liverpool	74	1,418	1.4	955	0.9	97	2	1
	Manchester	84	1,499	66.8	2,911	49.4	43	38	19
	Norwich	36	1,156	4.9	387	14.7	90	7	3
	Edinburgh	30	1,523	0.1	–	–	99	1	–
1850	Lichfield	12	1,060	94.7	1,161	80.3	7	49	44
	Dorset	52	508	39.6	598	14.7	70	22	9
	Liverpool	88	1,665	1.4	1,409	1.2	97	2	1
	Manchester	99	1,671	57.2	3,369	34.9	55	28	18
	Norwich	47	1,454	5.7	440	14.3	77	17	6
	Edinburgh	20	1,368	–	–	–	100	–	–
1860	Birmingham	10	1,091	93.1	1,473	79.4	8	49	44
	Lichfield	39	1,236	76.9	1,224	76.1	82	10	8
	Dorset	33	442	29.2	288	18.4	85	13	3
	Liverpool	73	1,803	1.1	1,550	1.2	95	3	2
	Manchester	118	1,839	46.7	4,219	27.2	70	18	12

	Norwich	22	1,339	2.0	386	7.8	77	22	1
	Edinburgh	21	1,031	–	–	–	100	–	–
1870	Birmingham	13	863	97.1	1,374	86.5	9	47	44
	Lichfield	41	1,032	65.9	896	58.0	93	5	3
	Weymouth	32	508	18.5	303	7.3	89	9	2
	Liverpool	80	2,026	0.4	599	0.3	98	2	–
	Manchester	102	1,375	11.7	3,704	6.2	89	7	4
	Norwich	24	1,374	2.0	459	3.3	64	36	–
	Edinburgh	30	1,229	–	–	–	100	0	0
1880	Birmingham	25	860	69.3	1,524	69.0	16	36	49
	Lichfield	57	916	43.0	883	43.0	95	3	2
	Weymouth	34	529	8.9	233	6.4	94	5	–
	Liverpool	70	2,315	0.4	637	0.2	98	2	–
	Manchester	94	1,489	5.6	4,693	1.7	93	4	3
	Norwich	23	1,382	0.4	435	1.6	99	–	–
	Edinburgh	29	1,162	–	–	–	100	–	–
1890	Birmingham	42	1,231	16.3	1,629	24.2	67	16	17
	Burton	43	488	4.5	364	1.6	100	–	–
	Liverpool	39	2,408	0.2	402	0.2	99	1	–
	Manchester	64	1,511	0.8	3,171	0.5	98	1	1
	Norwich	22	1,688	0.4	513	1.4	99	–	–
	Edinburgh	40	1,446	0.1	–	–	100	–	–
1900	Birmingham	35	1,545	8.7	1,603	6.7	91	6	3
	Burton	32	696	8.0	475	8.8	99	1	1
	Liverpool	28	2,275	–	359	0.3	100	–	–
	Manchester	39	1,509	0.1	2,995	0.1	100	–	–
	Norwich	28	7,374	0.01	761	0.1	100	–	–
	Edinburgh	35	1,327	–	–	–	100	–	–

[a] The Lichfield district had disappeared by 1890 and was replaced in part by one centred upon Burton upon Trent. Similarly, Dorset was replaced by Weymouth in the 1860s and Birmingham appears as a separate collection area by 1860.

Source: As Table 3.1. For year ending dates see Table 3.1.

be men of superior status and credit compared with the beer house keepers, the scale of their activity was larger and, when they brewed, the quality of their beer was usually better. Whereas in England and Wales in 1833 some 15,437 individuals (presumably mainly beer house keepers) paid the licence fee to brew up to fifty barrels a year, there were 25,990 who paid to produce between fifty and a thousand barrels apiece, the vast majority of whom were brewing victuallers.[9] The latter thus varied considerably in the scale of their operations from those brewing a barrel a week on average to those bordering on the activities of smaller commercial brewers who turned out twenty. In towns which were strongholds of victualler brewing they frequently drove a good business, often combining their operations with lodging house keeping in industrial towns and public catering in market centres. In the countryside they might also be small-scale farmers, specialising, by the nature of their occupation, in cattle dealing. Some with initiative made the transition to common brewers when local conditions were right. For example, in the Halifax area there were only six common brewers serving an almost entirely free trade in 1840; by 1880, at least twenty-six controlled over 90 per cent of the market. Most of these breweries established in the 1860s and 1870s were 'publican brewers who expanded to become common brewers supplying other outlets'. By 1895 half a dozen market leaders had emerged in the Halifax district, owning 284 tied houses between them. Fifteen other common brewers each owned fewer than ten public houses. Although the publican brewer was almost extinct in the Halifax area in the 1890s, the new breed of common brewers were often their descendants.[10]

Those who have looked at publican brewing in the nineteenth century have been almost exclusively preoccupied with explaining its geographical location. The position is set out in Table 3.2. Although limited for the sake of manageability to only half a dozen collection districts, it reveals a remarkable distribution pattern.

In London, Liverpool, Edinburgh and Norwich production by 1830 was almost entirely in the hands of common brewers: in the Midlands (the Lichfield figures are representative), West Yorkshire[11] and Man-

[9] *PP* (1834) XXIV, p. 173. 4th Report into the Excise (1834) Survey of Brewers. These figures almost fit those returns for 1833 which showed the quantities of malt brewed by the numbers of common brewers, victuallers and beer house keepers. The figures for the year ending 5.1.1832 are shown in Table 3.1.

[10] P. W. Robinson, 'The Emergence of the Common Brewer in the Halifax District', *Transactions of the Halifax Antiquarian Society*, 19 (1981), pp. 70–106.

[11] See Tables 1–3 in Sigsworth, *Brewing Trade*.

chester the publican brewer was predominant. Dorset represents a halfway house. Nationally, as Dr Baxter pointed out many years ago, there were some twenty-five excise collection districts where more than 67 per cent of all licensed victuallers brewed their own beer; conversely there were sixteen areas where fewer than 27 per cent of them did so. How do we account for these pronounced differences? Baxter believed brewing victuallers 'held greatest sway in the more remote parts of the country where transport facilities were poor and the new industrialisation was not felt'. Certainly the South-West, Wales and the adjoining English counties were their stronghold, but in Bristol, Coventry, Leeds and Sheffield they were similarly active. Where they failed to flourish as early as 1830 was in the eastern and southern counties (and oddly Cumberland), the heart of agrarian England.[12]

Eric Sigsworth attempted a more definitive explanation in his study of the Yorkshire brewing trade:

> nationally, in 1825, the extent of the common brewer's domination increases the nearer the excise collection is situated to London. On the whole, the farther west and north the collection, the less evident are the common brewer's activities and the greater the strength of the licensed victualler – the only exceptions to this strong tendency towards the geographical of wholesale or common brewing towards London in 1825 being the Liverpool, Northumberland, Cumberland, Durham, Hull, Whitby and Plymouth collections. As has been argued, a simple explanation of the rise of the common brewer couched in terms of the size of the local market fails to explain why this should have been retarded in the Birmingham, Sheffield, Leeds, Coventry and Derby collections, while already in 1825 the common brewer had come to dominate collections such as the Isle of Wight and Hampshire.[13]

Yet if he disposed of the size-of-market explanation, the exceptions seem so important as to upset his argument about the competitive pull exerted by the great London breweries. Moreover, there are other variations which defy his analysis. In Norfolk, the Norwich collection figures for 1830 show 90 per cent of output in and around the city was already in the hands of common brewers. In neighbouring Suffolk, 50 miles nearer London, they produced only 32 per cent, and 90 per cent

[12] J. Baxter, 'The Organisation of the Brewing Industry' (Ph.D. Thesis, London, 1945), pp. 44–50. Those collections with more than 67 per cent of brewing victuallers were Barnstaple, Bristol, Cornwall, Coventry, Derby, Essex (an obvious error), Exeter, Gloucester, Halifax, Hereford, Lancaster, Leeds, Lichfield, Lincoln, Northampton, Salop, Sheffield, Stafford, Stourbridge, Wales (4 districts), Worcester; those with fewer than 27 per cent of victuallers brewing for themselves were Cambridge, Canterbury, Cumberland, Durham, Hants, Hertford, Hull, Isle of Wight, Liverpool, Lynn, Newcastle, Norwich, Reading, Rochester, Surrey, Sussex.

[13] Sigsworth, *Brewing Trade*, pp. 6–7.

concentration was not achieved until the late 1870s.[14] In the end, Sigsworth, contrasting the predominance of publican brewing in the Halifax, Leeds and Sheffield districts with those of York, Hull and Whitby where the common brewer was already in the ascendant by 1830, rested his explanation upon the difficult state of communications 'in relatively hilly inland areas'. Admittedly beer was difficult to transport inland except by waterway before the coming of the railways, and undoubtedly good coastal shipping routes allowed common brewers in Edinburgh, Liverpool, Newcastle, Hull, Bristol, Great Yarmouth and North Kent to flourish and effectively remove the competition of their publican brethren. But communications in Leeds, Manchester and Birmingham were good enough to allow them to dominate the wool, cotton and hardware industries respectively by the late eighteenth century, and their populations grew at a rate which elsewhere would have encouraged rapid commercial brewing.

Any explanation of these differences in the scale of production seems to require consideration of a more complex set of factors than the spurt to competition delivered by the London brewers in the South-East together with regional transport advantages. These simply fail to explain marked contrasts as early as 1830, for example between neighbouring Liverpool and Manchester on the one hand, between Norfolk and Suffolk on the other. Clearly, the degree of public house control exerted by common brewers is important: in London, Liverpool, Norwich and Great Yarmouth it was already high in 1830, whereas in Birmingham, Manchester and Leeds it was almost non-existent. But explanations have concentrated upon the supply side. What of demand? Clearly, the traditions and economy of the working class, the prime consumers, were also important considerations. How else did publican brewing survive in Leeds well into the 1800s? The social structure of Birmingham, the classic city of the small master, encouraged a self-reliant publican brewing class similar in its standing to those of countless other employers around them. In 1873–4 no fewer than 97 per cent of victuallers and 99 per cent of beer house keepers in the city held a licence to brew.[15] Only after 1880, when an extraordinary 85 per cent of output was still brewed by publicans (see Table 3.2), was their economy smashed by the competition and commercial might of the new common brewers. Earlier, Sheffield and Manchester, as well as large areas of the

[14] Wilson, *Greene King*, p. 267.

[15] Crawford, Dunne and Thorne, *Birmingham Pubs*, p. 5. Their book provides the best account of the centre of publican brewing.

Black Country had supported a similar brewing structure. In early Victorian England, 'when the workman's only idea of play was drinking in a public house', there must have been enormous loyalty to publican brewers, themselves often one-time members of the local trade and known to everyone in the neighbourhood from birth.[16] And in the South and East of England the earlier emergence of the common brewer is best explained in relation to the barley and malt trade. All good malting barley was grown in this drier area, and those brewers who produced malt as well as beer derived benefits from this duality of business which allowed their breweries to expand. Already by 1830 there were towns in East Anglia, like King's Lynn, Norwich, Great Yarmouth and Ipswich, where common brewers were doing a trade of several thousands of barrels annually, owning their own maltings and many public houses. Good water carriage was also clearly significant in their success. These suggestions about early concentration of public house ownership by brewers, about different urban social and economic structures, and about the importance of the malt trade from North Yorkshire to Dorset are not presented as watertight explanations of the varying size of production units in brewing as between different cities and regions. Only with much more detailed local research, amongst the surviving deeds and correspondence surrounding the acquisition of these publican breweries, will definite answers be secured.[17]

II

For the London breweries the half-century after 1830 is something of a dark age. Charles Barclay's dozen 'power-loom' porter breweries (see p. 11) – familiar institutions from Peter Mathias's study – were exceptional features in the British brewing scene in 1830. Fifty years later differences in scale between them and the leading Burton, Dublin, Edinburgh and country brewers had largely disappeared. Not only was their output surpassed in some cases, but also they ran into increasingly acute difficulties in the thirty years before the First World War. What went wrong? The answers, entirely post-1880 in focus, are usually provided in terms of an intense competition in London and the burden upon their capital of ever-larger loans to publicans at a time when

[16] The quotation is from a working man writing in the *Birmingham Morning News* in 1871, quoted in Crawford, Dunne and Thorne, *Birmingham Pubs*, p. 5.

[17] See Wilson, *Greene King*, pp. 119–22 for an account of the types of early public houses they bought.

Table 3.3. *Brewing in the London excise collection district, 1831–80*

Year ending	Common brewers			Licensed victuallers			Persons licensed to sell beer[a]			Percentage brewed by		
	No.	Bushels brewed	Average[b] barrelage brewed	Total	No. brewing	Bushels brewed	Total	No. brewing	Bushels brewed	(1)	(2)	(3)
5. 1.1832	115	4,427,385	19,249	4,393	31	41,729	1,279	131	170,439	95	1	4
5. 1.1841	105	5,804,923	27,642	4,504	13	16,417	1,684	91	177,008	97	0.3	3
10.10.1850	72	5,628,901	39,089	4,346	2	1,881	2,209	64	104,583	98	0.03	2
10.10.1860	86	7,473,806	43,452	3,072	4	8,144	2,550	54	188,849	97	0.1	2
30. 9.1870	95	9,264,758	48,762	6,119	14	12,970	4,009	69	328,314	96	0.13	3
30. 9.1880	113	10,006,665	44,277	6,197	4	7,258	3,412	24	125,286	99	0.1	1

[a] After 1841 numbers are the total of those licensed to sell beer 'to be drunk on premises' and 'not to be drunk on premises'.
[b] Barrelages have been estimated by using the standard nineteenth-century formula of reckoning that 2 bushels of malt on average were required to produce a 36 gallon barrel of beer.
Source: PP (1831–2) XXXIV; (1841) XXVI; (1851) LIII; (1861) LVIII; (1871) LXII; (1881) LXXXIII.

consumption faltered. Do the problems of output, of competition and of capital which faced the big London brewers after 1880 have their origins in the previous fifty years? Sandwiched between their emergence as wonders of the first industrial age and their relative decline after 1860, this twilight period has been largely unexplored.

The dimensions of the London brewing industry in the half-century after 1830, drawn from the excise returns, are set out in Table 3.3. Unfortunately, the boundaries of the London collection district shifted between 1830 and 1880, and, since the excise officers' maps have not survived, it is impossible to trace their changes. But change they did, presumably in 1830, and also several times afterwards. Clearly always including the metropolitan area, the outlying boundaries seem to have been adjusted almost as frequently as their 'year ending' date. As statistics therefore they are neither more nor less reliable than most of those that economic historians rely upon. Nevertheless, they do underline several points quite clearly. First, the *average* size of a London brewery was roughly six times that of its country counterpart in 1830. Secondly, their output doubled between 1830 and 1850. What happened was not a rapid expansion of the biggest breweries, but rather that in the difficult trading years of the 1830s and early 1840s many smaller concerns went to the wall. And whereas elsewhere in England the number of common brewers grew appreciably between 1830 and 1850, in London, with traditionally high start-up costs, it was not easy for newcomers to break into an industry where more than 80 per cent of output was shared by a dozen brewers whose scale was unrivalled. Thirdly, brewing by licensed victuallers in London was already unimportant by 1830. It did not recover, since neither of the chief causes of this state – overwhelming competition from the great porter breweries and the high price of property – diminished. Any hopes that the government might have had in 1830 of prising open the oligopolistic London trade were quickly dashed. Beer house sellers never brewed more than a tiny 4 per cent of beer produced in the London collection district. It was exactly as Barclay and Buxton had prophesied in 1830: beer houses turned to them as sources of the best and cheapest supplies.

Although, therefore, the malt tax statistics do reveal sharp differences between the patterns of brewing in London and the provinces, averages obscure the polarity of scale between the capital's dozen great porter brewers and those numerous common breweries which were such a feature of eastern England. In 1829 there were eight London breweries producing in excess of 70,000 barrels (four produced 150,000 plus); of the fourteen unnamed brewers in England and Wales in 1831 yielding over 40,000 each it is difficult to identify with certainty a single one that did so outside London.[18] Only the capital, with its population of close on 2 million in 1830, could sustain this number of large-scale breweries. In fact a remarkable degree of concentration had been achieved as early as the 1780s. Then, the 'first twelve houses', all porter breweries, Mathias reckoned were producing over three-quarters of all strong beer sold in the capital: half a century later this had grown to 85 per cent.[19] The figure seems implausibly high when matched against the first post-Beer Act statistics, but the difficulty is not in demonstrating the degree of concentration in the capital which is evident enough, but in establishing whether this leading handful of brewers retained and increased their grip upon the metropolitan beer trade in the next half century.[20] To measure this we must first look at the expansion of this market before looking at the ways they met its changes and challenges.

Unquestionably the London beer trade offered brewers unrivalled opportunities in the fifty years after 1830. For the population of the capital grew by 150 per cent – a rate twice that achieved in the rest of England and Wales. Two important features stem from this. First, leading breweries failed to keep abreast of the rapidly expanding market on their doorstep: they supplied around two-thirds of the beer consumed in Greater London in 1880 in comparison with four-fifths half a century earlier. Moreover, there was a marked shift after the mid-century from porter to mild. This provided an opportunity not only for ale brewers in London but also for the more enterprising ones in Burton, Dublin, Edinburgh and other prime brewing centres, especially along the eastern seaboard, to obtain a strong foothold in the London trade when it was expanding at its fastest between the 1840s and the 1870s. When consumption everywhere dipped after 1880, and the porter brewers were forced into a renewed vigour by the new situation,

[18] Mathias, *Brewing Industry*, p. 552, *PP* (1834) XXIV, 4th Report into the Excise (1834) Survey of Brewers, p. 173, and 1885–6 return printed in *Country Brewers' Gazette* (1887), p. 112.

[19] Mathias, *Brewing Industry*, p. 26.

[20] In 1830, Mathias states the total of strong beer brewed in London was 1,441,000 barrels. A year later the output of beer of average gravity was 2,213,000 barrels. No doubt output jumped in 1831, but in 1830 the 'first twelve houses' produced 1,200,000 barrels (Barclay's estimate). Their output is unlikely to have jumped proportionately in the next year. Moreover, there were 115 common brewers in the London excise district in January 1832. On Mathias's figures, this left in 1830 only 241,500 barrels to be brewed by around 100 other brewers. An average output of 2,415 barrels seems implausably low, for the *national* average was 2,095 barrels in 1824 (Wilson, *Alcohol and the Nation*, p. 48).

Table 3.4. *Estimated output of the eleven leading London brewers, 1830–80 (in thousand barrels)*

Primarily porter brewers	*c.*1830	*c.*1880
Barclay Perkins	320	480
Truman Hanbury Buxton	230	580
Whitbread	190	250
Reid's	130	250
Combe Delafield	113	400
Calvert (later, City of London)	80	200
Hoare	70	200
	1,133	2,360
Primarily ale brewers		
Watneys	90	350
Mann, Crossman & Paulin	7	220
Charrington	15	470
Courage	10	250
	122	1,290
Total	1,255	3,650

Source: *c.*1830: Mathias, *Brewing Industry*, p. 552.
*c.*1880: Individual company records in the GLRO, Westminster and Whitbread Archives, and printed company histories.

the conditions were created to make the London market, as every brewery traveller lamented, intensely competitive. Second, the key to success in London was the ability to shift from brewing porter and vatted ales to a quicker maturing mild, sweet beer. The switch was far from untroubled and its ramifications provide the essential reality of the world of brewing in early and mid-Victorian London.

The capital's tradition of porter consumption in 1830 went back more than a century. Although country brewers did brew porter in small quantities, its production was very much a metropolitan speciality. The favourite London liquor possessed distinctive features. As a result of the use of high-roasted malts, it was dark and cloudy, and usually vatted for periods of nine months or more. Essentially it was a weaker, inferior stout, easily produced in bulk and ideally suited to the soft well-water of the capital. Because of its opaqueness it was not difficult for publicans to adulterate, and brewers themselves were adept at mixing and fining returns with fresh porter. There was some consumption of ale in the capital, but this was produced only by such brewers as Watneys, Courage and Charrington who specialised in mild ale production (Table 3.4), or brought along the Thames from such renowned centres as Burton, Derby, Dorchester, Faversham and Canterbury.

But already there had been a move away from porter. In 1818 Charles Barclay reckoned popular demand was for a milder beer and that porter was not kept for as long as formerly. Even if tastes in London appear to have been shifting in 1820, the leading brewers were almost totally committed to the production of porter. In 1831–7 Reid's proportion of porter to total sales was 87 per cent (98 per cent of its London trade), Truman's 82 per cent, and Whitbread's 85 per cent in 1835–6. Before 1835, when they began to brew mild ale, the latter's trade was entirely in porter (see Table 3.5). Truman had ventured into ale brewing two years earlier. What seems to have occurred is that in the 1830s, to accommodate this shift towards a lighter, but not essentially weaker, mild beer, the London porter brewers began to vary their production. Other brewers like Charrington, Courage, and Mann, Crossman & Paulin, who were principally small-scale ale brewers, were now able to increase their output rapidly. Courage soon gained an enviable reputation for mild and stout. At Charrington, 'the whole business seemed to be considered on a simple basis that Charringtons sold the best Mild Ale in London, and it was a great privilege for publicans to get on to their books'. The new beer houses allowed Mann, Crossman & Paulin's expansion; in 1850 they supplied around 500 beer houses and boasted the largest share in this area of the trade.[21] On the other hand, the switch of the great porter brewers to ale was remarkably slow: even in 1860 it represented only a quarter of Whitbread's porter trade in the capital; and Truman's and Reid's proportions were remarkably similar. From the evidence of these three breweries porter sales in London were largely stagnant between 1830 and 1860, showed a modest recovery in the 1860s, and then declined rapidly after 1870.

This hesitancy of the London porter brewers in embracing ale brewing in the face of a static market for porter gave the chance for ale brewers, in London and elsewhere, to break quite readily into the London market in the 1840s and 1850s. The lead of Charrington and Mann, Crossman & Paulin, Bass and Allsopp is well known. But the evidence of Lacon's Great Yarmouth brewers (see p. 118) provides fresh evidence of the ease with which it could be achieved. Lacon was well

[21] Quoted in *Brewer's Progress, 1757–1957* (1957), p. 38; SCHL into Acts for the Sale of Beer, *PP* (1850), XVIII, Qs, 139, 145. Evidence of Robert Crossman.

Table 3.5. *The London porter and ale sales of Whitbread, Reid's and Truman, 1833–80 (bulk barrels)*

	Whitbread			Reid's	Truman		
	1	2	3	4	5	6	7
Annual average	porter	ale	2 as % of 1	porter sale only	porter	ale	6 as % of 5
1830–4	174,629[a]	–	–	116,552	200,574	29,841[b]	14.8
1835–9	150,850	17,039	11.3	124,654	242,653	45,360	18.7
1840–4	145,292	25,938	17.9	131,840	219,329	51,994	23.7
1845–9	141,545	27,971	19.8	158,648	256,187	53,906	21.0
1850–4	129,580	30,304	23.4	152,375	260,425	63,795	24.5
1855–9	123,676	30,512	24.7	147,769	263,801	72,723	27.6
1860–4	130,876	38,945	33.6	163,404	278,749	94,064	33.7
1865–9	139,500	72,648	52.1	174,505	290,387	160,557	55.2
1870–4	134,966	96,655	71.6	144,828	266,455	221,566	83.1
1875–9	101,041	131,732	130.0	101,283	179,949	299,848	166.6

[a] 1832–4 only
[b] 1833–4 only
Source: Whitbread Rest Books, W/22 Whitbread Archive. Reid's Abstract of Rest 1809–87, GLRO, Acc. 75/108. Truman's Abstract of Rest Book 1781–1866, Acc. 73.36; Annual Totals 1867–1888, Acc. 73/36.

placed to satisfy the London market with its renowned mild ales. Indeed, it had probably done so since the Napoleonic Wars when Yarmouth became a major naval base and its breweries flourished, but the firm's ledger only discloses its scale from 1858 onwards. In that year Lacon were selling 42,838 barrels of mainly mild ale in the capital, which was no less than 80 per cent of their output. And the trade grew. It was never less than three-quarters of production. In 1871 it topped 100,000 barrels for the first time.[22]

Between 1830 and 1860 the London market, traditionally porter drinking, thus turned increasingly to the consumption of mild ales. They were variously supplied by ale brewers in London, who expanded rapidly in the 'free trade' in the 1840–70 period; by the porter brewers themselves who reluctantly shifted some of their production to ale; and by brewers, such as Lacon who were able to exploit their access to cheap transportation. It is clear that this consumption-led change in taste to

[22] Whitbread Archives, Lacon's Account Book, 197/239.

mild beers preceded the better-known invasion of the London trade by stronger, light, pale ales chiefly from Burton upon Trent in the late 1840s and 1850s (see pp. 93–5). Here it is necessary only to underline that these shifts in taste posed massive problems for the porter brewers. Why were they unable to respond with greater alacrity? Why did they not see off the likes of Lacon, Bass and Allsopp from their market? After all they possessed a remarkable record of achievement in every aspect of brewing between 1750 and 1830. The testimony of Charles Barclay in 1830 about the supremacy of London porter-brewing was wonderfully assured and confident.

Technology is really too grand a title for one of the main difficulties facing the porter brewers between 1830 and 1880. Supreme in the techniques of large-scale brewing at the outset, they did not fall behind their rivals. Evidence from their rest books (annual accounts of sales, stocks and profits) shows that their purchases of up-to-date utensils, steam-driven mashing machinery, and the latest refrigerators and ice-machines, for fully equipping integrated 'steam' breweries, were as forward as any in the industry.[23] Admittedly by the 1860s the breweries of Bass and Allsopp looked more impressive because of being largely new built, constantly expanding, unrivalled in their physical scale, and vigorously exploiting the railways.[24] The yards of the London breweries, still looking to the River Thames for transport, were in comparison decidedly cramped. Bass's brewery covered 140 acres in Burton, Barclay Perkins, the largest brewery in London, a mere 12. Even the uncritical Barnard gives the impression that the latter's Anchor Brewery in Southwark was inconvenient, having grown in a totally unplanned fashion. Other big brewers in London were similarly incommodious in their lay-outs and almost all of them required heavy capital expenditure to re-equip them in the 1880s. In contrast, prints of Bass's and Allsopp's breweries, reproduced everywhere, were icons of the new industrial age: they were the true images of massive Victorian growth rather than those symbols of the London brewing world, gigantic vats and dray horses. And, although production methods varied between London and Burton brewers, especially in fermentation, the former could brew as well as they had ever done by using good materials, absorbing the main results

23 Whitbread possess a splendid series running from 1798 to 1918. Each year, placing a valuation on the brewery, they listed any building alterations and machinery and equipment installed. Barclay Perkins, Truman and Reid's possess less complete runs.

24 See, for example, articles in the *Licensed Victuallers' Gazette*, 7 June 1873; 14 Nov. 1874, besides the well-known essays in Barnard, *Noted Breweries*.

of the 'scientific revolution' in brewing, and paying careful attention to the costs.

But if leadership in 'science' mattered little in an industry of tradition and variety, London's water supply was a problem. Traditionally porter was brewed with water from the Thames. Supposedly this gave it an inimitable character. This was a myth. All the London breweries sunk wells hundreds of feet deep in their yards. The water, once beneath the London clay, was soft, and with the use of dark malts they brewed a highly distinctive brown beer.[25] With this water it was also possible to brew a tolerably good mild ale. But when in the late 1840s and 1850s Burton ales swept the board in the capital, the London mild ale and porter brewers found that they could not brew comparable pale ale themselves, because London water with its higher carbonate and lower sulphur content produced a dull wort. All the superlatives of the Victorian beer writer were reserved for the colour and taste of Burton ales. A London brewer, writing in the late 1860s, acknowledged that when they first invaded the market in the boom of the late 1840s they were 'preeminent in quality, flavour, brilliancy and soundness'.[26] The London brewers faced a genuine problem.

Their first reaction – as it was elsewhere in England – was to produce an imitative pale ale themselves. Brewers passed backwards and forwards to Burton. They frantically analysed the London water and put additives to it. One brewer, giving his credential as being 'related to a great export brewer', added in 1844 3 lb of chloride of lime, 5 lb of subcarbonate of potash, 1 lb of carbonate of soda, 2 lb of common soda and 2 lb of Roach allum for 40 quarters of gyle. It was 'put into the first liquor [water] and boiled ½ hour and cooled down for Mashing'.[27] He swore by the result, but experiments of this nature were hit-and-miss affairs. More usually they were with sulphate of lime, but until the successful application of gypsum in the 1870s none of the experiments was successful – brewers' boasts notwithstanding.

The London brewers were therefore in a quandary. Most acknowledged the superiority of Burton's water in brewing pale ales, but some

25 Mathias, *Brewing Industry*, pp. 12–21 provides the best account.

26 Whitbread Archives, W15/42. This is the manuscript of a book compiled by an unknown brewer whose experience went back to 1825. 'Having spent nearly ten years at the Copperside at Combe & Delafields during which time I brewed 3172 Gyles, Mashed 363,439 quarters of malt and used 3,914,276 pounds of Hops which produced 1,233,683 Barrels of Brown Beer, 108,354 Barrels of Pale Beers. Total 1,347,037 Barrels.'

27 *Ibid.*

also believed that it was the Burton union system of fermentation, introduced in the 1840s, which was the real secret of their success. Again there was no consensus and some London brewers simply threw money at the problem. In the early 1870s, taking the lead of Ind Coope from Romford in 1856, Charrington, Mann, Crossman & Paulin, and Truman opened their own pale ale breweries in Burton (see pp. 96–8). In 1875 the *Licensed Victuallers' Gazette*, which ran a series of major articles on the nation's leading brewers, 'remarked that Messrs. Truman & Co. had learned how to turn to account the present prevailing mania for Burton ales. Their plan is alike simple and efficacious, and consists merely in going to Burton to make beer for the people to drink.' Courage took a rather more round about route. In 1872 they made an arrangement with Flowers of Stratford-upon-Avon to supply them with a fine pale ale. It did not work well because rail freights and double cartage costs in London were heavy, and therefore in 1886 they shifted their contract to Fremlins of Maidstone, who shipped some 32,000 barrels a year by sailing barge to Courage's wharf at Shad Thames. Only in 1903 did Courage take the final step and acquire Hall's brewery at Alton (Hampshire) with its seventy-seven tied houses and a local trade of 20,000 barrels a year. Shortly afterwards, 'the premises were rebuilt . . . and now challenge acceptance as a model brewery'.[28]

There was inertia amongst some of the porter brewers. Had the 'scientific revolution' in brewing come a generation earlier, the way forward might have been clearer. But locked into the world of porter (easier to produce than either a 'running' mild or pale ale), and with no means of brewing a consistent version of the latter in the 1850s and 1860s, momentum was lost. After a century of enormous success in large-scale brewing they were initially also dismissive of Bass's and Allsopp's advance in the 1850s. One London brewer put their view, succinctly, if crudely: 'you might brew ale in a piss pot, but porter must be in large quantities'.[29] Moreover, an absolute decline in the demand for porter was not really apparent until the 1870s. Indeed a modest recovery in the 1860s must have added to the porter brewers' general uncertainties. They could not bring themselves to scrap their vats, the real symbols of the porter trade, because there was no possibility of them producing in the 1850s and 1860s a 'running', bright, consistent pale ale with their water. In 1889 Barnard focused the problems facing them from the example of Mann, Crossman & Paulin:

[28] G. N. Hardinge, *The Development and Growth of Courage's Brewery* (1932), pp. 17–18.
[29] Whitbread Archives, W21/42, see note 26.

> These changes in the public trade are the cause of great expense to the brewer ... here for instance is a brewery in which, only a generation ago, were erected scores of vats ranging from 7,250 to 18,000 gallons capacity ... which have all been pulled down and no use found for them but cellar flaps and stillions. It is not only the disuse of these vats where the expense comes in, but the new ale required different treatment; for instead of being stored high up in columns of vats, it is now spread out in barrels on the ground floor, compelling the firm to buy ground right and left to meet the new demands.[30]

At Truman in 1875 there were 95 vats of various sizes, whilst at Barclay Perkins, 'although the old system of vatting has to a great extent gone out of use, it is by no means entirely abandoned'. Yet the latter brewery still housed an incredible 130 vats each of from 500 to 4,000 barrels capacity (see Plate 6).[31] These were impedimenta by the 1870s which Barnard realised were a real problem for the porter brewers. Their plant was often unsuitable for the production of running ales on a significant scale. Large settling-backs to clarify and settle the light, bitter ales required the space vacated by the vats. As a result, many London brewers had to rebuild large sections of their breweries from the mid-nineteenth century onwards.[32] Others, as we have seen, sought different solutions by opening branches in Burton. Reid, Meux and Whitbread had attempted to brew ale in London in old porter breweries. On the whole they did so without notable success. The uniquely surviving monthly minute books of Truman, commencing in 1884, reveal that for years their major problem was brewing in summer a consistent running beer that had more than a fortnight's life.[33] Frequently, they were in despair as their customers slipped away. Sometimes they hinted that their competitors, except Mann, Crossman & Paulin, were little more successful. Thirty years earlier the difficulty of brewing a 'running' beer in London must have been even greater. Certainly, it explains the genuine reluctance of the leading brewers to run down their porter trade, stagnant as it was in comparison with the burgeoning demand for mild and pale ales in Britain's fastest growing market.

In the 1850s and 1860s when the London brewers hesitated about which way to turn, their grip on the capital's market as a whole noticeably faltered. Having taken on the production of mild ale with tolerable success after 1830, when the taste for pale ales made extraordinary headway in the middle years of the century, ale and porter brewers alike

30 Barnard, *Noted Breweries*, I, p. 378.
31 *Licensed Victuallers' Gazette*, 16 Jan. 1875; 20 March 1875.
32 Barnard, *Noted Breweries*, I, pp. 245, 279, 371.
33 GLRO, Acc. 77.94, B/THB, Truman's Monthly Reports, 1884–1914.

briefly had no answer. Even the output of Mann, Crossman & Paulin, ale specialists and the fastest expanding brewery in London between the 1830s and mid 1860s, stagnated at around 200,000 barrels for the next two decades.

Undoubtedly, by the middle years of the nineteenth century the direction of the big London porter brewers, with eight or ten partners, was cumbersome. First, they were cumbersome because very large sums were advanced. In the 1830s their capital was amongst the largest of that subscribed in British industry. Individuals were providing sums, in some cases, of more than £100,000 each and, in addition, were credited with large 'surplus' capitals tied up in the business. When, for any reason, families wished to withdraw capital real problems could be created for both firm and family. Sir Benjamin Hobhouse, the senior partner of Whitbread, died in 1833; the conditions of the partnership were so constraining that it took almost ten years for his executors to withdraw the major portion of his £120,000 investment.[34] In the 1880s Truman had an even more acute problem. Henry Villebois, the direct Truman heir, possessed an interest of £141,560 (out of a total nominated capital of £423,000) plus a commensurate share of their £300,000 'surplus' capital. On his death in 1885 his family wished to withdraw his share; and there were other partners – three members of the Buxton family – whose commitment was thought to be questionable because of the impact of the tightening of the licensing laws, bad times and the cost of modernising the brewery.[35] These pressures precipitated the formation of Truman as a limited liability company. And again, the dissolution of the old partnerships was welcome in the mid-1880s because share-owning gave partners and their heirs a much greater flexibility in the distribution of their enormous assets. But, for two generations, while partnerships in such firms as Reid's, Barclay Perkins, Truman and Whitbread grew larger, constant preoccupation about the disposition of individual's assets led to unadventurous management.

Secondly, it became evident that many of the fastest growing country brewers, such as Bass, and some in London, for example Charrington, Courage and Hoare, were all more decisively run by not more than four partners. Of course, those London firms with around ten partners were always in practice actively managed by only two or three who were extremely well paid, lived on the premises, and headed a team of

[34] Whitbread Archives, W/36/95 Box UU.
[35] GLRO, Acc. 77.94, B/THB, Truman's Monthly Reports, 1884–1914.

salaried departmental managers. Nevertheless in terms of status they were often junior members of the partnership, constantly having to look over their shoulders for the approval of elderly, 'sleeping' partners, living in the country in great style and whose major preoccupations were financial and social. In 1828 Whitbread drew up a new twenty-year partnership agreement. Nine partners agreed to employ a capital of £440,000. Five of them, including the three largest subscribers and the two Whitbread representatives, were 'not to be obliged to see to the Management of the Brewery'.[36] This arrangement, traditional in concept, appears not to have worked well in a changing situation. The firm made little progress in the next thirty years. Indeed, a rare paper circulated amongst partners suggested it had been in decline to 1862. 'The question at issue is in fact this', it continued, seeking the opinion of all the partners as to the course to be pursued, 'whether we shall continue the policy of the last few years and extend our trade or whether we should return to the practice of many years previous and confine our transactions to much smaller limit.' They had now ample capital, the paper argued, 'for a good increase of the trade ... [it] is still 60,000 barrels short of what might be done in the Brewery, and it seems to us a most unnecessary waste to leave our large plant idle.'[37]

In fact Whitbread was not alone in its unadventurousness by the mid-century. Reid's, Barclay Perkins and Truman occupied the same league. Because their capitals were so large and invariably sustained by loans from family, friends and publicans alike, and these in turn were converted into numerous loans to tie trade, their accounts suggest they had become quasi-bankers. Admittedly they were adept, as they always had been, at producing porter and profit, but increasingly they were involved in the manipulation of loans and leases. For any vigorous extension of their trade beyond London there is little evidence before the 1870s. In comparison with the Burton brewers and their legion of imitators across Britain there was a general cautiousness.

Large partnerships and great traditions could induce somnolence. Barnard provides a wonderful, fleeting glimpse of this world. When he inspected the partners' private rooms at Truman – he was not invited to luncheon – he noted that they were hung with one of the best collections of big-game trophies to be found anywhere in Britain. He also noted that there were great spaces where the four Truman family portraits by Gainsborough (Baron Ferdinand de Rothschild had recently bought

36 Whitbread Archives, W/36/31.
37 *Ibid.*, endorsed 'Read to all the Partners on 26 July 1866'.

two of them) had hung for generations. This vignette perfectly captures the uneasy transition of the great London brewing dynasties into the rapidly changing situation of the 1880s.[38] From another angle, an account of Truman in 1875 provides a good flavour of the composition and limitations of their business arrangements:

> The present partners, then, are Sir Thomas Fowell Buxton, third baronet; Mr. Robert Hanbury, his son, Mr. Charles Addington Hanbury, and grandson; Mr. T. Fowell Buxton, his son, Mr. J. H. Buxton; Mr. Arthur Pryor, who has two sons in the firm; Mr. Edward North Buxton, and Mr. Bertram Buxton. In addition to these must be mentioned Henry Villebois, Esq., of Marham Hall, Norfolk, who is only a sleeping partner, but is the sole remaining representative of Sir Benjamin Truman. Mr. Villebois was for many years the master of the most celebrated pack of foxhounds in the Vale of White Horse, and now fills the same important office to his own hunt in Norfolk, where the Prince of Wales is a regular attendant.[39]

Few merchant banks, the highest status firms of the nineteenth century, boasted a more august ownership (see Plate 7). In terms of financial and business probity Truman belonged to the very best Victorian tradition. Theirs was the ideal form of organisation for steering a straight, unadventurous course. And in part the difficulties of London's great porter breweries were due to these cumbersome partnership structures. Truman had, as Barnard recorded, slipped from the 'top of the tree' with a production of 606,000 barrels in 1872 to 510,000 barrels in 1886–7.[40] Their minute books reveal that the firm was well run, but that it cherished traditional practices more than it faced up to problems of production and competition in the rapidly changing London beer market after 1880.

Bound within the confines of the declining popularity of its historic product, unable before the 1870s to produce a consistent pale ale to match the Burton beers which were in such great demand, possessing an unwieldy internal structure, concentrating upon production and relying very heavily upon massive loans to secure their retail outlets, the London brewers failed to keep abreast of developments in the mid-Victorian brewing trade. They were like aged battleships vulnerable to constant attack from Burton and the other brewing centres. By the 1880s they were no longer, as they had been half a century earlier, the market leaders in the quality of their products, in their large-scale system of production, in their financial and business structure, and

38 Barnard, *Noted Breweries*, I, pp. 176, 210–12.
39 *Licensed Victuallers' Gazette*, 16 Jan. 1875.
40 Barnard, *Noted Breweries*, I, p. 209.

(although less important) in technical and scientific innovation. Their performance in these years was not a good base from which to face the upheavals of the brewing industry in the 1885–1900 period and the difficult years which ensued to the outbreak of the Great War.

III

Burton upon Trent, like Bradford, Crewe and Middlesbrough, was one of those wonder towns of the nineteenth century, whose mushroom growth the Victorians traced with fascination and a plethora of statistics. In 1830 it was a slow-growing North Midlands community of fewer than 7,000 inhabitants, long famed for the quality of its beer, but whose seven or eight breweries together only produced 50,000 barrels a year – a total rather less than half the output of Combe Delafield alone, London's fifth largest brewery. Seventy years later the output of Burton's twenty-one brewing firms was 3,500,000 barrels, around 10 per cent of UK beer production. The town's population had reached 50,000, almost wholly supported by the beer industry which directly employed a workforce of 8,000.[41] Bass, 'the King of Brewers', was perhaps the best known firm in the British Empire. Burton was the capital of brewing (see Plate 10). Barnard found it in 1889 almost entirely a creation of the previous half century: 'All the principal establishments are closely packed together, and churchs, chapels and public houses plentifully abound. Nor are there any antiquities besides the Church and Abbey . . . All is brand new and shining.'[42] How had this transition – one of the most remarkable in all Victorian industry – taken place? Certainly it was a triumph few could have forecast in 1830.

Admittedly Burton's fame as a brewing centre went back more than two centuries. Its celebrated water, high in mineral content and almost free of organic traces, produced a fine strong ale which kept and, unusually, travelled well. And in the eighteenth century its handful of breweries had commenced a remarkable export trade, with the Baltic states by way of Hull. But the leaders of this trade, the Wilson, Sketchley, Bass, Evans and Worthington families, were as much speculators and merchants as they were brewers.[43] This resulted partly from the difficulties of a distant trade in a product as vulnerable as beer, partly

[41] Owen, *Development of Industry*, pp. 72–104. William Molyneux, *Burton-on-Trent: Its History, Its Waters, and Its Breweries* (1869) provides a good contemporary view of developments to the 1860s. See especially pp. 198–259.

[42] Barnard, *Noted Breweries*, II, p. 407.

[43] Owen, *Development of Industry*, pp. 32–67; Mathias, *Brewing Industry*, pp. 171–92.

from a dependence upon laborious communications via the River Trent and the Trent and Mersey Canal that led them into other ventures. In 1807 Napoleon's continental system dealt Burton's Baltic trade a near-mortal blow. It recovered partially after 1814 only to be finally extinguished by a sharp rise in Russian tariffs in 1822. The town reeled. Its breweries, none of which produced more than 5,000–6,000 barrels a year, contracted from thirteen in 1780 to five in the mid-1820s. Its population, at a period of rapid acceleration everywhere in Britain, hardly expanded. The first census recorded 6,044 souls in 1801; only 743 more were included thirty years later.

Yet those firms which did survive were forced to make important shifts in their market. Some Burton beer had always found its way to London. After 1807 it did so in increasing quantities, and Bass and Allsopp, the two principal survivors of the crisis, also tackled more vigorously the populous markets of Birmingham and South Lancashire. But the real fillip to renewal came from an unexpected quarter. An unusual trade in 'India Ale' had been conducted with the East India Company from at least the 1780s. It appears to have been dominated by the otherwise unremarkable firm of Abbot & Hodgson's Bow Brewery.[44] Barclay Perkins and some Scottish breweries had also entered the Indian market, albeit less successfully in the 1800s.[45] And when their Baltic trade finally collapsed in 1822, Bass and Allsopp made a rapid switch to the East Indies route. To do so they had to produce a new ale whose chief qualities were paleness and brightness – a beer quite different from the high-coloured, sweet, very strong beer the Russians had enjoyed. The evidence from Georges of Bristol's half-hearted experiments to brew 'India ale' in 1828 suggests that it was not difficult to improve upon Hodgson's beer. 'We neither like its thick and muddy appearance', wrote their senior partner to Willis and Earle in Calcutta, 'or (*sic*) rank bitter flavour.' Seven months later shipping twenty hogsheads of pale ale, he had 'made a slight alteration in the Ale by brewing it rather of a paler colour and more hop'd to make it as similar as possible to some samples of Allsopp's ale'.[46] But to reproduce another brewer's beer was by no means as simple as Georges implied. Mathias

[44] Molyneux, *Burton-on-Trent*, pp. 229–3 provides an early account of the development of India Pale Ale by Bass, Allsopp and Salt after 1823. Every subsequent description of the two great firms and the town repeated the standard description. Certainly it was a most important step because IPA became the forerunner of those bitter ales which sold so widely in Victorian Britain.

[45] Mathias, *Brewing Industry*, p. 190.

[46] Courage's Archives, 35740/GR/5, Georges' Foreign Letter Book (1818), Letters to Willis and Earle, Calcutta dated 14 May, 22 Dec. 1828.

Table 3.6. *Brewing in Burton upon Trent, 1831–1900*

Year	No. of breweries	Output (barrels)	Employees	Av. output per brewery in barrels
1831	9	50,000	200	5,550
1851	17	300,000	956[a]	17,650
1861	20	971,000	3,086[a]	48,550
1868	26	1,755,252	5,074	67,510
1888	31	3,025,000	8,215	97,580
1900[b]	21	3,500,000	8,000	166,670

[a] Not including clerical staff
[b] Approximate figures
Source: Owen, *Development of Industry in Burton-upon-Trent* (1978), p. 229.

concludes, 'Almost certainly, the virtues of Burton water enabled them to eclipse the original product in the trade which they had begun by imitating ... Burton "India Pale Ale" had the remarkable virtue of arriving pale, clear and sparkling in Calcutta, more successfully than any other.'[47] By 1832–3 Bass were shipping 5,250 barrels, Hodgson 3,900, and Allsopp 1,500 out of a total Bengal trade of 12,000.[48] The trade was of sufficient dimensions to revive the flagging fortunes of the two leading Burton brewers, but not to provide the momentum for Burton's remarkable growth after 1830 (see Table 3.6).

Of course, those forces examined in Chapter 2 – population growth, increasing real wages, the predilection of the new industrial labour force to spend its surplus earnings on the national beverage – were the bedrock of Burton's spectacular brewing edifice. But there were special features in the building itself. First, the town's water allowed its brewers to brew pale, bright, consistent beer – originally for the Indian market – which captured the nation's taste in the mid-nineteenth century. By the use of first-class materials, the union system of fermentation, and early attention to the science of brewing, Burton's leading brewers produced beers superior to vatted porters and stock ales. Adulteration and blending meant that the latter at point of sale were variable, at worst undrinkable. After 1815 they had had a thoroughly bad press.

47 Mathias, *Brewing Industry*, p. 192.
48 J. Bell, *A Comparative View of the External Commerce of Bengal* (1833), p. 14.

In the new cheap glassware, which replaced the old pewter, leather and pottery mugs after the 1840s, the Burton pale ales looked more appetising than a cloudy porter or murky vatted beer. *The Lancet* in 1852 pronounced it a restorative, 'a wine of malt'. Briefly, in the third quarter of the nineteenth century, few other brewers (and certainly not those in London) could imitate the exact qualities of the best Burton ales. As a result, their output grew by almost ten times between 1850 and 1875.

The second feature special to Burton related to innovations in retailing. However superior Burton's beers might be, they did not sell themselves, especially as they commanded premium prices. Exporting beer was a highly specialised, limited trade, beset with problems. Despite the Burton brewers' experience in handling this aspect of their business, to invade the entire British market from a remote North Midlands town required the development of a new retailing organisation. With the aid of the railways, Burton along with Guinness pioneered the agency system, for its expansion after the 1830s relied almost entirely upon the free trade. Loans to publicans and direct ownership of houses were virtually unknown. This system of agents and stores in all the larger towns of Britain was established in the half-century after 1830 (see pp. 151–68). Pioneered by the two leading firms of Bass and Allsopp, it appears to have developed informally even before the first railway came to the town in 1839. No other firms matched them in the scale and celerity of their growth. Together always accounting for around two-thirds of the town's beer output between the 1830s and 1880s, they stood head and shoulders above the rest. Unfortunately, their records have not survived in the detail necessary to reconstruct the key stages of their more important new departures. But sufficient is recoverable of Bass's history to trace its central contribution both to the Victorian brewing industry and to the rapid development of Burton upon Trent.[49]

As a firm Bass possessed everything by the 1880s (see Plate 30). It retailed a famed product in every country in the world. Its rapid growth and its profitability were by-words in Victorian Britain. Michael Thomas Bass (1799–1884), the architect of its greatness, was the doyen of Victorian brewers and a man of the utmost distinction in public and private life. Even Gladstone, no great ally of the trade, described the firm in 1880 as 'a permanent and respected institution of the country' and its proprietor as one who, 'both from his ability and his long

[49] C. C. Owen, *History of Bass*, forthcoming.

experience and skill in that branch of industry, stood at its head'.[50] Others were less restrained: *The British Mercury* believed Bass 'a mercantile colossus that has o'erstrided every similar institution in England, if not the world ... a monument to the energy of men'. *Vanity Fair*, standing Gladstone's assessment on its head, thought that Michael Thomas Bass's name would 'be remembered with gratitude when they [Gladstone and Disraeli] are utterly forgotten'.[51]

The firm of Bass certainly lived up to its reputation as a contemporary wonder. In 1881 its three breweries and thirty-nine malt houses in the town covered 145 acres. They consumed 300,000 quarters of malt a year – the produce of 75,000 acres of barley (not all British) and 36,000 cwt of hops which kept over 3,000 acres of hop gardens in cultivation. The breweries were powered by thirty-two steam engines. Nine locomotives, running on 12 miles of private track, conveyed brewing materials and beer round the breweries and to the town's railheads. Over half a million casks a year were renewed, repaired and cleansed by over 400 men and boys in a 'steam' cooperage (see Plate 9). In all, the firm employed 2,500, not counting managers, clerks, travellers and draymen in the agencies. Producing a million barrels a year, providing a revenue of £1,000 a day for the government from an annual turnover of £2,500,000, it was the biggest ale brewery in the world.[52] And to drive home this spiral of figures, wonders of the ancient world were introduced to conjure up visual stupendousness. The scale of the great pyramids and the walls of Babylon were easily exceeded by Bass's stock of casks. When Barnard marvelled at the firm's 600 foot hop store, its manager produced his Bible to prove that the building was 50 feet longer than Noah's Ark.[53]

Yet in 1830 Bass was producing a mere 8,480 barrels of beer. Tracing its origins back to 1777, like its chief Burton rivals, Allsopp and Thomas Salt, it had begun to produce a superior pale ale for export after 1823. Then its growth in the 1830s, exploiting the London, Midlands and

[50] Quoted in *The Financier*, March, 1900, p. 2. See also *North of England Farmer*, 15 May 1871; *Licensed Victuallers' Gazette* 14 Nov. 1874, pp. 2–7; *Licensed Victuallers' Almanack* (1881), pp. 97–101; *Arts and Sciences Album*, 22 Dec. 1886 (marked 'Refused to Pay' in Bass Museum); Barnard, *Noted Breweries*, I, pp. 1–77 for a selection of late nineteenth-century descriptions of Bass. K. Hawkins, *A History of Bass Charrington* (1978), pp. 8–15 provides a succinct modern account; C. C. Owen, a more extended one.

[51] *British Mercury*, 6 June 1879; *Vanity Fair*, 20 May 1871.

[52] Based upon the account of the firm in *Licensed Victuallers' Almanack* (1881), pp. 97–101.

[53] Barnard, *Noted Breweries*, I, p. 46.

Liverpool markets even before the railways, was exceptional for a small brewery. In 1837 it produced 31,500 barrels, at least a threefold expansion since the Beer Act.[54] Much of this trade had found its way along the Trent navigation and the Trent and Mersey Canal. Both provided slow, expensive means of transport. And it was a mode particularly subject to pilferage: bargemen broached the casks and topped them up with water. But in 1839 Burton was emancipated from the grip of decades of these delays, exorbitant costs and thefts. The Birmingham–Derby railway, opening in August of that year, connected Burton to the growing rail network at an early stage in both's development. To transport a ton of ale (rather less than five barrels) to London, formerly costing £3 for a journey of over a week, was now 15s (75p) for one taking only half a day.[55] The effect was immediate. Burton's total production of beer increased from around 70,000 barrels in 1840 to 300,000 ten years later; that of Bass, around 40,000 barrels at the end of the deep recession of 1837–42, had grown to 148,000 in 1853. Successful sales at the 1851 Great Exhibition inaugurated a most remarkable period of expansion the like of which the brewing industry had seen neither before nor since. In 1860 the firm produced 341,527 barrels, placing it alongside the largest London breweries; by 1876, brewing close on a million barrels a year, it was an undisputed world leader.

At the heart of Bass's success lay the demand for pale ale – usually forming around three-fifths of output in these years – and the agency system.[56] When national consumption rose rapidly in the third quarter of the nineteenth century, the railways distributed Bass's beer everywhere throughout the United Kingdom. Exports became proportionally less important, falling from a quarter of sales in the 1840s to a tenth in the 1860s. By the early 1850s, even with considerable expansion, the family's original brewery was inadequate. In 1853–4 Michael Thomas Bass, who succeeded his father in the running of the firm in 1827, constructed his Middle Brewery, ten years later a third, New Brewery, and then in 1876–8 the Old Brewery was demolished and completely rebuilt. And just as frequently similar great sets of maltings were constructed. By the late 1870s Bass ran twenty-eight malt houses in Burton and ten in Lincoln. The most recent set at Burton, built at Shobnall between 1872 and 1875, consisted of seven houses, each 240 by

[54] Bass Museum, F/12/5.
[55] For the development of transport from Burton, see Owen, *Development of Industry*, pp. 13–25.
[56] Owen, *History of Bass*, forthcoming.

90 feet, with four malting floors apiece. Like most things at Bass in the 1870s they were the biggest in the brewing world. In all these departures the drive was provided by M. T. Bass himself, although he was ably assisted by his Gretton and Ratcliff partners.

The only other brewing firm in Burton remotely to rival Bass in its dominance of the pale ale trade was Allsopps. From similar eighteenth-century origins, and with a comparable experience in the Baltic and Indian export trades, it matched Bass's moves after 1830 by the creation of a similar agency system. But, except between 1869 and 1876 when it enjoyed a particular sharp spurt, it was always a couple of steps behind Bass in terms of its barrelage, the scale of its two breweries and the size of its workforce. Yet with an output of close on 900,000 barrels at its peak in 1876, it was Britain's second largest brewery and the two together dominated brewing in Burton.[57] The firm faltered badly in the post-1879 recession. It was ill managed; its late acquisition of tied houses was ill considered; its public flotation was bungled (see pp. 303–4). To the casual visitor in Burton, all seemed well; but for the financial press, it had become, by the early 1890s, the prime example of how a brewery should not be run (see Plate 33).

The success of Bass and Allsopp before 1880 and the long tradition of small-scale brewing in Burton meant that many firms attempted to emulate a measure of their good fortune. Usually dreams outnumbered achievements. Nevertheless the number of breweries in the town increased appreciably: five in 1822; nine in 1834; seventeen in 1851; twenty-eight in 1875. Entry was not difficult and changes of ownership were frequent since the majority were small scale.[58] In the latter year, at the peak of Burton's pre-eminence in the British brewing industry, three-quarters of the firms produced fewer than 35,000 barrels each, whilst the top half-dozen breweries accounted for 88 per cent of output; Bass and Allsopp together concentrated 62 per cent of the town's beer production.[59] By 1880 there was a clear division between those breweries with Burton origins and those whose owners were attracted to Burton through their need to brew pale and bitter ales and by the magic of the town's reputation. Some of the breweries which had been long in

[57] There is no continuous series of Allsopp's barrelage available. A manuscript 'Burton Excise Returns' in the Bass archives suggests it grew from 555,000 in 1869 to 918,000 in 1876. Between 1883 and 1888 it collapsed dramatically, from 853,000 to 460,000 barrels according to the Excise Return and Owen, *Development of Industry*, p. 234.

[58] Owen, *Development of Industry*, pp. 73–104, 234.

[59] See copy of 'Burton Excise Returns', Bass plc. Owen, *Development of Industry*, p. 234 provides a table of Burton breweries and their output in 1888.

the town like Salt and Worthington grew steadily, the latter steered impressively after the 1880s by the shrewd management of W. P. Manners. And in the 1860s, the Burton Brewery Co., founded in 1843 and an unusually early incorporation of 1858, began to prosper. Typical of the smaller companies was Bindley which Barnard visited in 1889 (see Plate 11). Founded in 1873 by a Major Bindley, who had been twenty years with another Burton firm, Barnard conveys the distinct impression that this small, modern, pale ale brewery, with a 15,000–20,000 annual barrelage in the mid-1880s, was not really worth visiting.[60]

Conditions changed after the 1850s when a number of brewers from elsewhere in England decided to set up in the town. There were small migrants in the mid 1840s, for example William Middleton and Joseph Nunneley; much more notable was Ind Coope from Romford in Essex in 1856. Then curiously there was a hiatus in the brewing boom of the 1860s. Not until 1872 did Charrington acquire a Burton base, to be followed in the two succeeding years by Truman and Mann, Crossman & Paulin (see Plate 16). Certainly the reputation of Bass and Burton was at its height, but the three London brewers were remarkably slow in making their decision. Only mounting prosperity in Burton between 1860 and 1875 finally pushed them into action. In the late 1870s and 1880s a number of provincial firms followed the Londoners' lead, amongst them Boddingtons' (1875), A. B. Walker (1877) and Peter Walker (1880) both from Warrington, and Everard (*c.*1885) from Leicester.[61]

With the exception of Ind Coope, most of these migrants did not experience great success. Of course, in primarily producing pale ale for their firms elsewhere, they pursued a limited objective. Mann, Crossman & Paulin, Truman and the Walkers were not prepared to pump unlimited funds into their Burton subsidiaries. They simply wanted a good pale ale to push into their London and Lancashire pubs, and made

60 Barnard, *Noted Breweries*, II, pp. 407–18.

61 Owen, *Development of Industry*, pp. 80–2. The firm of Phillips & Sons Ltd was perhaps the most extraordinary. Originally a tiny brewery in Stony Stratford it moved to Northampton before 1860 where 'the business increased with unexampled rapidity, and the name and beers of Phillips Brothers became familiar throughout the country. But with something of that vaunting ambition which sometimes o'erleaps itself, the heads of the firm could not remain satisfied with local form, and not only established agencies in London and far distant provincial towns, but opened a branch brewery in Burton on a large scale' (*Licensed Victuallers' Gazette*, 9 Oct. 1875). In 1873 the Phillips family were ejected from their partnership by an unusually lively sleeping partner, S. L. Seckham, who sold the Burton brewery to Truman. Thomas Phillips bought a brewery with thirteen pubs in Newport (Mon.) which flourished in the booming border town. (*Phillips & Sons Ltd Jubilee, 1924.*)

no attempt to build up the networks of agencies which had carried Bass, Allsopp, Worthington and Salts to success. But even narrow objectives seemed elusive. Mann, Crossman & Paulin, according to Truman their great East End rivals, brewed the best mild ales in London. Yet in Burton they apparently never produced more than around 60,000 barrels at their Albion Brewery. In 1896 they placed it on the market. John Crossman dismissed their Burton venture: 'It came like a shooting star and quickly disappeared, paying the cost and leaving behind it a street named Crossman and a little church (endowed).' The firm's historian believed a more objective assessment of their decision to pull out of Burton would have been high transport costs and the London brewers' ability themselves to brew a reliable bitter ale by the 1890s.[62] Moreover, Truman's monthly minutes suggest that once the initial euphoria had worn off, their Burton scheme was little more successful than that of Mann, Crossman & Paulin, in spite of the fact that at their peak they brewed close on 150,000 barrels a year.[63] Certainly, after Ind Coope they were the largest 'migrant' brewers in Burton, selling around two-thirds of their output in their London pubs. Again, however, moving beer twice in Burton, then three times in London, together with rail and cartage costs, was an expensive business. And depression in the mid-1880s and an acute drop in Truman's sales in London between 1903 and 1911 meant that their Burton brewery ran well below capacity. At its best in the late 1890s, it produced a healthy 10 per cent profit, but there were years when the directors grumbled that it was not paying well and a report in 1898 concluded that its £150,000 capital might have been utilised more advantageously in London or Colchester. Even with a resident partner, management at a distance was not easy. Malt production was sometimes off target, and supplying public houses at 200 miles distance was not very profitable. At times their Burton beer was good. In 1886 their North Wales agent thought it 'the best in the market ... better than Bass and Allsopp'. But in London, publicans seldom shared his opinion, partly because the firm often blended its London and Burton ales – on their own admission not always successfully. But Truman were not the kind of firm to back out of its undertaking, and they continued brewing well below capacity, never realising the vision

62 H. Janes, *Albion Brewery, 1808–1958: The Story of Mann, Crossman & Paulin Ltd* (1958), pp. 55–64.

63 The following section is based upon Truman's Monthly Reports in GLRO, Acc. 77.94, B/THB. The Burton partner came across to London each month to produce a detailed written report of his activities.

of the early 1870s when the trio of bolder London brewers set up in Burton.

The town's emergence as Britain's premier brewing centre was a relatively brief affair. At the height of its success, after the period of extraordinary expansion enjoyed by Bass and Allsopp, it attracted brewers from London, Lancashire and the Midlands to share the secrets of its success. But by the 1880s Burton's paramountcy was being undermined. Per capita beer consumption declined. Brewers everywhere were producing a tolerable imitation of light, bitter Burton-type beers. And when they eliminated the free trade in the 1880s and 1890s by their purchase of public houses, the Burton brewers – themselves owning few houses and making few loans to publicans – found themselves excluded from their old markets. Moreover, the export trade gave them no comfort. Neglecting it in the great boom of the 1860s and 1870s, they later found that the trade had shifted away from the heavily hopped Burton ales to brighter lager-type beers (see pp. 174–6). There was, therefore, no shelter in overseas markets. The effects of all these changes were quickly felt in Burton. Between 1888 and 1900 the number of breweries in the town fell by a third. Only Bass, whose reputation and direction were unrivalled, and Worthington, whose tight management and early bottling achievements were exemplary, did tolerably well to 1914. Their success in these difficult years masked the fact that Burton's supremacy had come to an end by the 1890s.

IV

Although the great London and Burton breweries stole the headlines in the Victorian brewing press no history of the industry in the nineteenth century would be complete without an account, however brief, of Guinness and the Edinburgh brewers.[64] When Lynch and Vaizey wrote their pioneering *Guinness's Brewery in the Irish Economy, 1759–1876* (1960) they attempted to answer the question, amongst others, of 'why did a single brewery emerge to dominate the industry in Dublin and not in London or Burton or Edinburgh?'[65] For, although it had many parallels with Bass in its growth, Guinness's achievements were the

[64] This account of Guinness is based upon Lynch and Vaizey, *Guinness's Brewery in the Irish Economy, 1759–1876* and S. R. Dennison and O. MacDonagh's unpublished 'History of Guinness, 1886–1939', which Guinness plc allowed the authors to consult. Different in scope and detail, together they provide the best single account of a major brewery in Britain and Ireland.

[65] Lynch and Vaisey, *Guinness*, p. 7.

Table 3.7. *Sales of Guinness, 1830–1914 (bulk barrels of 36 gallons)*

Years	*Annual averages (barrels)*
1830–4	60,088
1835–9	76,524
1840–4	72,877
1845–9	92,385
1850–4	106,272
1855–9	150,219
1860–4	246,909
1865–9	341,572
1870–4	526,167
1875–9	654,359
1880–4	988,482
1885–9	1,269,104
1890–4	1,433,941
1895–9	1,589,769
1900–4	1,930,016
1905–9	2,163,115
1910–14	2,652,430

Source: Lynch and Vaizey, *Guinness's Brewery 1759–1876* (1960); Statistics records, Guinness, Park Royal.

more remarkable. These were principally in three spheres: in dominance of the Irish industry after the 1870s; in an increasingly successful incursion into the British beer market; in their unique methods of distribution of a couple of beers, porter in Ireland, and double stout in Britain. By the 1880s Guinness was the largest brewery in the world with an output of 1,350,000 bulk barrels, almost 60 per cent of total Irish output (see Table 3.7). Then, unlike almost all their major rivals in Britain, they never lost their momentum, even in the difficult years of the mid-1890s and post-1900. By 1914 Guinness brewed 2,842,740 bulk barrels, almost twice the amount of its nearest rival, Bass. In that year, the firm supplied 10.3 per cent of the United Kingdom beer market. Solely from a Dublin base, without amalgamations and without the support of a tied house network, it is an astonishing figure. Lynch and Vaizey's question was pertinent and, as they admitted, when dealing with aspects as nebulous as the demand for and quality of a particular beer, one not easily answered.

In many ways the background of brewing in Ireland was quite different from that in England. It was not simply that spirits were the basic liquor consumed but that the population of Ireland, despite its extremely rapid growth between 1800 and 1845, provided a generally unpromising market for common brewers. The Irish economy was sharply divided between a more prosperous eastern, maritime, anglicised sector, based on Dublin, Belfast, Waterford and Cork, and a backward, subsistence rural society to the west embracing at least two-thirds of the population. Here, Lynch and Vaizey maintained, there was basically no market before the 1850s. Not surprisingly in these circumstances the number of common brewers in Ireland in 1830 was only around one-tenth of their number in England and Wales. In 1832, 216 of them shared a total output of 771,632 barrels.[66] Much the most promising brewing centres were in Dublin and Cork, adjacent to the best barley growing regions in Ireland. Both were well served by coastal and, in the case of Dublin, canal communications. Indeed, towards the end of the period of the Napoleonic Wars prosperity (1800–15), Guinness brewed 66,000 barrels and the Cork brewers, Beamish & Crawford, an annual average of around 100,000 barrels between 1806 and 1815. On these figures, except for a small handful of London brewers, they were the largest common brewers in the United Kingdom. Most of their sales were of porter consumed by the artisan class in eastern Ireland (English exports to this region shrinking completely in the twenty years after 1793). But in 1816, with an acute post-war recession, trade withered dramatically. By 1820, Guinness's sales had fallen to 41 per cent of their 1815 peak; Beamish & Crawford's output in the late 1820s was running at three-fifths of its level twenty years earlier. For the Irish brewers, the 1820s was a worse decade than for their London counterparts. Only by 1833 had Guinness recovered its 1815 position.

It is at this stage that Guinness's similarities with Bass are most marked. The brewery faced fifteen lean years in the difficult period after 1815. Much of its trade, in 'town' porter, was in Dublin and its vicinity. Yet even with its chief partner, the second Arthur Guinness, increasingly immersed in the affairs of the Bank of Ireland, the firm began to turn to the English market as Irish migration eastwards accelerated in the post-war recession. The trade at first was small. In 1823 total Irish exports to Britain were a mere 1,686 barrels. Five years later they were just over 8,000. Guinness were early entrants, obtaining agencies for their stout in Liverpool and Bristol in 1824 and in London during the

[66] The pattern of brewing developed quite differently in Ireland after 1830. In 1852 there were ninety-six breweries and in 1900 about fifty. Although scattered thinly across Ireland, they never flourished in the west and in Ulster (Belfast, a great Victorian city, supported three in 1900). For real success a good English stout trade was essential, and Guinness squeezed its rivals hard in Dublin after 1870.

following year. To cater for the British market they produced a premium porter known either as Double or Extra Stout.[67] Like Burton pale ale, Dublin stout was recognised as something special. Possessing great stability, softness, mildness and viscosity, Guinness brewed theirs at 1079°, and in price it fell half-way between London porter and the best Burton pale ales. English brewers, envious of its success by the late 1830s, maintained that its prices were sustained by the superior opportunities for tax evasion in Ireland. Whatever the reasons, it sold extremely well. By 1840, 82 per cent of Guinness's output was of double stout. Tizard, no mean critic, thought these Dublin stouts were distinctive and of excellent quality.[68] And as the Irish market was wrecked by the 1837–42 recession, the great famines of 1845–51, and with some help from Father Mathew's celebrated Irish temperance mission, Guinness and the other leading Dublin and Cork brewers were forced increasingly to turn to the British market. By 1855 Guinness were selling 60,000 barrels of double stout in England, in contrast with 24,000 and a further 22,500 barrels of single porter in Ireland.

From this base, Guinness made a three-pronged advance. The British trade was extended, but the most notable progress occurred in Ireland. The coming of the railways in the 1850s and 1860s gradually transformed the old rural, subsistence economy. There were common breweries scattered thinly across the west and north (Belfast was never a significant brewing centre), but Guinness through their agents, and later their directly managed stores, captured a good deal of the growing consumption of beers in these areas. In the 1860s the Irish country trade became the fastest growing sector of Guinness's sales; and Limerick became the company's leading Irish agency. Coupled with their raid on the rural market was the extraordinary success of their porter sales in Dublin.[69] Between 1855 and 1880 these grew some sixteen fold; in 1880

67 Guinness's single porter, even cheaper than that retailed by the London brewers, was not sold in Britain except, for obvious reasons, in the Liverpool area. The argument was that bottlers and publicans would have mixed it with double stout (which they did in Ireland) to pass off as the latter. And sales of double stout were appreciably more profitable to Guinness.

68 Tizard, *Theory and Practice*, p. 484.

69 *Sales of Guinness Stout 1868–1886*

Thousands of bulk barrels (percentages of total in brackets)

Year	Total	Extra stout	Porter	Foreign
1868	350	235 (67.1)	115 (32.9)	n/a
1876	779	407 (52.2)	324 (41.6)	48 (6.2)
1886	1,217	513 (42.2)	622 (51.5)	82 (6.7)

Guinness's Irish sales were around 70 per cent of total output. Indeed, 1855 marks Guinness's take off. In the next twenty-one years output increased from 116,425 to 778,597 barrels. Guinness, like Bass in Burton, had become the predominant Irish brewer. As early as 1864, it produced more beer than the rest of Dublin's brewers put together, accounted for half Ireland's exports of beer, and had cornered a massive three-quarters of the Irish market outside Dublin. The brewery was completely rebuilt when output rocketed in the golden years from 1868 to 1876.

Their competitors in Dublin – for example like Manders, squeezed out of business in 1883 – and the London, Bristol and Liverpool brewers pondered long and hard on Guinness's ascendancy. It was in part explained by the consistency and quality of their product and the dynamic nature of their management. Stout, along with mild and pale ales, formed the great trilogy of Victorian beers and Guinness simply produced the best stout in the United Kingdom, and the capabilities of four generations of partners, active in the firm from 1759 to 1927, were perhaps unparalleled in the entire industry. Without exception they were intelligent, versatile, and good managers of men. Even Edward Cecil Guinness (1847–1927), the first Earl of Iveagh (see Plate 13), whose lifestyle was the *non plus ultra* of the Edwardian rich, and in marked contrast with that of his ancestors, retained a sharp eye and sure touch to guide the firm in the forty years after it went public in 1886. But it was in their outlook and practice that their business differed most from other leading British brewers. The firm maintained they had but one function, the production of beer. Even that was restricted to only three varieties, porter or single stout, double, and a matured export stout. They rejoiced in the free trade, they owned no more than a handful of pubs in Dublin, they provided no loans, they allowed those numerous firms and agents bottling and selling their beers to fix the retail price of Guinness, and they did not themselves believe in advertising beyond supplying a few obligatory show cards. All they attempted to do was seek means to improve their beer at the point of sale. After all, it was their product and ascendancy which gave them a bargaining position the Burton brewers ceased to enjoy after the 1880s. Most British brewers attempted to brew an imitative stout, but their attempts were less successful than with pale ales. Guinness vigorously pursued the 'exclusivity' clauses of their agreements with their bottlers and they did not concede discounts, like those Burton and London brewers who

1 'Publicans Sport for October' (1830): Wellington's Beer Act depicted here removing those brewers and publicans who relied upon adulterants in the production and sale of beer.

Key:

1 boiler house
2 copper house and hop back
3 malt bins and grist mill
4 mash tuns, mashing machine and brewer's office
5 engine house
6 cellars
7 water tanks
8–9 cooling squares and refrigerators
10–13 fermenting vessels
14 racking room
15 bottling stores
16 wine and spirit stores
17 loading-out bay

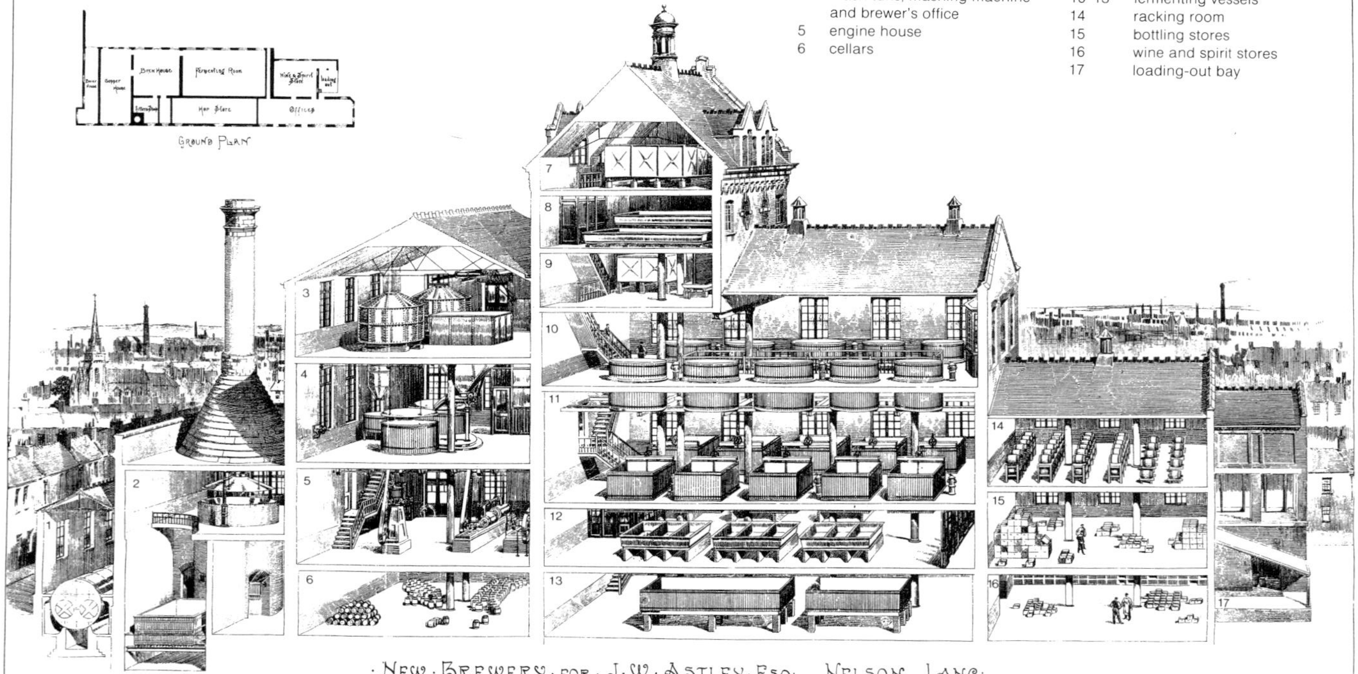

GROUND PLAN

·NEW·BREWERY·FOR·J·W·ASTLEY·ESQ: NELSON, LANC:

GEO: ADLAM·&·SONS, ENGINEERS & ARCHITECTS, BRISTOL.

PHOTO LITHO SPRAGUE & Cº Lᵀᴰ 4 & 5 EAST HARDING STREET, FETTER LANE, E.C.

3 Truman's union room, Burton upon Trent (1889). Introduced in the 1840s, and universally adopted in Burton, the union system of fermentation was believed to produce the finest pale ales.

4 Worthington's laboratory in 1889. The firm employed a succession of distinguished chemists, including H. T. Brown and G. H. Morris, from the 1860s.

5 The laboratory of Robert Deuchar Ltd, Duddingston Brewery, Edinburgh, *c.* 1945. A typical small brewery laboratory.

6 The porter vats of Barclay Perkins, *c.* 1850. In 1875, although the system of vatting had 'to a great extent gone out of use', the firm possessed almost 130 vats ranging in size from 500 to 4,000 barrels each.

7 The twelve partners of the great London firm of Truman Hanbury Buxton in 1886 at Hylands, Essex. *Back Row:* Sir T. F. Buxton Bt., J. H. Buxton, Arthur Pryor, E. N. Buxton, A. V. Pryor, J. H. Hanbury, Gerald Buxton, Robert Pryor; *Middle row:* Robert Pryor, snr., C. A. Hanbury, T. F. Buxton; *Front row:* E. S. Hanbury

8 The proprietors (*seated*) of H. Newton & Co.'s Penrith brewery *c.* 1890 with employees – a group poles apart from that of Truman. The workforce of the typical, small Victorian brewery was not large.

9 Bass's steam-cooperage in 1889. Bass employed over 300 men and boys to make and repair their stock of over half-a-million casks in the largest cooperage in Britain.

10 A general view of Burton upon Trent, the brewing capital of Britain, in 1873. Allsopp's brewery dominates the foreground (*Licensed Victuallers' Gazette*, 7 June 1873).

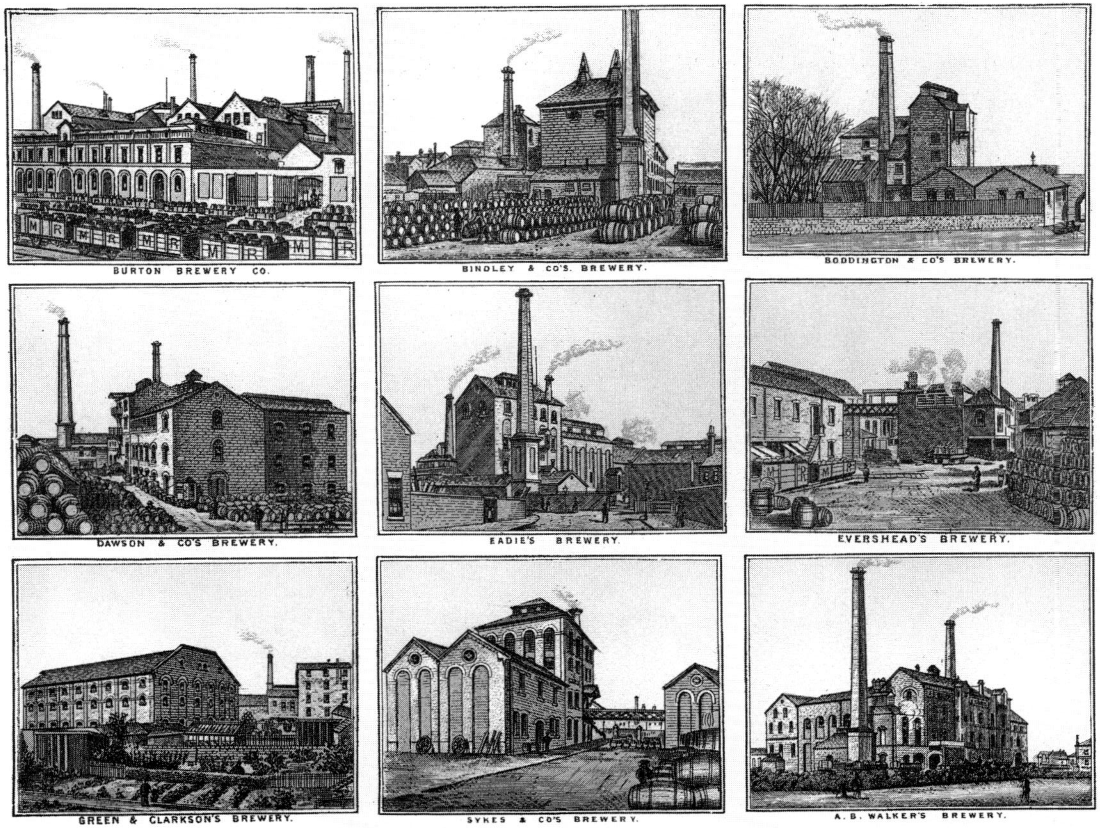

11 Nine of the smaller Burton breweries drawn by J. N. Tresise in 1888.

12 The east front of Lacon's Great Yarmouth brewery in 1894. Unless completely rebuilt like Eldridge Pope (see Plate 25) or John Smith's, most late-nineteenth-century breweries were a hotch-potch of buildings and styles. Extensive steam power had become universal in breweries by the 1860s.

13 A Spy cartoon of the first Earl of Iveagh (1847–1927). Chairman of Guinness and the doyen of Edwardian brewers, Lord Iveagh was a great socialite and philanthropist.

14 John Smith (1823–79). The son of a Leeds tanner, John Smith began brewing at Tadcaster in 1847. He was a characteristic, self-made Victorian brewer.

15 Sir Andrew Walker Bt. (1824–93) from a portrait *c.* 1870. He was later chairman of Peter Walker & Son of Warrington, the largest brewery in the north by the late 1860s. He bought a big Derbyshire estate and presented Liverpool with its magnificent art gallery, erected at a cost of £50,000.

16 Truman's Brewery and railway sidings, Burton upon Trent *c.* 1885. A decade earlier, Truman had begun brewing pale ale in Burton. Like all the town's breweries they depended upon first-rate rail facilities.

17. One of the stables at Guinness's St James' Gate Brewery, Dublin, *c.* 1910. Big stables of cart horses were features of breweries in the larger towns.

18 Guinness's loading wharf on the River Liffey, Dublin, *c.* 1910. The water-borne transport of beer around the coasts of the United Kingdom was a common sight in the 1830–1914 period.

19 'The Busy Bee': a steam wagon of W. H. Brakspear & Sons, Henley-on-Thames, *c.* 1905. Many brewers owned 'steamers' in the Edwardian period. Destructive of road surfaces, they were soon replaced by lighter motor lorries.

20 Drays and vans in the yard of Mitchells & Butlers' Cape Hill Brewery, Birmingham, about 1910.

21 The same yard some years later (*c.* 1928). The lorry has effectively replaced the horse-drawn dray. Almost all brewers commissioned photographs of their lorries and public houses in the inter-war years.

pushed a growing bottled trade, after the late 1880s. Guinness had become the pre-eminent firm in the United Kingdom's brewing industry by the mid-1880s, with a unique product, an unrivalled output, technical leadership and soaring profits.

V

It is tempting to write this brief section on the Scottish brewing industry backwards to capture best the events of the past 150 years. In the early 1960s the formation of Tennent Caledonian (later Bass) and the Scottish & Newcastle breweries brought together no fewer than fifteen of the principal Scottish breweries. None worthy of note escaped their embrace. All except the most vigorous – J. & R. Tennent of Glasgow, William Younger and William McEwan of Edinburgh, George Younger and James Calder of Alloa (and none of these had survived unscathed) – had endured what seems, at least in retrospect, unrelieved difficulties after 1900. Many, over-capitalised in the balmy 1890s, suffered in the sharp downturn in the industry's fortunes after 1900; wartime restrictions hit the Scotch strong beer market hardest; the inter-war years brought unparalleled unemployment, temperance and attrition in the traditional English and export markets; after 1945 worn out plant, low investment, over-capacity and the complete loss of foreign customers during the war years created the conditions which were to lead to the wholesale reformation of the Scottish industry in the early 1960s.[70] Those features which had previously set it apart – early bottling skills, vigorous exports, distinctive Scotch strong beer, and the skill to adapt best English and continental practices to local traditions – counted for little. Only in the second half of the nineteenth century did the industry enjoy the unclouded sunlight of success, when over a

70 This section is based upon the papers of J. & R. Tennent Ltd, William Younger & Co. Ltd, and William McEwan & Co. Ltd, the great trio of Scottish brewers. These are deposited in the Scottish Brewing Archive now at Glasgow University. Inevitably, I have drawn upon the writings of its former archivist, Charles McMaster, who edited a lively *Scottish Brewing Archive Newsletter*. This contains many articles on Scottish brewers and breweries. His 'The Scottish Constituent Brewery Companies of Scottish and Newcastle Breweries PLC' (n.d.), 'The Tennent Caledonian Breweries' (1985, with Tom Rutherford), and *Alloa Ale: A History of the Brewing Industry in Alloa* (1985) are useful. See also B. Bennison and J. P. Merrington, *The Centenary History of the Newcastle Breweries Ltd, 1890–1990* (1990). Barnard visited a number of Scottish breweries in his celebrated itineraries in 1888–90; but the essential monograph for the Scottish industry is Donnachie, *A History of the Brewing Industry in Scotland* (1979).

Table 3.8. *Beer production in Scotland, 1831–1914 (annual averages, in thousand standard barrels)*

1831–4	518	1875–9	1149
1835–9	574	1880–4	1138
1840–4	449	1885–9	1453
1845–9	469	1890–4	1749
1850–4	560	1895–9	2052
1855–9	612	1900–4	1981
1860–4	852	1905–9	1778
1865–9	1166	1910–14	1856
1870–4	1284		

Source: Wilson, *Alcohol and the Nation*, pp. 369–70.

hundred breweries flourished in Edinburgh, Glasgow, Alloa and many towns along the coast and deep estuaries of eastern Scotland, feeding a trade which grew from some 500,000 barrels around 1850 to over 2 million at its peak in 1899 (Table 3.8).

In the mid-nineteenth century the Scottish industry was not unlike that of Ireland, albeit after the 1850s the latter was always larger and no firm in Scotland ever possessed the grip of Guinness. But in its primarily east coast location, in the strength of the whisky trade in many areas, in the reliance upon free trade, and in the need to break into the English and export markets as a condition of growth, the Irish parallels are obvious. Even in 1850, when there were some 154 breweries in Scotland, concentration of production was evident. Although its population growth fell well behind Glasgow's in the nineteenth century, Edinburgh (always with around thirty breweries after 1825) remained very much the brewing stronghold of Scotland. Indeed as a reminder, and to her distaste, Queen Victoria's nearest and most evident neighbours at Holyrood were a number of breweries including the leading firm of William Younger. Glasgow's breweries, except for the historic firm of J. & R. Tennent, were neither so large nor so numerous.[71] And in Aberdeen and Dundee, lesser shadows of Glasgow, breweries remained generally small.[72] Only the Devanha Brewery in the former and Balling-

[71] It is difficult to reconcile the figures provided by Donnachie for the number of Glasgow's breweries. In 1825 trade directories reveal twenty-seven (pp. 31, 121); the excise collection figures give eighteen in 1832 (p. 127), only five in 1852 and nine in 1880 (p. 152). Presumably, many in 1825 were publican brewers although this is not made clear.

[72] Donnachie, *Brewing Industry*, p. 187.

hall in the latter reached national prominence, and these were easily overshadowed by the big Edinburgh and Alloa breweries. Alloa – the 'Burton of Scotland' for Barnard – was an industrial town on the Firth of Forth with some 11,000 inhabitants in 1890, boasting eight breweries in the second half of the nineteenth century, including Scotland's third largest brewery, George Younger. Already by 1845 Alloa produced 80,000 barrels of ale a year.[73] Edinburgh's dominance is underlined by three statistics: in 1832 its output of beer was almost five times that of Glasgow; in 1896 it was eleven times; and in the same year around 80 per cent of Scotland's beer was produced in the Edinburgh excise collection district.[74] Edinburgh, to echo Barnard, had become the Burton *and* London of Scotland's brewing industry rolled into one.

What set Edinburgh and Alloa apart? Again, qualities and supplies of good brewing water were important, although nearby supplies of Scotland's finest malting barleys from the Lothians, the Carse of Forth, and Fife were also a significant factor. The Scots of George IV liked their beer strong and sweet. The taste was an expensive one: only some 120,000 barrels were brewed in 1830; and when it retailed in England it was more costly even than Burton ale and well in advance of the price of Guinness and London porter. There were cheaper alternatives: porter, best brewed in Glasgow with its naturally soft water, were almost as popular there as in London. And for the impecunious, table beers were regularly brewed from a second mashing after the strong wort had been drawn off the mash tun. But when tastes in beer changed in the 1840s and 1850s, and working-class incomes in the industrial belt of Scotland advanced, Edinburgh, whose line of deep, hard-water wells stretched from Holyrood in the east of the city through the Canongate, the Cowgate and the Grassmarket to Fountainbridge in the west, and Alloa, similarly supplied with pure water by permeable strata from the neighbouring Ochils, were well placed to produce the Scottish version of pale ales. At their best these were fine beers. By 1890 William Younger's Holyrood brewery – 'an establishment as extensive as the Trent-side breweries' – was entirely given over to the production of pale ale.[75] The Alloa brewers had once been famed for their mild ales, yet by 1890 Barnard found that J. Calder & Co.'s speciality for the 'Home Trade'

[73] McMaster, *Alloa Ale*, p. 12.

[74] Donnachie, *Brewing Industry*, pp. 127, 187. But these 1896 figures are odd in that the Alloa brewers appear to be missing – unless they were included in the Edinburgh district.

[75] Barnard, *Noted Breweries*, III, pp. 18, 23. Edinburgh ale was brewed at their Abbey brewery, 300 yards away.

was a fine pale ale.[76] Similarly Ballinghall in Dundee, a firm whose output grew twelve times between 1850 and 1890, had by the latter date devoted half their production to pale ales. They were awarded medals at a string of Exhibitions between 1862 and 1890; Barnard considering them 'without being heady ... highly nutritious, bright and sparkling'.[77] The trade in strong Scotch ales did not diminish. Mashing at higher temperatures and fermenting longer at much lower heats, the best Scotch ales were very distinctive, although Andrew Smith, senior partner at William Younger & Co. (1851–69), thought that indifferent water – some wells were becoming polluted by the city's gas supplies – and a lightness with the malt explained the lack of success of some Edinburgh brewers.[78] But the market for strong Scotch beer was limited even where it was popular in eastern and lowland Scotland, in Newcastle and in London. These beers were expensive and too strong for all-year-round consumption. Disher's popular Ten Guinea Ale, 'the Burgundy of Scotland', was a potent brew of around 1100° gravity.[79] And whereas Barnard had found a wineglass of Ballinghall's old beer 'as much as we dared tackle', when he came to sample the Twelve Guinea Crown Ale of J. Fowler & Co. of Prestonpans he rationed himself to 'a tablespoon ... so rich, strong and old was this *seductive* drink'.[80]

The other factor explaining the dominance of Edinburgh and Alloa in the brewing industry of Victorian Scotland was their geographical position. Both had ready access to the eastern coastal trade, above all to London and Newcastle, but also to Aberdeen and Dundee, and via the Forth and Clyde Canal to Glasgow and Liverpool. The coming of the railways in Scotland had, therefore, somewhat less impact than elsewhere in the British brewing industry. The coastal transit of beer was cheaper. As Donnachie wrote of the London trade: 'Through most of the period [1850–1914] the bulk of shipments were sent coastwise, there being no particular cost advantage by rail.'[81] On the other hand, the railways allowed the Edinburgh and Alloa breweries, like Guinness

76 *Ibid.*, IV, p. 394.

77 *Ibid.*, III, p. 164.

78 'Further Excerpts from Andrew Smith's "Book of Notes on Brewing" 1834–1869' in *Scottish Brewing Archive Newsletter*, 13 (1988/9). Deteriorating water supplies and cramped sites in central Edinburgh led to no fewer than seven breweries setting up in greenfield sites within a single square mile at Craigmillar and Duddingston on the edge of Edinburgh in the late 1880s and 1890s. C. McMaster, 'The Breweries of Craigmillar and Duddingston' in *Scottish Brewing Archive Newsletter*, 9 (1987).

79 Barnard, *Noted Breweries*, IV, p. 384.

80 *Ibid.*, III, p. 164; IV, p. 362.

81 Donnachie, *Brewing Industry*, p. 220.

throughout Ireland, to invade the entire Scottish trade. As a consequence, many breweries disappeared: the 154 of 1850 had shrunk to ninety, thirty years later. In Dundee, for example, there were eighteen in 1800, of which four were wholesale brewers; in 1914 there was one.[82] And Dundee was a town of 175,000 inhabitants on the eve of the First World War. Those breweries which folded (and many more stumbled along until 1914) could not hold out against the consistent product, the discounts and the loans (Scotland's trade, although not as free as the brewers maintained, was not tied to the extent of the English market) which the larger Edinburgh and Alloa brewers negotiated with publicans. The Scottish industry had become in 1900, 'by then almost wholly dominated by larger firms'.[83]

The special feature of the handful scattered in Glasgow, Aberdeen, Dundee and Falkirk, as well as the leading brewers in Edinburgh and Alloa, was the ability to break out beyond their local markets. Because tied houses were by no means universal in Scotland – unlike in England, licences were issued annually to the individual publican rather than his house, and in any case most Scottish brewers operated on more restricted capitals – it was difficult for small breweries to sustain themselves by such means as they did in England to 1914. By the 1830s, however, the way forward for ambitious Scottish brewers was clear. Those who had notions of producing more than a few thousand barrels had to achieve growth by seeking out an English market and developing the export trade. Both avenues had eighteenth-century origins. By 1820, Younger of Edinburgh, Dudgeon of Dunbar and Meiklejohn of Alloa were the principal shippers of the 10,000 barrels of strong ale sold in England each year. But the growth in both markets was slow before 1850: in that year 21,000 barrels were exported abroad.[84] Real expansion in distant markets only came in the latter half of the nineteenth century. A brief diary of one of William Younger's travellers in North-East England in January–February 1843 provides a fascinating glimpse of the market and the problems it posed for those Scottish breweries who sought to develop a thriving English trade.[85] Newcastle upon Tyne was flourishing. It was an El Dorado for brewers – 'there is not a street

[82] Donnachie, *Brewing Industry*, p. 151; Barnard, *Noted Breweries*, III, p. 146. Donnachie (p. 215) maintains that small breweries 'dwindled in number rapidly after the 1880s' but this statement is not supported by his Table 57 (p. 151). The sharp contraction in numbers came after 1915.

[83] Donnachie, *Brewing Industry*, p. 151.

[84] *Ibid.*, pp. 132, 135.

[85] Scottish Brewing Archives, WY/5/12/1.

without some dozen public houses in it'. Carlisle and Leeds, by comparison, presented problems, for there the publicans largely brewed for themselves. And everywhere the Burton brewers, quicker off the mark than historians have recognised hitherto, were already making the running. Sunderland and Durham, he found, were 'strongholds of the Burton brewers'; in Newcastle, 'Burton ale seems to be as fashionable here as Porter in Aberdeen.' In Hull, York and Leeds, bottlers already monopolised the family trade with Burton beers. Indeed, in Leeds and the whole West Riding manufacturing area he felt nothing was to be done. In London the same pattern was evident: 'Burton Ales are taking the lead.' Younger were therefore unlikely to break into the bottlers' trade in the capital for, he surprisingly concluded, nothing was known of Edinburgh ale.

In the third quarter of the nineteenth century, however, when English consumption grew rapidly, the leading Edinburgh and Alloa brewers established a firm foot-hold via the agency system. In 1873 Younger had arrangements with fifteen: three in Scotland, three in Ireland, five in the North of England, and one each in London, Birmingham, Bristol and Swansea. They retailed six cask beers and the same number of bottling ales.[86] A few years later almost half their output was sold in Scotland and as much as a fifth each in Newcastle and London, though with some exports included in the capital's total. The other agencies provided modest outlets. Similarly, George Younger of Alloa had connections with six agencies in England and four in Ireland in the 1860s. In fact, however, all ran into problems after the late 1870s save for the Newcastle area. Here, in the region most appreciative of Scotch ales, they concentrated all their efforts into taking over two breweries in the 1890s. Nevertheless, Barnard found George Younger in 1889 with 'no local trade to speak of', without tied houses, and relying entirely upon those twin Victorian virtues, 'excellence and energy'.[87] They needed them because after the 1870s the English market, except on Tyneside, became increasingly difficult. Competition from local brewers, from Burton and from Guinness was overwhelming. Everywhere, the extension of the tied house system excluded the Scottish brewers. Only when they contemplated loans, made moves like George Younger in the 1890s or, like William Younger, employed ten salesmen in London and acquired tied prop-

[86] *Licensed Victuallers' Gazette*, 4 Jan. 1873.
[87] Barnard, *Noted Breweries*, I, p. 446.

erty in and around Newcastle, did they maintain a high level of English sales.[88]

But it was in exporting beer that Scotland's chief claim to fame lay in the nineteenth century. Since some Scotch beer was also exported from English ports the figures are minimum estimates. At its peak in the early 1890s, one-third of the United Kingdom's exports came from Scotland, although its total beer output never exceeded 6 per cent of the United Kingdom's share. It was a remarkable achievement because the export sector of the industry was much the most exacting area of retailing (see p. 169). Scotland's breakthrough came in the 1830s. In that decade small exports of beer to the West Indies, which had long been a feature of Scotland's trade, were superseded by sales in India and Australia. Growth was from 2,893 barrels in 1830 to 17,051 in 1841.[89] Tennent of Glasgow were the leading firm, but later William Younger and William McEwan (from the 1850s), both of Edinburgh, Aitken of Falkirk, and George Younger and J. Calder of Alloa joined them to form a tight caucus of Scottish exporters. By the 1890s when the trade was at its height and some 168,000 barrels were exported, McEwan held the palm. 'McEwans beer is a long way the best in the market, always regular and carries a splendid head', wrote H. J. Younger when he visited Australia in 1897. He found that there was a great deal of beer coming out, especially from 'the smaller fry' – Bernard and Robert Younger of Edinburgh, George Younger from Alloa. Their own beer, he was ashamed to admit, was the flattest to be found in Sydney. He resorted to the blackest imagery in describing the firm's prospects: 'Melbourne was purgatory, this is HELL pure and simple.' Again, he was forced to conclude, 'McEwans first and the rest nowhere.'[90]

Scotland's success in exporting beer was due to three factors. First, strong Scotch ales travelled reasonably well and the later pale ale trade was built on these foundations. Secondly, the leading Scottish brewers were good merchants – William McEwan, for example, coming from an Alloa ship-owning family – prepared to take infinite pains with their beers and the packaging, correspondence and remittances required to

[88] Donnachie, *Brewing Industry*, p. 217. Glasgow and Newcastle were the growth points of William Younger's trade between 1885 and 1900. The latter absorbed 34.5 per cent of sales in 1900; on the other hand, London's had fallen from 22 to 16 per cent. But William Younger was an exceptional Scottish firm, in both its size, producing around 400,000 barrels, and the high level of its English sales.

[89] *PP* Accounts and Papers, 1831 (60) XVII, p. 67; 1843 (175), LII, p. 229.

[90] Scottish Brewing Archive, WY/5/12/5 H.J. to W. Younger, 3, 12 Dec. 1897.

achieve quite small shipments to Latin America, India and Australia. Theirs was an expertise most English brewers neither possessed nor developed. The trade grew from old trading connections with Scottish merchants domiciled abroad. Thirdly, the Scots were pioneer bottlers. Beer was most reliably exported in the bottle and again, since the process was laborious, it required great commitment. Stray figures that survive are surprising. Between March 1862 and 1863 a dutiful clerk of J. & R. Tennent, Hugh McClean, counted the number of bottles the firm filled with porter, double stout and mild ale. His total reckoned from the tuns bottled was 1,011,523 dozen quarts and pints; by a calculation performed from the firm's four corking machines it was 1,020,194 dozens.[91] The discrepancy troubled McClean, but either way, at a period thirty years before bottling was supposedly becoming established, the figures are impressive. It was therefore not surprising that when Barnard visited the Falkirk brewery of James Aitken & Co., primarily an export brewer, he found their bottling department, a vast shed 450 by 65 feet, the biggest he had seen. He attributed the firm's success in Australia and the Colonies 'not only to the quality of their beer, but to the cleanly, perfect, and careful nature of their bottling'.[92]

The Scottish industry concentrated increasingly in Edinburgh and Alloa, was thus distinctive, at least for the handful of larger firms that stood comparison with the bigger English breweries, in its product, in its reliance upon exports and the English trade, and in the fact that it expanded largely upon the free trade. In these respects there were similarities with Burton. And in many ways, with increasing competition from local brewers rapidly tying their trade, it suffered a similar fate. As the export and English markets contracted, the leading Scottish brewers began to experience a sustained period of flatness in their affairs. And the rest never experienced that prosperity enjoyed by the more enterprising English country brewers.

VI

In considering the country brewers it will be useful to set out their number and size. The brewing licence returns provide reasonably accurate figures for the number of common brewers in Victorian Britain. Between 1840 and 1880 their numbers were remarkably stable, around or rather below 2,200. Only after 1880 was there any diminution: by

91 Scottish Brewing Archive, T2/11.
92 Barnard, *Noted Breweries*, I, p. 198.

Table 3.9. *Number of common brewers paying for licences in the UK, 1834–1914*

	No. of common brewers[a]								
Barrels	1834	1852	1861	1871	1881	1891	1901[b]	1911[b]	1914[b]
1,000–9,999	1,302	1,654	1,614	1,810	1,677	1,370	911	716	580
10,000–19,999	89	151	160	216	275	284	263	202	197
20,000–199,999	45	121	103	154	197	279	326	310	310
200,000–499,999			10	8	10	13	11	11	16
500,000–999,999				4	2	2	6	5	5
1,000,000–1,999,999					1	2	2	1	2
2,000,000+							1	1	1
Total	1,436	1,926	1,887	2,192	2,162	1,950	1,520	1,246	1,111

[a] NB Our definition of a common brewer is one who produced more than 1,000 barrels a year. In 1835 around 200 of those who produced less nevertheless considered themselves common brewers (see Table 3.2 column 1). At the margin, the distinction in size between common and publican brewers is not clear cut. But very few of the latter can have produced more than 1,000 barrels, and increasingly a 1,000 barrel output was a minimum scale of operation for a common brewer.

[b] Persons or firms licensed.

Source: 1834, XXIV Fourth Report of the Commission of Inquiry into the Excise Establishment, and into the Management and Collection of the Excise Revenue throughout the UK. Survey of Brewers; Accounts and Papers, 1863 LXVII, p. 101; 1872, LIV, p. 4; 1882, LXXIII, p. 32; 1892, LXXII, p. 80; 1902 XCIII, p. 101; 1912–13 LXVIII p. 644; 1914–16, LIV p. 414.

1900 they had declined by just under a third (31.8 per cent) in twenty years. But the interesting feature is not their stability to 1880, but the great increase in the output of individual breweries which took place. The details are given in Table 3.9.

Two important features emerge from the table. Small-scale brewers (i.e. those producing below 10,000 barrels) had certainly not been squeezed out after 1830; indeed they still accounted for a substantial 70 per cent of producers in 1891. Nevertheless, for a minority the scale of production was transformed. Almost 90 per cent of common brewers in 1834 had brewed less than 10,000 barrels, whereas a mere 1.1 per cent – sixteen breweries in all, of which at least half were big London porter producers – indicated that they turned out more than 40,000 barrels of strong beer a year. Of the mere handful of brewers in the provinces who crept into this category, none approached a 100,000 barrel output. Half a century later, thirty had achieved the latter figure. And no fewer than 137 brewed between 30,000 and 100,000 barrels, of which any amongst them might have expected, had they paid for the privilege, to find their enterprise recorded in Barnard's *Noted Breweries*.[93]

As this chapter has stressed, in an environment of strong market growth especially from 1860 to 1880, and with the private and publican brewers placed at an increasing disadvantage, the more energetic and competent common brewers flourished as never before. Selling about 7 million barrels in 1830, having eliminated their private and public competitors, their annual sales had reached almost 35 million in the years before 1914. It was a fivefold growth which signalled expansion even for the most hesitant brewer and opened up a veritable gold-mine for those of enterprise and vision. Yet those breweries that have become household names in the twentieth century are usually amalgamations of several, sometimes scores of, breweries which in their day had been celebrated in their localities. There is a temptation for those interested in the development of brewing therefore to assume that, in an industry of long roots, growth from the outset was smooth and regular, and that the great post-1880s firms had their origins in a single species similar, if smaller, to those nurtured in London and Burton. The fully grown trees of the 1990s, however, give little indication of their origins and growth-pattern more than a century ago. Above all, an account of what occurred in London and Burton bears little resemblance to developments elsewhere – at least before the 1860s.

Peter Mathias writes at the outset of his *Brewing Industry in England, 1700–1830* that 'much of the argument in other sections of this book is an elaboration of the implications of a 200,000 barrel annual production in fixed capital, cash, horses and drays, raw material costs, organisation and control'. His analysis possesses little relevance for the Georgian common brewer *outside London*.[94] It has not much more for their successors in the 1830–80 period, because only very exceptionally did

[93] He gives descriptions of his visits to 113 breweries in Great Britain and Ireland. A typically Victorian compilation, the volumes present repetitive, sycophantic accounts of the production process, contrasting the London, Burton, Edinburgh and Yorkshire variations in brewing practice. He expresses a clear preference for the new, lighter bitter ales; he has some difficulty in explaining recent scientific advances in intelligible laymen's terms. Unfortunately, since he relied entirely on the brewers' co-operation, the entries have virtually nothing to say about the public capitalisation of the companies going on around him, very little about sales or the acquisition of tied houses. In spite of excluding some notable provincial breweries, Barnard's volumes are useful as a kind of combined Burke's *Brewerage and Beerage*.

[94] Mathias, *Brewing Industry*, p. 25.

their output exceed half that which Whitbread and Barclay Perkins had achieved by 1800. Small, therefore, as the majority of country brewers in their operations might be, their firms possessed a considerable variety: in their origins, in their markets, in their possession of retail outlets, in the strength of their annual balances and the worth of their partners, and in their brewing techniques. In constructing a typology of those 2,000–2,200 country breweries that flourished in the half-century after the passing of the Beer Act, three categories are sustainable. First, there were those firms already enjoying a large trade in the 1830s and 1840s – sometimes, but not invariably, possessing the protection of a sizeable number of tied houses, and usually relying upon an extensive trade beyond their locality. Secondly, there were those firms which grew rapidly in the 1830–80 period from modest origins, vigorously exploiting the post-1830, free-trade beer market. Thirdly, there were newcomers to the industry who realised the opportunity of accelerating demand, technological change and ample profitability in the rapidly expanding Northern and Midland cities. Of course, breweries in each category might have achieved similar size by the 1890s. But it is instructive to analyse the means by which the leaders in each group grasped the extraordinary opportunities presented by urban growth and real wage increases in Victorian Britain, and in the process transformed the scale of brewing in the provinces.

Obvious market leaders in country brewing in the 1830s and 1840s are hard to find if only because producers of more than 20,000 barrels annually were rare. In 1830, there were only forty-five of them all told, and this included the great London brewers. Some thirty or so country breweries, however, set themselves apart at an early stage. What features did they share?

The first category comprises those breweries, principally in the South and East of England, which already controlled substantial numbers of public houses. Ownership of considerable tied estate houses is not an infallible indication of nineteenth-century brewery size, and only rarely do a brewery's records before the 1880s allow a close comparison of its tied estate and barrelage. But already by the 1830s there were firms whose pre-eminence, thrusting them into the top flight of provincial breweries turning out more than 20,000 barrels a year, depended upon their tied estate. Steward & Patteson of Norwich provides the best example.[95] Founded in 1793 by John Patteson, an aggressively entre-

95 This paragraph is based upon T. R. Gourvish, *Norfolk Beers from English Barley: A History of Steward & Patteson, 1793–1963* (Norwich, 1987), pp. 13–48.

preneurial member of the Norwich merchant elite in what was one of the largest cities of its day, the firm produced 20,000 barrels of strong beer annually by 1800. In 1837, following three notable amalgamations of breweries and tied properties, the firm owned around 250 pubs, of which no fewer than 183 were in Norwich itself. But its growth, in the depressed market conditions of the late 1830s and 1840s, did not falter. In 1841 it obtained some of the fifty-three pubs sold by the brewery at Coltishall, a famed malting centre 10 miles north of Norwich, for around £50,000; and four years later it leased the twenty-two pubs of Bell's Gorleston brewery, and bought the twenty-five attached to Paget's Yarmouth brewery. By the mid-1840s, when its Pockthorpe brewery was modernised, production must have stood at around 40,000 barrels. In its pattern of early acquisition, reflecting both the partners' drive and the number of houses already attached to numerous East Anglian breweries, Steward & Patteson underlines David Gutzke's contention that the 'brewers' rationale for rapidly accumulating tied houses emerged earlier, exhibited greater diversity, and owed more to long-term changes than historians have hitherto recognised'.[96]

Many firms followed Steward & Patteson's lead. In 1845 six other breweries in Norwich each owned between twenty-two and seventy-one public houses in the city alone; and in Hertfordshire at least two breweries there owned more than 100 houses each by the 1850s. Any hesitancy to acquire further pubs, when the proliferation of beer houses after 1830 led to a decline in public house prices, was over by 1837. When Thomas Cobbold retired from his Harwich brewery in 1837 some of his twenty-one tied properties sold for more than '50 years purchase of the rent', and neighbouring brewers 'were ... buyers of the great bulk of the property'.[97] This recovery in prices brought both breweries and public houses readily onto the market.[98]

What were the reasons for these early acquisitions of tied property from the south coast to the Wash? Partly it was an attempt to seek protection from the penetration by London brewers into this area.[99] Even small breweries, however, tucked well away from easy access by coast and river, had strings of public houses attached to them. When the

[96] D. W. Gutzke, *Protecting the Pub: Brewers and Publicans against Temperance* (1989), p. 20.

[97] *Bury and Norwich Post*, 12 July 1837.

[98] *Ibid.*, 31 May 1837; *Norfolk Chronicle*, 2 Sept. 1840; Wilson, *Greene King*, p. 62.

[99] For example, Whitbread shipped 5,000 barrels a year to Yarmouth in the 1790s and 3,000 to Norwich. Mathias, *Brewing Industry*, p. 142.

executors of Thomas Vipan sold his small brewery in sleepy Thetford in 1837 it had eighteen pubs scattered across the south-west Norfolk and west Suffolk countryside which realised £11,250.[100] Metropolitan porter was no threat, whether carted 80 miles down the London road or trundled 30 miles from the county town. Vipan was clearly a smaller version of the Norwich breweries, of a type (with its early reliance upon a tied trade) unknown in the Midlands and the North, but which probably after the 1840s became increasingly widespread elsewhere.[101] The most likely explanation is the profitability of joint brewing and malting ventures in this prime barley growing district, the 'early start' of many of these breweries with origins often going back into the eighteenth century, the nearby London example of retail control, and the ease with which public houses could be acquired, often on mortgage, by common brewers with adequate financial resources. Public houses in themselves were a sound investment, providing a regular rental and good security against further loans. Steward & Patteson, sited in a large town and unusually acquisitive, possessed few rivals, but it had many imitators in the South-East.

It was no accident that these brewers from the South-East were the pillars of the Country Brewers' Society in its formative years between 1822 and 1870.[102] Of course they were handy for the occasional meeting in London and the big annual dinner held there during Derby week, but it was their substance as considerable property owners which gave them standing and cohesion in the affairs of the Society. A handful were Members of Parliament, several were also bankers. And elsewhere, especially in the Thames Valley where tied houses were also a feature of the trade, similar sizeable historic brewers were evident. Just as the Stewards and the Pattesons were prominent in local affairs in Norwich, so were the Simonds in Reading, the Reids in Windsor, the Brakspears in Henley, the Bonham-Carters in Portsmouth and the Agg-Gardners

100 *Bury and Norwich Post*, 31 May 1837.

101 For example in the Thames Valley, Hampshire, Cheltenham and Bath. Shepherd, *Brakspear's Brewery* and T. A. B. Corley, 'Simonds' Brewery at Reading, 1760–1960', *Berkshire Archaeological Society*, 68 (1975–6), pp. 77–88 and his 'The Old Breweries of Berkshire, 1741–1984', *Berkshire Archaeological Society*, 71 (1981–2), pp. 79–87 provide well-documented examples of the continuous growth after 1830 from much smaller origins than the larger East Anglian and Hertfordshire examples. It would be useful to have similar studies of West Country breweries although prominent firms like Eldridge Pope and Hall & Woodhouse do not reveal a similar pattern, expanding into tied houses only after the 1870s.

102 Brewers' Society Library, 'Country Brewers' Society Minute Book No. 1'.

in Cheltenham.[103] All owned breweries with an early, flourishing, tied trade. There was an obvious hierarchy of country brewers, just as there was for landowners and farmers. Before 1870 these property rich brewers in the South and East were at the top of the tree, although their pre-eminence in this respect carried no long-term guarantee of permanence. Partnerships could develop a rentier mentality, especially in an area of Britain where opportunities were less than those in industrialised regions of the Midlands, the North and the central belt of Scotland. Early prominence in tied house acquisition was no warranty of subsequent growth. Most of them were overhauled in terms of output by newcomers in the northern towns in the 1870s and 1880s. These were crucial decades; for in them every brewery had to meet the challenges presented by changes in the organisation of companies, renewed competition from Burton, Dublin and London, and the application of science to brewing. Some breweries did so more wholeheartedly than others; and the drive of their owners and partners was a more significant factor than the size of past tied house growth.

The second type of large country brewer is essentially a variant upon the first. The distinctive feature of this group is a reliance upon excellent communications to develop a large extra-regional trade from an early date. In effect, theirs was a dependence not upon tied houses – although they might well rely upon these for their local base – but upon coastal shipping and first-rate river access before the coming of the railways in the 1840s (see Plate 18). Edinburgh's and Alloa's prominence in Scottish brewing and the dominance of Dublin, Wexford and Cork in Ireland underline how necessary good sea transport was for the success of many of the larger breweries in the post-1830 period. In England, brewers in the eastern seaports never achieved a similar supremacy, although the Great Yarmouth firm of Lacon, leading provincial brewers by the 1830s, exploited its coastal location and easy access to good malting barley to become East Anglia's leading Victorian brewery. Similarly, the estuarine position of Bagge of King's Lynn, Cobbold of Ipswich, Cobb of Margate and other north Kent breweries, and Georges in Bristol accounts for their early growth.[104]

Mathias uses Lacon as a good example of a brewery which grew by

[103] See note 101; for Agg-Gardner see the *Licensed Victuallers' Gazette*, 13 Feb. 1875; and Barnard, and P. Eley, *Portsmouth Breweries 1492–1847* (Portsmouth, 1988) for Pike Spicer's (Bonham-Carter) Portsmouth Brewery.

[104] For Cobbold and Cobb see the *Licensed Victuallers' Gazette*, 14 Aug., 4 Dec., 1875.

Table 3.10. *Sir Edmund Lacon & Co., sales of strong beer 1838–57 (in bulk barrels)*

1838	31,415	1843	38,948	1848	35,222	1853	36,450
1839	34,463	1844	37,845	1849	34,906	1854	40,096
1840	36,519	1845	36,199	1850	34,876	1855	43,399
1841	39,979	1846	34,561	1851	36,334	1856	46,818
1842	34,985	1847	34,361	1852	36,710	1857	49,401

Source: Whitbread Archives, 193/239. Sales of table beer are also given. They reached a peak of 3,483 barrels in 1847.

diversification.[105] With origins going back to at least the early 1740s, Edmund Lacon had acquired the brewery in 1786 and transformed it. Developing his interests from his central brewing business, his wealth by the early nineteenth century also depended upon retail malting, the coastal trade, ship-owning and banking.[106] Member of Parliament for the borough in 1812, he was rewarded with a baronetcy when he retired six years later. Unfortunately, the records of the firms do not allow us to pick up their output and their exploitation of their coastal site before the late 1830s. And, as so often, there is no correspondence to fill out the statistical record. Table 3.10 reveals that the firm was amongst the largest provincial brewers in the 1830s and that its output, like so many established breweries in the South and East of England, hardly grew before the mid-1850s. A stray draft letter suggests that its management in 1842 was not brisk, and the fact that it experienced static profits and a declining reserve from 1838 to 1850 (no details are provided after 1850) underlines this assertion.[107]

Then in 1858 a more detailed set of entries reveal quite remarkable statistics. They separate the firm's London trade from that of Yarmouth (the home trade) and its agencies – note that none relied upon the railways – Norwich, Bridlington (closed in 1863), Sunderland (in 1868) and Plymouth. They disclose that Norwich's market was virtually

105 Mathias, *Brewing Industry*, pp. 30, 46, 105, 119, 122, 323, 328–9, 390, 467. See also Wilson, *Greene King*, p. 14; Gourvish, *Norfolk Beers*, p. 38.

106 In 1786 Lacon owned twenty pubs valued from £150–£300 each; by 1811 he owned thirty-nine in Yarmouth and four outside, valued up to £2,000 apiece (Whitbread Archives, 197/222).

107 Whitbread Archives, 197/243, draft letter of W. Sterling Lacon dated 3 Feb. 1842, 'I am attacking the present management of the brewery . . .' [but then no details are given]. The partners withdrew £6,000 a year, 1838–50; an unusual overdraft in 1848 and the reserves showing a deficit to the tune of £902 in 1847 (they had been £18,776 in surplus in 1840) indicates that the late 1840s were difficult years for the firm.

Table 3.11. *Sir Edmund Lacon & Co., sales of strong beer 1858–74 (in bulk barrels)*

Year	In London	Per cent of total	Total sold
1858	42,838	79.6	53,790
1859	42,645	79.3	55,194
1860	41,660	76.8	54,242
1861	45,813	75.6	60,570
1862	48,805	75.7	64,465
1863	50,568	75.1	67,363
1864	57,577	76.6	75,158
1865	66,134	78.3	84,470
1866	69,547	76.9	90,946
1867	72,691	78.1	92,269
1868	86,081	81.0	106,211
1869	91,077	80.4	113,321
1870	92,967	80.8	121,195
1871	101,227	80.4	125,936
1872	–	–	–
1873	99,804	81.7	122,153
1874	108,770	79.7	136,548

Source: Whitbread Archives, 193/239 and 197/52. Figures for 1875–90 exist, albeit in a different form. Total barrelage reached its peak in 1874 and the percentage of sales in London fell to 54 per cent by 1886, although there was a distinct improvement in both sets of figures, 1887–9.

impenetrable by this stage; that the sales of Yarmouth beers in an unlikely Yorkshire resort and in Durham were always small; and that the Plymouth agency, probably opened in 1858, was a good one throughout the 1860s.[108] But the London figures are extraordinary. When Steward & Patteson had attempted to sell their beer in the capital in the early 1840s, their agent there told them that Lacon's ale beat their's hollow.[109] Presumably Lacon, with much easier coastal access to London, had long enjoyed this trade; but the sharp increase in output after 1854 must record a sudden spurt in its growth. In 1858 no fewer than 42,838 barrels of strong beer – 79.6 per cent of Lacon's total sales – were vended in the London market. Table 3.11 provides the figures until 1874.

[108] Only in 1868 did sales in Norwich exceed 400 barrels a year; often they were below 300. The Plymouth agency in the 1860s averaged sales of 1,393 barrels annually.
[109] Gourvish, *Norfolk Beers*, p. 38.

Historians of the industry have always acknowledged the penetration of the London market in the late 1840s and 1850s by the Burton, Dublin and, to a lesser extent, Edinburgh brewers. But Lacon's record, impressive by 1858 and growing by over 100 per cent between 1863 and 1871, reveals the potential and openness of the metropolitan beer trade in this boom decade. Clearly, trade was by no means confined to Bass and Allsopp, Guinness and William Younger. And, with Lacon, that trade was very much in their cheaper lines – above all a mild ale.[110] Yet it was remarkably profitable. Between 1872 and 1879 yearly profits averaged £25,855, providing 18.1 per cent on capital; from 1880 to 1889, £33,853, giving an annual return of 18.6 per cent. Lacon's notable achievement – albeit running into chillier competition after the late 1870s – was their exploitation of the free trade in London.[111] Other English breweries, notably in north Kent, similarly utilised their estuarine, river or canal-side positions to tap the London market. And Wethered of Marlow and Nevile Reid of Windsor, each producing 25,000–30,000 barrels, relied upon the Thames to convey their porters and beers to the capital; Jennings of Windsor, Simonds of Reading, Brakspear of Henley and Wells of Wallingford – smaller in comparison, although not in terms of country breweries elsewhere in the 1830s – similarly exploited their riverside locations.[112]

Bristol Brewery Georges appears at first sight similar to Lacon. In 1830 it was a leading provincial brewery, tracing its origins back into the early eighteenth century, with a prime city-centre site on the River Avon adjacent to all the facilities of a first-rate port. Again no correspondence survives, but an interpretation of its sales figures suggests that its performance before the late 1880s was in fact less impressive, and that it failed, or had less need, to exploit the advantages of superb natural communications in the manner of Lacon or the leading Edinburgh and Dublin breweries (Table 3.12).

Certainly growth before the mid 1860s was unremarkable. The Bristol excise district figures reveal that publican brewing remained strong until the 1870s; and Georges' 'country' sales figures show that after 1840 the firm made little inroad into the trade of rural publicans – that is, if the 'town'-'country' classification remained a true and unchanging bookkeeping distinction. Moreover, sales to Ireland and

[110] For example, in 1880 sales were: ale 25,630 barrels, X 75,210, XX 435, XXX 2,437, porter 853 and stout 870. Total 105,435 barrels (Whitbread Archives: 197/52).

[111] An account of 1838 suggests their 'home' trade relied upon no more than fifty pubs, although their tied estate may have grown steadily across the next half century.

[112] Corley, 'Old Breweries'.

Table 3.12. *Bristol Brewery Georges, beer sales, 1830–94 (annual average in barrels)*

Years	[1] Town	[2] Country	[3] [2] as % of [1]	[4] Total net sales
1830–4	10,242	8,203	80.1	18,389
1835–9	11,663	9,267	79.5	20,535
1840–4	13,923	8,784	63.1	22,227
1845–9	17,565	10,497	59.8	27,551
1850–4	19,191	8,678	45.2	27,328
1855–9	22,451	10,774	48.0	32,735
1860–4	19,096	6,763	35.5	25,475
1865–9	35,280	6,067	17.2	44,356
1870–4	52,470	5,995	11.4	59,559
1875–9	61,056	5,343	8.6	66,403
1880–4	61,710	4,788	7.6	65,196
1885–9	63,562	3,882	6.1	66,228
1890–4	111,558	2,943	2.6	111,826

Note: Total net sales = Town and country trade and bottled beer (to 1872) less all returns.
Source: Courage Archives (Bristol), LM/A/1.

London disappointed. Clearly, superb river and coastal communications were no guarantee of success. And Georges' early venture into the export trade underlines the formidable difficulties facing exporters of beer (see pp. 169–70).

Increasingly Georges relied upon its Bristol base. Possessing no large tied estate (the firm owned around seventy houses, mostly of recent acquisition, when it became a public company in 1886) it grew upon the 'free trade' of a great city whose population increased from 104,000 in 1831 to 222,000 sixty years later.[113] Again, like Lacon, there was a remarkable spurt forward in production between 1863 and 1873, when 'town' trade grew by a massive 196 per cent. It was this achievement, consolidated in the next fifteen years and then expanded by a highly competent management after 1886, that gave the brewery its reputation in the financial press of being the soundest provincial brewery in Britain.

[113] G. Channon, 'Georges and Brewing in Bristol', in C. E. Harvey and J. Press (eds.), *Studies in the Business History of Bristol* (1988).

In considering this second category of country breweries – those which grew principally upon the free trade – one important point needs emphasising at the outset. *All* breweries except Guinness, even in Scotland, acquired tied property after the 1880s. Admittedly some, like Tetley and Allsopp, did so comparatively late. But large and widespread holdings of pubs by the 1900s obscures the fact that many Victorian breweries could grow and flourish by the free trade with little or no tied house support, at least before the 1880s. And these were not confined to familiar examples of the biggest breweries in Burton, Scotland and Ireland. Indeed Greene King, in the heart of East Anglia, provides the classic example of an established brewery which grew by vigorous exploitation of the free trade.[114]

Tucked away in land-locked Bury St Edmunds and excluded from the benefits of industrial and urban expansion, it had nothing to nurture its growth beyond superb supplies of Britain's best malting barley on its doorstep and the drive of its ambitious, sole proprietor, Edward Greene (1815–91). An historic brewery, it had been owned by the Greene family for thirty years, before Edward Greene, on coming of age in 1836, acquired it from his father who had become increasingly involved in the ownership and management of sugar plantations in St Kitts. In the mid-1830s it produced little more than 2,000 barrels of strong beer, and, most unusually for an East Anglian brewery, the number of its tied houses could be counted on one hand. Forty years later, at the height of the beer boom in 1875, the brewery produced some 40,000 barrels. This twentyfold growth had been achieved, at least prior to 1868, entirely in the free trade as Edward Greene boasted when he was elected Member of Parliament for Bury in 1865. Producing basically two beers – a vatted strong Suffolk ale and an imitative Burton-type bitter – he had used the railways after the mid-1840s to push sales throughout East Anglia. By 1875 his beer had become 'the accepted and most popular "tap" from Watton and Wymondham in the north to Colchester and Bishops Stortford in the South, and from Ely and St Ives in the west to Framlingham and Woodbridge in the east'.[115] The expansion had been achieved by travellers working from Bury, Haverhill, Stowmarket, Sutton (near Ely) and two outlying stores in London and Wolverhampton. It was a profitable enterprise which allowed him to extend his brewery every ten years, buy a country estate in 1874, and

114 Wilson, *Greene King*, pp. 60–129 upon which the following paragraph is based.
115 *Bury and Norwich Post*, 17 April 1875 quoting an article from the *Licensed Victuallers' Gazette*.

acquire some ninety public houses between 1868 and the firm's merger with the neighbouring firm of F. W. King & Sons in 1887.

Other firms, some long established by 1830, grew similarly. Alfred Beer, the eponymous owner of Beer & Co., a famed Canterbury brewery, 'prides himself [in 1875] on the fact that, without exerting any pressure or resorting to any large extent on "tied houses" he has never lost a customer'.[116] Georges' growth before 1880 as we have seen was principally in the free trade in Bristol. And the Tadcaster Tower Brewery, which possessed scores of public houses in York acquired at an extravagant valuation at the height of the beer boom in the 1870s, recognised that its success in the following decade had been achieved not through its tied trade – the majority of its pubs in York did very badly in the 1880s – but in the neighbouring army canteens and free trade.[117] The centres of these latter activities were in the flourishing industrial areas of Castleford, Newcastle and Stockton-upon-Tees. Their exertions in the free trade were commonplace in the brewing world before the 1890s. And, of course, newcomers to wholesale brewing, of which there were large numbers before the 1880s, initially did not possess the capital to acquire tied houses on any scale. By no means all these newcomers found the easy route to success which they had imagined an elastic consumption and numerous examples of wealthy brewers could bring (see Plate 8). But many did, especially in the North and Midlands. It is the firm of J. Dymore Brown & Son of Reading, however, which provides the model of a small, free-trade brewery, of a type found everywhere in Victorian England before the 1880s.[118]

James Dymore Brown, from a local farming background, must have anticipated the post-Beer Act bonanza when he acquired a small retail brewery there in 1831. He was disappointed, for between 1832 and 1837 he produced on average only 1,100 barrels, little more than a prosperous brewing victualler would have turned out. With only two tied houses output grew painfully slowly in the depressed 1840s. Nevertheless, he acquired the contract of the Royal Berkshire Hospital in 1854, and ten years later built a new brewery and – inevitably in Berkshire with its superfluity of Royals – named it the Royal Albert. At first its output was around 3,000 barrels, but in the beer boom this had trebled by 1873 and

[116] *Licensed Victuallers' Gazette*, 22 May 1875.
[117] Bass (North): Tadcaster Tower Brewery, Partners' Diaries.
[118] T. A. B. Corley, 'A Small Berkshire Enterprise: J. Dymore Brown & Son 1831–1944', *Berkshire Archaeological Journal*, 69 (1977–8), pp. 73–80.

grown to 14,000 by 1887. Two-thirds of its trade was private, secured by the services of nine agents operating in towns stretching from Hungerford to Windsor, and from Oxford to Southampton. When James Dymore Brown died in 1899 he had made a comfortable fortune of £50,000. Incorporated in 1902, with a paid-up capital of £17,250, the firm thereafter struggled. But it provides a good vignette of these numerous small breweries that flourished by the free trade in the third quarter of the nineteenth century. Their origins and early existence are easily obscured by later public house acquisitions and eventual merger.

The third category of Victorian country brewers is largely to be found in the industrial heartland of England and Wales: the Midlands, the North and Glamorgan. Mostly these regions had been strongholds of publican brewing, although in towns like Liverpool, Leeds and Sheffield common brewing had modest Georgian roots. What they shared in the nineteenth century, however, was an extraordinary concentration of urban population growth. After the 1850s, therefore, when beer consumption increased rapidly, the fastest growing of all Victorian breweries outside Burton became located in those areas possessing the ideal conditions for mushroom growth. Essentially they were creations of the free trade, although when they formed limited liability companies in the 1880s and 1890s they had come very recently to own scores of pubs, beer houses, and off-licences both freehold and leasehold. Yet their development was distinct from breweries either in London and the South-East, long adept at tying their trades, or in Burton, Dublin and Edinburgh which had expanded by exploitation of distant markets. Here in south Lancashire, Tyneside, West Yorkshire, the Midlands and South Wales there was far less emphasis on tradition, much less reliance upon tied house ownership, and not much recourse to elaborate networks of agencies and bottling arrangements. Large markets were on the doorstep, creating some of the fastest growing of all Victorian brewing companies. Commenting on Groves & Whitnall's great Salford brewery, Barnard wrote, 'the population of the borough is over 220,000, that of Manchester being about 380,000; the total population within a radius of thirty miles exceeding that of an equal distance from Charing Cross'.[119]

Indeed, when he compiled his volumes he could barely conceal his surprise. Of course, his panegyrics about Whitbread and Barclay Perkins, Bass and Allsopp, Guinness and William Younger, and even

[119] Barnard, *Noted Breweries*, III, p. 185.

those idyllic, but now sizeable, breweries scattered across rural England, could have been anticipated. For as a Londoner he rose to the thrill of a great historic brewery, or one tucked away in a cathedral city or, best of all, one approached on a summer's day through hop fields and leafy lanes. But the passages about Peter Walker of Warrington, William Butler of Wolverhampton, John Smith's of Tadcaster, S. A. Brain of Cardiff, Joshua Tetley of Leeds, and Groves & Whitnall of Salford were surprising. All possessed, he indicated, large, up-to-date breweries equipped with laboratories and the latest brewing technology; they were wonders of the adaptation of steam and scale to the traditional processes. Their proprietors (see Plates 14 and 15) were go-ahead, able to attune production to local conditions and demands. They were model Victorian entrepreneurs. All these breweries had been founded within living memory and their growth was phenomenal. Peter Walker & Sons, perhaps the biggest English brewery outside London and Burton, had, by early, vigorous exploitation of the Liverpool market on their doorstep, increased the output of their Warrington brewery from 270,000 barrels in 1867 to 340,000 in 1889. The brewery had been founded as recently as 1846.[120] William Butler had built a new brewery on moving to Wolverhampton in 1874; its capacity of 400 barrels per week 'was considerably in excess of the trade at that time'. A second brewery was built in 1881; seven years later the firm could turn out 2,500 barrels a week.[121] Similarly John Smith had begun brewing in premises attached to an old coaching inn in Tadcaster. Forty years later, in the most handsome brewery in Yorkshire, his nephews were brewing 150,000 barrels a year.[122] Brain of Cardiff, Barnard found, had brewed only 100 barrels weekly at the beginning of the 1880s; now they finished 1,100 barrels. 'No brewery in the Kingdom', he thought, 'had increased its output as rapidly as this.'[123]

Certainly, Groves & Whitnall of Salford occupied the same first division. The founder W. P. G. Groves had had a fascinating career before he finally acquired a brewery of his own, at the age of 51, in 1868. A Londoner who had spent two years in Australia during the gold rush of the early 1850s, he ran a vinegar works in Manchester, was a brewers' traveller and eventually managed the small brewery he bought for £9,000 in 1868. It was a propitious year to buy a brewery, for trade

[120] Barnard, *Noted Breweries*, II, pp. 94–102. Barnard's entry is strangely brief and muted.
[121] Barnard, *Noted Breweries*, II, pp. 134–53.
[122] Barnard, *Noted Breweries*, III, pp. 2–47.
[123] Barnard, *Noted Breweries*, III, p. 480.

burgeoned in the great beer boom of the next decade. He rebuilt the old brewery, and added a most impressive new one in 1882–4. Most of the trade was free for in 1885 they owned only five fully licensed houses and forty-three beer houses. Their trade was around 150,000 barrels a year in 1889. Success, Barnard thought, was 'entirely due to the energy and enterprise of the firm'. Manchester drinkers paid great testimony to the fame of its mild ales, unsurpassed in the city.[124] Boddington's, Deakin (later the Manchester Brewery Co.) and Threlfall's, Groves's principal rivals in Manchester, developed similarly. Indeed, before the early 1880s their trade was larger.[125]

There were many other brewers which Barnard might have included, like Best, Robert Cain and Higsons in Liverpool, Vaux in Sunderland or Ansells and Mitchells in Birmingham.[126] They all grew on the same lines: a recent history, sometimes from public or beer house brewing origins; rapid growth after the 1860s, initially in the local free trade; application of the latest brewing techniques in breweries constantly expanded and re-built; and production of a range of beers, a strong ale or sweet mild depending on regional tastes, a London-type stout which became increasingly popular in late Victorian Britain, and Burton-style pale and bitter ales. Yet Barnard's laudatory essays on individual breweries omit two important features surrounding the growth of these large breweries. First, competition was fierce. Growth, certainly in the early 1880s, was never achieved as easily as he implied. Liverpool, Manchester, Birmingham, Leeds and, above all, Newcastle were full of brewers' agents and travellers pushing the beers of every sizeable Burton, Edinburgh, London and Dublin brewery, besides those of local competitors. In 1885 the Leeds traveller of the nearby Tadcaster Tower Brewery was in despair. 'Fifty-one Travellers turn out in Leeds every morning now', he reported, 'fifteen years ago there were only about a

124 For Groves and Whitnall, see Barnard, *Noted Breweries*, III, pp. 183–204 and *The History of the Brewery, 1835–1949* (Groves and Whitnall, 1949).

125 Henry Boddington had become proprietor of the Strangeways Brewery in 1853. Ten years later its output was 17,000 barrels; in 1872, 50,000 and in 1876 93,759, by which time it was the largest brewery in Manchester. See M. Jacobson, *200 Years of Beer: The Story of Boddingtons' Strangeways Brewery, 1778–1978* (1978).

126 For example his account of Barras of Newcastle upon Tyne, III, pp. 168–80 and of no fewer than five Sheffield breweries, III, pp. 269–344. But no better example of a good middle-sized brewery *c.*1890 is provided than that of J. W. Lees, Middleton Junction (Lancs). Lees was chairman of three other companies, sole proprietor of his brewery, first Mayor of Middleton; he had studied brewing chemistry in Liverpool and London, was his own architect of his new brewery (1876), set up a fine laboratory, possessed 2,000 volumes of scientific books in his private room. He had acquired 200 pubs (half were freehold), and served 300 free houses. 'It well illustrates', concluded Barnard, 'the economics of a large brewery.'

dozen.'[127] Secondly, Barnard's criterion for inclusion in his volumes was identifiable success. There were hundreds of breweries which did not on these grounds merit an entry. Not surprisingly, for there were ninety-two breweries alone in the Manchester excise collection district in 1880, and fifty in Sheffield.[128] Therefore brewing, at least to the 1880s, was always a more open industry than Barnard suggests. A recent survey of some two dozen Manchester breweries shows how frequently these smaller firms changed hands, and how easy it was to buy or rent premises, how easy it was to enter the trade.[129] Failure was as evident as success. Nevertheless, from the 1850s to the 1880s, golden opportunities were provided in these industrial areas for go-ahead entrants to the brewing industry. If they possessed a modest capital and the business skills to secure the rewards of mechanised brewing, and above all if they supplied consistently honest beers, good fortune was likely, if not guaranteed.

To conclude: the Victorian brewing scene was very varied. There were still, in 1880, over 2,000 breweries scattered everywhere across the United Kingdom. There was considerable geographical concentration in London, Dublin, Edinburgh, increasingly in the great industrial cities, and also in those 'brewing' towns, Burton upon Trent, Tadcaster, Alton, Wrexham and Newark, whose water supplies allowed them to brew easily the sparkling pale and bitter ales which were the test of every Victorian common brewer. There were also essential differences in scale and tradition. Some already by the 1880s brewed more than a million barrels a year and were amongst the great household names of British industry; some struggled to brew a thousand. But everywhere by the 1880s concentration was becoming evident. The boom years of the 1860s and 1870s were over; consumption dipped; the effects of the temperance movement began to bite. The larger breweries were rapidly eliminating those publican brewers which survived, increasingly tying the trade of pubs, beer houses and off-licences alike, and beginning to acquire their smaller commercial competitors. Private brewing was virtually extinct; publican brewing, except in a few areas, was becoming a curiosity; smaller breweries were beginning to struggle. The common brewer was the prime beneficiary of those extraordinary changes which the Beer Act and the industrialisation of Britain had unleashed in 1830.

127 Bass (North), Tadcaster Tower Brewery Partners' Diaries, August 1885.
128 J. Baxter, 'The Organisation of the Brewing Industry' (1945), p. 66.
129 A. Gall, *Manchester Breweries of Times Gone By* (1978–80).

4

Markets and distribution

In the nineteenth century most beer was sold locally through the traditional outlets of inns, taverns and alehouses, and after 1830, via beer shops and, still later, through off-licences. Yet to study this local distribution presents a problem. For in brewing, as in other industries, there is available to the historian far more evidence about production than about distribution and retailing. It is clear from surviving brewery records that partners and directors discussed the purchase of malts and hops, the quality of their beer, licensing, property acquisitions and finance much more frequently than they did retailing. There is little reference to those countless unrecorded contacts between the brewers and the publicans they served beyond, at best, columns of figures noting their transactions in barrels and dozens of bottles sold. Yet for the great majority of brewers the building up and maintaining of networks of outlets – ideally comprising the most respectable public houses with the largest regular trades in any district, usually over distances of not much more than a dozen miles – was at the very heart of their business. In some centres, however, long famed beyond their locality for their beers, a few brewers enjoyed a more distant, water-borne trade. The dramatic extension of this trade by the railways after 1830 brought about a revolution, opening up undreamt horizons in the industry for the likes of Michael Thomas Bass and the Guinnesses. The men who realised these opportunities for the more successful brewers, emulating Bass's and Guinness's lead, were the travellers, agents and store managers of the railway age, the unsung heroes of Victorian enterprise, and the subject of the middle section of this chapter. The final part considers the export of beer, never important for the industry as a whole.

I

The ideal, easy market for a common brewer was one in which he possessed the trade of scores of handily situated public houses. It meant that he could distribute his beer cheaply, keep a close eye on his outlets and, by the reputation of his beer, hope to increase his trade. Before the 1830s there were, of course, few towns and districts whose populations were sufficiently large to realise this vision. It is the London market that therefore provides the key example of early, large-scale distribution, in which the leading brewers at the outset of our period were each vending their beers through hundreds of public houses. Between 1750 and 1830, as Mathias has shown, the great London porter brewers came increasingly to control the retail distribution of beer through the 5,000 or so public houses in the capital.[1] Few London publicans, even in 1750, brewed on their premises; and their independence was increasingly undermined by the brewers' growing control. This was brought about by a complex surveillance system, enforced by the abroad coopers and abroad clerks (or collectors) of the brewers, covering monthly credits and price, and including nascent quality and stock controls. Pressures from the brewers increased after the 1790s when licences in London became restricted and the goodwill or premium payments on leases escalated in the inflationary French Wars (1793–1815). Brewers of every description began to tie retail outlets both by acquiring the leases of public houses themselves – almost all property in London, unlike the rest of the country, was leasehold – and, even more frequently, by loans made to publicans to enable them to pay for premiums, improvements and valuations.[2] The loan-tie, virtually unknown outside London, was already in place by 1830 for as many as half of London's publicans. It was almost entirely a creation of the special forces operating in the capital's property market.

This spacious, traditional world of drays, of abroad clerks, of loans and time-honoured relationships between independent publicans and the great paternalistic porter brewers was not swept away by the Beer Act. Indeed, it was not seriously undermined until the late 1880s. Only in the twenty-five years before the outbreak of the First World War were many of these features fundamentally altered. For the coming of the railways and the increasing ownership of retail outlets by brewers, at

[1] Mathias, *Brewing Industry*, pp. 99–138.

[2] See Mathias, p. 133 for a table showing the growth of the tied trade of London's three largest breweries, 1750–1830.

least before the mid-1890s, had less impact on the capital than elsewhere in Britain. Of course, it was not sealed off from these events entirely; and, on their production side especially, the London brewers responded to changes in taste and advances in brewing science and technology after the 1860s by rebuilding and re-equipping their breweries. On the other hand, the mechanism of sales and loans – indeed the entire distribution of beer in the metropolis – changed very little before 1880. As its population increased, however, the number of outlets grew at an unprecedented rate from the 5,000 or so that served the needs of thirsty Londoners throughout the Georgian period (see Table 3.3).

Temperance reformers and parliamentary committees-of-enquiry monitoring the drink trade liked to work out league tables comparing the number of public houses per head of population in industrial towns, seaports, cathedral cities and rural areas, with the number of proceedings for drunkenness.[3] Inevitably, no simple relationship existed between the two sets of figures, and in London the exercise would in any case be very misleading. For the London excise collection districts, whose boundaries were altered so frequently, never coincided with the Greater London census area. Moreover, there were considerable differences between the densities of public houses in various parts of the metropolis. Therefore only a general conclusion can be drawn. Between 1831 and 1870 the number of retail outlets within a shifting London excise collection district increased from 5,672 to 10,126 (78.5 per cent), whereas the population of Greater London grew from 1,907,000 to 3,890,000 (104 per cent). In fact before the 1870s there was little difficulty in obtaining new licences: 1,726 full licences to sell spirits and beer were granted by magistrates as well as the 4,000 sold to beer house keepers. Indeed, the construction of public houses appears to have been central to the strategies of developers in every area of London between the 1830s and the 1860s. *The Builder* described how in 1854,

> On the pastures lately set out for building you may see a double line of trenches with excavation either side . . . and a tavern of imposing elevation standing alone and quite complete, waiting the approaching rows of houses. The propinquity of these palaces to each other in Camden and Kentish New Towns is quite ridiculous. At a distance of 200 paces in every direction they glitter in sham splendour . . . In some instances one speculative builder, reserving all the angle plots, runs up half-a-dozen public houses; he obtains licences for all that he can, and lets or sells such at incredible prices or enormous rentals-: others he sells to adventuring publicans who try for the privilege, or, in case of failure, open as

[3] SCHL on Intemperance, second report, (1877) XI, appendices A–O, pp. 383–98; fourth report (1878) XIV, Tables 1–29, Figures 1–4, pp. 586–91.

beer shops at war with the Bench . . . from £2,000 to £3,000 is an ordinary price, and for good standings £5,000 to £8,000 is not infrequent.[4]

At first, most of these new public houses were almost indistinguishable from the terraces which surrounded them (see plate 36); by the beer boom of the 1860s and 1870s their design became increasingly distinct and vibrant.[5]

Although, therefore, the brewers' ledgers grew fatter with these new accounts, the distribution of beer within the capital as described by Mathias changed very little. Beer was primed in the brewery, delivered by the ubiquitous drays that cluttered the streets of inner London, and set up in the cellars of publicans by the abroad coopers. Orders and payments were collected and returns negotiated weekly by the abroad clerks. In two respects there were evident changes. The vast 108 gallon butts, weighing more than half a ton each when full, which had been a special feature of the London porter trade, were replaced by more manageable 36 gallon barrels in the 1850s. The sweet, mild ales had a much shorter life than that of the traditional porters which they increasingly replaced after the 1840s. In summer this was often no more than a fortnight. As a consequence, the retail cycle of the new 'running' beers became more problematic and frenetic for both brewer and publican alike. Yet at the heart of the relationship between the two groups were a couple of recurrent issues: loans and adulteration. Although the intensity of these might oscillate over half a century, their essential nature did not.

In 1830 Charles Barclay had estimated that half the capital's public houses were tied to the common brewers for their supplies.[6] Much the most usual form of tie was loans made by brewers to victuallers to allow them to acquire the leases of their public houses (Table 4.1). It was a beneficial system for both parties. The victualler, putting up some money himself, was saved the trouble of finding, and the cost of executing, a mortgage; and if his calculations about the house's barrelage were proved correct he was assured of, in good years at least, securing a reasonable, if hard-working livelihood. And the brewer in return procured the supply of porter and mild – pale ale not being tied at this stage. If the publican fell out with the brewer (usually about adulteration or the quality of beer) and was not in serious arrears with either his loan or beer payments, he could, at twenty-four hours notice, transfer his loan if

[4] *The Builder*, 25 Feb. 1854 quoted in M. Girouard, *Victorian Pubs* (1984 edn), p. 36.
[5] *Ibid.*, pp. 37–46.
[6] SCHC on Sale of Beer, *PP* (1830) X, p. 14.

Table 4.1. *The London tied trade of Barclay Perkins, Reid's and Whitbread, 1830–75*

	Barclay Perkins						*Reid's*						*Whitbread*					
Year	Owned	%	Loan	%	Free	%	Owned	%	Loan	%	Free	%	Owned	%	Loan	%	Free	%
1830	51	5.8	476	54.0	355	40.2	168	27.3	355	57.7	92	15.0	88	13.1	365	54.5	217	32.4
1835	44	5.0	462	53.0	354	41.2	142	23.7	338	56.2	121	21.2	95	14.0	310	45.7	273	40.3
1840	33	4.2	462	59.3	284	36.5	122	19.7	360	58.3	136	22.0	99	15.4	382	59.4	162	25.2
1845	40	5.0	457	57.6	297	37.4	120	18.2	406	61.6	133	20.2	110	16.3	366	54.1	200	29.6
1850	38	4.7	449	55.8	318	39.5	120	17.2	391	55.9	188	26.9	127	18.7	388	57.1	165	24.3
1855	36	4.4	442	54.0	340	41.6	107	15.7	378	55.4	197	28.9	108	15.6	343	49.5	242	34.9
1860	36	4.5	420	52.1	350	43.4	96	12.8	384	51.2	270	36.0	100	17.4	329	57.2	146	25.4
1865	34	4.7	390	53.4	306	41.9	76	9.2	394	47.8	355	43.0	79	13.7	353	61.3	144	25.0
1870	35	5.1	392	57.3	257	37.6	55	6.0	407	44.7	438	49.3	57	9.3	381	62.2	175	28.5
1875	29	4.4	396	59.9	236	35.7	52	6.0	391	44.8	430	49.2	36	6.3	419	73.0	119	20.7

Source: GLRO, Barclay Perkins, Capital Accounts Ledger 1801–75, Acc. 2305/1/394; Reid's Abstract Rest Books, 1809–87, Acc. 75.108; Whitbread Rest Books 1830–75, W/22.

Table 4.2. *Loans made to publicans by four leading London breweries, 1830–85*

Year	Barclay Perkins	Reid's	Truman Hanbury Buxton	Whitbread
	(£s)	(£s)	(£s)	(£s)
1830	332,572	317,799	232,952	316,407
1840	448,594	324,028	305,303	361,246
1850	491,035	361,007	358,985	363,703
1860	499,254	451,886	574,164	338,967
1870	541,542	496,534	–	542,962
1880	799,466	725,787	–	828,070
1885	1,027,059	806,454	1,214,282	952,744

Source: GLRO, Barclay Perkins Capital Account Rest Book 1801–75, Capital Account Rest Book, 1876–1912, Acc. 2305/1/394–395; Reid's Abstract Rest Books, 1809–87., Acc. 75.108; Truman Hanbury Buxton, Abstract Rest Books, 1781–1866, Acc. 73.36, Private Thursday Memoranda, 1857–93, Acc. 73.36; Whitbread Archive, Whitbread Rest Books 1830–85, W/22.

another brewer was willing to take it on. Blandishments to encourage publicans to shift suppliers, however, were seriously discouraged in a world in which brewers were considered to behave like gentlemen.

These loans, invariably carrying an interest rate of 5 per cent, were already numerous and extensive by 1830. In that year Whitbread, supplying 670 publicans in all, made 365 at an average of £869 each; Barclay Perkins, with 882 victuallers on their books, made 476 of £699 apiece.[7] Yet outright acquisition of the leases of public houses, in contrast with the considerable tied freehold estates which some country brewers built up, had never been extensive in London. Admittedly some brewers had been more acquisitive than others in this respect. A public house broker in 1830 maintained that some brewers disapproved of ownership: 'There are brewers who will not buy a house; other brewers will buy ... Messrs. Elliott buy a good many; Taylor buys a good many; Messrs. Barclay, Messrs. Whitbread and some others will not buy.'[8] The last two firms, taking a high-minded, free-trade stance, maintained that a brewery with a large tied estate was likely to brew an inferior beer.

It is clear, in terms of loans and, to a lesser extent, direct ownership, that between 1830 and 1870 the position of the larger London breweries remained basically unchanged.[9] Only when a publican was bankrupt or in severe difficulties did they reluctantly accept the lease. The situation for four main firms is shown in Table 4.2. As is evident, it hardly varied across forty years in each brewery. It was not a tight noose for the publican. Although the four big breweries had a tied trade of at least 50 per cent plus, this did not intensify once the immediate effects of the Beer Act wore off in the late 1830s. Moreover, loans were less restrictive agreements than those enjoyed by country brewers possessing large-scale freehold ownership of public houses. Certainly, the loan arrangements seem to have presented no real barrier to the penetration of 'foreign' mild and pale ales into the London market after the 1840s. And, in comparison with what occurred after 1890, the period was one of free trade.

There were two developments, however, which affected the position

7 Mathias, *Brewing Industry*, p. 133.

8 SCHC on Sale of Beer, *PP* (1830) X, p. 58.

9 D. M. Knox, 'The Development of the London Brewing Industry, 1830–1914, with special reference to Messrs. Whitbread and Company', Unpublished Oxford B.Litt. thesis (1956), p. 73. Oddly, the thesis is less good on Whitbread than in its excellent survey of the London industry from a wide variety of printed sources, principally Parliamentary Papers.

of the big brewers. First, the number of beer houses grew appreciably (see Table 3.3). In 1850 there were 2,200; by 1870 4,000. They provided an entry for enterprising mild ale brewers like Mann, Crossman & Paulin into the trade. Their Albion brewery supplied by 1850 no fewer than 500 beer houses in the capital which Robert Mann maintained were respectable (in stark contrast to police evidence) and – with bad debts of no more than 1.5 per cent – very loanworthy. They were, he maintained, 'generally speaking ... very independent of us. They can go where they please if we do not send them a good article.' Certainly Mann's endeavours to supply 'a good article' in their beer houses were still evident almost sixty years later. Truman reckoned that Mann had a 500,000 barrel trade in mild ale. No other brewery could match its fullness of taste. 'Other Brewers' houses', the partner despondently concluded, 'as well as our own, in good positions, are empty, while Mann's little houses, in out of the way back alleys, are full to overflowing, so much so that I have seen the customers obliged to consume their beer outside on the pavement ... if all the houses in the East End were free they would only sell Manns.'[10]

But the porter brewers did not, after an initial hesitancy, turn their backs on 'inferior', beer house outlets. In London, unlike in the countryside, they frequently did a good trade, some of as many as twelve or fifteen barrels a week. Although Mann, Crossman & Paulin possessed the largest trade in this sector of the market, Whitbread, Combe Delafield, Elliot and Reid's became increasingly active.[11] For example, the 670 victuallers listed by Whitbread in 1830 had become 775 in the following year. Presumably many of these additional customers were beer house sellers; in 1840 they supplied seventy-nine of them; ten years later eighty-seven. Yet large loans were not made to such customers, because without highly profitable spirit licences they were less good risks than the great City and West End taverns. In 1840 Whitbread lent £361,246 to the majority of its 643 victuallers; whereas their seventy-nine city beer houses had borrowed only £40 in all.[12] Robert Crossman, a decade later, suggested their rule of thumb for loans was between a fifth and a quarter of the valuation placed upon a beer house. Most brewers appear, given the reputation of beer house keepers for bad debts, more cautious than Robert Crossman. Truman by the mid-1880s

[10] SCHL on the Operation of the Acts for the Sale of Beer (1849–50) XVIII, pp. 1–15; GLRO, Acc. 77.94, B/THB, Monthly Reports, December 1903, March 1906, June–December 1908.

[11] SCHL on the Operation of the Acts for the Sale of Beer (1849–50), XVIII, pp. 10–12.

[12] Whitbread Archives, Rest Books W22/42–3, 52.

had a classification of their houses: loans to their first-class houses (they did not reveal their numbers) totalled £622,501, to second-class ones, £298,425, and to beer shops, £106,581. Although the loss per £1,000 lent for the past ten years had been £41, £64 and £141 respectively, the partner had to conclude, 'Contrary to my Expectations', that in terms of trade-per-£1,000-lent the beer houses came out of the exercise much the best.[13] Secondly, the size of loan tended to grow gradually over the years and this placed an increasing burden on the brewers' capital. They grew because public house values increased. Tenants improved their premises, moved on average every five years, and capitalised on their unexpired leases. Breweries had therefore to find larger loans, especially after the late 1860s as publicans remodelled their houses. Moreover, rates and licence duties increased appreciably as a consequence of the Valuation of the Metropolis Act (1869), providing for quinquennial revaluations and the price of houses was driven up sharply as the number of licences began to be restricted after legislation in 1869. Consequently, when costs rose sharply in the late 1860s and trade slumped in the 1880s, they had to beg the brewers to grant them bigger loans. And as competition increased, there was little the brewers could do but accede to this demand. In 1869 Whitbread's average loan to the 207 publicans in their 'East' ledger was £1,400 each; in 1888 it had more than doubled to £2,890.[14]

By the 1870s the loan problem was worrying the leading London brewers; by the mid-1880s it had become acute. Brewers were forced to raise more capital, either from their partners or, more frequently, from a wide variety of subscribers, including publicans (who deposited their savings), to finance increasing loans. In essentials these were proto-debentures secured by note and bond. Yet even when the brewers had made these increasingly expensive arrangements to secure their porter and mild trade, and, by the late 1880s, a growing pale ale trade, their hold over publicans was incomplete. Loans were transferred to other brewers; and the growing spectre of bad debts, as the effects of depression and declining consumption bit deeper, was even more worrying. The brewers, however, never considered ditching the system, unknown outside London, until the recession of the mid-1880s when the issue of loans, publican bankruptcies and increasing discounts came to a head. Indeed Truman used loan applications as an index of activity. When their beers were in a poor state, in the summer of 1884, they expressed

[13] GLRO, Acc. 77.94, B/THB, Monthly Reports, April, May 1885.
[14] Whitbread Archives, Rest Books, W/22/72, 91.

their worries that few proposals for new loans came in from publicans.[15] Then, brewers suddenly saw the way forward. By converting their partnerships to limited liability companies they could retain control of their firms and, by the issues of debenture shares to an eager public, move into the ownership of retail outlets on a scale never previously contemplated. Guinness's great flotation, in fact unrelated to any contemplated ownership in retail outlets, pointed the way in 1886. The rest followed. But in the previous decades the tendency for loans slowly to increase, and the brewers' preoccupation with negotiations and debt management, possibly diverted their attention from the wholesale exploitation of the London ale market. They seemed to be running in familiar grooves, inserting a piece of equipment here, renewing a vat and mash tun there, increasing the provision of casks and dray horses, but not adopting a new strategy that would exploit to the full the extraordinary opportunities of the London market in these years.

Servicing larger and larger loans clearly put pressure also upon publicans. When F. W. Thornton published a little handbook in 1885, *How to Purchase and Succeed in a Public House*, he acknowledged the 'liberal lending and liberal treatment' of the thirty 'London leading brewers' he listed. He also provided an interesting example for his readers. His licensed victualler, acquiring the fifty-year lease of a pub at a rental of £100 per annum could expect to pay £6,100 for the premium of the lease and goodwill, the valuation of the furnishings and stock, and the expense of the transaction. Typically, he would find £1,200 himself and borrow £4,200 from the brewers and £700 from the distillers who usually provided smaller loans for the spirits tie. Both would charge 5 per cent interest and exact exclusive dealing agreements. Therefore the publican had to pay at least £450 in interest charges, rent, rates and licence duty.[16] He was also responsible for making improvements which if he undertook them necessitated further loans. Thirty-five to forty years earlier these loans had been much smaller. Robert Crossman was of the opinion that if a gentleman's servant or mechanic, the usual entrants to the trade, had saved £300–£400 his firm would lend them £500 to £600 to take on the lease of a good beer house in the capital, although he believed a public house plying a similar trade, but with a full spirits licence, would cost £2,500.[17] When the beer trade boomed

[15] GLRO, Acc. 77.94, B/THB, Monthly Reports, August 1884.
[16] F. W. Thornton, *How to Purchase and Succeed in a Public House* (1885), pp. 8, 30–2.
[17] SCHL on the Operation of the Acts for the Sale of Beer (1849–50) XVIII, evidence of Robert Crossman, p. 6.

between the mid-1850s and the mid-1870s a flourishing tavern might well guarantee a good livelihood. It was from this assurance that the standing and independence of the London licensed victualler, always acknowledged to be higher than that of his country counterpart, was based.[18] When, however, depression and a check in consumption came in the late 1870s, and the price of pubs went on rising because of an almost total restriction on new licences, the situation was very different. Calculations like Thornton's, quoting some hypothetical average monthly trade, were easily upset in bad years like 1884–5. Moreover, publicans' margins were always tight.

The brewers' pricing of beer is discussed in Chapter 5, but it is necessary here to consider it in relation to the publicans' profits. The wholesale price of porter was reduced in October 1830 by 12s from 45s to 33s per barrel. The cheapest mild came down from 48s to 36s, although some brewers claimed theirs was as low as 30s and 33s respectively by the mid-century.[19] They remained unchanged until 1887 – except briefly in 1847, when malt prices rose sharply; and during the Crimean War when the malt tax was increased.[20] A 5 per cent discount was universal, and there was no concept of a 'wet rent' in London (see p. 208). The beer house keepers in London in 1850 sold porter at 3d a quart pot off the premises (most publicans did a large jug and bottle trade in Victorian Britain) and 4d on, although one claimed he sold it in his house for 1d a pint and 1d for a crust of bread and hunk of cheese.[21] At best, with no waste, a beer house keeper could

18 Thornton, *Purchase and Succeed*, pp. 29–30. Girouard, *Victorian Pubs*, pp. 94–101 provides examples of some leading late Victorian publican entrepreneurs. An article in *Truth* quoted in the *Country Brewers' Gazette* (1879), p. 236 reckoned, 'Metropolitan publicans have a thriving business, hence they can afford elaborate decoration of their premises, they borrow £4,000 from their brewer, and put up £1,000 – and usually clear £1,000 net profit a year after paying interest, etc.' Only a tiny handful at the height of the boom in the decade before 1876 can have realised these returns. Certainly, the London public house keepers were the first to organise themselves, forming the Licensed Victuallers' Protection Society in London in 1833. Within six months it had a membership of 900 metropolitan licensees who paid an annual subscription of half a guinea. Outside London, publicans did not form the Licensed Defence League of England and Wales until 1872. The London Society became the London Central Board in 1892 and led an independent existence until 1976 when it joined with the National Federation of Licensed Victuallers (which the Defence League had become) and the Amalgamated Licensed Retailers' Society to become the National Union of Licensed Victuallers. We are grateful to Mr Edward Guinness, the last president of the London Central Board, for this information.

19 *Report ... for the Sale of Beer* (1849–50), evidence of Robert Prosser and Samuel Mellis.

20 Knox, 'London Brewing Industry', pp. 51–7.

21 *Report ... for the Sale of Beer* (1849–50), evidence of Robert Crossman, Robert Prosser and Samuel Mellis, pp. 6, 16, 21–2.

expect a profit of 14s a barrel on his most popular sales of porter and mild. Admittedly licensed victuallers with better premises charged 1d a quart more, and margins were higher on the more expensive ales selling from 5d to 8d a quart pot and in those City and West End taverns which drove a good spirits trade. The case of Benjamin Bouch, a bragging Euston Square beer house seller is illuminating. He had begun trade with the proverbial shilling and, in his own estimation, stood 'more pre-eminent in the beer trade ... than any other individual in London, in the world I may say'. He paid £270 monthly to Elliot and Mann for the beer of his three houses, and contended that the 'profits are not immense'. Seventeen years of success in the business had enabled him to achieve his dream of 'a little cottage in the country, where there are no ill-conducted beer-houses'. He reckoned a metropolitan beer house keeper had to do a trade of twenty barrels a month 'for it to be a profitable speculation'.[22] And although examples were quoted of beer house keepers selling forty to sixty barrels a month, there were many who sold well below Bouch's twenty barrel threshold, for all brewers record considerable differences between their most thriving and least successful customers. By the 1880s the busiest houses were selling 150 barrels a month, others as few as ten.[23] Therefore small margins, recession and frequently bad management made a publican's existence a precarious one. It was also, in other respects, a tough existence. Setting aside problems of keeping an orderly house, the hours alone were horrendous: public houses in the 1860s were kept open 148 hours, beer houses 116 hours a week.

With these pressures of work and finance weighing heavily on the publican, it was perhaps not surprising that the adulteration of beer in London before the 1880s was a universal practice. Most contemporary commentators maintained that the beer turned out by the leading London brewers was soundly made from good materials. Even after the mid-1880s any spell of trouble with their beers meant that Truman's free-trade publicans and some of their own tied tenants placed their orders with Truman's rivals. The firm believed it was fatal to provide any pretext which would give an opportunity for another brewer's abroad clerks to get a toe-hold in their premises. After 1900, with sharply declining sales, they were mesmerised by Mann's ability to produce a superior mild. The London market was fiercely competitive

22 *Ibid.*, pp. 87–9.

23 GLRO, Acc. 77.94, B/THB, Monthly Reports, October 1888 records the purchase of five 'large houses; with monthly trades of 105 to 150 barrels (651 in all).

in terms of quality, if not price, for Victorian drinkers were exacting and knowledgeable about their beer. Robert Prosser, a brewer from St Georges-in-the-East, thought 'the working people particularly look more to the quality of the beer than they do the price'. A Truman's director stated in 1907. 'The Public ... are much more critical and observant of a change for better or for worse than ever we are.'[24] These were brewers' comments which would have been universally substantiated to 1914. Yet they had little direct control of their beer at the point of sale. Adulteration by publicans and the smaller, less scrupulous brewers was an old art which probably achieved its highest form in the two decades before 1830. And it was a practice which did not disappear for at least another half-century.

The revelation of two early treatises on the adulteration of food and drink, Accum's *Treatise on Adulterations of Food and Culinary Poisoning* (1820) with its arresting title page quotation, aimed at porter: 'There is Death in the Pot' (2 Kings 4:40), and Mitchell's *A Treatise on the Falsification of Food and the Chemical Means Employed to Detect Them* (1848), and the official enquiries into the liquor trades in 1819, 1850 and 1854 were frightening. Nothing was ever proved against the big London brewers (except Meux as long ago as 1812), but the charges laid against the publicans were formidable. John Mitchell told the Select Committee on the Adulteration of Food in 1855, that in analysing by 'chemical means' 200 samples of beer during the previous nine years he had not found one to be pure except some taken at source from the brewery.[25] An analytical chemist in the previous year reckoned that out of 150 samples of porter he had taken from various pubs in East London not one was within 20 per cent of its strength when it left the brewery.[26] A popular recipe for publicans was to dilute the beer by a third, adding four pounds of coarse sugar, one of salt and a choice of 'drugs' to give the porter a strong head.[27] There was an element of sensationalism in all this, a sustained attempt to discredit the beer houses. Much more usual was the mixing of beers. All brewers despaired that publicans mixed expensive with cheaper beers. Guinness in Ireland sold principally porter because they believed it would be pointless to sell the dearer extra stout: victuallers would simply mix it with porter and pass it off as stout. Conversely in England, their Dublin porter was sold only in Liverpool;

24 *Report ... for the Sale of Beer* (1849–50), p. 16; GLRO, Acc. 77.95, B/THB Monthly Reports.
25 Quoted in Burnett, *Plenty and Want*, p. 196.
26 Quoted in Hawkins, Thesis, p. 21.
27 Burnett, *Plenty and Want*, p. 195.

elsewhere Guinness thought it would be bought to dilute their more profitable extra stout.[28] And of course the brewers' collectors and abroad clerks attempted to stamp out the worst excesses by their constant vigilance. Certainly, these began to disappear with the passing of the Adulteration of Food, Drink and Drug Act (1872) which empowered borough councils to employ public analysts. Equally important was that the brewers themselves began to carry out their own analysis of returned beers. Truman as late as 1886 concluded from the evidence of their tests that many of their publicans were still diluting and sweetening their beers, although they recognised that publicans could not make a profit on beer sold at 3d a quart 'without reducing gravities'.[29] Therefore when in the autumn of 1886 the London publicans petitioned the Brewers' Company for a reduction in wholesale prices, those brewers who were members added an amendment to their Trade Rules, 'that an allowance of 3s per barrel in town may be made on Porter, X or XL ale, on condition of the customer selling his beer without adulteration, dilution, or mixing'.[30] Clearly, they were confident of their own chemists' reports and the cooperation of publicans and excise alike. The Truman minutes record no further mention of adulteration. Public awareness, above all effective analysis of beer by public analysts and the brewers' own chemists, had effectively stamped out one of the worst features of the London trade.

Although the London trade was uniquely concentrated and tied, the delivery of beer was still a complex and expensive operation for brewers. At its heart were their drays and draymen. As the supreme exemplars of muscular strength in an increasingly mechanised world, both horses and men remained powerful symbols of the time-honoured role of beer in the nation's life (see Plate 17). In London especially the reminder was ever present, for its brewers, unable to use the railways for their town deliveries, relied much more upon draught transport than producers elsewhere. Mathias reckoned that as a rough rule of thumb, a top London brewery around 1800 required a stable of at least fifty horses for every 100,000 barrels of beer it sold. Certainly, Barclay Perkins had 150 horses in the 1815–28 period when they produced 300,000 barrels; Truman 100 for an output of around 280,000 barrels in the mid-1830s.[31] By then in London at least, the use of mill horses had been entirely

[28] Dennison and McDonagh, 'History of Guinness 1886–1939', pp. 7–10.
[29] GLRO, Acc. 77.94, B/THB, Monthly Reports, November 1886, February 1887.
[30] Quoted in Knox, 'London Brewing Industry', p. 53.
[31] Mathias, *Brewing Industry*, p. 79; GLRO, Acc. 73.36, B/THB, Truman's Suggestion Books, 1835, 1837.

replaced by steam engines, but the number of draught horses went on increasing across the nineteenth century as barrelages grew. Whitbread in 1889, according to Barnard, employed 105 horses and eighty-three stablemen, wheelwrights and draymen directly connected with them. And by the end of the First World War they foddered 371 horses (as many as 150 apparently hired at £48 or £54 a year) of which 221 were used in London and the rest at their forty bottling stores scattered across Britain.[32] Truman's stables also grew: in the mid-1880s they were occupied by 175–80 horses; by 1902, 224. Even though, as their trade thereafter sharply declined – their success as bottlers was confined in comparison with Whitbread – they owned 150 in 1910.[33] No brewery employed more horse transport than Ind Coope of Romford. In 1899, with a vast family trade, four London stores from which they did a brisk trade with the city's bottlers, and no fewer than seventy-eight country depots they employed 543 horses and 370 light drays.[34] The second rank of London brewers also possessed considerable stables. Barnard noted that Hoare had room for seventy horses; the City of London, fifty; Savill (famed bottling brewers), seventy-eight; and Courage, eighty.[35] But the palm of London brewery stables went to Mann, Crossman & Paulin: Barnard reckoned they were 'the best arranged stables in any London brewery'. Built in 1885 on a lavish scale in white brick and slate, they had stalls that were equipped with semi-automatic feeding devices for their 105 horses. Barnard's usual description of stabling ran to no more than two or three sentences; Mann merited three pages.[36]

The horses themselves were both impressive – Mann's specimens drawn from the Eastern counties (Edward Mann having acquired a large South Norfolk estate in 1885) were mostly 17 hands high – and expensive. In 1800 a good dray horse had cost around £40; in the 1890s this had increased to between £80 and £100. In comparison with the prices of malt and other agricultural produce it was a large and almost unparalleled advance. Therefore the largest breweries had sums of £20,000 or more tied up in their horses alone; and with a replacement rate of at least 10 per cent a year, depreciation was rapid. Moreover, feed was similarly expensive. Between 1832 and 1844 Truman's horses

32 Barnard, *Noted Breweries*, II, p. 213; Whitbread Archives, W/15/73 ff. 95–6.

33 GLRO, Acc. 73.36, Private Thursday Memoranda Book (1891–1912), Acc. 77.94, Monthly Reports and Directors' Minutes, 17 Aug. 1911.

34 *Ind Coope & Co. Ltd Souvenir 1799–1899* (1899), p. 5.

35 Barnard, *Noted Breweries*, II, pp. 39–51, 293–309; III, pp. 48–67, 422–39.

36 Barnard, *Noted Breweries*, I, pp. 384–6.

cost on average £43.9 each a year to keep.[37] By 1912–13 Whitbread's cost £56 apiece, a sum which covered a large variety of feedstuffs, and farriers' and horsekeepers' wages.[38] But little expense was spared on two grounds. First, brewers' drays were a form of advertisement. There was a strong element of competition between breweries to turn out the smartest drays. Second, the work itself was heavy. The old low drays which had carried only three vast 108 gallon butts were replaced in the 1850s by ones capable of pulling either twelve or twenty barrels each, the larger load weighing around 4 tons when full. The latter therefore required two superb horses in peak condition to pull them. More usually, it took three. Yet the change seems to have brought little advance in productivity. A dray horse in 1830 was capable of delivering an average 2,000 barrels a year. In 1907–8 Truman's horses averaged only 1,953 barrels. On the other hand, between 1908 and 1914 Whitbread's London horses each carted between 3,756 and 4,201 barrels annually.[39] The figures, however, are not strictly comparable since by the 1900s the firm was making very regular, direct deliveries to its nine big London bottling stores.

Besides stabling costs, there were, of course, those of the draymen themselves. Again their numbers in the bigger breweries were impressive. Watney in 1873 employed ninety-five at an annual cost of £8,452, besides hiring some additionally; Barclay Perkins entertained a hundred of their draymen to lunch and dinner at Alexandra Palace in September 1875; Truman employed 117 in 1902, 93 in 1911.[40] By the latter date the firm, to the annoyance of its own draymen, were engaging increasing amounts of hired transport. Traditional methods for payments of draymen at Truman were so complex, covering sixteen separate tasks, that arrangements ran to seven pages in 1912. They were a paradise for the employment of clerks, and one director wearily concluded a long discussion about them that they were,'very complicated and it is quite time the matter was understood'.[41] Indeed such was their complexity they failed to note how they arrived at a fixed wage and estimation of the traditional 'tun' or 'butt' money paid by publicans to the draymen on delivery. On the other hand, they did record that Barclay's draymen

[37] GLRO, Acc. 73.36, B/THB, Private Memoranda Book 1891–1912; an entry for 1892 calculates that their horses cost £79 a year in keep and depreciation.

[38] Whitbread Archives, W/15/73, ff. 95–6.

[39] *Ibid.*, and GLRO, Truman's Private Memoranda Book, 1891–1912.

[40] Acc. 789, No. 903, Watney & Co. Papers re draymen at Stag Brewery, 1873, Westminster City Archives. *Licensed Victuallers' Gazette*, 2 Oct. 1875.

[41] GLRO, Acc. 73.94, B/THB A/122, Monthly Reports, 1908–38.

were paid between 40s and 50s plus 'butt' money (no other firm matched their rates) whereas Watney Combe Reid's five classes of draymen were paid between 24s and 43s. Thus each dray, with two men and two or three horses, was an expensive piece of equipment to keep on the road throughout the year. Truman, who had some sixty-five drays operating at this stage, found in 1902 they cost them £446 on average.[42] This meant that motor transport, even in its initial experimental phase, competed on roughly equal terms with draught transport costs (see pp. 302–3). And what is interesting in all these figures is that the cost of maintaining a brewery horse matched the wages of the draymen themselves. Indeed, Truman in 1892 reckoned a horse cost them 5s a day whilst their 'first' draymen received 4s 10d. Sir James Caird, contemplating the plight of the agricultural labourer in southern England forty years earlier, had thought it wrong that farmers should spend more per week on fattening a bullock than on the wages of one of their labourers.[43] Did the draymen, as they trundled along the streets of the capital, entertain similar thoughts about their vast charges?

More usually, of course, brewers worked out their transport costs per barrel.[44] Whitbread, for example, between 1904 and 1911 transported on average 486,676 barrels a year at 11.2d per barrel in their 'Town Trade'.[45] This represented about 60 per cent of their output; the rest was transported, notionally at the same cost, to their forty bottling stores. A stray reference in Truman's monthly minutes in 1902 suggests they did not quite match these figures, with costs of 1s 1d per barrel, or 5.15d per barrel per mile.

Journeys in London were clearly short-haul, but not all transport costs were incurred within the capital itself, for the larger brewers carried on 'country' trades. Comparatively, they were not large. Whitbread's between 1832 and 1849 was never more than 9.1 per cent of their town trade in these years.[46] Reid's did rather better. In the 1830s and 1840s their proportion of country to town trade was just over a third

42 The precise number was not disclosed. Barnard noted in 1889 that they had seventy-three drays and sixteen carts. In 1911, by which time trade had fallen to 456,937 from 547,189 barrels in 1902, they employed fifty drays, two motor lorries and an undisclosed amount of hired cartage.

43 J. Caird, *English Agriculture in 1850–51* (1852), p. 22.

44 There were other costs of transport, carting malt from the wharves and railway stations, the collection of empties and the carrying of dried spent grains, sugar and forage, but the main task of carrying malt was always added to brewing costs.

45 Whitbread Archives, W/15/73, ff. 27–8.

46 W/41/16.

(33.6 per cent).[47] Of course, in comparison with the sales of most other brewers at the time, these 'country' trades of the London brewers were in themselves quite extensive. Whitbread averaged 15,465 barrels in the years cited above; Reid's, whose rest books indicate only values of sales and stocks, must have had a country trade of at least 45,000 barrels since these sales averaged £88,818 a year in the 1840s. But the evidence also indicates that the country trade of neither firm grew in the railway age. Whitbread's had fallen by the 1880s to 7.8 per cent of its London sales; Reid's was running at 18.6 per cent in 1880–4 – a considerable fall in comparison with its position forty to fifty years earlier.

In fact, their failure to develop an extra-London trade does not rest with transport costs. Certainly these soon escalated with distance. Even in town, Truman delivered beer to Shoreditch from their Spitalfields brewery at 6d per barrel, whereas to cart it to Chiswick cost 1s 2d. Haulage from King's Cross station in the 1860s was costing 3s 6d per ton.[48] Beyond the metropolitan area, the lower costs of transport by water had to be balanced against the much faster turn-round of valuable casks by rail. The advantages of the latter were, in general, ones of convenience, not cost.[49] But these factors faced brewers everywhere. The real reason for the larger London brewers' failure to attack the country trade vigorously was almost certainly their preoccupation with servicing their complex loan business involving hundreds of publicans apiece. And although they had the largest beer market in the world on their doorstep, they had to meet the increasing competition of brewers from Burton, Dublin, Edinburgh and elsewhere selling good beers usually at large discounts. Almost all their energies were therefore concentrated upon retaining their existing market share, especially in their really popular lines, porter, sweet mild ales and single stouts. But because margins on these cheaper beers were smaller, they were not profitable to sell at distances from the capital. Nor, once porter went out of fashion, were these London beers in great demand, beyond a modest radius of the capital. Comparing the records of Truman with Bass, no mention in the 1880s and 1890s of an agency, beyond passing reference to depots in Chatham and Colchester, emerges in those of the former, whereas for Bass the management of their score of agencies and stores was the very life blood of their business. This mould of comparative

47 GLRO, Acc. 75.108, Abstract of Rests, 1809–87.

48 GLRO, Acc. 73.36, B/THB, Malt Ledger, 1855–69; Private Thursday Memoranda Book, 1891–1912.

49 E. Jones, 'A Private Transport Saving Calculation for the Brewers Truman Hanbury and Buxton, 1815–63', *Journal of Transport History*, 7 (1986), pp. 1–17.

Fig. 4.1 The location of Barclay Perkins's 'country customers', *c.* 1905. (*Source:* GLRO, Barclay Perkins's Country Customers Register, 1892–1908, Acc. 2305/1/519.)

inactivity by the major London brewers in beer markets outside the capital was only broken in the 1890s. And then in a novel form. Whitbread made a spectacular breakthrough by rapidly developing the first national bottling network (see pp. 299–301) in the twenty-five years before 1914. It was a triumph comparable with those achieved earlier by Bass, Allsopp and Guinness. And they did possess imitators: Barclay Perkins listed 115 country customers in the 1900s (see Fig. 4.1); Ind Coope, always an unusual firm in the scale of its family trade, boasted seventy-eight depots a few years earlier.[50]

But until the 1890s, most transport for the London brewers was short-haul. Indeed it remained so until 1914. Nevertheless, they were conscious of costs and the expense of constantly handling brewing materials and beer. For those who owned Burton subsidiaries the message was doubly underlined. Freighting ale by rail to London, then handling it twice, curtailed the whole Burton pale ale enterprise of the London brewers in the 1880s and 1890s. Even costs of around 1s a barrel to move beer in London, which compared very favourably with those breweries particularly in Burton whose sales had to be sustained by a rail network of agencies and stores, were a significant cost factor, at least for cheap porters and mild ales. This was especially true after 1900 when profits were sharply eroded by increased discounts and debt charges. Edward Buxton lectured Truman's directors in 1902:

> I need not repeat what I have perhaps too often said that it is of the utmost importance to secure sufficient trade near at hand to make more of the plant than we do at present. The advantages too will readily occur to you – more moderate discounts, less carriage, casks used oftener, bad debts avoided.[51]

Yet economies in this area, beyond the increasing hiring of transport after 1900, were not widely practised. Horses and drays were an important method of advertising when little was undertaken in other forms. Drays had therefore to be turned out in tip-top condition. Moreover, they were a special feature of the London brewing world in that brewers, like Londoners generally, perceived them as colourful, prized links between country and capital, the very epitome of the role of beer in London's life.

II

In complete contrast with the London porter brewers, with their great strings of metropolitan pubs, were those breweries which relied entirely

50 *Ind Coope & Co.. Ltd Souvenir 1799–1899* (1899), p. 12.
51 GLRO, Acc. 73.94, B/THB, Monthly Reports, April 1902.

upon the free trade for their existence and expansion. The Burton brewers, Guinness, and the likes of Tetley in Leeds provide the key models. Clearly, the factors in their success were quite different from their peers in London who concentrated upon loans as a response to competition and attempted to retain a hold on the rapidly expanding metropolitan beer market. Basically, these country brewers, whose vision set them apart from the hundreds who were content to confine their enterprise to their immediate localities, had to forge new methods of distribution to free their enterprises from the constraints traditionally placed upon them. Besides the usual endeavours to maintain the reputation and quality of their beers, they had to concede large discounts and construct a network of agencies and stores that would take full advantage of the changes which the railways brought to the sale and distribution of beer in Victorian Britain.

Beer never improved with travel. Admittedly, stouts, strong pale ales and the Scottish beers withstood the jolting of a boat or cart better than the weaker, less stable milds. Porters when they were soundly vatted were more robust. But even by rail, especially in the summer months, all beers deteriorated from the condition in which they left the brewery. There was no wonder in these circumstances that publicans employed a battery of prescriptions to revive the contents of their cellars, nor that an export trade was always difficult to develop. Condition was one reason that beer markets in Georgian Britain remained essentially local. The other reason, of course, was economic. To transport beer more than a few miles, even by waterway, added greatly to distribution costs. Sales of any quantity were invariably by the cheapest form of transport, coastal shipping. The costs of an expensive export ale or double stout might withstand the charges by other forms – as much as 12s a barrel between Burton and London by river and canal – but it was a different matter with porters or milds selling wholesale at around 33s–36s (minus discount).[52] Most London brewers at least seem to have felt that developing distant markets were at best frustrating, at worst not worth the candle. Orders were usually small, credit around 1830 was invariably extended to six months, debts were difficult to collect, the turnaround of casks was protracted, and the return of beers was near impossible in a trade where pilferage was rife. Surviving brewers' letter books reveal a deep despair with the state of affairs.[53]

[52] Owen, *Development of Industry*, p. 23 cites £3 a ton (i.e. almost five full 36 gallon barrels).

[53] See that of Sampson Hanbury quoted in Mathias, *Brewing Industry*, pp. 147–9.

Not surprisingly in these circumstances most brewers had to rely upon local distribution networks, either in the free trade, or by the ownership or leasing of pubs, or, most usually, by a mixture of both. The example of John Day & Sons of St Neots well illustrates the constraints transport imposed upon the vast majority of brewers in the 1830s.[54] Like many a brewer in the eastern counties, Day had acquired an early holding of pubs. In 1814 he owned thirty-four: eight in St Neots, three in Bedford, four in Biggleswade, and nineteen in the neighbouring villages. By 1836 the Days employed sixteen men in their brewery and wharf site in St Neots. A further twelve were solely engaged to convey beer and small quantities of porter, coal and a variety of miscellaneous goods. By the early 1830s the firm was producing around 5,000 barrels of beer a year which was distributed by road to customers in villages within an 18 mile radius of St Neots. Of the 5,917 barrels transported over land in 1834, 23 per cent was purchased by customers in the town compared with 58 per cent which was conveyed to outlets under 10 miles. The remaining 19 per cent was sold to customers in villages between 10 and 18 miles of St Neots. The ideal market for the sale of a low-value bulk product like beer was under 10 miles. Estimates of the number of journeys and barrels carried per delivery show that the average consignment of beer by Day consisted of seven barrels, conveyed by road carriage within 10 and 11 miles of St Neots. The sizeable inland navigation based upon the Great Ouse was available to them from their riverside wharf. They appear to have taken little advantage of it for their beer sales, although they dispatched between eight and fourteen barrels a week to London by road in the 1820s, orders probably commissioned through trading or familial links.

Similarly, Steward & Patteson, the great Norwich brewers, used their powerful city base from which to develop a trade out into the countryside in the first half of the nineteenth century. Unusually in this period, they acquired several country breweries in the process. And although they maintained a strong presence in the port of Great Yarmouth they were unsuccessful, at this stage, in pushing their trading frontiers beyond Norfolk. A brief foray into the London market in the late 1830s had failed by 1845.[55] With an expensive transit by wherry, and by steam packet from Yarmouth, the beer failed to maintain its condition on its

[54] This paragraph is based upon the day and trade books of John Day & Son (Acc./1299/1–6, Huntingdon Record Office). See chapter 5 of F. J. Wood's thesis on 'Inland Transport and Distribution in the Hinterland of King's Lynn, 1760–1840', Unpublished Cambridge Ph.D. thesis, 1992.

[55] Gourvish, *Norfolk Beers*, pp. 37–8.

arrival in London. The other large Norwich breweries, Morgan's, Bullard, Young, Weston and Crawshay likewise developed by forays into villages and small towns of Norfolk.[56] Purchase and lease of pubs was their usual method of acquisition and advance; the beer house in Norfolk was less prominent. Theirs were strategies entirely dictated by the problems of distributing beer any distance in the pre-railway age. It is unlikely that all the Norwich breweries put together sold more than a few score barrels outside Norfolk and north Suffolk before the 1850s.

Although brewers in large east coast ports like Edinburgh, Hull, King's Lynn and Yarmouth were well placed to push a sizeable London trade, others elsewhere were subject to the same constraints that confined the markets of the East Anglian breweries. When Henry Bentley, the son of a well-known Huddersfield brewer, set up the Eshaldwell brewery in 1828 at Woodlesford, 6 miles from Leeds, he had an acute appreciation of its location.[57] He chose a site between the busy River Aire, and the Leeds–London turnpike road. Within a couple of years he had built up a trade of 3,000 barrels which went on expanding because he vigorously attacked the nascent Leeds beer house trade after October 1830. Not surprisingly most of the 140 customers on Bentley's books in that year, all of them private or free-trade accounts, were from Leeds or in the industrial villages which crowded the river or turnpike. He acquired from an Allerton Bywater publican, William Pearson, a second-hand keel for £120; with it he shipped about a fifth of his output to a big Hull merchant, Thomas Sanderson. Yet even though the Leeds–London railway, opened in 1840, passed almost as close to the brewery as did the turnpike road, the firm's barrelage in 1850 was only just over 9,000 barrels. Marked expansion for Bentley's only came in the late 1860s and 1870s when beer consumption everywhere increased. The railways facilitated the growth of the beer market, they did not create it. And of course many breweries still remained essentially local, even though their trade grew rapidly after 1860. For as Britain's population in the industrial areas burgeoned after 1830, many urban concentrations were

[56] In 1845, Steward, Patteson, Finch & Co. owned 183 public houses in Norwich alone; Young, 71; Morgan's, 59; Westons, 32; Bullards, 32; Crawshays, 25 (together 72.1 per cent of the 558 public houses in Norwich: Gourvish, *Norfolk Beers*, p. 36).

[57] This paragraph is based upon a reconstruction of a year's trading account from Bentley's Sales Ledger (1828–32) in Whitbread Archives, 288/72; see also an MS 'Early History of the Brewery' which forms the basis of *A Famous Country Brewery 1828–1928* (1928) and Barnard *Noted Breweries*, III, pp. 247–53. It is Barnard that, unusually, disclosed Bentley's barrelages: 9,227 in 1850, 36,000 in 1870, 'nearly 100,000' in 1889.

created which provided similar opportunities to those presented earlier by the London beer market.

It was the markets of the Burton breweries which the railways most spectacularly freed. Here their impact was immediate. Although long a famed brewing centre, its progress before the 1820s had been slow (see pp. 89–94). Then its celebrated pale ales, first produced for export, rapidly caught on with middle-class drinkers in London, Liverpool and Birmingham in the 1820s and 1830s. Since they were expensive, they could, in some measure, withstand both the costs and upheavals of long canal and river journeys from the land-locked Midlands centre. The Burton industry's rapid growth after the mid-1830s meant that its leading brewers were poised to take immediate advantage of the new rail link with London in 1839. This did three things for the Burton brewers. First, as already mentioned, it reduced freight charges to London from around £3 a ton (almost five barrels) to 15s.[58] Rates to other centres crashed; the leading Burton partnerships then individually began to press the rail companies into further concessions for the bulk transport of malt, hops, beer and empty casks. Secondly, journey times were slashed; formerly taking up to three weeks for the circuitous canal route to London, they were reduced to twelve hours. Suddenly, Burton beer could be distributed nationwide cheaply and quickly in the 1840s and 1850s. For example Bass's *home* trade quadrupled within four years of the railway coming to Burton; again when the national rail network was almost in place, Bass's output, 145,177 barrels in 1855, incredibly *doubled* within the next three years. Domestic markets rapidly became more important than the distant Indian trade. The problem of pilferage seems to have disappeared. Thirdly, the railways transformed the carriage of materials and beers between brewery and malting sites in Burton itself. Perhaps no other town and industry in Victorian Britain demonstrated better the benefit of the railways.

Commentators on the industry in Burton were much struck by the importance thereto of the railways. An account in the *Licensed Victuallers' Gazette* in 1874 informed its readers that: 'something like 120,000 railway trucks [were employed], enough if all placed on a line of railways in a straight line now to reach from London to Liverpool and

[58] Owen, *Development of Industry*, p. 23. From the surviving Bass records, *average* costs of carriage per barrel can be determined, but not those to individual agencies. After the late 1860s these average costs appear to have been remarkably stable: 3s 2.7d per barrel in 1869–70, 3s 2.8d in 1884–5, 3s 5.0d in 1909–10.

back again'.,[59] Already Bass was the largest railway customer in the world.[60] By 1889 when Barnard visited Bass, the six company locomotives of 1874 had increased to ten, and the 6 miles of privately owned track to 12. Endearingly, with a child's delight, he 'steamed through the premises' – three breweries and thirty-seven maltings – journeys he repeated at Allsopp and Worthington with an equal glee.[61] At Bass, at its peak in the late 1890s, 600 trucks a day were employed.[62] Within a few hours these could be unloaded *inside* the company's great stores at St Pancras Station and the London docks in north Woolwich. Burton became a web of intercommunicating lines belonging to the four companies operating in the town, besides the 40 miles of private lines and the sidings of all but its smallest breweries (see Plate 16).

The railways also allowed the creation of agencies and stores which became the life-blood of the Burton breweries and the free trade after 1840. Indeed, they were the most significant feature of the distribution of beer in Victorian Britain, for the most enterprising breweries everywhere followed the lead of Bass, Allsopp and Guinness in creating them. Yet historians of the industry have ignored them. In all fairness so did most contemporaries. Barnard and all those contributors to the local press and trade journals, who could turn out competent, stereotyped articles about the bigger breweries and their owners, invariably waxed lyrical about the traditions of the industry and the ways in which science and technology had transformed the scale of production in the half-century after 1830. They barely mentioned demand and distribution. Descriptions were given of the London stores of the three or four biggest Burton breweries and the towns in which a firm's agencies were situated. The latter were simply lists, providing a selection of as many as twenty towns from Aberdeen to Plymouth and from Dover to Galway. When the *Burton Chronicle* tried its hand at a Barnard-style piece about Bass, its author wrote: 'To be the historian of its multitude of stores and its Home and Foreign Dependencies would require a large measure of time and fill many a tome.'[63] Of course its author shirked the task, but an outline of the agency system as classically developed in Burton and imitated elsewhere is essential to understand the remarkable growth of the leading breweries following the completion of a national rail network.

59 *Licensed Victuallers' Gazette*, 14 Nov. 1874; see also *North of England Farmer*, 13 May 1871 and the *Licensed Victuallers' Almanack* (1881), pp. 97–101.
60 *Retford Times*, 13 May 1876.
61 Barnard, *Noted Breweries*, I, pp. 45–119; II, pp. 121–71, 408–48.
62 *Institution of Mechanical Engineers*, 20 Sept. 1898.
63 *Burton Chronicle*, 19 Jan. 1899.

In fact, a reconstruction of any brewery's agency network is not easy because detailed records seldom survive for the pre-1880s period. Nevertheless it is certain that the lead in their creation was given by the Burton brewers. Bass and Allsopp were the key firms, although, since few of the latter firm's nineteenth-century papers remain, the former's role is possibly exaggerated. Certainly, the system has its origin in the pre-railway darknesses of the firm's history. They most probably had their antecedents in those arrangements, usual in the eighteenth century, whereby a trader on the spot would look after the interests of a distant manufacturer or merchant. As early as the 1780s Truman were attempting to channel their country trade through the accounts of half a dozen merchants accessible by good navigable connections, rather than through scores of small, individual customers. Agencies were therefore a response to the problems of opening up distant markets more profitably.[64] Possibly, they may also have owed something to those extraordinary networks of agencies that the early insurance companies ran, and that enabled a firm like the Norwich Union to thrust itself into national prominence after 1815. Generally, in an age in which traders, shopkeepers and even lawyers seldom made a living from a single interest, the commission agency was a popular means of boosting incomes. Not surprisingly, when Michael Thomas Bass succeeded his father he devised an agency network to expand the sales of his beers in England as well as overseas. His earliest agencies in London (*c.*1830), Liverpool (1830), Stoke-on-Trent (1835) and Birmingham were in place before the railway came to Burton in 1839. And within four years a valuation of Bass's stocks reveal that a further three had been added.[65] Those in London and Liverpool were much the most important. It is impossible to know their precise ties with Bass. The one in London almost certainly was a *store*, i.e. where Bass owned or rented the premises (at 49 Great Tower Street) and directly employed the agent or manager, clerk, traveller and storeman, and also its drays and horses. Arrangements in Liverpool were similar. But the other five at this stage were purely *agencies*, i.e. where Bass paid a small retaining salary, a commission on net cash sales and a percentage to cover the agent's cartage costs. There was then a distinction between stores and agencies: the former owned or rented and run by the brewery itself; the latter worked by an independent trader operating on a commission basis.

64 Mathias, *Brewing Industry*, pp. 147–8.
65 See note 71 below.

Unfortunately, the distinction was then frequently lost because both were alike loosely referred to as agencies, even in a firm's own records.

Worthington's brewery provides a good example of the setting-up and development of an agency network. Before the early 1860s their business centred upon the local trade and a London stores opened in 1854. Then, in the mid-1860s, they quickly expanded their agency business. In 1863 and 1864 one of the firm's four partners (all Worthingtons) wrote down their agency agreements in scruffy entries into their record of weekly 'board' meetings.[66] They reveal the construction of a rapid, ramshackle affair. Some two dozen names were mentioned, and although the record usually ran to a note of the commission and the security Worthington demanded, the venue of the agency was not invariably entered. The firm gave a commission of 12 per cent on cash sales, required a security, most often of £200, and made the agent responsible for a quarter of his bad debts. In some instances it is clear the initiative came not from Worthingtons but from the agent himself. If a salary was paid – for example William Callow & Co. of Manchester were paid £120 per annum and allowed £100 for their premises, half their rates, and a clerk's salary at 25s per week – then the commission fell to 7 per cent. Some agencies like those in the west of Scotland, Derby, Manchester, Lancashire, west Yorkshire and Newcastle upon Tyne clearly had potential; those in rural areas like Anglesey and Spilsby (Lincolnshire) did not. No further mention is made of their fate, although it is clear that Worthington's output, aided by a royal warranty to the Prince of Wales in 1866, grew rapidly after the 1860s – a growth fuelled by their agency network. In 1875 the firm advertised in the *Licensed Victualler's Gazette* that it had twenty-six agencies, six in the Midlands, ten in the North, four in the South of England, three in Wales, one in Scotland, and two in Ireland.[67]

As with all the major Burton breweries, Worthington's most important stores were in London. As early as 1875 it had two: one at St Pancras Station serving the Midland Railway connection; a second at Moorfields for the North-Western route. Together they were capable of storing between 3,000 and 4,000 barrels. Fifteen years later they had moved to Broad Street and were greatly expanded, using thirty horses to

66 This paragraph is constructed from Worthington's 'Board' Meetings, 1862–71 (Bass Museum, A/179).

67 *Licensed Victuallers' Gazette*, 2 Jan. 1875. Salt & Co. (Burton) had sixteen agencies in 1874, the Burton Brewery twenty-one in 1873. See *Licensed Victuallers' Gazette*, 12 Dec. 1874, 27 Sept. 1873. The opening and closing of agencies were regular features in the activities of the larger breweries.

deliver 1,000 barrels a week (around a quarter of Worthington's sales).[68] In Liverpool, on the other hand, the directors lamented in 1884 that trade had fallen from £33,000 a year in 1877 to £21,000. The firm was remarkably lenient with its agent, Jones, hinting he should take early retirement and appointing a second traveller to assist him. Of the trade of the other ten agencies in 1892 there is no record, but the twelve together in that year retailed 144,009 barrels as against 143,328 'direct'.[69] By the 1900s Worthington's sales had begun to be summarised in an extended printed annual return. In 1910, for example, a surprisingly high 58.5 per cent of barrelage was sold in the free trade (see Table 4.3). Worthington, who had vigorously acquired pubs after 1886, were still relying before 1914 on their agencies to retain a hold in the diminishing free-trade market and to push their 'Worthington E', a market leader in the expanding bottled beer trade.

If Worthington's records provide a rare indication of how a brewery could grow using an agency system, it was the example of Bass's model network which provided the inspiration for every aspiring Victorian brewer (see Plate 24).[70] Already by 1846, the agencies that M. T. Bass had set up in the 1830s and early 1840s were flourishing. They revealed how the expanding rail network might be utilised to retail nationally a distinctive, high-quality beer. In that year, 46.4 per cent of Bass's total sales of £154,670 were made from its Burton base, but no less than

[68] Barnard, *Noted Breweries*, I, p. 448.

[69] Bass Museum A/164, Worthington's Board Meetings, 1884; Private Minute Book 1892–3. The list extracted from stray references in the latter is possibly incomplete. It includes London, Liverpool, Hull, Newcastle, Stoke-on-Trent, Cardiff, Swansea, Manchester, Blackpool, Cheltenham, Gloucester and Birmingham. There are references in other years to ones in Leeds, Darlington, Plymouth, Cork and Antwerp.

Worthington's beer sales, 1889–1898 (in standard barrels)

	'Direct'		'Via stores' (agencies)	Sales plus stocks and beer allowances
1889	122,745		96,084	240,485
1890	128,797		111,770	263,664
1891	140,767		129,184	292,986
1892	143,328		144,009	319,869
1893	146,484		154,909	328,588
1894	136,229		158,415	322,687
1895	148,409		150,442	330,270
1896		321,148		362,458
1897		328,596		370,455
1898		–		380,020

[70] This section is based upon records in the Bass Museum and Owen, *History of Bass*, forthcoming.

Table 4.3. *Worthington's free and tied trade, 1910*

Trading area	Barrels	Percentage	Per cent tied	Per cent free
Home	67,264	17.4	49.9	50.1
Northern	145,282	37.5	45.1	54.9
Southern	161,679	41.7	34.6	65.4
Scotland	7,276	1.9	0	100
Ireland	1,749	0.5	100	0
Antwerp	4,398	1.1	100	0
Total	387,648	100.1	41.5	58.5

Source: Bass Museum, Worthington & Co. Agencies, F/15/1.

35.7 per cent from its London store, 6.8 per cent from Liverpool, and the rest vended via its five other agencies.[71] Of course, the London and Liverpool figures might well have included some exports, but the continuing feature was the place the London and south Lancashire stores held in Bass's trade, even when, as by 1860, the list of agencies had reached eleven.[72] Bass's London store was a massive enterprise in itself. In 1867 it was moved to the Midland Railway's great St Pancras Station. Here a lower floor, with street access, was given over to the storage of beer. Indeed, its consulting engineer, W. H. Barlow, using iron columns and girders to economise upon space, reckoned, 'the length of a beer barrel became the unit of measure, upon which all the arrangements of this floor were based'.[73] Bass's store alone housed 120,000 barrels and employed 150 men. And eventually, in the major cities of all the four countries of the United Kingdom, smaller versions of the London stores were set up by Bass. In 1890 there were twenty-two; in 1900, a peak of twenty-five. In the latter year the London agency did a trade of £840,950, Newcastle came next with almost £300,000, Liverpool, Manchester and Glasgow followed with just over £200,000 apiece, and five others (Stoke-on-Trent, Stockton-on-Tees, Plymouth, Leeds and Dublin) had sales of between £100,000 and

71 In order of importance, Wolverhampton, Stoke-on-Trent, Manchester, Birmingham, Bristol. Bass's trade through its London agency remained remarkably stable: between 1865 and 1874 it varied between 32.5 and 39 per cent of all Bass's beer dispatched by rail in the UK.

72 London, Liverpool, Manchester, Birmingham, Wolverhampton, Newcastle upon Tyne, Bristol, Stoke-on-Trent, Cork, Dublin and Edinburgh.

73 Quoted in J. Simmons, *St Pancras Station* (1968), p. 31.

£200,000.[74] Most provincial breweries would have been satisfied had their sales exceeded any *one* of these agencies.

Whatever their value as a substitute for description, such statistics cannot indicate the role of the agent in Bass's affairs. It was his vigour that created sales, his character that advertised Bass's presence in any of these two dozen centres. He was the firm's eyes and ears. Not only did he endlessly report upon the quality and condition of their beers, and manage the travellers, storemen and draymen in the store, but eventually he came to play a key role in their loans policy. Although they never matched the London brewers in this field, Bass began to supply loans to tie a fast-declining free trade after 1886. By 1897 these loans for the first time topped £1,000,000, of which £134,320 was lent in London. By 1911 Bass's involvement had reached a peak of £1,480,000. The London, Midlands and Newcastle agents were deeply involved in the negotiation of all these loans; they were also essential links in reporting back to Bass about the incursions and strategies which other breweries were employing in the industry's trade wars after the 1890s. As discounts (the chief competitive weapon) soared (see pp. 208–9), it was the agents and travellers who apprised the firm of the acute problems all brewers faced in the free trade after the 1890s. Of course involvement brought increasing recognition of the agent's role. It is possible to argue that Bass's London agent was the most important individual in the firm after Lord Burton himself. Certainly W. H. Bailey, the firm's London manager, believed he was (see Plate 22).[75] An incredible publicist in an age when self-importance was rife, no dinner or cricket match – and there were many – in the beer trade, either in London or Burton, was complete without a speech from him. When in Burton he stayed at Rangemoor with Lord Burton. His salary in the 1890s was a comfortable £1,500: well-deserved because he was instrumental in securing Bass's growing interest in the London restaurant and catering world and setting up their Belgian agency. When he retired in 1909, 400 members of the metropolitan drinks trade attended a dinner in his honour at the Victoria Hall. Bailey rose to the occasion, denouncing Lloyd George to thunderous applause, and recalling the 'good and bad times we had shared' and 'the bitter crusades of the past twenty years'.

[74] The other fifteen were in order of sales, Edinburgh, Hull, Sheffield, Belfast, Aberdeen, Brighton, Cork, Southampton, Bristol, Leicester, Birmingham, Exeter, Wolverhampton, Nottingham and North Wales.

[75] There are many references to W. H. Bailey in Bass's volumes of 'Scrapbooks' – essentially contemporary volumes of press-cuttings (Bass Museum, A/558). See also

John Shorthose, the Newcastle agent from 1851 to 1898, and in all sixty years with the firm, had an equal status (see Plate 23). A couple of letters he wrote to the firm in 1908 provide a wonderful, rare vignette of Victorian commercial life.[76] When he had gone to Newcastle in the year of the Great Exhibition, Bass had done 'very little trade' there.

Shortly afterwards I got a Horse and Dray, one cellarman and Horsekeeper and so we went on for a few years, increasing annually. We did all the delivering to customers by ourselves at very small incomes. From that time to the day I retired, not a person ever left the office to solicit an order, or to collect an account, I did it all myself.

He reckoned he had sold Bass £4,400,000 worth of beer, with 'scarcely mentionable' bad debts, in his forty-seven years at Newcastle. Given his assiduity, his calculations were probably correct. Trade there did grow from £2,000 a year in his first year, to £100,000 in 1873–4, and to £300,000 at the height of the late 1890s beer boom. In 1874 Bass had opened a store with a capacity of 10,000 barrels beneath the Forth goods station. Keeping beer at a constant temperature and installing Armstrong's hydraulic machinery for loading, it was the model Victorian beer store, run by a model agent.[77] In 1908, Shorthose recalled that Lord Burton believed, 'he was the best agent they had. I took this as a great compliment. I shall never forget it.' Now, although living very comfortably in Northumberland, it was clear he had miscalculated his longevity. Electing to take a lump sum of £5,600, he regretted that he had not taken the massive £800 a year pension offered to him. And like all old men he could, when faced with an unsympathetic new management, only lament changed times: 'Truly we do not live now in [the] days of my old and very esteemed friends, Michael Thomas Bass, Samuel Ratcliff and John Gretton.' But these were personal reflections. The agency system, created in Shorthose's own lifetime, had barely passed its zenith. It was at least for the biggest Burton brewers the elimination of the free trade and the motor lorry in the inter-war years which finally led to its dismemberment.

Few breweries besides Guinness maintained as extensive an agency

The Morning Advertiser, 15 Dec. 1909. The Museum has recently purchased a volume of Bailey's own cuttings.

76 Dated – Jan. and 14 Feb. 1908 in A/135 (John Lambrick, the Company Secretary's private box).

77 *Newcastle Chronicle*, 12 Nov. 1874. Bass's Newcastle trade was reported to be 3,500 barrels, Allsopp's 2,000.

system as that erected by the big Burton breweries, and none on the scale of Bass, Allsopp and Ind Coope. Yet it was the Bass model which clearly provided the example for all those breweries who aimed to expand beyond their own district by incursions into the free trade. The more enterprising Scottish breweries grew exactly in this way. Donnachie, generalising from the example of McEwan, represented the typical big Edinburgh and Glasgow brewery, around 1880 making half its sales locally, a quarter in the country trade, and the rest split between the English and export trades.[78] William Younger, the most prominent Scottish brewer, had erected a network of fourteen agencies by 1873 to achieve these ends: three each in Scotland and Ireland, and five in the North of England besides those in Birmingham, Bristol and London.[79] Unusually, as much as 35 per cent of its trade between 1880 and 1914 was in London, but then they employed no fewer than ten travellers there in 1890.[80] William Younger were exceptional, but smaller firms like Ballinghall of Dundee and James Calder of Alloa had stores in Newcastle and Liverpool, as well as Glasgow, and the Edinburgh and Leith Brewery Co. reputedly sold its beers principally in England.[81] And in England John Smith's of Tadcaster similarly expanded by erecting an agency network. A firm of recent growth, in a town which the Victorians liked to categorise as the Burton-of-the-North, it possessed sixteen offices and stores and twenty-two agencies in the 1880s, although its competitors maintained that a good deal of its success was due to the discounts of 20 per cent or more which they found difficult to match.[82] But the earliest surviving evidence of a firm which copied Bass's route to prominence comes from Tetley of Leeds. The largest Yorkshire brewery in 1870, it was an unusual firm in that its stronger arm, at least before the 1850s, was its malting business. Then two go-ahead partners, F. W. Tetley and his brother-in-law, Charles Ryder, transformed its fortunes in two decades by building a new brewery in the mid-1850s to brew a good IPA. Already in 1859 they produced a total output of almost 36,000 barrels. Three years later production really took off, by 1876 reaching a pre-1905 peak of 166,740 barrels.[83] Much of

[78] Donnachie, *Brewing Industry*, pp. 215–17.
[79] *Licensed Victuallers' Gazette*, 4 Jan. 1873.
[80] Donnachie, *Brewing Industry*, p. 221.
[81] Barnard, *Noted Breweries*, III, pp. 142–66; IV, pp. 384, 386–94.
[82] John Smith's Archives (Tadcaster), JA/M/6; comments made in the partners diaries of the Tadcaster Tower Brewery, see note 99 below.
[83] West Yorkshire Archives, Leeds, Tetley MSS. Box 40, Ale and Porter No. 4 Profit and Loss, 1858–77.

the early resurgence was due to their endeavours to set up a national distribution system in six cities, London, Dublin, Liverpool, Birmingham, Manchester and York.[84] For a northern brewery, especially in a citadel of publican brewing, it was a most unusual step (see Table 4.4). By 1859 its agency business was already impressive. Yet, unlike the Burton brewers, the early promise was not maintained. In London after 1880 it could not compete against the large advances made to publicans by the London and Burton producers, and a decade later against the Manchester brewers who began to purchase every free house on the market. Only in York, where the Tadcaster Tower Brewery owned the majority of pubs but brewed indifferent beers, was their market more or less maintained.[85] Tetley's sales did not reach their 1876 peak again before 1914, but at least they were fortunate in that they could switch their efforts in developing the great Leeds–Bradford beer market to achieve a good reputation and good profits throughout the period.

On the other hand some large breweries made no attempt to open agencies and stores: they simply used travellers, working from the brewery office, to service their tied trade and open up the free and private trades in their vicinity. Invariably, these breweries were in the largest conurbations and many of them were amongst the most profitable and fastest growing enterprises of the post-1860s expansion. Peter Walker of Warrington attacked the vast Liverpool market from one large city store. William Butler in Wolverhampton, Henry Mitchell in Birmingham, John Barras in Newcastle upon Tyne, Vaux in Sunderland, Brain in Cardiff, Groves & Whitnall in Manchester, the Nottingham Brewery, the five leading Sheffield breweries, the Vale Brewery in Darwin, Lees of Middleton (Lancs) all notably expanded by securing

Joshua Tetley: Barrels of Beer distributed by Rail and Dray, 1854–1877 (annual averages)

	Railway (1)	Dray (2)	Railway trade as percentage of total
1854	19,850	15,470	56
1860–4	15,073	20,831	42
1865–9	23,650	37,573	35
1870–4	29,976	63,872	32
1875–7	39,503	112,243	26

[84] C. Lackey, *Quality Pays ... The Story of Joshua Tetley & Son* (1985), p. 56.

[85] See also *A Century of Progress* (Joshua Tetley & Son Ltd 1923), p. 18 which exaggerates the collapse of the Manchester agency; Hawkins, *Bass Charrington*, p. 28.

Table 4.4. *Tetley's beer sales from its four major stores, 1859–1905 (annual averages in barrels)*

Year	Stores [i] London	[ii] Liverpool	[iii] Manchester	[iv] York	Total sales	Percentage of total sales cols. i–iv
1859	4,858	3,440	1,680	1,440	35,150	32.5
1860–4	3,004	2,087	1,646	1,336	35,908	22.5
1865–9	4,360	2,270	4.704	1,670	61,212	21.2
1870–4	5,000	2,194	7,892	2,440	93,852	18.7
1875–9	4,718	1,598	13,452	3,330	149,540	15.4
1880–4	3,476	1,630	12,514	2,724	134,522	15.1
1885–9	2,104	866	12,346	2,540	146,274	12.2
1890–4	1,472	700	8,366	2,666	141,536	9.3
1895–9	1,056	418	6,284	4,578	139,174	8.9
1900–5	315	208	5,018	5,389	147,190	7.4

Source: Joshua Tetley & Son, Ale and Porter Account Books, No. 4, 1857–76; No. 5, 1877–1905, West Yorkshire Archives, Leeds.

the ample markets on their own doorsteps.[86] Moreover, the beers of the North-East and Sheffield, strong and sweet, were of a character not appreciated elsewhere. They were primarily regional beers which agents elsewhere, however persuasive, would have failed to sell.

Georges of Bristol provides the best example of a brewery which flourished without recourse to agencies or a London store. The only mention in the company's minutes of an agency (South Wales) comes as late as 1909. Its long-held reputation as one of the soundest breweries in England was based upon its strong position in Bristol. By 1893 eight-ninths of its business was in the tied trade; four years later nineteenth-twentieths. In 1905 its travellers did little besides visit the firm's 440 houses and few private customers. Two years later its chairman could grandly declare 'my company has certainly no idea of hawking round beers for sale'. With £750,000 invested in pubs, they were going to do 'nothing to injure their interest'.[87]

A more usual distribution pattern was for brewers to use a mixture of agencies and stores to achieve local and regional aspirations. Some achieved growth basically by developing one big extra-regional interest. The north Kent breweries capitalised their access by sea to London as did Lacon from Yarmouth (although they also, without notable success, set up agencies in Norwich, Bridlington, Sunderland and Plymouth); Joule of Stone concentrated upon the Liverpool market as well as their own 158 public houses in Staffordshire; similarly the trade of Bentley's of Woodlesford was local except for their Manchester connection; Benskin's of Watford ran a big London depot.[88] On the other hand there were breweries that employed scores of agents on a commission basis. These agents, often wine and spirit merchants or grocers, were already numerous by the 1830s. Kelly's Directory lists twenty-eight ale and porter agents in Manchester in 1850; Gore's Directory included thirty-four in Liverpool seven years later; forty-eight were listed for Glasgow in 1870.[89] Even rural areas were well supplied: twenty-seven in Hampshire in 1878, and no fewer than eleven in the Oxfordshire market town of Banbury a couple of years later. Competition in Banbury must have been fierce: three retailed Burton ales, three represented Guinness, two

[86] The list is compiled from Barnard, *Noted Breweries* which includes (or in these cases ignores) agencies and stores; also the firms' in-house company histories, where they exist, have been checked.

[87] Courage Archives (Bristol), 35740 BG/9(C).

[88] Whitbread Archives, 197/239; Barnard, *Noted Breweries*, III, pp. 83–106, 247–53; IV, pp. 29–52.

[89] Donnachie, *Brewing Industry*, pp. 192–4.

Ind Coope, and three local breweries – Lewis & Ridley, Shipstone & Stour, and the Northampton Brewery – each possessed one in the town.[90] Therefore it was not difficult to find an agent anywhere in Britain to retail beer for an ambitious brewer. But there were problems beyond those of estimating profits and transport costs. The brewers wanted sureties, were hesitant to pay too large a retainer for a sole agency, or give too generous a discount. Above all, they worried about the bad debts a negligent agent failed to collect. Optimistic calculations on scraps of paper often turned to ashes when the agent's efforts did not match his promises and the trade of the district did not live up to expectations. Yet some breweries relied on whole posses of agents. Rogers in Bristol had eighty besides a London store; Watkins of Hereford had over 100 scattered across southern England, including one in the Channel Islands besides two stores in Cardiff and Swansea.[91] But none exceeded those employed by the Anglo-Bavarian Brewery, which after 1869 brewed, improbably, a lager-type beer in Shepton Mallet. Barnard records that beside several branch stores they had 250 selling agents scattered across the kingdom.[92] Their average sales for the brewery must have been very small. In 1903 Greene King had emerged as one of the largest breweries in East Anglia. Possessing five stores to service their tied and private trades by rail, they also employed thirty agents on commission. Together they sold no more than 3,000 barrels.[93] Possibly, when the free trade was more extensive before the 1890s, these agencies accounted for a larger share of Greene's trade; certainly by 1910 their role in the firm's distribution was much further in decline.

A middling position in the reliance upon an agency network between the examples of Lacon and Joule on the one hand, and the Anglo-Bavarian Brewery on the other, was occupied by firms such as Eldridge Pope. This Dorchester brewery had its antecedents in a wine and spirits-cum-publican brewing enterprise by the 1830s and 1840s. Like all West Country breweries it expanded very slowly. By 1870 when it came into the hands of the Popes, a well-to-do Dorset farming family, it probably produced no more than 10,000 barrels a year. Thereafter under the direction of Alfred Pope, a sharp solicitor, its expansion was

[90] *White's Directory of Hampshire* (1878); *Rusher's Directory* (1880). There were also eight brewers listed in Banbury, some of these small brewers also acted as agents and, later, bottlers.

[91] Barnard, *Noted Breweries*, II, pp. 329–30; III, pp. 513–22.

[92] *Ibid.* II, pp. 256–82.

[93] Wilson, *Greene King*, p. 136. In 1903 beer sales totalled 75,378 barrels, the peak of their 1887–1914 performance.

rapid. Constructing an impressive new green field brewery contiguous to the London South-Western railway in 1881, its sales had increased to 44,326 barrels by 1890 (see Plate 25). It was much the biggest brewery in the South-West, 'constituting probably the finest pile of buildings devoted to industrial purposes in the South of England'.[94] The basis of this expansion was not its 117 tied houses, but the depots which the firm opened in Bath, Winchester, Southampton, Portsmouth, Salisbury, Eastleigh, Bournemouth and Weymouth. Through them it drove a growing beer and wine and spirits trade on the coasts of Dorset and Hampshire. Other breweries like Cobbold of Ipswich, Steward & Patteson in Norwich, Simonds of Reading, Garton & Co. of Bristol, Hudson's of Pampisford (Cambs.), Robin of Brighton, the Phoenix Brewery of Dover, the Lion Brewery of Ashford, and Warwicks & Richardsons of Newark followed a similar route to regional dominance, each utilising a mixture of agencies and stores to serve their tied and extend their free trades.[95] In 1875 Agg-Gardner's Cheltenham Original Brewery had 'a distinction of its own, which specially marks it out for notice, for although not professing to vie with the more gigantic establishments of London and Burton, it has yet acquired for itself a reputation, extending for fifty miles in every direction of the highest possible character'.[96] The author of the account put this down to good beer and good treatment of its publicans. When the same writer turned his attention to the Northampton Brewery, like Agg-Gardner's owned by a single proprietor, he was more explicit about the role of its agencies. Listing nineteen with good river connections, he commented:

these agencies ... are all having to send in their account of sales, etc. every day, and to attend at the chief office once a month in order to have their accounts thoroughly examined. The result of this excellent system is that the percentage of bad debts at the agencies is remarkably small, while their cost averages less than the ordinary commission of a traveller. The agents, indeed, being without the independence so often very unwisely given them, might be more properly described as local travellers with offices.[97]

94 This section is based upon the unsorted archive of Eldridge Pope and their published history (an above average example of the species), J. Seekings, *Thomas Hardy's Brewer: The Story of Eldridge Pope & Co.* (Wimborne, *c.*1988).

95 For Cobbold, see the *Licensed Victuallers' Gazette*, 14 Aug. 1875; for Simonds, Corley, 'Simonds Brewery at Reading, 1760–1960' and *The Road to Worton Grange* (1980); for Steward & Patteson, Gourvish, *Norfolk Beers*; for the rest see their entries in Barnard, *Noted Breweries*.

96 *Licensed Victuallers' Gazette*, 13 Feb. 1875.

97 *Licensed Victuallers' Gazette*, 9 Oct. 1875. The agencies were at Rugby, Coventry, Leicester, Peterborough, Daventry, Kingscliffe, Harrow, Hitchin, Kettering, Deddington, Leighton Buzzard, Market Harborough, Wellingborough, Hinckley, Wansford, Stony Stratford, Thrapston, St Albans, Oxford, 'and other places'.

When R. S. Boddington visited a number of Edinburgh breweries in the New Year of 1882 he cryptically noted McEwan's agency arrangements: 'All paid servants – full control – sometimes loss at first establishment, but soon begins to pay.'[98] Clearly, there was a variety of experiences: in Burton, in the northern cities and in rural centres. No brewery, therefore, was quite typical in its distribution pattern. A great deal depended upon local conditions and the drive of the brewery partnership.

Surviving brewery records are only rarely sufficiently complete to reconstruct the precise arrangements between brewer and agent, to trace the evolution of agencies into stores, and to record their decline as the free trade withered rapidly after the 1880s with the brewers' success in tying their outlets. Lists of agencies, columns of barrelages unfold neither decisions nor strategies. It is only with the survival of so unique a record as the partners' diaries of the Tadcaster Tower Brewery that the detailed picture emerges.[99] To flesh out the general account in the foregoing pages, this section concludes with a brief survey of the way this brewery built up a network of agencies, stores and travellers to ease the tight margins imposed by the purchase of an over-priced business in the late 1870s.

The Tower Brewery was a curious one. Known originally as Hotham & Co., its origins in York went back a century and a half. It was sold with ninety tied houses – about one-third of the city's pubs – for £36,000 in 1875. Six months later the new partners acquired a further dozen houses; in 1879, fifty more, again almost all in York, at the inflated price of £63,000. The need to raise more capital brought in two more partners, both old Etonians of impeccable connections, who supplied £20,000 each.[100] Yet from that moment on the partnership was frequently in dire financial straits. Their brewery in George Street was a poor one, most of their tied houses were in an appalling state of repair attracting an appalling class of tenant. The details of disrepair, the

98 Whitbread Archives, W/405, Boddingtons' Diaries, 1869–82.

99 The following paragraphs are constructed from the diaries (at Bass North, Leeds) covering the years 1879–90. There is a gap from July 1881–November 1882. The diaries were compiled in fact *for* the perusal of the partners, who lived in and around York, by the manager, C. H. Tripp. Often calling on their way from the Yorkshire Club, the partners, especially R. H. Munro and the Hon. Reginald Parker, then made their comments in the margins, usually on the beer and horses. The diaries become less detailed after 1887, but they are, because of their length, compilation and purpose, a unique source for the historian of brewing in the late Victorian period. See also W. Swales, *The History of the Tower Brewery Tadcaster* (1991), which provides good illustrative material.

100 Sir Frederick Milner Bt., MP and the Hon. Reginald Parker, sixth son of the sixth Earl of Macclesfield.

catalogue of misdemeanours was endless. 'House in a filthy state'; 'the house and yard were simply disgracefully dirty, house wants painting outside and roof mending'; 'the place alive with vermin' – these were not untypical entries about their pubs, or that made about the tenant from Barmby Moor who 'came in quite drunk, stunk like a stoat'.[101] And when the directors brought together all their publicans for a meeting to discuss an increase in government duties, it was, unsurprisingly, 'rather drunken and disorderly'. In 1882, as if deliberately to distance themselves from this morass, the firm built a new brewery on the latest tower principle nine miles away in the Yorkshire brewing centre of Tadcaster. Visually impressive and with a North-Eastern railway connection, it was a managerial nightmare for the partners who continued to operate the business from their York office. Transport by rail to York cost 3s 6d a ton; control of a succession of head-brewers was difficult. For years they seemed incapable of brewing and racking bright 'running' beers which were in increasing vogue. Even worse was the brewery's financial plight. Mortgages, although easily raised amongst the partners' grand acquaintances, were numerous and after 1880 trade in York declined sharply.[102] For six long years it remained in the doldrums. In 1886 the manager recorded: 'Trade is awful in York: half of our Tied Houses are in a ruined state.' As evidence he quoted the turnover of fifty-four of them which had declined from £15,660 in 1877 to £11,923 in 1885. Only fifteen of their houses had shown an increase. Of their 150 or so houses with a total trade of £34,680 in the year ending 30 September 1885 a mere thirty-two had accounts with the brewery in excess of £300. One did a miserable trade of £16 a year; another £31.

The firm's only way to ease its tight margins – the result of inflated prices paid in the late 1870s for poor property and the acute recession in York after 1880 – was by exploiting the free trade. In November 1885 the manager made his policy clear:

> To increase therefore, with a falling trade at Home in their Tied Houses, we must 'look-a-field', the Firm wants to see 20,000 Blls. sold this year against 18,600 last! The question is where to go to?? What to do?? If a [rail freight] rate

[101] None had a more precipitate end than Mrs Metcalf of Stockton. In January 1884, after consultation with the police about reports of her heavy drinking, the manager visited her. She was 'much the worse for drink' and he persuaded her to give up the licence in a month. He was barely back in his office before it was reported that she had been 'found dead at the bottom of the stairs'. For its worst twenty tenants the brewery had an x, xx, xxx rating, just as it had for its beers.

[102] Mortgages were supplied by the third Earl of Durham (Swales, *Tower Brewery Tadcaster*, pp. 5–6); Lady Wenlock (£20,000) and also two of the vendors, William Hotham and James Melrose.

could be obtained suitable and a really good Buying Agent in London found who would give real security, here might be a centre?! we have written for quotations etc. And Liverpool has during the past fortnight come much under notice.[103]

In fact their options were severely limited. With prohibitive carriage rates of 23s 4d a ton to London, and the realisation that the only trade in Liverpool would be with beer houses, nothing was done. Moreover, although the firm was fortunate in that its well-connected partners could bring it the business of the military hospital, the prison and, above all, the army canteens at the new barracks at Strensall, 5 miles north of York, they could not afford to improve and rationalise their pubs in York, nor acquire additional tied property elsewhere except on a minimal scale. Even in the free trade their room for manœuvre was circumscribed by the competition of John Smith and Joshua Tetley. John Smith's offered 20 per cent plus discounts; Tetley brewed a much better product in Leeds, the obvious market for Tadcaster beers. Yet within these constraints the manager pursued a clear strategy which was adventurous in seeking out new opportunities. First, he set up a number of agents on a part-salaried, part-commission basis in a number of Yorkshire and North-East towns, with travellers working from four stores.[104] Secondly, he acquired three small, run-down breweries in areas where he could envisage expansion: Castleford, Wakefield and Grimsby.[105] The spartan pubs in and around Castleford, dependent upon workers from the potteries and mines, drove a brisk trade. Grimsby provided new opportunities, 'a nice seaport fishing Town: good streets, good houses, and mostly all new within the past 20 years'.

The calculations the firm made to arrive at its decisions are fascinating.

[103] For a time they discussed the possibilities of employing an ex-traveller of Tennent (Glasgow) who informed them that Scotch beers were unpopular in Liverpool and therefore left an opening for others, 'whereas there were fourteen Scotch Breweries pouring beer into Liverpool five years ago there are only five now'.

[104] The diaries are imprecise in their distinction between agencies and stores, agents and travellers. Agencies are mentioned in Scarborough, Goole, Hull and Doncaster. Initially the area was worked by travellers operating from York (across an enormous area), Hull, Darlington and, later, from stores at Wakefield, Castleford, Kirkstall (soon closed) and Grimsby. In 1887 the diaries record that there were ten travellers (not all full time) including ones working from Newcastle and Stockton.

[105] Mitchell Bros. of Castleford was bought with ten houses in September 1884 for £8,000. The Tower Brewery had to turn down five further Mitchell houses because the valuation was too high. In May 1885 they acquired Scott's Phoenix Brewery in Wakefield. It had an entirely free trade of only 2,700 barrels in 1884. The brewery was closed and F. Scott stayed on as a traveller on generous terms. A similar arrangement (which soon folded) was reached that same summer with the Sells' tiny Willow Brewery, Kirkstall, which had a trade of only thirty to forty barrels a week. In November 1887, after eighteen months of negotiations, Smith of Grimsby, with six freehold and twelve leasehold houses, was acquired for £12,927.

Table 4.5. *Net profit calculation of the Tadcaster Tower Brewery's ten Castleford houses, 1885*

	£		£
Expenses to work agency etc.	90	Sale of beer and stout in ten houses	3,000
Share of J. W. Green's salary[a]	100	Cost of materials to produce, 46 per cent	1,380
Rent of brewery and stores (at Castleford)	50	Gross profit of 54 per cent	£1,620
Repairs to ten houses	10		
Discount 5 per cent	145		
Rail carriage of 1,250 barrels or 250 tons at 4s	50		
Horse keep and harness repairs	50		
One drayman and allowance	60		
Office lad	25		
Bad debts 5 per cent	140		
Coal, finings and extra expenses at Tadcaster	100		
Annual net profit	800		
	£1,620		

[a] Green was paid £200 as the firm's Castleford traveller.
Source: Tadcaster Tower Brewery, Diary, 2 August 1884, Bass North, Leeds.

On any proposed venture, whether opening an agency or acquiring a struggling brewery, they estimated the free and tied trade (if any) and then performed a series of calculations on the costs of distribution to set against their gross profits (see pp. 180–2). Fortunately, the latter's margins were increasing because like all brewers they experienced the lowest brewing materials costs for more than a century, and in any case they skimped on both quantities and qualities of these. With materials and the excise duty together running at between 39 and 46 per cent of wholesale prices, they could then calculate their distribution costs and net profit. In 1885 they reached the profits of both the tied and free trade of Mitchell's Castleford brewery as shown in Table 4.5. The manager then performed a similar set of calculations (the great difference being the 15 per cent discount necessary) on the hypothetical free trade Green

the traveller might be expected to secure; one of twenty barrels a week would realise a net profit of £90 a year – double this trade, £680.[106] Of course all calculations could so easily be upset. Although Mitchell's beer was so bad it had not even been sold in some of their own houses, the Castleford drinkers did not take quickly to the Tower Brewery's beers, showing a marked preference for Tetley's or John Smith's. And J. W. Green, the Castleford traveller, at first sight 'rather a swell in his manner and way, but seemed a business man and well up to his work', turned out badly. Within six months he was sacked, for although he had built the free trade up to twenty barrels a week the loss on the account was reckoned to be £34 18s 6d. In his place, they appointed their Hull traveller at half Green's salary. Eventually, as trade generally picked up in the late 1880s and the firm's beers improved, the travellers working from Castleford, Wakefield, Grimsby, Darlington, Stockton and, eventually, Newcastle did turn round the fortunes of the brewery by their endeavours in the free trade. A total barrelage of 14,264 in the year ending 30 September 1884 had almost doubled to 27,549 in 1887–8. When the firm took its 100 employees to Scarborough for their annual outing, the manager, C. H. Tripp, addressing them, was so confident of the firm's successful incursions into the free trade that he could, in his experience, allay any fears about the growth of the tied trade generally. It was a difficult position to maintain in 1888, but it demonstrated the success of the firm's free-trade strategy in difficult years.[107]

There were other factors: an improvement in their beers and a growing army canteen trade. But the company's survival rested upon their expansion of the free trade, encouraged by increasing discounts and a concentration upon four distinct areas: Castleford-Wakefield; Grimsby; the string of Cleveland towns from Darlington to Saltburn-on-Sea; and Newcastle upon Tyne. Pipe-dreams about London, Liverpool and even Leeds were dismissed as the reality of transport costs, of small turnovers and of unbeatable competition sank home. 'Agents are a great bother' bemoaned the manager as their Leeds enterprise failed, but in reality the firm was saved by the exertions of its half-dozen more energetic travellers. A large concentration of tied houses was not the only way forward for brewers before the 1890s.

[106] Twenty-five barrels a week were calculated to return a net profit of £237; thirty barrels £352; thirty-five barrels £500. But these were quite large trades, and many an agency or stores failed because its trade was too small to justify its existence.

[107] *York Herald*, 17 Aug. 1888.

III

Much of Britain's wealth in the nineteenth century resulted from the extraordinary export performance of its key industries. Growth therein was to a considerable extent dependent upon overseas sales. This was true above all in textiles, but also in engineering, shipbuilding and, eventually, coal. In the brewing industry, however, exports can virtually be ignored. Never shipping more than around 3 per cent of output, it is the only major British industry in which the focus is almost entirely insular. The export of beer was nevertheless an old art. Wherever British settlers colonised land, in the East and West Indies, in America, in Ireland, and eventually in Australasia, a demand for the native drink of their homeland was established. Conditions on the spot, intemperate climates for brewing, and the absence of good materials, made the production of even tolerable imitations of London porter, Burton ale, Edinburgh strong beers and Dublin stouts impossible.

Of course, the difficulty came in shipping beers to arrive in anything like a drinkable condition. The problems of transporting a bulky, unstable product, difficult enough within Britain, were immense when transposed to the West and East Indies or Australasian markets. Condition was only one aspect of the question; price and protracted payments were almost equally insuperable issues. Not surprisingly most brewers steered clear of the export trade. The early, rare survival of Georges' foreign letter book (1818–35) reveals the reasons with great clarity.[108] Bristol brewers had long shipped modest quantities of ale and porter to the Mediterranean, Ireland and the West Indies.[109] Georges appear to have shared in this trade from around 1800, but with recession at home and brewing 'like all other trades much overdone at present [April 1820] it becomes very desirable to find sale for our surplus quantity [abroad].' They now attempted to secure outlets in Quebec, Boston, New York, Charleston and Rio de Janeiro, as well as expanding their established markets in Malta, Portugal, Jamaica, Trinidad and Barbados. Brewing a strong mild (Taunton ale) and a West India 'small' ale (in fact strong and pale) and briefly, in 1828, experimenting with a Burton-style IPA for the Calcutta market, they shipped both in bottle and in bulk. Since all were heavily hopped to provide a protracted fermentation, judgement of condition was paramount. If beer was too

108 Courage Archive, Bristol, 35740/GR/5, upon which this paragraph is based.

109 Mathias, *Brewing Industry*, p. 194. Total Bristol exports were between 3,000 and 7,000 barrels in the 1773–1820 period.

old, it drank 'harsh and without life', if 'too young, fresh and lively' it smashed the bottles in transit because their stoppers were strongly secured with copper or iron wire. Report of breakages and complaints about condition, whether in bottle or barrel, were frequent. One customer in Lisbon was advised to sell his sour porter as fine vinegar even though the colour was not right. Inevitably, the correspondence concentrates upon hitches in normal transactions, but the impression is conveyed that the financial aspects of the operation were as problematic as those in ensuring the beer arrived at its destination in a sound state. Prices were high,[110] not only to cover shipping and insurance costs and the non-return of casks and bottles, but because payments were delayed – on occasion for as long as five years. Customers were perpetually reminded about how Georges looked for quick returns rather than high profits and that 'the article we export has been paid for about *18 months* before we ship it, and therefore if we cannot expect to realize something in a modest and reasonable time our object in exporting to a foreign Market is at an end'. For years, their export trade continued in a half-hearted fashion, never exceeding a few hundred barrels annually, and after 1830, with new opportunities presented by the Beer Act, it collapsed completely.

Georges' venture is a study in failure: an account of how difficult it was for even a large brewery in a major port to export beer unless commitment was total. There were notable eighteenth-century successes: the Burton brewers in the Baltic trade; and the London porter brewers in Ireland before 1800.[111] But both collapsed during the Napoleonic Wars, and expertise gained in them was transferred to other markets, especially in India and Australia. But it was some time before real advances were made. Total exports of some 90,000 barrels in 1800 had fallen to 60,000 by 1830; by the 1840s they had increased to average around 146,000 barrels a year. Eventually, the London porter brewers, 'the great source for the movement of beer within England and abroad' in the Georgian period, were outdistanced by the leading Burton brewers, whose break-through, with their unsurpassable pale ales, into the Indian trade in the 1820s and 1830s is a familiar story.[112] By the 1840s Bass was exporting a quarter of their rapidly growing output; it

[110] Best double stout sold at £5 per hogshead (54 gallons) or £10 per butt (108 gallons), cask included. Bottled beer retailed at 8s or 2.5 to 3 American dollars per dozen. But their size is unclear for Georges reckoned quantities in tierces (42 gallons) which contained either seven or ten dozen large bottles.

[111] Mathias, *Brewing Industry*, pp. 151–92.

[112] *Ibid.*, pp. 149–50.

was two-fifths at its peak in 1844. Debts reveal that their principal markets were in India and Australia, although the detailed export figures show that beer was shipped world-wide, substantiating Bass's boast that by the 1870s their product could be found in every country in the globe. In 1872–3, for example, Bass shipped beer in bulk to fifty-eight different foreign destinations, ranging from one hogshead (the traditional 54 gallon unit of measurement in the export trade) to Persia to 7,036 in the United States. Allsopp in the same year sent their beers to forty-four foreign outlets, notifying the minimum shipment of a single cask to Sweden and Norway, Arabia, Madeira, Canary Islands, Tasmania and the west coast of South America, and recording, surprisingly, their largest shipment of 943 hogsheads to France.[113] Unfortunately the amounts of beer exported in bottle to each country are given in values not quantities, and therefore the amounts of bottled beer exported by any brewer are not calculable. Moreover, a large proportion of bottled beer was not exported directly by the brewers themselves but by semi-independent bottlers, principally in London and Liverpool. Guinness in 1913, for example, was imported into America by no fewer than twenty-three bottling firms, nine in Liverpool (which provided the best shipping services), six in London, two in Dublin and six in New York.[114] Similarly, Bass was exported in bottles by the great London bottlers, and presumably those smaller breweries that claimed to export beer in fact had their supplies handled by the export bottling firms.[115] For the export of beer demanded great expertise, commitment and capital. Only a minority of brewers and the biggest bottling firms possessed these features.

Above all it was the leading Burton firms, the Edinburgh and Alloa brewers, Guinness, and the London and Liverpool bottlers which persisted in the export markets. At its peak in the early 1890s, Bass exported 131,000 barrels, around 25 per cent of all beer exports (although only 10 per cent of its own output). Allsopp were well behind, in 1872–3 exporting in cask less than one quarter of their great rival. The Scottish brewers, shipping 21,000 barrels abroad in 1851, persisted more assiduously in the foreign beer trade than did the other sections of the United Kingdom brewing industry. By 1890, at 168,000 barrels, their exports accounted, as already mentioned, for almost one-third of

113 Owen, *History of Bass*, forthcoming. In 1872–3 Bass exported 36,058 hogsheads, Allsopp 8,139, other brewers 177,017.

114 Edward Guinness, 'Guinness in America, 1801–1945' (unpublished), p. 33.

115 Greene's beers, for instance, in the early 1880s were claimed to have found their way from Bury to San Francisco, Natal and Australia (Wilson, *Greene King*, p. 83).

the entire British overseas beer trade.[116] Guinness also possessed a good export record: 48,000 barrels in 1874, 75,000 in 1884.[117] The leading London brewers were more fitfully engaged in the foreign beer market. Before the 1890s the nearby European market did not present the opportunities of India and Australia, for there were flourishing brewing industries in Germany, Austria and the Netherlands. Moreover, porter, in comparison with premium pale ales, had limited overseas appeal. Some firms made an effort: Barclay Perkins, old hands in the export business, exported 13,667 barrels in 1835; Charrington briefly dangled their toes in the East Indies market in the late 1820s; Whitbread had a large and profitable contract trade, principally with India, in the 1850s and 1860s.[118]

In the decade 1854–63, Whitbread shipped some 308,234 barrels on contract to the 'East India Government'. The trade was chiefly in porter although some ale was consigned, and the orders were sizeable. One contract for porter and ale shipped to Karachi was for 38,073 barrels, and the average tender was for 9,632 barrels. Contract prices were high to cover the costs of casks, freight and insurance. On 22 July 1857 a tender for 6,150 barrels of porter at 58s 3d each to be shipped to Calcutta was accepted. The cost of the porter was 27s 2d. Margins were not always so generous: the contract price of 67s 2d for 9,000 barrels of ale for Karachi in December 1855 was only 20s 6.5d above Whitbread's cost of producing the beer in Chiswell Street. And profits, once the final transactions of cash, bills, drawbacks and profits on commission and exchange had been totalled, were variable. Some tenders turned out to be more profitable than the original calculations, others less. In addition, Whitbread were also selling beer in the Australasian and Cape markets besides occasional ventures elsewhere. On the other hand Truman appear to have had no direct involvement in the export trade at all, although, like other firms, their beers found their way overseas via the larger bottlers.

Nationally, the limited break-through in the export of beer came in the 1850s (see Appendix, Table III). In the late 1840s, after a decade of decline, it stagnated at around 136,000 barrels. Then growth in the 1850s was rapid. In 1859 it reached a peak of 614,000 barrels, a total not again exceeded until (and then very briefly) 1911–13. Therefore even

[116] Donnachie, *Brewing Industry*, pp. 222–3.
[117] Guinness, 'Guinness in America', p. 2.
[118] Mathias, *Brewing Industry*, pp. 190–1; W/21/66 Whitbread's Foreign Trade Ledger, 1853–1866.

the demonstrable success of the leading Burton, Edinburgh and Alloa brewers together with Guinness should not be exaggerated once this initial thrust, fuelled by pale ale, the fillip given by the early railways and the triumph of the Great Exhibition, was spent. Certainly, contemporary commentators by the 1880s presented the beer exporters with few bouquets.

There were two reasons for this poor performance after 1860. First, beer was simply too easy to sell in Britain before the 1880s. Rising consumption and the decline of publican brewing meant the vast majority of brewers never contemplated the export market. Even Bass and Allsopp ran in familiar grooves. Bass's exports as a proportion of output declined to around 10 per cent. There is evidence that in the years of its fastest expansion, in the mid 1840s, and in the great Burton boom from the late 1850s to the mid-1870s, domestic demand took precedence over the firm's foreign orders. Secondly, the problems which breweries like Georges encountered in the 1820s did not diminish even when communications and beers improved. On the one hand, the export performance of individual firms can seem quite impressive. On the other hand the written record, in so far as it survives, indicates exactly why most firms either steered clear of foreign markets or placed little confidence in them. That of Tennent, William Younger and Guinness reveals a constant series of complaints by agents and partners about unfavourable climate, high duties, gluts, cheap local substitutes, German competition, falsification, bad debts, litigation, and above all the brewery's lack of control over retail outlets in the West Indies, Australia or elsewhere. Beer was constantly reported flat, and agents deficient in enterprise and expertise.

The experiences in the Americas in 1875–6 of James Marshall, partner and trustee of J. & R. Tennent (Glasgow) and a man of enormous experience in shipping and the agency and export business, were not untypical of all those export brewers who made periodic journeys to find out for themselves how things were in remote parts.[119] In Buenos Aires in August 1875 he found 'prospects of this market not very sanguine for the present'. The familiar catalogue facing British brewers followed: high duties, falsification of trade marks, enormous stocks of

119 This paragraph is based upon Scottish Brewing Archive (Glasgow University), J. & R. Tennent's MSS. T2/12 copy letter book of James Marshall, 1875–6; T2/7 Production Book, 1875–9; T2/13 and 16; T3/6 Auditors' Reports. Also William Younger MSS., WY/5/12/5 letters of H. J. and A. Younger from Australia and Egypt. Guinness, 'Guinness in America'; Dennison and MacDonagh, History of Guinness, 1886–1939, Chapter five.

English beer, a scarcity of money. When he visited a local brewery he was not unimpressed with their techniques, pronouncing the beer 'insipid and thin although sound'. What unnerved him most was the brewery's prolific use of Bass and Tennent labels: 'the proprietor laughed derisively when the irregularity was pointed out and seemed to think it was rather a good joke. From a large chest he took out handfuls of our capsules [labels] ... and frankly admitted that these were what he used.' In Valparaiso, Marshall found the same glut of English and Scottish beers, the native beer, 'sound, a little dark in colour and *aley* flavour' costing just half the price of British imports. Only rarely, as in the 'principal hotel' in Santiago, did he find Tennent's beers in 'best order and condition'. Not surprisingly, only firms like Tennant, McEwan and George Younger with a long experience of the vagaries of the foreign beer trade and a profound knowledge of exporting in general, or ones with unsurpassed reputations like Bass and Guinness, really possessed the will to make the foreign beer-trade work. And even for them there were obvious barriers to sustained growth; whilst for most brewers the export trade was simply too much trouble to contemplate. Selling beer in Middlesbrough or Bournemouth was a far easier exercise than that encountered by James Marshall in Buenos Aires, or by A. T. Shand, Guinness's 'World Traveller' in America between 1899 and 1913, or by H. J. Younger in Australia in the mid-1890s.

Although the export trade – roughly estimated at around the output of a couple of large London breweries – stagnated after 1860 (falling as a percentage of total output, from 3.15 per cent in 1859 to reach a low point of 1.28 in 1878) it was not before the 1880s that this gave rise to extended comment in the brewing literature.[120] In 1885 the *Brewers' Journal* reckoned that exports should have been between 3 and 4 million barrels, or a reasonable one-tenth of the 30 million barrel consumption of 'our colonies and other countries with which we trade'. The journals blamed a few large companies for 'letting it slip through their fingers'.[121] A trade of 584,764 barrels in 1873 had fallen back to 420,301 in 1886. Here was decline in the performance of a noted industry, here

[120] The final section of this chapter is a shortened version of the first part of R. G. Wilson and T. R. Gourvish, 'The Foreign Dimensions of British Brewing (1880–1980)', in E. Aerts, L. M. Cullen, and R. G. Wilson, *The Production and Consumption of Alcoholic Beverages since the Late Middle Ages* (1990), pp. 120–37. See also M. D. Ripley, 'British Beer Abroad – A 300 Year Overview of Beer Exports', *The Brewer* (August 1986), pp. 295–8.

[121] *Brewers' Journal*, 15 Nov. 1885; see also 15 Oct. 1884.

again the spectre of German competition. Already by the early 1880s Germany was exporting more beer than the United Kingdom.[122]

The *Brewers' Journal*'s castigation of the large companies, Bass, Allsopp, Barclay Perkins and Guinness, was not misplaced for, as they proudly proclaimed, their wares were sold in every country in the world. 'Bottled Bass', trumpeted the *Brewers' Journal* in August 1882, 'has been found in every country where Englishmen had yet put foot.' Contemporaries did not blame the agency system of foreign sales, although consuls in the mid-1830s maintained British beer was too often unobtainable. They laid the problem at the door of the country's leading brewers. Trade journals could hardly accuse them directly of complacency, but they did point out their inability to match supply with foreign demand. In America and in the colonies – especially the all-important Australian and Indian markets – there was a remarkable switch in taste in the last quarter of the nineteenth century to German lager beers which British brewers made no attempt to satisfy. Pale ales which had swept the board in the 1850s remained Britain's chief export beers. But even these when bottled threw a sediment. They contained, according to a critic, 'too much alcohol, too much sediment, too much hops and too little gas'.[123] Demand abroad was increasingly for a weaker, carbonated, 'star bright' beer. German and American lagers fitted the bill; Britain's heavier beers did not. Of course, British brewers explained the falling away in terms of profit-eroding competition, heavy transport costs, and the fact that the Colonies as a consequence set up their own breweries. This was true of India and even Japan, as well as of Australia, Argentina and South Africa. But a fair summary of the situation in the 1880s would be that Britain's leading brewers, rather behind America in bottling technology, failed to produce a lager beer that would match German competition and sell readily in foreign markets. Instead they continued to rely upon their traditional pale ales and stouts. Yet as early as 1882, according to R. S. Boddington, when he visited Edinburgh a number of brewers told him that German beer was superseding Bass in bottled beer exports, although they claimed it was not affecting their trade.[124]

In the 1880s the discussion about declining beer exports became linked with the question of imports and the production of lager beers in

[122] *Ibid.*, 15 Sept. 1884 when it reckoned that for 1881 Germany exported 608,003 barrels and the United Kingdom, 458,319.
[123] *Ibid.*, 15 Feb. 1890.
[124] Whitbread Archive 405/10, Boddington's Diaries (1869–82), entries for 1–4 Jan. 1882.

Britain. In fact, imports remained small. The brewing journals could report gloomily about their propensity to increase year after year, unlike the export series, but even in 1887, when they had risen to 25,431 barrels, this was a mere 0.048 per cent of United Kingdom production.[125] Only in 1899 had they reached 50,000 barrels; and by 1913, 75,000. It was the output of a single brewery to be found in any English town of middling size. Although most of the imports came from Germany, there was little fear of the trade. In 1887 the *Brewers' Journal* scathingly confined the impact of foreign beers to 'the pressman's world – the City, Fleet Street and the West End'.[126] Certainly it was in London restaurants that the lager trade originated in the 1870s – not surprisingly since it was reckoned to be retailed at four times its price in Munich. British brewers were confident that it would remain beyond the reach of their main consumer, the British worker, who they believed would continue to demand a strong, nutritious, traditional, top-fermented beer.

Moreover, the last thing brewers wanted to do was switch production methods. They made good profits retailing traditional British beer. Their priorities, after 1880, were in extending their tied house outlets, taking over suitable competitors, and adapting some of the latest technology – not producing lager beer. Given these expenditures and the difficulties of assessing the British demand for lager in a pre-market research era, they were not prepared to face heavy capital costs, equipping lager breweries to cater for either the domestic or the uncertain foreign market. The lager system of production, which prospered in Germany in the 1840s and spread like fire in America after 1850, would have entailed enormous investment in new fermentation, ice-making and storage systems. Lager was produced slowly at low temperatures below 40°F. Although artificial ice-making to achieve these temperatures was possible by the 1880s, the lager brewer was fortunate if his turnover was achieved within four months. In Britain the brewers received their cash within four weeks of brewing the increasingly popular 'running' ales. With these sorts of considerations in mind, they turned their backs on lager production in the 1880s. The *Brewers' Journal* thought the issue was the 'ignis fatuus' of the brewing year in 1881. But the British brewers' conservatism and hesitancy certainly cost them any progress in the export trade beyond a remarkable incursion

[125] See for example, *Brewers' Journal*, 15 Aug. 1882; 15 Jan. 1887.
[126] *Ibid.*, 15 Jan. 1887; see also *Country Brewers' Gazette*, 9 Nov. 1881.

into the Belgian market after the 1890s and Guinness's improved performance, especially in America where Dublin Stout possessed a great reputation as a tonic.[127]

A few bold brewers did, however, take up the manufacture of lager. They were small, little-publicised affairs, and are therefore difficult to trace in the brewing literature. It is uncertain whether all of them, at least at the outset, brewed a true lager as opposed to a chilled pale ale. J. & R. Tennent and William Younger, though – significantly, both prominent in the export trade – were attempting to produce true lagers in Scotland in the early 1880s.[128] Fifteen years later there were four of these lager breweries.[129] Probably none of them brewed more than 20,000 barrels apiece. Reputedly they enjoyed an export trade. When, in 1917, the Wrexham Brewery was forced to dismiss its German brewer it claimed to export three-fifths of its output.[130] There were two more notable ventures: the German-owned, designed and managed Tottenham Brewery of 1882; and Allsopp, the most recklessly run brewery in England in the 1890s. The latter invested £80,000 in a 60,000 barrel plant in 1899, intending to capture the lager import trade. But none of these ventures, as the journals pointed out, achieved any degree of success beyond mere survival to 1914. As well as the brewers' refusal to

[127] All the leading Burton and London brewers possessed Belgian agents and sometimes stores by the 1890s. In 1909–13 exports to Belgium averaged 102,005 barrels; taking 16.4 per cent of beer exports, it was Britain's largest market. Guinness exports of foreign stout reached an all time peak of 157,500 barrels in 1912, although this was still only 5.7 per cent of their total beer sales. Their exports of 72,000 barrels (3.5 per cent of total sales) in 1904 was the lowest recorded in the period 1874–1914.

[128] See R. G. Wilson, 'The Introduction of Lager Brewing in Late-Victorian Britain', in *A Special Brew: Essays in Honour of Kristof Glamann*, (Odense, 1993).

[129] According to the *Brewers' Journal* when it commented about the construction of Allsopp's lager plant in 1899. The first was possibly the Anglo-Bavarian Brewery Co. at Shepton Mallett whose foundation went back to the early 1860s. (Barnard, *Noted Breweries* II, pp. 257–81). But the evidence from the journals is confusing. After 1873 they employed a German brewer, but their chief claim to fame was the string of prizes which they won between 1873 and 1880 for their pale ales at international brewery exhibitions. In July 1881 its brewery was reported to be undergoing extensive alterations which suggests it only turned to lager production then. The Wrexham Lager Beer Co. was registered in May 1881 and appears to have begun brewing before the company was restructured in 1885. There were two seemingly abortive attempts by lager brewing companies to acquire Grier's Eltham (Kent) brewery in 1881–2. In 1882 the *Brewers' Journal* (10 Oct.) reported at length on the Austro-Bavarian Lager Beer Co.'s extensive new lager brewery at Tottenham entirely run by Germans. But it seems to have died an early death. The Kaiser Lager Beer Co. (1884–90) and the English Lager Beer Brewery (1890–3) at Batheaston were also transient affairs. But J. & R. Tennent's enterprise at the Wellpark Brewery in Glasgow, reconstructed as a lager brewery in 1889–91, was more successful after they began lager brewing in 1885. William Younger were experimenting with lager production in Edinburgh between 1880 and 1884.

[130] *Brewers' Journal*, 15 Jan. 1917.

contemplate, still less to encourage, lager production in Britain, the increasingly anti-German mood of the country confirmed the British consumers' belief that their beer was best whatever the state of opinion elsewhere.

5

Costs, prices and profits

A discussion of costs, prices and profits brings us to the heart of the brewer's world. Basic economic concepts in themselves, their manipulation by the brewer was the means whereby he established his unique position in the society and economy of Victorian Britain. His costs, especially for malt, hops and horses, linked him to the agrarian centre of the country, the old Britain of farmers, markets and maltsters. At the other end of the economic process the ample profits realised by the sale of beer carried some brewers to the forefront of the new capitalist society, the arena of big business, parliamentary politics and the super-rich. Of course, by its nature the brewing industry was exceptional in the way that it straddled the new world of large-scale manufacture and the old, rooted in agriculture – spheres which drifted so relentlessly apart in Victorian Britain. Facing both ways in this fashion, the brewer was an unusual entrepreneur: half agriculturist, half industrialist; on the one hand conservative and traditional, on the other forced along by the pace of industrial and demographic change which transformed Victorian Britain. These wider concepts should not be obscured by the mechanism whereby the brewer viewed his costs, fixed his prices and calculated his profits. For there was a continuous link from the purchase of barley and hops to the steam yachts and grouse moors which the most successful brewers enjoyed.

I

At the outset of an analysis of costs it is necessary to underline two points. First, nineteenth-century brewers, unlike their late twentieth-century counterparts, were primarily producers of beer. Their profits might increasingly be secured by the ownership of their retail outlets, their turnover extended by the sale of wines, spirits and mineral waters, and, if they were small scale, by coals, hops and malt retailed to publican and private brewers, but they were not direct purveyors of leisure and food. The sale of beer was the great central prop of every brewer's business.[1] Secondly, brewers' manuals and journals provide no guide to the *economics* of brewing. Black and Southby, both *practical* guides and consequently the most widely consulted, confined their attention entirely to the mysteries of the art. They considered accounting, profitability and management to be discrete, private matters, taught during pupillage and learnt only by practice. Directives in these areas would have been considered presumptuous. But the gap means that the modern historian of the industry lacks guidance at this point. For company minutes, often continuous from the 1880s, chiefly record share and property transactions. Few letter books – never voluminous in a word-of-mouth industry – have survived. Reliance is therefore placed upon the private ledgers of partners and directors where comment is non-existent. And by their very privacy, they remain a less than revealing source.

Nevertheless, it is hard to imagine another industry in which partners could have monitored and logged costs more carefully or in greater detail.[2] Their basis was a common set of accounting procedures, already in place by 1830, and instilled into every brewery pupil and clerk. Besides keeping their inscrutable brewing books, brewers basically struck two accounts to facilitate their calculations of profitability: one aggregated manufacturing costs, the other trading or retailing expenses. Both sets summarised scores of pages detailing the buying and selling transactions of manufacture with hundreds, sometimes thousands, of people. Bass by the 1880s produced an annual *summary* of its accounts which in itself filled a substantial folio volume.

From his manufacturing account a brewer obtained a notional gross profit figure by subtracting costs of production, principally those of malt, hops (and after the 1860s sugar, maize and rice), excise duties,

1 Bass's beautifully detailed accounts indicate no wine, spirit or mineral water sales. More typically, Lacon's accounts show modest spirit sales throughout the period. In the early 1830s sales averaged 3,337 gallons a year. By 1892 the 'gross profit' on the ale account was declared at £37,598, on spirits at £1,714 (Whitbread Archive, 197/52,205). Of course, as brewers acquired more houses they began themselves to provide publicans with spirits, wines and mineral waters, eventually often enforcing exclusive ties for these items. In 1886, the Tadcaster Tower Brewery engaged a policeman who was on holiday to detect tenants who were dealing elsewhere for spirits. His commission was 10s for each 'conviction'. The firm's diaries also indicate that spirits were less profitable than beers: in 1884 they reckoned the gross profit to be 25 and 54 per cent respectively.

2 See P. Mathias, 'Brewing Archives: Their Nature and Use', in L. Richmond and A. Turton (eds.), *The Brewing Industry* (1990), pp. 23–31 and 'Historical Records of the Brewing Industry', *Archives* 7 (1965), pp. 2–10.

Table 5.1. *The gross profit of Lacon & Sons, year ending 30 Sept. 1891*

Brewing costs	Barrels	£	% on[a] sales	Sales barrels		£
Stock at 30.9.90	2,703	3,521	–	Freehouses]		
Malt (29,432 qts)]		50,286	31.8	Tied houses]	35,131	
Hops (2,146) cwt)]		13,086	8.28	Table beer]		
Isinglass (45 cwt)]	113,513	804	0.5	London	76,993	
Sugar (1,056 cwt)]		1,034	0.65		112,124	154,821
Sundries]		780	0.49	Grains		3,007
London stout and porter	441	924	0.58	Yeast		107
Brewhouse wages		6,083	3.85	Stock at 30.9.91	3,385	4,539
Brewhouse coals		2,005	1.26	Waste	1,149	
Excise duties		38,165	24.16			
Waste, returns and allowances		2,172	1.37			
Gross profit		43,614	27.61			
	116,658	£162,474	100.55		116,658	£162,474

Note: [a] These calculations were apparently performed by a partner and added later.
Source: Whitbread Archive, 197/53. Figures to nearest pound and barrel.

wages and returned beers from the firm's annual turnover. This gross profit figure, invariably cited in percentage terms, gave the brewer his first rough indication of profitability. The accounts also set out all costs as percentages of total sales, as shown in Lacon's accounts for 1891 (Table 5.1). These percentages revealed any improvement or deterioration in the prime cost of malt and hops, thus allowing comparisons to be made with previous years. The calculation of a gross profit figure seems to have been common practice among brewers; it was used as a basis, after the deduction of all retailing costs, for arriving at the potential net profitability of any pub or agency they acquired (see pp. 167–8). At Tadcaster Tower Brewery the gross profit was calculated monthly; at Lacon it was calculated annually. Although rates of profit

Table 5.2. *Lacon's brewing costs, 1890–1*

	£	Percentage of brewing costs (excluding excise)	Percentage of total cost (including excise)
Malt	50,236	65	44
Hops	13,086	17	11
Sugar	1,034	1	1
Coals	2,005	3	2
Wages	6,083	8	5
Waste etc.	2,172	3	2
Other items	2,508	3	2
Excise	38,165	–	33
	£115,289	100	100

Source: As Table 5.1.

varied, since breweries always differed in their styles and the degree to which they were milked for profit, Lacon's accounts reveal the universal shape of the industry's cost structure. They also underline the Victorian brewer's preoccupation with the prices of malt and hops and the levels of excise duty.

If Lacon's total costs of brewing in 1890–1 are isolated the heavy domination of raw material costs and the relative insignificance of labour costs is immediately underlined (see Table 5.2). The record of Bass's highly sophisticated accounting system, probably the summit of Victorian practice, has survived only in a truncated form but the 'Comparative Statement of Costs, Charges and Profits' reveals similar features to those of Lacons. For example, each barrel of Bass's beer in 1891–2 was sold for an average of £2 18s 5.387d. (including 6s 4.72d profit). Thirty-three manufacturing and retailing costs were itemised but the three key costs of malt and sugar, hops and excise duty alone totalled £1 3s 6.131d or 42.58 per cent of each barrel sold[3] (see Appendix, Table II). As brewers presented these calculations, the certainty that they had to be masters of the intricacies and mysteries of the malt and hop trades was brought home to them.

[3] Bass Museum, A/1145, accounting statistics 1887–94. Wrongly catalogued as those of Worthington & Co.

II

Brewers were keen to demonstrate the strength of their links with British agriculture especially when faced with a growing mountain of temperance criticism after the 1830s. A visitor to Bass's brewery in 1880, mulling over the figures Professor Leone Levi had produced for Michael Bass a decade earlier, reckoned that brewers in the United Kingdom consumed the produce of 1,946,000 acres of barley out of a total of 2,714,000 acres grown in 1878. Levi had calculated that the cultivation of land given over to production for the liquor trades alone employed 95,000 persons.[4] The great authority on the malting and barley trades, E. S. Beaven, estimated that in some years around 1900 as much as two-thirds of the British barley crop was malted.[5] Undoubtedly, throughout the nineteenth century the demand for malting barley was a principal prop of light-land arable farming in the east of Britain and was responsible for its improvement. When the import of cheap foreign grains totally undermined the profitability of cereal farming after 1870, brewers sustained the British barley crop better than millers and bakers did that of native wheats. Wheat acreages in the three great eastern cereal-growing counties, Lincolnshire, Norfolk and Suffolk, fell sharply in the twenty years of worst depression after 1874; those of barley marginally increased. Nevertheless, nationally, there was some contraction.[6] Brewers, however patriotic they might appear, sought out like other manufacturers the cheapest raw materials, turning increasingly to imported barleys from the Continent, North Africa and the Americas, especially, it was said, for bottled beers. Although the import figures do not distinguish quantities used in malting and those retained for animal feedstuffs, it is estimated that some 25–30 per cent of barley used in British beer production between

[4] See *A Glass of Pale Ale and A Visit to Burton* (1880), pp. 6–8 and L. Levi, *The Liquor Trades: A Report to M. T. Bass, Esq. M.P., on the Capital Invested and Number of Persons Employed Therein* (1871). The author of the former, working backwards from the malt consumption figures, reckoned that each acre of barley on average produced 30 bushels. This is possibly an underestimate compared with the first available yield statistics which from 1884–9 averaged 33.1 bushels (Mitchell and Deane, *Abstract*, p. 90). In 1872, the last year in which the return was made, corn used for distilling was 11,943,192 bushels or around one-fifth of that consumed in brewing.

[5] Quoted in J. Brown, *Steeped in Tradition: The Malting Industry since the Railway Age* (1983), p. 81.

[6] Between 1868 and 1914 the barley acreage fell from a peak of 2,667,000 acres in 1879 to 1,598,000 acres in 1911 (40.1 per cent), wheat from 3,630,000 acres in 1874 to 1,417,000 acres in 1895 (61.0 per cent). Mitchell and Deane, *Abstract*, p. 78.

the early 1880s and 1914 was of foreign origin.[7] Bass, who produced most of their own malt, appear to have relied on considerable amounts of French, Saale, Smyrna, Algerian and Californian barleys by the early 1890s; by the 1900s their dependence on English barley producers had almost ceased. Bass were bottled beer producers *par excellence*; producers of milds, like Truman, still obtained most of their malt from East Anglian sources. Moreover, after Gladstone's celebrated 'freeing' of the mash tun in 1880, when he shifted excise duties from malt to beer, brewers began to use increasing amounts of sugar and unmalted forms of grain (chiefly maize and rice) so that by 1914 these made up 18–19 per cent of the total brewing grist.[8]

It was in its connections with hop growing, however, that the brewing industry retained its most colourful link with British agriculture. Introduced into England as a commercial crop around 1525, hop cultivation became increasingly concentrated in half a dozen counties.[9] In Kent, Sussex, Surrey, Hampshire, Herefordshire and Worcestershire, there was continuous expansion from some 35,000 acres in 1800 to 50,000 in 1850 and a peak of 71,789 in 1878. Two-thirds of production was concentrated in Kent where on all except the smallest farms at least 10–12 acres of hops were grown. It was an unusual crop on several counts: it was expensive both to establish and to maintain because the ground had to be kept clean and well-manured and the plants supported by a scaffolding of poles, wires and strings; it required a vast army of casual labour for its brief harvest; and it possessed a single market – the brewing industry. In spite of the fact that growers could not shift easily in and out of hop cultivation – capital costs were high and the plants had a life of 15–30 years – its output was extremely variable as the crop was subject to an horrendous tripartite battery of wet weather, pests and, above all, the scourge of mildew and wilt which went largely unchecked before the late nineteenth century. In 1881 output was around 7 cwt per acre, in 1882 it collapsed to 1.8 cwt; prices even of the cheaper Weald of

[7] E. S. Beaven, 'Barley for Brewing since 1886', *Journal of the Institute of Brewing*, 46 (1936), pp. 488–9.

[8] Brown, *Steeped in Tradition*, p. 86. When world cereal prices collapsed after 1920, the inevitable occurred. By 1924, 39 per cent of barley malted in the United Kingdom was imported and eight years later when the situation for farmers was at its bleakest the figure exceeded 41 per cent. Thereafter there was some improvement as an advertising campaign supported by the Brewers' Society encouraged the purchase of British barleys.

[9] This brief account is based upon A. H. Burgess, *Hops: Botany, Cultivation and Utilization* (1964); Institute of Brewing, *An Introduction to Brewing Science and Technology*; Wilson, *Alcohol and the Nation*, pp. 65–74; R. Filmer, *Hops and Hop Picking* (1980); H. H. Parker, *The Hop Industry* (1934).

Kent hops rocketed from an average of £6 6s to £18 15s. Since profitability was so unpredictable, cultivation so concentrated and the crop so labour intensive, most brewers fought shy of direct involvement. There were exceptions. Courage, Guinness, Shepherd Neame and Whitbread (after 1920) later notably supplied themselves. In 1875, Beer & Co., the Canterbury brewers, claimed that every drop of beer they retailed was produced from the hops and barley they grew themselves.[10] And as late as 1950 Whitbread's Kentish hop gardens extended to 400 acres.[11] After the 1850s, however, the vast majority of brewers bought their requirements through hop merchants. As with barley, cultivation reached its zenith in the late 1870s. Already in the early 1860s there was mention of imports from Germany. The 1890 Select Committee examining the problems of the hop industry noted, in addition to the threat of increasing Bavarian imports, that beer was becoming significantly less hopped as vatted beers went out of fashion. In 1908 – as hop prices collapsed and a large rally in London had focused the plight of hop growers after 5,000 acres of Kentish gardens had been grubbed up within a few months – the brewers argued, somewhat disingenuously, that foreign imports (increasingly drawn from California in the decade before 1914) were essential for modern beers. Between 1880 and 1914 about a third of hop consumption was reckoned to be imported. Bass, the king of heavily hopped pale ale brewers, consumed an annual average of 23,775 cwt (costing £9.05 each) of English hops in the years 1889–94 against 15,341 cwt (£7.35) of imports. By 1900–5 the gap had been closed – 20,839 cwt (£7.27) of English hops against 20,483 cwt (£7.69) – and the price differential, marked in the former period, reversed. By 1909 hop cultivation in Britain was well under half its mid-1880 levels. Then, during the First World War, it collapsed further to a mere 16,000 acres in 1918.

Certainly brewers, increasingly on the defensive in their industry, were keen to put across their underpinning of the country's agriculture; after the 1870s the brewing journals spelt out the message forcibly and regularly. For individuals, however, it was not the wider impact of the industry that was their constant preoccupation, but the intricacies of malting production and economics.

Malt was the brewers' main raw material and their profits from year to year depended upon its price and quality.[12] Of course, the barley

[10] *Licensed Victuallers' Gazette*, 22 May 1875.

[11] *Whitbread's Brewery* (1951), pp. 43–4.

[12] The late Victorian bible of malting was H. Stopes, *Malt and Malting* (1885). Excellent recent guides to the history of the industry will be found in Mathias, *Brewing Industry*, pp. 387–474 and Brown, *Steeped in Tradition*. We are grateful to Christine M. Clark, a

harvest itself determined these in large measure. Maltsters required corn with firm, thin-skinned, starchy kernels, which when carefully malted – a process taking from fourteen to twenty-four days depending upon temperature and the type of malt made – produced the best maltose extracts and the best beers. Barleys of this type were ideally grown on light soils in a hot summer. Contrarywise, wet growing seasons and harvests meant a dearth of good malting barleys; and always there were marginal regions outside the eastern counties which in terms of climate and soil produced flinty, thick-skinned barleys high in nitrogenous content. These made inferior malts even in favourable summers. The skill of the maltster became one of selecting the best barleys available at the keenest prices. Indeed, some maltsters went so far as to maintain that the real test of their proficiency was in barley buying. This was achieved by good judgement and constant attention, aided by a continuous flow of market information. And the brewer was drawn centrally into this process. For malting, although a separate trade, was something of a Cinderella industry – small scale, technologically unimpressive, enslaved to the distilling and, above all, the brewing industries.

The industry encompassed three types of producer: the small maltsters, scattered across the countryside – especially before 1850 – who sold their output in small parcels to publican and home brewers; the sales maltsters who operated on a larger scale, producing malt to the direct order of the bigger brewers as well as making other sales; and the brewers who largely made their own malt. The comparative scale of operation of the three categories is impossible to assess. Yet, although the number of maltsters was squeezed hard after the 1840s and concentration thereby increased, the brewers' control of the industry was not relaxed.[13] Indeed, its grip hardened. Mathias maintained that at the beginning of the nineteenth century, 'the [separate] identity of maltster and brewer . . . was still almost universal'.[14] For common brewers in the widest definition of the barley growing counties from the Lothians to Wiltshire this distinction had never held; these brewers always largely

University of East Anglia Ph.D. student working on the malting industry in East Anglia, 1880–1960, for her comments on this section.

13 The number of maltsters' licences in England and Wales issued fell from around 10,000 in the early 1830s to under 4,000 by the late 1870s. Meanwhile, malt charged with duty grew from 32 to 53 million bushels. Wilson, *Alcohol and the Nation*, pp. 385–7; Mitchell and Deane, *Abstract*, pp. 248–9. Brown suggests that in 1902 brewer maltsters, at least by a head count, were 45 per cent of the total. In the interwar years they produced 40–45 per cent of malt consumed (*Steeped in Tradition*, p. 29).

14 Mathias, *Brewing Industry*, p. 467.

made their own malt. And the sales maltster, although his output grew appreciably over the century, became increasingly subject to the dictates of the big brewers driving hard bargains on price, quality and delivery in a highly competitive industry. For the London brewers and those in the industrial towns of the north (except Leeds, always a main malting centre), however, buying on commission was common practice. They were unlikely to malt on their own premises because traditional floor malting was an extremely space-consuming operation; labour costs were higher than in the countryside; and malt, lighter in weight than barley, was marginally cheaper to transport. Therefore malting largely took place in the best barley growing regions. The brewers financed the barley buying and the maltsters were paid a sum, usually around 5s a quarter, for their working costs and profits. Some brewers like Whitbread owned their own maltings in Norfolk to supply part of their needs; others, like Truman, placed yearly contracts with as many as ten large-scale maltsters in East Anglia. What the brewer liked to do was deal with several maltsters in order to obtain the best malt, spread his risks, and keep the maltsters on their toes. The malt was then moved as required by boats and, increasingly, by rail. Enormous quantities of malt from the eastern counties poured into London, Manchester and Liverpool on these terms.

Truman's monthly minute books provide a good view of their malting concerns in the thirty years after 1884. Three subjects dominate the entries: the acquisition of tied houses; the difficulties of brewing a consistently good mild ale in a highly competitive and discriminating market; and the necessity of getting malt supplies and qualities right. In some ways, the early nineteenth-century trade of the big London brewers had not changed much.[15] When in 1905 a director of Truman suggested they should buy more malt on the open market by forward contract, J. M. Hanbury, the director responsible for barley and malt, concluded, with some complacency, 'I venture to think that the existing arrangements would not have gone on for the last 100 years unless they had proved satisfactory.'[16] In other ways, things had changed out of all recognition. Already by 1888 Truman's mash tun contained 18 per cent malt substitute in the form of sugar; a decade later experiments were being made with 10 per cent maize. In 1905, the grist of their 'country'

[15] *Ibid.*, pp. 416–17, 458–62, 469–70.

[16] Hanbury and his predecessor, Robert Pryor, made long and sometimes rambling monthly reports on the barley and malt trades. They visited the maltings themselves at least annually, and made an annual report on the state of trade in January each year.

porter contained only 20 quarters of malt made by their own maltsters and four of these were of Californian origin – out of a total of 42. It included bought crystal and black malt as well as flaked oats, caramel and sugar. Yet the brew was pronounced 'very good'. And as they noted, every brewer in London by the late 1890s was undertaking similar experiments. Truman maintained it was 'without doing any harm to the beer', and that beers brewed without sugar were thinner, while conceding that brews solely of the best malt were necessary to maintain their best yeast strain.

Clearly, this increasing reliance upon malt substitutes and foreign barleys undermined the position of the maltster, especially in the 1880s and again after 1900 when beer consumption contracted. And the malt factor, however important a figure in Truman's arrangements around 1800, had no role by the 1880s. The firm by the latter date seems to have instructed eight to ten large-scale maltsters, chiefly in Norfolk, to make malt of the description and price they required, based upon three grades of English and one of foreign barley.[17] Total orders ran to around 100,000 quarters in any single year in the late 1890s and the key consideration was how much stock of malt should be held at the end of the malting season (early October–early May). Malt, if kept thoroughly dry and air-tight, had a life of as long as twelve months, and even older malts could be used for porter; but the chief factors were price and quality. If both were right, large stocks to see them through seven or eight months would be held. In other years like 1888, when English barleys were of poor quality, stocks diminished. By 1905–6, when production had contracted sharply over the previous half dozen years, stocks *exceeded* their annual net consumption. After calculating stocks and forecasting demand for the next season orders were placed between October and January; and the firm had built up a highly responsible relationship with its maltsters over a long period. Most of them depended upon Truman for the major part of their livelihood. In 1905–6, as stocks mounted, they had long heart searchings before ending their relationship with Mealing & Mills of Coltishall, conscious that they kept five out of seven of the firm's malt houses working. Otherwise, they lopped off a percentage of their orders from each of their other contractors. They stuck with the rather cumbersome com-

[17] In 1903–5 the prices (per quarter) of these barleys were given:

	A	B	C	Foreign
1903–4	31s 6d	27s	24s 1d	31s 2d
1904–5	30s	28s	27s 4d	21s

mission system rather than buying malt directly through the London market at Bear Quay, Queenhithe and Mark Lane, believing in the last resort that, 'there are so many tricks in the trade in making malt it is difficult to rely upon bought malt', and remaining 'very doubtful about the advisability of purchasing malt to any great extent instead of making it ourselves'[18] (i.e. on commission).

Even when English barley prices remained generally low after 1880, and blending of imported barleys and 'adjuncts' of maize and rice further reduced costs, Truman paid constant attention to the price and quality of their malts and the mechanisms that controlled them. Scientific analysis of the malt in their laboratory made the task easier and, thereby, control over the maltster even greater. But, by whatever means, obtaining good malt at favourable prices was of absolute importance to them in producing bulk mild ale. In the autumn of 1905 the analysis of their problems was simple: 'There can be no doubt at all that all our trouble this year, indifferent beer and the inability to meet the public trade, has been due to the bad quality of the malt.'

In the East and South of England, in Burton and in Scotland, most brewers made their own malt. By 1862 there were no fewer than 2,133 brewers who had taken out maltsters' licences.[19] They ran the gamut from publican brewers to Bass and, at least so far as the bigger commercial brewers were concerned, fell into two categories. In the barley growing counties brewers made all their own malt except when they sought to keep stocks high on reports of an indifferent barley harvest or they required small parcels of a particular type of malt. In the bigger breweries a partner or manager was responsible for barley purchases from farmers and corn merchants and for making the malt. He garnered market information and gained expertise just like any independent maltster. Sometimes the arrangements look inconvenient because the capacity of malt houses before the 1880s was quite small and therefore the ports and more accessible market towns of East Anglia were crowded with them. In Great Yarmouth there were forty-two in 1846,

18 In 1903 A. V. Pryor, the Burton director, rehearsed the arguments for buying malt rather than obtaining it on commission. They included better purchasing and stock controls, total responsibility resting with the maltster, and better qualities 'with no question of malt being delivered having been made from a different barley to what has been passed'.

19 Brown, *Steeped in Tradition*, pp. 28–9, i.e. out of a total of 5,458 licences. In 1913 the Maltsters' Association reckoned 50 per cent of brewers made at least some of their own malt. Together, this represented half the total of malt produced. (Information provided by Christine Clark.)

sixty-seven in 1880 – in both years worked by some ten concerns.[20] Similar, if smaller, concentrations, were to be found in Ipswich, Bury St Edmunds, Stowmarket, Mistley, King's Lynn, Norwich, Coltishall, Gainsborough, Grantham and Newark. Individual brewers occupied veritable warrens of malting premises. Cobbold, for example, ran twelve in Ipswich, three in Woodbridge and two in Stowmarket; Steward & Patteson's malt was made in sixteen separate malt houses in Norwich. Cartage and control cannot have been aided in these circumstances.

Elsewhere, malting operations were rather different. As Barnard recorded, the majority of brewers he visited made their own malt, with the exception of firms in the largest cities who, like the London brewers, had malt made on commission or, if they were smaller, bought directly from the maltster. The great Manchester brewers, Groves & Whitnall, for example had their malt made on commission in the Midland counties.[21] But even in such big brewing centres as Burton, Edinburgh and Tadcaster – indeed everywhere outside the eastern counties, Yorkshire and Kent – it is clear that brewers did not make all their own malt, especially in years when consumption of beer and imports of barley advanced sharply. William Younger, with maltings on six sites (total capacity, 110,000 quarters in the early 1890s) in and around Edinburgh, still purchased some best English and Scotch malts. Ind Coope in Burton did not make half their requirements.[22] Even Bass, whose malting operations were the largest in Britain, still bought some malt (see Table 5.3), in spite of the fact that between 1859 and 1875, when demand for Burton ales was insatiable, they built no fewer than eighteen extensive malt houses of the most up-to-date construction. Indeed, in 1878 they occupied twenty-eight malt houses in Burton and a further ten in Lincoln and Retford.[23] And as late as 1901–5 they built eight vast

[20] Information from the Yarmouth Poor Rate Books (Norfolk Record Office, Y/L1, 71–3; 175–7, 184; 228–231, 293) and those of other towns mentioned kindly supplied by Christine Clark.

[21] Barnard, *Noted Breweries*, III, p. 187. He included accounts of 113 breweries in his four volumes. Some 62 per cent appear to have made at least some of their own malt.

[22] *Ibid.*, II, pp. 9–16, 55. Other large breweries like John Smith's, with extensive maltings in South Milford, Thirsk and Leeds, and Tetley in Leeds, appear to have bought little malt besides that which they produced.

[23] By the late 1860s there were already over 100 malt houses in Burton. Except the great complexes owned by Bass and Allsopp they were generally small. The structural value of these two firms' malt houses accounted for 85 per cent of those assessed for rates in 1868. Some of the smaller breweries possessed no malting facilities in Burton. But by the 1890s the second-rank firms, as well as Bass and Allsopp, had notably increased their malting capacity.

Table 5.3. *Bass, Ratcliff & Gretton, summary of malting, 1889–1914*

Date (year ending 30 June)	[1] Malt made at Burton (quarters)	[2] Malt made at Retford and Lincoln (quarters)	[3] Malt bought (quarters)	[3] as a % of [1] and [2]
1889	186,834	47,552	15,702	6.7
1890	212,193	51,829	35,109	13.3
1891	208,671	48,518	62,556	24.3
1892	209,156	47,177	43,948	17.1
1893	218,895	43,441	53,775	20.5
1894	199,958	39,681	44,164	18.4
1895	216,803	40,024	37,674	14.7
1896	236,581	45,364	26,655	9.5
1897	242,283	46,290	37,494	13.0
1898	243,630	47,346	49,200	16.9
1899	231,873	46,689	86,773	31.2
1900	219,664	44,580	94,616	35.8
1901	227,751	47,664	111,510	40.5
1902	233,790	48,275	100,019	35.5
1903	238,895	48,036	85,735	29.9
1904	237,033	47,621	79,064	27.8
1905	239,721	45,570	38,050	13.3
1906	210,639	38,804	33,804	13.6
1907	208,665	49,791	40,876	15.8
1908	207,556	61,563	32,752	12.2
1909	203,998	58,636	25,778	15.9
1910	177,446	51,658	13,200	5.8
1911	187,839	54,609	2,414	1.0
1912	202,328	60,404	9,720	3.7
1913	202,179	58,241	7,234	2.8
1914	197,978	58,324	38,969	15.2

Source: Malt Books, Bass Museum. Figures in column 2 after 1905/6 relate to the Sleaford maltings. In addition, after 1906–7 around 9,000 quarters of malt were made on commission each year by Thompson's of Grantham.

malt houses at Sleaford at a cost of £340,000. With a continuous frontage of almost 1,000 feet (see Plate 26), they were the perfect statement of the role of brewing in Edwardian Britain – monumentally impressive, rooted in the land, yet convenient for the import of foreign barleys into the Lincolnshire ports.

Although Bass's malting enterprise was vast in scale, changes in malting for the average brewer before 1914 should not be exaggerated. The industry made little technical advance: there was some in the drying of barley, in the handling of corn and malt by elevator and conveyor, and in the kilning of malt. But the real advance of pneumatic malting from the Continent – large, slowly revolving drums or boxes which controlled heats and aeration – made little progress before 1914 although firms had experimented with them since the 1870s. Essentially, labour and building costs in Britain remained cheap and floor maltings produced malts best suited to British beers, whereas the new pneumatic method turned out malts ideal for lager and spirit distillation. Therefore, brewers, with few exceptions, stuck to traditional floor malting. Of course some brewers, like the maltsters themselves, built much bigger, more up-to-date maltings after the 1880s which concentrated production and included those small improvements in design and handling machinery made since the 1860s. Always accessible to the railways or sea, they were amongst the most distinctive industrial monuments of their age.

What were the economics of brewers producing their own malt? Above all, the advantage was one of quality control. Maltsters were never entirely to be trusted; they practised too many deceits. Ideally, the brewer bought his own barley and had it malted entirely under his supervision. Then he alone was responsible for quality. He also saved some of the 5s a quarter of the commission charged by maltsters, although, of course, he had to account for rent, fuel and labour charges when he himself made malt. Witnesses to the 1867 Select Committee on the Malt Tax reckoned these charges were of the order of 3s to 3s 6d per quarter.[24] And they did not grow much towards the end of the century because any increases in labour costs – not in themselves a large item – were offset by improvements in productivity following the introduction of handling machinery.[25] The trend of *barley* prices was markedly downwards after 1875, and though malt prices similarly declined (at Bass they fell from 12s 0d to 10s 2d per barrel between 1875 and 1896) astute purchases of barley, careful malting methods and tight control of stocks still remained the quickest route to profitable brewing. Indeed, as the discount war hotted up after the 1880s, malt margins were more important than ever. There was massive scope for savings as barley

[24] *PP* (1867/8) IX, pp. 282, 302, 309. For a few years (1866–74) Steward & Patteson recorded their average costs of production: they varied from 2s 3d to 3s 5d per quarter except in 1874 when they leapt to 4s 9d (NRO, BR1/118).

[25] At Bass in 1874/5 barley purchases formed 91 per cent of malting costs; by the 1900s these had fallen to 80 per cent.

imports grew, as experiments with adjuncts were permissible after Gladstone's 1880 budget, and as the cheaper bulk beers became less strong. Even in the low price years 1895–8, Bass's total malt and sugar costs still averaged £653,673 or around 18–19 per cent of 'total proceeds' (turnover).[26] And for every other brewer there was similar scope for savings and experiment since their gross profits were essentially determined by the price of malt.

Although hop costs – varying in all but the most exceptional years from around one-fifth to one-third of a brewer's malt bill – were appreciable, few brewers engaged in hop cultivation. The reasons were evident enough: a highly regional concentration, high costs of cultivation, highly volatile prices and profits. Moreover, the character of beer depended for its flavour upon the character of the malt brewed, rather than the variety and quality of hops used. For all these reasons, most brewers therefore dealt for their hop supplies with the Southwark merchants who traditionally controlled the trade.[27] Typically, the brewers, unlike in their malt requirements, dealt with only one or two merchants. Credit terms were generous – usually six months – and the merchants were therefore, like the maltsters, important financial props of the smaller brewers.

The hop trade was complex in its composition and credit networks, encompassing growers, factors who acted on their commission, and the Southwark merchants. The last bought only from the factors and provided a full range of hop varieties and qualities, both native and imported, for the brewers. Inevitably, given the speculative nature of the hop industry, the brewers made charges of excessive profiteering against the merchants, especially in the crisis years of 1854, 1860 and 1882, when hops advanced beyond £15 per cwt (see Appendix, Table VI) and there were periodic attempts by consortia of London brewers to deal directly with the growers or at least their factors.[28] But the schemes never worked. The firmly entrenched Southwark merchants provided a

26 Bass Museum, A/139 wrongly catalogued as Accounting Statistics of Worthington & Co. In 1875 malt costs were £970,070 or 39.25 per cent of turnover (although this of course included malt tax payments).

27 Mathias, *Brewing Industry*, pp. 475–533 provides a wonderfully detailed view of the hop industry and trade before 1830. For the 1830–1914 period see the reports from the two Select Committees on the Hop Industry, 1890 and 1908. Convenient summaries are to be found in the brewing journals on their publication, for example *Brewing Trade Review*, 1 Aug. 1908. See also Parker, *Hop Industry*.

28 See for example, *Brewing Trade Review*, 1 Nov. 1892. Truman's monthly minutes mention a hop 'syndicate' in 1898 comprising themselves, Barclay Perkins, Whitbread and Watneys. By 1902, it had broken down; Watneys were blamed.

valuable service and the brewers, as prices fell, held larger stocks. This was a response to the nature of the trade and the fact that hops had a life of as long as two years – even longer when cold storage became common after the 1890s. Truman usually held a year's supply and they also bought cheaper 'yearling', or one-year-old hops, to mix with those of the new season. And the import of hops and the changing nature of late nineteenth-century beers clearly affected prices in the brewers' favour. Whereas vatted porter and Bass's export beers had contained as much as 5 lb of hops per barrel in mid-century, rates fell sharply after 1882.[29] From 1886–7 to 1890–1 it was estimated that about 1 cwt of hops was employed for every forty-nine barrels of beer brewed; by 1901–2 to 1905–6 the proportion had fallen to 1 cwt to every fifty-six barrels.[30] In the years 1900 to 1914 Bass's average hopping rate per barrel fell from 1.9 lb to 1.7 lb per barrel. And everywhere brewers were similarly experimenting to reduce their hopping costs.

III

Apart from malt and hops, the other large item in the manufacturing costs of beer was the excise. In matters of taxation and control the relationship between the brewing industry and the government was a close and historic one. Mathias represented the brewer in the eighteenth century as 'encompassed about with regulations from the farmer's cart to the publican's pot'.[31] The industry was not unique in these taxes: salt, soap, paper, glass, leather, bricks and printed fabrics bore similar exactions. But it was the total contribution of the taxes upon malt and beer as well as hops that set the industry apart. By the early nineteenth century, 18 per cent of total national revenue was raised from the malt and beer taxes. Although the basis of taxation widened in the nineteenth century, taxation on all alcoholic beverages remained significant. At the height of their productiveness in 1879–80, 43.4 per cent of revenue was raised from taxes on liquor. When Government expenditure rose significantly after 1890, however, the proportion fell quite quickly. By 1919–20 it was down to 13.4 per cent, although, paradoxically, the industry felt the excise exactions more than ever between the Wars (see p. 341).

There were two central events for brewers in the taxation of their

[29] Mathias, *Brewing Industry*, p. 482; Wilson, *Alcohol and the Nation*, p. 71.
[30] *Brewing Trade Review*, 1 Aug. 1908.
[31] Mathias, *Brewing Industry*, p. 352.

Table 5.4. *Main changes in the excise duties on beer and materials used in its production, 1801–1914*

Date of change or imposition of duty	Rate of duty and basis of change
1801	Hop duty increased to 2½d per lb
1822	Malt duty reduced to 2s 7d per bushel
1830	Duties on beer repealed
1855	Malt duty increased to 4s per bushel
1856	Sugar duty on brewers' sugar raised to 6s 6d per cwt
1856	Malt duty reduced to 3s 8½d per bushel
1857	Brewers' sugar duty reduced to 3s 9d per cwt
1861	Hop duty reduced to 1½d per lb
1863	Hop duty repealed
1880	Malt and sugar duties abolished; beer duty of 6s 3d per standard barrel of thirty-six gallons at gravity of 1057° re-imposed
1889	Standard gravity reduced to 1055°, equal to increase of 2½d per barrel
1894	Beer duty increased to 6s 9d per barrel
1900	Beer duty increased to 7s 9d per barrel
1914	Beer duty increased to 23s per barrel

Source: Wilson, *Alcohol and the Nation*, pp. 320–1; *Brewers' Almanack*, 1940, p. 28.

product in this period: the repeal of the beer tax in 1830 and the malt impost half a century later (Table 5.4). In the former year the removal of the beer duty allowed brewers to lower their prices. For thirty-two years they paid a tax on malt of 2s 7d a bushel until during the Crimean War when it was increased briefly to 4s a bushel. Although the duty never regained its pre-war level it was reduced to 3s 8½d a bushel in 1856. In 1880 when Gladstone replaced the malt tax and sugar duties by a beer tax of 6s 3d on each barrel of standard gravity he thereby allowed brewers to use what materials they liked in the 'free' mash tun. This inaugurated a period of experiment in which brewers sought to brew more cheaply a bright, lighter and yet stable beer. But the 1880 beer tax was a hidden advance of almost a shilling on the malt duties. In 1900 it rose appreciably and – to the fury of the brewers who were facing difficult times – permanently. Bass's accounts reveal that duties averaged between 12.5 and 15 per cent of total turnover in the 1880–1914 period. Lacon calculated theirs as 24.16 per cent of net sales in 1890 or 33 per cent of manufacturing costs (Table 5.2). Before 1880, it is difficult to extrapolate the imposition because brewers invariably recorded malt prices inclusive of taxes. Since they generally used larger quantities of malt per barrel before 1880, the element cannot have been less in the previous fifty years. Yet, as Sir George Murray, Chairman of the Inland Revenue Board, politely reminded the Country Brewers' Society at its annual banquet in 1897, taxes on liquor were paid by consumers: 'Through your agency I am enabled to extract from the pockets of the people a sum of money ... and to do this without their knowing anything about it at all ... where ignorance produces such bliss, do you think it wise to enlighten?'[32]

Compared with the combined impact of malt, hops and excise, all other costs were small. Of these, brewery wages were the most important.[33] Brewing was, however, a highly capital-intensive industry; breweries themselves were not large, direct employers of labour. Admittedly, Leone Levi in 1871 had claimed that the industry, in the widest sense, was a large employer of labour. That was true, however, only if barley and hop cultivation, malting, and, above all, numbers engaged in running public houses were included. He estimated a total labour force of 846,000 for the industry. His figures are difficult to reconcile with other calculations. Those in the 1871 census – ignoring barley and hop growing – came to a total of 292,000 including 39,600 being directly employed in maltings and breweries.[34] The 1907 Census of Production suggests that this latter figure had almost doubled to

32 Quoted in Wilson, *Alcohol and the Nation*, p. 197.

33 Other items of significance in brewers' manufacturing accounts not discussed in the text above were isinglass (used in fining beers), brewing sugars and other adjuncts, coals, and waste and returns. Coals could be an appreciable item. Truman reckoned they used 16–18 tons of coal to brew every 1,000 barrels of beer. They kept a six weeks stock. Bass were using about 40,000 tons a year at 10s a ton in the same period for their malting and brewing operations at Burton alone. Some London brewers, whose water supplies were limited, had recourse to private and later municipal supplies. In general, brewers used 15–16 barrels of water for every barrel of beer brewed. Waste or beer returns were carefully monitored by all brewers. Indeed, the latter was always considered to be a real test of their success. Truman recorded in May 1898, 'the return book is the best barometer of the quality of the beer. For instance we have only had ten barrels of porter returned since Xmas out of a total of 40,000, this works out at 0.0023 per cent.' This was unusual: any figure under 1 per cent was considered good.

34 The figures are discussed in Wilson, *Alcohol and the Nation*, pp. 202–3.

79,680.[35] Of course, some breweries individually *were* large employers: Guinness in Dublin occupied a workforce of 3,457 in 1913; Bass, 2,560 men and boys and 200 clerks in 1887; Allsopp almost 1,600 in 1890. Truman and Barclay Perkins employed around 700 each.[36] Except for the three giant breweries, these figures were not large in comparison with the bigger textile mills and engineering works of late Victorian Britain. Middling size London breweries, like Hoare, Courage and the City of London – partly because they employed no maltsters – were run with around 200 men each. In the country, John Smith's of Tadcaster and William Butler of Wolverhampton employed similar numbers, although Tetley, Worthington and Ind Coope ran to around 500 each.[37] And a rising brewery like Brain of Cardiff, with an annual output of around 50,000 barrels, had only sixty-five men and thirteen travellers and clerks on its rolls.[38] Unfortunately, Barnard was not invariably clear about the strict division between the workforce and those employed as clerks, travellers and agents of each brewery he visited. The 1907 Census of Production made a division in breweries and maltings between 64,953 wage-earners and 14,727 salaried persons. It was an important distinction because the former were charged to manufacturing expenses, while the salaries of managers, clerks and travellers were included in distribution costs (see pp. 203–5).

It would be misleading to make calculations about labour productivity because employment rolls reveal an extremely heterogeneous workforce. Not all breweries employed maltsters, bottlers, agents, signboard painters and, by the 1890s, in some cases, tied house managers. This makes comparison difficult. Even a rough calculation of output per man from the barrelages and employees of the many breweries Barnard cites in the late 1880s would be largely meaningless. Moreover, labour costs were always far less significant than those of raw material and distribution costs (see Table 5.1 and Appendix, Table II). At least before the 1900s, brewers made little effort to economise on labour. When production and profits rose rapidly, workforces similarly expanded.[39] The record suggests a certain ease of approach. Barnard

35 Cd. 6320 (1912) Final Report of the First Census of Production of the United Kingdom (1907), p. 477.

36 Dennison and MacDonagh, 'History of Guinness, 1886–1939', chapter IX; Barnard, *Noted Breweries*, I, pp. 76, 161, 265. Truman employed 688 in 1902.

37 Barnard, *Noted Breweries*, II, pp. 51, 153, 309; III, pp. 46, 66, 244, 447.

38 Barnard, *Noted Breweries*, III, p. 484.

39 Bass grew from 338 men and twenty-nine boys in 1851 to a total of 1,834 in 1864; Edward Greene employed in 1851 eighteen men and three boys; thirty years later,

found the men at John Smith's 'not overworked'. As Truman's trade continued to decline in 1908, the managing director reported: 'I have spent many hours in trying to find a means of reducing the staff of labouring men inside the Brewery by one man, and I have failed to find it possible.' Worthington ran a tailor's shop 'whereby, by means of a sewing machine, slippers, jackets, flannel trousers, watchmen's coats, and cooler bags are made by four of the old employee's who have been maimed or injured on the establishment'.[40] These examples do not suggest streamlined workforces.

The heterogeneity of labour in the larger brewery – encompassing teams of men in malt houses, the brewhouse, the cooperage, the engineering or works departments, the bottling stores, loading out, deliveries and the stables – meant that control was strict and hierarchical and wages riddled with differentials. Managers and foremen enforced the former, an army of clerks the latter.[41] Two features stand out in any consideration of labour in the brewing industry: the continuity of employment and its extraordinary paternalism. Although there was a pronounced seasonal element before year-round brewing became common practice in the third quarter of the century,[42] and long afterwards in malting, generation followed generation of brewery servants just as partners did in management. All breweries could cite remarkable instances of the longevity of individuals' service and the attachments of families. The paternalism – a feature which ran like a deep vein through labour relations in all the larger Victorian industries – could be heavy handed. When an attempt was made to unionise brewery labour at Burton in 1892–3, it was represented as 'Beer, Beef and Excursions'.[43] All brewery workmen were allowed a ration during their breaks, usually of two or three pints daily – often of indifferent beer. Half stones of beef for the family and pounds of tea for the wife were regular Christmas gifts. And the great feature of brewery life by the late nineteenth century was the annual brewery excursion. None exceeded those at Bass in the 1890s which claimed to be the largest company outings in the

ninety men; the Tadcaster Tower witnessed mushroom growth in the 1880s from some thirty to over a hundred men in the six years, 1882–8.

[40] Barnard, *Noted Breweries*, III, p. 46; II, p. 421.

[41] For example, see the extract from the 'Yarmouth Punishment Book, 1901–16' of Steward & Patteson; Gourvish, *Norfolk Beers*, pp. 88–94.

[42] Many of Bass's 400 malt house labourers migrated from the Norfolk-Suffolk borders for the September–May season. G. E. Evans, *Where Beards Wag All: The Relevance of the Oral Tradition* (1970).

[43] See the long article on 'Organising the Labourers' from the *Morning Advertiser*, Jan. 1893 in Bass Museum 'Scrapbooks'.

world (see Plates 27 and 28). As many as seventeen trains conveyed the families of workers and staff alike, albeit separately, to different northern and eastern resorts. In 1895, no fewer than 10,000 went on the Blackpool excursion. Its 'Napoleonic' organiser, William Walker, planned the trips for close on half a century. In 1902 Truman reckoned its package of beer allowances, regular all-year-round work, sick pay, pensions, holidays, outings, 'presents' and extra accident pay was worth 6s a week although, stubbornly, the men would 'not realize what they do receive'. Guinness had established a Brewery Dispensary by the turn of the century that looked after the health and welfare of its 3,500 employees and their dependants.

Stripped of paternalism, were brewery wages generous? Undoubtedly, those of coopers and draymen were. The former were a highly skilled craft organisation, the latter worked very long hours. In London in the 1900s draymen were paid from 35s to 50s a week plus 'butt money'.[44] Their hours were incredibly long and unregulated; the work was heavy and the hazards of the job – injury and the customary free pint at every pub – only too evident. And in other departments also, foremen and more reliable workmen were well rewarded, but there were large numbers of labourers and boys employed in menial tasks throughout any large brewery who were not. Customarily, the labourers' rate appears to have been in the region of 2s above those of neighbouring agricultural workers (rates which varied considerably across Britain). By 1892 there were disputes at Bass about a labourers' rate of 17s, and a series of meetings between brewers were held in late 1913 to discuss 'the Labour question in Burton [which] has become a very grave one and may soon be critical'. Individual companies were instructed not to negotiate with the Union but settle a rate agreed amongst themselves. Maltsters' wages were advanced to 30s, unskilled labourers' to 23s for a fifty-four-hour week and a scale for youths fixed from 7s–20s.[45] Wages in London, of course, were higher. Truman paid their general labourers 25s and their building labourers 28s in 1905, although they reckoned they could get good men from the countryside at 22s. Hours eased from the sixty-hour week which was general in breweries in the 1860s. But even thirty years later Truman's men were working from 6 a.m. (cheap fares being unavailable after 6.30 a.m.) to

[44] Truman Monthly Minute books in 1911 categorised four classes (unspecified) of draymen, each performing sixteen different tasks. The system of payment that had grown up was so complex that the director confessed not to understand it. 'Butt or Tun money' was a customary payment for handling the massive 108 gallon barrels.

[45] Bass Museum, B/124: Burton Brewers' Meeting Minutes.

4.30 p.m., and to 12 noon at Saturdays. Yet even if labourers' wages appeared tight and hours long, attempts at unionisation outside London and Burton before the First World War were rare, for everywhere it was an uphill struggle in the face of the brewers' considered paternalism. Conditions were improved because canteens, libraries and, in the biggest non-metropolitan breweries, sporting facilities became usual. Many directors' and managers' wives ran Mothers' Meetings for those of the workforce. But above all the continuity of employment, pensions and annual bonuses – an old feature in breweries – holidays, finely tuned wage differentials, and a carefully engendered company loyalty guaranteed workforces which, in comparison with those in other industries, were remarkably quiescent and constant.

IV

Once brewers had accounted for their manufacturing costs to define their gross profit, they then debited a formidable array of distribution costs to arrive at the crucial net profit figure. Clearly, distribution costs varied a good deal, depending upon whether a brewery was small with a local trade or, by the late nineteenth century, had regional or even national aspirations. Again the accounts of Lacon's Great Yarmouth brewery in 1890–1 provide a guide to general practice, although all breweries applied slightly different charging conventions in their private ledgers because they drew slightly different distinctions between manufacturing and distribution costs (Table 5.5). The Bass accounts (Appendix, Table IV), working out costs of every item, are more detailed. Discounts and agency expenses – an increasing feature of all accounts, oddly omitted as a separate item in Lacon's balance sheet – are considered below (see pp. 207–9),[46] but the two items of casks and salaries require a brief discussion here.

If increasing amounts of beer were retailed in jars and bottles in the course of the nineteenth century, the vast majority of beer was sold wholesale in traditional wooden casks: butts, hogsheads, barrels, kilderkins and, an innovation of the 1880s in the family trade, firkins and pins.[47] Their construction in imported oak, usually from the Baltic, was a highly skilled, craft operation employing many men and apprentices in

[46] In the early 1880s the Tadcaster Tower Brewery reckoned that discounts and commission consumed 15 per cent of sales, carriage 10 per cent and bad debts 2½ per cent. Later, as gross profits increased discounts drifted to 25 per cent.

[47] See glossary under 'barrels'.

Table 5.5. *The distribution costs of Lacon & Sons for the year ending 30 Sept. 1891*

To expenses			By gross profit	£
Freight account	4,071		Ale account	43,614
Horse keep	943		Spirit account	1,464
Rents payable	2,314		Interest	268
Rates and taxes	1,575		Rents receivable	2,729
Fire insurance	185			
Salaries	2,444			48,075
Casks	1,256			
		12,788		
Trade expenses				
Water	927			
Gas	1,274			
Brewery	930			
Coopers' and engineers' wages	1,081			
Horses bought and stable costs	647			
Subscriptions	158			
Law and audit costs	438			
Bank and licence charges	163			
Postage, stationery, etc.	378			
Income tax	1,191			
		7,187		
Repairs to public houses	1,294			
Repairs to brewery, plant and machinery	3,267			
		4,561		
Bad debts		449		
Interest on partners' and other loans		1,451		
		26,436		
Net profit		21,639		
		48,075		

Source: Whitbread Archive 197/53. A partner calculated the net profit as 14.62 per cent or 4s 1d per barrel (excluding interest) or 13.7 per cent or 3s 10d per barrel (after charging interest).

the larger breweries. Casks were an item that fascinated Victorian brewery writers. The author of *A Glass of Pale Ale* listed those at Bass: 46,901 butts, 159,608 hogsheads (always used in the export trade), 139,763 barrels and 197,597 kilderkins. 'Babylon was a square of fifteen miles on the side – these casks would more than surround the walls three times!' Barnard, a decade later, found 518,121 casks including 68,597 of the newly introduced firkins. Their steam cooperage, employing 227 men and 46 boys, was *the* state-of-the-art cask manufactory in Britain. Even Bass's stave yard ran to 25 acres at Shobnall.[48] The great pyramids of empty casks in the yards of the larger breweries in Burton was one of the sights of Britain's brewing capital (see Plate 29). All this was rather exceptional. Only Guinness later matched Bass, by 1913 employing 294 coopers.[49] In London, Combe, with its big 500,000 barrelage, employed a hundred coopers and cask workers, but teams of thirty to fifty were more usual in the capital's breweries.[50] Neither coopers nor casks merited more than a bare mention in Truman's uniquely detailed Monthly Minute Books running from 1884 to 1914. Presumably, with a rapid turnover in a highly concentrated market, cask stocks and control was a lesser problem than in Burton, Dublin and Edinburgh, where the leading brewers largely depended upon a national rail network of deliveries.

At the other end of the scale, the Tadcaster Tower Brewery initially employed only three coopers to repair and un-head casks, buying its hogshead barrels at 20s–22s and its 36 gallon barrels at 15s–16s apiece in the 1880s. Nevertheless, its stock was not negligible. When an irate director went over from York to investigate the array of returned ale he was, 'perfectly disgusted . . . it was all lying about anyhow, bungs on the ground, leaking etc.'[51] He counted fifty hogsheads, 120 barrels and 'heaps of other sizes' of returns alone. Since barrels were expensive items, the value of casks could exceed the valuation of the brewery and its plant. They did at Bass in 1843.[52] In 1873 casks there were valued at a massive £200,000, although later there is evidence of smaller cask stocks, at least in relation to total beer sales, because their circulation was more rapid and more beer was bottled.

48 *A Glass of Pale Ale and A Visit to Burton* (1880), p. 12; Barnard, *Noted Breweries*, I, pp. 49–56.

49 Dennison and MacDonagh, 'History of Guinness', Chapter IX. In 1886 it had employed 155 men, boys and apprentices in the Dublin cooperage.

50 Barnard, *Noted Breweries*, I, p. 293.

51 Bass North (Leeds): Tadcaster Tower Brewery diaries, September 1885.

52 Owen, *History of Bass*, forthcoming. Property (£8,149) and plant (£9,876) were valued less than casks (£17,212) and staves (£5,963).

Other tasks besides the constructing and maintenance of casks were important. One test of a well-run brewery was the cleanliness and control of its casks. By the 1880s much of the former was done by steam and patent washing machines. It was an essential process because good, fresh casks were necessary in turning out good beer. And since they were in themselves expensive items, prone to theft, clerks had to devise effective control of them. Barnard, with barely concealed wonder, found in Bass's cask office thirty-five clerks 'whose duty it is to check the numbers of all casks going out and coming in, and this is done so systematically, that if a cask be away longer than is necessary, it can be traced immediately'.[53] Bass's arrangements were the epitome of cask control, underlining the importance all brewers paid to this part of their business.

Although salaries were a smaller item of distribution costs than the making and maintenance of a good stock of casks, a consideration of them takes us to the centre of brewery administration and, more generally, to a vital stratum of Victorian society. For the remarkable material progress of the middle classes between 1830 and 1914 is nowhere better illustrated than by briefly looking at the conditions and salaries in breweries of their managers, clerks and brewers. Always it is a settled world, hierarchical, observing strict divisions between staff and workers, dull in its routines, but comfortable in its rewards and the guarantee of continuous employment.

Numbers were significant. The 1907 Census of Production listed 14,727 salaried staff in breweries. Guinness, the biggest company, employed fifteen brewers, nine senior managers including the Company Secretary, Head Engineer and Chemist, 285 'no. 1' staff, 203 'no. 2', ten 'other' and fifty-four 'Lady clerks'.[54] Even middling breweries employed two or three brewers, half a dozen departmental managers and twenty or thirty clerks. Boddingtons' in 1875, for example, employed a head-brewer and three assistants, twenty clerks, six travellers and six collectors.[55] Barnard invariably poked his head into the offices of the breweries he visited, giving their dimensions, stating the number of clerks and, sometimes, commenting on the sumptuousness of the accommodation. Material rewards were excellent and posts keenly sought. Guinness in the 1890s paid its brewers on an eighteen-point

[53] Barnard, *Noted Breweries*, I, p. 107 where there is an illustration of the 96 × 29 feet cask office.

[54] Dennison and MacDonagh, 'History of Guinness', chapter XI.

[55] Whitbread Archive 405/21 Boddingtons' salary book.

annual scale from £100 to £1,000 a year, with higher salaries for its Head and Second Brewers. These were revised upwards in 1900, and again in 1903 to attract first-class scientists. In 1889 there was a new scale for the five grades of 'no. 1' staff and six for the 'no. 2', salaries ranging from £40 to £700. These payments were always matched in the top dozen London breweries which traditionally had paid the biggest salaries. Reid's thirty-two staff in 1866 averaged salaries of £315, a figure exceeding those of the thirty-eight on the eve of its amalgamation with Watney and Combe in 1898.[56] The new combine rewarded its most senior management well: in 1905 the chief secretary was paid £1,500; the town trade manager, £2,000; its big Mortlake depot manager, £1,000. C. H. Tripp (whose diary entries for the Tadcaster Tower Brewery have been so revealing about brewery life) received £4,000 a year when, as general manager, he went to Ind Coope to revive their flagging fortunes in the early 1900s.[57]

In the country, salaries of course were less. Those of clerks at Boddingtons' in 1875 varied from the £14 6s paid to an assistant to the £262 10s received by the managing clerk. In addition, all were paid 10 per cent bonuses. And those travellers, agents and collectors, whose efforts were so crucial to the success of breweries, were even better rewarded with their commissions, expenses and free houses.[58] Boddingtons' chief traveller was paid £505 plus bonus in 1875, a sum more than twice that of the head brewer. These excellent salaries rewarded service and success. But there were other bonds reinforcing the paternalism and hierarchies which were such a striking feature of the larger breweries. When the families of the richer brewers became prominent in local life, their elections to public office, as well as their celebrations, marriages

[56] Westminster City Archives, Acc./789/26 clerks' salary book, 1866–98. High salaries for clerks and managers in London were matched by salaries paid to partners. The six partners of Truman drew from £800 to £5,000 apiece in early 1866, the senior managing partner drawing a salary which was not exceeded by directors until a century later.

[57] *Brewing Trade Review*, 1 May 1896, 1 June 1905 and 1 May 1908. He went to Burton as general manager 1893–6, was promoted to managing director of Ind Coope in 1897 and rewarded by a seven-year contract of £4,000 per annum. This was renewed, but when Ind Coope ran into serious problems in 1905–8 he agreed to take a cut of £1,000. He resigned as joint managing director in 1913. He was also chairman of the British Pure Yeast Co. and the Diamond Soda Water Co., and a director of the Crystal Palace Co. Above all, Tripp was a tireless self-publicist.

[58] Tripp defined the onerous duties of travellers at Tadcaster Tower in 1880: in each public house they were to examine the cellars and the beer; report on the cleanliness of the house, its utensils and glasses; count the casks on the premises and, if tenants, check that they were not buying their spirits elsewhere. They were to visit their York pubs weekly, their country pubs monthly. Written reports were to be entered in a book for examination by the partners.

and deaths, were recorded in immensely decorous detail by the provincial press. The staff were admitted to the margins of this world, proud of their attachment both to the brewery and to its owners.

V

Costs have been discussed in some detail because a consideration of the way brewers arrived at their net profits was complex in an industry embracing excise duties as well as an unusually wide range of distributive expenses. Moreover, it has been necessary to stress the industry's close relations with agriculture since barley and hops formed such a high proportion of the manufacturing costs of beer. Prices can be considered more briefly. What considerations surrounded the brewer's decisions in arriving at the wholesale costs of his beers? Was there collusion between brewers about prices, especially when those of brewing materials fell appreciably after 1880?

One of the most remarkable features of the brewing industry in this period is that the price of beer remained essentially unchanged. Only in 1847 when malt prices soared, when additional duties were imposed during the Crimean War, when in 1886 prices in London were reduced by 3s a barrel, and in the summer of 1909, were prices significantly adjusted across sections of the trade.[59] Moreover, both in 1847 and 1909 the increase, by no means sanctioned by all brewers, was of the briefest duration. There were two key prices, that of porter and of the cheapest mild. The removal of the beer duty in 1830 allowed the London brewers to reduce the former to 33s (from 45s) and mild to 36s (Table 5.6). Discounts in London at this stage were minimal: 3d in the pound traditionally paid as pin money to the publican's wife. Price material in the provinces is difficult to come by; that of Henry Bentley's newly established brewery at Woodlesford near Leeds suggests that his beer tariff, invariably quoted per gallon, ranged from 1s 3d to 1s 10d before 11 October 1830, was slashed to 10d from 1s 6d for three months and then, with mounting bad debts, settled at 1s to 1s 6d. His best-selling mild ale and porter were delivered at 36s a barrel.[60] Then for eighty years these prices remained remarkably stable. What were the causes?

First, the price of malt (see appendix, Table V) never rose to the levels

[59] Knox, 'London Brewing Industry', pp. 51–3.
[60] Whitbread Archive, 288/72.104, Henry Bentley, Sales Ledger (1828–32) and cash book (1828–31).

Table 5.6. *Wholesale and retail price of beer after 1830*

Wholesale price per barrel (shillings)	Retail price per quart pot (pence)	Gross profit to publican per barrel (shillings)
30	3	6
33	3½	9
36	4	12
48	6	24
60	8	36

experienced during the French Wars (1793–1815) and the immediate post-war period. They fluctuated quite widely to the 1860s, and then experienced a secular downturn to the mid-1890s and – for farmers – a painfully slow recovery to 1914. Moreover, the price of hops, although demonstrating the volatility inherent in their cultivation and marketing, did not on average reach those attained in the early nineteenth century. Secondly, duties remained essentially unchanged for half a century after 1830. And even when they advanced steadily from 1900 the price of materials still continued at levels that did not merit a rise in beer prices. When a number of brewers, incensed by the government's proposed tax increases on the industry in the budget of 1909, advanced their prices, they were unable to sustain them for more than four months.[61] Whatever troubles the brewers faced after 1900, the answer, in the face of government hostility, declining consumption and intense competition, was not a price rise. Thirdly, 1830 marked a return to price stability which brewers welcomed. The inflation and high duties of the 1795–1830 period had meant frequent price changes, but they were exceptional years of stormy interlude between the earlier Georgian and Victorian periods. Lastly, free trade worked. After 1830 there were too many producers and outlets for brewers to combine effectively to advance prices when those of barley and hops increased. Brewers had to live with temporarily reduced profits and await a good harvest. When Bass in 1860, faced with a sharp increase in malt and hop costs, raised

[61] See pp. 292–4 below. On 24 February 1909 a meeting, minuted by Truman, with Cosmo Bonsor in the chair and attended by nine other 'friends' to discuss the public house trade in London could not agree price increases. The problem Truman centred upon was the dual pricing of beer in tied and free houses and their level in the former. Therefore when on 1 July 1909 some brewers increased prices there was, inevitably, disagreement. Whitbread, rightly, argued the move was premature and three months later the Parliamentary Committee of the Brewers' Society diplomatically urged the brewers to lower them.

prices by 6s a barrel, their sales fell by 20 per cent. Similarly, six years later, when they attempted an increase of 3s, their trade dwindled by 13 per cent.[62] Collective action outside the great London porter brewers was non-existent; that of individual brewers was positively suicidal.

For fifty years therefore, but especially from the late 1850s to the mid-1870s, as general prices, the standard of living and the demand for beer all advanced, beer prices remained stable. Profit margins in years of low raw-material costs were good and rapidly increasing output for many brewers eased those margins. After 1880 conditions in the beer market changed quite rapidly: consumption declined in some years, and the cost of brewing materials slumped. Yet the price of beer remained essentially unchanged. Indeed, in real terms it became increasingly expensive – which explains in part the years of poor trade in the early and mid-1880s, in the early 1890s and in the 1900s, and accounts for the popularity of the cheapest beers. Had free trade been trampled to death in the rush to tie trade? Temperance critics, unable to contemplate cheaper beer, nonetheless argued that profitability in the industry was excessive. But the question of beer prices after 1880 is more complex than their invariably crude analysis suggests.

The cheapest beers were retailed at 3½d or 4d a quart. Any meaningful reduction to stimulate consumption would have meant one of ½d a pint or 12s a barrel. Brewers' profits, averaging (except in the most abnormal year) between 6s and 9s per barrel would have been largely wiped out by even a 6s a barrel reduction. Of course, not all beers sold on such tight margins as porter and cheap mild. The premium Burton ales were retailed at around 60s–66s a barrel; of course their material costs were much higher both in terms of quantity-per-barrel brewed and in the quality of the malts and hops used. Yet all brewers of any scale produced eight to ten beers with a considerable variation of price (3½d to 8d per quart: good stouts and bitters retailing at around 6d a quart, an export ale at 8d). The more expensive beers sold in smaller quantities, often of no more than a few hundred barrels apiece, but the spread meant that brewers had more manœuvrability with prices than the stable prices of their best-selling lines, whether porter, mild, pale ale or stout, suggest. In this situation the stress was on quality and reputation. A good brewer guarded them with his life, for these were the features that sold beer in Victorian Britain – not its comparative price.

There was, therefore, every incentive to leave the price of beer

62 Hawkins, 'Brewing Industry', p. 46.

unchanged after 1880. In fact, the brewers were forced to concede increasingly large discounts. Again, the ability to do this was made possible because low brewing material costs ensured a higher gross profit margin. Indeed the low cost of malt and often of hops was at the heart of changes after the 1880s. Truman believed it allowed the frenetic acquisition of tied property in London in the 1890s. Certainly, brewers were able to charge their distribution accounts with additional items so long as manufacturing costs eased, prices remained stable, and output did not continuously decline. Above all, they allowed discounts to ease and borrowings to increase. It is the former that concerns us here. Brewers had always operated cash discounts but until the 1840s these remained small. The agency system of the Burton brewers pioneered growth by discounts, and by the 1860s any brewery wishing to expand vigorously in the free trade was offering discounts in the region of 10–15 per cent.[63] By the 1880s recession discounts of 20–25 per cent and more were not uncommon. These were limited to the free trade. In the tied trade discounts of 5 per cent – also common in London by the mid-century – appear universal in the second half of the nineteenth century. In the country, but not London, this gave rise to the concept of the 'wet' and 'dry' rent. Brewers charged low rents for their pubs, often well below the market rate. These were known as 'dry' rents, and brewers recouped an economic return on their outlay and for the maintenance of their pubs by allowing tied tenants only a 5 per cent discount in contrast with the much larger rebates conceded in the free trade. The difference in charges per barrel made to tenants *above* the price paid in the free trade was the 'wet' rent.

There were inherent problems in the system. It allowed free houses to compete well and forced tied tenants to sell cheap, thereby eroding their small margins even further. To attract trade, publicans began the practice of the 'long pull' – selling well over the measure for the same price – a custom tied tenants could ill afford.[64] Yet dilution and adulteration, the old resort of distressed publicans, seem to have been increasingly stamped out after the mid-1880s as analysis became common, and the brewers fought long and hard to remove the practice of the 'long pull'. Mounting discounts in the 1880s and 1890s therefore

[63] Joshua Tetley & Son, Ale and Porter Account Books, No. 4, 1858–76, West Yorkshire Archives, Leeds.

[64] C. H. Tripp discussed the problem in some detail in the Tadcaster Tower Brewery diaries in August 1887. Selling cheap mild at 4d a quart and best at 5d, tenants were ill equipped to sell greatly over measure in response to the free trade which was sustained by 25 per cent discounts.

became a further incentive for country brewers to acquire pubs. In London, where loan tie arrangements were different and the brewers did not concede increased discounts, additional pressures were put on their accounts because loans escalated and publican insolvencies began to rise. In these circumstances, both in the country and in the capital, every effort was made by brewers after 1880 to maintain traditional price levels.[65]

One more point in relation to prices needs stressing. Brewers were extremely secretive about their accounts. Only the partners and the most senior managers were allowed to see the final balance sheet entered in locked private ledgers, putting together gross and net profit figures. Of course, price lists were common property although advertising was minimal to the 1900s. Nevertheless, crucial matters like general and quantity discounts and credit terms were confidential to partners, agents and travellers. The latter two, reporting back on every aspect of retailing and competition, were the eyes and ears of the brewers at the cliff-face of sales. These points about confidentiality and the individual brewer's independence in adjusting his discounts and terms in the face of competition – even if it was unwise to move far on the wholesale prices of his best-selling beers – are particularly relevant to any consideration of the brewers' collective action about prices in Victorian Britain.

To the 1880s, the brewers' interests were represented by two organisations, the London Brewers' Company and the Country Brewers' Society. The former, dominated by the biggest London firms, was an historic body incorporated in 1437.[66] By the eighteenth century its affairs were laxly run. Only after 1795 was its authority revived, when the Committee of the Porter Brewers, a body loosely attached to the Company through meeting in its Hall and utilising the services of its clerk, began in effect to fix the price of porter in London during the upheavals of the French Wars. In the early Victorian period, although its courts were initially no more frequent, the Company, or more

[65] Except in 1886 when the London brewers conceded a 3s a barrel reduction on condition that publicans – encouraged both by the excise and the Licensed Victuallers' Association – would discontinue the practices of adulteration, dilution and the 'long pull'. Knox, 'London Brewing Industry', pp. 40–1.

[66] This paragraph is based upon the Brewers' Company Trade Committee Book 1830–92 (Guildhall Library, MS.5468) and its Court Minute Books, 1881–92, 1892–1903, 1903–18 (MS.5445/39–41); Knox 'London Brewing Industry', Chapter 2; M. Ball, *The Worshipful Company of Brewers* (1977). Mathias, *Brewing Industry*, pp. 228–43 provides a detailed account of the Committee of the Porter Brewers, 1795–1830.

precisely its Brewing Trade Committee, does seem to have been effective in maintaining, at least to the 1880s, collective action on prices, discounts and practices in the metropolitan beer trade. The minute books reveal little action or discussion. The dozen big brewers ruled the roost; the rest, whether members of the Company or not, were unable to cut prices further and survive. Apparently, they fell in with the ruling oligarchy's directives. Yet it would be misleading to suggest that price maintenance was the chief function of the Company. The core of its existence, like most Victorian livery companies, was its charitable – especially educational – work, the management of its considerable income, and its calendar of dinners.[67] When the real crunch came in the London beer market in the late 1880s, with discussions about the Burton brewers' big discounts, and above all the size of loans and the scramble for property, the Company's easy authority disintegrated. Truman's monthly minutes reveal how a semblance of co-operation was maintained, but now behind the façade, the old gentlemanly partners' world, undermined by distrust and rivalry, had fallen apart. In the face of intense competition, the brewers went their own way in matters of property acquisition. In fact as the industry generally faced increasing hostility, the Company became far more assiduous in its activities, taking on the much wider defence of the trade in the capital. As a consequence its efforts became enmeshed with those of the National Trade Defence Fund (formed in 1888 and changing its name to Association in 1900), the London Brewers' Association and the Country Brewers' Society.[68] Discussion about prices and trade practices became lost in this enormous agenda.

In the country, there was little if any collective action on prices. The Country Brewers' Society, founded in 1822 (see pp. 13–14), was for the first fifty years of its existence dominated by a few score brewers

[67] It ran Aldenham School, the Dame Alice Owen schools in Islington and Alderman James Hickson's school at Barking. The Company's income was £18,840 in 1884 which, apart from the 'Great Twelve', made it the wealthiest of the minor companies.

[68] But Andrew Motion, chairman of the Cannon Brewery and one of the country's most forward looking brewers in the 1900s, was dismissive of the Brewing Company's new role. In 1906 he thought 'it was time . . . [it] became something more than a name'. The following year he was more specific:

> the greatest danger to the Trade laid within and not outside. It had always been so, and he spoke of the deplorable organisation, or rather want of organisation of their Trade. Naturally, in time of stress and danger, they turned to the head – Brewers' Hall – a place to which every London brewer should belong . . . and what did they find? Out of fifty brewers in the London area, only nine, including that firm, were members, and why was that? Because the rules were absolutely out of date, and because the older members were wedded to the autocratic ideas of a quarter of a century ago.

(*Brewing Trade Review*, 1 March 1906; 1 March 1907.)

drawn from the South and East of England.[69] Action was largely confined to consuming an annual dinner in Derby week and paying their guinea subscriptions many years in arrears. In the early 1840s, a settled period in the trade, it almost collapsed. Only in 1855 was there any discussion of beer prices, and although it produced a list to reflect the increase in malt duty and liaised with the victuallers, it clearly had little faith, or indeed belief, that its recommendations would be followed. Then in the twenty years after 1869 it was transformed in the face of mounting attacks on the industry. It supported a series of journals which became the brewers' effective mouthpiece; it became affiliated with the county associations of brewers' bodies which proliferated in the 1880s and existed in every English county (save Cornwall), Wales and Scotland to co-ordinate local political pressure; it raised funds to defend the industry in and out of Parliament.[70] It was never entirely representative before 1904 when the Brewers' Society was formed to amalgamate the three big brewing interest groups, the Country Brewers, the Burton and the London Brewers' Associations.[71] Again, the political task of the past thirty years had been a massive one. Price discussions seem not to have extended beyond general fears about the government's determination to load the industry with additional taxation and restrictions. Even in the county brewers' associations, although detailed pricing discussions if they did take place apparently went unrecorded, meetings concentrated upon the defence of the industry and political organisation at local level. It was the steep rises in duty after 1914 that led to collective action on pricing. Brewers, by participation and by reading the journals, became better informed about the national industry and its changing shape and problems. A study of their trading associations between 1870 and 1914, however, does not support the conclusion that there was effective, collusive action on the pricing of beer. All the evidence points to an intensifying competition on discounts and terms.

69 This section is based upon the Society's minute books in the Brewers' Society Library. A detailed account of its political activities, and indeed of all the other trade organisations, for the 1870–1914 period, will be found in Gutzke, *Protecting the Pub*.

70 The official organs of the Country Brewers' Society were the *Brewers' Guardian* (1871–8), succeeded by the *Country Brewers' Gazette* (1878–86) and then the *Brewing Trade Review* after 1886. These journals and the *Brewers' Journal* were a milestone in the industry. Not only did they inform brewers on the politics of the industry, but above all they made them aware of scientific advances in brewing.

71 In 1883 only 15 per cent of common brewers (i.e. brewing over 1,000 barrels annually) were members of the Country Brewers' Society; in 1900 39 per cent, and by 1910, following the formation of the Brewers' Society, 60 per cent. Gutzke, *Protecting the Pub*, pp. 64, 231.

VI

The profitability of individual breweries, and ultimately of the brewing industry, in Victorian Britain, is difficult to determine. It would take a bold historian of accountancy to calculate profits with certainty, because items, entered or disguised, and conventions, employed or undisclosed, a century and a half ago remain hidden to us now. Moreover, before company accounts were widely accessible after 1885, brewery writers never discussed the subject. Even in the late 1880s Barnard omitted all mention of them. Like barrelages they were a closed topic. Nevertheless, critics of the brewing industry in the later nineteenth century and thereafter have been certain that profits from the sale of beer rained effortlessly down into the brewers' coffers. No other business venture, it was believed, save perhaps banking, provided a surer route to a fortune in Victorian Britain. There are elements of truth in these assertions if examples are carefully selected. But strictly as a return on capital, profits were not excessive nor were they achieved, as these pages have suggested, without effort. A well-run brewery was, as Mathias revealed for Georgian London or as Barnard demonstrated nationally in the late 1880s, a fine business enterprise on any terms.

It is clear that brewers had several rules-of-thumb to estimate the rough profitability of firms employed in the industry. After the 1830s, with static prices, these approximate calculations did not alter much. Something in the order of a 10 per cent return on capital, in addition to the 5 per cent interest upon it paid quarterly – and which they might have expected as a return from the safest investment – was the aim across the life of a partnership, good years compensating bad. In 1867 S. C. Whitbread set out the returns on partners' capital for the previous fifty years. As Table 5.7 shows, they were much the same in 1858–67 as in 1818–27, despite the intervening fluctuations. The real determinant of this profitability was not increased sales – they reached the level of 1832 in only four years before 1860 – but the variable costs of malt and hops (see Appendix, Tables V, VI). In 1855–6, when malt prices and duties advanced, profits (£7,103) were as small as 1.75 per cent; in 1824–5 they had reached a record 16.75 per cent after the lowest run of malt and hop prices for thirty years. The decade after 1837 was one of poor returns, with yearly profits paid to the partners averaging only £22,425; yet three good years (1870–3), when an advance in sales coincided with favourable brewing material costs,

Table 5.7. *Whitbread: percentage return on partners' capital, 1818–67*

Year ending 30 June									
1818	7.0	1828	10.0	1838	4.875	1848	7.5	1858	7.75
1819	10.5	1829	10.0	1839	7.0	1849	10.5	1859	13.4375
1820	10.0	1830	3.75	1840	4.375	1850	8.25	1860	12.9375
1821	10.25	1831	6.875	1841	6.5	1851	11.25	1861	2.375
1822	12.75	1832	6.875	1842	6.25	1852	10.0	1862	6.4375
1823	11.75	1833	6.375	1843	8.375	1853	7.875	1863	11.875
1824	11.75	1834	8.5	1844	7.5	1854	12.5	1864	12.6875
1825	16.75	1835	7.25	1845	3.875	1855	9.25	1865	14.75
1826	6.0	1836	7.125	1846	5.5	1856	1.75	1866	14.0
1827	15.25	1837	6.375	1847	4.25	1857	7.1875	1867	6.40625
10-year average	11.1875		7.3125		5.875		8.5625		10.25

Figures originally in fractions, converted to decimals. This return was in addition to 5 per cent interest, paid quarterly.
Source: Whitbread Archive: Box UU.

transformed the partnership's fortunes as profits leapt beyond £80,000.[72] The business had to generate sufficient profit to pay not only the interest on partners' capital but also that due on all those loans made by partners, their family and friends, publicans and clubs, and, sometimes, banks. To sustain very large capitals and loans, breweries had to realise large profits.

Another rule-of-thumb about profitability was that net profits should exceed 5s per barrel on sales or, as Truman put it in 1885, return 2s 6d average profit for every pound of gross takings. These were the roughest guides. A profit of 5s per barrel on large sales of porter or mild was good; on best pale ale it would be indifferent. Because the pivot of brewing profitability was raw material prices, the brewer's only defence against total vulnerability was the astute management of stocks. Nevertheless, these casual estimates of profitability are helpful. A modest brewery turning out 40,000 barrels a year could expect annual average profits of around £10,000 across the life of a partnership. And after 1880, providing they kept a tight rein on discounts and borrowing, the lowest malt prices for over a century allowed brewers larger returns. A brief run of

72 Whitbread Archive, Private Ledgers, W/17/1–4.

Mann, Crossmann & Paulin's sales, capital, profits and loans between 1847 and 1868 demonstrates the utility of the profit-per-barrel guide. Their return on capital looks absurdly high, but if worked out as profits per barrel – 4s 4d on an annual average barrelage of 97,777 barrels between 1847 and 1856 and 3s 10d (loans escalating after 1858 and presumably acting as a drag on profits) between 1858 and 1867 – the result, for their big sales of cheap mild ale, makes the rule-of-thumb seem very plausible.[73]

Outside London, the evidence about profitability is much scrappier for the fifty years before presentation of accounts to shareholders became commonplace. The great exceptions were Guinness, Bass and Allsopp. Bass's record after the early 1840s was unparalleled in Britain. As a return on partners' capital, profits averaged 25.3 per cent between 1843 and 1852 and 17.4 per cent in the following decade. It is unclear whether, in addition, 5 per cent interest had been paid on these capitals. Either way, they were ample, and unlike Whitbread they were earned on a rapidly expanding capital which reflected total assets employed fairly closely. In 1843 partners' capital and reserves were £63,183; twenty years later they had multiplied almost thirteen times to £848,455.[74] Yet fluctuations in profits were still marked: indeed they oscillated far more widely than those of Whitbread. In 1849 profits reached a dizzy 48.9 per cent; six years later a loss of 11.4 per cent was declared. Bass's record, and Allsopp's too at this stage, was exceptional because they were pioneering the sale of highly profitable premium ales on a national agency system. Demand for the best Burton ales seemed insatiable in the 1840–80 period.

But the indications from other partnerships of country brewers before the 1880s, scrappy and indeterminate as these often are, suggest that profits were more modest than those of Bass. Of course, as capital costs grew from 1860 with the rapid expansion of the larger breweries, profits were sufficiently large to finance this growth because most of it was based upon retained profits. Before 1860 profits were generally lower and more variable. Lacon – the early evidence is restricted to the years 1838–50 – appear to have solved this problem of fluctuation with some ingenuity. Each year, on a capital of £53,339, they paid £6,000 to the partners' account and £1,200 to a reserve fund: in all 13.5 per cent on capital. These constant payments were met, if profits dipped, from a reserve fund which itself varied from £18,776 in credit in 1840 to a

[73] Courage Archive (Bristol), Private ledgers MA/A/1. The figures for 1857 are missing.
[74] Owen, *History of Bass*, forthcoming.

deficit of £902 in 1847 following three difficult trading years (sales were running at around 36,000 barrels in the 1840s). By the 1870s, barrelages had more than trebled in some years and profits had similarly risen, varying from £17,723 in 1874 to £35,663 two years later.[75] The accounts of Georges of Bristol, equally incomplete, suggest the same experience: two decades of difficulty in the 1830s and 1840s; sharply rising prosperity for twenty years before flotation in the late 1880s. In the 1830s and 1840s the firm was troubled by large stocks and large bad debts. In addition, its loans often approached one-third of its capital of £56,000–£60,000. Both were serviced at 4 per cent interest, and then a modest dividend, usually of £3,000 but rising to £9,000 in a good year, was added. Over twenty years later, profits averaged almost £39,000 in the fifteen years before incorporation in early 1888. The key to this prosperity was growth – barrelages were running at roughly three times the 1830s–40s level after 1870 – and to declining malt prices.[76]

Few surviving brewery accounts cover the whole 1830–70 period. The more numerous sets, usually relating to partnerships on the eve of incorporation, underline the post-1865 surge in profits enjoyed by Lacon and Georges. Simonds of Reading more than doubled its output from 28,600 barrels in 1866 to 57,000 in 1871 and its profits rose sharply to exceed, sometimes comfortably, £10,000 in every year from 1868 to 1874; Edward Greene, in the decade before the incorporation of his firm with F. W. King's, returned a profit of 12–16 per cent on a capital which grew from £144,000 to £196,000 in the last years of partnership; Cobbold of Ipswich, whose earnings were generated as much from their thriving wines and spirits and malting business as from brewing, returned profits which averaged £11,249 in the decade after 1876 when its partners declared a capital of £65,376 (although this did not include their 220 houses whose rents were £5,000 in 1876); again Eldridge Pope's profits rose very sharply from the early 1880s, and in every year but one from 1887 to 1914 returned sums in advance of £30,000 on sales of 40,000–65,000 barrels.[77] In Scotland, material on profits is even scarcer. J. & R. Tennent's profits seem modest indeed in the 1880s, with a return

75 Whitbread Archive, 197/52–3, 78, 239.

76 Courage (Bristol), Georges' Private Ledgers 35740/GR/3a–b. In 1873 and 1974 malt costs (including duty) averaged £74,955; by 1886 and 1887 they had fallen to £25,218. The great surge in hop prices in 1882 cut profits from £42,000 to £33,000.

77 Corley, 'Simonds Brewery', pp. 81–2; Wilson, *Greene King*, p. 268; Ipswich and East Suffolk Record office, HA/231/1/3, 12–13. Cobbold's profits did not really take off until 1896–1900 when they trebled to £41,507 in five years; Eldridge Pope (Dorchester) Private ledgers, 1873–9, 1890–1916. Again, the brewery, like Cobbold, ran an unusually flourishing wines and spirits trade. In 1895 and between 1900 and 1911 profits exceeded £40,000. Steward & Patteson between 1886 and 1895 returned a profit of 10.4 per cent

of never more than 10 per cent and usually nearer 5 per cent on the very large capital required to run their exceptional export trade. They were also launching lager production in this decade.[78] T & J. Barnard in their company prospectus declared average profits of £15,033 on average sales of 57,977 barrels in the 1890–5 period.[79] Their profits, advertised as perfectly adequate in the prospectus, were less than a farthing (¼d) per pint.

The profitability of the industry after 1885 is discussed in detail in Chapter 7, in the context of the incorporation of most of the larger companies, the scramble to acquire tied property, and the down-turn in fortunes of the industry after 1900. Here, it is necessary only to stress that for many breweries (except those in London, where the cost of property and publicans' insolvencies gave rise to serious problems in the 1900s) the profitability of the 1865–85 years continued. It was achieved above all by the decline in the price of raw materials and by paying increasing attention to paring all those costs identified in their manufacturing and distribution statements, as consumption was checked and the government's attitude to the industry hardened after 1900. Thereby good returns on capital were ensured for the majority of the new companies. Dividend payments on ordinary shares, as good a guide to profitability as other forms of calculation, demonstrate this (see Table 7.2, p. 308). Those of Guinness and Bass continued their extraordinary progress. The former's total profits from its incorporation in 1886 to 1914 amounted to over £25 million, of which the ordinary shareholders received £15.4 million, the preference and debenture holders together £4.9 million, and the reserves £4.3 million.[80] Dividends on the ordinary shares (including payment of tax) rose from 15.4 to 35.7 per cent. Bass in 1896 and 1897 paid dividends of 30 per cent and in six wonderful years between 1896 and 1902 net profits exceeded £500,000 annually.[81] Both enterprises were totally exceptional. Duncan's *Brewery Manual* calculated (the figures including 31 foreign companies) for its investors in 1895 that:

3 companies paid 20 per cent or over
5 companies paid 15 per cent or under 20 per cent
39 companies paid 10 per cent or under 15 per cent
62 companies paid 5 per cent or under 10 per cent
47 companies paid under 5 per cent (32 paying no dividend).

to its partners in addition to generating substantial retentions for development (Gourvish, *Norfolk Beers*, pp. 57–8).

78 Scottish Brewing Archive, T/3/3 and 6.

79 Scottish Brewing Archive, S/2/1.

80 Dennison and MacDonagh, 'History of Guinness, 1886–1939', chapter III.

81 Owen, *History of Bass*, forthcoming.

Some of these companies included in the *Manual* had been speculatively floated in the late 1880s, on dubious profit forecasts. Had Duncan had access to the balance sheets of those private limited companies which sought no stock exchange quotation, dividends in the table would have been higher. After the early 1900s, as he dolefully reported, conditions in the industry hardened. For some breweries like Eldridge Pope or the Hull Brewery there was no check in profitability throughout the decade. Others briefly stumbled; even Bass's dividends fell briefly below 10 per cent in 1909–12; and those of others, principally the London brewers, Allsopp and Ind Coope, withered to nothing. Everything depended upon tight management, the level of loans undertaken to secure expansion (especially in tied house acquisition in the late 1880s and again in the late 1890s), and the control of discounts and bad debts. If all three were right then profits after the late 1880s at least to the early 1900s could still be as generous as in the preceding twenty years. Only after 1902 did brewers experience their worst run of profits, and for even longer periods than in the early Victorian years.

VII

To analyse scraps of information from partners' private ledgers 150 years ago and runs of dividends after the 1880s is to reveal only one, albeit the most significant, dimension of wealth generated in the brewing industry. Contemporaries viewed the matter differently. Alfred Barnard did not tackle Lord Burton, the Riley-Smiths or the great London brewers about their returns on capital; but, like others at all levels of Victorian society, he was fascinated by the riches which that capital generated for its owners. Sometimes the wealth was of recent origin; more often it was the result of generations of involvement in the industry. Always, however, Barnard noted the mansions the profits had purchased, the offices the owners and directors held. Big manicured gardens and big mayoral chains, all now captured by camera, were omnipresent symbols of the brewers' wealth. In the concluding section of this chapter these other aspects of profitability are briefly examined.

In his well-known studies of the wealth in Britain since the Industrial Revolution, W. D. Rubinstein showed that brewers formed one of the largest groups of all non-landed millionaires as represented by the declared value of their estates at death.[82] Between 1809 and 1939 he

[82] See especially, *Men of Property: The Very Wealthy in Britain since the Industrial Revolution* (1981), pp. 62–5, 86–91. Rubinstein's method takes no account of wealth made and given away over a lifetime. It is also biased towards testamentary calculations only.

identified thirty-three millionaires and fifty half-millionaires who had made their fortunes in the industry. Throughout, its power to generate wealth remained impressive; between 1880 and 1899 only banking and merchant banking together equalled its record of producing millionaires. And they were a very rare species in Victorian Britain. Some were household names: M. T. Bass (1799–1884) and his son, the first Lord Burton (1837–1909), and their partners Richard Ratcliff (1830–98) and John Gretton (1833–98). The last left nearly £3 million, a striking testimony to the great riches England's premier brewery had generated over sixty years. A. O. Worthington (1844–1918) was another Burton millionaire whose firm was nationally known. So too were William McEwan (1827–1913), Sir Benjamin Guinness (1798–1868), the first Earl of Iveagh (1847–1927) – Britain's second richest man in the entire period studied by Rubinstein – James Watney (1800–84) and his son and namesake (1832–86), and Sir Henry Meux, Bt. (1817–83). Other London brewers, the Hanburys, Courages, Whitbreads, Barclays, Charringtons, Combes and Buxtons, jostled to appear regularly as half-millionaires in the brewers' riches stakes. Some other names were less predictable: Sir Andrew Walker, first baronet (1824–93), of Peter Walker & Sons of Warrington, left £2.877 million; Edwin Pope (1845–1928), an original partner of Eldridge Pope, left more than half that amount after more than half a century's careful accumulation from the family's Dorchester brewery. And further down the scale, middling breweries generated ample wealth for their owners across a lifetime's endeavour: C. F. Young of the Wandsworth Brewery left £348,915 in 1890; Edward Greene of Bury St Edmunds a similar sum in the following year; W. T. Hewitt of the Tower Brewery, Grimsby, in 1902, £447,357; O. H. McMullen of Hertford, £138,893 in 1913.[83] But these fortunes, trumpeting the wealth of brewers, were exceptional. The industry contained firms of all sizes in this period; similarly probate valuation of partners and directors, recorded faithfully for the readers of the *Brewers' Journal* after 1870, were equally varied. A study of them reveals that a large majority of brewers were leaving estates to their heirs worth tens, not hundreds, of thousand pounds. Even on this score they were very comfortably off by the standards of their day, but well in the wake of the selection of the super-rich recorded above. For example J. A. Hardcastle of the Writtle Brewery, chairman of the Country

[83] Details taken from the monthly record of wills in the *Brewing Trade Review*. See also the estates of the Country Brewers' committee members who died before 1900 in Gutzke, *Protecting the Pub*, p. 90.

Brewers' Society in 1864 and one-time Liberal MP for Bury St Edmunds, left only £7,333 on his death in 1900. But it was a rare brewer who lost all. When A. O. Stopes, one-time chairman of the Colchester Brewing Co., died in 1916, his widow, supposedly penniless, begged help with his funeral expenses.[84]

As many brewers liked to point out in their speeches on the hustings, revealing a now uncommon attitude of mind, great wealth brought great responsibility.[85] Partly this was exercised through the paternalism which was extended to the welfare of their workforces, partly in their wider charitable effort.[86] Some of the latter was spectacular: Lord Burton reputedly gave over £200,000 to charity in his life-time, in addition to endowing Burton with two large churches, its municipal offices and a bridge over the River Trent; William McEwan built the magnificent McEwan Hall for Edinburgh University; Sir Andrew Walker gave Liverpool its splendid Walker Art Gallery; Lord Iveagh presented Kenwood and its contents to the nation on his death in 1927, gave £250,000 to inaugurate the Lister Institute of Preventative Medicine, and founded charitable trusts in Britain and Ireland. Many a Victorian hospital relied upon the support of its local breweries, many a Victorian church was built or restored from the profits of demon drink. For the four owning families of Bass, church construction was an obligatory exercise.[87]

Of course, not all the brewers' riches were spent so publicly or so piously. The first call was a good establishment. Again, some were ostentatious. Lord Burton and his father three times rebuilt or extended Rangemoor near Burton to live in ducal style. The son collected fashionable eighteenth-century portraits; Sir Joseph Paxton's 'genius

84 *Brewing Trade Review*, 1 Aug. 1900; information from Mr M. D. Ripley.

85 See for example the speech made by M. T. Bass when his portrait was presented to Derby Corporation, *Burton Chronicle*, 1 Dec. 1870 and his *Times* obituary, 1 May 1884. His benefactions were not restricted to Burton since he was MP for Derby, 1848–83. He presented his constituency with a recreation ground, swimming bath, free library and art gallery. The *Licensed Victuallers' Gazette* (2 May 1874) remained unimpressed, commenting it was 'some feathers being given back by the man who had taken the goose'.

86 Mostly, this charity was expended on the families of the brewery workforce. But some was more extensive. Lady Constance Combe gave an annual 'scrumptious meat tea and entertainment' for 500 children from the 'night courts, alleys and slums' of East London (*Brewers' Trade Review*, 1 Feb. 1896); Lord Burton on the wedding of his only child in 1894 gave a tea for 16,000 children in Burton and his employees 5s each to spend.

87 The Bass family built two Burton churches, and one at Rangemoor, the Grettons were active at Stapleford, the Ratcliffs at Stanford and even the junior partners, the Clays, built Newburgh church.

... made of the Rangemoor gardens and conservatories a veritable paradise'.[88] He also owned, after 1884, Chesterfield House in London and rented a famous Scottish estate, Glenquoich. Inevitably, he entertained Edward VII in all three. But the Bass's at this stage were not major landowners. M. T. Bass owned 2,283 acres scattered in five counties in 1883; Lord Burton acquired little more.[89] Rubinstein represented the post-Industrial Revolution new rich as reluctant 'to purchase land on a vast scale in the manner of their predecessors'.[90] His generalisation, if applied to the brewing industry, centres upon a definition of 'vast'. Because brewers had close ties with agriculture they more easily identified with its society and ethos. Therefore the richest frequently acquired land, sometimes on a considerable scale. H. T. Tennent (1863–90) reputedly spent a massive £200,000 on a Perthshire estate when he came of age; his elder brother owned both a Borders and a Sussex estate.[91] H. J. Younger bought one in Argyllshire for £84,750 in 1889; and although William McEwan lived unostentatiously in Edinburgh and London, his daughter, heiress and socialite hostess, the Hon. Mrs Ronald Greville, certainly did not at Polesden Lacey.[92] Sir Andrew Walker of Warrington bought 5,000 Derbyshire acres when he married, as his second wife, the daughter of a Derbyshire landowner in 1887.[93] Lord Iveagh acquired the Elveden estate from the executors of the Maharajah Duleep Singh in 1894. With its 23,000 acres, vast house, and the best shoot in England, its hospitality and management became legendary. Nearby, the Manns re-established their Norfolk roots when they acquired a sizeable south Norfolk estate around 1885; Charles F. Ryder (1856–1942), partner and shareholder in Joshua Tetley & Son, 'in middle life invested largely in farm lands and became possessed of about 20,000 acres in Suffolk and Cambridgeshire and about 5,000 acres in Yorkshire'.[94] With their brewing profits to sustain them, these families were the envy of the old landed gentry whose fortunes, if they lacked an alternative source of income, went into serious decline with the onset of prolonged agricultural depression after 1880. Partly because large-scale landownership no longer made economic sense, it became possible to make progress in county society without this traditional passport.

88 Barnard, *Noted Breweries*, I, p. 17.
89 J. Bateman, *The Great Landowners of Great Britain and Ireland* (1971 edn), p. 28.
90 W. D. Rubinstein, *Men of Property* (1981), p. 218.
91 C. McMaster and T. Rutherford, *The Tennent Caledonian Breweries* (1985), n.p.
92 *Dictionary of Scottish Business Biography*, II (1990), pp. 42–4, 77.
93 Barnard, *Noted Breweries*, II, p. 97.
94 From his obituary in the *Yorkshire Post* quoted in Lackey, *Quality Pays*, p. 71; G. Martelli, *The Elveden Enterprise* (1952).

Therefore brewers, like other entrants to this world, were content with a smaller, more manageable model estate. In this sense, brewers were seldom amongst those large landowners who found their way into the pages of John Bateman's *Great Landowners*. Nevertheless, their tendency to farm a few hundred acres and to enjoy rural pursuits remained greater than amongst captains of other industries.[95]

Some brewers, since they could afford both the time, and the expense of a London house, became, as they had in the Georgian period, Members of Parliament. Often they served for long periods, but there were seldom more than a score at any one time, except when the numbers of directors of brewing companies briefly swelled their ranks after 1886.[96] By December 1910 there were sixteen in all, no more than there had been in the late 1860s. To 1885 they were of mixed persuasion; after the Liberal–Unionist split, almost invariably Conservative. Contemporaries holding Liberal and temperance opinions exaggerated their impact and represented them as some kind of sinister cabal, frustrating through their power and wealth every move to curb the trade. Especially in Burton, local pride proclaimed the brewers' political clout. In 1868 the rhyme ran,

> Unfranchised Burton – stronger than the free,
> Great Birmingham returns no more than three;
> Yet five true senators are sent by thee,
> To teach mankind the Brewers' ABC.[97]

In 1878 the defeated MP for Tamworth who lost to M. T. Bass's second son, Hamar, thought, 'if a donkey with a barrel on its back bearing the names of Bass or Allsopp had contended the seat it would have won'.[98] But the most recent account, by David Gutzke, of the brewers' political influence has questioned it both in terms of their lack of cohesion as a group defending the industry and in the relative paucity of their financial support for its interest groups. He has even accused them of apathy.[99] Certainly, most brewers were unimpressive members. M. T.

95 Bateman, from the basis of the 'Return of Owners of Land, 1872–3', verified the entries of all those owners who possessed more than 3,000 acres of land. He also included, in footnotes of lesser detail, owners of 2,000–3,000 acres.

96 A list of MPs who were brewers between 1832 and 1914 will be found in D. Gutzke, 'Rhetoric and Reality: The Political Influence of British Brewers, 1832–1914', *Parliamentary History*, 9 (1990), pp. 78–115.

97 S. C. Allsopp (later 2nd Lord Hindhip) and M. A. Bass (later 1st Lord Burton) were MPs for East Staffordshire; M. T. Bass for Derby; G. H. Allsopp for Droitwich and O. E. Coope for Middlesex.

98 Quoted in Owen, *History of Bass*, forthcoming.

99 Gutzke, 'Rhetoric', p. 102.

Bass and George Younger, first Viscount Younger of Leckie and Chairman of the Conservative Party (1916–23), were exceptional. William McEwan, one of the shrewdest brewers of his generation, and Liberal Member for Central Edinburgh between 1886 and 1900, made little impact at Westminster.[100] And the rest were far more effective on home ground than in the House of Commons. Yet membership set the seal on their careers and provided a near certain route to a baronetcy. Their aim was the satisfaction of local status, not the pursuit of national political influence.

And most brewers were active in politics at the local level. Many became mayors, aldermen, county councillors and were tireless in local administration.[101] Often they also enjoyed being Justices of the Peace, and deputy-lieutenants and colonels in the local militia, whilst the more established and elevated became High Sheriffs of their counties. These offices were sometimes combined with mastership of foxhounds. Shooting and, for the wealthiest, steam yachting – *the* status pursuit for the Victorian and Edwardian super-rich – were also popular. Brewing could provide a plutocratic social calendar few other industries matched. Sir Walter Greene (1842–1920), from his 1,200 acre Suffolk estate, combined his ferocious stag hunting and steam yachting diary with membership of Parliament and chairmanship of the family brewers (see Plate 31). He enjoyed his £20,000 income from the brewery to the full, although this meant he often never went near it for weeks on end.[102] Others, like Frederick Gretton (1840–82), Hamar Bass (1843–98) and his son Sir William Bass (1879–1952), upset this easy balance between business and pleasure. Gretton, who owned an immensely lucrative one-eighth share in Bass in the 1870s and early 1880s, carried off his 16-year-old mistress to Paris with an abandon that would have riveted the tabloid press of today. On his death in 1882 he left, besides her, fifty-five racehorses, a 283 ton steam yacht stacked to the gunnels with champagne, and debts – easily met from the disposal of his assets – of £120,000. M. T. Bass's son and grandson, both Harrow educated and married into the peerage, lived on the grandest scale in Staffordshire, London and Newmarket. Both were addicted to the turf and, in effect, excluded from the firm. By 1913 their extravagance had outrun even the

[100] *Dictionary of Scottish Business Biography*, II (1990), pp. 42–3.

[101] For example the careers of James Hole in Newark and E. W. Lake in Bury St Edmunds (*Brewing Trade Review*, 1 June 1914; Wilson, *Greene King*, pp. 169–71).

[102] Wilson, *Greene King*, pp. 179–81, 188–9, 197–8. For his yachting exploits, see R. G. Wilson, 'Badge for the Age: Diary of an Edwardian Steam-Yacht Owner', *Country Life*, 7 Aug. 1986, pp. 446–8.

resources of the Basses and Sir William had to sell his homes and horses.[103] Such colourful footnotes to Victorian society spell out some of the ways in which the entrepreneurial talents of families could be dissipated.

Inevitably, as the honours system widened in the late nineteenth century, brewers were rewarded for their political and charitable efforts by knighthoods, baronetcies and peerages. The 'beerage' became a British institution. In fact, it always remained restricted. Burton upon Trent generated three peerages: Lord Burton (created 1886), Lord Hindlip (Allsopp, 1886) and Lord Gretton (1944); Guinness two, Lord Ardilaun (1880) and Lord, later Earl of, Iveagh (1891, 1919). Two later peerages were conferred on Sir Gilbert Greenall Bart. (Lord Daresbury, 1927) and George Younger of Alloa (Viscount Younger of Leckie, 1923). But the strict 'beerage' in effect extended to many brewers who were rewarded with baronetcies or who remained institutions in their counties like the Whitbreads in Bedfordshire or the Hanburys and Meuxs in Hertfordshire.[104] Some married into the peerage, and even a self-made brewer like Sir Andrew Walker took, as his second wife in 1887, a Maid of Honour to Queen Victoria. Others belonged to well-established county dynasties, like the Cobbolds of Ipswich; others, such as the Courages in North Yorkshire, set about founding them. Yet other brewers like the equally wealthy Georges and Vaughans in Bristol, or the Morses and Stewards in Norwich, remained essentially members of an old urban elite. Social advance was a matter of taste, ambition and resources.

All this suggests that brewers were easily accepted in county society by the late nineteenth century. And details of their schools and clubs, marriages, activities in gentlemanly sports and politics apparently underlines this. Yet even in the top echelons there was a little unease, generated by the envy of an increasingly impoverished old landed society, which underlines the prickly path newcomers from an industrial background – even one as established as brewing – had to tread when they entered the coveted portals of the old gentry. When Sir James Agg-Gardner, socially well connected, educated at Harrow and

103 These details are taken from the Private Box and voluminous Scrapbooks in the Bass Museum A135 and 558.

104 Brewing baronetcies included, Allsopp (1880), Bagge (1867), Bass (1882), Bonsor (1925), Buxton (1840), Greenall (1876), Greene (1900), Guinness (1867), Hobhouse (Whitbread, 1812), Holder (Midland Brewery Co., 1898), Holt (1916), Lacon (1818), Majoribanks (Meux, 1866; 1881 Baron Tweedmouth), Mann (1905), Meux (1831), Walker (1886), Wigram (Reid's, 1805) and Younger (1911).

Trinity College, Cambridge, and many times MP for Cheltenham, wrote his autobiography, only once did he mention his brewing connection in 246 pages of parliamentary name-dropping (See Plate 32).[105] Similarly, Sir Walter Greene's daughter wrote, in the late 1930s, an account of her life in East Anglia and London over seventy years. It was never published, but it is immensely revealing about attitudes. The references to hunting, county balls, her father's and grandfather's membership of Parliament are copious. Yet never once could she bring herself to declare the source of their advancement.[106] In these circumstances some brewers, like the Greenes, claimed ancient descent. The Allsopps sought refuge in a knight of the time of Richard I. This was too much for their arch rivals, the Basses. The compiler of their scrapbooks, which included many items on their competitors, wrote 'blurb' in the margin of the newspaper account tracing the Allsopps' illustrious descent.[107]

It is difficult to know the extent to which the brewers' rigorous pursuit of political and social advancement and those leisure pursuits which their ample time and income allowed took the edge off their entrepreneurship, blinkered their vision and endowed them with conservative values. It is all too easy to make judgements from the standpoint of the 1990s, just as it is unwise to introduce international comparisons given that British brewers, with a handful of exceptions, were never involved in an export trade. Beer was very much an industry of British dimensions. Moreover, only the minority of large brewers were self-made men; many knew nothing but material comfort from the cradle to the grave. Clearly, there were brewers like Frederick Gretton and Hamar Bass who assumed the habits of the aristocracy and took to the turf in what is believed to be classic fashion. But enterprise has never been inherited at birth. Indeed, their respective brothers, John Gretton and Lord Burton, although showing a penchant for grand living, were immensely capable in continuing the extraordinary success M. T. Bass had established. And there were brewers from similar backgrounds like Lord Iveagh or Cosmo Bonsor, both old Etonians, who were good businessmen on any count. Others from totally different backgrounds, like Sir William Waters Butler, W. P. Manners or even Sir John Ellerman, who came into the industry with a wide perspective in the 1880s,

[105] J. Agg-Gardner, *Some Parliamentary Recollections* (1927). For an autobiography it began unpromisingly, 'Personal History is not of much interest' (p. 12).

[106] The typescript was kindly lent by a member of the Greene family through the auspices of the late Dr Raymond Greene.

[107] *Evening News and Post*, 5 Nov. 1890 in Bass Scrapbook/558.

achieved similar entrepreneurial goals. All possessed drive and foresight, sometimes taking on the defence and development of the industry as well as the running of their own firm. Lord Iveagh operated at the pinnacle of Edwardian society; W. P. Manners enjoyed it very little. Certainly, the industry allowed partners and directors ample time and money, if they were inclined that way, for social and political pursuits. It was an old tradition that owners, on successfully launching their sons into the firm, should largely withdraw to enjoy their wealth. Yet with all these caveats about the quest for social advance in an undistracted British fashion, some impressive business enterprises were created in the British brewing industry. Those of Guinness, Whitbread, Bass, McEwan and William Younger and their countless 'country' imitators were the true monuments to the skills of brewers.

6

Partnerships, companies and capital, 1830–1885

Most firms in 1830 were owned by families, partners or, in the parlance of the day, sole proprietors. Because there were tens of thousands of enterprises in the brewing industry, from the struggling beer house seller to the big London breweries it is difficult to generalise about entry into the industry and the way in which the typical brewery was managed by its owners. Of course, since publican brewing continued with reasonable buoyancy to the 1870s it was possible for the one-time servant who had nurtured his savings, the small-scale maltster, the ubiquitous tenant farmer and shopkeeper, all with a taste for a rasher speculation, to begin brewing with a few hundred pounds. A tiny minority made the transition to become successful common brewers, especially in the larger industrial towns of the Midlands and North where the market for beer grew fastest. And certainly the studies of brewing at county and city level indicate large numbers of small common brewers before the 1880s who drifted in and out of brewery partnerships with a frequency that defied the numerous trade directories of the day.[1]

If it is necessary to stress that entry was not as exclusive as a quick roll-call of Victorian brewers might at first suggest and that generalisations about representative brewers and breweries invariably require qualification, the tendency, at least with the majority of common breweries, was for capital requirements to become larger as their scale grew and their holdings of tied property multiplied. This usually meant that the successful brewer after 1830 had either inherited and expanded a family enterprise or invested considerable capital in the purchase of a brewery or partnership. More rarely had he emerged from the fringe territory of the publican-cum-smaller common brewer. The first part of this chapter examines these features amongst the leading London and

[1] See for example, Gall, *Manchester Breweries of Times Gone By* (Parts 1 and 2, Swinton, 1978–80); H. Poole, *Here for the Beer, A Gazetteer of the Breweries of Hertfordshire* (1984).

country brewers between the passing of the Beer Act and the first rush by brewers to seek the benefits of limited liability in the mid-1880s.

I

The inflationary French Wars (1793–1815) had forced great changes within the partnerships of the big London porter brewers. Essentially, the need to hold larger stocks of malt, hops and casks as the scale of production increased and the cost of tying more trade by direct acquisition of pubs, or, more usually, extending loans to publicans, brought in larger numbers of partners to supply additional capital. In 1830, Barclay Perkins had eight, Truman six and Whitbread nine. Meux, at the height of its expansionary phase in 1810 had, untypically, no fewer than twenty.[2] Many of these 'new' partners were bankers or financiers: (Sir) Benjamin Hobhouse and William Wilshere, bankers in Bath and Hitchin respectively, joined Whitbread in 1800 and 1816; Sir Robert Wigram, an East India Company mogul, brought £60,000 into Meux in 1798–9; the close-knit Quaker banking network of the Barclay, Gurney and Hanbury families played a prominent role in the two largest breweries of the first half of the nineteenth century, Barclay Perkins and Truman.

Yet when the pressures of rapid growth and inflation eased there was no cut-back in the numbers of partners admitted to share the profits of the largest London breweries. Production in many of these did not increase much in the two decades after 1830 and any additional demands for capital could be met by either retaining a larger proportion of profits or, more usually, by borrowing from the partners, their friends, their publicans, and the savings clubs run from some of their pubs. These were old practices which continued to the 1880s. In this sphere the Beer Act made no break. For example, the profits of Barclay Perkins were shared by nine partners in 1837–40, twelve in 1847–53 and eleven in 1873–8.[3] Invariably they were members of the great Quaker clan of Barclay, Gurney and Bevan, with a scattering of Perkins and, after 1873, Scrivens. No more than five families shared the firm's generous profits between 1781 and 1896 when it became a limited company; only thirty-four individual partners ever attached their signature to the rest books in all these years.

[2] Mathias, *Brewing Industry*, p. 301. The paragraph is based upon his enormously detailed 'Finance and the Entrepreneur' chapters, pp. 252–338.

[3] Taken from lists of the partners who signed the annual rest. (GLRO, Acc. 2305/1/1, Barclay Perkins Partners' Record Book.)

Similarly, Whitbread was run by a succession of partnerships between 1799 and 1889. After the original deed of 1799, new ones were drawn up in 1800, 1812, 1816, 1827, 1840, 1860 and 1869 to admit replacement partners on the decease or withdrawal of others.[4] Again there were only thirty partners in ninety years. And they were almost entirely confined to the Whitbread, Godman, Hobhouse, Martineau, Shaw-Lefevre (Viscount Eversley) and Worsley families. In fact, individual partners were not called upon to supply significantly more capital in 1880 than they had done half a century earlier. In 1833 two Whitbreads, two Godmans, three Martineaus and a Hobhouse found £393,000 (it had been £440,000 in 1827), ranging from £100,000 supplied by James Godman senior to £12,500 by the youngest Martineau. Thirty years later the partners in 1865 reckoned the firm had been run on unadventurous lines for decades, and although they were themselves prepared to find more capital, there had been no expansion to encourage them to do so. By 1875 things were beginning to change. In fact the firm's capital in 1869 had increased only to £475,000 (shared by ten partners, whose holdings ranged from 147 to 912 £100 shares) and the principals were still members of the Whitbread and Godman families, although the value of the firm's assets had grown – at conservative valuations – from £646,000 in 1833 to £928,000 in 1875. The means to finance these came from deposits totalling £245,000 and the partners' retained or 'surplus' capital of £133,850 which attracted interest at 5 per cent. It was from these two sources that a large proportion of the firm's £588,120 loans to publicans were made.

Truman's accounts reveal similar features, although before the 1860s the firm possessed a more vigorous set of partners than those in Whitbread. The difference was essentially one of tradition and outlook. Whitbread was run by three families: the Whitbreads, who were great Bedfordshire landowners of almost a century's standing, the Godmans, who were rentiers, and the Martineaus, who were practical maltsters and brewers. The combination was a recipe for caution. On the other hand, Truman and Barclay Perkins partners were more adventurous. Thomas Fowell Buxton's 'Book of Observations' (1811–16) and the firm's 'Suggestion Book' indicates that none of the larger London brewers was better run than Truman before the 1860s.[5] Buxton's early

[4] This paragraph is constructed from the Whitbread Rest Books (W/22), the partnership deeds and a typescript 'The Early Partnerships of Whitbread and Co.'

[5] The following section on Truman is based upon the firm's papers, especially GLRO, Acc. 73.36, T. F. Buxton's Book of Observations 1811–16, Suggestions Book 1825–51, annual Rests for the years discussed and Clerks' Statistics 1819–45.

plan for improving profits was simple: 'this great and invaluable secret is – making our Beer the best in Town'. Reputation – paramount in a fickle, competitive trade – was 'better to acquire now by good beer, than to have to seek it then by gifts, and loans and purchases of leases'. The great anti-slavery leader was obsessive about quality and statistics, and his principles for careful management were clearly imbibed by partners in the 1830s and 1840s. The 'Suggestion Book' is full of careful calculations about savings in every aspect of brewing costs. And occasionally there are sterner entries about the need for the precise observation of them, and about the workforce generally, indicating that good management could be achieved within these large, grand partnerships.

Yet the evidence about Truman's partners' financial management is perhaps more ambiguous. As men of great wealth and status they had no apparent difficulties in supplying the extra capital which allowed the firm's output to grow from 200,000 barrels in 1831 to 455,000 in 1853: an impressive achievement, making it latterly the largest trade of any brewery in the United Kingdom, and leading to a peak of 616,458 barrels in 1875. But, unlike general practice in British industry, whereby growth was financed by the plough-back of profits, the big London breweries, each operating the unique loan-tie to secure the trade of their publicans, raised additional capital to expand the system by means best described as those of quasi-bankers. Their responses to the growth of the capital's mid-Victorian beer market reflected these arrangements. In other words their approach was different from those of the rapidly expanding country brewers, whose capital was largely internally generated in more tightly focused partnerships.

The capital raised by Truman's partners – the numbers increased from five to six in the 1830s and 1840s, and from eight to ten in the 1860s and 1870s – remained unchanged at £423,000 until 1872 (Table 6.1).[6] To sustain both growth and publican loans they resorted to increased borrowing. In 1830 this totalled £294,750 and was raised from a spectrum of lenders selected to sustain the brewery's interests. There was a balance between the resources of the partners within their wider family networks and those of the firm's thriftier publicans and drinkers. The sum of £71,290 was provided by the deposits of eighty-six 'victuallers in trade', £37,320 by fifty-nine 'persons out of trade'. The partners themselves were credited with £122,282 (largely in the names of J. T.

[6] When the 1 July 1872 rest was discussed, the partners agreed to add £423,000, their fixed loans of £434,750, together with £82,250 from the Contingency Fund to form a capital of £940,000.

Table 6.1. *Capital and loan capital of Truman Hanbury Buxton, 1830–76*

	Capital (i)	Partners' fixed loan (ii)	Victuallers (iii)	Persons out of trade (iv)	Partners' loans (v)	Private loans (vi)	Via private ledger[a] (vii)	Societies (viii)	Total (iii–viii)
1830	423,000	124,007	71,290	37,320	122,282	52,271	7,617	3,970	294,750
1838	423,000	38,500	87,575	98,518	175,000	33,417	46,780	4,413	445,703
1846	423,000	75,200	135,680	118,506	117,050	54,022	216,000	9,386	650,644
1860	423,000	289,050	184,230	154,306	124,501	64,237	149,260	7,392	683,926
1868	423,000	223,001	146,557	165,867	223,101	94,035	186,400	6,587	822,567
1876	940,000	58,750[b]	202,413	257,924	307,800	110,818	118,502	6,613	1,004,070

[a] Includes Savings Banks.

[b] From 1 July 1872, the partners agreed to transfer the fixed loan (£434,750) to the capital belonging to the partners, and £82,250 of the contingency fund to the total capital (£940,000).

Source: GLRO, Acc. 73.36, Truman's Rest Books, 1830–4, 1838–40, 1844–50, 1860–76.

22 W. H. Bailey (1847–1926), 'the prince of agents'. Bailey, a great self-publicist, was Bass's London manager from 1888 to 1909.

23 John Shorthose in 1894. Bass's Newcastle agent from 1851 to 1898, he claimed to have sold £4.4 million worth of beer in these forty-seven years.

24 Some of the ale stores and offices at Bass's agencies, *c*. 1900.

25 A view of Eldridge Pope's Dorchester brewery in 1881. Built on a green-field site, it was one of the most impressive industrial structures in the West Country.

26 The Sleaford maltings of Bass, Ratcliff & Gretton, built 1903–6. These produced around 60,000 quarters of malt a year or one-fifth of the total brewed by the company. With their 1000 ft frontage, Pevsner says: 'for sheer impressiveness little in English industrial architecture can equal the scale of this building'.

27 Bass's trip to Blackpool, 1911. The passengers of the No. 1 train (see Plate 28). The annual excursion was a great feature of life in many breweries in the 1880–1914 period.

29 Stack of 10,000 hogsheads at Bass's Dixie Ale Bank, Burton upon Trent, *c.* 1885. On the left, un-headed barrels await steam cleansing.

Train Arrangements.

"Punctuality is the Soul of Business."

The Route Map at the back of this Sheet will enable you to follow the Journey throughout.

ALL THE TRAINS will Start from Burton Railway Station (St. Paul's side Platform), and, on returning, from the EXCURSION PLATFORMS (Queen Street), adjoining the Talbot Road Station, BLACKPOOL. For Views see pages 4 and 11, and also at the back of this Sheet.

NOTE.—HAVE YOUR TICKETS READY.—All persons will be required to show their Railway Ticket at the **Doors at the Main Entrance**, and at the **Barriers** at the top of the steps, at **Burton** Station, **and none but Excursionists travelling by these Trains will be allowed upon the Platforms.** The tickets will also be examined at the Platform **Barriers** at **Blackpool** before leaving for Burton, and must be given up at the **Barriers** at **Burton Station AT NIGHT.** Persons using the Barton and Walton and Branstone Train, and the Tutbury Special, will, of course, show their Tickets in the morning, and give them up at night when alighting at their own Station. See page 9.

The Foremen and Men employed in the Various Departments, with their Wives and all others for whom they have obtained Tickets, must travel by their OWN Train—both going and returning—as under:—

No. of Train.	DEPARTMENT, &c.	OUTWARD JOURNEY Depart Burton	OUTWARD JOURNEY Arrive Blackpool.	No. of Platform at which you arrive and from which you depart.	RETURN JOURNEY Depart Blackpool	RETURN JOURNEY Arrive Burton
		A.M.	A.M.		P.M.	P.M.
1	Mr. Hodgkinson—Stables and Mr. Ollis Coppersmiths, Platelayers, Tailors, Cloggers, and Wireworkers ..	**4.0**	7.30	9	**8.0**	11.30
2	Mr. R. W. Clubb—Repairing Cooperage	**4.10**	7.40	8	**8.10**	11.45
3	Mr. R. W. Clubb—Steam Cooperage, ... Mr. Elson .. .. Mr. Ollis—Plumbers	**4.20**	7.50	7	**8.20**	11.50
4	Mr. J. Clubb—Middle Yard and Shobnall	**4.30**	8.5	6	**8.30**	MIDNIGHT. 12.0
5	Mr. J. Clubb—except Middle Yard and Shobnall . Mr. Ollis—Fitters	**4.40**	8.10	5	**8.40**	A.M. 12.10
6	Old Brewery—Mr. Ollis—Shobnall and Shobnall Old Brewery	**4.50**	8.20	4	**8.50**	12.20
7	New Brewery and Gas and Electric Works ..	**5.0**	8.30	3	**9.0**	12.30
8	Middle Brewery .. .. Mr. Ollis—Bricklayers and Painters	**5.15**	8.45	2	**9.10**	12.40
9	Mr. Williamson—Railway Department	**5.25**	9.5	1	**9.20**	12.50
10	Grain Department	**5.35**	9.15	9	**9.30**	1.5
11	Mr. Dearle .. .. Mr. Ollis—Office and Joiners	**5.45**	9.25	8	**9.40**	1.15
12	The Customers .. .. This Train will take up and set down Customers at WILLINGTON and at DERBY.	**5.55**	9.35	7	**9.50**	1.25
13	The Estate, Farm, Gardens and Stables at Rangemore and Byrkley .. .. .. This Train ONLY will take up and set down at BARTON and WALTON and BRANSTONE.	**6.5**	9.45	6	**9.55**	1.35
14	Local Special from Tutbury.	**6.15**	9.55	5	**10.10**	1.40
15	Mr. Ollis—Blacksmiths, Excavators, and Wheelwrights This Train will take up and set down Passengers at Willington, and at Derby. Derby Passengers (except Customers) must travel by this Train—both ways.	**6.25**	10.5	4	**10.20**	1.50
16	Clerks	**6.35**	10.20	3	**10.25**	2.0
17	Mr. Walters and Friends	**6.45**	10.30	2	**10.40**	2.25

Placards will be found affixed to each Train, both at Burton and Blackpool, plainly indicating the **number** of the Train. There will also be Boards—with the number of each Train—placed on the Indicator at the **bottom of the steps** leading to the Platform (to the **Right** hand) at Burton. Prominent Notices will also be found over each of the **Excursion Platforms at Blackpool**. For Views see over, and pages 4 and 11.

SPECIAL NOTE.—Third Class Passengers **must** travel—**10 in each Compartment—5 on each side**—the same as ordinary passengers—and this must be **strictly carried out in all the Trains** to accommodate the Passengers.

VERY URGENT.—It is **imperative** that all persons should **Travel both Ways** by their **Own Train**, and most urgently does this apply to the **Earlier** Trains on the **Return** Journey. The Lancashire and Yorkshire Railway Company are most particular about you travelling by your **own** Train, and seeing **Your Ticket**, so be fully prepared at Blackpool at night.

☞ **Remember to bring ALL your Railway Tickets, and have them ready at Burton and Blackpool Stations.**

For Views of the Excursion Platforms at Talbot Road Station, Blackpool, our Special Cloak Room, Lavatories and Way Out, see back of this Sheet, and pages 4 and 11; and for the direct way from Talbot Road Ordinary Station to these Excursion Platforms—see page 11.

For Special Tramway arrangements at Burton, and from and to Gresley and Ashby—see pages 13 and 14, and Special Note at side of this Sheet.

SPECIAL NOTES

TUTBURY.—As the last train in now timed to arrive at Burton at **2-25** a.m., it is hoped that the Tutbury Local Special will be run as under, instead of as stated on page 9, viz:—

Leave	Burton	2-30 a.m. (Saturday).
Arrive	Stretton and Clay Mills ...	2-35 ,,
,,	Rolleston	2-40 ,,
,,	Tutbury	2-50 ,,

GRESLEY.—A Car will also leave Gresley Station at **4-25** a.m., calling at the "Rising Sun," Swadlincote, &c, and return from Burton Station about **2-30** a.m, (Saturday). FARES, each way, from Gresley Station, **10d.**; "Rising Sun," **8d.**; and from other places as stated on page 14.

ASHBY.—The Return Car to Ashby will probably be able to leave at **2-30** a.m. (Saturday) instead of at 2-45 as stated on page 14.

28 The train arrangements for Bass's 1911 trip. In some years the trains conveyed 10,000 employees, families and friends. Bass issued a special illustrated brochure; William Walters organised the trips with Napoleonic vision for almost fifty years.

30 King Edward VII, assisted by Bass's head-brewer, Cornelius O'Sullivan, FRS, opening the malt-hoppers to start a special brew – the King's Ale – on 22 February 1902.

31 Sir Walter Greene Bt. (1842–1920) of Greene King seen at the wheel of his 460 ton steam-yacht, *RYS Agatha*. A typically rich brewer, Sir Walter was addicted to hunting, carriage-driving and his succession of steam-yachts – *the* status symbol of Edwardian society.

32 Sir James Agg-Gardner (1846–1927). Sole proprietor and later chairman of the Original Brewery, Cheltenham. Educated at Harrow and Trinity College, Cambridge, he represented Cheltenham in many parliaments between 1874 and 1927.

CITY LIFE
No. 15. Vol. I.]
WEDNESDAY, MARCH 12, 1890.
[Price One Penny.
REGISTERED FOR TRANSMISSION ABROAD.]
LONDON AND
WESTMINSTER BANK
POOR OLD ALLSOPP!
The Directors of the London and Westminster Bank allotted the shares of Allsopp, Limited. Mr. R. J. Ashton was allotted 1,500, Messrs. Benecke had 1,000 shares, Mr. J. N. Bullen had 2,000, Mr. F. J. Edlemann 3,000, Sir P. G. Julyan 3,000, Lord Magheramorne 5,000, Mr. F. H. Norman 1,000. All these gentlemen are London and Westminster Directors, and have all sold their shares—at least, their names do not now appear on the register. They have, in fact, turned up Allsopp. (See p. 114.)
VIRTUOUS BANK DIRECTOR: I can't have you here, my good fellow. It's true I once did some business with you, but now—well, you've fallen so low I must really ask you to go away!

33 'Poor Old Allsopp' (1890). In this cartoon, a director of the London and Westminster Bank (it had allocated Allsopp's shares in 1887) moves on a collapsed Allsopp after their dividends crashed in 1889–90.

34 The 'Crown', Cricklewood, before its refurbishment by the Cannon Brewery in 1898. Cannon acquired and improved some of the biggest public houses in London in the late 1890s.

35 The same house, *c.* 1930 – some thirty years after its 'Jacobean' face-lift.

36 Watneys' 'The Queen's Arms', Peckham (*c.* 1890), a typical end-of-terrace London public house. Note the fine show-boards, the main one incorporating the firm's stag emblem.

37 The bar of the 'Dover Castle', Westminster Bridge Road (1895), opulent in glass, mahogany and gasoliers.

38 The 'Crooked Billet', Newcastle upon Tyne (*c.* 1898). Opposite Armstrong-Whitworth Co.'s works, it sold for £15,700 in 1896. It was cited in Rowntree and Sherwell, *Temperance Problem*, as an example of the insane prices for which public houses changed hands in the late 1890s.

39 Ind Coope's 'Portland Beer Stores', 12 Horner Road, Sheffield (*c.* 1910). There were almost 18,000 of these beer off-licences scattered across England and Wales at the end of the First World War.

40 Bottling plant, Brakspear's Brewery, Henley-on-Thames (*c*. 1900). Although many breweries introduced bottling from the 1890s, this plant was a far cry from those of Worthington, Whitbread and the big independent contract bottlers.

41 The vast crowd of demonstrators against the 1908 Licensing Bill marching towards Hyde Park, 27 September 1908. *The Daily Graphic* estimated the crowd as numbering 750,000.

Villebois and Robert Pryor) and their 'private friends' with £52,271. These were invariably family trusts or the deposits of Hanbury, Buxton, Pryor connections, except for £7,617 placed by 'Savings Banks'. In addition, twenty-four friendly societies ranging from the 'Thoughtful Sisters' to the 'Sons of Prudence', and presumably run from the larger Truman pubs, were credited with £3,970. On the other hand, there were 'loans out of trade' of £32,868 (besides those made to publicans) and £2,000 lent to ten of the pawnbrokers who were such essential props of working-class budgets in the East End. It is a nice irony: immensely upright Quaker brewers making loans to sustain the drink culture of the poorest in the 1830s.

Over the years, borrowings grew: to £650,644 in 1846, and to £1,004,070 in 1876. Those sources tapped in 1830 expanded. The number of publicans in and out of trade who made deposits increased; as did the partners' surplus capital, reserves or 'fixed loans' (i.e. attracting 5 per cent interest) as Truman designated them. Moreover, deposits by saving banks grew – they were £118,502 in 1876 – besides loans made by the partners themselves or their family and friends. But what is equally of interest in this expansion of capital is the investments the firm made as its profits accelerated.

Breweries by their nature were always cash-rich ventures. Of course provision had to be made for the great seasonal purchases of malt and hops, but in summer their cash flow was positive. Already in June 1838 the firm had £20,000 deposited with two bill brokers and £10,000 in Long Annuities. By 1846, a year of heady speculation, investment had mushroomed. No less than £100,000 was placed with Overend Gurney, and £50,000 with another broker, Bruce & Co. In addition £40,000 was invested in three railway companies, £20,000 with the Liverpool Paving Co., £7,449 in American ventures, and £30,000 as a loan made to George Hudson, the Railway King. In these high-feather conditions, the credit extended to three pawnbrokers was restricted to £350.

How far fingers were burnt with the Hudson connection is uncertain, but the 1860 rest book still recorded £75,000 'cash at brokers' (including £55,000 with Overend Gurney), £47,418 cash 'at Home and Bank', and £4,000 at 'Country Banks'. There was also £218,753 in twenty investments which were beginning to look like a typical big Victorian investment portfolio with British and foreign railway shares, Exchequer Bills and municipal loans prominent. The £8,100 lent to Lambeth Vestry underlined the firm's local links. In 1876 investments totalled £361,922.

The quasi-banking nature of the firm is clear. Its ample profits were by no means all extracted annually but allowed to accumulate as 'fixed loans' in proportion to each partner's shares. Further loans were made by the richer partners as well as those advanced in the name of family trusts and nominee accounts. In addition, the firm attracted substantial deposits, easily placed and withdrawn, from publicans, friendly societies and savings banks. Indeed, capital was more plentiful than could be consumed in Truman's brewing activities. Partners therefore sought an outlet for it in other investments. Not surprisingly, the management of loans and investments became their chief function. Of course, they realised that progress was not to be made without brewing consistently good beer, but much of the day-to-day running of the firm could be left to a couple of junior partners and the departmental managers. At Truman the key figure was the head brewer, George Gow, an immensely loyal servant of the firm from 1822 to 1855. The 'clerks statistics 1819–45' volume reveals others, John Raffety, William Adams and James Young all encouraged by generous salaries and 'presents', but Gow's salary best indicates the dependence the partners placed upon him – raised from £525 to £835 in 1832, and eventually reaching £1,815 between 1850 and 1855 when he left abruptly 'owing to peculiar circumstances' with a £400 pension. But in 1834 one of the partners could write, 'we are perfectly satisfied with Gow's zeal and hearty interest in our welfare. We think there is not a man in London equal to him.' Praise indeed, and clearly reflected in Truman's sale figures in these years. His competence meant that the principal partners could oversee the complex finances of the firm and enjoy a way of life of the utmost comfort in Essex and Hertfordshire. Indeed, this was no different from that of partners in the biggest London banks. And of course it was quite impossible for newcomers to break into this most select of business coteries. Family connection was everything. All loans, besides those readily accepted from publicans and savings banks, were drawn from the family networks of Villebois, Hanbury, Buxton and Pryor. Above all, because the potential supply was plentiful, partners were restricted entirely to direct male descendants. There was then a gentle weeding-out process which selected for advancement those most interested in the brewery's affairs. Nevertheless, it was only too easy for middle-aged partners to live upon their ample profits and interest and, without a second thought, spend their days hunting, shooting and socialising, managing their estates and farms, and joining the gentry and clergy in the running of county administrations.[7]

Other breweries of note and tradition in the capital were similarly run as large partnerships. If Barclay Perkins, Truman and Whitbread, whose partners were by-words for wealth and probity, jostled for position at the top of the tree, in London's business elite, there were others who scrabbled for a foothold immediately beneath them. The firms of Combe, Elliot, Watney & Co., Reid's, Meux, Calvert (City of London Brewery after 1860) and Hoare were almost equally celebrated institutions.[8] They were owned and run by the same partnership structures, there was the same reliance upon junior partners and well-paid managers, brewers and confidential clerks to keep the breweries running efficiently on a day-to-day basis, the same need to provide generous publican loans and capital to sustain ventures which, in comparison with all except Guinness, Bass and Allsopp, were exceptionally large brewing ventures even in the 1880s. Of course there were differences in style and management, just as there were between Truman and Whitbread. Reid's and Hoare possessed great reputations for their porters and stouts, Watney and Combe for their ales. The latter also had strong distilling interests. Reid's, with eleven partners in 1850, possessed the largest partnership structure of any British brewery. Watneys by the 1860s was essentially run by a single family which, in James Watney (1800–84), possessed one of the toughest father figures of any Victorian brewery. But in all of them there was the same stress upon tradition and exclusiveness. Only rarely were newcomers accepted into partnerships, and then their financial and business credentials had to be immaculate. James Watney, who bought in 1837 a quarter share (for a term of fourteen or twenty-one years as the parties might agree) in Elliott's historic Stag Brewery, Pimlico, came from a family of millers in the Wandsworth area, who had seen their milling, baking and distilling ventures burgeon after the 1780s.[9] Within five years he and his brother Daniel had £160,000 invested in the brewery. When in 1852 a further

[7] The best account of the social range of an early Victorian brewer is to be found in G. Curtis, *A Chronicle of Small Beer* (1970), a book based upon the diaries of John Izzard Pryor (1774–1861), a member of the famous Baldock brewing family. His brothers Robert and Arthur were partners in Truman Hanbury Buxton for many years.

[8] This section is based upon the invaluable Reid's 'Abstract of Rests', GLRO, Acc. 75.108 and Watney's archive in the Westminster City Archive, Acc. 789. Barnard provides an account of each brewery around 1890 and Hurford Janes, *The Red Barrel: A History of Watney Mann* (1963) attempted to piece together a sustained account of the Watney, Combe and Reid's breweries before their amalgamation in 1898.

[9] Janes, *Red Barrel*, pp. 96–103.

partner's widow withdrew her late husband's £111,000 capital and loans, Joseph Bonsor and John Tanqueray were brought into a new partnership to supply additional capital. The former, from Nottinghamshire, had many business interests; the latter was both a Bedfordshire landowner and a partner in a neighbouring distillery.[10]

But most partners in these half-dozen breweries were drawn from the hard core of their owners' families. Provision was made for one generation to introduce another of sons and nephews as the occasion arose; in interests and status they were no different from those of the top three London breweries. Amongst the senior partners were MPs, Lord Mayors of London, art collectors, bankers and masters of foxhounds. Others were prominent in the affairs of the East India Company; John Elliott was a Fellow of the Royal Society.[11] They were plutocrats, equally at home in the capital's banking, commercial and political circles, or in the Home Counties of Surtees, pursuing the fox, breeding fat cattle, and growing exotic fruits at vast expense.

Certainly, it was a world of tradition. Colonel Oswald Serocold, a great-nephew of the Wigrams (who together with the Reids and Allfreys formed the ownership and management of Reid's Clerkenwell brewery in the nineteenth century), recollected: 'When I first entered the business [1886], and indeed until the 1890s, the wearing of top hats by directors, office staff and brewers was compulsory. In the case of Reid and Company I remember that a fine of a guinea was imposed on anyone entering the brewing room without observing this rule.'[12] He also commented upon the firm's obsession with secrecy in both the brew house and the offices. There was resort to coded thermometer scales and partly faked entries in the brewing books; as in other firms, only the partners were allowed to see the accounts. In such an environment innovation did not permeate the partnerships easily.

Occasionally, there was a hiccough as direction passed from one generation to another. Edward Delafield, a junior partner with £79,200 invested in Combe Delafield, frittered away £100,000 on the Theatre Royal Covent Garden, the Royal Italian Opera and a Belgian singer in the early 1840s. His capital was a loss to the firm, although his repu-

10 Janes, *Red Barrel*, p. 119.

11 Janes, *Red Barrel passim*, provides good examples from the Watney Combe Reid partnerships; see also R. Wigram, *Biographical Notes Relating to Certain Members of the Wigram Family* (1912). Unusually, Frederick du Cane Godman, a director of Whitbread, was joint editor of the massive 63-volume *Biologia Centralia-Americana*. There is a monument to him in the Natural History Museum.

12 Quoted in W. P. Serocold (ed.), *The Story of Watneys* (1949), pp. 18–19.

tation was not.[13] But his uncle and senior partner, Harvey Combe, seemingly learnt few lessons from the débâcle, for when he died in 1858 succession amongst the partners was not clear cut. Unusually, his two brewers, James Groves and William Dell, had been given just before his death one-fifth of his shares to ensure the smooth working of the brewery. For his nephews and heirs, Richard and Charles Combe, had not been trained as brewers; the former enjoyed his 1,500 acre estate; the latter had been on active service in India for twenty years. The hiatus allowed Joseph Bonsor to seize his opportunity. He increased his holding to a massive £370,000, becoming senior partner, and, with his son Cosmo, steering Combe to greater achievements.[14] Barnard noted it had become London's second brewery; Cosmo was the architect of the great amalgamation in 1898 of Watney Combe Reid.

The key problem in partnerships was ensuring continuity of direction across generations. Capacity in businesses, unlike the fortunes made in them, was not invariably inherited. This brought periodic strains which no partnership deed, however carefully worded, could prevent. Moreover, senior partners, anxious to enjoy the fruits of their inheritance and labours, devolved day-to-day management to juniors and senior salaried staff. At the level of the highly routinised procedures of brewing, of the purchase of materials, of distribution, and of public house loans, management by the big London partnerships was first rate, and control by ledgers and clerks was meticulous. But in matters of strategy, because senior partners reviewed their firms' finances with a rentier mentality, worrying about family loans and trusts, partnerships were less efficient. In addition, the problems created when partners or their heirs wished to withdraw their capital (see pp. 86–9) sometimes took a long time to resolve and provided an inducement for the move to company status in the 1880s. But in the 1830–80 period, withdrawal could lead to the introduction of more enterprising partners like the Bonsors and James Watney. Nevertheless, the entire partnership system, considered in terms of recruiting ability, was something of a lottery.

Not all London breweries were run on these highly traditional, spacious lines. It is easy to forget that there were tiers of second- and third-rate breweries below the dozen top enterprises which dominated brewing in the capital and its environs. The excise officials recorded 115

13 See Edward T. Delafield's letters to his uncle, Harvey Combe, and related papers in Westminster City Archive, Acc. 789/751–764.

14 Janes, *Red Barrel*, pp. 120–1.

common breweries in the London collection district in 1831, 113 in 1880. These smaller breweries often struggled, prospered when times were good, admitted new partners, and occasionally came up for sale. Gardner's Cannon Brewery in Clerkenwell, thirteenth in the list of 107 London brewers in 1837 (brewing around 60,000 barrels a year), was sold in 1863 with fifty-eight public houses, principally leasehold, for a total valuation of £110,102. The new owners, George Hanbury and Barclay Field, were hop factors, cousins and, most importantly, grandsons of Osgood Hanbury, a leading Truman partner.[15] Clearly, since working capital had also to be found, entry at this level was not cheap. Nor was it elsewhere, as the size of almost all breweries in the capital grew in the Victorian period. More rarely, complete newcomers entered the brewing scene. A new brewery at Stratford, built up after 1855 by the two Savill brothers, was an unusual venture. Entirely financed within a partnership confined to them, Barnard found in 1890 that it was flourishing with an output in the region of 150,000 barrels.[16]

There were also tightly run family firms like J. & R. Farnell of Isleworth, Charrington and Courage, whose partners were drawn from single family proprietorships. Until publican loans burgeoned in the 1860s and 1870s, they were run on middling capitals. J. & R. Farnell of Isleworth had seen the valuation of its brewing concern grow rapidly to £120,000 by the 1830s; Charrington's capital grew from £110,000 to £168,000 between 1839 and 1860; Courage's partners divided one of £155,150 in 1851.[17] Of course, the supply of direct male heirs and the avoidance of major injections of new capital were crucial factors in allowing these enterprises to remain within the control of a single family. Since, however, they shared increasingly large profits, they were able both to secure expansion and restrict their distribution within a tightly defined family circle.

The most thrusting brewery in London in the generation after the Beer Act, however, followed a course of expansion more usually seen in large provincial cities during the brewing boom of the 1860s and 1870s. James Mann, a migrant from Norfolk, bought with his partner the struggling Albion Brewery at the Mile End turnpike gate in Bethnal Green for £2,420 in 1819.[18] Its output was a mere 1,730 barrels. Mann

[15] F. A. King, *The Story of the Cannon Brewery* (1951), pp. 6–7.

[16] Barnard, *Noted Breweries*, III, pp. 422–39.

[17] H. Janes, *Albion Brewery 1808–1958. The Story of Mann, Crossman & Paulin Ltd* (1958), pp. 18–19; L. A. G. Strong, *Brewer's Progress, 1757–1957* (1957), p. 52; G. N. Hardinge, *The Development and Growth of Courage's Brewery* (1932), p. 11.

[18] This paragraph is based upon Janes, *Albion Brewery*.

transformed the brewery within the next twenty years so that by the early 1840s he had built up a remarkable trade of around 60,000 barrels almost entirely through the new beer house outlets. Yet when he died in 1846, the firm, like many a partnership in this situation, was thrown into a deep managerial crisis. Of his three sons, one had predeceased him by three weeks; the eldest, such was the profitability of a good brewery, had already bought an estate in Northamptonshire and was uninterested in an East End business; the youngest had barely reached his majority. Through a remote family connection, two brewers from Berwick-upon-Tweed, Robert Crossman and Thomas Paulin, were therefore, brought into the firm to form the partnership of Mann, Crossman & Paulin. Both men, who had worked at Farnell's Isleworth brewery in the late 1820s and early 1830s, were from textbook self-help backgrounds. The valuation of the brewery in 1846 was £54,907: Crossman could afford a quarter share, Paulin an eighth. Mann's were fortunate in that Robert Crossman was one of the most enterprising brewers in mid-Victorian London. By the early 1860s the firm enjoyed an output of around 220,000 barrels, with profits in a good year in excess of £40,000. A decade later, when sales had stabilised, six partners, some from the second and third generations, contributed a capital of £400,000. Except in style and the origins of its partners, Mann, Crossman & Paulin had become comparable with the greatest London breweries. Yet with its strong beer house connections and rapid growth from unpromising origins and location, it was an unusual enterprise amongst the leading London breweries. Elsewhere such progress was more usual.

II

Because there were always more than 2,000 *common* breweries in the 1830–80 period, with tens of thousands of individual partners involved in their ownership, it is not easy to single out the typical country brewery partnership in these years. For in their origins, in the provision of capital and in their enterprise, they varied enormously. It is possible to sustain a quadruple division. First, there were those partnerships already well established, particularly in the South and East of England. Many prospered, some of them, like Bass and Allsopp, spectacularly; almost all of them enjoyed expansion in the boom years of the 1860s and 1870s. To these we shall return in more detail, because they illustrate the fundamental features of country brewing partnerships. But the others merit a moment's attention. The second category includes many

Victorian brewing concerns, especially in those areas that were strongholds of publican brewing, whose origins were modest but which by the plough-back of profits and a tough, clear management line broke clear of their countless local competitors. And because their roots were in the industrial heartland of Britain, some of these breweries were large enterprises by the 1880s. Examples abound in Barnard; a few stray facts about others can be derived from slender company histories.[19] Two brief examples here must suffice to epitomise the history of many Northern and Midlands breweries which were flourishing by the 1890s. Joseph Holt's Cheetham (Manchester) brewery traces its origins to a humble beer house around 1849. Acquiring almost a pub a year in the 1860s and 1870s, it expanded very rapidly between the late 1880s and early 1900s when around a hundred more were bought. The father of Joseph Holt (1813–86), the founder, had been an Unsworth weaver's child; his son Edward (1849–1928) was created a baronet in 1916.[20] Such was the transforming power of brewing. In Tadcaster the entire town was energised by the activities of the Smiths. Yet their credentials as brewers were recent and modest. John Smith, the 24-year-old son of a Meanwood (Leeds) tanner, had bought in 1847 a Tadcaster coaching inn which brewed its own beer (see Plate 14). The early records of the firm do not survive, but it is clear that by brewing a first-class range of beers sold at generous discounts in the West Riding industrial towns, he, his brother and his nephews (who were trained in the brewery) put Tadcaster on the brewing map. The nephews, Riley-Smiths by this stage, entertained Barnard in royal style in 1890; as well they might, on profits topping £50,000 in a good year. When in 1892 the firm went public, its prospectus claimed, in a shower of superlatives, that it was a brewery 'of the most perfect description ... the most modern and complete in the North of England'. Indisputably, it was valued with its tied houses at £357,030.[21] There was little of tradition here. Neither

[19] See the entries in Barnard, *Noted Breweries* for Peter Walker (Warrington), W. Butler (Wolverhampton), Groves & Whitnall (Manchester), Soames (Wrexham), Hardy & Hanson (Nottingham), Halliwell (Bolton). See also the Supplement of the *Burton Daily Mail*, 3 Aug. 1906 for W. Butler. He was an iron-worker, who kept an off-licence and brewed in his spare time in the 1840s. Forty years later he was brewing 100,000 barrels a year. The early history of Boddingtons', Matthew Brown, the Burton Wood brewery, Chesters (Manchester) and Mitchells (Lancaster) reveal similar origins and growth patterns.

[20] N. Richardson, *A History of Joseph Holt* (1984).

[21] This information is supplied by Mr G. Tattershall-Walker, a former director, who has created a small museum and archive in the old brewery at Tadcaster. Virtually no records survive for the pre-1892 period. The early directors' minute books of the new

Holt nor Smith could claim the benefits of an expensive education, training or inherited wealth; nor could they rely upon established partners. They ploughed their profits into their ventures, they bought property wisely, they seized their chance in an expanding market; their sons and nephews enjoyed great riches. Many a Northern and Midlands brewery shared a similar history.

The third category of brewery, those owned by a single proprietor, were a rarer species. Breweries in the North, like those of Joseph Holt, John Crook at Darwen and J. W. Lees of Middleton Junction, flourished through the energies of a sole owner.[22] And there were other more historic breweries like Agg-Gardner's in Cheltenham and S. L. Seckham's Northampton Brewery Co. whose ownership was similarly concentrated.[23] Agg-Gardner's, the *Licensed Victualler's Gazette* claimed in 1875, was 'the largest brewery in England, and probably therefore in the world, which is the sole and entire property of one man'. Clearly what made them different was the reliance they necessarily had to place upon their general manager and head-brewer. Indeed, when J. T. Agg-Gardner (1846–1928) was a minor and a ward of Chancery, the Court would only confirm the brewery's manager on an enormous security of £36,000.[24] Devolved management continued because Agg-Gardner was MP for Cheltenham for many years after 1874 (see Plate 32). These breweries worked well enough if the proprietor had drive. Agg-Gardner did not and, in this situation, the widening of the firm's ownership and management when it secured limited liability in 1888 removed some uncertainties.

The fourth category of brewery isolated an unusual entrant to the industry, the gentleman brewer. In the section below on country brewing partnerships it is argued that, as in London, the level of profitability and ease in raising money ensured an unusual continuity within the industry. It was in these conditions difficult to secure a good partnership. Yet by the 1870s the profitability of brewing was being trumpeted to all. Therefore there were a number of gentlemen, even aristocratic entrants to the trade, attracted by its wealth-generating potential and seeming ease of management. Barnard noted that the

company (JA/B/63–4) are singularly uninformative beyond details of property transactions and transfers of debenture shares.

22 Barnard, *Noted Breweries*, IV, pp. 229–33, 446–61.

23 *Licensed Victuallers' Gazette*, 13 Feb.; 9 Oct. 1875.

24 *Licensed Victuallers' Gazette*, 13 Feb. 1875. See also Wilson, *Greene King*, pp. 60–95 for the long period after 1836 when Edward Greene ran his Bury St Edmund's brewery as sole proprietor.

Trent Valley Brewery Co. had been founded by 'a company of gentlemen in Lichfield in the year 1875, when there was such a demand for Burton ales, who determined that the building and plant should be erected in the best possible manner and fitted with modern appliances regardless of cost'.[25] Others possessed more elevated partners. Robert Tennant (1827–1900) bought the Brunswick Brewery, Leeds, in 1873. A member of an old Dales family, he was a one-time Leeds solicitor, then, successively, flax-spinner, brewer, MP for Leeds (1874–80), a director of the Great Northern Railway, and chairman of several coal and iron companies.[26] His partners in the brewing venture had impeccable Yorkshire connections: R. D. Marshall, by then a Lakeland landowner, was a grandson of the pioneer industrialist, John Marshall; the Hon. Cecil Duncombe was the younger son of the second Lord Feversham. 'None of these gentlemen had previously had any connection with the brewery or breweries', commented the *Licensed Victuallers' Gazette* in its laudatory piece on the brewery. Indeed, Tennant had become a speculator, and on a large scale. 'Small enterprises had no attraction for him; he always dealt in big figures', wrote the *Yorkshire Post* on his death.[27] Similarly, John David Beverley Faber (1854–1932), who transformed Strong of Romsey after the 1880s into one of the leading breweries in the South of England, belonged very firmly to that Victorian upper-middle-class elite whose tentacles embraced big business, banking, the law and landownership.[28] The Brains who acquired the Old Brewery in Cardiff in 1882, and who undertook a programme of headlong expansion in the Welsh boom town in the next decade, were members of an old Gloucestershire family, again with banking connections.[29] But those aristocrats who joined Hotham's York brewery (the Tadcaster Tower, or Snobs brewery as it was locally known, after 1882) in 1879 possessed no such business acumen. In 1879 Sir Frederick

[25] Barnard, *Noted Breweries*, IV, pp. 124–34.

[26] *Licensed Victuallers' Gazette*, 4 Sept. 1875.

[27] Quoted in H. Owen, *Stanhope, Atkinson, Haddon and Shaw: Four North Country Families* (privately printed, 1985), p. 191. Tennant was an unusually interesting man. He undertook the obligatory entertainment of the Prince of Wales at his Ross-shire shooting lodge; he wrote books on Sardinia and British Guinea; he had interests in the US and Canada; he was involved in proposals to build a grand hotel and pleasure park at the Niagara Falls.

[28] See Burke's *Landed Gentry* (1937 edn), 'Faber late of Ampfield House'. Faber's mother was a member of the Beckett-Denison families and sister of the first Lord Grimthorpe. His two elder brothers were both raised to the peerage: Lord Faber was senior partner in Beckett's Bank, a railway director and MP; Lord Wittenham was also a partner in the bank and a Member of Parliament for twenty years.

[29] Barnard, *Noted Breweries*, III, pp. 466–84.

Milner, seventh baronet, and the Hon. Reginald Parker, sixth son of the Earl of Macclesfield, each became partners in the brewery, each putting up £20,000 to buy fifty overpriced York pubs. Further finance was provided by the third Earl of Durham and in 1882, when a new brewery was built at Tadcaster, the Hon. George Dawnay was admitted to the partnership. All four were connected by marriage, all had been to Eton, all were more interested in the Turf than in the intricacies of brewing. Of the quartet, only Parker put in anything like a regular appearance at the brewery, but most of his considerable efforts to secure the army canteen trade around York were conducted from the deep armchairs of the smoking room of the Yorkshire Club.[30] Three of Lord Tollemache's nine sons bought the Ipswich brewery of Charles Cullingham in 1888 for £100,000. Their father, the owner of two great romantic houses, Peckforton and Helmingham, was, according to the family chronicler, 'horrified and considered it degrading to the name of Tollemache'. But again generalisation, even restricted to this handful of breweries, is difficult. For Strong and Brain were highly successful breweries; so was Tollemache, in its way, in Ipswich.[31]

These three categories of breweries were not, however, typical of partnerships existing in the industry between the 1830s and the 1880s in much of Britain. For most sizeable towns from Dorset to Northumberland, in Burton upon Trent, Liverpool, Edinburgh, Alloa and Glasgow, possessed classic, established country brewing partnerships. Again, almost invariably these were closed. Profits were ample and, therefore, as in London, not to be shared by outsiders or salaried staff unless there was a crisis in continuity or in the provision of capital. And because these brewers were men of fortune, often with considerable public house investments, their sons and nephews underwent an expensive training. Most frequently in the early Victorian period their early education had been acquired in the local grammar school or some private establishment. William Lucas, a well-read, sixth-generation brewer from Hitchin, went from John Dyer's School in the town to one at Fishponds near Bristol before, unusually, commencing a five years' training with Edward and Frederick Smith, Quaker chemists in the

30 W. Swales, *The History of the Tower Brewery Tadcaster* (1991). Ethel, Lady Thomson, *Clifton Lodge* (1955), provides a fascinating view of her father, the Hon. Reginald Parker, and family.

31 The brewery had sixty-nine tied houses of various descriptions and a London adjunct. Major-General Devereux-Hamilton Tollemache (*The Tollemaches of Helmingham and Ham, Ipswich* (1949), pp. 171–2) considered 'the brewery had been a brilliant financial success and the courage of a younger brother's venture [it was effectively run by the Hon. Douglas Tollemache] has proved a blessing to the whole family'.

Haymarket, London. That was in 1819 and his father paid the Smiths a £250 premium; he was a model apprentice, regularly attending Brade's and Faraday's lectures at the Royal Institution.[32] Those brewers of grander status like the Lacons of Yarmouth, the Cobbolds of Ipswich and the Agg-Gardners of Cheltenham educated their sons in the major public schools. And by the 1860s, as the number and reputation of the latter grew, many other brewers were sending their sons to them. Edward Greene (1815–91) and his three brothers (one became a distinguished Governor of the Bank of England) were all educated at Bury St Edmunds Grammar School in the 1820s and 1830s; but Edward's only son Walter (1842–1920), always destined for the family brewery, went, following a year at his father's reputable old school, to Rugby.[33] Such was the case with Archibald and George Brakspear of Henley-on-Thames, 'After a spell at Henley Grammar School they had both been sent to one of the new public schools for the gentry, Marlborough.'[34] Robert Tennant had been educated at Leeds Grammar School. But his seven sons went either to Rugby or to Harrow in the 1860s and 1870s.[35] Sometimes, because sons were numerous and the partnership succession not clear cut, they had spells at university. Tennant's eldest son went from Rugby to Christchurch, Oxford; George Henry Morse (1857–1931), the second son of Steward & Patteson's senior partner, was educated with a view to finding a post in the Public Works Engineering Department in India.[36] Only when his elder brother became seriously ill was he recalled to the Norwich brewery.

The education of the four sons of John Izzard Pryor (1774–1861), a wealthy Baldock brewer, is particularly instructive about patterns of education in prosperous country partnerships. The first three were educated at Charles Blomfield's private school in Bury St Edmunds. Since it was old established and Blomfield's eldest son became Bishop of London in 1828 the school was unusually prestigious amongst private academies. The two eldest sons, John (1800–53) and Morris (1804–71), were already effectively running the brewery by the time their father began to keep a diary in 1827. No mention is made of their training: most likely it was at Truman where both the diarist's two younger

[32] G. E. Bryant and G. P. Baker (eds.), *A Quaker Journal, being the Diary and Reminiscences of William Lucas of Hitchin (1804–1861)* (1934), I, pp. 43–54.

[33] Wilson, *Greene King*, pp. 47, 112.

[34] Sheppard, *Brakspear's Brewery*, p. 71.

[35] *Licensed Victuallers' Gazette*, 4 Sept. 1875; *Burke's Landed Gentry* (1937 edn), Tennant of Arncliffe Cote late of Chapel House and Tennant of Hatfield Peverel.

[36] Gourvish, *Norfolk Beers*, pp. 49–50.

brothers and a nephew were partners. But the third son Alfred (1811–76) was a problem. The father discussed his prospects at Bury with James Blomfield in 1828:

> [I] explained to him my intentions respecting my son remaining only half a year longer and that I wished him to pay particular attention to the Mathematics, Mensuration, Merchants' Accounts, Surveying and the use of the globes, and to resume his dancing. He is therefore not to attend at Dr. Malkins [the Grammar School] this half which will allow him time for other studies. This plan is pretty generally adopted for those boys not intended for either of the universities.[37]

But Alfred was slow to settle down. He spent four idle years at Cley Hall, the family's recently acquired Hertfordshire estate, before his father decided to spend £1,000 on sending him for two years training with an English merchant in Hamburg. In fact Alfred had been in Germany almost three years when, in the summer of 1836, his father planned to buy the Hatfield brewery, primarily with a view to making 'a capital settlement' for him. In fact the diarist got cold feet about the venture. It was not the total capital outlay of £40,000 that troubled him, so much as his two elder sons being reluctant to join any enterprise with Alfred. For in the midst of the scheme they had to reveal to their father that he had 'got into a detestable scrape in London with a diseased female'.[38] Six months later the brewery unexpectedly came back on the market; this time the two brothers took the lead in acquiring the Hatfield brewery. Yet they could have had no more faith in Alfred's training as a brewer than they had in his morals, for, however much the vocation flowed in Pryor veins, his apprenticeship was sketchy indeed. Entry to the brewery was fixed for Lady Day 1837. Only on 12 February was it 'arranged with Morris for Alfred to go to Baldock on Tuesday to accompany them to Hitchin market, and to begin to acquire a knowledge of the Brewery Department by getting up to brew with Mr. Tranter and go through the whole process for several brewings; and at other times accompany their clerk Robins to the public houses belonging to the Hatfield Brewery to become acquainted with the publicans'.[39] Three days later, John Izzard noted with some relief: 'I found him with his apron on and looking like a brewer. He seems to like it very well.'[40] Alfred was then 26. After the trials of this costly risk, not surprisingly, the fourth son (by a second marriage) Frederick (1822–60) was pre-

[37] Curtis, *Chronicle of Small Beer*, p. 25.
[38] *Ibid.*, p. 29.
[39] *Ibid.*, p. 31.
[40] *Ibid.*, p. 32.

pared, via Winchester and New College, Oxford for the church. It was an expensive education, but the outcome promised a smaller capital expenditure.

Alfred Pryor's lax training was unusual, although his father's schemes for his four sons were not. Some young brewers received their practical instruction under the surveillance of their father, their uncles and the head-brewer. The system was too insular and it became increasingly common practice for them to be sent, usually for one or two years, to another brewery of reputation. Normally, this was arranged through family and friendship networks. Moreover, some head-brewers possessed special renown for their skills in training both those pupils destined for the family firm and those who would earn their living as professional brewers. Indeed, in some breweries, pupil fees made a significant contribution towards the high salary of the head-brewer. For example, Edward Greene trained three of his nephews in the brewery in the 1860s and could boast in 1875 that he had trained the brewers at Georges; Mann, Crossman & Paulin in Burton; Charrington; and 'one of the largest brewers in Ireland'. On the other hand his son Walter was sent in 1860, after Rugby, to learn foreign languages in Paris and then undertake his training at Brighton with 'a noted brewer' (Tamplin).[41] C. F. Tetley, a third-generation member of the famous Leeds brewing family, went, after Leeds Grammar School, Harrow and Trinity College, Cambridge, for a spell to H. & V. Nicholls of Lewisham and Nevile Reid of Windsor;[42] and when the Popes shifted from farming to brewing, two of the three brothers were sent to Tetley and to Benskin's in Watford.[43] Twentieth-century recipients recall that such training was very variable.

There was probably little that was systematic in this instruction. Its main aspect was the exposition of brewing skills 'at the copper-side', whilst other parts of the brewing business were acquired practically: the buying of barley, the making of malt, the judging of hops, the keeping of accounts and the understanding of every aspect of distribution. Above all, at least in the better run breweries, they were instructed in the two essentials of brewery management: first, to achieve maximum profitability, by paying scrupulous attention to economies in every aspect of production and sales; secondly, and much more nebulous, the need to judge character and credentials in a business where personal contacts

[41] Wilson, *Greene King*, pp. 83, 112.
[42] Lackey, *Quality Pays*, p. 59.
[43] Seekings, *Thomas Hardy's Brewer*, p. 32.

with a wide range of merchants, dealers, agents, travellers and publicans were paramount. In the period before the 1880s brewers maintained that this hands-on training was unsurpassed; and even when college based courses in brewing science (see pp. 60–3) made many aspects of it increasingly obsolete, the pupillage system had its fierce champions to 1914 and beyond.

On the completion of their training, and after a quite short period of assimilation into the family brewery, they were admitted to partnerships. In general, the larger the partnership the longer they had to wait. Whereas Walter Greene was allowed a share of his father's profits at the age of 20, those in the great London partnerships or firms like Steward & Patteson had to wait longer. And some fathers were less indulgent than Edward Greene as a matter of principle. Of course, salaries of a few hundred pounds were paid for their services when they were assigned, if the firm was sizeable, to one of the three main branches of their calling: the barley, malt and hop departments; brewing; or sales and distribution. Then, when the opportunity arose, and providing their application was not totally wanting, they were accepted into a full partnership with specific responsibilities. Their share of the firm's capital was usually quite small; normally a few thousand pounds provided by their father, father-in-law or uncles, whose shares proportionately contracted. Then over the term of the partnership, often of twenty years duration in breweries, their own share was built up by the retention of 'surplus' earnings and, eventually, inheritance. Steward & Patteson provide a classic case-study. In 1863 Henry Patteson was appointed senior managing partner with a salary of £700; his two juniors, Donald and Walter Steward, were paid £400 each. Yet the three of them together owned a mere 12.25 per cent of the firm's £40,000 capital. There were no fewer than six 'sleeping' partners skimming the cream of its ample profits. Twenty years later, on the execution of the next partnership agreement, however, Patteson and his son shared 21 per cent of the £140,000 capital and Donald Steward, 18.5 per cent.[44] Similarly, when C. F. Tetley joined his father and uncle in 1879, the latters' share of the firm's capital was a massive £273,396, his a mere £6,714.[45] Young partners usually worked hard. Paid managers' salaries, they often lived on the premises and were expected to overlook every aspect of the business. When Simonds of Reading underwent 'a sustained rate of expansion' after the mid-1860s:

[44] Gourvish, *Norfolk Beers*, pp. 43, 49–52.
[45] Lackey, *Quality Pays*, p. 60.

the strain on the three partners must have been considerable, however. They were forever writing letters, often in their own hand, making sure that publicans, branch offices at home and abroad, and refreshment-room and pier managers were kept on their toes. Thus they brought in two nephews in the 1870s, to specialise in the increasingly complex secretarial work.[46]

When Edward Greene became an MP and sounded off in Suffolk about the efficacy of the work ethic, he recalled that between 1830 and 1842 'he never, save on one occasion [his marriage], missed being the first in the morning in the brewery to superintend the commencement of the day's labours'.[47] Later, as breweries grew in size, relatively inexperienced partners were able to draw upon the skills of both a salaried general manager and a head-brewer. Greene possessed neither in the 1830s; thirty years later when he was in Parliament, he relied upon his manager, William Pead. 'With supreme control of the office and the books, with a supervising power over the whole establishment', Pead was paid a salary of £800 in addition to a share of the malting profits.[48] These managers, like those of the Purser and Geoghegan families at Guinness's brewery, were advanced only after years of proving themselves. And in some breweries where partners were old or inattentive or both, the manager, head-brewer or occasionally the firm's solicitor came to wield effective control.[49]

What other routes were there into these highly profitable brewing partnerships besides inheritance and connection? Almost none. Breweries did come up for sale. In the 1830s and 1840s, when the Beer Act and general depression upset established interests, this was an occurrence of some frequency.[50] But there always was a regular trickle of sales as brewing families died out, partnerships got into difficulties or owners simply decided to realise their assets. Most never reached public auction and those that did were almost invariably bought by established brewers. The Hatfield Brewery which John Izzard Pryor bought in 1837 is a case in point. In the end he had to pay £31,000 for the brewery, whose barrelage had fallen from a three-year average of 7,600 to 6,000 in 1836–7. In fact, with working capital, his three sons had to find £40,000. But Pryor could orchestrate his family connections. His brother-in-law,

[46] Corley, *The Road to Worton Grange*, p. 6.

[47] *Bury and Norwich Post*, 17 April 1875; for Greene's attitude to work see Wilson, *Greene King*, pp. 77–8.

[48] *Ibid.*, p. 114.

[49] For example the career of W. P. Manners at Worthington or William Sykes at John Smith's.

[50] *Bury and Norwich Post*, 16 Aug. 1835; 13 May, 12 July, 26 Sept., 11 Oct. 1837; 2 April 1838; Gourvish, *Norfolk Beers*, pp. 39–40, 48, 66.

Joseph Morris, an Ampthill brewer, lent £8,000; his brother Robert, a wealthy bachelor partner in Truman, £10,000; and two elder sons found £10,000 apiece from their stake in the Baldock brewery.[51] And when, in turn, the Baldock brewery itself was sold with 122 tied houses at a valuation of £81,904 in 1853 immediately following John Pryor's death, it was bought by the two nephews of the Royston brewer, John Phillips. They found half the price; the other remained on mortgage to the Pryors at 4 per cent.[52] Even the modest Halifax Stone Trough Brewery sold in 1881 for £50,000 was purchased by a neighbouring brewer, John Taylor Ramsden.[53]

In terms of competition and of experience in the industry it is easy to see why these breweries which came up for sale were usually bought by established brewers. For they could borrow easily. Like the Pryors, they could draw upon the savings of relatives and friends ready to place them in the family enterprise at 4.5 or 5 per cent. Moreover, since they were owners of considerable amounts of freehold property, they could, like landowners, easily raise mortgages. Not all did, of course. But with well-heeled family networks and the ability to borrow easily – and some like the Cobbs, Simonds, Cobbolds, Agg-Gardners and Lacons were in addition country bankers – it was easy for them to keep afloat and extend their undertakings.[54] Perhaps in no other industry was continuity therefore such a feature. Certainly, it was unlike the textile industries where ease of both entrance and exit was a feature of every trade cycle in the Victorian period.

This is not to deny that bankruptcies amongst brewers' partnerships took place, that even in the South and East there were brewers, often from farming, malting and publican backgrounds, whose origins were relatively modest and whose enterprises slipped in and out of the trade directories which were such a feature of Victorian business life. But the most notable feature of brewing partnerships was undoubtedly the

51 Curtis, *Chronicle of Small Beer*, pp. 31–2. Alfred Pryor was not a successful brewer: the firm was sold on his death to his son for £29,442. The brewery was acquired in 1920 by Benskin's with 107 pubs.

52 *Ibid.*, pp. 206–7. John Pryor had two sons at Eton; his brother Morris (who had no sons) felt incapable of running the brewery until his nephew could take over, and their father, almost 80, was powerless to do so. See also Wilson, *Greene King*, pp. 228–9.

53 Robinson, 'The Emergence of the Common Brewer in the Halifax District', p. 89.

54 Banks also appear in brewery accounts as short-term lenders, principally providing overdraft facilities when brewers were busily buying barley, malt and hops during the October–March season. At other times in the year balances built up. Truman's and Greene's breweries reveal exactly this pattern in the 1870s and 1880s; Lacon's accounts between 1863 and 1872 show an extraordinarily large 'balance at bank' on 30 November each year; 1869 was not untypical: £83,558 plus £27,897 on deposit.

growth of capital investment across the 1830–86 period. The progression was not smooth for it concentrated very much in the years after 1860. Increases were reflected in three areas of the partners' private ledgers: the value of the brewing premises and utensils; tied house investment; and stocks of barley, malt, hops, beer and casks. Costs and profits were discussed in Chapter 5. Here it is only necessary to reflect that growth was not entirely mirrored in increases in the *subscribed* capital of the partnerships. Profits were retained to fund expenditure in each of the three areas above. Moreover since valuations, especially of premises and utensils and of tied house property (at least before sharp advances in its price in the 1870s), were historic, most partnerships undervalued their assets. Nevertheless the increase across this 1830–80 period was often impressive. At Bass it was spectacular. In round figures, partners' capital grew from £29,000 in 1827 to £3,200,000 in 1880. Although this was an exceptional performance in absolute amounts, some smaller firms could almost equal it in their rates of growth. These were sustained by capitals generated from profits rather than loans, at least before the price of tied property began to rise sharply from the mid-1870s. When Joshua Tetley commenced renting his Leeds brewery in 1822, its fixtures were valued at only £400. Admittedly, his flourishing malting business sustained the new brewery in its early years. But by 1841 his capital was valued at £23,933; by 1870 three partners were credited with £280,110.[55] And Tetley owned no tied property at this stage. Likewise Edward Greene bought his small, historic brewery with its land-locked, rural market and little if any tied property from his father in 1836. With a trade of 2,000 barrels he cannot have repaid him more than a few thousand pounds in the next decade. Yet when he joined forces with his pushy neighbour Fred King in 1886 Greene's capital account stood at £195,963. He had bought pubs freely after 1870 but only after 1883 did his mortgage account exceed £4,250.[56] And breweries established later enjoyed a similar success. The Mansfield brewery founded in 1855 by a practical brewer, a farmer and a maltster was initially a tiny affair with a capital probably no more than £2,000. In 1873 this had grown to £12,000; in 1901 its three partners shared £162,444.[57]

If a judgement about the enterprise of partners was simply a reflection

[55] Lackey, *Quality Pays*, pp. 14, 49, 60.
[56] Wilson, *Greene King*, pp. 61–3, 268.
[57] P. Bristow, *The Mansfield Brew* (1976), pp. 20, 25, 51.

of these increases in the valuation of breweries, then the matter would be easily settled. Success in material terms was there for all to see. And looking at the careers of Robert Crossman, Cosmo Bonsor, Michael Thomas Bass, the Guinnesses, William McEwan, Peter and Andrew Walker of Warrington and Edward Greene to take but a handful, all in their different ways are textbook examples of the entrepreneurial ideal in their innovation, drive and vision. Other brewers clearly did not possess these attributes in equal measure. The Pryors of Baldock, William Lucas of Hitchin, J. Agg-Gardner in Cheltenham ran prosperous breweries in more familiar ways. The aristocratic partners of the Tadcaster Tower Brewery were more likely to be found on the grouse moor or race course than in their brewery. But there was always a spectrum of enterprise in brewing as in any other industry. Indeed, it seems odd that economic historians should examine the key contribution of enterprise in economic growth, whether in Britain, America or Europe, imagining that there is some prescriptive, national ideal for business behaviour. In the British brewing industry this was especially unlikely. Brewers, especially country brewers, faced both ways: they were businessmen; they were frequently also landowners and farmers. It is too easy, however, to follow Martin Wiener's thesis, nowhere more applicable than in brewing, that the edge of British enterprise was blunted through its leaders' conforming to the values of the landed ruling elite.[58] It is arguable that the ethos of that elite changed as it was permeated by the mores of Victorian capitalism. Moreover, in brewing, recognition must be taken of the competitiveness of the industry before 1900. Brewers could not stand still. Admittedly, there was a rentier mentality especially amongst the great London brewers; everywhere breweries could be effectively run on a day-to-day basis by head-brewers and general managers with routine guidance from partners; the industry flourished without a great export trade; individual brewers could survive not because they were managerially adroit, but because they brewed good beer. But the achievements of Bass, Guinness and McEwan and, on a lesser plane, those of leading country brewers show that some brewery partners deserve their place alongside leaders from other industries in any hall of fame devoted to British business enterprise in the Victorian period.

[58] M. Wiener, *English Culture and the Decline of the Industrial Spirit 1850–1980* (1981).

III

On 25 October 1886 the death knell of the British brewing partnership was sounded. Guinness was sold to the public for £6 million. Scenes in the City were unprecedented. Two days earlier, in the stampede to obtain prospectuses, the outer office doors of Baring, the share-issuers, were broken 'by the pushing crowds of clerks, agents, messengers and City men'.[59] The subscription lists were closed within an hour of opening on the 25th; a fortnight later Sir Edward Guinness reported that the amount applied for had been an extraordinary £130,000,000. The stock market and the brewing industry were convulsed. In its wake during the next few years, there was a rush by almost every major brewery to convert to limited liability and to issue shares to raise money from the public. The structure and policy, although not the management, of the brewing industry in Britain were transformed. Like all revolutionary changes its roots ran deeper than the dramatic events of October 1886. Those on the surface, the impact of recession in the early 1880s on the industry, were a tangled affair. Its two deeper tap roots, changes in company law going back to the 1850s and the rush to buy public houses following licensing restrictions in the early 1870s, are best laid bare first.

The impact of changes in company law in Victorian business has been discussed at length elsewhere.[60] Between 1844 and 1856 there were important advances in the law relating to both companies and to stock exchange practice. Legislation necessarily followed the extraordinary speculative activity surrounding the rapid expansion of the British railway network in the 1840s. The provisions of corporate law, previously enjoyed only by public utilities or by private Act of Parliament, were extended to manufacturing industry. Firms could share the benefits of limited liability simply by filing minimal documentation with the Registrar of Joint Stock Companies under the Acts of 1856 and 1862. Suddenly, 'English company legislation [had] become the most permissive in Europe'.[61] Not surprisingly, therefore, the benefits of limited

59 *The Daily News*, 26 Oct. 1886.

60 H. A. Shannon, 'The Coming of General Limited Liability', *Economic History*, 2 (1931); 'The Limited Companies of 1866–1883', *Economic History Review*, 4 (1933); J. B. Jeffreys, 'The Denomination and Character of Shares, 1855–1885', *Economic History Review*, 16 (1946); P. L. Payne, 'The Emergence of the Large-Scale Company in Great Britain, 1870–1914', *Economic History Review*, 2nd ser. 20 (1967) and his introduction to L. Richmond and B. Stockford, *Company Archives: The Survey of the Records of 1000 of the First Registered Companies in England and Wales* (1986).

61 P. L. Cottrell, *The Finance and Organisation of English Manufacturing Industry* (1980), p. 52.

liability were hotly debated in the 1850s, and the record of failure in the next thirty years of many of the early public companies underlined the disquiet.[62] Few industries, since in brewing bankruptcies were rare and firms prized their reputations, eschewed the provisions of the Companies Act more. By 1886 a mere score or so of breweries were registered under the Acts. None was notable, and most were struggling, with overcapitalisation and bad management the chief culprits of their misfortune.[63] Certainly, Checkland's contention that the partnership system, the key form of business organisation in Britain's early industrialisation, collapsed because it seriously restricted the growth of business, 'made for discontinuity', was 'most cumbersome' and 'very risky', seems too sweeping when applied to brewing.[64] Partnerships steered the industry through the fastest period of growth it had ever experienced in the 1860s and 1870s with few of these consequences. Indeed, there was general distrust amongst brewers of the new companies that were established. When, in 1880, it was rumoured that Bass was to be converted into a limited company, the *Country Brewers' Gazette* 'gave it little credence as we share the common belief that the conversion of an old firm into a company must be treated with suspicion'.[65]

What changed these attitudes so rapidly after 1886? Most historians of the industry are agreed it was the supply and price of pubs after 1869.[66] In that year the Liberal government – persuaded by temperance advocates, the growing prevalence of drunkenness and the long

62 Shannon, 'Limited Companies of 1866–1883' and his 'The First 5000 Limited Companies and their Duration', *Economic History*, 2 (1932).

63 The Burton Brewery Co. (1858) and the Kirkstall Brewery Co. provide examples of mismanaged early companies (Hawkins, pp. 88–91). In 1879 a London stockbroker listed only the shares of ten brewery companies of which three were London ventures, the City of London (formerly Calvert's brewery (1860)), Lion (1865) and New Westminster (1873). The leading provincial firms were the Burton Brewery Co. (1858) and Birkenhead Brewery (1868). At least another ten limited joint stock brewery companies existed but their shares were unquoted, at least in London (*Country Brewers' Gazette*, 7 Jan. 1880). Between 1882 and 1885 there was a low level of company flotations during the general recession. Watneys' incorporation with a capital of £2,000,000 in 1885 marked the up-turn.

64 S. G. Checkland, *The Rise of Industrial Society in England, 1815–1885* (1964), p. 107.

65 *Country Brewers' Gazette*, 18 Feb. 1880. Bass in fact became a *private* limited company on 31 January 1880, despite there being no such entity in law. Its 32,000 shares of £100 each were entirely shared by the eight partners. In October 1880 Greenall, Whitley & Co. of St Helens were similarly converted. The capital of £700,000 was taken up by the existing partners dividing 700 shares of £1,000 each.

66 J. Vaizey, 'The Brewing Industry', in P. L. Cook (ed.), *Effects of Mergers: Six Studies* (1958), pp. 401–7; K. H. Hawkins and C. L. Pass, *The Brewing Industry: A Study in Industrial Organisation and Public Policy* (1979), pp. 18–19, 25–8; Payne, 'The Large-Scale Company', pp. 530–1.

Table 6.2. *Number of victuallers, beer house sellers and on-licences per head of population in England and Wales, 1831–1911*

	Number of licences		Total	Population per on-licence
	Publican	Beer on-licences		
1831	50,547	31,937	82,484	168
1841	57,768	33,844	91,612	174
1851	59,676	35,808	95,484	188
1861	64,923	42,773	107,696	186
1871	70,294	42,590	112,884	201
1881	71,814	35,096	106,910	243
1891	73,394	31,612	105,006	276
1901	73,784	29,064	102,848	316
1911	63,574	27,012	90,586	398

Source: Wilson, *Alcohol and the Nation*, p. 236.

campaign against beer houses – passed a temporary measure (made permanent three years later)[67] handing over the issue of future retail beer and wine on-licences to the control of the magistracy. Protection was given to existing beer houses (known henceforth as the pre-69 beer houses) and new beer off-licences could only be refused on specified grounds. What happened, as the important select committee of the House of Lords pointed out in great detail in 1878, was that the number of beer houses declined quite sharply, and magistrates became increasingly vigilant about the issue of licences for new public houses and post-69 beer houses. Since the population was still increasing rapidly, the effect upon the number of retail pubs per capita was marked (see Table 6.2). Moreover, a series of judgements culminated in the famous case of *Sharp v. Wakefield* (lost by the Trade in the House of Lords in 1891), when Lord Halsbury, the Lord Chancellor, ruled that under the Alehouse Act of 1828, 'the grant of a licence is expressly within the discretion of the magistrates'.[68] In effect, it meant that magistrates could refuse the licences of those inns they believed were not required.

[67] H. A. Bruce's more drastic licensing bill of 1871 was 'impractical and unpopular', giving 'mortal offence to the Trade'. It was withdrawn but the temporary acts of 1869–70 were confirmed by the Licensing Act in 1872. For a longer account, see R. Shannon, *The Crisis of Imperialism* (1976), p. 92; R. C. K. Ensor, *England, 1870–1914* (1936), pp. 21–2; H. J. Hanham, *Elections and Party Management* (1978), pp. 222–6.

[68] Quoted in Wilson, *Alcohol and the Nation*, p. 108.

Undoubtedly, after 1880, brewers became resigned if not reconciled to the fact that the number of public houses would remain at best fixed. And, inevitably, given these market forces, they argued that the price of pubs must rise. In these circumstances, breweries began to tie increasingly expensive retail outlets at an unprecedented rate once the gloomiest years of the mid-1880s were over. This is the accepted, orthodox account. Before 1880, Kevin Hawkins writes, 'there is no evidence of a deliberate attempt by the brewers at this stage to get control of the retail trade'.[69] Recently, this interpretation has been questioned by David Gutzke, who suggests that the *majority* of brewers – the exceptions being the market leaders in Burton, Dublin and Edinburgh – were busily acquiring property from the inception of the beer house in the 1830s, and that the feature of the half-century from 1830 to 1880 was the steady build up of tied property.[70] It is a sensible argument, particularly for developments in the South and East of England, backed by much empirical evidence. Partnerships regularly ploughed surplus profits into pubs; they were a good investment in themselves, especially since they provided first-rate collateral for the negotiation of loans and overdrafts. Nevertheless, the price of pubs rose sharply in the 1870s, and far fiercer competition was experienced when consumption declined after 1876. In the pursuit of forward integration by brewers, the 1870s mark a watershed.

If it is an identifiable turning-point in terms of the numbers and prices of pubs, the ramifications for brewers were more complex than historians have suggested when making calculations about property prices and numbers of pubs per head of population. For brewers faced an increasingly hostile world in the 1870s and 1880s as the temperance movement gained momentum. Naturally, they expressed sharp opposition to prohibition schemes, high taxation, and the wilder excesses of the movement and its leaders. Yet the realisation grew that they had to live with the impact of the movement on a day-to-day basis. Since, however, most transactions between brewers and publicans were conducted in a face-to-face situation, the record of what actually occurred is incomplete. Where a rare view is afforded, as in Truman's monthly minutes or the remarkable diaries of the Tadcaster Tower Brewery, it is clear that there were other issues at stake in the 1880s for brewers besides the diminishing supply of free-trade pubs. Truman's response to problems was to secure first-class houses. Surprisingly for the part-

69 Hawkins, 'Brewing Industry', pp. 62–3.
70 Gutzke, *Protecting the Pub*, pp. 18–29.

ners these did not guarantee a better return, but they argued that in terms of the firm's reputation if a real squeeze in licensing came as a result of temperance legislation, then first-class houses with good tenants and respectable customers were most likely to survive the holocaust. 'Our whole existence', wrote J. H. Buxton, 'depends on our reputation and our kudos, and to deal with the best publicans, and lend our money on the best security ought to be our aim.'[71] Their renewed acquisition of tied houses was the only form of protection they could envisage against an uncertain future. On the other hand, the partners and manager of the Tadcaster Tower Brewery, owning scores of houses in and around York, made every effort to suppress drunkenness in the pubs they supplied; they rid themselves of tenants of bad reputation; they sought out the best publicans they could to replace them; they reminded them of the law; they co-operated with the police and magistracy. These responses to temperance pressures mark the beginning of the public house improvement movement. They also show that brewers were keen to acquire houses both to protect licences and to ensure their own reputation. An estate of good tied houses underlined the good management of a brewery in its widest sense.

The other aspect of the more hostile world facing brewers after 1880 was the general recession, which hit the industry hard in the decade after 1876. As suggested, it was the short-term cause of the dramatic shift to limited liability after 1886. Overall, beer output declined sharply by some 18 per cent from peak to trough, 1876–83. The year 1879 was a bad one; the three from 1883–5 were no better. Truman noted at Christmas, 1884: 'Dullness seems to pervade every town in England ... even Messrs. Bass & Co. at this the chief brewing season in the year are not in full work. This is owing to the great and universal Depression of English Trade in the country, and the extreme poverty of the working classes.' In York the slump appears to have been deeper and longer than in London. In July 1886, just when summer sales should have been at their height, the manager of the Tadcaster Tower Brewery noted, 'our own houses are doing wretchedly badly as regards trade. Much worse than last year.' In one respect brewers exaggerated. Profitability,

[71] GLRO, Acc. 77.94, B/THB, Monthly Reports 1884–91, April–May 1885. The partners discussed at length the reasons for concentrating upon the better end of the trade. Local Option was likely to ruin the small pub most. They also argued by example: Combes who had concentrated upon first-class houses had done 'very well'. They drew out a general conclusion, 'with any trade, if a firm has the reputation that the inferior customers deal with them, a man will not willingly deal with a firm of such reputation *because it injures his own*'.

although often stagnant, was not so badly affected, as malt prices, although not those of hops,[72] fell to the lowest levels brewers ever remembered. In another sense they did not exaggerate, for competition, in the declining beer market, appreciably hardened. After two decades of expansion, over-capacity in many breweries was a problem. But the brewers did not directly reduce the price of beer; those, like the Burton brewers and John Smith's, with few if any pubs, increased their discounts to 20 or even 25 per cent. This had a profound impact on the entire trade. Free houses with discounts of these proportions could compete better than tied houses where discounts were traditionally 5 per cent; they resorted to the 'long pull', the tied tenant seriously cutting his margins in an attempt to match the blandishments of the free trade. Therefore to meet the competition of big discounts offered by the 'national' brewers like Bass and Allsopp or, locally, those breweries who expanded by giving generous discounts, brewers resorted to tying arrangements with a renewed vigour. Quickly, as it had not been before the 1880s, the whole movement became compulsive and frenetic. Hawkins and Pass summarise it as 'a domino effect'.[73] Everywhere brewers needed to tie firmly the free trade which remained to protect themselves against the inroads of massive discounts, the consequence of cheap barley prices and stagnant output. Limited liability and public ownership of shares suddenly offered the way forward. By converting partnerships to company status, breweries, by the sale of shares, could raise the necessary capital to buy property on an unprecedented scale. The jigsaw of developing company law, temperance and licensing policy, and the effects of the 1876–85 recession, suddenly fitted together as prosperity returned in 1886. The success of Guinness's conversion removed fears and offered solutions to these problems which had increasingly worried brewers in the previous decade.

During the years 1885–1900 all the bigger partnerships became limited liability companies, the largest of which raised capital on the stock market to modernise their breweries and, above all, acquire the freeholds and leases of public houses. By 1906, when the operation had largely run its course, 307 brewery companies with capital valued at £186,842,000 were publicly quoted in Burdett's *Official Intelligence*.[74]

[72] These reached record levels after the failure of the 1882 hop harvest. This led to increased imports, and acute problems for brewers in 1883, and is possibly one explanation for the low level of company flotations in 1883–4.

[73] Hawkins and Pass, *Brewing Industry*, p. 28.

[74] H. W. Macrosty, *The Trust Movement in British Industry* (1902), pp. 243–5. But see note 93 below.

The movement was concentrated in two periods of frenzied flotation, 1886–90 and 1895–9.

Underlying both was the perceived prosperity of the industry. The *Country Brewers' Gazette* summarised the views of many financial commentators: 'the profitable nature of breweries is proverbial; many of the richest men amongst us have accumulated their fortunes through the steady growth of this industry . . . many of the firms lately "converted" have been in successful existence and have passed through a course of expanding business for 50, 80 or even a hundred years'.[75] The industry was, *The Standard* opined succinctly, 'a veritable gold mine'.[76] Moreover, the brewers themselves liked the conversion arrangements. First, they ensured the spread of ownership in a controversial industry. One with tens of thousands of debenture holders, encompassing widows and orphans as well as speculators, was easier to defend than one in which ownership was confined solely in the hands of the brewers. Moreover, not only did the arrangements allow them to realise their assets if they wished, but also capitalisation allowed them to share more easily their greatly increased disposable wealth. In most cases the partnership's assets were sold to the new limited liability *company*, the directors of which – and these most frequently were the old partners – normally retained the ordinary or voting shares and sold to the public a proportion of preference and, more commonly, the debenture or loan capital shares. The latter, easily raised on the collateral of the brewery and, especially, of freehold tied property, were a highly cost-effective means of raising substantial sums of long-term loan capital. Again, the accommodation was one which was a considerable advance upon those made for borrowings in the old partnerships. With the level of speculation and the utility of arrangements for brewery partners, it was not surprising that the flotations attracted enormous interest both within and without the industry.

Yet in an industry of around 2,000 firms, ranging from amongst the largest concerns in British industry to tiny, unmodernised breweries whose partners were intimidated by the pace and cost of change, the courses whereby they took company status differed widely. The majority of the smaller firms took no part in the speculative activities of these years.[77] Remaining as partnerships, they simply became increasingly

[75] *Country Brewers' Gazette*, 1 March 1889.

[76] *The Standard*, 10 August 1888.

[77] For example Simpson of Baldock which, in the century after 1858, had an unchanging output of around 20,000 barrels entirely geared to its 125 pubs. It did not become a limited company until 1936. Wilson, *Greene King*, pp. 228–9.

vulnerable to the attentions of the larger breweries. The latter, driven by intense competition and the need at least to maintain output by aggressive forward integration, sought the benefits of company legislation and the improved stock market mechanisms for raising industrial capital. Not all large breweries did so in the same way. Some from the outset put a proportion (the London Stock Exchange rule was that at least two-thirds of any class of share had to be publicly traded if the company was to receive a listing) of loan capital on the market. These were the earliest brewery companies, numbering 167 in 1895 and 339 in 1900.[78] Others took company status but publicly marketed none of their shares according to the rules of the London Stock Exchange. Anxious to retain total family control, they were essentially *private* limited companies, although until 1908 there was no difference in law between them and the *public* companies. Then a clause of the Companies (Consolidation) Act of 1908 stipulated that any limited company with more than fifty shareholders must provide for an unrestricted transfer of shares.

Four brief case-studies bring out these different arrangements clearly. The example of Guinness makes a good starting point. The Guinness flotation was unusual in its scale, in the fact that a merchant bank was involved (Barings' first venture into a domestic industrial issue) and in that two-thirds of the *equity* was sold.[79] The principal reason for incorporation was not, as with most brewery companies, the need to find large amounts of loan capital for development, but to allow its proprietor, Sir Edward Guinness (later first Earl of Iveagh), to ease his managerial burdens and convert his enormous stake. A board of seven directors was constituted and a price of £6,000,000 fixed. In fact, through Barings' inexperience, the affair was both badly thought out and badly managed. Unusually at this stage in company formation, details about sales, profits and stock were full; and in fairness to Barings, who were unduly pessimistic about the flotation, Guinness owned no public houses and therefore, as *The Economist* pointed out, a large valuation had to be made of the firm's goodwill.[80] Nevertheless, with Barings and three other banks taking large allotments, besides Sir Edward's one third share of the equity, most of the 6,000 successful

[78] Duncan's *Manual of British and Foreign Brewery Companies for 1895 and 1900.*

[79] This paragraph is based upon Chapter 2 of Dennison and MacDonagh, 'History of Guinness'.

[80] 'Goodwill' is defined as the difference between a company's assets and its nominal capital. Contemporary accounting practice reckoned it should not exceed two to three times a brewery's annual net profits.

applicants (13,000 supposedly were disappointed) had to be content with two or three shares each. And the brewing trade itself felt it was passed over; this was important in view of Guinness's marketing solely through a network of agents and bottlers. Moreover, Sir Edward himself was buying large numbers of shares in the open market a few months later at prices almost double those made at allotment. But none of the strictures made by the press or the trade in the months after October 1886 had the slightest impact. For profits were better than those indicated in the prospectus; and the price paid was far from excessive. After interest payments, profits were running at around £500,000 in the 1890s, dividends on the ordinary shares were 15 per cent, and a massive reserve fund of £295,000 and a depreciation one of £200,000 had been created by 1894. With these resources, the development of the largest brewery in the world could go on unchecked to the Great War, and its flotation became the bell wether for those of all brewery companies.[81]

The example of John Smith's of Tadcaster represents the most common form of brewery flotation – that in which the equity capital was entirely retained by the original partners who, as directors of the new company, raised substantial sums of loan capital by the sale of preference and debenture stocks. Barnard, who had a good feel for the standing of a brewery, could pen no more laudatory sketch than that he reserved for this firm.[82] Certainly, it was matched by few in its profitability. When it was incorporated in August 1892, the two vending partners, H. H. and F. Riley-Smith took the whole of the nominal capital of the new company: £295,000 in shares and £5,000 in cash. The assets acquired by the company were valued at £357,030; there was no valuation for goodwill, and no promotion money had been paid.[83] Immediately the new company raised £200,000 in 4 per cent debentures, 'the whole to be *retained in, and used for, the development and extension of the business*, and no part thereof ... is payable to Messrs. Riley-Smith in respect of the purchase'. Since profits averaged £26,247 in the three years 1889–91, the interest payment of £8,000 caused few searchings. In April 1895, the company raised a further £150,000 in 5

[81] Even the manager of the Tadcaster Tower Brewery devoted a whole page of his diary to record the details of Guinness's incorporation and concluded with envy, 'It must be a remarkable Business. They have not a single Tied House, or one single Loan!'

[82] Barnard, *Noted Breweries*, III, pp. 2–47.

[83] Prospectus dated 12 Aug. 1892. The company had 223 licensed premises, of which 108 were freehold, valued at £181,937, of which one-third (by value) had been acquired since 1 Jan. 1892.

per cent cumulative preference shares, the directors retaining one-third of them.[84] Evidently the debenture capital had been well spent: the company controlled 512 licensed properties; profits for the year ending 30 September 1894 amounted to £37,971; assets were valued at £607,162. And the boom for Smith's accelerated. Profits spiralled, averaging £81,128 in the four years 1899–1902; dividends on the ordinary shares reached 27 per cent in 1901; a healthy £25,000 was transferred to reserves each year. Therefore the company could easily afford to raise a further £200,000 in debentures in 1896 and again in 1902, accept large loans from the Riley-Smith brothers, and issue further preference shares in 1899. Control of the company was entirely maintained by the Riley-Smiths. Non-voting debenture and preference-share capital, easily raised at a useful premium, allowed it to pursue a period of headlong growth. Nowhere did the new stock market arrangements in the brewing industry work better in these years, although Georges, Threlfall's, Eldridge Pope and Phipps of Northampton, for example, pursued similar gilded paths.

Citing Guinness and John Smith's might suggest nothing was easier than to achieve growth between 1885 and 1900. But not all companies went into incorporation enjoying the same conditions. Everything went right at John Smith's because the company possessed a superb modern brewery (1882) in a famed brewing centre; it was long experienced in retailing good beers across the North of England at generous discounts; its accounts were encumbered neither by an inflated goodwill valuation nor previous mortgages. Yet there were brewery companies floated at the height of the speculation manias which were ill conceived, ill managed and ill financed. Several ran into almost immediate trouble. Duncan noted in his *Brewery Manual* (1895) that of the 198 companies he listed (including thirty-one foreign ventures), thirty-two 'failed to remunerate their Ordinary shareholders with any dividend'.[85] The Plymouth Breweries Co. provides a good example.[86] Incorporated in October 1889, the venture was the creation of a promoter who acquired five breweries in Plymouth and its vicinity. These were acquired by the company at the inflated price of £317,650 paid in cash. The directors then raised £90,000 in ordinary shares, £90,000 in 5 per cent preference

[84] Prospectus dated 22 April 1895. Other details in this paragraph are taken from the first directors' minute book, Courage Archive, Tadcaster, JA/B/63.
[85] Duncan's *Brewery Manual* (1895), p. vi.
[86] The rest of this paragraph is based upon the papers of the brewery in Courage Archives (Bristol), DA/A/90, C/1, C/15 etc.

shares, and £180,000 in 5 per cent debentures.[87] Everything went wrong from the outset. The five directors including the chairman, the Earl of Cork and Orrery, were not large shareholders, and they possessed few managerial or financial skills; profits, inflated in the 1889 prospectus, plummeted after 1890; interest payments were an impossible burden because the price paid was £90,000 too high; the five breweries proved difficult to amalgamate, partly because substantial work was required to modernise the main Regent Brewery. In 1892 the annual report – desperately seeking excuses – had recourse, besides the brewers' standard explanation of a cold summer and increased brewing costs, 'to the disastrous effects of the blizzard in March last [1891], both to trade and to property'. No dividends were paid on the ordinary shares in the years 1891–3. There were no reserves. The investigation committee appointed by the shareholders in 1892 recommended writing down the 9,000 £10 ordinary shares to £3 each and reducing the interest of both the debenture and preference issues. The whole half-baked scheme was a far cry from John Smith's incorporation.

Other amalgamations of breweries similarly brought together during the 1886–90 flotation boom – Bristol United Breweries (1889), Newcastle Breweries Ltd (1890), Wolverhampton & Dudley Breweries (1890), and Bentley's Yorkshire Breweries (1892) – were far more successful ventures.[88] Price, location and management were the key variables. But there were other companies, like Plymouth Breweries Ltd, whose finances were too highly geared from the outset. The oft-quoted example of Allsopp, floated in 1887 on a fast-diminishing output, overpriced and badly managed, was the classic example of a brewery – in this case a household name – which became a byword for financial folly (see Plate 33).[89] Others were scattered across Britain.[90]

87 Applications totalling £260,070 for the debenture issue were received, £178,390 for the preference and £227,860 for the ordinary shares. As a result of the tough decisions taken in 1892–3 about writing down share capital and closing four of the five breweries, modest profitability was achieved after 1894.

88 For the Newcastle Breweries amalgamation, see Bennison and Merrington, *Newcastle Breweries Ltd 1890–1990*, pp. 14–20.

89 A brief account will be found in Hawkins and Pass, *Brewing Industry*, pp. 32–3, a longer one in T. R. Gourvish and R. G. Wilson, 'Profitability in the Brewing Industry, 1885–1914', *Business History*, 27 (1985), pp. 146–65, and an extended one in Hawkins, 'Brewing Industry'.

90 Ones that had failed, in some years at least before 1894, to pay an ordinary dividend were the Barnsley Brewery Co. (1888), Bath Brewery Ltd (1889), Burton & Lincoln Breweries (1889), Chesters' Brewery Co. (Manchester, 1888), Colchester Brewery Co. (1886), Daniell & Sons' Breweries (Colchester, 1887), Edinburgh Limited Breweries (1889), Hammond's Bradford Brewery Co. (1889), Northampton Brewery Co. (1887), Nottingham Brewery (1887), Stretton's Derby Brewery (1890).

Their numbers increased sharply after 1900 when the second great expansionary phase of brewery capitalisation ran into diminished consumption and government hostility (see pp. 292–4). But the division between sheep and goats in the industry was apparent from the outset of the first speculative boom in 1886. John Smith's and the Plymouth Breweries were always distinct species.

In addition there was a large number of breweries, by no means all of them small concerns, which became incorporated as limited liability companies but which did not have resort to the stock market, seeking a quotation for any class of their shares. They simply registered their Memoranda and Articles of Association at Companies House, allotted their shares amongst the partners' families, kept their directors' minute books with variable degrees of informativeness, produced an annual balance sheet for the few shareholders, and conducted, in some cases, what must be the shortest company annual general meetings on record. Their affairs remained essentially private, entirely family driven. The fourth case-study, the Suffolk firm of Greene King, illustrates this class of brewery well.[91] When the neighbouring firms of Edward Greene and F. W. King were amalgamated in June 1887 to reduce competition, they sought incorporation to divide the capital of the two principals and the three members of the next generation who ran the firm. The large capitalisation of the company, £555,000, allowed for considerable future growth. Tangible assets were valued at £360,000 and a very generous one-third goodwill valuation of £180,000 on the two partnerships' free trade was added. Five individuals and a trust nominee shared £200,000 ordinary shares, £200,000 5 per cent preferences and £155,000 debentures. Only £14,500 of the latter were raised amongst 'friends' in and around Bury St Edmunds to buy a small brewery on the Essex borders. But the capitalisation of such a large goodwill calculation caused no problems in a family company. For the brewery was superbly managed by Edward Lake; dividends on equity ranged between 8 and 10 per cent before 1914; and the stock of tied houses grew from 148 in 1887 to 389 at its pre-1914 peak, financed from reserves and a mere £40,000 in additional debentures. The mechanism of the 'private' company worked admirably in capable hands. Edward Greene and Fred King

91 Wilson, *Greene King*, pp. 122–9, 144–9. Other examples of large firms which remained essentially private to 1914 were Tetley (incorporated 1897), Eldridge Pope (1897), Cobbold (1924), Lacon (1894), Steward & Patteson (1895), Greenall Whitley (1880, 1952), Brakspear (1896). All of them by incorporation already owned big strings of tied houses; indeed in 1892 Greenall Whitley and Steward & Patteson were the largest owners of tied licensed property in Britain.

were able to realise their wealth locked into the old partnerships and to continue to control their company and families.[92] Not until 1927 were the shares of this large company publicly quoted. Other firms, already with great caches of tied public houses, like Steward & Patteson, Cobbold, Lacon and Greenall Whitley, expanded smoothly, operating their companies by essentially 'private' mechanisms.

These four case-studies illustrate the different approaches to incorporations by brewers between 1885 and 1900. They underline variants between companies in terms of management, profitability and the conditions whereby old partnerships were converted. This last point brings us to consider the nature of the great speculative booms of 1886–90 and 1895–9. By the end of 1885 there were not more than twenty brewery companies with publicly issued capital of £5,000,000. For 1890 Duncan's *Brewery Manual* lists 139 British firms with a capital of £69,000,000 (including loans and mortgages) and for 1901, when the second great surge had abated, 353 firms had issued £188,000,000 of shares. These are maximum estimates;[93] and rather more than one-half of the sums was vendors' capital, i.e. shares allotted to partners on the

[92] Edward Greene had five children, F. W. King eleven, and E. W. Lake, the managing director from 1887 to 1920, thirteen. Of course, all the sons could neither share in the management of the firm nor benefit directly from its largesse. But F. W. King set up a large family trust with his shares and the five children of Sir Walter Greene (1842–1920) lived in considerable style chiefly on their brewery dividends. Within forty years the company's shares were spread across the Greene, King and Lake families in a manner impossible in the old partnership arrangements.

[93] Hawkins and Pass reckon there were twenty public companies created before 1886, eighty-five incorporated between 1886 and 1892 and 149, 1893–1900 (*Brewing Industry*, p. 29). These figures are taken from Duncan's *Brewery Manual*. They appear to have omitted those companies listed in Duncan which returned 'incomplete Details or no Reports'. K. Watson 'Industrial Finance in the UK: The Brewing Experience, 1880–1913' (unpublished Oxford D.Phil. thesis, 1990), pp. 94, 113 included the following table constructed from Burdett's *Official Intelligence*:

The number of wholesale brewers, corporate brewers and the capital subscribed in brewing companies

Year	(1) Common brewers	(2) Brewing companies	(2) Total public capital in brewing (£)
1885	2,399	17	4,703,680
1890	2,330	111	59,868,002
1895	1,922	143	80,009,860
1905	1,732	316	186,786,087

Both Duncan and Burdett possess their own idiosyncrasies and are only as complete as the material returned to them by individual companies. The authors are grateful to Dr Watson for allowing them to use this table and her figures above.

sale of their firms. Katherine Watson, in a careful calculation, reckons that capital created and called by brewery companies (*excluding vendors' shares*) was £32,368,116 (35.7 per cent) in 1886–90 and £44,446,834 (49 per cent) in 1895–9 out of a total of £90,688,961 for the years 1885–1905 inclusive. This indicates the scale of 'public' contribution and the concentration within two five-year periods. She concludes that as early as 1890 the largest firms dominating the industry were already public companies, that the corporate sector greatly increased its hold in the late 1890s flotation boom, and that, 'rather than failing the domestic brewing industry by restricting the finance available, if anything, the public capital market provided it with too much support'.[94] Certainly, in both periods, especially in the first, speculators outside the industry forced the pace of conversion. Brewers were not reluctant to sell and convert; indeed *The Statist* commented in 1888:

> The years 1886–88 will appear in financial history as the beer company fever ... the brewers have been wise in their generation, and seized the best opportunity for selling properties at top prices. In the secret recesses of their hearts 'the trade' had a nervous apprehension of legislative measures adverse to brewers' interests, and just when they were anxious to sell, an obliging public became eager to assume the proprietorship of mash tun and vats ... such people would follow a leader blindly, the bigger the premium, the more enthusiastically they would plunge into a partnership in a business of which they knew nothing.[95]

The paper exaggerated. Most breweries wanted to buy more licensed property, modernise their breweries and capitalise their wealth. But not all could withstand the blandishments of company promoters attracted by the speculative conditions surrounding the industry after 1886. The autobiography of one of these, H. Osborne O'Hagan, survives.[96] It is a highly selective survey of his involvement, for some of the companies he helped construct were more successful than others. But he does show how a network of stockbrokers, solicitors and accountants were drawn into the action. Most interesting was the involvement of key accounting and broker firms. J. R. Ellerman, the great entrepreneur who began his business life as an accountant, was involved in at least eight complex flotations, sometimes in association with O'Hagan.[97] And there were 'front men' like Hector Gurdon-Rebow of Wivenhoe Park, Colchester,

94 Watson, 'Industrial Finance', p. 105.
95 *The Statist*, 13 Oct. 1888.
96 H. O. O'Hagan, *Leaves from my Life* (1929), I, pp. 240–58.
97 Edinburgh United Breweries (1889), Hull Brewery Co. (1888), Leeds and Wakefield Breweries (1889), Moors' and Robson's Breweries (1888), Nixey, Coleclough & Baxter Ltd (1890), Springwell Brewery (1888), Stretton's Derby Brewery (1890) and Wolverhampton & Dudley Breweries (1890).

who in 1891 was director of no fewer than eleven new brewery companies, most of which had been formed with the ministrations of O'Hagan and Ellerman.[98] At worst the various promoters watered capital by creating excessive goodwill valuations and provided inadequate or misleading information in their prospectuses, invariably omitting barrelages and providing generous definitions of net profit. But the appetite of the investing public for brewery stock, in spite of cautions regularly administered by *The Economist*, *The Statist* and *The Times*, was insatiable in the late 1880s. Just as in the past, during canal and railway construction, the profits of a few key companies, like Guinness and Bass or such local stalwarts as Georges and John Smith's, carried the movement rapidly forward. By mid-1888 it had, as *The Statist* noted, reached fever pitch. One day in late March 1889 there was even a knock at the door of the Tadcaster Tower Brewery offices: 'a Mr. Jas. Sully of 70 Queen Victoria Street called yesterday ... and had some visionary scheme of Brewery Amalgamations in the West Riding: viz, Simpsons and others. He said he had £3,000,000 at his back and will give 12 years purchase for any Brewery's nett annual profits.'[99] Mr Sully was indeed scraping the barrel. Such was the demand for brewery shares that the attention of promoters and investors turned overseas as the supply of British brewery companies offering ordinary and preference shares failed to satisfy the demand in 1888–90.

Briefly, therefore, in these years a number of Continental and Colonial and above all American breweries were acquired by English syndicates of investors. With a faster rate of growth than the British brewing industry (production quadrupled to 26 million barrels between 1875 and 1892), making also extraordinary strides forward in technology in the 1880s, and undergoing a similar movement of company incorporation to the British industry, American breweries looked ripe for acquisition. Between 1888 and 1892 at least thirty-one breweries with a capital of some £20,000,000 were acquired by English registered com-

[98] In 1895 he was chairman of Daniell & Sons (Colchester, 1887), Manchester Brewery Co. (1888) and Tamplin & Sons (Brighton, 1889); he was also a director of Hull Brewery Co. (1888) and Farnham United Breweries (1889).

[99] Bass North (Leeds), Tadcaster Tower Brewery diaries, entry for 21 March 1889. No more was heard of the scheme, but in June 1886 the manager had noted that Sykes of Batley was trying to form his brewery into a company, with others, through a London promoter; in Feb. 1887, 'most important communication from Henry Bentley & Co. to form a syndicate in London' (no details were given). And two of the directors were caught up in the speculation: the Hon. Reginald Parker was a director of the Emerald & Phoenix (New York) besides the Springwell Brewery (Heckmondwike); R. H. Munro became a director of two American breweries.

panies.[100] A number of *financiers* formed syndicates to acquire American breweries, the shares of which they placed on the London Stock Exchange. They were not ventures by British *brewers* keen to acquire a foothold in the American industry. Nevertheless, a number of individual brewery directors, often prominent as Members of Parliament, like Sir Harry Bullard, the Norwich brewer and MP (he was chairman of Ohlsson's Cape and the Milwaukee and Chicago Breweries), fronted these companies. The management was retained in American hands, but each of them set up what were in effect advisory boards in London which kept foreign shareholders informed. *The Brewers' Journal* comforted its readers in March 1890, when the financial press began 'to depreciate the value of American breweries' that 'those who have invested money in American breweries need not forget that these undertakings are now controlled by some of the most eminent English brewers whose names alone afford a sufficient guarantee of absolute integrity and sound business capacity'. Other references, and the participation of J. R. Ellerman (involved in no fewer than four companies) and H. Osborne O'Hagan, suggest that promoters played a more prominent role than the brewers in the rush to acquire American brewery shares in 1889. There was a similar, if smaller, involvement in buying Canadian, Australian, South African and European breweries in the boom of 1888–90. But by 1893, with acute recession in both America and Australia, many of the investors, who cheerfully expected the 15 per cent returns that glowing company prospectuses based upon accounts of the very prosperous years 1886–9 promised, had their fingers burned. Shares were trading way below par, dividends went unpaid, conditions were slow to ease.

And in Britain in the early 1890s, the first brewery flotation boom also ran out of steam. Dividends fell; the *Sharp v. Wakefield* judgement threatened licences for which there was no prospect of compensation; nationally, beer consumption was stagnant in the 1890–4 period as the depression of the 1876–85 years returned; and the collapse of foreign brewing company share prices in 1891–2 had a knock-on effect. Only in 1895, as the domestic boom of the late 1890s developed, did prosperity

[100] For the American industry, see S. Baron, *Brewed in America: A History of Beer and Ale in the United States* (1962); T. C. Cochran, *The Pabst Brewing Company* (1948); W. L. Downard, *The Cincinnati Brewing Industry: A Social and Economic History* (1973); M. Wilkins, *The History of Foreign Investment in the United States to 1914* (1989), pp. 324–31. Cochran, pp. 405–6, provides a list of twenty-four 'syndicate breweries' and *The Brewers' Journal* lists twenty-two companies 'formed in England to carry on breweries in America' in May 1892. Others appear in the journal literature: fifteen were floated in 1889 alone, seven in 1890.

return. Then the years 1896–9 were the most extraordinary the industry had ever experienced. The number of incorporations more than doubled. This time the movement was more internally driven: less equity capital was issued, and a massive amount of debenture shares sold instead to fuel a frenzied period of property speculation.[101] It is this scramble for tied houses as it affected the London, Burton and country brewers to which we must now turn.

[101] In 1885–9 ordinary shares formed 24.3 per cent of capital created and called by brewing companies, 10.7 per cent in 1895–9, whereas the figures for debentures were 40.7 per cent and 66.1 per cent respectively. Watson, 'Industrial Finance', p. 113.

7

The scramble for property and its aftermath, 1885–1914

The best-known feature of the Victorian brewing industry is the brewers' success in the 1880s and 1890s in transforming the retailing of beer. By the wholesale acquisition of tied houses in these years they became extensive property owners and, by a variety of agreements, increasingly restricted their new tenants. The sheer scale and speed of the operation affected their organization, management and competitive position. And inevitably it led in the 1890s to increasing attacks on their 'monopolistic' interests.[1] The industry's troubles in the 1900s, indeed continuous rumblings ever since about the nature of its tied trade, have their origins in 'the scramble for property' in the last two decades of the nineteenth century.

In fact, the statistical parameters of the scale of their acquisition are unclear. Even in the 1950s the exact proportion of public houses owned by the brewers is speculative (see pp. 408–9). In the late nineteenth century calculations are even more in the nature of guesswork. There is no good reason for accepting Hawkins's and Pass's estimate that 50 per cent of on-licences were owned by brewers in 1870 and 90 per cent in 1900.[2] Both seem too high in the light of later calculations. And even when the evidence appears firmer with the 1892 parliamentary return of on-licence owners, the data are incomplete.[3] Further, partial details of

1 The discussion about these issues informs the nine volumes of the Royal Commission on Liquor Licensing Laws (1896–9). See especially the evidence of E. N. Buxton (Truman) E. Lubbock (Whitbread), T. W. Lovibond, (Newcastle Breweries), J. G. Groves (Groves & Whitnall), E. Ellis (Peter Walker), T. J. Down (Greenall Whitley), in *PP* Liquor Licensing Laws (1898) XXXVI, pp. 281–300, 317–19, 375–409.

2 Seemingly based upon estimates of total public house valuations in 1869 (Levi) and the amount invested by companies in tied property in 1900. Hawkins and Pass, *Brewing Industry*, p. 27 and Hawkins 'Brewing Industry', chapter 2 where his 90 per cent calculation is for the year 1914.

3 *PP* Accounts and Papers (1892) LXVIII, pp. 147–275. Return Relating to On-Licences. The return lists the owners of *two* or more on-licences compiled by clerks to justices in licensing districts in England and Wales. The detail is fascinating: those areas, Herefordshire, Cornwall, Devon, Somerset, Gloucestershire, Shropshire, Wales,

the brewers' control of pubs in the 1890s are to be found in the voluminous evidence to the Royal Commission on Liquor Licensing Laws (1896–9). In such towns as Manchester, Liverpool, Bristol, Plymouth and Hull 90 per cent of the beer trade was indeed tied to brewers. But there was a real difference between rural and urban experience, between the practices of brewers in London, Burton and the country.

I

Historians of the industry, following D. M. Knox's survey of the tied house system in London, have maintained that brewers in the capital showed no interest in the ownership of public houses before 1885 or even, arguably, until 1892.[4] Of course the larger brewers had since the 1800s secured at least half their trade by the unique London loan-tie (see pp. 128–37). They continued these arrangements unchanged, but, partly because the size of loan grew and then escalated after 1870, they appear neither to have tied more trade nor owned more leaseholds in 1880 than they had half a century earlier. In this respect they were unlike their country counterparts. Their problems in the mid-Victorian period had been the shift to ale brewing, the integration of beer houses into their organisations and, for some, the acquisition of subsidiary breweries in Burton. But in the 1880s, when consumption was checked, there were unresolved problems: the sheer cost of loans as London property prices spiralled; the incomplete nature of the tie, and its growing complexities;[5]

Worcestershire, Northumberland, and the East and North Riding of Yorkshire where the brewers *owned* few houses in comparison with East Anglia and the South-East of England are immediately evident, as is the contrast between rural and urban in this respect. But the degree of tied property *controlled* by brewers is seriously underestimated. First, all owners of *single* houses are omitted. Secondly, and more importantly, many owners are included who of course *leased* their houses to brewers. Some landowners, like the Dukes of Devonshire, Bedford and Rutland owned dozens of pubs. Like other owners of and investors in public house property they most probably leased their properties to brewers. Therefore serious underestimates (especially in the North-West) can be made of the tied estate of brewers like Groves & Whitnall, who *leased* almost as many pubs and beer houses as they owned. And the figures seem low when compared with the individual records of firms. For example, Greene King is credited with owning 181 pubs. In fact the firm controlled 274 tied houses in May 1892. Figures for the big London brewers are, by the same process, underestimated. Nevertheless, there were seventy-six brewing companies who owned over 100 licensed properties each, amounting in total to 12,614 houses (12 per cent of the total number of public houses. See Hawkins and Pass, *Brewing Industry*, p. 30.

4 D. M. Knox, 'The Development of the Tied-House System in London', *Oxford Economic Papers*, 10 (1958), see especially pp. 74, 77. Her evidence is taken principally from Whitbread's records.

5 I.e., mortgages granted to some individual publicans by the London brewer for mild and porter, the distiller for wines and spirits, and the Burton brewer for pale ales. The

and the increasingly unrealistic discounts offered by the Burton and some country brewers in the capital's free trade. When trade was bad these discounts could touch 30, even 40 per cent. Yet since the leading brewers were of great repute, capital does not seem to have been too difficult to raise. When, however, total loans for the biggest brewers passed the million pounds barrier in the 1880s they began inevitably to ponder the wisdom of the loan tie. Might it not be more advantageous, especially given the ease of raising debenture-share capital via the new company structure, to acquire leaseholds themselves and forge a tighter tie with publicans?

E. N. Buxton, the immensely able director of Truman, giving evidence to the Royal Commission on Liquor Licensing Laws in June 1897, was precise about both the causation and the chronology of the London brewers' shift in practices:

At that time [four to five years ago] it was not so common as it is now for brewing firms to own public houses themselves – at least in London. The pressure of competition has wrought a great change in the last few years, and for the purpose of keeping their trade together all brewing firms have sought to purchase licences in the open market. They would, in fact, have lost their trade unless they had done so.[6]

A study of Truman's monthly reports, however, suggests that the turning point in policy came in the first company conversion boom of 1886–90.[7] For Truman two key issues coloured their thinking. First there were the accelerating costs of loans. In the summer of 1888 the firm noted, 'loans are something enormous and as they increase constantly our risks are greater'. Whitbread were quoted as lending £24,000 on two East End houses; in 1890 Truman made a 'huge loan' of £23,000 on the 'Beaconsfield' at Hammersmith. Moreover, they lamented that they were having to lend publicans the *whole* purchase price of leases, a practice they would not have condoned a few years previously. Secondly, the company was obsessed, seemingly following the lead of Combe, about acquiring 'first-class' houses as an insurance policy against future legislation removing the licences of the worst grades of houses. By the autumn of 1888 Buxton was stating Truman's collective views: 'I . . . believe that it is well to secure our position by the purchase

publican himself made a smaller contribution (E. N. Buxton reckoned it was 23 per cent of the average premium in 1892). Arrangements therefore became administratively difficult and, because publicans overstretched themselves, short lived. It is arguable that the whole loan-tie system was disintegrating in the late 1880s.

6 *PP* (1898) XXXVI, Q. 35,009.

7 The following section is based upon the reports in GLRO, Acc. 77.94, B/THB.

of first rate houses for ourselves tying the trade. It will mean the investment of a lot of capital but it tends to do away with the Evils of Brewers' Competition.' The firm paid £69,710 for the purchase of five houses with an average length of lease of 47.4 years. Buxton's comment at the conclusion of the transaction was: 'the competition for these large houses is becoming severe and this will not cease till they are all owned by the large brewers'. In these circumstances prices rose sharply and the old conventions recognised formally within the Brewers' Company broke down. Truman mentioned that Courage were lending £450,000 to the Brewery Assets Corporation, 'a syndicate formed to purchase a large number of Public houses including some of ours. The Company may not float but this action of Courage's is a direct infraction of a resolution of Brewers' Hall.'

When the speculative boom surrounding the flotation of British and foreign brewing companies burst in 1891, Truman's purchase of leases apparently dried up. But their loan account continued to grow, and when in late 1893 prosperity returned to fuel the great domestic boom of the late 1890s, some remarkable prices for pubs were recorded. The Cannon Brewery, 'pushing their trade very hard', paid £42,000 for the 'Princess Alice' at Forest Gate; Truman expended half that amount on the 'Roebuck' at Chiswick. In November Buxton noted that his company had spent £190,000 since July. He recommended a further issue of debenture capital. The raising of loan capital and the scramble for property had become self-generating. Yet Truman could not jump off the escalator. As Buxton explained.

> I do not think we can properly say that it is time to hold our hands. On the contrary *now is our opportunity*, and unless we take advantage of it as occasions serve, without rushing, to secure the remainder of our trade, others will do so. The operation is a necessary one to ensure the permanence of our trade. At present we have tied rather more than two thirds of our trade. What will it cost to tie the remainder? After careful consideration of this question with Reeve [Manager], I put the answer to it at about £350,000; but it must not be supposed that it is at all likely that we can accomplish such a complete result in the next two years. I think that £250,000 more will very likely be required in that period.

Such calculations quickly became redundant as pub prices continued to spiral. In 1897 two were sold in Barking Road for £112,000. Truman had considered offering £102,000. 'It is evident', commented Buxton, 'that all our rivals in trade have convinced themselves that, however reluctantly, they must follow these high prices.' The fever reached its peak in 1897–9. Disappointed, Truman realised that their heavy capital expenditure did not result in markedly increased beer sales. From time to time they lamented that they simply spent to stand still. In fact, their trade advanced modestly in the 1890s although by 1898 they had tied 83 per cent of their trade.[8] The cost, they reckoned, was £1,100,000. And at the conclusion of the boom in 1899, the company took stock of its actions.

It is clear that the interest on this capital must be paid to the detriment of our profit. Yet if we had not made this gigantic effort we should have lost trade very heavily instead of gaining a little. It is admitted that the purchases made in recent years are beyond their intrinsic value. We must aim at bringing them down in our books to something like their intrinsic or old value.[9]

In this uniquely detailed surviving account of the scramble for property in the 1890s, as seen through the eyes of Truman's directors, it is the force of competition and the ease with which loans could be raised that stand out. When the firm was incorporated in 1889, the partners had received all the 12,150 £100 ordinary shares and one-third of the £1,200,000 4 per cent debenture stock. In 1897–8, a further £1.6 million of capital had been raised. Yet the old loans to publicans, in the easy financial conditions and the buoyant beer market of the late 1890s, also increased: from £1,441,896 in 1893 to £1,733,043 in 1900.[10] Change and tradition walked hand in hand.

The other big London breweries, drawn into the whirlpool of competition, reacted very similarly to events. For example, Whitbread was transformed in the 1890s. Incorporated in 1889, with a nominal share capital of £1,250,000, the firm issued debenture stock of £750,000. By 1901 this total capital of £2,000,000 had doubled, with debentures alone running at £2,000,000. Its leasehold and freehold properties, valued at only £26,430 in 1886, had increased, largely after 1893, to almost £2,000,000 by 1907. No fewer than five breweries were acquired between 1891 and 1902, principally because the firm saw their purchase as the cheapest means of buying houses.[11] As at Truman, the traditional forms of finance, loans and deposits did not wither away. Indeed, until 1905 they increased.[12] Also, the number of their *freehold* properties,

[8] See Appendix, Table II.
[9] The estimate was that their investment in public houses should be written down by around £500,000 across ten years.
[10] By 1914 these had fallen back to £634,026.
[11] (1891) H. & V. Nicholl, Lewisham; (1896) Gripper Brothers, Tottenham; (1898) Abridge Brewery, Essex; (1899) Matthews & Canning, Chelsea; (1902) Jones & Co., Bromley.
[12] Town trade loans grew from £1,649,088 in 1896 to a peak of £2,340,829 in 1901. After 1905 they declined rapidly to £626,904 in 1914. Deposits reached a peak of £996,410 in

thirty in 1893, had grown to 278 by 1910. Therefore Whitbread, partly also because their bottling venture was so successful (see p. 300), saw their barrelage burgeon. It more than doubled from 381,026 in 1890 to 778,152 in 1905. Other firms similarly fuelled the public house boom in the metropolis. The Cannon Brewery, enthusiastically seeking the protection of the tied house, saw its capital increase from £800,000 on incorporation in 1895 to £3,000,000 four years later. Its historian maintained that when its dynamic managing director, Andrew Motion, 'began to buy licensed property on a large scale for the output of the Cannon, he elaborated a system which was copied more and more by other breweries'.[13] Certainly, no other company was more prominent in buying grade one houses at higher prices (see Plates 34 and 35). Barclay Perkins was capitalised in 1896 at over £4 million, again with a large preference and debenture share issue. After Guinness, it was the biggest brewery capitalisation.[14] Both paled, however, beside the amalgamation of three great city breweries at the height of the boom in 1898. Watney Combe Reid, the brainchild of Cosmo Bonsor, with a capital of £15,000,000, was the largest British company of its day; and with a public preference and debenture share issue of £5,754,204 at 3.5–4 per cent it again, inevitably, fuelled pub prices.[15]

As a result of the London brewers' perceived need to protect themselves, of the ready availability of cheap money, of low raw material prices and good profits, and of the general domestic boom which swept Britain from 1894, the London beer trade became far more extensively and firmly tied than ever the old system of publican loans financed by deposits had guaranteed. Between 1895 and 1902 leaseholds were brought up at the rate of around 500 a year. Truman had tied 90 per cent of their trade by the turn of the century; other firms, buying pubs with the same exuberance, must have achieved similar results. The cost, easily countenanced in the high-feather conditions of the late 1890s, was massive. Calculations about barrelages, turnover and profits of individual houses, usually so carefully appraised by travellers, managers and

1900; by 1914 they had fallen to £148,724. (Whitbread Archives, W/8/1 Balance Sheets and Accounts.)

13 F. A. King, *The Story of the Cannon Brewery, 1751–1951* (1951), p. 12.

14 Gourvish and Wilson, 'Profitability in the Brewing Industry', pp. 149–50. Barclay Perkins came into the public house market very late indeed compared with Truman, Watneys and the Cannon Brewery. In 1896 their 'value of leases' was only £107,920. By 1902 it had grown almost to £700,000 and topped £1 million by 1911. (GLRO, Acc. 2305/1/394–5, Capital Accounts Rest 1801–1912).

15 GLRO, Acc. 78/989, 'Prospectus of Watney Combe Reid & Co., 7 July 1898' and H. Janes, *The Red Barrel: A History of Watney Mann* (1963), pp. 144–52.

directors, seem to have been set aside as company outbid company with, briefly, undreamt supplies of capital at their command. Then after 1900 in a different economic climate, the doubts, which directors had put behind them at the zenith of the boom, materialised many-fold. Conditions in the London beer trade were indeed bleak to 1914.

II

The agency system of the Burton brewers worked well until the changed conditions of the 1880s. Then, increasingly shut out of other brewers' tied houses as the free trade contracted, and with their sales undermined by every brewer attempting to brew an imitative pale ale, they had to reconsider their position. With cheap barley and malt prices ruling in the 1880s and therefore with generous gross profit margins, they responded initially by offering increased discounts: 20–25 per cent became general. But neither of the above forces relented, and eventually, as the stock of free houses began to dry up, the Burton brewers were forced very late into acquiring a hastily constructed protective shield.

It is clear that their initial response to the contraction of beer sales in the 1880s, to other brewers' production of *cheaper* pale ales, and to accelerated purchase of tied houses, was, reluctantly, to offer bigger price discounts. Of course, this added to the intense competition between the Burton brewers themselves. Bass possessed the strongest position, in the sheer scale of its operations and with an unparalleled reputation for its beers and its probity. In the mid-1890s it attempted to force its bottlers, like those of Guinness, into exclusive agreements. Nevertheless the position of the market leaders was being constantly eroded by the smaller brewers offering larger discounts. In 1891 Worthington noted that Allsopp were offering 22 per cent in South Wales, Thomas Salt 25 per cent in Manchester and Scotland, Evershed 27 per cent, Thompson, Charrington and Ind Coope, 22–27 per cent in the Potteries, and the ubiquitous Tadcaster Brewery Co. 30–35 per cent generally.[16] A few months earlier they recorded with weary resignation that, 'the Burton Houses are just as ready as ever to outbid us in discounts'.[17] Worthington's minute books reveal that they and Bass remained arch rivals throughout the 1890s and beyond in London, Hull and elsewhere in matters of loans and discounts. At one stage, a

[16] Bass Archives, A/106, Worthington and Co.'s Minute Books, no. 3 (1891–2).
[17] *Ibid.*, quoting letter of their London manager, 12 Nov. 1890.

dispute about a restaurateur in Liverpool passing off Worthington as Bass to gain a further 2 per cent discount ended in the law courts and press. Normally, a seething hostility persisted.

The discount war was self-defeating. As brewers tied their houses and attempted to remove the Burton pale ale supply, the latter trade contracted. Bass sold 10 per cent less beer in the 1880s, Allsopp 25 per cent. And although their trade, like Worthington's, recovered in the 1890s, the small brewers in Burton were, according to Kevin Hawkins, in 'a parlous state'.[18] But the discount disputes, in effect a price war, never abated. Those of Bass grew between 1888 and 1899 from a massive £403,728 to £685,276 or from an average of 9s 5.7d to 10s 6.1d per barrel. Worthington's similarly expanded from £99,952 in 1889 to £153,251 in 1898. There is no doubt that in the capital in the late 1890s the leading Burton brewers in competition with themselves and their London rivals were sucked into a highly speculative and complex property spiral of which they, momentarily, lost control.

Problems for the Burton brewers became particularly acute in London in the mid-1880s and again in the 1895–9 boom because so much pale ale was sold in the capital. Although Bass, and presumably Allsopp, had begun to make modest loans earlier to tie their pale ale trade, Worthington made none before 1887. As late as 1886 they had written to their London manager, 'we cannot see any reason for altering our previous determination not to grant loans'. Obviously, changing conditions in the London beer market forced their hand. Initially, Worthington's loans in London were not large. Like those of the Burton brewers generally, they were usually in the £1,000–£5,000 range. Invariably they were made in conjunction with a London brewer (making much larger loans for the porter and mild tie), often the vendor, sometimes an insurance company, and a private investor. As many as five charges could be listed against the mortgage of the lease or freehold. Discounts were negotiated (Worthington usually acting with the Cannon Brewery and applying what they called 'the Motion scale'), the cash input of the publican stated, and barrelages calculated. The new arrangements were clearly testing for brewery managements, especially when speculation became rife. Publicans in London were a mobile species; there were many sharp middlemen involved in the sale of leases, ready to take a quick profit as premiums escalated; brewers tied their trade and then, sometimes quickly, sold their newly acquired properties

[18] Hawkins, 'Brewing Industry', p. 189.

on to public house investors; increasing sums were raised to refurbish houses in the 1890s employing mirrors, plate glass, mahogany and brass with *fin de siècle* abandon (see Plate 37).[19] Although the tenant paid for these improvements, it was the brewers who either made the loan at 5 per cent or bought the lease and attempted to recoup his investment by charging an enhanced rent. Bass's loans, of which the majority before 1907 were in London, grew fast: from under £150,000 in 1880, to over £550,000 in 1889 and £1,402,000 in 1900–1.

Few Burton brewers *owned* pubs in London before the mid-1890s. Even Bass owned only twenty-seven *nationwide* in 1883 and only fourteen in London in 1892. Allsopp owned none in 1887 and their chairman at the company's first annual general meeting stated, 'they do not intend to'.[20] But with brewers everywhere buying pubs in the late 1880s and debenture issues making purchases easy, the policy of the Burton brewers began to shift. In 1889 the Burton Brewery Co. reckoned it had been forced to spend £116,000 on sixty-five houses in 1888–9 because it had lost 235 customers when other brewers had purchased these houses and tied their trade. In the same year, Worthington observed that brewers had begun to buy houses in Swansea. Ind Coope had recently acquired four, A. B. Walker twelve and Truman three. Therefore they themselves contemplated 'any proposals [laid] before us from time to time'. In London, Worthington began to record their anxiety in November 1895, 'Mr. Manners [managing director] brought before the Board the serious position recently. Come about by the action of many London Brewers who are buying houses out and out and securing the whole of the malt trade – to the exclusion of all Burton beers.' Manners was particularly concerned that the Cannon Brewery was, 'buying houses in all directions' and 'insisting upon loanees (in a very large measure) taking the beers produced by them'.[21] At first, he lamented the seriousness of Worthington's position and the breakdown of their arrangements with the Cannon Brewery; by the summer of 1896 they themselves had begun to buy London pubs.[22] A few months later,

19 Examples of 'selling on' are to be found in Truman's minutes and also in accounts of Worthington's association with Andrew Motion of the Cannon Brewery, who appears to have been the prime mover in these schemes. In 1893 Worthington's manager, negotiating a £3,000 loan for Ross & Davis of the 'Southampton', noted they had spent £7,600 on 'Fittings, Furniture and Decoration'.

20 Reported in *Country Brewers' Gazette* (1888), p. 424, quoted in Gourvish and Wilson, 'Profitability', p. 153.

21 *The Financial Times*, 9 Dec. 1889; 23 Jan. 1890; Bass Archives, A/60 Worthington & Co.'s minutes, entries for 28 Nov. 1895, 11 May, 11 June 1896 and 4 Jan. 1897.

22 The 'Crown and Anchor', Finsbury Pavement, for £65,000; The 'Priory', Clapton, for £40,500.

Bass's London agent, W. H. Bailey, reported events back to the company secretary, John Lambrick, in Burton:

> Worthingtons are giving big prices. They gave £40,000 for 'The Priory' at Clapton, £63,000 for our 'Woolpack' at Moorgate, £40,000 or more [£65,000] for the House under their offices in Finsbury Pavement and a huge price (don't know figure) for Raggett's in Jermyn Street.
>
> They resell a tied house and I hear they are working jointly with Nicholson's. Of course these last will work with anybody for their own advantage – as they have been so heavily hit by the boom.

And he concluded with the sober wisdom that prevailed generally at Bass: 'By and by we shall have the slump.'[23] Prophetic words, and certainly not heeded at Allsopp. By the mid 1890s with an improvement in their affairs they began completely to reverse their previous policy. In 1898 'the policy of securing trade by the purchase of, and investments in, licensed properties has been so successful' that they proposed raising £950,000 to acquire more.[24] In 1897–1900 Allsopp went into the market with a folly no other brewery matched. *The Economist* considered the prices they paid 'insane';[25] Allsopp proclaimed, in a moment of rare insight, 'they were sowing in order that they might reap'.[26] In three years the company increased its share issue by an extraordinary £3,250,000 to fund this headlong expansion.

In fact, the scale of purchase needed to achieve total protection was an impossible goal for the leading Burton brewers. Allsopp had acquired 363 houses by 1900 only after massive expenditure, and Bass over 500, principally in Wales, south Lancashire and the Potteries.[27] In addition, they continued to operate generous discounts to secure trade and, like the London breweries, to negotiate publican loans from their agencies. Allsopp had £1.7 million of trade loans in 1900, Bass £1.4 million in the

[23] Bass Archives, A/135, Private Box, W. H. Bailey to J. Lambrick, 10 Feb. 1897.

[24] Stock Exchange Company Reports, Allsopp circular dated 12 March 1898.

[25] *The Economist* (1900), p. 1265. In June 1898 W. H. Bailey reported two pubs, the 'Angel', Victoria and the 'Rockingham', with 999 year leases changing hands for a truly incredible £325,000. Truman had agreed loans of £150,000 on these, the vendor (Brinkley, who had given £220,000 for them recently) £90,000. Bass, who had made a loan of £40,000 to Brinkley, 'lost a trade of £8,000 a year at one blow and a splendid bottled trade but I declined to ask you to lend a solitary sixpence in such a case as this'.

[26] *Country Brewers' Gazette* (1899), p. 626.

[27] Hawkins, 'Brewing Industry', p. 190 (the figure of 1200 cited in Hawkins and Pass, *Brewing Industry*, p. 32 must be erroneous, for in 1914 they owned 461: Owen, *Development of Industry*, p. 95). Bass's purchases had been far more provident: although they issued £1.8 million preference and debenture shares in 1888–91, there was only one further modest issue of £560,000 3½ per cent debentures in 1897.

same year.[28] But the Burton brewers, especially the smaller companies, continued to remain highly vulnerable because their exposure to the free trade was still marked. Bass's London trade, for example, contracted from 36 per cent of its total sales in 1890 to 26 by 1900 and Worthington made 57.4 per cent of its sales of 404,753 barrels as late as 1911 in the free trade.[29] Yet the latter firm showed that advances could be made by the vigorous marketing of their bottled beers. They saw their total sales expand from 240,000 in 1889 to over 400,000 for the first time in 1911. Elsewhere in Burton experiences were very different. The 'scramble for property' had not provided the guarantee of protection it briefly promised in the late 1890s. Burton's brewers, whose numbers declined from thirty-one in 1888 to seventeen in 1911, were hit even harder than their London counterparts in the down-turn of the industry's fortunes in the 1900s.

III

The country brewers enjoyed a different experience from the London and Burton brewers in the rapid acquisition of tied property in the 1880s and 1890s. Few could have contemplated either the loans or the prices which were paid in the capital. Except in its suburbs, they stood aside. Moreover, their purchase of houses was unlike that of the leading Burton brewers. The latter created far-flung, almost unplanned, semi-national collections which were built up from their various agencies across the country. On the other hand, for country brewers, concentration and selectivity was the recipe for success. Of course not all brewers made shrewd purchases in equal measure, but those breweries that flourished in the difficult years from 1900 to 1914 and beyond had invariably bought wisely or, like Guinness, not bought at all.

Some breweries, especially in the South and East, as we have seen, had built up considerable stocks of tied houses by the early 1880s. This was fortunate, for agricultural depression in the 1880s and 1890s meant that trading conditions were far less buoyant for them than for brewers in the industrial and mining heartlands of the Midlands, South Wales, Northern England and Central Scotland. Even here brewers from the

28 The interesting feature of Bass's loans is that before 1900 they were principally in the London trade; by 1907 those made in the provinces predominated. They began to include substantial loans to other brewers – in London, Newcastle upon Tyne, Hull, Plymouth, Bolton, Manchester and even Burton – to tie the pale ale trade.

29 Bass Archives, F/15/1, Worthington Co.'s Agency Book, 1906–11. In 1906 it had been 59.1 per cent.

1860s had been buying houses and negotiating short- and long-term leases, and making modest loans to tie their trade. But two features, besides the response to recession in the industry after 1876, and increasing fears about licence restriction, undoubtedly hotted up the pace from the mid-1880s: the rapid incorporation of partnerships and what Hawkins and Pass term the 'domino' effect.[30] The two were closely linked.

Whether or not they discussed conditions in the industry at meetings of the Country Brewers' Society and the local Brewing Associations, or eagerly read their trade journals, all company chairmen made similar pronouncements at their annual general meetings in the 1885–1900 period. That made by Henry Boddington in Manchester in February 1889 is representative, except in his passage on free trade. In Manchester this must have been obligatory; elsewhere it was usually skipped.

> The freehold and long leasehold property held by the firm was valued at the large sum of £178,037. Considerable purchases had been made under this head during the year. The directors regretted to find that, in the brewing trade, Free-trade was less and less possible. Free-trade placed brewers on their mettle, and made them produce a good article in order to succeed, but when the directors found houses which were occupied by their customers in the market they were obliged to purchase the houses if the price was reasonable, or other brewers would do so and take away trade.[31]

But if these utterances made after incorporation by brewery chairmen up and down the country were very similar on the need to buy tied property, real differences existed in practice. In moves to acquire a substantial tied estate a good deal depended upon the vision and drive of the directorate: some felt more vulnerable than others; some had more ample resources; some were prepared to borrow more adventurously. In Scotland, because the nature of the licence was different, the tied house system did not 'generally prevail' according to those who gave evidence to the Royal Commission on the Liquor Licensing Laws between 1896 and 1899. Nevertheless some Scottish brewers began to acquire houses in the North-East of England, although more usually they developed the loan-tie. If the great Edinburgh firm of William Younger & Co. was typical, their moves were late and low key.[32] In the rural areas of the

[30] Hawkins and Pass, *Brewing Industry*, p. 28.

[31] *Courier*, 28 Feb. 1889 (newspaper cutting in Boddingtons' Breweries Ltd Minute Book 1 in Whitbread Archives, 1/13).

[32] Donnachie, *Brewing Industry in Scotland*, pp. 194–6. But in comparison with the firm's barrelage and with those made by London and Burton brewers they were indeed modest. In 1904 at their peak they were only £66,750.

South-West of England and the western half of the country generally, purchases of freeholds came in the 1890s boom. And everywhere brewers had to rid themselves of their old rule-of-thumb calculations about pub prices and reluctance to make loans to tenants.

By 1900 some very impressive estates of tied houses had been built up by the country brewers. The 1892 return, made before the greatest period of activity in 1895–9, showed that in England and Wales seventy-six breweries *owned* more than 100 licensed houses each; and of the eleven biggest owners, each with more than 200 houses, all were country brewers.[33] Most usually, these breweries owned and leased scores of houses before incorporation and then, by the issue of debenture capital, went headlong into the market especially during the late 1890s. John Smith's Tadcaster Brewery Co. for example, was incorporated by the Riley-Smith brothers in August 1892. They owned 119 fully licensed pubs, beer houses and off-licences (a fair number of which had been bought in the previous eight months), tying sixty-six similar properties by lease and yearly tenancy, and a further thirty-eight 'by means of loans or otherwise'.[34] In all there were 223 licensed premises attached to the business. Immediately, they issued £200,000 debenture stock at 4 per cent to acquire more, and by April 1895, when £150,000 5 per cent cumulative preference shares were issued,'the Company at the present time has under its control 512 licensed properties'. The moves had placed its trade 'upon a very stable and secure foundation'. Similarly, Bents spent £585,000 in the 1890s on buying new property; Henry Mitchell & Co. Ltd quickly built up control of over 200 houses by 1892; Lacon, with 352 tied houses in 1897, had 504 (including 126 off licences) in 1904.[35]

Few breweries matched Georges Bristol Brewery's attempts to achieve growth by public house purchase in the five years after their incorporation in 1888. The brewery had marked time for much of the

[33] Hawkins and Pass, *Brewing Industry*, p. 30. Of those seventy-six companies only ten were based in London and two in Burton; together the seventy-six companies owned 12,614 houses or 12 per cent of the total stock in England and Wales. The largest owners were Greenall Whitley & Co. (681 houses), Steward & Patteson (473), Peter Walker & Sons Ltd (410), Bristol Brewery Georges Ltd (350), Colchester Brewery Co. (289), Truman (267), Bullard & Co. (260), Watney & Co. (258), Phipps & Co. (242), Thwaites & Co. (219), Boddingtons' Breweries Ltd (212). See note 3 for the limitations of the 1892 return.

[34] Courage (Tadcaster), John Smith's Tadcaster Brewery Co. Ltd Prospectus, 12 August 1892 and 22 April 1895. The value of public houses in 1892 was reckoned at £119,908 of which £62,029 had been purchased (or agreed) since 1 Jan. 1892. The 1895 prospectus provided little detail about its properties.

[35] K. Hawkins, *Bass Charrington*, pp. 28, 44; Whitbread Archives, 197/119.

1870s and 1880s.[36] Although profits were ample, beer sales in 1887 equalled those of 1873. Then with incorporation, the old management was transformed. Modestly capitalised at £300,000, the company in the next few years issued £162,000 worth of debenture stock and a further £300,000 of ordinary and preference shares at considerable premiums. Owning around seventy houses on incorporation, the directors went into the public house market with gusto in 1888–93. The Bedminster Brewery was bought in 1889, and throughout these years the company was buying and leasing houses and making loans. In a busy period in late 1888–early 1889 it was acquiring pubs at the rate of two dozen a month. The minute books are full of property transactions: beer and the brewery were rarely mentioned. Barrelages and profits doubled in three years over their levels in the 1870s and 1880s. By early 1892 Georges owned 380 houses and leased a further 120. The book value of these had increased from £89,103 in 1889 to £501,480 in 1893. The 1892 survey revealed that Georges owned no fewer than 289 houses in Bristol alone. It was a record of concentration matched by no other brewery in England. By 1893 the company, only very recently enjoying the free trade which persisted generally in Bristol and the West Country, had tied 89 per cent of its trade. Three years later the proportion was 94 per cent. Georges were unusual in that they had largely curtailed their property buying as early as 1893. They did not look much beyond the Bristol region except in South Wales; they made numerous, but invariably small, loans; and they paid a dividend of 15 per cent plus throughout the 1890s. In 1889, at the first annual general meeting, C. E. A. George had stated: 'he took it that a tied trade was an absolutely safe trade, a safe dividend paying trade for the proprietors'. Bristol Brewery Georges & Co. Ltd observed this text throughout the 1890s. They were the supreme exemplars of a company who had acquired tied property generously and wisely. They had a defined policy; they knew when to stop.

Most country brewers made similar moves. Simonds of Reading, although they relied increasingly upon army canteen contracts, doubled their stock of tied houses to 158 between 1872 and 1896.[37] Thomas Phillips, who had acquired a tiny Newport (Monmouth) brewery with four owned pubs and nine on annual tenancies in 1874, had 125 by their

[36] This paragraph is based upon the minute books of the company, the Reports of the Directors, Georges' balance sheets, and the unusually detailed 'Report of the Proceedings of the Annual Meeting of Shareholders' 1889 ff. These ran to four or five closely printed pages each year – supposedly to counter misrepresentation in the press.

[37] Corley, 'Simonds Brewery at Reading', p. 83.

jubilee fifty years later.[38] In Newark, Warwicks & Richardsons in a prospectus of 1907 stated that they had bought sixty-eight pubs since 1888. It claimed to have 111 freehold houses besides seventeen on long leases and seventy-four on short lease and yearly tenancies. Many of them were sited in urban centres: Newcastle, Grantham, Nottingham, Peterborough, Doncaster, Lincoln, Hull, Grimsby and Leicester.[39] Even in areas in which publican brewing had flourished into the 1880s public house proprietorship witnessed a rapid change. In 1897, 89 per cent of Halifax's trade was tied, principally to six breweries.[40] Again, Tetley, which had flourished in the Leeds free trade for seventy years, shifted its policy in the early 1890s. In 1890 it possessed two pubs, in 1904, 185 – although two-thirds of their market was still in the free trade.[41]

As a consequence of these concerted moves, pub prices, especially during the 1895–9 boom, rose sharply. Conditions were exactly right. Consumption surged sharply forward again; profits, with low brewing material prices, were good; money was cheap. The race by brewers to acquire the last free houses and vulnerable small breweries was on. Although prices in the provinces never touched those recorded in London, there were sharp advances. In Lancashire, beer houses in large villages were reported to be changing hands for £5,000 apiece in 1895; two year's later, although Warwicks & Richardsons's country pubs were valued by a Lincoln firm at £700–£1,000 each, those in Grimsby and Nottingham were estimated to be worth as much as £8,000.[42] Rowntree and Sherwell, attacking the 'monopoly' value conferred by an on-licence on property, provided some remarkable examples. The 'Crooked Billet', opposite Armstrong Whitworth's works, had fetched £15,800 in 1896 (see Plate 38). Even then, it was pulled down and rebuilt. Forty years earlier it had changed hands for £900. Similarly, the 'Ord Arms' opposite Armstrong's new works had sold for £28,100. As Rowntree pointed out, the Twizell estate in the same county with a good mansion and 700 acres had made only £25,000.[43] Even in depressed Suffolk, competition from the Norwich brewers, Watneys and Whitbread, was

[38] *Phillips and Sons Ltd. Jubilee 1924*, pp. 5–6, 10.
[39] Courage (Tadcaster), JD/C/15.
[40] Robinson, 'Emergence of the Common Brewer in the Halifax District', pp. 77–9.
[41] C. F. Tetley, *A Century of Progress* (1923); Lackey, *Quality Pays*, pp. 64–6; Hawkins, p. 174.
[42] Hawkins, *Bass Charrington*, p. 44; Courage (Tadcaster), JD/E/2, valuation by Vickers & Shaw, Lincoln.
[43] Rowntree and Sherwell, *Temperance Problem*, pp. 516–19.

driving up prices in the market towns by 1896–7. Greene King were paying £3,500–£4,000 for properties which would have cost them little more than one-third of that a decade earlier.[44]

In these conditions, sensible purchase was a real test of managerial skills. Few were as successful as Edward Lake, the managing director of Greene King. In 1898 he wrote in his annual report,

> It is interesting to note that during the eleven years which have elapsed since the formation of the Company no less than £157,602 has been expended on the purchase of 157 houses. Only £41,000 of this has been met by debentures. The rest of this amount has been found net of Profits and by the amount written off Machinery and the reduction of Capital in Book Debts, Beer, Malt, Hops etc.[45]

Few brewers had Edward Lake's light touch with loan capital in the 1890s. Moreover, as he and many other brewers lamented, purchase did not guarantee an enlarged trade, for often they were expensively tying houses formerly served in the free trade or secured by lease or annual tenancy. And some brewers put together collections of licensed properties that were too far from their home base to manage profitably. For example, Arnold, Perrett & Co. Ltd of Gloucester bought two Devonshire breweries with eighty-four houses in 1889 and 1893; in 1896, in order to concentrate trade, both were sold to Starkey, Knight & Co.[46] Also brewers' calculations about licensed property values, usually reckoned to be five times the value of the house's annual beer turnover, were upset in the price spiral. It became increasingly rare for rentals to provide a 5 per cent return on capital, especially since they took no account of repairs and depreciation.

Of course there were small breweries which could take little part in the bonanza of the 1890s beyond buying the odd beer house and the out-of-the-way pub. As the free trade contracted they became the prey, albeit invariably quiescent, of larger breweries everywhere. With stocks often of no more than a score of houses they nevertheless provided, in their release of new trade, the means for larger brewers to extend their capacity. The Tadcaster Tower Brewery, whose schemes always outran its resources, advertised in the *Yorkshire Post* in 1886,

> To small brewers and others – A large and well-known firm of Yorkshire Brewers – knowing the utter impossibility it is for small brewers to make

[44] Wilson, *Greene King*, p. 138.
[45] *Ibid.*, p. 146.
[46] Hawkins, 'Brewing Industry', p. 207 and his *Bass Charrington*, pp. 41–2.

headway and to make any profits at the present time – will be glad to hear from all and any such brewers with a view to amalgamation or purchase.[47]

As a result of similar, more discreet moves the number of breweries fell sharply in the thirty years after 1885 (see Table 3.9). And others survived without expanding their tied trade. In Hertfordshire, eleven leading brewers had tied 46.5 per cent of the county's trade (1,453 houses) in 1892; a decade later they controlled 74.5 per cent (1,566).[48] But only five of these, swallowing up the county's smallest breweries and every free house which came onto the market, expanded their ownership. The position of the rest remained essentially unchanged.

IV

What were the effects of the rapid growth of the tied trade in these years? They were not so harmful to competition as numerous critics averred. The old days of dumping inferior beer in a firm's tied houses had, if they ever existed, passed. Brewers, when asked questions about these practices by the Peel Commission in 1896–9, seemed genuinely insulted by them. In 1892 there were fifteen breweries which *owned* more than a hundred pubs each in nine towns. And only in eight, all of them small except Warrington, did a *single* brewery *own* more than half of the town's tied property. Of course the situation changed between the 1892 return and 1900. But there was, except in rural areas and the smaller towns, fierce competition between brewers. In London it was unrelenting to 1914, and a perusal of company minute books suggests that in towns like Edinburgh, Newcastle, Liverpool and Leeds it was equally fierce. Even in Norwich, long overrun with tied licensed property, five breweries maintained cut-throat competition. In Bristol there was fierce rivalry between its two leading breweries, both controlling hundreds of tied houses in the city. The scramble for property between 1885 and 1900 did not make collusion easier. Brewers might increasingly co-operate in matters of excise, materials and licences, and undoubtedly the brewing journals and discussion in the Country Brewers' Associations made them better informed on a whole range of

[47] *Yorkshire Post*, 15 May 1886 and *Yorkshire Gazette*, 12 June 1886. The manager C. H. Tripp wrote in the brewery diary, 'no York paper has ever before produced such an advertisement'.

[48] Those breweries which notably expanded were McMullen (54 to 139), Benskin's (36 to 201), Pryor Reid (21 to 137), Askey & White (29 to 71), Lucas (16 to 43). The tables from returns of 1892 and 1902 are analysed in Hawkins, 'Brewing Industry', pp. 175–6. They are, of course, lists of *owned* property and do not include those held on lease and annual tenancy.

issues, but in matters of property, finance and competition breweries remained highly secretive organisations.

Whereas, in the past, publicans had in theory been able to shift their suppliers with ease, they were in 1900 firmly tied by agreement and loan not only for their beer but also for tobacco, spirits, wines and aerated waters – often all supplied by the brewery. It is possible to overestimate the publican's freedom in an exaggerated free-trade past. Outside London, loans (admittedly, small ones) were made, and webs of debts inevitably tied publicans. Even independent publican brewers were constrained by the credit networks of maltster and brewer alike. By the end of the century competition between brewers to retain the free trade had largely shifted to competition between publicans. This put the brewers on their mettle. A brewery's reputation now depended not only on its beers but also on its pubs. These had to be improved, good tenants selected, a reputation in the community cultivated and, in today's parlance, a good 'corporate-image' created. Critics of the industry failed to realise the way the onus of respectability had shifted to the brewer. Moreover, although in the 1890s brewers like Georges imagined they were constructing impregnable tied fortresses into which they could retreat, conditions in the industry after 1900, above all the animus of the Liberal government (itself in part fired by the excesses of the 1895–1900 boom), meant the dream was never perfectly realised.

After 1900, conditions in the brewing industry changed with remarkable rapidity. And we have an unprecedented view of them because the chairmen of the new companies now had to compile yearly reports and address their shareholders at annual general meetings. Many, because incorporation in practice meant little diffusion of shareholding, remained private affairs, but the larger companies, and some others with preference and debenture shareholders, were obliged to hold annual meetings at which they presented their reports and accounts. Of course, these occasions were carefully orchestrated, and chairmen sometimes hid unpalatable items in the accounts and glossed over managerial misjudgements. Some spoke with remarkable brevity; others, especially on the subject of the government's treatment of the trade, provide extended accounts of the industry's plight in these troubled years.[49] As a result, individual companies – indeed the industry

[49] The best accounts are those provided by the chairmen of Watney Combe Reid, Barclay Perkins, the Cannon and New Westminster breweries in London, Bristol Brewery Georges, Mitchells & Butlers (Birmingham), J. W. Cameron (Hartlepool), Newcastle Breweries. The chairmen of Bass, Guinness and the leading Scottish breweries were, at least as reported in the *Brewing Trade Review*, 'Companies Meetings' section, relatively

generally – were opened up to the scrutiny of the financial, local and trade press. When things went badly wrong between 1900 and 1914, especially in the London and Burton breweries, the spotlight was turned upon them. Shareholders' meetings were more frequent and often acrimonious. The old days of total secrecy maintained within partnerships had passed, at least for the leading companies.

How, from these reports, did brewers view the industry in the Edwardian period? There were many points of consensus. All were agreed that there were real pressures upon working-class standards of living in these years. Consumption of beer fell in every year from 1899 to 1909: in England, by some 14 per cent. Even with good summers, as in 1908, demand did not revive. Although Percy Gates of the New Westminster Brewery represented 1908 as a 'most anxious year' with the industry exposed to 'the crest of the wave of temperance', brewers firmly believed that demand would spring back once employment and wages advanced.[50] Given that consumption did revive in 1910–13, their analysis was fundamentally correct. Moreover, they admitted that traditional patterns of working-class expenditure were changing. Other consumer industries, with the development of a mass market in ready-made clothing and shoes, machine-produced furniture and packaged foodstuffs, began seriously to compete with spending on alcohol; music halls, football and cheap railway excursions flourished; in London and the largest cities the extension of suburbs undermined the trade of once crowded, central drinking establishments. Brewers experienced this pressure on wages and the impact of all these changes in a marked shift to bottled and cheaper beers, increasingly retailed through off-licences, grocers shops, clubs and, in some urban areas, by 'family' brewers and agents hawking beer from door to door. It was ironic that just as the brewers had virtually completed their ownership of tied houses, the popularity of the public house, that old citadel of working-class leisure, declined. Even in deepest Suffolk, Edward Lake warned the Greene King directorate in 1904 that, 'there seemed a tendency among the public not to use the Public Houses as formerly'.[51] The real shift in the

uninformative. Those of Allsopp's Ind Coope and Meux provide long accounts of the restructuring of companies *in extremis*.'

For a detailed survey of the trade, compiled from the collective actions of the brewers and retailers in the 1875–1914 period as seen through the (Country) Brewers' Society, the Brewers' Company, the National Trade Defence Association, brewers' associations in various counties and the retailers' organisations, see D. W. Gutzke, *Protecting the Pub*.

50 *Brewing Trade Review*, 1 Feb. 1909.

51 Wilson, *Greene King*, p. 131.

role of the public house came in the inter-war years (see pp. 418–37), but the origins are rooted in the Edwardian period.

Of course, some brewers blamed the temperance lobby for their plight. The mere mention of its two principal spokesmen in Parliament, Sir Wilfred Lawson and Sir Thomas Whittaker, could induce apoplexy in the mildest brewery director. But publicly, brewers were sufficiently adroit to condemn drunkenness. By providing good beer in well-run public houses and anticipating a return of working-class prosperity, they believed their affairs would again flourish.[52] Yet if brewers could rationally explain their misfortunes – usually tending to have a collective amnesia about their participation in 'the scramble for property' in the late 1890s – what they could not forgive was the action of the government. All their difficulties in the 1900s were laid at its door. Therefore, before the contrasting fortunes of breweries are assessed, it is necessary to outline the basis of conflict between the government and the industry in these years.[53]

V

The dispute focused upon two issues: the extinction of surplus on-licences, and the government's increasing propensity to tax the industry. Both were clearly central to profitability, and both had an increased impact as beer consumption slumped and the industry's earnings faltered after 1900.

Discussions about extensive reform of the licensing system went back to Bruce's abortive Bill of 1871 (see p. 252).[54] The crux of the problem, given the reformers' objective of restricting licences to one per 1,000 population in urban districts and one per 600 in rural areas, was one of compensation. How far, if at all, should the owners be reimbursed for their loss when on-licences were removed from premises? Discussions centred upon the concept of the 'monopoly' value that the licence

[52] For the 'improved public house' movement see G. B. Wilson, *The 'Improved Public-House': Is It a Day-Dream or a Smoke-Screen?* (United Kingdom Alliance, n.d.). Early proponents of the movement amongst brewers were Robert Cain & Sons, Liverpool, Peter Walker & Son, Warrington and, above all, Mitchells & Butlers, Birmingham. See for example W. Waters Butler's speech reported in *Brewing Trade Review*, 1 Dec. 1901.

[53] The fullest survey will be found in Gutzke, *Protecting the Pub*. See also D. M. Fahey, 'Brewers, Publicans and Working-Class Drinkers: Pressure Group Politics in Late Victorian and Edwardian England', *Histoire Sociale/Social History*, 13 (1980), pp. 85–103 and A. E. Dingle, *The Campaign for Prohibition in Victorian England: The United Kingdom Alliance, 1872–1895* (1980). Rowntree and Sherwell, *The Temperance Problem* and Wilson, *Alcohol and the Nation* are also useful guides.

[54] For a summary of the Bill's main proposals, see Wilson, *Alcohol and the Nation*, p. 106.

conferred and the 'time limit' within which compensation would be paid for licences to be rescinded. There were other issues which the brewers faced in these years, above all Local Option (in effect prohibition in any district where a two-thirds majority of ratepayers voted for the abolition of its public houses), Sunday Closing (achieved, partially, in Scotland in 1853, in Ireland in 1878 and in Wales in 1881), and the discussion of experiments like the Gothenburg scheme and the proposals of the Bishop of Chester in the early 1890s.[55]

Traditionally, both historians and Liberal politicians have viewed the late nineteenth-century temperance question as a confrontation between an immensely rich and politically strong caucus of brewers facing a variety of temperance bodies essentially less well organised and well heeled.[56] More recently, this view has been contested in studies arguing that the drink trades, as brewers enforced the tie, were increasingly divided and were frugal in their support of their trading organisations. Only in the early 1890s was effort sufficiently co-ordinated to wreck Local Option schemes. The real strength of the trade was the scale of its contribution to government taxation, the numbers employed in the drink and related industries, and the wealth and standing of its leaders in Parliament and society.[57] Certainly there is the impression that the industry could live with its temperance detractors between 1870 and 1900. R. B. Weir concludes of these years, 'Temperance had promised much and delivered little.'[58] Truman, who possessed the best set of political antennae in the trade in the 1890s, were clearly troubled with the prospect of restrictive legislation in the early part of the decade but they eventually realised there were so many bills and schemes 'flying around' that it was 'not likely that anything very drastic will be

55 The Gothenburg system (1865) was concerned with the municipalisation of the spirits trade. Joseph Chamberlain took up the theme in 1877. In 1892 the Bishop of Chester drew attention to the failings of ordinary temperance reform. In a letter to *The Times* in August 1892 he advocated State control of public houses, reform which promoted the sale of non-alcoholic beverages and provision of improved recreational facilities. Rowntree and Sherwell, *Temperance Problem*, pp. 569–71; *Brewing Trade Review*, Oct. 1892, p. 297; *Brewers' Journal*, Oct. 1894, pp. 546–9. Also see J. R. Greenaway, 'Bishops, Brewers and the Liquor Question in England, 1890–1914', *Historical Magazine of the Protestant Episcopal Church*, 53 (1984), pp. 61–75, and 'The Drink Problem back on the Political Agenda', *Political Quarterly*, 61 (1980), pp. 80–92.

56 For a convenient summary of the literature, see R. B. Weir, 'Obsessed with Moderation: The Drink Trades (1870–1920)', *British Journal of Addiction*, 79 (1984), pp. 93–107.

57 See especially Gutzke, *Protecting the Pub*.

58 Weir, 'Obsessed with Moderation', p. 97.

carried'.[59] And when the Local Option Bill was defeated and a Conservative government returned in 1895 there was a massive sense of relief amongst brewers.

Nevertheless the licensing issue did not go away. *Sharp v. Wakefield* (1891) had confirmed the magistrates' powers to remove licences without compensation for reasons other than the misconduct of licensees. As brewers acquired more and more houses this right increasingly troubled them. Although many brewers were themselves Justices of the Peace, they were excluded from the annual licensing sessions. The same omission was not observed by their temperance opponents. Especially in the boroughs, and sometimes backed by chief constables and inspectors of police holding similar views, brewers felt temperance magistrates could unfairly press home their drink animus in licensing affairs. In fact, the number of licences did not fall sharply before 1900. The picture, however, is somewhat obscured because although the total of pre-1869 beershops did fall, it was a decline partly compensated for by a rapid growth of off-licences which the magistrates (such was their view of the public house as the bastion of drunkenness) encouraged.[60] Moreover, much to the brewers' chagrin, the number of clubs also grew appreciably in the thirty years before 1914.[61] Yet full on-licences contracted only marginally from 68,358 in 1869 to 67,071 in 1902. The effect was that the number of persons per on-licence increased from 223:1 in 1875 to 324:1 in 1906 – a considerable shift, yet a figure far adrift from temperance goals. The brewers were not opposed to these trends. Restriction maintained the prices of tied property; and there was a realisation, particularly in Birmingham and Liverpool, that licences were too numerous. And in Birmingham from the late 1890s, and later in other towns, brewers co-operated with magistrates in 'surrender' schemes.[62] But

59 GLRO, acc. 77.94, B/THB, Trumans' Monthly Reports, 1890–5.

60 Wilson, *Alcohol and the Nation*, Table 25, pp. 394–406.

61 These were predominantly working-class clubs. The number of all clubs increased from 1,982 in 1887 to 8,738 in 1914. In the latter year 1,613 of these with 489,000 members were affiliated to the Working Men's Clubs and Institute Union. See Wilson, *Alcohol and the Nation*, pp. 134–47, 384, and Gutzke, *Protecting the Pub*, pp. 192–203. Gutzke maintains the brewers were the principal backers of clubs. Yet brewery chairmen, for example those of J. W. Cameron and Newcastle Breweries, roundly denounced them in the 1900s. They disliked their competition, their lack of magisterial regulation and their payment of minimum registration duties. Of course, small family brewers might have realised an opportunity, but leading London and country brewers certainly attacked their growth after 1900.

62 The Birmingham Surrender Scheme was a voluntary compensation scheme created in 1897 by a group of brewers in Birmingham, and members of the Birmingham Licensing Committee, notably Sir William Waters Butler of Mitchells & Butlers, and Arthur Chamberlain. The Birmingham Brewers and Licensing Magistrates formed the Bir-

nowhere were they prepared to see a wholesale removal of licences without proper compensation.

Unfortunately the Peel Commission (on the Liquor Licensing Laws, 1896–9) did not grasp the nettle of compensation, or indeed any others. Sitting for 133 days spread over more than two years, and interviewing 250 witnesses who provided enough evidence to fill nine stout volumes, the Commission ended in 'complete disarray'.[63] Its moderate chairman, Viscount Peel, became a temperance convert and, with anti-drink members of the Commission, produced a long minority report calling for the suppression of 40,000 licences within a seven-year time limit. The briefer majority report, containing the views of the trade, admitted the need for fewer licences and proposed moderate limitation with full compensation, paid for by the trade, and with no time limit. Discussion of the Reports and action by the government was abandoned at the onset of the Boer War. And when in 1902 the government did pass a Licensing Act to give effect to some of the recommendations of the Peel Commission regarding off-licences, clubs and habitual drunkenness, it ducked the crucial issue of compensation. But the magistrates were less shy, and in surprising quarters. In that same year the Farnham Bench refused to renew nine out of the forty-five licence renewals which came before its brewster sessions. The Birmingham surrender scheme had been reported with growing interest, but when the zealous Surrey magistrates operated the full letter of the 1872 Act to impose restriction without compensation, brewing interests were badly shaken. In 1903, 240 licences in England and Wales were refused – well above the average of the past five years. Mr Armine Bevan addressed the shareholders of the Newcastle Breweries in December in sombre mood: 'In consequence of the extreme position taken up by the licensing magistrates of certain districts, great anxiety has been caused your directors during the past year. The renewals of five licences were refused.'[64] Thoroughly alarmed, the brewers brought 'strong political pressure' to bear on the Conservative government to pass the Licensing Act of 1904.[65]

mingham Property Co. which purchased old run-down public houses in the centre of the city and built 'fewer but better' houses on the outskirts. The scheme was quickly adopted by licensing magistrates in towns such as Sheffield, while other towns like Blackburn, for example, introduced their own schemes. With the introduction of the Licensing Act in 1904, the scheme soon drew to a close, by which date 183 public houses had been closed at a total cost of £173,738. *Brewing Trade Review*, Oct. 1898, pp. 359–60; Sept. 1904, p. 428.

63 Gutzke, *Protecting the Pub*, p. 128.

64 *Brewing Trade Review*, 1 Jan. 1904. Three were regained on appeal, but the whole process was time consuming and expensive.

65 Wilson, *Alcohol and the Nation*, p. 110.

In fact, like the Old Age Pensions Act of 1908, the matter of compensation had been under discussion for at least thirty years and more. Balfour simply grasped a large and mature nettle in 1904. For the brewers the Act was an important piece of legislation placing the removal of licences on a proper footing. The element of uncertainty in actions like those of the Farnham magistrates was removed. Closures, except those made on the specific grounds of ill-conduct or structural unsoundness, were to be compensated for from a fund levied upon all licensed properties. The government made wild estimates that as many as 2,500 houses would be closed annually, but since the brewers in effect were charged with the levy on each of their houses it was clear that the size of the fund would limit the pace of public house closure. In the event, 600 on-licences per year on average were removed under the Act between 1905 and 1935.[66] The temperance, non-conformist wing of the Liberal Party was incensed, immediately labelling the legislation as the 'Brewers' Endowment Fund'. Remembering the crazy speculation of pub prices in the late 1890s, and believing the brewers and the Conservatives to be hand in glove, they were, after 1904, doubly intent upon tightening the screws of taxation and restriction upon the industry.

How did the brewers themselves view the Act? At first, there were deep misgivings. Any notion of 'endowment' was, of course, rejected. 'The Mutual Burial Fund' was their label for the legislation.[67] It was, reckoned the chairman (A. R. Motion) of the Cannon Brewery, 'a costly process to help to exterminate ourselves'.[68] For the levy was raised entirely on the trade. Directors represented it as one more burden imposed by Conservative and Liberal governments alike, and calculated its impact as a percentage of their ordinary dividends, for they argued that it bypassed the preference and debenture stockholders. But there were more percipient brewers who from the outset welcomed the legislation. Henry Mitchell, chairman of Mitchells & Butlers, 'thought it was an Act honestly intended to meet the requirements of the case, and if fairly administered should work beneficially both ways'.[69] Costing the firm £10,000, he estimated the ordinary shareholders would in future forego 2 per cent of their dividends. Moreover, when in 1907–9 the industry was menaced with further impositions of a more drastic character, brewers everywhere began to warm to the compensation scheme.

[66] *Ibid.*, p. 111.

[67] S. O. Nevile, *Seventy Rolling Years* (1958), p. 56.

[68] *Brewing Trade Review*, 1 March 1905.

[69] *Brewing Trade Review*, 1 Sept. 1905; see also the comments of E. T. Hargraves of Stretton's Derby Brewery, 1 Jan. 1906.

Strong of Romsey 'thought the weeding out of some of the smaller licensed properties would be an ultimate benefit'.[70] Suddenly, company minute books detail at length careful calculations and discussions with the compensation committees of Quarter Sessions about the closure of houses and, in some areas, the negotiation of new licences in return. Given time, brewers argued that the Act would work. In less than three years, the chairman of Wilson's Manchester Brewery calculated that over 300 pubs had been closed in the city.[71] Edward Lake of Greene King in 1911 gave the real clue as to why brewers finally approved the Act. An addict of statistics in pre-pocket calculator days, he informed his handful of shareholders that since 1904 the sale of their delicensed properties had realised £17,034: £11,071 in compensation and £5,963 on their subsequent sale. The levy had amounted to only £9,299.[72] These were neat sums in difficult years. In Suffolk, the pubs closed were marginal affairs in terms of their tiny barrelages; in urban areas managing directors lamented that closure with compensation meant the loss of significant trade.

Although the outcome of both the Peel Commission (if the conclusions of the minority report are ignored) and the 1904 Act was not shattering for brewers, they nevertheless represented themselves as an industry hounded, taxed and controlled by government to a degree no other was. Partly they lamented the rapid advance in local rateable values of pubs and breweries,[73] but their real complaints were reserved for the steady advance of 'imperial' taxation. Two items were raised year in year out, by both the brewers' trade organisation and individual companies. The first was an additional duty of 3d per barrel, added in 1890 supposedly to enable County Councils to compensate licence holders, but in fact spent upon technical education. This was no palliative at all to the brewers. The second, more serious, was a further duty of 1s per barrel in 1900 to fund the Boer War. Duties of 6s 3d per standard barrel charged by Gladstone in his re-introduction of the beer duty in 1880 now stood at 7s 9d. And the shilling duty was not removed when peace resumed. In the light of the taxation to be levied upon the industry during the Great War (see pp. 318–19), the brewers' constant

70 Whitbread Archive, 324/114, Strong and Co.'s Minute Books, 28 Nov. 1905.

71 *Brewing Trade Review*, 1 May 1907; see also E. W. Gifford's speech to the shareholders of Barclay Perkins, 1 July 1908.

72 Wilson, *Greene King*, pp. 142–4, where he discusses in detail the working of the Act; see also Gourvish, *Norfolk Beers*, p. 73 and Gutzke, *Protecting the Pub*, pp. 155–7.

73 In London they were reckoned to have risen by 55 per cent between 1898 and 1908 (*Brewing Trade Review*, 1 July 1908).

reiteration of their problems seems excessive.[74] With firm pressure on consumption and profitability after 1900, the continuation of the shilling duty was represented as one more nail banged by the government into the industry's coffin. The City of London Brewery believed it cost their ordinary shareholders 1 per cent in dividends; the Wenlock Brewery reckoned that, together with the compensation levy and an increase in sugar duties, it deprived its shareholders of 4 per cent in all.[75] 'For every £1 of net profit the Company earned', estimated James Agg-Gardner of the Cheltenham Original Brewery, 'it gave 15s. to the State. He knew of no other trade or business in this or any other country that made a like contribution.'[76] Of course, brewers naturally stressed the government's malign role in troubled times; it largely absolved them of charges of bad management.

All this discontent, heaped on politicians of all persuasions, suddenly seemed as nothing as the Liberal government, after an unexpected respite whilst it dealt with other aspects of its legislative programme, prepared a new Licensing Bill in late 1907. Introduced into the Commons in the following May, it shook the brewing industry to its foundations. *The Brewers' Journal*, in its annual review of the trade in January 1909, reckoned 'the past year had undoubtedly been the worst that the brewing trade has experienced within modern times at least'. For only a nonagenarian brewer could have recalled the passing of the 1830 Beer Act. Winston Churchill, with frankness, summarised the motivation behind the bill as 'a measure of plunder to satisfy political spite'.[77] Certainly, the industry saw it as one imposed by 'a teetotal-ridden Government', acting from vindictiveness. The main purpose of the Bill was to accelerate greatly the reduction of on-licences, but its real threat was the assumption by the state of the monopoly value of all on-licences. At the end of a time-limit of fourteen years, a national Licence Committee would issue licences on the payment of the equivalent of their monopoly value. In the mean time compensation would be less generous and referenda on local option would be encouraged. Every temperance strategem of the previous forty years seemed to have a place in the Bill. The brewers reeled. 'There never was a Bill so tainted with

[74] For a good example of a speech outlining brewers' difficulties in these years, see the *Brewing Trade Review*, 1 Jan. 1904 for the statement of the chairman of Newcastle Breweries. But most made similar speeches. Presumably they read each others, and the gloom multiplied.

[75] *Brewing Trade Review*, 1 March 1904; 1 Jan. 1907.

[76] *Brewing Trade Review*, 1 Dec. 1904.

[77] Quoted in a speech of H. Cosmo Bonsor, *Brewing Trade Review*, 1 Sept. 1908.

dishonesty, that so smacked of confiscation', stated Percy Gates, the chairman of the New Westminster Brewery Co.[78] His theme of theft was reiterated by every brewer in Britain. Although the Brewers' Society, the National Trade Defence and Allied Brewery Traders' Associations 'mobilized public opinion with well tried tactics: mass meetings, petitions and deputations', individual breweries were paralysed (see Plate 41).[79] Many companies felt unable to declare an interim dividend; work on pubs and breweries was suspended; the incorporation of new companies virtually ceased. Things were so bad that Sir Gilbert Greenall, chairman of Greenall Whitley, resigned the Mastership of the Belvoir Hunt in the spring of 1908 with knowledge of the Bill's 'drastic nature, and that if it became law he could not continue the heavy expense of his office'.[80] Moreover, the menace of the Bill was exacerbated by depression in 1908. Beer consumption fell while the price of brewing materials remained high. Although the Bill passed its second and third readings in the Commons with handsome majorities, it was defeated, to the delight of the industry, by the Lords in November 1908.

But any respite for the industry was brief. In reality it could expect nothing but further retaliation. The government chose its weapons in the budget of 1909. As Leif Jones, a Temperance MP, put it, 'while the Licensing Bill chastised the Trade with whips, the Chancellor of the Exchequer would chastise it with scorpions'.[81] In his budget to fund social reform, Lloyd George imposed additional burdens on the trade to the tune of some £4 million, by increasing duties on both breweries and public houses. Breweries, formerly paying a nominal licence of £1 to brew, were now taxed at the rate of 12s per fifty barrels beyond the first 100; retail licences were approximately trebled.[82] In addition, spirit duties were increased from 11s to 14s 9d. Again the provisions, along with the rest of 'the People's Budget', were rejected by the House of Lords. The election of January 1910 was called to resolve the constitutional crisis; and the budget of that year reimposed the government's additional taxes on the trade.

In the short term, all was gloom. 'The year just closed', wrote the editor of the *Brewers' Journal* in January 1910, 'will undoubtedly go

78 *Brewing Trade Review*, 1 July 1908.
79 Gutzke, *Protecting the Pub*, p. 168.
80 *Brewing Trade Review*, 1 April 1908, p. 257.
81 Quoted in *Brewing Trade Review*, 1 July 1909, p. 325.
82 Overall, brewers paid £800,000 rather than £11,000 in licence fees. Guinness, the United Kingdom's largest brewery, paid £25,600. (Gutzke, *Protecting the Pub*, pp. 173–4).

down to history as the blackest, without exception, in the annals of the brewing and licensed trade.' The chairman of Newcastle Breweries spelt out for his shareholders the problems facing the industry at the end of 1909:

They were all in a state of uncertainty. The year under review had not been a favourable one. They had been suffering – firstly, from the uncertainty and anxiety as to the future; secondly, from the threats of increased taxation, which if carried out, might have made it impossible to ever pay a dividend again on the ordinary shares; thirdly, from the increased cost of malt and hops; fourthly, from the bad state of trade in the district; and lastly, from the growing competition of clubs.

Then the brewers began to count the cost of the budget's impositions. All commented upon the increasing exactions of government: often it added up to 60 per cent of earnings.[83] Counting the Boer War shilling duty, the compensation fund levy, and the extra licence duties exacted in the 1909 budget, the chairman of Newcastle Breweries maintained it 'represented a dividend of over 10 per cent on the ordinary capital, leaving but 2 per cent for distribution'.[84] Watney Combe Reid disclosed that the retail licence tax cost them £106,000 in 1910–11, the licence to brew, £10,000.[85]

In fact, prospects improved more quickly than the trade believed possible. A new Licensing Act was approved in 1910 to consolidate those passed between 1828 and 1904, but the menacing clauses of the 1908 Licensing Bill were not revived. Nor were the retail licence duties so swingeing as brewers feared. In the event the old pre-budget revenue of £1.9 million was doubled rather than trebled and brewers found salvation by contesting the rating valuations of their public houses on the grounds that their value was diminished by the additional duty. In some cases rate reductions were as much as increases in duty. Only in London were exactions unequal. With one-ninth of the population, its publicans paid about one-third (£550,000) of the extra tax in the first year of its existence.[86] But the real cause of the brewers' brief Indian summer before the Great War was an increase in consumption, not the government's armed neutrality after 1910. Between 1909 (whose truly

[83] See the speech by the chairman of Hoare & Co., *Brewing Trade Review*, 1 Aug. 1911.
[84] *Brewing Trade Review*, 1 Jan. 1911.
[85] *Ibid.*, 1 Sept. 1911.
[86] Formerly paying a maximum £60 duty, the larger houses were faced with bills of £300 plus. Ninety per cent of publicans could not find the additional taxation and came to the brewers for aid. It was one more problem for London brewers, wearied by a decade of struggle.

appalling summer some brewers compared with 1879) and 1913 consumption advanced in the United Kingdom by over 3 million barrels. It was the last surge that most brewers would experience.

VI

Conditions for brewers in London were exceptionally bad between 1900 and 1914. Edward Giffard of Barclay Perkins, speaking in 1911, believed, 'during the past few years the licensed trade in London had been more depressed than in any other part of the United Kingdom'.[87] As a result, when brewers came to analyse their plight they had resort to a wide range of explanations. Of course, like brewers everywhere, they blamed the government. Indeed in the years 1907–10 they mentioned little else. Taxation eroded net profits and dividends, and in London the impact of increased licence duties fell disproportionately upon the big, highly assessed, metropolitan pubs. But all breweries faced the increased local and central taxation of these years, although none performed so badly as those in London. What was the nature of their special difficulties?

Nationally, the decline in beer sales was sharp. *The Statist* calculated that between 1900 and 1908 per capita consumption of beer fell by 18.2 per cent.[88] Brewers were adamant that the cause was a sluggish economy, not the triumph of temperance. And undoubtedly, acute recession in Edwardian Britain appeared to hit beer sales harder in London than in the Midlands and industrial North. The years 1902–5 and 1908–9 were singled out by London brewers as being especially difficult. Andrew Motion of the Cannon Brewery, with a quarter of a century's experience, had 'never known anything like the badness of trade generally' in 1904.[89] Indeed, there was little respite during the decade in unemployment (particularly in the building trades), short time, and the squeeze upon real wages. Money was short; the overwhelming demand was for the cheapest, least-profitable, mild beers. As a consequence, barrelages fell, and they did so earlier in London than elsewhere. The boom of the late 1890s faded fast in 1900. Watney Combe Reid, with unusual frankness, admitted to a fall of 74,000 barrels – a massive 1,400 barrels a week – between 1899 and 1901. Truman noted

[87] *Brewing Trade Review*, 1 May 1911. This section on the London breweries is based upon company reports extracted from the *Brewing Trade Review* and the records of Truman and Whitbread.

[88] *The Statist*, 17 April 1909.

[89] *Brewing Trade Review*, 1 March 1905.

a severe drop in trade by the autumn of 1901. The arsenic scare and the Boer War were blamed.[90] But throughout the 1900s London breweries regularly reported annual declines in barrelages of between 2 and 7 per cent. Truman's output fell by 120,175 barrels (19.1 per cent) in the 1900–5 quinquennium; Meux suffered a quite exceptional contraction of 45.75 per cent between 1898 and 1905.

Behind this pattern of declining barrelages there were features experienced in London with an intensity unknown elsewhere. The trade of its great central pubs, lavishly rebuilt in the 1880s and 1890s, was undermined by the shift of population to the suburbs. If the tramways were responsible for the removal of some custom, more ominous was the switch to bottled beer. Pins, firkins and jars sold from public houses and by 'family' brewers had been a feature of the late Victorian beer trade. After 1900 they were largely replaced by quart and pint glass bottles sold increasingly from off-licences by grocers. The London brewers complained bitterly of the competition and small profits of the bottled beer trade, although it was the one notable growth area of their business. And they lamented the way it undermined the more profitable cask trade of the pubs they had so recently acquired. When Cosmo Bonsor discussed the decline in the London public house trade with representatives of five other breweries at Watneys in February 1909, the nine 'friends' present concluded that it was due to the decrease in spending power, the stringency of the law, bottled beer, and other attractions like clubs and music halls.[91]

It was this erosion of the capital's public houses, acquired and improved so expensively with the brewers' money, that was at the crux of the London brewers' difficulties. Properties were vastly overvalued in company accounts at 1900 prices; tenants, with a dwindling trade, could repay neither the interest on their loans nor the rents they had nego-

[90] In November 1900 traces of arsenic were found in sugar used to manufacture beer by brewers in Manchester and the Salford districts. This immediately led to the appointment of a Royal Commission on Arsenical Poisoning in 1901. Over 3,000 cases were reported, seventy of which were fatal. The arsenic outbreak could not have come at a worse time. In May 1901, advocates of the Pure Beer Bill – which aimed to protect the consumer from the use of deleterious substances in the manufacture of beer – passed its second reading in the House of Commons by a majority of 100. Quick action by the brewers in the withdrawal and destruction of contaminated beer in addition to a recommendation by the Country Brewers' Society that its members adopt an immediate policy of testing all raw materials used in brewing, restored public confidence. In July 1901, the Commission concluded in its First Report that it was satisfied that the brewers had improved their procedures for detecting contaminated beer. A few days later the Pure Beer Bill was withdrawn. *Royal Commission on Arsenical Poisoning*, 1st Report, 26 July 1901. Also see the *Country Brewers' Society Annual Report 1900–1901.*

[91] GLRO, A122, B/THB, Truman's Monthly Reports, 1908–38.

tiated. Therefore the brewers had to pay both heavy charges of debenture interest and preference stock, issued so freely in the 1890s, at the same time as they had to write off massive bad debts for their tenants and scale down public house assets and goodwill valuations in their balance sheets. All this had to be achieved in the face of dwindling sales and increasing taxation. Producing consistently good beer – the brewer's old problem – suddenly seemed easy in comparison. Certainly, chairmen often commented on the excellence of their beers in contrast with the state of their finances.

Watney Combe Reid provides the most interesting case study in the London trade, partly because its chairman, Cosmo Bonsor, publicly discussed the problems of the firm with a frankness no other London brewer matched. In the first half-dozen years after incorporation (1898) it was clear that the amalgamation had not worked: few economies were made and the management, in the face of dwindling sales and mounting financial problems, was incapable of effecting rationalisation. The real problem, as Bonsor revealed in 1903 and 1904, was the weight of interest charges and mounting bad debts. The latter especially caused problems because publicans could not meet their rent and interest obligations contracted in the boom. In 1910 Bonsor believed:

> the whole reduction of their profit during the last ten years was owing to the inability of their customers to pay their interest and their rents; they had had to write off a great deal of interest and rent in the past as bad, and that, of course, had its natural effect on the depreciation of their securities.[92]

Already in the year 1902–3, £90,000 was reserved for bad and doubtful debts and loans; in the following year, the fund exceeded £100,000. At the annual general meeting, Bonsor analysed the problem which faced every large brewer in London to a greater or lesser degree:

> We carry on two businesses, and practically every brewery in London carries on two businesses. In the first place, naturally, we are manufacturers and sellers of beer. That part of our business is as good as it ever was; but it is the other portion of our business, in which we deal in the securities of licensed houses and in financing our customers, that we have made a loss upon. Practically our manufacture as brewers is good; but the financial portion of our business is not so good.[93]

This was a typical Bonsor understatement. In December 1905, after a stormy annual general meeting when bad debts totalling £480,000 in five years were revealed, the firm's ordinary stock was reduced by 75 per

[92] *Brewing Trade Review*, 1 Sept. 1910.
[93] *Brewing Trade Review*, 1 Sept. 1904.

cent from £3.2 million to £0.8 million.[94] Yet in most subsequent years no dividend was paid on these shares. But Watney Combe Reid's problems were not exceptional in that they were shared by every large London brewer in the 1900s. The Cannon and City of London breweries, which had returned good dividends to 1904–5, paid none by 1909–10. Many were forced to reduce their capital. By March 1908 the directors of the Lion Brewery had written down the valuation of their public houses and loans (£890,000) by over £200,000 from reserves. In the same year Hoare wrote off over £800,000 of their capital and completely restructured their shareholdings. Two years later, they were seriously discussing amalgamation with the City of London Brewery. Meux's problems were in a class of their own. With a thoroughly out-of-date and incommodious brewery, unmodernised houses, and its directors' initiatives thoroughly circumscribed by the concentration of share ownership in the hands of Lady Meux and Lord Tweedmouth, it failed for years either to find a new brewery site or to restructure its capital to account for collapsed property prices.[95]

Meux's management was exceptionally poor, but even well-run firms like Truman, Barclay Perkins and Whitbread, whose capitalisations had been modest and acquisition of public houses moderately restrained, did badly. Truman agonised over their problems in late 1905, confronted with a close-on 20 per cent fall in sales over the previous five years. Typically, they thought their beers were to blame, but they also imagined that other brewers provided bigger discounts, pushed their bottled and jar trades harder, and had acquired new trade, often in suburbia, by purchasing small breweries. Economies in manufacture and investment in bottling plant and depots, however, were insufficient, and in 1910 the firm wrote down its ordinary shares and reserves by £1 million. Barclay Perkins's estimated rate of return fell from 8 per cent in 1897 to only 2.3 per cent in 1910. Ordinary share dividends declined from 12 per cent to zero, and a painful capital reconstruction was forced on the company in 1911. The ordinary shares were written down to 1 per cent of their nominal value, and the preference shares were reduced to 40 per cent of their original value.[96] And this was in a year when barrelage increased by 40,000. Whitbread faced identical problems to Watney Combe Reid, although its chairman was more discreet than Cosmo Bonsor. For the firm's accounts reveal that an average £130,000

[94] *Brewing Trade Review*, 1 Sept., 1 Dec. 1905.
[95] *Brewing Trade Review*, 1 April 1906; 1 April 1908; 1 May 1909.
[96] Gourvish and Wilson, 'Profitability', pp. 149–52.

was written off public houses and loans between 1903 and 1912 as valuations of the former plummeted and insolvency of the latter spiralled. But under the capable direction of Edgar Lubbock, Whitbread enjoyed an immensely successful venture into bottling. Barrelage grew every year from 1889 to 1906, from 336,052 to 834,021 barrels.[97] It was a truly remarkable performance; it meant the firm could ride out the storm after 1900 far more easily than all their competitors, perhaps save Mann. Even so, by 1911 the dividend on its ordinary shares had fallen to ½ per cent. This at least was typical of the dismal returns shareholders experienced in their holding of London brewery stocks after 1900.

But behind the gloomy balance sheets, the inevitable accounts of widows and orphans deprived of their incomes, and the arguments about capital restructuring, significant changes in the London brewing world were taking place. Much the most important was in bottling. Bottling beer was an old art. Vaizey maintained it was an unimportant aspect of trade before 1914.[98] He was wrong. As already shown, the triumph of Bass, Allsopp and Guinness was created upon bottling. Much of this was done by independent bottling firms. Bass's export beers were bottled by no fewer than seventeen firms in London by the late 1870s. One of them, M. B. Foster & Sons (whose links with Bass went back to 1830), with vast stores at Woolwich and Marylebone, had claims to be the world's biggest bottling company. Similarly, sales of Guinness were vigorously pushed by independent bottlers tied by 'exclusive' agreements. The Scottish brewers were also early masters of the specialism; but in the 1890s and 1900s techniques largely imported from lager breweries in America revolutionised bottling by chilling, filtering, carbonisation and pasteurisation. By these means *all* beers could be bottled fresh, star bright and without sediment. There were other innovations, such as mass-produced cheap glass bottles, bottle washers, and corking and labelling machines.[99] Once laborious

[97] Whitbread, W/41/16. The 'Brewers' Memorandum Book' contains a large number of statistics relating to various activities, 1889–1913.

[98] J. Vaizey, *The Brewing Industry, 1886–1952* (1960), p. 5. Bass brewed an average of 770,000 barrels of pale ale a year for the home trade between 1900 and 1905, approximately 75 per cent of which was in bottled form. (Hawkins, *Bass Charrington*, p. 51; Owen, *History of Bass*, forthcoming). For an account of M. & B. Foster, see *Licensed Victuallers' Gazette*, 3 Jan. 1874. The Marylebone Road stores employed 200–300 men 'in the busy season' and had capacity for 3 million returned bottles and 1,500 butts of Bass's beers. The Woolwich export stores employed 300–400. Each store, even by 1875, possessed mechanical washers, fillers, and steam and hydraulic lifts.

[99] See the article by F. E. Lott, 'Bottled Beers', in the *Journal of the Federated Institute of Brewing* (1901), pp. 191–208 and a series of articles on 'Bottling' by 'an old contributor' in *Brewing Trade Review* (1905).

Table 7.1. *Barrels of beer bottled by Whitbread, 1870–1910*

1870	1,293
1880	10,264
1890	31,782
1895	66,115
1900	140,984
1905	245,599
1910	353,936

Source: N. B. Redman, 'Whitbread and Bottled Beer, 1869–1930', *The Brewer* (March 1991), p. 110.

processes, initially pursued by the exporters of beers, were transformed. Many provincial brewers, who had long bottled Guinness and Bass and who also often manufactured mineral waters for which there was a great vogue in Victorian Britain, began to bottle their own beers in the 1890s (see Plate 40).[100] In London, the lead was given much earlier by Whitbread. Its progress after it commenced operations in 1869 was remarkable, leaving its competitors far behind (see Table 7.1). Whitbread's venture in its way was as singular as those of Bass and Guinness. Like them it differentiated its product by a carefully guarded registered trade mark. It was spending in 1903, according to Truman, £12,000 on 'station advertising', a sum equal to almost two-thirds of the annual amount expended by the trade organisations in the defence of the industry at the height of the struggle with the Liberal government in 1908–9.[101] In 1912 the firm bottled as much as 439,532 barrels, or 45 per cent of its output. It did so from a series of bottling stores and depots opened rapidly on a nationwide basis after 1891. By 1914 there were forty-six of these, ten in London (some housed in small breweries the firm had acquired), twenty-six scattered across England, two in Wales, three in Scotland, four in Belgium and one in France. Those in London were large affairs in themselves, some costing close on £40,000 each.[102]

No other London brewery approached Whitbread's great enterprise, whereby 'the public were able to obtain their beer anywhere in England

[100] Steward & Patteson began in 1894, Greene King in 1897. By 1913 the latter were bottling 5,045 barrels a year. Wilson, *Greene King*, pp. 153–4.

[101] Gutzke, *Protecting the Pub*, p. 234.

[102] This section is based upon N. B. Redman, 'Whitbread and Bottled Beer, 1869–1930', *The Brewer* (March 1991), pp. 106–13 and the 'Brewers' Memorandum Book', see note 97 above.

at 2/6 per dozen'.[103] For bottling was clearly perceived by the other big London brewers as being something beneath their dignity and best left to small 'family' brewers and independent bottlers. Because it was highly competitive, with a large free-trade element, and labour intensive, brewers maintained it was unprofitable in comparison with the cask trade. 'It is', said Cosmo Bonsor of Watney Combe Reid in 1905, 'a trade into which we have been forced to a certain extent.' A shareholder reckoned that one of the reasons the firm was doing so badly was that it had gone into bottling late.[104] But Truman's reports indicate that few London brewers had followed Whitbread's early lead. They reveal that seven had commenced bottling in 1903 and four in the following year, including Barclay Perkins, and with Charrington poised to begin. Whitbread, Mann and Allsopp were considered Truman's great rivals, although they also respected Fremlins (Maidstone) who had been the first to chill successfully and filter beer commercially. Three years later the picture was rather different: Barclay Perkins had 'collapsed after a good start'; Mann was 'steadily decreasing'; the beers of Taylor Walker, with many of their own off-licences, were 'very popular'; and Fremlins were Truman's 'chief competitors' with 'excellent beers' retailed at good prices. Yet Whitbread were the clear market leaders. 'Those breweries', Truman commented,'who have opened suburban depots have been uniformly successful. Whitbreads now have eight such depots.' By 1911 Truman had five of these outlets and a total bottling trade of 42,000 barrels.[105]

Although Truman's records show that they commenced bottling in the late 1880s, they did so with none of the vision Whitbread employed to create a national bottling network. In 1890 they constructed a new bottling store, but consistently protested throughout the 1890s that the investment was not profitable. By 1894 they were bottling 11,000 barrels a year and employing at the season's peak, forty-two men and seventy-three boys a week. Four years later, the trade had grown to 26,052 barrels, 18,368 of which were freighted from their Burton brewery. This was almost a decade before the surge in bottling which swept the London trade in the mid-1900s. Then, with large discounts in the free trade, there was a perpetual price war. By 1911 Truman's assessment of

103 GLRO, Acc. 77.94, B/THB, Truman's Monthly Reports. This paragraph is based upon the random observations made in the reports about their bottling operations from 1889 to 1911.

104 *Brewing Trade Review*, 1 Sept. 1905, 1 Jan. 1906.

105 In the year ending 31 March 1911, 400,255 dozen (47.25 per cent) had been sold in the free trade, 446,784 dozen (52.75 per cent) in Truman's on- and off-licences.

their bottling venture was that although they had seen the trade grow to over 40,000 barrels a year (just over one-tenth of Whitbread's sales) and had acquired five bottling depots in outer London, the returns had not been very profitable. But there could be no release, for bottling allowed access to the free trade, and in any case drinking habits themselves were changing: 'the public have found out the advantage of beer in glass delivered to their homes' (see Plate 39). It was for these reasons that the London brewers, with the exception of Whitbread, somewhat reluctantly began bottling. In the inter-war years it was the central activity in an otherwise declining industry. Its origins, however, are rooted very firmly in the pre-1914 period.

The other development, the introduction of motorised transport, was less significant. Again, however, a central feature of the industry in the post-1918 period has its roots fixed in the Edwardian years when brewers began to experiment with motor transport. For the many carting tasks needed by brewers, the limits of horse-drawn transport, in terms of capacity and distance, were obvious. But motorised transport, swifter in itself, permitted deliveries from the brewery over much longer distances without transferring goods from one form of transport to another. For the carriage of bottled beer, mineral waters and spirits, lorries were especially advantageous. Before 1914 this new form of transport was in a highly experimental phase (see Plate 19). Initially, steam wagons outnumbered those propelled by internal combustion engines, although they were hard on the roads and Truman found they caused 'considerable annoyance ... through ashes thrown from the chimney'. Greene King conducted feasibility surveys between 1908 and 1913; Greenall Whitley introduced lorries in 1908; Tetley commenced operations in 1912. When a critical shareholder accused directors of the Colchester Brewery Co. in 1913 of 'being antiquated and more or less referring to the time of Adam than the present day', he cited as an instance their failure to introduce motors.[106]

In London, Truman's and Mann's trials in this field went back to 1902–3. By 1906 the former were hiring three lorries. Whitbread, they disclosed, 'will soon have six motors and during the last two years they have considerably reduced their dray horses'. Truman's stables were also depleted, but more as a result of dwindling trade. They were uncertain about the economies effected, for although lorries were cheaper per ton-mile, they concluded 'it is impossible to compare the

[106] Wilson, *Greene King*, pp. 154–5; Slater, *A Brewer's Tale*, p. 163; Lackey, *Quality Pays*, p. 73.

two because long distances and suitable work is especially chosen for the motor work (see Plate 20).[107] Certainly, there was not a great shift to them before 1914, although there were proposals to provide each of the abroad clerks with a car and driver in 1908. Courage made no move to introduce motors before 1916.[108] In experiments with motor transport and the equipment of bottling stores, the London brewers made modest steps forward in the Edwardian period. The pace was undoubtedly slowed by their dismal financial prospects in these years.

VII

The problems of the Burton brewers were of a different nature from those of their London peers. They were more acute and in essence twofold. First, the tying of trade everywhere seriously squeezed the free trade upon which they had depended. Their purchase of public houses was late, costly and inadequate. They therefore had to have resort to increasingly large discounts. Even these were immaterial where tenants were obliged to exclude Burton beers. In London especially, where the bottled pale ale trade remained free into the 1890s, sales collapsed.[109] Secondly, every sizeable brewery successfully imitated and bottled its own version of traditional Burton beers. These forces, evident in the 1890s, but masked by the 1895–1900 boom, returned with renewed intensity after 1900. A crossroads was reached when Mann, Crossman & Paulin withdrew from Burton in 1898, leasing their houses to Thomas Salt and Ind Coope. Between 1889 and 1911, the number of breweries in the town fell sharply and on the eve of the First World War thirteen small breweries were idle.

Nor did the larger ones survive easily. Allsopp remained in a terrible plight after 1900, thereby illustrating the perils of generous company flotation, unthinking public house acquisition, the acute nature of 'the Burton problem', and the crucial role of management.[110] In 1887 it had been capitalised at the peak of the post-Guinness flotation euphoria. With an unparalleled goodwill valuation of eight times its average net profits, any details of the firm's declining barrelage since the early 1880s

107 GLRO, A122, B/THB, Truman's Monthly Reports, 1908–38, and scattered earlier references in the reports.
108 Hardinge, *Courage's Brewery*, p. 23.
109 Bass's London agency sales fell from 36 per cent of all agency sales in 1889/90 to 26 per cent in 1900 and 22.5 per cent by 1909.
110 See Gourvish and Wilson, 'Profitability' pp. 151–4, but much the best and fullest version of Allsopp's troubles between the 1880s and 1914 appears in Hawkins's thesis which was written 'with particular reference to Samuel Allsopp and Sons Ltd'.

had been omitted from its prospectus. Holding out the promise of an 8 per cent dividend, it paid none to its incensed ordinary shareholders in 1889–91. Matters improved in the good years of the mid- and late-1890s, but by 1900 the company was in the direst financial straits. An analysis of Allsopp's reports and comment in the brewing press reveals two inescapable forces. First, a point already touched upon, is the fierce competition the company faced. The discount war was one of attrition. Year after year Allsopp's chairman made brief reference to the crucial decline in sales; 4 per cent in 1900–1, 3 per cent in 1901–2, 7 per cent in 1904–5. By 1910 sales had fallen by 40 per cent across the decade, to well under half their early 1880s peak. It was this consistent fall in sales that ate away at already frayed profit margins. Secondly, the company almost doubled its employed capital between 1896 and 1900 from £3.95 million to £7.73 million. Customer loans were granted and public houses purchased with true abandon. It also equipped a £60,000 lager brewery to capture the tiny British lager trade, expanded its wines business, bought hotels and casinos, and spent £200,000 upon the Southend Kursaal. In three years the company increased its share issue by an extraordinary £3.25 million to fund this foolish, headlong expansion. The crash came quickly. Net profits as a percentage of capital employed fell from 6.7 per cent to 2.7 per cent between 1896 and 1900; fixed interest charges consumed an excessive proportion of gross profit; management expenses, especially on discounts and distribution, were not contained. By 1901 its accounts showed a deficiency of £1.43 million. Eventually, after much argument, the firm's capital was written down by this amount in 1905, and, again, in 1912, halved from £5.031 million to £2.536 million to reduce interest bearing capital. Even so, a massively overvalued goodwill valuation of £850,000 showed in the accounts.

The old directors had been removed in 1900, and the new chairman, J. F. Remnant, attempted the impossible task of turning round the firm's affairs in the most difficult decade brewers had experienced. Allsopp suffered enormous overcapacity, but, with no resources, it could only discuss terms with other Burton firms which were equally troubled – Thomas Salt, the Burton Brewery Co. and Ind Coope. None paid any dividends, and all courted the attention of receivers. At various times between 1906 and 1912 each held serious discussions about amalgamation with Allsopp. These broke down on the details of shareholders' rights and collapsed public house valuations. In 1910–12 there were even desultory talks with Bass, but the latter's directors could not agree on the price to be paid. Briefly, in 1911–12, Allsopp, at the insistence of the debenture shareholders, was itself in the hands of the receiver. Faced with these reversals, J. Stewart resigned in 1912 and was replaced by J. J. Calder from Archibald Arrol of Alloa. Calder brought a new dynamism to Allsopp's affairs. In 1913 he just beat Mitchells & Butlers to acquire Showell's of Birmingham, another badly managed casualty of the 1900s, but lost the Burton Brewery Co. to Worthington because his firm was unable to afford an adequate offer.

Allsopp provided a true enough parable for brewers in the 1900s, yet its fate was not shared by its principal rivals, Bass and Worthington. They faced exactly the same exposure to the free trade, and one that pub purchase would not solve. In 1900 Allsopp revealed that around 63 per cent of their trade remained untied in spite of their acquisition of around 400 pubs: a figure identical to that disclosed by Ind Coope in their talks with Allsopp in 1911.[111] Bass's and Worthington's position was essentially the same. The latter still enjoyed a tied trade of only 41.5 per cent in 1910.[112] Moreover, Bass saw its sales fall by over 26 per cent between 1902 and 1910; its goodwill was reduced by £560,000 from reserves as a precaution against a rapacious government in 1908. Yet the company remained essentially strong. And Worthington, with a thoroughly tough managing director, W. P. Manners, bucked the Burton trend. Brewing good beer and pushing their bottled beer and agency accounts hard by big discounts, their sales barely dipped in 1908–9.[113] The key to success in Burton, as elsewhere, was clearly sound finance and sound management. The former universally hinged upon a firm's record and restraint in the 1895–1900 boom; the latter was less easy to predict.

VIII

Historians of brewing have tended to present the industry's management as conservative and secretive, one in which the drive to go public introduced virtually no change in ownership, structure and management. There is a good deal of truth in this. Most companies went public

111 *Brewing Trade Review*, 1 August 1911.

112 Bass Museum, F/15/1, Worthington & Co.'s Agency Statistics.

113 Worthington's Sales, 1906–1911 (in bulk barrels, year ending 30 Sept.)

1906	326,250
1907	392,233
1908	383,297
1909	379,838
1910	387,648
1911	404,752

in a legal sense only. Control of ordinary shares did not pass from the original brewery owners, and in many cases only a proportion of preference and debenture shares were released to a grasping public in the 1886–90 flotation boom and the scramble for property in 1894–1900. After 1902 those breweries which had over-extended themselves paid the price. Dwindling profits forced them often to pass dividends even on their preference shares and reorganise their capital structures in order to bring them into line with sharply declining public house and good-will valuations.

Although this account represents accurately enough what occurred in London and Burton, it does not exactly fit the picture elsewhere. It is not that management in the country was superior, nor that conditions in the industry were easier there, but that the 'special' problems of the London and Burton brewers discussed above did not apply in the same degree. Nevertheless, there were country brewers whose records after 1900 were as dismal as those of Watney Combe Reid, Hoare, and Barclay Perkins in London or Allsopp and Thomas Salt in Burton. Some like the Heavitree Brewery (Exeter), Arnold Perrett, the Colchester Brewery Co., Stocks (Halifax), Showell's (Birmingham), and the Manchester Brewery Co., soon ran into severe problems. The Leeds & Batley brewery never paid any ordinary dividend after its incorporation and its houses were leased to Ind Coope. In the most difficult years, 1908–9, they were joined by other recently profitable ventures – Groves & Whitnall, Bents, the Plymouth Brewery Co., the Tadcaster Tower, and in Scotland, Steel Coulson (Glasgow) and Archibald Arrol (Alloa). By 1909 and 1910 there were ninety brewery companies that paid no dividends on their ordinary shares.[114] It was a reversal none had anticipated a decade earlier. However, there were many more breweries whose profits continued to produce a good return for the owners of their share capital: Guinness (with reserves of £2.5 million, paying a 27 per cent dividend in 1907–8), Georges and the Bristol United Brewery, Threlfall's, Mitchells & Butlers, J. W. Cameron, Strong of Romsey, the Hull Brewery, Phipps of Northampton, Steward & Patteson and Greene King in East Anglia, and in Scotland, McEwan and William Younger. What was their secret? Good luck? Local conditions? Superior management?

Local conditions of trade and unemployment are at first sight important explanations of performance. Chairmen accounted for declining

[114] *Brewing Trade Review*, 1 Jan. 1911.

profitability, after their ritual castigations of the temperance movement and the Liberal government, in these terms. The Newcastle Breweries' sharply reduced dividends of 1909–10 were partly explained by the very depressed state of trade on Tyneside. Sir John Ellerman, chairman of J. W. Cameron (Hartlepool), reporting dividends of 14 per cent for 1912, put their good results down to the fact that, 'the district they served had had, notwithstanding strikes, a very prosperous period. Trade was booming ... everything pointed to great activity there in the coming year.'[115] Increasing unemployment seems to have explained reductions in output of up to 10 per cent in any two years. Yet all brewers faced these historic problems whether their breweries were primarily urban or rural, or predominantly reliant upon the prosperity of a single industry. It is arguable that an increasingly 'tied' market protected them from worse fluctuations. Moreover, all brewers faced the problem of changing drinking habits. Chairmen puzzled over this and, since the issue was not clear-cut, came up with explanations which today appear tentative in our market-researched, statistics-ridden age. David Faber, the unusually able chairman of Strong of Romsey, thought their decrease of trade in 1905 could be

> attributed mainly to the want of employment amongst almost every class of worker, and to the bad times that prevailed. He also thought the habits of the people had altered to some extent, less beer and spirits were consumed, more money being spent on Games like football and similar attractions, all classes travelled more and in the towns very many cheap forms of amusement had been provided.

By 1912 his explanation was vaguer. 'The times are different – your old toper who would sit in the public house until closing time is gradually dying out and is not being replaced. Popular amusements such as picture shows have multiplied.'[116] As Faber realised, it was unwise for brewers to deplore these changes, at least in public. And given that brewers everywhere experienced similar vagaries of unemployment and social change, it is management explanations that provide the prime reason for variations in profit performance.

Of what did good management in brewing consist? Very seldom was it innovating drive. All brewers pursued, to a greater or lesser degree, the same path of modest technical innovation in achieving reliability of their beers, in bottling, in motorised transport, in tying their outlets by purchase, and in achieving growth by amalgamation or the purchase of

[115] *Brewing Trade Review*, 1 Jan. 1911; 1 Jan. 1913.
[116] Whitbread Archive 324/114, Strong & Co. Minute Books, 28 Nov. 1905, 5 Nov. 1912.

Table 7.2. *Brewing profits 1897–1914: ordinary dividends and 'net rate of return on capital'; selected companies*

Year[a]	London companies				Burton		West		East Anglia				Midlands		North of England							
	Whitbread		Barclay Perkins		Allsopp		Georges Bristol		Greene King		Steward & Patteson		Phipps Northampton		Bent's Liverpool		Hull		Barnsley		Bentley's Leeds	
	O	RR	O	RR	O	RR	O	RR	O	RR	O	RR	O	RR	O	RR	O	RR	O	RR	O	RR
1897	13	5.8*	12	8.0	3.5	5.0*	19	13.0	8	6.8	6	6.6	20	10.4*	8	8.4	10	–	0	6.3	6	5.3
1898	13	6.7	13	6.5	0	3.0	18.5	13.0	8	8.0	6.5	7.0	20	11.0	9	7.4*	11.25	8.5	6	6.7	6	5.3
1899	13	6.7	12	6.1	0	–	18.5	13.1	9	8.0	6.5	7.8	23	10.6	10	7.7	11.25	8.1	8	7.6	6	4.8*
1900	12	–	10	5.5	0	2.2	18.5	13.2	9	7.5	7	8.3	17.5	8.9*	10	7.0	11.25	8.1	9	8.2	6	5.1
1901	12	6.2*	9	5.2	0	2.4	18.5	12.5	10	7.3	7.5	7.7	15	8.5	10	6.0	11.25	7.8	10	8.6	4	4.9
1902	11	6.0	9	5.4	0	2.6**	18.5	12.9	10	7.3	8	7.8	15	8.6	10	5.0*	11.25	8.0	10	8.7	1.5	4.1
1903	11	5.9	6	4.5	0	2.1	18.5	12.3	10	7.4	9	9.4	15	8 .5	7	4.8	11.25	8.3	10	8.7	4	5.1
1904	8	5.0	5	4.0	0	2.0	17	11.5	10	7.0	10	9.6	11.25	7.9	5	4.8	11.25	8.4	10	10.9	5	5.2
1905	5	4.4	5	4.3	0	1.8	15	10.9	10	6.6	10	9.4	10	–	3	4.4	12	8.9	10	8.6	4	4.9
1906	5	4.4	3	3.8	0	−0.8	15	11.0	10	6.8	12	11.1	10	7.7	3	5.0	13.5	10.0	10	10.3	3	4.6
1907	3[b]	4.4	1	3.4	0	−0.1	15	10.8	10	6.4	12	11.6	11	8.2	3	5.3	13.5	10.6	10	10.9	4	4.9
1908	2[b]	4.1	0	3.3	0	–	12	10.8	10	6.3	13	12.6	11	8.6	0	4.8	13.5	10.3	10	12.3	4	4.9
1909	2[b]	4.6	0	2.9	0	–	12	10.3	10	5.8	13	11.3	11	8.6	0	4.7	13.5	10.4	10	9.5	4	4.5
1910	2[b]	3.4	0	2.3	0	–	10	9.0	10	5.8	23[c]	8.5	10	8.7	0	3.3	13.5	10.5	10	12.6	2	4.1
1911	0.5	3.5	0	6.1**	0	–	10	10.2	10	7.7**	13	11.7	11	9.0	0	5.0	13.5	9.7	10	14.5	3	4.8
1912	0.5	3.2	0	5.1	0	–	10	9.8	10	6.1	13	10.1	12	8.9	0	4.7	13.5	9.8	10	15.2	4	4.8
1913	0.5	3.2	0	5.0	0	–**	11	11.0	10	7.2	25[c]	10.9	13	9.3	0	5.1	13.5	11.4	10	9.0	5.5	5.1
1914	0.5	3.2	0	5.3	0	2.4	11	12.3	10	7.7	12	13.6	13	9.7	0	5.6	13.5	10.7	10	9.9	6	5.6

Key: O Ordinary dividend; RR Rate of return; * Increase in capital of 20 per cent and over; ** Write-down of capital of 20 per cent and over

Notes: [a] Year is nearest calender year (year to 30 June 1887 taken as 1886). [b] Small shareholders (up to £10,000) received 5 per cent. [c] With bonus. Capital/profits data are difficult to compare owing to the immense variety in accounting practices, differences in capital structure (gearing, interest rates), etc.

An attempt has been made to standardise on the basis of the following definitions: 'net profit': after working costs, depreciation, taxes, but before interest, debenture interest; 'capital': nominal value share capital and debentures plus (where given) outstanding mortgages and loans.

Source: Gourvish and Wilson, 'Profitability in the Brewing Industry, 1885–1914', *Business History*, 27 (July 1985), 165.

small breweries. It was the way in which they pursued these aims in financial terms, however, that was significant. Financial conservatism in the 1880s and 1890s – the acquisition of a defined trading area at an early stage, the purchase of houses principally out of profits, the creation of a healthy reserve against which losses and revaluations after 1902 could be written off – was all-important. However, those firms that allowed too generous a valuation of goodwill,[117] that created no appreciable reserve fund, that issued debentures freely on the calculations of profitability in the heady late 1890s, courted disaster for their shareholders in the difficult years after 1902. C. P. Wood, chairman of the Springwell Brewery (Heckmondwike), 'rejoiced that the Company had not yielded to the craze of the boom, which had been the downfall of many companies'.[118] Local conditions might exacerbate trends, but the difference between those breweries whose profitability faltered badly and those which survived almost unscathed even in the 1908–10 period is accounted for by wise managerial and sound financial decisions taken a decade or more earlier. The variations in experience are illustrated in Table 7.2 which gives ordinary dividends and net rates of return for a selection of eleven companies.

A typology of the profitability of country breweries in Edwardian Britain falls, therefore, into three categories. First, there were those that had already by the 1880s acquired a good stock of public houses, like Greenall Whitley and Steward & Patteson. Secondly, a number of breweries prudently bought public houses and other breweries throughout the 1880s and 1890s out of profits and without resort to large debenture issues. The management of these breweries – like Greene King, Strong and the Hull Brewery for example – was capable and forward looking. Lastly, there were those breweries that were generously capitalised in the 1880s and 1890s, that issued debentures freely, or that bought together unwieldy amalgamations of breweries, like Arnold Perrett, Showell's, the Leeds & Wakefield Brewery, and the Colchester Brewery Co. After 1902 these ran into serious difficulties. The first two categories, however, came through a testing decade largely unscathed.

Most brewers liked to maintain that they had little room for managerial manœuvre. With raw materials costs, and excise and licence duties

117 i.e., the difference between a company's share and loan capital and the total value of its assets. Brewing accountants reckoned it should not exceed three years' purchase of a company's net profits. Allsopp in 1887 was an unparalleled eight years, and even then its assets were valued generously.

118 *Brewing Trade Review*, 1 July 1906.

running at about two-thirds of total outlay, with a negligible export trade for the vast majority of them, and with retailing governed by the state of employment and the clemency of the seasons, they asserted they were at the mercy of the grain and hop harvest, the weather, the trade cycle and the government. In fact the contribution of management was an important ingredient in a brewery's success. George McKay of the St Leonard's Brewery reckoned that, 'bad management as much as bad water can ruin a brewery'.[119] The Cheltenham Original Brewing Co. provides a quotable example to illustrate this point. An unwieldy amalgamation of breweries in Cheltenham and Hereford in 1888, it possessed in the early 1890s a capital of £200,000 plus debentures, loans and mortgages of £214,500. In 1901–2 it paid a healthy 8 per cent on its ordinary capital. Four years later it generated insufficient profits to pay any dividend at all on these shares. The company reacted quickly. It sought 'the expert advice of the Managing Director of an important brewery in the East of England . . . Mr. Lake. They hoped by the aid of his expert knowledge of brewery management . . . to introduce reforms and retrenchments in the management and expenditure of the brewery that would augment its profits and increase its future prosperity.'[120] By 1912–13 Edward Lake, the managing director of Greene King, had pulled affairs round sufficiently for the Cheltenham company to pay a 5 per cent dividend again. His reputation was based upon the meticulous detail of his management at Greene King.[121] Like all successful brewers, he was concerned with careful accounting, working out meticulously his profit per barrel each year so that he could trim margins at all stages of production. And although all brewers in the pre-1900 period had followed very similar working apprenticeships, not all of them had learned the same lessons of careful management. For the style of breweries varied considerably. Many had flourished in the years of great expansion of the 1850–80 period and again in the 1890s. It was this easily won prosperity that attracted so much hostility to the industry. Affluence also encouraged ingrained attitudes.

Initially, brewery management did not change much in the 1885–1900 period. In all breweries employing more than 50–60 men or

[119] Quoted in Donnachie, *Brewing Industry*, p. 190. See also the *Country Brewers' Gazette* (1891), p. 670 for the Burton Brewing Co.'s annual general meeting: 'Since the appointment of their new general manager a very marked improvement had taken place in the character of the ales and the economy of manufacture, with the result that trade had received a very healthy and continuous impetus.'

[120] COBC annual reports in *Stock Exchange Year Book*; *The Brewers' Journal* (1906), p. 730.

[121] Wilson, *Greene King*, pp. 130–71.

producing more than 20–30,000 barrels, the chief departments – malting, brewing, retailing, tied property – remained somewhat autonomous, and those in charge of them were preoccupied with the details of their carefully delineated responsibilities. They required therefore a capable, wholly committed managing director to impose policy, especially after 1900. Edward Lake did this both at Greene King and at the Cheltenham Original Brewing Co. The directors of Mitchells & Butlers and David Faber of Strong were similarly successful. The latter pursued a clear policy of economy and concentration after 1900, also improving the firm's public houses and developing the bottling of their beers. He adapted a growing firm to changed circumstances. Others, like Georges, remained cautious and traditional, returning excellent profits throughout the Edwardian period. But it became notably more difficult to remain in the old, familiar grooves after 1900. Even a proud firm like Lacon dismissed its manager in 1912 and reorganised 'the entire management of the firm' on the advice of Sir Richard Garton, a director of several brewing and sugar companies, who was himself appointed 'advisory director' of Lacon the following year.[122]

Of course, the sudden truncation of the speculative boom of the late 1890s had revealed some appalling cases of mismanagement. None exceeded Allsopp. The principal directors were Members of Parliament, caught in the richest threads of late Victorian society, believing that the conditions of the 1860s and 1870s and the pre-eminence of their brewery would last forever. They were unmoved by the public criticism of their conduct at what were the liveliest annual general meetings in the industry. In 1891 one shareholder maintained that Allsopp, 'was the worst managed concern in Burton or elsewhere'. Even the shareholders' committee was powerless: 'Why one of the committee who was sent to Burton to look after the shareholders' interests spent more of his time discussing sporting dogs with the Hon. George Allsopp [great laughter and hisses]. How many homes had been wrecked by the mismanagement of Allsopp's business?'[123] Watney Combe Reid, an amalgamation of three great firms, effected no significant economies. In 1902 it dismissed its managing director (Phillips) and three others, and engaged (Sir) Richard Garton to run the firm. Cosmo Bonsor, the chairman, spoke with some hyperbole of harnessing 'new energy and ripened experience'. The shareholders seemed less convinced as sales

[122] Whitbread Archive, 197/34, Minute Book of E. Lacon & Co. Ltd.
[123] *Country Brewers' Gazette* (1891), pp. 558–9.

plummeted.[124] Showell's (Birmingham) revealed a deficit of £431,612 in its balance sheet in 1904. The advisory committee appointed to look into the company's affairs revealed that 'the downfall of the business was due largely to gross mismanagement and reckless extravagance'. Properties were overvalued, profits 'grossly overstated'. It recommended the dismissal of all directors responsible for the management prior to October 1903 (and this has a modern ring) although they were themselves ignorant of the chairman's and general manager's 'frauds', they 'must learn that they would be held responsible for lack of ordinary business precautions'.[125] And even a solid provincial firm like Morgan's of Norwich, whose chairman could explain dwindling profits with some eloquence as the natural consequence of increasing government intervention and taxation, revealed, on closer inspection, serious management deficiencies. In 1906 the firm employed a Mr Crosier Bailey of Charles Street, Mayfair, to report on the management. His review of the five directors was devastating. The chairman was old and infirm; his deputy was often away in South Africa; the third was only modestly capable; the fourth, also head-brewer, was overstretched and in any case had little 'serious business capacity'; and the fifth, although competent, usually attended just twice a week from 11 a.m. to 3 p.m. Here was a business, with a capital approaching £750,000, whose management depended four days out of six entirely upon the head-brewer. Bailey concluded: 'It is impossible to imagine for a moment that any business ... can be pulled out of trouble by such management as this (it would be grotesque if it were not so serious).'[126]

Breweries had always experienced management crises of these dimensions, and the spectrum of ability had run from the likes of Edward Lake and David Faber to the Hon. George Allsopp, but they had been hidden within partnership structures. After 1900, the presence of shareholders and auditors made them more difficult to contain. And conditions after

[124] *Brewing Trade Review*, 1 Sept. 1902. Truman were uncharacteristically critical of Watneys in May 1902. They thought Bonsor and Phillips were tied up with Garton in the sale of saccharum (a brewing sugar); they considered the firm 'bankrupt'; 'there are only about two of the whole lot of directors who know what honour or truth is'. Truman smarted because Watneys had ill-used them in the formation of a hops syndicate.

[125] *Brewing Trade Review*, 1 Dec. 1904.

[126] Norfolk Record Office, BR 160/29, 'Mr. Bailey's Memo'. We are grateful to Christine Clark for this reference. Eldridge Pope's management – conservative and indecisive since the 1900s – was equally shaky by the 1914–18 War. At one board meeting no decision about a bonus and pay rise could be reached because Edwin Pope declined to vote and George Pope was unable to hear (Seekings, *Thomas Hardy's Brewer*, pp. 71–2).

1900 were hard, with aspects of the trade changing quite quickly. Certainly, a larger tied trade did not make management easier between 1900 and 1914, for all brewers had to face major issues, decreasing sales, excess capacity, the pursuit of amalgamation, the improvement of houses in the face of a hostile government and magistracy, and the introduction of bottled beer and motorised transport. Such factors, as well as financial exigencies, forced changes upon brewery managements. They were limited because brewing remained largely an insider's world, where connection and tradition counted for everything. A typical instance was when Lacon of Great Yarmouth sought an amalgamation with Youngs, Crawshay & Youngs of Norwich. In terms of malting facilities and market combination it made sound economic sense. Discussions were amicable, but Lacon were informed that Mr Youngs, the aged, principal shareholder, objected – or at least the other directors thought he did. Charles Crawshay wrote apologetically, 'I fancy his head is rather queer and if he had been younger he would have felt more able to negotiate with you.' This was the old world of unaccountable partners. In reality in Edwardian Britain – like the sunlit days of horses, old topers and a vast cask trade of strong beer – it was passing for many brewers.

PART 2

THE BREWING INDUSTRY 1914–1980

8

Production and consumption, 1914–1955

This chapter, the first of three dealing with the events of 1914–55, examines the implications for British brewing of a series of major demand and supply fluctuations associated with war, recession and economic growth. It begins with an evaluation of the effects on the industry of the First World War.

I

As the First World War progressed, it came to be regarded as an unqualified misfortune by Britain's brewers. The small number of exporting businesses quickly lost their markets in the United States, India, Australia, and what little they sent to continental Europe, chiefly to the ale-loving Belgians. For these firms post-war recovery proved to be a slow and painful process.[1] The vast bulk of the industry supplied the home market, of course, and here too the War introduced problems on a broad front, intensifying the existing trend towards lower levels of beer consumption. Moreover, these problems affected all brewers, whether they possessed national, regional or local status. Higher costs, stimulated by increased taxation, input shortages and general inflationary pressures, were combined with a reduction in the quality of materials used in brewing. At the same time, controls were imposed both on the volume of output and on its strength, i.e. the specific gravity of the beer to be brewed. Nor was this all. Consumption was restricted by means of the twin mechanisms of price control and much tighter licensing regulations. Brewing and retailing in key munitions areas such as Carlisle were nationalised (see pp. 324–6). Much of the blame for the wartime squeeze on brewing could thus be directed at government intervention. Although controls were imposed on all industries,

[1] No market recovered its pre-war position, and exports to Australia and the United States all but disappeared after 1918.

brewing felt them more keenly than most. Not only was intervention more wide ranging; it was also undertaken in a climate of hostility to the trade actively promoted by no less prominent a temperance supporter than Lloyd George. Brewers did not forgive his jibes, made early in the War, about the evils of alcohol, when he claimed that excessive drinking was prejudicing industrial production. 'Drink', he thundered in a speech at Bangor in February 1915, 'is doing us more damage in the war than all the German submarines put together ... We are fighting Germany, Austria, and Drink; and as far as I can see the greatest of these three deadly foes is Drink.'[2]

For over two centuries the industry had been considered fair prey for wartime Chancellors of the Exchequer.[3] It was therefore no surprise that one of the earliest of the numerous steps taken by the government involved unprecedented levels of exaction. In November 1914 the beer duty was increased from 7s 9d (£0.3875) to 23s (£1.15) per 'standard' barrel (i.e. of 1055° gravity), and successive increases took it to £1.25 per barrel by April 1917. It was doubled a year later, then raised to £3.50 and £5.00 in April 1919 and April 1920 respectively, by which time it produced £123 million (1920–1), compared with only £13.6 million in 1913–14. The increase in the tax burden over the period 1914–20 in *real* terms (i.e. allowing for wartime inflation) was of the order of 430 per cent.[4] Nor was there much amelioration after 1920. The only concession made was in April 1923 when a rebate of £1 per

[2] An examination of the evidence gathered by Lloyd George suggests that his claim that drink was responsible for significant lost production was nebulous: John Turner, 'State Purchase of the Liquor Trade in the First World War', *Historical Journal*, 23 (September 1980), 597–9; David Lloyd George, speech at Bangor, 28 February 1915, and address to deputation of shipbuilders, 29 March 1915, reported in *The Times*, 1 and 30 March 1915, and cf. also *War Memoirs of David Lloyd George* (1933), I, pp. 322–8. His remarks have been much quoted in the secondary literature, including the numerous surveys of the control period. Note, in particular, Henry Carter, *The Control of the Drink Trade in Britain: A Contribution to National Efficiency During the Great War 1915–1918* (2nd edn, 1919); Thomas N. Carver, *Government Control of the Liquor Business in Great Britain and the United States* (New York, 1919); Arthur Shadwell, *Drink in 1914–1922* (1923); and more recently, G. B. Wilson, *Alcohol and the Nation* (1940); Sir Sydney O. Nevile, *Seventy Rolling Years* (1958); Norman Longmate, *The Water Drinkers* (1968); Michael E. Rose, 'The Success of Social Reform? The Central Control Board (Liquor Traffic), 1915–21', in M. R. D. Foot (ed.), *War and Society* (1973), pp. 71–84; and Derek H. Aldcroft, 'Control of the Liquor Trade in Great Britain 1914–21', in W. H. Chaloner and Barrie M. Ratcliffe (eds.), *Trade and Transport* (Manchester, 1977), pp. 242–57.

[3] Mathias, *Brewing Industry in England*, pp. 356–7, 369.

[4] Shadwell, *Drink*, p. 86; duties in money terms deflated by retail price index in C. H. Feinstein, *National Income, Expenditure and Output of the United Kingdom, 1855–1965* (Cambridge, 1972), T140.

bulk (i.e. selling) barrel was granted, but this left the duty well above the April 1919 level.[5]

As German submarines took their toll of British merchant shipping in 1915, the government responded by restricting brewing output, and reducing raw material usage by placing limits on the strength of beer to be brewed. Both steps were designed to economise on the industry's import requirements, but they could also be regarded as an encouragement to sobriety as part of the war effort. Legislation in August and December 1916 limited production to 85 per cent of the dutiable output of 29.9 million standard barrels in the year ending 31 March 1916, but at the same time it gave brewers the option of accepting a reduction to 70 per cent of the output in the year to 30 September 1914 (36.2 million), indicating a maximum annual output of about 25.3 million barrels.[6] It was a testimony to the work of the brewing lobby, led by the Brewers' Society and the National Trade Defence Association, that the medicine was kept as palatable as it was. Walter Runciman, President of the Board of Trade, had faced considerable criticism from brewers both inside and outside the House of Commons, and it was the Brewers' Society which had negotiated the option of applying the reduction to pre-war output. The legislation as amended postponed the date of calculating a production balance for each brewery from 30 September 1916 to 31 March 1917, causing a civil servant in the Ministry of Food to observe that there existed a 'moral understanding' between the brewers and the Board of Trade that there would be no further interventions for at least a year, i.e. until April 1917.[7] As William Beveridge, then Second Secretary in the Food Ministry, later recalled sardonically, 'the protracted and laborious discussion aroused by this far from drastic measure was perhaps typical of the spirit of . . . 1916'.[8]

As the supply situation worsened the government's strategy became more determined. In March 1917 Lord Davenport, the Food Controller appointed by Lloyd George's more hawkish Coalition Government to

5 For brewers of higher gravity beer. The April 1923 rebate gave proportionately greater relief to brewers of *lower* gravity beers. For example, for a brewer of 1055° beer the £1 rebate represented a reduction of 20 per cent, but for a brewer of 1037° beer it amounted to a 30 per cent cut and brought his tax bill close to that of April 1919.

6 Output of Beer (Restriction) Acts, 1916, c.26, c.57; BS, Annual Report for Year Ended 30 September 1916, pp. 31–6, BS.

7 BS Law Committee Minutes, 1 March 1916, General Meeting, 26 April 1916, BS; H. F. Paul, notes with draft of Report dealing with the use of Cereals in Brewing and Distilling, 1 January 1917, Beveridge Papers on Food Control, 1916–17, Vol. 2 No. 12, Coll. Misc. 92, BLPES; L. Margaret Barnett, *British Food Policy During the First World War* (1985), p. 84.

8 Sir William Beveridge, *British Food Control* (1928), p. 18.

Table 8.1. *UK beer production in standard and bulk barrels, 1913–20, with average gravity*

Year[a]	Standard barrelage (millions)	Bulk barrelage (millions)	Bulk as % of Standard	Average Gravity (Degrees)
1913	36.1	37.6	104	1052.80°
1914[b]	36.2	–		
1914	33.1	34.8	105	1052.35°
1915	30.3	32.1	106	1051.88°
1916	26.6	30.2	113	1048.54°
1917	13.8	19.1	138	1039.81°
1918	12.9	23.3	180	1030.55°
1919	25.1	35.0	140	1039.41°
1920	26.7	34.5	129	1042.61°

Source: BS, *Statistical Handbook 1988*, p. 7; *Annual Reports of Commissioners for Customs and Excise.*
Note: Production is beer charged with duty.
[a] 1913 = Year ending 31 March 1914, *et seq.*
[b] Year ending 30 September 1914.

apply a firmer policy of food conservation, introduced an order limiting brewing output to a mere 28 per cent of the pre-war level or a third of that in 1915–16, with effect from 1 April. This indicated a reduction to about 10 million standard barrels for 1917–18.[9] The new target was accompanied by restrictions on malting, the requisitioning of barley and control of the hop market.[10] In fact, the reduction to 10 million barrels was never made, and the actual output for 1917–18 was some 13.8 million (see Table 8.1). This was due in part to the earmarking of additional output for military canteens. But the decisive factor was undoubtedly the relaxation of output control in the second half of 1917. Here the realities facing Lloyd George and the prohibition lobby were fully exposed. Whereas in 1915 drink was identified as a greater menace than the enemy in limiting vital industrial production, two years later

[9] Intoxicating Liquor (Output & Delivery) Order, 29 March 1917, 1917, No. 270; War Cabinet Minutes, 12 and 23 January, 14 February 1917, CAB23/1, PRO. Exports were also terminated. For further detail see Beveridge, *Food Control*, pp. 100–1, and Barnett, *Food Policy*, pp. 105–6.

[10] On malt and barley restrictions see DOR Orders, 1917, No. 51, 132, 159, 259, 345 and 364 (26 January, 3 and 20 February, 21 March, 12 and 16 April). On hops see 1917, No. 914 and 925 (31 August and 3 September), and Nevile, *Seventy Rolling Years*, pp. 88–92.

came the realisation, fully documented in the Reports of the Commission of Enquiry into Industrial Unrest in July 1917 and carefully explained to the House of Commons by the Home Secretary, that the shortage of alcohol in general, and of beer in particular, had been a major factor in fomenting industrial unrest in the summer of 1917. The government thus faced a dilemma. It had to allow brewing output to rise, but at the same time wished to stabilise or even reduce the industry's cereal consumption. The solution lay in the notorious 'Government Ale', a term applied, much to government annoyance, to the low alcohol beer established by the new regulations. From the second half of 1917 a new order permitted an increase in the maximum standard barrelage of 20 per cent (and, at the Food Controller's discretion, up to 33⅓ per cent), but stipulated that brewers accepting the increase should brew at least half of their total production at a gravity of no more than 1036° (about 3.5 per cent alcohol by volume).[11] Brewers again had been active behind the scenes. The increase appears to have owed its origin to a suggestion made to Lloyd George by Colonel John Gretton, Chairman of Bass, Ratcliff & Gretton.[12] Furthermore, the subsequent raising of the gravity figure to 1042°, in October 1917, was undertaken after complaints from leading producers of higher gravity beers, notably Guinness.[13] Nevertheless, Britain's brewers acquiesced

11 Intoxicating Liquor (Output & Delivery) Order No. 2, 7 July 1917, 1917, No. 700. Brewers who accepted the 20 per cent increase also had to restrict the gravity of the remaining half of their output to that used in the quarter beginning 1 July 1916. The 13⅓ per cent increase was intended for munitions and agricultural areas. On the impact of drink shortages on social unrest see *Commission of Enquiry into Industrial Unrest. Summary of the Reports by the Rt Hon. G. N. Barnes, M. P.*, 17 July 1917, *PP* (1917–18) XV, Cd.8696, and Sir George Cave (Home Secretary), statement, 5 July 1917, *Parl. Deb. (Commons)*, 5th ser. Vol. 95 (Session 1917), c.1416f.

12 Cf. Gretton-Lloyd George, 'Suggestions for Dealing with the Present Beer Situation', June 1917, Beveridge Papers on Food Control, Vol. 2 No. 34, BLPES. The memo is attributed to 'Major Gretton', but, given the role of Col. John Gretton in the brewers' negotiations with government, it is likely that he, and not his younger brother and fellow Bass director, Major Hugh Frederic Gretton, was its author. Gretton suggested an output increase of 33⅓ per cent with a gravity of about 1037°, and the idea was subsequently considered by the Cabinet: Minutes, 21 June 1917, CAB23/3, PRO.

13 Intoxicating Liquor (Output & Delivery) Order No. 3, 15 October 1917, 1917, No. 1059; *Brewers' Journal*, July, September and October 1917, pp. 270, 356, 393. Ironically in view of Gretton's initiative, Bass was among the half-dozen or so leading firms which declined to brew with a 1036° restriction. See W. W. Butler, memo on 'Shortage of Beer', 9 August 1917, Lord D'Abernon's Papers, H0185/265, PRO. Pressure exerted by Guinness and the Irish brewers probably tipped the balance. Irish beer gravities were traditionally high – 1065° in 1910 cf. 1052° in Great Britain – and English-bottled Guinness Extra Stout had a gravity of 1072°. Brewing was also more central to Ireland's agriculture. See Sir H. Duke (Chief Secretary for Ireland), memo to Cabinet on 'Concessions to Irish Brewers as to Increase in Output', 30 June 1917, Lord D'Abernon's Cabinet Papers, H0185/266, PRO; Draft papers on 'Restriction of

in a major reduction in the industry's consumption of raw materials, which fell to about a half of the pre-war level.

In March 1918 a further restriction on output was announced for the following year, accompanied by fresh controls on malting. Both moves were made in order to reduce brewing's import needs and to free barley for use in bread. A critical factor now was the pressure exerted by the United States for total prohibition. Herbert Hoover, the Food Administrator, issued veiled threats from the middle of 1917 that an increase in American grain exports to Britain would be difficult to secure unless domestic brewing were halted. The suggestion was examined by the Cabinet, but fears of unrest tipped the balance in favour of a reduction in gravity.[14] From April 1918 production was limited to 10,720,000 standard barrels, plus 1,120,000 for munitions areas and 750,000 for army and navy canteens. The beer was to be brewed at a low average gravity of 1030°, an exception being made for the canteens, and for Ireland, where the gravity was fixed at 1045°.[15] Thus, in the year ending March 1919 the standard barrelage fell to its lowest level, under 13 million barrels, but the quantity of beer produced was 80 per cent higher than this (Table 8.1). By this time steps were being taken to deregulate the industry, and in July 1919 output control ceased, although an average permitted gravity remained in force: 1044° for Great Britain, 1051° for Ireland.[16] But in spite of the relaxation of controls, recovery was limited, as the data for 1919 and 1920 indicate. Although there was some restoration of the strength of beer brewed, the standard barrelage remained about 25–30 per cent lower than in 1914 and even in terms of bulk barrels post-war production failed to match pre-war levels (Table 8.1).

During the second half of the war, price control was also applied. The retail price of beer had doubled in the period 1914–16, reaching 4d for an ordinary pint of draught beer in a public bar, and there were further increases with the tighter output controls imposed in the first half of

Brewing', 1 January 1917, Beveridge Papers on Food Control, Vol. 2 No. 14, BLPES; *Brewers' Journal*, August 1917, p. 335; Wilson, *Alcohol and the Nation*, p. 58.

[14] Herbert Hoover–William Goode, cable, 11 May 1917, Beveridge Papers, Vol. 2 No. 36, BLPES; Sir Joseph Maclay (Shipping Minister), memo to Cabinet, 22 January 1918, Lord Rhondda (Food Controller), memo to Cabinet on 'Continuance of Brewing', 7 March 1918, and War Cabinet Minutes, 8 March 1918, CAB23/5, H0185/266, PRO. The issue is examined in depth by Barnett, *Food Policy*, pp. 163–80.

[15] Intoxicating Liquor (Output & Delivery) Order, 19 March 1918, 1918, No. 339. Malting was restricted by Order, 26 February 1918, 1918, No. 225.

[16] Intoxicating Liquor (Output & Delivery) Order No. 2, 21 July 1919, 1919, No. 927, and see also Order, 5 February 1919, 1919, No. 104.

1917. The government responded in October of that year by fixing maximum prices of 4d a pint for beer under 1036° in gravity, and 5d for beer in the range 1036–42°. In March 1918 these prices were applied to lower gravities, while subsequent adjustments in February and July 1919 and April 1920 set maxima for the entire range of gravities and for bottled beers. These controls were not abandoned until the end of August 1921.[17] Clearly, then, the package of government restrictions represented a considerable assault upon beer, which remained highly priced in relation to its pre-war quality and strength. Most brewers complained gloomily about 'Government Ale'. Some went so far as to attach the name to the weaker beers on sale in their pubs, and the government became so concerned about this form of marketing that it inserted a clause in the price fixing order of October 1917 preventing brewers from advertising beer of under 1036° in gravity as 'Government Ale' or 'Government Beer', or implying in any way that the beer had been brewed under state direction, a requirement repeated in subsequent orders.[18]

Much the most enduring feature of wartime regulation was associated with the government's efforts to solve the 'drink problem' by means of prohibition or nationalisation. Measures taken under the Defence of the Realm Act introduced draconian reductions in the permitted hours of serving alcohol in retail outlets, while the 'Carlisle Experiment' involved the state purchase and management of breweries and public houses in certain key munitions areas. Both elements, which continued in large measure in peacetime under the terms of the Licensing Act of 1921, remained as long-term monuments to the interventionism of Lloyd George and the temperance lobby, even if the ultimate

[17] See Beer (Prices & Description) Orders, 15 October 1917, 1917, No. 1058; 19 March 1918, 1918, No. 343; 5 February 1919, 1919, No. 103; 12 July 1919 no. 565; 10 April 1920, 1920, No. 540. Controls on bottled beer prices were introduced in the February 1919 Order. Public bar prices for draught beer in 1919–21 were:

Price (pint)	Gravity Feb. 1919	Gravity July 1919	Gravity Apr. 1920
2d	–	– 1019°	–
3d	– 1022°	1020–6°	– 1019°
4d	1023–8°	1027–32°	1020–6°
5d	1029–34°	1033–8°	1027–32°
6d	1035–41°	1039–45°	1033–8°
7d	1042–9°	1046–53°	1039–45°
8d	1050° +	1054° +	1046–53°
9d	–	–	1054° +

[18] *Ibid.*; War Cabinet Minutes, 28 October 1917, CAB23/4, PRO. The practice of naming beer 'Government ale' appears to have originated in London. Cf. *Brewers' Journal*, November 1917, p. 428.

goals of either prohibition or complete state purchase went unrealised.[19]

In brief, the circumstances were as follows. Powers to close public houses and/or restrict opening hours were given first to military and naval authorities, then to civil authorities, in August 1914. The early impact of these measures was felt in particular in London, where the evening closing time became 10 p.m., instead of 12.30 a.m., in October. In the following year controls became much more widespread, thanks to the orders issued by a newly constituted government body, the Central Control Board (Liquor Traffic), established in June 1915. In large areas of the country, including most of Scotland and the North of England, opening hours were substantially reduced, from 16 to 17 hours (19½ in London) to 5½ hours on weekdays, with a compulsory 'afternoon break' in serving, and evening closing set at 9–9.30 p.m.[20] Retail abuses, such as the provision of credit, 'treating' and the 'long pull', were also tackled.[21] By the end of 1915 restrictions of this kind had been applied to about half of Great Britain, and by the end of the war about 94 per cent of Britain's population had been affected.[22] Nor was this all. Alarming reports of increased drunkenness in and around Carlisle, where a large munitions factory was being built, led the Central Control Board, in a series of steps begun in January 1916, to take the town's four breweries into public ownership, together with some 235 licensed properties in the Carlisle, Gretna and Annan areas. Similar worries about drinking near the ordnance factory at Enfield Lock, near London, and the naval base at Invergordon, in Cromarty Firth, resulted in the nationalisation of a further forty-four properties in the first half of 1916. Compensation for these actions amounted to about £900,000.[23]

The significance of these interventions by the Control Board is still a matter for debate. Certainly, the widespread restriction of opening hours led to a dramatic decline in the overt signs of excessive drinking,

19 The state management of the Carlisle brewery and its associated licensed properties in the Carlisle and Cromarty areas was not abandoned until 1974 (following an Act of 1971). More liberal licensing hours, including afternoon opening, were not introduced until 1977 in Scotland and 1988 in England and Wales.

20 Sunday hours were reduced from 6–7 to 5: Carter, *Drink Trade*, pp. 35–6, 136–7, 145.

21 The 'long pull' was a generous over-measure provided by certain publicans to attract trade. *Ibid.*, pp. 157–61.

22 38.5 million out of a total population of 41 million: *ibid.*, p. 134.

23 Sir Edgar Sanders, General Manager, Carlisle, Address to Members of the House of Commons, 25 February 1920, H0185/23, PRO; *Report of the Committee on the Disinterested Management of Public Houses (Southborough Committee)*, May 1927, *PP* (1927) X, Cmd.2862, p. 13. The Maryport Brewery, with its *full* tied estate (those in Carlisle had already been nationalised), was subsequently added to the scheme from 1917, and the final total of acquisitions was close to 400. The Enfield Lock pubs were returned to the private sector in 1923.

as was readily observable in London in 1914–15.[24] On the other hand, the State's venture into the trade, an experimental application of the hypothesis that 'disinterested management', both at the production and retailing stages, would cut beer and spirits consumption and end the 'evils of drink', was more ambiguous in its impact.[25] The number of convictions for drunkenness did fall sharply in the controlled areas, and efforts to rationalise and improve public houses received widespread publicity, drawing a stream of visitors to Carlisle in the immediate post-war period.[26] A policy of 'fewer and better' pubs was vigorously pursued, encouraged by the brewing representatives on the Control Board, Sydney Nevile, and William Waters Butler, chairman of the prosperous Birmingham firm of Mitchells & Butlers (Plates 43 and 44).[27] By 1920 the number of licensed properties in Carlisle had been cut by over 40 per cent, and there were reductions of a similar order of magnitude elsewhere in the nationalised districts.[28] Butler's firm had been notable for its move into directly managed public houses before the War, and this change was made in Carlisle, where competing houses and the worst, male-only, drinking dens were eliminated. 'Undesirable' practices, such as the use of spirit 'chasers', Sunday drinking and the consumption of spirits on Saturdays, were prohibited. Emphasis was placed upon the civilising influences of food, non-alcoholic drinks, facilities for women, games and entertainment. These features were incorporated in new or reconstructed 'model' pubs, such as the 'Gretna Tavern' of July 1916.[29]

The rationalisation of Carlisle's breweries, only one of which was being used by 1920, together with the reduction in retail outlets, represented a clear message to private sector brewers from state management, a microcosm of the vogue for 'rationalisation' in wartime industries and

24 Carver, *Government Control*, p. 119; Carter, *Drink Trade*, pp. 36, 247.

25 Balanced judgements are not made easy by the fact that the most detailed accounts of the Control Board's operations were written by temperance supporters, such as the Rev. Henry Carter, a member of the Board, Arthur Shadwell (see note 2 above), the Rev. Wilson Stuart, *Drink Nationalization and its Results* (1927), and J. Rowntree and A. Sherwell, *State Purchase of the Liquor Trade* (1919).

26 For visits to Carlisle see H0185/22 and 23, PRO; Rose, 'Central Control Board', 80–1. Visitors included interested country brewers such as the Lakes of Greene King in 1919: Wilson, *Greene King*, p. 200.

27 Butler, born in a Butler's pub, was appointed in January 1916, and Nevile, a brewer with Brandon's of Putney, joined the Board in July 1917. Nevile later had a distinguished career with Whitbread & Co. as a managing director from 1919.

28 Sanders, Address, 1920, H0185/23, PRO; *Central Control Board (Liquor Traffic). Carlisle and District. General Manager's Report 1918*, 1919, *PP* (1919) XXIV, Cmd.137, pp. 2–3; *Southborough Committee Report*, 1927, p. 13.

29 Carter, *Drink Trade*, pp. 214–20; Rose, 'Central Control Board', 78–9.

a pointer to the policies which would be required in the context of reduced demand for beer in peacetime. Indeed, Butler's enthusiasm for the Carlisle experiment was such that he declared himself a staunch advocate of full nationalisation, much to the consternation of his colleagues in the trade.[30] On the other hand, sceptics were able to point out that most of the alleged benefits of state management were spurious. The incidence of drunkenness, for example, declined sharply everywhere – convictions fell by 84 per cent in England and Wales between 1914 and 1918 – and marked improvement could be found in 'private sector' ports and munitions areas such as Liverpool, Portsmouth and Cardiff quite as much as in Carlisle, where the problem had been turned into a public scare by the sudden, but temporary, influx of 15–16,000 navvies. The trend towards greater sobriety had been evident before the War, and its intensification in wartime was the product of state control rather than state management, a consequence of more expensive, weaker beer in short supply, sold at restricted times.[31] Nor could it be argued that state intervention had transformed the production process. At Carlisle's remaining brewery, concern about the quality of the beer was such that Butler and Nevile were called in to offer advice in 1922. Their investigations uncovered defects at every stage of production, in fermenting, fining, the dry-kilning of barley, and refrigeration. The Home Office, which had assumed responsibility for the Carlisle 'experiment' in 1921, responded by appointing Dr E. R. Moritz, a leading brewing expert, as a consultant.[32]

Nevertheless, the establishment of the Central Control Board, and the enthusiasm for state purchase of the liquor trade shown by Lord D'Abernon, its chairman, and colleagues such as Waters Butler, Philip Snowden and Henry Carter,[33] represented the highpoint of the government's flirtation with the nationalisation issue. How serious the Cabinet was in its intentions is not easy to gauge, despite a careful examination of

[30] Hawkins, *Bass Charrington*, pp. 71–3; Nevile, *Seventy Rolling Years*, p. 103.

[31] Convictions for drunkenness fell by 71 per cent in Carlisle, 1914–18, and by 79 per cent in Liverpool, 61 per cent in Cardiff and 89 per cent in Portsmouth. *Licensing Statistics, PP* (1914–16) LIV, Cd.7981, 1919, LI, Cmd.352; *Central Control Board (Liquor Traffic). General Manager's Report, 1918*, PP (1919) XXIV, Cmd.137, p. 8. Cf. *inter alia*, Stuart, *Drink Nationalization*, pp. 10ff., George E. G. Catlin, *Liquor Control* (1931), p. 183, Shadwell, *Drink*, pp. 89–91, 142–4.

[32] H.O. file on Appointment of Brewing Experts, 1922–42, HO185/27; Brewing Expert, Reports, 1922–3, HO185/28, PRO. Large private sector breweries were not free of such problems, of course. At Whitbread's Chiswell St brewery, one of the largest in the country, Dr Mortitz was engaged on a similar mission in 1923–5: Whitbread & Co. Board Minutes, W/23/3, Whitbread & Co. plc.

[33] Sir Henry Vincent, Lord D'Abernon, had been Governor of the Imperial Ottoman Bank; Philip Snowden was a leading temperance sympathiser in the Labour Party; the Rev. Henry Carter was secretary of the Wesleyan Methodist Temperance Committee.

the available evidence.[34] While there were firm supporters of the policy, others, more firmly in the grip of temperance propaganda, insisted upon prohibition. And in a Cabinet not uniform in its sobriety, there were other Ministers who probably did not care about either course of action. The government twice examined the implications of nationalisation – in 1915 and again in 1917. On the first occasion the issue was orchestrated by Lloyd George, then Chancellor of the Exchequer, who appears to have been convinced that drink was responsible for the faltering munitions effort.[35] After he had sounded out leading Conservatives and representatives of the brewers, he obtained a preliminary estimate of the cost of acquiring the trade from a leading accountant of the day, Sir William Plender.[36] The Cabinet then established advisory committees for England and Wales and for Scotland, to examine the financial arrangements needed for either state purchase or regulation with compensation. The English committee, which was led by Herbert Samuel and included Philip Snowden among its members, reckoned that the cost of purchase would be about £250 million, and concluded that the best method of acquiring the assets would be to exchange them for 4 per cent government stock. In the first instance quoted securities would be bought on the basis of their average price over the three years to 30 June 1914.[37] The scheme came to nothing, of course. Lloyd George claimed that the cost was found to be too high, although he also blamed the opposition – which contained such strange bedfellows as staunch prohibitionists and Conservative brewing interests – for its abandonment.[38] However, many of his Liberal colleagues were hostile, and an additional consideration was undoubtedly the time and trouble it would have taken to survey and value the assets of such a large and dispersed industry,

34 Turner, 'State Purchase', 589–615, who provides the most authoritative account, notes, re the events of 1915, that 'The exact significance of drink in this hectic activity is difficult even yet to discern' (596).

35 Lloyd George organised a meeting with trade unionists, the shipbuilders' delegation (see note 2 above), and obtained pledges of wartime abstinence from King George V and Lord Kitchener. Lloyd George, *War Memoirs*, I, pp. 328–30, Shadwell, *Drink*, pp. 13–15, and Carter, *Drink Trade*, pp. 41–2, 48–51.

36 Plender provided a preliminary estimate of £320 million, which was subsequently amended to £225 million. Lloyd George, *War Memoirs*, I, p. 330; Turner, 'State Purchase', 599.

37 *Report of the Advisory Committee on Proposals for the State Purchase of the Licensed Liquor Trade (England & Wales)*, April 1915, *PP* (1916) XII, Cd.8283. The Scottish Committee, led by T. McKinnon Wood, was unable to provide a cost estimate owing to the special circumstances affecting that country, viz. (1) the absence of compensation for withdrawn licences cf. England & Wales (1904 Act); (2) the absence of tied houses; and (3) the provision of a local option to establish 'dry' areas (Act of 1913) from 1920. See *Report ... Licensed Liquor Trade (Scotland)*, April 1915, *PP* (1916) XII, Cd.8319. The Reports were not published until July 1916.

38 Lloyd George, *War Memoirs*, I, pp. 331–4.

with some 3,700 brewers (including publican-brewers) and 111,000 on-licensed properties.[39] It may well have been that the threat of state purchase was a convenient stick with which to beat the brewers into accepting tighter controls and the country into accepting more draconian wartime measures. Events moved swiftly, but it is certainly true that the work of the advisory committees took place at a time when the government, in the space of a few weeks, swung between the idea of state purchase and the introduction of swingeing increases in liquor taxes (including punitive rates for higher gravity beers), and the setting up of a control mechanism via amendments to the Defence of the Realm Regulations and a Control Board.[40] And yet those brewers whom Lloyd George consulted, such as Sir George Younger and Waters Butler, apparently found the prospect of a total buy-out at pre-war valuations more attractive than that of continuing to trade independently but menaced by irksome controls.[41]

More prominence was given to state purchase in 1917, when the need for drastic curbs on brewing was accepted by a wider group of policy-makers. The Control Board's declared enthusiasm for nationalisation, expressed in December 1916 and January 1917, was considered by the War Cabinet, and although no immediate action was taken, a Home Office committee was appointed in the following month to examine the implications of restricting alcohol output. This offered two schemes: purchase; and full control without purchase.[42] In June three committees, for England and Wales, Scotland and Ireland, were appointed to consider the financial aspects. The subsequent reports, published in 1918, revealed no unsurmountable obstacles to nationalisation, but showed that the cost had escalated. For England and Wales the price had risen to at least £350 million at pre-war valuations, excluding spirits, while the total cost was thought to be in the region of £400–500

[39] In the year ending 31 March 1914 there were 3,746 UK licences for sale issued (about 2,500 to publican-brewers (see Table 8.5) below)), and on 1 January 1914 there were 87,660 on-licences in England and Wales. In Scotland there were 6,708 pubs and inns, and in Ireland 16,679 pubs and beer houses. *Report of Commissioners of Customs and Excise, England and Wales, for year ending 31 March 1919, PP* (1919) XIII, Cmd.503, p. 47; *State Purchase and Control of Liquor Trade. Reports of the English, Scotch and Irish Committees*, 1918, *PP* (1918) XI, Cd.9042, pp. 40, 57, 70.

[40] Turner, 'State Purchase', 601–6, and cf. Lord Beaverbrook, *Politicians and the War 1914–1916*, I (1928), p. 67. The liquor tax measures, included in the 1915 budget proposals, were amended in the Commons, with the proposal to tax higher gravity beers being defeated by the Irish.

[41] Turner, 'State Purchase', 602–4. It should be noted that the larger enterprises had more to gain from a state buy-out than the smaller, country brewers, a point conceded by Butler.

[42] Turner, 'State Purchase', 607–9. The Committee, chaired by the Home Secretary, Sir George Cave, included brewing representatives such as Sir George Younger, Col. John Gretton and Frank Whitbread.

million.[43] By this time, of course, the government had turned to control through gravity restrictions.

Lloyd George, now Prime Minister, maintained that the brewing lobby's opposition was a key factor in the abandonment of state purchase for a second time. 'It is a powerful trade', he told the Commons in February 1917, 'and no one knows better than my old colleagues and myself what it can accomplish when its interests are menaced.'[44] In his *War Memoirs* he recalled that 'alcohol is a refractory citizen, and as he has a multitude of friends everywhere he soon made trouble'.[45] In fact, unpalatable as it may have been, many brewers were quite prepared to accept state purchase, provided that parliamentary consent were obtained and the terms were 'just and equitable'. It was the brewers' insistence that the state either compensated the industry for wartime control on the basis of pre-war profits or bought the assets at pre-war valuations that pushed the coalition government into a corner. Prominent in the manœuvring, which was not without its ambiguities, were Butler and Younger, now Conservative Party chairman. They persuaded Lord Milner, who had been charged with the task of drawing up a draft bill, to make generous concessions. His proposals provided for immediate control with compensation on the basis of pre-war profits, and subsequent post-war purchase. Gretton also played a decisive part, since his proposal for an increase in beer output with a gravity reduction (see p.321) supplied Lloyd George with a convenient and much cheaper alternative course of action.[46]

Government control had taken the sting out of the drink question. By 1920 the appetite for extending the Carlisle scheme to the country as a whole had diminished, political support was at best lukewarm, and the cost, according to Snowden, had risen to £1,000 million.[47] Lord D'Abernon, who resigned as Control Board chairman in the same year, made a final attempt to press the case for nationalisation in March 1921 when he gave advice to a Cabinet committee appointed to examine post-war

[43] *Reports of the English, Scotch and Irish Committees*, 1918, cit. Compensation was based on so many years' purchase of the net profits in specified pre-war years. The formula varied from committee to committee, that for England and Wales (chaired by Lord Sumner) favouring fifteen years' purchase of average net profits in the four years 1910/11–1913/14. The principle of adequate compensation had been strengthened in July 1917 when the Cannon Brewery successfully pursued an action in the High Court against the Central Control Board over compensation for the compulsory acquisition of the 'Ordnance Arms' at Enfield Lock: *The Times*, 1 August 1917.

[44] *Parl. Deb. (Commons)*, Vol. 90 (Session 1917), 23 February 1917, c.1611.

[45] Lloyd George, *War Memoirs*, III, p. 1,334.

[46] Turner, 'State Purchase', 609–12.

[47] Snowden, *The Times*, 26 June 1920, cited in Aldcroft, 'Control of liquor trade', 249.

liquor control. State purchase, he argued, was fully justified by brewing's 'ill-regulated competition', the Gresham's Law of public houses, in which the good was driven out by the bad, and the lack of capital for reorganisation. Above all, the industry was inefficient: 'Like a tortoise – it is well equipped to resist outside attack but its internal arrangements are deplorable.'[48] However, the Committee, whose chairman was H. A. L. Fisher of the Board of Education, rightly saw that nationalisation would not command sufficient support in the Commons now that it had more of a right-wing composition since the 1918 Election, although it did recommend that Carlisle should remain in the public sector, at least for the present.[49] The subsequent Licensing Act of 1921 set the broad conditions under which brewing would operate for the next fifty years. Purchase by the state was firmly rejected, and the Control Board was abolished. But the state-owned assets were merely transferred to the Home and Scottish Offices, and licensing hours, though relaxed a little, retained much of their wartime limits. Weekday hours were set at eight to nine hours, with afternoon closing compulsory, and five-hour opening on Sundays remained unchanged.[50]

II

How did the war affect brewing enterprise? In addition to the difficulties arising from state controls, loss of manpower as brewery workers first volunteered and then were conscripted likewise threatened production (Plate 42). Many companies found that their patriotism was more than echoed by their workforce. At Tetley of Leeds, for example, 261 or 43 per cent of a total staff of 613 were lost to war service, while at Whitbread in London, a return of March 1916 showed that of an eligible male staff of 1,066, 456 (43 per cent) had enlisted, 305 (29 per cent) had been attested and 132 had been rejected. A post-war board minute noted that altogether 1,071 staff and employees had joined the forces.[51] Similar figures were reported by Bass and Watney Combe Reid. Even in strife-torn Dublin, Guinness lost 600 men, a sixth of its brewery workers. Country brewers suffered comparable losses to their smaller

48 Lord D'Abernon, memo on 'Drink Traffic', 24 March 1921, in Cabinet Committee on Liquor Control, 1921, CAB27/150, PRO.

49 *Ibid.* meetings, 5, 18, 20 and 21 April 1921. One of the members of the Committee, the Attorney-General, Sir Gordon Hewart, subsequently led a parliamentary conference which drew up draft legislation. Aldcroft, 'Control of liquor trade', 253.

50 Licensing Act, 1921, 11 & 12 Geo V c.42.

51 Lackey, *Quality Pays*, p. 74; Whitbread & Co., Statement on 'Male Staff', 3 March 1916, Board Minutes, 27 March 1916, 2 December 1918, W/23/3, W&Co.

workforces.[52] Production problems, caused by these difficulties and by raw material controls, proved to be a severe challenge for brewers used to more stable conditions on the supply side; many of them, facing an uncertain future full of temperance gloom and doom, simply went out of business or sold out. The number of licences issued to UK brewers ('brewers for sale') fell from 3,746 in 1913–14 to 2,914 in 1919–20, a reduction of 22 per cent.[53] Physical output fell sharply, causing particular anxiety in those companies supplying a large tied estate. Thus, Bass, Ratcliff & Gretton of Burton saw its bulk barrelage cut from 1,103,561 in 1915–16 to only 518,637 in 1917–18, a reduction of 47 per cent, and its average gravity fell from 1061.9° to 1054.5° and then to only 1043.9° in 1918–19.[54] In London, output at Whitbread's Chiswell Street brewery fell by 54 per cent from 1913–14 to 1917–18, from 900,636 barrels to 413,112. In Dublin, sales of Guinness were halved from 3.0 to 1.5 million bulk barrels, while the gravity of its Extra Stout fell from 1074° in 1916 to 1049° (1054° from 1919).[55] Moreover, firms in a less central position than those in Burton, London and Dublin were certainly not unaffected. Country brewers may have avoided some of the severe disruptions characteristic of the industrial North and Midlands, but they shared the experience of considerable falls in output. In Bury St Edmunds, for example, Greene King's output fell by 23 per cent from 1914–15 to 1918–19, from 75,142 to 58,568 bulk barrels, while in Norwich, Steward & Patteson brewed only 67,351 bulk barrels in 1917–18, 45 per cent fewer than the 122,852 in 1913–14, and the average gravity was only 1033.1° compared with 1057.5° in the immediate pre-war years.[56] The directors of some companies expressed their fears in their minute books. The hapless firm of Samuel Allsopp & Sons, unable to pay an ordinary dividend from 1901 to 1918, found it extremely hard to keep within the government-imposed production

52 Watney Combe Reid reported a figure of 1,051, Bass 1,250 (36 per cent of its 3,519 strong workforce) and Mitchells & Butlers 1,192. Serocold, *The Story of Watneys*, p. 65; Owen, *History of Bass*, forthcoming; Mitchells & Butlers, Annual Report for Year Ended 30 June 1919, cit. in *Brewing Trade Review*, September 1919, p. 258; Dennison and MacDonagh, *History of Guinness*, Ch.XI. Of the country brewers, Thomas Wethered of Marlow had seventy employees serving by December 1916, Annual General Meeting, 15 December 1916, W/357/36, W&Co.

53 *Report of Commissioners of Customs and Excise for year ended 31 March 1920*, *PP* (1920) XIII, Cmd.1082, p. 52. 'Brewers for sale' were licensed to produce and sell beer.

54 Bass, Ratcliff & Gretton, Comparative Brewing Statements, 1901–19, Ref.150, Bass plc.

55 Whitbread & Co., Production Statistics, W/44/1–2, W&Co.; Dennison and MacDonagh, 'History of Guinness', Ch.XI. Whitbread's average gravity fell from 1052° in 1916–17 to 1044.7° in 1917–18 and 1030.0° in 1918–19.

56 Wilson, *Greene King*, p. 272; Gourvish, *Norfolk Beers*, pp. 98, 179.

limits, and in 1917 was preaching the virtues of a collective response to the industry's problems.[57]

However, it is difficult to find evidence of low profitability to match the brewers' gloomy prognostications, other than in firms which were already experiencing difficulties as a result of the pre-war rush to buy licensed properties. For the majority of brewing companies, whether large or small, urban or rural, the War first made only a marginal difference to profit levels, then offered a welcome bonanza. The enforced move to weaker beer lowered unit costs; demand, sustained by full employment and the absence of peacetime leisure pursuits, did not fall despite the sharp rise in beer prices. Nor did the government's tax demands, which included an Excess Profits Duty initially set at 50 per cent on profits earned above the pre-war level, make much of a dent in the improvement in earnings.[58] Consequently, a general advance in profits was observable, particularly from 1917. A rough indication of the position may be obtained from an analysis of the ordinary dividends (taking account of cash bonuses and capitalised reserves) declared by twenty-four 'representative' companies. Annual averages weighted by the size of ordinary share capital reveal an increase from 9.5 per cent in 1910–13 to 9.8 per cent in 1914–16 and 17.3 per cent in 1917–20.[59] The return on share capital and debentures, a proxy measure of the return on net assets, confirms this picture.[60]

Of course, individual company fortunes varied considerably, and the

[57] Samuel Allsopp & Sons Board Minutes, 12 October and 8 November 1916, 31 January, 1 March, 19 April and 3 May 1917, Minute Book 10, Allied Breweries Ltd.

[58] The rate of Excess Profits Duty was subsequently set at 60 per cent in 1916, 80 per cent in 1917, 40 per cent in 1919, and 60 per cent in 1920 (when a Corporation Profits Tax of 5 per cent also applied). However, treatment of companies was fairly generous. The pre-war standard (against which the excess was calculated) was taken to be 6 per cent for companies earning less than this, and other concessions applied to the calculation, including the pooling of accounting periods. See BS Circular on 'Finance (No. 2) Act 1915', 5 January 1916, BS.

[59] This is a weighted average, which reflects the experience of Bass, Guinness, Mitchells & Butlers and Whitbread (who account for 60 per cent of the total nominal ordinary share capital of the twenty-four companies in 1917–20). An unweighted average yields percentages of 7.2, 7.7 and 13.3 for the same periods. See Appendix, Table IX for details.

[60] The average percentage rate of return (excluding capitalised bonuses) was:

1910–13: 5.5
1914–16: 5.7
1917–20: 7.6

The correlation with ordinary dividends (excluding capitalised bonuses, 7.2, 7.7, 11.4) is 1.00.

Table 8.2. *Company profitability (ordinary dividends), 1910–20 (annual averages)*

Company		Ordinary dividends		
		1910–13	1914–16	1917–20
Archibald Arrol & Sons	Alloa	0.0	0.0	0.0
Meux's Brewery Co.	London	0.0	0.0	0.6
Whitbread & Co.	London	1.0	1.5	7.8
Colchester Brewing Co.	Colchester	1.3	4.0	7.4
Newcastle Breweries	Newcastle	5.4	9.3	15.0[22.5][a]
Boddingtons' Breweries	Manchester	5.8	7.0	13.3
Style & Winch	Maidstone	6.5	11.0	12.8[14.6][a]
Mitchells & Butlers	Birmingham	15.0	15.0	13.1[26.9][a]
Arthur Guinness Son & Co.	Dublin	16.3	14.7	22.0
Steward & Patteson	Norwich	18.5	13.3	9.8[15.3][a]
Weighted average (24 companies)		9.5	9.8	14.9[17.3][a]

[a] takes account of capitalisation of reserves as bonus shares.
Source: See Appendix, Table IX.

dispersion around 'average' profits was large.[61] The selection of results in Table 8.2 bears this out. In terms of ordinary dividend payments companies such as Arrol of Alloa failed to make headway, while Meux of London was able to make only one distribution to shareholders, in 1919, and that on a much reduced capital. But for the majority of companies which had suffered difficulties before 1914, nil or very low dividends were transformed into respectable returns in the later years of the war. In Table 8.2 the experience of Whitbread and the Colchester Brewing Co. illustrates this, and the experience was shared by a number of others, including Tadcaster Tower, the Springwell Brewery of Heckmondwike, Huggins & Co. and John Lovibond of London, and the St Anne's Well Brewery in Exeter.[62] At the other end of the scale, soundly

[61] For example, the standard deviation around the unweighted mean of ordinary dividends in 1917–20 (13.3 per cent) was 8.1.

[62] Company results:

Tadcaster Tower	0.0% 1906–9	3.6% 1910–14	10.2% 1915–19
Springwell Brwy	0.0% 1908–17	9.0% 1918–19	
Huggins & Co.	0.0% 1908–12	2.2% 1913–16	15.0% 1917–19
Lovibond & Sons	0.0% 1912–16	7.5% 1917–19	
St Anne's Well	0.0% 1910–11	4.6% 1912–16	10.0% 1917–19

The Manual of British and Foreign Brewery Companies for 1920 (1920), *passim.*

based firms were able not only to maintain double-figure dividends but also to build up reserves strong enough to permit a portion of these to be distributed in cash or in bonus shares. Thus, in 1918 Guinness gave £20 in 5 per cent War Loan Stock for each £100 Stock, and Steward & Patteson of Norwich trebled its ordinary share capital by offering two new shares for each one held. The Birmingham firm of Mitchells & Butlers belied its chairman's enthusiasm for nationalisation by paying a steady 15 per cent from 1910 to 1916, after which it made no less than three bonus share issues: one for two in 1917 and 1918, and one for one in 1920. Those with the confidence to match their cash reserves seized opportunities to grow by acquisition. In Bristol, for example, Georges bought forty public houses from John Arnold & Sons of Wickwar in 1917 and about a hundred from Welton Breweries in the following year.[63] Other sizeable expansions included the takeover of the Midland and Holder's breweries by Mitchells & Butlers in 1918–19.[64] Cameron, Newcastle, Style & Winch and Tamplin also made purchases at the end of the war.[65] Country brewers, encouraged no doubt by all the wartime talk of industrial rationalisation, participated in the process too. In 1919–21 Strong of Romsey bought three breweries in Andover, Totton and Bere Regis, the prelude to further acquisitions in the inter-war years, while Greene King also bought three breweries, together with their 128 pubs, in Bury, Sudbury and Haverhill, thereby increasing their tied estate by a not inconsiderable 28 per cent.[66] Even those companies which were still finding it difficult to pay ordinary dividends saw a healthy upturn in trading profits. For example, Barclay Perkins increased its profits from £139,000 in 1914–15 to £246,000 in 1917–18 and £396,000 in 1919–20 – an increase in real terms of about 40 per cent from 1914/15–1919/20 – and were able to improve the distribution to holders of 10 per cent cumulative preference shares from an average of only 2.875 per cent in 1910–13 to 4.17 per cent in 1914–16 and a high 16.25 per cent in 1917–20.[67]

Thus, when the historian of the Leeds firm of Joshua Tetley & Son observed that it had 'bucked the trend' by doubling its profits from

[63] *Ibid.*, p. 98.

[64] Mitchells & Butlers Annual Report for Year Ended 30 June 1919 and 1920, cit. in *Brewers' Journal*, September 1919, p. 356, August 1920, p. 359.

[65] *Manual of British Brewery Companies* (1920), pp. 105, 194, 235, 237.

[66] H. A. Monckton, *Whitbread's Breweries* (1984), pp. 44–5; Wilson, *Greene King*, pp. 166, 168, 270, 278.

[67] *Stock Exchanges, London & Provincial. Ten Year Record* Nos. 10 (1916), 16 (1924); Barclay Perkins Annual Reports for Year Ended 31 March 1915, 1918, 1920, cit. in *Brewers' Journal*, August 1915, p. 445, September 1918, p. 299, July 1920, p. 307.

£60,000 in 1913 to £124,000 six years later, he was wrong on two counts. First, since retail prices also doubled over the same period, there was no improvement in constant values. Second, Tetley's performance was disappointing in comparison with many brewers, whose profits outpaced the rate of inflation. In fact, a national estimate of brewing company profits showed a considerable increase from £9.97 million in 1913–14 to £32.4 million in 1919–20, a rise of 54 per cent in real terms.[68] With all their pessimism and political manœuvrings, the brewers emerged from the war in better shape than when they had entered it. The Central Control Board and the Carlisle scheme had drawn the teeth of the temperance movement without damaging beer consumption too much, while the overall impact of government controls was to protect and even enhance profits. The real challenge was to come in the more difficult demand conditions of the next twenty years, when the shift to lower consumption levels was sustained.

III

In the inter-war years brewers faced a more challenging market environment than they had experienced for a century. First, alternative leisure activities, released from wartime restraints, emerged to compete with drinking, and consumers increasingly looked beyond the confines of the traditional public house. Sports, both spectator and participatory, the cinema, the radio, coffee bars and ice cream parlours: all offered competition, while the government's retention of high beer duties made beer relatively expensive as retail prices fell after 1920. An impressive rate of housebuilding, which involved the creation of 4.5 million new units between 1919 and 1939, left a gap between areas already well stocked with pubs and the new areas of suburban settlement. More important still, people appeared to be drinking less and less often. The statistics of convictions for drunkenness, though an inadequate measure of the extent of the social problem itself, suggested that the British had become more sober. The fall in the number of convictions during the war, from 183,800 or 49.7 per 10,000 in 1914 to 29,100 (7.9 per 10,000) in 1918 was halted briefly, and there was an increase to 95,800 (26.5) in 1920. But convictions then fell steadily to a low point of 30,100 (7.5) in

68 Profits of £29 million in 1920–1 represented a more modest increase of 19 per cent in real terms over 1913–14. Lackey, *Quality Pays*, p. 72; Feinstein, *National Income*, T140; *Brewers' Almanack 1919*, p. 103, *1940*, p. 132; Aldcroft, 'Control of liquor trade', 245.

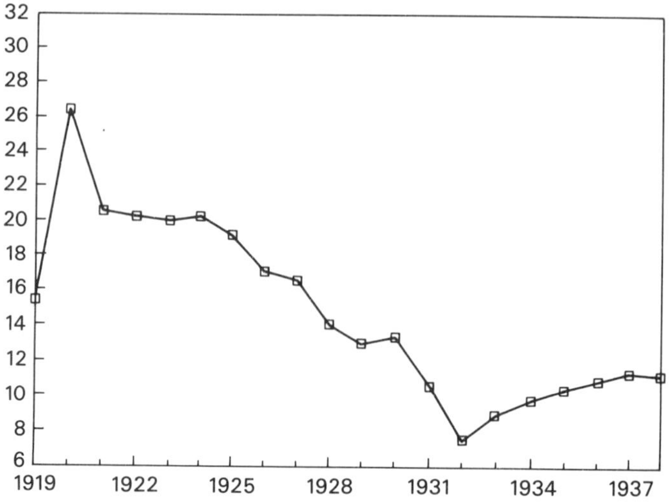

Fig. 8.1 Convictions for drunkenness in England and Wales per 10,000 population, 1919–38 (*Source: Brewers' Almanack 1940*, p. 112; see Appendix, Table VII.)

1932, and although rising thereafter, the 1938 figure of 46,600 (11.3 per 10,000) was much lower than those of pre-war years (see England and Wales data in Fig. 8.1).[69] Of course, there was more to such statistics than a change in social behaviour. The toll taken by the First World War on the lives of young men was heavy, robbing the brewing industry of about 0.7 million potential customers, most of them under the age of 35.[70] But even if they had lived, many of them would have had little excess income at their disposal in the economic environment which followed the short post-war boom in 1919–20. That important segment of the market, the demand for beer and spirits from males working in heavy industry, was hit severely by the depressed state of Britain's staple industries in the 1920s and 1930s, affecting brewers in Lancashire and Yorkshire, the North-East, South Wales, and the central lowland belt of Scotland, in particular. In these areas the emergence of a growing club trade, offering cheaper beer and entertainment to customers with tighter budgets, presented the tied public houses with considerable competition in the large, working-class market. By 1939 there were over

[69] *Brewers' Almanack 1940*, p. 112.
[70] J. M. Winter, *The Great War and the British People* (1985), p. 81. Of the casualties, 86 per cent were under the age of 35.

18,000 clubs in the UK, nearly double the number in 1914; they made up about 20 per cent of the total number of on-licensed premises.[71]

In the circumstances, it is scarcely surprising that both the production and consumption of beer should exhibit a tendency to fall, although the pattern was more complex than a simple decline, and indeed it followed that indicated by convictions for drunkenness.[72] Beer output in the UK (excluding southern Ireland) fell from about 31.5 million bulk barrels in 1919 to just under 24 million barrels in 1922, a reduction of about a quarter. Production then firmed up a little, settling at 25–6 million barrels for the rest of the decade. Then the demand restraints and higher taxation associated with the economic crisis of 1931 caused production to fall by some 30 per cent to under 18 million barrels in 1932. This was followed by a steady recovery, which saw production rise to 24.7 million barrels in 1938. Nevertheless, average output in the 1930s was lower than in the 1920s: for example, bulk barrelage in the six years 1933–8 was 13 per cent down on the corresponding period in the 1920s (see Fig. 8.2 and data in Appendix, Table VIII). Production expressed in standard barrels of 1055° followed the same trends very closely, as Fig. 8.2 indicates, although since post-war brewing gravities remained well below the 'standard' the measure was much lower in absolute terms than the bulk data, of course.[73] Fluctuations in average gravity also intensified the contrast between the 1920s and the 1930s. Gravities edged upwards in the 1920s, peaking at 1043.17° in 1928. A fall to 1039.52° in 1932, stimulated by an increase in the beer duty, was halted, but the subsequent recovery was weak. Consequently, the fall in standard barrelage was more marked than that for bulk barrelage – 17 per cent lower in 1933–8 than in 1923–8 (Appendix, Table VIII).

Data on domestic *consumption* are difficult to derive with complete confidence, owing to problems in extracting information on domestic production, exports and retained imports on the same basis. The picture is further complicated by the fact that Guinness's beer, sent to Britain from the Dublin brewery, was counted as domestic production until

[71] BS, *UK Statistical Handbook 1980*, p. 64.

[72] Production in bulk barrels fell by 1.65 per cent p.a., 1919–38 (log linear equation: LogY = 35.1 −0.0165X, adj. r_2 = 0.46), and in standard barrels by 1.82 per cent p.a. (LogY = 38.1 −0.0182X, adj. r_2 = 0.48). Rank order correlation coefficients of convictions for drunkenness in England and Wales per 10,000 population and UK bulk and standard barrel production were 0.76 and 0.86 respectively.

[73] The correlation coefficient of bulk output and standard output for 1919/20–1938/9 was 0.968.

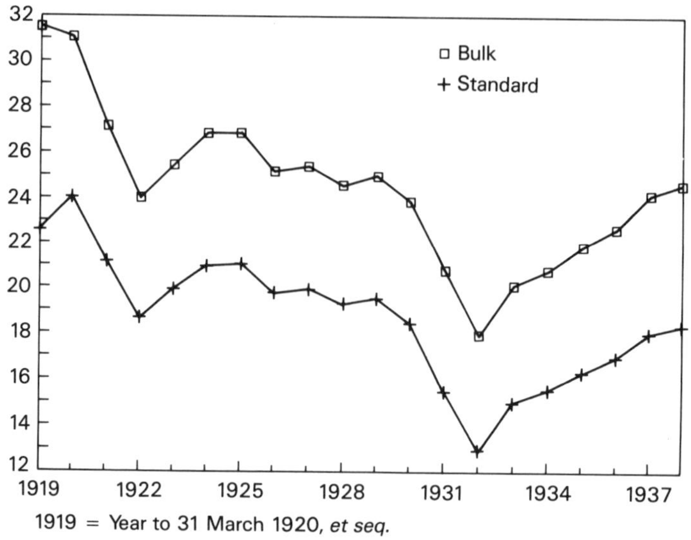

Fig. 8.2 UK beer production (beer charged with duty, excluding Eire) in millions of bulk and standard barrels, 1919–38. (*Source: Customs and Excise Reports*; *Brewers' Almanack*; see Appendix, Table VIII.)

1922 and as imports thereafter. This 'trade' amounted to over a million barrels per annum until Guinness's London brewery at Park Royal began brewing in earnest in 1937.[74] Our estimates are based on production in Great Britain and Northern Ireland plus retained imports less exports, in standard barrels. The necessary adjustments to the production series on this basis are not great, however. Retained imports averaged only 1,310,386 barrels per annum over the period, most of them coming from the Irish Republic. Indeed, total imports (including re-exports) other than those from Eire were negligible after 1922: only 31,000 standard barrels a year in 1923–38, compared with a total of 1,358,000. They were largely confined to such specialities as bottled lagers from Carlsberg and Beck intended for the restaurant and club trade in the West End of London and similar outlets in the major provincial cities. Furthermore, export volumes more than halved in the

[74] Imports from Eire (including re-exports) amounted to 1,327,290 standard barrels p.a., 1923–38; Board of Trade, *Annual Statements of Trade*. Sales of Guinness in the UK (excluding N. Ireland) amounted to 1.21 million bulk barrels p.a., 1923–38: Guinness Statistics Department, 'Sales of Guinness in Great Britain – Calendar Years, 1921–66', Guinness Archives, Park Royal (GPR).

inter-war period, falling from an average of 623,000 barrels per annum in 1909–13 to only 290,000 barrels in 1924–8 and 270,000 in 1934–8.[75] Established exporters such as Bass, Guinness and Whitbread continued to sell their bottled stout and pale ales abroad, if at lower volumes, and there were a half-dozen producers of lager for both the home and export markets, notably J. & R. Tennent of Glasgow, Barclay Perkins of London (from 1922), Red Tower, Wrexham, John Jeffrey of Edinburgh, and Archibald Arrol of Alloa, brewers from 1927 of the successful Graham's Golden Lager brand. Indeed, such was the strength of this small but vociferous group that complaints of dumping by continental producers in the 1930s persuaded the government to introduce a special surtax of £1 a bulk barrel on non-Empire beer with effect from April 1936.[76] However, British beer consumption essentially reflected the satisfaction of local tastes for traditional, if increasingly lighter, beers. It is therefore no surprise to find that our estimates follow the pattern exhibited by domestic production very closely indeed, nor that they match alternative estimates, such as those of Stone and Rowe.[77] The assessment of consumption trends becomes more revealing if we produce data for the *standard* barrelage on a *per capita* basis. Here, the contrast between the pre-war and inter-war periods is much sharper. Fig. 8.3 illustrates this. Although the importance of short-term changes – falls in 1920–2 and 1929–32, recoveries in 1922–4 and 1932–7 – should not be ignored, the overall trend was clearly downward.[78] And a per capita consumption which averaged 13.1 gallons in 1931–8 was a far cry from pre-war levels of, for example, 32.2 gallons in 1899 and 27.5 gallons in 1913.[79]

Some of the factors responsible for this decline have already been explored in outline; others require more attention. Though social changes – the boom in tea shops, for example – were clearly relevant, so also were relative prices. While the general level of prices fell, retail

[75] Data on imports (including re-exports) and exports here are for calendar years and are taken from the *Annual Statements of Trade*. There are no data on *retained* imports identifying country of origin.

[76] Wilson and Gourvish, 'Foreign Dimensions', p. 128.

[77] Correlation coefficients of our estimates and those in Stone (adding an observation for 1919 from Prest) and the *Brewers' Almanack* are 0.965 and 0.975 respectively. See Richard Stone, *The Measurement of Consumers' Expenditure and Behaviour in the United Kingdom 1920–1938* (Cambridge, 1954), I, p. 188; Prest, *Consumers' Expenditure*, p. 76; *Brewers' Almanack 1940*, p. 99.

[78] A log linear regression indicates a fall of 2.15 per cent p.a. Equation: $\text{LogY} = 44.2 - 0.0215\text{X}$, adj. $r_2 = 0.58$. Consumption per head of those aged 15 and over fell by 2.62 per cent p.a.: $\text{LogY} = 53.6 - 0.0262\text{X}$, adj. $r_2 = 0.67$.

[79] *Brewers' Almanack 1940*, p. 99.

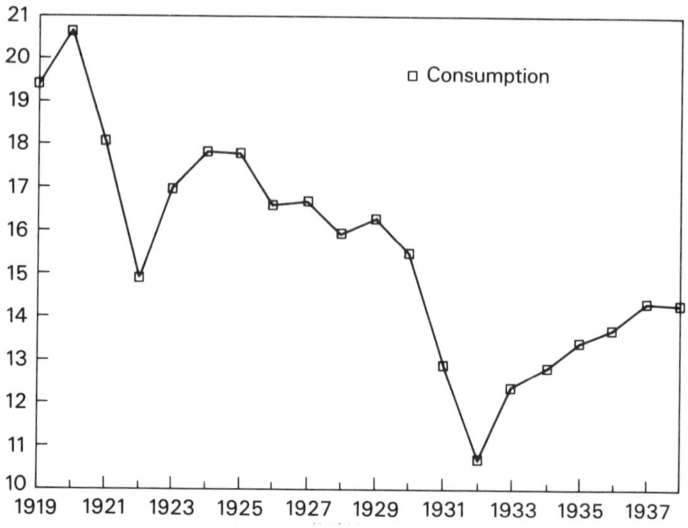

Fig. 8.3 UK beer consumption in standard gallons per capita (excluding Eire), 1919–38. (*Source:* see Appendix, Table VIII.)

prices of beer and spirits were virtually stationary.[80] For draught beer that price was apparently 6d (2.5p) a pint, the only exceptions being a higher price when the beer duty was high, i.e. before the introduction of a £1 rebate per bulk barrel in April 1923, and following the increase of the £5 duty per standard barrel by the Labour government in response to the economic crisis – to £5.15 in April 1930, and £6.70 in September 1931 (in force until April 1933). Given the sharp fall in retail prices, 44 per cent from 1920 to 1933 and still 37 per cent lower in 1938 than in 1920, it is quite clear that beer became more and more expensive relative to a wide range of goods until retail prices began to recover after 1933. The price of beer may have been some 40 per cent higher in real terms in 1931–3 than in 1920–3 and was still 25 per cent higher in 1934–8 (Table 8.3), at a time when leisure substitutes were more readily available.[81] Price was not the only determinant of consumer choice of course. The inter-war years also saw a rise in the popularity of bottled beer, which was more expensive than draught. Its share of the home market increased from about 10 per cent in 1920 to about 20 per cent in

[80] Prest, *Consumers' Expenditure*, p. 8, referring to an increase in tobacco consumption, temperance propaganda and the introduction of tea shops.

[81] Note: Stone's estimates of average beer prices may underestimate the price increases introduced by brewers in response to the rise in duties of 1930–1.

Table 8.3. *The retail price of draught beer, 1920–38*

Period	Unit price (per pint)	Index 1920–3 = 100	Retail price index 1920–3 = 100	Beer price index in constant 1920–3 prices
1920–3	6.75d	100.0	100.0	100.0
1924–30	6.00d	88.9	81.0	109.8
1931–3	6.53d	96.7	69.1	139.9
1934–8	6.00d	88.9	71.3	124.7

Source: Calculated from Richard Stone, *The Measurement of Consumers' Expenditure and Behaviour in the United Kingdom 1920–1938* (Cambridge, 1954), I, p. 189, and C. H. Feinstein, *National Income, Expenditure and Output of the United Kingdom, 1855–1965* (Cambridge, 1972), T140.

1939.[82] Nevertheless, there is much force in Richard Stone's conclusion that 'the whole variation in beer consumption can be very largely explained by changes in the relative price of beer'.[83] Consumers' expenditure, after making due allowance for bottled beer, fell from £268 million per annum in 1920–3 to £196 million in 1930–8, a reduction of 37 per cent; in constant 1920–3 prices the fall was more pronounced, amounting to 47 per cent.[84]

The fall in consumption, most visible during the depressed years of 1931–3, shaped the climate in which the brewing industry traded in the inter-war years. The brewers expressed particular concern, and even anger, about the increases in the beer duty in 1930–1. To judge from the editorials in the brewing journals the industry was facing its nadir in 1931 and 1932, and the entire blame could be laid at the feet of the Labour Chancellor, Philip Snowden. No doubt paying off temperance as well as party political scores, the *Brewers' Journal* attacked Snowden for his 'grave blunder' in raising the duty by over a third in 1930–1, arguing that the 1931 crisis had fallen 'with especial severity' upon the industry (cf. Plate 45). The *Brewing Trade Review* in its leader of January 1933 claimed that the result had been reduced profits for most companies.[85]

82 Stone, *Measurement of Consumers' Expenditure*, pp. 176, 178, 182, 189, 270. Alternative estimates of the bottled beer market, projected backwards from the post-1945 period, suggested that market-share was about 25 per cent in 1939. Cf. Wilson and Gourvish, 'Foreign Dimensions', 129.

83 Stone, *Measurement of Consumers' Expenditure*, p. 178.

84 Calculated from *ibid.*, p. 189 and Feinstein, *National Income*, T140.

85 *Brewers' Journal*, January 1932, pp. 3, 7; January 1934, p. 1; *Brewing Trade Review*, January 1933, p. 2.

In fact, the situation was much more complex than this. As *The Economist* was quick to point out, for much of the twenties the brewing industry enjoyed 'exceptional prosperity during a period of general trade depression and large scale unemployment'. The setbacks of 1930–2 not only were temporary, but were attributable to depression as well as higher taxation, and 'in the majority of cases the ordinary shareholder continued to draw dividends'. Performance over the rest of the thirties was stable and sound.[86] As in the First World War, the well-organised brewing companies, whatever their size, were able to prosper.

The impact on the industry of recession and higher beer duties was real enough. *The Economist* noted that the profits of eight selected companies fell by 11.5 per cent between 1930 and 1932, while the Exchequer estimate of brewing industry profits painted an even gloomier picture, revealing a fall from £26 million in 1930 to £23 million in 1932 and only £16 million in 1933, over a third lower than in 1930.[87] Certainly, declining fortunes were characteristic of our selected companies in Lancashire and the North-East – Boddingtons' of Manchester, Matthew Brown of Blackburn, Newcastle Breweries, and J. W. Cameron of Hartlepool (see Table 8.4). Matthew Brown was particularly hard hit, being unable to pay an ordinary dividend in the period 1932–6 after years of double-figure distributions, while Newcastle's profits, after meeting debenture interest, slumped from £69,700 in 1929–30 to *minus* £13,400 in 1931–2, necessitating a passed dividend in that year. Similar difficulties were experienced by William Hancock of Cardiff, Hammond's Bradford Brewery, and Massey's of Burnley.[88] On the other hand, some companies continued to trade well in the same areas, notably Bent's of Liverpool, and several firms held their net profits position and maintained, or even raised, ordinary dividends through the worst of the depression. This was true of Bass, Guinness and Whitbread among those with claims to a national market, of Bristol Brewery Georges among the strong regional brewers, and of some of the smaller companies, such as Greene King, Russells & Wrangham of Malton, and Archibald Arrol, the latter ending a quarter-century drought of dividends after Allsopp gained control of the company in

[86] *The Economist*, 31 October 1925, pp. 697–8, 20 August 1932, p. 363, 4 November 1933, p. 872, 13 August 1938, p. 327.
[87] *Ibid.*, 13 August 1938, p. 327; *Brewers' Almanack 1940*, p. 132.
[88] Information from *Manual of British Brewery Companies*, 1930–37/8; Hawkins, *Bass Charrington*, p. 92.

1930 (Table 8.4).[89] The accounts of the Bristol concern show a trading profit which increased steadily from £222,000 in 1927–8 to £381,000 in 1936–7, a rise of over 70 per cent.[90] Thus the effects of the depression, readily detectable in lower output and sales figures for many companies, were not necessarily translated into lower profits, whether gross or net, and were rarely expressed in markedly lower dividends, especially when these were averaged out over quinquennia. The annual average ordinary dividend declared by twenty-five 'representative' companies[91] fell very slightly from 1924–8 to 1929–33, but the overall trend was clearly upward. The unweighted average (making allowance for capitalised bonuses) increased from 11.1 per cent in 1921–3 to 18.1 per cent in 1934–8; the weighted average increased from 16.4 to 25.9 per cent (see Table 8.4).

Obviously, calculations like these must be regarded with a degree of caution. Brewery profits are difficult to assess, with gross profits dependent on accounting conventions which varied from company to company, and where the allocation of margins between products and departments and between the production and retailing sides of the business was often arbitrary.[92] Dividends are at best an imperfect indicator of overall profitability, as they may be influenced by corporate decisions relating to gearing, reserves and depreciation provision, for example. A number of companies, reluctant to reveal their true profit position, used depreciation and other devices to reduce sums prior to publishing a profit figure. For example, when H. & G. Simonds of Reading was negotiating to buy the Newport business of Phillips & Sons (a limited company since 1892) in 1949, the latter's auditors admitted that for some considerable time 'the addition to P & L Balance per the printed Report was purposely kept down to a small figure, and was arrived at after very substantial sums had been "tucked away" ... the avowed policy of the Phillips & Sons Board being to make the published figures as uninformative as possible!' The chief accountant of Simonds responded first by noting that the accounts 'certainly were uninformative in no small degree, perhaps even more so than the old Accounts of the great firm of Bass!' He added: 'I purposely refrain from entering into

89 *Brewery Manual*, 1937–8, p. 59. On Bent's of Liverpool see Hawkins, *Bass Charrington*, pp. 93–4.

90 Bristol Brewery Georges Reports and Accounts, 1888–1955, CA/C/1, Courage Archive, Bristol.

91 From 1934 ordinary dividends for Allsopp were replaced by those for Ind Coope & Allsopp. For full details see Appendix, Table IX.

92 Cf. Vaizey, *Brewing Industry*, p. 73n, 131ff. Vaizey attempted profit calculations for 1920–38 and 1946–53 but did not consider them very robust.

Table 8.4. *Company profitability (ordinary dividends), 1921–38 (annual averages)*

Company		Ordinary dividends			
		1921–3	1924–8	1929–33	1934–8
Arrol	Alloa	0.0	0.0	8.5	8.2
Newcastle	Newcastle	6.7	7.6	5.2	11.9
Whitbread	London	9.0	11.1	14.2	18.0
Bass, Ratcliff & Gretton	Burton upon Trent	11.0	14.8	17.0	23.2
Greene King	Bury St Edmunds	12.8	15.5	16.8	20.8
Russells & Wrangham	Malton	13.0	13.8	15.0	19.6
Boddingtons'	Manchester	14.0	14.6	9.1	8.5
Matthew Brown	Blackburn	14.7	13.6	6.1	3.3
Bristol Brewery Georges	Bristol	17.8	18.8	20.0	18.4[25.6][a]
J. W. Cameron	Hartlepool	22.5	15.0	7.9	8.9[10.4][a]
Guinness	Dublin/London	27.0	29.2[43.8][a]	32.3[48.3][a]	28.6[42.9][a]
25-company average (unweighted)		11.1	14.2[a]	15.1[a]	18.1[a]
25-company average (weighted)		16.4	24.8[a]	24.4[a]	25.9[a]

[a] Takes account of capitalisation of reserves as bonus shares.
Source: See Appendix, Table IX.

any argument concerning the "tucking away" of substantial sums before disclosing the net profit, as we ourselves have likewise adopted this procedure in the past to the extent of really huge amounts which no doubt will surprise you.'[93] Nevertheless, with all the caveats which must apply, a further test, using the rate of return on paid-up capital, broadly confirms a position of sound trading.[94] If some shudders went through the industry in the early 1930s – hardly surprising given a 34 per cent increase in taxation coupled with a 30 per cent fall in consumption, 1930–2 – brewing weathered the storm well and kept its shareholders content.

This remarkable stability in profits, achieved in spite of the depressing state of demand, was clear evidence of the strength of brewers' financial reserves. However, *The Economist* later attacked the industry for its conservatism and lack of enterprise. The consumption trends of the 1920s and 1930s were regarded as insufficiently harsh to jolt the brewers from their self-satisfied torpor. Good profits could be distributed because companies merely plodded along, doing little to transform the industry, whether in terms of organisational structure, technology, products, marketing or the standards of retail outlets. Consequently, the inter-war years are often seen as relatively quiet, sandwiched between two more significant periods of change: the rush to incorporate and to acquire public houses from the 1880s to *c.*1900; and the 'merger mania' of the late 1950s and 1960s, with the accompanying moves into keg bitter and draught lager beers and the adoption of more aggressive, national brand advertising.[95] *The Economist*'s view, while it has its

93 R. C. L. Thomas of Walter Hunter, Bartlett, Thomas & Co., Newport (Auditors) – A. G. Richardson, Chief Accountant of H. & G. Simonds, 8 January 1949 and reply, 13 January 1949, Phillips & Sons correspondence files, BD/C/23, Courage.

94 The results of four companies (unweighted annual average for Arrol, Bass, Newcastle and Whitbread) were:

Period	Rate of return on capital* (%)	Ordinary dividends (%)
1921–3	5.0	6.7
1924–8	5.9	8.2
1929–33	6.3	11.2
1934–8	7.1	15.3

* nominal value of share capital/debentures

Whitbread's net profits as percentage of capital = 1921–3: 6.71 (cf. ord. div. 9.00); 1924–8: 7.88 (cf. 11.13); 1929–33: 10.47 (cf.14.20); and 1934–8: 11.46 (cf. 18.00).

The Exchequer estimates of brewing profits provided the following averages (£m): 1921–3: 23.67; 1924–8: 24.74; 1929–33: 22.90; 1934–8: 25.40. *Brewers' Almanack 1940*, p. 132.

95 Note *The Economist*'s much-quoted observation about the 1950s: 'traditionalist, paternalistic, inbred, secretive ... A picturesque dinosaur. A declining industry', 19 September 1964, p. 1,144, cited for example in Hawkins, *Bass Charrington*, p. 137.

elements of truth, is misleading. The inter-war years saw a variety of responses by companies seeking competitive advantage under stagnant demand conditions. Some sought to strengthen product differentiation by building up brand loyalty through marketing analysis and advertising (e.g. Guinness and Whitbread); others moved to exploit economies of scale in production by picking up assets from companies willing to sell and then rationalising productive capacity (e.g. Meux, Ind Coope).[96] Most companies with any pretensions to being progressive invested in bottling plant and motorised distribution (Plate 21), took action to improve the location, standards and management of their public houses, and dabbled with advertising.

Furthermore, concentration in brewing has been a continuous feature of the twentieth century, with movement towards higher levels of concentration. The number of brewers licensed to sell beer in the UK (excluding Eire) fell from 2,464 in 1921 to 1,502 in 1928 and only 840 in 1939; the number of brewing companies more than halved, from 941 (including Eire) in 1920 to only 428 twenty years later.[97] Brewing shared fully in the heightened merger activity characteristic of British manufacturing in the 1920s and 1930s.[98] Hawkins and Pass's calculation from the *Stock Exchange Year Book* data reveals that in the period 1915–35 283 quoted companies acquired 261 firms, 227 of them in 1919–32.[99] It is therefore no surprise to find that of our 'representative' group of twenty-five companies, no less than nineteen were engaged in taking over smaller firms between the wars, averaging at least three acquisitions each, while five companies were themselves the subject of a takeover, three of them by another company within the group.[100] The subject will be analysed in more depth in the following chapter. At this stage it should be observed that the motivation for company acquisitions changed substantially after 1920. In the immediate post-war years cash-rich companies had bought breweries to expand their retailing base. After 1920 the emphasis was firmly upon the rationalisation of productive capacity in circumstances of reduced demand. Activity was particularly evident in Burton and London, where problems of over-

[96] Both Meux and Ind Coope concentrated brewing production in London, at breweries at Nine Elms and Romford respectively.

[97] *Customs and Excise Reports*; BS, *UK Statistical Handbook 1980*, p. 88.

[98] Leslie Hannah, *The Rise of the Corporate Economy* (1983), p. 178.

[99] Hawkins and Pass, *Brewing Industry*, p. 48.

[100] Takeovers within the group of twenty-five companies were: Colchester, by Ind Coope, 1925; Style & Winch, by Barclay Perkins, 1929; Arrol, by Allsopp, 1930. McEwan became part of Scottish Brewers in 1931, and Allsopp merged with Ind Coope in 1934.

capacity were most pressing in the 1920s. In Burton, Bass had produced nearly 1.3 million barrels in 1913/14 and 1.5 million (at a reduced gravity) in 1920/1. Output then fell by about 28 per cent to an average of 1.06 million per annum, 1922–6, a decline matched by both domestic and export sales. The company responded first by merging with Worthington in 1926 and then proceeded to take over two more Burton brewers, Thomas Salt and James Eadie, in 1927 and 1933 (though in the case of Worthington, much the largest acquisition, little rationalisation took place before the 1950s). Even so, production fell sharply in the Depression (from 1.02 million barrels in 1928/9 to only 0.72 million, 1931/2, a fall of 29 per cent).[101] Allsopp and Ind Coope also responded positively to market conditions with a policy of acquisition. The former gained control of breweries in Birmingham, Derby and Oxford in the late 1920s and in Lichfield and Alloa in 1930 (Plate 46); the latter, already established in both Burton and Romford in London, bought breweries over a wider area stretching from Leeds to Rochester. The two enlarged companies came together in another Burton merger in 1934. The shareholders were promised 'considerable' savings in joint production and selling; the managing director, J. J. Calder, explained the situation more graphically, claiming to have told an Ind Coope director: 'You have had a difficult task building up Ind Coope's who have 1,600 Houses, and I have built up Allsopp's with 1,800 Houses. There is only a wall between our Breweries. Do you not think it would be wise for us to join forces?'[102]

London also saw considerable activity. In 1930 Taylor Walker acquired control of the Cannon Brewery, and three years later Charrington bought Hoare & Co. However, most of the mergers involved the purchase of small or medium-sized concerns by the major companies, notably Whitbread and Watney Combe Reid. Whitbread was particularly active in the 1920s, responding to a pronounced fall in output and sales. From 1920 to 1927 production declined from 675,600 barrels to 466,600, a reduction of 31 per cent, and total sales (including sales of Bass and Guinness) fell from 737,000 barrels to 493,500, a fall of 33 per cent (sales of Whitbread's own beers fell by 32 per cent, from 659,000 to

[101] Bass, Ratcliff & Gretton, Brewing Statements, 1913–42, M/B/39, and Comparative Agency Sales, 1916–38, C15, C22, C30, Bass.

[102] Samuel Allsopp & Sons, Letter to Holders of Preference Stock and Ordinary Shares, 30 April 1934, printed in *The Times*, 25 May 1934, in Ind Coope & Allsopp merger file, C/F/2/55, and Transcription of the Recording made by J. J. Calder at his home, 1 December 1959, Allied Archive, Burton. The number of brewing firms in Burton fell from seventeen in 1911 to nine in 1927, five in 1945 and four in 1950. Owen, *Development of Industry*, p. 103, and *History of Bass*, forthcoming.

445,000 barrels).[103] The company acquired the Notting Hill and Forest Hill breweries in London in 1920 and 1923 respectively. It then made two major purchases in Kent, of Frederick Leney & Co. in 1927 and Jude, Hanbury & Co. in 1929, which brought in over 400 pubs. At the same time, proposals put to Whitbread to buy other breweries, including Cannon (see above), two in Brighton and one in Maidstone, were rejected.[104] Important changes in production and selling strategies followed these acquisitions. The purchase of the Forest Hill Brewery, one of the pioneers in manufacturing filtered and carbonated or 'bright' bottled beer, encouraged Whitbread to develop the product, while through the acquisition of Jude Hanbury it also bought that company's major innovation – the distinctive milk stout, Mackeson, which was then promoted successfully on a national scale. Furthermore, by building up its tied estate it was able to reduce its heavy dependence on the free trade, which by 1938 accounted for only 39 per cent of its sales.[105] The difficulties in the domestic market also led Whitbread to strengthen its presence in Belgium, despite adverse export trends. It had established its first bottling plant there in 1904, and had opened three more by 1914, when sales, predominantly of Extra Stout, were running at 17,000 barrels a year. Retail outlets were subsequently acquired, and sales rose to 22,200 barrels per annum, 1920–5, over 4 per cent of total Whitbread sales (excluding Bass and Guinness).[106] Indeed, the recognition of the need to rationalise production and increase tied estates was particularly strong in London. In the early 1920s Whitbread conducted a survey of its corporate competitors within a 30 mile radius of its

[103] Whitbread & Co. Trade Figures (Draught & Bottled), 1920–32, W/15/75A, Production data, W/44/2 and W/15/24, W&Co.

[104] Whitbread & Co. Board Minutes, 26 February and 14 May 1923, 25 October and 13 December 1926, 14 February, 24 October, and 12 December 1927, 12 March, 30 July, 29 October and 11 December 1928; 'Particulars of a Brewery in Kent which has been offered to Whitbread & Co. Ltd.', 23 June 1927; 'Draft Memorandum (Printed) of Amalgamation of Whitbread & Co. and The Cannon Brewery Co.', 10 April 1928, Minutes, 12 April 1928; Memorandum on 'Proposed Amalgamation of Leney's with Another Concern', 8 March 1929, Minutes, 18 March 1929, W/23/3 and 4, W&Co. See also Berry Ritchie, *An Uncommon Brewer: The Story of Whitbread 1742–1992* (1992), pp. 92–3.

[105] Whitbread & Co. Board Minutes, 14 May 1924, 15 March and 21 June 1926, and 12 March 1928; 'Allocation of Trade', 1938 and 1945, Whitbread & Co. Board Papers, 1945–7, W/23/12, W&Co.; Nevile, *Seventy Rolling Years*, pp. 201–4. Mackeson & Co. had been bought by H. & G. Simonds in 1920 and was sold to Jude, Hanbury in 1929.

[106] Whitbread & Co. Trade Figures, 1920/1–1932, W/15/75A, Beer Sold Statistics, W/15/39, 52–4, and Notes on P.H.G.'s (Grundy) Annual Visit to Belgium, September 1930, 12 September 1930, Nevile Papers, W/40/4, W&Co.

Chiswell Street brewery. Eighty-nine companies were listed; by 1939 only thirty-four of them remained.[107]

There was still room for smaller companies in the market, of course. Falling raw material prices cushioned the blow of sluggish demand, and with wholesale (and retail) prices holding up, margins increased. The price of barley fell from an average of 65.7p a cwt in 1920–8 to 42.8p in 1929–37, a reduction of 34 per cent; that of hops fell from £11.31 a cwt in 1924–8 to £8.55 in 1929–33 (a fall of 24 per cent), prodding the growers into creating a marketing scheme (see p. 362) which from 1934 established a fixed price of £9 a cwt.[108] Several country brewers exploited the growth potential in the more buoyant South and South-East. Strong & Co. of Romsey, H. & G. Simonds, Brickwood & Co. of Portsmouth and Greene King all took advantage of offers for sale to secure their production by acquiring breweries with their tied houses. Strong, under the firm direction of its able chairman, David Faber, pursued a determined rationalisation policy to an extent that was unusual among brewers. Having bought seven breweries stretching from Andover and Petersfield to Southampton and Poole over the period 1920–34, it then concentrated production at a single, modernised brewery in Romsey.[109] The level of concentration in brewing, if at this stage lower than in many manufacturing industries, was thus increasing steadily on a broad front. The leading brewers sought to strengthen their national distribution networks and exploited the growing popularity of bottled beer, with its higher margins, and the improvement and relatively lower cost of transport. Regional brewers responded by seeking to tie additional outlets and to supply these with their own bottled brands. The full extent of the change is difficult to measure precisely. Brewers' Licence returns for 1914 reveal the extent of concentration on a production basis (Table 8.5). Unfortunately, this was the last published return, but given the very much smaller number of brewers in 1939 (840) there is every indication that the category producing under 1,000 barrels a year had all but disappeared. Brewers' Society information on the ten largest companies reveals that their share of output volume increased from about 25 per cent of total output volume in 1914 to 40 per cent by 1939. The average production of brewers for sale rose from about 11,000 barrels (bulk) in 1921 to nearly

[107] 'List of Breweries Within a Radius of 30 Miles of the City', n.d. (*c.*1922), Nevile Papers, W/40/3, W&Co.

[108] *Brewers' Almanack 1940*, pp. 72, 74. Barley prices are for calendar years.

[109] Strong & Co. Annual General Meetings, Chairman's Statements, 1920–30, 324/116, W&Co.

Table 8.5. *UK Wholesale Brewers, Year ending 30 September 1914*

No. of brewers producing	
Under 1,000 barrels	2,536
1,000–9,999	580
10,000–19,999	197
20,000–99,999	280
100,000–499,999	46
500,000 +	8
Total	3,647

Source: Brewers' Almanack 1920, p. 117.
Note: Most of those brewing under 1,000 barrels were publican-brewers.

28,000 in 1938, at a time when output in the industry fell by 18 per cent.[110]

The changes in consumption patterns and drinking habits also stimulated the first efforts to improve advertising and marketing responses. Although relatively modest in the aggregate and predominantly local in character, advertising was taken up by most companies. Active promotion of the three leading brands of bottled beer, Guinness, Bass and Whitbread, was certainly evident. Guinness, who alone of the major brewers had rejected a tied house strategy in the UK, felt more vulnerable to reduced demand in the 1920s, although in fact its loss of sales volume was little worse than that of Bass and Whitbread – 34 per cent, 1920–6, compared with 32 per cent for Bass and 31 per cent for Whitbread.[111] Nevertheless there were justifiable fears about future demand for the company's products, given the sharp decline in the popularity of porter and the fact that its Extra Stout, now much weaker than it had been before the war, was little stronger than the stouts manufactured by competitors. Guinness, like Bass, had relied on strength as well as quality for market penetration, but the duty concession of 1923 (£1 rebate per *bulk* barrel) put producers of stronger beers at a financial disadvantage compared with lower gravity brewers. Thus, in 1927 Guinness decided to embark on a pilot advertising scheme in Scotland. A leading London agency, S. H. Benson, was employed, and Martin

[110] Calculated from production data (excluding Eire), cit. above; *Customs and Excise Reports*; BS, *UK Statistical Handbook 1980*, p. 88; and private information from BS.
[111] Guinness Statistics Department, 'Sales in Great Britain in Bulk Barrels, 1908–46', GPR. For Bass and Whitbread see notes 101 and 103.

Pick, brother of Frank Pick of London Transport, was appointed as advertising manager. The success of this experiment, which began in April 1928 with the slogan 'Guinness Is Good For You', led to a vigorous national campaign, launched with press advertising in England in February 1929. The health properties of Extra Stout were emphasised; thousands of medical practitioners were canvassed for their endorsement of the idea that Guinness was good for nerves, digestion, insomnia and tiredness. The product was also firmly associated with sporting activities such as golf and cricket thanks to Bateman cartoons. Having spent an impressive £229,000 in 1929 the company agreed advertising budgets of £275–290,000 a year in the 1930s, and with witty and amusing copy made strong progress in the medium (Plate 47).[112] Needing to promote a single product through the free trade, Guinness's marketing strategy was clear enough. For other companies with national status, marketing was more complex. Sizeable tied estates were built up, and the pressure to spend large sums on advertising was not so great. For example, the estimated expenditure on *press* advertising by Guinness in 1933 was £115,000, twice as much as the next largest spender, Bass (£54,000), and three times more than Worthington (£34,000).[113] Watney and Bass made progress with well-known slogans such as 'What We Want is Watney's' and 'Great Stuff this Bass'. Whitbread, encouraged by its recently appointed joint managing director, Sydney Nevile, ran a special press campaign in London in the early 1920s, using Industrial Publicity Service Ltd, and increased its spending on advertising from £37,000 in 1920 to £53,000 in 1923. By 1932 the figure had risen to £73,000, and it increased over the rest of the decade. The advertising of bottled beer for home consumption was given prominence (see Plate 48).[114] Regional brewers, who did not have national market pretensions, were content with much smaller budgets. Bristol Brewery Georges, for example, spent about £4,000–5,000 a year on general and public house advertising in the 1920s, and about £5–6,000

112 Dennison and MacDonagh, 'History of Guinness', Ch.12; Brian Sibley, *The Book of Guinness Advertising* (Enfield, 1985), pp. 15–16, 37–40, 56; F. G. Wigglesworth, 'The Evolution of Guinness Advertising', *Journal of Advertising History*, 3 (March 1980), 14–15.

113 Legion Publishing Co., *Statistical Review of Press Advertising*, I–II (1933–4). The reported expenditure of Whitbread and Watney was only £8,000 and £4,500 respectively.

114 Whitbread advertising expenditure data, 1920/1, 1923/4 and 1924/5, and 1932, in Nevile Papers, W/40/1 and 2, W&Co., and Ritchie, *Uncommon Brewer*, pp. 97–100. On Watney's advertising see Serocold, *Watneys*, pp. 48–53.

on general advertising in the late 1930s. In the aggregate, the brewing companies' total expenditure was modest in relation to sales.[115]

But it was the Collective Advertising Campaign orchestrated by the Brewers' Society from 1933 which took the eye. The idea, which was not new, was given impetus by the industry's difficulties in the early 1930s. The sharp fall in consumption which accompanied higher beer duties in 1931–3 caused widespread alarm in the trade, and the Society campaigned vigorously for a reduction in duty. In April 1933, the Chancellor, Neville Chamberlain, introduced a new scale of duties: £1.20 per barrel of 1027° gravity or less, plus 10p for each degree above 1027°. For brewers of 1040° beer, the norm in the 1930s, this represented a tax reduction of over 35 per cent (£3.87 to £2.50 per barrel), bringing the duty below that levied in 1923–30 (£2.64).[116] However, Chamberlain asked for a *quid pro quo* from the brewers: a price reduction of 1d a pint; a 2° increase in average gravity; and a promise to raise output and use more home-grown barley.[117] Welcome as the new duties were, fears were expressed that the *quid pro quo* would be difficult to deliver. Beer appeared to have lost its position as the 'national beverage'; the product was believed to have become a drink primarily for middle-aged and elderly men. Under Sydney Nevile's direction the Brewers' Society appointed the London Press Exchange as advertising agents to organise a national campaign to promote beer. Launched in December 1933 with the slogan 'Beer is Best', this was financed by a levy on Society members according to output.[118] The initiative proved successful from the start, and few problems were encountered. The temperance interest responded with a slogan of its own, 'Beer is Best Left Alone', but this made little headway. Some brewers expressed doubts about the campaign, none more so than Guinness, who feared that a slogan emphasising 'beer' would prejudice the consumption of stout. There was little evidence to support this view, in fact.[119] The brewers' cam-

[115] Bristol Brewery Georges Board Minutes, 1921–38, *passim*, BG9(e)–(k), Bristol Record Office; Nicholas Kaldor and Rodney Silverman, *A Statistical Analysis of Advertising Expenditure and of the Revenue of the Press* (Cambridge, 1948), pp. 31, 144–8 (estimates for 1935).

[116] *Brewers' Almanack 1940*, p. 27.

[117] 'History of the Collective Advertising Campaign', memo for Brewers' Society Advertising Sub-Committee, 11 June 1947, BS.

[118] Initially 3d per bulk barrel. About 80 per cent of the brewers (by barrelage) supported the campaign. See BS Advertising Sub-Committee Minutes, 4 May 1933; Report on 'National Campaign for Advertising Beer', 11 May 1933; BS Annual Report for Year ended 30 September 1934, pp. 5–7; File 8/1/2, BS.

[119] BS Advertising Sub-Committee Minutes, 8 November 1933, Advertising Consultative Committee Minutes, 20 April 1936, BS; Dennison and MacDonagh, 'History of

paign, planned on a one-year basis, was renewed annually and ran without interruption until the war (when the advertising space was placed at the government's disposal). Expenditure over the period 1933–8 amounted to £833,000 or £139,000 per annum. It was one of the largest co-operative ventures of its day.[120]

'Beer is Best', with its emphasis on the wholesomeness of ingredients, the relationship between beer and sport and recreation, and the role of the public house as a social centre, represented a middle-class, status-raising focus for the product. The Society's campaigns, which were executed by Major G. Harrison of London Press Exchange and the publicity agents, Editorial Services Ltd, led by Sir Basil Clarke, embraced not only conventional advertising – newspapers, posters, bus and tram bills, etc. – but also a song, a film and a revue. Furthermore, the Society was anxious from the start that 'drawings of family groups should not depict a lower social status than that of a middle class family'.[121] All this suggests weaknesses as well as strengths in the marketing effort. Sophisticated market research was as ill developed in brewing as it was in much of British manufacturing. When Guinness turned to Benson's for help, the latter sent investigators into the pubs to ask consumers why they drank the product. Other brewers relied on instinct and prejudice. There was much argument when Whitbread contemplated replacing naturally conditioned bottled beer, on which the reputation of its celebrated pale ale was based, with carbonated beer. A memorandum of October 1921 in Sydney Nevile's papers gives some idea of the nature of the early debate.

It is inconceivable [wrote the anonymous author of the memorandum] 'that anyone who drinks beer thoughtfully could really prefer artificially conditioned beer. The difference is that between freshly made tea and tea made with tepid water. It is the difference between butter and margarine. It is the difference between the clear reasoning of H. G. Wells and the diatribe of an angry woman.

Guinness', Ch.13. At the beginning of the campaign some difficulties were caused by the wording of the appeal to the brewers, which drew attention to the need to attract younger drinkers, and implied that advertising revenue might influence editorial opinion. See Nevile, *Seventy Rolling Years*, pp. 222–3.

120 'History of the Collective Advertising Campaign', 1947, and data in File 8/1/2, BS; Kaldor and Silverman, *Advertising Expenditure*, pp. 29–30. Kaldor and Silverman give data for co-operative *press* advertising for 1935 and 1938, which indicate expenditure by the Brewers' Society of £78,500 and £64,300 respectively. The actual expenditure (year to end November) was £71,820 and £63,017, and total expenditure, including poster advertising amounted to £152,275 and £131,166: BS file, 8/1/2, BS.

121 BS Advertising Sub-Committee Minutes, 19 December 1934, and 8/1/2, BS. In 1937 the Society's advertising agents, London Press Exchange, were replaced by W. S. Crawford. BS Advertising Executive Committee Minutes, 18 November 1937, BS.

It is the difference between real beer and sham beer ... It is impossible to consider anything except naturally matured beer.

This was a view which turned out to be considerably wide of the mark.[122]

The brewers were, however, aware of the market research conducted by others in the 1930s. The Brewers' Society subscribed to the *John Bull* readership surveys of the food, drink, etc. market conducted by its publishers, Odhams Press, in 1933 and 1938. Based on postal questionnaires, the first census investigated preferences for bottled beer consumed at home. It identified thirty-nine leading brands and gave Guinness a remarkable 38.1 per cent share of these *brand* preferences, followed by Bass with 8.2 per cent and Whitbread with 6.4 per cent. The same companies' shares of *all* preferences (including unspecified brands) were 21.5, 4.6 and 3.6 per cent respectively (Table 8.6). Five years later a further survey produced brand shares (thirty-seven bottled brands) of 14.5 per cent for Guinness (suggesting that the company's dominance in 1933 had been overstated), 9.5 per cent for Bass, and 8.5 per cent for Whitbread; market shares were put at 8.0, 5.2 and 3.6. The other major brands identified were Watney, Davenport of Birmingham, Tetley (Leeds), Mitchells & Butlers, Hammerton of London, Mann, Crossman & Paulin (London) and Worthington (Table 8.6). The 1938 study also looked at public house preferences (i.e. draught and bottled beer), and here the ranking was clearly different. Bass was the market leader, with 13.1 per cent of the fifty brand preferences and 6.9 per cent of the total market. William Younger of Edinburgh, Ansells of Birmingham, Walker of Warrington and Burton (part of Walker Cain) and Taylor Walker of London emerged as major brands (Table 8.6). Supplementary reports supplied to the Brewers' Society gave information about leading brands in particular areas of the country. Watney emerged as the leading brand in London and the South-East, Steward & Patteson of Norwich in the Eastern Counties, Mitchells & Butlers in the West Midlands, Shipstone of Nottingham in the East Midlands, Tetley in the West Riding and Younger in Scotland.[123]

How much use of this material was made by the Society and its members is not clear. What is clear, however, is that before the war the industry was worried about the changing nature of demand and activity

[122] Anon., memo on 'Beer', 18 October 1921, Nevile Papers, W/40/1, W&Co. This is not to imply that Sydney Nevile's assessments of the trade and its trends were as crude, of course.

[123] The Second John Bull Census (1938), supplementary report for Brewers' Society.

Table 8.6. *Brands and market preferences for beer (consumed at home and on licensed premises), 1933 and 1938*

	Beer consumed at home					Beer consumed on licensed premises		
	1933			1938			1938	
Brand	% of 39 brands	% of total	Brand	% of 37 brands	% of total	Brand	% of 50 brands	% of total
Guinness	38.1	21.5	Guinness	14.5	8.0	Bass	13.1	6.9
Bass	8.2	4.6	Bass	9.5	5.2	Guinness	7.6	4.0
Whitbread	6.4	3.6	Whitbread	6.5	3.6	Watney	5.0	2.6
Mitchells & Butlers	3.7	2.1	Watney Combe Reid	6.3	3.5	Tetley	4.9	2.6
Hammerton	3.1	1.8	Davenport	5.3	2.9	Mitchells & Butlers	4.4	2.3
Watney Combe Reid	2.9	1.6	Tetley	4.7	2.6	Younger	4.2	2.2
Mann, Crossman & Paulin	2.7	1.5	Hammerton	4.5	2.5	Worthington	4.1	2.1
Worthington	2.6	1.5	Worthington	4.1	2.3	Ansells	3.7	1.9
Davenport	2.5	1.4	Mitchells & Butlers	3.7	2.1	Walker	3.7	1.9
Tetley	2.5	1.4	Mann, Crossman & Paulin	3.0	1.7	Taylor Walker	3.1	1.6
Number specifying brands	4,426			1,395			1,813	
Number consuming product	7,832			2,515			3,459	

Source: The John Bull Census and the Food and Beverages Market (Odhams Press, 1933); The Second John Bull Census. Report on Confectionery, Drinks, Tobacco, Dog Food, Photography, Cycling and Hobbies (Odhams Press, 1938), general and individual reports.

encouraged fresh responses. But marketing and market research certainly remained limited in sophistication. When London Press Exchange were invited to tender for a post-war resumption of collective advertising in 1947 they stated bluntly that 'no systematic effort has ever been made by your Industry, as an industry, to build up by means of market research a living library of facts about consumer habits and trends'.[124] This was a matter for the post-war years.

IV

In many ways, the Second World War created conditions similar to those produced by the First World War. Raw material and labour shortages, higher prices, pervasive government controls and much higher levels of taxation were characteristic of both conflicts. But there were also marked differences. Intervention was sometimes much firmer than in the First World War, notably in the area of taxation. The beer duty was raised to very high levels indeed, the base rate of £1.20 per barrel of 1027° being doubled on the outbreak of war, and then increased again in April and July 1940, April 1942 and 1943, and April 1944, when the rate reached £7.03, 486 per cent higher than the pre-war figure. At the same time the incremental duty of 10p per degree (above 1027°) was increased to 26p. Thus, brewers of 1040° beer experienced a 317 per cent increase in the taxation per barrel, from £2.50 to £10.42. Further rises in the austerity period, in November 1947 and April 1948, took the basic rate to £8.94, 645 per cent above the pre-war duty, or 339 per cent in real terms (the incremental rate rose to 33p). The 1040° brewer's tax burden was now 430 per cent higher than before the war (212 per cent in real terms). There was no amelioration at all until the budgets of April 1949 and 1950, and even then the duty remained higher than that of 1944–7.[125] Furthermore, the Excess Profits Tax levied during the Second World War was a much stiffer impost than its predecessor, Excess Profits Duty. The initial rate was set at 60 per cent of assessed profits, but this was soon raised to 100 per cent from April 1940, and it remained at that level until 1946. Recognition that the tax might discourage companies from raising output caused the Cabinet, in January 1941, to offer them the return of 20 per cent (less Income Tax) as a

[124] London Press Exchange, 'Proposals for an Advertising Campaign for the Brewers' Society', 1947, Appdx. 1E, BS.

[125] Except for weak beer in the gravity range 1027–30°. *Brewers' Almanack 1958*, pp. 114–15; BS, *UK Statistical Handbook 1980*, p. 54; Feinstein, *National Income*, T140.

post-war credit to finance reconstruction.[126] Nevertheless, taxation on company profits, in addition to income tax, was retained by post-war governments. A peacetime Profits Tax, introduced in 1947, with initial rates of 10 per cent on undistributed profits and 25 per cent on distributed profits, was to prove an additional burden for brewers, as for other companies.[127] A higher tax burden certainly resulted in higher retail prices for beer, since by this time duty made up about 70 per cent of the final price. *The Economist* reckoned that the average price of a pint of draught beer increased from 5d (2.1p) to 1s (5.0p) during the War; the Brewers' Society's calculations of the average price of draught bitter reveal an increase from 7d (2.9p) in 1939 to 1s 0¾d (5.3p) in 1943 and 1s 3¾d (6.6p) in 1947, a rise in real terms of 33 and 44 per cent respectively.[128]

War damage and transport restrictions brought new problems in the Second World War. Bombing destroyed many public houses, particularly in London and other major targets such as Liverpool, Newcastle, Portsmouth and Coventry, and forced some brewers, for example Morgan's of Norwich, to cease brewing.[129] Brewers also suffered from the wartime restrictions on motor fuel, since most companies had abandoned the horse for the motor lorry in the 1920s and 1930s. For regional and local distribution the Ministry of Food and the Brewers' Society collaborated in encouraging voluntary local economies, for example by the temporary exchange of public houses between brewers. In 1943 a more assertive zoning scheme, drawn up jointly by both parties, was introduced. This required each of eighty-eight zones in the UK to supply its own needs as far as possible, and sought to eliminate cross-haulage within zones by asking publicans to take beer from the nearest available source, thereby weakening tied house arrangements. Control was undertaken by Divisional Food Officers.[130] A notable

126 Finance Acts 1939 and 1940, 2 & 3 Geo VI c.109, 3 & 4 Geo VI c.29; W. K. Hancock and M. M. Gowing, *British War Economy* (1949), pp. 163, 327, 340. The EPT rate was cut to 60 per cent at the beginning of 1946, then abolished at the end of the year. *Brewers' Almanack 1949*, p. 305.

127 See F. W. Paish, *Business Finance* (1965 edn), pp. 65–7, for details of subsequent adjustments.

128 *The Economist*, 18 September 1943, 8 and 15 December 1945, cit. in Vaizey, *Brewing Industry*, pp. 39, 42; BS, *UK Statistical Handbook 1988*, p. 41; Feinstein, *National Income*, T140.

129 Gourvish, *Norfolk Beers*, p. 137; BS, Annual Report 1943–4, p. 14, BS. On Watney's losses see Serocold, *Watneys*, p. 74.

130 BS, Annual Reports, 1940–1, p. 13, 1941–2, p. 6, 1942–3, pp. 7–8, BS; R. J. Hammond, *Food. Vol. I. The Growth of Policy* (1951), pp. 340–3; Vaizey, *Brewing Industry*, pp. 42–3.

exception was made of the 'national' and 'distributive' brewers, such as Guinness, Bass, Whitbread, Watney and Younger, which made considerable use of the railways to move beer economically over relatively long distances in bulk; this traffic accounted for about half of the ton-mileage of beer carried in 1941. Even here, of course, national transport difficulties demanded economies. However, those imposed on the leading brewers appear to have fallen well short of the draconian, and the contribution they made to overall transport savings was negligible, especially as brewing output rose (see p. 359). Some traffic was diverted to rail and more horses were used, but motor transport remained the dominant mode for beer distribution.[131]

In other ways the Second World War proved to be less harsh for the brewers. There was no Lloyd George to plague them; temperance protests were muted and ineffective; licensing hours remained largely undisturbed; there was no question of *direct* control by the government on the 'Carlisle' model, though the vestiges of that relic of the First World War persisted; and there was little talk of nationalisation, outside a small circle of Labour politicians angry about the brewers' unwavering support for the Conservative Party.[132] A spirit of co-operation prevailed, both between the brewers and government and among the brewers themselves.[133] More important still, exhortations to prohibit or ration brewing were firmly resisted. Government ministers such as Lord Woolton, Minister of Food (1940–3), were happy to equate brewing with the war effort, safe in the belief that the population was much more temperate. The reported incidence of drunkenness in England and Wales, for example, fell steadily from 12.8 per 10,000 population in 1939 to 9.9 in 1941, 6.6 in 1943, and reached a low point of 5.0 in 1946.[134] And the Prime Minister, Churchill, was fully in favour of

[131] A comparison of the years ending 30 September 1941 and 1943 revealed that the proportion of total traffic (barrelage) sent by road had fallen only slightly, from 84 to 80 per cent. BS, Memo on 'Transport Economy by Breweries', 11 December 1943, BS File on 'Wartime Transport', 6/5/3, BS. See also BS Annual Report, 1943–4, pp. 8–9, BS; Hammond, *Food*, pp. 343–4.

[132] Cf. John Parker, 'Should we nationalise beer?', *Labour Forum*, 1 No. 2 (January–March 1947), 2–4. Parker's response was stimulated by anti-Labour slogans in the summer of 1946, when beer was in short supply:

We've got no beer, we've got no stout,
You put 'em in, you put 'em out.

[133] Early evidence of brewery co-operation was the agreement, signed by eight companies in the West of England in June 1940, which provided for mutual assistance in the event of bombing: Agreement signed by Bristol Brewery Georges, Ushers, Cheltenham Original and others, 26 June 1940, CA/C/119, Courage.

[134] Lord Woolton, *The Memoirs of the Rt. Hon. the Earl of Woolton* (1959), pp. 242–3; Wilson, *Greene King*, p. 207; *Brewers' Almanack 1958*, p. 96. Data are for 'charges

42 Brewing in the First World War: the use of female labour. Women rolling out barrels at J. & R. Tennent's Wellpark Brewery (date unknown).

43 Sir William Waters Butler (1866–1939), chairman of Mitchells & Butlers (1914–39), in 1926. Butler, one of the leading brewers of his day, was a pioneer of the 'improved public house' and a member of the Central Control Board (Liquor Traffic), 1916–21. Born in a public house, he was chairman of the Brewers' Society, 1907–8.

44 Sir Sydney Oswald Nevile (1873–1969), of Whitbread, opening the 'Lord Morrison of Lambeth' in Wandsworth on 16 October 1962, with Lord (Herbert) and Lady Morrison. Nevile, like Butler, was a firm believer in improved public houses. A director of Whitbread for fifty years (1919–69), and a managing director for thirty (1919–49), he was a major figure in the industry for much of the century. He was chairman of the Brewers' Society, 1938–40, and of the National Trade Defence Association, 1946–8 (see his autobiography, *Seventy Rolling Years* (1958).

It's the first time you've ever seen me angry but really—! When are they going to reduce the beer duty so that I can reduce the price to you of
WILLIAM YOUNGER'S
Scotch Ale
BUY BRITISH BEER
Branches at London, Glasgow, Manchester, Leeds, Newcastle, Middlesbrough and Belfast.

45 Brewers' protests at the increase in beer duty in Philip Snowden's budgets of April 1930 and September 1931: advertisement for William Younger's Scotch Ale (*Daily Express*, 6 March 1932).

46 Samuel Allsopp & Sons board of directors, with associated brewers, at the Recreation Ground, Burton, on 10 July 1929 (*left to right, standing:* E. C. Quilter; E. T. Hargraves (Stretton's Derby Brewery); G. D. Atkinson (Brampton's Brewery); Selkirk Wells (joint managing director); *sitting:* James Davenport (deputy-chairman); Sir William Peat (chairman); John J. Calder (joint managing director); Lord Remnant). Allsopp merged with Ind Coope in 1934.

47 Guinness's inter-war advertising: 'A Guinness a Day', *c.* 1930. Guinness dominated beer brand advertising in the inter-war years.

48 Whitbread's inter-war advertising: appeal to housewives, *Evening Standard*, 16 July 1935, from the Sydney Nevile papers.

49 and 50 Brewing managers and offices. Bristol Brewery Georges: managing director and brewing staff, *c.* 1945 (*left to right, standing:* A. Bishop; R. J. Roles; S. Allen; *sitting:* R. Crawford; Arthur Hadley, managing director; F. Long). F. A. Simonds, chairman of H. & G. Simonds, Reading, and secretary, 1951.

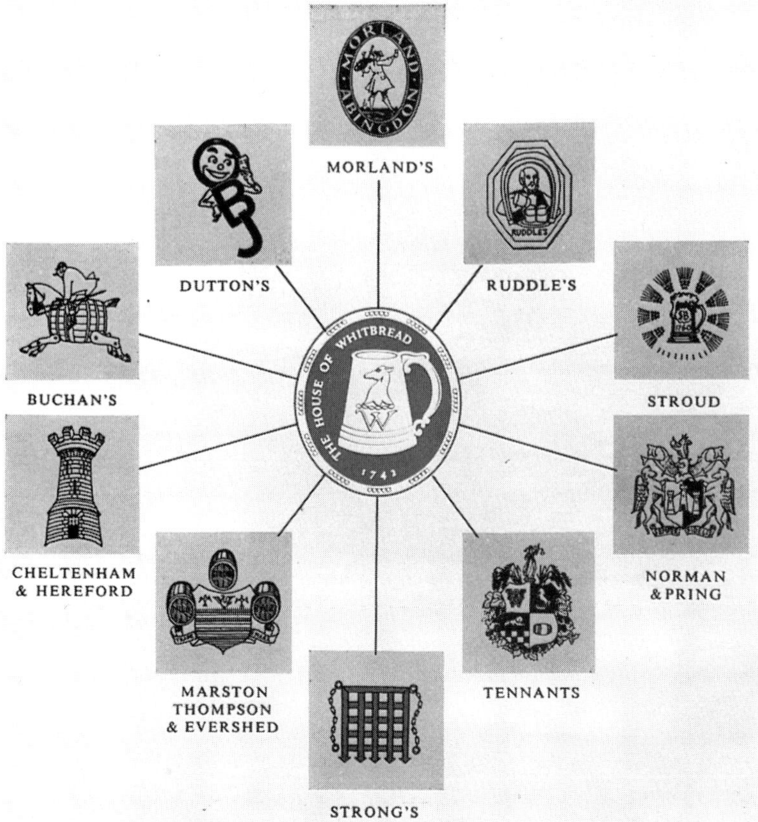

Brewery Companies associated with Whitbread

Andrew Buchan's Breweries Ltd, Rhymney, Monmouthshire
Cheltenham & Hereford Breweries Ltd, Cheltenham, Gloucestershire
Dutton's Blackburn Brewery Ltd, Blackburn, Lancashire
Marston, Thompson & Evershed Ltd, Burton-on-Trent, Staffordshire
Morland & Co Ltd, Abingdon, Berkshire
Norman & Pring Ltd, Exeter, Devonshire
G. Ruddle & Co Ltd, Oakham, Rutland
Strong & Co of Romsey Ltd, Romsey, Hampshire
Stroud Brewery Co Ltd, Stroud, Gloucestershire
Tennant Bros Ltd, Sheffield, Yorkshire

4

51 The Whitbread 'umbrella' in 1956 (Whitbread Annual Report, 1956). Of the ten independent companies shown to be sheltering under the umbrella, seven were subsequently taken over by Whitbread: Tennant Bros., 1961; Norman & Pring, 1962; West Country Breweries (Cheltenham & Hereford, Stroud), 1963; Dutton's, 1964; Rhymney (Buchan's), 1966; and Strong, 1968.

52 'Perpendicular drinking': The 'Nag's Head', Covent Garden, in 1951 (from *House of Whitbread*, Summer 1951).

53 and 54 The 'Improved Public House'. Progressive brewers invested in improved public houses in the inter-war years, and Mitchells & Butlers of Birmingham were notable enthusiasts (see Chapter 10). The 'Traveller's Rest', Northfield, Birmingham (Mitchells & Butlers), before and after (1929). (From Mitchells & Butlers, *Fifty Years of Brewing, 1879–1929.*)

55 and 56 The 'Improved Public House': the 'Holly Bush' (Mitchells & Butlers), Hagley Road in 1937: view from the bowling green; the Gentlemen's Smoke Room.

57 The 'Improved Public House': 'The Downham Tavern', London, in 1930 (*Brewers' Journal*, June 1930). The 'Downham', built by Barclay Perkins in 1930 at a cost of over £50,000, was a huge housing-estate pub with the full range of improvements, including a hall where Shakespearean plays were staged.

58 The limits of catering in the inter-war public house: the 'Terminus Hotel', Bristol, *c.* 1927.

No wonder everyone's asking for SKOL
the light dry Lager
Order plenty of SKOL
for the Whitsun rush!

In the trade press, the brewers of SKOL lager admit that they aim to capture the support of the teenagers -- girls as well as boys.

59 and 60 Early lager advertising, designed to appeal to the young and to women: Skol advertisement, 1960, included in a study of advertising by the Christian Economic and Social Research Foundation, October 1960; Harp and the 'Cool Blonde Lager', 1964.

"THERE MUST BE SUMMAT GOOD ON TELLY TONIGHT"

61 The increase in the take-home trade: Andy Capp and 'There must be summat good on't Telly tonight', *Daily Mirror*, 18 October 1958.

maintaining the supply of beer to the armed forces, a desire put into action by the Brewers' Society through its Beer for Troops Committee, established in July 1942.[135] All this meant that there were no swingeing controls on output, as there had been in the First World War. In fact, brewers actually increased both their bulk and standard barrelage, as Table 8.7 indicates. Bulk barrelage increased by 21 per cent from 1938 to 1941, fell back a little in the following year, then rose steadily to 1945, by which time output was 32 per cent higher than in 1938. Average gravity fell by about 15 per cent, from just under 1041° to about 1034.6° in the latter years of the War, but the reduction was insufficient to prevent a modest rise in standard barrelage (1055°) of 12 per cent from 1938 to 1945 (Table 8.7). Beer may have been weaker on average than it had ever been (with the exception of the worst year of the First World War, 1918 (1030.55°)), but physical volume, at 32.65 million bulk barrels, was the highest recorded output since 1914.[136] The contrast with spirits was marked; consumption of British-manufactured products, measured in proof gallons, fell by 25 per cent from 1938 to 1945.[137]

A rising output should not be taken to imply that the brewers had an easy time with raw material supplies and input costs. Scarcity produced higher prices and, as in the First World War, there was an extensive range of government controls embracing, *inter alia*, barley, sugar, hops and beer gravity. Barley, the major item of input costs, had already been the subject of government intervention. A commitment was obtained from the brewers in 1933 to buy as much home-grown barley as possible (see p. 352), and in 1935 to buy at least 7.5 million cwt, a promise which was fulfilled.[138] Then in July 1939 the government introduced an interim marketing scheme, whereby the brewers and the Exchequer

proved' not 'convictions', as with the pre-1939 data. Of course, the fall in the incidence of drunkenness on this basis may also reflect changes in policing practice (greater tolerance during the War) as well as changes in social behaviour.

135 Churchill's response to Alexander's request for more beer for the troops in Italy in 1944 has been much quoted: 'Good. Press on. Make sure that the beer – four pints a week – goes to the troops under the fire of the enemy before any of the parties in the rear get a drop.' Cf. Janes, *The Red Barrel*, p. 170. On the Beer for Troops Committee, chaired by F. A. Simonds, see BS, Annual Reports, 1941/2–45/6, *passim.*

136 Making allowance for the inclusion of Eire in statistics before 1922. *Standard* barrelage was the highest since 1925.

137 From 9.176 million to 6.913 million. *Brewers' Almanack 1958*, p. 75. However, consumption of foreign and colonial spirits increased from 1.273 million to 2.031 million proof gallons over the same period, so the *overall* reduction was 14 per cent. *Ibid.*, p. 78.

138 *Brewers' Almanack 1940*, pp. 69–71. The action was taken to prevent an additional import duty being placed on malting barley. By 1939 purchases had risen to 9.527 million cwt.

Table 8.7. *UK beer production in standard and bulk barrels, 1938–45, with average gravity*

Year[a]	Standard barrelage (millions)	Index 1938 = 100	Bulk barrelage (millions)	Index 1938 = 100	Average gravity (degrees)	Index 1938 = 100
1938	18.4	100	24.7	100	1040.93	100
1940	18.7	102	25.4	103	1040.62	99
1941	18.4	100	26.2	106	1038.51	94
1942	19.3	105	29.9	121	1035.53	87
1943	18.3	100	29.3	119	1034.34	84
1944	19.2	105	30.5	124	1034.63	84
1945	19.7	112	32.7	132	1034.72	85

[a] 1938 = Year ending 31 March 1939, *et seq.*
Source: Customs and Excise Reports, summarised in *Brewers' Almanack 1958*, p. 50. Production is output charged with duty.

jointly agreed to support the domestic price if it failed to exceed 8s 1d (40p) a cwt.[139] However, the scheme was soon made redundant by wartime restrictions, notably by an immediate embargo on imported barley for brewing, and it was abandoned in the autumn. From 1940 the Minister of Food, consulting with the brewers through a Technical Adviser, Hugh Paul, and a Brewing Advisory Committee (1940–3), controlled the distribution of barley for malting, and brewers were required to peg their standard barrelage to the level of the year ending 30 September 1939.[140] In the Second World War the government made it clear that it preferred gravity reductions to a fall in physical output; a cut of 10 per cent in 1938/9 gravity levels was ordered from February 1941, and this was amended to 15 per cent in January 1942 (except for brewers whose average gravity was already below 1030° (1032° from June 1945), a concession negotiated by the Brewers' Society).[141] As Table 8.7 suggests, the government's requirements were met by the industry until supply problems eased in 1944–5. Barley prices were left to the market at first, but a massive increase in 1941, provoked by a poor crop, saw the weighted average price (England and Wales) rise to £1.81 a cwt in the year to 31 August 1942, compared with only 42p in 1938/9, and prices as high as £3.75 a cwt were reported. From July 1942 a maximum price ex-farm of £1.75 a cwt was imposed by the government, a figure subsequently reduced to £1.38 for the 1943 crop. Average prices fell to £1.25 a cwt by 1944, although it should be noted that the acreage under barley, a profitable crop for farmers during the war, had doubled in six years (1938–44).[142]

Supply problems for brewers were at their worst in 1942–3, when the country's cereal and shipping difficulties were greatest. With sugar

139 The levy on brewers was to be 1s per standard barrel, the rate falling by ½d for each 1d rise in price above 8s 1d; the subsidy to farmers was to be 30s an acre at 8s 1d, falling by 1s 3d an acre for each 1d rise in price above 8s 1d. See BS, Annual Report, 1939–40, p. 8, *Brewers' Almanack 1940*, pp. 74–7. The actual price in 1939–40 (weighted average) was 14/4d. a cwt.

140 BS, Annual Reports, 1939–40, pp. 7–9, 1940–1, pp. 5–8, 44; Hammond, *Food*, I, pp. 83–5. Barley distribution was organised through permits issued by the Ministry of Food, whereby an initial allocation (at first 70 per cent of requirements, later 60 per cent, then 80 per cent) was granted; supplementary requests were monitored later in the purchasing year. The Brewing Advisory Committee was appointed by the Ministry but consisted of Brewers' Society Council members, including E. L. D. Lake (Greene King), Sydney Nevile (Whitbread), F. Nicholson (Vaux), F. A. Simonds (H. & G. Simonds), Sir Richard Wells (Charles Wells), and C. J. Newbold (Guinness).

141 BS, Annual Reports, 1940–1, pp. 6, 16, 1941–2, pp. 3–4, BS.

142 *Ibid.*, 1940–1, pp. 8–9, 1941–2, pp. 4–5, 1942–3, pp. 4–5; *Brewers' Almanack 1946*, pp. 53, 55 (reference is to the weighted average price of home-grown barley used for all purposes). Price regulation remained in force until 1953.

rationed from April 1940 (brewers were limited to about 70 per cent of their pre-war usage) and supplies of malt, irrespective of barley stocks, affected by labour shortages in the maltings, brewers were asked to use flaked barley and flaked maize in 1941–2. Then, during the general supply crisis of early 1943, Hugh Paul suggested that the brewers turn to inferior substitutes such as flaked oats and even dried potatoes, in order to reduce their barley demand by 10 per cent. With the full co-operation of the Brewers' Society, the industry reduced its barley consumption by the stipulated amount in six months.[143] Hops were less important than malt in brewing's total production costs, but were nonetheless a key ingredient in providing stability, flavour and aroma, a role given added relevance by the enforced dilution of barley in the mash-tun. As with barley, the product had been affected by government intervention before the war. Control introduced in the First World War, which involved *inter alia* the reduction of the 37,000 acres under hops by half, was retained until 1925. In that year continuing fears of over-production and low prices encouraged a co-operative venture, English Hop Growers, but this failed to discipline the market and was wound up in 1929. From 1932 a marketing scheme was operated under the terms of the Agricultural Marketing Act (1931); as amended in 1934, it not only set an average price (£9 a cwt) but operated five-year production quotas and collected an annual levy (initially 50p per cwt) to support the market. A new scheme was negotiated just before the war.[144] The declaration of hostilities did not disturb this apparatus, but a government embargo on imported hops (which had been limited to 15 per cent of total domestic demand under the Scheme of 1934) disrupted the market, as did the restriction of hop acreage to its pre-war level of 18,800 acres until 1943, and the loss of about 18 per cent of the 1940 output in London bombing. Only 75 per cent of brewers' contracts were honoured in 1941, and a special distribution scheme had to be introduced. In June of the same year the Brewers' Society responded to an instruction from the Ministry of Food and directed its members to reduce hopping rates by 20 per cent. This initiative was successful, and home producers were able to satisfy 95 per cent of the industry's

[143] BS, Annual Reports, 1939–40, p. 9, 1940–1, pp. 9–10, 1941–2, pp. 4–6, 1942–3, p. 5, BS; Hammond, *Food*, III (1962), pp. 25, 576–7; Bird, *History of the Institute of Brewing*, pp. 60–1.

[144] The history of hop control, and the complexities of the Hops Marketing Schemes of 1932, 1934 and 1939 are set out in *Brewers' Almanack 1940*, pp. 59–67. The 1939 Scheme raised the average price to £9.50 a cwt. and the import quota to 17.5 per cent. See also Parker, *The Hop Industry*, and Burgess, *Hops*, pp. 242ff.

requirements in 1943. However, prices reached £20 a cwt in 1944, and there were renewed problems of supply in 1944–5.[145]

All breweries had to contend with the challenge of maintaining a regular supply of beer of adequate quality to tied houses and regular customers. At the brewery the shortage of labour was just as acute as it had been in the First World War, while transport difficulties hampered distribution to a far greater extent than in 1914–18. It is also clear that the smaller breweries found the technical problems of responding to lower hopping rates and the shortage of malt very severe indeed. A number of them decided to close or sell their businesses to a neighbouring concern. Even comparatively well-placed regional companies such as Greene King, led by that doyen of the Brewers' Society, the redoubtable Major E. L. D. Lake, experienced problems in stabilising beers at low gravities and in finding adequate supplies of containers.[146] On the other hand, weaker beers meant lower costs per unit of volume and helped to counteract the effect of higher input prices. As in the First World War, the industry's pre-tax profits soared, aided by the cessation of investment and maintenance of breweries and public houses. It should also be noted that the government was anxious to co-operate with its brewers as far as possible. The role of the Brewers' Society in acting as the industry's spokesman, and its success in obtaining a series of concessions for its members on matters ranging from the requisitioning of vehicles, the treatment of deferred repairs and compensation for war damage to licence duty relief, the supply of timber for casks and the price of brewers' grains, were significantly different from the uphill struggle in 1914–18.[147]

The impact of wartime production on consumption trends, particularly in the longer term, is more difficult to assess. There could have been few complaints from customers about overall supply, although scarcity was evident from time to time, particularly in industrial areas formerly depressed but revived by war production. However, the quality and strength of draught beers left considerable room for improvement, and may well have stimulated a distrust of the darker draught beers (such as mild) and a corresponding preference for bottled beers after the war. Direct evidence in support of this hypothesis is

[145] The average price in 1945 was £21 a cwt. *Brewers' Almanack 1950*, p. 65; BS, Annual Reports, 1940/1–44/5, *passim*, BS. A new hops marketing scheme began in 1950.

[146] Cf. Wilson, *Greene King*, pp. 207–10.

[147] Cf. Hammond, *Food*, I, p. 268; Vaizey, *Brewing Industry*, pp. 40–1. The details are outlined in the Society's Annual Reports.

rather elusive, but there are strong hints in the trade press.[148] It is certainly true that during the war the public house re-established its central place in British leisure activity, but this was primarily a situation caused by lack of alternatives rather than positive preferences. And given the postponement of essential repairs and maintenance, the satisfaction of consumer needs after the war was to present brewers with an enormous challenge in investment terms.

More important for long-term consumption patterns was the persistence of various constraints long after the war had ended. In many ways the difficulties facing the industry in the austerity period of the late 1940s and early 1950s were more acute than they had been in 1939–45. Not only did raw material shortages and high taxation continue to affect brewing, but they were accompanied by output restrictions which were far more onerous than those experienced during the war. In 1946 the world-wide food crisis caused the Labour government to restrict the supply of grain for brewing purposes. In May the industry was limited to 85 per cent of its standard barrelage in the year to 30 September 1945, a restriction which was to apply to each individual brewery. This represented a significant departure from wartime practice, where virement of output between breweries had been permitted. Three months later a further cut in average gravity, of 10 per cent, was ordered, together with a reduction in the minimum average from 1032° to 1030°. After lobbying by the trade some concessions were obtained. The Minister of Food agreed to change the base-year to that ending 31 March 1946, and in May 1947 the gravity restriction was withdrawn.[149] But the relief proved limited and temporary. Many companies could not increase their gravities, since they were hard pressed to maintain bulk supplies, and the Brewers' Society, which had been given a small reserve barrelage (86,000) by the Minister in May 1946 in order to iron out allocative inequalities, found itself quite unable to meet the numerous claims upon it.[150] The situation was then aggravated by the economic crisis of 1947, with its fuel cuts, coal rationing and attendant disruption. On top of this the government ordered a 25 per cent cut in sugar consumption from January 1948 as part of its curb on dollar spending. With the Ministry of Food unwilling to release extra barley, a

148 Cf. *Brewers' Journal*, March 1946, pp. 284–5, July 1949, p. 309; *Brewing Trade Review*, June 1948, pp. 376–7, April 1950, pp. 226–7.

149 BS, Annual Reports, 1945–6, pp. 4–5, 1946–7, pp. 4–5, BS.

150 *Ibid.* 1946–7, pp. 5–6, 1947–8, p. 11. The reserve had initially been provided because the Ministry of Food had gone further than original government intentions in imposing an 85 per cent cut (cf. 90 per cent).

further reduction in brewing output was ordered, from 85 to 82 per cent of the 1945–6 baseline. Complaints about its impact on individual breweries merely provoked a further cut in January 1949 to 78 per cent, with 4 per cent being added to the Brewers' Society's reserve. Accompanying these changes, the increases in beer duty in November 1947 and April 1948 added 2d (0.8p) to the retail price of beer. All this meant that there could be no swift improvement in the supply and quality of the product, and the perpetuation of 'wartime' beer, with shortages in industrial areas such as the West Midlands, aggravated critical reactions from consumers.[151]

Accompanying the restrictions on output were equally burdensome controls on investment and maintenance. In 1944 a Home Office committee reported that in England and Wales alone 1,600 licensed premises had been closed by enemy action to the end of August 1943,[152] and many thousands more were deteriorating badly owing to lack of maintenance. Prudent brewers had built up sizeable reserve funds to cover post-war property improvement, and there had been considerable discussion in the trade press about the public house of the future under the banner of reconstruction. But the limitations imposed by building licensing prevented them from achieving very much before the mid-1950s, and even where licences were granted there remained the frequent disruptions caused by labour and material shortages in the building industry.[153] In the space of three years after 1945 the overall climate facing the brewers had changed radically. Matters were not improved by allegations of excessive profit-taking which circulated in 1948, nor by a Licensing Bill in the same year which initially proposed to place large areas in the vicinity of New Towns under state management. The Brewers' Society, in its annual report for 1948–9, was moved to claim, though with scant regard for history, that the trade now faced 'attacks more virulent than it has ever had to face before'.[154] By the time

151 *Ibid.* 1946–7, pp. 9–10, 1947–8, pp. 3–5, 12, 1948–9, pp. 17–18. On criticisms of beer shortages see *Brewing Trade Review*, September 1948, p. 564. The sugar control required brewers to cut their usage from 90 per cent of the 1939 level (fixed in September 1945) to 74 per cent (71.7 per cent from January 1950). BS, Annual Report, 1949–50, p. 21, BS.

152 *Report of the Committee on War Damaged Licensed Premises and Reconstruction* (Morris Committee), February 1944, Cmnd.6504, p. 56.

153 On reconstruction discussions and the public house, see *Brewers' Journal*, May–November 1943, *passim*.

154 BS, Annual Report, 1948–9, p. 4. Criticisms of high profits related to the 1946–7 results, £47.5 million gross in aggregate: *ibid.*, 1947–8, pp. 10–11, and see below, p. 370. On the Licensing Act 1949 see *Brewing Trade Review*, September 1949, pp. 672–3, 692ff.

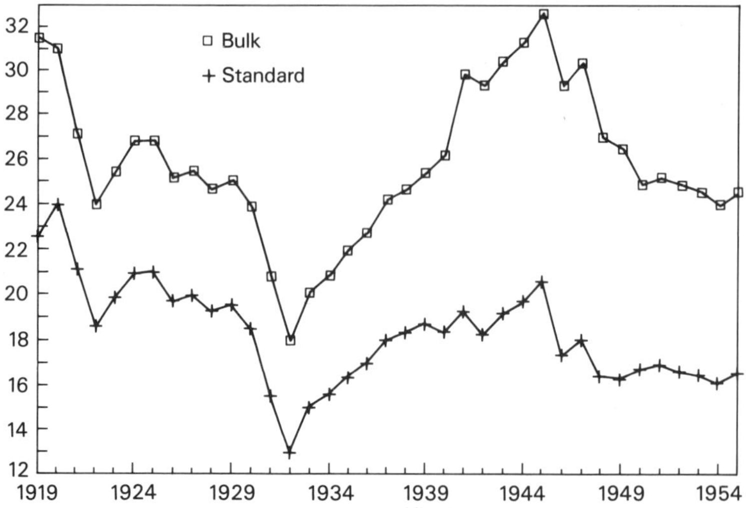

Fig. 8.4 UK beer production (beer charged with duty, excluding Eire) in millions of standard and bulk barrels, 1919–55. (*Source: Customs and Excise Reports*; see Appendix, Table VIII.)

conditions eased, and the government was prepared to lighten the burden of the beer duty a little, domestic demand had begun to decline. In the Budget of April 1949 the duty was reduced by 21s (£1.05) a barrel, but since this was accompanied by an enforced price reduction of 1d (0.4p) a pint, the industry estimated it was out of pocket to the tune of 3s (15p) a barrel.[155] In the following year, the base rate was cut by 2s 6d (12.5p) and applied to beers of 1030° gravity, instead of 1027°; incremental rates were then applied to beers of 3° extra gravity without extra duty. At the same time the restriction on average gravity was removed. The limit on output was retained, however, but as the Brewers' Society admitted, this was 'largely academic'.[156] In Table 8.8 the effect of government intervention is clearly evident. Standard barrelage fell by 16 per cent in 1946 compared with 1945, bulk barrelage by 10 per cent, and average gravity by 6 per cent. A modest recovery in 1947 was followed by cuts which took both standard and bulk barrelage to about 80 per cent of the 1945 levels. The reduction of duties in 1949–50 had no impact at all. Bulk barrelage slipped to 76 per cent of the 1945 figure in 1950 and remained at this level into the mid-1950s.

[155] BS, Annual Report, 1948–9, p. 6, BS.
[156] *Ibid.* 1949–50, p. 21, 1950–1, p. 3.

Table 8.8. *UK beer production in standard and bulk barrels, 1945–55, with average gravity*

Year[a]	Standard barrelage (millions)	Index 1945 = 100	Bulk barrelage (millions)	Index 1945 = 100	Average gravity (degrees)	Index 1945 = 100
1945	20.6	100	32.7	100	1034.72	100
1946	17.3	84	29.3	90	1032.59	94
1947	18.1	88	30.4	93	1032.66	94
1948	16.4	80	27.0	83	1033.43	96
1949	16.3	79	26.5	81	1033.88	98
1950	16.7	81	24.9	76	1036.99	107
1951	17.0	82	25.2	77	1037.07	107
1952	16.7	81	24.9	76	1036.87	106
1953	16.5	80	24.6	75	1036.97	106
1954	16.2	78	23.9	73	1037.13	107
1955	16.6	81	24.6	75	1037.22	107

[a] 1945 = Year to 31 March 1946 *et seq.*
Source: Appendix, Table VIII.

Because the brewers increased their average gravities by about 7 per cent from 1945 to 1950, standard barrelage stabilised at about 81 per cent of the 1945 figure. But an annual average output of 16.6 million barrels (standard) in 1950–5 was reminiscent of the worst years of the 1930s rather than a reflection of post-war recovery. From the perspective of the mid-1950s the war period appeared as a temporary 'blip' in the slow but steady decline in output.[157] Only by reducing average gravity was the bulk output of the 1920s matched in the early 1950s (Fig. 8.4).

Production and consumption patterns were very similar, since both exports and imports were slow to recover from wartime restrictions. In terms of both standard and bulk barrels, retained imports and exports failed to equal inter-war figures.[158] The published data on consumption made for depressing reading. Changes in the data presented in the Customs and Excise Reports make a long-run series difficult to construct on the basis adopted earlier (see pp. 337–9). But a series using consumption data derived from the net duty paid figures (rather than the quantity charged with duty) shows a clear downward trend from 1938 to 1955, from 14.2 standard gallons per head to 12.0 (see Fig. 8.5).[159] Results such as these certainly worried some of the more far-sighted brewers, who were well aware that quality and supply problems since 1939 had tended to alienate many beer drinkers. The industry may not have been nationalised, like coal, electricity and the railways, but it shared many of the characteristics of the public sector. Controlled in peacetime and taxed extremely heavily, it also faced a disturbing market environment.

Concern about projected demand was one thing; current financial results were another. As we saw in earlier periods, such anxieties were not translated into results as shown in company balance sheets, although profit figures were undoubtedly magnified by postponed maintenance

[157] Production in standard barrels fell by 1.04 per cent p.a., 1938–55 and by 0.57 per cent p.a. over the longer period, 1919–55; bulk barrelage fell by 0.82 per cent p.a. 1938–55. The equations are:

$\text{Log}Y = 23.1 - 0.01040X$, adj. $r_2 = 0.54$;
$\text{Log}Y = 14.0 - 0.00575X$, adj. $r_2 = 0.24$;
$\text{Log}Y = 19.3 - 0.00821X$, adj. $r_2 = 0.14$.

[158] Correlation coefficients are: production and consumption in standard barrels, 1938–55: 0.994; bulk barrels: 0.997.

[159] See *Brewers' Almanack 1958*, p. 51. The Customs and Excise data exclude information on exports after the year 1950–1. A log linear equation for consumption per capita in standard gallons produces a growth-rate of −1.54 per cent p.a., 1938–55. The equation is: $\text{Log}Y = 32.5 - 0.0154X$, adj. $r_2 = 0.61$.

Table 8.9. *Company profitability (ordinary dividends), 1939–55 (annual averages)*

	Ordinary dividends		
Company	1939–45	1946–50	1951–5
Maclay	0.0	0.0	0.0
Barclay Perkins	5.2	6.8	8.1
Boddingtons'	8.7	15.0	15.9
Steward & Patteson	12.5	15.0	14.9[15.4][a]
Joshua Tetley	12.7	16.0	14.7[15.9][a]
Whitbread	17.3	20.4[27.6][a]	22.7[73.9][a]
Bass	20.7	24.8	38.9
Mitchells & Butlers	21.0	21.5	17.3
Guinness	27.6	29.6	22.2[27.8][a]
All 25 companies (unweighted)	14.6	18.5[a]	21.4[a]
All 25 companies (weighted)	18.8	22.2[a]	28.1[a]

[a] Takes account of capitalisation of reserves as bonus shares.
Source: Appendix, Table IX.

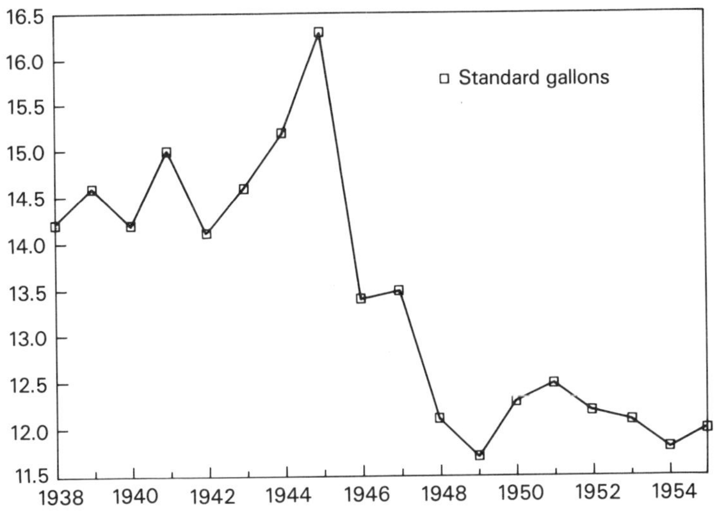

Fig. 8.5 UK beer consumption in standard gallons per capita, 1938–55 (*Source:* see Appendix, Table VIII.)

and investment. The Exchequer figures of brewing profits appeared to give support to the critics, showing a steady rise in profits (before income tax) from £25.5 million in 1938–9 to £48.5 million in 1947–8. However, the after-tax figures were more modest, showing a rise from £17 to £24.2 million, then, in 1949–50, the last year for which data were published, a sharp fall to £15 million. Given the fact that prices rose substantially (by 80 per cent, 1938–49), it is clear that brewing profits failed to maintain pre-war levels in real terms, though there were fewer enterprises to share in the aggregate.[160] Whatever the interpretation which supporters and opponents placed on such results, it is quite clear that ordinary dividends remained extremely healthy, and by resisting any temptation to make generous distributions in wartime most companies were able to maintain their figures during the austerity period. An unweighted average of ordinary dividends for twenty-five companies (allowing for capitalised bonuses) reveals a rise from 14.6 per cent in 1939–45 to 18.5 per cent in 1946–50 and 21.4 per cent in 1951–5; the weighted average, which reflects the success of companies such as Bass, Guinness, Ind Coope and Whitbread, increased from 18.8 per cent to 22.2 and 28.1 per cent (Table 8.9). The only breweries in our 'representative' group to show comparatively modest dividends were Maclay (which paid nothing) and Barclay Perkins. The results may be flattering in that they relate profits to the historical value of assets, but there is nothing to suggest that alternative measures of profitability would challenge these findings.[161] Concentration of brewing resources

[160] *Ibid.*, pp. 69, 184 and Feinstein, *National Income*, T140. After-tax profits in constant 1938 prices amounted to:

Year	Profits	Profits per brewer
1938/9	£17.0m.	£19,209
1947/8	£14.9m.	£23,840
1949/50	£8.3m.	£14,638

[161] Several tests were undertaken. The results for Bass, Whitbread and Bristol Brewery Georges (unweighted annual averages) were:

Period	Rate of return on capital*	Ordinary dividends (%)
1946–50	12.15	21.85
1951–5	14.40	25.94

* = distribution on share capital and debentures

A comparison of net profits and other data yielded the following:

Period	Net profits/ capital (%)	Rate of return (%)	Ordinary dividends (%)
Bass 1946–50	10.20	11.38	24.80
1951–5	15.25	16.44	38.90
Whitbread 1946–50	11.69	10.08	20.35
1951–5	11.48	14.35	22.73

again provides some of the answers to the conundrum. The number of brewers ('brewers for sale') continued to fall, from 840 in 1939 to 680 in 1945 and only 426 in 1955. Gloom about war and austerity conditions no doubt encouraged several smaller companies to give up, as did the increasing market penetration of larger brewers producing national bottled beers. For example, Cleator Moor Brewery was bought by Matthew Brown in 1947, Soames of Spalding by Steward & Patteson in 1949, and George Beer & Rigden by Fremlins, also in 1949. Companies such as these, who decided to cease trading, gave opportunities to the more adventurous post-war companies, notably Hammonds United and J. W. Green, which expanded by making several purchases. Many companies talked about the possibility of merging without taking action, not least Joshua Tetley and John Smith's in 1945.[162] Opportunities for scale economies, which sustained the players left in the game, are indicated by the fact that the number of full on-licences remained more or less constant over the same period: 81,881 in 1939, 81,428 in 1954.[163] The experience of the successful national and the smaller regional brewers could differ markedly. As shown in Table 8.8, UK bulk beer production fell by 25 per cent, 1945–55; but while Guinness sales in Great Britain actually increased by 14 per cent, and the production of Bass increased by 7 per cent, the sales of Wadworth of Devizes, for example, fell by over 70 per cent.[164]

The contrast between the pressures provided by government intervention, high taxation and falling demand on the one hand, and the absence of complaints from shareholders on the other, is thus a persistent theme. Profits remained reasonably healthy, and as Hawkins and Pass have observed, the brewers were persuaded to 'temper commercial

[162] John Smith's Tadcaster Board Minutes, 26 March 1945, JA/C/5. John Smith's, Tadcaster.

[163] *Brewers' Almanack 1958*, p. 69; BS, *UK Statistical Handbook 1980*, p. 64.

[164] Data:

Company	Production/sales (blls) 1945	1955	% change
Guinness	1,723,000	1,960,000	+14
Bass, R. & G.	937,000	999,800	+ 7
Ind Coope & A.	1,100,000	901,000	−18
Mitchells & B.	963,000	794,000	−18
Wadworth	21,700	6,100	−72

Source: Guinness, 'Sales ... 1921–66', GPR; Bass, production data, cit. in Owen, *History of Bass*, forthcoming (data include beer brewed for Worthington; sales of Bass beer fell by about 18 per cent); Ind Coope & Allsopp, 'Net Bulk Production, All Breweries', F/108/A17, Allied; Mitchells & Butlers, Sales Analyses, 'B2', Cape Hill, Birmingham; Wadworth, 'Summary Book, 1945–74', Wadworth & Co. Devizes. It is not clear whether the Wadworth data refer to draught sales only or to draught and bottled. Wadworth's fortunes revived dramatically in the 1960s following a successful trading agreement with Scottish & Newcastle and the popularity of its '6X' bitter.

instincts with a sense of social responsibility'.[165] The situation goes a long way to explain the relaxed, gentlemanly approach to business, and such matters as takeovers, investment and marketing, which characterised the brewing industry before the late 1950s, as will be made clear in Chapter 9.

[165] Hawkins and Pass, *Brewing Industry*, p. 46.

9

Organisation and management – a 'picturesque dinosaur'?

I

How distinctive was the brewers' industrial management before the mid-1950s? Was there an identifiable 'brewing style' in the way in which they organised and managed their companies in the forty years after 1914? At first sight, we might be tempted to conclude that the industry was the exemplar of everything that has been considered defective or, at the very least, inhibiting in British manufacturing since the late nineteenth century. A strong family orientation and a cosy, amateur style, reflected in a 'club' atmosphere in the boardroom, was characteristic of most, if not all, breweries in the first half of the twentieth century, as it had been in the second half of the nineteenth. Some of the attitudes and patterns of behaviour developed in Victorian Britain and described in Part I of this book survived two World Wars, even if not entirely unscathed. Notions of 'gentlemanly' conduct certainly persisted. Brewers were expected to behave according to an informal code which included the idea that acquisitions and mergers should be pursued in a restrained, non-aggressive manner, that expanding companies had an obligation to retain staff affected by such activities and, above all, that a brewer had an obligation to his community, for whom beer was the traditional lubricant at events where politics, religion, charitable fund-raising, sport and recreation intermingled.[1] The code of conduct was also reflected in more routine business decisions, such as the recruitment and training of staff, where co-operation between brewers was common, and could be detected in informal collusion over wage-rates and pricing (e.g. through the Brewers' Federation Council). That a

[1] Cf. Vaizey, *Brewing Industry*, p. 151, and on 'gentlemanly' conduct more generally, D. C. Coleman, 'Gentleman and Players', *Economic History Review*, 2nd ser. 26 (February 1973), 92–116, and T. R. Gourvish, 'British Business and the Transition to a Corporate Economy: Entrepreneurship and Management Structures', *Business History*, 29 (October 1987), 18–45.

rather self-contained environment existed is clearly acknowledged; whether it was accompanied by or is evidence of a quiescent, conservative and generally unenterprising performance is quite another matter. *The Economist* certainly thought the two went together when in 1964 it criticised the industry's record over the 1950s: 'Traditionalist, paternalistic, inbred, secretive – Britain's brewing industry slumbered through the nineteen fifties, hogging over £1,000 million of capital . . . A picturesque dinosaur. A declining industry'. Nor, it was implied, did this situation represent a sudden deterioration from an earlier record of energy and enterprise. What happened in the 1950s was, apparently, more of the same.[2] Such a verdict was rarely if ever to be found in commissioned histories celebrating a brewing centenary or a longer anniversary. But it was expressed by economic and financial critics, and particularly those whose perspectives were shaped by the changes which affected the industry from the 1960s.[3]

It is not difficult to find evidence, from the smaller breweries in particular, which points to a rather relaxed style of management. Helped by the retention of a production process which was not subject to dramatic technological change – a feature shared with confectionery, for example – and cushioned in the retail trade by distribution to tied public houses, brewers could survive without displaying exceptional entrepreneurial qualities. Determination combined with a degree of competence was sufficient to sustain an individual brewer for as long as he chose to remain trading. Company histories are full of such men, and a considerable length of service was not uncommon. Thus, William Wyper, secretary and joint managing director (1919–31) of T. & J. Bernard of Edinburgh and J. S. Pringle, chairman and managing director (1932–59) of the same firm each served the company for fifty years; at Henley-on-Thames Brakspear's brewery was sustained by John Chalcraft, managing director (1928–69) and chairman (1970–4), who had first joined the company in 1914. In Norwich the management of Steward & Patteson was dominated by Sir George H. Morse and Charles H. Finch. Morse joined the brewery in 1878, Finch in 1885. They both became founding directors on the firm's incorporation in 1895 and served until 1931 and 1945, totals of fifty-three and sixty years respectively. Another Morse, Arthur, joined Steward & Patteson in

2 *The Economist*, 19 September 1964.
3 E.g. Graham Turner, *Business in Britain* (1969), pp. 271–2.

1898 and was a director from 1904 to 1957.[4] This is not to imply that continuity of management was necessarily a weakness, but the frequency with which brewers acted for long periods as chairmen or managing directors suggests that age was no barrier to the retention of control. Indeed, it may be significant that many brewery mergers or sales took place only after the retirement or death of such long-serving figures.[5]

A typical example of a small to medium-sized brewery was the South Midlands firm of Hunt, Edmunds & Co. of Banbury. Registered in 1896 and a private company until 1950, it controlled about 270 tied houses from the 1930s and had a paid-up capital with debentures of £343,000 from 1932 (£321,000 in 1950).[6] The company deserves our attention because it has been the subject of a scathing, if affectionate, account of its relaxed management at board level by an insider, Lance Harman, who was its managing director from 1952 and chairman from 1956. Born in 1909, Harman was educated at Uppingham and Christ's College, Cambridge. He joined the board in 1945 after qualifying as a surveyor and working as a land agent for Alfred Savill & Sons. If he is to be believed, his introduction to senior management procedures at Banbury was rather curious, to say the least:

> This is what I found when I first visited the brewery to discuss my future with the managing director. On arrival I was led to a door which said 'Board Room' ... The room, which was dark and dismal, consisted of a side-board with several bottles and glasses on it, six chairs surrounding a large table, at the head of which sat a charming looking gentleman ... There wasn't a piece of paper, pen or any such triviality one might expect to see in an office of the managing director or a business the size of our brewery. It struck me that this scene was a bit odd, but I assumed the gentleman was so efficient that he gave all instructions by word of mouth ...
>
> The managing director ... then explained that the chairman was spending some of the time on military duty in Ireland, and was only occasionally at the brewery and then for short periods ... I ventured to say that he must have a lot to do and have a busy time. To my surprise he said, 'Oh no, if you are managing director here it's not the work you have to do but just being here in case something happens'. I then asked whether anything had happened while the chairman had been away on military duty. The answer was 'No, nothing which I have had to deal with. We have Raymond here and he deals with everything' ...

4 T. & J. Bernard Directors' Annual Reports, 1920–60, and Board Minutes, 19 August 1959, TJB5/1 and 5/2/5, Scottish Brewing Archive, Glasgow University (SBA); Sheppard, *Brakspear's Brewery*, p. 187; Gourvish, *Norfolk Beers*, pp. 49–54, 71, 125.

5 Death duties were often a cause of sale or merger.

6 From 1925 to 1952 a profit-pooling agreement with Hitchman & Co. of Chipping Norton was operated through a holding company, H. E. H. Ltd. Hunt, Edmunds had 190 pubs, Hitchman eighty. *Stock Exchange Year-Book, 1939–55*, passim.

Ronnie [the managing director], who had by now produced *Sporting Life* from his pocket, said, 'Raymond is our secretary. If you want to know anything ask him'. Raymond then retired and Ronnie said he must ring his bookmaker ... that was the end of my first experience of the family brewery ... I had not had any experience of 'Big Business' so couldn't be expected to understand how it was conducted.

Harman's first day at work as assistant managing director was equally disconcerting:

I was asked to appear at 11 o'clock in the morning, not before, as Raymond wouldn't be ready to see the directors before that time. I arrived at the board room at the appointed hour and found Ronnie again at action stations by the telephone, reading *Sporting Life*, while Maurice [the chairman] was writing letters ... This situation prevailed till twelve noon, when Ronnie picked up the favoured house telephone and bellowed to Raymond to come and dish out gin and sherry. This, it was explained, was a favourite aperitif before lunch in the Midlands. Gin and sherry were followed by lunch, after that a sip of vintage port and finally another short sit down in the board room, then home. Besides not wanting the directors' presence before 11 o'clock in the morning, Raymond also liked them to leave no later than 3 o'clock in the afternoon. He found them a hindrance before and after these times.[7]

As Harman describes it, the brewery had for some time been managed with the bare minimum of senior management staff, under the supervision of an intelligent, but scarcely executive, board of directors. The day-to-day running of the business was left to the company secretary and a head-brewer, apparently a womanising ex-boxer known as 'The Wizard'.[8]

Clearly, Harman's account must be taken with a sizeable pinch of salt, but there is corroboration of elements in it from other sources. Surviving photographs of boardrooms and directors' offices, for example, suggest a gentle pace (see Plates 49 and 50), although one must be careful not to jump to conclusions. It is also the case that many brewing companies had a lovable eccentric in their midst. At Greene King, Rayment's brewery of Furneux Pelham was acquired in 1931 and from 1937 was managed by Captain Neville Lake. A naval man, Lake ran the brewery for some thirty years just as if it were a frigate. However, his disconcerting naval style did not prevent him from making a successful assault on the club trade.[9] Donald C. Steward of Steward & Patteson was a less dynamic eccentric. He had joined the office staff in 1928 at the

[7] C. L. Harman, *Cheers, Sir! From the Vicarage to the Brewery* (Cheddar, 1987), pp. 75–8.
[8] Harmon, *Cheers, Sir*, pp. 79–90.
[9] Wilson, *Greene King*, pp. 188–9, 203.

age of twenty after an education at Radley and Cambridge, became a director in 1936, and remained so until the company was taken over by Watney Mann in 1963. A convivial figure when visiting tenants or representing Steward & Patteson at sporting events, his appearance at the brewery was sporadic. Stories about him abound. It has been said that the chairman once wrote to him enclosing a map showing the way to the brewery. Whenever a takeover was in the offing, Donald was apparently wheeled out to show prospective purchasers over the property; this was usually sufficient to cause a withdrawal of interest.[10] Further allegations of somnolence and complacency have been levelled at more important concerns too. In the 1960s the managing director of Guinness, Dr Arthur Hughes, was quoted as admitting that life at the Dublin brewery had been 'almost offensively easy' before the war. Some thought that these conditions persisted for many years afterwards. In the 1970s there were still signs that Guinness was a public company behaving like a family business. Production-orientated, it lacked cohesive management at the top; its divisions were run by barons presiding over a hotch-potch of businesses of the most diverse and sometimes bizarre character.[11]

It would, of course, be foolish to rely on anecdotes when seeking to analyse such a large and complex industry. In the first half of this book it has been made quite clear that brewing encompassed a wide range of enterprises with differing levels of sophistication. The expansion in Britain and overseas of larger firms such as Bass, Guinness and Whitbread and the export activities of Scottish companies such as William McEwan and William Younger were spectacularly successful by contemporary standards and were not inhibited by family-dominated ownership and management. Indeed, these firms, in extending their market areas and combining production with distribution and retailing functions displayed many of the characteristics which Alfred Chandler considered so important in the rise of the modern corporation in the United States.[12] The larger brewing companies, then, provide a good example of the fact that family firms *per se* do not preclude a clear business strategy, a sound organisational structure, and the build-up of competent and carefully supervised managerial hierarchies. We should

[10] Gourvish, *Norfolk Beers*, p. 126; interviews with former Steward & Patteson directors.
[11] Turner, *Business in Britain*, p. 272; *The Financial Times*, 6 June 1990, p. 8. See also Nick Kochan and Hugh Pym, *The Guinness Affair – Anatomy of a Scandal* (1987).
[12] Alfred D. Chandler, Jr., *The Visible Hand: The Management Revolution in American Business* (Cambridge, Mass., 1977), and see pp. 89–110.

not assume that there is anything intrinsically disadvantageous about family-dominated enterprise.[13]

Nor should we fall into the tempting trap of assuming that, the large successful firms apart, the brewing industry was complacently and even badly run. Of course, brewing had a definable style. The links with the landed gentry and the senior ranks of the armed forces imparted a squirearchical atmosphere in the boardroom. Brewers invariably sent their sons to major public schools, Sandhurst and Oxbridge, and tended to recruit outsiders from the same institutions although, as will be shown below, they were not inimical to the rise of managers from the secretariat or brewing room. In the inter-war years Hunt, Edmunds & Co. was managed by a colonel, a rear-admiral and a JP; four of the five directors of Nuttall's Blackburn brewery were JPs; Ansells of Birmingham had a lieutenant-colonel as chairman, a major and a captain in a board of six directors. This emphasis should not be misconstrued, however. It should be noted that elsewhere in business retired military figures and pillars of local government and society could be found in similar numbers.[14] The specialisation and success of firms where economies of scale in production and sales were clearly exploited obviously take the eye, but we should not ignore the fact that capable management was evident in some of the smaller and medium-sized companies. Georges of Bristol, Strong of Romsey, Greene King at Bury St Edmunds and J. W. Green of Luton all spring to mind, but there were others too.[15] After all, to survive and, above all to expand and prosper in the industry after 1914, given the ups and downs of war, recession, depressed demand and higher tax regimes, was not automatic; and if most firms were able to enjoy the cushioning of a tied estate, then this estate had first to be built up prudently and then managed carefully. The search for a sustainable quality in beer, via improvements based on pasteurisation, packaging and transport, was a matter for most brewing companies, whether large, medium or small.

Analysis of brewing company capitalisation clearly reveals the indus-

[13] Cf. concluding discussion in Kesaji Kobayashi and Hidemasa Morikawa (eds.), *Development of Managerial Enterprise* (Tokyo, 1986), pp. 282–5 and reviews of Chandler's *Scale and Scope: The Dynamics of Industrial Capitalism* (Cambridge, Mass., 1990), e.g. by Leslie Hannah, *Business History*, 33 (April 1991), 297–309.

[14] *Manual of British Brewery Companies*, 1938–9.

[15] For Georges and Greene King see Channon, 'Georges and Brewing in Bristol', pp. 165ff., and Wilson, *Greene King*. For Strong and J. W. Green see Alfred Rose, *Personalities and Progress (1858–1969): The Story of Strong & Co. of Romsey Limited* (Ringwood, Hants, n.d.), and Martyn Cornell, 'The Brewmaster's Story', *Bedfordshire Magazine* (Summer 1981), 13ff., copies in Whitbread Archive (W&Co).

Table 9.1. *Structure of the brewing industry*, c. *1919, 1955*

Enterprise type	Capitalisation[a]	1919 Number		1919 %		1955 Number		1955 %	
Very large national and regional	£2,000,000 and over	16		4		47		13	
Large regional	£1,000,000–£1,999,999	20		5		46		13	
Regional	£500,000–£999,999	66		17		58		16	
Medium-sized local	£300,000–£499,999	72		18		64		18	
Small local	£150,000–£299,999	109	290	28	74	144	208	40	58
Very small local	Under £150,000	109		28					
Total		392		100		359		100	

Notes: [a] Paid-up nominal share capital plus debenture stock.
Percentages rounded to nearest whole number.
Companies quoted include subsidiaries and companies retaining status after merger.
Source: Manual of British Brewery Companies, 1920, 1956.

try's diversity (see Table 9.1). In 1919 there were sixteen companies which could be considered very large, each with a paid-up capital (including debentures) of £2 million and over. They comprised the three national/exporting brewers, Bass, Guinness and Whitbread; seven London/South-East companies, Barclay Perkins, Cannon, Charrington, Courage, Mann, Crossman & Paulin, Truman Hanbury Buxton, and Watney Combe Reid (at £10.5 million the largest of all on this basis); and the six largest regional brewers, the quasi-national Allsopp and Ind Coope from Burton, Mitchells & Butlers (Birmingham), and Threlfall's, Peter Walker and Robert Cain from Lancashire. These were among the top fifty or so manufacturing companies in Britain.[16] Next came twenty large regionals, each with a capital between £1 and £2 million, including the Scottish exporting brewers, William McEwan and William Younger, who were also building up a national market in Britain, Worthington, which distributed nationally, Benskin's of Watford, Phipps (Northampton), Lacon of Great Yarmouth, Bent's (Liverpool), Groves & Whitnall of Salford, Bentley's (Leeds), John Smith of Tadcaster, and Newcastle. Below these were the smaller regional companies with capitals of £0.5–£1 million. There were sixty-six of them in 1919, 17 per cent of the companies listed. They included Ansells, Boddingtons', Bristol Brewery Georges, Cameron, Eldridge Pope of Dorchester, and Greene King. What is striking about Table 9.1, however, is that while there were 102 companies, 26 per cent of the total, in the top three categories, the rest of the industry was made up of medium-sized and small local firms. There were seventy-two (18 per cent) in the medium-sized category – companies such as Barnsley, Cheltenham Original, McMullen of Hertford, and Thomas Wethered of Marlow. This left 218 companies, 56 per cent of the total, with capitals under £300,000, and half of these were relatively small concerns with a capitalisation below £150,000. They ranged from brewers with regional pretensions, such as Matthew Brown, Hall & Woodhouse and

[16] This claim is based on ranking by nominal value of paid-up share capital and debentures. A similar ranking for 1905 produced by Peter Payne (nominal value of 'issued shares, debentures, mortgages, loans and deposits') had seventeen brewery companies in the top fifty manufacturing companies – the sixteen referred to here for 1919 *minus* Robert Cain and Mitchells & Butlers *plus* City of London, Hoare, and Wilson's: 'The Emergence of the Large-Scale Company in Great Britain, 1870–1914', *Economic History Review*, 2nd ser. 20 (1967), 539–40. It should be noted that rankings based on the market value of traded securities show far fewer breweries in the top fifty. Chandler's recent listing, based in large measure on Hannah's earlier work, has only three in the top fifty, but sixteen in the top 133 – the sixteen in our list *minus* Ind Coope and Robert Cain *plus* John Smith and Walker & Homfrays: Chandler, *Scale and Scope*, pp. 688–9, and cf. Hannah, *Corporate Economy*, pp. 188–90.

Mackeson, to modest concerns with a distribution area rarely exceeding 20 miles, brewers such as Alton Court of Ross-on-Wye (capital: £52,280), Hook Norton, near Banbury (£59,500), and Paine of St Neot's (£66,300). Indeed, the dominance of smaller firms was probably greater than that shown in Table 9.1, since information on the capital structure of several private companies and brewing partnerships was not reported.[17] Moreover, the data for 1955 show that even after some thirty-five years of acquisition and merger in the industry, the numerical preponderance of smaller firms was still evident. There were now forty-seven companies of national/large regional status, including twenty-seven with capitals exceeding £4 million, led by Watney Combe Reid (£17.5 million), Ind Coope & Allsopp (£16.2), Courage & Barclay (£15.8), Guinness (£14.5) and Charrington (£12.5).[18] Then there were forty-six regional companies with capitals of £1–2 million, considerably more than in 1919. The increase reflected the expansion of companies such as Boddingtons', Bristol Brewery Georges and Steward & Patteson. But there were still 144 companies, 40 per cent of the total, with capitals under £300,000. Although some of these were companies of convenience (e.g. subsidiary property or investment companies), most of them were genuine brewers serving primarily local markets. They included companies such as Hook Norton (whose capital was the same as in 1919), Adnams of Southwold (capital: £144,000), Jennings of Cockermouth (£100,000), and St Anne's Well of Exeter (£177,000). Brewers such as these each produced about 10–20,000 barrels a year and owned up to fifty tied houses, in marked contrast to the leading companies, which owned over 1,000 houses and brewed over 1 million barrels a year.[19]

17 *Manual of British Brewery Companies*, 1920. In 1919–20 there were 2,914 brewers licensed for sale in the UK (including Ireland), 941 of them organised in companies. BS, *UK Statistical Handbook 1980*, p. 88. Hawkins and Pass, *Brewing Industry*, p. 49, used information in the *Stock Exchange Year-Book* for 1927, 1936 and 1942, but the lowest sub-division given was 'below £1 million'. On this basis there were 318 companies (87 per cent) in this category in 1927 and 221 (74 per cent) in 1942, and forty-seven companies (13 per cent) with capitals of £1 million and above in 1927, and seventy-seven companies (26 per cent) in 1942.

18 *Manual of British Brewery Companies*, 1956. It should be noted that some double-counting has been incorporated into the data, since constituent and subsidiary companies were often included. In 1955–6 there were 426 brewers licensed for sale, about 300 of which were organised in *active* brewing companies. BS, *UK Statistical Handbook 1980*, p. 88.

19 In fact, Adnams had seventy-two public houses by 1955 and St Anne's Well sixty-six houses: *Stock Exchange Year-Book*, 1956. Vaizey lists 340 companies in England and Wales in 1952. Of these 138 owned one to fifty pubs (195 companies owned 1–100 pubs) while twelve companies owned 901 + (six owned 1,001 +): Hawkins and Pass, *Brewing Industry*, p. 76. Data collected by Guinness's statistical department show a

We must conclude, then, that in relation to organisation, decision-making and control, the demands made of brewing directors and managers varied considerably with the size of company, and with the extent and range of the market area served. Some elements may have been common to most, if not all, firms, but while economies of scale were clearly evident as breweries expanded, managerial capability was quickly tested, one of many examples of what Edith Penrose has called 'the managerial limits to growth'.[20] The balance between a brewery's tied and free-trade sales, the willingness to distribute both cask and bottled beers beyond a given radius (say 30 miles), and the approach to export opportunities were all relevant. After the First World War at least half of all brewing companies were potentially available for purchase. They faced the challenge of either growing to a more economic size in production terms, or establishing a business strategy based on survival. They could also, of course, decide to cease trading. The choice depended on the nature of the individual firm, the quality and ambitions of its directors and managers, and – not to be underestimated – chance factors of location and market character (remote rural locations often provided market niches for smaller breweries such as Adnams and Hook Norton). Inevitably, in business history more is known about the larger and relatively successful breweries. This bias, often acknowledged but rarely taken into account, should be kept firmly in mind when reading the remainder of this chapter. It should be emphasised that until the 1950s brewers of modest size and pretensions were more typical of the industry than the leading national and regional companies. And since the management challenge facing brewers located in small country towns and serving under 100 public houses was less demanding than that confronting the much larger companies, it was scarcely surprising that some of the more relaxed, even eccentric traits of organisation and management in the industry should be found in enterprises which advanced tentatively and unaggressively in the period under examination.

slightly higher concentration level. In January 1953 eleven companies owned over 1,000 on-licensed premises: Ind Coope & Allsopp, 3,197; Watney Combe Reid, 1,605; Charrington, 1,564; Walker Cain, 1,397, H. & G. Simonds, 1,342; Bass, 1,128; Greenall Whitley, 1,099; Courage, 1,020; J. W. Green, 1,010; Ansells, 1,008; and Barclay Perkins, 1,003. Guinness Trade statistics, Park Royal, London. Four companies brewed over 1 million barrels in 1939 and 1950.

[20] Edith T. Penrose, *The Theory of the Growth of the Firm* (Oxford, 1959, 2nd edn, 1980).

II

The extent of family participation in brewery ownership and management varied from company to company and changed with time. The industry's adoption of limited liability status in the later nineteenth century was strengthened after 1914. Not only did more private partnership firms seek incorporation, but many of the existing private companies, where the bulk of the capital was retained by the original owners and their families, obtained public company status as their needs for capital increased, or they faced a financial crisis resulting from the death of a major shareholder.[21] Thus, despite the disappearance of numerous firms by sale or merger, the number of brewing companies listed in the *Stock Exchange Year-Book*, which had been about 350 in 1919, was still over 250 in 1956.[22] However, the trend towards public incorporation, common to many branches of British manufacture, does not appear to have been accompanied by dramatic changes in the type of organisation and management structure employed in the industry. Alfred Chandler's recent assessment of the industry in the period to 1919 (and apparently beyond) is unequivocal. Although his judgements are based on a rather narrow range of secondary sources, he argues persuasively that brewing management was very much more personal in character than in other family-dominated sectors such as confectionery and branded food products. In fact, the reasons for moving to corporate status seem to have been primarily financial and legal, rather than managerial. What Chandler calls a 'partnership' form of management predominated; directors acted very much as managing partners, taking responsibility for the major departments of the business – purchasing and production (malting, brewing), sales and retailing (tied public houses), and so on. Only in those companies with a national or international market to supply did a managerial hierarchy develop below board level. Even here – Chandler singles out Bass, Worthington, Watney and, above all, Guinness – a family presence on the board

21 Steward & Patteson in Norwich sought public company status in 1936 after the death of the principal shareholder, Sir George Morse. Gourvish, *Norfolk Beers*, p. 133. Among the companies which converted from private to public were Cobbold (1924), Greene King (1926), Taylor Walker (1927), Devenish (1936), Hammerton (1937), John Jeffrey (1938), Norman & Pring (1944), Joseph Holt (1951), and Greenall Whitley (1952). *Stock Exchange Year-Book*, 1956.

22 *Ibid.*, 1919, 1956. The exact numbers – 348 and 259 – must be treated with reserve since it is not always possible to identify the company function in the brief listings provided in the *Year-Book*.

remained significant, in terms of both ownership and participation in executive management.[23]

How satisfactory is Chandler's assessment when applied to the four decades after the First World War? Clearly, we must distinguish between ownership, and the dominance of key strategic decision-making which this could provide, and day-to-day executive management. It is evident that the extent of personal ownership in brewing companies varied considerably. A study of equity capital in a range of larger firms in 1936, cited by John Vaizey, reveals this variation. Thus, family ownership of the ordinary share capital in the managerially more developed Bass and Guinness amounted to 52 and 32 per cent respectively, but in Mitchells & Butlers the figure was 14 per cent, and in Ind Coope & Allsopp only 3 per cent.[24] Both Whitbread and Guinness maintained a strong family involvement in spite of considerable corporate growth. Whitbread, whose ordinary shares were held by the participating families until 1948, retained control after a public offer by splitting the shares, altering the voting rights and establishing an investment company (see pp. 401–2). In Guinness, although the holdings of individual family members diminished, total family holdings were maintained into the 1980s, there being a gentleman's agreement that shares were not to be sold to outsiders.[25]

There were similar variations among smaller companies. The directors of Strong of Romsey held 96 per cent of the ordinary capital in the mid-1920s and although control was diluted after David Faber's death in 1931 they retained a solid majority (some 75 per cent) until they were bought out by a financial group in 1943. On the other hand, Boddingtons' directors owned only 10–11 per cent of the ordinary shares in the 1930s and the direct family only 27–8 per cent.[26] In Scotland, William McEwan was a further example of the continuing strength of family control, despite production growth and the penetration of international markets. Like Guinness, it was exporting its beers all over the world well before the end of the nineteenth century, but the firm continued to function very much as a private company until its merger with William

23 Chandler, *Scale and Scope*, pp. 266–7.

24 Beesley, PhD thesis, Birmingham, 1952, cit. Vaizey, *Brewing Industry*, pp. 60–1. The other companies were Walker Cain (24 per cent family-owned), Watney (15 per cent). It has not been possible to verify Vaizey's reference, because Birmingham University has been unable to trace the thesis.

25 Jonathan Guinness, 'Why we took to Ernest', *Evening Standard*, 28 August 1990, p. 7.

26 Strong & Co. Shareholders' Register, 1925–36, Register of Deferred Ordinary Shareholders, 1936–43, 324/151, 153; Boddingtons' Register of Shareholders, 1933, 1938, 405/52, 57, W&Co.

Younger to form Scottish Brewers Ltd in 1931. On incorporation in 1889 all the ordinary share capital of £500,000 was retained by the founder, William McEwan, who held 87 per cent, and his nephews, William and Robert Younger of Alloa. On McEwan's death in 1913 the bulk of his holding, nearly two-thirds of the voting shares, passed to his daughter, the Hon. Mrs Greville, of Polesden Lacey (see p. 220).[27] One of the more unusual examples of family control among the leading brewing firms was the fact that during the 1920s the active McEwan directors, who after William Younger's retirement in 1924 were all executives from outside the McEwan and Younger families, were obliged to seek the endorsement of this celebrated socialite in the South of England before major decisions could be taken.[28]

Elsewhere, as generation succeeded generation, the most likely occurrence was a decline in the proportion of the ordinary stock held by active representatives of the founding family or families. However, it was much easier to maintain a family presence on the board of directors. In many companies such a presence persisted long after the loss of a formal voting majority. Moreover, unless the shareholders could be mobilised to vote on particular issues – which was a remote prospect – the possession of three or four seats on the board was usually sufficient to ensure control. In Steward & Patteson, for example, the ordinary stock held by the founding directors, all members of the original families, amounted to 67 per cent of the total in 1895. This holding fell to 48 per cent by 1920 and 28 per cent by 1936, but no outsiders were elected to the board until 1949.[29] In fact, in most of our twenty-five 'representative' companies (see Appendix, Table IX), whether large or small, a family presence was retained. This is clear from an analysis of directors

[27] From 1889 two executive directors held 500 shares each. William McEwan Ordinary Share Register, 1889, SN/M/8/10/21, SBA. See also Ian Donnachie, 'William McEwan', in Anthony Slaven and Sydney Checkland (eds.), *Dictionary of Scottish Business Biography 1860–1960. Vol. 2: Processing, Distribution, Services* (Aberdeen, 1990), pp. 42–4. In 1913 Mrs Greville owned 33,000 shares (66 per cent), the Youngers 14,000 (28 per cent), and the executive directors 3,000 (6 per cent). In 1924 Mrs Greville transferred 1,000 of her shares to additional executive directors. McEwan Share Registers, 1913, *et seq.* SN/M/8/10/23, 24, SBA.

[28] McEwan Private Minute Book 1918, Record of Salaries, 2 March 1920, SN/M/5/9, and Board Minutes, 21 October 1924, SN/M/5/2/1, SBA. On Mrs Greville's social life, and, in particular, her friendship with King Edward VII, George V and VI, and the Duke and Duchess of Windsor, see *inter alia*, Sir Philip Magnus, *King Edward the Seventh* (1964), p. 317, S. E. D. Fortescue, *People and Places, Great and Little Bookham* (1978), pp. 67–70, and Sir Osbert Sitwell, *Laughter in the Next Room* (1949), pp. 43–5, 155–8.

[29] In fact, the first 'outsider' was Hugh Peacock of Soames, a Spalding brewery taken over by Steward & Patteson in 1949. Gourvish, *Norfolk Beers*, pp. 69, 125, 152–5.

in 1920 and 1955, derived from the *Manual of British Brewery Companies*. The Mitchell and Butler families, for example, retained four seats on the board of Mitchells & Butlers in the two years analysed, although their potential voting strength was weakened by an increase in the size of the board from nine to thirteen members. The Barclays and the Perkins held four directorships in Barclay Perkins, where there was a board of eight in 1920, and three in a board of eleven in 1955.[30] At Guinness, the eleven-strong board of 1920 contained four members of the family; in 1955 there were five in a board of thirteen, three of them women.[31] In some companies representation was increased. Thus, the Riley-Smiths provided only one of the five directors of John Smith's (Tadcaster) in 1920, but two of the six in 1955, and there were similar increases in the participation of the Boddington and Tetley families in their companies.[32] At Whitbread & Co., three members of the Whitbread family were on the board in 1920 and 1955, while the total number of directors fell from ten to seven. However, the essential point is that the company was structured around a set of partnerships, as it had been in the nineteenth century, involving the Whitbread, Martineau and Godman families, among others. On this basis the Whitbread board was composed almost entirely of founding family members, and the only 'outsider' to be recruited was Sydney Nevile, who joined the company in 1919.[33]

In other companies the participation of the founding family or families declined, either for personal reasons, such as the lack of suitable heirs, or for business reasons, including the disruption caused by financial crisis or takeover by another brewery or, more positively, as a result of substantial expansion. The lack of heirs, coupled with the willingness to recruit managers as directors, weakened the family presence in William McEwan, J. W. Green of Luton, and Bristol Brewery Georges, for example, while financial and/or merger elements had the same effect

[30] *Manual of British Brewery Companies*, 1921, 1956. The Woodhouses held all four seats on the board of Hall & Woodhouse in 1920, and four out of five in 1955; the Russells provided three of the four directors of Russells & Wrangham in 1920, two of five in 1955.

[31] Maureen, Marchioness of Dufferin and Ava, the Lady Patricia Lennox-Boyd, and the Lady Honor Svejdar. *Manual*, 1956. In the 200+ companies which issued balance sheets in 1920 and 1955, there were five and seventeen female directors respectively.

[32] The Boddington family provided three of the five directors in 1920, four of five in 1955, while the Tetleys provided four of the five directors of Joshua Tetley in 1920, six of nine in 1955. *Manual*, 1921, 1956.

[33] *Ibid.* and information in Whitbread Archive.

at Allsopp, Arrol, Colchester, Style & Winch and Tamplin.[34] Of course, the reduced participation of founding families could be made up by recruiting an extended family – nephews, cousins, in-laws – or by adding representatives of breweries which had been acquired. Greene King provides a very good example of the way in which a family-dominated board could be maintained by this means. The Greenes and the Kings provided three of the seven directors in 1920 and only one, the chairman, Sir Edward Greene, in 1955. However, with the addition of the Lakes (related to the Greenes), the Bridges (related to the Kings), the Clarkes and the Olivers (whose breweries had been acquired in 1917 and 1919 respectively), all seven directors could be regarded as 'family' in 1920, and seven of the nine could be so regarded in 1955. Only two were 'outsiders' in the mid-1950s: T. H. Veasey, family solicitor to the Simpsons of Baldock, whose brewery was purchased by Greene King in 1954; and General Sir Miles Dempsey, chairman of H. & G. Simonds of Reading, who joined the board in 1953 at Sir Edward Greene's request, and was to play an important part in preserving the company's independence.[35] Indeed, the role of 'outsiders' acting as 'insiders' in family-run breweries should not be underestimated, as is demonstrated by the contribution of directors such as Lt. Col. George B. Winch of Style & Winch, who on the acquisition of his brewery by Barclay Perkins in 1929 joined the latter's board and exerted a considerable influence on company policy in the 1930s.[36] Nevertheless, continuity of direction was the most marked feature of brewing. An analysis of the composition of the representative companies' boards in 1920, 1938/9 and 1955 reveals that no less than 42 per cent of the directors of 1920 remained in post in 1938/9, while 35 per cent of the directors of 1938/9 were still on the board in 1955. A dozen directors served throughout the period. They included the redoubtable Sir Sydney Nevile of Whitbread; Rupert Guinness, 2nd Earl of Iveagh, chairman of Guinness, 1927–62; Major C. A. C. Perkins of Barclay Perkins; F. G. Brakspear; Sir

[34] *Manual*, 1921, 1956. Arrol was acquired by Allsopp in 1930, Allsopp merged with Ind Coope in 1934, Ind Coope gained control of Colchester in 1925, Barclay Perkins bought Style & Winch in 1929, and Watney Combe Reid acquired Tamplin in 1953.

[35] *Ibid.* and Wilson, *Greene King*, pp. 166–8, 186–7, 225–6, 229, 321n.

[36] On Winch's efforts as deputy-chairman and joint managing director to reform Barclay Perkins's management and brewing strategy see, *inter alia*, his confidential 136-page report of 31 October 1936, and references to his earlier efforts, e.g. in June 1931, in a report by H. L. Grimston of June 1939, Acc. 2305/1/132/10/1, and 1/131/3, GLRO. Winch was Chairman of the Brewers' Society, 1925–7.

Edward Greene; and Col. Charles H. Tetley, chairman of Joshua Tetley, 1934–53.[37]

This is not to conclude that there was anything particularly exceptional in such tales of long service in British brewing, nor to argue that continuity at board level prevented management change. Continuity of leadership at the top was evident in several branches of British manufacturing, for example in industries such as steel and hosiery and, indeed, in American manufacturing.[38] Of course, where family participation encouraged such a continuity, it produced enterprises which were scarcely a fertile environment for innovation and organisational change; but this does not mean that long-serving directors produced a complete ossification of organisation and management practices. In the first place, there was a variety of corporate experiences. Continuity of direction, while strong in companies such as Whitbread and Joshua Tetley, for example, was much weaker in others, including Meux, Colchester, Newcastle and McEwan.[39] Second, and more importantly, changes in the composition of the boards were evident in most companies, whether the turnover of directors was high or low. A calculation based on information on over 200 companies identified by the *Manual of Brewery Companies* (section I) as issuing balance sheets reveals a tendency for boards to become larger and to recruit more and more managers as executive or managing directors. The average size of a brewing company board increased from 4.6 directors in 1919 to 5.9 in 1954; the number of companies with a board of ten or more increased from one (Whitbread) to twelve; the proportion of companies with named managing directors almost doubled from 33 to 62 per cent; and the proportion identifying head-brewers as directors increased from nil to 22 per cent.[40]

The statistics, then, suggest that there were some very real changes in the way brewery companies were organised at the top. The use of

[37] *Manual*, 1921, 1939/40, 1956 (data for twenty-five companies (Allsopp = Ind Coope & Allsopp, 1939/40, 1956; Arrol excluded in 1956); Nevile, *Seventy Rolling Years*; Lackey, *Quality Pays*, p. 122; Sheppard, *Brakspear's*, pp. 86–7; *Who Was Who*.

[38] Cf. Charlotte Erickson, *British Industrialists: Steel and Hosiery, 1850–1950* (Cambridge, 1959), pp. 77, 137. Erickson found that in steel leaders in office in 1905–25 had on average seventeen years at the top, and in 1935–47 fifteen years; in hosiery those in office in 1930 were at the top for an average of 18.5 years.

[39] *Manual*, 1921, 1939/40, 1956.

[40] *Ibid.* 1920, 1955. The number of companies surveyed was 226 and 206 respectively. A caveat needs to be inserted with the results. The fact that a company did not identify a director as a managing director or identify a director as a head brewer does not *prove* that such figures were absent. Nevertheless, the change in *Manual* listings does provide a lower-bound estimate of the shift in emphasis.

managing directors and the recruitment of senior executives to the board were not new elements in the 1920s, of course. Before the First World War Whitbread had six managing directors, Guinness four, and they could be found listed in medium-sized concerns such as Bristol Brewery Georges. But on the whole these executive directors, who took responsibility for broad areas of the business – raw material purchasing, production, distribution and so on – were drawn from the ranks of the founding families, indicating, as Chandler suggests, a perpetuation of 'personal' or 'partnership management'. In many companies this tradition persisted. At Whitbread, for example, five of the six managing directors were recruited from the families in the inter-war years, although they included managers with some experience outside the industry. Percival Grundy came to Whitbread in 1889 after working as a clerk in the Bank of England; he became secretary in 1896, and joined the board ten years later. Cecil Lubbock worked in the civil service after an education at Eton and Trinity College, Oxford before becoming a Whitbread director in 1901.[41] In several companies it was the practice of the leading family director to combine the posts of chairman and managing director, as, for example, William Younger at McEwan (1913–24), and Robert Boddington at Boddingtons' (1908–30).[42]

What is apparent, however, is that after the First World War in particular there was an increase in the number of managing directors drawn from outside the ranks of the founding companies, and often from outside the company, and that the process involved the injection of a greater professionalisation in executive management. The introduction of trained brewers, secretaries, lawyers and, later, accountants to brewing boards gave companies more of the skills necessary to the effective supervision of a modern business enterprise. It helped to broaden horizons which, for many family brewers, were shaped by a

[41] *House of Whitbread*, June and December 1921, October 1931, October 1933, W&Co. Cecil Lubbock was a director of numerous concerns, including (in 1920) the Bank of England, Northern Assurance, Provident Accident & Guarantee, and the Hudson's Bay Co. *Directory of Directors*, 1921.

[42] Robert Slater Boddington (1862–1930) was a director for forty-seven years and managing director for forty-two years (salary in 1919: £1,500 p.a.); William Younger (1857–1925), a founding director of William McEwan, was effectively in charge of the company from 1902 (salary £3,000, from 1919 £5,000). Jacobson, *200 Years of Beer*, pp. 63–4, 66; Ian Donnachie, 'William Younger', in Slaven and Checkland (eds.), *Dictionary of Scottish Business Biography*, p. 78; *Brewing Trade Review*, October 1925, p. 397; McEwan Private Minute Book, SN/M/5/9, SBA; Boddingtons' Salary Book, 1919, 405/23, W&Co.

classical education at a major or minor public school and a fleeting association with the sporting and social joys, as well as the intellectual challenge, of an Oxbridge college. Above all, a wider recruitment in management helped to resolve the problem of succession in many an established family firm in the doldrums. This phenomenon was not unique to brewing. As Donald Coleman has shown in his history of the textile firm, Courtaulds, succession problems in the 1890s were largely resolved by the appointment of two able managers from outside the family and company. Henry Tetley and Thomas Latham went on to dominate Courtaulds for the next quarter-century.[43] In the brewing industry this solution was anticipated in some of the major and emerging companies. Before 1914 Guinness had appointed a managing director from outside the family – first C. D. La Touche (1902–13), then Col. H. W. Renny-Tailyour (1913–19) – and up to four assistant managing directors, most of them outsiders. The practice continued under C. E. Sutton (managing director, 1919–27), T. B. Case (1927–41), C. J. Newbold (1941–6) and Sir Hugh Beaver (1946–60). Together the managing director and his assistants formed a group of executive directors – in essence an executive board – which met much more regularly than the full board and effectively ran the company.[44] The managing directors' backgrounds were diverse. La Touche had been a brewer, Renny-Tailyour an engineer, and Sutton a partner in a firm of Dublin solicitors. Case and Newbold were products of Guinness's policy of recruiting Oxbridge science graduates to the Dublin brewhouse from the 1890s. Beaver, who was arguably the most gifted and certainly the most distinguished of the six managers, joined the company in 1945 after a successful career as a consulting engineer (he was a partner in Sir Alexander Gibb & Partners) and a key wartime position as Director-General of the Ministry of Works (1940–5).[45]

Other companies also turned to outsiders to fill leading managerial positions before 1914. Barclay Perkins may have been run as a family business, with two of its pre-incorporation partners of the 1890s serving

[43] D. C. Coleman, 'Sir Thomas Paul Latham' and 'Henry Greenwood Tetley', in David J. Jeremy and C. Shaw (eds.), *Dictionary of Business Biography*, III (1985), pp. 662–4, V (1986), pp. 470–2.

[44] Dennison and MacDonagh, 'History of Guinness'. Newbold was Chairman of the Brewers' Society, 1942–5.

[45] Beaver (1890–1967) was educated at Wellington College. He was a founding member of the Council of the British Institute of Management in 1950 and chairman in 1951–4. In 1957–9 he was president of the FBI. Ibid.; Tom Corran, 'Sir Hugh Eyre Campbell Beaver', Jeremy and Shaw, *DBB*, I, (1984), pp. 234–6; *Brewing Trade Review*, January 1950, p. 95; Beaver papers, MSS. 200/F/3/P5/11/1, MRC.

as directors from the company's foundation in 1896 until 1948 and 1950 respectively.[46] But it also appointed its secretary, Edward Giffard, managing director in 1902, a post he combined with that of chairman from 1908 to 1933. Subsequent executive directors included H. L. Grimston, a managing director from 1918 to 1946; R. W. R. Law, the company's head-brewer from 1920, who was a director in the period 1934–47; and Col. T. B. Bunting, a chartered accountant who became secretary in 1931 and in 1945 joined the board to take charge of sales to the free trade.[47] In Bristol, Georges Brewery was effectively managed by executives turned directors both before and after the First World War. The locus of power was not immediately clear from the register of directors. A member of the George family acted as chairman for most of the company's existence, with Christopher George holding the position from 1919 to 1952. But the real authority lay elsewhere. The estate manager, Wilfrid Bisdee, became a director in 1891 and, with the head-brewer Arthur Terry, acted as joint managing director from 1907. Appointed sole managing director in 1913, Bisdee dominated the company's strategic decision-making until 1929.[48] He was quickly followed by Arthur Hadley, who had come to Georges in 1908 after a pupillage at Mitchells & Butlers and practical experience of two other breweries. Head-brewer from 1913, he became a director in 1927 and joint managing director two years' later. From 1932 to 1948 he combined the posts of head-brewer and sole managing director, dominating the company's affairs very much as Bisdee had done (Plate 49). His son, Arthur Cecil, who had become a director in 1941, succeeded him in two posts and went on to act as chairman and managing director from 1953 to 1961, when the company was taken over by Courage, Barclay & Simonds.[49]

[46] The two long-serving directors were Lt.-Col. H. F. Barclay, partner 1892, director 1896, chairman, Brewers' Society, 1913–14, died 1948; and Granville Bevan, a direct descendant of Sylvanus Bevan, partner in the brewery in 1772–1801, who was a partner 1890, director 1896, and died in 1950. There was also Major Charles A. C. Perkins (1875–1960). Educated at Eton, he joined the brewery company in 1892 and was a director from 1902 to 1955 and managing director, 1933–48. *Courage & Barclay Journal*, April 1960, p. 10.

[47] Grimston was head of 'town trade', 1917, an assistant managing director, 1918–33, and managing director, 1933–46. Law was also chairman and managing director of Plymouth Breweries, 1938–71. Bunting was chairman of the Brewers' Society 1961–3. Barclay Perkins, Reports for AGMs, 1930–54, *passim*, Board Minutes, 14 December 1916, 3 January 1918, 23 March 1933, 24 January 1946, Acc. 2305/1/12, 23, 28, GLRO.

[48] *Western Daily Press*, 17 September 1952, Courage plc archive; Channon, 'Georges and Brewing in Bristol', 173.

[49] Bristol Brewery Georges Board Minutes, 12 November 1908, 2 October 1941, 35740/BG/9(c) and (m); Salary Books, 1924–48, BG/22(b) and (c), Bristol Record Office; Reports & Accounts, 1940–60, Reports, *passim*, CA/C/1, Courage plc; *Brewing Trade Review*, February 1949, p. 129.

Our case-studies indicate that increasingly recourse was made to this modified form of family management. At J. W. Green of Luton the transfer of power from family to professional management was more clear-cut. The founder of the business, John William Green, bought the brewery in 1869 when he was only 22 years of age. On the firm's incorporation in 1897 he took the chair, a position he held until his retirement in 1930. His sons, Sidney (1930–2) and Harold (1932–5, 1935–7, 1942–4) enjoyed brief spells at the top and a grandson, Col. J. B. S. Tabor, joined the board in 1932 and became a joint managing director in 1935, a post he held for some twenty-five years. But in 1935 the company was reconstituted as a public company with an expanded capital, the move forced by the Green family's financial problems after the founder's death in 1932. The change brought with it a larger, more professional, board. Three managing directors were appointed: Tabor; W. W. Merchant, the long-serving brewery manager, who had become a director in 1917 and had managed the business since 1930; and Percival Lovell, secretary since 1926 and a director from 1932. They were soon joined by a 'new blood' appointee, Bernard Dixon, the company's head-brewer since 1932.[50] Over the next twenty years, before J. W. Green experienced a further reorganisation by merging with Flower & Sons of Stratford-upon-Avon in 1954, these three executive directors dominated the management. Merchant was chairman and joint managing director from 1937 until his death in 1942; Lovell was secretary and joint managing director, 1935–44 and a director until 1954; and Dixon, ultimately the most influential of the three, became a managing director in 1940 and acted as chairman and joint managing director (with Tabor) from 1947 to 1954, continuing in these posts with the reorganised company, Flowers Breweries, until ousted by the Flowers faction in 1958 (see pp. 490–2). Under Dixon's leadership the company anticipated later trends in the industry by embarking upon an aggressive policy of brewery acquisitions and launching a new product, carbonated and filtered 'keg' beer. Dixon had ambitions to turn Green's into a national brewing concern. He made it clear that while the strategic direction of the company remained in his hands, he needed able

[50] J. W. Green Board Minutes, 25 September 1917, 22 August 1930, 29 September and 23 November 1932, 3 June, 11 September and 26 November 1935; Report to AGM, 14 December 1932, 75/1, 3–5, W&Co.; *The Times*, 12 December 1935. Tabor, educated at Malvern and Pembroke College, became a pupil in 1929. He was a joint managing director from 1935 to 1967, and was chairman of Flowers for a few months before his death in July 1967: Flowers Breweries Board Minutes, 27 April 1967, 74/5, *Whitbread News*, August 1967, W&Co.

lieutenants to support him. In his chairman's statement of 1952 he declared that the promotion of executives to board level was a conscious company policy. It ensured 'that the Group has always available a cadre of young executives of proven worth and with the necessary knowledge of all departments to make certain of continuity of management of the type required for the successful administration of a company of this kind'.[51]

There were many companies like J. W. Green which made the transition from a family-based to a more professional top management in the period 1914–55. In the process, a number of major business leaders emerged. Some of them, men such as Nevile, Giffard, Beaver (see above) and Sir Richard Garton (Watney Combe Reid), joined leading family brewers such as Francis Pelham Whitbread and Sir William Waters Butler (Mitchells & Butlers) in not only successfully managing their companies but also acting as spokesmen for the industry.[52] Others became more prominent by assuming managerial responsibility for more than one brewery. This caught the eye in an industry where multiple directorships were comparatively rare (excepting those which came naturally with loose mergers such as Bass/Worthington and Barclay Perkins/Style & Winch or the establishment of subsidiary companies). Two of the early figures of this kind were, interestingly, both chartered accountants by training. James H. Stephens of Meux had a wide range of interests. In 1920 he was also a director of the Bath, Border, Cornbrook and Tadcaster Tower breweries, as well as the Yorkshire Insurance Co. and the British & North European Bank. In the mid 1930s, towards the end of his career, he was chairman of Meux and Cornbrook, vice-chairman of Booth's Distilleries, chairman of Burberry and Colonial Wharves, and a director of Lanarkshire Steel and numerous hotel concerns, including the Ritz, the Carlton and the Hyde Park.[53]

51 Bernard Dixon, Statement for J. W. Green AGM, 18 December 1952, 75/1; Board Minutes, 21 April 1937, 13 November 1940, 11 February 1942, 12 April 1944, 75/5, 6, W&Co. Dixon had been head-brewer at Greene King's Panton (Cambridge) brewery when the company won the Champion Challenge Cup at the Brewers' Exhibition of 1931. He pioneered a number of technical developments, including enzymic malt and the Redox tank treatment system: Wilson, *Greene King*, p. 321n.; Bass, File on 'Flowers', 1955, Cape Hill, Birmingham.

52 Kevin Hawkins, 'Sir William Waters Butler', Tom Corran, 'Sir Richard Charles Garton', and David J. Jeremy, 'Francis Pelham Whitbread', in Jeremy and Shaw, *DBB*, I (1984), pp. 533–5, II (1984), pp. 491–3, and V (1986), pp. 769–74. Garton (1857–1934) was educated at Owen's College, Manchester, and Marburg University. He joined the Watney board in 1902 and was chairman, 1928–32 and deputy-chairman, 1932–4.

53 James Henry Stephens (1862–1937): *Directory of Directors*, 1921, 1936; *Who Was Who*.

Frank (later Sir Frank) Nicholson, the managing director of C. Vaux (later Vaux & Associated Breweries), was another accountant-turned-brewer with wider interests. In 1920 he was also chairman and managing director of Lorimer & Clark of Edinburgh, and a director of a number of non-brewing companies; in the mid 1930s he was also deputy-chairman of Ind Coope & Allsopp and a director of some of its subsidiaries, including Allsopp and Arrol.[54] Later, Harry Bradfer-Lawrence of Hammond's Bradford Brewery, and two directors of Greene King, General Sir Miles Dempsey (see above) and Harold Lake, had similar responsibilities. Bradfer-Lawrence, a chartered land agent from Norfolk, moved to Ripon and became managing director of Hammond's in 1935. He proved to be an early enthusiast of growth by merger. As acting chairman from 1942, and chairman and joint managing director two years later, he widened the company's horizons by organising a series of takeovers. In 1946 the company changed its name to Hammonds United to mark his success in making two sizeable acquisitions: Bentley & Shaw of Huddersfield; and the Tadcaster Tower Brewery. But he was also a director of both Ind Coope & Allsopp and Vaux & Associated Breweries and of Guardian Assurance.[55] Of the Greene King directors, Dempsey, as we have already noted, was chairman of H. & G. Simonds (1953–63); from 1955 to 1969 he was also chairman of Greene King.[56] Lake's range of interests was one of the most extensive in the industry. Son of E. W. Lake and younger brother of E. L. D. Lake, he was educated at Uppingham and Oriel College, Oxford, and practised as a solicitor at Lincoln's Inn before training as a brewer at Rayment in 1912. In 1914 he joined Greene King, becoming secretary in 1919 and a director three years later. After finding his sphere of influence confined by his brother's position as managing director, he left Bury in 1937 to take up the post of assistant managing director at Benskin's of Watford. In 1939 he became chairman and managing director of Morland of Abingdon, and was also appointed to the boards of Wilson's (Manchester) and the Cheltenham Original

[54] Frank Nicholson (1875–1952), Kt. 1943, chairman, Brewers' Society, 1921–5 and 1930–1: *Directory of Directors*, 1921, 1936, 1951, *Who Was Who*.

[55] Bradfer-Lawrence (1887–1965) was chairman of the Brewers' Society, 1957–8. Hammonds signed a reciprocal trading agreement with Ind Coope in 1948. Hammonds Bradford Brewery/Hammonds United Board Minutes, 30 May 1935, 21 May 1936, 27 June 1940, 17 December 1942, 26 June 1944, Bass North, Leeds; *Directory of Directors*, 1951; *Brewing Trade Review*, November 1965, p. 679; Hawkins, *Bass Charrington*, pp. 99–100, 124.

[56] Dempsey (1896–1969) was also deputy-chairman of Courage, Barclay & Simonds, 1961–6 after the merger of 1960. Wilson, *Greene King*, p. 321n.

Brewery (later Cheltenham & Hereford). Reappointed a Greene King director in 1947 after his brother's death, he was, in the early to mid 1950s, chairman of Morland, Cheltenham & Hereford and Wilson & Walker, and a director of the latter's subsidiaries, Manchester Breweries, Wilson's and Walker & Homfrays.[57]

These 'interlocking' directorships were essentially personal in character, although some of the arrangements indicated an informal understanding between the breweries concerned, which sometimes culminated in a formal merger (Lorimer & Clark was acquired by Vaux in 1946, for example). But at the very end of our period there were the first signs of more formal, institutionalised interlocking agreements, and a quite new phenomenon in brewing, the hostile takeover bid. By 1955, when merger activity began to accelerate, some of the smaller breweries, especially those sitting on under-valued, under-utilised assets, expressed concern that predatory bids, particularly from non-brewing interests, might threaten their independent existence. A number of them actively sought an alliance with a larger brewer who would agree to provide a measure of protection and preserve the *status quo*. In 1955 Strong of Romsey, Morland (Abingdon), Norman & Pring of Exeter, and Cheltenham & Hereford Breweries aligned themselves with Whitbread in this way. Whitbread purchased a significant bloc of shares and obtained representation on the boards of directors. The chairman, Col. W. H. Whitbread, became a director of all four companies. Subsequently, the process was repeated several times. The Annual Report for 1956, produced in May 1957, referred to six more companies as being associated with it: Andrew Buchan's of Rhymney, Dutton's Blackburn Brewery, Marston, Thompson & Evershed of Burton, the Stroud Brewery, Tennant Brothers of Sheffield, and G. Ruddle of Oakham. The company also had investments in several other breweries, including Courage & Barclay, Hammonds, Hope & Anchor, Newcastle and Truman.[58] This, then, was the origin of what became known as the 'Whitbread umbrella' (see Plate 51). The small companies hoped that

57 Lake (1882–1960) was chairman of the Brewers' Society, 1951–2. *Directory of Directors*, 1956; Wilson, *Greene King*, pp. 215–16, 321n.

58 Strong & Co. Board Minutes, 17 February 1955, 324/122, Whitbread & Co., Directors' Report, AGM for 1956, p. 4, W/8/97, Norman & Pring, Register of Directors, 1948–55, 55/20, Dutton's Register of Directors, 1908–66, 175/15, Cheltenham & Hereford Board Minutes, 30 December 1955, 121/7, Stroud Brewery Board Minutes, 1 February 1957, 149/52, W&Co.; *Brewery Manual*, 1956; Hawkins, *Bass Charrington*, pp. 116–17; *Investors' Chronicle*, 7 and 14 January, 12 May 1956; pp. 11, 127, 457; 22 February and 1 March 1957, pp. 577, 658; *The Times*, 9 March 1957, p. 12; *The Economist*, 23 March and 13 July 1957, pp. 1,016–17, 156–7.

Whitbread would prove to be a bulwark against unwelcome takeover bids, and although this appears to have been the case the situation also made it more likely that the companies would be swallowed up by Whitbread itself. In fact, the 'umbrella' was the mechanism by which Whitbread eventually transformed itself from a company with a strong base in London and the South-East into a truly national giant (see Chapter 11).

In 1955 Whitbread's activities were still very much the exception to the rule. Brewing boards were predominantly local and where multiple directorships occurred they were confined in the main to control of direct subsidiaries. It should not be assumed that all brewers were parochial to the extent of eschewing non-brewing interests. The lists of directors of our twenty-five selected companies show that about 30 per cent of the directors held non-brewing directorships, a proportion which remained remarkably constant over the three years analysed: 1920, 1938/9 and 1955. Banking, insurance and investment trusts were favoured, some of these linkages owing their origins to family-based business activities of long vintage – for example, Barclay Perkins and Barclays Bank, Steward & Patteson and the Norwich Union, Cameron and Ellerman Lines, Debenture Securities Investment and the London General Investment Trust.[59] Some brewing directors sat on the boards of several companies. James Davenport of Allsopp was a director of fifteen other companies in 1920, and seventeen in 1938/9 (Plate 46); in 1955 H. Davenport Price of Cameron sat on twenty-six other boards, Ronald Nutting of Guinness on twenty-four, and W. L. Barrows (Mitchells & Butlers) on sixteen.[60] Impressive as these portfolios were,

[59] Note L. E. D. Bevan and Barclays Bank (1955), George Morse, C. H. Finch and Norwich Union (1920), Sir John Ellerman and later Cameron directors and Ellerman Lines, Debenture Securities Investment, and London General Investment Trust (1920–55). Other banking links included Guinness and the Bank of England, Royal Bank of Scotland (1920), Whitbread and Bank of England (1920), Barclay Perkins and Westminster, Meux and Lloyds and Midland, Ind Coope and Midland, Bass and National Provincial (1955).

[60] James Davenport (1875–1945) was well known in the City. Secretary from 1908 of the Brewery Investment Trust, he was in the 1930s managing director of one of the leading financial trust companies, General Investors & Trustees, and also of Cardinal Investment Trust. A director of Samuel Allsopp, 1913–34, he remained on the board of its subsidiary, Allsopp Brewery Investments, after 1934, and was a director of numerous companies including Nitrate Securities Trust, Spiers & Pond, Singapore Traction, Lothbury Assets & Land, and Egyptian Consolidated Lands. H. Davenport Price (1890–1958), was a solicitor and director of publishing and investment companies; William L. Barrows (1905–76) was a chartered accountant, and partner in Howard Smith Thompson (Birmingham and London) and Price Waterhouse; A. R. Nutting (1888–1964), educated at Eton and Trinity Hall, Oxford, was governor of the Bank of Ireland, 1926–30 and chairman of Westinghouse Brake & Signal Co. 1944–62. *Who Was Who*; *Directory of Directors*.

they were not typical of the industry as a whole. Even in our twenty-five company selection, which contains a bias in favour of the larger companies, 70 per cent of all directors confined their activities to their own companies.

III

Given the evidence of a change to a more executive management style, how far was it accompanied by operational innovations in managerial hierarchies (if that is not too pretentious a term in view of the relatively small staffs needed to run an average brewery)? This question is by no means easy to answer with confidence. Brewing archives, like many other business records, do not easily lend themselves to such an analysis, and existing company histories often skate over the issue or imply that a rather crude, personal style of management persisted with little alteration until the 1960s. Kevin Hawkins's book on *Bass Charrington* is a good example. Critical of the merger of Bass and Worthington in 1927 as 'the biggest non-merger in the history of the brewing industry', he explains that 'the two companies continued to run more or less independently of each other', but nowhere does he tell us exactly how Bass and Worthington managed the production, distribution and sale of their beers. The precise nature of their managerial hierarchies, the directors' areas of responsibility, the functions and status of the salaried staffs, the reporting lines and the control of managers and agents in the breweries' national distribution networks, the presence (or absence) of accounting and financial expertise in decision-making and control systems – all remain a mystery.[61] Admittedly, this agenda is a considerable one, and to generalise with authority about the industry as a whole, having first investigated in depth the management structure and operations of several companies, is, given the present state of knowledge, beyond the scope of this book.

Nevertheless, some clear pointers to brewing's organisation and management do emerge from a more modest study of our representative companies. For example, Barclay Perkins provides a number of insights into the strengths and weaknesses of a larger metropolitan brewery in the period to the mid-1950s. On the one hand, there is evidence of a relatively sophisticated grasp of the realities of operating below capacity

[61] Hawkins, *Bass Charrington*, pp. 89–90. What is needed is something for Britain to complement the American work of R. Beniger, *The Control Revolution* (Cambridge, Mass., 1986) and JoAnne Yates, *Control through Communication* (Baltimore, 1989).

in the depressed demand conditions of the inter-war years, and an awareness that the merger with Style & Winch in 1929 offered opportunities to concentrate resources and effect economies. On the other hand, there was little dynamism at the top to drive radical policies home, and there was much to criticise in the company's internal arrangements. The details are as follows. Having merged with Style & Winch and its associated companies, Dartford Brewery and the Royal Brewery, Brentford, Barclay Perkins now faced the problem of running both its antiquated Southwark brewery and Style & Winch's Maidstone brewery below capacity. The new board, influenced by activists such as Col. G. B. Winch and H. L. Grimston, sought ways of reducing costs and at the same time improving the quality of the brewing plant. Winch, in particular, argued that opportunities to capitalise on the merger were being missed, and pressed for a radical solution to brewing over-capacity.[62] In 1931 London Press Exchange were employed as consultants to evaluate Barclay Perkins's sales organisation, and four years later Price Waterhouse, the company's auditors, were asked to investigate the entire organisational structure of the four constituent companies, focusing in particular upon the advantages and disadvantages of a full centralisation of brewing. Two schemes – one to brew at Southwark, the other to brew at Maidstone – were then assessed.[63] Shortly afterwards, Barclay Perkins entered into negotiations with J. J. Calder, joint managing director of Ind Coope & Allsopp (which controlled Arrol of Alloa), with a view to concentrating the two companies' lager production at Alloa.[64] Winch also produced, in 1936, a lengthy report which not only evaluated a number of bold strategic options for Barclay Perkins, including the buying-in of beer from another London brewer and the possibility of another merger, but also made numerous detailed suggestions for tighter control of costs.[65] The sophistication of this work

[62] H. L. Grimston, Report to Barclay Perkins Chairman and Directors, June 1939 (refers to Winch in 1931), Acc. 2305/1/131/3, Barclay Perkins Board Minutes, 20 June 1935, Acc. 2305/1/24, GLRO.

[63] London Press Exchange, Report on 'Barclay Perkins & Co. Sales Organisation', June 1931, Acc. 2305/1/130/4; Price Waterhouse, Report on 'Organisation, including Concentration of Brewing', 24 May 1935, 1/133/7/1–3; Barclay Perkins Board Minutes, 17 October 1935, Managing Directors' Committee Minutes, 16 December 1935, 1/24, 25/1; Sub-Committee Minutes and Reports, 1935–6, 1/133/6, 1/61, GLRO. Price Waterhouse had already been asked in 1931 to adjudicate on bottling charges to constituent companies: Barclay Perkins Board Minutes, 19 March and 2 April 1931, Acc. 2305/1/22, GLRO.

[64] Barclay Perkins Managing Directors' Committee Minutes, 20 December 1937, Acc. 2305/1/25/1; J. J. Calder–G. B. Winch, 6 July 1939, and Report on 'Proposed Amalgamation of Lager Interests', 11 July 1939, 1/131/1/1, 2, GLRO.

[65] G. B. Winch, confidential report, 31 October 1936, cit.

is not in doubt. Policy options were carefully evaluated with a full analysis of alternative production and distribution costs, and some calculations were produced by accountants acting as consultants.[66]

However, for all this effort, and the appointment of numerous investigative sub-committees, little was done. The company, after taking advice from Barings, realised that the financing of a completely new brewery in the late 1930s would be difficult. Most of the reports were then shelved.[67] Furthermore, the consultants' investigations revealed how the company actually operated behind the rhetoric and ambition of its more dynamic directors. There was much to support the view that Barclay Perkins was still operating with 'partnership management'. The various departments – tied trade, free trade, exports, bottling, etc. – operated on a personal management basis as self-contained units with reporting lines blurred by the joint responsibility of executive directors and heads of department. As Price Waterhouse noted, 'the various departments are conducted almost as a set of independent concerns with little or no regard to the interests of the Company as a whole'.[68] Not for the first or last time, the consultants pressed the company to issue an organisational chart.[69] Opportunities for rationalisation were also being missed. Both London Press Exchange and Price Waterhouse criticised Barclay Perkins for a product range that was too large in relation to sales volume. The company (excluding Style & Winch, etc.) supplied about 360 tied public houses in the mid-1930s, mainly in the London area, but distributed no less than sixteen different ales and sixteen bottled beer brands, together with seven 'foreign' beers (Guinness, etc.). Of these the 5d Mild Ale represented 31 per cent of total production of about 296,000 barrels, while all milds accounted for 44 per cent of the total. Style & Winch, on the other hand, brewed only eight beers. The company had 1,650 free-trade customers on its books, but the average trade was small, and expansion was inhibited by the use of independent bottling agents, who handled the product lines of several brewers.[70] The only real improvement to come from the merger before the Second World War was the decision to supply the London trade of

66 Barclay Perkins Board Minutes, 28 January 1937, Managing Directors' Committee Minutes, 30 December 1937, Acc. 2305/1/25/1; Mason & Co. (chartered accountants specialising in breweries), Report on 'Cost of Brewing 500,000 barrels at Maidstone', 16 May 1939, 1/132/7; Price Waterhouse-Grimston, 17 July 1939, 1/132/6/2, GLRO.

67 Barclay Perkins Board Minutes, 17 October 1935, 19 March 1936, Managing Directors' Committee Minutes, 30 December 1937, Acc. 2305/1/24, 25/1, GLRO.

68 Price Waterhouse, Report, p. 27.

69 London Press Exchange, Report, p. 4.

70 *Ibid.*, pp. 5ff.; Price Waterhouse Report, 1935, Exhibit 2, Acc. 2305/1/133/7/3, GLRO.

the constituent companies from one source: Southwark for beer, Battersea for wines and spirits. Otherwise, organisational separation was maintained, with the retention of four boards of directors.[71]

A similar mix of elements existed at Whitbread. That the company possessed competence and imagination at the top is not in doubt, as the contributions of Sydney Nevile and, later, Col. W. H. Whitbread and F. O. A. G. Bennett demonstrate. That the business presented a considerable organisational challenge as it grew from the 1920s is also not in doubt. By the mid-1950s the company owned about 850 public houses, distributed bottled beer nationally via its forty depots to 65,000 retail outlets, and exported to sixty countries.[72] But the way in which the directors ran the business differed little from that of Barclay Perkins, as Nevile discovered when he joined the company in 1919, and as later management papers reveal. With little formal education – he became a pupil brewer at the age of 14 – Nevile was appointed to a board dominated by four old Etonians. He found a distinct emphasis upon 'historic methods and usages'. The practice of recruiting junior directors from the owning families was maintained in the inter-war years and beyond. And the Kent companies acquired by merger in the late 1920s – Frederick Leney, Jude Hanbury and Mackeson – enjoyed a fair measure of autonomy in matters of brewing and public house management.[73]

As at Barclay Perkins, Whitbread took steps to modify the organisation in response to expanded operations and management anxieties in the 1920s. In 1927, with trade at a low ebb, Nevile argued vigorously for an improvement in the selling and public house management functions. J. S. Eagles, general manager of the Carlisle State Brewery, was then appointed to advise on the supervision of pubs and on the retail organisation generally. At the same time, Whitbread followed Nevile's recommendation that financial advice was required and engaged Mason & Co. to act as financial consultants.[74] Ten years later he pressed for the establishment of an additional directors' meeting. The intention here was to give the managing directors time to 'discuss without interruption

[71] Price Waterhouse Report, 1935, p. 29. On the company's position at the time of the merger with Courage in 1955 – it owned 1,034 pubs by this time, for example – see Peat Marwick Mitchell, Report, 21 March 1955, Acc. 2305/8/42/1, GLRO.

[72] Col. W. H. Whitbread, 'Review of 1955', *House of Whitbread* (Autumn 1956), pp. 7–15, W&Co.

[73] Nevile, *Seventy Rolling Years*, pp. 23–4, 142–7, 205; Nevile papers, W/40/7–20, W&Co. See also Ritchie, *Uncommon Brewer*, pp. 85, 91.

[74] Whitbread Board Minutes, 24 October and 12 December 1927, W/23/4, W&Co. Eagles, educated at Marlborough and Magdalen College, Oxford, was a civil servant before joining the brewing industry.

matters of policy, major matters requiring decision, etc. in order to make decisions and to have a record of what has been decided'. It was clearly implied that this had been lacking in the company earlier and that internal lines of communication, particularly those involving directors, needed to be improved.[75] In May 1937 a Managing Directors' Committee began to meet on a weekly basis; within two years it had reviewed the working of most of the major departments. After the war, the committee's deliberations became known as 'policy meetings'.[76] From the late 1940s Whitbread impressed financial analysts with its 'personal leadership, teamwork, technical perfection and ... post-war sales organisation'. The promotion of a national trade in bottled beer based on four strong brands – Pale Ale, Mackeson, Forest Brown and Stout – attention to export opportunities, and an extensive modernisation of brewing departments were identified as company strengths. The success of reciprocal trading agreements with Ind Coope (1951) and Truman Hanbury Buxton (1954) in extending the market penetration of Mackeson and other brands was also noted with approval. The key to the company's post-war emergence lay in a 'younger generation' in top management: 'the managing directors, who are all in their forties or early fifties, work in close association with an expert staff, which includes some of the most able and leading technicians in the trade'.[77]

Of course, there were limits to the changes introduced at Whitbread before the 1950s. The company continued to set great store by its family atmosphere, as exemplified in its magazine, *The House of Whitbread*, and, in common with many breweries, the business was conservatively managed. Its capital was undervalued for a considerable period and the distribution of profits was cautious. The paid-up share capital remained unchanged at £1.989 million (nominal value) from 1908 to 1949, generous provision was made for depreciation, and substantial reserves were built up – over £5 million, including £2 million in hidden reserves, by 1948. Furthermore, family control was retained even after the company became fully public in 1948 and in the following year increased its share capital to £4.038 million by means of a two-for-one bonus issue.[78] After

[75] Nevile, memo, 13 May 1937, Nevile papers, W/40/6, W&Co.

[76] Whitbread Managing Directors' Committee Minutes, 21 May 1937 *et seq*. W/23/11, W&Co. Referred to as 'Board Meetings' in 1945–6, the gatherings became known as 'Policy Meetings' from 6 February 1946: W/23/13, W&Co.

[77] 'What puts the "head" on Whitbreads?', *Investors' Chronicle*, 10 July 1954, p. 102.

[78] Whitbread Reports & Accounts, 1908–49. At 31 December 1948 there were cash reserves of £3,062,000. A 'Special Reserve' of £2,048,800 including £1,576,510 represented by excess depreciation provisions in the past, was written back into the account

lengthy negotiations with the representatives of the numerous family trusts a quarter of the ordinary share capital was placed on the market, underwritten jointly by Barings and Schroders.[79] However, the *status quo* was maintained by splitting the ordinary shares into 'A' shares (80 per cent of the capital, one share one vote) and 'B' shares (20 per cent, one share 20 votes), with most of the latter held by the families.[80] When a further bonus issue (of one for two) was made in 1954, increasing the ordinary capital to £4.949 million and the total share capital to £5.574 million, the possibility of an eventual loss of control emerged. This was pre-empted by using the device of an investment company. Whitbread Investment Co., a wholly owned subsidiary, was established in March 1956 (it became a public company a month later) to acquire the brewery shares held by Whitbread as a consequence of its 'umbrella' policy. In the 1960s the Investment Co. acquired most of the 'B' stock and sufficient of the 'A' stock to ensure a controlling interest.[81]

Thus, while some significant advances were apparent in the running of Whitbread by 1955, the company remained consciously and proudly a family firm, its chairman, Col. Whitbread (Plate 67), 'an outspoken advocate of the importance of the family as the fundamental unit in Britain's industrial structure'.[82] Like Barclay Perkins, Whitbread had no carefully formulated strategy for development. As F. O. A. G. Bennett, a managing director from 1949, recalled: 'There was no particular desire to push up profits nor was there any wish to acquire other brewers. There was, however, an urge to become widely known for its products in the free trade and in off-licences. The push for this type of expansion probably stemmed as much from the managers of the

and distributed as a bonus issue in August 1949. *Investors' Chronicle*, 23 July 1949, p. 220.

79 According to the offer document the decision to make the offer was prompted by 'estate duty and high taxation': Whitbread & Co., Offer for Sale, 29 June 1948, *The Times Book of New Issues of Public Companies*, Jan–June 1948, p. 483, Guildhall Library. Four prominent shareholders died in the 1940s: F. P. Whitbread (1941), S. H. Whitbread (1944), H. W. Whitbread (1947) and G. W. Godman (1947). On the negotiations with the family trustees see Whitbread Policy Meeting Minutes, 1946–8, *passim*, W/23/13–15, W&Co.

80 Each £100 ordinary share was split into 80 £1 'A' shares and 400 1s (5p) 'B' shares. They were then converted into £1 and 5s (25p) stock (the latter with five votes). A quarter of each was offered to the public at 88s (£4.40) and 22s (£1.10) respectively. In the offer document it was stated that the directors would continue to hold 60 per cent of the 'B' Stock: Offer, 29 June 1948, cit. Debentures amounting to £1.75 million were also issued, mostly to replace existing stock.

81 'Notes on a conversation with F. O. A. G. Bennett, 4 March 1985', Whitbread Reports & Accounts, 1954–7, W&Co., and information from C. W. Strickland of Whitbread. For further details see Chapter 11.

82 Editor's Diary, *House of Whitbread*, Spring 1956, p. 3, W&Co.

business as from the Directors and shareholders'. Even the 'umbrella' was a reactive process, with Harold Lake of Cheltenham & Hereford approaching Col. Whitbread for help in countering a threat to the former's independence from a financial group.[83]

A similar combination of traditional management, continuity of personnel, both at board and executive management level, and modest improvement, was evident in Burton at Bass.[84] In 1914 the company, led by Col. Sir John (from 1944 Lord) Gretton, operated very much as it had in the past, via a board composed of long-serving family members. Of the eight directors, there were two Grettons, two Ratcliffs and two Clays, sons of pre-incorporation partners who had served for an average of seventeen years (altogether they went on to average thirty-four years' service). Some directors were recruited from the executive or from outside – John Lambrick, the company secretary (a director, 1909–26), Frank Garrard (1913–19), and Claude Burt (1915–46), from Allsopp's, another former secretary – but there is no evidence to suggest that they injected exceptional vigour or new ideas into the enterprise. Although some improvements were made on the production side in the 1920s (electrification, steel conditioning tanks and cask-washing machinery, for example) and stakes were taken in other companies in order to secure market-share (e.g. in Wilson's of Manchester, and the Wenlock Brewery), caution was the watchword, and it seems that the company was losing ground to its Burton rival, Worthington, in depressed trading conditions before the two companies merged in 1927. The merger seems to have been inspired by Arthur Manners of Worthington, who quickly became the dominant figure in the post-merger management of both companies. Worthington's fortunes had been transformed earlier by the appointment of new blood from within its executive: William Posnette Manners, who joined the brewery as an office boy in 1862 and became chairman in 1894; Horace Tabberer Brown, the head-brewer, who became one of the leading brewing chemists of his day; and Cecil Ball, the general manager, who joined the board in 1918. William Manners and his son, Arthur, who joined the company in 1903, combined considerable ability with entrepreneurial drive, autocracy and social ambition. But from 1927 Arthur Manners displayed the same continuity and caution as had generations of leading family brewers. Some

83 Bennett, 'Notes'; Whitbread Report & Accounts, 1955. Bennett was deputy-chairman of Whitbread, 1959–72, chairman, 1972–7, and chairman of the Brewers' Society, 1972–4.

84 This section is derived from Bass records, Burton; Owen, *History of Bass*, forthcoming; Hawkins, *Bass Charrington*.

improvements from merger were claimed, for example in distribution, though they were rather limited, and there was co-operation in bottled beer production, with Bass brewing some of the Worthington beers. But there is no evidence of organisational or managerial innovation, and another acquired company, James Eadie, also enjoyed a fair amount of autonomy after its acquisition in 1933, as did the other subsidiaries.

The reconstituted board of 1927 continued to serve until the Second World War. In 1945 Lord Gretton stepped down as chairman of Bass after nearly fifty-two years on the board, following a minor squabble with Manners, who became chairman and managing director. Gretton was quickly followed by others of the old guard: Percy Ratcliff, who resigned in 1946 after forty-three years as a director; Claude Burt (1946, after thirty-one years); and James A. Eadie (1947, fourteen years). By the late 1940s Bass was in essence a Manners-dominated concern, the family providing no fewer than four of the six directors in 1948, for example. But this domination of the boardroom was not reflected in the Bass and Worthington organisations lower down. There was considerable departmental duplication and a variety of working practices. Brewing continued at a number of antiquated, often cramped, sites in Burton, using largely traditional methods. In the demand conditions prevailing after 1945 there was an urgent need for rationalisation combined with improved distribution and a joint Bass–Worthington marketing strategy. This is not to say that these exigencies were unknown at board level, but no one was prepared to tackle them head on. Instead Bass was living on past glories. Its sales fell by 18 per cent between 1945 and 1954, though group sales held up thanks to the greater popularity of Worthington bottled beers. By the early 1950s there was considerable concern among institutional investors about falling sales and managerial inertia. In 1953 Sir James Grigg, a distinguished former civil servant and politician,[85] was asked to join the board, and Manners was persuaded to step down. However, no vigorous personality took Manners's place, the chairmanship falling to a 'caretaker', Cecil Ball, a long-serving directorial colleague of Manners.

Bass in many ways presents a paradox. From the outside the company enjoyed a considerable reputation for the quality of its beers and was generally regarded by other brewers as being well managed. But while it had an impressive agency network and a managerial hierarchy, its organisational development was distinctly limited and serious market-

[85] Grigg was by this time a director of Imperial Tobacco, Distillers, National Provincial Bank, Prudential Assurance and Westinghouse.

ing problems had surfaced by the mid 1950s. It took a further merger, with Mitchells & Butlers in 1961, to shake the company out of its torpor.

Among the smaller companies, Bristol Brewery Georges appears to have maintained its position as a sound regional concern, conservatively but competently managed. The sound profit record built up in the late nineteenth century was continued, and growth was steady if unspectacular to 1956, when Georges merged with its chief rival in Bristol, Bristol United. The surviving records indicate how closely the business was controlled by the active directors and departmental heads. Regular reports were received by the board on finance and the cash position from the chief accountant, on production and sales from the head-brewer and managing director, and on public houses from the surveyor and estate manager. The quality of many of these reports is, from a late twentieth-century standpoint, impressive. The board was able to use them to monitor all aspects of production, distribution and retailing and to keep a careful eye on sales trends, costs and margins, etc. Everything suggests an enterprise which was managed successfully.[86] And if nepotism was common here as elsewhere in brewing, it was accompanied by a determination that sons following fathers should possess the necessary education and training. Thus, when Wilfrid Bisdee died the board informed his widow that her son, then at Marlborough, would need to do two years' training with another brewery if he wished to enter the company. If he decided to go to University the board's view was that 'Cambridge, where he could take a Scientific or Chemistry degree, or failing these Mathematics, would be best. In any case it was the Board's wish that he should go to another Brewery, if fitted to take up the Brewing side of the business, or start with a Chartered Accountant's office, or alternatively take some Business Training Course where he could learn accountancy, Book-keeping, shorthand, typing, etc.'[87]

By 1955, then, there were signs that some breweries had adapted their operations to suit twentieth-century demand conditions and made some management changes to reflect the greater concern with financial matters. These modifications were far from dramatic; nor did they necessarily conflict with an emphasis on the family, either in terms of ownership or control. At the same time, it must be recognised that to accept the idea of total stagnation, unimaginative conservatism, a failure

[86] Bristol Brewery Georges, Reports Guard Books, 1936–62, 35740/BG/25(a)–(d), Bristol RO; Bristol Brewery Georges Board Minutes, e.g. 1948–51, Acc. 2305/68/1/1, GLRO.

[87] Bristol Brewery Georges Private Board Minutes, 21 April 1932, 2 March 1933, Acc. 2305/68/6/1, GLRO.

to respond at all to the managerial challenges of twentieth-century manufacturing and retailing, would be foolish. Brewers in their public pronouncements could (and still can) be disarmingly casual in describing their affairs. As already observed (pp. 375–7) they sometimes take delight in anecdotes implying an absence of managerial supervision, hard work and professional standards. Thus, to find it noted that in 1945 the brewer in charge of Guinness's hop farm in Kent had not visited the property since 1923 should not be taken as proof positive that the company everywhere was run in a lax, amateurish fashion.[88] A further reference to J. W. Green of Luton is appropriate here. It might well be wondered how a fairly small provincial concern, with an administrative staff, including junior clerks and typists, of barely forty people, could grow in the space of five years, from 1948 to 1952, by taking over seven breweries and over 700 pubs, into an empire of 1,000 pubs stretching from Sunderland in the north to Tunbridge Wells in the south. Board meetings after the war frequently referred to negotiations with five, ten or even fifteen separate companies. J. W. Green once contemplated buying a brewery in the Isle of Wight. On abandoning the idea they were anxious to make it known that they would look at companies 'however remotely situated they might appear from the home premises at Luton'.[89] The answer lay in determined leadership at the top, due attention to executive appointments, including an accountant, transport manager, laboratory assistant and (from 1951) a company statistician. When the company was reconstituted in 1935 (see p. 392), Richard Ottley, a director of Erlangers, the merchant bankers, joined the board, beginning a close relationship which was vital to the financing of Green's expansionist ambitions.[90] The capacity to respond positively to post-war challenges could also be identified at Greene King and Steward & Patteson.[91]

The 'picturesque dinosaur' seen by *The Economist* is an unduly harsh judgement of the brewing industry. Advances in management techniques and in organisation were far from spectacular in British industry as a whole before the 1960s (ICI and Unilever not excepted); brewers were by no means the only people to feel vulnerable to predatory takeovers from the mid-1950s; and it is hard to expect radical responses

88 Edward Guinness, *The Guinness Book of Guinness, 1935–1985* (Enfield, 1988), p. 154.
89 J. W. Green Board Minutes, 9 February 1949, 75/6, W&Co. On takeover negotiations with other companies, it should be noted that eleven different breweries were discussed at the meeting on 27 August 1953, 75/7, W&Co.
90 *Ibid.*, 9 October 1946, 28 June, 30 August and 29 November 1951.
91 Wilson, *Greene King*; Gourvish, *Norfolk Beers*.

in an industry lacking the stimulus of sudden demand changes or production transforming innovation. Companies tended to be production orientated, with a lack of marketing in the modern sense. Financial management was rather weak, and employment policies were distinctly paternalistic in character before the universal recognition of trade unions. The situation certainly changed in the 1950s. However, the dramatic 'revolution' that affected the industry from the second half of the 1950s should not obscure the progress which was made by most of the leading firms in adapting the family enterprise to the environment of increased competition, over-capacity, and the opportunities offered by acquisition and merger.

10

The sale of beer, 1914–1955

I

In the period 1914–55 beer was sold primarily in public houses, the majority of which had become tied to specific wholesale brewers. Reliable estimates of the exact proportions are difficult to find. In 1927 the Southborough Committee on the Disinterested Management of Public Houses reckoned that 90 per cent of existing licences were tied to brewers. Four years later the Royal Commission on Licensing (England and Wales) reported that the proportion of on-licences owned by brewers was estimated to be 'as high as 95 per cent'.[1] Assessments of the position twenty years later were equally speculative. In 1953 Arthur Seldon thought that English and Welsh brewers owned about 85 per cent of the 73,000 on-licensed premises, while John Vaizey, apparently referring to the year 1950, put the figure at 95 per cent.[2] All these estimates appear to be a little high. One of the few authoritative statements, based on the results of a Brewers' Society questionnaire, indicates that in 1948, 75 per cent of the on-licences in England and Wales, and 40 per cent of the off-licences, were owned or leased by the brewers. The total number of on- and off-licences tied was 63,700, 67 per cent of the 95,000 properties.[3]

Vaizey provided more detailed information on the nature of the beer market in 1950. Ranking beer sales by type of retail outlet, on the basis of brewers' returns, he found that 85 per cent of the beer sold in Britain was sold in public houses and off-licences, and only 10 per cent was

[1] *Report of the Committee on the Disinterested Management of Public Houses* [Southborough Committee], May 1927, *PP* (1927) X, Cmd.2862, p. 8; *Report of the Royal Commission on Licensing (England & Wales), 1929–31, December 1931, PP* (1931–2) XI, Cmd.3988, p. 66.

[2] Arthur Seldon, 'The British Brewing Industry', *Lloyds Bank Review* (October 1953), 33; Vaizey, *Brewing Industry*, p. 69.

[3] BS Statement on 'Tied House System', 5 December 1949, based on replies to Circular 36/48, BS File on 'Tied and Free Trade', 1949, BS.

consumed in clubs. Sales in tied premises accounted for 75 per cent of the market (70 per cent in public houses, 5 per cent in off-licences). The largest single market category was 'local beer', i.e. locally produced beer, which accounted for 73 per cent of total sales, and the largest category by outlet was 'local beer sold in tied public houses', which accounted for 57 per cent.[4]

Was this picture of local, brewer-dominated retailing markedly different in, say, 1914 or 1939? The answer is almost certainly no, although the market environment was neither uniform nor static. In Scotland, for example, where licensing arrangements were quite different, the tied public house was virtually unknown in 1914, and although brewery acquisitions gathered pace after 1939, free houses continued to dominate. Vaizey claimed that 80 per cent of Scottish pubs were tied in 1950, compared with 95 per cent in England and Wales, but this must be wrong. The results of the Brewers' Society survey of 1948 indicated that brewers owned only 28 per cent of full on-licences in Scotland, while in England and Wales the figure was 75 per cent, a situation which persisted into the mid-1960s.[5] Changes over time are more difficult to chart. While the process of public house acquisition, driven by falling demand and the breweries' resultant excess capacity, led in one direction, the rise of the small but significant number of major brewers, who promoted their national brands through the free trade, the clubs and the tied houses of other brewers, led in another direction. The balance between these two elements is difficult to determine, but it is unlikely that the broad picture of brewer domination in the early 1950s was radically different thirty or forty years earlier.

If ownership and sales patterns changed relatively slowly, there were tensions in the trade over the period which presented a challenge to the industry's existing distribution and retailing operations. As shown in Chapter 8 (pp. 335–40), the demand situation facing brewers after 1914 was rather gloomy. Production and consumption fluctuated, sometimes quite sharply, as in 1929–33, and the World Wars provided numerous problems affecting both demand and supply, although there were also periods of relative stability, for example in the 1920s and from the late 1940s to the mid-1950s. But the bald fact was that by pre-1914 stan-

4 Vaizey, *Brewing Industry*, p. 69.

5 *Ibid.*, pp. 69–70, 74; Brewers' Association of Scotland, Return, 10 January 1949 (this response to circular 36/48 referred to 1,596 owned or leased on-licences), BS File, 1949. The Monopolies Commission's *Beer: A Report on the Supply of Beer*, April 1969, produced data for 1966 which showed that 28 per cent of Scottish premises were tied, cf. 87 per cent in England and Wales: *PP* (1968–9) XL, pp. 49–50.

Table 10.1. *UK beer production (excluding Eire), 1913–55 (annual averages)*

Year[a]	Production bulk barrels (millions)	Index 1913 = 100	Production standard barrels (millions)	Index 1913 = 100	Standard production per capita (gallons)	Index 1913 = 100
1913	33.8	100.0	32.5	100.0	28.6	100.0
1919	31.5	93.2	22.6	69.5	18.6	65.0
1922–9	25.4	75.1	19.9	61.2	15.9	55.6
1935–9	23.8	70.4	17.7	54.5	13.5	47.2
1950–5	24.7	73.1	16.6	51.2	11.8	41.3

[a] 1913 = Year to 31 March 1914 *et seq.*

Source: 1913 data: *Brewers' Almanack 1940* (Great Britain/all Ireland *minus* 10 per cent); 1919–55: Appendix Table VIII.

dards the market had shrunk. Bulk production (beer of any gravity) in the UK (excluding Eire), which had amounted to about 33.8 million barrels in 1913 and 31.5 million in 1919, only once reached this level – in 1945 – and was in general about 25–30 per cent lower than in 1913, excluding the exceptional circumstances of the Second World War (see Table 10.1). Moreover, the position appeared to be much worse when assessed in relation to a product of 'standard' (i.e. 1055° gravity) strength and expressed in per capita terms. 'Standard' production in the UK, 32.5 million barrels in 1913, fell to 22.6 million in 1919 and deteriorated further thereafter. Compared with 1913 the decline was about 40–50 per cent. The fall in production per capita was of the order of 45–60 per cent (Table 10.1). It is scarcely surprising then that the more market conscious brewers appeared edgy about the appearance of any form of competition in the retail trade, however marginal such challenges may appear to historians at half a century's distance. Thus, the emergence of a more substantial club trade may have offered some companies an opportunity to supply additional outlets at a time when licences were being surrendered under the 1904 Licensing Act (see Chapter 7). But the development also represented a threat both to the tied house and to market share as well, since in the 1920s some of the larger federations of clubs, such as the Leeds & District Clubs (1919) and the Northern Clubs' Federation (1920), began to brew on their own account. There was also some concern about the steps taken by brewers such as Davenports of Birmingham to distribute bottled beers direct to consumers' homes. Finally, the concept of the public house itself came under scrutiny, encouraged by the proselytising activities of the Carlisle State Management Scheme (see Chapter 8) and the movement for the 'Improved Public House'. All this stimulated a debate about whether the traditional pub should be replaced by a multi-purpose leisure centre providing food, recreation, meeting-rooms, etc. as well as alcoholic refreshment. These elements are examined in more detail below.

II

The penetration of the club trade could be detected in crude terms by brewers who consulted the published licensing statistics. It was immediately clear that after the First World War the number of licensed premises and, in particular, the number of publicans' on-licensed premises had fallen (see Table 10.2). Figures for England and Wales

Table 10.2. *Liquor licences and clubs, 1913–55 (England and Wales, 1913–55, UK, 1923–55)*

Year[a]	England and Wales					United Kingdom			
	Publicans'[b] on-licences	All on-licences	Off-licences	Clubs	Total	All on-licences	Off-licences	Clubs	Total
1913	62,104	87,660	23,408	8,738	119,806	–	–	–	–
1923	58,887	80,987	22,135	11,471	114,593	89,943	26,580	12,097	128,590
1949	56,112	73,572	21,995	17,362	112,929	81,881	24,793	18,139	124,813
1945	55,875	72,960	21,599	15,590	110,149	81,417	24,155	16,359	121,931
1955[a]	60,670	71,244	23,548	21,164	115,956	79,669	26,094	22,355	129,762

[a] Year to 31 December (1955 is year to 30 June).
[b] All drinks.
Source: Licensing Statistics.

revealed the decline in the latter to have been about 5 per cent by 1923, 10 per cent by 1939. With the number of off-licences also falling – by 5 per cent to 1923, 6 per cent by 1939 – attention was firmly focused upon the increase in the number of registered clubs, which doubled from 8,738 in 1913 to 17,362 in 1939. Although numbers fell during the Second World War, by 10 per cent, there was a sharp post-war recovery. By 1955 there were 21,164 clubs, 36 per cent more than in 1945, and this sector had increased its share of the total number of outlets from 7 per cent in 1913 to 18 per cent. The UK picture was very similar; the number of clubs increased by 37 per cent, 1945–55, and their share of total outlets in 1955 was 17 per cent (Table 10.2).

The significance of this trend should be clearly understood, however. The brewing trade certainly expressed anxiety about the growth of clubs, although more often than not the protests came from publicans worried about competitors whose licensing restrictions were less onerous and whose prices were lower. Reporting on evidence submitted to it in 1929–31, the Royal Commission on Licensing suggested that the club had become 'a formidable competitor to licensed premises'.[6] The wholesale brewers had regarded the clubs as offering a market opportunity during the tighter demand conditions of the inter-war years, and some companies built up a very extensive trade. In London, for example, Whitbread were supplying 3,920 clubs in 1948, compared with 808 tied houses, while Ind Coope & Allsopp, who had 2,679 tied houses, were distributing beer to 1,590 clubs.[7] However, even the brewers had some cause for concern, in this instance as a result of the emergence of club breweries, which were born out of dissatisfaction with high prices and beer shortages during the First World War (see pp. 319–23) and were encouraged by the co-operative aspirations of the Working Men's Clubs and Institute Union (CIU).[8] The most important of these, the Northern Clubs' Federation Brewery of Newcastle, sold about 26,000 bulk barrels per annum in the late 1920s, 78,000 (including bottled beer,

6 *Report of Royal Commission on Licensing*, 1931, p. 67, also referred to in Wilson, *Alcohol and the Nation*, p. 146.

7 Brewery statements on 'Hotels, Tied Houses and Clubs' (response to circular 36/48), 1949, BS File, 1949. Other major suppliers of clubs were H. & G. Simonds (1,277), Mitchells & Butlers (997), Samuel Smith (815), and Hammonds (810).

8 The CIU, which had been founded in 1862, had 1,613 clubs affiliated to it by 1914, representing a membership of 525,838. See The Freedom Association, *Handbook for Speakers and Writers on the (So-Called) Temperance Question* (8th edn, 1929), p. 485; Ted Elkins, Jr., *So They Brewed Their Own Beer* (Newcastle, 1970), pp. 8–18; B. R. Bennison, 'The Economic and Social Origins of the Northern Clubs' Federation Brewery: Some Preliminary Thoughts', *Newcastle Polytechnic School of Economics Staff Paper*, December 1984; extract from *Newcastle Journal*, 30 November 1957, BS File on 'Club Breweries', 1957–8, BS.

started in 1934) in the late 1930s, and 210,000 in 1955–6, by which time sales to some 425 clubs amounted to £3.4 million.[9] In all the seven co-operative club breweries produced about 300,000 barrels a year for over 1,000 clubs in the early 1950s, an output equivalent to that of one medium-sized brewery and representing about 1.2 per cent of total UK production. In the prevailing conditions of brewing over-capacity and a highly controlled retail market, the reduction in the free trade arising from clubs being 'tied' to their own breweries (to the extent of about 10 per cent of the overall club demand for liquor) was scarcely welcomed by brewers in the areas most affected – the North-East of England, Lancashire and Yorkshire, the East Midlands and South Wales.[10] Indeed, the growth of the two leading breweries, the Northern Clubs' Federation and the South Wales & Monmouthshire, was sufficient to prod the Brewers' Society into examining the potential threat to conventional distribution, in inquiries of 1952 and 1957–8. Here, particular reference was made to the attractiveness of the rebates or 'divvy' paid to member clubs and to the extensive loans made by the Federation Brewery to its affiliated clubs – £891,000 in total by March 1956. Fears were expressed that the brewers' hold on the club trade would be weakened significantly were the Co-operative Wholesale Society to purchase a major brewery.[11]

In the event these fears proved groundless; and the overall challenge to brewers' markets should not be overstated. With the exception of the prize-winning Federation Brewery, the club breweries were unable to match the quality of the beer produced by the wholesale brewers. Nor was the clubs' share of licensed premises fully reflected in market-share. They made up 13–18 per cent of the total number of outlets in the ten years after 1945, but only about 8–10 per cent of the beer sold.[12] In any case, the expansion of club licences did not take place

[9] Northern Clubs' Federation Brewery Half-Yearly Report & Accounts, 30 July 1938, 30 September 1949, 31 March 1956, BS. Bulk barrelages are annual averages for 1927–9, 1936–8 and 1955–6, with estimates for bottled beer based on the assumption that sales were in 6 oz bottles in the late 1930s and in half-pint bottles, 1955–6.

[10] In 1945–6 the members of the Association of Club Breweries sold 265,000 barrels of draught beer to 944 clubs, and in the following year 247,000 barrels; in 1950–1, 272,000 barrels were sold to 1,042 clubs. See Association of Club Breweries, Annual Report for years ended 31 July 1946 and 1947, in Topic Collection TC85, Box 2C, Tom Harrisson Mass-Observation Archive, University of Sussex (hereafter MO); Sir Robert Ewbank, memo on 'Club Breweries', 18 April 1952, BS File, 1957–8.

[11] Ewbank, memo, 1952; Northern Clubs' Federation Brewery Half-Yearly Report and Accounts to 31 March 1956; BS Council Minutes, 16 July 1958, BS memo on 'Club Breweries', 5 November 1958, BS File, 1957–8.

[12] Ewbank, memo, 1952; BS memo, 5 November 1958; Table 10.1. The clubs' share of liquor sales in the inter-war years was about 5–7 per cent: J. Baxter, 'The Organisation

simply at the expense of public houses and off-licences. Ever since the Licensing Act of 1904 had offered compensation for surrendered licences in England and Wales, brewers had been rationalising their more marginal outlets. Over the period 1914–55, 11,621 licences were 'refused with compensation', equivalent to 77 per cent of the net decrease in licences; the compensation payments totalled £19.3 million.[13] Furthermore, the post-war increase in clubs was more than matched by an increase in publicans' on- and off-licences. Over the period 1945–55 these increased by 9 per cent, or by 4,800 and 1,950 respectively, reaching the highest levels since the First World War and exceeding the increase of 5,600 in the number of clubs (Table 10.2).[14] The overall impact of the club is therefore difficult to gauge. As a rival to the public house, there is no doubt that it offered potent competition in some areas. As Table 10.3 shows, there were significant numbers of clubs in certain counties and county boroughs in both 1938 and 1955. Although numerical strength was not fully reflected in sales levels, the data invite the suggestion that in some cases the clubs' 'market-share' may have been as high as 25–40 per cent. Club memberships were also substantial. Estimates for the UK suggest a total membership of 4.45 million in 1929 and 6.98 million in 1955.[15] Of course, a large number of club members were either irregular attenders or non-drinkers, and such figures may not mean a great deal. But it does appear that by the inter-war years the club represented a very real challenge to the public house in the working-class market, and that this challenge intensified after the Second World War. Here, a more telling statistic is the fact that by 1930 0.9 million people belonged to the 2,660 clubs affiliated to the CIU, where liquor consumption was higher than in the average club, and by 1946 the figures had risen to 1.7 million and 3,000 respectively.[16] The factors explaining the increase in popularity of the

of the Brewing Industry', London University Ph.D. thesis, 1945, p. 255. Baxter also notes that the clubs' numerical strength was not fully reflected in sales, but exaggerates the gulf by comparing sales share with the ratio of club numbers to on-licences (and not club numbers as percentage of on-licences *and* clubs).

13 *Brewers' Almanack 1960*, pp. 88, 168; *Licensing Statistics, 1923 (England & Wales)*, Cmd.2257, p. vi.

14 Here it should be noted that the increase in publicans' or all drinks on-licences was encouraged by legislation facilitating the conversion of more limited on-licences into full ones, viz. the Finance Act, 1947, s.73, and the Licensing Act, 1953, s.7.

15 Estimates derived from Return of Clubs and Members, 1932, cit. in Wilson, *Alcohol and the Nation*, p. 141 (England & Wales, *c.*1929, 13,513 clubs, 4,222,113 members: multiplier = 312.4].

16 Wilson, *Alcohol and the Nation*, p. 142; Mass-Observation, Report on Drinking Habits, August 1948, p. 153, File 3029, MO.

Table 10.3. *Clubs and on-licensed premises in selected counties and county boroughs, 1938 and 1955*

County/county borough	31 December 1938 (i) Registered clubs	(ii) On-licences	30 June 1955 (i) as % of (i) + (ii) %	(i) Registered clubs	(ii) On-licences	(i) as % of (i) + (ii) %
West Riding Yorks	1,985	2,379	45	1,054	2,424	30
Surrey	662	1,235	35	774	1,255	38
Middlesex	597	1,103	35	734	1,118	40
Northumberland and Durham	567	1,926	23	707	1,913	37
London (Metropolitan Police District)	1,503	4,969	23	1,524	4,589	25
Birmingham	345	957	26	470	912	34
Huddersfield	118	211	36	111	193	37
Newcastle	115	324	26	159	304	34
Coventry	100	242	29	226	355	36
Middlesbrough	54	104	34	58	99	37
ENGLAND and WALES	16,951	73,920	19	21,164	71,244	23

Source: Brewers' Almanack 1940, p. 109; *1959*, p. 93.

working- and lower-middle-class club in the first half of the twentieth century deserve some attention, although they are not easy to pin down precisely owing to the paucity of good market research before the 1960s. However, what is available suggests that while the public house and the club were complementary in leisure activities, after the Second World War preferences for the latter were not only strong, but were based on much more than the price of drink. A major survey of drinking habits in 1947–8, conducted for Guinness by Mass-Observation, the social research body, found that 68 per cent of those interviewed who used both pubs and clubs expressed a preference for the club, while only 22 per cent favoured the pub.[17] The advantages of the pub, identified as including a varied clientele and the provision of better quality drink, were apparently outweighed by the stability, conviviality and good recreational facilities offered by the club. The report concluded that 'Drink, as so often before, is an incidental, and the clubgoer in particular regards it as of far less importance than the social activities. For the clubgoer is on the whole the casual drinker, and the serious drinker who appreciates his beer on its own merits alone is content in his pub and his home without bothering about clubs.'[18] Whatever the validity of this compilation of preferences and prejudices – the findings appeared to play down thc extent of heavy drinking in clubs, for example[19] – a number of public house tenants responded to club competition by turning all or part of their premises into quasi-clubs offering exclusivity and a range of social activities – outings, games, raffles, etc. – to a defined group of customers.[20] Thus, while the club trade was still small in terms of aggregate liquor consumption, its growth was one of the elements which forced brewers to think more seriously than before about public house environments and facilities.

Compared with the threat from clubs the increasing tendency to

17 Mass-Observation, Report on Drinking Habits, p. 176. The Report, which was based on wide-ranging studies of London (Tottenham, Fulham, Dagenham, East End), Birmingham (Aston), Bolton, Middlesbrough, York, Blaina and Exmoor in March 1947–8, found that 70 per cent of club-goers interviewed also went to pubs.

18 *Ibid.*, p. 178 and see also pp. 148, 163, 176–7. The Report defined the 'serious drinker' as one interested primarily in the *quality* of the drink, and the 'casual drinker' as one who regarded drink as a necessary incidental to other activities. *Ibid.*, pp. 11–12.

19 *Ibid.*, p. 163, and see also Mass-Observation, Preliminary Report on Drinking Habits, July 1948, p. 28, File 3016, and Topic Collection TC85, Box 14, Drunkenness Survey 1950–1 (refs. to Leicester and Nottingham), MO. The notion that clubs discouraged heavy drinking was contradicted by references to the attractiveness of drinking out of normal licensing hours and to the practice of giving members rebates in the form of beer. Cf. Report on Drinking Habits, cit. p. 166, MO, and Courtenay C. Weeks (ed.), *Proceedings of 20th International Congress on Alcoholism* (1934), pp. 196–7.

20 E.g. the 'Vane', Middlesbrough: MO Report, pp. 106, 178.

consume beer at home provoked only a muted response from the trade. After all, the brewers had reacted to the phenomenon, a reflection of changing consumer behaviour reinforced by the effects of temperance propaganda portraying the pub as a stigmatised drinking-den, by supplying, and often, tying, off-licensed premises. Some companies built up a considerable trade with free off-licences. Whitbread, for example, were supplying 8,622 such customers in 1948, Watney had 1,713 and Tollemache of Ipswich 1,210.[21] Others established a large chain of tied off-licences. Mann, Crossman & Paulin, for example, owned 450 in 1948 compared with 696 on-licensed premises, Whitbread had 402 (and 808 on-licences), Mitchells & Butlers 358 (873), and Ansells 304 (850).[22] The direct supply of beer from the brewery to the home was tried by one or two breweries before the First World War, at a time when the long-established 'private trade' of most brewers was disappearing. A notable participant here was Davenports of Birmingham, which started home deliveries in 1904 and provoked the opposition of both retailers and wholesalers in the city. By 1939 the company could boast of over 250,000 customers supplied via a network of depots.[23] However, operational problems, notably the losses of bottles and crates, ensured that few brewers were tempted to emulate Davenports. Thus, the challenge to conventional on- and off-licence distribution was minimal before the emergence of the large supermarkets in the late 1950s.[24]

III

A more important, and more enduring, element was the threat to the trade posed by the movement to secure an 'improved public house'. With its roots in the nineteenth century, in the temperance and quasi-temperance charities which encouraged moderation in drinking habits and the provision of food and non-alcoholic drinks in public houses, it gathered pace with the threat of prohibition, nationalisation or local

21 Truman had 1,331 free-trade off-licence customers, Mann, Crossman & Paulin 1,407, and Ind Coope & Allsopp 770. Brewery Statements, 1949, BS. No returns were made by Bass and Guinness, each of which supplied a large free trade.

22 Ind Coope & Allsopp owned 352 off-licences. *Ibid.*

23 *Birmingham Weekly Post*, 20 November 1953, press cutting, BS; Alan Crawford, Michael Dunn and Robert Thorne, *Birmingham Pubs 1880–1939* (Gloucester, 1986), pp. 69–70.

24 Gutzke, *Protecting the Pub*, pp. 205–12; John Mark, 'Changes in the British Brewing Industry in the Twentieth Century', in D. J. Oddy and D. S. Miller (eds.), *Diet and Health in Modern Britain* (1985), pp. 81, 98–100.

option during the early part of the First World War and with the introduction in 1916 of the Carlisle State Management Scheme (see Chapter 8). Pressure for change came from several quarters. Pioneering social reformers, most of them with religious affiliations, emerged at the turn of the century to offer an alternative to the prohibitionist policies of the strict temperance groups. The People's Refreshment House Association of 1896, and the Central Public House Trust Association of 1901, with its constituent county trusts, focused upon the acquisition and management of public houses on 'disinterested' lines, i.e. they would have no direct financial interest in promoting the sale of liquor. Moderation in alcoholic consumption was to be secured by a change in the way public houses were run. The problem of excessive drinking was laid at the door of the tied, and in particular the tied tenanted, house. Managers, rather than tenants, were to be employed, who would be given financial incentives to promote the sale of food and non-alcoholic drinks. The conception of the state management scheme in Carlisle owed much to these ideas and, in turn, the activities of the state gave added impetus to the voluntary sector in the inter-war years.[25]

The scale of this intervention was modest in the aggregate, although the publicity it attracted was out of all proportion to the numbers of public houses affected. In 1925 it was reported that fifteen trust companies were managing 267 pubs in Great Britain, while in addition Trust Houses Ltd, a separate and more commercial enterprise formed in 1919 after the Hertfordshire Trust had severed its links with the Central Trust, operated another 174 pubs. Four years later the Royal Commission on Licensing stated that the trust companies held a total of 428 licences.[26] Other bodies active in the inter-war years were propagandist and had little to do with direct management of houses. The True Temperance Association, with its associated branches, and the Fellowship of Freedom and Reform, for example, were in general sympathetic to the brewers and wished to see the industry reform itself,

25 Most of the Trusts worked to a self-imposed dividend limitation, following the philanthropic housing associations. See, *inter alia*, Robert Thorne, 'The Movement for Public House Reform 1892–1914', in Oddy and Miller, *Diet and Health*, pp. 238–45; Ernest E. Williams, *The New Public House* (1924), pp. 63ff.; Ernest Selley, *The English Public House As It Is* (1927), pp. 69–108; Jean Wakeman, *Trust House Britain* (1963), pp. 12–14; *Brewing Trade Review*, January 1904, p. 29.

26 Figure of 267 pubs given in Central Trust's report for 1924, summarised in *Brewers' Journal*, August 1925, p. 388, and reproduced in *Report of Committee on Disinterested Management*, 1927, pp. 6–8; *Report of Royal Commission on Licensing*, 1931, p. 78.

with the help of appropriate legislation.[27] A more interventionist group, although on a small scale, was the Association for the Promotion of Restaurant Public Houses in Poor Districts (also known as the Restaurant Public Houses Association), which was founded by Louise Sotham and Edith Neville, among others, in 1923. This distinguished itself from the trusts, which in the main were operating with country hotels and inns, by emphasising the need to improve pubs in the poorer, inner-city areas. With the help of sympathetic London brewers such as Barclay Perkins, Watney and Whitbread, the Association took on the management of a number of houses in the capital on an experimental basis.[28] In all about 500 pubs were managed under the 'social reform' banner in the 1930s, representing an investment in licensed property of about £2 million.[29]

The inter-war debate was very much focused through these reform groups, and through the Southborough Committee (1927) and the Royal Commission on Licensing (1931), on which the reformers were represented and to which they gave evidence. Numerous public house improvement Bills, which were introduced in the Commons between 1908 and 1933, sought to tackle the problem of excessive drinking. Those presented from 1919 onwards made provision for licence-holders to apply for an improved public house certificate, which would confer specified privileges, and the right of appeal to Quarter Sessions in the event of rejection or withdrawal. Although these Bills failed to progress, they probably influenced the attitude of licensing justices and certainly acted as a counterweight to the equally vigorous Bill-promoting activity of temperance groups intent on giving communities the right of 'local veto'.[30] There was thus a strong thrust towards 'disinterested management' and 'the improved public house' as the policies best designed to tackle the problem of excessive drinking and ward off temperance zeal. The Southborough Committee and the Royal Commission gave expression to the opposing views of improvers and abstentionists. Indeed, the

[27] The True Temperance Association was founded in 1908. See Williams, *New Public House*, pp. 66–79, Thorne, 'Public House Reform', pp. 248–9. On the Fellowship of Freedom and Reform, founded in 1920, see *Brewers' Journal*, December 1920, p. 497, Williams, *New Public House*, p. 79, and Selley, *English Public House*, p. 121. There are numerous references to both in the trade and press.

[28] *Report of Committee on Disinterested Management*, 1927, p. 20; Nevile, *Seventy Rolling Years*, pp. 180–3; *Brewing Trade Review*, January 1927, p. 10, May 1954, p. 299.

[29] These approximate figures are based on an observation by the Southborough Committee that about 450 pubs were managed by the Trusts and the capital employed was approx. £2 million: *Report of Committee on Disinterested Management*, 1927, p. 7.

[30] There were thirteen Commons Bills dealing with the improved public house, 1908–33, and twenty-five temperance Bills (local option, veto, prohibition, etc.).

majority report of the Royal Commission was very much a charter for public house improvement. It sought to encourage the acceptance of larger, more spacious premises with ample seating, and the provision of food and recreational facilities. Drinking habits deemed undesirable were to be discouraged: purchasing liquor direct from a bar; drinking standing up at the bar ('perpendicular drinking'); and drinking in confined spaces (an end to 'snugs' and 'snuggeries'). 'There were still', it complained, 'large numbers of houses, particularly in industrial districts, which are poor and cramped in structure, gloomy, often insufficiently ventilated ... the predominating, and very often the exclusive, emphasis is on the sale of intoxicants.' Its ideal solution was 'to make the public house ... a place where the public can obtain general refreshment, of whatever variety they choose, in decent, pleasant and comfortable surroundings'.[31] Reform was also promoted by several books on public house improvement, notably by Ernest Williams and Ernest Selley, and subsequently by brewing architects and designers such as Basil Oliver and Francis Yorke.[32]

The Carlisle State Management Scheme also served as a showpiece for those anxious to promote improvement, particularly in the early 1920s. The majority of its licensed properties were managed; the provision of food received considerable emphasis; and several of the small, unsavoury drinking dens were replaced by larger pubs on model reformed lines. The lasting effects of this initiative were more limited than its more enthusiastic supporters were prepared to concede. However the work of the management team at Carlisle, and in particular the first architect, Harry Redfern, did much to persuade the sceptics, both in the brewing industry and among the licensing authorities, that public house planning was desirable.[33]

Aside from all this propaganda there was pressure for change coming from the trade itself. In Birmingham, for example, much progress was made before 1914 with the policy of 'fewer but better' houses advocated by companies such as Mitchells & Butlers and Ansells and by such brewers as Sir William Waters Butler. Widespread publicity was given to the establishment in 1897 of the Birmingham Property Co., a consor-

[31] *Report of Royal Commission on Licensing*, 1931, pp. 45–7.

[32] Williams, *New Public House*; Selley, *English Public House*; Basil Oliver, *The Modern Public House* (1934) and *The Renaissance of the English Public House* (1947); Francis W. B. Yorke, *The Planning and Equipment of Public Houses* (1949).

[33] Oliver, *Renaissance*, pp. 20, 58–9; *Central Control Board (Liquor Traffic). General Manager's Report for Year ending 31st December, 1919*, p. 4, *PP* (1920) XX; R. M. Punnett, 'State Management of the Liquor Trade', *Public Administration*, 44 (Summer 1966), 195.

tium of local brewers which operated a voluntary compensation scheme to facilitate the surrender of licences on small, run-down, inner-city pubs affected by slum clearance. After the 1904 Licensing Act introduced a statutory compensation scheme, the brewers developed an informal *quid pro quo* arrangement with the licensing bench by which licences were surrendered in return for a smaller number of new licences for larger pubs in the expanding suburbs. By 1925 it was reported that 557 pubs had been closed on voluntary initiative, together with a further 300 under the 1904 Act.[34] Mitchells & Butlers, which gave up about 300 of these licences, became a dominant force in the Birmingham market as a result and, more than most brewers, moved enthusiastically into managed, rather than tenanted, houses (see p. 441). The new pubs were architecturally impressive and well appointed, with gardens, bowling greens, meeting rooms, and provision for families and cars (Plates 53–6).[35] Further signs of enlightenment on the part of licensing magistrates and brewers were later found in Leeds, Middlesbrough and the county of Middlesex.[36]

London was also a focal point for early responses to the attack on the trade before the First World War. Sydney Nevile, then with Brandon's of Putney, recalled that he had been prompted to consider public house reform by the Liberals' temperance-inspired Licensing Bill of 1908 (see pp. 292–3), and had realised that in seeking to improve the image of the pub 'there was no conflict between the permanent commercial interest of the brewing trade and the best interests of the public'.[37] He found like-minded brewers in Edwyn Barclay (Barclay Perkins), Frank Mason (Charrington) and Frank Whitbread and Cecil Lubbock (Whitbread). Whitbread went so far as to establish, in 1904, a separate company, the Central Catering Co., to supply cooked food to its public houses, but the initiative was premature, and the business was wound up after three years with losses to Whitbread of at least £12,500.[38] Nevertheless, in

34 *Brewing Trade Review*, September 1925, p. 355 and see also *ibid.*, October 1897, p. 348, October 1898, pp. 359–60.

35 Oliver, *Renaissance*, pp. 80–6; Thorne, 'Public House Reform', pp. 246–7; Crawford *et al.*, *Birmingham Pubs*, pp. 48–57; Mitchells & Butlers, *Fifty Years of Brewing 1879–1929* (Birmingham, 1929), pp. 58–95.

36 Williams, *New Public House*, pp. 84ff.; Selley, *English Public House*, p. 53; *Brewing Trade Review*, February 1923, p. 71; Freedom Association, *Handbook*, pp. 448–50.

37 Nevile, *Seventy Rolling Years*, p. 65.

38 A sum of £12,500 was shown as outstanding in the final entry of the company's private ledger on 9 January 1907, Central Catering Co. Private Ledger, CC/3, W&Co. However, Nevile put the losses at £50,000: *Seventy Rolling Years*, pp. 69–70. On the company's problems, e.g. a low take-up rate for food, operational problems, and

spite of the fact that the licensing climate was far from supportive in London, limited experiments were entertained, for example, by Charrington in the south-east of the city, while in the west, Fuller, Smith & Turner and the Royal Brewery, Brentford were able to rebuild or enlarge some houses.[39] The more difficult circumstances of the war (see Chapter 8) then gave impetus to the brewers' reforming activity. Nevile, together with Sir Richard Garton and Col. Oswald Serocold of Watney Combe Reid, Frank Whitbread, and Edward Giffard (Barclay Perkins), met in 1917 to formulate constructive proposals. Five principles were drawn up and endorsed by the parliamentary sub-committee of the Brewers' Society in January 1918: a faith in consumer choice; opposition to state intervention; support for a uniform licensing system with the right of appeal; the linkage of licence rationalisation with public house improvement and 'removal', i.e. the transfer of licences from overcrowded areas to expanding districts; and an endorsement of larger premises with greater social amenities. A licensing reform sub-committee was then established which with a similar body from the National Trade Defence Association (wholesalers and retailers) mounted a publicity campaign for reform under the slogan 'Service with Sobriety'. Efficiency of service, the suppression of excessive drinking, and support for reforming legislation were tenets of the new faith.[40] It was accepted that 'the licensed house should aim at providing refreshments and social amenities for both sexes and all classes of the community'.[41] In this way the brewers combined strategic and practical considerations. They sought to deflect temperance opposition and at the same time encourage reforms which were compatible with the retention of private sector control of the industry. As Nevile rightly observed, 'social duty' coincided neatly with 'self interest': 'a contented, sober,

competition from costermongers in the East End, see Whitbread Board Minutes, 24 October 1905, 30 October 1906, 22 January 1907, W/23/2, W&Co.

39 Nevile, *Seventy Rolling Years*, pp. 70–1; Freedom Association, *Handbook*, p. 460.

40 BS General Committee Minutes, 20 December 1917, Parliamentary Sub-committee Minutes, 3 and 21 January 1918; National Trade Defence Association General Committee Minutes, 1 February 1918; Joint meeting of BS Licensing Reform Sub-committee, NTDA, and Guarantee Fund Trustees (a brewers' lobby), 19 February 1918, 12 May 1919, BS. The BS Reform Sub-committee comprised Nevile, Edwyn Barclay, Frank Nicholson (Vaux), and E. Threlfall Hopkins (J. Jordan, Oldbury, later Wilson's). The lobby promoted two Licensing Bills, introduced in the Commons by John Gretton of Bass: Nevile, *Seventy Rolling Years*, pp. 121–33, *PP* (1920) III, p. 229, (1921) II, p. 429.

41 Gerald Miller, 'A Forward Movement. Public House Improvement', 17 February 1936, BS.

well-catered-for public house population is a sure source of monetary profit as well as a commendable social unit'.[42]

The brewers' activities gathered pace in the 1920s and 1930s. Improvers were emboldened by a growing awareness that the Carlisle experiment had run out of steam. The long-term impact of the state scheme was disappointing, in relation both to the percentage of pubs improved and to the extent of food sales, a situation publicised by the Southborough Committee in 1927.[43] Furthermore, the policy was also part of a necessary response to changing consumption patterns, demographic change and social trends. The improved, multi-functional public house was regarded as an asset by brewers concerned about declining per capita beer consumption, the dislocation caused to retailing by suburban resettlement, and the competition offered by clubs and by non-alcoholic leisure facilities such as coffee shops and milk bars. Brewers in London were particularly prominent, and the trade press made much of the efforts of Barclay Perkins, Charrington, Courage, Truman, Watney, Whitbread and Benskin's of Watford, among others. Improvements were organised in several ways. Large public houses were built in newly developed areas, often with a *quid pro quo* extracted by the licensing authorities in the form of surrendered licences on smaller, older properties elsewhere. Several of the larger houses were established in conjunction with the rehousing schemes of London County Council. At the same time, brewers were anxious to demonstrate their social responsibility and flexibility of response by co-operating actively with reforming charities and trusts. Some initiatives were clearly aimed at the middle-class market, notably the roadhouses, with their imposing architectural features and lavish facilities, including first-class restaurants. This work was usually organised by the brewers' own architects and building gangs.

Barclay Perkins, Watney Combe Reid and Whitbread caught the eye with the range of their activities. Barclay Perkins established a chain of improved houses – 'Anchor Taverns' – while Whitbread formed a new company, the Improved Public House Co. of 1920, as a vehicle for the retail management of its large new houses. Starting in modest fashion with control of four existing pubs, it owned seventeen properties and was responsible for managing thirty-two others for

[42] Nevile, *Seventy Rolling Years*, p. 174.

[43] *Report of Committee on Disinterested Management*, 1927, pp. 14–19, and see also Hawkins, 'Brewing Industry', pp. 470–1.

Whitbread by 1939–40.[44] Watney acquired a reputation for both the scale of its rebuilding programme and its attention to architectural style.[45] All three companies built large pubs for London's new housing estates, for example at Bellingham, Downham and Becontree.[46] They also proved to be particularly receptive to reforming ideas, running houses on 'disinterested management' lines and offering others to bodies such as the Restaurant Public Houses Association, which, as noted earlier, was formed in 1923 to encourage the introduction of reforming principles to working-class pubs in inner-city areas. In that year Barclay Perkins opened such a pub, the 'Rose' in Camberwell. Hailed as 'a great experiment on [*sic*] the psychology of the working man', it was designed to 'encourage the consumption by the public of food and liquor at separate tables served by waiters and waitresses, and generally to make the premises more of the nature of a refreshment house'.[47] A manager was appointed to promote food sales, but there was some embarrassment when he absconded within four months leaving debts of £300.[48] The prohibition of perpendicular drinking was a condition imposed at the company's huge pub on the Downham estate near Bromley. Opened in 1930, the 'Downham Tavern' had no bars; embracing the full panoply of 'improvement', it included a massive hall and later acquired distinction for the staging of Shakespearean plays (see Plate 57).[49]

Barclay Perkins, Watney and Whitbread also offered some London pubs to the Restaurant Public Houses Association to be managed on an experimental basis. Whitbread provided three: the 'King's Head', Cumberland Market, in 1925; the 'Tavistock', Stibbington Street,

44 Oliver, *Modern Public House*, pp. 18, 20–3; Nevile, *Seventy Rolling Years*, pp. 141, 147; Improved Public House Co. Accounts, year ended 30 September 1940, IPH/12, and Nevile papers on 'Improved Public House Co., 1920–3', W/40/34, W&Co.

45 E.g. 'Windsor Castle', Victoria; 'Belle Vue', Clapham Common; 'Mitre', Holland Park Avenue. See Oliver, *Modern Public House*, pp. 23–5; *Renaissance*, pp. 94–5; Serocold, *Watneys*, pp. 76–8; *Brewers' Journal*, September 1933, p. 464; *Brewing Trade Review*, September 1937, p. 357.

46 E.g. Barclay Perkins's 'Fellowship Inn', Bellingham; 'Downham Tavern', Downham; and 'Cherry Tree', Becontree; and Whitbread's 'Robin Hood', Becontree. See *Brewers' Journal*, July 1924, pp. 357–8, June 1930, pp. 319–21.

47 *Brewers' Journal*, April 1923, pp. 180–1; *Brewing Trade Review*, April 1923, p. 186; Edward Giffard, speech on opening the 'Rose', n.d. but = 21 March 1923, Acc. 2305/1/1053/33, GLRO.

48 Barclay Perkins Board Minutes, 4 September 1922, 22 March and 20 August 1923, Acc. 2305/1/16, GLRO.

49 *Brewing Trade Review*, June 1930, pp. 373–4; *Brewers' Journal*, June 1930, pp. 319–21, December 1937, p. 595; Oliver, *Renaissance*, pp. 164–6; LCC Housing Book, May 1937, pp. 226–7, 28–75 LCC, GLRO. The 'Warrington Hotel' in Maida Vale even had an indoor miniature golf course: *Brewers' Journal*, October 1930, p. 547.

Somers Town, in 1927; and the 'Anchor', also in Stibbington Street, which was rebuilt in 1929 and managed for the Association by Rev. Basil Jellicoe of the St Pancras Housing Society.[50] The Association hoped to demonstrate the viability of an extended scheme to be undertaken by the brewers themselves, and after a conference in 1928 a draft Bill was prepared with the intention of securing a more sympathetic licensing system.[51] Little headway was made, however, and since the financial results of the experimental management were rather mixed (see below), the Association turned its attention instead to the idea of a training scheme for public house staff. A pilot project in 1932, supported by the three brewers, was converted into a more substantial scheme two years later. Backed by the Ministry of Labour and supported by initial donations from the Brewers' Company and individual firms, the Association had trained 160 men by February 1935. Over thirty public houses were made available by ten companies.[52] Clearly, such policies were driven by the brewers' desire for goodwill from social workers vulnerable to prohibitionist arguments as well as a genuine wish to improve public house management and widen the retail market. A similar strategy lay behind attempts to increase the provision of food in pubs generally. Whitbread in particular were prominent here, making much of the fact that in the first half of the 1920s they had invested over £200,000 in establishing a full meals service in 282 (49 per cent) of their 580 houses, 101 (17 per cent) of which were equipped with separate dining rooms.[53] By 1948 they were selling meals and snacks in 87 per cent of their 570 pubs, with set meals provided in 24 per cent.[54]

Reforming zeal was by no means confined to the leading London brewers. Benskin's of Watford, for example, came to prominence as a Home Counties concern on the strength of its considerable investment

[50] Nevile Papers on 'Restaurant Public Houses Association, 1925–34', including S.O. Nevile–Edith Neville correspondence, e.g. 3 July 1925, 5 November 1926, and Basil Jellicoe (ed.), *Housing Happenings*, 2 (1929), pp. 23–4, W/40/36, W&Co.; *Brewing Trade Review*, January 1927, p. 10.

[51] Memorandum on the Conference with the Restaurant Public Houses Association, 3 May 1928 and follow-up correspondence, e.g. Nevile–Cecil Charrington, 5 November 1928; C.W.A. (Arnett), 'A Bill', n.d., W/40/36, W&Co.

[52] Minutes of Special Meeting of the [RPHA] Executive Committee and representatives of the brewers, 22 May 1934 and other papers, W/40/36, W&Co.; Barclay Perkins, papers on '"Cross Keys", Blackfriars, 1935', Acc. 2305/1/1009/68, 70, 74, 81–3, 102, 108, etc. The companies involved initially were Barclay Perkins, Watney and Whitbread, followed by Courage, Mann Crossman & Paulin, Meux, Truman, Fuller, Smith & Turner, and two pub-owning companies, Levy & Franks and Trust Houses.

[53] *Brewing Trade Review*, July 1926, p. 262, November 1927, p. 444.

[54] J. S. Eagles, note on 'Catering in Whitbread Houses', March 1948, in Nevile Papers on 'Whitbread Public House Committee, 1946–8', W/40/24, W&Co.

in houses on London's periphery. It attracted acclaim for the 'sumptuous' quality of pubs such as the 'Berkeley Arms', Cranford, the 'Myllet Arms', Perivale and the 'Comet', Hatfield, designed by the company's architect, E. B. Musman.[55] Improvement was emulated by a score of provincial companies in Birmingham, Brighton, Cardiff, Liverpool, and even in some country districts, where Basil Oliver himself designed pubs for Greene King, and where Flower & Son of Stratford-upon-Avon were also prominent.[56]

The aggregate impact of all the various efforts to improve public houses is difficult to quantify fully, as has been recognised elsewhere.[57] There are sporadic references in the trade press to spending levels at certain times, both by individual companies and by the industry as a whole. Thus, at the company level, the firm of Peter Walker (Warrington) & Robert Cain was reported to have spent £370,000 excluding maintenance and renewals on 380 of its pubs in the five years 1925–30, while Watney Combe Reid put its expenditure on rebuilding and alterations at £181,000 for the year 1925–6 alone. The same company was later reported to have spent £3.78 million (£165,000 p.a.) on major rebuilding and alterations (over £1,500) affecting 561 properties in the period 1918–40; the largest pub-owning company, Ind Coope & Allsopp, spent £953,000 (£191,000 p.a.) on similar projects (over £1,000) for 228 properties in 1934–9.[58] In 1932 the *Brewers' Journal* gave two estimates of aggregate expenditure. In July it noted that about £21 million had been spent 'since the war', and in November remarked that £25 million had been spent 'since 1918'.[59] Both estimates probably owed their origin to data collected by the Brewers' Society for the periods 1922–6 and 1927–30 and made known to the Royal Commission

55 Oliver, *Renaissance*, pp. 101–2, 132–3; *Brewers' Journal*, July 1937, p. 342; *Brewing Trade Review*, April 1932, pp. 167–9, November 1936, p. 493; Col. W. H. Briggs, Chairman's speech to Benskin's Watford Brewery AGM, 12 November 1937, C/V/188, Allied.

56 Particularly active were Mitchells & Butlers (Birmingham), Kemp Town (Brighton), S. A. Brain (Cardiff), Bent's (Liverpool), Greenall Whitley (Warrington), John Smith's (Tadcaster), Walker Cain (Warrington and Liverpool), Flower (Stratford upon Avon), and Greene King (Bury St Edmunds). See Oliver, *Modern Public House*, pp. 32–3, *Renaissance*, pp. 107–20, 142–4; Wilson, *Greene King*, pp. 200–1; *Brewers' Journal*, September 1954, p. 407; *Brewing Trade Review*, October 1932, pp. 418–19, March 1935, p. 137.

57 Hawkins, 'Brewing Industry', pp. 485–6.

58 Serocold, *Watneys*, p. 77; Ind Coope & Allsopp, Rebuilding and Alterations data, 1934–40, 27 November 1951, C/F/2/51, Allied; *Brewing Trade Review*, December 1930, p. 657, *Brewers' Journal*, September 1926, p. 393, December 1930, p. 695.

59 *Brewers' Journal*, July and November 1932, pp. 369, 587, and see also September 1933, p. 464.

Table 10.4. *Estimates of expenditure on public house improvement in England and Wales, 1922–55 (current prices)*

Period	Breweries: Canvassed	Returned	Total Expenditure £	Public houses owned	Public houses improved	% improved	Expenditure per house £	Expenditure per annum £
1922–6	513	324[a]	12,365,139	47,224	13,542	29	913	2,473,028
1927–30[b]	102	84	8,613,763	27,680	6,581	24	1,309	2,461,075
1922–30			20,978,902		20,123		1,043	2,468,106
			Capital improvements			Maintenance/repairs		
			£			£		£
1954–5	100%[c]	100%[c]	13,337,987	–	5,626	24,541,339	–	18,939,663

[a] Reported as 329 to *Royal Commission on Licensing (England & Wales), 1929–31.*
[b] To June 1930.
[c] Information based on 90 per cent response rate grossed up to 100 per cent. *Off*-licences are included.
Source: Brewers' Society, 'Expenditure on Improving Licensed Houses', November 1930, and memo. on 'Public House Improvement' for Survey Committee, 13 December 1960, BS.

on Licensing. The information was used to refute suggestions that the brewers had done little to improve their properties. The industry was stung by one claim in particular, that made by Lord Balfour of Burleigh, an advocate of nationalisation. Introducing his Liquor (Disinterested Ownership and Management) Bill in the Lords in 1928, he had asserted that 'something like 75 or 80 per cent of the public-houses in this country come under [the] category of "slum-pub"'. The results of the first survey were published in a Brewers' Society brochure entitled *The Modern Public House.*[60] This revealed that in the five years ending in 1926, 324 of 513 companies canvassed had reported a total expenditure of £13.4 million on 13,500 pubs and beer houses, an average of £913 per outlet (see Table 10.4). A second survey covering the 3½ years to June 1930 showed that a smaller number of companies – eighty-four – had spent £8.6 million on 6,600 houses, an average of £1,309 per house (Table 10.4). With an expenditure of nearly £21 million on 20,000 pubs over eight years, based on limited returns, the brewers could scarcely be accused of neglecting the cause of improvement.[61] Unfortunately no further surveys appear to have been undertaken by the Brewers' Society until that conducted by its Survey Committee for the period 1954–60.[62] However, it is reasonable to assume that spending levels in the 1930s were at least as high as those in the 1920s.

Quite what we are to make of such data, and the likely returns to public house investment, is far from clear. The restrictions on building during the Second World War and the post-war austerity period undoubtedly represented a serious setback to the efforts to improve licensed properties. In addition to the interruption to new building, a considerable backlog of repairs and renewals was produced. Brewers were also excluded from taking early advantage of new town development by legislation in 1949 which provided for state management of licensed premises in such areas.[63] Although the Brewers'

60 Lord Balfour of Burleigh, *Parl. Deb. (Lords)*, 5th ser. Vol. 71 (Session 1928), 20 June 1928, c.583–4 (and see also *Brewing Trade Review*, September 1928, pp. 324–5; *Brewers' Journal*, July 1928, pp. 305–7); BS, *The Modern Public House* (October 1928), p. 2, and *Brewers' Journal*, September 1928, p. 435. Note that the data here are described as relating to '1923–7' and not '1922–6' as shown in BS files and subsequently (see note to Table 10.4).

61 For information passed to the Royal Commission on Licensing see F. P. Whitbread, *Minority Report, Royal Commission on Licensing (England and Wales)*, 21 December 1931, para. 32, *PP* (1931–2) XI, Cmd.3988.

62 BS memo on 'Public House Improvement', for Survey Committee, 13 December 1960, BS.

63 BS, Report for Year ended 31 March 1949, p. 22; BS; *Brewers' Journal*, August 1951, p. 409.

Society survey of 1960 revealed that by the mid-1950s spending on public houses and off-licences was fairly high – £13.3 million on capital improvements, £24.5 million on maintenance in 1954–5 (Table 10.4) – qualitative evidence suggests that there was a great deal still to be done to bring public house estates up to the standard demanded by the post-war consumer. The scale of the problem may be gauged by referring to the experience of one of the large London brewers, Watney Mann. Reviewing the position in 1959, the company stated that over 70 per cent of its licensed properties had been destroyed or substantially damaged during the War. Restrictions on building activity meant that annual expenditure on new building and major alterations had been limited to £232,000 per annum in 1943–54; in the period 1954–8 the figure had almost trebled to £663,000 p.a.[64]

It should also be emphasised that there was a considerable difference between best and worst practice in the industry, and that the absolute scale of improvement, i.e. in terms of the percentage of properties affected, was not as substantial as the trade's more enthusiastic supporters liked to believe. A detailed breakdown of spending by the eighty-four companies which reported for 1927–30 makes this clear. While at one end of the scale there were six companies which spent £300,000 or more over the 3½ year period – one company spent over £1.2 million – at the other there were five companies which each spent under £15,000. Six brewers improved 200 pubs or more; another six improved fewer than fifteen. Expenditure per house also varied considerably. Seven companies reported an expenditure of £3,000 per house and above – one of them spent £108,160 on twenty-four pubs, an average of £4,507 each – but twelve companies spent under £500 per house. One brewer reported spending something on all of his 107 properties, while nine revealed that they had improved under 10 per cent of their estates. The most common response was rather modest. Thus, 67 per cent of the companies spent £1,500 or less per house in improving 74 per cent of the pubs covered by the survey; 70 per cent of the companies improved under 30 per cent of their estates. Given that this was at a time when Barclay Perkins spent over £50,000 on the 'Downham Tavern' (1930) and Watney £83,000 on the 'Windsor Castle' (1928), and when it cost Whitbread £7,700 (£10,900 with other items) to rebuild the 'Anchor', its 'slum-pub' in Somers Town for the Restaurant Public Houses

[64] Simon Combe (Chairman, Watney Mann), Report to Ordinary Shareholders, 8 September 1959, Courage. For a general view see Edward Reed (Newcastle Breweries), 'A Note on the Brewing Industry', 4 May 1950, BS.

Table 10.5. *Average annual sales volumes (in bulk barrels) of draught and bottled beer in selected 'improved' and 'unimproved' Whitbread public houses, 1930s and 1955*

Public house	1930s			1955	
1. 'Improved'[a]	Draught	Bottled[b]		Draught	Bottled[b]
'Robin Hood', Becontree	1,840	1,048	[1935–8]	977	1,532
'Rest Hotel', Kenton	1,124	652	[1932–7]	n.a.	n.a.
'Rose and Crown', Tooting	1,079	315	[1933–7]	459	352
'Welcome Inn', Eltham	994	416	[1928–36]	468	636
'White Hart', Tottenham	984	291	[1932–7]	347	469
'Grapes', Hayes	551	235	[1932–7]	686	628
'Valley Hotel', Caterham	584	113	[1934–7]	198	154
2. 'Unimproved'[a]					
Average of nineteen 'unimproved' houses in Centre and South Walks	409	89	[1933–8]	168	154

[a] The category 'improved' is as defined by the company. This is not to suggest that no expenditure was undertaken on 'unimproved' houses.

[b] Bottled beer data given in barrel equivalents.

Source: Whitbread & Co. Estate & Trade Ledgers, W/13/30, 32–4, 42, 63, 74–5, 80, 91; Whitbread Properties Trade Ledger, W/14/3; Whitbread & Co. Quarterly Sales Figures, 1955, W/15/89–92, W&Co.

Association in 1929, then average practice as revealed by the Brewers' Society survey was more limited than the improvement lobby cared to admit.[65]

The results of the industry's improvement effort also appear to have been mixed, not only in terms of financial return but also in terms of consumer reaction. It is true that many of London's new, 'improved' public houses quickly returned impressive sales figures, three or four times higher than those of the average tied house in the capital. Data for Whitbread houses, shown in Table 10.5, make this clear. The 'Robin Hood' in Becontree, for example, returned remarkable average annual figures of 1,840 barrels of draught and 1,000 barrels of bottled beer in 1935–8, and there was a good trade in Kenton and Eltham. On the other hand, some ventures were less productive, as with the 'Valley Hotel' at Caterham, and it is doubtful whether the higher barrelages from the new houses fully compensated brewers for the loss of trade on low barrelage, loss-making pubs whose licences had been surrendered.[66] Taking into account the high initial capital cost of the new, large houses, and higher running costs, particularly in the staffing of managed houses, it is unlikely that such outlets produced average margins on turnover or an average return for the trade on capital employed. Frank Nicholson of Vaux certainly suggested as much in his evidence to the Royal Commission on Licensing of 1929–31, while Nevile recalled that at Whitbread it was 'some years' before the 'White Hart' at Tottenham, which had been built to 'elaborate' standards at a cost of well over £35,000, returned as much as 5 per cent.[67] Such views are supported by evidence on the fortunes of Whitbread's subsidiary, the Improved Public House Co. This concern made losses in the early years of its existence, £7,600 in all in 1921–3, largely due to the fact that its initial choice of houses for management was ill-conceived. It was 1930 before the company broke even on a cumulative basis, and thereafter profits were modest: net profits averaged £2,300 per annum in 1931–40, £8,400 in 1949–55. Detailed accounts for the year ending September 1940 reveal that its seventeen owned houses returned a gross profit of £62,600 on a turnover

[65] Barclay Perkins Board Minutes, 3 November 1930, Acc. 2305/1/22, GLRO; Watney Combe Reid Board Minutes, 18 Aug. 1926 and 1929–30, *passim*, Courage (Serocold, *Watneys*, p. 77, put the cost at £95,000 but the Minutes indicate that the original tender of 89,468 was reduced to £74,818, with subsequent additions in 1929–30 amounting to £8,082); Nevile–Jellicoe, 9 July 1931, W/40/36, W&Co.

[66] A point made by Hawkins, 'Brewing Industry', p. 485 citing the experience of Mitchells & Butlers.

[67] Nicholson, evidence to *Royal Commission on Licensing (England and Wales)*, 14 March 1930, Vol. I, Q.14,497; Nevile, *Seventy Rolling Years*, pp. 177–8.

of £223,800, but a net profit of only £6,900 (3.1 per cent of turnover), or £990 per house. Losses on other properties managed for Whitbread reduced the overall net profit to a mere £3,300.[68] Food sales were scarcely impressive, either. The seventeen owned houses took under £11,000 in 1939–40, only 5 per cent of their total turnover.[69] Nor were Whitbread's dealings with the Restaurant Public Houses Association remunerative. The experiments in Cumberland Market and Somers Town may have been successful in terms of public relations, but, in Nevile's words, were 'hardly commercial'. The 'Anchor', for example, sold over 700 barrels of beer in 1930, returning a small profit to the company of £347. But smaller pubs were cheaper to run with tenants rather than managers, and the accounts for 1933–4 revealed that on the three pubs the Association had made an operating loss of £1,772, a sum which was met by Whitbread.[70] In the absence of comprehensive information, it is difficult to weigh up all the financial elements of the brewers' improvement policies of the inter-war years. But it is safe to say that if such an investment was a necessary strategic response from companies seeking to retain or extend market-share in more difficult trading conditions, then the short- to medium-term returns were not particularly high.

Given the results, it is understandable that the policy was not pursued more vigorously. In the first place, licensing authorities continued to be deaf to brewers' pleas for permission to extend premises or relocate houses. A series of battles fought by leading brewers with licensing justices indicated the scale of the problem facing the would-be improver. In 1921, for example, a dispute between Whitbread and Wandsworth Licensing Justices was taken to the High Court. The company objected to the authorities' refusal to give consent to the rebuilding of a Tooting beer house unless another licence were surrendered, and the Court found in its favour.[71] That difficulties persisted is clear from a legal ruling in 1938, which arose from the anxiety of the Commissioners of Customs and Excise to obtain monopoly value

[68] Nevile Papers on 'Improved Public House Committee, 1920–3', W/40/34, and Improved Public House Co. balance sheets and accounts, 1921–58, and in particular accounts for year ending 30 September 1940, IPH/12, W&Co.

[69] *Ibid.*

[70] Memo on 'Anchor', Stibbington Street, 8 July 1931, Nevile–Jellicoe, 9 July 1931, Arnett–Nevile, 18 June 1934, W/40/36, W&Co.

[71] 'Rose and Crown', Tooting: Nevile, *Seventy Rolling Years*, pp. 168–70; *Brewers' Journal*, April 1921, p. 161. It should be noted that Section 71 of the Licensing Act of 1919 required the consent of the licensing justices to be obtained before any alterations or improvements to existing public houses could be undertaken.

(payable on new licences, see p. 5) when public houses were altered or enlarged. In *Rex v. Weston-super-mare Licensing Justices, ex parte Powell*, the High Court upheld the decision of the local justices that they had no power to permit alterations or extensions to existing licensed premises unless a new licence were obtained. This decision plainly dismayed the trade, and although it was quickly overturned in the Court of Appeal, it was symptomatic of the obstructive environment in which brewers had had to operate.[72] The scale of the problem may be gauged by a further reference to the licensing statistics (see p. 416). The 11,621 on-licences surrendered in England and Wales in 1914–55 were paralleled by a mere 3,300 'removals', i.e. transfers of a licence from one location to another, over the same period.[73]

In any case, it soon became clear that the large, barrack-type pub was no answer to consumer requirements in what had become a more complex leisure market. Many of the improvements sponsored by reformers were resented and resisted by the drinking public, and if that public was rather middle aged and elderly, as the brewers believed in the 1930s, then there was no firm evidence to support the idea that the young were any better disposed to waiter-service, cooked food, Shakespearean plays and miniature golf courses. Some brewers realised this at an early stage. Thus, in 1933, Lt.-Col. E. N. Buxton, a director of Truman Hanbury Buxton, one of the improving companies, deplored the loss of personal service in the large pubs, and noted the preference for ordering drinks at the bar and the distinct limits to the customers' desire to consume food (Plate 58).[74] Indeed, the Royal Commission on Licensing had itself conceded that 'perpendicular drinking' was 'an ingrained national custom' (Plate 52); like watching football from a standing terrace, it was slow to die.[75] In the late 1930s the trade press was full of condemnations of 'palace', 'luxury liner' and 'freak' public houses, and from the perspective of the latter stages of the Second World War the *Brewers' Journal* was able to state that 'there is universal approval in Trade circles of the view that there should be a relatively large number of moderate-sized houses rather than a small number of large houses. Public-house patrons share the view because they like the

[72] 'Three Queens Hotel', Weston-super-mare: *Brewers' Journal*, November 1938, pp. 578–9, 584–5, and BS, Annual Report for year ending 30 September 1939, pp. 14–15, BS.

[73] *Brewers' Almanack 1960*, p. 89.

[74] Lt.-Col. E. N. Buxton, Oxford House address, 5 March 1933, reported in *The Black Eagle Magazine*, July 1933, pp. 11–15, and the *Brewing Trade Review*, September 1933, pp. 360–1.

[75] *Report of Royal Commission on Licensing*, 1931, p. 47.

pub to be homely, individual and personal.'[76] Later a survey by the Central Statistical Office of beer prices and expenditure in 1951 revealed that the predominant form of drinking was still public bar drinking, and that beer bought with food or snacks accounted for only 6 per cent of the total outlay on the product.[77]

The brewers' response was also economic. Larger pubs had higher overheads per barrel sold, and they suffered more severely from the reduction in demand during the depression of the early 1930s. Waiter service and other elements of improvement were more costly to provide than the more limited but personal service of the tenanted pub. Consumer preferences accentuated the differences between the two types of retail outlet. The situation was readily apparent at Barclay Perkins's 'Downham Tavern', initially the only pub serving a population of 29,000. Given its high operating costs – there were thirty-five staff and three dozen lavatories, for example – it relied for its profitability on a monopoly position. When in 1937 Watney obtained a licence for a new pub, to be run with conventional bar service, half a mile away, Barclay Perkins responded immediately by obtaining authority to convert the 'Downham' to the same mode of operation.[78] The *Brewers' Journal* noted that 'the spontaneous revolt of the public at Downham against notions of public-house improvement imposed at the behest of people who have never entered a public-house as customers in their lives carries a lesson'.[79] Equally, the comparative costs of 'improved' and 'unimproved' houses provided an equally apposite lesson for the trade.

The retail market did exhibit some changes by the mid-1950s. More women could be found in pubs, a feature encouraged by the greater purchasing power of female workers during the Second World War. There was also evidence that more middle-class customers were being attracted into the better-appointed premises. Brewers also accepted the facilities had to be modified if younger drinkers were to become pub-goers. But the resistance to change characteristic of the bulk of the working-class market before the 1960s combined with the physical constraints of post-war building controls and raw material shortages to

[76] *Brewers' Journal*, June 1943, p. 502, and for earlier references see *ibid.*, April 1933, pp. 169–70, December 1938, p. 610.

[77] W. F. F. Kemsley and David Ginsburg, Preliminary Report for CSO on 'Beer Prices, Expenditure on Beer, and Drinking Habits', 1951 (based on a study of 2,858 people in May–June 1951), Tables 7, 8, 12, RG23/216, PRO: 52 per cent of male expenditure was incurred in public bars.

[78] Barclay Perkins Board Minutes, 6 May and 17 June 1937, and papers on 'Alterations to the "Downham Tavern", 1936–9', Acc. 2305/1/25, 2305/1/1011, GLRO.

[79] *Brewers' Journal*, December 1937, p. 595.

Table 10.6. *Brewers' tied estates and free-trade distribution, 1948/9*

Brewing company	Barrelage distributed to on/off licensed premises		Tied estate	Tenanted	Managed
	Tied estate %	free trade/clubs canteens %	(numbers)	%	%
All (Brewers' Society Survey)[a]	69	31	54,940	83	17
Average of 22 Companies[b]	73	27	12,914	82	18
Barclay Perkins	88	12	1,005	96	4
Boddingtons'	99.9	0.1	209	75	25
Brakspear	93	7	141	97	3
Bristol Brewery Georges	94	6	756	98	2
Matthew Brown	87	13	550	93	7
Cameron	93	7	362	93	7
Eldridge Pope	81	19	192	92	8
J. W. Green	89	11	358	100	0
Greene King	88	12	502	82	18
Hall & Woodhouse	95	5	140	100	0
Ind Coope & Allsopp	68	32	2,697	79	21
McEwan	19	81	57	7	93
Meux	90	10	341	75	25
Mitchells & Butlers	77	23	873	14	86
Newcastle	85	15	324	59	41
Russells & Wrangham	37	63	93	90	10
H. & G. Simonds	63	37	1,222	94	6
John Smith's	74	26	842	75	25
Steward & Patteson	95	5	614	99.8	0.2
Strong	91	9	468	92	8
Tetley	64	36	378	86	14
Whitbread	51	49	808	96	4

[a] Barrelage data include Scotland, tied estate data are for England and Wales only.
[b] Companies = earlier selection of twenty-five, excluding Bass, Guinness and Tamplin (who made no returns) and Arrol, Colchester, and Style & Winch (the subject of takeovers), but adding Simonds, Strong and Eldridge Pope.

encourage brewers to exercise caution in their modernisation of public houses. It was accepted that preferences were still largely traditional in nature, that a satisfying environment was as important as the quality and price of drink in consumers' choice of drinking place.[80]

IV

The brewers' management of their retail trade, and the economics of retailing, are difficult to pin down satisfactorily for any period before the 1960s, when we have the benefit of the Reports of the Prices and Incomes Board (1966) and Monopolies Commission (1969). Company practices clearly varied widely. Some brewers relied very heavily on their tied trade, which gave them steadier, forecastable sales together with a greater control of product quality at the point of sale; others specialised in the free and club trades, thriving in a more competitive environment characterised by lower wholesale margins; and a handful of large companies with a 'national' market built up an extensive network of distribution and bottling facilities. There were also brewers who pioneered the system of 'management', that is the replacement of tenant-publicans with salaried managers. The comparative economics of the two systems of retailing, which require a detailed knowledge of brewers' 'dry' (property) and 'wet' (beer) rent practices for their tenanted houses, as well as the operating costs of managed houses, are by no means easy to unravel for a single company, let alone for an entire industry. Here again, company procedures, founded on decades of local custom, varied a great deal, and, frustratingly for the historian, were rarely articulated in an accessible form, such as a board minute or a manager's report. In the circumstances, what follows is no more than a very rough indication of the major developments in the forty years to 1955.

As noted earlier, most brewers tended to distribute beer (and in smaller volumes wines and spirits) to a locally based tied estate. The Brewers' Society survey of the retail trade in 1948/9 makes this clear (see pp. 408–9). From our selection of companies, no less than fourteen of the remaining twenty-two depended on their tied trade for over 80 per cent of their sales (Table 10.6). Of these, Boddingtons', Hall & Woodhouse, and Steward & Patteson distributed 95 per cent or more of

80 Cf. *Brewers' Journal*, May and June 1943, pp. 416–17, 499–504; July 1945, pp. 600–3; Edward Reed, 'The People's Pub', December 1949, BS; Mass-Observation, Report on Drinking Habits, pp. 46–54, 70–6, 132–42, MO.

their beer to their own on- and off-licences, and others, such as Brakspear, Bristol Brewery Georges, Cameron, Strong and Meux, were not far behind. On the other hand, McEwan sold 81 per cent of its beer to the free trade and Whitbread 49 per cent, while Russells & Wrangham, a small Yorkshire brewery with a relatively large number of club accounts, sold 63 per cent outside the tie (Table 10.6), a feature it shared with Timothy Taylor of Keighley (69 per cent), Samuel Smith of Tadcaster (62 per cent), and Hope & Anchor Breweries of Sheffield (58 per cent). The free trade clearly meant more in counties such as Yorkshire, since both Tetley (36 per cent) and John Smith's (26 per cent) also had a substantial free trade. It was also important in Scotland, Wales and the South-West. In Scotland, for example, in addition to McEwan, Maclay of Alloa (69 per cent), John Jeffrey of Edinburgh (90 per cent), William Younger (69 per cent) and a number of smaller concerns relied on free-trade customers for more than half of their sales volumes.[81] Nor was there necessarily a correlation between size and free-trade dependence. The two largest owners of tied on-licences in the selected companies, Ind Coope & Allsopp (2,679) and H. & G. Simonds of Reading (1,222), distributed about a third of their barrelages to the free trade (Table 10.6). And two of the prominent 'national' brewers, Guinness and Bass, who made no returns to the Brewers' Society questionnaire, were also free-trade specialists. Guinness had only one tied house in Great Britain and therefore all of its British sales may be regarded as 'free'. A considerable portion of its trade went into the tied estates of other brewers, secured via an extensive distribution network serving bottling plants, including those of independent bottling companies. A survey of the English market in 1933 revealed that nearly 80 per cent of the Guinness sold was distributed to tied outlets, and that over half was bottled by brewer bottlers. By this means Guinness increased the market-share of its beer (at this time mainly bottled Extra Stout) from 2.7 per cent of total British and Guinness production in 1912–14 to 5.4 per cent in 1931–3 and 7.9 per cent in 1954–6.[82] Bass also relied heavily on the distribution of bottled ales via an agency network –

[81] BS, Brewery Statements, 1949, BS. Other companies with a large free trade included: Andrew Buchan (Rhymney); Fern Vale (Rhondda); Webbs (Aberbeeg); Wrexham Lager Brewery; Blundall (Plymouth); Venning (Liskeard); Shepherd Neame (Faversham); Star (Eastbourne); Frederick Smith (Birmingham); James Aitchison (Edinburgh).

[82] Arthur Guinness & Co., Volume of Miscellaneous Trade Statistics, and memo on 'Guinness Wholesale and Retail Prices in England', 25 January 1934, GPR. The sales survey of 1933 showed that 78.5 per cent of English Guinness was sold in tied outlets and that 57.25 per cent had been bottled by brewer bottlers.

it operated with twenty-five of these in the 1920s and twenty-two in the 1930s. London was the most important market, its agency there handling 18 per cent of the company's UK sales volume in 1933–7 and 15 per cent in 1947–9.[83] How reliant it was on the free trade is less certain. Hawkins has claimed that most Bass pubs in the 1920s were managed, and that 'less than 10 per cent' of its barrelage was sold through them.[84] However, this appears to exaggerate Bass's reliance on the free trade, particularly after its merger activity over the decade. A considerable tied estate was certainly built up, such that by January 1953 the company was reported to own 1,128 on-licensed premises and 200 off-licences. It is therefore likely that at the time of the Brewers' Society survey the company's tied:free ratio was nearer to 40:60 than 10:90.[85]

For substantial owners of public houses the relative profitability of tenanted and managed outlets became a matter for debate after 1914. Managed houses were consonant with the reforming zeal represented by the Carlisle State Management Scheme and the initiatives of social reformers, while the larger houses opened by reforming brewers invited operation by salaried managers since they were beyond the capital resources and managerial capacities of a single tenant and his/her family. On the other hand, management could be a costly way to run a pub when the trade was modest or uncertain. With a tenancy, the 'dry' rent paid on the property was nominal, for most pubs between £50 and £200 a year, a figure based loosely on the extent of trade, the value of the property or the amenity value of the tenant's living accommodation. A perusal of brewing company records reveals a tendency for rents to rise, though change was gradual. For twenty Whitbread pubs, for example, the average rent paid was £151 in 1938 and £168 in 1957, while for eighteen John Smith's pubs in Yorkshire it was £35 in 1921, £41.50 in 1938 and £64 in 1955.[86] The Brewers' Society survey of 1948/9 discovered that for thirty-four representative companies the average rent was £115 a year. London rents were higher – Watneys averaged £397, Whitbread £201 and Courage £193 – while the rents in some country

83 Bass, Comparative Statements of Sales, 1926–53, C30, B134–5, Bass.
84 Hawkins, *Bass Charrington*, p. 89.
85 Guinness, 'Number of Licensed Houses owned by Principal Brewers in Great Britain (including houses owned by subsidiaries)', January 1953, Trade Department Volume of Great Britain Brewing Statistics, GPR. Bass had 1,128 on- and 200 off-licences. At 250 barrels per outlet, the tied trade would be 332,000 barrels, or 40 per cent of Bass's UK sales in 1952 (837,000 barrels).
86 Whitbread Estate Trade Ledgers Centre Walks, 1935–42, 1938–47, 1956–60, W/13/30, 32, 35, W&Co; John Smith's Public House Ledgers, JA/S/16, 20, John Smith's, Tadcaster.

districts were very low indeed – £15 for Greene King, £19 for Hall, Cutlack & Harlock of Ely, and £26 for Andrew Buchan of Rhymney.[87] The greater part of the profit to the brewer came from the difference between production cost and the wholesale price of the beer, which for tied tenants was augmented by a 'wet' rent, that is a premium paid over the price which the brewer charged a retailer in the free trade. A managed house would provide no 'dry' rent, but the brewer would collect the entire wholesale and retail mark-up, that is, the difference between the retail price and the production/distribution cost. On the other hand, the pub's total running costs would fall to the brewer. Hawkins has argued that direct management was preferable to tenancy arrangements because it enhanced the rate of return on capital. Claiming that management specialists such as Mitchells & Butlers and Bent's had a higher rate of return on their capital than the companies which relied on tenancies, he suggests that the tenancy system was a suboptimal form of retailing in a profit sense, and that the token 'dry' rents symbolised a chronic under-exploitation of brewers' properties. The *Statist*, quoted by Hawkins, put it simply: 'the traditional and the paternal have tempered the commercial'.[88] It may be that the management system was potentially more profitable, but it was inappropriate for the smaller pub; and in the period under examination tenants were easier to find and were frequently more reliable than managers. If, however, we leave aside other arguments – that brewers should have disposed of outlets which were too small to manage profitably or else let the properties at commercial rents for purposes other than brewing – the choice of retailing system, it must be admitted, was often a matter of fine judgement if profit-maximisation were the objective. What is clear is that long-run organisational preferences triumphed over short-run commercial ones. The 'dry/wet' rent system may have established a rather cosy relationship between brewer and tenant, but it was also a flexible system which facilitated ease of entry into the trade; and, by

[87] BS, Memo on 'Tied House System' (responses to circulars 36/48 and 31C/49), 5 December 1949, BS. The Society erroneously put the average at £116 (it was £115.2). The mean of the companies' mean rents was £89.70, and the standard deviation was £80.95. The thirty-four companies were: Simonds, Morland, Mitchells & Butlers, Hall, Cutlack & Harlock, Plymouth Breweries, Wethered, Vaux, Hardy's, Tennant Bros., Hammonds United, Benskin's, Cheltenham & Hereford, Bristol Brewery Georges, Bristol United, Thwaites, Peter Walker, Threlfall's, Truman Hanbury Buxton, Whitbread, Watney, Courage, Taylor Walker, Boddingtons', Andrew Buchan's, Greene King, Northampton, Newcastle, Trouncer (Shrewsbury), William Hancock, Friary Holroyd & Healy, Tetley, John Smith's, Ind Coope & Allsopp, and Usher's.

[88] *Statist*, September 1952, cit. in Hawkins, *Bass Charrington*, p. 119.

adjusting the total rental paid according to turnover, it protected the tenant when trade was low or falling and rewarded the brewer when trade increased. The strength of the licensed victuallers' lobby was another influence. It is safe to assume that the traditional tenancy system was rarely abandoned unless a good case could be made for a change.[89]

A shift from tenancy to management certainly took place in the period after 1914, but it tended to be a characteristic of particular locations and particular firms and therefore had defined limits. It is clear from the final report of the Royal Commission on Liquor Licensing Laws of 1897–9 that brewers' pubs in Liverpool were primarily managed in the 1890s, while in Birmingham too the system was gaining ground. In both places the legacy of past retailing, where private pub owners and pub-owning companies had been more common, was important, but so too was the sympathetic attitude to the idea of occupancy by salaried managers shown by licensing magistrates in these areas.[90] Elsewhere, however, tied tenancies were the predominant form. Frank Nicholson of Vaux, in his evidence to the Royal Commission on Licensing in March 1930, claimed that in 1925 only 6,000 or 7.5 per cent of the on-licenses in England and Wales were under management.[91] The proportion increased over the next decade. Companies such as Mitchells & Butlers, Ansells and Bent's, along with Burton brewers such as Bass, moved enthusiastically into retailing by management. In the early 1920s Mitchells & Butlers were managing about 60 per cent of their on- and off-licences, and the proportion rose to 86 per cent over the next twenty years or so.[92] Calculations made by Guinness's statistical department at Park Royal, which carried out a great deal of market intelligence work in the inter-war years, found that managed houses accounted for 18 per cent of brewers' English and Welsh on-licences in 1934 and 1935. In three areas, based on Guinness's travelling districts, the proportion was shown to be markedly higher: Cardiff (70 per cent), Birmingham (48 per cent) and Newcastle (48 per cent).[93]

89 Cf. Nicholson, evidence to the *Royal Commission on Licensing*, 14 March 1930, QQ.14,531–46.

90 *Final Report of Royal Commission on Liquor Licensing Laws*, 1899, *PP* (1899) XXXV, p. 96, and evidence of Capt. J. W. N. Bower, 13 April 1897, *PP* (1898) XXXVI, QQ.26,337–54; Hawkins, *Bass Charrington*, p. 84n. Of 2,078 Liverpool pubs in 1892, 1,057 were brewer-managed and 218 brewer-tenanted.

91 Nicholson, *Royal Commission on Licensing*, Q.14,531. Nicholson did not distinguish between tied and free houses in making his calculation.

92 Hawkins, *Bass Charrington*, p. 83.

93 Guinness, 'Number of "On" Licences in England & Wales, Subdivided into Travelling Districts', 1934 and 1935, in Volume of Miscellaneous Trade Statistics, GPR. The coverage and reliability of the information by district is not entirely certain. The

The available evidence suggests that the proportion of managed houses – about 18 per cent of brewers' pubs (about 13 per cent of the total number of on-licences) – remained more or less fixed over the next twenty-five years. Thus, the Brewers' Society survey of 1948/9 produced a percentage of 17 per cent for England and Wales, while for our selection of twenty-two companies the figure was 18 per cent (Table 10.6). A later survey by the Society carried out in 1960 found the proportion to be much the same, viz. 19 per cent.[94] Company returns revealed a wide variation, of course. Tenancy specialists predominated. Of the twenty-two companies listed in Table 10.6, thirteen had tenants in 90 per cent or more of their pubs. J. W. Green and Hall & Woodhouse ran all their houses by tenancy, while Steward & Patteson had tenants in all but one of its 614 houses. A tenancy return of 100 per cent was also recorded by other companies, such as Phipps of Northampton, which had 486 houses, and by smaller brewers such as McMullen (Hertford), Ridley (Hartford End, Essex), Ruddle (Oakham) and Arkell (Swindon). At the other end of the scale, McEwan managed no less than 93 per cent of its properties, Mitchells & Butlers 86 per cent, and Newcastle 41 per cent (Table 10.6). Elsewhere, management specialists included Ansells in Birmingham (80 per cent), and Higson's (87 per cent) and Threlfall's (80 per cent) in Liverpool. In Scotland, the smaller concern of Maclay in Alloa managed all of its dozen pubs. The survey underlines the point that managed houses tended to be preferred by certain brewers in Birmingham, Lancashire, the North-East and the West Midlands. Here, economic depression, which made it harder to attract tenants, was as important as the brewers' search for higher profits.[95]

The only overall indication of the economics of tied retailing before the 1960s comes from the Brewers' Society survey of 1948/9, which was conducted in response to attacks on the industry and the tied house system at the time of the passage of the Licensing Bill of 1948 (which became the Licensing Act, 1949). As the Society's circular of December 1948 noted, 'the Action Committee finds itself at a disadvantage in refuting what appear to be obvious mis-statements because there are no reliable figures available as to the real extent of the tied house system,

Newcastle district, for example, was reported to have 70 per cent of tied houses managed in 1934, but only 48 per cent a year later. The Liverpool district was shown to have only 16.8 per cent of the houses managed in 1934 (16.7 per cent in 1935).

[94] BS, Memo on 'The Tied House System', for Survey Committee, 12 April 1960, BS. The proportion of brewers' on- and off-licences managed was 17 per cent in 1949 and 21 per cent in 1960.

[95] Brewers' Society, Brewery Statements, 1949, BS and cf. Nicholson, *Royal Commission on Licensing*, Q.14,532.

Table 10.7. *Tied house rents and imputed costs (England and Wales), 1949*

	per house £	per barrel p		Estimated E & W aggregate £
Revenue:				
'Dry' rent	116[a]	33.8	(6s 9d)	5,290,000[a]
Costs:				
Maintenance	165	47.5	(9s 6d)	7,524,000
Rates/licence duty	19	5.4	(1s 1d)	866,000
Schedule A Tax	49	14.2	(2s 10d)	2,234,000
Total	233	67.1	(13s 5d)	10,624,000
'Loss' to be recovered via 'wet' rent	117	33.3	(6s 8d)	5,334,000
Co. variation (34 companies):				
Highest	507	119.6	(23s 11d)	
Lowest	+49[b]	+12.5[b]	(+2s 6d)[b]	
Mean of means	136.7	44.6	(8s 11d)	
Standard deviation	97.4	29.7	(5s 11d)	

[a]True average per house: £115.2 (aggregate £5,253,000).
[b]Figure positive, i.e. 'dry' rent exceeded costs.
Source: Brewers' Society, Memo on 'Tied House System', 5 December 1949, BS.

the management system, and the volume of trade which passes through the clubs'.[96] Calculations made on the basis of detailed returns from thirty-four companies, taking into account further information supplied in response to a follow-up circular of July 1949,[97] revealed some of the basic economics of tied tenancies, and in particular the extent to which 'dry' rents failed to cover the brewers' basic public house costs (Table 10.7).

With average 'dry' rents of £116 per house (in fact £115 on the Society's own figures) or 33.8p per barrel, the shortfall after providing for mainte-

[96] BS, Circular on 'Hotels, Tied Houses and Clubs' (36/48), 21 December 1948, BS. A Private Member's Bill to abolish tied houses was introduced, but failed to secure a second reading.

[97] BS, Circular on 'Tied Houses' (31C/49), 20 July 1949, BS. Originally, forty companies were selected, but five were ruled out because their information on repairs was considered unreliable, while the data on two associated companies could not be separated.

nance, rates, licence duty and Schedule 'A' Tax was put at £117, or 33.3p per barrel, a 'loss' which was to be recovered from 'wet' rent payments by the tenant. The experience of individual companies varied widely. In seven cases the difference between the dry rent and reported costs amounted to £200 a house (and in one instance – Newcastle Breweries – was as high as £507), while for six companies the margin was under £60. On a barrelage basis three companies had a shortfall of £1 or more, while for six companies it was under 15d. One company – Courage – showed a positive balance of £49 per house and 12½d per barrel.[98]

The 'wet' rent charged to tenants was thus an important part of the profit calculation for most brewers. Unfortunately, information on the subject is patchy, and meaningful averages are difficult to construct, since rents varied from product to product and from tenant to tenant. At Joshua Tetley's, for example, the wet rent charged to Leeds tenants in the early 1950s was 6s (30p) a barrel, a level which was sufficient to cover the reported shortfall between the dry rent and basic costs of 4s 3d (21p) in 1949; Manchester tenants, on the other hand, paid only 4s (20p).[99] If we assume that an average wet rent of 10s (50p) a barrel was charged at this time – the figure was suggested to the Royal Commission by Nicholson in 1930 – then for over half of the thirty-four breweries surveyed this would have been sufficient to cover the shortfall between the dry rent and outgoings.[100] Given the crucial importance of wholesale profits, supplemented by wet rents, in brewers' tied houses, it is scarcely surprising to find that the tie, which before 1914 had been confined in the main to draught beer, was extended from the 1920s to embrace not only bottled beer, but 'foreign' beers (bottled beers from other brewers, e.g. Guinness), wines and spirits and, in many cases, soft drinks. The move was a consequence of the companies' more determined entry into bottling, wines and spirits merchanting, and mineral water production, but it was also stimulated by cheaper distribution costs, which arose from the more intensive use of motor lorries.[101] Concentration levels

98 Companies with a shortfall of £200 a pub or more: Simonds, Mitchells & Butlers, Wethered, Thwaites, Andrew Buchan's, Northampton, and Newcastle; less than £60 a pub: Peter Walker, Watney, Courage, Taylor Walker, Friary Holroyd, and John Smith's. Companies with a shortfall of £1 a barrel or more: Simonds, Andrew Buchan's and Newcastle; under 15p: Peter Walker, Truman, Whitbread, Watney, Taylor Walker, and John Smith's. BS, Memo. on 'Tied House System', 5 December 1949, BS.

99 Peat Marwick Mitchell, Report on Joshua Tetley Accounts for year ending 30 September 1955, p. 13, Tetley, Leeds; BS, Memo, 5 December 1949.

100 BS, Memo, December 1949; Nicholson, *Royal Commission on Licensing*, Q.14,545.

101 On the significance of the tie see, for example, chairman's statement to Watney Combe Reid AGM, 22 September 1949, Courage Archive.

also increased after the War. The on-licences owned by the leading eighteen English companies amounted to 26 per cent of the total in England and Wales in 1949 and 32 per cent in 1955.[102] In 1949 the Brewers' Society sponsored a 'model tenancy', by which the tie was to be confined to alcoholic drinks. The publican would be free to buy other products where he chose, and in return he would undertake to bear the running costs of his pub. However, the evidence suggests that this made little headway. Market forces pointed in the opposite direction, in fact.[103]

Some features of the modern British brewing industry – a tendency to higher concentration, a shift to packaged (i.e. bottled) beer, a wider awareness of the pros and cons of managed vs. tenanted houses, and a recognition of the need to invest considerable sums in tied houses – had emerged by the mid-1950s. But in the main, traditional retailing practices persisted, and the tied house system served to protect the market shares of the smaller, locally based brewing concerns. The situation was not necessarily disadvantageous to either the industry or the consumer. The tied house system and the companies' preference for tenancies – a preference often shared by customers – had many advantages. Although it is doubtful whether profits were being maximised as a result, it should not be assumed that the system lacked a rationale, that it was merely an antiquated way of trading waiting for management consultants and accountants to sweep it aside. The 'brewing revolution' of the next twenty-five years was to transform the industry in so many ways, but it left the tied tenancy as the predominant form of on-licensed property.[104]

The build-up of the industry's vertical integration was as much a consequence of the strict control of licensed premises, and the problems of distributing a bulky product over large distances, which made companies anxious to secure access to the market, as it was a search for realising scale economies and greater market-share. Paradoxically, the emerging national brewers sought expansion outside the tie, by promoting heavily advertised bottled beer brands. Once the tied system had been established, large sums were invested in improvements to the premises, which cemented the relationship between producer and retailer. Competition was blunted by the system, as it was by regional

102 *Brewers' Almanack 1960*; Guinness, 'Number of Licensed houses owned ...', January 1955, GPR.

103 *Brewing Trade Review*, August and September 1949, pp. 576, 688.

104 In 1979 72 per cent of tied houses were tenanted. BS, *UK Statistical Handbook 1980*, p. 65.

collusion over minimum beer prices,[105] but it was certainly not eradicated, and the early 1950s saw signs of a more intense oligopolistic competition. The tied house was still the predominant form of retail outlet, but well-established rivals to it were more prominent in the early 1950s than they had been a half-century earlier: drinking at home, national bottled brands and the challenge of alternative leisure activities. Furthermore, public house standards clearly had to move with the times, a fact of life for tied trade brewers for many decades. Those companies which had failed to improve their pubs in the gloomy demand conditions of the inter-war period found their problems compounded by years of forced inactivity from 1939 to 1955. In many cases the under-investment was so great that acquisition by a more enterprising brewer became the only logical course of action. The *Statist* was not only echoing past debates but looking forward to future problems when it declared in 1952: 'the economic implications of all this is that brewers who have traditionally regarded themselves as brewers first and last may have to consider themselves increasingly as owners of property'.[106]

105 Cf. Vaizey, *Brewing Industry*, pp. 156–7. Evidence of collusion may be found in the minutes of county brewers' associations.

106 'Economic Trends in the Brewing Industry', *Statist*, 1952, p. 10.

11

Merger mania, 1955–1980

I

The merger 'mania' of the 1960s and early 1970s was not of course confined to the brewing industry; it was a national phenomenon. In the period 1959–73 no fewer than 12,800 of the larger British firms disappeared through merger, a rate of 856 per annum, compared with only 291 per annum in 1954–8, and 460 per annum in 1974–80.[1] Particularly high levels were recorded in 1964–5, 1968 and 1972–3. In manufacturing, which accounted for about 60 per cent of this reported activity,[2] thirty-nine of the top 200 manufacturing firms in 1964 had experienced an acquisition or merger by 1969, and twenty-two of the top 200 in 1969 had experienced a merger by 1972.[3] By 1968 the hundred largest firms controlled 41 per cent of net output, compared with only 22 per cent in 1949 and 27 per cent in 1953; in retailing, multiple stores accounted for 37 per cent of total turnover in 1971, compared with 22 per cent in 1950.[4] Since most of the mergers were horizontal in nature, concentration levels increased substantially in most industries. For example, the employment share of the three largest enterprises in the average manufacturing industry increased from 32 per cent in 1958 to 41 per cent in 1968 and 42 percent in 1973.[5] In short, the late 1960s and

1 Data taken from *Economic Trends*, April 1963, November 1965, and *Business Monitor MQ7*, 1981. Major breaks in the data before 1969 mean that any long-run assessment of merger activity can only be approximate.

2 According to Leslie Hannah, in the period 1959–73 no less than 8,066 manufacturing firms disappeared through merger, 538 per annum, compared with only 1,695 (154 p.a.) in 1948–58; the capital value (in constant 1961 share prices) of these firms was £6,563 million (£438m. p.a.) in 1959–73 and £1,235 million (£124m. p.a.) in 1949–58. Hannah, *Corporate Economy*, pp. 176–7. The caveat in note 1 also applies here.

3 Alan Hughes, 'The Impact of Merger: A Survey of Empirical Evidence for the UK', in James Fairburn and John Kay (eds.), *Mergers and Merger Policy* (1988), p. 37.

4 S. J. Prais, *The Evolution of Giant Firms in Britain* (Cambridge, 1976), p. 4; B. W. E. Alford, *British Economic Performance 1945–1975* (1988), p. 60.

5 The share of product sales of the top five firms in the average manufacturing industry increased from 55 per cent in 1958 to 63 per cent in 1968 (65 per cent in 1975). P. E. Hart and R. Clarke, *Concentration in British Industry* (Cambridge, 1980), pp. 95–6.

Table 11.1. *Brewing industry concentration, 1952–80*

Year	Concentration measures: Share of top five enterprises in: quoted assets %	net output %	employment %	retail outlets %	Number of: Brewing companies	Breweries
1952	21	–	–	–	–	524
1954	–	18	19	–	305	479
1955	–	–	–	11	–	460
1957	24	–	–	–	–	416
1958	–	23	22	–	–	399
1960	–	–	–	21	247	358
1963	–	42	49	–	–	304
1967	63	–	–	–	117	243
1968	–	62	61	–	117	220[a]
1973	–	69	61	38[b]	88	162
1980	–	55[c]	53[c]	–	81	142

[a] Break in series – from 1969 estimated by Brewers' Society
[b] Data for 1974
[c] Data for 1979
Source: P. E. Hart, 'Concentration in the United Kingdom', University of Reading Discussion Papers in Economics No. 24, June 1970, pp. 9–10, 32–3; Hawkins and Pass, *Brewing Industry*, p. 64; K. Cowling *et al.*, *Mergers and Economic Performance* (Cambridge, 1980), pp. 215–16; BS, *UK Statistical Handbook 1980*, p. 88; Guinness, 'Number of Licensed Houses owned by Principal Brewers', January 1955, August 1960, Trade Dept Statistics, GA; *Census of Industrial Production*, 1973, 1979.

early 1970s were the second stage (the first having been in the 1920s) in a process of concentration and company growth which has been labelled 'the rise of the corporate economy'.[6]

The brewing industry was one of the most prominent industries in this process, as the data in Table 11.1 demonstrate. The quoted assets of the top five brewing enterprises increased from 21 per cent of the industry's total in 1952 to 24 per cent in 1957, then jumped to 63 per cent by 1967. The share of the top five companies in both net output and employment increased in similar vein from 23 and 22 per cent respectively in 1958 to 62 and 61 per cent respectively by 1968. In 1955

[6] Hannah, *Corporate Economy*, Chs. 7 and 10.

the top five brewers owned 11 per cent of Britain's licensed retail outlets. Five years later this had almost doubled, and by 1974 it had reached 38 per cent. In consequence, the number of brewing companies and their breweries contracted sharply. The number of breweries, i.e. production sites, fell from 479 in 1954 to 162 in 1973, a fall of no less than 66 per cent. The company casualty rate was slightly higher, with a fall from 305 in 1954 to 88 in 1973, a reduction of 71 per cent. There then followed a period of stabilisation, and in fact the concentration ratio for the top five firms fell to about 53–55 per cent by 1979.

In one element the brewing industry diverged from the national picture, that is in the timing of the decisive period of change. This came earlier in brewing, in the late 1950s and early 1960s, rather than in the late 1960s and early 1970s. According to Hawkins and Pass, of ninety-eight mergers no less than thirty-five occurred in the period 1959–61.[7] The more complete data used here confirm this finding, showing that of 164 mergers in the period 1958–72, seventy-five or 46 per cent took place in 1959–61 (see Appendix, Table X).[8] Heralded by the entry into British brewing of the Canadian brewing entrepreneur E. P. Taylor, who used Hope & Anchor Breweries as a base for expansion, by the merger of Watneys and Mann, Crossman & Paulin in 1958, and the much-publicised unsuccessful bid for Watney Mann by Charles Clore of Sears Holdings in the following year (see pp. 460–4), the next five years saw significant and enduring company formations. First, there was the merger of Hope & Anchor, Hammonds United and John Jeffrey to form Northern Breweries in 1960; the new company, subsequently called United Breweries, expanded by means of further acquisitions before its merger with Charrington in 1962. Then, also in 1960, Courage & Barclay merged with H. & G. Simonds, and Scottish & Newcastle Breweries was created. In 1961 there were two important mergers: that of Bass and Mitchells & Butlers; and the combination of Ind Coope, Tetley Walker and Ansells (the new company being renamed Allied Breweries at the end of 1962). Finally, Whitbread made its first moves to formalise the relationship with companies in its 'umbrella'. These mergers produced the 'Big Six' which, with Guinness, dominated British brewing for three decades (see Appendix, Table X). By 1967, at the time of the Monopolies Commission inquiry into beer, the seven companies – Allied, Bass Charrington (the product of a merger of the two companies in that year), Courage, Guinness, Scottish

[7] Hawkins and Pass, *Brewing Industry*, pp. 64–5.
[8] Data are for the number of firm disappearances by merger.

& Newcastle, Watney and Whitbread – accounted for 73 per cent of total UK beer production, and this share had increased to 80 per cent by 1972.[9] Most of the mergers were horizontal in nature, although the motive was often to acquire additional retail outlets rather than to add productive capacity and therefore the moves could be considered 'quasi-vertical' from the brewing standpoint. And four of the biggest mergers, Grand Met/Truman (1971), Grand Met/Watney Mann (1972), Imperial Group/Courage (also in 1972) and Allied/Lyons (1978) were conglomerate mergers linking brewing with a range of leisure and consumer product interests. There were also horizontal mergers in continental Europe. In the 1960s Watney Mann acquired substantial interests in Belgium, while Allied did the same in Holland.[10] Rationalisation and greater scale economies in production were obvious consequences of the merger activity. The Big Six (excluding Guinness) closed fifty-four or 44 per cent of their 122 breweries over the period 1958–70, for example, and average production per brewery plant rose accordingly. The average output per company increased four-fold from 1958 to 1973, and the average per brewery by nearly as much.[11]

II

Why did the mergers occur? Here, we must distinguish between general economic influences and factors specific to brewing. Because the merger wave was a national, indeed an international phenomenon, economists and historians have pointed to common causes of higher levels of concentration in post-war developed economies. These include: the existence of a buoyant stock market, which facilitated mergers via an exchange of shares rather than a cash purchase; the search for scale

[9] Monopolies Commission, *Report on the Supply of Beer* (1969), p. 5; Anthony Cockerill, 'The Merger Movement in the Brewing Industry', *The Brewer*, March 1977, p. 82. The Big Seven still accounted for about 80 per cent of the market at the end of the 1980s: cf. Monopolies and Mergers Commission, *The Supply of Beer. A Report on the Supply of Beer for Retail Sale in the United Kingdom*, March 1989, PP (1988–9) Cm.651, p. 3.

[10] Allied Breweries became the second largest brewer in Holland after acquiring d'Oranjeboom and De Drie Boefizers (Breda) in 1968, while Watneys purchased three Belgian breweries, Jules Delbruyere (1966), Vandenheuvel (1968) and Maes (1969), making it the third largest in Belgium. *Brewing Trade Review*, February 1966, p. 99, March and September 1968, pp. 200, 694–5, September 1969, p. 868; *The Times*, 10 March 1969; *The Economist*, 8 November 1969, p. 77; *Brewing Review*, March 1973, p. 163.

[11] Average production per company (barrels), 1958: 96,000; 1973: 420,514; per brewery: 1958: 60,150, 1973: 228,395. Cockerill, 'Merger Movement', pp. 82, 87.

economies; and the determination of leading companies to retain market-share, or indeed to increase market power, through the suppression of competition, motives stimulated by the challenge of trading in world markets which had become increasingly dominated by powerful multinational conglomerates. In the UK the actions of successive governments served both to encourage and discourage corporate competition. On the one hand, there was an attack on restrictive practices, and cartels in particular, embodied in legislation of 1956, and the abandonment of resale price maintenance in retailing in 1964. On the other hand, there was a pragmatic, even permissive, attitude to concentration itself. Thus, while the Monopolies Commission (established in 1948) extended its sphere of influence in 1965 in order to ensure that mergers as well as monopolies did not infringe the public interest, the creation of the Industrial Reconstruction Corporation in the following year represented a positive encouragement to mergers in industries where the government believed that greater concentration held the key to improved international competitiveness. Both types of government reaction, it may be argued, stimulated a higher level of merger activity.[12] Entrepreneurial responses were also significant. The emergence of takeover specialists such as Clore, who were attracted to companies which had failed to realise the full potential of their assets, and property assets in particular, evidently fuelled the 'mania', as did the growing divorce of ownership and control in larger companies, which came with the decline of family management. Both factors helped to create what has been described as a 'market mechanism for corporate control', whereby in the course of hostile takeover bids shareholders were in effect wooed by competing groups, each of which claimed that its victory would lead to improved results.[13]

In brewing, these features were clearly present, but there were also aspects peculiar to the industry. The most important were changes in demand. In the 1950s UK beer consumption was static at the 25 million bulk barrel level. Then, with little or no change in the average gravity of

[12] Under the Fair Trading Act, 1973, the Monopolies Commission became the Monopolies and Mergers Commission. See, *inter alia*, B. S. Yamey, *Resale Price Maintenance* (1966), pp. 258ff.; Hannah, *Corporate Economy*, p. 148; Alister Sutherland, 'The Management of Mergers Policy', in Alex Cairncross (ed.), *The Managed Economy* (Oxford, 1970), pp. 106–34; James Fairburn, 'The Evolution of Merger Policy in Britain', in Fairburn and Kay (eds.), *Mergers*, pp. 193–6.

[13] Hannah, *Corporate Economy*, p. 150; 'Introduction', Fairburn and Kay, *Mergers*, pp. 1–2.

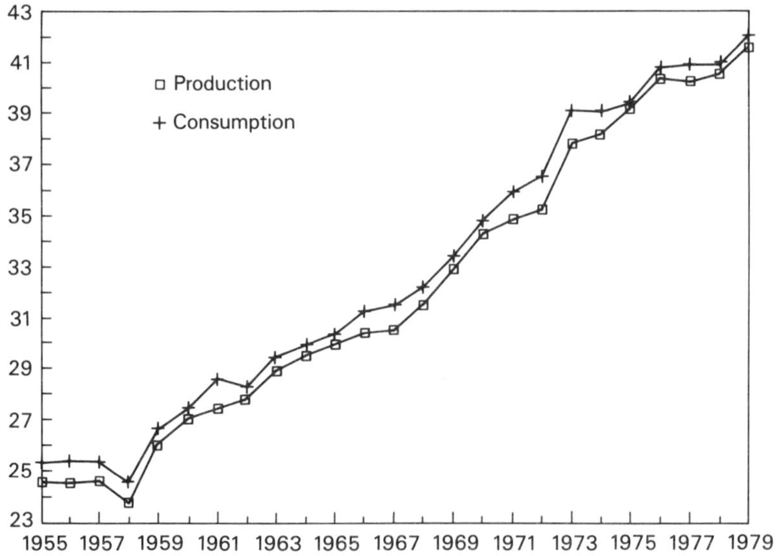

Fig. 11.1 UK beer production and consumption in bulk barrels (millions), 1955–79. (*Source:* see Appendix, Table XI, cols. 1 and 3.)

beer,[14] there followed a prolonged rise from a low point of 24.6 million barrels in 1958 to 42.1 million in 1979, an increase of 71 per cent, or 2.5 per cent per annum (see Fig. 11.1 and Appendix, Table XI). This expansion of the market was part of a general increase in the consumption of alcoholic drinks. Indeed, wines, spirits and cider exhibited much higher growth rates: over the period 1955–79, the thirst for these products increased by 7.4, 5.2 and 4.3 per cent per annum respectively, compared with 2.4 per cent for beer (see Fig. 11.2). While the significant merger activity of 1959–61 may be seen as the product of uncertainty, even gloom, about the future size of the market, later mergers were sustained by optimism about demand prospects in the industry. In fact, beer consumption was particularly buoyant towards the end of the merger wave. It grew by 3.5 per cent a year over the period 1967–73.[15]

As in earlier periods, almost all of the demand for beer was satisfied

[14] Average gravity of beer consumed 1955–79 was 1037.41° (high 1037.74°, low 1036.86°, SD = 0.26°); the average gravity of domestic production was 1037.38° (high 1037.70°, low 1036.87°, SD = 0.26°).

[15] Consumption increased from 31.52 million barrels in 1967 to 39.20 million barrels in 1973. After the oil crisis of 1973, and its accompanying high inflation, growth was slower: 1.2 per cent p.a., 1973–9. See Appendix, Table XI.

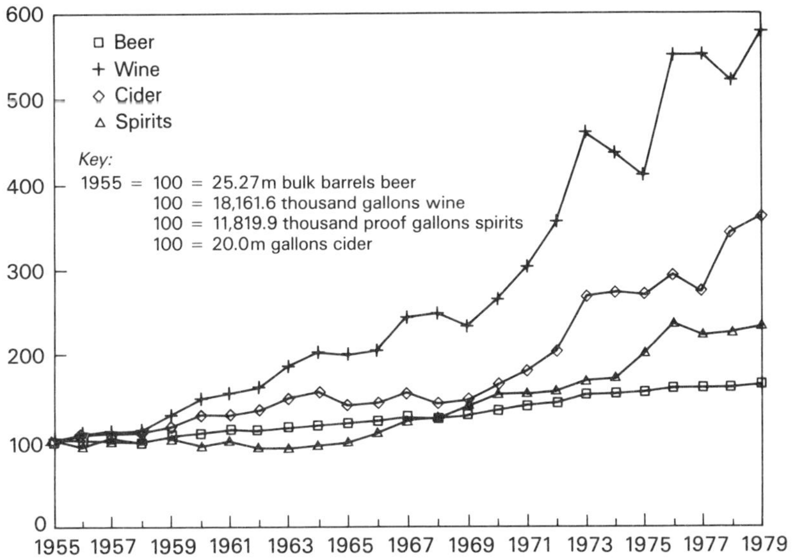

Fig. 11.2 UK alcohol consumption by product, 1955–79 (1955 = 100). (*Source:* see Appendix, Table XI, col. 3; BS, *UK Statistical Handbook 1980*, pp. 28, 38, 42.)

by domestic production. Both imports and exports remained relatively insignificant. Imports released for home consumption averaged 1.45 million bulk barrels per annum, 1955–79, about 4.4 per cent of home production, while exports averaged 0.37 million barrels, 1.1 per cent of production, over the same period.[16] There was a little growth in these areas. Imports of Dublin Guinness, which had dominated imports into the United Kingdom since the establishment of the Irish Republic, remained fairly constant in absolute terms, but their percentage of total imports slipped steadily over time as imports of lager beer increased; the growth of imports, which amounted to 5.3 per cent a year, 1962–73 (compared with a rate of only 0.3 per cent p.a., 1955–62), was largely explained by the fact that some of the rising demand for lager after 1960 (see p. 458) was met by imports from Holland and Denmark. Once these countries' principal products – Heineken and Carlsberg

[16] There are no fully satisfactory series of imports and exports over the period 1955–80. Here, imports = 'imports released for home consumption', while export data, derived from the *Annual Statements of Trade*, include re-exports from 1970. For details see Appendix, Table XII.

Table 11.2. *Alcohol and beer consumption, and consumption per head, 1955–79 (1955 = 100)*

Year	Consumption (volume)		Consumption per head	
	Alcohol[a]	Beer	Alcohol[a]	Beer
1955	100	100	100	100
1979	237	176	215	151

[a]Weighted consumption expressed in gallons of 100% alcohol, using the formula in BS, *Statistical Handbook 1990*, p. 36. Unweighted volumes (spirits at 70° proof) = 1979: 179, 164 (p.c.)
Source: BS, *UK Statistical Handbook 1980*, pp. 12, 28, 38, 42.

Lager – began to be brewed under licence at new breweries opened in the UK by Whitbread at Luton in 1969 and by Carlsberg/Watneys at Northampton in 1973, imports fell away again.[17] In any case, import growth was accompanied by an increase in British exports, notably to Belgium and the USA. At half a million barrels a year in 1973–7 they were twice as high as in the 1950s and early 1960s.[18] However, the foreign trade in beer was far too small to produce a divergence between consumption and production; the two series followed each other very closely indeed, as Fig. 11.1 indicates.[19] The difficulty of shipping beer in bulk internationally, which was reflected fully in transport costs, together with excise duties on imported beer, meant that the increase in demand produced obvious and relatively unchallenged market opportunities for domestic brewers, whose growth strategies were clearly influenced by it after the early 1960s.

Why did demand for alcohol rise in the 1960s and 1970s? In part it was a consequence of a growth in population, and in part a response to the greater prosperity which came with higher rates of economic growth

[17] Imports from Eire amounted to 1.2 million barrels p.a. in both 1953–7 and 1973–7, but the share of total imports fell from 92 to 64 per cent (the advent of Draught Guinness, produced at Park Royal, was a further element in the decline). Imports from Denmark and Holland grew from 95,000 barrels p.a. (7 per cent of the total) in 1953–7 to 428,000 (24 per cent in 1968–72, then fell back to 366,000 barrels (19 per cent) in 1973–7, and were negligible from 1978. Wilson and Gourvish, 'Foreign Dimensions of British Brewing', p. 137.

[18] Exports averaged 247,000 barrels p.a., 1953–7 and 497,000 p.a., 1973–7. Exports to Belgium increased from 61,000 barrels p.a., 1953–7 to 200,000 barrels, 1973–7, those to USA from negligible amounts to 55,000 barrels. In the latter period Belgium took 40 per cent of the total exported, the USA 11 per cent. *Ibid.*, p. 136.

[19] Correlation Coefficient of the two series = 0.999.

after a decade and a half of austerity. The UK population increased by 10 per cent in the period 1955–79, from 50.9 to 56.2 million, while the number aged 15 and over increased by 12 per cent, from 39.3 to 44.2 million. Thus, as Table 11.2 shows, consumption per head grew less rapidly than total consumption. At the same time, consumers enjoyed greater purchasing power. Consumers' expenditure increased by 2.5 per cent a year in real terms from 1959 to 1979.[20] But there was more to it than that. The proportion of total expenditure represented by alcohol purchases, which had fallen steadily in the 1950s, then increased, from 5.6 per cent in 1959 to 7.3 per cent in 1979, while spending on beer alone increased from 3.4 to 3.8 per cent.[21] The reasons are various. It appears that some deepening of the market took place, with increased consumption among those who had not previously been regarded as significant consumers of alcohol. They included the middle class, women and the young, groups which now attracted interest from sociologists and market researchers alike. The youth market was stimulated by a 'youth culture' based on American developments, not least of which was the appearance of specialist popular music, films, clothes, and subsequently alcoholic and non-alcoholic drinks such as lager and Coca Cola (Plates 59 and 60).[22] Furthermore, this segment of the market was larger than it had been in the inter-war years. The 'bulge' generation, born in the latter stages of the war and the immediate post-war years, reached drinking age in the early 1960s, and a 'baby boom' in the late fifties and early sixties meant more potential customers for the brewers in the seventies. Thus, the numbers in the 15–24 age group increased by over a third, from 6.6 million or 13 per cent of the population in 1951 to 9.0 million or 16 per cent in 1981.[23]

New consumers of alcohol, particularly those from the middle class, especially women, who might well have been inhibited about the prospect of visiting a pre-war public house, were undoubtedly encouraged by the liberalisation of licensing and by the introduction of new products. The Licensing Acts of 1961 and 1964 represented the first general revision of licensing arrangements for forty years. By introducing a new

[20] Calculated from CSO, *Economic Trends. Annual Supplement 1991*, p. 35.

[21] Calculated from data given in BS, *Statistical Handbook 1990*, pp. 37–8. The percentages derived vary from those given in CSO, *Social Trends* – e.g. for 1979: alcohol 7.7 per cent, beer 4.2 per cent.

[22] See, *inter alia*, John Street, 'Youth Culture and the Emergence of Popular Music', in Terry Gourvish and Alan O'Day (eds.), *Britain Since 1945* (1991), pp. 305–13; Iain Chambers, *Urban Rhythms: Pop Music and Popular Culture* (1985).

[23] CSO, *Annual Abstract of Statistics.*

Table 11.3. *Licensed premises in the United Kingdom, 1951–89*

Year	Full on	Restricted on	Clubs	Off-licences	Total
1951	81,824	–	20,568	26,172	128,564
1955	79,669	–	22,355	26,094	128,118
1959	77,984	–	24,624	26,199	128,807
1962	76,786	2,914	24,146	27,764	131,610
1970	73,690	10,898	28,205	31,776	144,569
1979	75,741	20,504	32,697	41,097	170,039
1989[a]	83,000	31,300	33,600	51,600	199,500

[a]estimated
Source: BS, *Statistical Handbook 1990*, p. 54.

Table 11.4. *Supermarkets, superstores, and off-licence provision, 1958–79*

Year	Supermarkets[a]	Superstores[b]	All Grocery Outlets
1958	175	2[1963]	–
1979	7,130	237	–
1979 % with off-licences	89	100	67

[a]Stores with a selling area of at least 2,000 sq ft.
[b]Stores with a selling area of at least 25,000 sq ft.
Source: Supermarket Association of Great Britain, *Licences for Supermarkets?* (July 1965), p. 1; Jordan & Sons, *Supermarkets and Superstores* (1981), p. ix; Institute of Grocery Distribution Research Services, *Superstores Growth and Trading Profile* (November 1982); information from Jane Le Cluse, *The Grocer*, 1991.

type of licence for restaurants and hotels – the 'restricted on-licence' – the 1961 Act encouraged an increase in the number of on-licences, as Table 11.3 indicates. The new licences grew rapidly in popularity. In 1962 there were 2,900 of them, in 1970 over 10,000, and by 1979 20,500, roughly equivalent to the net growth in total on-licences. The Acts also promoted growth in the number of off-licences by facilitating their appearance in food shops with more liberal opening hours. In 1959 there were 26,200 off-licences, much the same number as in 1951; by 1979 there were 41,100.[24] The emergence of the large food supermarkets with their own off-licences was the key development, stimulating a new business in take-home alcohol purchases. The number of supermarkets and superstores increased from under 250 in the late 1950s to nearly 7,500 by 1979, when the vast majority had off-licences (Table 11.4). The process was encouraged by the general abandonment of resale price maintenance in 1964, and the formal acceptance that abolition applied to liquor two years later.[25] Thus, not only had the public more licensed premises to choose from – 170,000 by 1979, a third more than in 1959 – but there were also new types of outlet which appealed to housewives, and others who had not previously used the older types of retail outlet.[26] The change was reflected in a shift to take-home sales (Plate 61). This was more pronounced with wines and spirits than it was with beer, but even with the latter take-home sales increased from about 5 per cent of total sales in 1960 to 8 per cent in 1970 and 12 per cent in 1980. Supermarkets accounted for about half of this business.[27]

New products and shifts in packaging were also associated with the period of rising demand. Here, developments may be seen as both causes and consequences of merger activity among brewers. First of all, the development of 'keg' beers – brewery-conditioned beers which were filtered, pasteurised and carbonated – reversed the trend from draught to bottled beer, by giving the consumer all the advantages of bottled beer – consistency, brightness, carbonation and a longer shelf-life – in a draught ale.[28] Pioneered on a small scale by Watneys in the 1930s, and

[24] Licensing Act, 1961, 9 & 10 Eliz.II c.61, 1964 c.26 (consolidating measure), and see also BS, *Licensing Act 1961. A Summary of the Changes in Licensing Law* (n.d.).

[25] Gwylmor P. Williams, *Social Effects of the Ending of Resale Price Maintenance of Alcoholic Beverages 1966 to 1967* (1968).

[26] 'The Lady Carries the Can', *The Red Hand* (Ind Coope), Christmas 1959, pp. 1–3; 'Watney's Comprehensive Take-Home Survey', *Brewing Trade Review*, August 1972, p. 271.

[27] Information for 1970 and 1980 from NEDO (Brewing Sector Working Group), *Market Prospects and the Implications for Employment* (1983), p. 4. An inquiry of 1985 put take-home sales at about 15 per cent in 1985, cf. 8 per cent in 1975, and also pointed out that the number of off-licences associated with grocery retailing had increased from just over 50 per cent of the total in 1972 to just over 70 per cent by 1983. Monopolies and Mergers Commission, *Scottish & Newcastle Breweries PLC and Matthew Brown PLC: A Report on the Proposed Merger*, November 1985, PP (1985–6) Cmnd.9645, p. 13.

[28] 'Keg' beer is bulk-conditioned or brewery-conditioned beer, distinct from traditional cask-conditioned ale through the removal of yeast by filtering, and also (where appropriate) by pasteurisation and carbonation, to produce a beer with a long life. The definition is, however, approximate, and as the Foods Standards Committee conceded in 1977, 'We had great difficulty in distinguishing as a clearly defined category the product known as keg beer'. MAFF, *Food Standards Committee Report on Beer*, FSC/REP/68, 1977, pp. 35–6, and see also Arnold Hill (former Flowers brewer), 'The

Table 11.5. *Beer sales volumes by beer type and type of package, 1960–89 (percentages)*

Year	Beer type		Type of package			
	Ale/ stout	Lager	Draught	Returnable bottles	Non-returnable cans	Non-returnable bottles
1960	99.0	1.0	64.0	34.0	2.0	
1964	98.0	2.0	68.0	30.0	2.0	
1969	94.0	6.0	71.0	27.0	2.0	
1974	83.6	16.4	73.8	19.7	5.9	0.6
1979	70.9	29.1	78.4	11.1	10.0	0.5
1984	61.1	38.9	78.2	6.8	12.9	2.1
1989	49.6	50.4	72.1	6.4	18.5	2.9

Source: BS, *Statistical Handbook 1990*, p. 17.

developed and successfully marketed in the UK by J. W. Green/ Flowers Breweries as Flowers Keg in 1954, the product rapidly gained ground when adopted by the larger brewers, notably by Watneys (Red Barrel, promoted vigorously from the late 1950s) and Ind Coope Tetley Ansell/Allied (Double Diamond, 1962). Second, the increasing popularity of lager also gave a boost to the draught beer market. Led by Ind Coope, with its Skol brand of 1959, lager sales increased from minute proportions to 2 per cent of the British market by 1964 (see Table 11.5). But the really significant change came in the mid-1960s when draught lagers were introduced. Here the pioneer was Harp Lager Ltd, a British-Irish consortium of 1961 led by Guinness and including Courage, Barclay & Simonds, Scottish & Newcastle and Bass, Mitchells & Butlers. The introduction of Draught Harp after test marketing in Scotland, Manchester and Bristol not only increased the brand's share of the lager market to a leading 25 per cent but helped to increase general sales of draught beer, from 64 per cent of total beer sales in 1960 to 78 per cent by 1979 (Table 11.5).[29] Finally, there was a shift to cans

Development of Keg Beer', typescript, n.d., BS. There are also problems in defining a 'keg' container, since many containers are used for both cask-conditioned and brewery-conditioned beer. A working definition of 'keg' is a pressurised container working at a pressure of up to 60 psi: *Brewing Trade Review*, February 1976, p. 51.

[29] Harp Lager Technical Committee Minutes, 8 May 1963, 11 March 1964, GPR; *Guinness Time*, Autumn 1968, pp. 3–10. See also *Brewers' Journal*, April and Novem-

and, to a lesser extent, non-returnable bottles, sales of which exceeded 10 per cent of the market by 1979 and 20 per cent a decade later. All this meant that sales in conventional bottles, the great success of the twentieth century in brewing, fell away. Beer sold in returnable bottles had over a third of the market in 1960; thereafter its share dwindled steadily, to 11 per cent in 1979 and only 6 per cent in 1989 (Table 11.5).[30]

These various changes in demand and in the nature of sales outlets and products invited a vigorous response from brewers. Not all companies possessed the financial and managerial resources to exploit them. The more cautious, having done very little to change either their product range or the quality of their tied houses, were vulnerable to takeover as the advertised national brands began to threaten local and regional sales. Furthermore, post-war company legislation helped to tip the balance in favour of would-be acquirers. The Companies Acts of 1947 and 1948 forced limited companies to improve their accounting methods and disclose much more information about their financial circumstances than hitherto, giving prospective purchasers a greater insight into asset values and financial performance. Although the secretive, staunchly independent, family brewer could keep such items as barrelage and trading patterns to himself, he could no longer hide behind the complete screen of privacy that had protected him in the pre-war years. Indeed, a much greater amount of disclosure was required by subsequent legislation, notably the Companies Act of 1967.[31] In 1955 Cheltenham & Hereford Breweries had sought the shelter of Whitbread's reassuring 'umbrella' in the wake of an unwelcome bid from non-brewing interests (see p. 395). Vulnerability to bids from predators who knew (like Clore in his bid for Watney Mann) that brewers were sitting on under-valued property assets, increased substantially in the 1960s, as financial disclosure became greater, forcing many a brewer to consider an agreed inter-brewery merger as a defensive option. The rise in property values associated with scarcity in city centres as Britain experienced a sustained consumer boom from the mid-1950s, and the operations of professional property speculators, increased the vulnerability to hostile takeover bids of those brewers with considerable property portfolios in the centres of such cities as London,

ber 1961, pp. 158, 551–2, December 1962, p. 643; *Brewing Trade Review*, November 1958, pp. 710–14, April 1962, pp. 354–7, July and August 1963, pp. 420–2, 464–5, October 1966, p. 709, March and December 1968, pp. 207, 941.

30 The refusal of supermarkets to handle returnable beer bottles was clearly a critical element.

31 Companies Acts, 1947, 1948, 1967, and *Sweet & Maxwell's Companies Acts* (1980).

Birmingham, Manchester and Leeds. In the event, the number of hostile bids was remarkably small; but the fear that these might materialise acted as a considerable spur to brewing mergers (see pp. 464–73).

Thus, the volatility of the brewing market in the 1960s and 1970s, the need to respond to modern, segmented market conditions, the growing importance of the 'free trade' outside the brewer-owned public house, represented by developments such as supermarket off-licences, and the need to improve product ranges and public houses to satisfy the demands of differing groups of customers, added up to a formidable list of challenges for any brewer. For some, particularly those whose managements had been stretched by the legacy of earlier mergers, it was plainly too much. Several family brewing businesses had clearly reached the 'managerial limits to growth' identified by Edith Penrose.[32] They had no desire to carry on trading under the more complex conditions of the 1960s, and, for them, an invited merger bid was an obvious solution to their difficulties. For others, it was a means to inject much-needed investment into the business. Here, managements which otherwise may have been soundly based, reached *financial* limits to growth. A number of medium-sized regional companies found themselves in this position in the 1960s. Like Hammonds United, which combined with others to form Northern Breweries in 1960, and Flowers Breweries and Dutton's of Blackburn, which merged with Whitbread in 1962 and 1964 respectively, they were anxious to improve their public houses and product ranges but had exhausted their own investible resources. A suitable merger was one way of unlocking investment and at the same time permitting both rationalisation and the extension of brand penetration.[33]

III

The basic steps in the emergence of the 'Big Six' pub-owning brewers are summarised in Table 11.6. Although different combinations of the various influences conducive to mergers were at work in each case and at different stages of the process, some common themes are evident. They include defensive anxiety, and the search for national status through the acquisition of retail outlets. Emulation of others was also important. Here, two events were especially decisive. The first was Clore's bid for

[32] Penrose, *Growth of the Firm*.
[33] *The Economist*, 28 April 1962, p. 373, 18 July 1964, p. 292.

Table 11.6. *The emergence of the 'Big Six', 1955–72*

Company	Major mergers
Allied (Ind Coope)	Benskin's (1957), Taylor Walker (1959), Tetley Walker/Ansells (1961), Friary Meux (1964)
Bass	Mitchells & Butlers (1961), Bent's (1967), Charrington United (1967)
Courage	Barclay Perkins (1955), H. & G. Simonds (1960), Bristol Brewery Georges (1961), John Smith's (1970)
Scottish & Newcastle	Scottish Brewers and Newcastle Breweries (1960)
Watneys	Mann, Crossman & Paulin (1958), Phipps, Wilson & Walker, Ushers (1960), Steward & Patteson, Bullard (1963), Drybrough (1965), Samuel Webster (1972)
Whitbread	Tennant Bros. (1961), Flowers (1962), West Country (1963), Dutton's (1964), Threlfalls Chesters, Fremlins (1967), Strong (1968), Brickwoods (1971)

Source: Appendix, Table X.

Watney Mann in 1959; the other was the rapid expansion of E. P. Taylor's brewing interests in Britain, which received particular attention when his United Breweries made an uninvited bid for Bristol Brewery Georges in 1961. Both require some attention.

When Charles Clore offered £20.7 million in cash for 75 per cent of Watney Mann's £9,047,620 equity in May 1959 it came as a complete surprise to directors, shareholders and financial pundits alike. After all, Watneys was not an ultra-conservative brewing lamb for the slaughter, but had shown considerable enterprise in moving in the required direction of retail expansion, rationalisation and property development. It had secured a strong base in London and the South-East through a process of acquisition, buying four breweries in 1947–55 – Alton (1947), Charles Hammerton (Stockwell) (1951), Tamplin's of Brighton (1953) and Henty & Constable (Chichester) (1955). Only the previous year it had become one of the biggest brewers in the UK by merging with fellow London brewers, Mann, Crossman & Paulin, to form Watney Mann, a combine with 3,670 pubs. The motive here was clear. As early as 1954 Watney had accepted that although planning restrictions prevented it from developing its Stag Brewery site in Pimlico for brewing, the opportunity for property development was considerable.

Indeed, in 1954–5 Watney's chairman, Simon Combe, had encouraged a serious merger proposal involving Mann, Crossman & Paulin and the stagnating Bass, Ratcliff & Gretton, the combination to be financed in large measure by the sale of the Pimlico site to the government. In the event the negotiations with both Bass and the government came to nothing.[34] But in 1958 Watney went ahead with a merger with Mann, the move being very much driven by the need to find extra brewing capacity, given the decision to cease brewing in Pimlico (production stopped in April 1959), and plans were well advanced to sell the site lease. The company had also decided to establish a separate, wholly owned property subsidiary to exploit the development potential of properties no longer required as licensed premises (Plate 64). All this was made known by Simon Combe ten days before Clore's bid.[35] It is scarcely surprising, then, that this hostile bid from a non-brewer was resisted strongly. But to some extent the move might have been foreseen, since there was a sizeable difference between the book value of Watney's assets, which had last been valued in 1929, and their current market value.[36] Such discrepancies had been evident before, for example in the merger negotiations between Friary Holroyd & Healy of Guildford and Meux, the London brewers, in 1956.[37] Furthermore, Clore had established a considerable reputation via Sears Holdings, his shoes, hosiery machinery and shipbuilding conglomerate, for acquiring under-exploited assets, releasing asset values by sale and lease-back methods and then extracting higher profit levels from high-street properties.[38]

[34] The negotiations began with a proposal that one of Bass's subsidiaries, the Wenlock Brewery in London, should be closed and the pubs supplied by Watney in return for the latter's agreement to sell Bass in its pubs. A more ambitious scheme to establish a tripartite holding company was then worked up. The major stumbling-block in the several negotiations which followed was that neither Watney nor Bass wished to be absorbed by, or subservient to, the other. Instead a new trading agreement was signed in 1958, after the Watney Mann merger, and an exchange of directors was agreed. Combe and Michael Webster joined the Bass board and C. A. Ball and Arthur Manners became Watney Mann directors. Hawkins, *Bass Charrington*, p. 168; Bass, 'Z' File, 1954–9, Bass Cape Hill (Birmingham).

[35] Watney Combe Reid Board Minutes, 6 February 1958, GMet; *Statist*, 30 May 1959; *Investors' Chronicle*, 27 November 1959; *Daily Sketch*, 26 May 1959; Simon Combe, letter to Watney Mann ordinary stockholders, 8 September 1959, GMet.

[36] The bid of 45s a share, with the promise that shareholders would retain 25 per cent of their holding after splitting into 5s shares, represented a bid of 60s a share, and could be compared with a 'book value price' which financial analysts put at around 47s. The book value of Watney Mann's assets was £27.2 million, which the company later reckoned to be an under-valuation of £6.79 million. *The Economist*, 30 May 1959; Combe, letter, September 1959.

[37] *Investors' Chronicle*, 6 October 1956.

[38] On Clore and Sears Holdings see Leonard Sainer, 'Sir Charles Clore', *Dictionary of Business Biography*, I (1984), pp. 697–700; Charles Gordon, *The Two Tycoons: A*

For a time the atmosphere was very tense. A meeting of leading brewers was held at the Brewers' Society to discuss the implications of the bid, and Watney Mann went to the lengths of changing its bankers after discovering that Lloyds had assisted Clore in building up his stake.[39] But soon afterwards, in June, the bid was withdrawn, after 'friendly discussions' between the parties. The association of Simon Combe, whose pedigree embraced Eton, the Guards, White's Club and marriage to the Earl of Leicester's sister, and Clore, the Jewish Eastender, had never seemed very likely (Plates 62 and 63). And, in any case, the market determined the outcome. The £1 shares rose from a pre-bid price of 51s 3d (£2.56) to a high of 77s (£3.85), well above the offer price of 60s (£3), and Clore, who had been interested primarily in the Pimlico site, was unwilling to increase his price to an unrealistic level, and was quite content to take his profit.[40] Nevertheless, the failed bid was an important landmark in the establishment of the 'Big Six'. Certainly, it galvanised Watney Mann into more concerted activity. The company rapidly widened its horizons by acquiring breweries with large tied estates in Northampton (Phipps Northampton), Manchester (Wilson & Walker) and Trowbridge (Ushers), all in 1960. They were followed by important acquisitions in Norwich (Steward & Patteson, Bullard) in 1963 and Edinburgh (Drybrough) in 1965. In the process Watney Mann's tied estate doubled in size. At the same time, the company pursued Clore's tactics. It duly established its property company in 1959, transferred to it properties valued at £4.65 million and proceeded to exploit their development potential. In nine years' trading prior to a merger with Star (Great Britain) Holdings the property company's pre-tax profits rose from £205,000 to £570,000.[41] Watney's strategy was not without flaws, however. By buying breweries with large rural estates such as Steward & Patteson (which owned about

Personal Memoir of Jack Cotton and Charles Clore (1984), p. 53; David Clutterbuck and Marion Devine, *Clore: The Man and his Millions* (1987), pp. 81–3; *Investors' Chronicle*, 25 July 1958, 29 May 1959; *The Financial Times*, 27 May 1959; Hawkins, *Bass Charrington*, pp. 121–3.

39 Notes of a Meeting of Survey Committee held at the Brewers' Society, 27 May 1959, BS File on 'Takeovers and mergers', 1/15/1, BS; Arthur Guinness Son & Co. Board Minutes, 2 June 1959, GPR; Watney Combe Reid Board Minutes, 11 June 1959, GMet. Sears had used Lloyds Nominees to acquire shares, while Lloyds had also lent money to Sears: *Daily Mail*, 4 June 1959. The *News Chronicle*, 27 May 1959, noted that the crisis was such that on receiving notice of the bid Simon Combe 'issued an urgent call to his fellow directors ... They answered it at once, some of them missing the outing of the London Brewers' Golfing Society'.

40 *Evening Standard*, 26 May 1959; *The Economist*, 27 June 1959.

41 Watney Mann Property Co. Reports and Accounts, 1960–9, and supporting papers, GMet/FBG.

1,400, mostly low-barrelage pubs at the time of the takeover) it made post-merger rationalisation activity more protracted, and its relative tardiness in entering the draught lager market was something to regret. Nevertheless, no-one could deny that Watney Mann had transformed itself from a large regional into a national brewer in the space of four years after the Clore bid.[42]

But the bid also had a ripple effect on other large brewers, particularly those with large metropolitan estates, who were forced to re-evaluate their business strategies. It is perhaps too much to see the contemporaneous merger of Ind Coope and Taylor Walker in 1959 as a response to Clore. This was, after all, announced only a week after Clore's bid, and for Ind Coope the strengthening of its presence in the London market was a prime motivation, as it had been when it acquired Benskin's of Watford two years earlier. Nevertheless, the timing probably owed something at least to Clore's intervention, and rationalisation was put more firmly on the expanded company's agenda.[43] Indeed, the bid for Watney Mann may well have persuaded others such as Courage and Whitbread to pursue a more determined policy of expansion. And most of the brewers paused for thought in 1959. The Clore bid, which was followed soon afterwards by an unsuccessful (and fraudulent) bid for the Ely brewery, Cardiff by a London banking firm, H. Jasper & Co.,[44] alerted brewers to the fact that if they did not continue with merger activity, pursuing economies of scale, a wider market and the full exploitation of their assets, then other parties from outside the industry would do it for them. This can be seen in the brewers' deliberations at the Brewers' Society. Among ideas thrown up in the wake of the Clore bid was a proposal (Simon Combe) that groups of five or six companies should place their most valuable properties in separate holding companies. The brewers also turned to Barings for advice on mergers and property asset management. As Col. Bill Whit-

[42] Gourvish, *Norfolk Beers*, pp. 148, 156–8; Watney Mann & Truman, Business Plan 1977/78–1981/82, February 1978, GMet/FBG.

[43] Edward Thompson, Chairman of Ind Coope, stressed that the merger was 'a traditional and normal brewer's merger, which is not related to other things that have been happening': *The Times*, 4 June 1959.

[44] Jasper & Co. bought the Ely Brewery for £1.8 million in September 1959, and a new board was established. Within days it was revealed that the Jasper Group was unable to finance the purchase and the Fraud Squad was called in to investigate. Harry Jasper and his colleagues resigned from the Ely board and the company was subsequently acquired by the Rhymney Brewery for £1.75 million. Ely Brewery Press Cuttings Books, 1949–60, 220/3, W&Co. The full ramifications of the fraud, which involved the illegal use of building society funds by Herbert Murray and Friedrich Grunwald, is outlined in George Bull and Anthony Vice, *Bid for Power* (3rd ed., 1961), pp. 268–79.

bread put it, 'Our only hope for the industry is to integrate, or else disintegrate'.[45]

If Clore caused the metropolitan brewers disquiet, then the activities of E. P. Taylor, in building up a brewing empire in Britain, had a much more substantial impact on the industry as a whole. Eddie Taylor was one of Canada's most successful entrepreneurs (Plate 65). Born in Ottawa in 1901 and educated at McGill University, where he obtained a degree in mechanical engineering, he first dabbled in transport (taxis and buses) until he had more enduring success with his grandfather's modest Ontario brewery. This he built up in the 1920s and 1930s into a combine later known as Canadian Breweries, and after his wartime experiences had given him access to a wider, more international stage, he was, by the early 1950s, actively seeking investment opportunities outside Ontario, notably via a takeover bid for Northern Breweries of Montreal.[46] In fact, in Taylor's early dealings with Britain's brewers, it seems that the initiative came from the British side, from two lager-producing companies looking to expand exports. One of them was a major brewery. In the autumn of 1950 Edward Thompson, Chairman of Ind Coope, visited Canada with the intention of buying into the industry, and identified the ailing Northern Breweries as a prime candidate for investment. Discovering that Taylor had already made a bid for the company, and with the active encouragement of Quebec's largest brewer, Molson's Brewery, which was anxious to exclude Taylor, he sought government approval for a proposal that Ind Coope should purchase Canadian Breweries' stake in Northern. When in March 1952 it emerged that Canadian's bid had succeeded, and that Northern was to be reconstituted, Thompson turned his attention instead to the possibility of an exchange of shares with Canadian itself.[47]

Ironically in view of subsequent attitudes by British brewers,

[45] BS Meeting, 27 May 1959; Lord Gretton, note on meeting of 16 June 1959, 19 June 1959, Bass Cape Hill; papers in BS File 1/15/1, BS; and *Morning Advertiser*, 27 May 1959.

[46] In 1941 Churchill appointed Taylor President of the British Supply Council in North America; after the war he established the holding company Argus Corporation. On Taylor see obituary, *The Times*, 16 May 1989, *The Daily Telegraph*, 20 May 1989; Robert Bothwell and William Kilbourn, *C.D. Howe: a Biography* (Toronto, 1980), pp. 10, 107, 149–53.

[47] Edward Thompson, 'Memorandum on the Canadian Brewing Industry', 11 March 1952, and correspondence 4–26 March 1952; Thompson–Sir Henry Hancock, 27 March 1952; Thompson, 'Memorandum No. 2 on Canadian Breweries Ltd.', 24 June 1952, E. P. Taylor–Thompson, 16 July 1952, Ministry of Agriculture and Fisheries Supply Department Papers: Cereal Group, Capital Issues Committee File, MAF84/52, PRO.

Thompson appears to have got on well with Taylor, exchanging views with him about the latter's great passion, racehorses, and thanking him for the 'very friendly, candid and sympathetic way in which you listened to a complete stranger, and the generous spirit which permitted me to explore my ideas with you'.[48] However, the scepticism of the Treasury and the Capital Issues Committee, voiced at a time of investment shortages at home and strict foreign exchange controls, prevented any progress being made. The Treasury position was clear. Sir Leslie Rowan, Treasury Second Secretary, confirmed the view of Sir Henry Hancock, Permanent Secretary of the Ministry of Food, that 'we could not make dollars available for investment by way of the purchase of a mere shareholding in an existing enterprise. Any scheme with this as its basis would be quite unacceptable'. However, Whitehall had no objection to 'an active partnership with a Canadian firm with the prospects of earnings ...' and this opened the way for alternative proposals.[49]

While Thompson was pursuing his negotiations with Taylor, another brewer came into the reckoning, the much smaller Hope & Anchor Breweries of Sheffield. Dismissed rather perfunctorily by Thompson as this 'small stout firm',[50] Hope & Anchor had ambitions which stretched far beyond its size. Led by a dynamic managing director, Tom Carter, it had begun lager production in 1947 and had concluded a trading agreement with the Manchester lager brewers, Red Tower, but was particularly anxious to promote a more traditional British product, Jubilee Stout, in Canada. As early as 1949 it examined prospects in the North American market and entered into exploratory talks with Taylor. A reciprocal brewing scheme was presented to the Board of Trade in March 1950; it secured the provisional approval of the Bank of England in September, before Ind Coope's expression of interest in Canada.[51] After an abortive search for an English brewery to brew lager – Hope & Anchor failed in its attempt to buy control of Red Tower – and further difficulties in persuading the British authorities to ratify the scheme, approval for a brewing and trading agreement was finally secured in

48 Thompson–Taylor, 28 May 1952, MAF84/52, PRO.

49 Sir Leslie Rowan-Hancock, 8 April 1952, Hancock–Thompson, 17 April 1952, and see also Herbert Brittain–Hancock, 13 September 1952, MAF84/52, PRO.

50 Thompson–Hancock, 21 April 1952, MAF84/52, PRO.

51 Hope & Anchor Board Minutes, 17 January, 21 March and 6 July 1949, 8 February 1950; 'Review of Negotiations on Reciprocal Trade Agreement – Canadian Breweries Ltd – Hope & Anchor Breweries Ltd'. 1949–51, Bass North, Leeds; J. T. Davies–D. W. Peall, 13 September 1951, MAF84/52, PRO. See also H. D. Watts, 'Lager Brewing in Britain', *Geography*, 60 (April 1975), 143.

1952.[52] The two companies set up subsidiary companies in each other's countries to market brands produced under licence. Canadian Breweries agreed to produce and distribute Jubilee Stout in Canada, while Hope & Anchor arranged to brew and distribute Carling Black Label Lager in Sheffield. The agreement, and its relevance to the establishment of the Taylor empire, have already been described in detail by Kevin Hawkins.[53] He shows that both parties were quickly dissatisfied with the agreement, and that both, it could be argued, had entered it on the basis of a misconceived strategy. Hope & Anchor was mistaken in its belief that the Canadian market would accept a dark, heavy beer, while Taylor was disappointed with the low sales of his lager, having failed to appreciate that, with the overall demand for lager modest in the 1950s, the tied house system made it difficult to sell the beer outside Hope & Anchor's own moderate estate of 166 pubs (1957 figure). Once he realised that the acquisition of breweries and their pubs was the appropriate strategy for widening the market for his product the way was open for an aggressive policy of expansion.[54]

Few were to play this game better than Taylor. By 1957 he had built up a sizeable minority stake in Hope & Anchor, and was quickly able to exploit its weakness. In the following year gloomy results from the company's Canadian venture raised serious doubts about its future viability, while at home there was concern about the difficulties in widening the market for Jubilee Stout. Having overstretched itself financially, it was happy to sign a new agreement with Canadian Breweries. In June 1959 Taylor agreed to take over the British company's ailing Canadian operation and in an exchange of shares obtained control of 30 per cent of its equity.[55] Hope & Anchor then became the springboard for his penetration of the British industry. After widespread canvassing, and negotiations with a large number of companies in 1959, he created Northern Breweries in February 1960, by merging Hope & Anchor, John Jeffrey & Co., the Edinburgh lager brewers, and Hammonds United Breweries. The new combine was a sizeable regional company with assets of £17 million, owing largely to the fact that Hammonds, under the direction of H. L. Bradfer-Lawrence, had itself

52 A plan to buy the Palatine Bottling Company's 15 per cent shareholding in Red Tower proved too expensive. Hope & Anchor Board Minutes, 20 and 27 March 1950, 10 December 1951, 13 February and 20 May 1952, Bass North. Red Tower was acquired by Scottish Brewers in 1956.

53 Hawkins, *Bass Charrington*, pp. 124–60; *Brewing Trade Review*, August 1952, p. 684.

54 Cf. Carling's Brewery of Canada Board Minutes, 14 September 1955, Bass North.

55 Hope & Anchor Board Minutes, 16 September 1957, 27 January, 28 February, 5 and 8 May, 29 September 1958, 4 June 1959, Bass North.

expanded considerably since the war.[56] In the course of 1960 Taylor, now deputy chairman of Northern (Bradfer-Lawrence had become chairman), used his base in Edinburgh to bring in five more Scottish brewers, George Younger, Fowler, Murray, Calder and Aitken (see Appendix, Table X). A subsidiary management company, United Caledonian, was formed to handle these interests, and the main company was re-named United Breweries in October. Breweries in Wales and Northern Ireland were also purchased.[57] The changes in Scotland were particularly dramatic. In the space of a few months, its brewing industry, which had been hit by stiffer competition in traditional export markets, had shed its informal arrangements and become highly concentrated. The largest merger involved Scottish Brewers, which acquired three smaller companies, Bernard, Morison and Robert Younger, and then joined with Newcastle Breweries to form Scottish & Newcastle in April 1960.[58] It is quite clear that this action was a response to the activities of Northern Breweries and Vaux.[59]

The establishment of United in such a short time had a considerable impact on the brewing industry. Some of the smaller and medium-sized regional companies clearly felt that they needed to combine in order to counter Taylor's moves. This certainly explains the acquisition in 1960 of Melbourne Breweries[60] by Joshua Tetley, and Tetley's simultaneous merger with Walker Cain of Warrington, since both Melbourne and Walker Cain had first been approached by Taylor. The acquisition by Vaux of Steel Coulson and Thomas Usher in 1959–60 and the Scottish Brewers' mergers may also have been a defensive response to Taylor's predatory ambitions. He certainly frightened the Cardiff brewers William Hancock with the directness of his approach, for almost immediately afterwards the company invited Bass to take an 'umbrella'

[56] Hawkins, *Bass Charrington*, pp. 124–5, 130–6. Hammonds United had acquired two small brewers in 1956 and three more in 1959 (see Appendix, Table X); by this time it too was financially stretched.

[57] The breweries were Webbs (Aberbeeg) and the Ulster Brewery.

[58] Donnachie, *Brewing Industry in Scotland*, pp. 239–42; V. Dickie, 'The Effects of Mergers on the Brewing Industry in Scotland', B.A. dissertation, Heriot-Watt University, 1981.

[59] William McEwan Younger, statement on 'Scottish & Newcastle Breweries', 17 October 1960, Scottish & Newcastle Merger File, S&N. Vaux acquired Steel Coulson and Thomas Usher in 1959 and John Wright (Perth) in 1961. See Appendix, Table X.

[60] Melbourne was formerly Leeds & Wakefield (it changed its name just before it acquired Russells & Wrangham in 1958 (this brewery was subsequently sold by ICTA to Cameron)). The company had been included in the early talks (codename: PENAM) leading to the formation of Northern Breweries. Hawkins, *Bass Charrington*, pp. 130–1; *Investors' Chronicle*, 6 December 1957, 14 February 1958.

holding in the company. There were also lessons for those who thought that such 'avoiding action' would insulate them from unwelcome bids, or that trading agreements and 'umbrella' stakes brought companies irrevocably within a particular sphere of influence. After all, Ind Coope had had a long relationship with Hammonds, and had secured a new trading agreement, together with an exchange of directors, in 1948. However, this had not prevented the latter from joining Taylor's camp, a decision which must have annoyed Edward Thompson.[61] There is no doubt at all that Taylor's personable but brash style irritated the old guard in brewing. One former company director, recalling Taylor's activities in 1958–9, observed that he 'had been driving round the United Kingdom and bursting in upon startled directors ... with only the slimmest of introductions, suggesting mergers with the eloquence of a carbon paper salesman'.[62]

However, it was Taylor's hostile bid for Bristol Brewery Georges in 1961, with the intervention of Courage, Barclay & Simonds as white knight to Taylor's black knight, that really alerted the industry to the strong possibility that the rush to merge would culminate in the establishment of only a handful of brewing groups. Georges, who had merged with a sizeable local rival, Bristol United, in 1956, was one of the few large regionals in the West of England which remained independent, a fact not lost on Taylor. At the end of January he offered the shareholders about £15.5 million for the share capital, a figure comfortably in excess of the existing market value (about £12 million). Soon afterwards Courage, Barclay & Simonds intervened with a counter-offer of about £18 million. Both bids were left on the table while the Georges directors waited for the results of a property revaluation. When this indicated that their assets were worth 'in excess of £13 million' they decided to recommend acceptance of Courage's offer. Taylor's United then attempted to do a deal with Courage, offering to take 25 per cent of Georges' tied estate together with its Shepton Mallet brewery, but this was firmly rejected. By the time United was in a position to make an

61 When Thompson resigned from the Hammonds board, he cited the fact that Ind Coope had links with Labatt of Canada which might conflict with the new Northern group: Hammonds United Board Minutes, 15/16 February 1960, Bass North. Other examples of minority stake-holders failing to prevent a sale to another brewer include Bass and Wilson & Walker (acquired by Watney Mann, 1960), Whitbread and Wells & Winch (acquired by Greene King, 1961), and Whitbread, Bass and Hewitt Brothers of Grimsby (merged with United, 1962). Hawkins, *Bass Charrington*, pp. 150, 166; *Investors' Chronicle*, 8 December 1961, 19 January 1962.

62 A. Avis, 'Anatomy of a Merger', typescript account of formation of Northern Breweries, n.d.

improved offer – of about £19.5 million – in March, over half of the Georges shareholders had already accepted Courage's terms. Following discussions with their merchant bank advisers, Warburgs, Georges agreed to the offer proceeding, having received an undertaking from Courage that it would improve its offer by 8s (40p) in cash per share to reflect the rise in market price since the offer had first been made. The final offer was worth about £19 million.[63]

This takeover had significant implications for the industry. Not only had Taylor launched the first predatory bid by a brewer, breaking established conventions, but in the words of the *Investors' Chronicle*, 'trading considerations [had] fairly obviously gone by the board', with Courage being persuaded to pay considerably over the odds for its acquisition.[64] The investment press made much of the family brewers' antipathy for Taylor. Certainly, his assurances to Georges about its post-merger future seemed every bit as reassuring on paper as the promises made by Courage, or indeed those made to others by Whitbread or Ind Coope – the protection of employment and continued operation of the local plant, 'decentralised management directed by regional boards, with only a small group in the parent company to co-ordinate policies to the benefit of all concerned ... strong representation from your Board at policy making level'.[65] However, there was little enthusiasm for United among the Georges directors, and Courage, with Guinness's financial support, was clearly anxious to keep United

[63] Courage, Barclay & Simonds Board Minutes, 10 March 1961, Courage/FBG; Bristol Brewery Georges Board Minutes, 9–17 February, 9–10 March 1961, Acc. 2305/68/4, and Courage, Barclay & Simonds Sundry Acquisition Papers: Bristol Brewery Georges, Acc. 2305/26/74/3/1, GLRO; *The Economist*, 4 and 18 February, 11 March 1961; Hawkins, *Bass Charrington*, p. 145. The share capital was: £2,158,337 Ord. and £365,968 6 per cent Pref. United offered eleven 6 per cent Pref. for ten Georges Pref. and eight 5s Ord. shares and £2 cash for each Georges £1 Ord. Courage offered fourteen 5 per cent Pref. for each ten Georges Pref. and five Ord. and £3 cash for each Georges Ord. United's revised offer was twelve for ten Pref., and eight for one Ord. plus £4 cash.

[64] *Investors' Chronicle*, 10 March and 7 April 1961; *The Economist*, 8 April 1961. The United-Courage battle for Georges was not the first contested merger between brewers. In 1956 significant opposition emerged when Friary, Holroyd & Healy merged with Meux. Over a third of Meux shareholders, feeling the terms were inadequate, resisted the bid, and the situation was exploited by two other brewers, Flowers and Ind Coope. Flowers built up a 10 per cent stake in Meux, used it to negotiate a trading agreement by which Flowers Keg was introduced into Meux's managed houses in London, and then consented to the merger. It sold its holding in 1958. Ind Coope acquired about 12 per cent of Friary Meux, presumably from 'dissident' Meux shareholders, and also negotiated a trading agreement. See *Investors' Chronicle*, 21 July, 1 September–6 October 1956, 5 and 12 July 1957, 7 February and 1 August 1958, 4 August 1961; Flowers Board Minutes, 1956, 1958, 74/2, 74/3, W&Co.

[65] E. P. Taylor–A. C. Hadley (Chairman, BBG), 2 February 1961, CA/C/125, Courage.

out of the South.[66] Sound commercial judgements helped to reinforce personal prejudices at Georges. The arguments advanced by Courage, in criticising United's empire as too thinly spread, emphasising the value of its connection with Guinness's Harp Lager consortium, its stronger financial position, and its ability to effect post-merger economies owing to the existence of common trading areas, must have carried weight with the Bristol company and its advisers.[67]

In fact, the implications went much further than this. Some brewers, notably Guinness, feared that if Taylor succeeded in building up a very large company he would not only disturb the industry's reciprocal trading arrangements – vital to a company such as Guinness, which was seeking to build up sales of Harp Lager and Draught Guinness – but also upset the British government's relatively tolerant attitude to the industry.[68] But most companies now realised that mergers involving medium-sized regionals were insufficient, and that the process would have to go much further. The surprise announcement in April 1961 that Ind Coope had joined with Tetley Walker and Ansells to form Ind Coope Tetley Ansell (ICTA), Britain's largest brewing group with 9,500 pubs, was clearly a reaction to what Taylor was attempting (Plate 66). Not only was it a defensive combination based on decentralised independent managements – what Thompson called a 'Commonwealth of Brewers' – without immediate plans to rationalise plant and outlets, but it was also a move to protect the new group's Skol lager interests from attack by Carling and Harp, in Thompson's words the 'battle of the lagers'.[69] It was from this point that Britain's brewers became much more ambitious in their own negotiations, bringing into play national brewers such as Bass and Whitbread, who hitherto had relied more on brands than retail outlets for their status and had determinedly stood apart from the early merger rush. Thus, in March–May 1961 there were serious talks between Courage, Bass and Mitchells & Butlers, which were aimed at preventing the latter from falling to Taylor. Once again apprehensiveness about the future market for lager appeared to be a catalyst. Courage and Guinness had persuaded Mitchells & Butlers to join the Harp consortium a week after the Courage/Georges merger had been

[66] Courage Acquisition Papers, strategy statement, 1 February 1961, etc. Acc. 2305/26/74/3/1, GLRO. On Guinness's support for Courage see Arthur Guinness Son & Co. Board Minutes, 23 March, 19 May and 7 June 1961, GPR.

[67] Courage strategy statement, February 1961.

[68] Cf. Lord Boyd, Guinness Board Minutes, 23 March and 7 June 1961, GPR.

[69] *Investors' Chronicle*, 7 April 1961; *The Economist*, 8 April 1961; letter to members of ICTA from chairmen, 26 April 1961; Ind Coope Chairman's Committee of Executive Directors Minutes, 28 March 1960, 2 January 1961, Allied.

Table 11.7. *Leading brewing companies, ranked by tied estate (on-licences), 1963–70*

Company	1963 Tied estate	Nominal capital £m	Market value £m	Company	1967 Tied estate	Nominal capital £m	Market value £m	Company	1970 Tied estate	Nominal capital £m	Market value £m
Allied	9,300	90.4	177.3	Bass Charr	10,230	80.7	243.2	Bass Charr	9,450	149.4	330.0
Watney Mann	5,500	43.8	103.5	Allied	8,250	128.1	234.7	Whitbread	8,280	145.5	186.1
Charr Utd	5,000	43.1	92.7	Whitbread	7,376	104.8	127.8	Allied	8,250	157.7	297.3
CB&S	4,800	45.3	76.3	Watney Mann	6,667	84.8	144.7	Watney Mann	6,135	86.0	146.6
BM&B	4,100	33.0	96.0	CB&S	4,418	57.1	94.4	Courage	6,000	70.1	140.8
Whitbread	3,500	40.6	95.2	S&N	2,076	64.8	127.0	S&N	1,700	87.3	169.8
S&N	1,700	44.9	92.1	Guinness	2[a]	26.5	102.2	Guinness	2[a]	26.5	134.0
Guinness	2[a]	19.5	94.0								

[a] Guinness's tied estate = Castle Inn, Bodiam and Guinness Club House, Park Royal.

Key:

BM&B	Bass, Mitchells & Butlers
Bass Charr	Bass Charrington
CB&S	Courage, Barclay & Simonds
Charr Utd	Charrington United
S&N	Scottish & Newcastle

Source: Investors' Chronicle, 30 August 1963, 20 October 1967, 13 November 1970; *Stock Exchange Year-Book*, 1964–72; *Stock Exchange Official Daily List*, 1 October 1963 and 1970, 2 October 1967.

resolved, and this was accompanied by trading agreements with a number of other brewers, including Hunt Edmunds and Flowers. On hearing of Bass's interest in Mitchells & Butlers, Courage explored the possibility of a tripartite grouping before Bass took the initiative and decided to merge with the Birmingham company.[70] At the same time Whitbread began to strengthen its hold on the seventeen companies under its 'umbrella'. It built up its equity stake in some of the more important ones from 10 to 25–30 per cent, absorbed Tennant of Sheffield at the end of 1961, and followed this in 1962 with the acquisition of Flowers (Stratford & Luton), Norman & Pring (Exeter) and Starkey, Knight & Ford of Bridgwater. West Country Brewers (formerly Cheltenham & Hereford) was taken over in 1963.[71] A major step towards higher concentration was taken in April 1962 when United merged with Charrington. This provided Taylor with a sizeable partner whose complementary geography – Charrington traded in London and the South – at last gave him the national status he desired.[72] The Glasgow lager brewer, J. & R. Tennent, was added in May 1963.[73] By this time the industry was clearly dominated by seven companies, eight including Guinness (see Table 11.7).

Merger activity was much quieter over the next three years. The only substantial acquisitions were Allied's takeover of Friary Meux in 1964 and Charrington United's purchase of Massey's of Burnley in 1966. However, the period saw Whitbread grow steadily in terms of tied estate by bringing several more of its 'umbrella' companies under formal ownership – notably Dutton's of Blackburn, Threlfalls Chesters and Fremlins (see Table 11.6). In the process it became a truly national

70 Courage, Barclay & Simonds Board Minutes, 24 May 1961, Courage/FBG; Guinness Executive Directors Minutes, 13 March and 1 August 1961, 28 June 1962, GPR; Confidential Report to Directors, Courage, Barclay & Simonds, 24 May 1961, Courage Papers, Acc. 2305/26/68/2, GLRO. There was some apprehension on Courage's part about joining with Bass. As the report noted, 'the Chairman of B[ass] is noted for not being the most approachable person ... the individuals concerned may not necessarily be those with whom one would choose to live on a desert isle!' On the Bass, Mitchells & Butlers merger see Hawkins, *Bass Charrington*, pp. 160–70 (though there is no ref. to the Courage/Harp discussions), and *The Economist*, 10 May 1961.

71 *Investors' Chronicle*, 4 August and 8 December 1961, 4 May 1962.

72 *Investors' Chronicle*, 13 April 1962; *The Economist*, 14 April 1962; Hawkins, *Bass Charrington*, pp. 155–60; Charrington had bought three small companies in 1960–1, notably Brutton Mitchell Toms, which it acquired after a takeover battle with Courage, Barclay & Simonds.

73 Hawkins, *Bass Charrington*, pp. 175–6. Scottish & Newcastle had contemplated a takeover of Tennent in 1962, with Guinness taking a minority stake. However, S&N feared that the scheme would draw the Government's attention to its dominance of Scottish brewing, and it was shelved. Guinness (Confidential) Board Minutes, 22 May, 1 and 12 June, 19 October 1962, GPR. See also p. 483.

brewer. In 1967 the last pieces in the Big Six jigsaw were put in place when Bass, Mitchells & Butlers, having won a battle with Watney Mann for Bent's of Liverpool, went on to join forces with Taylor's Charrington United to create a combine of over 10,000 on-licensed premises, 2,000 more than Allied and 3,000 more than Whitbread (Table 11.7).[74] The last three years of the decade saw further acquisitions by Whitbread, including Bentley's and Strong in 1968, and by Bass Charrington, which added Joule, William Hancock and William Stones, also in 1968 (Appendix, Table X). By 1970 the top five companies controlled 38,000 on-licences (Table 11.7), over half of the total number of full-on licences.

IV

If the 1960s saw the establishment of the Big Six, the 1970s saw the first conglomerate mergers in brewing. Courage, having absorbed John Smith's of Tadcaster in 1970, merged with Imperial Tobacco two years later. Watney Mann, having lost its battle for Truman to Grand Metropolitan Hotels in 1971, was itself taken over by Grand Met in the following year. Finally, Allied Breweries, having failed both to merge with Unilever in 1969 and to capture Trust House Forte, the hotel chain, in 1971, acquired the restaurants and food company J. Lyons & Co. in 1978. This shift of emphasis in merger activity, from several transactions involving only brewers to a limited number of conglomerate mergers linking brewing with food, tobacco, hotels and restaurants, was a reflection of the growing competition for the consumer in the leisure market in the 1970s. It also demonstrated a greater awareness that if public houses were to justify their existence and maximise returns they should be places of more general entertainment rather than merely a point of sale for liquor.[75]

The intrusion of Maxwell Joseph and Grand Met into the brewing world was if anything more alarming to the industry's establishment than that of either Clore or Taylor. Taylor had in fact returned to Canada when Grand Met launched its takeover bid for the last non-aligned brewer of sizeable dimensions left in London, Truman Hanbury Buxton. An old-fashioned firm, its tied estate had changed very little in twenty years (about 950 public houses in 1950, 1,080 twenty years later), and it was brewing about 300,000 barrels per annum in the mid-1960s.

[74] *Investors' Chronicle*, 20 October 1967, and see also 9 and 16 June 1967; Hawkins, *Bass Charrington*, pp. 174, 191–202.

[75] Hawkins and Pass, *Brewing Industry*, p. 85.

Just before the takeover, however, the company had taken steps to inject vigour into its management. Sandy Pease from the merchant bankers Morgan Grenfell became chairman, George Duncan was appointed chief executive, and Anthony Tennant took charge of marketing. Pre-tax profits increased by 32 per cent, 1966–70. Furthermore, a major rationalisation and rebuilding scheme was well under way. The Brick Lane brewery had been completely rebuilt at a cost of £4.5 million. Brewing at Burton was abandoned, and the scattered tied estate of seventy-three pubs in the North and Midlands was sold to Courage in return for thirty-six London houses and £580,000 in cash. In 1971, then, Truman was clearly in a much healthier state than its current level of profits implied. In Brick Lane it had a brand-new, low-cost production facility which could not be fully utilised with existing tied house demand and was bound therefore to attract attention from others.[76] This point was certainly not lost on Joseph, whose hotels and leisure company, having made substantial acquisitions in 1969–70, viz. Express Dairies, Berni Inns and Mecca, was anxious to diversify further into brewing and pubs.[77] The takeover bid was enlivened by the entry of Watney Mann as a rival, by a much publicised split in the Truman board over the merits of the two bidders, and a flurry of activity, involving numerous banking and broking firms, as bid and counter-bid drove the price up.[78]

The details were as follows. In June 1971 Joseph asked Whitbread if it would sell its 10.7 per cent holding in Truman.[79] Having received a rebuff the Grand Met chairman made a direct offer for the company in the following month. Truman responded by asking Whitbread and Courage for their support, but neither was prepared to intervene, and it was Watney Mann which expressed its intention of making a counter offer. As offer and counter-offer were mounted over the next two months, it was clear not only that there was relatively little to choose between the bids but that the board was itself split in half, a faction led

[76] *Investors' Chronicle*, 13 November 1970; *Investors' Review*, 22 May 1971; *Brewing Trade Review*, January 1971, p. 74; Kathleen Burk, *Morgan Grenfell 1838–1988* (Oxford, 1989), p. 192; Truman Hanbury Buxton Brewing Agenda Book, 1963–5 (output 331,219 blls, 1963/4, 347,595 blls, 1964/5), GMet/FBG.

[77] *Investors' Review*, 24 September 1971; W. J. Reader and J. Slinn, 'History of Grand Metropolitan', unpublished typescript, Ch.5.

[78] The firms were: Morgan Grenfell, Guinness Mahon, and Warburgs (bankers); de Zoete & Bevan, Cazenove, and Panmure Gordon (brokers). Freshfields (lawyers) were also engaged as advisers.

[79] Truman also had a stake in Whitbread: its holding of 'B' shares amounted to 12 per cent in 1957: *The Financial Times*, 13 June 1957.

by George Duncan preferring Watney and another in favour of Grand Met. The issue was not only that of whether or not to try and keep Truman within the 'brewing family' but of weighing up the prospects of the extra business offered by Grand Met against Watney's promise of substantial economies from rationalisation. There were other complications. Truman's advisers, Morgan Grenfell, had been unduly pessimistic in arguing at the outset that the company, whose ordinary shares stood at a pre-bid price of 254p, would be unable to defend a bid of 300p. Grand Met's first bid of £34 million valued the shares at 311.5p, and the final offer was worth about 460p. These developments cast a shadow of doubt on Pease's position at Truman, which was further compromised by the fact that he altered his personal preference from Watney to Grand Met during the negotiations. There were other elements of disquiet too, not least the allegation by Watney supporters that its shares had been sold on the market to depress its share price and thereby reduce the value of its current bid (the rival bids were based primarily on an exchange of shares). In a close-run contest for control Grand Met secured just enough support to win.[80] The episode demonstrated how a determined competition for a company could increase the acquisition price considerably and in the process induce both bidders to dilute their equity earnings in order to succeed. The successful offer of £50 million gave Truman a high price/earnings ratio of 32 on exit (the ratio was normally in the range 15–20), which provided its purchasers with a substantial management challenge.[81]

With Truman under his belt, Joseph quickly turned to Watney Mann itself.[82] The latter was determined to preserve its independence, and had high hopes of a reorganised management team based round Michael Webster and Truman refugee George Duncan.[83] However, after an even fiercer if less complex battle stretching over four months in 1972, the company was eventually forced to accept an offer worth about £435

[80] *The Financial Times*, 2 July 1971; *Investors' Review*, 24 September 1971; Truman Hanbury Buxton Board Minutes, 4, 5, and 29 July, 12/13, 16 and 26 August 1971, GMet/FBG. A more detailed account is provided in Reader and Slinn, 'History of Grand Met', Ch.5.

[81] *The Economist*, 28 August and 23 October 1971. Given uncertainty about the real value and profit potential of Truman's London properties, however, it was not certain that the price of £50 million was necessarily too high.

[82] In fact, Grand Met had started to buy Watneys shares in August 1971, before the Truman takeover was finalised, while Rothschilds began to buy shares on Grand Met's behalf from June 1971. Reader and Slinn, 'History of Grand Met', Ch.5.

[83] Webster succeeded D. P. Crossman as chairman in 1970 (Crossman had succeeded Simon Combe in 1965). Duncan joined Watneys in November 1971.

million, much the highest takeover price then paid in the UK.[84] For Grand Met, the prospect of securing brewing economies once offered to Truman by Watney was attractive, but there was much more to the transaction than that. Watney had recently acquired brewing interests in Belgium and in 1972 a major international drinks concern, International Distillers & Vintners. The acquisition of Watney Mann and its associated companies gave the new Grand Met conglomerate an international dimension in the drinks and leisure industries, an important consideration at a time when the prospect of Britain's entry into the European Common Market was very real. Presumably these considerations outweighed the increase in gearing and doubts in the investment press about future profit levels for what became Britain's twelfth largest company.[85]

Courage's merger with Imperial Tobacco in the same year was also a surprise, in that a merger with the complementary brewing group Scottish & Newcastle had been confidently forecast by the market for some time. In fact, S & N had approached Courage with a proposal in June 1972. The arguments in favour rested on the advantages of improving national coverage by linking S & N's brands with Courage's distribution, and the opportunities for Courage to secure a rationalisation of production. But the Courage board doubted that 'Scottish Courage' could earn substantially more than the two companies separately, and as a junior partner in the scheme it was disappointed by S & N's insistence that the Head Office be in Edinburgh. It was also clear to both sides that given the Scottish company's superiority in production and marketing Courage would have to face some uncomfortable post-merger adjustments.[86] Almost immediately, Courage turned instead to Imperial, whose offer of August 1972 topped anything which S & N was prepared to contemplate. Opportunities for larger groups in the European market were an influence, and there was much talk of 'broadening the trading base'. But what really carried weight with Imperial was the need to diversify out of tobacco, which provided 80 per cent of its profits

84 There were some complications, in fact, including a counter-bid from the Rank Organisation, rejected by Watney Mann, and support buying from Whitbread. *Investors' Chronicle*, 19 and 26 May 1972; *The Economist*, 27 May 1972; *Investors' Review*, 2 June 1972; Reader and Slinn, 'History of Grand Met', Ch.5.

85 *Investors' Chronicle*, 19 May and 23 June 1972; *The Economist*, 20 May and 26 June 1972; *Investors' Review*, 30 June 1972.

86 Courage Board Minutes, 6 July and 2 August 1972, Courage/FBG; Scottish & Newcastle Board Minutes, 20 July 1972 and Confidential Minute, 31 August 1972, S&N. The negotiations also referred to opportunities for greater co-operation in selling Harp lager and whisky.

and where demand was being depressed by an increasingly hostile medical and social environment (the company had already bought food interests such as Golden Wonder Crisps, HP Sauce and Ross Foods in the period 1965–70).[87] Grand Met's acquisition of Watney was also a stimulus. Given the uncertainty that such a merger had introduced, Courage could see advantage in retaining a substantial amount of autonomy as a division of Imperial.[88]

In contrast, Allied Breweries' early attempts to diversify were not so successful. In November 1968 an adventurous and imaginative plan to merge with Unilever had been announced, with apparent agreement on both sides. The scheme anticipated an association of food and drink interests on a global scale. Unilever had brewing interests in Spain (in association with Heineken) and Africa (Ghana, Nigeria, Sierra Leone and Chad, via the United Africa Company). Allied had just bought two Dutch breweries and the major drinks company, Showerings, and had turned Skol, its lager brand, into an international brewing venture.[89] For Allied, access to Unilever's international network and cash support appeared to be the major attraction, though there was much talk of the benefits of utilising Unilever's marketing expertise. But the proposal was referred to the Monopolies Commission and by the time that body had given the merger its blessing, in June 1969, there had been a cooling on both sides. The Commission, which at the same time ruled against a merger of Rank and De la Rue, had questioned the likelihood of the promised marketing benefits, and had also expressed qualms about the impact of such mergers on managerial efficiency and financial strength. This view was also shared by the merchant bankers and consultants which offered advice to the Allied board.[90] Undoubtedly, the major stumbling block was the movement in Stock Exchange values over the

87 *Brewing Review*, September 1972, p. 325; *Investors' Chronicle*, 22 September 1972; Hawkins and Pass, *Brewing Industry*, p. 86. Sir John Partridge, chairman of Imperial Tobacco, had argued that a merger with Courage would reduce his company's profit-dependence on tobacco from 80 to 62 per cent: Courage Board Minutes, 2 August 1972, Courage/FBG.

88 Richard Courage–Sir John Partridge correspondence, 7 August 1972, Courage Board Minutes, 10 August 1972, Courage/FBG.

89 Skol International, a Bermuda-based company, was established in 1964 by Allied, Labatt (Canada), Pripp (Sweden) and Unibra (Belgium). Brewers from Portugal and Austria joined in 1965, and there were licensing agreements for brewing in Spain, Holland, Australia and New Zealand. By 1973 Skol was brewed in eighteen countries and distributed to thirty-five. Wilson and Gourvish, 'Foreign Dimensions', p. 132.

90 Allied Board Minutes, 28 November 1968, 6 May 1969, Allied-Lyons. Advice was taken from Barings, Rothschilds, Peat Marwick Mitchell and Merrett Cyriax. It was also rumoured that the Showerings representatives on the Allied board were more sceptical about Unilever than Sir Derek Pritchard, the chairman.

seven month period. Allied's share price rose while Unilever's fell, and this made it extremely unlikely that the latter would be able to make an attractive offer.[91] A less ambitious proposal by Allied to strengthen its hotel interests by acquiring Trust House Forte in 1971 also came to nothing, though it left the brewing company with a 21.6 per cent stake, which was eventually disposed of in August 1978, a month before the successful merger with J. Lyons. The company also had similar disappointments with a number of attempts to expand in brewing in the late 1960s, and notably a scheme to acquire a major brewer under the codename 'CALYPSO' (Charrington United?), which was abandoned in June 1967.[92] The successful Allied-Lyons merger of 1978 was a loose association on the holding company principle, and the investment press failed to see the logic of the move, referring to 'size for size's sake' and 'the fallacy of the big merger concept'. But in linking drinks and hotels with cakes, biscuits, ice cream, tea, coffee and catering on a considerable and international scale it produced a conglomerate to rank with Grand Met/Watney six years earlier.[93]

These mergers of the 1970s, then, were a reflection of considerable change within the brewing industry. The cosy, self-enclosed world had gone, and the appearance not only of large brewing companies with large public house estates but also of conglomerates with interlocking leisure interests worried both the government and consumer groups, a concern expressed in the inquiries of, *inter alia*, the Monopolies Commission in 1966–9, the Erroll Committee in 1972, and the Monopolies and Mergers Commission in 1987–9 (see pp. 570, 596–8). The changes were both an expression of and a stimulus to a fundamental change from a production-led to a marketing-led approach in the industry, to an emphasis on the use of alcohol in a wider leisure context, and the full exploitation of property assets. Whether, as investment sceptics

91 Allied Board Minutes, 6 June 1969, Allied-Lyons; Monopolies Commission, *Unilever Ltd and Allied Breweries Ltd. A Report on the Proposed Merger*, 9 June 1969, *PP* (1968–9 LX, HC297; *Investors' Chronicle*, 6 December 1968, 31 January, 13 and 27 June 1969; W. J. Reader, *Fifty Years of Unilever 1930–1980* (1980), pp. 79–81; Fairbairn, 'Evolution of Merger Policy', pp. 199–200.

92 The company was not identified, but appears to have been Charrington United, which turned to Bass immediately after the 'CALYPSO' talks broke down on 1 June 1967: Allied Board Minutes, 1 June 1967, Allied-Lyons; Hawkins, *Bass Charrington*, pp. 199–200. There were other merger discussions in 1969–70 under the codenames 'X', 'Y' and 'WD': Allied Board Minutes, 6 May and 18 November 1969, 16 December 1970.

93 Allied Board Minutes, 3 and 22 August 1978, Allied-Lyons; *The Economist*, 23 October 1971; Allied-Lyons Group Report and Accounts to 3 March 1979, p. 33; *Investors' Chronicle*, 11 August, 1 September 1978; *Investors' Review*, 18–31 August 1978.

doubted, there would be immediate gains via rationalisation, management improvements or 'synergistic' operations was less clear.

V

The merger mania did not embrace all companies. A quite different strategy was pursued by Guinness. No mergers were created and no tied houses were acquired. Instead the company maintained its presence in Britain's increasingly concentrated retail market by paying assiduous attention to its trading agreements with other brewers, maintaining its brand advertising, and developing new products. Guinness enjoyed considerable success with Harp Lager, which was introduced to the market in 1961 and grew in popularity when sold as a draught beer from 1964. The company also did well with Draught Guinness, which enjoyed greater market penetration after 1959, when the introduction of 'Easy Serve' casks improved its dispense in pubs. Both were keg beers, and Guinness fostered co-operation among British keg producers by encouraging the formation of a Pressurised Beers Liaison Committee in 1961.[94] Progress was made by means of a determined strategy of alliances with other brewers. With Harp Lager, Guinness established a strong consortium of Courage, Barclay & Simonds in the South, Mitchells & Butlers (later Bass, Mitchells & Butlers) in the Midlands, and Scottish & Newcastle in the North. Brewing was undertaken at Dundalk, London and Manchester, and subsequently at new, jointly financed breweries at Alton (opened in 1963) and Edinburgh (1971). The consortium was reorganised as a holding company in 1967, and there were further changes when Bass left in 1970, Greene King and Wolverhampton & Dudley joined in 1975–6, and Courage and Scottish & Newcastle withdrew to become franchisees in 1979.[95] Harp soon ousted Skol as the leading lager brand, establishing a 25 per cent market-share by the late 1960s, though this declined later with the challenge of

[94] J. R. Moore, 'History of Draught Guinness', typescript, 1974, pp. 41–2, GPR.

[95] The original marketing/production companies were Ireland (100 per cent Guinness owned), South (Guinness 45 per cent, CB&S 45 per cent, BM&B 10 percent), and North (Guinness 50 per cent, S&N 50 per cent). The 1967 holding company was Guinness 50 per cent, CB&S 22.5 per cent, S&N 22.5 per cent, BM&B 5 per cent, and from 1970 Guinness 50 per cent, CB&S 25 per cent, S&N 25 per cent. In 1975–6 Greene King and Wolverhampton & Dudley each acquired about 2 per cent with the other partners each holding 32 per cent. After a further reorganisation in 1979, holdings were Guinness 70 per cent, GK 20 per cent, W&D 10 per cent. Guinness approached several other companies in relation to Harp in 1961–2, including Greenall Whitley, John Smith, Tetley Walker and Whitbread.

Heineken and Carlsberg in particular (Carlsberg followed Guinness in establishing a non-pub-owning lager brewery in Britain – at Northampton). Sales increased to 1.5 million bulk barrels in 1974, 2 million in 1976.[96] Draught Guinness helped to steady a declining demand for stout. With 2,500 outlets supplying 71,000 bulk barrels in 1959/60, demand for this product grew steadily, such that by 1972/3 1,003,000 barrels were sold in 48,500 outlets.[97] Guinness also exhibited enterprise elsewhere, opening six breweries in the third world in 1963–74, in Nigeria, Malaysia, Cameroun, Ghana and Jamaica,[98] and diversifying at home, with interests in a variety of sectors, including pharmaceuticals, confectionery, plastics and general trading.[99]

Guinness's keg beers, and the policies adopted to gain them entry into the tied houses of other brewers, were central to the retention of the company's 7–8 per cent share of the UK market. The strategy was recognised to be important at a relatively early stage. In May 1950 Sir Hugh Beaver, the managing director, informed the board that with the strong possibility of higher concentration levels in Britain 'we shall have to prepare for greater competition from the larger groups'.[100] The company responded in several ways. In the 1950s particular attention was paid to production quality, shelf-life and good trading terms. When merger activity intensified later on, a wider range of policies was required. When the opportunity arose steps were taken to limit competition in the stout market. In 1960, for example, when Simon Combe of Watney Mann offered to give up the 'Reid's Stout' brand, Guinness agreed to pay the company £200,000, hoping that Watney might agree to take Draught Guinness and Harp in return. However, Watney had already undertaken to exchange Red Barrel for Ind Coope's Skol and was unwilling to break an embargo placed on Draught Guinness by London brewers anxious to retain their share of draught beer sales in public houses. It was at this stage that Guinness decided to pursue a

96 Edward Guinness, 'The lager phenomenon', *Brewing Review*, January–February 1978, pp. 6–9; *Guinness Time*, Autumn 1968, pp. 3–10; *Harp Record*, Spring 1977, pp. 8–9; Guinness Reports and Accounts, 1964, p. 5, 1967, pp. 25–8.

97 Moore, 'Draught Guinness', appendix.

98 Guinness Reports and Accounts, 1963–80. There was also an attempt to brew in the USA. In 1948 Guinness acquired Burke's brewery in New York, but abandoned the project six years later after poor results. 'Guinness in America', *Guinness Time*, Christmas 1948, pp. 5–8; Dr A. J. Hughes, taped interview; Guinness Board Minutes, 5 September 1950, 4 December 1952, 29 March 1954, GPR.

99 The record here was not so successful. Cf. K. Bhaskar, 'Three Case Studies – Guinness, Spillers and Nestlés', in J. M. Samuels (ed.), *Readings on Mergers and Takeovers* (1972), pp. 98–107.

100 Guinness Board Minutes, 23 May 1950, GPR.

more assertive strategy with its new products.[101] In more general terms, Guinness decided to intensify its quasi-umbrella policy, whereby it offered loans to smaller companies, often in conjunction with revised trading arrangements, and was prepared to give financial assistance to strengthen companies which were threatened with an unwelcome merger. In the late 1950s loans of £50,000–100,000 had been made to independents such as McMullen, Bateman and Wadworth to help finance expansion or improvements. In the next decade similar amounts were loaned to several companies but on a *quid pro quo* basis, i.e. in return for concessions for Draught Guinness or in recognition of earlier co-operation. For example, agreements were made with Brickwoods, Burtonwood, Fuller, Smith & Turner, Gibbs Mew, Hall & Woodhouse, Ruddle, Thwaites, and the Northern Clubs' Federation.[102]

As the merger movement gathered pace and the stakes became higher, Guinness was forced to consider more extensive support to larger companies. This became clear in 1961–2. As already mentioned, it was prepared early in 1961 to give support to Courage in its battle with United for Bristol Brewery Georges; Courage not only joined in the Harp consortium but subsequently helped Guinness to break the London embargo on Draught Guinness in 1963.[103] Then in April Charrington invited Guinness to buy a 6 per cent stake in its equity in order to strengthen its position against a possible bid. Guinness asked in return that Charrington take Harp Larger in all of its pubs and Draught Guinness in a minimum of 500 outlets of Guinness's choice. The negotiations broke down, however, and in the following year Charrington merged with United.[104] The episode caused Guinness to re-evaluate its general strategy. Lord Boyd, now managing director, asked his colleagues whether 'serious consideration' should not 'be given to changing the company's traditional policy of refraining from large scale

[101] Moore, 'Draught Guinness', p. 41; Guinness Board Minutes, 12 February, 17 March, 2 June and 7 December 1960; Guinness Executive Directors Meetings, 12 February 1960, 4 and 31 January 1961, GPR; ICTA Board Minutes, 22 March 1962, Allied-Lyons.

[102] Harp supplied all the lager requirements of Burtonwood, Fuller, Smith & Turner and Gibbs Mew. Guinness Executive Directors Meetings, 11 June 1957, 29 August 1960, 2 October 1961; Guinness Board Minutes, 17 July 1967–6 May 1968, *passim*; *Harp Record*, Spring 1977, p. 8; Moore, 'Draught Guinness', p. 58, GPR.

[103] Courage was offered discounted trade terms to take Draught Guinness. See Courage, Barclay & Simonds Board Minutes, 2 October 1962, 5 February 1963, Courage/FBG; Guinness Executive Directors Minutes, 29 June 1962, Guinness Special Board Minutes, 23 July 1962, 5, 12 and 26 February 1963, Guinness Board Minutes, 21 March and 9 October 1963, GPR.

[104] The proposal involved 475,000 shares costing about £2.47 million. Guinness Executive Directors Minutes, 17, 24 and 25 April, 23 May 1961, GPR.

association or consortium with other brewers'. But his fellow directors reiterated the view that they should only take an interest in other breweries when it was to their trade advantage to do so.[105] Sometimes this produced a delicate situation, as for example when Ind Coope was involved, since Guinness was working closely with this company in Ireland (where a joint marketing company – Irish Ale Breweries – had been established), or when negotiations brought in Whitbread, with whom Guinness had entered into joint advertising of Guinness and Mackeson.[106] There were also fears about E. P. Taylor's intentions in the Irish market, and more specifically his interest in Beamish & Crawford in 1962.[107] But the existence of such complications did not prevent Guinness from making proposals to independent companies. In 1963, for example, shortly before J. Nimmo of Castle Eden agreed to merge with Whitbread, a Guinness representative offered the company financial assistance if it wished to preserve its independence.[108] And the Guinness board minutes certainly indicate a willingness to consider more substantial interventions, for example in relation to Greenall Whitley and J. & R. Tennent in 1962, and, with a more successful outcome, Greene King in the same year, where a protective 'umbrella' stake was taken in return for a trading agreement for Harp and Draught Guinness (see p. 495).[109] Guinness could not offer reciprocal trading terms, of course, but the advantage of dealing with the company was that it was not acquisitive. Moreover, it could offer a lager product which was far superior to the top-fermented, straw-coloured beers which some of the smaller companies tried to sell as lager. At this stage its Harp Lager and Draught Guinness were not directly competitive with the independents' own draught ales. With such stratagems Guinness showed that it was possible for at least one large brewing company to retain its position in the national market without purchasing a large tied estate.

VI

Mergers were resisted elsewhere too. A handful of regional companies preserved their independence, notably Greenall Whitley, Wolverhamp-

105 Guinness Executive Directors Minutes, 17 April 1961, GPR.
106 The beers were advertised with the slogan 'Keep it Dark'.
107 Cf. Guinness Executive Directors Minutes, 10 September 1962, GPR. Beamish & Crawford was acquired by Taylor's Canadian Breweries in the same year.
108 J. Nimmo & Son Board Minutes, 27 June 1963, 118/3, W&Co.
109 Guinness Executive Directors Minutes, 10 October 1961, 10 April 1962; Board Minutes, 6 December 1961, 30 May 1962; Special Board Minutes, 1 and 5 June, 12

ton & Dudley, Vaux, Marston, Matthew Brown, Greene King and Boddingtons' – the latter resisting a bid from Allied in 1969 with the help of the Whitbread 'umbrella' (see p. 490). In addition, a number of 'local' brewers, that is companies producing around 100,000 barrels per annum or less, continued to trade, sometimes quite successfully, under the new conditions. They included Fuller, Smith & Turner and Youngs in London; Charles Wells of Bedford; Hydes' and Joseph Holt in Manchester; Eldridge Pope and Hall & Woodhouse in the South-West; and smaller companies such as Maclay of Alloa, Adnams of Southwold, George Bateman of Wainfleet, and Hook Norton. All survived the predatory activities of the expanding large regionals and emerging nationals. How did they survive? What elements worked to safeguard the independence of the family breweries which remained?

Geographical location is sometimes cited as a key element. There were pockets of resistance in some of the more isolated areas, notably in Dorset, where a low-barrelage rural trade (though boosted by a growing holiday demand) encouraged the survival of three companies – Eldridge Pope, Hall & Woodhouse and Palmer of Bridport. Moreover, would-be acquirers such as Edward Thompson and E. P. Taylor would have found it difficult to find places such as Wainfleet and Hook Norton on a map. Here it might be argued that neither the trade nor the pubs were sufficiently attractive to a potential buyer. On the other hand, some independents continued to operate successfully in metropolitan areas, while the modest trade of the average East Anglian pub did not deter Watney Mann from acquiring Bullard and Steward & Patteson in 1963. There was clearly more to continuing independence than the existence of an unpromising market area. Relative size, coupled with the nature of the brewer's control of his business, was a more important element in the equation. As the *Investors' Chronicle* noted in 1967, independence was more likely to remain in those 'small- to medium-sized concerns operating within a fairly narrow range, and therefore able to keep expenses at a minimum level while cashing in on the loyalty of their customers'.[110] Insights into what was important emerge from a study of the fortunes of similarly placed firms, some of which survived and some of which disappeared. Here, a combination of factors, family, financial, entrepreneurial and strategic, was at work.

It is clear that financial control of the business was a necessary,

and 19 October 1962; GPR; Courage, Barclay & Simonds Board Minutes, 5 June 1962, Courage/FBG.

[110] *Investors' Chronicle*, 28 July 1967.

though not a sufficient, condition for independent status. There were varying degrees of control. The dwindling number of private limited companies with no Stock Exchange listing, such as Samuel Smith of Tadcaster, Bateman and Hook Norton, were clearly immune from an unwelcome attack.[111] But there were also alternative financial strategies for those companies which had sought to expand with the support of the capital market. A cluster of semi-private or quasi-public companies with a Stock Exchange listing had emerged. These continued, as they had done in the inter-war years, to offer preference shares and/or debenture stock to the market, but retained all or a majority of the ordinary share capital in the hands of directors, family and friends. In 1967, for example, at the time of the Bass Charrington merger, this was the case with Hall & Woodhouse, which had been converted from a public company into a private company in 1935 but had publicly quoted debenture stock, and S. A. Brain (Cardiff), Brakspear and George Gale (Horndean), where the whole of the ordinary capital was retained. Control was also secured by some of the larger companies, such as Daniel Thwaites of Blackburn (100 per cent retained) and Burtonwood of Warrington, a public company from 1964 (72 per cent owned or controlled, reduced to 43 per cent by 1980).[112]

Where such an operation became difficult to sustain – through either the proliferation of family shareholders, the death of a major shareholder, or an unwillingness to finance growth through borrowing, a different course of action was required. A number of companies split their equity into two classes of share, altering the voting rights in the process. It will be recalled that in 1948 Whitbread had set something of a precedent by splitting its ordinary shares into 'A' and 'B' shares, keeping voting power predominantly in family hands (pp. 401–2). In the early fifties three local companies and one regional company pursued a similar course of action. In 1951 splitting was undertaken by Eldridge Pope and Fuller, Smith & Turner, both, it appears, as a result of advice offered by the brewery accountants, Mason's. They were followed in 1953 by Young & Co. of Wandsworth.[113] In the case of Eldridge Pope, private company status was threatened by the frailty of a

[111] Hook Norton had a long-standing link with Burtonwood (Forshaws). The Gilchrist family (Ian, Mary, William) acquired the bulk of the Hook Norton ordinary share capital in December 1960. Ian Gilchrist was managing director (later chairman) of Burtonwood. Hook Norton, Burtonwood (Forshaws) Share Registers, 1950–79, Companies House.

[112] *Stock Exchange Year-Book*, 1968, 1980/1.

[113] *Ibid.*, 1955. Mason's were auditors to Fuller, while W. F. Symonds of Mason's was an Eldridge Pope director. Interview with Philip Pope, 11 June 1991.

major shareholder, Rolph Pope (who died in November 1951) and the desire of certain members of the family to realise their investment in the brewery. The directors, having first contemplated keeping the ordinary shares in private hands and offering only the preference shares to the market, failed to find a satisfactory scheme for doing this. Instead, in October 1951 they split the £250,000 ordinary capital into 'A' shares, which were to have an unrestricted market but very limited voting rights, and 'B' shares, which had full voting rights but could only be sold to members and friends of the Pope family. In this way full control was exercised. In 1954, the directors held 50 per cent of the 'B' shares, in 1978 54 per cent; family ownership amounted to 74 and 56 per cent respectively in the same years. As Philip Pope recalled: 'Frequently, various people – other brewers – approached me and said: "Wouldn't you like to be taken over?" And with reasonable politeness a very definite "No" was the answer. And, you see, after 1951 one could say definitely "No" because, as long as the family didn't want it they couldn't get in'.[114] A few months later, Fuller split each of its 6,000 £100 ordinary shares into fifty £1 'A' and 200 5s 'B' shares, each having one vote; in 1980 the directors and their families still owned or controlled 91 per cent of the latter.[115] Two years later Young's conducted a similar operation, their £230,000 ordinary capital being divided into £92,000 'A' and £138,000 'B'. The latter shares (60 per cent of the total) were privately held, with the directors and their families owning about 85 per cent. From 1964 the shares were also used as the vehicle for an employee profit-sharing scheme.[116] The result was that in such companies predators were unable to buy voting shares unless the Board invited them to do so.[117] Companies such as Hunt Edmunds, on the other hand, did not remain in such a secure position, for they were encouraged to go fully public in order to finance essential development. As the chairman, C. L. Harman, recalled: 'This may have been the right advice, but by now we had become more than attractive to other larger breweries and, being on the open market, it enabled them to buy our

[114] Eldridge Pope Board Minutes, 23 October and 11 December 1950, 15 January, 19 February and 19 November 1951, Eldridge Pope & Co.; Seekings, *Thomas Hardy's Brewer*, p. 103; Eldridge Pope Shareholders Registers, 1954, 1978, Companies House; Interview with Philip Pope.

[115] *Stock Exchange Year-Book*, 1955, 1980/1.

[116] *Ibid.*; interview with John Young, 17 October 1989; information from C. A. Sandland, company secretary, Young & Co.'s Brewery.

[117] However, the company's staunch independence seems to have wavered in the mid-1960s, since it made an informal approach to Allied in 1966: Allied Board Minutes, 17 November 1966, Allied-Lyons.

62 and 63 Merger mania, 1959. Charles Clore, chairman of Sears Holdings, shook the brewing industry when as a complete outsider he launched a bid (ultimately unsuccessful) for Watney Mann. Watneys were a progressive but traditional company, whose chairman, Simon Combe, had a brewing pedigree which stretched back to the 1780s. Charles Clore (1904–79), in his Mayfair office, 5 June 1959; Simon Harvey Combe (1903–65), chairman of Watney Mann (1951–65), portrait by Derek Hill, 1961–2. Combe was chairman of the Brewers' Society, 1955–6.

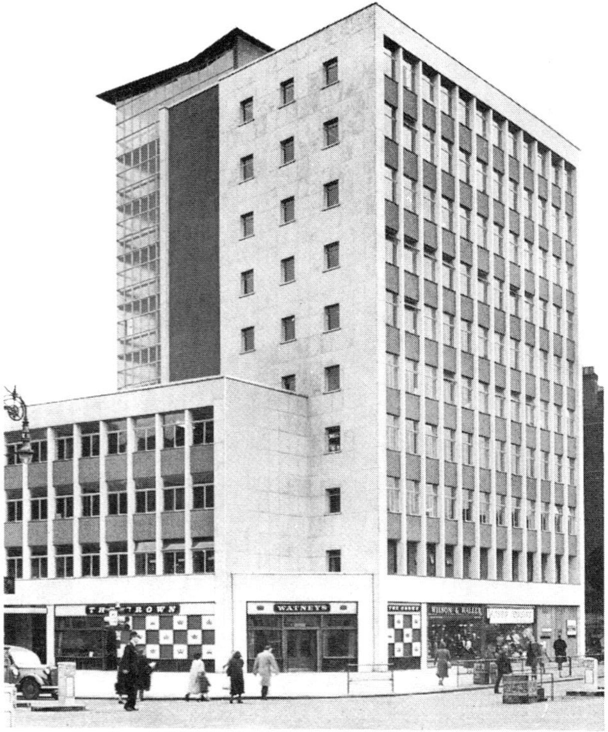

64 Watney Mann's property development: the 'Crown', Edgware Road, 1959 (from *Watney Mann Annual Report*, 1959)

65 E. P. (Edward Plunket) Taylor (1901–89), king of brewery concentration: portrait by James Gunn, 1954. Taylor, born in Ottawa, built up Canadian Breweries and the Carling Black Label brand in the inter-war years, then turned to the UK in the 1950s. He established Northern (later United) Breweries in 1960, and engineered mergers with Charrington in 1962 and Bass in 1967. A great supporter of horse racing, his horse *Northern Dancer* won the Kentucky Derby in 1964.

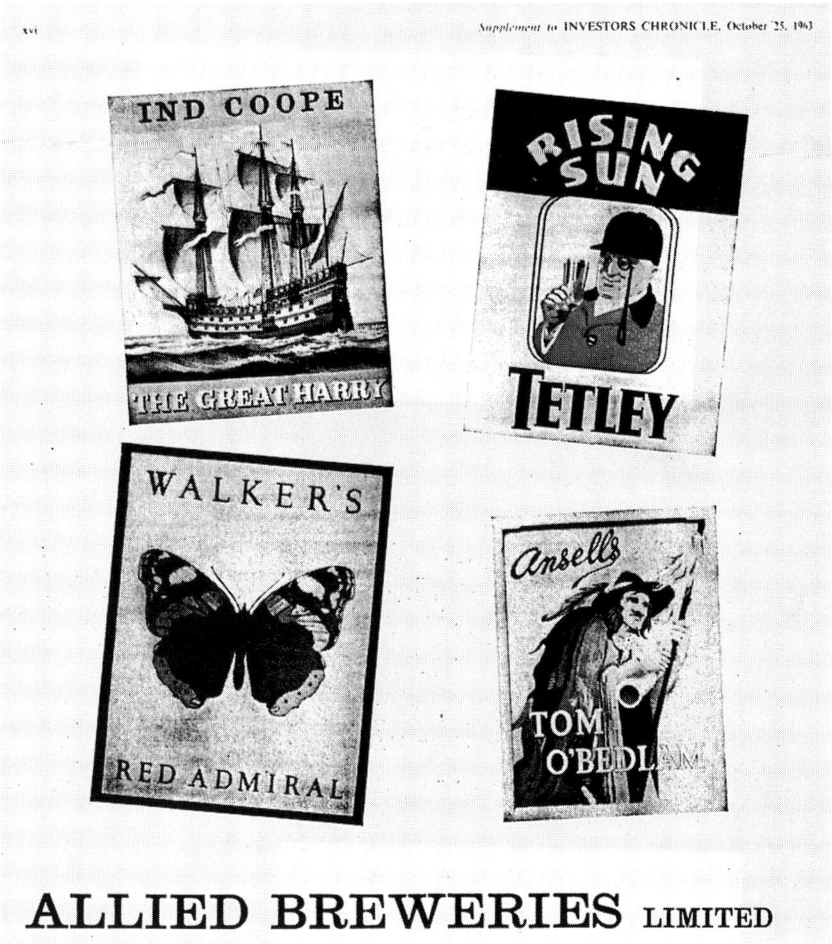

66 The constituent companies of Allied Breweries, 1963 (Supplement to *Investors' Chronicle*, 25 October 1963).

67 Col. William Henry ('Bill') Whitbread (born 1900), at Warren Mere, Surrey, *c.* 1957. Bill Whitbread was essentially a family brewer. Nevertheless, as chairman of Whitbread from 1944 to 1971 he was, with Alex Bennett, the architect of his company's modernisation and its growth through acquisition in the 1960s. A versatile, energetic figure, he rode in two Grand Nationals.

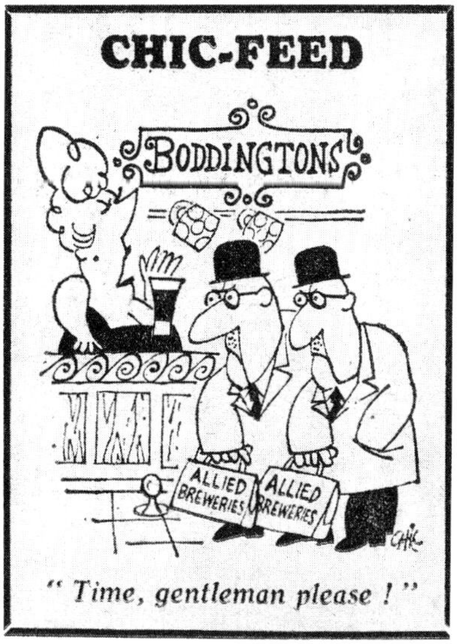

68 'Time, Gentlemen, Please': the Allied/Boddingtons' takeover battle, 1970 (*Daily Express*, 18 February 1970). Boddingtons' successfully resisted Allied's attempts to acquire control.

69 A mega-brewery in the 1980s: Courage's Berkshire Brewery, Reading, in 1980.

NO TALKING
TO BOTTLE SIGHTERS

70 and 71 Bottling. Small brewery bottling line: John Jeffrey's brewery, Edinburgh, in the 1950s; modern bottling line: Carlsberg's Northampton Brewery, 1974.

72 The copper room: J. W. Green, Luton, October 1935.

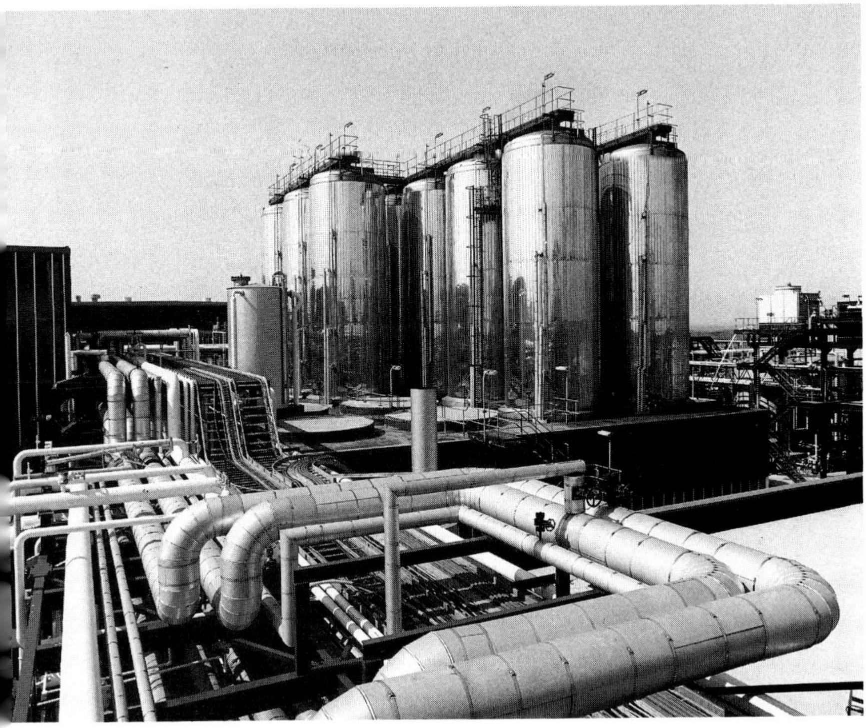

73 Modern fermentation: Bass Charrington's Runcorn Brewery, 1974. All the major breweries turned from open-vessel fermentation to the use of large, closed fermenters.

74 Watneys' ill-fated 'Red Revolution': advertisement, reproduced in *Campaign*, 19 October 1979.

75 A modern brewing board in traditional surroundings. Whitbread board of directors, in the boardroom, Chiswell Street, London, in 1978 (*left to right:* R. E. Gillah; C. H. Tidbury; A. J. J. Simonds-Gooding; R. N. Farrington; J. M. Clutterbuck; M. C. Findlay; F. O. A. G. Bennett; G. R. Seymour; A. G. Knight; A. McQuillan).

76 Sir Alan Walker (1911–78), chairman and chief executive, Bass Charrington (1963–76), in 1975. Walker took Mitchells & Butlers to prominence, then revived the old firm of Bass after its merger with M&B in 1961 and with E. P. Taylor's Charrington United in 1967.

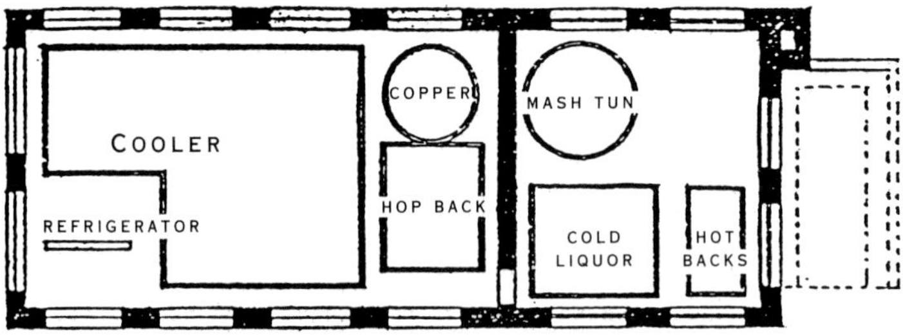

PLAN

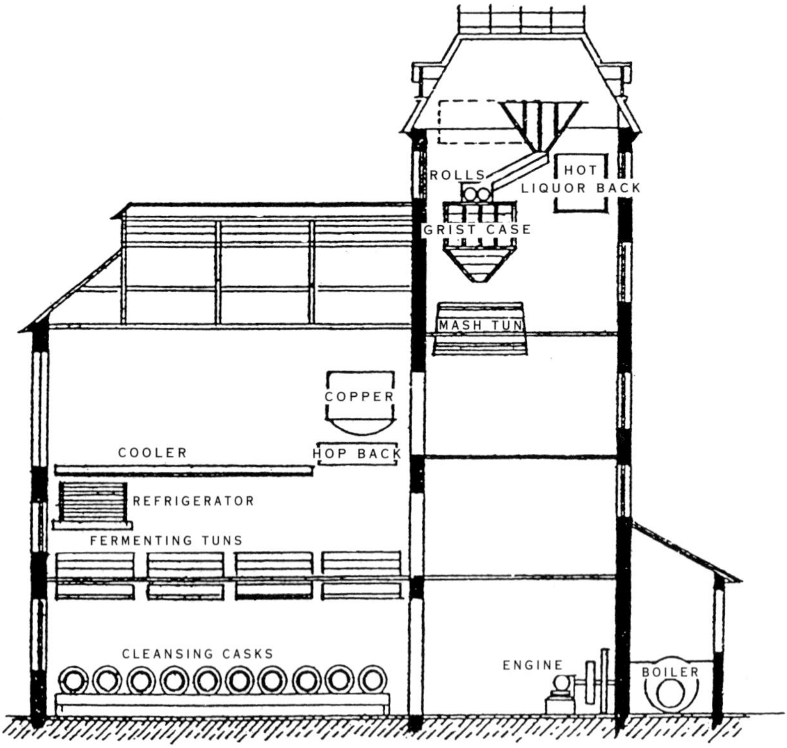

SECTION

5 0 5 10 20 25 30

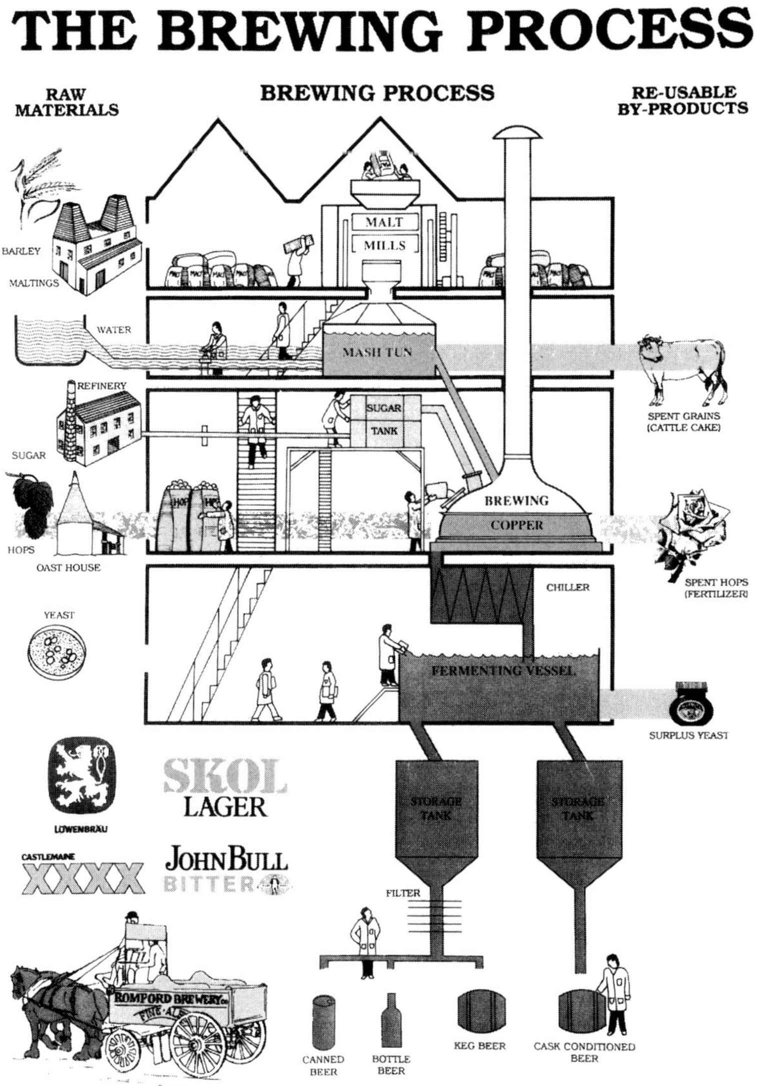

77 and 78 The continuance of the basic brewing process. A small brewery, *c*. 1880 (from George Scamell and Frederick Colyer, *Breweries and Maltings* (1880); Allied's Romford Brewery, *c*. 1970.

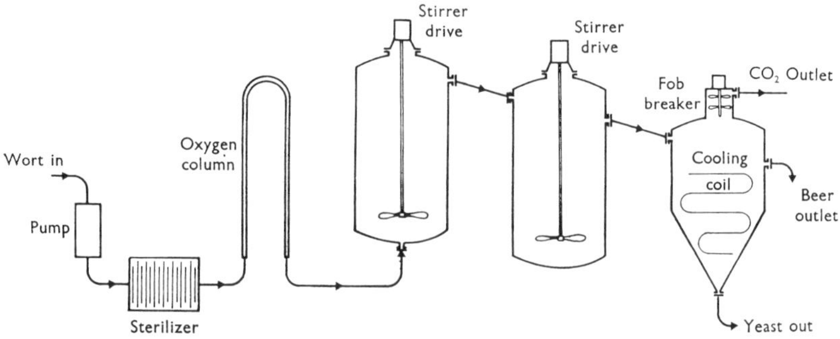

Fig. 1.—General flowsheet of continuous fermentation.

79 Continuous fermentation: process diagram, 1970 (*Journal of the Institute of Brewing* (1970), p. 173).

80 Brewery transport during fuel rationing: Truman's dray at the 'Princess of Prussia', Prescott St, London, E1, in the 1940s. Drays enjoyed a brief revival when motor transport was requisitioned during the war and afterwards a return to motor transport was inhibited by fuel rationing.

81 Brewery yard of Joshua Tetley & Sons, in the 1940s (from C. Lackey, *Quality Pays*).

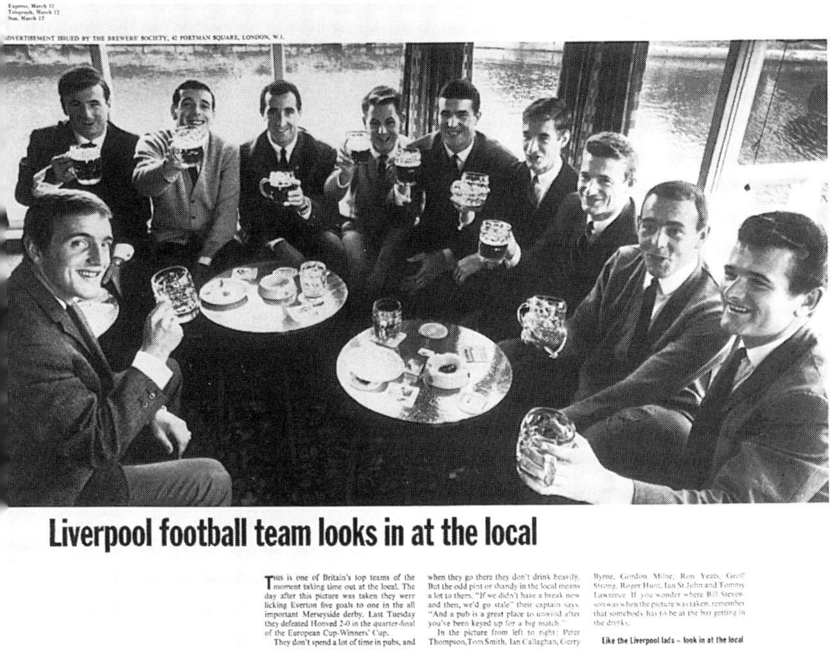

Express, March 12
Telegraph, March 12
Sun, March 12
ADVERTISEMENT ISSUED BY THE BREWERS' SOCIETY, 42 PORTMAN SQUARE, LONDON, W.1.
Liverpool football team looks in at the local
This is one of Britain's top teams of the moment taking time out at the local. The day after this picture was taken they were licking Everton five goals to one in the all important Merseyside derby. Last Tuesday they defeated Honved 2-0 in the quarter-final of the European Cup-Winners' Cup.
They don't spend a lot of time in pubs, and when they go there they don't drink heavily. But the odd pint or shandy in the local means a lot to them. "If we didn't have a break now and then, we'd go stale" their captain says. "And a pub is a great place to unwind after you've been keyed up for a big match."
In the picture from left to right: Peter Thompson, Tom Smith, Ian Callaghan, Gerry Byrne, Gordon Milne, Ron Yeats, Geoff Strong, Roger Hunt, Ian St John and Tommy Lawrence. If you wonder where Bill Stevenson was when the picture was taken, remember that somebody has to be at the bar getting in the drinks.
Like the Liverpool lads – look in at the local

82 Brewers' Society advertising campaign: 'Look in at the Local', the Liverpool football team, March 1966.

83 The 'Packaged Pint': Wimbledon tennis final shown on public house colour television set: the 'Welcome Inn', Eltham, 7 July 1969 (the 'Welcome Inn' was one of Whitbread's 'Improved Public Houses' in the inter-war years (see Table 10.5)).

shares as they became available. Eventually we were forced into being taken over, particularly through a Canadian brewer who had acquired, under nominee names, a comparatively large number of our ordinary shares'. The company was taken over by Bass, Mitchells & Butlers in 1965.[118]

Ordinary share splitting was also undertaken by the biggest regional company to remain independent – Greenall Whitley & Co. of Warrington, which in 1967 was the largest pub owner outside the Big Six, with 1,592 on-licences. A private company from 1908 to 1952, by which time it had built up its tied estate from 700 to 1,200 pubs, Greenall became a public company and enlarged its capital by capitalising its reserves. The ordinary share capital was increased from £662,000 to £808,302, and the shares were divided into 2.94 million 5s shares (£734,820) with one vote each, and 1.47 million 'A' 1s shares (£73,482) with four votes each. Both classes of share were quoted and a portion of each – 9.9 per cent – was offered to the market. But the move ensured that the 'A' shares, only 9 per cent of the equity and largely retained by family interests, represented two-thirds of the voting strength. Nearly thirty years later, in 1980, the 'A' shares, now 6.5 per cent of the equity, still commanded 25.8 per cent of the votes.[119] On the other hand, John Smith's of Tadcaster, close behind Greenall with 1,536 pubs in 1967, diluted its control in 1953 when, having increased its ordinary capital from £960,000 to £2,200,000 by capitalising reserves (in 1949 and 1953), it offered £1 million, i.e. 45 per cent, to the public.[120] The extent of a company's gearing may also have affected its ability to withstand pressures to merge. It is interesting to observe that a number of companies which were able to maintain independence through the 1970s had low gearing ratios (ordinary: preference/debenture). They included Matthew Brown, Burtonwood, Everards, Maclay and Thwaites, for example, which had no loan capital at all in 1967 (or in 1980), and had gearing ratios better than 66:34, and Adnams, Eldridge Pope, Greene King, and Wolverhampton & Dudley, which had ratios of 55:45 or

118 Harman, *Cheers Sir!*, p. 106; Hawkins, *Bass Charrington*, p. 195.

119 *Stock Exchange Year-Book*, 1955, 1980/1; *Investors' Chronicle*, 13 December 1952. Greenall Whitley's change to public company status followed its purchase of Shrewsbury & Wem Breweries in 1951. See J. Norman Slater, *A Brewer's Tale. The Story of Greenall Whitley & Co. Ltd through Two Centuries* (Warrington, 1980), pp. 189–92. The company did not always feel secure. In 1962 Guinness was informed that the directors were worried that a Greenall family trust, which owned about 40 per cent of the equity, might be sold. Guinness Board Minutes, 30 May 1962, GPR, and see above, n. 95.

120 *Stock Exchange Year-Book*, 1955; *Investors' Chronicle*, 16 May 1953.

better. On the other hand, some of the breweries which disappeared had a fairly high level of fixed interest capital when they were taken over, for example, Hammonds United (35:65), Meux and Hope & Anchor (both 37:63). And some of the larger companies became vulnerable when their gearing increased. Charrington United, for example, was identified by the financial press in this regard in the mid-1960s. Its gearing ratio slipped from 65:35 in 1962 to 40:60 immediately prior to the merger with Bass in 1967.[121]

Taking refuge inside Whitbread's umbrella was another financial option available to independents from the mid-1950s, of course. However, the companies which did so had mixed fortunes. A number of them continued to trade independently in our period, with Whitbread securing trading agreements and a minority holding. This was true of some of Whitbread's early (pre-1961) investments, Marston, Thompson & Evershed, Morland and Ruddle, as well as companies which were invested in later, such as Boddingtons', Brakspear, Matthew Brown, Buckley, Devenish, Hardy's Kimberley (Hardys & Hansons), Joseph Holt and Vaux.[122] Others had a quite different experience, as we have already indicated. In all, twenty-three companies were acquired in the period 1961–71 (see Appendix, Table X). Does this mean, then, that in the words of one brewer, the 'umbrella' was 'a bit of a con'?[123] Some breweries clearly thought so and were determined to keep Whitbread out at any price. Others thought quite differently. It is true that Whitbread had much to gain from a full merger with its associated companies. Loose associations, while helping Whitbread to maintain the market-share of its national brands such as Mackeson, did not enable it to realise economies of scale, the fuller utilisation of existing brewing capacity or other advantages arising from rationalisation. A complete merger offered such prospects and, in some cases, extra brewing capacity without the need for new construction. The acquisitions of Tennant and West Country Breweries were certainly affected by these

[121] *Stock Exchange Year-Book*, 1968, 1980–1; *Investors' Chronicle*, 15 April 1965. The analogy should not be pushed too far, however, since the independent Young & Co. had a ratio of 23–77 in 1967, while John Smith's, prior to its merger with Courage in 1970, had a ratio of 64–36.

[122] Five of these companies – Ruddle, Boddingtons', Buckley's, Matthew Brown and Devenish – were the subject of mergers or takeovers in the 1980s. The Whitbread Investment Company impressed many independent brewers, who could see its advantages, not least in terms of company taxation. Cf. Joshua Tetley & Son, Report on 'Trade Investments', 2 June 1956, Allied (Tetley), Leeds.

[123] Interview with Philip Pope.

considerations, for example.[124] Furthermore, it was extremely likely (though not inevitable) that the building up of a sizeable minority stake meant that an eventual takeover by Whitbread would be difficult to resist. But from the standpoint of the independents, absorption by Whitbread also offered several advantages and it seems that in most cases this course of action was requested by the umbrella companies themselves for various reasons, including problems in paying death duties, market difficulties, a bid from another large brewer, and the advantages to the smaller company of combined production and selling arrangements.[125]

Where a company was trading successfully and was determined to retain its independence then the 'umbrella' did not work against it. This is evident in the experience of Boddingtons' Breweries in 1961–2 and 1969. The company had always been vulnerable in the sense that the Boddington family's control of the equity had been weak since the 1920s (see p. 384). On the first occasion a crisis was caused by the merger of Ind Coope, Tetley Walker and Ansells in April 1961, which left the new company, ICTA, in control of a quarter of Boddingtons' equity through stakes built up in nominee accounts since the late 1950s.[126] Fearing for its independence Boddingtons' approached Whitbread for assistance. The latter purchased a minority holding, initially 4.1 per cent, in May, and increased this to about 6.3 per cent by the end of the year. Then Col. Bill Whitbread and Alex Bennett managed to persuade Derek Pritchard, a managing director of ICTA, that the best course of action was for each to establish a trading agreement with Boddingtons', with a promise that neither would compromise the Manchester firm's independence. Two 25-year agreements were duly signed in 1962 providing for the sale of national bottled beers in Boddingtons' houses and Boddingtons' undertook to brew some draught beer for Whitbread at its Strangeways

[124] Cf. Tennant Brothers Board Minutes, 13 September–4 December 1961, 38/13, W&Co.

[125] With Tennant the threat of a takeover by other brewers led Whitbread to propose a merger in not entirely amicable circumstances. First, Tennant had merger discussions with Flowers, then received a serious bid from Charrington. Tennant Board Minutes, 16 May–8 November 1961, 38/13, W&Co. The experience of Nimmo of Castle Eden was different. Led by Mrs E. D. Trechman (née Nimmo) as chairman since 1952, the company faced anxiety caused by the desire of some shareholders to realise their assets: Board Minutes, 13 December 1962, 6 September 1963, 118/3, W&Co.

[126] There were five nominee accounts, Lloyds Bank (Manchester), West Castle (Liverpool), Westmore (Birmingham), West Nominees, and Midland Bank (Princes Street), with a combined holding of 123,239 shares (24.6 per cent) in April 1961. The Boddingtons' directors held only 4.3 per cent. Boddingtons' Breweries Shareholders Register, 13 April 1961, Companies House.

brewery.[127] There was clearly great rejoicing in Manchester at Whitbread's intervention. As Geoffrey Boddington explained, in a letter to Bennett: 'The shares of my brother's trusts were sold to you for 131/9. I was very grateful to you for buying them'; Ewart Boddington told Bennett: 'We are all *so* relieved at Boddingtons! It is impossible for us to express our thanks to your Chairman and you adequately but only to say that our future has been secured as a result of your help'.[128] By 1963 Whitbread had increased its holding to 11.3 per cent, while Allied held 26.1 per cent.[129] Six years later Pritchard, now chairman and chief executive of Allied, surprised the Boddingtons' board by announcing that his company intended to mount a takeover bid. Once again Col. Bill came to the rescue (Plate 68). Both Allied and Whitbread bought in the market, and the former managed to build up its holding to 40 per cent (including securities promised). However, the turning point came when a major institutional shareholder, Britannic Assurance (8.5 per cent), rejected the Allied offers, and insufficient support was obtained. Allied's 36 per cent stake in the company was subsequently offered for sale in April 1971. Whitbread increased its holding to 25 per cent, and Bennett joined the Boddingtons' board. Clearly, the 'umbrella' could function to maintain independent companies if the circumstances were favourable.[130]

The ingredients were quite different in the case of Flowers Breweries. Here was a good example of the dilemma facing an aspiring regional whose financial and management problems led it first into a trading agreement, then into a firm place under the 'umbrella', and finally into a

127 Boddingtons' Register of Share Transfers, 13 April 1961–11 April 1962, Companies House; Boddingtons' Board Minutes 1961–2, Alderley Edge; ICTA Board Minutes, 18 January 1962, Allied-Lyons; Whitbread, statement of Boddingtons' share transactions, 21 April 1987 (information from C. W. Strickland); *Investors' Chronicle*, 2 February 1962; F. O. A. G. Bennett, draft letter to Derek Pritchard, 23 January 1962, Boddingtons Papers, 405/117, W&Co.

128 Letters to Bennett from Ewart, Geoffrey and John Boddington, all 31 January 1962, 405/117, W&Co. The Board Minutes show that the shares of Richard, Evelyn and C. G. Boddington were sold to Whitbread for 111s 9d: Minutes, 28 March 1962, Bodd.

129 Boddingtons' ordinary share capital was doubled in 1963 to £1 million after the takeover of Richard Clarke & Co., of Stockport. Boddingtons' Share Allotments, 26 April 1963, and Register, 30 April 1964, Companies House.

130 Boddingtons' Board Minutes, 19 December 1969, 21 January and 3 February 1970, 31 March and 4 May 1971, Bodd.; Allied Board Minutes, 19 February 1970, Allied-Lyons; Boddingtons' Shareholders Register, 16 April 1970, 17 February 1971, 12 April 1972, Companies House. See also *Investors' Chronicle*, 13 February 1970; Jacobson, *Boddingtons' Strangeways Brewery*, pp. 76–7. On Allied's difficulties in disposing of its shares, see Allied Board Minutes, 2 April, 28 May, 23 June and 21 July 1970, Allied-Lyons.

full merger with Whitbread. When Flowers of Stratford merged with J. W. Green of Luton to form Flowers Breweries in 1954, Whitbread acquired a small stake (about 2 per cent) in the new company. Five years later, when the board ousted its chairman and managing director, Bernard Dixon, after a fundamental disagreement over company strategy, it signed a trading agreement with Whitbread. A much larger investment of nearly £1 million followed, making 11 per cent of the equity in all by January 1962; and shortly after that a full takeover was agreed.[131]

Why did *this* company, which had pretensions to be a quasi-national brewer with a strong brand – Flowers Keg – disappear so quickly? First, its very expansion had weakened it financially, and, more importantly, had diluted family control. Second, there was an absence of strong, competent management from family members. At Luton the Green family was represented by the rentier interest of Winifred Green, and for some years the company had been run by Bernard Dixon, a dynamic brewer-manager whose appetite for growth by merger suggested an ambition to be a second Bradfer-Lawrence if not a second E. P. Taylor (see pp. 392–4). At Stratford overspending on new brewing plant in the early 1950s had exposed the limitations of family management by Fordham and Dennis Flower. The intervention of another Flower, Evadne Lloyd, who had been a director since 1943, resulted in the installation of a new team led by Mrs Lloyd's brother-in-law, Pen Lloyd, as managing director. But further embarrassments under the new regime – not least with the quality of the beer – led the company into the arms of Bernard Dixon.[132] However, this second 'palace revolution' produced no long-term stability. A merger of complementary regionals might have been expected to produce a much stronger company. But over the next five years the strains of trading against a background of falling demand and national brand penetration and, above all, the costs of launching keg beer, brought financial pressures. By 1957 it was clear that Dixon wanted to focus more on Luton rather than on Stratford as a brewing centre. The anxieties of the Flowers' interest on this score (at the time of the merger the two companies had agreed that brewing would be maintained at Stratford for at least twenty

131 Whitbread Investment Company investments, 1987 (from C. W. Strickland); Flowers Breweries Shareholders Registers, 1954–62, Companies House.

132 Flower & Sons Board Minutes, 15 February 1950–29 March 1954, Private Minute Book, 24 October 1950–18 December 1953, 110/6–7, J. W. Green Board Minutes, 25 June, 27 August, 29 December 1953; 4 February 1954, 75/7, W&Co.; Interview with Mrs Evadne Lloyd, 5 July 1991.

years) and fears about the company's future gearing persuaded the Flower family directors to seek an alliance with Whitbread.[133] After an acrimonious boardroom struggle Dixon was forced to resign and after exploring a number of options involving Simonds, Brickwoods, Ushers, Tennant and Greene King, among others, the company duly signed a 25-year trading agreement with Whitbread in July 1959.[134] A full merger came about when it did because the umbrella arrangement proved fragile for a fairly large public company with a proliferation of small shareholders, in which the directors held only a small percentage of the equity (about 2 per cent by January 1962). By this time merger speculation had raised the share price, and it was rumoured that E. P. Taylor had built up a stake. There was apparently some support for an amalgamation with Watney Mann, but in the end a merger with Whitbread was really the only logical course of action.[135] A not dissimilar configuration of events – not so dramatic perhaps, but equally telling in terms of lost independence – may be observed in Whitbread's changing relationship with Dutton's.[136]

If financial control was important, the attitude and quality of brewery management was crucial; and where that management was dominated by a brewing family or families, then the quality of family members was critical. For Hall & Woodhouse and Eldridge Pope, for example, there was never any thought in the minds of family managers that the business would be sold. According to Philip Pope, a director from 1931 and chairman in 1974–82, 'there must be family loyalty, and family pride in the business', and Eldridge Pope had both in large measures. Frank Pike, company secretary at Hall & Woodhouse from 1954, and sales director from 1961, recalled that 'this brewery has always been very family conscious ... I don't think there was any thought in their mind that they were going to be taken over'. Conservative financial management plus care with appointments cemented this attitude. As Pope noted, 'It is no good just giving people jobs. One of the sons goes

133 Flowers Breweries Board Minutes, 1954–8, 74/2, W&Co.; Interview with Evadne Lloyd.

134 Flowers Breweries Board Minutes, 1957–9, and in particular 20 November 1957–6 May 1958, 25 September–4 November 1958, 16 June–30 July 1959, 74/2, 3, W&Co.; *Investors' Chronicle*, 26 December 1958. Flowers had exploratory talks with Usher's (in which it had a stake), prior to the latter's agreement with Watney Mann; Brickwoods (a move encouraged by Whitbread); Simonds (where a bid was contemplated before the latter's association with Courage & Barclay); Greene King (see below), and Tennant (see above).

135 Flowers Board Minutes, 25 April 1962, 74/3, W&Co.; interview with Evadne Lloyd; *The Economist*, 28 April 1962.

136 Bennett, interview, 1985, W&Co.; *Investors' Chronicle*, 17 July 1964.

probably into a fashionable regiment for ten or twenty years. He then retires from the army and expects a job in the brewery. Sometimes that just doesn't work because they haven't got any business acumen at all'. Pike observed that at Hall & Woodhouse 'there was never any financial crisis. We adopted a very conservative dividend policy ... all the thoughts were we've got to build the business up and keep going without getting too large, without over-stretching overselves'.[137]

At Alloa the situation was somewhat different. Maclay may have been just as determined to stay independent as the brewers in Dorset, but here the major family shareholders – first the Frasers, then the Shepherds – put the management of the company in the hands of professional managers. In addition, a major brewer held a substantial portion of the equity. In 1959, after Maclay had sold its pubs in the North of England to Hammonds United, the latter obtained a 28 per cent holding, an investment which was passed on to Northern, United, Charrington United, and the latter's Scottish subsidiary, Tennent Caledonian (later part of Bass Charrington).[138] Independence was not compromised, however. As George King, company secretary and subsequently managing director, observed, 'it wasn't the sort of asset that they could realise to make a lot of money out of, so it eventually became regarded by them as simply a minor investment in a minor player which to do anything with wasn't going to make any significant difference to them anyway. So they just left it alone'. The family investors, whose money came from the wholesale grocery business, Fraser & Carmichael, held 64 per cent of the ordinary stock in 1959–61, and were happy to support independent status as long as no crisis developed. Their direct involvement in the brewery's management was very much at arms length, however. James How Shepherd, chairman and managing director until 1962, when he was well into his eighties, 'did his managing directing', as King has asserted, like James Fraser before him, 'by catching the train from Dunfermline to Alloa one day a week, walking down, arriving here about half-past nine ... he would sit in this office and do his managing directing until – what? – four o'clock then take the train back to Dunfermline. That was one day a week'. His successor, Fraser Shep-

137 Interview with Philip Pope, and with Frank Pike, 2 July 1991. Pike was Hall & Woodhouse's company secretary, 1954–62, sales director, 1961–71, and administrative director, 1971–83.

138 Hammonds United Joint Managing Directors Minutes, 3 November 1958–12 January 1959, Bass North; Maclay Dividend Book, 1955–61, Maclay & Co. Hammonds bought Maclay pubs in 1956–8: Hammonds United Board Minutes, 28 June 1956, 26 September and 24 October 1958, Bass North. The Bass stake was 29.3 per cent in 1978: Dickie, dissertation, Table 9.

herd, did much the same, except that he travelled by car. The real management was the responsibility of an executive, George Reid, the former secretary (who became joint managing director, managing director and then chairman), and the head-brewer on the brewing side. A similar situation obtained when Helen Shepherd succeeded Reid as chairman in 1978, with Jack Cubitt, then King, as managing director. Merger enquiries were made from time to time, but, according to King, 'none of them were welcomed nor pursued'. Charles Ritchie, the head-brewer, claimed that 'approaches that were made could be dismissed within either hours or days'. Of course, Maclay was a small concern, whose modest financial position was scarcely enticing for a would-be purchaser.[139]

Some of the larger, regional companies had an equally fierce determination to resist merger. Greene King's historian refers to its 'collective tenacity', strengthened by the appointment of Sir Miles Dempsey (see p. 387), but he also makes the point that directorial resolution on its own was insufficient; companies of this size had to protect their regional base and retain market share through modernisation and improved marketing, although without laying themselves open to acquisition. Here, Whitbread's surprise acquisition in 1954 of Dale of Cambridge, a company regarded as lying within Greene King's sphere of influence, appears to have acted as a catalyst. The company signed a trading agreement with Whitbread, then pursued a modest merger programme of its own, acquiring Simpson's in 1954, Mauldon in 1958, and Wells & Winch (in which Whitbread had a 10 per cent stake) in 1961.[140] It also trod a careful path in its dealings with the nationals. An unsigned typescript has survived, revealing the company's thoughts in June 1959 when the prospect of a loose merger with Simonds and Flowers was being discussed (see p. 492). In it the author identified three objects: to maintain the *status quo*; to safeguard employment; and to protect the shareholders' interests. There were three possible courses of action: to amalgamate with other companies; to make the company 'unattractive to an outside bidder'; and to do nothing. The idea of a merger with Simonds and Flowers was rejected on the grounds that Greene King would be 'very much the smallest [and therefore weakest]

[139] Interview with George King and Charles Ritchie, 20 May 1991. Bernard Dixon of Flowers told his Board that Maclay was on the market in 1957: Flowers Board Minutes, 31 January 1957, 74/2, W&Co. This may not have been true, however, since Dixon also claimed that Hammonds United was amenable to a bid, which seems unlikely: *ibid.*, 29 November 1956.

[140] Wilson, *Greene King*, pp. 226–33.

partner'; to do nothing was a possibility, the company arguing that its geographical position made it difficult for a purchaser to secure immediate post-merger economies, for example by supplying its pubs from another brewery (an over-optimistic view, of course, as subsequent events in the industry have demonstrated). The best course of action, it was felt, was to look at ways of making the company a more unattractive merger proposition. Here, the possibility of an 'umbrella'-type arrangement, though *not* with Whitbread, was explored. Courage and Guinness were identified as potential partners, as were Schweppes and Flowers, and the idea of linking up with a continental brewer was also raised, since the author of the document stated perceptively that 'I should not be at all surprised to see a very great increase in the popularity of the Continental type beers in the next 20 years'. With control of the company by family and friends weakening (in 1959 they held about 50 per cent of the equity), the merits of creating an additional share trust to operate an employee share-owning scheme were also explored.[141]

These ideas were clearly speculative rather than expressions of firm policy, though it is clear that some progress was made with them after 1959. The acquisition of Wells & Winch certainly strengthened Greene King's market position, and there was evidence of competent management in the marketing of new beers and wines and spirits and the development of the tied estate. Although E. P. Taylor and Bass Charrington acquired an 'unfriendly' minority stake of 11.2 per cent (it was disposed of in 1971), it was balanced by a friendlier holding by Guinness, which owed its origin to a trading agreement of 1962 involving the supply of Draught Guinness and Harp Lager to Greene King pubs (the company later joined the Harp consortium, in 1975). The motive was simple. Greene King, fearing a takeover, was 'anxious to have a substantial part of their equity in safe hands to strengthen the company against ... attack'.[142] Greene King has continued to trade profitably on its own, in contrast with so many of its neighbours, such as Steward & Patteson, Bullard, and Lacon. Steward & Patteson may have seen off E. P. Taylor when he paid a surprise visit to the brewery and was

[141] *Ibid.*, p. 232; Greene King, unsigned policy document, 8 June 1959; Flowers Board Minutes, 28 May, 25 June, 27 August 1959, 74/3 W&Co.

[142] Guinness initially agreed to take a 5 per cent holding, but it rejected Greene King's request that it provide a chairman. Guinness Board Minutes, 6 December 1961; Executive Directors Minutes, 10 October 1961, 28 February, 13 March 1962; J. R. Moore, 'History of Draught Guinness', typescript, 1974, p. 45, GPR; Wilson, *Greene King*, pp. 234–60, 322. The precise historiography of the Guinness and Bass holdings is obscured by the use of nominee accounts.

confronted by Donald Steward,[143] but the company was less successful with Watney Mann. Though a much larger company than Greene King in the early 1960s it had stretched its financial resources when it acquired East Anglian Breweries of Ely in 1957 and then participated in a rationalisation of Norwich brewing in 1961. Together with Bullard it purchased Morgan's in order to divide up the tied estate, but the two companies made a major tactical blunder by selling the brewery, which was much the most modern of the three, to Watney Mann. Watney then used the new base to increase market-share in the region, swallowing up both Steward & Patteson and Bullard within two years.[144] As Martin Corke of Greene King has rightly observed, one of the secrets of survival lay in not making serious mistakes.[145] Another, as Flower & Sons discovered, was to manage the business effectively with familial support. The directors' private minute book of the early 1950s, with its record of acrimonious meetings held far away from the Stratford brewery in the comfortable surroundings of London's Savoy, Mayfair and Grosvenor Hotels, gave every indication that independent status would not be protected for very long.[146]

Financial strength, control of the equity, family determination, an absence of serious mistakes – all were essential ingredients for independence. But so too was a measure of entrepreneurial flair. Companies which could see market niches to exploit found it much easier to survive. For Eldridge Pope, for example, strength in the 1960s and 1970s rested on a flourishing wines and spirits business (as early as 1938–9 this accounted for 38 per cent of total turnover), specialisation in bottling, a quick response to the demand for lager, and particular attention to maintaining income from its tied estate.[147] For Hall & Woodhouse, it was the free trade which provided niche opportunities. Though small, the company showed particular enterprise when it provided beers for distribution via Littlewoods Mail Order catalogue in the early 1960s. Later on, it wooed 'real ale' customers with its distinctive, bitter beers, developed a range of lagers, including an alcohol-free product, and had some success in extending its canning facilities, distributing Skona lager and its Panda Soft Drinks brands on a national

[143] According to the story, Steward mistook Taylor for a wheelwright who had done some inferior work on the prized horse drays. Moore, 'Draught Guinness', pp. 44–5.

[144] Gourvish, *Norfolk Beers*, pp. 158–66.

[145] Interview with Martin Corke, 18 October 1990.

[146] Flower & Sons Private Board Minutes, 1950–3, 110/7, W&Co.

[147] Seekings, *Thomas Hardy's Brewer*, pp. 106–24; interview with Philip Pope; Reports and Accounts, 1974–6; Eldridge Pope, Private Ledger, 1926–39, EP.

scale.[148] And sound profits came with such enterprise. It is interesting that a recent study found that higher profits were characteristic of local and minor regional companies where concentration elsewhere may have actually helped to cut competition in their localities.[149]

By 1980, then, the structure of the brewing industry had changed markedly from that of twenty-five years earlier. It had seen the creation of a handful of very large firms which had started to coalesce in response to falling demand and the need to improve capacity utilisation and secure economies of scale in production and distribution; the process then proceeded on the basis of two decades of increasing demand, in which consumer tastes for beer and, indeed, for alcoholic drinks in general, changed radically in relation to both product-type and the location of drinking. The result was the emergence of the Big Six pub-owning companies, three of them linked up in the 1970s with other products in conglomerates (Watney Mann, Courage and Allied). There were also three brand-based brewing companies with no pubs, or 'Brewers Without Tied Estate' as they were later known: Guinness, the Harp venture and Carlsberg of Northampton. Smaller, independent brewers could and did survive, sometimes by luck, more often by shrewd judgement. In the next chapter we explore the effects of the merger activity of 1955–80 on the industry, and examine in particular prices, profits and productivity.

148 Hurford Janes, *Hall & Woodhouse 1777–1977: Independent Family Brewers* (1977), pp. 72–9; interview with Frank Pike, and Pike, letter to authors, 25 October 1991; Hall & Woodhouse Reports and Accounts, 1977–80.

149 Hugh Hope-Stone, 'Market-Share and Profitability in the UK Brewing Industry', *Thames Polytechnic Business Papers*, No.4 (1985), p. 12.

12

Profits, productivity and prices

I

The impact of amalgamation and merger activity upon organisation, the management of production and distribution, inter-company transactions, and productivity levels is a key issue in the modern history of British brewing. So too is the influence of a more highly concentrated industrial structure on retail prices and profit levels. Both issues are difficult to analyse adequately, given the presence of other variables in the equation, notably fluctuations in demand, changes in consumer tastes and legislative changes affecting licensing. Furthermore, the problem of securing access to suitable business records adds a further element of difficulty. Nevertheless, a considerable amount of work has been carried out by professional economists and financial analysts, and this work must be tested against the material available from the industry's archives.[1]

Economists have devoted much attention to the impact of modern mergers, focusing in particular upon their implications for post-merger efficiency and profitability. While they have recognised that mergers can be beneficial in such matters as the exploitation of technical economies of scale and the spreading of overhead costs, they have also pointed out that higher concentration in an industry may reduce economic efficiency, for example, by increasing a company's ability to tolerate inefficiency, or by facilitating price increases and excess profits through the wielding of an expanded market-power. Furthermore, empirical investigations into the impact of company acquisitions on subsequent profitability, a proxy for efficiency, have tended to be gloomy. Studies of the 1950s by Singh and of the 1960s by Newbould, Utton, Meeks and

[1] Some companies, notably Allied, Courage/Fosters, Guinness, Scottish & Newcastle and Whitbread, granted access to Board Minutes (and in some instances other papers) for the period 1955–80.

Kumar, based on company accounts, suggest that the average profitability of the enlarged firms was more likely to fall than to rise, or was lower than those firms which relied on internal growth.[2] Some of this research shows that the situation persisted for some time after a merger took place. Geoffrey Meeks, in his book *Disappointing Marriage*, examined the fortunes of 213 merged companies in the period 1964–72. More than half of them were found to have experienced a decline in profitability in each of the first seven years after merger.[3]

Of course, objections may easily be raised about the methodology and data employed in such studies. Profitability as revealed in company accounts is not a very rigorous test of 'efficiency', and some scholars have argued that the results are more equivocal if we use alternative measures, such as stock market performance.[4] Nevertheless, an agnostic view of the benefits of mergers has been supported by case studies, notably those assembled by Keith Cowling *et al.* for the late 1960s. Here, the authors were unable to sustain the hypothesis that mergers were either a necessary or a sufficient condition for economic gain. They found that in many cases, efficiency did not improve; in some cases it declined; and in others it improved but by no more than one would have forecast in the absence of merger. In short, efficiency gains from mergers were 'generally not found'.[5] And these disappointing results can be linked with the companies' response to the challenge of the

2 A. Singh, *Takeovers* (Cambridge, 1971), esp. pp. 162–6; G. D. Newbould, *Management and Merger Activity* (Liverpool, 1970); M. A. Utton, 'On Measuring the Effects of Industrial Mergers', *Scottish Journal of Political Economy*, 21 (February 1974), 13–28; G. Meeks, *Disappointing Marriage: A Study of the Gains from Merger* (Cambridge, 1977), esp. pp. 18–25; M. S. Kumar, *Growth, Acquisition and Investment* (Cambridge, 1984), p. 180. The results of these studies are summarised in Secretary of State for Prices and Consumer Protection, *A Review of Monopolies and Mergers Policy. A Consultative Document*, May 1978, *PP* (1977–8) XXIV, Cmnd.7198, pp. 17–19, 100–5, and more recently in Brian Chiplin and Mike Wright, 'The Logic of Mergers', *Institute of Economic Affairs Hobart Paper*, 107 (1987), and J. G. Walshe, 'Industrial Organization and Competition Policy', in N. F. R. Crafts and Nicholas Woodward (eds.), *The British Economy Since 1945* (Oxford, 1991), p. 353.

3 The results for the actual year of merger revealed increased profits, while those for years six and seven, where the population of companies was small, were not statistically significant. Meeks, *Disappointing Marriage*, pp. 18–25.

4 Cf. G. Meeks and J. G. Meeks, 'Profitability Measures as Indicators of Post-Merger Efficiency', *Journal of Industrial Economics*, 29 (June 1981), 335–44, and Brian Sturgess and Peter Weale, 'Merger Performance Evaluation: An Empirical Analysis of a Sample of UK Firms', *Journal of Economic Studies*, 11 (1984), 33–44. See also Roger Clarke, Stephen Davies and Michael Waterson, 'The Profitability – Concentration Relation: Market-Power or Efficiency?', *Journal of Industrial Economics*, 32 (June 1984), 435–50, who argue that if profitability increases in more highly concentrated industries it may well be that firms in such industries are more likely to employ collusive strategies.

5 Keith Cowling, Paul Stoneman *et al.*, *Mergers and Economic Performance* (Cambridge, 1980), esp. pp. 168, 370.

post-merger environment, in terms of both organisational and business demands. Derek Channon, for example, in his book on strategy and structure in British industry, has associated mergers with the introduction by the larger companies of a strategy of diversification together with the half-hearted adoption of the multidivisional form of organisation.[6] This is important. Doubts about the extent of post-merger efficiency must necessarily raise questions about the quality and completeness of the British organisational response in these areas, particularly in relation to managerial control of disparate activities and the rationalisation of production facilities and distribution networks.[7] In general, then, mergers led to increased market-power, but this does not seem to have been reflected in internal efficiency, at least in the short to medium term. The evidence for the 1950s and 1960s in particular indicates that higher concentration was followed by a reduction in competitive pressures rather than an improvement in efficiency.[8]

How does brewing fit into the general picture? First of all, diversification as a corporate strategy was limited, although the major companies certainly acquired more substantial interests in associated drinks products sold in public houses – wines, spirits and soft drinks. For example, Ind Coope/Allied acquired Victoria Wine (1961), Bristol Vintners (1965), Showerings Vine Products and Whiteways (1968) and David Sandeman (1970), becoming the largest wholesaler and retailer of wines and spirits in the UK, while Watney Mann's acquisition of International Distillers & Vintners (IDV) in 1972 brought the brewer a number of leading brands and businesses, including Croft, Gilbeys, J & B Rare Scotch, Peter Dominic, Justerini & Brooks and Westminster Wine. Whitbread was also a noted diversifier, acquiring the soft drinks manufacturer R. White in 1969, Long John whisky in 1975, and a 79 per cent stake in the German wine firm Langenbach in 1974. By 1980 Allied-Lyons, Grand Met and Whitbread derived sizeable earnings from wines and spirits: respectively 40, 20 and 11 per cent of total profits.[9] And the entry of Grand Metropolitan and Imperial Tobacco

[6] Derek F. Channon, *The Strategy and Structure of British Enterprise* (1972), esp. pp. 236–42. The significance of diversification should not be exaggerated. For example, Meeks's findings hold good for both diversifying and non-diversifying firms.

[7] On the impact of the multidivisional form of organisation in Britain see Peter Steer and John Cable, 'Internal Organization and Profit: An Empirical Analysis of Large UK Companies', *Journal of Industrial Economics*, 27 (September 1978), 13–29.

[8] Cf. Hannah, *Corporate Economy*, pp. 153, 155, 162.

[9] John Cavanagh and Frederick F. Clairmonte, *Alcoholic Beverages: Dimensions of Corporate Power* (1985), p. 63; Appendix, Table X. Courage added Charles Kinloch

into the industry was not only a major feature of the 1970s; it also encouraged brewers to consider further diversifications in the leisure industry (broadly defined), as well as producing a number of post-merger management difficulties (see pp. 529–30). However, as was seen in the previous chapter, diversification was not the prime motive in brewing mergers and takeovers. The main thrust of such activity was the horizontal merger, which in most years was the dominant type of merger throughout the economy.[10]

A point of divergence from general studies is the fact that economic analyses of post-merger performance in brewing tend to focus more upon productivity measures than upon profitability. This is unsurprising. Given the significance of tied estates to the brewers – the Monopolies Commission in 1969 estimated that 60 per cent of total brewing capital was represented by licensed property – rates of return on capital are difficult to interpret, since the results in large measure hinge upon the frequency and accuracy with which companies revalued their properties. Such valuations, as the Commission noted, were normally based upon internal estimates of the expected profits from retailing, and with this procedure actual returns tend to reflect the level of return forecast by the business.[11] But in any case, measures of productivity, however crude, are to be preferred to profitability data as a guide to the efficiency with which factors of production were deployed. This said, what few profit studies there are tend to confirm the results for post-merger British companies as a whole. Thus, Robert Jones, writing in the *Statist* in 1964, noted that brewery share prices reflected an upward turn in profits in the industry from the late 1950s but contended that the brewers with the best profit records were not the large companies which had grown by merger but the smaller concerns. A simple calculation was provided in support of this view. Five of the largest companies – Allied; Bass, Mitchells & Butlers; Courage, Barclay & Simonds; Watney Mann; Whitbread – had increased their properties by 69 per cent over the period 1959–64, but equity earnings rose by only 36 per cent; at the same time nineteen smaller brewers, including Boddingtons', Cameron, Friary Meux, Lacon and Wolverhampton & Dudley, increased their properties by only 26 per cent but raised their equity earnings by 49 per

(1957), Arthur Cooper (via Simonds) (1960), Saccone & Speed (1961), and Wine Trades Consortium (1973).

10 Cf. Walshe, 'Industrial Organization', p. 350.

11 Monopolies Commission, *A Report on the Supply of Beer*, 1969, p. 75; Price Commission, *Beer Prices and Margins*, Report No. 31, 1977, p. 17; Hawkins and Pass, *Brewing Industry*, pp. 108–10.

cent.[12] In 1977 the Price Commission, in its report on *Beer Prices and Margins*, set aside its initial scepticism about interpreting rates of return and argued that in 1976 returns were higher for the small brewers and regionals than for the large, national brewers. The variation was shown to be much greater if the return to brewing and wholesaling only (i.e. excluding retailing) was considered. Profits expressed as a percentage of capital employed were 32 per cent for the large brewers, 46 per cent for the regionals and 53 per cent for the small brewers.[13] A more sophisticated enquiry conducted in 1985 by Hugh Hope-Stone for the period 1972–82 again contrasted the more modest profit record of the large companies with that of some of the independents. Relatively low rates of return on investment, including property, were found for Allied, Bass, Courage and Whitbread – though also for Young's, Greenall Whitley and Vaux. On the other hand, much higher returns were made by Matthew Brown, Boddingtons', Greene King, Thwaites and Wolverhampton & Dudley. Locally based firms with low market-shares were the most profitable concerns.[14]

The studies certainly linked the variation in corporate profitability to the merger process, although it was by no means the only factor identified. Jones suggested first of all that the merging companies had spent too much on the companies they acquired, though the evidence in support of this allegation was rather insubstantial. He went on to argue that some mergers had been pursued for the sake of size alone, and that because many breweries were run by individualistic family managements they could not be fitted into a large streamlined group without considerable friction.[15] Hope-Stone also advanced a number of explanations. The national brewers had the burden of large-scale investment in keg and lager plants in the late 1960s and 1970s, which took time to reflect itself in rate of return. The smaller regional and local brewers, on the other hand, tended to specialise in cask-conditioned beer, and here they were encouraged by the lobbying of the Campaign for Real Ale

[12] Robert Jones, 'Where Have All the Merger Benefits Gone?', *Statist*, 2 October 1964, p. 41 (also cit. in Hawkins and Pass, *Brewing Industry*, p. 115). A diagram on p. 42 gives the property increase of the Big Five companies as *169* per cent, but this appears to be an error.

[13] Price Commission, *Beer Prices*, pp. 18–20. Returns on total capital were: large 10 per cent; regionals 13 per cent; small 15 per cent.

[14] Hope-Stone, 'Profitability', 1–18. Hope-Stone conducted tests using the return on investment with and without property, and the return on equity.

[15] Hawkins and Pass note that Jones justified his argument by reference to the fact that several breweries had been bought at below average earnings yields. This of course begs the question of property valuation. *Brewing Industry*, p. 162.

(CAMRA), and by their comparatively low distribution and promotion costs, which offset higher production costs. It was also pointed out that although the process of mergers and acquisitions was largely complete by 1972, the diversification strategies pursued by some brewers in the late 1970s produced a short-term drain on profitability, affecting the rate of return of large companies such as Allied-Lyons and Guinness.[16] Plausible as these findings appear to be, there remains the problem of the relative frequency with which companies revalued their assets. This point has been emphasised by Hawkins and Pass, who provide two measures of the rate of return for eight and thirteen companies in selected years between 1968 and 1976. The results indicate that a tardiness to revalue properties had the effect of inflating rates of return for several of the smaller companies, such as Boddingtons', Matthew Brown, Greene King, Davenport, Mansfield and Wolverhampton & Dudley.[17] A further complication was the lack of a standardised method of allocating internal costs. Clearly, profit data need to be treated with considerable caution.

Efficiency studies provide a much better indication of the operational impact of merger and acquisition strategies in the industry. In particular, they endorse the claim that the larger companies failed for some considerable time to obtain the scale economies which theory asserts should have been realisable. The best-known study is that of Cowling and his team, who provide a measure of total factor productivity both for the industry as a whole and for six of the largest companies in the period 1955–72. Their 'k' statistic, that is the total factor requirement per unit of output, makes for a gloomy conclusion. Far from falling, it rose steadily, averaging over 2 per cent per annum.[18] The data for the six major companies are more difficult to interpret, since the 'k' statistic fluctuated considerably in some cases. However, the results certainly

[16] Hope-Stone, 'Profitability', 12–15.

[17] Hawkins and Pass, *Brewing Industry*, pp. 108–10. This point is also emphasised by Bryan Carsberg, 'The Economic Interpretation of Accounting Information', in BS, *Beer Prices and Margins. A Response to the Price Commission* (September 1977), pp. 23–6.

[18] Graham C. Hall, 'The Effects of Mergers on the Brewing Industry', Warwick University Centre for Industrial Economic and Business Research, Discussion Paper No. 74 (April 1977), pp. 21–3; Cowling *et al.*, *Mergers*, pp. 219–20. The data presented in the final study (Cowling) differ slightly from those in the interim study (Hall). Estimated annual growth rates for 1955–72 are: 2.14 per cent (Cowling), 2.27 per cent (Hall). It should also be noted that the reliability of the findings is weakened by the admitted difficulty of collecting authoritative data on wholesale prices.

Table 12.1. *Average output/capacity per plant of the largest brewing companies, 1966–85 (in million barrels)*

Company	1966		1970		1974		1980		1985	
	No. of plants	Output per plant	No. of plants	Capacity per plant[a]	No. of plants	Capacity per plant[a]	No. of plants	Output per plant	No. of plants	Output per plant
Allied	11	0.418	9	0.600	8	0.748	7	n.a.	6	0.779
Bass M&B/Bass Charr	6	0.468	21	0.305	13	0.575	13	n.a.	13	0.644
Charrington Utd	15	0.178	–	–	–	–	–	–		
Courage	8	0.195	6	0.367	8	0.421	6	n.a.	3	1.057
Guinness	1	1.559	1	1.700	1	1.700	1	1.323	1	1.046[b]
S & N	4	0.594	3	0.933	3	1.233	4	1.190	4	0.972
Watneys	12	0.238	11	0.282	8	0.655	7	n.a.	6	0.535
Whitbread	14	0.194	18	0.228	17	0.264	16	n.a.	8	0.503
Total/average	71	0.298	69	0.380	58	0.551	54	n.a.	41	0.692

NB It is not clear how the Carlsberg and Harp breweries were handled in the 1970 and 1974 estimates. The average capacity of the four Harp breweries was about 0.6m blls in 1977, about 0.7m in 1980.

[a] Capacity data approximate: in known cases, output exceeded estimated capacity. Guinness output was 1.811m blls in 1970, 1.945m in 1974; S & N output was 1.017m blls in 1970, 1.367m in 1974.

[b] Excludes Harp.

Source: 1966: *Brewery Manual 1967*, market intelligence from BS, Papers for MC enquiry, 1967, 1/1/9, and company information; 1970: Cockerill and Rainnie estimates, cited in Hall, 'Effects of Mergers', 1977, p. 15; 1974: Osborne estimates, cited in Hall, p. 15 and Cowling *et al.*, *Mergers*, p. 218; 1980: *Brewery Manual 1980/1*, and company information; 1985: MMC, *The Supply of Beer*, March 1989, Cm.651, p. 330.

point in the same direction.[19] The work on plant scale also indicates a failure to achieve theoretical best practice. In the mid-1960s Anthony Cockerill developed a 'cost-engineering approach' in order to estimate economies of scale in brewing. By 1975 he was claiming, in a joint paper with G. F. Rainnie, that the greater proportion of cost savings was obtained when brewing plants achieved an annual production of one million bulk barrels, which represented the minimum efficient scale or MES. Two years later he changed the figure to 1.2 million barrels.[20] Whether either figure is an accurate indication of the MES is a matter for argument, particularly since there appears to be a trade-off between lower production costs and higher distribution costs;[21] moreover, there are other factors which need to be taken into account, for example the ability of a company to handle (i.e. store and distribute) the production of plants working at maximum capacity.[22] However, it is certainly true that British breweries fell far short of the recommended MES. Thus, although the average annual production per brewery rose more than six-fold between 1950 and 1980, this was from a low base of only 44,000 bulk barrels in 1950. The average in 1980 of 272,000 barrels was less than a quarter of Cockerill's suggested MES of 1.2 million.[23]

19 Hall, 'Effects of Mergers', pp. 24–6; Cowling *et al.*, *Mergers*, pp. 220–3. Additional data for 1973 and 1974 appear to indicate an improvement in efficiency, however.

20 The MES represented the output where a doubling of scale would result in a reduction in total unit costs of 5 per cent or less. A. J. Cockerill's early work appeared in an unpublished progress report, 'Economies of Scale in the British Brewing Industry', December 1965, BS. It was summarised in C. F. Pratten, *Economies of Scale in Manufacturing Industry* (Cambridge, 1971), pp. 73–6. The 1975 study, A. J. Cockerill and G. F. Rainnie, 'Concentration and Economies of Scale in the Brewing Industry', has been cited by a number of authorities, notably by Cowling, *Mergers*, pp. 217–18, and S. J. Prais, *Productivity and Industrial Structure. A Statistical Study of Manufacturing Industry in Britain, Germany and the United States* (Cambridge, 1981), p. 112. Cockerill himself presented a revised version in 'Economies of Scale, Industrial Structure and Efficiency: The Brewing Industry in Nine Nations', in A. P. Jacquemin and H. W. de Jong (eds.), *Welfare Aspects of Industrial Markets* (Leiden, 1977), pp. 273–302.

21 A point made, for example, by Hall, 'Effects of Mergers', pp. 11–16, and by Prais, *Productivity*, p. 112. Cockerill himself subsequently drew a distinction between the MES of production – 1.2 million blls – and the overall MES including transport – put at 0.61 million: Cockerill, 'Economies of Scale', pp. 291–3. Hall had other criticisms, casting doubt on the industry's production engineers, and suggesting that production costs might behave differently with different types of production mix.

22 I am grateful to Mr Jim Dickson of Scottish & Newcastle Breweries for this point. Maximum production is *not* the maximum weekly output x 52. Vessels have to be cleaned and maintained, and brewers may wish to switch between beer types to satisfy consumer demand. Cf. NEDO Brewing Sector Working Group, Report on 'Investment and Efficiency in the Brewing Industry', January 1978, p. 6, BS.

23 Data are only approximate. They are derived by dividing UK beer production by the number of breweries listed in BS, *Statistical Handbook 1988*, pp. 14, 76 (the 1980 figure excludes about sixty new micro and pub breweries).

Table 12.2. *UK brewery investments, acquisitions and closures by the largest companies, 1966–85*

Brewery co.:	New breweries	Major rebuilds (selected)	No. of breweries in 1966	Breweries acquired 1966–85	Total acq'd	Closures/transfers 1966–72	Closures/transfers 1973–80	Closures/transfers 1981–5	Total 1966–85	No. of breweries 1980	No. of breweries 1985
Allied		Romford (£5m+) Burton (£12m+) Warrington	11	1	12	4	1	1	6	7	6
Bass Charr	Runcorn 1973 (£20m)	Burton (£12m)	21	7	28	10	5	0	15	13	13
Carlsberg	Northampton[a] 1973 (£14m)		0	1	1	0	0	0	0	1	1
Courage	Reading 1980 (£90m)	Bristol (£4.7m)	8	5	13	4	3	3	10	6	3
Guinness			1	0	1	0	0	0	0	1	1
Harp Lager	Alton 1963	Edinburgh[b] (£2.6m)	3	1	4	0	4	0	4	0	0
S&N		Edinburgh[b] (£2.6m) Tyne (£9m) Edinburgh[c] (£13m)	4	2	6	1	0	1	2	4	4
Watneys/ Grand Met	Northampton[a] 1973	Norwich (£2m) Edinburgh (£1m)	12	4	16	6	3	1	10	7	6
Whitbread	Luton 1969 (£7m) Samlesbury 1972 (£5m) Magor 1979 (£46m)		14	22	36	16	4	8	28	16	8

[a] Northampton Brewery, built jointly by Carlsberg and Watneys/Grand Met.
[b] Holyrood Brewery, rebuilt by S & N and Harp Lager Ltd.
[c] Rebuilding of the Old Fountain Brewery, Edinburgh.

More significantly, the average capacity of the breweries owned by the seven or eight largest companies also remained lower than the suggested ideal. In the mid 1960s, when Cockerill first began his studies, the average output of the eight largest breweries amounted to a mere 0.3 million barrels per plant (1966 estimate, Table 12.1). Only Guinness, whose production was concentrated on stout, exceeded the minimum efficient scale; its Park Royal brewery in London produced 1.6 million barrels in 1966. By contrast, the twenty-four brewing plants owned by Courage and Whitbread, companies whose product-mix was diverse, were averaging under 200,000 barrels. Nevertheless, the evidence does reveal a tendency to greater scale in brewing, as more of the smaller, older breweries were closed and production was concentrated on new investment in larger plants, with lager manufacture a priority. Between 1966 and 1980 the Big Seven closed no less than fifty-seven breweries, while seven new production sites were opened at Luton, Alton, Northampton, Samlesbury, Runcorn, Magor and Reading (see Table 12.2 and Plate 69). In 1974 two companies, Guinness and Scottish & Newcastle, exceeded Cockerill's MES, and by 1985 they had been joined by Courage. The overall average per plant increased to 0.55 million barrels in 1974 and 0.69 million in 1985. On the other hand, quite small plants could and did continue brewing, while two of the larger-scale breweries disappointed and were closed. Several local and regional breweries survived with single plants producing 20–50,000 barrels per annum in the mid-1980s, companies such as Adnams, Arkell, Bateman, Brakspear, Elgood, Holt and Hook Norton. Regional companies with multiple plants, such as Boddingtons', Greenall Whitley and Greene King, averaged only 130–330,000 barrels per plant. And, of course, this was also reflected in the survival of smaller breweries within the empires of the Big Seven. All but Guinness continued to operate at least one brewery producing 500,000 barrels or less. Eight produced 200,000 barrels or less: Bass's Cannon Brewery at Sheffield; Scottish & Newcastle's Home Brewery in Nottingham; Watneys' Ruddles Brewery; and Whitbread's breweries at Cheltenham, Castle Eden, Marlow, Sheffield and Faversham.[24]

Bass and Whitbread proceeded with more caution than the others. Not only did these companies have to contend with the legacy of having

[24] Data are for 1987 (Home was taken over by S & N in 1986) and are derived from Citicorp Scrimgeour Vickers (Ian Shackleton and Colin Humphreys), *Brewers Today. A Review of the UK Brewing Industry*, October 1987. *Please note*: Company barrelage data collected by the BS are confidential and have not been released to the authors.

acquired a number of relatively small concerns, but they also accepted the need to retain local breweries where consumer preference for local beers was strong. Although they increased the average scale of their brewing – Whitbread closed half of its breweries between 1980 and 1985 – their average output per plant was only 0.64 and 0.5 million respectively in 1985 (Table 12.1). A simple condemnation of the brewers on the grounds that they failed to take advantage of scale economy opportunities after mergers begs the question. Was there an optimal operational scale, taking into account all relevant factors, including transport costs (which became a more critical consideration after the oil crisis of 1973) as well as consumer tastes and product mixes? High gravity brewing, which was employed by most of the larger companies from the mid-1970s, made it possible to satisfy additional demand, for example at seasonal peaks, with existing capacity. There was also the point that some of the new larger plants opened in the 1970s proved a headache for brewery managements to run effectively. At Luton and Runcorn (Preston Brook), for example, Whitbread and Bass encountered substantial industrial relations problems which had not existed at some of their older sites, and experienced sharp rises in transport costs as they attempted to supply a large and dispersed tied estate from a single source. Both were subsequently closed, in 1984 and 1991 respectively.[25] It may be that management ineffectiveness contributed to these problems; but there is at least a prima facie case for arguing that the optimal practical scale of brewing given all considerations, including marketing and distribution, fell far short of the level contained in the books of academic observers. Here, an appeal to international comparisons is also instructive. In the early 1970s, for example, the average output per plant was much greater in the United States and in Holland than in Britain. In those countries, the level of concentration was very high, the product range was limited, and canning levels were substantial. On the other hand, British brewers were operating on a scale far higher than that in leading beer-producing countries such as Belgium and (West) Germany; and, indeed, in such other countries as France and Italy. The hypothesis that the industry 'failed' to attain 'ideal' levels of production clearly raises more questions than it resolves.[26]

[25] H. D. Watts, 'Understanding Plant Closures. The UK Brewing Industry', *Geography*, 76 (October 1991), 327–9. On Whitbread's problems at Luton see Whitbread Board Minutes, 1971–80 *passim*, and esp. 12 September 1978.

[26] Cockerill, 'Economies of Scale', pp. 295–6. See also John Sutton, *Sunk Costs and Market Structure: Price Competition, Advertising, and the Evolution of Concentration* (Cambridge, Mass., 1991).

II

How did brewers approach the challenge of containing production and total costs as companies grew in size? Earlier in this book (see Chapter 5, pp. 181–96) an analysis of the profile of brewing costs placed emphasis on the relative insignificance of labour costs, at least in the production process itself. Later, reference was made to the growing importance of excise duties, especially from 1914 onwards (pp. 318–19, 340–2). In this context, economists and others have made use of the data collected for the several inquiries into the brewing industry, inspired by public or governmental concern about beer prices, concentration and monopoly, and the tied house system. The report of the National Board for Prices and Incomes on *Costs, Prices & Profits in the Brewing Industry* in 1966 included a breakdown of brewing costs for 1964–5, based on data for forty companies (Table 12.3). This indicated that the overall position had changed very little since the 1930s. Excise duties now accounted for over 60 per cent of total costs,[27] while production labour costs made up only 7 per cent.

Whatever brewers did to contain the costs over which they had control, the plain fact was that excise duties were by far the largest cost component. At the time of the Prices and Incomes Board enquiry, they represented 43 per cent of the wholesale selling price of beer, and a decade later, when the Price Commission examined the industry, they made up 36 per cent over the period 1974–7, 48 per cent if VAT is included.[28] There was little the brewers could do to alleviate tax burdens, given the determination of successive governments to retain a considerable source of public revenue. The lobbying of the Brewers' Society and other groups in the industry may have had some impact on the absolute levels of duty, but the fluctuations which occurred probably owed as much to the inflation policies of government as to anything else. The evidence indicates that the tax burden fell after the 1950s. The duty of £10.09 per barrel (or 3.5p a pint) of 1037° beer set in April 1950, though lower than the peak rate of £12.26 of 1948–9, was nevertheless high, and it remained in force until 1959, when it was reduced to £7.91 (2.75p a pint). And although there were regular increases in duty in the 1960s, annually over the period 1964–8, they were insufficient to return

27 The Monopolies Commission Report of 1969 reported the duty to be 58 per cent of total costs (minus beer purchased) in December 1962, 60 per cent in September 1966, and 61 per cent in September 1967: *Supply of Beer*, p. 179.

28 National Board for Prices and Incomes, Report No. 13 on *Costs, Prices & Profits in the Brewing Industry*, April 1966, Cmnd.2965, p. 4; Price Commission, *Beer Prices*, p. 5.

Table 12.3. *Composition of UK brewing costs, 1964–5*

Component	Overall costs %	Production/distribution costs (excl. excise)[a] %
Raw materials	8.6	22.3 [23]
Production labour	7.1	18.4 [17]
Depreciation	2.9	7.5 [7]
Other costs	12.9	33.4 [35]
Total production costs	31.5	81.6 [82]
Excise duty	61.4	– –
Distribution costs	7.1	18.4 [18]
Total costs[b]	100.0	100.0 [100]

[a] Rounded figures given by NBPI, p. 5.
[b] Costs exclude purchases of beer.
Source: Calculated from National Board for Prices and Incomes, Report on *Costs, Prices and Profits in the Brewing Industry*, April 1966, Cmnd.2965, pp. 4–5 (cf. also Pratten, *Economies of Scale*, 1971, p. 74 and Hawkins and Pass, *Brewing Industry*, p. 99).

the industry to 1950s levels in real terms. Furthermore, there were no increases at all in 1968–72, and the rate was cut in 1973 when VAT was introduced. Consequently, in real terms, the 1959 duty was only 53 per cent of its 1950 level. It then rose to 67 per cent by 1968, but fell back to 51 per cent in 1972 and (with VAT) was only 50 per cent of the 1950 value in 1980 (see Appendix, Table XIII). A similar picture emerges if the excise duty collected is expressed as a percentage of consumers' expenditure on beer. On this basis the duty amounted to 49 per cent over the period 1950–8. It then fell to 38 per cent in 1960–8 and to 29.6 per cent by 1972. The combined burden of excise and VAT, which amounted to 29.8 per cent of consumers' expenditure in 1973, remained at around this level until VAT was doubled (from 8 to 15 per cent) in June 1979. As a result the percentage jumped to 33 in 1980, but the proportion was still much lower than in the years before 1959.[29]

Whatever the fluctuations, it is clear that taxation remained a major component of costs and therefore of final price. The excise rate per barrel was also much higher than in the other major producing coun-

[29] Data taken from BS, *UK Statistical Handbook 1980*, p. 53, and *Statistical Handbook 1988*, pp. 38, 44–5.

tries.[30] This said, it is difficult to gauge what effects the tax regime had on the response of brewing managements to other costs. Because the excise duty was a flat-rate tax on a given gravity of beer there were no savings with additional volume, and companies who were able to secure reductions in unit costs through increased scale experienced a rise in the proportion of their total costs taken up by tax. John Mark has suggested that a high level of duty may have lessened the incentive to economise on raw materials, for example, since they remained a low proportion of total costs – only 8.6 per cent in 1964–5 (Table 12.3) – an element which may have favoured the smaller independents. On the other hand, high duties also served to keep the proportion of transport costs low – distribution making up only just over 7 per cent of total costs in 1964–5 (Table 12.3) – and this may have encouraged the larger companies to extend the area of distribution from larger plants. Another consideration was the wastage allowance. The Customs and Excise, in determining the actual duty payable, gave the brewers an allowance for wastage of 6 per cent of brewing wort. The true wastage rate for an individual brewery was very difficult to determine, given process dilution and the over-filling of containers, but there was clearly a considerable incentive to keep wastage below the 6 per cent figure. The evidence suggests that many companies did so. Estimates prepared by the Brewers' Society for 1971–8 suggested that wastage levels were between 2.5 and 3.8 per cent of total volume, with an average of 3.1 per cent. Two types of brewer appeared to gain from the system: the large producer using more modern equipment; and the smaller producer specialising in traditional draught beer, who lost no beer in kegging, bottling and canning. The combined net effect of these several elements is difficult to calculate. Some factors worked to the advantage of the larger brewers; others plainly did not.[31]

This emphasis on the excise should not be taken to imply that brewing costs were either unimportant or neglected by brewery managements. Whatever their proportion of total costs, substantial costs *were* within the control of managers and, as was noted earlier, the competent (and successful) brewers always monitored their production

[30] Except Ireland. See BS, 'Beer Taxation Comparison', *Brewing Industry Information*, No. 2 (November 1974); Graham Bannock, *The Smaller Business in Britain and Germany* (1976), p. 93; Cockerill, 'Economies of Scale', p. 290.

[31] C. W. Thurman, Report to the BS Beer Duty Committee, 9 May 1980, BS; John Mark, 'The British Brewing Industry', *Lloyds Bank Review*, 112 (April 1974), 41; Hall, 'Effects of Mergers', p. 12n. Note that the 6 per cent wastage allowance, like the excise duty, related to beer volume at a given strength (degrees of original gravity).

costs very carefully indeed (see Chapter 5, pp. 180–2). The post-war period was certainly no exception, though no doubt the cut-and-thrust of merger and takeover activity may have served to distract brewing room staff. As Table 12.3 indicates, labour inputs in the mid 1960s were not inconsiderable, if excise duties are disregarded. Production labour costs amounted to 18 per cent of production/distribution costs, and since labour accounted for over 60 per cent of distribution costs, overall labour costs amounted to 29 per cent of the total for production and distribution.[32] And the sums involved were far from small. Allied Breweries, for example, the largest brewing enterprise in the mid-1960s, was spending £7–8 million per annum on labour (and associated) production costs.[33] In a paper submitted by the industry to the National Board for Prices and Incomes in 1969, the aggregate expenditure on wages and salaries of seven major companies, representing 50 per cent of the industry's output, was stated to be £38.4 million in 1964 and £51 million in 1969, respectively 32 and 34 per cent of total production and distribution costs (excluding excise duty).[34] Here was an area where brewery modernisation and the building of new plants could effect cost savings and hence productivity gains. Cockerill's calculations indicated that a new brewery with a 0.5 million barrel capacity could reduce the unit labour cost of production by 78 per cent, a saving which more than offset higher depreciation charges on the new capital investment.[35] Moving to a higher scale of production also had dramatic implications for labour costs, it was argued. Unit labour cost in a 1 million barrel plant was under half that in a 200,000 barrel brewery, and a quarter of that in a 100,000 barrel brewery.[36] Savings with additional scale were also greater for keg and draught beer than for bottled and canned products.[37]

[32] The NBPI Report stated that distribution labour made up 11 per cent, and other distribution costs 7 per cent, of total costs (excluding excise).

[33] Allied Breweries (UK), Trends 1972/73, February 1974, Allied.

[34] BS, 'Justification for an increase in the Price of Beer', 22 July 1969, p. 11, BS. The seven companies were: Allied, Courage, Scottish & Newcastle, Truman Hanbury Buxton, Vaux, Watney Mann and Whitbread.

[35] Cockerill, cit. in Pratten, *Economies of Scale*, pp. 73–4.

Costs: £ per barrel

	New brewery	Old brewery
Labour	0.33	1.53
Depreciation	1.43	0.45

[36] *Ibid.*, p. 75. *Overall* production costs in a 1 million barrel plant were only 15 per cent lower than in a 200,000 plant, however. Hall, 'Effects of Mergers', p. 13.

[37] Cockerill shows that in moving from a capacity of 0.61 million to 1.83 million barrels, the unit costs of keg/draught fall by 39 per cent, cf. 31 per cent for canned beers and 25 per cent for bottled beers. Cockerill, 'Economies of Scale', p. 287.

Table 12.4. *Labour productivity in brewing and malting, 1958–80*

Year	Employees per establishment (nos.)	Net output per employee (constant 1958 prices) (£)	Average annual growth (%)
1958	118	1,977	
1963	150	2,235	2.5
1968	210	2,728	4.1
1973	321	3,465	4.9
1980	261	3,686	0.9

Source: Appendix, Table XIV.

How successfully did British brewers take advantage of these opportunities? The evidence is rather mixed, which is scarcely surprising since much of it is permeated with the adversarial debate between industry and public bodies which characterised the 1960s and 1970s. There is no doubt at all that brewing increased its labour productivity as the concentration of production proceeded. Data for brewing and malting, derived from the Censuses of Production, indicate that the number of employees per establishment rose from 118 in 1958 to 321 in 1973, when merger activity died down, then fell back to 261 in 1980, as firms focused their attention more upon internal labour economies (Table 12.4). Labour productivity, measured as net output per employee at constant prices, increased by 2.9 per cent per annum, 1958–80, and growth was particularly high in the period 1968–73, when the annual rate was nearly 5 per cent (Table 12.4). In comparison with manufacturing industry as a whole, these results were respectable. Productivity growth in brewing for 1958–80 equalled that in manufacturing, while in absolute terms it was almost twice as high: £1,977 compared with £1,009 in 1958, and £20,818 compared with £10,803 in 1980.[38]

On the other hand, there were grounds for disappointment too. Many commentators have observed a disparity between productivity levels in British manufacturing and those in other leading countries, notably the

38 Net output (in constant 1958 prices) per employee in manufacturing also increased by 2.9 per cent p.a., 1958–80 (£1,009; £1,912). *Census of Production*, 1958–80; CSO, *Economic Trends. Annual Supplement 1991*, p. 6 (GDP deflator, factor cost).

United States and Germany.[39] Brewing is certainly no exception, as a number of economists have pointed out. Unfortunately, strict comparisons are difficult to make for a number of reasons. The extent of beer wholesaling, brewing methods (e.g. fermentation times) and product-mixes differ substantially in the three countries. There are also marked variations in the estimates which have been produced.[40] Nevertheless, the differences between German and British productivity are significant given the fact that average plant size in Britain was about six times higher. For example, Jon Prais has noted that while in the mid-1930s German brewing productivity (physical output per head) was a third lower than in Britain, by 1972 it was 7 per cent *higher*.[41] Other estimates consider the difference to be much greater than this.[42] Furthermore, American productivity continued to surge ahead of that in Britain. In the mid-1930s output per head was double the British figure; in 1972 it was nearly four times greater.[43]

These findings invite explanations for Britain's 'lag' in brewing productivity. Whatever else may be relevant here, it would seem that brewing exhibited two of the most pertinent deficiencies characteristic of British manufacturing as a whole: low capital productivity; and a retarding framework of industrial relations. As to capital productivity, there is no doubt that brewery managers responded well to the need to

[39] Cf. N. F. R. Crafts, 'Economic Growth', in Crafts and Woodward (eds.), *British Economy Since 1945*, pp. 262–3.

[40] Some elements serve to depress Britain's comparative position, while others work to her advantage. Thus while British calculations include labour used in distribution (which is excluded in German data, for example), countries such as the United States and Germany package (i.e. bottle or can) more beer, which requires more labour. Cf. Economists Advisory Group (Graham Bannock and Alan Doran), Report to BS on 'Productivity in Brewing in the UK, US, and West Germany', December 1977, pp. 1–5, BS.

[41] Prais, *Productivity*, pp. 115–16, cit. L. Rostas, 'Industrial Production, Productivity and Distribution in Britain, Germany and the United States', *Economic Journal*, 53 (April 1943), 46. On plant size cf. Cockerill, 'Economies of Scale', pp. 275, 280.

[42] Bannock and Doran, for example, suggest that German output per worker was 18 per cent higher in 1972 and 15 per cent higher over the period 1964–73: Economists Advisory Group, Report, 1977, p. 6, BS. A separate comparison for 1975 suggested that German *value-added* per worker was 25 per cent higher than in the UK: A. E. Bollard, 'Pint-Sized Production: Small Firms in the Brewing Industry', *Alternative Industrial Framework for the UK Report No. 1* (Interim Technology Development Group, 1982), p. 9.

[43] Prais used Rostas's provisional estimate for 1935, which put the difference at 64 per cent; however, Rostas published revised data allowing for different barrel sizes and bottling, which made the difference 102 per cent. See Prais, *Productivity*, pp. 115–16; L. Rostas, *Comparative Productivity in British and American Industry* (Cambridge, 1948), p. 108. The calculations of Bannock and Doran reveal American output per head to be 3.67 times greater than British output in 1972 and 2.91 times greater in 1964–73. Economists Advisory Group, Report, 1977, p. 6, BS.

modernise their plants in the 1960s and 1970s. As Table 12.2 shows, all the major brewers embarked on substantial investment programmes, and some built completely new plants on greenfield sites, e.g. Harp (Guinness/Courage), Carlsberg/Watneys, Bass, Courage and Whitbread. And the data on investment/turnover ratios and investment per employee, drawn from the Censuses of Production, indicate that brewing's investment record was much higher than average.[44] Rather it is the effectiveness of some of this investment which must be challenged. Existing studies indicate that the returns to this new investment were sub-optimal despite promising market conditions. The work of Wragg and Robertson, which covered the period 1963–73, identified brewing as one of a small number of industries where a comparatively high growth in labour productivity was combined with a relatively low growth in total factor productivity. The explanation lay in a much higher than average growth in capital per head. In brewing, then, capital was apparently being used 'excessively and inefficiently', even though an analysis of labour productivity growth suggested that the industry was 'in the forefront of increased efficiency'.[45] Some of this 'inefficiency' was certainly the result of the changing product mix in British brewing. A considerable amount of brewery investment had been directed away from ale bottling and into lager manufacture and draught ale conditioning (chilling and pasteurising), which did not have a dramatic impact upon physical output per employee.[46] At the same time consumer loyalty to local brands acted as a brake upon efficient plant utilisation. Nevertheless, a substantial element in the industry's comparative weakness in productivity was that it exhibited a more common failing of British manufacturing, viz. higher manning levels, the reten-

[44] Cf. Hawkins and Pass, *Brewing Industry*, p. 101, and Bannock, *Smaller Business*, p. 118. Total net capital expenditure in 1979–81 was high at 15 per cent of gross output value: Abby Ghobadian, *The Effects of New Technological Change on Shift Work in the Brewing Industry* (Aldershot, 1986), p. 169.

[45] Richard Wragg and James Robertson, 'Post-war Trends in Employment, Productivity, Output, Labour Costs and Prices by Industry in the United Kingdom', *Department of Employment Research Paper* No. 3 (June 1978), pp. 18, 88, 91, and see also Prais, *Productivity*, p. 346n and Eric Batstone, *The Reform of Workplace Industrial Relations: Theory, Myth and Evidence* (Oxford, 1988), pp. 138–40. Wragg and Robertson's data showed that 67 per cent of labour productivity growth in brewing was explained by an increased capital–labour ratio. Annual growth rates, 1963–73:

	Brewing	All industries
Labour prod.	6.6%	4.2%
Capital prod.	−0.6%	−0.2%
TFP	1.6%	2.7%

[46] Cf. Economists Advisory Group, Report, 1977, pp. 15–16, BS.

tion of restrictive practices, and weak management control of labour processes.[47]

Industrial relations are thus particularly relevant when assessing brewing's comparative productivity performance. To a considerable extent the difficulties of the 1960s and 1970s were shared by British industry as a whole. They were fuelled by inflation and also by more formalised bargaining procedures, the latter being a consequence of government efforts to reform industrial relations on the one hand and to enforce prices and incomes policies on the other.[48] But the problems were exacerbated by factors peculiar to brewing. The hectic merger activity of 1958–73 encouraged labour unrest associated with the rationalisation of work practices and the concentration of production on larger sites. This unrest was itself further stimulated by the process of unionisation, as the leading unions attempted to challenge a deep-rooted tradition of paternalism. A comparatively low level of union representation reinforced by decades of paternalism was the key feature of industrial relations in brewing for much of the period covered by this book.[49] The situation had been encouraged by the brewers' appeals to respectability and social responsibility, but it was also reinforced at the breweries by the fact that the workforce was made up of a large number of fairly small groups of workers, each with differentiated skills and functions (see p. 198). Indeed, the brewers' response to increased militancy in 1913–14 and demands for more formal collective bargaining during the First World War was to increase welfare provision. The efforts of Watney Combe Reid in this regard were given publicity at the time of the General Strike (1926), but it is clear that most brewers fostered close personal relations with their employees.[50] Little seems to have changed before the late 1930s. At Mitchells & Butlers of Birmingham, for example, there was apparently no reference to trade unions when the company imposed a wage cut in the wake of the depression in December 1932, nor when it was restored six months later, and the first mention of the Transport and General Workers' Union (TGWU) in the board minutes was in September 1938. The same company acted like many a brewer when it proudly held a spectacular smoking concert in

[47] See, for example, C. F. Pratten and A. G. Atkinson, 'The Use of Manpower in British Manufacturing Industry', *Department of Employment Gazette* (June 1976), pp. 571–6.

[48] See, for example, Chris Wrigley, 'Trade Unions, the Government and the Economy', in Gourvish and O'Day (eds.), *Britain Since 1945*, pp. 59–87.

[49] Robert Fitzgerald, *British Labour Management and Industrial Welfare 1846–1939* (1988), pp. 137–48.

[50] *Ibid.*, pp. 144–5.

1938 to express its appreciation of twenty-nine employees with forty years' service or more, including the chairman, Sir William Waters Butler, and 250 employees with service of twenty-five years and more.[51] By this time, however, growing union recruitment was forcing many brewers to accept some kind of union recognition. In Scotland, for example, the TGWU was pressing hard for recognition in 1936–7, and although many firms were reluctant to take this step the principle was conceded at a general meeting of the Brewers' Association of Scotland in December 1937. This was followed by a meeting of twelve Edinburgh companies and the TGWU in March 1938 in which the union was recognised and a wide-ranging agreement on pay and conditions was reached.[52]

While wage negotiations remained a matter for local brewers' associations after the War, evidence of changed conditions was provided by the first formal interest shown by the Brewers' Society in industrial relations. This came in 1946, after the TGWU had lobbied the Ministry of Labour about the establishment of a national agreement on hours and wages. Although the idea was firmly resisted by the industry, the Society decided to set up a sub-committee on hours and wages to act as a facts-gathering body. The sub-committee, which first met in December 1946, was converted into an Industrial Relations Committee in the following year. It proceeded to exercise a monitoring role in relation to pay and conditions, making general recommendations on such matters as work-study and incentive schemes and suggesting pay guidelines for the area associations.[53] The extent of union penetration, which increased further with the tighter labour markets of the 1950s and the more volatile economic conditions of the 1960s, can be gauged from the evidence gathered by the Industrial Relations Committee. An initial questionnaire, the results of which were considered in February 1947, revealed that 'the great majority of brewery employees did not belong to trade unions'. But it was evident that unionism was strong in several

[51] Mitchells & Butlers Notices, 30 December 1932, 30 June 1933, Board Minutes, 5 January and 1 June 1933, 15 September 1938, Bass plc (Cape Hill, Birmingham); Mitchells & Butlers Smoking Concert Programme, 9 December 1938, with lists of long-serving employees at 30 November 1937, Sandwell Local Studies Centre, Smethwick Library, ref. 2530.

[52] Brewers' Association of Scotland, Committee Minutes, 9 June and 9 July 1937; General Meeting, 14 December 1937; Meeting of Edinburgh Brewers and TGWU, Minutes, 25 March 1938, Brewers' Association of Scotland, Edinburgh.

[53] BS Council Minutes, 16 May, 19 June, 21 November and 11 December 1946, 16 April 1947; BS Industrial Relations Committee Minutes, 13 April 1948; BS Annual Report 1946–7, pp. 7, 19–20, BS. On work study see BS Industrial Relations Committee Minutes, 12 April 1960; BS Annual Report 1959–60, pp. 20–1, BS.

areas (Nottingham, Staffordshire, Warwickshire, Yorkshire, South Wales and Scotland), and that the larger companies were being unionised. Thus, seventy-five companies, who together accounted for 44 per cent of the beer produced, had dealings with the TGWU.[54] In 1950 twenty associations reported no formal dealings with the unions; by 1965 this figure had fallen to thirteen.[55] At the same time the intensified merger activity, together with a higher level of capital investment, produced instability in working practices in an industry where custom was strong. As the unions gathered strength they were sometimes able to institute a 'leapfrogging' process of pay awards by playing off one area against another. Some brewers, for example those in London, conducted negotiations as a group, and on several occasions the Society's committee considered the idea of moving to national collective bargaining through a Joint Industrial Council. However, each time this was resisted.[56] Most problems, then, remained fundamentally a matter for individual companies to settle.

The concentration of brewing into larger plants by the major companies had the effect of raising the profile of distribution by road; and since breweries operated their own transport fleets it brought them into conflict with the principal union, the TGWU. Labour disputes, accounts of which had rarely been reported in the pages of board minute books, intruded more and more into the discussions of senior management. Difficulties were particularly evident at the mega-breweries such as Luton and Runcorn, which were close to car assembly plants and therefore affected by greater union militancy and the special characteristics of the local labour market. That there was room for improvement was admitted in the 1977 Report of NEDO's Brewing Sector Working Group, which pointed to the problems caused by outmoded collective agreements, defective payments systems and the serious underutilisation of vehicles and manpower, and called for greater flexibility of working.[57] There were also problems with retail staff as the major

[54] BS Council Minutes, 18 February 1947, BS.

[55] BS, Reports on 'Hours, Wages and Conditions in the Brewing Industry', 31 July 1950, 31 January 1960, Industrial Relations Committee Papers, BS.

[56] Cf. BS Industrial Relations Committee Paper on 'Functions of the Committee', dated 17 February 1960, and Committee Minutes, 16 February and 13 December 1960, 19 January and 19 October 1965, BS.

[57] NEDO Brewing Sector Working Group (chairman: D. Holden-Brown (Allied)), Report on *Brewing* (May 1977), pp. 15–16, also cit. by Prais, *Productivity*, p. 120. A further report in 1983 noted some improvement in distribution efficiency, but attributed it to the pressures created by the downturn in beer consumption after 1979 rather than to any positive response. NEDO BSWG, *The Outlook for the Brewing Industry. Market Prospects and the Implications for Employment* (1983), p. 22.

companies sought to place more emphasis upon management rather than tenancies in their tied public houses.[58] Statistical data support these observations. Union density in the food and drink sector increased from 43 per cent in 1948 to 65 per cent in 1979 (compared with 45 and 55 per cent in industry as a whole).[59] An analysis of the number of work stoppages per 100,000 employees in 1970–5 revealed brewing and malting to have a much higher incidence than both manufacturing and all industry (including services).[60] These disputes were not in general protracted, but at a time when industry was transforming its corporate structure and modernising production and distribution facilities on a considerable scale it was clearly disturbing to be beset by a comparatively large number of minor disputes.[61]

III

The response of the industry to the challenge of reorganisation and rationalisation in the wake of merger was not regarded sympathetically by public bodies. Successive reports of the National Board for Prices and Incomes (1966, 1969), the Monopolies Commission (1969) and the Price Commission (1977) were highly critical of the larger companies in particular, and with each report there was little sign of a better understanding of the way in which the industry functioned in wholesaling and retailing terms. One of the recurring themes raised by these quasi-governmental agencies was that the major brewers, far from reorganising effectively, had passed on the costs of post-merger adjustment to the consumer in the form of higher prices for beer, wines, spirits and soft drinks. Thus, the National Board for Prices and Incomes argued in 1966 that the bulk of the industry's cost increases had already been covered by price increases and, further, that the tied house system had reduced competition and enabled the brewers to withhold from the consumer

58 See Kevin Hawkins, 'Brewer–Licensee Relations: A Case-Study in the Growth of Collective Bargaining and White-Collar Militancy', in N. H. Cuthbert and K. H. Hawkins (eds.), *Company Industrial Relations Policies: The Management of Industrial Relations in the 1970s* (1973), p. 115.

59 Robert Price and George S. Bain, 'Union Growth in Britain: Retrospect and Prospect', *British Journal of Industrial Relations*, 21 (1983), 46–7, 54.

60 38.8 cf. 22.9 (manufacturing) and 12.4 (all industries). C. T. B. Smith *et al.*, *Strikes in Britain* (1978), cit. in Ghobadian, *New Technological Change*, pp. 28–30.

61 The number of days lost per 1,000 employees in brewing was lower at 484.6 than manufacturing (819.7) and all industry (586.6). *Ibid.* Other evidence points in the same direction, e.g. strike data for 1949–73, cit. in J. W. Durcan *et al.*, *Strikes in Post-War Britain. A Study of Stoppages of Work due to Industrial Disputes, 1946–73* (1983), p. 176.

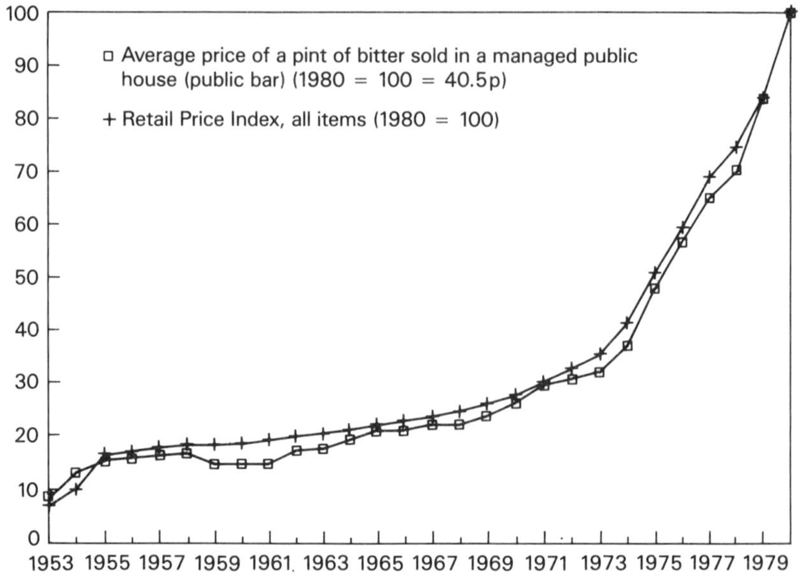

Fig. 12.1 Beer price and retail price indices, 1939–80. (*Source:* BS, *Statistical Handbook 1991*, p. 41; CSO, *Economic Trends 1991*, p. 128; *The British Economy: Key Statistics 1900–1970*, p. 8.)

the cost reductions associated with brewing innovation.[62] Then, in 1977, the Price Commission attacked the larger companies for their price increases in the mid-1970s, observing that while their prices were higher than those of the smaller brewers their profit margins were lower.[63] And successive reports urged the brewers to make a more exact distinction between wholesaling and retailing activities in their pricing, and in the evaluation of rates of return, despite the industry's repeated assertion that the business was an integrated one, and that the internal transfer prices used to 'sell' beer to brewers' pubs were not intended to reflect the real benefit of the retail outlets to the business as a whole.[64]

What validity was there in these criticisms? The first point to make is

[62] NBPI, *Costs, Prices & Profits*, pp. 7, 13–14. This observation inspired a reference to the Monopolies Commission.

[63] Price Commission, *Beer Prices*, pp. 9, 13, 41.

[64] NBPI, *Costs, Prices & Profits*, p. 14; Price Commission, *Beer Prices*, pp. 18–23, 44; BS, *Beer Prices and Margins. Response to the Price Commission* (September 1977), pp. 6–7; CBI, Comment on 'Price Commission Report on Beer Prices and Margins', September 1977, p. 4, BS.

that the pricing mechanisms in the industry were complex. British beer was certainly not a homogeneous product; nor was there uniformity in the sales outlets. The brewers were thus able to claim with justification that the retail price of beer sold in on-licensed premises represented payment for a 'package deal', including the amenities in which the brewers had invested (Plate 83).[65] Furthermore, careful reading of the reports reveals little evidence that beer prices, whether wholesale or retail, were found to be historically high, or rising significantly faster than retail prices as a whole.[66] Indeed, when Allied (in 1978) and Whitbread (in 1979) made applications to the Price Commission to raise prices, the Commission after thorough investigation concluded that margins were fairly low and that the increases were merited.[67] Were prices high in 1980? The data assembled by the Brewers' Society on the price of bitter sold in the public bar of a managed house, although subject to reservations about how far as a single figure it could adequately capture the variety of the industry's pricing, is nevertheless important in demonstrating how over the longer term the price of beer rose very much in line with retail prices as a whole (see Fig. 12.1). The growth rate of the beer price over the period 1939–80 was 5.67 per cent per annum, while that of retail prices was 5.94 per cent.[68] On the other hand, the series does give some support to critics who argued that the price of beer had outpaced the rate of inflation since the merger activity of the late 1950s, and, in particular, during the 1970s. Thus, the 6p (1s 2½d) pint of 1959–61 had become 13p by 1973 and 40.5p by 1980, an increase of 575 per cent (9.07 per cent per annum, 1960–80), while general prices increased by 436 per cent (8.28 per cent per annum).[69] Whether the gap was covered by an improvement in the 'package' of amenities provided is, of course, a matter for argument.

65 See BS, Draft statement on 'Prices and Incomes Board Report No. 13', 27 May 1966, pp. 1–2, BS, Memo on 'Organisation, Structure and Practices of the British Brewing Industry', 1 July 1968, p. 38, BS and subsequent documentation.

66 NBPI, Report No. 136 on *Beer Prices*, November 1969, Cmnd.4227, pp. 25–6; Price Commission, *Beer Prices*, p. 41.

67 Price Commission, Report on *Allied Breweries (UK) Limited – Brewing and Wholesaling of Beer and Sales in Managed Houses*, 26 April 1978, p. 32, and on *Whitbread and Company Limited – Wholesale Prices and Prices in Managed Houses of Beer, Wines, Spirits, Soft Drinks and Ciders*, 12 June 1979, p. 43. More reservations were expressed about Bass's intended price increases in *Bass Limited – Wholesale Prices of Beer and Prices in Managed Houses*, 12 June 1979, pp. 4, 37–8.

68 The two series have a correlation coefficient of 0.997 for 1939–80. BS, *Statistical Handbook 1988*, p. 41; RPI from CSO, *Economic Trends. Annual Supplement 1991*, p. 128 and London & Cambridge Economic Service, *The British Economy. Key Statistics 1900–1970* (1973), p. 8.

69 Calculated from *ibid*.

IV

The final section of this chapter deals with the industry's organisational responses to post-merger conditions. Here there is an opportunity to put flesh onto the bones of the economic studies referred to above, to examine the managerial dynamics underpinning decision-making in relation to investment, production, the labour force and marketing. Here, too, there is a vast general literature which chronicles the failings of British industry as a whole. It refers to the reluctance of companies to adopt the multidivisional form of organisation and to the persistence in large companies of either an over-centralised divisional structure or a loose holding-company form. It also condemns the cosy, 'clubby' atmosphere of British boardrooms in which management innovations such as corporate planning, management accounting and investment appraisal techniques were regarded with suspicion until the late 1960s and arguably beyond.[70] Post-merger strategies are customarily associated with a number of managerial constraints or shortcomings: the continuance of paternalism; an unwillingness to prune ruthlessly both white- and blue-collar staff; a defensive attitude in which the structures of the companies merged or amalgamated were retained intact long after the formal transfer of ownership; and uncertainty about the appropriate organisational structure for control in large companies, a situation which encouraged lurches towards centralisation followed by equally violent lurches toward decentralisation.[71]

How does brewing fit into this gloomy general picture? From what has already been observed, it would be difficult to argue that brewing was an exception to the rule of post-war adjustment by British business enterprise. Brewing companies, large and small, shared many of the organisational characteristics of British manufacturing companies, and their adoption of modern corporate forms appears to have been no quicker nor more comprehensive than that of companies in other sectors. And yet it is also apparent from the business records of individual companies that by 1980 many brewery companies had done much to transform their organisations, control methods and management accounting.

[70] See e.g. Channon, *Strategy and Structure*; Hannah, *Corporate Economy*; Coleman, 'Gentlemen and Players', 92–116; Gourvish, 'British Business and the Transition to a Corporate Economy', 18–45.

[71] See e.g. Cowling, *Mergers*, etc.

It is a commonplace when referring to modern corporate responses to observe that organisational difficulties multiplied when mergers or amalgamations were complex. Reference to the very different histories of, for example, Scottish & Newcastle Breweries on the one hand, and Allied Breweries on the other, makes this clear. The amalgamation of Scottish & Newcastle was essentially an end-on combination of complementary brewing and retailing interests in Scotland and the North-East, although the contemporary acquisition of some smaller Edinburgh companies necessitated some rationalisation (see Chapter 11, p. 468). In consequence, recourse to a holding-company structure with two main subsidiaries, one in Edinburgh, the other in Newcastle, made obvious operational sense. It is true that trading operations in the North-East were quickly integrated under Newcastle's control and the wines and spirits businesses were combined. But in essence much went on as before. The chairman, William McEwan Younger, outlining the circumstances of the merger in 1960, saw it as both a drastic and a final step: 'We consider it extremely unlikely that any merger with any other company will even be contemplated.' In 1963 he explained to shareholders that 'it is now generally appreciated that the benefits to be gathered from mergers ... take longer to realise than was previously thought, and perhaps than we anticipated ... if amalgamations and expansion proceed at too rapid a rate it must almost inevitably strain managerial resources to the full, with consequences which may be harmful'.[72]

To a considerable degree Scottish & Newcastle's business strategy reflected its organisational caution. No further mergers were made before the 1980s, and the company's tied estate remained much the same over the longer term. Amounting to 1,459 houses in 1961, the estate reached 1,652 by 1973/4, then fell back with rationalisations to 1,472 in 1979/80.[73] Expansion rested upon exploitation of a small number of leading ale brands which were promoted in the free trade – Newcastle Brown Ale, McEwan's Export and Younger's Tartan – and participation in the Harp consortium. The company certainly outperformed the market. Its UK sales increased from 2.44 million barrels in 1965/6 to 4.62 million ten years later, an increase of an impressive 89 per cent; sales to the free trade grew by no less than 150 per cent, from 1.43

72 W. M. Younger, statement on 'Scottish & Newcastle Breweries', 17 October 1960, p. 2, S&N Merger File, S&N; Younger, statement with S&N Report & Accounts for year ending 30 April 1963, p. 3.

73 Information from S&N.

to 3.58 million barrels. This compared very favourably with a growth in UK consumption of only 29 per cent.[74] However, Scottish & Newcastle's strategy began to falter in the mid-1970s, and signs of weakness were recognised by the company in 1972 when, having contemplated a merger with Courage, it found itself outbid by Imperial Tobacco (see pp. 477–8). The problems which were identified included an over-dependence on the wholesaling of beer, the lack of lager brands, a limited presence in the more prosperous South-East, and more intense competition in the free trade.[75] To rectify these weaknesses, the company gave more encouragement to diversification, expanding its Thistle Hotels subsidiary (formed in 1965). In the beer market it introduced its own lager brands, McEwan's and Kestrel, and placed more emphasis on managed houses. To support this, a new, more centralised divisional structure was introduced in 1978, in which the organisation was divided into a beer (production/wholesaling) company and an inns (retailing) company. However, it survived for only four years, being jettisoned in favour of a decentralised, regional structure for distribution, selling and public house management. These changes may have been unsettling, but they were scarcely drastic adjustments in a business which was fairly straightforward, and where a clearly understood corporate strategy was pursued systematically and on the whole consistently for twenty years.[76]

The difficulties facing some of the other large companies, however, were of a different order of magnitude. Brewers such as Allied, Bass, Watney Mann and Whitbread acquired large and heterogeneous tied estates and collections of production facilities, many of them small and ramshackle. The organisational challenge facing the senior managers of ICTA in 1961, for example, was considerable and it was scarcely a surprise that a loose federative structure was first adopted. Justified by the chairman Edward Thompson as 'a Commonwealth of Brewers' (see p. 471), it was no more than making a virtue out of necessity, given the traditions and entrenched managements of Ind Coope, Tetley Walker and Ansells, and their constituent companies. Indeed, two of the three amalgamating companies had themselves experienced a major merger in the previous two years – Ind Coope and Taylor Walker

74 S&N sales data, 1964/5–84/5, 7 May 1985, S&N. A distinguishing feature of 'Tartan' was that it was invariably served cool.

75 S&N, confidential memo on 'Proposed Merger with Courage', S&N Board Minutes, 31 August 1972, S&N.

76 Bennison and Merrington, *Newcastle Breweries*, pp. 96, 100; S&N strategy documents, S&N.

(1959), Joshua Tetley and Walker Cain (1960). Difficulties were mitigated by the fact that as with Scottish & Newcastle the merger was one of complementary regional concerns, but the scale of the new company was very different. ICTA (Allied) was a merger of three of the ten largest brewers of the day, and the UK's largest brewing company until Bass Charrington was formed in 1967. Furthermore, there was an urgent need to rationalise both production and retailing facilities, particularly in areas where the constituent companies overlapped, while progress in management accounting was inhibited by the considerable variety of internal accounting procedures in use.[77] The new company pronounced itself pleased with its initial financial results, and could point to some progress in rationalisation. The main board surmounted early barriers to the integration of Joshua Tetley and Walker Cain, which had not proceeded very far before the ICTA merger. The first steps were taken to integrate the hotels, soft drinks and wines and spirits businesses of the three constituents, and modifications were made to the boundaries of their tied house estates, notably in 1963 in relation to Ind Coope and Tetley Walker in the North of England, and to Ind Coope and Ansells in the Midlands and South Wales.[78] Production (net brewings) increased from 3.7 million barrels in 1960/1 to 4.7 million in 1966/7, an increase of 27 per cent, and before-tax profits improved substantially, rising from £12.7 million in 1960/1 to £20.3 million in 1966/7, an increase in real terms of 19 per cent.[79] But it is clear that for some time each of the three individual companies continued to operate as autonomous enterprises and that radical changes were limited before 1969.[80]

In 1969 the company replaced its decentralised organisation with a much more centralised structure. There were several catalysts in 1968: the purchase of a major British wine company, Showerings Vine Products and Whiteways; the acquisition of two Dutch breweries, D'Oranjeboom and Breda; a proposal to merge with Unilever (see p. 478); a

77 Peat Marwick Mitchell, Report on 'ICTA Ltd', 24 August 1961, F/30/1, Allied.

78 ICTA/Allied, Report and Accounts, 1962–4; ICTA Board Minutes, 19 October, 16 November, 14 December 1961; Allied Board Minutes, 20 June, 18 July, 21 November 1963, 20 February 1964; Ind Coope Board Minutes, 4 July 1963, Allied; *Investors' Chronicle*, 7 February 1964.

79 Allied Breweries (UK), Trends 1973/4, January 1975; CSO, *Economic Trends 1991 Supplement*, p. 6 (GDP deflator). Sales figures are more ambiguous. Sales of 'Allied beers' increased by 26 per cent, 1960/1–66/7, but 'total sales (minus shandy and cider)' increased by only 13 per cent. (Allied, Report and Accounts, 1968, has pre-tax profits of £11.9m for 1960/1 (adjusted for 52 weeks) and £20.9m for 1966/7 (53 weeks).

80 Cf. ICTA Minutes, 13 June 1961, Allied Minutes, 19 December 1963, Allied.

change at the top, with Sir Edward Thompson retiring as chairman and chief executive in favour of Sir Derek Pritchard; and anxiety about the future of the tied house system given the deliberations of the Monopolies Commission.[81] But the overriding concern was to strengthen the Beer Division. Here, it was argued, the existing organisation was ill equipped to promote Allied's corporate strategy, which required the centralisation of planning and production in order to ensure the vigorous promotion of national brands such as Draught Double Diamond, Skol Lager and Long Life.[82] Senior executives conceded that 'of the problems which have arisen so far the most difficult has been the forging of a united entity of one Beer Division because tradition and what has been the practice and custom in the past has tended to influence reactions and (perhaps unconsciously) to encourage unilateral action at various levels of management. On this ground alone, a complete break with the past ... seems justified.'[83] The central board had sought to exercise control through operating and capital expenditure committees, and via functional directors appointed in 1962 to handle brewing, finance, marketing and retail sales.[84] But they had failed to establish consistency of action in the constituent companies, where the number of subsidiaries added to the complexity of operation (Allied had no less than 247 subsidiary companies in 1969).[85]

Under Pritchard's leadership the management consultants, Production-Engineering, were appointed to assist the company in creating a new organisation.[86] Three divisions were established: Beer and Hotels; Wines Spirits and Soft Drinks; and International. Both Beer and Wines Spirits etc. were unified under holding companies, the latter under the direction of Showerings. But the main change was undoubtedly in the beer division, where a new holding company, known from April 1970 as Allied Breweries (UK), was given overall responsibility for beer production and sales within the group. The intention was to exercise firmer control of the subsidiaries below it, principally the five management or

[81] On the latter see *Ibid.*, 20 July 1967.

[82] Cf. *Ibid.*, 5 January 1967, 18 March 1969; Chief Executive, Allied Breweries (UK), letter to employees, 3 April 1970, Allied.

[83] Memo on 'AB (UK) and its five management companies', 13 February 1970, F/29/4, Allied.

[84] ICTA Minutes, 13 June 1961, 21 June, 19 July, 20 September and 22 November 1962, Allied. A number of adjustments were made to the functional directorate before the new organisation was established, notably the appointment of vice-chairmen in 1967 (with the combination of marketing and retail sales) and a director of corporate affairs in 1968: Allied Minutes, 20 July 1967, 19 September 1968, Allied.

[85] *Ibid.*, 21 July 1966, 18 May 1967, 24 July 1969.

[86] *Ibid.*, 18 March, 17 June and 24 July 1969.

trading companies, viz. Ind Coope, Tetley, Ansells, Ind Coope (Scotland) and Allied Breweries (Production).[87] The new organisation was introduced in the name of administrative economy and centralised management, the aim being to shorten lines of communication and to integrate corporate planning, national marketing and control processes.[88] But the main impact over time was to separate decision-making in beer production from that in beer sales. This was soon to have unfortunate results for the group.

In 1978 the company reintroduced a decentralised regime. Once again, a major acquisition coincided with the move, the company merging with the food conglomerate J. Lyons & Co. (the name Allied-Lyons was adopted in 1981). However, this time organisational change was initiated *before* the merger, in response to perceived defects in the existing organisation, and in particular to the realisation that it had become inadequate in the face of market developments from the mid-1970s. The rise of the consumer group CAMRA at that time had encouraged a return to regional, cask-conditioned beers, contributing substantially to a growing complexity in the beer market. But an organisation which had effectively separated production and distribution from sales was ill prepared to respond quickly to local market signals, and there was some evidence that Allied's major national brands were beginning to lose market-share. The company's monitoring of sales and profits supported this. Group pre-tax profits fell by 26 per cent in real terms from 1969/70 to 1977/8, the contribution of Allied Breweries (UK) falling from 75 to 57 per cent. Over the same period Allied's share of the UK beer market fell from 15.5 to 14.0 per cent.[89] Sales of Double Diamond slumped by 60 per cent between 1971/2 and 1977/8, the losses being particularly severe in the Tetley and Ansells areas.[90] The Allied board had become dissatisfied with both the holding company, Allied Breweries (UK), and the trading companies. The former, it was asserted, had proved weak in financial control, investment appraisal and management accounting. It had neglected the finance and personnel functions and given distribution too low a priority, allowing it to 'atrophy'. At the same time, the latter were criticised for being inadequately motivated and for losing touch with the Group's objectives. The

87 *Ibid.*, 24 July and 16 September 1969, 3 March and 2 April 1970.
88 Allied, Report and Accounts, 1968–9, pp. 4, 26–7.
89 Allied Breweries (UK), Trends, 1977/8, Allied; CSO, *Economic Trends 1991 Supplement*, p. 6. On Board concern see Allied Board Minutes, 31 January 1978, Allied.
90 Double Diamond sales fell from 1,224,000 barrels to 489,000: Allied Breweries (UK), Trends, 1977/8, 1981/2. See also Allied Minutes, 20 June 1978, Allied.

directors of the trading companies received strong criticism. They had, it was believed, 'undermined ... morale and commitment in professional, production and distribution management'.[91] These views were echoed in the Price Commission's contemporaneous report on Allied.[92] There was also concern about the management of industrial relations. Rising labour costs and an intensification of industrial relations problems culminated in major strikes at Warrington (Tetley Walker) in 1979 and Birmingham (Ansells) in 1981.[93]

Early action to break up the over-centralised beer division came in 1975, when the trading company in Scotland, Ind Coope (Scotland), was given greater autonomy.[94] In January 1978 the Allied board expressed its intention to apply a 'profit-centred' approach to the beer division as a whole, and the main changes were effected by the time of the merger with Lyons in September.[95] There were five divisions: Beer; Wines Spirits and Soft Drinks; Food; International; and Hotels (Embassy Hotels).[96] In the first, Allied Breweries (UK) became a true holding company, confining its activities to controlling capital, setting objectives and monitoring performance. Lower down, responsibility for production, distribution and sales was combined at the profit-centred companies of Ind Coope, Ansells, Joshua Tetley, Tetley Walker and Ind Coope (Scotland). Here, managers were given bottom-line responsibility, the intention clearly being to make them more responsive to market signals and profit opportunities. In all, twelve profit-centres were listed under the Beer Division in the company's annual report for 1979.[97] To support the new structure, management accounting was

91 Allied Breweries (UK) Executive Committee Minutes, 20 March 1978, and see also Allied Breweries (UK) Minutes, 26 January and 15 March 1978.

92 Price Commission, *Allied Breweries (UK)*, 1978, pp. 1, 7.

93 See Allied, Reports and Accounts, 1977–9, p. 12; David P. Waddington, *Trouble Brewing. A Social Psychological Analysis of the Ansells Brewery Dispute* (Aldershot, 1987), *passim*.

94 Allied Breweries (UK) Minutes, 27 March 1975, Allied.

95 Allied Board Minutes, 16 and 31 January, 28 March, 20 June, 3 and 22 August 1978, Allied.

96 These were soon reduced to three, for the International Division was broken up and the Hotels company transferred to the Food Division. Allied-Lyons, Reports and Accounts, 1979–80, p. 3.

97 In addition to the companies listed in the text, separate profit centres were established for the Burton and Wrexham breweries, retailing sub-divisions in the West (Halls) and Aylesbury, for the take-home trade (Ind Coope (Home Sales)), and for hops and malting. Allied, Reports and Accounts, 1977–9, p. 11. The Ind Coope company was itself transformed into a holding company with six subsidiaries: *Ibid.*, 1979–80, p. 6.

given particular emphasis and improvements were pursued in finance, personnel and distribution.[98]

The experiences of Bass, Courage, Watney Mann and Whitbread generally followed a similar course, although their reactions differed both in scale and scope. Variations emerged partly because in 1972 Watney and Courage became part of the non-brewing conglomerates, Grand Metropolitan and Imperial; and partly because corporate styles and the personalities of key business leaders differed. At Watney Mann, for example, the pace of post-merger rationalisation was relatively gentle at first. Under Simon Combe (chairman to 1965), and then Peter Crossman and Michael Webster, the company operated on a loose, holding-company principle.[99] Diverse companies located at varying distances from the Pimlico head offices, in Whitechapel, Brighton, Norwich, Trowbridge, Manchester and Edinburgh, retained their production facilities and the local managements were left more or less undisturbed. Some changes were made. In 1966 the three Norwich brewery companies – Morgan, Bullard and Steward & Patteson – were grouped together as Watney Mann (East Anglia). Three years later there was a further grouping of production companies, this time in the South-East. Production at Mortlake, Whitechapel, Alton and Brighton was managed by a new subsidiary, Watney Mann (London & Home Counties). In addition, functional control was strengthened at the centre, and more ominously, perhaps, a production plan of 1970 emphasised the need to concentrate future production in London and Manchester. In the main, however, the company honoured its pledges to keep local managements intact.[100]

Similar promises were made by Maxwell Joseph when Grand Met took over Truman in 1971 and Watney Mann in the following year, but the post-merger outcome was very different. By this time, a number of flaws in Watneys' strategic armoury had begun to surface. The company's emphasis on its keg bitter brand Red Barrel in the 1960s had prevented it from developing its own lager. Belatedly it signed an agreement with Carlsberg in 1970 to construct a new lager brewery at Northampton, but delays and financial difficulties produced discord with its Danish partner. The company's attempt to replace Red Barrel with Red, which was promoted aggressively in 1971–2 as the 'Red

[98] Allied Breweries (UK) Minutes, 27 January 1978; paper on 'Finance – General Commentary', 7 November 1978, Allied.

[99] Crossman was chairman, 1965–70; Webster was vice-chairman, 1965–70 and chairman, 1970–2.

[100] Watney Mann Report & Accounts, 1969, p. 3.

Revolution' (see Plate 74), proved to be a spectacular failure and attracted the attention of the fledgling consumer group CAMRA. Finally there was concern about the low profitability of some of the company's overseas investments, notably the Vandenheuvel-Ixelberg Brewery in Belgium and the Angevin wine companies. Grand Met also faced the task of rationalising the overlapping production and retailing facilities in the South-East owned by Watney and Truman, its other and apparently better-managed subsidiary. The response of Joseph and his team was both speedier and more radical than was usual in the industry. The Watney Mann board was immediately pruned of many of its old brewing family representatives and reduced in size. A more focused team, led by Joseph as chairman and Stanley Grinstead, a managing director of Grand Met, then set about redistributing the assets of its brewing acquisitions, much to the consternation of their former senior managers. After consultants had investigated Grand Met's brewing in 1973, the subsidiary companies were merged under a new holding company, Watney Mann & Truman Holdings. The new organisation was a significant innovation. Brewing and wholesale distribution were separated from retailing, the former as Watney Mann & Truman Brewing [WMTB], the latter as Chef & Brewer. Grinstead replaced Webster as chief executive of the holding company in October 1974. Two years later, under Allen Sheppard's direction, the pendulum swung back towards decentralisation.[101] Fully recognising the need to respond to local tastes in beer, WMTB established nine regional companies; a 'controlled delegation' process was set in motion, and several 'real ale' brands were reintroduced.[102] The company went on to pursue a number of specified strategic objectives, including the recovery of lost market-share, the improvement of public houses, flexible wholesale pricing, and manpower rationalisation. Here, then, was a case where takeover by a non-brewing group produced a quicker and more determined shake-up than had been customary.[103]

At Whitbread the challenge presented to top management as the company expanded was daunting. In the period 1961–71 no fewer than twenty-three brewing companies were acquired, both large and small,

[101] Decentralisation had been encouraged by Anthony Tennant in 1975. See WMTB Board Minutes, 2 April 1975, Courage (FBG).

[102] The companies were: London; Southern; Manns; Wilson's; Norwich; West; Webster; Drybrough; and Truman.

[103] This section has been derived from *Brewery Manual, 1966–80/1*; *Investors' Chronicle, passim*; Michael Webster interview, in *Business Administration*, May 1970, 45–7; analysts' reports; WMTB papers in Courage (FBG); and Reader and Slinn, 'History of Grand Met'.

stretching from Exeter to Ramsgate, Edinburgh to Great Yarmouth, and Barrow to Rhymney. It is clear that great strains were placed on the personal management style characterised by Col. Bill Whitbread, chairman from 1944. In 1967 he stepped down as managing director in favour of Alex Bennett, who became chief executive. Then, on his retirement as chairman in 1971, the opportunity was taken to streamline and strengthen the executive, following advice from the management consultants Urwick Orr. Nevertheless, many brewing subsidiaries were left for some time with their local managements, in accordance with promises made on merger, and the main board appeared to outsiders to be rather large and unwieldy, numbering twenty-two in 1967, thirty-seven in 1980, and with its three types of director – ordinary, managing and technical (from 1972 chairman/deputy-chairman, executive, non-executive and specialist) (Plate 75). There was a great deal to do in the 1970s, under the leadership of Alex Bennett, chairman 1971–8, and Charles Tidbury, chairman 1978–84, to rationalise production, reduce the organisational span, introduce strategic planning and exhibit the hallmarks of the large modern corporation. The evidence suggests that Whitbread performed impressively in that decade. A strategy for the rationalisation of production was formulated. Equity earnings increased steadily. By 1980 the company had established a reputation as an aggressive marketeer.[104]

The organisation of Bass was also transformed in our period. Here, too, the retention of local managements was very much in line with central thinking, and both Bass, Mitchells & Butlers (BM&B, formed in 1961), and Charrington United, which merged with it in 1967, embraced the holding-company structure. However, it is clear that under the dynamic leadership of Alan Walker, chief executive of BM&B from 1961 and chairman and chief executive from 1963 (Plate 76), the degree of control exerted at the centre over such matters as product strategy, marketing, finance and investment appears to have been much firmer than in most contemporary brewing companies of this size. The new company's geographical concentration in the Midlands undoubtedly helped here, as did the fact that the corporate styles of the two constituents differed considerably and demanded attention. Under Walker's direction Mitchells & Butlers had become an extremely efficient beer producer and tied trade specialist; Bass, on the other hand, had a much more secure footing in the free trade but in other areas was more

[104] See *Brewery Manual, 1968–80/1*; Whitbread Board Minutes, 1971–80 *passim*, esp. 7 July 1971, 10 April 1979; Ritchie, *Uncommon Brewer*, pp. 121ff.

complacent.[105] Walker's insistence on early returns from the 1961 merger, supported by reports from the consultants Production-Engineering, was clear evidence of his more positive approach.[106] How far intention was translated into immediate action (for example in the rationalisation of marketing organisations and production facilities) is less clear. But the pace of change certainly accelerated after the death of Sir James Grigg, chairman of BM&B, in 1963, and in the mid-1960s the company's rationalisation of marketing functions under a regional company structure took the eye.[107] The situation was made even more challenging when BM&B merged with Charrington United in 1967, since the latter was widely dispersed and less centralised. Both E. P. Taylor and Alan Walker personified bold management, and their collective energies were applied to the problem of organisation with considerable success. However, their presence did not prevent the companies from making strategic mistakes.[108] Nevertheless, as far as the shareholders and the City were concerned, proof of the pudding was in increased equity earnings following both mergers. Thanks to leadership at the top from Walker and from Derek Palmar, who succeeded him as chairman and chief executive of Bass Charrington in 1976, a company (Bass) which in the early 1950s was generally regarded as being weak and somewhat in the doldrums was by the late 1970s accepted as being very soundly managed.[109]

By 1980, then, it was clear that over the previous decade or so the larger brewing companies had tackled only hesitantly and with much trial and error such urgent problems as the structure and role of the main board, the handling of subsidiaries, the relationship between core and peripheral activities, as well as corporate planning, investment appraisal and management accounting. There was no shortage of dynamic leaders at the top, men such as Walker and Palmar of Bass, Bennett and Tidbury at Whitbread, or Grinstead, Tennant and Sheppard at Grand Met. There were successes, but the impression remains

105 Cf. Hawkins, *Bass Charrington*, p. 179.

106 Cf. Production-Engineering, Report No. 1 on 'Mitchells & Butlers Ltd', April 1961, and Report on 'Some Implications of the Bass, Mitchells & Butlers Merger', 23 January 1962, Bass Cape Hill.

107 BM&B, 'Memorandum on Regional Administrative Reorganisation', 25 February 1965, Bass Cape Hill; Hawkins, *Bass Charrington*, p. 179.

108 With hindsight we may criticise Charrington United's investment in growth through acquisition using the subsidiary Hare Place Investments (Hawkins, *Bass Charrington*, pp. 201–2) and Bass Charrington's investment in the 2.5 million bll Runcorn brewery in 1975 (see pp. 556–7).

109 Cf. Hawkins, *Bass Charrington*, pp. 222–8; Owen, History of Bass; analysts' reports.

that the strength of tradition in brewing, the legacy of family management and consumer loyalties, generally acted as a brake on rapid progress in responding to problems of size and post-merger adjustment.

13

Technology and retailing

I

Of all the elements contributing to the transformation of the modern brewing industry, technology is perhaps the least known and certainly the least understood by the consumer. The essential nature of beer, and the way it is brewed, has remained largely unchanged in the twentieth century. Malted grains, primarily barley, are mashed using warm water to release fermentable sugars. The sugar solution, brewer's wort, is separated from the grains, and the resultant liquid is then boiled with hops. The wort, having been cooled, is then fermented using yeast (see pp. 47–58). Indeed, what is striking is the superficial similarity of the nineteenth- and late twentieth-century charts depicting the brewing process (prior to the final stages of conditioning and packaging) (see Fig. 13.1 and Plates 2, 77 and 78). In terms of research, the years *c.* 1900–50 have been described by R. G. Anderson of Allied as a 'barren period', sandwiched between two 'golden ages', the first in 1870–1900, the second from the early 1950s to the 1970s. The same writer, reviewing the progress of brewing science and technology over the longer term, suggests that in the twentieth century the industry 'had remained essentially conservative when compared with some other industries'.[1] This view is something of an exaggeration. It is true that research had a low profile in many breweries until cost accountants began to quantify the savings achieved by the researching companies. But there *were* important changes in brewing technology, for example in the pasteurisation and filtration of bottled beer and in plant breeding. If they were introduced only gradually and often rather anonymously in the first half

[1] R. G. Anderson, 'The Pattern of Brewing Research: A Personal View of the History of Brewing Chemistry in the British Isles', *Journal of the Institute of Brewing*, 98 (March–April 1992), 96–100, 105.

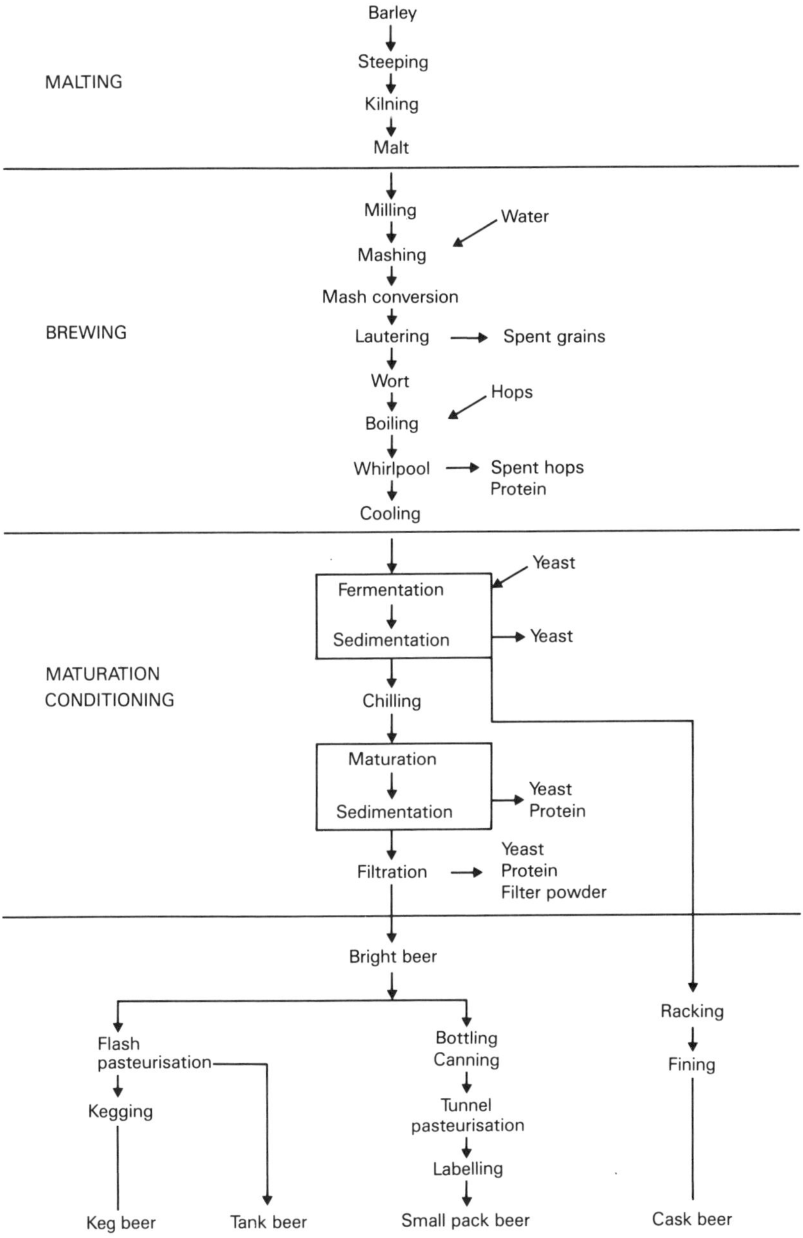

Source: Brewers' Society.

Fig. 13.1 The modern brewing process.

of the century, they certainly became more apparent as they gathered pace after 1960.

The contention that little dramatic happened in the first half of the century should not be allowed to devalue the progress which was made in establishing a research environment in the industry. The work of company laboratories on hops and barley was given support and focus through the Institute of Brewing, which was reconstituted in 1904 and assumed a wider role under the encouragement of leading brewers such as Sydney Nevile, Frank Whitbread and William Waters Butler. Projects were undertaken at Rothamsted, Wye College and elsewhere, with the active co-operation of such companies as Guinness, Truman, Watneys, Whitbread and William Younger. The work was concerned primarily with investigations of the chemical properties of barley and hops, but some research in the 1930s dealt with more practical subjects, for example the material for beer pipes and the problem of effluent disposal.[2] Education and training was also given encouragement through the Institute's sponsorship of initiatives in higher and further education, notably at Birmingham University, Heriot-Watt College in Edinburgh, Sir John Cass Technical College, London, and the Manchester College of Technology.[3] An Operative Brewers' Guild, known as the Incorporated Brewers' Guild from 1929, was also active among company brewers in stimulating an appreciation of the importance of technological change.[4]

Information on the operations of individual companies is more difficult to chart. Guinness was employing a large staff of brewing chemists by the 1930s, by which time it had established an outstanding reputation for research into barley and hops. But this was very much an exceptional response at the time, and in any case the secrecy surrounding its work limited the dissemination of its scientists' findings.[5] The industry as a whole endeavoured to understand more fully the basic micro-biological and bio-chemical processes in brewing, but most of this work tended to lack focus or practical application. Instead, the progress that was made

[2] See W. H. Bird, *A History of the Institute of Brewing* (1955), pp. 1–84 *passim*, and Sir Gilbert T. Morgan, 'Research Activities of the Institute of Brewing', *Journal of the Institute of Brewing*, 46 (April 1940), 133–50.

[3] Bird, *Institute of Brewing*, pp. 28–30, 55–9.

[4] *Brewers' Guardian: 100 Years of British Brewing*, September 1971, pp. 147–8; *Incorporated Brewers' Guild Directory 1991*, pp. 9–17.

[5] Stella V. Cunliffe, Presidential Address, Royal Statistical Society, 12 November 1975, *Journal of the Royal Statistical Society*, Series A, 139 Part 1 (1976), 3; J. F. Brown, *Guinness and Hops* (1980), pp. 16–26; *Journal of the Institute of Brewing*, 37 (1921), 249; 48 (1942), 7–8; 53 (1947), 6–8.

tended to come from a desire to achieve quality, consistency and economy in production through continuous adjustments to brewing techniques, that is, via technical adjustments to familiar processes rather than from scientific discovery. Some changes may be acknowledged. In the inter-war years some brewing companies achieved better raw material utilisation and adopted improved control methods derived from earlier scientific work, as, for example, in the practical application of the knowledge that low-nitrogen barleys gave higher yields in malting. But elsewhere, practice was more empirical, and there were few advances in the field of fermentation. Before 1950, then, brewing and malting processes went on virtually unchanged in many breweries, and what research work there was was fragmentary and largely divorced from commercial pressures.[6]

There were those who appreciated the importance of commercial application of scientific advances. Here, the contributions of Richard Seligman, founder of the brewery equipment manufacturers, APV, Arthur Cosbie of Truman, and John Ford of William Younger caught the eye.[7] Seligman's 'Paraflow' heat exchanger of 1923 cooled the beer wort more efficiently and hygienically, an advance which was readily apparent. By 1940 it seems that over 300 were in use in British breweries. Walter Scott's yeast pressing process was another important development, while the introduction of first aluminium, then stainless steel, vessels took place on a limited scale.[8] But the more conspicuous improvements came at the conditioning and distribution stages, in the pasteurisation and filtering of bottled beer, the early development of conditioned beer in bulk, the introduction of mechanised bottling lines, the canning of beer from the mid-1930s, and motorised delivery, which gathered pace in the 1920s. Watney Combe Reid was prominent in conditioning beer in bulk. In 1929 the firm bought a Berndorf Pasteu-

[6] J. O. Harris, 'Changes in British Brewing Techniques', and A. H. Cook, 'Brewing Research', *Brewers' Guardian*, September 1971, pp. 105, 141–2; E. S. Beavan, *Barley: Fifty Years of Observation and Experiment* (1947), pp. 116–18; I. A. Preece, *The Biochemistry of Brewing* (Edinburgh, 1954), pp. 4ff., 116–23.

[7] Anderson, 'Pattern of Brewing Research', 98–9. On Seligman see *Journal of the Institute of Brewing*, 33 (1927), 225–7; 35 (1929), 10–11; 78 (1972), 442–3, and G. A. Dummett, *From Little Acorns: A History of the A.P.V. Company Limited* (1981), pp. 1–181, *passim*; on Cosbie see Bird, *Institute of Brewing*, pp. 55, 82; *Brewers' Journal*, June 1951, p. 319; *Journal of the Institute of Brewing*, 58 (1952), 7; on Ford see *Journal of the Institute of Brewing*, 38 (1941), 301–43; 40 (1944), 161–3. Anderson also mentions William Gosset (Guinness), inventor of the significance test 't'; Edwin Beavan and Herbert Hunter (barley research), and John Shinwell (Beamish & Crawford, then Whitbread).

[8] *Journal of the Institute of Brewing*, 33 (1927), 225–7; *Brewing Trade Review*, May 1935, pp. 195–6; Dummett, *From Little Acorns*, pp. 57, 81.

riser and began to export naturally conditioned beer which was then chilled, filtered and pasteurised and distributed in 5 gallon stainless steel containers.[9] Other companies attracted attention by introducing more advanced bottled beer pasteurisers, notably Hoare & Co. of Smithfield in London, which introduced an auto-feed liquor-spraying machine in 1930.[10] Such technical changes and, in particular, incremental improvements in production were often regarded by brewing companies as commercial secrets, and consequently it is difficult to discover exactly how much progress was made. But the received wisdom was that there were few significant breakthroughs either in basic research or in major technical adjustments to production processes before the 1950s.[11]

Scientific research into brewing became more thorough and sophisticated after the Second World War. Here, a significant development was the establishment in 1951 of the Brewing Industry Research Foundation, at Nutfield in Surrey.[12] The new institution, promoted by enthusiasts such as Seligman (APV), Julian Baker (Watney Combe Reid) and C. J. Newbold (Guinness), was established on the joint initiative of the Brewers' Society and the Institute of Brewing and was funded by the industry through the Society. The capital cost was £233,000, and annual research expenditure, which amounted to £77,000 in 1952, rose steadily to £123,000 in 1960, £211,000 in 1970 and £815,000 in 1980, or £114,000 in 1952 prices. In all, £7.7 million in current prices was spent in the period 1955–80.[13] Under the direction of Sir Ian Heilbron, Professor of Organic Chemistry at Imperial College London, and Dr Arthur Cook, the Foundation carried out important scientific research into most aspects of brewing. In association with Guinness, Courage & Barclay and APV, it undertook pioneering work on continuous brewing and, in particular, continuous wort production and fermentation. Later it was active in promoting high-gravity brewing, a technique which secured significant energy savings by brewing and fermenting at relatively high specific gravities

[9] R. O. Darling, 'From Barrels to Bulk Tanks', *Brewers' Guardian*, September 1971, pp. 128–9; Hurford Janes, *Red Barrel*, p. 163.

[10] *Brewing Trade Review*, November 1930, pp. 610–11.

[11] Anderson, 'Pattern of Brewing Research', 99–100; *Journal of the Institute of Brewing*, 40 (1934), 1; 54 (1948), 136.

[12] From 1976 known as the Brewing Research Foundation.

[13] Brewers' Society Council Minutes, 18 October 1950, Research Committee Minutes, 13 March 1951, 17 March 1953, 16 March 1954, 14 June 1960, BS; A. D. Portno, 'Brewing Research Foundation. Twenty-Five Years of Brewing Research', *Journal of the Institute of Brewing*, 89 (May–June 1989), 146–8.

and then diluting the beer in the final stages of processing. The Foundation developed a more complete understanding of the biochemistry of barley (and notably the role of oxygen in germination), hop chemistry (also in association with Guinness) and yeast nutrition and growth. Research was also carried out on the definition of beer quality and components of flavour. Although the Foundation's interests lay squarely in scientific research, it emphasised the practical application of advances in knowledge to brewing production. Research activity was also stimulated elsewhere, at Birmingham University and Heriot-Watt, while the major companies expanded their laboratory facilities, notably at Guinness, which opened new laboratories at Park Royal in 1955, Allied, which did the same at Burton in 1964, Bass, and Scottish & Newcastle.[14] The research environment in the industry from the 1950s was altogether more co-operative and less secretive, and the volume of research output unprecedentedly high.[15] A cost-benefit analysis of twenty-five years of research conducted in 1980 concluded that economic benefits to the industry totalling £859 million (in 1980 prices) had resulted, the contribution of the Brewing Research Foundation amounting to 19 per cent or £164 million, on an expenditure (in 1980 prices) of £19.6 million over the period 1955–80.[16]

In the twenty-five years after 1950, research and commercial development proceeded very much hand in hand. If the environment seemed to have been research-led, it should also be recognised that brewing companies, and the large ones in particular, were very much more receptive to new ideas and their application than they had been before the War. The factors inducing change are familiar and have been discussed elsewhere: the changing tastes of consumers, and notably the receptiveness to keg beer and lager in the 1960s and 1970s; the merger mania, which led to the establishment of very large firms and in turn invited scale economies in production and the technological methods to exploit them; and the search for labour-saving and energy-saving capital equipment which followed the rise in labour and energy costs from the mid-1960s.

But whatever the stimuli, successful technological change demanded an appropriate response from scientists, brewing companies and manufacturers, and here it is clear that developments were underpinned by

[14] *Guinness Time*, 8 (Autumn 1955), pp. 5–7; Allied Breweries, Report & Accounts, 1964, p. 7.

[15] Anderson, 'Pattern of Brewing Research', 100, 103; *Journal of the Institute of Brewing*, 65 (1959), 144–54.

[16] Portno, 'Brewing Research Foundation', 146–8.

fundamental interdisciplinary work and greatly improved production control techniques. In relation to raw materials, the fundamentals of the malting process were mastered and significant improvements in efficiency attained. In the 1960s a better understanding of the germination process led to the introduction of interrupted steeping and 'air-rests' to allow oxygen to permeate the barley and facilitate respiration. In the following decade work on gibberellic acid, derived from a fungus, led to its widespread use as a supplement to encourage germination.[17] Finally, Geoffrey Palmer's 'abrasion' process, where the barley husk and outer layers were scarified prior to malting, had the remarkable consequence of accelerating malting by producing an improved penetration of water and gibberellic acid.[18] All this led to the halving of malting times and malting loss (see Table 13.1). The savings to the industry arising from all research in barley/malting, including the selection of new barleys (notably Proctor and Maris Otter), malting with difficult barleys, reduced storage, etc., were put at £142 million (£5.67 million per annum) in 1955–80 at 1980 prices.[19]

If enhanced malting produced benefits, there is no doubt that improved hop utilisation produced still more, indeed the greatest savings. The cost-benefit study of 1980 concluded that in the period 1955–80 £365 million (£14.6 million p.a.), or over 40 per cent of total benefits, had been derived from improved bitterness recovery, lower storage costs and hop breeding advances.[20] Certain technological developments were especially important. First, identification of the iso α-acid resin as the agent of bitterness encouraged the breeding of new varieties (such as Wye Challenger and Wye Target) with a higher α content – average levels were increased from under 4 to about 8 per cent.[21] In

[17] It was estimated that by 1970 gibberellic acid, derived from the fungus *gibberella fujikuroi*, was being used in 73 per cent of British malting production: G. F. Ray, 'The Application of Gibberellic Acid in Malting', in L. Nabseth and G. F. Ray, *The Diffusion of New Industrial Processes: An International Study* (Cambridge, 1974), p. 219. Most of the acid was manufactured by ICI.

[18] Charles Dalgleish, '25 Years of Brewing Research', *Brewing Review*, March 1976, pp. 109–11; J. R. Hudson, 'Recent Developments in Brewing Technology', *Brewers' Guardian*, 1976, p. 31 and 'Expanding Brewing Technology', *Journal of the Institute of Brewing*, 89 (May–June 1983), 191. On Palmer's work see *ibid.*, 75 (1969), 536–41, 76 (1970), 65–8.

[19] Portno, 'Brewing Research Foundation', 147. Guinness, in particular, was prominent in developing barley crosses, in association with the Plant Breeding Institute at Cambridge.

[20] *Ibid.*

[21] From the farming/brewing perspective, hop varieties which were resistant to wilt were important, and these tended to have a higher α-acid content. Interview with R. T. Kerslake (Guinness), 24 March 1992.

consequence, there was a considerable decrease in hop usage in Britain; in the thirty years to 1980 this fell by over a third (Table 13.1) and the hop acreage fell by 36 per cent.[22] Then, in the 1970s the development of hop pellets helped to maintain the quality of hops under conditions of storage, while hop extracts, and isomerised extracts in particular, enabled hopping to be introduced after wort boiling and, indeed, after fermentation.[23] In this work the Foundation was supported by companies such as Guinness and Allied, which with Stafford Allen (later Bush Boake Allen) formed a consortium in 1966 to work on extracts.[24] The commercial impact was rather limited at first, however. Extracts were difficult to use effectively unless breweries replaced their traditional hop backs and fermenters with whirlpool separators and conical fermenters (see below). In addition, it was not clear that the savings in raw materials justified the cost of switching production methods, particularly for beers which required subtle flavours. As late as 1981/2 whole hops still accounted for over half (56 per cent) of the hops used in British brewing.[25] Isomerised hop extracts offered energy savings but because in modern plants new hop separators were more effective than before, the cost differential per barrel was too low to provide a sufficient incentive. Consequently their use was largely confined to bringing bitterness levels up to specified requirements after hop boiling. In 1976 a more promising extract was developed by the Foundation in association with the Distillers' Company. This was produced by extraction with liquid carbon dioxide instead of organic solvents and since it was free of unwanted residues (tannins, hard resins, etc.) it promised a more

22 The British hop acreage amounted to 22,000 in 1950 and 14,000 in 1980. Since then there has been a sharp reduction and the 1990 acreage was only 9,600. *Brewers' Almanack 1958*, p. 62; BS, *UK Statistical Handbook 1983*, p. 24; information from MAFF. Hop usage also fell because brewers were able to achieve greater stability in their lower gravity beers, and because there was a widespread belief that English hops were unsuitable for lager production.

23 M. Sprackling, 'The Economics of Using Isomerised Hop Extracts', *The Brewer*, February 1971, pp. 38–40; Interview with Dr A. H. Button, 12 February 1992. The storage of hop cones was improved with the introduction of cold storage.

24 Brown, *Guinness and Hops*, pp. 47–8; Guinness General Purposes Committee Minutes, 6 April–1 June 1965, GPR. Pripp of Sweden and Labatt of Canada were also members of the consortium, which was colloquially known as 'GABBA'. The new extracts were marketed under the name 'Lupania' from 1968. Guinness, which found that hop extract beers produced too much bitterness, confined the use of concentrates to the production of Foreign Extra Stout abroad and as a back-up in London and Dublin. Guinness Board Minutes, 23 March 1961, GPR.

25 Hudson, 'Recent Developments', p. 33; BS, *Statistical Handbook 1988*, p. 19. Pelletisation made foreign hops cheaper to import, and Czech and Bavarian varieties were preferred in much of the British lager brewing in the 1960s and 1970s.

Table 13.1. *Technological economies in brewing, 1950–80*

Process	1950	1980
Malting processing time	9–12 days (14 days)[a]	4–5 days
Malting loss	10%	3–4.5% (5%)[a]
Hop usage (cwt)	233,000	150,000
Hops' α-acid content	3–4%	8.0%
Wort boiling evaporation	10–15%	5–10%
Fermentation time	7–10 days	3.5–7 days

[a] Alternative figures derived from J. R. Hudson, 'Expanding Brewing Technology', *Journal of the Institute of Brewing*, 89 (May–June 1983), 189.
Source: B. Atkinson, 'Requirement for Innovatory Research in Support of Malting and Brewing', *Journal of the Institute of Brewing*, 89 (May–June 1983), 160; *Brewery Manual*, 1955, p. 13, 1983, p. 29; information from Isobel Tucker, English Hops Products Ltd, March 1992.

cost-effective application.[26] Nevertheless, extracts remained essentially adjuncts to the hopping process, where pelletised hops proved to be the most attractive proposition. By 1981/2 they accounted for 40 per cent of the hop ingredients used (by weight), while extracts amounted to only 4 per cent (including 0.4 per cent in isomerised form).[27]

Further economic benefits – amounting to some £175 million or £5 million per annum, 20 per cent of the total in 1955–80 – were estimated to have been derived from improvements to the basic brewing processes of wort production and fermentation.[28] Here, the major developments were faster mashing times; the use of higher temperatures in wort boiling, which reduced loss through evaporation and economised on energy use; and the introduction of conical fermenters, which provided much faster fermentation under more hygienic conditions (see Table 13.1). In addition, there was the adoption after 1975 of high-gravity brewing; and the elimination of warm conditioning in maturation.

[26] P. R. Ashurst, 'Hop Extracts', *Brewers' Guild Journal*, 55 (December 1969), 620–36; Hudson, 'Expanding Brewing Technology', 189–90; J. O. Harris, 'Brewing Technology of the Future', *The Brewer*, June 1978, p. 214; D. R. Laws *et al.*, 'Preparation of Hop Extracts Without Using Organic Solvents', *Journal of the Institute of Brewing*, 83 (1977), 39–40; B. Atkinson, *English Hops* 2(3) (May 1982), 6–11; J. S. Hough, *The Biotechnology of Malting and Brewing* (Cambridge, 1985), pp. 78–85; Interview with Dr Button.

[27] BS, *UK Statistical Handbook 1983*, p. 22. In 1987/8 the percentages were: whole hops: 29 per cent; pellets: 68 per cent; extracts: 3 per cent. See BS, *Statistical Handbook 1988*, p. 19.

[28] Portno, 'Brewing Research Foundation', 147.

Many of the innovations had a long pedigree: the conical fermenter, for example, was part of a Swiss brewing system developed by Dr L. Nathan in the 1920s and promoted in Britain in 1930.[29] Although taken up by one or two brewers in Britain, notably Walker & Homfrays of Manchester, it lay dormant until post-1960 conditions, and in particular the shift to larger-scale batch production of lager and pasteurised ales, encouraged its adoption. But it is also quite clear that this, together with many of the other innovations in wort production and fermentation, emerged as a spin-off from the determined work on continuous brewing and, in particular, continuous fermentation, which began under Foundation auspices from 1956. The search for an economic continuous-flow production system was taken up enthusiastically by APV, Guinness, Watneys, Bass and others, and it was supported by some of the industry's leading scientists, such as Laurence Bishop and Cyril Rainbow.[30] Ultimately, the R & D work proved disappointing; but beneficial results emerged in the form of superior techniques in batch production, which matched the marketing requirements of the late 1970s, shaped by consumer support for the retention of local traditional beers and a variety of beer types.

British research in continuous production began at the end of the war when a floating brewery was built to provide beer to troops in the Far East. In 1946 the 'Davy Jones Brewery', located on *MV Menestheus*, produced a 1037° mild beer using distilled sea water, malt extract, hop concentrate and an enclosed 'pressure' fermentation system. Lance McMullen of Guinness acted as technical adviser and the head-brewer was George Brown of Truman Hanbury Buxton.[31] The results were quite promising, but little further appears to have been attempted until 1956, when research began under Foundation auspices on continuous wort boiling, mashing and fermentation. The work was supported energetically by APV, Guinness and Courage, and by mid-1961 an APV continuous mashing system had completed a six-month production run

[29] L. Nathan, 'Improvements in the Fermentation and Maturation of Beers', *Journal of the Institute of Brewing*, 36 (1930), 538–42; *Brewers' Journal*, December 1930, pp. 712–13. Nathan's first patent for the fermenter was taken out in 1908. D. R. Maule, 'Reflections on Cylindro-Conical Fermenters', *The Brewer*, June 1977, p. 204.

[30] Cf. L. Bishop, 'A System of Continuous Fermentation', *Journal of the Institute of Brewing*, 76 (1970), 172–80, and 'A Conspectus of Brewing Progress', *ibid.*, 77 (1971), 12–24; C. Rainbow, 'A Century of Brewing Microbiology', *ibid.* 83 (Jan–Feb. 1977), 9–14; *ibid.*, 94 (1988), 299–300; Anderson, 'Pattern of Brewing Research', 101.

[31] See L. McMullen, letter to Director of Victualling, 4 January 1946, George Brown, 'Report on the Functioning of the Brewery Unit on TSMV "Menestheus" ...', 1946; Ken Morison, letter 22 March 1979, and other papers in BS, File on 'Floating Brewery', BS.

in Guinness's Park Royal brewery.[32] The parties operated as a consortium until 1964, by which time Guinness alone had spent about £0.75 million.[33] Brewing scientists were keen to exploit developments in biotechnology, but the initiative was also driven by the companies' anxiety to secure faster and less labour-intensive production. Guinness subsequently withdrew from the work,[34] but others saw possibilities in the continuous fermentation of ale. Several new types of equipment were developed, notably a multi-tank system (Plate 79), installed by Watney Mann, and APV's tower fermenter, first installed in Bass, Mitchells & Butlers' Cape Hill Brewery in 1964.[35] In 1970 Bishops reported that continuous fermentation was being employed successfully in four of Watneys' breweries (two in London, one in Edinburgh and one in Cork) with a total capacity of one million barrels. Savings in labour of 30 per cent were claimed, and it was also reported that Watneys' noted strong ale, Stingo, could now be produced in two days rather than the nine months it took using traditional methods with open, shallow fermenters and conditioning vessels.[36] Bass and Watney Mann & Truman, in particular, persisted with the system in the 1970s, and the latter, under Bishop's influence, could claim to be the UK's most innovative and technically advanced brewer.[37] There appears to be no reliable estimate of how much beer was actually produced by continuous methods, but one source suggests that at one time some 4 per cent of Britain's production (about 1.5 million barrels) was being made in a continuous process using tower fermenters. Bass alone was producing around 400,000 barrels a year in the mid 1970s.[38] In the end, the

32 Courage & Barclay Board Minutes, 4 June and 3 December 1959, FBG; BS Research Committee Minutes, 19 March 1957, 17 November 1959, 14 June 1960, BS; Guinness Board Minutes, 10 March and 27 November 1961 (C. J. Virden's Notes), GPR; Dummett, *From Little Acorns*, p. 197. On the stimulus for research into continuous brewing, including work at Porton Down on penicillin and brewing research in New Zealand and Canada, see Button, 'Changes in Fermentation Techniques', p. 114; Robert Bud, 'Biotechnology and the Chemical Engineer: A Case Study in the History of Continuous Brewing', *International Industrial Biotechnology*, 9(6) (1989), 18–19.

33 C. K. Mill, memo. 13 August 1965, Guinness Statistical Dept File 00965/8, GPR.

34 Guinness had been developing an accelerated batch process in Dublin, and the company was also disturbed by the dubiety of the patent position. See Guinness General Purposes Committee Minutes, 18 July 1963, GPR.

35 Dummett, *From Little Acorns*, p. 198; Bishop, 'Continuous Fermentation', 173; A. W. Seddon, 'Continuous Fermentation in a Tower. Experiences in Establishing Large Scale Commercial Production', *The Brewer*, March 1976, pp. 72–3.

36 Bishop, 'Continuous Fermentation', 175, 178, 180.

37 Cf. A. D. Portno, 'Continuous Fermentation – Past, Present and Future', *Brewing Review*, April 1976, 170–5; Obituary of Laurence Bishop, *Journal of the Institute of Brewing*, 94 (1988), 300.

38 Bud, 'Biotechnology', 19, citing Hough, *Biotechnology*, pp. 125–6; Seddon, 'Continuous Fermentation', p. 73.

new process did not offer sufficiently attractive savings to justify it. Costs were found to increase dramatically if production was halted, for example when changing to a different beer type, and the system also required more complex control procedures and a more technically competent labour force to manage production in such a sterile environment. With the uncertainty in the mid-1970s about the future balance of ale and lager demand there was reduced enthusiasm for combining fermenting and conditioning in one vessel. In any case, most brewers became sceptical about the flavour of many of the new beers manufactured in this way.[39] However, research was certainly not wasted. It helped to stimulate more general improvements in batch production with lower running costs: automated control; the replacement of the single mash tun by the mash tun and lauter tun or mash filter to separate spent grains; the use of steam heating in wort boiling; the widespread use of deep conical fermenters (with 1–2,000 barrel capacities) with new yeast strains (Plate 73); centrifugal clarification; and automatic 'in-place' cleaning of vessels. Undoubtedly, this is where the industry secured considerable savings as well as improving product quality and consistency.[40] The earlier ingenious if potentially unhygienic methods of fermentation such as the Burton Union and the Yorkshire Stone Square (see pp. 56–7), which had been retained by some breweries to produce distinctive ales with special yeasts, were abandoned.[41]

The research work also facilitated the adoption of high-gravity brewing, in which beer wort was produced at high specific gravities (usually up to 1060°) and then diluted to requirements. Here, motivation was provided by a revised system of charging excise duty on beer, introduced in March 1974, which removed the bulk barrel rebate and thus the penalty on higher gravity brewing.[42] Higher energy costs also afforded a stimulus, encouraging brewers to seek ways of avoiding the

[39] Bud, 'Biotechnology', 20; Hough, *Biotechnology*, p. 126; J. O. Harris, 'Brewing Technology of the Future', *The Brewer*, June 1978, p. 213; Maule, 'Reflections', pp. 204–8; Dummett, *From Little Acorns*, p. 226; interview with Dr Button.

[40] Cf. Dalgleish, 'Twenty-Five Years', p. 110; Hudson, 'Expanding Brewing Technology', p. 191; D. J. Dickinson, 'Some Aspects of Modern Brewery Engineering', *The Brewer*, January 1973, pp. 13–14; L. McMullen, memo on 'Continuous Brewing', 13 July 1965, 000965/8, G. W. Barton, memo on 'Continuous Brewing Research in P.R.D.', February 1967, Guinness file (unnumbered), GPR.

[41] The Yorkshire stone square system used a flocculent yeast, the Burton Union a non-flocculent strain. R. W. Ricketts, 'Review of Fermentation Systems', *Brewers' Guardian*, July 1970, pp. 44, 46; J. S. Hough, D. E. Briggs and R. Stevens, *Malting and Brewing Science* (1971), pp. 522–3.

[42] Until March 1974 there was a rebate of £1 per barrel. Thereafter duty on beer above 1030° was levied at a linear rate.

cumbersome and therefore expensive handling of large bulks of water. The result was an increase in through-put for a given size of brewery and lower processing costs. One estimate of high-gravity brewing at a gravity of 1060° for sale at 1040° put the net revenue savings at 5 per cent plus a net saving in capital of 9 per cent.[43] The shift in production method was impressive in some cases. In February 1977, for example, the Allied board was informed that the company would soon be high-gravity brewing at the rate of 1 million barrels per annum.[44] Total production by high-gravity methods amounted to about 8 million barrels, or 20 per cent of total UK production by 1980.[45]

In fact, it is clear that brewing experienced a host of new developments, not all of which can be discussed here. They affected all stages of the production and distribution processes, and although it is not always easy to assess their impact in precise terms it is clear that the overall result was to give beer a more consistent quality at the point of sale. The changes included: the use of solid cereal adjuncts such as wheat flour in the grist and experiments with green malt concentrates; the introduction of liquid adjuncts such as dextrose syrups for uniformity and consistency; the use of seaweed extracts (alginates) in wort boiling; the replacement of cellulose/asbestos filters by Kieselguhr (diatomaceous earth) filters; anti-haze treatments, including the use of proteolytic enzymes and adsorbents such as nylon, polyvinylpolypyrrolidone (PVPP) and silica; antioxidants; and action to restrict the unwanted production of diacetyl and nitrosamines.[46] At the same time, there were numerous improvements at the post-conditioning stage: a switch to faster, fully automated bottling and canning lines (the latter with process rates of 1,000–1,400 cans per minute by the mid-1970s (Plates 70 and 71); palletised handling, including the use of hi-cone carry-packs; and the use of carbon dioxide to preserve and dispense beers. The most important change was undoubtedly the appearance of new containers such as aluminium and stainless steel casks, which were more easily cleaned and required little maintenance. By 1980 wooden barrels had all

43 C. Whitworth, 'High Gravity Brewing', *The Brewer*, November 1980, p. 339. See also P. J. Hawkins, 'High Gravity Brewing', *Brewers' Guardian*, May 1975, pp. 46–7; Hudson, 'Recent Developments', p. 35.

44 Allied Board Minutes, 1 February 1977, Allied.

45 Based on 1060° wort reduced to 1040°, and calculated from information provided by C. W. Thurman of BS.

46 Cf. BS, Annual Report, 1967–8, p. 15; 1977–8, p. 25; 1978–9, pp. 21, 27; 1980–1, p. 32; 1981–2, p. 30; Hough, *Biotechnology*, pp. 65–70, 140–6; Jeffrey Patton, *Additives, Adulterants and Contaminants in Beer* (Swimbridge, Devon, 1989), pp. 77ff.; interview with Dr Button.

but disappeared. There was a revolution in packaged beer too, with the introduction of ring-pull cans (from 1964), and non-returnable (including wide-mouth) bottles. Thus, while in 1968 94 per cent of the packaged beer sold was in returnable bottles, by 1979 the figure had shrunk to only 16 per cent, with 78 per cent sold in cans.[47] In short, the carpenter and the coppersmith were replaced by the steel fabricator and the glass and plastic technologist, and many brewers of the old pre-war school would have found a modern brewery such as Samlesbury and Runcorn an unfamiliar place.

But how extensive was the diffusion of the new brewing technologies? Clearly, the changes were led by the large companies. Some of the new equipment, for example the massive 8,106 barrel fermenter installed by APV in Guinness's Dublin brewery in 1959, and the larger systems manufactured by the refrigeration specialists, Porter-Lancastrian Ltd, were beyond the resources of the local and small regional companies.[48] On the other hand, it should not be assumed that only the large companies were in the forefront of research and new technology. Tollemache & Cobbold of Ipswich, for example, carried out some important work on malt/wheat flour grists, and Steward & Patteson of Norwich researched re-steeping in pneumatic maltings in the early 1960s.[49] J. W. Green of Luton, under the guidance of Bernard Dixon, who had patented an enzymic malt process, was in the forefront of the introduction of 'keg' ales.[50] George Gale of Horndean may have been a small brewer, but it found the resources to purchase an APV bulk pasteuriser in 1961.[51] And Mitchells & Butlers attracted considerable attention in the trade when, just before its merger with Bass, it built the first 'block' brewhouse in Britain at Cape Hill and produced ale wort via the continental practice of segregated conversion and lautering.[52] Clearly, when the major companies moved from an emphasis on bottled ale to the production of draught ale and lager, the capital investment required was considerable. Smaller companies could avoid this by retaining their

47 John Cobring, 'The Bottle v Can – the Beer Market', *The Brewer*, July 1980, p. 212; Arnold Coward, 'A Review of Packaging Development', *ibid.*, March 1974, pp. 100, 102.

48 Dummett, *From Little Acorns*, p. 205.

49 P. A. S. Scully and M. J. Lloyd, 'Further Developments in the Use of Wheat and Barley', *Brewers' Guild Journal*, 53 (November 1967), 559–64; Button, interview; Gourvish, *Norfolk Beers*, p. 156; M. Riviere, 'Practical Application of Resteeping in a Pneumatic Drum Malting', *Journal of the Institute of Brewing*, 67 (1961), 55–7.

50 Arnold Hill, 'The Development of Keg Beer', BS typescript, pp. 6–8

51 *Brewing Trade Review*, July 1961, pp. 781–2.

52 *Brewers' Journal*, January 1961, pp. 14–15; Harris, 'Changes in British Brewing Techniques', p. 106.

traditional methods of brewing of course, but here too there were quality imperatives. By 1980 it was clear that even in the more backward companies a major transformation in production and handling had taken place. Malting had been improved; many breweries were producing lager with bottom fermentation; there was more automation; aluminium and stainless steel had largely replaced wood; beer was being sold in disposable bottles and cans, and distributed in bulk in tanker lorries.

The higher quality and consistency of the new beers did not appeal to all consumers, however. In many a test the new products were heavily criticised. When, for example, APV test-marketed beer made with a continuous wort boiler in the pubs of the Northampton Brewery Co., the product was roundly condemned for tasting like 'nail varnish'.[53] And while a leading head-brewer in 1971 could anticipate with enthusiasm the demise of the 'unhygienic leather bucket type beer engines with lead piping', the traditional ale-drinker clung tenaciously to beer drawn by hand pump.[54] A brewing chemist's 'off-flavour' (something to be eliminated) might be a desired 'flavour' to diehard beer drinkers. Just as consumer tastes represented a check on the move to larger-scale production (see pp. 503–8), so the technological changes made possible by successful R & D came up against CAMRA and its demands for traditional beer and wider consumer choice. Brewers made considerable progress in the thirty years after 1950, but they had to strike a balance between science and tradition, and between lower operating costs and higher capital costs. As Professor Isaac Preece of Heriot-Watt put it, the industry should be seeking 'to understand its raw materials ... utilise these raw materials with the utmost economy ... [but, above all] to present an acceptable product to a public which covers the whole gamut from undiscerning to pernickety: to please the public which drinks merely by eye, as much as that section which drinks by eye, nose and palate'.[55]

II

During the years from 1955 to 1980 an equally important, though perhaps less obvious, revolution took place in distribution, bringing changes as dramatic as those achieved at the production stage. Brewers'

[53] Dummett, *From Little Acorns*, p. 156.
[54] Darling, 'Barrels to Bulk Tanks', p. 131.
[55] Preece, *Brewers' Guild Journal*, 50 (January 1964), 11.

Society enquiries in the 1940s revealed that brewers were using a mix of road and rail transport, as well as a considerable number of horse-drawn vehicles (Plate 81). A survey of brewing's motor transport in November 1945, based on returns from 236 companies, discovered that the industry owned about 5,000 C-licensed vehicles (see Table 13.2) and that sixty-nine companies intended to use some of them beyond a 60-mile radius once wartime restrictions were lifted. At the top end of the scale there were eighteen companies which owned fifty or more vehicles, including seven owning over 100. However, the scale of vehicle ownership did not correlate closely with company size and national status. Thus, the seven largest vehicle owners included Watneys, with 240, Charrington (123), Walker Cain (117) and Ansells (110), but there were also smaller companies – Davenports of Birmingham (135), Fremlins of Maidstone (111), and Friary Holroyd & Healey of Guildford (103). Furthermore, smaller regionals such as John Smith's and Greene King had sixty-eight and fifty-three vehicles respectively, more than Ind Coope & Allsopp (forty-five), while nationals such as Bass and Guinness owned only twenty-seven and seven lorries respectively. At the bottom of the list four brewers had no road vehicles at all, while 108, that is nearly half of the companies surveyed, owned fewer than ten. They included Arrol and Hook Norton, with one vehicle each, John Young (two), Maclay (four) and Hall & Woodhouse (seven). The mean ownership was 18.5 (Table 13.2).[56] The deployment of horses also varied widely. An analysis of 1945, based upon an inquiry four years earlier, revealed that 143 companies used horses for an average of 15 per cent of their road deliveries (Table 13.2). Two companies used horses for all their road deliveries: Daniel Fielding of Halifax, and Nock & Co.[57] But it is also clear that at this time London brewers with a dense network of public houses found horses economic for short-distance deliveries, and there was higher than average utilisation by Courage (17.5 per cent), Truman and Taylor Walker (both 25 per cent), Mann, Crossman & Paulin (52 per cent; Plate 80) and Young's of Wandsworth (57 per cent). Usage was also high in some provincial areas – for example at J. W. Green of Luton and Lacon of Yarmouth (both 20 per cent), Tollemache

[56] BS, memo on 'Transport. Summary of Replies to Circular 29/45', n.d., BS file on 'Transport', 6/4/1, and BS Parliamentary Committee Minutes, 12 December 1945, BS. Some important companies made no return. They included Whitbread, Barclay Perkins and Mitchells & Butlers.

[57] BS, Memo on 'Horse Transport (ex 20/41)', based on replies to BS Circular 20/41 on 'Transport: Delivery of Beer', 23 June 1941, BS. The survey was undertaken at the request of the Ministry of Food. The provenance of Nock & Co. is not known.

Table 13.2. *Brewery motor vehicles and horse deliveries, 1945*

Companies with 'C' licensed vehicles [a] (frequency distribution)			Percentage of companies' road deliveries made by horse (frequency distribution)		
No. of vehicles	No. of companies owning vehicles		%	No of companies	
0	4		0	0	
1–9	108		1–9	54	
10–24	71		10–19	44	
25–49	35		20–9	29	
50+	18		30–9	10	
			40+	6	
Total	236		Total	143	
Total vehicles owned	Mean no. of vehicles owned	SD		Mean	SD
4,362	18.5	26.7		14.8	13.9

'C' licences = licences for firms carrying only their own goods.
Source: Brewers' Society memo on 'Transport. Summary of replies to Circular 29/45', n.d., and return on 'Horse Transport (ex 20/41)', 4 June 1945, BS File on 'Transport', 6/4/1, BS.

of Ipswich (24 per cent), Everards of Leicester (25 per cent) and Tetley of Leeds (27 per cent).[58] There was also a limited amount of water transport (both coastal and inland waterway), which received renewed attention under wartime conditions.[59]

The picture quickly changed in the 1950s, once wartime restrictions and petrol rationing were removed. In the first place, the distribution of beer by rail, which had formed a considerable element in the transport of beer by 'national' companies such as Bass, Ind Coope and Guinness, fell away rapidly, and had all but disappeared by the late-1960s. Surveys of the balance of road and rail transport were undertaken by the Brewers' Society in 1941 and 1942, when the Ministry of Food encouraged the industry to economise in its use of transport, and again in 1956, when the industry submitted objections to the British Transport Com-

[58] *Ibid.*
[59] Cf. BS note on 'Transport: Delivery of Beer', July 1941, which noted that weekly deliveries by water had amounted to 8,718 barrels in May 1941 (based on returns from 365 brewers), BS File on 'Wartime – Transport', 6/5/3, BS.

mission's draft new merchandise charges scheme.[60] Unfortunately, the results of the latter have not survived (it is not at all clear that the enquiry was proceeded with), but a summary of the replies to a Society circular in 1941, though measuring distribution which was clearly affected by the exigencies of war, may be regarded as broadly illustrative of the position. Based on returns from 387 brewers, it revealed that 90 per cent of the 2.4 million barrels delivered in May 1941 were sent by road, and that nearly three-quarters of the road deliveries were dispatched over short distances (of up to 15 miles radius). Rail was still dominant over longer distances: it was responsible for 54 per cent of the barrelage sent over 30 miles, and 75 per cent of that over 50 miles.[61]

Road transport then quickly achieved dominance in the industry, as it did with most general merchandise traffic. By 1979, 98 per cent of food, drink and tobacco ton-mileage was being carried by road.[62] The interruption to services during the rail strike of 1955 created uncertainty, as did subsequent trade union disputes, while the introduction of new freight charges in 1957 scarcely encouraged customer loyalty in an industry concerned not only about higher charges but also about a variety of special circumstances, including the procedure for estimating consignment weights and the cost of returning empty wagons.[63] However, four other factors were more important in promoting the shift from rail to road. First, the railways, under Beeching's leadership, accelerated the decline of their wagon-load traffic (including beer consignments), by placing a greater emphasis upon cost reduction at the expense of quality of service. Second, the post-1958 merger mania (see Chapter 11) produced new company formations with opportunities for

60 BS Circular 3/56 on 'Railway Freight Charges', 2 February 1956, and BS Transport Sub-committee Minutes, 1955–6; T. R. Gourvish, *British Railways 1948–73: A Business History* (Cambridge, 1986), pp. 184–5.

61 BS, Memo on 'Transport: Delivery of Beer (Summary of 387 Replies ... Representing 88.6% of Total Barrelage)', 31 July 1941, BS File 6/5/3, and BS Circular 20/41, 23 June 1941, BS File 6/4/1, BS. It should be noted that (i) the enquiry was based on barrels sent, not ton-mileages; (ii) data for two large rail users, Bass/Worthington and Ind Coope & Allsopp, were not included.

62 For all goods, road's share of total ton-mileage (or tonne-kilometres) was 53 per cent. *Report of the Inquiry into Lorries, People and the Environment* (Armitage Report) (December 1980), p. 8 and see also pp. 4–10; Department of Transport, *Transport Statistics Great Britain 1991* (September 1991), p. 48.

63 See British Transport Commission (Railway Merchandise) Charges Scheme, 1957: Minutes of Evidence before the Transport Tribunal and, in particular, the evidence of Eric Blain, 20 January 1956, and Bruce Lewis (Guinness), 25 January 1956, Vol.2 pp. 639–44, MT80/16 PRO, and BS, 'Statement of Objections ...', 9 May 1955 and other papers in BS File 6/4/1, and BS Materials Committee Minutes, 18 September 1956, BS. Other issues worrying the brewers included rates for road-rail tanks, and private siding rebates.

rationalisation and the improvement of distribution. Third, the provision of motorways, which began with the opening of the M1 in 1959, encouraged the large-scale trunking of beer by road. There were 600 miles of motorway within a decade and 1,600 by 1980.[64] Finally, the economics of longer-distance road transport was transformed by the improvements in road-freight technology. Larger, heavier and faster lorries were introduced, with a greater deployment of articulated types. The average gross weight of goods vehicles increased steadily, from 5 tonnes in the late 1940s to 16–28 tonnes by the late 1960s, while the number of articulated vehicles increased to over 100,000 (21 per cent of heavy goods vehicles) by 1980.[65] Tanker lorries with 80 barrel capacities carried beer in bulk from the early 1950s, while improved lorries of the open platform type were deployed for deliveries of beer in kegs, or in pallets of bottles and cans. Here the most significant events were the increase in the weight limit to 24.4 tonnes in 1955 and 32.5 tonnes in 1964 (38 tonnes in 1983), and the increase in permitted speeds – for heavy goods vehicles from 20 to 30 mph in 1957, 40 mph in 1963, and 50/60 mph in 1984 – while most lorries were allowed to use motorways from 1959 to 1971 without special speed restriction.[66] In consequence the average length of haul by road increased markedly – for merchandise as a whole from 22 miles in 1953 to 43 miles by 1979, for food, drink and tobacco from 31 miles in 1962 to 47 miles in 1977, and a much greater volume of road traffic was handled without a dramatic increase in the number of lorries.[67]

One cannot be other than impressed by the speed with which the major brewers effected the change from rail to road distribution. Bass had operated over a 26 mile railway network in Burton, marshalling train-loads of beer which were sent over the British Railways system in substantial quantities until the late 1960s. As late as 1962 sixteen major freight services (about ninety trains in all) were assembled each week in

[64] Gourvish, *British Railways*, pp. 493–7; *AAS*, 1980, 1990.

[65] D. G. Rhys, *The Motor Industry: An Economic Survey* (1972), p. 347; Dept of Transport, *Transport Statistics*.

[66] A general maximum speed limit of 70 mph was introduced on motorways in 1965 (in 1966 vehicles pulling trailers were limited to 40 mph). HGVs without trailers were limited to 60 mph in 1971, and from 1984 their maximum speed on dual carriageways was set at 50 mph. See *Statutory Instruments*, 1971, no. 601; *Report of the Inquiry into Lorries, People and the Environment* (December 1980), p. 5; M. A. Cundill and B. A. Shane, 'Trends in Road Goods Traffic 1962–77', *Transport and Road Research Laboratory Supplementary Report 572* (1980), pp. 1–2; information from Louise Wright and C. J. Curson, Department of Transport.

[67] Armitage Report, 1980, pp. 5, 7; Cundill and Shane, 'Trends', p. 4. Here 'Food, Drink & Tobacco' excludes cereals, fruit and vegetables, etc.

Table 13.3. *Bass/Worthington beer consignments in bulk barrels, 1927–69*

Period (annual averages)	Consignments (barrels)	Proportion by: rail %	road %	Tank/ total %	Tank traffic by: rail %	road %
1927–39[a]	861,181	90.0	10.0	–	–	–
1947–55	774,633	80.1	19.9	–	–	–
1950	901,625	82.7	17.3	–	–	–
1953	744,772	80.0	20.0	–	–	–
1956[b]	1,358,575	72.0	28.0	13.2	45.7	54.3
1959	1,420,839	56.0	44.0	16.8	11.9	88.1
1962	1,381,666	42.7	57.3	19.2	7.2	92.8
1965	1,271,184	21.9	78.1	28.7	2.1	97.9
1967	1,317,070	12.0	88.0	39.3	1.6	98.4
1969	1,591,425	6.1	93.9	43.0	0.4	99.6

[a] Bass only 1927–55 and calendar years.
[b] From 1956 Bass/Worthington and year ending in September.
Source: Bass/Worthington Burton Barrelage ledger, 1924–69, Bass plc.

Burton to take beer to all parts of Great Britain.[68] The shift from rail to road in Bass/Worthington deliveries can be seen in Table 13.3. Before the war Bass had sent 90 per cent of its barrelage by rail and the figure was still 80 per cent as late as 1953. The proportion fell rapidly from the mid-1950s, and was only 12 per cent in 1967 when the company decided to close its private rail operation. Two years later rail traffic had dwindled to a mere 6 per cent of the barrelage consigned. The increasing importance of bulk deliveries in tanks was a major factor in the change. In 1956 beer sent out in tanks amounted to only 13 per cent of total traffic and it was shared by road and rail in the proportion 54-46. Within three years the road–rail split had shifted to 88–12, and by 1969, when tank traffic made up 43 per cent of the total traffic, the rail share was negligible (Table 13.3). By this time Bass, with its recently acquired partner Charrington United, owned a substantial fleet of motor vehicles, about 4,200 in all.[69] Other leading companies also moved out

68 There were 16 miles of privately owned track plus running powers over an additional 10 miles of British Rail track. See R. C. Riley, 'A Night on the Beer', in G. F. Allen (ed.), *Trains Illustrated Annual* (1962), pp. 59–61; Ian P. Peaty, *Brewery Railways* (Newton Abbot, *c.* 1985), pp. 21, 30; Ben Ward, typescript history of Bass, pp. 46–8, Bass plc.

69 Figure quoted by Roger Denniss, in *Bass Brewers News*, September 1991, p. 4.

of private railway operations in the 1960s, for example Mitchells & Butlers in 1962, Ind Coope (Romford) in 1963 and Marstons in 1964.[70]

Guinness had more reason to use rail for long-distance distribution, since it distributed to brewers rather than to public houses. Supplementary road transport was provided by independent road hauliers. For example, Thomas Allen was employed to undertake the company's deliveries in the London area, while after the nationalisation of long-distance road haulage in 1947, British Road Services, the public sector carrier, was used to make deliveries to the Midlands and East Anglia. However, the shift to bulk tank distribution from the mid-1940s favoured road transport, and this development prompted the company to take a direct interest in road distribution. Park Royal Transport, a wholly owned subsidiary of Guinness which had been established as early as 1935, purchased eight tanker lorries from Thomas Allen in 1949 and quickly built up a sizeable fleet. In 1955 it took over Thomas Allen's Park Royal operations and a year later it was renamed Guinness Transport Ltd to reflect its wider role. By this time it owned seventy-one tankers and eighteen platform lorries (in 1964 there were seventy-five and thirty respectively). About 80 per cent of the beer produced at Park Royal was distributed in 40 and 80 barrel tanks, and most of it went by road. The railways were not abandoned. Guinness purchased nine road-rail tankers for bulk distribution in 1949 and in the early 1950s British Railways was still carrying Guinness to a number of locations, notably South Wales, the West of England and Newcastle (the latter meriting a twice-weekly service). However, rail distribution was reduced after the transport subsidiary was integrated into the brewing company in 1967.[71]

Ironically, the move to road transport, which had been encouraged in part at least by the disruptions caused by labour disputes on the railways, brought its own industrial relations problems. The substantial shift to road encouraged the recruitment of brewery workers to the Transport and General Workers' Union, and, as noted earlier (see pp. 517–18), this union was often at the forefront of disputes in the industry. In fact, higher drivers' wages were largely responsible for a

[70] Peaty, *Brewery Railways*, pp. 21–2, 51.

[71] The move was made for industrial relations reasons. Park Royal/Guinness Transport Board Minutes, 19 March 1935, 20 December 1948, 24 May 1949, 29 March 1955, 20 June 1956, 25 June 1957, 15 February 1967; *Guinness Time*, Spring 1950, p. 1; Summer 1952, pp. 5–7; Summer 1954, pp. 20–2; Summer 1955, p. 16; Summer 1957, pp. 4–7; Christmas 1964, pp. 4–8, GPR; *The First Hundred Years of Thomas Allen (Ltd)* (n.d. [1954]), pp. 36–7; Edward Guinness (ed.), *Guinness Book of Guinness*, pp. 350–2; Interview with R. T. Kerslake.

rise in vehicle operating costs, which increased generally by about 20–50 per cent in real terms between 1962 and 1977.[72] On top of this, road transport operations were affected by periodic fuel crises, as, for example, in 1956,[73] by sudden hikes in fuel costs, notably during the 1973 oil crisis, and by new government regulations designed to improve the quality of owner-operated vehicles (for example in the Transport Act of 1968). There were also periodic attempts to encourage the diversion of freight traffic from road to rail for environmental reasons. In the Transport Act of 1968 there was a quantity licensing scheme, by which goods carried by road vehicles of over 16 tons for distances above 100 miles were to be transferred to the railways, although this was not in fact implemented. In the late 1970s there were further expressions of alarm about the environmental costs of road freight movements, for example in the Green Paper on *Transport Policy* of July 1976, and (more controversially) in the Armitage Report on *Lorries, People and the Environment* of December 1980.[74] Although very little was done to redirect freight movements onto the railways these political moves created anxiety in an industry now firmly committed to road transport. Further anxieties came after Britain joined the EEC in 1973, which required responses to a further set of complex regulations governing road transport. Thus, the difficulties of operating substantial haulage fleets in the 1970s, within a regulatory framework which was becoming extremely complex, and with numerous disruptions caused by labour disputes (culminating in the road haulage strike of 1979), were such that the leading brewers established a special informal group to discuss them. The '"75" Club', as it was known, consisted of the distribution directors of the major brewers, supplemented in due course by the transport managers of the leading regional brewers. From 1975 it met regularly to discuss transport issues of mutual concern.[75]

There was much to discuss in this forum, but the principal challenge for management – that of matching production concentration, marketing changes and distribution – was a matter for the individual companies. It may be inferred that by 1980 the distribution of beer had become more efficient, faster and more reliable than before, and

72 Cundill and Shane, 'Trends', p. 15. Cf. also *Brewers' Guardian*, June 1970, p. 46.

73 See BS Circular 17/56 on 'Oil Supply Restrictions and Petrol Rationing', 26 November 1956, and Brewing Materials Committee Minutes, 11 December 1956, BS.

74 Department of Environment, *Transport Policy* (July 1976), Vol.1, pp. 3–4, 26–7, 65, 89–91; Armitage Report, December 1980, esp. Ch. 3. The latter made a strong case for the introduction of heavier lorries.

75 BS File 6/4/1, BS.

although there was periodic concern over rising costs, there was no evidence to suggest that the railways could offer a cheaper service of similar quality. Under these circumstances, the central task of the distribution manager was to ensure that the transport function was fully integrated with his company's production and marketing strategies. For the smaller companies distributing over a compact geographical area from a single brewery, the operation was comparatively straightforward. For others, and in particular the larger companies facing the reorganisation of beer portfolios in the wake of merger, the challenge was of an altogether different order. Here, the main features were: first, moves made by the leading companies such as Bass, Courage, Scottish & Newcastle and Whitbread to shift a considerable proportion of their production to new, larger breweries built on greenfield sites located to take advantage of the emerging motorway network; second, an increase in the number of beer brands marketed nationally or inter-regionally and exchanged by brewers; and third, the tendency to separate production and packaging locations as concentration proceeded. Because these trends served to increase the volume of road transport in brewing, as they did in the food and drink sector as a whole, they made transport logistics more critical in the flow from raw material assembly to final consumer.[76] The strategies pursued from the mid-1960s, before the demand changes stimulated by the consumer reactions of CAMRA and other groups were fully evident, may have made sense with contemporary market projections, but they became rather fragile with the passage of time. Some of the bolder production strategies based upon perceived efficiencies of scale have been noted earlier, namely the opening of Whitbread's new brewery at Luton, and the Bass Charrington brewery at Runcorn (see pp. 507–8). The latter, for example, was part of the company's long-range production plan of 1969, which proposed the construction of a new brewery with a capacity of 2.4 million barrels and the closure of sixteen production sites. The plan emerged from a determined management initiative, code-named 'BC-1982', to secure beer production and distribution at the lowest cost by 1982. Much was made of Runcorn's location at a nodal point on Britain's road and rail trunk routes, and there were high expectations of cheaper distribution via British Rail's Freightliner services. But the other assumptions upon which the decision rested were less certain: that all beers were to be processed and nationally distributed; and that all beers could be pro-

[76] Cf. Linda Saunders (Freight Unit, GLC), 'Freight Transport in the Brewing Industry', November 1976, BS.

duced at any location. On this basis the 'minimum cost system' was one where up to 9.75 million barrels per annum would be produced at a location near Liverpool and distributed through sixteen depots. The new, more modest brewery was opened in 1974. However, as time went on the production-distribution paradigm shifted, favouring the distribution of regionally brewed beers from more than one site, while the additional costs and industrial relations exposure of distributing over a wide area from a single location became more difficult to justify.[77]

The challenge of the 1970s in particular was how to match the concentration of production, marketing changes and efficient distribution at a time of high inflation and worsening industrial relations. As brewery-operated road transport became a more critical element in corporate strategies it demanded managerial flexibility and an end to restrictive practices in responding to changing market conditions, shifts in brand penetration and the changing mix of beer types. One should not underestimate the size of the task, given contemporary social conditions in the 1970s, but the concern expressed in 1977 by the National Economic Development Office about transport management in the brewing industry (see p. 518), and the conferences which were convened on its initiative in 1979 and 1980, suggest that at the end of our period much remained to be achieved.[78]

III

The principal changes in the market for, and retailing of, alcoholic drinks in Britain since 1955 have already been identified (see pp. 451–9). First, there was a steady growth in demand from under 25 million barrels in 1958 to over 42 million in 1979. Second, there was the appearance of new products and fundamental changes in packaging: the shift to brewery-conditioned draught beers, first bitter ('keg'), then lager, and an accompanying decline in the market-share of bottled beers. Finally, although the tied house continued to dominate public house retailing, there was a significant growth in the free trade, in pubs, clubs and off-licences. The increase in take-home sales, which supermarkets increasingly controlled, encouraged a shift to canned beers. Data for 1960 and 1980 provide a clear demonstration of the changes

77 See F. J. Yardley's papers, Bass Cape Hill (Birmingham). The Runcorn brewery was closed in 1991.

78 Cf. Report on NEDO Brewing Distribution Conference, Manchester, 28 March 1980, BS.

Table 13.4. *The beer market, 1960–80*

Category	1960	1980
Ale/stout	99%	69%
Lager	1%	31%
Draught beers	64%	79%
Mild	[39%]	[11%]
Bitter	[25%]	[44%]
Lager	[0%]	[24%]
Returnable bottles	34%	10%
Cans	1%	10%

Source: BS, *Statistical Handbook 1988*, p. 18; BS estimates.

(Table 13.4). The period also saw a marked reduction in the total number of beer brands – from 3,000 in 1966 to under 1,500 a decade later[79] – although this reduced figure was still large by international standards. The 1960s and 1970s were dominated by the leading keg and lager beers of the major producers: Double Diamond (Allied), Worthington 'E' (Bass), Courage Tavern, Draught Guinness, Tartan (S&N), Watneys' Red Barrel and Whitbread Tankard; and the lagers, Skol (Allied), Harp (Guinness and others), Carling and Tennent (Bass Charrington), Carlsberg (Watneys) and Heineken and Stella Artois (Whitbread). Over the rest of the market, the demand for cask-conditioned bitter and mild beers was protected to a certain extent by tied house sales, although these tended to decline whenever advertised national brands were introduced into pubs. The competition between major suppliers for market-share was consequently much fiercer than it had been before 1960, indeed fiercer than at any time since the battle for the London market at the turn of the century.

Marketing and advertising activity both reflected and encouraged these changes. The 1960s and 1970s saw important developments. While the Brewers' Society continued to publicise beer-drinking and the public house with its annual, 'collective advertising' campaigns, as it had done since 1933, there was a general increase in the advertising activity of individual companies, stimulated by the use of television in media advertising and supported by a greater and more sophisticated

[79] Citicorp Scrimgeour Vickers, *Brewers Today* (1987), p. 11.

use of market research techniques. Corporate, 'prestige' advertising gave way increasingly to the promotion of single brands (although for one of the leading companies – Guinness – the two went hand in hand). This led to both a variety and a volatility in product promotion and in the type of advertising deployed, a feature facilitated by the regional structure of independent television.

The Brewers' Society continued to emphasise the sociability of the public house and the nourishing qualities of beer. Using S. H. Benson as advertising agents from 1953 its campaign placed emphasis on 'Good Wholesome Beer' and 'Beer – the Best Long Drink in the World'. The greater part of the allocated subscriptions was used in press advertising to 1954 (Table 13.5). When from 1955 the Society decided to augment its activity by a further levy on its members, made in response to anxieties about declining consumption, a poster campaign was included, together with a limited amount of advertising on Radio Luxemburg.[80] In the period 1957–63 'outdoor advertising' was the most popular medium, although the Society made its first use of television (in 1959 when the Society held its mock 'beer' election[81]). By this time, demand for beer was picking up again, and on the advice of Alan Seaward, Duncan Simonds and other members of the Society's Publicity Sub-committee the emphasis was redirected to the public house (e.g. with the slogan 'Look in at the Local'; Plate 82).[82] From October 1963 resources were concentrated largely on television advertising, although the press was the chosen medium during the 1968/9 campaigns (Table 13.5), while the industry awaited the report of the Monopolies Commission. New agents, Doyle Dane Bernbach, were employed in the last campaign in 1969–70, which used television to emphasise the virtues of the 'Packaged Pint' (Plate 83). But at this stage two leading members of the Society expressed their unwillingness to continue with the scheme, and there was a recognition that generic advertising had lost its force with the growing segmentation of the drinks market and the emphasis

80 A Stargazers recording, 'Good Wholesome Beer', was played on Radio Luxemburg. The extended scheme was confined to England and Wales after a more ambitious scheme, including Scotland, had failed to attract support in 1954. See BS, Annual Report 1954–5, pp. 13–14 and File on 'Collective Advertising', 8/1/1 (circulars 2/54, 9/54, 22/54, 5/55). Support for the extended scheme from members, initially about 73 per cent, had reached 92 per cent by 1958.

81 Participating pubs asked customers to vote for draught or bottled beers. See BS, Annual Report 1958–9, p. 13, BS.

82 BS Publicity Sub-committee Minutes, 21 October 1959, 19 November 1963, Publicity Committee Minutes, 16 January and 16 October 1962; BS Annual Report, 1962–3, pp. 16–17, BS.

Table 13.5. *Brewers' Society collective advertising campaigns, 1948–70*

Year ending 30 September (ann. averages)	Expenditure [£]	Deployment: Posters %	Press %	TV %	Radio %
1948–54	126,000	–	85	–	–
1955–6	254,000	46	50	–	3
1957–63	334,000	58	37	1.5	0.5
1964–7	379,000	–	23	73	–
1968–9	292,000	–	94	–	–
1970	254,000	–	–	97	–
Total: 1948–70	6,089,000	26	46	23	0.4

Source: Appendix, Table XV.

on brands. The Society turned its attention to public relations, giving its publicity committee that name in April 1970. Collective advertising then ceased.[83] Nevertheless, the successive campaigns had been far from insubstantial. In all £6 million was spent in the twenty-two years to 1970 (Table 13.5).

Corporate advertising was on a much larger scale, of course. Table 13.6 provides an indication of aggregate expenditure over the period (and see Appendix, Table XVI for full data). Spending on beer advertising increased from an estimated £2.2 million in 1955 to £33.4 million in 1979, an increase in real terms of some 191 per cent. Media advertising (i.e. press and television) grew somewhat faster than this, 250 per cent in real terms, 1955–79. Growth was particularly pronounced in the period 1955–60 and 1965–70, when the new keg and lager brands were being heavily promoted by the six large pub-owning companies which with Guinness had come to dominate the industry. And the move to television advertising was critical: as early as 1960 it amounted to 30 per cent of total advertising expenditure, and a decade later the figure was 65 per cent (these proportions were much greater than for UK advertising as a whole). The amount of beer advertising also increased faster than total UK advertising, notably in the 1960s, even if it remained at under 2 per cent of the total spent). Although the precise relationship

[83] BS, Annual Report, 1969–70, p. 31 and file on 'Collective Advertising', 8/1/2, BS. Advertising was resumed in 1982/3, in the wake of recession and falling demand. A £750,000 campaign was launched with the theme 'You should have been in the Pub last night'.

Table 13.6. *Indices of beer and total UK advertising expenditures, 1955–79 (in constant 1979 prices, 1955 = 100)*

Year	Beer advertising expenditure: constant 1979 prices: All sources	'Media' (Press/TV)	Total UK advertising expenditure (constant 1979 prices) All sources	TV expenditure as % total expenditure Beer %	All advertising %	Beer advertising expenditure as % of UK total %
1955	100	100	100	5	1	1.25
1960	181	206	161	30	22	1.42
1965	193	233	183	56	24	1.33
1970	291	344	186	65	23	1.97
1975	265	358	176	75	24	1.89
1979	291	350	234	60[a]	22[a]	1.86

[a] ITV industrial dispute, August–October 1979.
Source: Appendix, Table XVI.

between advertising and corporate concentration is difficult to pin down and has been the subject of academic debate,[84] in British brewing it is quite clear that the two elements went together. The period of fastest advertising growth – the 1960s – coincided with the establishment of the major brewing companies, while a stabilisation in real advertising expenditure came in the 1970s when the industry's corporate structure settled down. An additional, non-economic element in the 1970s was the expression of public anxiety about increased alcohol consumption, and in particular a concern, difficult to prove statistically, that advertising was influencing consumption, particularly among the young. Early lager advertising had certainly been aimed at women and young people. In 1975 both the Advertising Standards Authority and the Independent Broadcasting Authority introduced codes of practice for alcohol advertising, and in 1978 the latter made its rules on television advertising more severe. Appeals to the young (defined by the IBA as the under-25s) were prohibited, and advertisers were prevented from associating alcohol consumption with either sexual prowess, social success or physical strength. These moves certainly caused anxiety in the industry,

84 Cf. Brian Chiplin, Brian Sturgess and John Dunning, *Economics of Advertising* (1981), pp. 113, 129; Robert B. Ekelund, Jr. and David S. Saurman, *Advertising and the Market Process: A Modern Economic View* (San Francisco, 1988), pp. 97ff., and Keith Cowling *et al.*, *Advertising and Economic Behaviour* (1975), pp. 195–6.

Table 13.7. *Selected beer advertisers (press and TV), 1955–79*

Year	Leading advertisers (%) Big Seven companies[a]	No.1 advertiser		No.2 advertiser		Lager advertising
1955	54	Guinness	24	Whitbread	12	–
1960	66	Guinness	17	Ind Coope	16	19
1965	71	Guinness	19	Watney Mann	14	10
1970	90	Bass Charr	22	Guinness	21	18
1975	92.5	Guinness	21	Allied	17	29
1979	94	Guinness	20	Watneys/GMet	16	37

[a]Percentages include allocation of lager brands to relevant company.
Source: Appendix, Table XVII.

and they probably encouraged brewers to stabilise their real advertising expenditures.[85]

It is quite clear that most of the aggregate expenditure on beer advertising was undertaken by the largest companies. The Big Seven increased their share of the total spent on media advertising from 54 per cent in 1955 to 71 per cent in 1965 and 90–94 per cent in the 1970s, the increase being a direct consequence of corporate expansion, notably the creation of Bass Charrington and the emergence of Courage and Scottish & Newcastle as major national advertisers, and the emphasis on keg and lager brands (Table 13.7).[86] Guinness, dependent to a considerable extent on sales in the tied houses of other brewers, was a dominant advertiser throughout; indeed, it spent far more per barrel than any

[85] Advertising Standards Authority, *The British Code of Advertising Practice*, February 1975; Independent Broadcasting Authority, *Code of Advertising Standards and Practice*, September 1975, October 1978. The Codes were in part a response to the anxiety expressed by the Erroll Committee in 1972: *Report of the Departmental Committee on Liquor Licensing (Erroll Committee)*, December 1972, *PP* (1972–3) XIV, Cmnd.5154, pp. 45–6, and see also Williams and Brake, *Drink in Great Britain*, pp. 204–5. Most academic research indicates that advertising has had very little impact on alcohol consumption in the UK except at the brand level. Cf. Mike Waterson, *Advertising and Alcohol Abuse* (Advertising Association, 1983), p. 5; Martyn Duffy, 'The Effect of Advertising on the Total Consumption of Alcoholic Drinks in the UK: Some Econometric Evidence', *Journal of Advertising History*, 1 (1982), 105–18; P. W. Kyle, 'The Impact of Advertising Markets', *ibid.*, 345–59; Reginald G. Smart, 'Does Alcohol Advertising Affect Overall Consumption? A Review of Empirical Studies', *Journal of Studies on Alcohol*, 49 (1988), 314–23.

[86] Scottish & Newcastle was notable for its success in promoting Newcastle Brown Ale as a national beer, in an 'unfashionable' sector of the market which was dwindling.

other company.[87] Other companies fluctuated in the rankings with the fortunes of their brands, and with the extent of reciprocal agreements, which freed them from the need to advertise beers important to their tied house sales. Guinness and Ind Coope/Allied were the only companies to be found among the top four media advertisers in all the years surveyed. Others – Bass Charrington, Watneys and Whitbread – experienced fluctuations in their advertising budgets with the development of specific brands. Watneys, for example, was in the top four in 1960 and 1965, when it promoted Red Barrel strongly. It then invested £2 million in Red in 1971–4, but the brand failed to please consumers and expenditure was terminated abruptly in 1975.[88] Four years later, the company was back among the top four promoting its more successful lager brands, Carlsberg and Holsten (see Appendix, Table XVII). In the period 1963–73 Allied spent half of its £22 million advertising budget on only two brands: Double Diamond (£7.3 million) and Skol (£4 million).[89]

At the other end of the scale, very limited funds were spent on the modest advertising of a multiplicity of ale brands, using posters and the local press. The estimates of press/television advertising published by the statistical reviews for 1960 reveal the wide disparity. While Guinness spent about £523,000 (and a total of £1.25 million on all advertising[90]), no expenditure was reported for several smaller and medium-sized concerns, such as Adnams, Hydes, King & Barnes, Greene King and Marston's. And even regional brewers such as Greenall Whitley and Vaux made only modest expenditures – £13,000 and £8,000 respectively. A decade later a similar picture was apparent. The reported expenditure on media advertising by Bass Charrington was £1.7 million, Guinness spent £1.6 million, and Allied £1.5 million; but Vaux spent a mere £35,000, Greene King only £6,700, while the advertising of Greenall Whitley, Adnams and King & Barnes was too small to be recorded separately.[91] Some smaller brewers did show more initiative in media advertising. Burtonwood of Warrington was one of the first companies to use television in 1956, and it was followed in 1960, for example, by Gibbs Mew of Salisbury and Hall &

87 Cf. W. Greenwell *et al.*, *The Brewing Industry. Quarterly Commentary*, August 1976, p. 13; *Morning Advertiser*, 13 November 1980.
88 Greenwell, *Quarterly Commentary*, August 1976, p. 14.
89 Allied Breweries (UK), 'Trends 1972/3', p. 11, Allied.
90 Cf. R. Harris and A. Seldon, *Advertising in Action* (1962), pp. 160–4.
91 Legion Publishing Co., *Statistical Review of Press Advertising*, 29–30, (1960–1); Media Records Ltd., *Statistical Review of Independent Television Advertising*, 5–6 (1960–1); Register-MEAL Ltd, data for 1970.

Woodhouse. However, the estimated sums involved were very small – under £5,000 in each case.[92] The spending on *types* of beer also fluctuated. In 1960, for example, lager accounted for 19 per cent of media advertising; five years later the total had fallen to only 10 per cent, when the limits of bottled lager penetration were reached, and the promotion of keg beers was dominant, led by Allied with Double Diamond and Watney Mann with Red Barrel. By 1970, however, lager advertising, now focused on the draught market, had recovered to 18 per cent; it then doubled to 37 per cent of the total in 1979 (Table 13.7). The focus of attention certainly shifted to lager brands in the 1970s, when a revived interest in local, cask-conditioned beers began to affect the popularity of some of the national, brewery-conditioned, ale brands (see below). Certainly, the proportion of total advertising expenditure spent on lager remained much higher than the product's market-share, though the gap was closing by 1979,[93] and, in the process, home-produced lager replaced foreign-brewed lager as the dominant product. Only 35 per cent of lager consumption in 1955, it had risen to 71 per cent by 1965, and 96 per cent by 1980.[94]

It is extremely difficult to generalise about the advertising strategies of the brewing companies, given the material at our disposal. Their activities certainly increased awareness of the new beers and brands, but equally, advertising effort was required to create or expand demand for 'up-market' beers which were being produced by the heavy investment in new plant and new breweries or to satisfy licensing agreements with continental lager brand-owners. Furthermore, brand advertising was aimed not only at the consumer directly but at the smaller brewers who were either unable or unprepared to make the investment necessary to produce and promote keg and lager beers of the requisite quality and consistency. Advertising also acted as a means of redirecting demand within tied houses as well as the free trade. For example, brewers such as Watney Mann and Whitbread, which had inherited a large number of ale brands with the acquisition of smaller companies in the 1960s, advertised major brands to facilitate the phasing out of local brands with

[92] Media Records, *Statistical Review of Independent Television Advertising*, 1, 5–6 (1956, 1960–1).

[93]

	Lager: Share of advertising	Market share
1960	19%	1%
1970	18%	7%
1979	37%	29%

[94] C. W. Thurman, note on 'The Lager Market', 11 December 1978, BS; 1980 figure estimated from data in BS statistical handbooks.

more limited sales. This can be seen, for example, in the promotion of Red Barrel and the less successful Red and Starlight in East Anglia and the West of England in the early seventies, and the promotion of Whitbread Tankard (from 1955) and the cask-conditioned Trophy Bitter (from 1968) by Whitbread. In this way, advertising and product rationalisation were closely linked.[95]

What is clear is that the major companies became aware of, and made increasing use of, market intelligence and market research techniques and services. As a consequence, advertising became more sophisticated and better directed to particular markets, taking careful account of regional variations in drinking patterns and choices of drink. The Brewer's Society itself commissioned regular studies of attitudes to drink and the public house, notably a series undertaken by MORI in 1973–81.[96] And the major companies employed most, if not all, of the market research agencies at one time or another to investigate market segments, ranging from the work done by Gallup and Mass-Observation for Guinness in 1951–2 to the marketing consultancy provided by the aptly named Booz Allen & Hamilton for Courage/Imperial in the late 1970s.[97] United Breweries (subsequently Charrington United) appears to have been a particular enthusiast of market research. In the early 1960s it commissioned several studies from Marplan, British Market Research Bureau and others which dealt, *inter alia*, with the Scottish market, lager drinking and lager brands, and regional variations in Scotland, Yorkshire and Southern England. These revealed important insights into changing demand patterns, notably the appeal of lager among women and the young, the association by consumers of particular brands with attributes such as alcoholic strength, social class and sex, and the early penetration of lager, and Tennents in particular, in Scotland's working-class market.[98] With a wider understanding of

95 Reader and Slinn, 'Grand Met History', Chapter 5; Whitbread Board Minutes, 23 February 1961, 10 March 1964, 29 April 1969, 5 May 1970, 14 December 1971, 23 May 1972, W&Co.

96 In 1973, 1975, 1978 and 1981.

97 On Guinness see Guinness Board Minutes, 12 and 27 February 1951, GPR, and Sibley, *Guinness Advertising*, p. 143 and *Guinness Book of Guinness*, pp. 248–9. For Courage see Courage Board Minutes, 7 December 1978, Fosters Brewing Group (FBG).

98 See studies in J. Walter Thompson archive, e.g. Marplan, 'Report on a Study of the Image of Lager and Lager Brands in Scotland, England and Wales', December 1961, and 'Report on a Survey of the Drinking Habits and Attitudes of Beer Drinkers in Yorkshire', October 1962; BMRB, 'Export Ale', February 1961, 'Stout Survey', January 1962, and 'Report on a survey of the Scottish market for beer', March 1963; Lonsdale-Hands, 'A Study in the Consumer Market for Beer in South England', November 1963; J. Walter Thompson, 'A Look at the Pub in the Affluent Society', August 1964. Our thanks to J. Walter Thompson and to Bass plc for allowing us access

the market came a wider range of directed advertising, including corporate sponsorship and advertising at the point of sale. Conspicuous here was Whitbread's support of horse-racing and ocean racing (Mackeson/Whitbread Gold Cup, Round the World Yacht Race), Tennent Caledonian's series of 'Lager Lovelies' on its canned beers, the Skol 6-Day Cycle Race, and the *Guinness Book of Records* (1955 *et seq.*).[99]

The stimulus for much of this effort was the change in consumer behaviour. First of all, the late 1950s and 1960s saw changes on a national basis, in which keg beer made a considerable dent in the market-share of draught mild, brown ale and bottled stout, while lager gained rapidly in popularity (though from a very low base), particularly among female drinkers and the 18–24 age-group.[100] In the 1970s, on the other hand, consumer markets generally began to fragment. Of relevance here was the rise of self-service shopping, the segmentation of leisure activities, the increased popularity of entertainment clubs in industrial areas and the greater importance of entertainment in the home. There was an increasing tendency for groups of consumers to express themselves through a range of self-contained, and often mutually exclusive, patterns of life or 'life-styles'. In this environment the purchase for home consumption of beer in disposable packs (together with wines and other drinks) provided a substantial threat to the market-share (beer only) of public houses, which fell from over 80 per cent in 1955 to 78 per cent in 1967, 73 per cent in 1970 and 63 per cent a decade later.[101] Beer thus followed a general trend towards brand promotion in a more segmented market. A potent symbol of the change was consumer resistance to Watney Mann's attempt in 1971 to promote a uniform bitter brand – Red – and to turn its tied houses into a 'brand' by painting them red – the ill-fated 'Red Revolution'.[102] More positively, it was seen in the use of advertising techniques which gave particular brands real or assumed special characteristics or 'unique selling propositions', and a close association with consumer life-styles

to these files. Other companies also made use of similar research. Note, for example, Ind Coope/Allied: Mass-Observation, Report on 'Lager Drinking', 1962, File 4067, MO, and 'National Study of Wine Drinking December 1967', February 1968, Allied.

99 IPC, 'The UK Beer Market', September 1977, p. 137; Charles Schofield and Anthony Kamm, *Lager Lovelies: The Story Behind the Glamour* (Glasgow, 1984); Allied, 'Skol Brand Plan 1974/5', Allied; Sibley, *Guinness Advertising*, p. 127.

100 On women, see Rosemary Scott, *The Female Consumer* (1976), pp. 162–3.

101 Data for 1955 estimated from Chapter 10; for 1967 from Monopolies Commission, *Report*, 1969, p. 48; for other years from information provided by Chris Thurman of the BS.

102 Reader and Slinn, 'Grand Met History', Chapter 8.

and aspirations.[103] Guinness, of course, had been doing this for some time (see p. 351). A long-term relationship with Benson's dating back to 1927 produced, in the 1950s, posters proclaiming 'Guinness for Strength' as well as the continued use of animals in a whimsical manner. But with the appointment in 1957 of George Wigglesworth as managing director of Public Attitude Surveys (a Guinness subsidiary) and Alan Wood as advertising manager in 1961 a more hard-sell approach was adopted. Then in 1969 the company moved its UK account to J. Walter Thompson, and embarked on a series of more stylish, better directed and more aggressive selling campaigns. Television advertising was used to particular effect and a more conscious appeal was made to younger drinkers, including women.[104] But there were others, too, and in particular, Frank Wood and Anthony Simonds-Gooding's imaginative promotion of Heineken from 1974 with the slogan 'Refreshes the Parts No Other Beers Can Reach'.[105] Guinness and Heineken advertising, followed later by Harp, John Smith's (Courage), Tennent (Bass) and others, were pertinent examples of the change in marketing emphasis.

The emergence of the Campaign for Real Ale (CAMRA) in 1971 and its subsequent growth into a major consumer organisation were further influences upon brewing marketing in the 1970s. Ironically, this middle-class pressure group began to stress the virtues of traditional mild and bitter at a time when the working class was turning to 'up-market' keg beers and lager. Backed by Christopher Hutt, author of *The Death of the English Pub*, and Richard Boston, who contributed a weekly column on beer in the *Guardian*, CAMRA exploited self-defined *causes célèbres*, such as the closure of Joule's Stone brewery by Bass in 1973 and the demise of Barnsley Bitter a year later in the wake of the Courage–John Smith's merger in 1970, to feed anxiety among traditional ale drinkers about homogeneity and a lack of choice. The nostalgic appeal to local and regional tastes was timely in that it coincided with and responded to the vigorous promotion of uniform keg and lager brands.[106] It is easy to exaggerate the impact of CAMRA among beer

103 T. R. Nevett, *Advertising in Britain: A History* (1982), p. 179, citing Rosser Reeves, *Reality in Advertising* (1961).

104 Guinness Board Minutes, 15 June 1965, 25 and 28 March 1969, GPR; Sibley, *Guinness Advertising*, pp. 143–85; *Guinness Book of Guinness*, pp. 217–19, 354–6, 452.

105 See Peter Mayle, *Thirsty Work: Ten Years of Heineken Advertising* (1983). Our thanks to Shirley Braithwaite of Bryant Jackson Communications for this reference.

106 See CAMRA, *What's Brewing*, April–November 1974; Christopher Hutt, *The Death of the English Pub* (1973); Richard Boston, *Beer and Skittles* (1976), pp. 95ff. CAMRA eclipsed a longer-established but rather arcane body, the Society for the Preservation

drinkers generally. A MORI study for the Brewers' Society in 1975 revealed that only 12 per cent of those interviewed had heard of it, and cask-conditioned beers were only about 17 per cent of the total market in 1980.[107] But CAMRA did help to retain a firm niche in the market for traditional beers, despite the comparative difficulty of transporting and serving this type of product. In consequence, several of the smaller brewers enjoyed an unexpected boost in the 1970s, just at the time when it seemed that they would no longer be able to maintain their position in the market. The popularity of 'real ale' presented a considerable lifeline to small independents such as Adnams, Brain, Harvey & Son, Timothy Taylor, Wadworth and Young's. It no doubt rescued many a company which, faced with either a massive investment programme to facilitate the brewing of new beers or a sales agreement with a major producer of keg and lager, had come close to throwing in the towel.[108] At the same time, it forced a response from the national brewers. By 1980 they clearly accepted that the emphasis on national keg beers had been overdone, and that the market was not a homogeneous whole receptive to very limited numbers of brands. The continuing popularity of beer among middle-class consumers, which CAMRA helped to nurture, resulted in a redirection of the marketing strategies of the Big Six. Companies such as Allied and Watney Mann & Truman (Grand Met), which had pressed national products too vigorously, stepped back and reintroduced local brand names, though these were not necessarily brewed in the locality. Thus, by 1980 the six national companies were selling about eighty brands of cask-conditioned beer. The names of Allied subsidiaries such as the Aylesbury Brewing Co., Benskin's, Friary Meux, Halls, Taylor Walker and Peter Walker were back on the bar counter, while Watneys reintroduced Ushers, Mann's and Tamplin's and produced local beers for the Norfolk market.[109]

of Beers from the Wood, which had been established by 'disgruntled beer drinkers' at the 'Rising Sun', Epsom, in December 1963.

107 MORI, 'Attitudes to the British Brewing Industry', 1975, p. vii; Rowe and Pitman, *Quarterly Report*, June 1980, p. 9 (data for 1979).

108 Cf. Mike Dunn, *Local Brew: Traditional Breweries and Their Ales* (1986), pp. 32–3; John Mark, 'Changes in British Brewing', 85.

109 CAMRA, *Good Beer Guide 1981* (St Albans, 1981). Rowe and Pitman, *Quarterly Report*, June 1980, p. 11 list seventy-four brands, but this does not appear to be complete. On middle-class consumption, note the observation of the Erroll Committee Report, based on an OPCS Survey, that regular beer drinkers were just as numerous among the middle class (39 per cent) as among skilled manual (36 per cent) and unskilled manual (42 per cent) workers. Report, 1972, p. 58.

IV

Imaginative strategies in marketing were all the more critical because it rapidly became clear to brewers that while the tied public house remained the principal source of alcohol sales in the UK, spending therein was in relative decline at a time of considerable inflation. Public house turnover appears to have increased by only 3 per cent in real terms between 1964 and 1979, a record which compared unfavourably with the growth of the market as a whole – beer consumption rose by 41 per cent over the same period. Furthermore, real public house turnover actually fell by 10 per cent, 1973–9, compared with a 7 per cent rise in beer consumption.[110] And since turnover was a composite of several elements – drinks other than beer, food, machine income (see below), etc. – it is clear that sales of beer itself were under pressure in this period. Other factors combined to challenge the pub as the centre of social drinking. First, there was the simple fact that the number of pubs declined relative to other licensed premises (on and off) in the 1960s and 1970s. While the number of full on-licences remained fairly static at about 76,000 between 1960 and 1980, the number of clubs increased by a third to 33,000 and the new category of 'restricted' on-licence for restaurants, small hotels, etc., which had been introduced by the 1961 Licensing Act, numbered 22,000 in 1980. In addition, the number of off-licences increased by over 60 per cent to 42,000 (see pp. 456–7). Second, there was a greater awareness of the social consequences of drinking outside the home. Campaigns against drinking and driving gathered pace in the 1960s, culminating in the introduction of the breathalyser test in 1967. The number of tests carried out in Great Britain increased to 184,000 by 1980, three times more than in 1968, the first full year of its operation, while the number of convictions for drinking and driving also increased threefold to 79,000 (car mileage rose by only 44 per cent).[111] Convictions for drunkenness, which totalled 61,000 or 12.4 per 10,000 of the population in 1955, climbed to 94,000 or

110

	Indices: UK beer consumption	Public house turnover (real terms)
1964	100	100
1973	131	114
1979	141	103

Source: BS, *UK Statistical Handbook 1980*, pp. 12, 81.

111 BS, *UK Statistical Handbook 1983*, pp. 70–1, and information from Jean Wilson (Scottish Office). There was a thirteenfold increase in the number of convictions for drinking and driving between 1958 and 1980.

17.6 per 10,000 in 1962, and although fluctuating thereafter were considerably higher at 136,000 or 25 per 10,000 by 1980.[112] Furthermore, public house standards of comfort came under more intense scrutiny as alternative recipients of leisure spending flourished, including the club, coffee and wine bars, restaurants, sporting activities, home improvements (DIY) and more holidays (especially those taken overseas, which helped to encourage the demand for wine). The marketing environment was also made more difficult by publicly expressed concern about pricing in pubs and the tied house system generally as an alleged competitive restraint. This was expressed in a succession of inquiries by the National Board for Prices and Incomes (1966 and 1969), the Monopolies Commission (1969), the Erroll Committee on Liquor Licensing (England and Wales, 1972) and the Price Commission (1977). Counter-arguments by the industry that the price charged for beer and other drinks in pubs represented payment for a 'package' of amenities put further pressure on brewers to justify the system by maintaining and improving standards and amenities and therefore investment in their tied estates over a period when turnover was sluggish.

Awareness of the challenge all this presented to the traditional organisation of the trade, and in particular the relationship between the brewer and his retailers, whether tenants or managers, came quite early on in our period. In 1957 Sir Sydney Nevile, stalwart supporter of the National Trade Defence [from 1956 Development] Association, the body representing both brewers and retailers, raised the question of public house standards of service at the Brewers' Society. However, his proposal for a training scheme for licensees failed to attract support. Four years later, when the Licensing Act established a special licensing category for restaurants, small hotels, etc., thereby appearing to threaten the retail position of the public house, he had more success. The industry's retailers, he argued, were poorly trained. They were failing in particular to respond adequately to customer's demand for food (less than 12 per cent of brewer-owned pubs provided meals), while the continued dominance of the tenancy system (80 per cent of tied houses were still tenanted at low 'dry' rents) prevented brewers from exerting full control over standards of decor and furnishing. In May 1961 the Society's Survey Committee appointed a sub-committee, with Lord Boyd (Guinness) as chairman, to consider the 'improvement of retail service'. Its final report, in January 1963, recommended the

[112] BS, *UK Statistical Handbook 1983*, pp. 69, 76.

expansion of NTDA training courses for staff, an acceleration of pub modernisation and rationalisation programmes (the building of a new 'social centre' pub in Hatfield New Town by Guinness and McMullen was drawn to the sub-committee's attention), and a reduction in the vast difference in brewer control between managed and tenanted premises.[113]

However, these bold proposals fell on rather deaf ears. The implied threat to brewers' retailing quickly subsided with buoyant demand, good profits and growing opportunities in the free trade for the brand-building companies. Merger activity and post-merger managerial responses also consumed the attention of the industry. It was not until the Report of the Monopolies Commission in 1969 that the brewers were induced to return to the question of public house management and control. The Commission, as we have seen, was critical of the tied house system, regarding it as a competitive restraint which was not essential to the 'success of a modern large brewing and distribution unit'. It noted, in particular, that higher concentration had produced larger local monopolies of on-licensed premises; the dominance of Bristol by Courage and of Birmingham by Bass and Allied was singled out.[114] In the following year Nicholas Ridley, a junior minister at the Department of Trade and Industry, asked for information on local/regional monopolies and for proposals to reduce them.[115] Merrett Cyriax Associates, engaged by the Brewers' Society as consultants to examine the question, began by defining monopoly as a situation where a single brewer held a third or more of on-licences. A preliminary report in October 1970 identified 130 local authority areas with such a monopoly. A revised report, in January 1971, was clearly intended for consumption by the DTI. This adopted a more 'realistic' definition of monopoly, which was limited to areas with a population of at least 100,000 where one brewer enjoyed 50 per cent of the sales; to achieve this, it was contended, he would need to

[113] Sir Sydney Nevile, 'Note on Trade Policy', March 1961; Major-General Sir Reginald Scoones (Director, BS), note, 11 April 1961; BS Survey Committee Minutes, 16 May 1961; Sub-committee report on 'Improving Service to the Public', February 1963, BS; Nevile, *Seventy Rolling Years*, pp. 38, 145, 263–5. The report also advocated a pensions scheme for tenants and a grading system for pubs offering food.

[114] Monopolies Commission, *Supply of Beer*, 1969, pp. 52, 105; and see also 'Public Policies in Relation to the Brewing Industry', MMC, *Scottish & Newcastle Breweries PLC and Matthew Brown PLC: A Report on the Proposed Merger*, November 1985, *PP* (1985–6) Cmnd.9645, Appdx 2.3. The Commission accepted that concentrated, 'monopolistic' supply had been a characteristic of many small breweries in the past before the emergence of the Big Six. *Ibid.*, 106–7.

[115] Nicholas Ridley, written answer, 9 December 1970, *Parl. Deb. (Commons)*, 5th ser. vol. 808 (Session 1970–1), *132*.

own at least 69 per cent of the on-licences. Even so, there were important locations where ownership was concentrated in this manner: Bristol, Ipswich, Norwich, Northampton, Portsmouth, St Helens and West Bromwich. In December 1970 the Society gave the government an undertaking to encourage the elimination of such monopolies, and went on to formulate a code of best practice covering brewers' relationships with tied tenants.[116] By this time, in fact, action by individual brewers was being taken to effect 'pub swops'. In the period 1969–72 eight such arrangements were reported to the Society. Most of them were comparatively modest in scope, but two, a Truman–Courage deal in 1970 and one involving Courage and Watneys in October 1971, were more ambitious, transferring the ownership of 262 pubs in all, including sixty-eight in Bristol and forty-three in Norwich.[117]

In overall terms action was limited, however, and the crisis passed. The Erroll Committee took up the recommendation of the Monopolies Commission that licensing be 'substantially relaxed', and went on to argue that both on- and off-licences be made easier to obtain, opening hours more flexible, the age limit for drinking lowered from 18 to 17, and children given greater access to licensed premises. The Committee's ideas were too radical for governmental and public opinion, it appears, and nothing was done. In Scotland, however, the laws were relaxed, somewhat surprisingly in view of the greater incidence of alcoholism there. Following a similar report, that of the Clayson Committee in 1973, Sunday opening and longer opening hours were introduced in 1977.[118] Once again it took external criticism, in the shape of further inquiries, a preliminary report by the EEC on the tied house system in 1975 (part of extensive investigations into European brewing), and the report of the Price Commission in 1977, together with lobbying

[116] This advocated *inter alia* the tenant's freedom to buy non-beer items outside the tie, the prohibition of restrictive covenants on the sale of public houses, and encouragement of longer leases. See BS, *A Statement by the Brewers' Society*, 1 December 1970, and BS, 'Code of Practice on Tenants' Security', BS Law Committee Minutes, 16 August 1972, BS; MMC, *Scottish & Newcastle*, 1985, Appdx 2.3.

[117] In October 1971 Courage transferred sixty-eight Bristol pubs to Watneys; Watneys transferred forty-three Norwich pubs, seventeen in Northampton and twenty-five in Brighton to Courage. BS, paper on 'Local Concentration', 1976, Competition Sub-Committee file, 1975–7, BS.

[118] Action fell far short of the Committee's recommendations. See Erroll Committee, Report, 1972, pp. 269–82; Scottish Home and Health Department, *Report of the Departmental Committee on Scottish Licensing Law* (Clayson Committee), August 1973, *PP* (1972–3) XV, Cmnd.5354, pp. 227–41; Licensing (Scotland) Act 1976, 1976, c.66, 15 November 1976; MMC, *Scottish & Newcastle*, 1985, Appdx 2.3.

by CAMRA, to generate internal adjustments to the industry's retailing structure. Action in furtherance of EEC doubts about the 'tie' was postponed. But in August 1976 CAMRA requested the Office of Fair Trading to refer Allied's control of public houses in the northern Home Counties to the Monopolies and Mergers Commission. It followed this up with a similar complaint about monopolies enjoyed by each of the other large companies. CAMRA claimed that Allied owned 65 per cent of pubs in specified parts of Hertfordshire, Bedfordshire and Buckinghamshire, while Courage was found to own 64 per cent of the on-licences in Avon and Watney Mann & Truman a similar proportion of those in Norfolk.[119]

This produced an immediate response. In 1977 Allied, Bass and Courage exchanged 437 public houses in Bristol, the West Midlands, Thames Valley and Chilterns.[120] The Brewers' Society then made renewed efforts to encourage a response from its members. In May 1978 it gave an undertaking to John Silkin and Roy Hattersley, respectively Minister of Agriculture and Secretary of State for Prices and Consumer Protection, that it would carry out a systematic survey of the undue concentration of brewery-owned public houses and advance specific proposals for their elimination. Defining 'undue concentration' on this occasion as ownership above 50 per cent in areas with populations of at least 100,000 (estimated share of sales = 35 per cent), it discovered seventeen cases in all, eleven involving national companies, and six involving regional brewers.[121] In the autumn the Society was able to reassure the Minister that the brewers concerned had promised to take steps to bring ownership down below 50 per cent, though they were careful to stress that action involving 1,000 pubs could not be instantaneous. Nevertheless, by the end of October 1980 six of the eleven cases concerning nationals and one of the six involving regionals had been eliminated, while considerable progress had been made towards the 50 per cent norm in the remaining areas. In this way, the more conspicuous examples of

119 CAMRA, 'Request for a Reference to the Monopolies and Mergers Commission of a Local Monopoly in the Supply of Beer', August 1976 and other papers, BS.

120 Hoare Govett, *Brewing*, April 1979, p. 9.

121 The cases were: Norfolk, Northamptonshire (Watney Mann & Truman); Birmingham, Sandwell and Walsall (Bass Charrington); Gloucestershire, Portsmouth and Luton (Whitbread); South Tyneside (S&N); Dacorum (Herts.) and Aylesbury Vale (Allied); Halton, Vale Royal, Warrington and St Helens (Greenall Whitley); Blackburn (Thwaites); and Ipswich (Tollemache & Cobbold). BS, 'Local Concentrations of Ownership of Public Houses: Exchanges of Draught Ales', October 1978, BS; MMC, *Scottish & Newcastle*, 1985, Appdx 2.3.

single-brewer concentration in retailing were tackled.[122] The Society also reaffirmed its support for best-practice tenancies.[123]

Whatever the Society's pronouncements about brewer–tenant relationships, it is clear that there were tensions between the two elements of the trade in the 1970s. In spite of rising demand overall, the tenanted tied house came under increasing pressure, particularly from the larger brewers, who were anxious to service their large capitals by turning all their properties into profit-centres. This emerged, for example, in the unpublished Report of the Cairncross Committee in October 1971. In the wake of the Monopolies Commission Report of 1969 and the appointment of the Erroll Committee, the Brewers' Society had asked a committee, led by Sir Alec Cairncross, to report on the value to the industry of the tied house system and on the implications of any relaxation in licensing arrangements. Its report, which noted the steady if slow decline in the value of tied houses to the larger brewers, was critical of the industry's internal management accounting procedures in retailing. In particular, it criticised the way in which the acquisition of additional retail outlets was justified on a marginal sales basis. This, it was argued, had led to the retention of large numbers of unprofitable or low-profit public houses, thus depressing average rates of return on an investment (in 1970) of £1,000 million.[124] The data it collected, together with information gathered subsequently by the Brewers' Society, certainly pointed in this direction. Tenanted public house sales accounted for 64 per cent of total brewery sales in 1964, 39 per cent in 1970 and only 27 per cent in 1979. In spite of a closure rate of 1,000 per annum gross, 800 net, many pubs were still being retained as much for social as for economic reasons. In 1970 10 per cent of the public houses were selling under 100 barrels a year; and 38 per cent under 200 barrels. There was also a considerable difference between tenanted and managed house sales (Table 13.8). Finally, the average 'dry' rent on a tenanted house, which the Cairncross Committee

[122] Roy Hattersley, Written Answer, 11 December 1978, *Parl. Deb. (Commons)*, 5th ser. vol.960 (Session 1978–9), 74; BS, Memo on 'Pub Swaps and Ale Exchanges', 3 November 1981, BS.

[123] C. W. Thurman, Note, 12 February 1975; Report of BS Competition Sub-Committee, 5 July 1977, BS. A revised 'Code of Practice on Tenants' Security' was issued by the BS in May 1981. It is reproduced in MMC, *Elders IXL Ltd and Allied-Lyons PLC: A Report on the Proposed Merger*, September 1986, *PP* (1985–6) Cmnd.9892, Appendix 4.2.

[124] Cairncross Committee, Report to the Brewers' Society on 'The Value of the Tied Estate', October 1971, Box 1/I, BS. The other members of the Committee were William Brown, Walter Bull, George Cyriax and John Pears.

Table 13.8. *Average public house barrelages, rents and margins, 1967–79*

Year	Average sales (barrels)			Average rents (tenanted)				Average brewery repairs
	Tenanted	Managed	All	Dry	Wet	Total		
1967	–	–	–	£168	£198	£366		£302
1970	265	533	331	£224	£206	£430		£314
				Dry (+ repair element)[a]		Dry (no repair element)	Wet	
1970[b]	333	644	–	£330		£938	£231	£378
1973	–	–	–	£433		£1,221	£260	£583
1979	330	680	–	–		–	–	–

[a] Tenant undertakes some repairs.
[b] 1970/73/79 data for England and Wales only, from BS Retail Operations Questionnaire Results, BS.
Source: 1967–70: Cairncross Committee Report, October 1971, BS.

claimed amounted to only about 1 per cent of book value,[125] remained as low as it had been in 1949 (cf. pp. 439–40). Furthermore, such rents failed to cover repair costs by a fair amount, and provided only modest average margins when 'wet' rents and/or contributions to repairs were included in the calculation (Table 13.8). While the force of the Report evaporated with the tame outcome to the Erroll Committee's deliberations, it nevertheless contained some trenchant (if not always sustainable) observations about brewing retailing. In particular, it pointed out the considerable differences between large and small brewers, and argued vigorously for substantial programmes of rationalisation and investment.

The trade associations' main concern at this time was to defend the tied house system, in which the industry was investing substantially in the late 1970s.[126] Asked to support its defence by Roy Hattersley's Department in 1977, the Brewers' Society offered two principal arguments. First, the importance of such properties had declined. Tied public houses amounted to 48 per cent of all licensed premises (includ-

125 *Ibid.*, p. 33.
126 Brewers spent £266 million on retailing in 1980, most of it on tied properties. C. W. Thurman, 'The Structure and Role of the British Alcoholic Drinks Industry', in Marcus Grant, Martin Plant and Alan Williams (eds.), *Economics and Alcohol: Consumption and Controls* (1983), p. 253.

ing clubs) in 1967, but only 36 per cent by 1976 (and 32 per cent by 1979); their market-share (beer only) fell from about 65 per cent in 1967 to 52 per cent by 1976 (and 50 per cent by 1979).[127] Second, the system, though not without its defects, had considerable advantages. It enabled the brewers to pursue low-cost production and distribution strategies, and to pass savings onto the consumer in the form of lower prices and higher levels of investment in pubs. As the Brewers' Society emphasised, the tied house benefited beer drinkers by giving them a wider choice of beer and retail outlet than would have been the case with a fully competitive retail market. The Society warned the government that an abandonment of the system would cause considerable damage to smaller brewers, a wholesale closure of outlets, particularly in rural areas, and increased rents for tenants. The higher distribution costs which the bigger brewers would have to meet with a less predictable market would produce higher prices and a reduction in consumer choice, notably of the more perishable cask-conditioned beers.[128] Given the warnings of internal documents such as the Cairncross Report, there is no reason to believe that this was a brewers' bluff. But although the argument was won in the short term, the competitiveness of on-licence retailing was a subject to which the government would return with some vigour in the following decade.

Given publicly expressed anxieties about the tied house system from the later 1960s it was essential for brewers not only to defend their interests but to maximise retailing revenue. In fact, considerable progress was made in exploiting the full potential of the public house. With overall turnover rather sluggish (see above), novel elements of the 'packaged pint' assumed greater importance. The brewing companies, both large and small, quickly recognised the value of relatively new sources of income: food, music and electronic games; and gaming machines. And these elements were regarded with more enthusiasm by the larger brewers as they came to regard their primary function as owners of retail properties rather than as beer producers. Progress towards satisfying Nevile's aspirations for public house catering were steady, if not spectacular, in the 1960s, and brisker in the following decade. This coincided with a switch in emphasis from the single design of pub popular with brewers such as Watney Mann in the late 1960s to a variety of specific 'themes', targeted at particular groups of drinkers. There were also moves to place the larger houses under direct manage-

[127] Estimated from information in BS Retail Operations Questionnaires, 1971–9, BS.
[128] BS, Paper on 'The Tied House System', March 1978, BS.

ment. Thus, the percentage of brewer-owned pubs which were managed increased from 24 per cent in 1967 to 29 per cent by 1980, by which time food sales accounted for about 12 per cent of public house turnover, a notable change compared with the situation in the early 1950s (see p. 435).[129]

Special attention was given to the installation of music, juke boxes, electronic games and fruit machines (technically Amusement With Prizes or AWP machines). These items not only made substantial contributions to retail income; they also required little or no attention from licensees. The AWP machines were the most lucrative, though their introduction into licensed premises was hindered by restrictive and often complicated legislation, and the industry's trade associations made much of the difference in the treatment of clubs and public houses. Before 1960, any form of gambling, including the use of 'one-armed bandits', was prohibited on licensed premises.[130] However, in that year the Betting and Gaming Act introduced a more liberal regime. First, it sanctioned the playing of darts, dominoes, etc. for stakes on licensed premises. Second, it provided for the introduction of gaming machines in clubs, though not in pubs, while a rather ambiguous section dealing separately with AWP machines allowed their use in 'commercial' premises provided that a local authority licence were obtained and that both stakes and prizes did not exceed 1s (5p).[131] This latter part of the legislation was clearly intended to apply to funfairs, amusement arcades and the like, but some brewers and publicans were encouraged to introduce AWP machines, particularly where the competition from clubs was strong. The Brewers' Society was concerned about their impact on the image of the public house, particularly in the wake of Nevile's efforts. But a survey of its members in 1963 revealed that although a majority of brewers (about 80 per cent) was prepared to support a resolution opposing AWPs in principle, many companies had already begun to introduce them into their pubs. In addition, some tenants had acquired machines without obtaining their landlord's

129 Citicorp, *Brewers Today*, pp. 4, 7.

130 Licensing Act, 1953, 1 & 2 Eliz.II, c.46, 31 July 1953, s.141. Some exceptions were made for small lotteries under Acts of 1956 and 1959.

131 Betting and Gaming Act, 1960, 8 & 9 Eliz.II c.60, reaffirmed by the Betting Gaming and Lotteries Act, 1963, 11 & 12 Eliz.II c.2. An amending Act in 1964 limited the maximum value of a non-cash prize to 5s (25p): Betting Gaming and Lotteries (Amusement with Prizes) Act, 1964. There appears to have been some initial confusion about the maximum permitted stake in *coin*-operated (as opposed to *token*-operated) AWPs.

permission.[132] In the circumstances the Society decided to adopt a neutral if rather unenthusiastic stance. Similar equivocation was shown towards the introduction of contraceptive machines.[133]

The Gaming Act of 1968 strengthened controls over a growing business. It established a supervisory Gaming Board for Great Britain, and made a clearer distinction between the higher-prize 'jackpot' machines permitted in the clubs, whose profits were used to subsidise beer prices, and the more modest AWP machines permitted in pubs and elsewhere (defined by Section 34 of the Act and by subsequent guidelines).[134] Gradually, under pressure from the brewing industry and the licensed victuallers, who continued to complain about the disparity between clubs and pubs, the limits on AWP stakes and prizes were raised. The 5p maximum stake was doubled in 1981, while the cash prize limit was increased to 10p in 1969, 20p in 1976 and £1 in 1981.[135] But in spite of strong representations from the trade to the Royal Commission on Gambling of 1978, the distinction between clubs and pubs was retained.[136]

Notwithstanding the handicaps, AWP machines proved popular in public houses and by the end of the 1970s the majority of these outlets had such installations. The total number of AWPs licensed in pubs and other premises increased from 72,800 in 1972 to 121,000 eight years later.[137] In fact the AWP machine became an extremely important addition to public house profits. This can be seen in the seriousness with which brewers fought to retain their share of machine income, which appeared to be excluded by the provisions of the 1968 Gaming Act,[138] and subsequently in their determined negotiations with retailers (e.g. through the National Federation (later Union) of Licensed Victuallers) about the division of profits.[139] The evidence shows that machines were

[132] See BS File on 'Retail: Gaming, 1949–72', 7/8/1, BS.

[133] BS, Annual Report, 1963–4, pp. 10–11, 16–17, BS.

[134] Gaming Act 1968, c.65, 25 October 1968. The Act also transferred responsibility for licensing pub machines from local authorities to the licensing justices.

[135] The maximum for non-money prizes was £2. See BS, Annual Report, 1970–1, pp. 32–3 and information in BS File on 'Retail: Gaming, 1972–81', 7/8/2, BS.

[136] See *Final Report of Royal Commission on Gambling*, July 1978, *PP* (1977–8) VII, Cmnd.7200, vol.II, pp. 381–5, 392–4. The Commission recommended that cash prizes in AWPs be raised to £1, and accepted BS arguments that tokens should be abandoned.

[137] BS, *UK Statistical Handbook 1983*, p. 75. There were 41,300 licensed 'jackpot' machines in 1980.

[138] The Act prevented machine *suppliers* from sharing in machine profits. Brewers retained their profit-shares by ceasing to supply machines directly. See BS, Annual Report, 1969–70, p. 13.

[139] See information in 7/8/2, BS.

a substantial source of profits in low-barrelage houses, particularly in rural areas, where the returns frequently exceeded dry rents. They were also an important source of corporate income generally. For example, Allied Breweries' machine income doubled from £1.25 million in 1971 to £2.59 million in 1974, by which time it was a third of rental income and 9 per cent of the Beer Division's before-tax profits. Six years later the income was nearly £13 million, very close to that derived from rents.[140] A similar income was enjoyed by Courage – £2.53 million per annum, 1973–7; by 1979 the company was planning a diversification into amusement arcades.[141] And in 1979/80 Watney Mann & Truman Brewers derived no less than 18 per cent of their trading profit from machine income, £9.3 million in a total of £51.1 million, nearly as much as net rents (£10.1 million).[142] In the depressed conditions of the late 1970s this revenue was critical to those brewers who relied heavily on tied trade income.

The transformation in brewing marketing and retailing was considerable in the quarter-century ending in 1980. There were new products; a change in the balance of tied and free sales which came with shifts in consumer behaviour; a volatility in the market which saw the popularity of bottled beer give way to draught, first as keg bitter and then, when 'traditional', cask-conditioned ales made a revival in the later 1970s, as lager; the growing complexity and sophistication of the drinks market, with its implications for brand advertising and the character of public houses; and a general concern about the tied house system, and about the medical and behavioural costs of alcohol consumption, which encouraged a defensive but ameliorative response from the trade.[143] This brewing revolution, with its increasing concentration, new technology, some scale economies, and an intensifying product differentiation accompanied by higher advertising expenditure, was not unique to Britain,[144] and in the circumstances it is no surprise to find that the British companies were both willing and able to change. Of course, an

140 Allied Breweries (UK), 'Trends 1972/3–1980/1', Allied.

141 Courage Executive Committee Minutes, 2 July and 10 September 1979 (Codename 'Fidelis'), Courage Archive, FBG.

142 Information on WMTB from Courage Archive, FBG.

143 As early as 1960 the BS encouraged its members to display warning notices about excessive drinking and driving. It continued to promote responsible and moderate drinking, e.g. in 1975 with its 'Don't Have One For the Road', campaign.

144 Cf. evidence for the US, including F. M. Scherer, *Industrial Market Structure and Economic Performance* (Chicago, 1980); Victor J. Tremblay, 'Scale Economies, Technological Change, and Firm-Cost Asymmetries in the US Brewing Industry', *Quarterly Review of Economics and Business*, 27 no.2 (Summer 1987), 71–86.

environment in which overall demand was rising provided a considerable encouragement. This was absent in the 1980s when the difficulties facing the trade were to become more acute.

14

Postscript

It seems sensible to conclude by taking note of some of the changes which have been experienced by the brewing industry since 1980. The following brief account, derived in the main from secondary sources, is intended to provide a short, general narrative of the industry's fortunes in the 1980s, together with references to the responses of its leading firms and the trade associations at a difficult time in the industry's history. It is not, however, part of our remit to explain the complex factors surrounding the reference of 'the supply of beer for retail sale' to the Monopolies and Mergers Commission in 1986 nor the events which have followed its recommendations of March 1989.[1]

I

The first point to emphasise is that the demand for beer, though not the demand for alcoholic drinks generally, fell sharply in the 1979–81 recession and did not recover thereafter. As Table 14.1 shows, domestic beer production fell from 41.7 million barrels in 1979 to 36.6 million in 1982, a reduction of 12 per cent, and then stabilised at around this level. Over the same period beer consumption fell by a similar amount, 11 per cent, from 42.1 to 37.4 million barrels, but then made a slight recovery, reaching 38.2 in 1990. Consumption of alcohol as a whole, including wines and spirits, was more buoyant; although the demand for spirits fell, that for wine soared, increasing by no less than 67 per cent (58 per cent in per capita terms), 1979–90, while cider sales increased by 43 per cent, 1980–3.[2] As a result, total consumption of alcoholic drinks fell by a

[1] Monopolies and Mergers Commission, *The Supply of Beer: A Report on the Supply of Beer for Retail Sale in the United Kingdom*, March 1989, *PP* (1988–9) Cm.651.

[2] Cider sales increased from 46.5 million galls in 1980 to 66.7 million galls in 1983. The data for wine are for 'wine of fresh grape'. 'Made-wine' amounted to 12 per cent of total wine consumption in 1979, but only 8 per cent 1985–90. BS, *Statistical Handbook 1991*, pp. 23, 31.

Table 14.1. *Beer production and consumption, 1979–90*

Year	UK beer production[a] m. barrels	UK beer consumption[a] m. barrels	UK beer consumption per capita 1979=100= 217.1 pints (121.3 litres)	UK wine consumption per capita 1979=100= 8.1 litres	UK alcohol consumption per capita 1979=100= 7.7 litres (100° proof)
1979	41.7	42.1	100	100	100
1982	36.6	37.4	89	107	91
1986	36.2	37.3	89	140	96
1990	36.1	38.2	89	158	97

[a] Data = for 12 months ending 31 March in year following.
Source: BS, *Statistical Handbook 1991*, pp. 7, 15, 34, 36, and info. from BS. See Appendix, Table XI.

mere 3–4 per cent in the late 1980s, though beer showed a decline of 11 per cent, clearly coming off worst (Table 14.1).

Why was this? The decrease in beer drinking, while not dramatic in comparison with the post-1945 period or, indeed, with earlier periods, was the consequence of economic trends, reinforced by demographic and social change. Britain's manufacturing decline produced a corresponding decline in beer consumption by unskilled and semi-skilled manufacturing workers, who tended to be high-volume, 'session' drinkers of beer, particularly in the industrial towns. Official figures of unemployment, which stood at 1 million in October 1979, had jumped to 2.6 million by October 1982 and reached 3 million three years later. The effects were worst in traditional areas of heavy beer drinking; in the West Midlands and in Yorkshire and Humberside, for example, unemployment increased by 225 and 215 per cent respectively, 1979–85, compared with the national average increase of 189 per cent.[3] The downturn in beer consumption may also be explained in part by the product's loss of competitive edge during the 1979–82 recession. In this period consumers' disposable income was squeezed but the price of beer, influenced to a considerable extent by government beer duty and VAT, increased in real terms. Thus, the duty was raised by 90 per cent from 1978 to 1982, and VAT was increased from 8 to 15 per cent in June 1979. In consequence the retail price of beer increased by about 80–90

[3] Data = number of claimants at UB offices, adjusted for seasonality: *Annual Abstract of Statistics, 1992*, p. 117.

Table 14.2. *Beer duty and prices, 1978–90 (1980 = 100)*

Year	Beer duty	Beer prices (current):		Beer price (in constant 1980 prices)	
	1980 = 9.15p[a]	i: Pub 1980 = 40.5p[b]	ii: DOE[c]	ii: DOE[c]	iii: Pub (net of duty and VAT) 1980 = 26.07p
1978	82	70	73	97	100
1980	100	100	100	100	100
1982	156	133	134	110	102
1986	198	186	179	123	125
1990	223	272	232	123	153

[a] Duty on beer of 1037°.
[b] BS data on public bar (managed house) price of pint of bitter.
[c] Department of Employment series.
Source: BS, *Statistical Handbook 1991*, pp. 37, 41–2, 45, and see Appendix, Table XVIII.

per cent, or by about 13 per cent in real terms (Table 14.2). Then, during the economic upswing of 1982–6, beer duty increased to a level which was nearly double that of 1980, and by 1986 prices were 23 per cent higher in real terms. Pub prices increased by a little more; indeed, an average pub price, net of duty and VAT, was 25 per cent higher in real terms in 1986 compared with 1980 (Table 14.2). At the same time, demand for wine was given a boost by the insistence of the European Community that excise duties on alcoholic drinks be harmonised under Article 95 of the Treaty of Rome. In 1983 the European Court of Justice ruled that the UK had failed to fulfil its obligations by taxing imported table wine more heavily than UK-produced beer. In consequence the 1984 Budget increased the beer duty but made a substantial reduction in the duty on table wine.

The shift away from beer was also the product of demographic and social influences. Consumer preference for wine is usually attributed to a demonstration of greater sophistication by older drinkers, but affluent younger drinkers also turned to wine, particularly during the post-1982 boom.[4] In both young and old, there was a reaction to the perceived consequences of prolonged beer drinking on waistlines in a society turning more and more to positive health intervention, as seen by

[4] Cf. Public Attitude Surveys for the BS, July 1984, Tables 3a, 27a; 1992, Table 55/1.

popular enthusiasm for jogging, marathon runs, slimming and 'healthier' foods. There was also some anti-alcohol lobbying on health grounds in the late 1970s and early 1980s, together with renewed efforts to curb drinking and driving. Furthermore, media attention was given to the anti-social behaviour of young people after drinking, using the pejorative appellation 'lager louts'. Here, such excesses were associated, rightly or wrongly, with the consumption of beer rather than other alcoholic drinks. Demographic changes – an ageing society and fewer 15 to 24-year-olds in the population – also tended to work against beer and in favour of wine.[5]

In these circumstances, it was essential for brewers to react positively to the changing climate in British society, and the evidence suggests that they did so. First of all, the industry campaigned vigorously for more flexible licensing hours, which were extended to England and Wales in August 1988.[6] Second, the activities of the Brewers' Society indicated a growing concern to encourage responsible, moderate drinking and to discourage drinking and driving. In 1975 a Social Problems of Alcohol Committee was established, which worked with the Public Relations Committee in numerous campaigns aimed at curbing under-age drinking – for example, the 'Under 18 Rule' (1977), 'Play the Game' (1981), a Thinkstrip for schools and posters for the National Association of Youth Clubs (1978). The Society continued its attack on drinking and driving with the mass distribution to pubs of posters and beer mats, bearing slogans such as 'I'm Driving' (1975/6), 'Be Sensible Be Safe' (1978), and 'Banned – You Could Be One Drink Away' (1981), and the 'Wheelwatch' campaign of 1987–90. It also co-operated fully with the Department of Transport's own initiatives in the late 1970s. In 1981 the industry's remaining public house compensation funds (see pp. 289–91) were used to establish an Alcohol Education and Research Council, while in the same year the Society's 'Operation Counterstroke' sought to promote within its membership a more sophisticated awareness of the dangers of alcohol abuse.[7] New bodies also contributed to this climate: the Centre for Information on Beverage Alcohol, founded in 1986,

5 *Ibid.* and population data from *Annual Abstract of Statistics*, 1990, 1992. The percentage of those aged 60+ in the UK rose from 19.0 per cent in 1971 to 20.7 per cent in 1991; the number of 15–24-year-olds fell by 11.5 per cent, 1986–91.

6 The Licensing Act of 1988 (1988 c. 17) permitted the weekday opening of licensed premises for up to twelve hours between 11 a.m. and 11 p.m., with an extension of the Sunday afternoon closing time from 2 p.m. to 3 p.m.

7 BS, position paper on 'The Use and Misuse of Alcohol in the UK', 1978, BS Council Minutes, 13 December 1978, and *ibid.* 5 November 1978, 11 February and 11 November 1981, BS; Licensing (Alcohol Education and Research) Act, 2 July 1981, 1981 c. 28.

Table 14.3. *Composition of the beer market 1979–90 (%s)*

Year	Lager	Ale/ Stout	Draught	Bottles Ret.	Bottles Non-ret.	Cans
1979	29.1	70.9	78.4	11.1	0.5	10.0
1986[a]	43.5	56.5	75.8	6.3	2.7	15.2
1990	51.4	48.6	71.6	5.6	3.4	19.3

[a] No- and low-alcohol beers included from 1985.
Source: BS, *Statistical Handbook 1991*, p. 17.

which acted as an information clearing house and was funded by some of the world's major brewers and alcoholic drinks companies;[8] and the Portman Group, launched in 1989 by eight of the UK's leading drinks companies, which set out to reduce alcohol misuse and promote sensible drinking.[9] At the same time, the brewers played their part by developing new products, made possible by improved technology. First, there were the alcohol-free beers (not exceeding 0.05 per cent abv), such as Barbican, launched by Bass in 1980, and Guinness's Kaliber of 1986, which was ultimately more successful; then came low-alcohol beers (0.05–1.2 per cent abv), notably, among the lagers, Tennents LA (Bass, 1987) and Swan Light (Allied, 1988), and bitter ales led by Whitbread's White Label (1987).[10]

For many aspects of the brewing industry the last decade has seen a continuation of trends already evident in Chapters 11–13. In the beer market, lager clearly continued on its upward path and remained the exception in a sluggish sales environment. Accounting for less than a third of total sales by volume in 1979, it represented 44 per cent by 1986 and over half (51 per cent) by 1990. The continuing shift to this product was assisted by the successful introduction to the UK market of new brands from Australia and America. Foremost here were the Australian draught lagers: Fosters, first introduced by Watney Mann & Truman (Grand Met) in 1981; and Castlemaine XXXX, launched by Allied

8 Sponsoring companies included Allied-Lyons, Guinness, Whitbread, Anheuser-Busch and Heineken.

9 The sponsoring companies were: Allied-Lyons, Bass, Courage, Guinness, IDV, S&N, Seagram and Whitbread. See *Brewing Review*, January 1990, p. 11, and The Portman Group, *A Strategy for Sensible Drinking* (1992).

10 Some of the smaller independents were active in the NAB and LAB developments, e.g. Elgood and Shepherd Neame. See *Brewing Review*, January 1990, p. 6.

three years later, in May 1984. Both were supported by witty advertising campaigns. In addition, more limited market penetration was achieved by Budweiser, the leading brand of the American brewing giant, Anheuser-Busch, which became a popular packaged beer in association with Watneys/Grand Met from 1985, and Miller Lite, brewed and distributed by Courage from 1986.[11] The market-share of both draught and bottled beers declined slowly, while beer sold in cans almost doubled its share from 10 per cent in 1979 to nearly 20 per cent by 1990 (Table 14.3). This trend was assisted by the development of a 'draught beer in a can' or 'in-can system' (ICS). Pioneered by Guinness in 1988, and followed by Whitbread (Boddingtons'), Bass and others, this technological innovation produced canned beer which sought to replicate the type of beer served in a pub.[12]

II

The basic structure of the industry remained much as it had been in the 1970s, although there were echoes of the late 1950s in corporate responses to recession and falling demand. These took the form of additional rationalisation moves, and changes of ownership at the conglomerate level. The six large, pub-owning brewers retained their identities and strengthened their market-position. By 1985 Allied, Bass, Courage, Scottish & Newcastle, Watneys and Whitbread accounted for about 76 per cent of UK brewing turnover and 73 per cent of production, and owned 73 per cent of the industry's tied houses (Table 14.4). There were also two major brewers without a tied estate: Guinness; and Carlsberg, which maintained its links with Watneys/Grand Met but was from 1975 a wholly owned subsidiary of United Breweries (Carlsberg and Tuborg) of Copenhagen. If these are added to the Big Six, then the top eight companies accounted for no less than 85 per cent

[11] Citicorp, *Brewers Today*, 1987, pp. 13, 15–16; *The Brewer*, *passim*; MMC, *Elders IXL Ltd and Allied-Lyons PLC: A Report on the Proposed Merger*, September 1986, *PP* (1985–6) Cmnd.9892, p. 28. Fosters was brewed under licence from Carlton and United Breweries (taken over by Elders IXL in 1983), Castlemaine XXXX under licence from Castlemaine Tooheys.

[12] Different technologies have been developed to produce 'draught beer in a can'. Generally, beer is packaged in a mixed-gas system of carbon dioxide and nitrogen. The carbon dioxide content is lower than is usual in canned beer, being more typical of that found in draught beer. The added nitrogen maintains in-can pressure and produces a relatively stable creamy head. Several of the developed technologies involve the use of an ICS (in-can system). This is a plastic insert or 'widget' which promotes small bubble formation.

of total turnover in 1985 and 81 per cent of production.[13] For one company, however, stability was somewhat illusory. Courage experienced the more disconcerting effects of being part of a multi-product conglomerate, when its owners, Imperial Group, were acquired by Hanson Trust in April 1986. Within seven months Hanson sold on the brewing assets to Elders IXL of Australia, owners of the Fosters brand.[14]

As demand fell rationalisation of brewing capacity became more urgent. The number of established breweries fell from 142 in 1980 to 117 in 1986, a reduction of 18 per cent.[15] Closures were particularly evident in Whitbread, which had not pruned its productive units very vigorously before 1980, but closed half of its sixteen breweries in the space of three years (1981–4). Elsewhere Allied-Lyons shut its Ansells (Birmingham) plant in 1981, Courage closed four breweries in 1980–4, Grand Met (Watney Mann & Truman) shut its Norwich and Manchester (Wilson's) breweries in 1985 and 1986 respectively, and Scottish & Newcastle ceased brewing at its Holyrood site in Edinburgh in 1986.[16] The numbers employed in the production side of the industry (including malting) were also pruned substantially. There were only 35,300 in 1986, half that in 1973 and 34 per cent below the figure for 1980. Further productivity gains meant that net output per employee (in constant prices) increased by a third, 1980–6.[17] Diversification was also pursued more energetically by the large companies, particularly in wines and spirits, food, and general retailing, though by no means all of these transactions remained permanent. Guinness, for example, which had discarded a number of peripheral ventures, concentrated its efforts on spirits by acquiring Bells Whisky in 1985 and Distillers in the following year. It also obtained assets in health foods and spas and in newspaper and general retailing (Martins, Meeson, McColl). Whitbread

13 The 'Brewer Without a Tied Estate' category was isolated by the MMC in its 1989 Report. The other BWTE was the Northern Clubs Federation Brewery. Harp Lager, which by the mid-1980s was 75 per cent owned by Guinness, was not distinguished separately by the MMC.

14 *Courage News*, May and October 1986.

15 BS, *Statistical Handbook 1991*, p. 79. Numbers are for breweries established before 1 January 1971.

16 In addition, Allied closed two plants in Edinburgh after acquisition: Lorimer (Vaux) in 1980 and Drybrough in 1986. The closed Courage breweries were at Reading (Bridge Street, 1980, following the move to the Berkshire Brewery), London (Horsleydown, 1981), Newark (1983) and Plymouth (1984). CAMRA, *Good Beer Guide*, *passim*, and esp. *1985*, p. 35; Sheppards Research, *Decades of Change*, June 1990, p. 8.

17 Net output per employee: 1980: £3,686; 1986: £4,862 (in constant 1958 prices). See Appendix, Table XIV, and CSO Business Monitor, *Census of Production: Brewing and Malting*, 1989, PA427, p. 8.

Table 14.4. *Corporate structure of brewing, 1985–6 (selected companies ranked by turnover)*

Company	Turnover (£m) 1986	Profits before tax (£m) 1986	Tied houses (no.) 1986	Estimated production (barrels) 1985
1. Major pub-owning (6):	9,328 [76%]		33,608 [73%]	26,884,000 [73%]
Bass	2,710	310.4	7,405	8,369,000
Watneys[a]	1,858	n.a.	6,222	3,210,000
Whitbread	1,554	158.9	6,464	4,020,000
Allied[b]	1,539	157.5	6,748	4,676,000
Courage[c]	839	102.7	5,012	3,170,000
Scottish & Newcastle	828	90.3	1,757	3,439,000
2. Brewers without tied estate (3):	1,127 [9%]		nil [0%]	3,141,000 [9%]
Guinness[d]	932	72.0	nil	1,400,000
Carlsberg	195	34.6	nil	1,500,000
3. Regional (12):	1,210 [10%]		7,561 [16%]	4,556,000 [12%]
Greenall Whitley	387	35.3	1,695	1,100,000
Vaux	164	17.5	577	540,000
Wolverhampton & Dudley	113	18.7	729	525,000
Greene King	94	12.5	764	288,000
Boddingtons'	87	14.4	516	390,000
Marston, Thompson & Evershed	72	11.4	841	400,000

4. Local (41):	605 [5%]		4,822 [10%]	2,120,000 [6%]
Hall & Woodhouse (Blandford)	58	3.8	169	300,000
Young (Wandsworth)	41	3.6	139	180,000
Burtonwood (Warrington)	31	2.7	280	120,000
Eldridge Pope (Dorchester)	29	3.3	181	90,000
Wadworth (Devizes)	18	1.9	138	80,000
Joseph Holt (Manchester)	11	3.3	93	80,000
Adnams (Southwold)	10	0.9	64	50,000
Maclay (Alloa)	8	0.5	28	20,000
Hook Norton (nr. Banbury)	3	0.3	31	20,00C
Batham (Brierley Hill)	n.a.	n.a.	8	3,00C

[a] Data for Watney Mann & Truman plus Consumer Services (Grand Met).
[b] Allied Breweries Divn of Allied-Lyons.
[c] Imperial Brewing & Leisure, 11 months only to 27 Sept. 1986 (Hanson Trust/Elders IXL).
[d] Data for Guinness Brewing activity only.

Source: MMC, *The Supply of Beer*, March 1989, *PP* (1989–90) Cm.951 (Matthew Brown separated from S&N), supported by additional information drawn from Citicorp, *Brewers Today*, 1987; Flemings Research, *Directory of Regional Brewers*, September 1988; L. Messel, *Directory of Regional Brewers*, November 1985, December 1987.

moved strongly into restaurants with Beefeater, Pizza Hut (a joint venture with PepsiCo), and TGI Friday. Courage/Imperial also diversified, building up the Harvester, Happy Eater and Welcome Break catering chains together with Finlays the newsagents. Bass and Scottish & Newcastle developed their hotel chains, Crest and Thistle. With the beer market sluggish, it clearly made sense to diversify into other leisure and related activities, even if in the late 1980s corporate strategies often changed and many of these acquired assets were disposed of or exchanged.[18]

For the other brewers, it was a major challenge to hold on to market-share given the dullness of overall demand and the increasing importance in national sales of lager and the take-home trade, which favoured the larger companies. Unsurprisingly, their numbers diminished further after 1980. In that year there were eighty-one companies; six years later, the number had fallen to sixty-eight. Of these, eight were large, and twelve could be considered regional brewers, leaving the others as local concerns. The twelve regionals, which included companies such as Greenall Whitley, Marston, Vaux and Wolverhampton & Dudley (see Table 14.4), accounted for about 12 per cent of production and 10 per cent of sales, though their reputation for traditional bitter gave them a higher share (18 per cent) of ale production.[19] Then came fifty or so local brewers (the Monopolies and Mergers Commission (MMC) in fact identified forty-one in this category), with 6 per cent of production and 5 per cent of turnover. These companies ranged from fairly sizeable concerns such as Tollemache & Cobbold, Samuel Smith and Burtonwood, which owned 300 or so public houses each, to quite small ones, such as Batham of Brierley Hill and Donnington of Stow-on-the-Wold, which were not much larger than the largest of the micro-breweries (see p. 591). In fact by 1985 the industry had wel-

[18] Guinness sold its newsagents and health foods business in 1987. Hanson sold Harvester and Happy Eater to Trust House Forte in 1986. Bass sold Crest Hotels to Trust House Forte and bought Holiday Inns in 1990. Whitbread bought James Burroughs (distillers) in 1987, integrated it with its existing distilling business, Long John International, then sold the assets to Allied-Lyons in 1989. Scottish & Newcastle sold Thistle Hotels and bought Centre Parcs (holiday villages) in 1989. Information from Company Reports and Accounts. Bass was also prominent in betting shops (Coral, 1981) and AWPs (Barcrest, Paymaster).

[19] MMC, *Supply of Beer*, 1989, Cm.651, p. 17 (Matthew Brown was included as part of S&N in the MMC analysis, although the merger did not take place until 1987; the two companies' data have been separated here, with Matthew Brown included in the regional category). Note that the MMC published sales data which gave the regionals a 12 per cent share (presumably 13 per cent with Matthew Brown). The regionals not listed in Table 14.4 were: Matthew Brown, Cameron, Devenish, Mansfield, Robinson and Thwaites.

comed several new entrants, in both production and retailing. About 175 brewing publicans and micro-breweries had been attracted into the trade by the fashion among beer-drinking aficionados for 'real ale'. The newcomers, with echoes of the Victorian publican brewer, were a mixed bunch. At one end of the scale there were the home-brew pubs, about eighty in 1985, many of whom used malt extract in their brewing process; at the other there were more substantial enterprises, including David Bruce's chain of seven 'Firkin' pubs in London, and brewers such as Ringwood in Hampshire (1978), Butcombe in Avon (1978), Archers of Swindon (1979), Woodforde in Norfolk (1981), and Banks & Taylor (Shefford, Bedfordshire) and Burton Bridge (both 1982). The latter enterprises supplied beer not only to two or three tied houses each but also to 30–100 free-trade customers.[20] However, their aggregate production was very small, probably no more than 0.25 per cent of total production in 1985.[21] Clearly they posed no threat to the major companies.

The years after 1980 also saw a resurgence of merger activity. Many transactions were agreed between the parties, but it was the unsuccessful bids, three of which were referred to the MMC, which caught the eye (see Table 14.5). Declining demand made all brewers aware of the need to 'protect the mash tun', i.e. maintain production, by increasing the number of retail outlets. The large brewers could do this in a number of ways, for example by selling heavily advertised national brands in the free and take-home trades. But regional brewers, with their more limited resources, were encouraged to employ the traditional method of protecting output, that is the purchase of smaller companies for their public houses. Thus, in 1982–4 there were significant acquisitions by companies in the North-West, Boddingtons', Matthew Brown, Robinson and Thwaites, and in the Midlands by Marston, although Wolverhampton & Dudley's attempt to swallow Davenport was thwarted. In 1985 Boddingtons' and Mansfield made sizeable purchases, while Davenport was acquired by Greenall Whitley (Table 14.5). Corporate defensiveness was once again the order of the day, particularly among the smaller brewers vulnerable to a bid.

The moves which provoked most anxiety in regulatory circles involved the national brewers. Of these, Scottish & Newcastle was in the

20 CAMRA, *Good Beer Guide 1986*; Brian Glover, 'The Growth of the Micro-Breweries', in Roger Protz and Tony Millns (eds.), *Called to the Bar: An Account of the First 21 Years of the Campaign for Real Ale* (St Albans, 1992), pp. 101–7.

21 Estimated from information in *Good Beer Guide 1986*.

Table 14.5. *Brewing bids and mergers, 1982–6*

Year	Bidding company	Subject of bid	Result	Price	No. of pubs
1982	Boddingtons'	Oldham	Acquired	£23m	84
	Robinson	Hartley	Acquired	£?	55
1983	Wolv. & Dudley	Davenports	Contested/failed		
1984	S&N	Cameron	Lapsed on MMC ref.		
	Matthew Brown	Theakston	Acquired	£3m	6
	Marston	Border	Acquired	£13m	170
	Thwaites	Yates & Jackson	Acquired	£7m	39
1985	S&N	Matthew Brown	Contested/referred (MMC)/Failed[a]		
	Mansfield	North Country	Acquired	£42m	225
	Boddingtons'	Higson	Acquired	£28m	160
	Greenall Whitley	Simpkiss	Acquired	£2m	15
	Elders IXL	Allied-Lyons	Contested/referred (MMC)/Failed		
1986	Devenish	Inn Leisure	Merger	£30m	–
	Greenall Whitley	Davenports	Acquired	£38m	123
	S&N	Home	Acquired	£120m	457
	Grand Met	Ruddle	Acquired	£13m	0
	Elders IXL	Courage	Acquired	£1,400m	5,012

[a] Matthew Brown acquired by S&N in 1987.
Source: The Brewer; misc. analysts' reports.

most vulnerable position, since it was by far the smallest in terms of public houses owned (about 1,350 in 1983). In 1984 it attempted to acquire its North-East neighbour, Cameron, but withdrew the proposal when it was referred to the MMC. In the following year it turned its attention to Matthew Brown of Blackburn, but this bid, which was also referred to the MMC, was fiercely resisted by the latter. The company was finally successful in 1986 when it bought Home Brewery of Nottingham with 450 pubs in 1986, and, having obtained the blessing of the MMC, took over Matthew Brown at the second attempt at the end of 1987. The attitude of the MMC had been made plain when it cleared the Scottish & Newcastle bid for Matthew Brown in November 1985. Stating that 'in the interests of healthy competition ... it [was] desirable that there should continue to be viable and vigorous regional brewers', it could find 'no material advantages to the public interest arising from the proposed merger'. On the other hand, the Commission conceded that 'the question before us is whether the merger may be expected to operate against the public interest, and in our view there are not sufficient grounds for such an expectation'.[22] Similar anxieties, reinforced by concern about merger strategies which rested on heavy borrowing, were provoked by the intervention in the British market of the Australian brewing conglomerate, Elders IXL. In November 1985 it launched an ambitious bid for Allied-Lyons, having built up a 6 per cent stake. The proposal was referred to the MMC, which, reporting in September 1986, took ten months to decide that it was not against the public interest. But Allied-Lyons defeated the bid, taking pre-emptive action by acquiring the Canadian spirits company Hiram Walker. In the meantime Elders had turned its attention to Courage (Imperial Brewing), which it agreed to buy from Hanson Trust for £1.4 billion in September 1986. This undoubtedly helped to shape the agenda for the MMC inquiry into the level of competitiveness in the industry in 1986–9.[23]

Concern about increased concentration in brewing was combined with a continuing interest in retail price trends to stimulate government enquiries into the role of tied houses in maintaining brewers' incomes in a flat market. The contention of the Price Commission in 1977 that the larger brewers exerted price leadership via their managed public houses was repeated in the 1980s, for example by the MMC when considering the S&N/Matthew Brown merger proposal in 1985.[24] And the government's concern about competitiveness in retailing was given added emphasis by the European Commission's continuing interest in the structure of brewing at the retail level. When Britain joined the European Economic Community in 1972 exclusive purchasing agreements – the 'tie' – were permitted under Regulation 67/67 of 1967, renewed in 1972, which granted specified industries, including brewing, 'block exemption' from Article 85 (1) of the Treaty of Rome. In the 1970s the EEC undertook extensive further inquiries into conditions in all countries; these included an investigation of the British case in 1974–5. Although 'block exemption' was renewed by Regulation 1984/83 of July

22 MMC, *Scottish & Newcastle Breweries PLC and Matthew Brown PLC: A Report on the Proposed Merger*, November 1985, *PP* (1985–6) Cmnd.9645, pp. 64, 67.

23 The purchase was completed in November 1986. MMC, *Elders IXL Ltd and Allied-Lyons PLC: A Report on the Proposed Merger*, September 1986, *PP* (1985–6) Cmnd.9892, p. 88; *Elders IXL Ltd and Grand Metropolitan PLC: A Report on the Merger Situations*, October 1990, *PP* (1990–1) Cm.1227, p. 24; S. J. Gray and M. C. McDermot, *Mega-Merger Mayhem: Takeover Strategies, Battles and Controls* (1989), pp. 75–85.

24 MMC, *Scottish & Newcastle*, 1985, Cmnd.9645, p. 9.

1983, and the EC accepted the argument that the tied system made beer distribution more efficient, the long period of investigation, coupled with the hearing of a case on the tie before the European Court of Justice in 1976–7 – the 'Concordia' case[25] – made the industry nervous. And the renewal (until 1997) of block exemption was made subject to specified conditions. These were: first, that the maximum duration of an exclusive tie for beer was to be ten years (or the length of the tenancy if longer); second, that where other specified drinks were tied the maximum duration was to be five years (or the length of the tenancy if longer); third, that products other than drinks could not be tied. Tenants were free to use alternative sources of supply for all drinks except beer where more advantageous conditions could be obtained; they were also free to buy special packaged beers and even non-tied draught beers from outside suppliers under certain circumstances. The Regulation did not come into force until 1 January 1989, but all new agreements signed from 1 January 1984 were subject to it.[26]

In government circles, the regulation was welcomed as encouraging more competition in brewing retailing, but there is no doubt that it added to the existing instability in the marketing environment. The growth in popularity of lager, and the emergence of market 'segments' – average gravity, premium gravity and specialist beers – stimulated competition through the promotion of new brands, coupled with public house investment. The continuing debate about the advantages and disadvantages of the tie was an additional stimulus. The large brewers paid particular attention to the promotion of their draught lager brands in a period of sluggish demand. They also strove to maintain and improve public house standards in order to retain customers, the larger pub-owners aiming particular houses at specified segments of the drinking public (the so-called 'theme-pub'). Investment in brewery-owned pubs was indeed substantial during the 1980s: £2,655 million, 1981–6

[25] The case concerned a twenty-five-year loan-tie agreement of 1966 between the Concordia Brewery of Belgium and the proprietors of a café. New owners attempted to buy outside the tie, appealing to Article 85 of the Rome Treaty. The European Court found in the brewery's favour, ruling that agreements to which two undertakings from one Member State were party benefited from block exemption in the same way as agreements between parties in different Member States. See BS Competition Sub-Committee Papers, 1976–7.

[26] See summaries in MMC, *Scottish & Newcastle*, 1985, Cmnd.9645, Appendix 2.3, and *Elders IXL*, 1986, Cmnd.9892, Appendix 4.3. Tenants could buy draught beer outside the tie if it was a customary practice, or, if a new decision, did not result in a fall in sales of beers covered by the tie.

(at 1987 prices).[27] There was also a more ruthless attitude to outlets with a low turnover, a policy reinforced by the rise in property values during the mid-1980s boom and later by the fall in income during the post-1989 recession.

III

This long view of the British brewing industry over a century and a half has highlighted the persistence of issues which were as pressing in 1980 (and indeed 1986) as they were in 1830. Indeed, the opinion of one industrial analyst in 1988 that 'The UK brewing industry is currently very much at the cross-roads'[28] could have been advanced equally well in 1830, 1907–9, 1915, 1932, 1959 or 1969. Common elements at all these dates include brewers' anxieties about government regulation, the excise, the changing level of demand, and the maintenance of public house custom. Public anxieties, expressed through government and other bodies, have also shown continuity: prices, particularly pub prices; the implications for the consumer of the emergence of large brewing companies and a higher degree of integration, vertical and horizontal; and, periodically, the behavioural and health effects of alcohol. Yet there must be doubts about the value of this regulatory activity despite its abundance – there were no fewer than fifteen official reports in the twenty years 1966–86, a state of 'perpetual audit' equal to any experienced by a nationalised industry.[29] For example, most of the inquiries neglected the fact that high levels of horizontal concentration were characteristic of brewing industries in nearly all mature economies. Indeed, by international standards Britain's horizontal concentration was comparatively modest; and the choice of beer brands was much bigger than that available to consumers in Australia, Canada and the United States, where concentration was considerable and the 'tie' was prohibited.[30] Furthermore, the British consumer by and large did not share the official outrage during those periods when beer prices outpaced the retail price index. Consumer preferences were not shaped

[27] Paragon Communications (for BS), *The Brewing Industry: Leading Leisure in Britain* (1989), p. 8.

[28] Goldman Sachs International Research, *The UK Brewer*, May 1988, p. 11.

[29] There were five MC/MMC reports, seven from NBPI/PC, one from NEDO, and the Erroll and Clayson reports. The term 'perpetual audit' was coined by Sir Peter Parker when referring to experience of British Rail. Gourvish, *British Railways*, 1986, p. 570.

[30] In Britain the top three companies have a market-share of about 50 per cent. This is to be compared with Australia (top two: 90 percent), Canada (three: 96 per cent), USA (five: 91 per cent), Belgium (two: 90 per cent) and France (three: 82 per cent).

merely by a narrow consideration of relative prices. Change stemmed more from a variety of market forces than from government intervention. The increase, for example, in the free and take-home trades reduced the importance of the brewer-owned pub. By 1986 it accounted for only about 46 per cent of beer sales and represented only 32 per cent of the total number of on-licensed premises and clubs.[31]

One of our major themes, then, is the interplay between profit-making enterprise (and brewing by and large has been a very profitable activity despite periods of recession and uncertainty) and the social regulation of a popular alcoholic drink. But another is the long-standing tension between supply and demand, which has sometimes retarded the progress of the industry in an economic sense. For the producing companies, the economics of brewing have increasingly favoured the large-scale production of a smaller number of uniform, stable beers, and their distribution over a considerable market-area. Although this has been accepted happily by many consumers, there are others for whom the essential ingredient in beer drinking is a choice of distinctive beers from a multiplicity of local or regional sources. A similar tension exists in distribution and retailing. Economies of scale in production have not been easy to replicate in distribution; but, in any case, cask-conditioned beers do not travel well in comparison with brewery-conditioned beers. And attempts to apply uniformity, and presumably scale economies, to chains of public houses have sometimes foundered on the rock of consumer resistance, with its appeals to the retention of the 'traditional local'. It is quite clear that beer drinking, while naturally subject to social trends, changing tastes and mass-production and marketing, not only remains a major feature of Britain's way of life, but can also defy the simpler prescriptions of the brewing accountant and economist. This fact is important in an industry where the corporate culture has changed considerably since the Second World War. For two centuries brewing for retail sale was an investment and an occupation for gentlemen; now, like publishing, which in some ways it resembles, it has been transformed by mergers and market change, and is dominated by accountants, business strategists and management consultants.

In 1986 the MMC inquiry into the trade promised to upset the industry's cornerstone, the tied house system. Its majority report in March 1989 concluded that a 'complex monopoly' existed in brewing which operated against the public interest and that the degree of vertical

[31] BS, *Statistical Handbook 1991*, p. 54; Barclays de Zoete Wedd Research, *UK – Brewing*, December 1988.

integration should be reduced in order to encourage lower retail prices and improved consumer choice. The MMC recommended that no brewer should tie more than 2,000 on-licensed outlets, anticipating the disposal of some 22,000 properties worth £7 billion; that public house tenants should be free to buy a 'guest' draught beer outside the tie, together with all non-beer drinks, low-alcohol and alcohol-free beers; and that there should be no new tied loans.[32] The Department of Trade and Industry endorsed the report and shortly afterwards confirmed the MMC's opposition to a proposed merger of Elders (Courage) and Scottish & Newcastle.[33] The industry condemned the proposals as a 'charter for chaos', arguing that the MMC had failed to understand the market and that its proposals would damage smaller brewers quite as much as larger ones and result in a substantial reduction in the number of public houses.[34]

After considerable wrangling the government watered down the MMC's proposals. Nevertheless, its two Beer Orders of December 1989 promised a radical reform of the industry's integrative structure. The first addressed the loan-tie. It required brewers to allow the recipients of loans to give three months' notice of termination and prohibited the sale of licensed premises with restrictions on their use.[35] The second required brewers owning more than 2,000 full on-licences either to dispose of their brewery business or to dispose of or free the tie on *half* of the number in excess of 2,000 (about 11,000 properties in all) by 31 October 1992. From 1 May 1990 the same brewers were required to allow tied premises to sell a 'guest' cask-conditioned draught beer and to buy non-beer drinks and alcohol-free and low-alcohol beers outside the tie. The Order also applied to groups of companies related by equity

[32] MMC, *Supply of Beer*, 1989, Cm.651, pp. 283, 288, 293–4. The report also recommended greater protection for tenants, the removal of restrictions on future use when on-licensed premises were sold, and a requirement that brewers publish and adhere to wholesale price lists. A minority report (strictly, a 'note of dissent') from the trade union representative, L. A. Mills, expressed opposition to the public house and loan-tie recommendations.

[33] MMC, *Elders IXL Ltd and Scottish & Newcastle Breweries PLC: A Report on the Merger Situation*, March 1989, *PP* (1988–9) Cm.654; Francis Maude (Parliamentary Under-Secretary of State, Corporate Affairs), written answer, 21 March 1989, *Parl. Deb. (Commons)*, 6th ser. vol. 149 (Session 1988–9), c. 494–5; Lord Young (Secretary of State, Trade & Industry), 14 June 1989, *Parl. Deb. (Lords)*, 5th ser. vol. 508 (Session 1988–9), c. 1431–5; Francis Maude, written answer, 26 May 1989, *Parl. Deb. (Commons)*, 6th ser. vol. 153 (Session 1988–9), c. 775.

[34] BS, Press Release, 21 March 1989.

[35] *The Supply of Beer (Loan Ties, Licensed Premises and Wholesale Prices) Order 1989*, SI 1989 No. 2258, 1 December 1989. The Order also required brewers to publish wholesale price lists for beer.

holdings of 15 per cent or more; this was a move to prevent circumvention of the Order by demerging, but it was also a tilt at the 'umbrella' holdings of companies such as Whitbread.[36]

The effects of the Orders, reinforced by recession and the collapse of the property market, may well be substantial. At the time of writing, the responses have taken several forms. There has been: a proposal to create a substantial merger (Allied-Carlsberg);[37] a major exchange of breweries and pubs by Grand Met and Fosters Brewing Group (Elders); a cessation of brewing by leading regional brewers (Boddingtons', Greenall Whitley and Devenish);[38] a series of brewery closures;[39] heightened tension between the landlords and tenants of public houses; a considerable number of public house closures; and rising retail prices.[40] All this suggests a substantial threat to the long-standing link between brewing production and retailing, one of the major themes in this history. It also underlines the fact that the government's intervention, however well intentioned, was probably ill conceived, as so often before, and has failed to heed some of the most crucial features of the industry.

Since on these recent matters we lack the historian's customary weapon, hindsight, we can offer little more than the observation that only time will tell whether the present crisis facing the trade will turn out to be worse than that perceived at the time of the Beer Act of 1830, or during the temperance attacks of the late-Victorian period. It may well be that current difficulties will seem modest in comparison with the disastrous results of the speculative boom at the turn of the century, or with Lloyd George's attacks upon the trade in 1908–16. What is clear is that brewing has frequently attracted government intervention because it manufactures a popular but potentially hazardous drink and has been a major source of government revenue since the sixteenth century. In the post-war period government interest has intensified chiefly because there has been more anxiety about the degree of horizontal and vertical integration. Indeed, over the twentieth century as a whole, change has

36 *The Supply of Beer (Tied Estate) Order 1989*, SI 1989 No. 2390, 19 December 1989.

37 This has now been confirmed.

38 Boddingtons' sold its Manchester and Liverpool breweries to Whitbread in 1989, having closed its Oldham plant in 1988. Greenall Whitley ceased brewing at its three breweries in 1990–1. Devenish sold its brewery in a MBO in 1991.

39 Bass closed Runcorn and Wolverhampton in 1991; Whitbread closed Salford (1989) and Faversham (1990), in addition to Wethered's (Marlow) in 1988. Scottish & Newcastle closed the Matthew Brown (Blackburn) brewery in 1990, in addition to Carlisle (1987) and Workington (1988), and Grand Met shut the Truman Brick Lane plant in 1988.

40 Beer prices rose by 20 per cent in real terms, 1987–91. MMC, *Allied-Lyons PLC and Carlsberg A/S: A Report on the Proposed Joint Venture*, July 1992, *PP* (1991–2) Cm.2029, p. 31.

been more rapid in relation to corporate concentration, the creation of national brands, the disappearance of companies and their beers, and the fragmentation of drinking habits at the retail level. But the basic elements have endured. Beer drinking and pubs remain popular. In spite of substantial changes – catering, juke boxes, discos and AWP machines – the pub is still 'the best run outlet for selling beer anywhere in the world'.[41] Although far fewer in number than in 1830, there are still determined independent brewers producing distinctive beers; and, in spite of the flight from mild ale and the increasing popularity of lager, there is still a considerable variety in the types of beer brewed in Britain. The essential diversity in the industry in production and marketing can still be discerned, even if it has been tempered by recent developments.

41 Charles Tidbury (Whitbread), cited in Asa Briggs, 'Beer and Society: A Major Theme in English History', *The Brewer*, August 1983, p. 318.

Appendix

Table I. *Beer consumption and expenditure in England and Wales, 1831–1913*

Year	Output[a] (million gallons)	Gallons per capita	Total expenditure[b] (£m)	Expenditure per capita (£)	Real Wages (allowing for unemployment) 1850=100
1831	470	33.6	35.3	2.52	–
1832	463	32.7	34.7	2.45	–
1833	480	33.5	36.0	2.51	–
1834	518	35.7	38.9	2.68	–
1835	534	36.3	40.0	2.72	–
1836	553	37.0	41.5	2.78	–
1837	523	34.6	39.2	2.60	–
1838	527	34.5	39.5	2.58	–
1839	532	34.3	39.9	2.57	–
1840	527	33.5	39.5	2.51	–
1841	489	30.7	36.7	2.30	–
1842	479	29.7	35.9	2.23	–
1843	475	29.1	35.6	2.18	–
1844	491	29.7	36.8	2.23	–
1845	493	29.5	37.0	2.21	–
1846	537	31.7	40.3	2.38	–
1847	490	28.6	36.8	2.15	–
1848	491	28.3	36.8	2.12	–
1849	494	28.1	37.1	2.11	–
1850	501	28.2	37.6	2.12	100
1851	534	29.7	40.1	2.23	102
1852	543	29.9	40.7	2.24	100
1853	582	31.6	43.7	2.37	107
1854	528	28.4	39.6	2.13	97
1855	500	26.5	37.5	1.99	94

Table I. (*cont.*)

Year	Output[a] (million gallons)	Gallons per capita	Total expenditure[b] (£m)	Expenditure per capita (£)	Real Wages (allowing for unemployment) 1850=100
1856	550	28.9	41.3	2.17	95
1857	582	30.2	43.7	2.27	94
1858	580	29.8	43.5	2.23	94
1859	610	31.0	45.8	2.33	104
1860	648	32.6	48.6	2.44	105
1861	610	30.3	45.8	2.28	99
1862	629	30.9	47.2	2.32	100
1863	644	31.2	48.3	2.34	107
1864	694	33.2	52.1	2.49	118
1865	745	35.2	55.9	2.64	120
1866	806	37.7	60.5	2.83	117
1867	769	35.5	57.7	2.66	105
1868	781	35.6	58.6	2.67	105
1869	791	35.6	59.3	2.67	111
1870	795	35.3	59.6	2.65	118
1871	832	36.5	62.4	2.74	125
1872	894	38.7	67.1	2.91	126
1873	933	39.9	70.0	2.99	132
1874	965	40.7	72.4	3.05	136
1875	983	40.9	73.7	3.07	138
1876	1,028	42.2	77.1	3.16	136
1877	1,017	41.2	76.3	3.09	132
1878	1,018	40.7	76.4	3.05	128
1879	952	37.5	71.4	2.81	126
1880	977	38.0	73.3	2.85	132
1881	863	33.1	64.7	2.48	136
1882	870	33.0	65.3	2.48	138
1883	843	31.7	63.2	2.37	142
1884	872	32.4	65.4	2.43	138
1885	886	32.5	66.5	2.44	140
1886	888	32.3	66.6	2.42	142
1887	903	32.4	67.7	2.43	149
1888	904	32.1	67.8	2.41	155
1889	939	33.0	70.4	2.47	161
1890	976	33.9	73.2	2.54	169
1891	989	34.0	74.2	2.55	166
1892	984	33.4	73.8	2.51	159
1893	984	33.1	73.8	2.48	161

Table I. (*cont.*)

Year	Output[a] (million gallons)	Gallons per capita	Total expenditure[b] (£m)	Expenditure per capita (£)	Real Wages (allowing for unemployment) 1850=100
1894	986	32.8	74.0	2.46	165
1895	999	32.8	75.0	2.46	170
1896	1,049	34.1	78.7	2.55	177
1897	1,081	34.7	81.1	2.60	176
1898	1,105	35.1	82.9	2.63	176
1899	1,142	35.8	85.7	2.69	183
1900	1,117	34.6	83.8	2.60	184
1901	1,092	33.5	81.9	2.51	181
1902	1,086	33.0	81.5	2.47	176
1903	1,078	32.2	80.5	2.42	–
1904	1,053	31.3	79.0	2.35	–
1905	1,023	30.1	76.7	2.26	–
1906	1,037	30.2	77.8	2.27	–
1907	1,030	29.7	77.3	2.23	–
1908	1,006	28.7	75.5	2.15	–
1909	977	27.6	73.3	2.07	–
1910	990	27.7	74.3	2.08	–
1911	1,027	28.4	77.0	2.13	–
1912	1,013	27.9	76.0	2.09	–
1913	1,050	28.7	78.8	2.15	–

Notes:

[a] Output is given in standard barrels to 1899, bulk barrels, 1900–13. Wilson's observation (p. 58) was that the standard gravity of 1055° was near the average brewed before 1900: 'it is probable that the "bulk" barrelage did not greatly exceed the "standard" barrelage prior to that date'. These are not *consumption* figures; therefore exports (the figures are incomplete before 1840) are subtracted from output totals; imports (negligible before 1880) are added after 1880. No calculation can be made of the net trade balance in beer with Scotland and Ireland: it was increasingly negative.

[b] Total expenditure is calculated on two premises. First, that the price of beer did not change between 1830 and 1914. A. R. Prest based his calculations upon this fact when he estimated expenditure upon alcohol from 1870 to 1914 (*Consumers' Expenditure in the United Kingdom, 1900–1919*, pp. 75–88). Reid's London brewery recorded only three changes between 1830 and 1887 when after 11 October 1830 porter was reduced from 45s to 33s per barrel. In 1846 the firm failed to make a price increase of 5s stick (31 Dec. 1846–8 Feb. 1847); during the Crimean War prices were advanced by 3s a barrel (11 May 1854–23 June 1856); in 1887 it was reduced by 3s to 30s. The London porter brewers advanced and

Notes to Table I (*cont.*)

lowered prices in unison. Secondly, estimates are made on the average price of 1s 6d per gallon. Prest's calculations are based upon one of 1s 8d per gallon (p. 78). He selected this with no great conviction: contemporaries, partly motivated by the strength of their temperance convictions, varied between 1s 4d, 1s 6d and 1s 8d. I have selected the middle price; 1s 8d per gallon is certainly too high for the pre-1870 period. Porter and cheap mild sold wholesale for 33s a barrel throughout the 1830–1914 period (less a 5 per cent discount). Charging 4d a quart pot or 1s 4d a gallon gave the publican a theoretical profit of 15s a barrel. Probably the major portion of English beer – the cheapest porter and mild – was sold at this price. But the new pale ales, stouts and 'old' beers were more expensive and consequently sold in smaller quantities: 1s 6d per gallon takes account of this, although after 1880 there was a growing tendency for drinkers to consume the more expensive brands, especially in the competitive London trade as publicans provided the 'long pull' (which in effect lowered prices by as much as 25 per cent in difficult trading conditions) and began to sell bottled beer on an appreciable scale.

Source: Wilson, *Alcohol and the Nation*, pp. 369–70; Mitchell and Deane, *Abstract*, pp. 8–10, 343–5.

Table II. *Bass's barrelage statement showing the cost, charges, proceeds and profit per barrel on 1,132,075 ¾ barrels brewed and the percentage of the cost, charges and profit to the total proceeds for the year ending 30 June 1908*

Credit			Average per Barrel	
Percentage of total proceeds		Cost	Uncontrollable	Controllable
		£ s d	s d	s d
17.784	To Cost of Bought and Own made Malt, Saccharum	588,363 12 1	10 4.734	
5.505	To Hops	182,115 11 9	3 2.609	
0.388	To Returned Ale	12,838 16 6		2.722
0.740	To Coal	24,489 9 7		5.191
14.570	To Excise Duty	482,026 11 6	8 6.189	
18.561	To Discount and Allowances	614,067 11 3	10 10.182	
0.885	To Bad Debts and Losses on Consignments	29,294 6 6		6.210
0.346	To Casks knocked down lost and depreciation	11,438 8 4		2.424
1.315	To Cask repairs painting and branding. Shives. Pegs	43,490 13 3		9.220
5.793	To Carriage of Ale to Customers and Agencies	191,544 16 7	3 4.632	
0.223	To Railway Expenses	7,384 5 4		1.566
1.530	To Depreciation of Freeholds and Leaseholds and exceptional expenditure written off	50,606 11 5		10.729

0.340	To Depreciation of Plant	11,256	18	4		2.386
1.655	To Repairs to Premises and Plant	54,756	11	4		11.609
0.166	To Expenses of Engineers' Department unapportioned	5,493	16	1		1.164
0.641	To Tools Implements and Stores Breweries, Middle Yard	21,202	14	5		4.494
1.562	To Salaries, Pensions and Gratuities (excluding Agency Department Salaries and Gratuities)	51,667	0	9		10.954
5.517	To Agency Expenses (excluding Advertising and Showcards)	182,542	14	4	3	2.700
0.154	To Travelling Expenses. Burton	5,085	0	1		1,078
2.351	To Wages, Breweries, Middle Yard, Forwarding and Sundries	77,777	12	1	1	4.488
0.392	To Allowance, Ale to Men – Breweries Middle Yard and Shobnall	12,985	7	11		2.753
0.447	To Horses Carts and Horsekeep	14,776	12	0		3.132
2.234	To Advertising and Showcards. Burton and Agencies	73,916	3	2	1	3.671
0.360	To Labels and Stationery	11,920	19	5		2.528
0.098	To Insurance	3,234	3	1		0.685
0.528	To Sundries	17,461	8	8		3.702
1.205	To Petty Cash and Income Tax	39,874	2	10		8.453
3.756	To Losses on Loans and Reserves	124,271	18	2	2	2.345
0.573	To Depreciation of Stocks and Shares	18,957	8	1		4.018
0.425	To Rents Payable	14,078	7	11		2.985
0.681	To Rates and Taxes and Compensation Fund Charges	22,545	16	9		4.780

Table II. (*cont*).

Credit				Average per Barrel	
Percentage of total proceeds			Cost	Uncontrollable	Controllable
			£ s d	s d	s d
0.357	To	Interest Payable	11,810 3 10		2.504
8.918	To	Profit	295,045 15 8		5 2.550
100.000			£3,308,432 9s	£1 16s 4.346d	£1 2s 1.041d
				£2 18s 5.387d	

Debit				
			Proceeds	Average per Barrel
			£ s d	£ s d
	By	Proceeds of Ale and Beer	3,138,216 13 3	2 15 5.302
	By	Proceeds of Grains	36,344 16 4	7.705
	By	Proceeds of Barm and Hops	2,808 8 10	0.595
	By	Excise Drawbacks	13,070 6 11	2.771
	By	Sundry Rents Receivable	44,833 5 10	9.505
	By	Interest and Dividends Receivable	73,097 4 4	1 3.496
	By	Transfer Fees	61 13 6	0.013
			£3,308,432 9s	£2 18s 5.387d

Source: Bass's Statistics, A/139, Bass Museum.

Table III. *Quantities and values of beer exported from and imported into the United Kingdom, 1830–1914*

Calendar year	Exports barrels	value (£)	Imports barrels	value (£)
1830	61,272	212,564	2,377	6,410
1831	53,058	161,768	1,962	5,360
1832	67,980	204,001	1,875	5,204
1833	69,774	206,935	1,860	4,943
1834	62,430	186,321	2,392	6,144
1835	77,274	229,824	3,172	8,150
1836	90,882	270,915	2,796	7,168
1837	93,528	273,122	4,056	9,889
1838	119,962	317,359	5,573	10,750
1839	135,078	384,324	2,693	6,863
1840	149,670	422,222	2,777	7,215
1841	148,099	360,420	2,730	6,945
1842	141,313	343,740	3,408	9,240
1843	146,339	383,131	3,701	10,204
1844	169,829	437,373	5,334	13,073
1845	156,743	439,066	3,474	9,559
1846	133,382	381,799	4,492	12,330
1847	134,004	403,759	4,028	11,071
1848	136,723	410,472	5,139	14,146
1849	135,691	418,325	4,629	12,751
1850	182,479	558,794	2,895	7,902
1851	190,777	577,142	3,339	9,217
1852	244,115	754,627	2,739	7,526
1853	377,857	1,291,357	3,354	9,229
1854	398,941	1,314,810	3,029	8,082
1855	384,718	1,398,885	2,444	6,457
1856	410,392	1,455,043	2,084	5,179
1857	435,334	1,592,267	3,123	6,903
1858	533,828	1,851,755	2,989	7,744
1859	614,136	2,116,373	3,238	8,569
1860	534,827	1,868,144	3,593	9,533
1861	378,461	1,411,205	3,030	7,707
1862	464,827	1,595,654	2,629	6,971
1863	491,631	1,746,238	1,567	10,051
1864	498,981	1,841,637	3,957	23,179
1865	561,907	2,060,976	3,279	30,498
1866	564,176	2,057,553	2,577	15,491
1867	518,838	1,910,850	2,699	15,771
1868	496,646	1,869,183	4,318	18,232
1869	495,110	1,892,716	3,387	16,748

Table III. (*cont.*)

Calendar year	Exports barrels	value (£)	Imports barrels	value (£)
1870	521,199	1,881,673	5,057	24,391
1871	483,120	1,853,733	4,265	22,311
1872	522,080	2,085,430	4,381	20,317
1873	584,939	2,422,020	4,888	23,441
1874	559,413	2,449,035	4,619	24,394
1875	504,511	2,094,672	4,739	24,808
1876	484,919	1,922,972	5,105	26,706
1877	460,818	1,901,399	5,965	28,788
1878	411,669	1,760,692	6,196	26,069
1879	412,392	1,755,331	7,183	28,135
1880	412,192	1,733,505	10,742	38,690
1881	421,651	1,727,337	13,945	44,111
1882	437,273	1,869,095	18,888	54,946
1883	456,109	1,820,259	22,289	59,615
1884	437,241	1,641,975	24,246	62,403
1885	436,765	1,645,333	23,348	60,786
1886	420,290	1,582,773	24,736	64,558
1887	440,867	1,678,360	27,068	72,150
1888	447,940	1,705,368	28,392	74,749
1889	495,926	1,857,946	33,184	86,191
1890	503,221	1,874,886	35,081	92,120
1891	462,519	1,694,567	38,265	96,786
1892	451,972	1,651,486	40,193	96,553
1893	414,650	1,508,885	43,763	105,660
1894	412,590	1,463,107	43,121	105,264
1895	432,742	1,523,703	44,399	108,088
1896	462,960	1,592,435	45,180	113,592
1897	470,827	1,621,472	46,177	116,834
1898	476,424	1,623,183	46,874	117,507
1899	485,032	1,663,555	50,680	132,101
1900	510,843	1,760,552	53,220	154,070
1901	522,889	1,782,898	56,127	163,843
1902	525,316	1,786,300	57,294	157,015
1903	510,896	1,749,783	56,329	154,956
1904	518,367	1,727,749	54,118	154,321
1905	520,990	1,722,210	56,605	153,430
1906	544,014	1,815,620	58,577	158,650
1907[a]	604,794	1,885,918	54,035	149,637
1908	551,051	1,697,703	56,470	160,535
1909	572,142	1,742,368	51,458	152,770
1910	590,346	1,793,185	55,028	158,007

Table III. (*cont.*)

Calendar year	Exports barrels	value (£)	Imports barrels	value (£)
1911	625,512	1,954,150	66,082	188,524
1912	670,293	2,158,184	65,870	190,983
1913	655,461	2,134,703	75,801	220,092
1914	539,269	1,769,378	63,280	182,213

Notes:
[a] From 1907 in barrels of 36 gallons at standard gravity of 1055°.
NB: Import figures 1830–86 represent total imports of beer including mum and spruce and all other sorts. Export figures for 1830–40 have been converted from tuns (216 gallons) into 36 gallon barrels as have import figures for 1830–64.
Source: For Exports, 1830–40 see Exports Ledgers, CUST 9/17–27 PRO; Exports 1841–1914 are from G. B. Wilson, *Alcohol and the Nation* (1940), Table 16, p. 373. For import figures 1830–87 see Import Ledgers CUST 5/19–137 *passim*, CUST 4/41 for 1854 only, PRO. For 1888–1914 see *Statistical Abstracts for the United Kingdom*, 49 (1902); 62 (1915).

Table IV. *Barrels of beer brewed by five leading London breweries, 1830–1914*

Year	Barclay Perkins	Truman Hanbury Buxton[a]	Mann, Crossman & Paulin	Reid's	Whitbread[b]
1830	262,252	171,978	....	132,366	....
1831	330,528	199,486	....	154,631	....
1832	343,328	234,665	....	166,515	204,455
1833	315,784	226,924	....	150,865	187,070
1834	343,569	254,650	....	169,246	180,474
1835	382,083	280,075	....	181,187	186,206
1836	378,109	329,333	....	194,656	190,005
1837	354,360	303,590	....	162,840	180,512
1838	375,466	310,193	....	178,919	179,975
1839	405,819	320,675	....	171,650	183,468
1840	400,838	338,773	....	195,169	191,980
1841	382,047	314,474	....	187,722	185,084
1842	395,871	327,939	....	186,672	185,895
1843	389,835	344,342	....	194,442	183,058
1844	378,502	325,516	....	189,808	190,526
1845	396,784	369,020	....	227,306	183,296
1846	417,659	384,555	....	239,655	194,029
1847	417,998	383,993	41,470	233,795	187,852
1848	398,691	383,353	86,230	205,892	184,930
1849	395,820	358,997	92,454	205,203	182,513
1850	397,360	388,475	97,802	213,345	177,555
1851	419,430	401,863	101,899	215,255	173,311
1852	420,475	379,119	110,390	219,519	176,097
1853	441,199	455,477	115,576	223,308	206,040
1854	421,319	425,498	111,250	215,442	207,689
1855	357,836	363,554	106,363	179,217	225,578
1856	409,574	408,468	114,241	207,204	177,860
1857	437,948	429,871	123,823	230,964	172,907
1858	442,146	472,044	125,365	236,855	197,355
1859	425,494	451,693	130,292	245,240	223,758
1860	421,286	457,796	128,179	288,597	242,848
1861	373,043	449,274	135,243	234,104	169,419
1862	383,436	479,922	152,929	259,142	193,233
1863	418,461	479,742	176,490	268,542	220,665
1864	415,721	520,945	187,587	273,069	204,154
1865	415,142	537,180	203,117	277,757	236,418
1866	428,000	596,769	206,276	295,574	231,496
1867	423,444	554,955	201,014	274,299	235,665
1868	405,622	595,639	217,078	288,611	238,975
1869	409,327	534,949	227,027	272,253	231,904

Table IV. (*cont.*)

Year	Barclay Perkins	Truman Hanbury Buxton[a]	Mann, Crossman & Paulin	Reid's	Whitbread[b]
1870	410,710	509,447	217,575	264,753	225,600
1871	....	533,477	222,120	273,386	241,149
1872	407,874	559,137	240,111	262,266	250,360
1873	....	607,896	237,684	240,912	266,085
1874	....	605,393	250,957	244,036	253,563
1875	....	616,458	237,553	235,596	248,960
1876	....	618,240	238,436	208,685	251,981
1877	....	574,186	229,756	210,313	250,509
1878	....	542,518	235,798	268,631	246,256
1879	....	501,937	221,780	274,036	243,042
1880	....	456,393	231,942	274,146	249,744
1881	....	440,198	234,349	274,655	260,566
1882	....	423,830	232,405	286,806	280,612
1883	....	391,604	223,253	283,591	274,636
1884	....	440,230	228,800	284,909	301,381
1885	500,576	398,040	236,817	271,150	300,931
1886	494,928	382,657	247,388	250,835	286,750
1887	510,032	400,569	269,583	251,884	309,538
1888	500,398	420,202	268,697	....	322,688
1889	502,656	426,140	293,602	....	336,052
1890	522,645	453,336	293,845	....	357,878
1891	522,717	455,101	304,007	....	394,878
1892	532,958	448,494	300,350	....	426,722
1893	552,382	452,406	311,040	....	437,561
1894	....	423,082	321,310	....	442,347
1895	....	424,158	360,603	....	449,298
1896	....	462,327	410,286	....	476,626
1897	....	441,949	423,381	....	520,642
1898	....	459,805	441,921	....	573,176
1899	580,213	494,196	476,121	....	607,128
1900	589,201	505,341	500,029	....	693,706
1901	573,302	480,552	557,403	....	726,622
1902	541,822	454,533	593,694	....	744,855
1903	539,153	435,843	624,718	....	774,034
1904	534,284	439,439	644,162	....	783,924
1905	549,634	421,349	672,104	....	792,957
1906	560,103	391,923	657,161	....	816,664
1907	555,370	374,558	650,254	....	834,021
1908	527,716	355,110	625,130	....	808,237
1909	525,854	363,262	601,363	....	811,850
1910	500,205	365,520	590,608	....	800,011

Table IV. (*cont.*)

Year	Barclay Perkins	Truman Hanbury Buxton[a]	Mann, Crossman & Paulin	Reid's	Whitbread[b]
1911	549,841	398,385	630,417	....	852,806
1912	589,543	435,101	619,058	....	928,477
1913	....	441,858	611,704	....	850,756
1914	....	427,961	609,623	....	845,857

[a] Barrels sold from 1894
[b] Barrels sold
Source: Barclay Perkins, Acc. 2305/1/394 Capital Accounts Rest 1801–75; Acc. 2305/1/395 Capital Accounts Rest 1875–1912, GLRO. Truman Hanbury Buxton, Acc. 73.36 B(THB) Abstract Rest Book, 1781–1866; Reid & Co. Acc. 75.108, Abstract of Rest, 1809–87, GLRO. Mann, Crossman & Paulin, Mann's Private Ledgers 1846–1961, MA/A/1–MA/A/20, Courage Archive. Whitbread, Trade Books, W/15/70, Whitbread Archive.

Table V. *Truman Hanbury Buxton: average price of malt purchased, 1830–1914*

Year ending 30 June	Average price of Malt per quarter s d		s d
1830	60 9	1873	59 6
1831	64 6	1874	60 7
1832	68 10	1875	65 5
1833	59 9	1876	60 1
1834	60 2	1877	55 11
1835	58 2	1878	62 1
1836	57 10	1879	60 7
1837	60 9	1880	57 8
1838	58 1	1881	45 2
1839	58 10	1882	36 3
1840	42 6	1883	37
1841	65	1884	39 2
1842	58	1885	37 1
1843	53 4	1886	36
1844	56 9	1887	31 1
1845	63 3	1888	33
1846	58 3	1889	32 1
1847	65 10	1890	34
1848	62 5	1891	32 6
1849	58	1892	33 6
1850	57 8	1893	32 6
1851	49 9	1894	31 9
1852	53 9	1895	29
1853	56 5	1896	27 6
1854	67	1897	29 1
1855	71 6	1898	30 6
1856	69 10	1899	30 7
1857	68	1900	29 7
1858	66 10	1901	38 11
1859	64 2	1902	30
1860	62 2	1903	30
1861	63	1904	30
1862	64	1905	30 3
1863	59 1	1906	31 3
1864	61 2	1907	30 9
1865	...	1908	31 10
1866	55	1909	36 4
1867	65 11	1910	36 6
1868	62 2	1911	35
1869	66 10	1912	37 7
1870	61 6	1913	39 6
1871	59 2	1914	38 10
1872	58 10		

Note: The malt duty of 3s 8½d per bushel was replaced by one on beer in the Budget of 1880.
Source: Truman Hanbury Buxton Acc. 73.36 B(THB) Rest Book, 1781–1866; Annual Totals, 1867–89; Acc. 79.94 Abstract Rest Book, 1889–1915, GLRO.

Table VI. *Hop prices, 1830–1912*

Year	Acreage	Total grown	Imports	Exports	Estimated consumption	Average prices per cwt in shillings: Weald of Kent	Mid and East Kent
		Cwt	*Cwt*	*Cwt*	*Cwt*	s	s
1830	46,726	164,839	77	2,908	276,353	192	215
1831	47,129	325,893	Nil	4,399	346,552	106	130
1832	47,101	259,093	99	6,725	325,773	150	189
1833	49,187	292,386	Nil	14,839	355,744	145	168
1834	51,263	353,459	470	7,776	367,683	120	147
1835	53,816	438,274	Nil	9,784	377,174	92	120
1836	55,422	373,883	Nil	7,032	403,867	120	145
1837	56,323	332,993	Nil	3,966	361,048	88	110
1838	55,045	319,653	46	8,581	300,540	92	120
1839	52,305	383,023	Nil	15,576	354,126	66	95
1840	44,085	63,526	106	8,291	382,317	270	294
1841	45,769	272,358	34	3,553	312,090	135	160
1842	43,720	316,358	Nil	5,918	308,596	95	126
1843	43,156	248,774	27	2,633	306,838	126	153
1844	44,485	261,474	267	1,411	23,504	145	175
1845	48,058	294,417	726	2,078	316,348	145	176
1846	51,048	452,714	3,283	4,581	378,302	93	119
1847	52,328	402,985	1,467	4,888	302,529	72	100
1848	49,232	395,928	385	3,396	327,508	62	95
1849	42,798	148,668	5,271	2,835	343,016	147	178
1850	43,127	433,372	6,840	4,367	363,209	86	110
1851	43,244	241,454	461	9,005	358,663	138	162
1852	46,157	456,272	309	8,689	366,867	88	116
1853	49,367	283,497	42,315	8,856	377,662	226	265
1854	53,825	88,188	119,677	12,047	385,107	330	400
1855	57,757	743,047	24,662	19,180	392,953	105	147
1856	54,527	498,829	15,987	16,280	374,157	82	112
1857	50,974	426,049	18,711	13,322	436,689	78	110
1858	47,601	474,331	13,000	40,260	459,422	65	95
1859	45,665	611,579	2,220	12,392	427,512	84	112
1860	46,271	99,667	68,918	9,178	454,020	340	395
1861	47,911	213,857	149,176	9,321	436,037	162	187
1862	49,688	320,000	133,791	89,927	446,190	148	190
1863	51,395	300,000	147,281	23,416	448,245	105	147
1864	53,122	300,000	98,656	25,891	476,795	126	160

Table VI. (*cont.*)

Year	Acreage	Total grown	Imports	Exports	Estimated consumption	Average prices per cwt in shillings: Weald of Kent	Average prices per cwt in shillings: Mid and East Kent
		Cwt	*Cwt*	*Cwt*	*Cwt*	s	s
1865	54,849	600,000	82,479	24,288	503,278	105	148
1866	56,562	300,000	85,647	36,088	566,709	188	225
1867	64,273	240,000	296,117	21,291	562,648	180	218
1868	64,435	470,000	231,720	26,190	542,451	75	109
1869	61,785	270,000	322,515	16,940	547,827	108	148
1870	60,580	700,000	127,853	21,913	568,910	63	95
1871	60,022	350,000	218,664	15,272	589,994	189	240
1872	61,926	640,000	135,965	37,779	631,038	84	115
1873	63,276	540,000	122,729	38,353	664,620	130	153
1874	65,799	300,000	145,994	11,234	684,000	168	200
1875	69,171	700,000	256,444	18,087	692,285	93	122
1876	69,909	440,000	167,366	37,612	720,523	145	175
1877	71,239	460,000	250,039	19,132	714,039	88	115
1878	71,789	700,000	168,834	17,324	716,156	73	102
1879	67,671	160,000	262,765	9,508	664,443	189	220
1880	66,698	440,000	195,987	20,892	686,219	83	105
1881	64,943	455,000	147,559	23,190	613,153	126	150
1882	65,619	120,000	319,620	14,094	491,967	375	420
1883	68,016	560,000	129,900	22,812	488,060	135	162
1884	69,259	420,000	256,777	18,256	502,317	130	160
1885	71,327	509,170	266,952	14,458	492,935	80	103
1886	70,127	776,144	153,759	69,323	493,624	56	82
1887	63,709	457,515	145,122	27,760	504,285	80	100
1888	58,494	281,291	216,606	14,811	504,460	160	203
1889	57,724	497,811	200,690	18,089	542,898	63	85
1890	54,551	283,629	188,028	12,372	568,492	200	258
1891	56,148	436,716	195,264	9,740	573,028	126	152
1892	56,259	413,259	187,507	10,702	572,505	135	158
1893	57,564	414,929	204,392	18,748	573,291	135	150
1894	59,535	636,846	189,155	20,839	574,691	57	88
1895	58,940	553,396	217,161	13,132	565,687	56	90
1896	54,217	453,188	207,041	13,303	604,035	60	95
1897	50,863	411,086	164,154	15,491	610,751	70	105
1898	49,735	356,598	244,136	20,389	636,283	140	155
1899	51,743	661,426	180,233	14,700	651,753	65	80
1900	51,308	347,894	198,494	18,585	662,339	117	138

Table VI. (*cont.*)

Year	Acreage	Total grown	Imports	Exports	Estimated consumption	Average prices per cwt in shillings: Weald of Kent	Average prices per cwt in shillings: Mid and East Kent
		Cwt	*Cwt*	*Cwt*	*Cwt*	s	s
1901	51,127	649,387	116,042	22,702	649,903	56	68
1902	48,031	311,041	191,324	23,236	688,703	138	155
1903	47,938	421,068	113,998	30,279	670,521	105	140
1904	47,799	282,330	313,667	20,069	641,836	185	200
1905	48,967	695,943	108,953	25,675	595,908	60	75
1906	46,722	245,688	232,619	14,741	610,381	115	132
1907	44,938	374,129	202,324	17,204	610,334	75	90
1908	38,921	470,761	279,916	22,234	601,258	54	68
1909	32,539	214,484	140,777	22,209	586,578	165	168
1910	32,886	302,675	176,781	13,676	589,788	100	110
1911	33,056	328,023	169,184	67,017	614,373	205	220
1912	34,829	373,438	243,886	20,614	589,796	126	135

Source: Brewers' Journal, Special Supplement, May 1913.
Note: Average prices are also given for Sussex 1830–1912, and for Worcester and Hereford from 1889 only.

Table VII. *Drunkenness convictions/charges proved in England and Wales per 10,000 population, 1910–55*

Year	Convictions	Year	Convictions
1910	45.2	1933	9.0
1911	48.0	1934	9.8
1912	50.3	1935	10.4
1913	50.1	1936	10.9
1914	49.7	1937	11.4
1915	36.7	1938[a]	11.3
1916	22.7	1939	12.8
1917	12.5	1940	11.4
1918	7.9	1941	9.9
1919	15.4	1942	6.9
1920	26.5	1943	6.6
1921	20.5	1944	5.5
1922	20.2	1945	5.4
1923	20.0	1946	5.0
1924	20.3	1947	5.9
1925	19.2	1948	7.6
1926	17.1	1949[b]	8.1
1927	16.6	1950	10.9
1928	14.1	1951	12.3
1929	13.0	1952	12.3
1930	13.4	1953	12.2
1931	10.6	1954	12.0
1932	7.5	1955	12.2

[a] Data to 1938 are for 'convictions'. From 1939–48 'charges proved' are given, as the figures of 'convictions' were not available.
[b] From 1949 onwards data are for convictions and include all cases which would formerly have been described as 'charges proved'.
Source: Brewers' Almanack 1940, p. 112; *1958*, p. 96.

Table VIII. *UK beer statistics (excluding Eire), 1919–55*

Year	Production (charged with duty):		Average gravity (beer charged with duty): (degrees)	Consumption (beer charged with duty):			Consumption	
	in bulk barrels (millions)	in standard barrels 1055° gravity (millions)		in standard barrels (millions)	in gallons per head	in gallons per head of population aged 15 and over	in bulk barrels (millions)	in gallons per head
1919	31.543	22.604	1039.41	23.55	19.34	27.30		
1920	31.054	24.057	1042.61	25.05	20.66	28.72		
1921	27.161	21.162	1042.88	22.07	18.05	25.06		
1922	23.949	18.564	1042.72	18.31	14.87	20.58		
1923	25.425	19.890	1043.04	21.02	16.99	23.39		
1924	26.827	20.954	1042.97	22.23	17.82	24.41		
1925	26.839	21.034	1043.10	22.26	17.78	24.23		
1926	25.168	19.745	1043.14	20.82	16.57	22.46		
1927	25.435	19.962	1043.17	21.03	16.68	22.48		
1928	24.608	19.253	1043.07	20.16	15.92	21.36		
1929	25.062	19.551	1042.90	20.66	16.28	21.70		
1930	23.900	18.488	1042.54	19.71	15.47	20.50		
1931	20.791	15.514	1041.04	16.55	12.93	17.08		
1932	17.950	12.899	1039.52	13.81	10.73	14.14		
1933	20.182	15.043	1040.99	16.05	12.42	16.35		
1934	20.865	15.578	1041.06	16.64	12.84	16.89		
1935	21.970	16.387	1041.02	17.50	13.44	17.52		

1936	22.724	16.985	1041.10	17.97	13.74	17.78		
1937	24.206	18.056	1041.02	18.87 NDP	14.37 NDP	18.48	NDP	NDP
1938	24.675	18.364	1040.93	18.89/18.729	14.32/14.2	18.35	25.026	18.8
1939	25.367	18.739	1040.62	19.276	14.6		25.915	20.3
1940	26.204	18.351	1038.51	18.848	14.2		26.564	21.3
1941	29.861	19.295	1035.53	19.897	15.0		30.399	24.7
1942	29.297	18.294	1034.34	18.715	14.1		29.809	24.5
1943	30.478	19.194	1034.63	19.382	14.6		30.701	23.2
1944	31.333	19.678	1034.54	20.090	15.2		31.797	25.0
1945	32.650	20.612	1034.72	21.331	16.3		33.627	25.6
1946	29.261	17.344	1032.59	18.078	13.4		30.086	22.3
1947	30.409	18.061	1032.66	18.396	13.5		30.871	22.6
1948	26.990	16.410	1033.43	17.009	12.1		27.924	21.9
1949	26.514	16.337	1033.88	16.596	11.7		26.781	19.3
1950	24.892	16.739	1036.99	17.256	12.3		25.733	18.4
1951	25.156	16.959	1037.07	17.366	12.5		25.633	18.4
1952	24.883	16.681	1036.87	17.061	12.2		25.362	18.2
1953	24.582	16.525	1036.97	17.008	12.1		25.220	18.0
1954	23.934	16.162	1037.13	16.705	11.8		24.648	17.4
1955	24.551	16.618	1037.22	17.187	12.0		25.266	17.8

Note: 1919 = Year to 31 March 1920, *et seq.*
NDP Consumption figures based on Net Duty Paid data.
Source: Customs and Excise Reports; *Brewers' Almanack.*

Table IX. *Ordinary dividends of twenty-five 'representative' companies, 1910–55*

	1910–13	1914–16	1917–20	1921–3	1924–8	1929–33	1934–8	1939–45	1946–50	1951–5
1	0.00	0.00	4.50†	9.33†	9.00†	8.80	7.60	5.21	6.80	8.10
2	0.00	0.00	0.63†	3.39†	13.60†[16.60]**	11.50 [23.00]**	10.60[21.20]**	8.57	9.80	10.60
3	0.97#	1.50	7.75	9.00	11.13	14.20	18.00	17.29	20.35[27.55]*	22.73[73.90]*
4	6.50	11.00	12.81 [14.58]*	10.00	15.50	23.00	18.00	10.93	15.40	9.60
5	6.00	7.00	11.38	14.17	15.00	11.10	10.00	10.18	17.00	26.16
6	10.25	11.00	15.45	17.78	18.80	20.00	18.40[25.60]*	18.00	20.40	16.20[17.12]*
7	3.06	5.17	10.00	12.67	13.40 [20.80]*	13.40 [26.80]*	15.50[31.00]*	15.00	19.30	19.50
8	6.13	6.00	7.75	7.83	11.20	11.50	10.80	10.00	11.20	10.00
9	8.50	8.00	15.50 [18.00]*	10.00	23.50	17.60	17.30[21.95]**	27.60	20.00	18.00[19.00]*
10	1.25	4.00	7.44	5.83	8.20	11.42	11.65	15.36	24.00	21.50
11	10.00	10.33	12.00	12.83	15.50	16.80	20.80	18.43	23.05	22.60
12	18.50	13.33	9.75 [15.25]*	5.50	6.30	7.20	11.90[13.57]*	12.50	15.00	14.90[15.38]**
13	0.00	0.00	2.88†	3.58†	5.90†	8.30	26.00	23.00	29.50	15.60[30.00]*
14	8.25	12.33	14.00 [15.38]*	11.00	14.80	17.00	23.20	20.71	24.80	38.90
15	15.00	15.00	13.13 [26.88]*	10.00	13.20	13.40 [16.08]*	18.70[23.34]*	21.00	21.50	17.30
16	5.75	7.00	13.25	14.00	14.60	9.10	8.50	8.71	15.00	15.90
17	6.75	7.00	13.00 [14.88]*	14.67	13.60	6.10	3.30	10.71	19.00	18.30[27.50]*
18	–	–	–	–	–	14.80■	12.40[26.20]*	12.71	16.00	14.70[15.85]*
19	15.40	11.70	22.50 [34.88]*	16.17	15.40 [17.40]*	9.20 [18.40]*	12.80[25.60]*	16.18	22.50[25.25]*	13.60[23.92]*
20	7.25	7.00	9.75	13.00	13.80	15.00	19.60	20.71	32.17	13.32[37.33]*
21	13.63	17.33	20.25	22.50	14.95	7.90	8.90[10.40]*	7.79	10.30	10.50
22	5.38	9.33	15.00 [22.50]*	6.67	7.60	5.20	11.90	16.64	18.00	13.02[21.74]*
23	0.00	0.00	0.00	0.00	0.00	8.50	8.23	0.00	0.00	0.00
24	7.13	7.00	13.13	10.00	10.00	10.60	12.90	8.93	11.44	14.40
25	16.25	14.67	22.00◆	27.00	29.20 [43.80]*	32.30 [48.30]*	28.60[42.90]*	27.57	29.60	22.20[27.80]*
Ave 1	7.16	7.74	11.41	11.12	13.09	12.95	14.62	14.55	18.08	16.31
Ave 2	7.16	7.74	13.34	11.12	14.22	15.07	18.09	14.55	18.48	21.38
Ave 3	9.54	9.81	14.91	16.41	19.17	18.06	19.27	18.84	21.68	18.64
Ave 4	9.54	9.81	17.25	16.41	24.77	24.43	25.94	18.84	22.24	28.07

Key:

* Calculation takes account of the capitalisation of reserves as bonus shares (* ordinary; ** ordinary and preference). The ordinary dividend is recalculated to reflect the equivalent dividend on the original capital. Thus, the effect of a 1 for 1 (or 100 per cent) bonus distribution would be to double the declared ordinary dividend in following years. E.g. if a company pays 10 per cent; 10 per cent + 1 for 1 bonus; and 5 per cent, the calculation with bonus would be: 10 per cent; 10 per cent; and 10 per cent. The calculations start from scratch in 1921; and again in 1939.

† Calculation takes into account the writing-down of capital.

Includes effect of bonus of 3 per cent paid to small shareholders (holding under £10,000) in 1910.

◆ Includes special bonus of £20 in 5 per cent War Stock for each £100 Ordinary Stock in 1918.

■ Information available from 1930 (1929–33 = average of 1930–3).

Averages:
1 = Unweighted Ave (excl. bonuses)
2 = Unweighted Ave (with bonuses)
3 = Weighted Ave (excl. bonuses)
4 = Weighted Ave (with bonuses)

Companies:

	Company	Location	Region	
1	Barclay Perkins	London	London	(1)
2	Meux	London	London	(1)
3	Whitbread	London	London	(1)
4	Style & Winch/Fremlins[a]	Maidstone	SE	(2)
5	Tamplin's	Brighton	SE	(2)
6	Bristol Brewery Georges	Bristol	West	(3)
7	Hall & Woodhouse	Blandford Forum	West	(3)
8	Brakspear	Henley	West	(3)
9	J. W. Green (Flowers)	Luton	ECos	(4)
10	Colchester/Paine[a]	Colchester/St Neots	ECos	(4)
11	Greene King	Bury St Edmunds	ECos	(4)
12	Steward & Patteson	Norwich	ECos	(4)
13	Allsopp/Ind Coope & A.[a]	Burton	Mid	(5)
14	Bass, Ratcliff & Gretton	Burton	Mid	(5)
15	Mitchells & Butlers	Birmingham	Mid	(5)
16	Boddingtons'	Manchester	NW/NW	(6)

Table IX. (*cont.*)

	Company	Location	Region	
17	Matthew Brown	Blackburn	NW/NW	(6)
18	Joshua Tetley	Leeds	York	(7)
19	John Smith's Tadcaster	Tadcaster	York	(7)
20	Russells & Wrangham	Malton	York	(7)
21	Cameron	Hartlepool	NE	(8)
22	Newcastle	Newcastle	NE	(8)
23	Arrol/Maclay[a]	Alloa	Scot	(9)
24	Wm McEwan/Scottish Brewers[a]	Edinburgh	Scot	(9)
25	Guinness	Dublin	Ire	(10)

Regions:

1	London	6	North-West/North Wales
2	South-East	7	York
3	West	8	North-East
4	Eastern Counties	9	Scotland
5	Midland	10	Ireland

[a] Company changes:

4	Style & Winch 1910–38; Fremlins 1939–55
10	Colchester 1910–38; Paine 1939–55
13	Allsopp 1910–33; Ind Coope & Allsopp 1934–55
23	Arrol 1910–38; Maclay 1939–55
24	Wm McEwan 1910–38; Scottish Brewers 1939–55

Sources: Stock Exchange Official Intelligence, *Stock Exchange Year Book*, 1910ff.; *Manual of British Brewery Companies*, 1914ff. No adjustments have been made for Income Tax.

Table X. *Chronology of brewery mergers, 1955–80*

Year	Acquiring company	Acquired company	Eventual destination 1980
1. Acquired British Breweries			
1955	Warwicks & Richardsons	Brampton	Courage/Imperial
1955	Warwicks & Richardsons	Smith's (Oundle)	Courage/Imperial
1955	Frome United	Lamb Brewery	Whitbread and Watneys/Grand Met
1955	Ushers (Wiltshire)	Arnold & Hancock	Watneys/Grand Met
1955	Mansfield Brewery	Hornby's	Mansfield Brewery
1955	J. W. Cameron	John J. Hunt	Ellerman Lines
1955	Jeffrey Aitchison	McLennan & Urquhart	Bass
1955	Whitbread	Dale & Co.	Whitbread
1955	Ind Coope	Cowley Bros.	Allied-Lyons
1955	Courage	Barclay Perkins	Courage/Imperial
1956	Stroud Brewery	Alton Court	Whitbread
1956	Taylor Walker	Chesham & Brackley	Allied-Lyons
1956	J. W. Cameron	J. Fryer & Sons	Ellerman Lines
1956	Newcastle Breweries	James Deuchar	S&N
1956	Bristol Brewery Georges	Bristol United	Courage/Imperial
1956	Courage & Barclay	Reffells Bexley Brewery	Courage/Imperial
1956	W. Butler	Frederick Smith	Bass
1956	Bullard	Youngs, Crawshay & Youngs	Watneys/Grand Met
1956	Hammonds United	Bentley's Old Brewery	Bass
1956	Hammonds United	John Richdale	Bass
1956	Hope & Anchor	Truswells	Bass
1956	Shepherd Neame	E. Mason & Co.	Shepherd Neame
1956	Thwaites (Daniel)	Preston Breweries	Thwaites (Daniel)
1956	Workington Brewery	Armstrong & Dickie	Matthew Brown
1956	Hope & Anchor	Openshaws	Bass
1956	Tennant Bros.	Clarkson's Old Brewery	Whitbread
1956	Scottish Brewers	Red Tower Lager Brewery	S&N
1956	Wadworth	Long Acre Brewery	Wadworth
1956	Friary Holroyd & Healy's Breweries	Meux	Allied-Lyons
1957	Ushers (Wiltshire) and Stroud Brewery	Frome & Lamb	Whitbread and Watneys/Grand Met
1957	Ind Coope	Benskin's	Allied-Lyons
1957	Steward & Patteson	East Anglian Breweries	Watneys/Grand Met
1957	J. A. Devenish	Vallance's Brewery	Devenish
1957	Webster (Samuel) & Sons	John Ainley	Watneys/Grand Met
1957	Starkey, Knight & Ford	Holt Brothers	Whitbread
1957	Hull Brewery	Hartley's Brewery	Northern Foods

Table X. (*cont.*)

Year	Acquiring company	Acquired company	Eventual destination 1980
1957	Tollemache	Cobbold	Ellerman Lines
1957	Phipps	Northampton Brewery	Watneys/Grand Met
1957	Cheltenham & Hereford	Spreckley Brothers	Whitbread
1958	Tennant Bros.	Worksop & Retford	Whitbread
1958	Truman Hanbury Buxton	Daniell & Sons	Watneys/Grand Met
1958	Melbourne (Leeds)	Russells & Wrangham	Allied-Lyons
1958	Marston, Thompson & Evershed	Taylor's Eagle Brewery	Marston, Thompson & Evershed
1958	Drybrough	Mackay	Watneys/Grand Met
1958	Whitbread	Scarsdale	Whitbread
1958	Watney Combe Reid	Mann, Crossman & Paulin	Watneys/Grand Met
1958	Ind Coope	Hambridge Brewery Ltd	Allied-Lyons
1958	John Smith's	Whitworth Son & Nephew	Courage/Imperial
1958	Greene King	J. C. Mauldon & Sons	Greene King
1959	Hope & Anchor	Welcome (Oldham)	Bass
1959	J. W. Cameron	West Auckland Brewery	Ellerman Lines
1959	Cheltenham & Hereford	Stroud Brewery	Whitbread
1959	Dutton's Blackburn	Penrith Breweries	Whitbread
1959	Dutton's Blackburn	Crown	Whitbread
1959	Friary Meux	George Peters	Allied-Lyons
1959	Newcastle Breweries	John Rowell	S&N
1959	Guinness (Belfast)	Cairnes (Drogheda)	Guinness
1959	Ind Coope	Taylor Walker	Allied-Lyons
1959	Mitchells & Butlers	Atkinsons	Bass
1959	Courage & Barclay	Nicholsons	Courage/Imperial
1959	Vaux & Son	Thomas Usher & Son	Vaux
1959	Vaux & Son	Steel Coulson	Vaux
1959	Hammonds United	John Aitchison	Bass
1959	Hammonds United	R. F. Case	Bass
1959	Hammonds United	Westoe	Bass
1959	George Younger & Co.	Blair	Bass
1959	Tetley Walker	Wm Whitaker	Allied-Lyons
1959	Greenall Whitley	Shrewsbury & Wem	Greenall Whitley
1959	Greenall Whitley	Magee Marshall	Greenall Whitley
1959	Wolverhampton & Dudley	Broadway Brewery	Wolverhampton & Dudley
1959	Rhymney Breweries	Ely Brewery	Whitbread
1960	Charrington	Brutton, Mitchell & Toms	Bass
1960	Courage & Barclay	H. & G. Simonds	Courage/Imperial
1960	J. A. Devenish	John Groves & Sons	Devenish
1960	Wm. Hancock	David Roberts	Bass

Table X. (*cont.*)

Year	Acquiring company	Acquired company	Eventual destination 1980
1960	Fremlins	F. Leney & Sons (Whitbread)	Whitbread
1960	Ind Coope	Beverley's	Allied-Lyons
1960	Hewitt Bros.	Moors & Robson	Bass
1960	J. & R. Tennent	MacLachlan & Co.	Bass
1960	Joshua Tetley	Walker Cain	Allied-Lyons
1960	Tetley Walker	Melbourne (Leeds)	Allied-Lyons
1960	Hammonds United	G. S. Heath	Bass
1960	Northern Breweries	Hammonds United Hope & Anchor John Jeffrey	Bass
1960	United Breweries	George Younger	Bass
1960	United Breweries	John Fowler	Bass
1960	United Breweries	William Murray	Bass
1960	United Breweries	James Calder	Bass
1960	United Breweries	James Aitken	Bass
1960	United Breweries	Webbs (Aberbeeg)	Bass
1960	United Breweries	Ulster	Bass
1960	Watney Mann	Phipps & Co.	Watneys/Grand Met
1960	Watney Mann	Wilson & Walker	Watneys/Grand Met
1960	Watney Mann	Ushers	Watneys/Grand Met
1960	Mitchells & Butlers	W. Butler	Bass
1960	Scottish Brewers	Thomas & James Bernard	S&N
1960	Scottish Brewers	J. & J. Morison	S&N
1960	Scottish Brewers	Robert Younger	S&N
1960	Scottish Brewers	Newcastle Breweries	S&N
1960	Wolverhampton & Dudley	H. Newnam & Sons	Wolverhampton & Dudley
1961	J. W. Cameron	Russells & Wrangham	Ellerman Lines
1961	Steward & Patteson and Bullard & Son	Morgan's	Watneys/Grand Met
1961	John Smith's	Barnsley	Courage/Imperial
1961	John Smith's	Yates's Castle	Courage/Imperial
1961	Marston, Thompson & Evershed	W. T. Rothwell	Marston, Thompson & Evershed
1961	Greenall Whitley	Groves & Whitnall	Greenall Whitley
1961	Threlfall's	Chesters	Whitbread
1961	Greene King	Wells & Winch	Greene King
1961	Courage, B & S	Bristol Brewery Georges	Courage/Imperial
1961	Whitbread	Tennant Bros.	Whitbread
1961	Whitbread	J. R. Fielder	Whitbread

Table X. (*cont.*)

Year	Acquiring company	Acquired company	Eventual destination 1980
1961	ICTA	Ind Coope Tetley Walker Ansells	Allied-Lyons
1961	Bass	Mitchells & Butlers	Bass
1961	Bass, M & B	Wenlock	Bass
1961	Watney Mann	Morgan's (brewing only)	Watneys/Grand Met
1961	Watney Mann	St Leonard's	Watneys/Grand Met
1961	United Breweries	Cornbrook	Bass
1961	United Breweries	Catterall & Swarbricks	Bass
1961	Samuel Webster	Daniel Fielding	Watneys/Grand Met
1961	Davenport & Sons	Dares Brewery	Davenports
1961	Vaux & Sons	John Wright & Son	Vaux
1962	John Smith's	Warwicks & Richardsons	Courage/Imperial
1962	United Breweries	Hewitt Bros.	Bass
1962	Threlfalls Chesters	Birkenhead Brewery	Whitbread
1962	Bass M & B	Fussells	Bass
1962	Marston, Thompson & Evershed	W. A. Smith	Marston, Thompson & Evershed
1962	Boddingtons'	Richard Clarke	Boddingtons'
1962	Whitbread	Norman & Pring	Whitbread
1962	Whitbread	Flowers Breweries	Whitbread
1962	Whitbread	Starkey, Knight & Ford	Whitbread
1962	Charrington	United Breweries	Bass
1962	Charrington United	Hardy's Crown Brewery	Bass
1962	Courage, B & S	Clinch & Co.	Courage/Imperial
1962	Courage, B & S	Harman's Uxbridge Brewery	Courage/Imperial
1963	Whitbread	West Country Breweries	Whitbread
1963	Whitbread	J. Nimmo	Whitbread
1963	Charrington United	J. & R. Tennent	Bass
1963	Courage, B & S	Charles Beasley	Courage/Imperial
1963	Watney Mann	Steward & Patteson Bullard & Son	Watneys/Grand Met
1963	Hall & Woodhouse	Matthews	Hall & Woodhouse
1963	Charles Wells	Abington Brewery	Charles Wells
1964	Whitbread	Dutton's Blackburn	Whitbread
1964	Allied Breweries	Friary Meux	Allied-Lyons
1964	Allied Breweries	Thomas Ramsden & Son	Allied-Lyons
1964	Bass, M & B	Hunt, Edmunds	Bass
1964	Bass, M & B	Thomas Morgan & Sons	Bass
1964	Bass, M & B	G.F. & A. Brown (houses only)	Bass

Table X. (*cont.*)

Year	Acquiring company	Acquired company	Eventual destination 1980
1964	Charrington United	Woodheads	Bass
1965	J. Joule & Sons	James Norris	Bass
1965	Charrington United	Dunmow Brewery	Bass
1965	Charrington United	Offilers' Brewery	Bass
1965	Courage	Star Brewery	Courage/Imperial
1965	Watney Mann	Drybrough	Watneys/Grand Met
1965	Allied Breweries	Blatch's Theale Brewery	Allied-Lyons
1965	Allied Breweries	Charles Rose	Allied-Lyons
1965	Strong	W.B. Mew Langton	Whitbread
1965	Whitbread	E. Lacon	Whitbread
1966	Greenall Whitley	Wrekin	Greenall Whitley
1966	Whitbread	Rhymney	Whitbread
1966	Whitbread	James Thompson	Whitbread
1966	Whitbread	Southam's Brewery	Whitbread
1966	Charrington United	Massey's Burnley	Bass
1966	Samuel Webster	J. Hey	Watneys/Grand Met
1967	Whitbread	Evan Evans Bevan	Whitbread
1967	Whitbread	(Archibald) Campbell Hope & King	Whitbread
1967	Whitbread	Threlfalls Chesters	Whitbread
1967	Whitbread	Isaac Tucker	Whitbread
1967	Whitbread	Fremlins	Whitbread
1967	Bass, M & B	Bent's	Bass
1967	Bass, M & B	Charrington United	Bass
1967	Watney Mann	Beverley Brothers	Watneys/Grand Met
1967	Courage, B & S	James Hole	Courage/Imperial
1967	Allied Breweries	J.W. Hemingway	Allied-Lyons
1968	Burtonwood	J.B. Almond	Burtonwood Brewery (Forshaws)
1968	Whitbread	Cobb	Whitbread
1968	Whitbread	Bentley's Yorkshire	Whitbread
1968	Whitbread	Richard Whitaker	Whitbread
1968	Whitbread	John Young	Whitbread
1968	Whitbread	Combined Breweries (Holding)	Whitbread
1968	Whitbread	Strong	Whitbread
1968	Courage, B & S	G. E. Brown (Jersey)	Courage/Imperial
1968	Bass Charrington	Joule & Sons	Bass
1968	Bass Charrington	William Hancock	Bass
1968	Bass Charrington	W. Stones	Bass
1968	Bass Charrington	Welsh Brewers	Bass
1968	Watney Mann	Ballingall (houses only)	Watneys/Grand Met

Table X. (*cont.*)

Year	Acquiring company	Acquired company	Eventual destination 1980
1969	Wadworth	Garne & Sons	Wadworth
1970	Courage, B & S	John Smith's Tadcaster	Courage/Imperial
1971	Boddingtons'	J.G. Swales & Co. (houses only)	Boddingtons'
1971	Whitbread	Brickwoods	Whitbread
1971	Courage, B & S	Plymouth Breweries	Courage/Imperial
1971*	Grand Met Hotels	Truman Hanbury Buxton	Watneys/Grand Met
1972	Allied Breweries	Aylesbury Brewery	Allied-Lyons
1972	Watney Mann	Samuel Webster & Sons	Watneys/Grand Met
1972*	Clydesdale Commonwealth Hotels	Dudgeon (Belhaven)	Belhaven
1972*	Imperial Tobacco Group	Courage, B & S	Courage Imperial
1972*	Grand Met Hotels	Watney Mann	Watneys/Grand Met
1972*	Northern Dairies	Hull Brewery	Northern Foods
1973	Greenall Whitley	Shrewsbury & Wem	Greenall Whitley
1973	Vaux & Sons	S. H. Ward	Vaux
1974	Theakston	Carlisle & District State Management	Theakston
1974	Higson's Brewery	James Mellor & Sons	Higson's Brewery
1975	Ellerman Lines	J. W. Cameron	Ellerman Lines
1975	Matthew Brown	Workington	Matthew Brown
1975	Northern Clubs' Fed	Yorkshire Clubs'	Northern Clubs' Fed.
1977	Ellerman Lines	Tollemache & Cobbold	Ellerman Lines
1978	Vaux & Sons	W. M. Darley	Vaux
1978	Greenall Whitley	James Shipstone & Sons	Greenall Whitley
1978	Watneys/Grand Met	Alnwick	Watneys/Grand Met
1980	Allied Breweries	Lorimer's	Allied-Lyons

* acquiring company not a brewer

2. Mergers where the acquired company = a major European brewery

1966	Watney Mann	Jules Delbruyère (Belgium)	Watneys/Grand Met
1968	Watney Mann	Vandenheuvel (Belgium)	Watneys/Grand Met
1968	Allied Breweries	d'Oranjeboom (Holland)	Allied-Lyons
1968	Allied Breweries	De Drie Boefizers (Breda Holland)	Allied-Lyons
1969	Watney Mann	Maes (Belgium)	Watneys/Grand Met
1970	Bass	Lamot	Bass
1974	Vaux & Sons	Liefman's	Vaux
1977	WMT/Grand Met	Stern Brauerei	Watneys/Grand Met

Table X. (*cont.*)

Year	Acquiring company	Acquired company	Eventual destination 1980
3. Selected mergers where the acquired company = non-brewing company			
1957	Courage	Charles Kinloch	Courage/Imperial
1959	Ind Coope	J. & R. Phillips	Allied-Lyons
1959	Ind Coope	Alperton Bottling Co.	Allied-Lyons
1961	ICTA	Victoria Wine	Allied-Lyons
1961	Courage	Saccone & Speed	Courage/Imperial
1961	S&N	Charles MacKinley	S&N
1961	Charrington	People's Refreshment House Association	Bass
1964	Bass, M & B	Lyle & Kinahan	Bass
1964	Bass, M & B	Old Bushmills Distillery	Bass
1965	Whitbread	Thresher	Whitbread
1965	Allied Breweries	Bristol Vintners	Allied-Lyons
1965	Courage, B & S	Sheffield & District Public House Trust Co.	Courage/Imperial
1968	Allied Breweries	Showerings, Vine Products and Whiteways	Allied-Lyons
1969	Whitbread	R. White & Sons	Whitbread
1970	Allied Breweries	David Sandeman & Son	Allied-Lyons
1970	Allied Breweries	British Wine Co.	Allied-Lyons
1972	Watney Mann	International Distillers & Vintners	Watneys/Grand Met
1972	Guinness	Croft Inns	Guinness
1973	Allied Breweries	Wine Ways	Allied-Lyons
1975	Whitbread	Long John Int.	Whitbread
1978	Allied Breweries	J. Lyons	Allied-Lyons

Table XI. *UK beer statistics, 1955–90*

Year	Production (charged with duty) Bulk barrels (million)	Average gravity (degrees)	Consumption (NDP) in bulk barrels (millions)	Consumption in pints per head	Consumption in pints per head of population aged 15 and over
1955	24.551	1037.22	25.266	142.8	185.3
1956	24.507	1037.42	25.394	142.9	185.8
1957	24.648	1037.48	25.367	142.1	185.0
1958	23.784	1037.52	24.562	137.0	175.5
1959	26.115	1037.25	26.647	147.7	192.5
1960	27.098	1037.41	27.496	151.2	197.1
1961	27.496	1037.70	28.639	156.2	203.9
1962	27.813	1037.70	28.307	155.8	199.0
1963	28.964	1037.66	29.478	158.3	205.7
1964	29.528	1037.67	29.908	159.5	207.3
1965	29.988	1037.63	30.358	160.8	209.3
1966	30.418	1037.46	31.282	164.8	214.9
1967	30.528	1037.36	31.522	165.1	215.8
1968	31.554	1037.14	32.212	167.8	220.3
1969	32.941	1036.94	33.463	173.5	228.3
1970	34.360	1036.87	34.925	180.5	237.7
1971	34.969	1036.88	36.062	186.9	246.9
1972	35.338	1036.99	36.620	189.0	249.4
1973	37.894	1037.14	39.204	201.9	265.4
1974	38.239	1037.33	39.109	201.3	263.1
1975	39.201	1037.46	39.445	203.7	264.9
1976	40.404	1037.46	40.838	210.3	268.0
1977	40.279	1037.63	40.931	210.7	271.9
1978	40.596	1037.58	40.953	211.2 †	270.8 †
1979	41.701	1037.56	42.114	217.0/217.1	276.7/276.4
1980	38.991	1037.33	40.029	208.2	263.7
1981	37.054	1037.24	37.332	198.8	250.4
1982	36.575	1037.22	37.400	193.3	242.1
1983	36.965	1037.37	38.183	195.7	244.0
1984	36.644	1037.36	37.764	195.1	242.3
1985	36.174	1037.55	37.526	193.8	240.0
1986	36.239	1037.97	37.343	193.1	238.5
1987	37.202	1037.66	38.993	194.3	239.5
1988	36.382	1037.82	38.326	195.1	240.5
1989	36.499	1038.0	38.469	194.4	239.7
1990	36.132	1037.7	38.217	194.0	239.2

Note: 1955 = year to 31 March 1956, *et seq.*
NDP = Net Duty Paid basis.
† Revised series derived from 'Production adjusted for overseas trade' on a calendar year basis.
Source: BS, *UK Statistical Handbook 1980*, p. 47; *1991*, pp. 7, 34–5.

Table XII. *UK Beer imports and exports, in million bulk barrels, 1955–90*

Year	Imports[a]	Imports[b]	'Exports'[a]	Exports[b]	Re-exports
1955	1.15	1.30	0.43	0.23	0.13
1956	1.22	1.41	0.34	0.24	0.15
1957	1.20	1.42	0.49	0.24	0.18
1958	1.17	1.40	0.38	0.25	0.20
1959	1.27	1.50	0.74	0.21	0.19
1960	1.21	1.50	0.81	0.22	0.21
1961	1.23	1.56	0.09	0.25	0.26
1962	1.17	1.44	0.67	0.28	0.22
1963	1.24	1.41	0.72	0.39	0.17
1964	1.24	1.45	0.86	0.38	0.17
1965	1.27	1.42	0.90	0.37	0.14
1966	1.33	1.47	0.47	0.33	0.08
1967	1.40	1.53	0.40	0.30	0.07
1968	1.43	1.62	0.78	0.34	0.09
1969	1.47	1.61	0.94	0.37	0.10
1970	1.63	1.72	1.06	0.41	[c]
1971	1.94	2.01	0.85	0.45	
1972	1.88	2.06	0.60	0.43	
1973	2.15	2.36	0.83	0.45	
1974	1.66	1.83	0.80	0.44	
1975	1.68	1.81	1.43	0.54	
1976	1.72	1.88	1.30	0.52	
1977	1.46	1.56	0.81	0.53	
1978	1.45	1.56	1.01	0.49	
1979	1.58	1.68	1.17	0.48	
1980	1.41	1.58	0.37	0.46	
1981	1.35	1.63	1.07	0.44	
1982	1.45	1.67	0.63	0.42	
1983	1.61	1.88	0.39	0.46	
1984	1.79	2.05	0.67	0.52	
1985	1.91	2.25	0.55	0.60	
1986	2.01	2.36	0.91	0.62	
1987	2.19	2.50	0.40	0.70	
1988	2.72	2.66		0.75	
1989	2.80	2.77		0.82	
1990	3.08	3.10		0.99	

Key:
Imports [a] Released for Home Consumption (Net Duty Paid) year ending 31 March 1956 = 1955 *et seq.*
Imports [b] Imports entering the Country (including re-imports from 1987), Calendar year.
Exports [a] 'Production charged with duty' *less* 'UK production minus exports' (NDP basis), yr ending 31 March.
Exports [b] Exports of Home-produced beers, Calendar year (includes re-exports from Jan 1970).
[c] Re-exports included in Exports [b] series.
Source: BS, *UK Statistical Handbook 1983*, pp. 12–13; *1988*, pp. 7, 9–10, 14; *1991*, pp. 7, 9–10; *Brewers' Almanack 1962*, p. 59; *1963*, p. 59; *1971*, p. 56.

Table XIII. *Excise duty and VAT on beer, in current and constant prices, 1950–80 (selected years)*

Year	Duty per barrel 1037°	Duty/VAT per pint 1037°		Index 1959 = 100	Index 1959 = 100	Index 1950 = 100	Index 1950 = 100
	current prices	current prices	1959 prices	current prices	constant prices	current prices	constant prices
April 1950	£10.09	3.50p	5.17p	127	188	100	100
April 1959	£7.91	2.75p	2.75p	100	100	79	53
November 1968	£13.46	4.67p	3.47p	170	126	134	67
1972	£13.46	4.67p	2.64p	170	96	134	51
April 1973	£8.93	4.30p[a]	2.22p[a]	156	81	123	43
March 1980	£26.34	14.43p[a]	2.59p[a]	525	94	412	50

[a] Includes VAT.

Note:

In real terms, the excise duty on beer was much lower in the years after 1959 than in the 1950s. The April 1950 rate of £10.09 per barrel of 1037° beer was operative until April 1959, when it was reduced to £7.91. Thereafter, regular increases in duty, annually over the period 1964–8, produced a 70 per cent increase, 26 per cent in real terms, compared with 1959, but the level was still only two-thirds of the pre-1959 rate. And because there was no increase in duty over the period 1968–72, inflation eroded this increase. The reduction in duty in 1973, in consequence of the introduction of VAT, lowered the real value still further, and it was only in 1980 that the combined tax burden (duty + VAT) approached the 1972 level again.

Source: BS, *Statistical Handbook 1991*, pp. 41, 45, 48; CSO, *Economic Trends 1991*, p. 6.

Table XIV. *Labour productivity in brewing and malting, 1954–80*

Year	Establishments (no.)	Employees (no.)	Employees per establishment (no.)	Net output (£m.)	Net output per employee (£)	Net output per employee (1958 prices) (£)	Index (1958 = 100)
1954	–	68,700	–	101.8	1,482	1,773	90
1958	674	79,300	117.7	156.7	1,977	1,977	100
1963	578	86,800	150.2	218.4	2,514	2,235	113
1968	383	80,400	209.9	293.2	3,645	2,728	138
1973	223	71,600	321.1	488.3	6,822	3,465	175
1980	205	53,500	261.0	1,113.4	20,818	3,686	186

Source: Census of Production, 1954–80; CSO, *Economic Trends*, 1991, p. 6 (GDP deflator, factor cost).

Table XV. *Brewers' Society collective advertising campaigns, 1948–70*

Year ending 30 September (ann. averages)	Allocated subscriptions (£)	Extended subscriptions (£)	Expenditure (£)	Deployment: Posters %	Press %	TV %	Radio %
1948	80,000	–	75,000	–	92	–	–
1949–54	128,000	–	135,000	–	84	–	–
1955	120,000	91,000	174,000	40	57	–	3
1956	120,000	182,000	333,000	49	46	–	3
1957–8	120,000	196,000	312,000	66	30	–	2
1959–63	120,000	223,000	343,000	55	39	2	–
1964–7	120,000	265,000	379,000	–	23	73	–
1968–9	120,000	159,000	292,000	–	94	–	–
1970	120,000	147,000	254,000	–	–	97	–
Total:							
1948–54	851,000	–	887,000	–	85	–	–
1955–70	1,920,000	3,007,000	5,202,000	30	39	27	0.5

Source: BS File on 'Collective Advertising', 8/1/2, BS.

Table XVI. *Beer advertising expenditure, 1955–79 (in current and constant prices)*

Year	Beer advertising expenditure in current prices: All Sources	Beer advertising expenditure in current prices: 'Media' (Press/TV)	TV as % of All	Indices 1955 = 100 current prices: All	Indices 1955 = 100 current prices: Press/TV	Indices 1955 = 100 constant 1979 prices: All	Indices 1955 = 100 constant 1979 prices: Press/TV	Total UK advertising expenditure current prices	Total UK advertising expenditure constant 1979 prices 1955=100	Total UK advertising expenditure TV as % of All
1955	£2.200m	£1.318m	5%[a]	100	100	100	100	£176m	100	1
1960	£4.585m	£3.125m	30%	208	237	181	206	£323m	161	22
1965	£5.786m	£4.166m	56%	263	316	193	233	£435m	183	24
1970	£10.900m	£7.726m	65%	495	586	291	344	£544m	186	23
1975	£18.330m	£14.804m	75%	832	1123	265	358	£967m	176	24
1979	£33.400m	£24.047m	60%[b]	1518	1825	291	350	£2137m	234	22[b]

[a] Estimated on the assumption that 40 per cent of TV expenditure September 1955–April 1956 was made in 1955.
[b] ITV industrial dispute, August–October 1979.
Source: Legion Publishing Co., *Statistical Review of Press Advertising*, 24–5, 29–30 (1955–6, 1960–1); Media Records Ltd, *Statistical Review of Independent Television Advertising*, 1, 5–6 (1956, 1960–1); *Statistical Review of Press and TV Advertising*, 34–5 (1965–6); Register-MEAL Ltd, data for 1970–9; Advertising Association, *Advertising Statistics Year Book* (1987) (advertising deflator); estimates of S. H. Benson and Poster Publicity Ltd.

Table XVII. *Selected beer advertisers (press and TV), 1955–79*

Year	Leading advertisers (%)									
	Guinness	Ind Coope/ Allied	Bass	Charrington	Whitbread	Watneys/ Grand Met	Brewers' Society	Courage/ Imperial	S&N	Lager
1955	24	7.5	5	0.3	12	4	7	1.3	–	–
1960	16 (17[a])	16	6	3	13	8	3	0.1	3	19
1965	18 (19[a])	7.5	7	9	7.5	14	9	3	4	10
			Bass Charrington							
1970	18 (21[a])	19	22		8 (10[b])	8	3	6	4	18
1975	17 (21[a])	19	13		8 (14[b])	8 (11[c])	0	7.5	9	29
1979	14 (20[a])	14 (14[e])	12 (13[d])		2 (13[c])	6 (16[c])	0	9	9	37

[a] Harp advertising allocated to Guinness from 1960, Kronenbourg in 1979.
[b] Heineken advertising allocated to Whitbread from 1970, Stella Artois from 1975, Kaltenburg and Heldenbrau in 1979.
[c] Carlsberg advertising allocated to Watneys/Grand Met from 1975, Holsten in 1979.
[d] Tuborg advertising allocated to Bass Charrington in 1979.
[e] Lowenbrau advertising allocated to Allied in 1979.
Source: As Table 13.6.

Table XVIII. *Consumers' expenditure, beer duty and prices, 1978–90 (1980 = 100)*

Year	Consumers' expenditure (current prices all items) 1980 = 100	Beer duty per pint[a]	Beerprice: i: Pub[b]	ii: DOE[c] Jan. 1987 = 100	iii: Pub net of Duty/VAT	Retail price index 1980 = 100	Beer price (in constant 1980 prices) i] 1980 = 100	ii]	iii]
1978	72	7.46p	28.5p	39.5	18.94p	75	70	73	73
1980	100	9.15p	40.5p	54.4	26.07p	100	100	100	100
1982	122	14.30p	54.0p	72.9	32.68p	122	109	110	102
1986	173	18.08p	75.5p	97.3	47.60p	146	127	123	125
1990	195	20.39p	110.0p	126.4	75.31p	189	144	123	153

[a] Duty on beer of 1037°.
[b] Public bar (managed house) price of pint of bitter (lager prices: 1980, 47.0p; 1982, 62.5p; 1986, 86.0p). The 1990 figure is provided by the DOE and is not confined to public bar prices.
[c] Department of Employment series (bitter/lager).
Source: BS, *Statistical Handbook 1991*, pp. 37, 41–2, 45. NB The data used here differ from those cited in Monopolies and Mergers Commission, *The Supply of Beer*, March 1989, Cm.651, p. 57.

Glossary of Terms

abroad clerks Travellers for the London breweries. They obtained orders, checked stocks and collected cash paid by the publicans on monthly credit.

abroad coopers Again, term applied in London. They 'fined' beer in the publicans' cellars, checked that it was in a saleable condition and made arrangements for the return of stale beer.

ale and beer Originally ale was a liquor made from an infusion of malt by fermentation, as opposed to beer, which was made by the same process but flavoured with hops. By the eighteenth century 'beer' and 'ale' were being used interchangeably to denote such drinks with little or no colour, in contrast with 'stout' and 'porter' which were black or dark in colour due to additions of roasted malt or caramel. 'Beer' as used by the brewer, denoted the whole class of fermented drinks made from malted barley, including 'stout' and 'porter'.

alginates Seaweed extracts used in wort boiling to encourage the precipitation and coagulation of proteins and tannins.

anti-oxidant Reducing agent added to bottled beer to delay or prevent oxidation.

attenuation The percentage reduction in the wort's specific gravity caused by the transformation of its sugars into alcohol and carbon dioxide gas through fermentation.

barley abrasion Scarification of barley husk and underlying layers prior to malting, to facilitate action of gibberellic acid and water.

barrel and cask Originally, a hooped oak vessel for the storage and transport of draught beer. The following sizes were common:

Butt	108 gallons
Puncheon	72 gallons
Hogshead	54 gallons
Tierce	42 gallons
Barrel	36 gallons
Kilderkin	18 gallons
Firkin	9 gallons
Pin	4½ gallons

beer (see ale)

brewery-conditioned beer Draught beer conditioned (e.g. by chilling, filtering and carbonating) in the brewery; also called keg beer.

Burton Union System A method of fermentation in large casks fitted to 'swan neck' pipes through which the surplus yeast works out into troughs. Introduced in Burton in the 1840s, it became widespread for the production of pale ales.

bushel (and quarter) A unit of measurement for barley and malt (56 lb for barley, 42 lb for malt). Roughly, two bushels of malt produced a barrel of beer. A quarter contained eight bushels.

cask-conditioned beer Beer which is conditioned naturally in the cask; also called 'real ale'.

centrifugal clarification Process used to remove suspended solids in beer using centrifugal force.

cleansing The removal of yeast from beer when the main fermentation has been completed.

common brewer 'Commercial' or 'wholesale' brewer as opposed to the publican or beer-house brewer. For the purposes of this book defined as one who produced more than 1,000 barrels a year.

continuous fermentation Long-run fermentation method, using either a tower or a serial stirred tank system.

cooler or cooling squares Shallow vessel usually constructed in wood into which the hot wort was run after the hops had been removed. Late nineteenth-century brewers were divided about its use, relying increasingly upon refrigerating (water-cooling) machinery. Cooler now a vessel for storing hot wort on its passage between hop back and the wort refrigerators.

copper Vessel in which the wort is boiled with hops.

decoction mashing Similar to infusion mashing, but with a lower initial temperature. The temperature is then raised in stages by boiling a portion of the mash and adding it back to the rest.

diacetyl Chemical with a butterscotch flavour produced during brewing process.

enzymic malt Lightly kilned malt which ensures the survival of a high percentage of the enzymes.

fermentation The conversion of the wort sugar into alcohol and carbon dioxide caused by a complex series of chemical reactions set up by various substances secreted by yeast.

filtration Liquid–solid separation.

finings Jelly-like material added to the beer before racking which, falling to the bottom of the vat, drags down floating particles so that the beer racked is clear and bright. Traditionally a mixture of isinglass (prepared from the dried swim bladder of the sturgeon) and old beer.

gibberellic acid Microbiological product (plant growth hormone) extracted from a fungus (*gibberella fujikuroi*) which accelerates barley germination.

goods The ground malts in the mash tun.

grist Screened and ground malt grains ready for mashing; a quantity of ground malt sufficient for one mashing.

heat exchanger Equipment which facilitates the rapid heating or cooling of wort or beer.

high-gravity brewing Advanced brewing method where beer is brewed at high original gravity and then diluted at the processing stage in order to maximise the use of the brewing plant.

hop back or hop jack A large vessel with a perforated false bottom to separate the spent hops from the wort after boiling.

hop extract Bitter resins and oils extracted from hops by either organic solvents or liquid carbon dioxide.

in-can system Plastic moulded chamber insert ('widget') which promotes small bubble formation in canned 'draught beer'.

isomerised hop extract Hop extract in which the alpha-acids have been converted into the bitter iso-alpha acids. It is added to beer after fermentation.

Kieselguhr filter Filter which uses finely powdered sedimentary silica.

lager Generic term for bottom-fermented beer subjected to a cold conditioning period.

lauter tun Large vessel in which mash is allowed to settle and the grains are removed from the sweet wort by a straining process.

lautering Process of separating or filtering spent grains from wort.

liquor Term used throughout the brewing industry for water used in the brewing process.

long pull Common stratagem of publicans in the late nineteenth century to attract custom by serving over-measure quantities.

mash tun The vessel in which the malt is mashed with hot liquor. A second or, rarely, third mash is made by adding further liquor to the goods after the sweet wort from the first mash has been run off.

monopoly value The additional value conferred upon a public house in respect of the licence attached to it.

nitrosamines Potentially carcinogenic compounds.

original gravity The specific gravity of the wort prior to fermentation at the temperature under consideration as compared with the density of water at 4°C – conventionally given the value of 1.000. It is a measure of the total amount of solids dissolved in the wort.

pasteurisation The application of heat to bottled, canned or kegged beer for the purpose of stabilising it biologically, stopping fermentation and prolonging shelf life. In Britain, cask-conditioned beers are, by definition, not pasteurised.

pitching	The addition of yeast from a previous brewing to the cooled hopped wort.
polyvinyl-polyrrolidone (pvpp)	Substance added to beer. By absorbing reactive polyphenols it discourages haze formation.
porter or entire	A dark, cheap beer, especially popular in London in the eighteenth and nineteenth centuries.
proteolytic enzyme	Enzyme which breaks down protein, reducing the potential to form haze.
racking	The process of transferring fermented beer from the maturation vat into containers – bottles, can, casks or kegs.
racking square	Large vessel from which beer is racked off.
'running' beers	The late nineteenth century term for a quick maturing, usually mild beer. Sometimes known as 'summer' ales.
skimmer	The vessel in which the yeast is removed or skimmed from beer after the main fermentation. Also called a 'round' or 'ponto'.
sparging	The practice introduced in the early nineteenth century of spraying the goods left in the mash tun after the wort has been run off, in order to extract as much fermentable matter as possible.
stout	Heavily hopped beer brewed from full-flavoured malts, often with an addition of caramel. Dark in colour, 'stout' was first used by Guinness at the beginning of the nineteenth century in the sense of 'stouter porter'.
table or small beer	A weak, low-alcohol beer brewed from the second or third mashing.
vat	A large vessel in which beer is stored and matured.
wet rent	Term used by brewers whereby they charge a higher wholesale price to their tenants than they charge to the free trade. In effect, tenants were compensated by the traditionally low 'dry rent' terms on which they rented their houses from the brewers.
whirlpool separator	Device to separate and remove spent hops and proteinaceous material.

yeast A microscopic unicellular plant secreting various substances which turn maltose or wort sugar into alcohol and carbon dioxide. Brewers' yeast has special properties which make it easy to handle in the brewing process.

Yorkshire square Another variant (see Burton Union System) for fermenting beers in two sets of stone or slate squares placed above each other. Much prized in the nineteenth century in the regions bordering the Pennines.

Bibliography

1. MANUSCRIPT SOURCES (BREWING INDUSTRY)

Note: a fuller listing of most of the brewing sources used in this study is given in Lesley Richmond and Alison Turton (eds.), *The Brewing Industry: A Guide to Historical Records* (Manchester, 1990).

Allied Breweries (Burton)

Records of: Samuel Allsopp & Sons; Archibald Arrol; Benskin's; Ind Coope; Ind Coope & Allsopp; Allied Breweries (UK); Tetley Walker

Allied: Joshua Tetley & Son (Leeds)

Company records

Allied-Lyons plc (London)

ICTA, Allied Breweries, Allied-Lyons minute books, 1961–80

Bass Brewers (Museum, Burton)

Records of: Bass, Ratcliff & Gretton; Worthington; James Eadie; John Joule & Sons

Manuscript history of 'Bass, Ratcliff & Gretton', by Ben Ward

Manuscript history of 'Bass Ratcliff & Gretton', by Colin C. Owen (subsequently published as '*The Greatest Brewery in the World*' (Chesterfield, 1992))

Bass Brewers, Cape Hill (Birmingham)

Records of: Mitchells & Butlers; Bass, Ratcliff & Gretton; Bass Mitchells & Butlers; Bass Charrington

Bass North (Leeds)

Records of: Hammonds Bradford Brewery; Hammonds United; Hope & Anchor; Carling's Brewery of Canada; Tadcaster Tower; Northern Breweries; United Breweries

Boddington Group plc (Alderley Edge)

Boddingtons' minute books, 1887–1980

Brewers' Association of Scotland (Edinburgh)

Association minute books and papers, 1931–45, 1960–80

Brewers' Society (London)

Society council and committee minutes, reports, papers, etc

Bristol Record Office

Records of: Bristol Brewery Georges; Bristol United

Companies House, London

Shareholders registers, and returns, etc. for: Boddingtons' Breweries; Burtonwood; Eldridge Pope; Flower & Sons; Flowers Breweries; Hook Norton; Wadworth

Courage Ltd (Bristol)

Records of: Bristol Brewery Georges; Bristol United; Oakhill Brewery; Octagon Brewery; Phillips & Sons; Plymouth Breweries; H. & G. Simonds

Courage: John Smith's Tadcaster Brewery

Records of: John Smith's; Warwicks & Richardsons

Eldridge Pope & Co. (Dorchester)

Company minutes and papers, to 1963

Fosters Brewing Group (Staines)

Minute-books (*c.*1955–80) of Courage & Barclay; Courage Barclay & Simonds; Courage; Watney Mann & Truman Brewers

Grand Metropolitan plc

Records of: Truman Hanbury Buxton; Watney Combe Reid (at Brick Lane, London, since transferred)

Manuscript history of Grand Metropolitan, by W. J. Reader and Judy Slinn, 1992

Greater London Record Office

Records of: Barclay Perkins; Bristol Brewery Georges; Courage & Co.; Watney; Watney Combe Reid; Watney Mann; Mann, Crossman & Paulin; Meux; Reid's Brewery; Truman Hanbury Buxton

Greene King (Bury St Edmunds and Biggleswade)

Records of: Greene King; Simpson's; Wells & Winch

Guinness (Park Royal)

Records of Guinness and associated companies, including Harp, Park Royal/Guinness Transport, to 1980

Manuscript history of 'Guinness, 1886–1939', by S. R. Dennison and O. MacDonagh, *c.*1965.

Manuscript history of 'Draught Guinness', by J. R. Moore, 1974
Manuscript history of 'Guinness in America', by Edward Guinness

Suffolk Record Office, Ipswich

Records of Tollemache & Cobbold

Maclay & Co., Alloa

Dividend Book, 1955–61

Norfolk Record Office, Norwich

Records of: Bullard; Steward & Patteson; Youngs, Crawshay & Youngs

Sandwell Local Studies Centre, Smethwick

Records of Mitchells & Butlers

Scottish Brewing Archive, Glasgow (formerly Edinburgh)

Records of: Archibald Arrol; T. & J. Bernard; William McEwan; Maclay; Newcastle Breweries; Scottish Brewers; J. & R. Tennent; Robert Younger; William Younger

Wadworth & Co., Devizes

Company records to 1980

West Yorkshire Archives, Leeds

Records of Joshua Tetley & Son

Westminster City Archives

Records of: Watney Combe Reid; Watney Mann; Mann, Crossman & Paulin, Reid's Brewery

Whitbread plc

Records of: Whitbread & Co., and associated companies, viz. Alton Court Brewery; George Beer & Rigden; Bentley's Yorkshire Breweries; Boddingtons'; Cheltenham & Hereford; Ely Brewery; Flower & Sons; Flowers Breweries; J. W. Green; Improved Public House Co.; Lacon; Mackeson; Norman & Pring; J. Nimmo; Restaurant Public Houses Association; Strong; Stroud; Tennant Brothers; West Country Breweries
Manuscript history of 'The Story of Whitbread and Co. PLC, 1742–1990', by N. B. Redman

2. MANUSCRIPT SOURCES (OTHER)

Advertising Association Library

Register-MEAL data on beer advertising expenditure

British Library of Political and Economic Science, LSE

Beveridge papers on food control

Tom Harrisson Mass-Observation Archive, University of Sussex

Reports on beer, drinking habits, public houses

Modern Records Centre

Sir Hugh Beaver FBI papers, MSS.200

Public Record Office

Cabinet Papers

Customs and Excise Ledgers (CUST 5, 9)

Home Office papers on Central Control Board/State Management Scheme (HO45, 185, 190)

Ministry of Agriculture and Fisheries Supply Department: Cereal Group papers (MAF84)

Central Statistical Office papers (RG23)

Ministry of Transport papers: Transport Tribunal proceedings (MT80)

J. Walter Thompson, London

Consumer surveys for United Breweries, Charrington United, Tennent Caledonian, and Bass Charrington

3. PARLIAMENTARY PAPERS AND OFFICIAL PUBLICATIONS

Evidence of Select Committee ... [on] Police of the Metropolis, 1817, VII

Report of Select Committee ... [on] Public Breweries, 1818, III

Minutes of Evidence taken before the Select Committee on Public Breweries, 1819, V

Report of Select Committee ... [on] the Sale of Beer by Retail, 1830, X

Report of Select Committee ... [on] Expediency of Admitting the Use of Molasses in Breweries and Distilleries, 1831, VII

Account of Numbers of Persons in UK licensed as Brewers and Victuallers, 1831–2, XXXIV; 1841, XXVI; 1851, LIII; 1852–3, XCIX; 1861, LVIII; 1870, LX; 1872, LIV; 1881, LXXXIII; 1882, LXIV; 1890–1, LXXVII; 1892, LXXII; 1901, LXIX; 1902, XCIII; 1912–13, LXVIII; 1914–16, LIV

Report of Select Committee ... [on] the State and Management of Houses in which Beer is sold by Retail, 1833, XV

Report of Select Committee ... [on] Drunkenness, 1834, VIII

Report of Commissioners ... [on] Excise Establishment, 1834, XXIV

Report of Select Committee H.L. ... [on] Sale of Beer, 1850, XVIII

Report of Select Committee ... [on] Malt Tax, 1867, XI, 1867–8, IX

Select Committee H.L. ... [on] Intemperance, 1877, XI; 1878, XIV; 1879–9, X

Royal Commission on Liquor Licensing Laws, 1897, XXXIV, C.8355, XXVI, C.8356, XXXV, C.8523; 1898, XXXVI, C.8693–4, XXXVII, C.8695–6, XXXVIII, C.8821–2, C.8979, C.8980; 1899, XXXIV, C.9075, XXXV, C.9076, C.9379

Report of Departmental Committee ... [on] Beer Materials, 1899, XXX, C.9171–2

Reports of the Royal Commission on Arsenical Poisoning, 1901, X, Cd.692; 1904, IX, Cd.1845, 1848, 1869

Report of the Advisory Committee on Proposals for the State Purchase of the Licensed Liquor Trade (England & Wales), April 1915, 1916, XII, Cd.8283; (*Scotland*), April 1915, 1916, XII, Cd.8319

Commission of Enquiry into Industrial Unrest. Summary of the Reports by the Rt. Hon. G.N. Barnes, M.P., 17 July 1917, 1917–18, XV, Cd.8696

Licensing Statistics, 1914–16, LIV, Cd.7981; 1919, LI, Cmd.352; 1924, XXIV, Cmd.2257

Central Control Board (Liquor Traffic). Carlisle and District. General Manager's Reports, 1918, 1919, XXIV, Cmd.137, *1919*; 1920, XX

Report of the Committee on the Disinterested Management of Public Houses (Southborough Committee), May 1927, 1927, X, Cmd.2862

Report of the Royal Commission on Licensing (England & Wales), 1929–31, December 1931, 1931–2, XI, Cmd.3988

National Board for Prices and Incomes, Report No. 13 on *Costs, Prices and Profits in the Brewing Industry*, April 1966, 1966–7, Cmnd. 2965

Monopolies Commission, *Beer: A Report on the Supply of Beer*, April 1969, 1968–9, XL, HC216

Monopolies Commission, *Unilever Ltd and Allied Breweries Ltd: A Report on the Proposed Mergers and General Observations on Mergers*, 9 June 1969, 1968–9, LX, HC297

Report of the Departmental Committee on Liquor Licensing (Erroll Committee), December 1972, 1972–3, XIV, Cmnd.5154

Scottish Home and Health Department, *Report of the Departmental Committee on Scottish Licensing Law* (Clayson Committee), August 1973, 1972–3, XV, Cmnd.5354

Ministry of Agriculture, Fisheries and Food, *Food Standards Committee Report on Beer*, 1977

Price Commission, *Beer Prices and Margins*, Report No. 31, 1977

Final Report on Royal Commission on Gambling, July 1978, 1977–8, VII, Cmnd. 7200

Secretary of State for Prices and Incomes, *A Review of Monopolies and Mergers Policy: A Consultative Document*, May 1978, 1977–8, XXIV, Cmnd.7198

Price Commission, *Allied Breweries (UK) Limited – Brewing and Wholesaling of Beer and Sales in Managed Houses*, 26 April 1978

Price Commission, *Whitbread and Company Limited – Wholesale Prices and Prices in Managed Houses of Beer, Wines, Spirits, Soft Drinks and Ciders*, 12 June 1979

Price Commission, *Bass Limited – Wholesale Prices of Beer and Prices in Managed Houses*, 12 June 1979

Monopolies and Mergers Commission, *Scottish & Newcastle Breweries PLC and Matthew Brown PLC: A Report on the Proposed Merger*, November 1985, 1985–6, Cmnd.9645

Monopolies and Mergers Commission, *Elders IXL Ltd and Allied-Lyons PLC. A Report on the Proposed Merger*, September 1986, 1985–6, Cmnd.9892

Elders IXL Ltd and Scottish & Newcastle Breweries PLC: A Report on the Merger Situation, March 1989, 1988–9, Cm.654
Monopolies and Mergers Commission, *The Supply of Beer: A Report on the Supply of Beer for Retail Sale in the United Kingdom*, March 1989, 1988–9, Cm.651
Monopolies and Mergers Commission, *Elders IXL Ltd and Grand Metropolitan PLC: A Report on the Merger Situations*, October 1990, 1990–1, Cm.1227
Monopolies and Mergers Commission, *Allied-Lyons PLC and Carlsberg A/S: A Report on the Proposed Joint Venture*, July 1992, 1991–2, Cm.2029.

Statutory Instruments and Orders, including:
The Supply of Beer (Loan Ties, Licensed Premises and Wholesale Prices) Order 1989, SI, 1989 No.2258, 1 December 1989
The Supply of Beer (Tied Estate) Order 1989, SI 1989 No.2390, 19 December 1989

Parliamentary debates (Hansard)
Board of Trade, *Annual Statements of Trade*
Business Statistics Office, *Business Monitor MO7*, 1981, etc.
Census of Production, 1907, 1935, 1954, ff.
Central Statistical Office, *Annual Abstract of Statistics*
Economic Trends
Social Trends
Customs and Excise, *Annual Reports*
Department of Transport, *Transport Statistics Great Britain*
Report of the Inquiry into Lorries, People and the Environment (Armitage Report) (December 1980)
Department of Environment, *Transport Policy* (July 1976), Vol. I
Gaming Board for Great Britain: Reports, 1969–71
NEDO BSWG, *Report on Investment and Efficiency in the Brewing Industry*, January 1978
The Outlook for the Brewing Industry: Market Prospects and the Implications for Employment (1983)
Commission of the European Communities, *A Study of the Evolution of Concentration in the Beverages Industry for the UK*, Pt 1 (April 1977)
Advertising Standards Authority, *The British Code of Advertising Practice*, February 1975
Independent Broadcasting Authority, *Code of Advertising Standards and Practice*, September 1975, October 1978

4. BREWING JOURNALS, ETC.

Brewing Trade Review, 1886–1972
Brewing Review, 1972–92
The Brewer, 1971–92
Brewers' Journal, 1864–1963
Brewers' Almanack, 1894–1971
Brewers' Guardian, 1871–1992

Brewers' Guild Journal, 1958–70
Country Brewers' Gazette, 1877–1931
Courage and Barclay Journal, 1960
Courage News, 1986
(Duncan's) Manual of British and Foreign Brewery Companies, 1889–1992
Transactions of the Laboratory Club, 1887–90
Transactions of the Institute of Brewing, 1890–4
Journal of the Federated Institute of Brewing, 1895–1903
Journal of the Institute of Brewing, 1904–92
Incorporated Brewers' Guild Directory, 1991
Brewers' Society Statistical Handbooks, 1973–92
Brewers' Society International Statistical Handbook, 1979–83
Licensed Victuallers' Gazette
Licensed Victuallers' Almanack
CAMRA, *What's Brewing?*, 1971–92
Black Eagle Magazine, 1929–38
Hand in Hand, 1919–31
The Red Barrel, 1932–72
House of Whitbread, 1920–63
Whitbread News, 1962–92
Harp Record, 1973–9
Guinness Time, 1947–75
The Red Hand, 1959
Morning Advertiser, 1795–1992

5. OTHER JOURNALS, NEWSPAPERS

Burdett's Official Intelligence, Burton Chronicle, Burton Evening News, Burton Evening Post, The Daily Telegraph, Directory of Directors, The Economist, The Financial Times, Investors' Chronicle, Investors' Review, Statistical Review of Press (and TV) Advertising, Statist, Stock Exchange Year-Book, Stock Exchange Official Daily List, The Times, The Times Book of New Issues, Who Was Who

6. UNIVERSITY THESES AND DISSERTATIONS

J. Baxter, 'The Organisation of the Brewing Industry', University of London Ph.D., 1945
V. Dickie, 'The Effects of Mergers on the Brewing Industry in Scotland', Heriot Watt B.A., 1981
K. H. Hawkins, 'The Conduct and Development of the Brewing Industry in England and Wales, 1880–1938. A Study of the Role of Entrepreneurship in determining Business Strategy, with particular reference to Samuel Allsopp & Sons Ltd.', University of Bradford Ph.D., 1981
D. M. Knox, 'The Development of the London Brewing Industry, 1830–1914, with Special Reference to Whitbread and Company', University of Oxford B.Litt., 1956
Rachel Lovatt, 'Changing Industry – Changing Theory. A Study of Ind Coope Burton Brewery Ltd', Bristol Polytechnic B.A., 1989

K. Watson, 'Industrial Finance in the UK: The Brewing Experience, 1880–1913', University of Oxford D.Phil. 1990
F. J. Wood, 'Inland Transport and Distribution in the Hinterland of King's Lynn, 1760–1840', University of Cambridge Ph.D., 1992

7. SECONDARY WORKS, PUBLISHED BEFORE 1914
(place of publication: London, unless stated)

F. Accum, *Treatise on Adulterations of Food and Culinary Poisoning* (1820)
J. L. Baker, *The Brewing Industry* (1905)
A. Barnard, *Noted Breweries of Great Britain and Ireland*, 4 vols. (1889–91)
R. D. Baxter, *The Taxation of the United Kingdom* (1869)
J. Bickerdyke, *The Curiosities of Ale and Beer* (1889)
W. Black, *A Practical Treatise in Brewing* (4th edn, 1849)
C. Buxton, *Memorials of Sir Thomas Fowell Buxton, Bart.* (1848)
F. Faulkner, *The Art of Brewing* (1875)
W. Ford, *An Historical Account of the Malt Trade and Laws* (1849)
A Glass of Pale Ale and A Visit to Burton (Burton, 1880)
Ind Coope and Co. Ltd Souvenir, 1799–1899 (1899)
L. Levi, *The Liquor Trades: A Report to M. T. Bass Esq. M.P., on The Capital Invested and Number of Persons Employed Therein* (1871)
Consumption of Spirits, Beer, and Wine, in its relation to Licences, Drunkenness, and Crime: A Report to M. T. Bass (1872)
H. W. Macrosty, *The Trust Movement in British Industry* (1902)
W. Molyneux, *Burton-on-Trent: Its History, Its Waters and Its Breweries* (1869)
E. R. Moritz and G. H. Morris, *A Text Book of the Science of Brewing* (1891)
John Pitt, *How to Brew Good Beer* (1859)
E. A. Pratt, *The Licensed Trade: An Independent Survey* (1907)
J. Rowntree and A. Sherwell, *The Temperance Problem and Social Reform* (9th edn, 1901)
P. Snowden, *Socialism and the Drink Question* (1908)
E. R. Southby, *A Systematic Handbook of Practical Brewing* (2nd edn, 1885)
H. Stopes, *Malt and Malting* (1885)
F. W. Thornton, *How to Purchase and Succeed in a Public House* (1885)
W. L. Tizard, *The Theory and Practice of Brewing* (2nd edn, 1846)
A Voice from the Mash Tun (1845)
Sidney and Beatrice Webb, *The History of Liquor Licensing Principally from 1700 to 1830* (1903)
R. Wigram, *Biographical Notes Relating to Certain Members of the Wigram Family* (1912)

8. SECONDARY WORKS, PUBLISHED AFTER 1914
(place of publication: London, unless stated)

Mark Abrams, *The Teenage Consumer* (London Press Exchange, July 1959)
J. Agg-Gardner, *Some Parliamentary Recollections* (1927)
Derek H. Aldcroft, 'Control of the Liquor Trade in Great Britain 1914–21', in

W. H. Chaloner and Barrie M. Ratcliffe (eds.), *Trade and Transport* (Manchester, 1977)
B. W. E. Alford, *British Economic Performance 1945–1975* (1988)
R. G. Anderson, 'The Pattern of Brewing Research: A Personal View of the History of Brewing Chemistry in the British Isles', *Journal of the Institute of Brewing*, 98 (1992)
P. R. Ashurst, 'Hop Extracts', *Brewers' Guild Journal*, 55 (1969)
B. Atkinson, *English Hops* (1982)
'Requirements for Innovatory Research in Support of Malting and Brewing', *Journal of the Institute of Brewing*, 89 (May–June 1983)
M. Ball, *The Worshipful Company of Brewers* (1977)
Graham Bannock, *The Smaller Business in Britain and Germany* (1976)
L. Margaret Barnett, *British Food Policy During the First World War* (1985)
S. W. Baron, *Brewed in America: A History of Beer and Ale in the United States* (Boston, Mass., 1962)
Eric Batstone, *The Reform of Workplace Industrial Relations: Theory, Myth and Evidence* (Oxford, 1988)
E. S. Beavan, *Barley: Fifty Years of Observation and Experiment* (1947)
'Barley for Brewing since 1886', *Journal of the Institute of Brewing*, 46 (1936)
R. Beniger, *The Control Revolution* (Cambridge, Mass., 1986)
Brian R. Bennison, 'The Economic and Social Origins of the Northern Clubs' Federation Brewery: Some Preliminary Thoughts', *Newcastle Polytechnic School of Economics Staff Paper*, December 1984
Brian R. Bennison and James P. Merrington, *The Centenary History of the Newcastle Breweries Ltd, 1890–1990* (Edinburgh, 1990)
[Bentleys], *A Famous Country Brewery, 1828–1928* (Leeds, 1928)
Sir William Beveridge, *British Food Control* (1928)
K. Bhaskar, 'Three Case Studies – Guinness, Spillers and Nestlés', in J. M. Samuels (ed.), *Readings on Mergers and Takeovers* (1972)
W. H. Bird, *A History of the Institute of Brewing* (1955)
L. Bishop, 'A Conspectus of Brewing Progress', *Journal of the Institute of Brewing*, 77 (1971)
'A System of Continuous Fermentation', *Journal of the Institute of Brewing*, 76 (1970)
A. E. Bollard, 'Pint-Sized Production: Small Firms in the Brewing Industry', *Alternative Industrial Framework for the U.K. Report No. 1* (Interim Technology Development Group, 1982)
Richard Boston, *Beer and Skittles* (1976)
Robert Bothwell and William Kilbourn, *C. D. Howe: A Biography* (Toronto, 1980)
Brewers' Guardian: 100 Years of British Brewing (1971)
Asa Briggs, 'Beer and Society: A Major Theme in English History', *The Brewer* (August 1983)
P. Bristow, *The Mansfield Brew* (Ringwood, 1976)
H. T. Brown, 'Reminiscences of Fifty Years Experience of the Application of Scientific Method to Brewing Practice', *Journal of the Institute of Brewing*, 22 (1916)

J. Brown, *Steeped in Tradition: The Malting Industry since the Railway Age* (Reading, 1983)

J. F. Brown, *Guinness and Hops* (1980)

G. E. Bryant and G. P. Baker (eds.), *A Quaker Journal, being the Diary and Reminiscences of William Lucas of Hitchin (1804–1861)* (2 vols., 1934)

Robert Bud, 'Biotechnology and the Chemical Engineer: A Case Study in the History of Continuous Brewing', *International Industrial Biotechnology*, 9(6) (1989)

George Bull and Anthony Vice, *Bid for Power* (3rd edn, 1961)

A. H. Burgess, *Hops: Botany, Cultivation and Utilization* (1964)

W. L. Burn, *The Age of Equipoise* (1964)

J. Burnett, *Plenty and Want* (1966)

A. H. Button, 'Changes in Fermentation Techniques', *Brewers' Guardian* (September 1971)

CAMRA, *Good Beer Guide* (St Albans, 1974–92)

Henry Carter, *The Control of the Drink Trade in Britain: A Contribution to National Efficiency During the Great War 1915–1918* (2nd edn, 1919)

Thomas N. Carver, *Government Control of the Liquor Business in Great Britain and the United States* (New York, 1919)

George E. G. Catlin, *Liquor Control* (1931)

John Cavanagh and Frederick F. Clairmonte, *Alcoholic Beverages: Dimensions of Corporate Power* (1985)

Alfred D. Chandler, Jr, *Scale and Scope: The Dynamics of Industrial Capitalism* (Cambridge, Mass., 1990)

The Visible Hand: The Management Revolution in American Business (Cambridge, Mass., 1977)

Derek F. Channon, *The Strategy and Structure of British Enterprise* (1973)

Geoffrey Channon, 'Georges and Brewing in Bristol', in C. E. Harvey and J. Press (eds.), *Studies in the Business History of Bristol* (Bristol, 1988)

S. G. Checkland, *The Rise of Industrial Society in England, 1815–1885* (1964)

Brian Chiplin, Brian Sturgess and John Dunning, *Economics of Advertising* (1981)

Brian Chiplin and Mike Wright, 'The Logic of Mergers', *Institute of Economic Affairs Hobart Paper*, No.107, 1987

Christian Economic and Social Research Foundation, *Ten Years of Advertising Alcohol* (June 1969)

P. Clark, *The English Alehouse: A Social History, 1200–1830* (1983)

Roger Clarke, Stephen Davies and Michael Waterson, 'The Profitability–Concentration Relation: Market-Power or Efficiency?', *Journal of Industrial Economics*, 32 (1984)

David Clutterbuck and Marion Devine, *Clore: The Man and his Millions* (1987)

John Cobring, 'The Bottle v Can – the Beer Market', *The Brewer* (July 1980)

T. C. Cochran, *The Pabst Brewing Company* (New York, 1948)

A. J. Cockerill, 'Economies of Scale, Industrial Structure and Efficiency: The Brewing Industry in Nine Nations', in A. P. Jacquemin and H. W.L de Jong (eds.), *Welfare Aspects of Industrial Markets* (Leiden, 1977)

D. C. Coleman, 'Gentlemen and Players', *Economic History Review*, 2nd ser. 26 (February 1973)

A. H. Cook, 'Brewing Research', *Brewers' Guardian* (September 1971)

P. Lesley Cook, *Effects of Mergers: Six Studies* (1958)

T. A. B. Corley, 'A Small Berkshire Enterprise: J. Dymore Brown and Son, 1831–1944', *Berkshire Archaeological Journal*, 69 (1977–8)

'Simonds' Brewery at Reading, 1760–1960', *Berkshire Archaeological Journal*, 68 (1975–6)

'The Old Breweries of Berkshire, 1741–1984', *Berkshire Archaeological Journal*, 71 (1981–2)

The Road to Worton Grange: Simonds' and Courage's Brewery at Reading 1785–1980 (Reading, 1980)

Martyn Cornell, 'The Brewmaster's Story', *Bedfordshire Magazine* (Summer 1981)

H. S. Corran, *A History of Brewing* (Newton Abbot, 1975)

P. L. Cottrell, *The Finance and Organisation of English Manufacturing Industry* (1980)

Arnold Coward, 'A Review of Packaging Development', *The Brewer* (March 1974)

Keith Cowling, John Cable, *et al.*, *Advertising and Economic Behaviour* (1975)

Keith Cowling, Paul Stoneman, *et al.*, *Mergers and Economic Performance* (Cambridge, 1980)

N. F. R. Crafts and Nicholas Woodward (eds.), *The British Economy since 1945* (Oxford, 1991)

Alan Crawford, Michael Dunn and Robert Thorne, *Birmingham Pubs 1880–1939* (Gloucester, 1986)

M. A. Cundill and B. A. Shane, 'Trends in Road Goods Traffic 1962–77', *Transport and Road Research Laboratory Supplementary Report 572* (1980)

Stella V. Cunliffe, Presidential Address, *Journal of the Royal Statistical Society*, Series A, 139 Part 1 (1976)

G. Curtis, *A Chronicle of Small Beer* (1970)

N. H. Cuthbert and K. H. Hawkins (eds.), *Company Industrial Relations Policies: The Management of Industrial Relations in the 1970s* (1973)

Charles Dalgleish, '25 Years of Brewing Research', *Brewing Review* (March 1976)

R. O. Darling, 'From Barrels to Bulk Tanks', *Brewers' Guardian* (September 1971)

D. J. Dickinson, 'Some Aspects of Modern Brewing Engineering', *The Brewer* (January 1973)

A. E. Dingle, 'Drink and Working Class Living Standards in Britain, 1870–1914', *Economic History Review*, 2nd ser. 25 (1972)

The Campaign for Prohibition in Victorian England: The United Kingdom Alliance, 1872–1895 (1980)

Ian Donnachie, *A History of the Brewing Industry in Scotland* (Edinburgh, 1979)

W. L. Downard, *The Cincinnati Brewing Industry: A Social and Economic History* (Athens, Ohio, 1973)

Martin Duffy, 'The Effect of Advertising on the Total Consumption of Alcoholic Drinks in the UK: Some Econometric Evidence', *Journal of Advertising History*, 1 (1982)

G. A. Dummett, *From Little Acorns: A History of the A.P.V. Company Limited* (1981)

Mike Dunn, *Local Brew: Traditional Breweries and Their Ales* (1986)

J. W. Durcan *et al.*, *Strikes in Post-war Britain: A Study of Stoppages of Work due to Industrial Disputes, 1946–73* (1983)

Robert B. Ekelund, Jr and David S. Saurman, *Advertising and the Market Process: A Modern Economic View* (San Francisco, 1988)

P. Eley, *Portsmouth Breweries, 1492–1847* (Portsmouth, 1988)

Ted Elkins, Jr, *So They Brewed Their Own Beer* (Newcastle, 1970)

Aytoun Ellis, *Yorkshire Magnet: The Story of John Smith's Tadcaster Brewery* (1953)

Charlotte Erickson, *British Industrialists: Steel and Hosiery, 1850–1950* (Cambridge, 1959)

G. E. Evans, *Where Beards Wag All: The Relevance of the Oral Tradition* (1970)

D. M. Fahey, 'Brewers, Publicans and Working-Class Drinkers: Pressure Group Politics in Late Victorian and Edwardian England', *Histoire Sociale/Social History*, 13 (1980)

James Fairburn and John Kay (eds.), *Mergers and Merger Policy* (1988)

C. H. Feinstein, *National Income, Expenditure and Output of the United Kingdom, 1855–1965* (Cambridge, 1972)

R. Filmer, *Hops and Hop Picking* (1980)

Robert Fitzgerald, *British Labour Management and Industrial Welfare, 1846–1939* (1988)

M. W. Flinn, 'Trends in Real Wages, 1750–1850', *Economic History Review*, 2nd ser. 25 (1972)

M. P. Fogarty, *Further Studies in Industrial Organisation* (1948)

Freedom Association, *Handbook for Speakers and Writers on the (So-Called) Temperance Question* (8th edn, 1929)

A. Gall, *Manchester Breweries of Times Gone By* (Manchester, 1978–80)

Abby Ghobadian, *The Effects of New Technological Change on Shift Work in the Brewing Industry* (Aldershot, 1986)

M. Girouard, *Victorian Pubs* (1973)

K. Glamann, *Jacobsen of Carlsberg: Brewer and Philanthropist* (Copenhagen, 1991)

Charles Gordon, *The Two Tycoons: A Personal Memoir of Jack Cotton and Charles Clore* (1984)

T. R. Gourvish, 'British Business and the Transition to a Corporate Economy: Entrepreneurship and Management Structures', *Business History*, 29 (October 1987)

Norfolk Beers from English Barley: A History of Steward & Patteson, 1793–1963 (Norwich, 1987)

T. R. Gourvish and Alan O'Day (eds.), *Britain Since 1945* (1991)

T. R. Gourvish and R. G. Wilson, 'Profitability in the Brewing Industry, 1885–1914', *Business History*, 27 (July 1985)

S. J. Gray and M. C. McDermot, *Mega-Merger Mayhem: Takeover Strategies, Battles and Controls* (1989)
Christopher Grayling, *Manchester Ales and Porter: The History of Holt's Brewery* (Manchester, 1985)
J. R. Greenaway, 'Bishops, Brewers and the Liquor Question in England, 1890–1914', *Historical Magazine of the Protestant Episcopal Church*, 53 (1984)
'The Drink Problem back on the Political Agenda', *Political Quarterly*, 61 (1990)
[Groves and Whitnall], *The History of the Brewery, 1835–1949* (Manchester, 1949)
Edward Guinness, *The Guinness Book of Guinness, 1935–1985* (Enfield, 1988)
David W. Gutzke, *Protecting the Pub: Brewers and Publicans against Temperance* (Woodbridge, Suffolk, 1989)
'Rhetoric and Reality: The Political Influence of British Brewers, 1832–1914', *Parliamentary History*, 9 (1990)
'The Social Status of Landed Brewers since 1840', *Histoire Sociale/Social History*, 17 no.3 (May 1984)
Graham C. Hall, 'The Effects of Mergers on the Brewing Industry', Warwick University Centre for Industrial Economic and Business Research Discussion Paper No.74 (April 1977)
Leslie Hannah, *The Rise of the Corporate Economy* (2nd edn, 1983)
G. N. Hardinge, *The Development and Growth of Courage's Brewery* (privately printed, 1932)
C. L. Harman, *Cheers, Sir! From the Vicarage to the Brewery* (Cheddar, 1987)
J. O. Harris, 'Brewing Technology of the Future', *The Brewer* (June 1978)
'Changes in British Brewing Techniques', *Brewers' Guardian* (September 1971)
R. Harris and A. Seldon, *Advertising in Action* (1962)
B. Harrison, *Drink and the Victorians* (1971)
'Pubs', in H. J. Dyos and M. Wolff (eds.), *The Victorian City: Images and Realities*, I (1973)
B. Harrison and B. Trinder, 'Drink and Sobriety: An Early Victorian County Town: Banbury, 1830–60', *English Historical Review: Supplement*, 4 (1969)
P. E. Hart and R. Clarke, *Concentration in British Industry* (Cambridge, 1980)
Kevin Hawkins, 'Brewer–Licensee Relations: A Case Study in the Growth of Collective Bargaining and White Collar Militancy', in N. H. Cuthbert and K. H. Hawkins (eds.), *Company Industrial Relations Policies: The Management of Industrial Relations in the 1970s* (1973)
A History of Bass Charrington (Oxford, 1978)
Kevin Hawkins and C. L. Pass, *The Brewing Industry: A Study in Industrial Organisation and Public Policy* (1979)
Kevin Hawkins and Rosemary Radcliffe, 'Competition in the Brewing Industry', *Journal of Industrial Economics*, 20 (1971)
P. J. Hawkins, 'High Gravity Brewing', *Brewers' Guardian* (May 1975)
B. Hilton, *The Age of Atonement: The Influence of Evangelism on Social and Economic Thought, 1795–1865* (Oxford, 1988)

Corn, Cash and Commerce: The Economic Policies of the Tory Governments, 1815–1830 (Oxford, 1977)
Hugh Hope-Stone, 'Market-Share and Profitability in the UK Brewing Industry', *Thames Polytechnic Business Papers*, No. 4 (1985)
J. S. Hough, *The Biotechnology of Malting and Brewing* (Cambridge, 1985)
J. S. Hough, D. E. Briggs and R. Stevens, *Malting and Brewing Science* (1971)
J. R. Hudson, 'Expanding Brewing Technology', *Journal of the Institute of Brewing*, 89 (1983)
'Recent Developments in Brewing Technology', *Brewers' Guardian* (1976)
Christopher Hutt, *The Death of the English Pub* (1973)
Arthur Ingram, *Trucks in Britain: Brewery Transport* (Wellington, Somerset, 1991)
[Institute of Brewing], *An Introduction to Brewing Science and Technology* (n.d.)
Michael Jacobson, *The Cliff Brewery, 1723–1973* (Ipswich, 1973)
200 Years of Beer: The Story of Boddingtons' Strangeways Brewery 1778–1978 (Manchester, 1978)
A. P. Jacquemin and H. W. de Jong (eds.), *Welfare Aspects of Industrial Markets* (Leiden, 1977)
Hurford Janes, *Albion Brewery, 1808–1958: The Story of Mann, Crossman & Paulin Ltd* (1958)
Hall & Woodhouse 1777–1977: Independent Family Brewers (1977)
The Red Barrel: A History of Watney Mann (1963)
J. B. Jeffreys, 'The Denomination and Character of Shares, 1855–1885', *Economic History Review*, 16 (1946)
Basil Jellicoe (ed.), *Housing Happenings*, 2 (1929)
David J. Jeremy and Christine Shaw (eds.), *Dictionary of Business Biography* (5 vols., 1984–6)
E. Jones, 'A Private Transport Saving Calculation for the Brewers Truman Hanbury and Buxton, 1815–1863', *Journal of Transport History*, 3rd ser. 7 (1986)
Robert Jones, 'Where Have All the Merger Benefits Gone?', *Statist* (October 1964)
Jordan & Sons, *Supermarkets and Superstores* (1981)
Nicholas Kaldor and Rodney Silverman, *A Statistical Analysis of Advertising Expenditure and of the Revenue of the Press* (Cambridge, 1948)
D. Keir, *The Younger Centuries: The Story of William Younger and Co., 1749–1949* (1951)
F. A. King, *The Story of the Cannon Brewery, 1751–1951* (1951)
D. M. Knox, 'The Development of the Tied-House System in London', *Oxford Economic Papers*, 10 (1958)
Kesaji Kobayashi and Hidemasa Morikawa (eds.), *Development of Managerial Enterprise* (Tokyo, 1986)
Nick Kochan and Hugh Pym, *The Guinness Affair – Anatomy of a Scandal* (1987)
M. S. Kumar, *Growth, Acquisition and Investment* (Cambridge, 1984)
P. W. Kyle, 'The Impact of Advertising Markets', *Journal of Advertising History*, 1 (1982)

Clifford Lackey, *Quality Pays ... The Story of Joshua Tetley & Son* (Ascot, 1985)
W. R. Lambert, *Drink and Sobriety in Victorian Wales c.1820–c.1895* (Cardiff, 1983)
D. R. Laws *et al.*, 'Preparation of Hop Extracts Without Using Organic Solvents', *Journal of the Institute of Brewing*, 83 (1977)
David Lloyd George, *War Memoirs of David Lloyd George*, I (1933)
H. Lloyd-Hind, 'Pasteur to 1936 – An Account of the Development of Science in Brewing', *Journal of the Institute of Brewing*, 43 (1937)
Brewing Science and Practice (1938–40)
A. A. Locke, *The Hanbury Family* (2 vols., 1916)
London and Cambridge Economic Service, *The British Economy: Key Statistics 1900–1970* (1973)
Norman Longmate, *The Water Drinkers* (1968)
P. Lynch and J. Vaizey, *Guinness's Brewery in the Irish Economy, 1759–1876* (Cambridge, 1960)
Tony McGuinness, 'An Econometric Analysis of Total Demand for Alcoholic Beverages in the U.K., 1956–75', *Journal of Industrial Economics*, 39 (September 1980)
C. McMaster, *Alloa Ale: A History of the Brewing Industry in Alloa* (Edinburgh, 1985)
P. Mandler, 'Tories and Paupers: Christian Political Economy and the Making of the New Poor Law', *The Historical Journal*, 33 (1990)
John Mark, 'The British Brewing Industry', *Lloyds Bank Review*, 112 (April 1974)
'Changes in the British Brewing Industry in the Twentieth Century', in D. J. Oddy and D. S. Miller (eds.), *Diet and Health in Modern Britain* (1985)
J. Mason, '"Account for Beer": An Investigation into the Accounting Practice of Three Northamptonshire Breweries, 1882 to 1914', *Accounting History*, 1 and 2 (1981)
Peter Mathias, 'Brewing Archives: Their Nature and Use', in L. Richmond and A. Turton (eds.), *The Brewing Industry: A Guide to Historical Records* (Manchester, 1990)
The Brewing Industry in England, 1700–1830 (Cambridge, 1959)
'The Brewing Industry, Temperance and Politics', *The Historical Journal*, 1 (1958)
D. R. Maule, 'Reflections on Cylindro-Conical Fermenters', *The Brewer* (June 1977)
Peter Mayle, *Thirsty Work: Ten Years of Heineken Advertising* (1983)
G. Meeks, *Disappointing Marriage: A Study of the Gains from Merger* (Cambridge, 1977)
G. Meeks and J. G. Meeks, 'Profitability Measures as Indicators of Post-Merger Efficiency', *Journal of Industrial Economics*, 29 (June 1981)
H. Meller, *Leisure and the Changing City, 1870–1914* (1976)
William Mennell, *Takeover: The Growth of Monopoly in Britain 1951–61* (1962)
B. R. Mitchell and P. Deane, *Abstract of British Historical Statistics* (Cambridge, 1962)

Mitchells & Butlers, *Fifty Years of Brewing 1879–1929* (Birmingham, 1929)
H. A. Monckton, *A History of English Ale and Beer* (1966)
A History of the English Public House (1969)
Whitbread's Breweries (1984)
Sir Gilbert T. Morgan, 'Research Activities of the Institute of Brewing', *Journal of the Institute of Brewing*, 46 (1940)
L. Nabseth and G. F. Ray, *The Diffusion of New Industrial Processes: An International Study* (Cambridge, 1974)
L. Nathan, 'Improvements in the Fermentation and Maturation of Beers', *Journal of the Institute of Brewing*, 36 (1930)
T. R. Nevett, *Advertising in Britain: A History* (1982)
Sir Sydney O. Nevile, *Seventy Rolling Years* (1958)
G. D. Newbould, *Management and Merger Activity* (Liverpool, 1970)
Francis Noel-Baker, *Report on Drink Advertising* (February 1964)
N. T. C., *The Drink Pocket Book 1992* (Henley, 1991)
H. Osborne O'Hagan, *Leaves from My Life* (2 vols., 1929)
Basil Oliver, *The Modern Public House* (1934)
The Renaissance of the English Public House (1947)
H. D. O'Sullivan (ed.), *The Life and Works of C. O'Sullivan F. R. S.* (Guernsey, 1934)
C. C. Owen, *The Development of Industry in Burton-upon-Trent* (Chichester, 1978)
H. H. Parker, *The Hop Industry* (1934)
Jeffrey Patton, *Additives, Adulterants and Contaminants in Beer* (Swimbridge, Devon, 1989)
P. L. Payne, 'The Emergence of the Large-Scale Company in Great Britain, 1870–1914', *Economic History Review*, 2nd ser. 20 (1967)
Ian P. Peaty, *Brewery Railways* (Newton Abbot, *c.*1985)
Edith T. Penrose, *The Theory of the Growth of the Firm* (Oxford, 1959, 2nd edn, 1980)
Phillips and Sons Ltd. [Newport Mon.] Jubilee, 1924
H. Poole, *Here for the Beer: A Gazetteer of the Breweries of Hertfordshire* (Watford, 1984)
A. D. Portno, 'Brewing Research Foundation. Twenty-Five Years of Brewing Research', *Journal of the Institute of Brewing*, 89 (May–June, 1989)
'Continuous Fermentation – Past, Present and Future', *Brewing Review* (April 1976)
S. J. Prais, *The Evolution of Giant Firms in Britain* (Cambridge, 1976)
Productivity and Industrial Structure: A Statistical Study of Manufacturing Industry in Britain, Germany and the United States (Cambridge, 1981)
C. F. Pratten, *Economies of Scale in Manufacturing Industry* (Cambridge, 1971)
C. F. Pratten and A. G. Atkinson, 'The Use of Manpower in British Manufacturing Industry', *Department of Employment Gazette* (June 1976)
I. A. Preece, *The Biochemistry of Brewing* (Edinburgh, 1954)
A. R. Prest, *Consumers' Expenditure in the United Kingdom, 1900–1919* (1954)
Robert Price and George S. Bain, 'Union Growth in Britain: Retrospect and Prospect', *British Journal of Industrial Relations*, 21 (1983)

Roger Protz and Tony Millns (eds.), *Called to the Bar: An Account of the First 21 Years of the Campaign for Real Ale* (St Albans, 1992)
J. Pudney, *A Draught of Contentment: The Story of the Courage Group* (1971)
R. M. Punnett, 'State Management of the Liquor Trade', *Public Administration*, 44 (Summer 1966)
C. Rainbow, 'A Century of Brewing Microbiology', *Journal of the Institute of Brewing*, 94 (1988)
G. F. Ray, 'The Application of Gibberellic Acid in Malting', in L. Nasbeth and G. F. Ray, *The Diffusion of New Industrial Processes: An International Study* (Cambridge, 1974)
W. J. Reader, *Fifty Years of Unilever, 1930–1980* (1980)
N. B. Redman, 'Whitbread and Bottled Beer, 1869–1930', *The Brewer* (March 1991)
Rosser Reeves, *Reality in Advertising* (1961)
D. G. Rhys, *The Motor Industry: An Economic Survey* (1972)
N. Richardson, *A History of Joseph Holt* (Manchester, 1984)
L. Richmond and B. Stockford, *Company Archives: The Survey of the Records of 1000 of the First Registered Companies in England and Wales* (Aldershot, 1986)
L. Richmond and A. Turton (eds.), *The Brewing Industry: A Guide to Historical Records* (Manchester, 1990)
R. W. Ricketts, 'Review of Fermentation Systems', *Brewers' Guardian* (July 1970)
M. D. Ripley, 'British Beer Abroad – a 300 Year Overview of Beer Exports', *The Brewer* (August 1986)
B. Ritchie, *An Uncommon Brewer: The Story of Whitbread, 1742–1992* (1992)
M. Riviere, 'Practical Application of Resteeping in a Pneumatic Drum Malting', *Journal of the Institute of Brewing*, 67 (1961)
P. W. Robinson, 'The Emergence of the Common Brewer in the Halifax District', *Transactions of the Halifax Antiquarian Society*, 19 (1981)
Alfred Rose, *Personalities and Progress (1858–1969): The Story of Strong & Co. of Romsey Limited* (Ringwood, Hants, n.d.)
Michael E. Rose, 'The Success of Social Reform? The Central Control Board (Liquor Traffic), 1915–21', in M. R. D. Foot (ed.), *War and Society* (1973)
L. Rostas, *Comparative Productivity in British and American Industry* (Cambridge, 1948)
'Industrial Production, Productivity and Distribution in Britain, Germany and the United States', *Economic Journal*, 53 (1943)
J. Rowntree and A. Sherwell, *State Purchase of the Liquor Trade* (1919)
W. R. Rubenstein, *Men of Property: The Very Wealthy in Britain since the Industrial Revolution* (1981)
Charles Schofield and Anthony Kamm, *Lager Lovelies: The Story Behind the Glamour* (Glasgow, 1984)
Rosemary Scott, *The Female Consumer* (1976)
P. A. S. Scully and M. J. Lloyd, 'Further Developments in the Use of Wheat and Barley', *Brewers' Guild Journal*, 53 (1967)

A. W. Seddon, 'Continuous Fermentation in a Tower. Experiences in Establishing Large Scale Commercial Production', *The Brewer* (March 1976)
John Seekings, *Thomas Hardy's Brewer: The Story of Eldridge, Pope & Co.* (Wimborne, Dorset, *c.*1988)
Arthur Seldon, 'The British Brewing Industry', *Lloyds Bank Review* (October 1953)
Ernest Selley, *The English Public House As It Is* (1927)
W. P. Serocold (ed.), *The Story of Watneys* (1949)
Arthur Shadwell, *Drink in 1914–1922* (1923)
H. A. Shannon, 'The Coming of General Limited Liability', *Economic History*, 2 (1931)
'The First 5000 Limited Companies and their Duration', *Economic History*, 2 (1932)
'The Limited Companies of 1866–1883', *Economic History Review*, 4 (1933)
Francis Sheppard, *Brakspear's Brewery, Henley-on-Thames, 1779–1979* (Henley, 1979)
Brian Sibley, *The Book of Guinness Advertising* (Enfield, 1985)
E. Sigsworth, 'The Brewing Trade during the Industrial Revolution: The Case of Yorkshire', *Borthwick Papers*, 31 (1967)
J. Simmons, *St Pancras Station* (1968)
A. Singh, *Takeovers* (Cambridge, 1971)
J. N. Slater, *A Brewer's Tale: The Story of Greenall Whitley and Co. Ltd through Two Centuries* (Warrington, 1980)
Anthony Slaven and Sydney Checkland (eds.), *Dictionary of Scottish Business Biography 1860–1960* (Aberdeen, 2 vols., 1986, 1990)
Reginald G. Smart, 'Does Alcohol Advertising Affect Overall Consumption? A Review of Empirical Studies', *Journal of Studies on Alcohol*, 49 (1988)
C. T. B. Smith *et al.*, *Strikes in Britain* (1978)
M. Sprackling, 'The Economics of Using Isomerised Hop Extracts', *The Brewer* (February 1971)
Peter Steer and John Cable, 'Internal Organization and Profit: An Empirical Analysis of Large UK Companies', *Journal of Industrial Economics*, 27 (1978)
L. A. G. Strong, *Brewer's Progress, 1757–1957* (privately printed, 1957)
R. Wilson Stuart, *Drink Nationalization and its Results* (1927)
Brian Sturgess and Peter Weale, 'Merger Performance Evaluation: An Empirical Analysis of a Sample of UK Firms', *Journal of Economic Studies*, 11 (1984)
Supermarket Association of Great Britain, *Licences for Supermarkets?* (July 1965)
Alec Sutherland, 'The Management of Mergers Policy', in Alec Cairncross (ed.), *The Managed Economy* (Oxford, 1970)
W. Swales, *The History of the Tower Brewery Tadcaster* (Leeds, 1991)
C. F. Tetley, *A Century of Progress* (Leeds, 1923)
Robert Thorne, 'The Movement for Public House Reform 1892–1914', in D. J. Oddy and D. S. Miller, *Diet and Health in Modern Britain* (1985)
Chris Thurman, 'The Structure and Role of the British Alcoholic Drinks

Industry', in Marcus Grant, Martin Plant and Alan Williams (eds.), *Economics and Alcohol: Consumption and Controls* (1983)

M. F. Tighe, 'A Gazetteer of Hampshire Breweries', *Proceedings of the Hampshire Field Club*, 27 (1972)

Graham Turner, *Business in Britain* (1969)

John Turner, 'State Purchase of the Liquor Trade in the First World War', *The Historical Journal*, 23 (September 1980)

M. A. Utton, 'On Measuring the Effects of Industrial Mergers', *Scottish Journal of Political Economy*, 21 (February 1974)

J. E. Vaizey, *The Brewing Industry, 1886–1952* (1960)

David P. Waddington, *Trouble Brewing: A Social Psychological Analysis of the Ansells Brewery Dispute* (Aldershot, 1987)

J. G. Walshe, 'Industrial Organization and Competition Policy', in N. F. R. Crafts and Nicholas Woodward (eds.), *British Economy Since 1945* (Oxford, 1991)

Mike Waterson, *Advertising and Alcohol Abuse* (Advertising Association, 1983)

H. D. Watts, 'Lager Brewing in Britain', *Geography*, 60 (April 1975)

'Market Areas and Spatial Rationalization: The British Brewing Industry after 1945', *Tijdschrift voor Economische en Social Geografie*, 68 (1977)

'Understanding Plant Closures. The UK Brewing Industry' *Geography*, 76 (1991)

Michael Webster, interview, *Business Administration* (May 1970)

Courtenay C. Weeks (ed.), *Proceedings of the 20th International Congress on Alcoholism* (1934)

Leonard W. Weiss, 'An Evaluation of Mergers in Six Industries', *Review of Economics and Statistics*, 47 (May 1965)

R. B. Weir, 'The Drink Trades', in Roy Church (ed.), *The Dynamics of Victorian Business* (1980)

'Obsessed with Moderation: The Drink Trades (1870–1930)', *British Journal of Addiction*, 79 (1984)

R. W. Westbrook, *The Valuation of Licensed Premises* (1983)

[Whitbread], *Whitbread's Brewery* (1951)

C. Whitworth, 'High Gravity Brewing', *The Brewer* (November 1980)

M. Wiener, *English Culture and the Decline of the Industrial Spirit, 1850–1980* (1981)

F. G. Wigglesworth, 'The Evolution of Guinness Advertising', *Journal of Advertising History*, 3 (March 1980)

Ernest E. Williams, *The New Public House* (1924)

Gwylmor P. Williams, *Social Effects of the Ending of Resale Price Maintenance of Alcoholic Beverages 1966 to 1967* (1968)

Gwylmor P. Williams and George T. Brake, *Drink in Great Britain 1900 to 1979* (*c.*1980)

G. B. Wilson, *Alcohol and the Nation* (1940)

The 'Improved Public House': Is it a Day-Dream or a Smoke-Screen? (n.d.)

Richard G. Wilson, *Greene King: A Business and Family History* (1983)

'The British Brewing Industry since 1750', in L. Richmond and A. Turton (eds.), *The Brewing Industry* (Manchester, 1990)

Richard G. Wilson and Terry R. Gourvish, 'The Foreign Dimensions of British Brewing (1880–1980)', in Erik Aerts, Louis M. Cullen and Richard G. Wilson (eds.), *Production, Marketing and Consumption of Alcoholic Beverages since the Late Middle Ages* (Leuven, 1990)

Richard Wragg and James Robertson, 'Post-war Trends in Employment, Productivity, Output, Labour Costs and Prices by Industry in the United Kingdom', *Department of Employment Research Paper* No. 3 (June 1978)

B. S. Yamey, *Resale Price Maintenance* (1966)

JoAnne Yates, *Control through Communication* (Baltimore, Md., 1989)

Francis W. B. Yorke, *The Planning and Equipment of Public Houses* (1949)

9. ANALYSTS' REPORTS

Barclays de Zoete Wedd Research, *UK – Brewing* (December 1988)

Citicorp Scrimgeour Vickers, *Brewers Today: A Review of the UK Brewing Industry* (October 1987)

Euromonitor, *The Beer Report 1982* (1982)

Flemings Research, *Directory of Regional Brewers* (September 1988, October 1991)

Goldman Sachs International Research, *The UK Brewer* (May 1988)

W. Greenwell & Co., *The Brewing Industry: Quarterly Commentary*

Grieveson Grant Investment Research, *The Beer Market* (November 1984)

Hoare Govett, *Brewing* (April 1979)

IPC, *The U.K. Beer Market* (September 1977)

L. Messell, *Directory of National Brewers* (May 1987); *Regional Brewers* (November 1985, December 1987)

Panmure Gordon, *The Brewing Industry* (1968)

Rowe and Pitman, *Quarterly Report* (June 1980, etc.)

Shearson Lehmann Securities, *Review of Regional Brewers* (December 1987)

Sheppards Research, *Decades of Change* (June 1990)

Index

Abbot & Hodgson (Bow), 90
Aberdeen, 104, 106, 107, 156 n 74
Abridge & Son (Essex), 271 n 11
abroad clerks, 128, 130, 140, 303, 638
abroad coopers, 128, 130, 638
accounts, 180, 205, 209, 212–17, 227–37, 257–66, 271–2, 332–5, 342–5, 368–70, 378–81, 426–33, 439–40, 442–4, 461, 463, 485–8, 501–3, 509–12
Accum, Frederick, 139
Adams, William, 232
Adnams (Southwold), 381, 382, 484, 487, 507, 563, 568, 589
adulteration of beer, 6–7, 12, 59, 79, 91, 130, 138–9, 208, 209 n 65, 296
Adulteration of Food, Drink and Drug Act (1872), 140
Adulteration of Food, Select Committee on the (1855), 139
advertising, 39, 102, 146, 300, 345–6, 350–6, 558–68, 634–6, Pls. 45, 47, 48, 59, 60, 74, 82
Advertising Standards Authority, 561
Africa, 172, 478
age limits, 572
agents and agency system, 92, 94, 95, 97, 100, 101, 108, 117, 118, 125, 127, 144, 147, 151–2, 154–9, 161, 166, 168, 175, 200, 203, 204, 273
Agg-Gardner, Sir James, 223–4, 239, 249, Pl. 32.
Agg-Gardner (Cheltenham), 239
Agg-Gardner family, 115–16, 163, 242, 247
Aitchison, James (Edinburgh), 438 n 81
Aitken, James, & Co. (Falkirk), 109, 110, 468
alcohol abuse, 584–5, *see also* drunkenness
Alcohol Education and Research Council, 584
alcohol-free beers, 585
ale: Burton pale ales, 32, 41, 43, 46, 54, 170–3, 274, 277; India Pale Ale (IPA), 90–1, 158, 169, 170; light ales, 48, 58; mild ales, 42, 43, 69, 78, 80–2, 85–6, 134, 137–8, 144, 205, 363, 558; pale ales, 41, 43, 46, 54, 56, 57, 82, 130, 170–3, 175, 303; 'running' ales, 45, 46, 49, 50, 54, 55, 57, 59, 62, 85, 130, 165, 176, 642; Scottish pale ales, 105, 106, 109; *see also* beer; Campaign for Real Ale; porter
alginates, 546, 638
Allen, Stafford, 541
Allen, Thomas, 554
Allfrey family, 234
Allied (Allied Breweries, 1962–78; Allied-Lyons 1978–): advertising, 562–4, 568, 636; Calypso, 479; costs, 512; diversification, 500, 590 n 18; and games machines, 579; high-gravity brewing, 546; and imported beers, 585; labour relations, 528; low-alcohol beer, 585; market-position, 586; mergers and takeovers, 449, 450, 473, 478–9, 490, 497, 525, 527, 528, 592–3, 598, Pls. 66, 68; and public house monopolies, 573; prices, 521, 528; production, 504, 588; profits, 501, 502, 503, 588; rationalisation, 587; rebuilt breweries, 506; research, 539, 541; structure, 523, 525–9; tied estate, 472, 474, 524, 573, 586, 588; turnover, 588
Allied Brewery Traders' Association, 293
Alloa, 103–10, 116, 171, 173, 241
Allsopp, Samuel, & Sons, 123, 331; advertising, 39; agency system, 95, 97, 151, 152, 158; bottling, 299; brewery, Pl. 10; development of, 95–6; discounts, 255, 273, 304; distribution, 45, 151; exports, 91, 93, 95, 171, 173, 175; flotation, 95, 260, 303; free trade, 305; IPA, 90; labour force, 197; lager, 177, 304; loans, 276, 304; maltings, 190 n 23;

management, 95, 303, 311, 387, 394, Pl. 46; output, 331–2; profits, 214, 217, 308, 309 n 117, 620–2; problems of, 274, 285 n 49, 303–5; sales in Birmingham, 90, sales in London, 82, 119; size of brewery, 82; stores, 92; success of, 80, 84, 146, 237; takeovers, 342, 346 n 100, 347; tied estate, 121, 275, 276, 303–5; *see also* Ind Coope & Allsopp
Allsopp, George, 312
Allsopp Brewery Investments, 396 n 60
Allsopp family, 224
Alton, Hants, 50, 126
Alton Court Brewery Co. (Ross-on-Wye), 381
Amalgamated Licensed Retailers' Society, 137 n 8
amalgamations, *see* mergers; takeovers
America, South, 110, 169, 173–4
Amusement With Prizes (AWP) machines, 577–9
'Anchor Taverns', 424
Anderson, R. G., 534
Angevin wine company, 530
Anglo-Bavarian Brewery Co (Shepton Mallet), 162, 177 n 129
Anheuser-Busch, 585 n 8, 586
Ansells (Birmingham), 125; capitalisation, 380; closure, 587; labour relations, 528; management, 378, 528; market preference, 354, 355; mergers, 449, 524, 527; off-licence trade, 418; public house improvements, 421; tied estate, 382 n 19, 418, 441, 442, 525; transport, 549
antioxidants, 546, 638
Aluminium Plant and Vessel Co., 537, 538, 543, 544, 547, 548
Archers (Swindon), 591
Arkell (Swindon), 442, 507
armed forces, beer supplied to, 122, 168, 241, 280, 320, 322, 359
Armitage Report (1980), 555
Armstrong, H. E., 60
Arnold, John, & Sons (Wickwar), 334
Arnold, Perrett & Co. (Gloucester), 282, 306, 309
Arrol, Archibald (Alloa): distribution and transport, 549; Graham's Golden Lager, 339; management, 305, 387, 394; takeover, 346 n 100, 398; profits, 306, 333, 342–5, 620, 622
arsenic poisoning, 296
Askey & White, 283 n 48
Association of Club Breweries, 414 n 10
Association for the Promotion of Restaurant Public Houses in Poor Districts, 420, 425–6
Astley, J. W. (Nelson, Lancs.), Pl. 2
attemperators, 58
Australia: breweries in, 175, 265, 585, 587; exports to, 44, 109, 110, 169–75, 317; imports from, 585
Austria, brewing industry in, 172
Aylesbury Brewing Co., 568

Babington, Charles, 61
bacteria, 58–9
Bacterium Club, 60
Bagge (King's Lynn), 116
Bagge family, 223 n 104
Bailey, Crosier, 312
Bailey, W. H., 156, 276, Pl. 22
Baker, Julian, 46, 538
Balfour, Rt. Hon. A. J., 290
Balfour of Burleigh, Lord, 429
Ball, Cecil A., 403, 404, 462
Ballinghall & Co. (Dundee), 104–5, 106, 158
Banbury, 161–2
banking, 117, 227, 231–4, 247, 396, 399, 402, 463–4, 478
bankruptcies, 247, 251
Banks & Taylor (Shefford, Beds.), 591
Barclay, Charles, 11–13, 69, 75, 77, 78 n 20, 80, 82, 130
Barclay, Edwyn, 422, 423 n 40
Barclay, H. F., 391 n 46
Barclay & Simonds, 458, 469
Barclay family, 218, 227, 386
Barclay Perkins, 6–7, 42, 123: Anchor Brewery, 82, 85, 398; 'Anchor Taverns', 424; banking links, 396; bottling, 301; capitalisation, 272, 380; country trade, 145, 146; in difficulties, 284 n 49, 298; exports, 90, 172, 175; free trade, 436; hops, 193; incorporation, 227; labour force, 197; lager, 339; loans, 132, 133; management, 86, 87, 227, 228, 233, 386, 387, 390–1, 397–9; mergers and takeovers, 346 n 100, 387, 393, 398; production, 20, 79, 113, 610–12; profits, 308, 334, 369, 370, 620–1; public house building and improvements, 420, 422, 424–6, 430, 435; rest books, 82 n 23; tied estate, 131–3, 382 n 19, 399, 436; transport, 140, 142; vats, Pl. 6
Baring Brothers & Co., 251, 257, 399, 402, 464, 478 n 90
barley: cultivation, 186; drying, 192; flaked, 362; government controls on, 320, 322, 359, 362; imported, 188–9, 192–3, 361; prices, 188–9, 192–3, 205, 206, 255, 273, 349, 361; research on, 59, 536, 539; supply of, 75, 105, 121, 183

Barlow, W. H., 155

Barnard, Alfred, 42, 45, 50, 55, 60, 66, 84, 85, 87–9, 93, 103 n 70, 105, 106, 110, 112, 123, 124–6, 141, 143, 151, 190, 197, 202, 203, 212, 217, 235, 236, 238, 239, 258

Barnsley Brewery Co., 260 n 90, 308, 380, 567

Barras, J., & Co. (Newcastle upon Tyne), 159

barrelage, bulk and standard, 23–6, 318–22, 331, 337–9, 359, 360, 366–8, 602

barrels, 130, 546, 639, Pl. 29, *see also* casks

Barrows, W. L., 396

Bass (Bass, Ratcliff & Gretton, 1835–1961; Bass, Mitchells & Butlers, 1961–7; Bass Charrington, 1967–79; Bass, 1979–), 123: accounts, 180, 182, 196, 200, 343, 604–6; advertising and market research, 39, 350–1, 354–5, 562–3, 567, 636; agents and agency system, 94, 95, 97, 144, 151, 152, 154–8, 161, 276, 438–9, Pls. 23, 24; and alcohol abuse, 585 n 9; alcohol-free and low-alcohol beer, 585; banking links, 396 n 59; bottlers and bottling, 273, 299, 300, 438; breweries, 94, 506, 515, 544, 556; capitalisation, 380, 384, 472; casks, 202, 203, Pl. 9; coal consumption, 196 n 33; costs, 604–6; in difficulties, 254, 274, 284 n 49, 305; discounts, 255, 276; distribution and transport, 45, 150–2, 358, 438, 550, 552–3, 556; diversification, 590; beer duties, 196; excursions, 198–9, Pls. 27, 28; exports, 89–91, 93, 150, 170–1, 173, 174–5, 299, 339, 377; fermenter, 544; free trade, 438–9, 531; gravities, 331; growth of, 92–5; Harp consortium, 458, 480; hops, 185, 194; imported barley, 184; industrial relations, 508; IPA, 90–1; King's Ale, Pl. 30; labour force, 197, 199, 330; loans, 274–7; malt and maltings, 94, 190–3, Pl. 26; management, 86, 95, 383, 403, 404, 531–2; market-position, 586; mergers and takeovers, 347, 393, 405, 449, 462, 471, 473, 474, 485, 487, 488, 493, 495, 525, 531, 532; output, 321, 331, 347, 371, 404, 504; prices, 206–7; production, 588; profits, 214, 216, 217, 248, 264, 332 n 59, 333, 342, 344, 345 n 94, 369, 370, 502, 588, 604–6, 620–1; railway, 93, 151; research, 539, 543; sales in Birmingham, 90; sales in London, 82, 119, 277; size of brewery, 82, 93; stores and store managers, 92, 144, 151, 152, 155, 157; success of, 80, 84, 89–95, 98, 146, 237, 249; survey of industry, 28, 183; tied estate, 156, 274, 275, 276, 382 n 19, 439, 441, 472, 501, 524, 573, 586, 588; transport, 549; turnover, 588; umbrella, 468; water supply, 49

Bass, Hamar, 221, 222, 224

Bass, M. A. (1st Lord Burton), 156–7, 218–20, 223–4

Bass, M. T., 28, 92–5, 127, 152, 154, 157, 183, 218, 219 n 85, 220–2, 249

Bass, Mitchells & Butlers, formed, 449, 473

Bass, Sir William, 222–3

Bass Charrington, formed, 449, 485, 488, 525

Bass family, 89, 218, 223 n 104

Bass-Worthington merger, 393, 397, 403–4

Bateman, George (Wainfleet), 482, 484, 485, 507

Bath, 163

Bath Brewery Ltd, 260 n 90

Batham, Daniel, & Son (Brierley Hill), 589, 590

Baxter, Dudley, 35

Baxter, J., 73

Beamish & Crawford (Cork), 100, 483

Beaumont, J. T. B., 5 n 8

Beavan, E. S., 183

Beaver, Sir Hugh, 390, 393, 481

Beck's lager, 338

Becontree estate, London, 425

Bedminster Bridge Brewery (Bristol), 280

Beefeater, 590

beer: adulteration of, 6–7, 12, 59, 79, 91, 130, 138–9, 208, 209 n 65, 296; analysis of, 139–40, 208; blending of, 91, 97; colouring of, 7, 188; distribution of, 127–78, 200–1, 205, 358, 512, 548–57; narcotic effect of, 44, 58; returned, 140, 147, 181, 196 n 33, 202; Scotch strong beer, 103, 106, 107, 108, 109, 147; strength, 43–4, 46–7, *see also* specific gravity; summer brewed, 56, 85, 147; 'table' or 'small', 33, 105, 642; tastes in types of, 40–7; winter-brewed, 41, 48; *see also* ale; beer brands; beer duties; bottled beers; consumption of beer per capita; exports; porter; prices, of beers; production; specific gravity; stout

Beer, Alfred, 122

Beer, George, & Rigden (Faversham), 371

Beer Acts: (1823), 7, 8; (1830), 3–22, 29, 30, 65, 69, 126, 128, 170, 227, 246, Pl. 1; (1834), 17
Beer & Co. (Canterbury), 122, 185
beer brands, 523–4, 526, 568, 585–6; Barbican, 585; Budweiser, 586; Carling Black Label, 467, 471, 558; Castlemaine XXXX, 585; Courage Tavern, 558; Double Diamond, 458, 526, 527, 558, 563, 564; Flowers Keg, 458, 491; Graham's Golden Lager, 339; Heineken, 453–4, 480, 558, 567; Kaliber, 585; Kestrel, 524; Long Life, 526; McEwan's Export, 523, 524; Manns, 568; Miller Lite, 586; Newcastle Brown Ale, 523; Skol lager, 458, 471, 478, 480, 481, 526, 558, 563, 566, Pl. 59; Skona lager, 496; Stingo, 544; Swan Light, 585; Tennents LA, 585; Watneys Red, 529, 558, 563, 565, 566; Watneys Red Barrel, 458, 481, 529, 558, 563–5; Watneys Starlight, 565; Whitbread Forest Brown, 401; Whitbread Tankard, 558, 565; Whitbread Trophy Bitter, 565; Whitbread White Label, 585; Worthington E, 154, 558; Younger's Tartan, 523, 558
beer duties: (1813–30), 9–14; abolished (1830), 21, 23, 65, 195, 205, 206; reimposed (1880), 24, 26, 46, 65, 184, 194–6, 291; (1914–90), 318, 335, 342, 352, 356, 365, 366, 545, 582–3, 632, 637, Pl. 45; *see also* taxation of the industry
beer house keepers, 16–17, 67–71, 72, 77, 129, 134, 137–8
beer houses, 3, 14–20, 69, 134, 149, 252, 281
'Beer is Best' campaign, 352–3
Belfast, 100 n 66, 101, 156 n 74
Belgium: bottlers, 300; breweries in, 450, 477, 508, 530; exports to, 156, 177, 300, 317, 348, 454
Bellingham estate, London, 425
Bell's Brewery (Gorleston), 114
Bells Whisky, 587
Bennet, Henry, 5, 8
Bennett, F. O. A. G. (Alex), 400, 402, 489, 490, 531, 532
Benskin's (Watford), 161, 247 n 51, 283 n 48, 380, 394, 424, 426, 440 n 82, 464, 568
Benson, S. H., advertising agency, 350, 353, 559, 567
Bent's (Liverpool), 279, 307, 380, 440, 441, 474
Bentley, Henry, 20, 21, 149, 264 n 99
Bentley & Shaw (Huddersfield), 49, 66 n 6, 394
Bentley's (Bentley's Yorkshire Breweries) (Woodlesford), 41, 161, 205, 260, 308, 380, 474
Bernard, T. & J. (Edinburgh), 216, 374, 468
Best (Liverpool), 125, 308
Betting and Gaming Act (1960), 577
Bevan, Armine, 289
Bevan, Granville, 391 n 46
Bevan, L. E. D., 396 n 59
Bevan, Sylvanus, 391 n 46
Bevan family, 227
Beveridge, Sir William, 319
Bindley (Burton upon Trent), 96
Birkenhead Brewery, 251 n 63
Birmingham: agencies in, 108, 125, 152, 155 n 71, 156 n 74, 158, 159; beer houses in, 19, 74; Burton beers in, 90, 150, 152; common brewers in, 73, 74; drunkenness statistics, 33, 44; 'fewer but better' policy, 421; Institute of Brewing in, 61; licensed victuallers in, 74, 441, 442; preferred beers in, 44; publican brewers in, 74
Birmingham Property Co., 288 n 62, 421
Birmingham Surrender Scheme, 288 n 62, 289
Birmingham University, 61–2, 536, 539
Bisdee, Wilfrid, 391, 405
Bishop, Laurence, 543, 544
Black, W., 47, 52, 54, 55, 180
Blackburn surrender scheme, 289
Blomfield, Charles, 242
Blomfield, James, 243
Blundall (Plymouth), 438 n 81
Boddington, Ewart, 490
Boddington, Geoffrey, 490
Boddington, Henry, 278
Boddington, Robert S., 164, 175, 389
Boddington family, 386, 489
Boddingtons', 125, 238 n 19: agencies, 204; in Burton upon Trent, 96; capitalisation, 380, 381, 384; cessation of brewing, 598; free trade, 436; independence preserved, 484, 489–90; labour force, 203, 204; management, 389; production, 507, 588; profits, 333, 342, 344, 369, 502, 503, 588, 620–1; Strangeways brewery, 489–90; takeovers, 591, 592, Pl. 68; tied estate, 279 n 33, 436, 437, 440 n 82, 501, 588; trading agreements, 488
Boer War, 289, 291, 294, 296
Bonham-Carter family, 115

Bonsor, Cosmo, 206 n 61, 224, 235, 249, 272, 292 n 77, 296–8, 301, 311, 312 n 124
Bonsor, Joseph, 234, 235
Bonsor family, 223 n 104
Booth, Charles, 36
Booz Allen & Hamilton, 565
Border Breweries (Wrexham), 592
Boston, Richard, 567
Böttinger, Henry, 59
bottled beers: advertising of, 351, 445; bottling process, plants and stores, 141, 171, 273, 299, 303, 346, 437, 537, 546, Pls. 40, 70, 71; demand for, 45, 46, 62, 103, 108, 285, 296, 305, 313, 340, 349, 354, 363, 401, 411, 446; development of, 146, 272, 299–303, 307, 348; export of, 110, 171; independent bottlers, 171, 299; returnable and non-returnable bottles, 458, 459, 547; transport of, 302–3, 349, 585
Bouch, Benjamin, 138
Bournemouth, 163
Bow Brewery, 90
Boyd of Merton, Lord, 482
Bradfer-Lawrence, H. L., 394, 467, 468
Brain, S. A., & Co. (Cardiff), 46, 124, 159, 197, 240, 241, 485, 568
Brakspear, Archibald, 242
Brakspear, F. G., 387
Brakspear, George, 242
Brakspear, Robert, 56
Brakspear, W. H., & Sons (Henley), 119, 374, 436, 438, 485, 488, 507, 620–1, Pls. 19, 40
Brakspear family, 115
Brandon's (Putney) Brewery, 422
breathalyser, 569
Brede, Sussex, 17
breweries: 'Big Seven', 450 n 9, 507, 562, 588; 'Big Six', 449, 450, 460–3, 497, 560, 586; management of, 86–9, 117, 120, 136, 164–8, 180, 213, 217, 226–67, 282, 303, 305–13, 372–407, 492–7, 522–33, 586–93; rationalisation of, 324, 346–50, 398–9, 415, 500, 506–8, 516, 519, 525, 552, 567, 574, 586–7, 598; sale of, 246–7, 334, 371; *see also* mergers
brewers: education of, 61–3, 241–5, 378, 389–90, 405, 536, 570–1; wealth of, 217–25; *see also* country brewers
Brewers' Assets Corporation, 270
Brewers' Association of Scotland, 517
Brewers' Company, 140, 209–10, 270, 285 n 49
Brewers' Federation Council, 373
Brewers' Guardian, 211 n 70
Brewers' Hall, 6, 209
Brewers' Journal, 58, 174–5, 176, 211 n 70, 218, 292, 293, 341, 427, 434, 435
Brewers' Society, xix, 285 n 49: advertising and market research, 352–4, 559, 560, 568, 634, 636, Pl. 82; and barley consumption, 362; Beer for Troops Committee, 359; and beer prices, 357, 521; and club breweries, 415; and excise duties, 509; formed, 211; and games machines, 577–8; and gravities, 361, 366; Industrial Relations Committee, 517–18; and licensing, 293; and mergers and takeovers, 463, 464; model tenancy, 445; *The Modern Public House*, 429; 'Operation Counterstroke', 584; parliamentary sub-committee, 423; and public house standards, 570; Public Relations Committee, 584; research, 538; and reserve barrelage, 364, 365; Social Problems of Alcohol Committee, 584; spokesman for industry, 363; surveys and statistics, 349, 408, 409, 427, 429–30, 432, 437–9, 442, 565; and tied houses, 571–6; and transport, 548–50; and wartime restrictions, 319, 362, 364, 365; and wastage levels, 511; *see also* Country Brewers' Society (to 1904)
brewing: capital structure, 100, 103, 226–66, 309, 332–4, 343–5, 375–85, 448–9, 461, 463, 467, 469–70, 472, 475–6, 479, 485–8, 491–2, 495–6, 501–3, 506; concentration, 110–12, 331, 346–50, 370–1, 447–51, 460–80, 498, 507, 508, 516–17, 557, 571, 593, 595; corporate structure, 523, 588–9; costs, 179–207, 509–19, *see also* barley, brewing materials, hops, malt, malting, transport; cottage brewing, 65; economies of scale, 505–8; efficiency, 503–7; manuals, 47, 52, 54, 55, 180, 216–17, 259, 262; mechanisation of, 51–5; overcapacity, 103, 255, 304, 313, 346–7, 398, 409, 414; technology, 47–8, 58–63, 89, 91, 116, 129, 151, 189, 245, 534–48; *see also* management; rationalisation
Brewing Advisory Committee, 361
Brewing Industry Research Foundation, 538, 539, 541, 543
brewing materials: availability of, 331, 356, 364; imports of, 183–5, 188–9, 192–3, 361, 362; price of, 8, 10, 47, 179–89, 205, 216, 272, 510; *see also* barley; hops; maize; malt; oats; rice; sugar; wheat

brewing process, 44–5, 47–63, 534–48, Pls. 2, 77, 78; anti-haze treatments, 546; attenuation, 56, 57, 638; boiling, 47, 53, 548; chilling, 62, 299, 301, 538; conditioning, 537–8, 557, 639; continuous brewing, 538, 542–4; cooling, 54–5, 63, 537, 639; decoction system, 53; filtered beers and filtering, 45, 62, 299, 301, 348, 457, 534, 537–8, 546, 641; fining, 57; high-gravity brewing, 508, 538–9, 542, 545–6, 640; mashing, 47, 51–3, 82, 105, 106; racking, 57, 642; settling, 57, 85; skimming, 57; sparging, 52, 642; *see also* brewing, technology; fermentation systems
Brewing Trade Committee, 210
Brewing Trade Review, 61, 211 n 70, 292 n 74, 341
Brickwood & Co. (Portsmouth), 349, 482, 492
Bridges family, 387
Bridlington, 117, 161
Brighton, agencies in, 156
Bristol: agencies in, 100, 108, 155 nn 71 and 72, 156 n 74, 158; brewers in, 73, 74, 119, 469–71; tied trade, 268, 572–3
Bristol Brewery Georges & Co., 119–20: advertising, 351–2; agency, 161; brewers, 244; capitalisation, 380, 381, 469–70; co-operation during war, 358 n 133; in difficulties, 284 n 49; distribution, 116; exports, 119–20, 169–70, 173; free trade, 436; incorporation, 259, 279, 280; IPA, 169; management, 120, 311, 378, 386, 389, 391, 405, Pl. 49; mergers and takeovers, 334, 391, 405, 461, 469–71, 482; production, 21, 41, 91; profits, 215, 264, 306, 308, 342, 343, 344, 620–1; tied trade, 161, 279–80, 283, 284, 436, 438, 440 n 82
Bristol United Breweries, 260, 405, 440 n 82, 469
Bristol Vintners, 500
Britannic Assurance, 490
British Market Research Bureau, 565
British Road Services, 554
British School of Brewing and Malting, Birmingham, 61
British Transport Commission, 550–1
British United Brewery, 306
Brougham, Lord, 6, 8
Brown, Adrian, 59, 61
Brown, George, 543
Brown, Horace Tabberer, 59, 62, 403
Brown, Matthew (Blackburn), 238 n 19: capitalisation, 380; in difficulties, 342; free and tied trade, 436; independence preserved, 484, 487, 488; mergers and takeovers, 371, 590–3; profits, 502, 503, 620, 622
Bruce, David, 591
Bruce & Co., 231
Bruce's Bill (1871), 286
Brunswick Brewery (Leeds), 240
Buchan, Andrew (Rhymney), 395, 438 n 81, 440, 444 n 98
Buckley's (Llanelli), 488
Bullard, Sir Henry, 265
Bullard & Sons (Norwich), 149, 279 n 33, 463, 484, 495, 496, 529
Bunting, T. B., 391
Burn, W. L., 3
Burnett, John, 29
Burroughs, James, 590
Burt, Claude, 403, 404
Burton & Lincoln Breweries, 260 n 90
Burton Brewers' Association, 211
Burton Brewery Co., 96, 251 n 63, 275, 304, 305, 310
Burton Bridge brewery, 591
Burton Chronicle, 151
Burton pale ales, *see* ale
Burton union system, *see* fermentation systems
Burton upon Trent: brewing science in, 59–61, 539; growth of, 89–98; London and other brewers' subsidiaries in, 84–5, 96, 98, 146, 268; rationalisation, 347; water quality, 50, 83, 89, 91, 126
Burtonwood brewery (Warrington), 238 n 19, 482, 485, 487, 563, 589, 590
Bury St Edmunds, 121, 190
Bush Boake Allen, 541
Butcombe brewery (Avon), 591
Butler, Sir William Waters, 62, 124, 224, 288 n 62, 325, 326, 328, 329, 393, 421, 517, 536, Pl. 43
Butler, William (Wolverhampton), 124, 159, 197, 238 n 19
Butler family, 386
butts, *see* barrels *and* casks
Buxton, Bertram, 88
Buxton, Edward North, 88, 146, 267 n 1, 269, 270, 434
Buxton, J. H., 88, 254
Buxton, Thomas Fowell, 11, 13, 40–1, 77, 88, 228
Buxton family, 86, 218, 223 n 105, 231, 232

Cain, Robert, & Sons (Liverpool), 125, 286, 380
Caird, Sir James, 143

Cairncross Committee, 574, 576
Calder, J. J., 305, 347, 398
Calder, James, & Co. (Alloa), 103, 105, 109, 158, 468
Callow, William, & Co., agents (Manchester), 153
Calvert, Charles, 11
Calvert & Co., 6, 7, 48, 79, 233, *see also* City of London Brewery Co.
Cameron, J. W., & Co. (West Hartlepool): capitalisation, 380; and clubs, 288 n 61; in difficulties, 284 n 49; free and tied trade, 436, 438; market share, 590 n 19; profits, 306, 307, 342, 344, 620, 622; takeovers, 334, 592; tied estate, 436, 438, 501
Campaign for Real Ale (CAMRA), 502–3, 527, 530, 548, 567, 568, 573
Canada, breweries in, 265, 449
Canadian Breweries, 465, 467, 483 n 107
Cannon Brewery (Clerkenwell), 236, 270, 272, 274, 275, 284 n 49, 298, 347, 380
Cannon Brewery (Sheffield), 507
cans, 508, 537, 546–7, 557, 558, 585, 586, 641
Canterbury, 80
capital structure, *see* brewing
carbonated beers, 45, 55, 57, 62, 299, 348, 457, 546
Cardiff, 162, 326, 441
Carling Black Label Lager, 467, 471, 558
Carlisle: drunkenness in, 324–5; publican brewers in, 108
'Carlisle Experiment' (State Management Scheme), 317, 323–6, 329–30, 335, 411, 419, 421, 424, 439
Carlisle State Brewery, 400
Carlsberg: advertising, 563; brewery, 59, 453–4, 481, 504, 506, 515, 529, Pl. 71; free trade, 497, 586; imported, 338; merger, 598; production and profits, 558, 588
Carter, Rev. Henry, 325 n 25, 326
Carter, Tom, 466
Case, T. B., 390
casks, 59, 93, 144, 147, 150, 200–3, 546, 639, *see also* barrels
Castleford, 166–8
Catholic Emancipation Act (1828), 11
Cazenove, 475 n 78
Census of Production (1907), 196, 197, 203; (1954–80), 515, 633
Central Catering Co., 422
Central Control Board (Liquor Traffic), 324, 326, 328, 330, 335
Central Public House Trust Association, 419
Central Statistical Office, 435
Centre for Information on Beverage Alcohol, 584–5
Centre Parcs, 590 n 18
Chalcraft, John, 374
Chamberlain, Arthur, 288 n 62
Chamberlain, Rt. Hon. Sir Austen, 39–40
Chamberlain, Rt. Hon. Joseph, 287
Chamberlain, Rt. Hon. Neville, 352
Chandler, Alfred D. Jr., 377, 380 n 16, 383, 384, 389
Channon, Derek, 500
charity, 210, 219
Charrington (Charrington & Co., 1766–1962; Charrington United, 1962–7): advertising and market research, 565, 636; bottling, 301; brewers, 244; in Burton upon Trent, 84, 96; capitalisation, 380, 381; discounts, 273; distribution and transport, 549, 553; exports, 172; management, 86, 236; mergers and takeovers, 347, 449, 473, 474, 479, 482, 488, 531, 532; production, 79, 80, 504; tied estate, 382 n 19, 422–4, 472, 493
Charrington family, 218
Checkland, S. G., 251
Chef & Brewer, 530
Cheltenham & Hereford Breweries, 395, 403, 440 n 82, 459, 473
Cheltenham Original Brewery Co., 163, 310, 311, 358 n 133, 380, 394–5, *see also* Agg-Gardner
Chester, Bishop of, 287
Chesterfield House, London, 220
Chesters Brewery Co. (Manchester), 238 n 19, 260 n 90
Churchill, Rt. Hon. Sir Winston, 292, 358, 359 n 135
cider consumption, 581
cider duty, 14
City of London Brewery Co., 141, 197, 233, 251 n 63, 292, 298, 380 n 16, *see also* Calvert brewery
CIU, *see* Working Men's Clubs and Institute Union
Clarke, Sir Basil, 353
Clarke family, 387
Clay family, 219 n 87, 403
Clayson Committee, 572
Cleator Moor Brewing Co. (Cumberland), 371
clerks, 128, 130, 140, 197, 203, 204, 233, 303
Clore, Charles, 449, 451, 459–65, Pl. 62
closures, *see* breweries, rationalisation

clubs: brewing own beer, 411, 413, 414; competition with public houses, 285, 288, 289, 294, 296, 336–7, 409, 411–17, 424, 437, 443, 557, 569; number of, 414–16, 456; tied, 414
coal, 179, 181–2, 196 n 33
Cobb & Co. (Margate), 42, 116
Cobb family, 247
Cobbett, William, 64–5
Cobbold, Thomas, 114
Cobbold (Ipswich), 116, 163, 190, 215, 261 n 91, 262, 383 n 21
Cobbold family, 223, 242, 247
Cockerill, Anthony, 505, 507, 512
Colchester Brewery Co., 219, 260 n 90, 279 n 33, 302, 306, 309, 333, 346, n 100, 387, 388, 620–2
Coleman, Donald, 390
Coleridge, Lord Chief Justice, 27
Collective Advertising Campaigns, 352–3, 558–60, 634
colonies: breweries in, 264–5; *see also* exports
Coltishall, Norfolk, 114, 190
Combe, Charles, 235
Combe, Lady Constance, 219 n 86
Combe, Harvey, 235
Combe, Richard, 235
Combe, Simon, 462–4, 481, 529, Pl. 63
Combe Delafield & Co. (London), 79, 83 n 26, 89, 134, 202, 233–5, 254 n 71, 269
Combe family, 218
Committee of the Porter Brewers, 209
Committee on the Disinterested Management of Public Houses (1927), 408, 420, 424
Committee on Sale of Beer (1833), 42
Committee on Public Breweries (1818), 6
Committee on the Police of the Metropolis (1816–17), 5, 6
Committee on the Sale of Beer by Retail (1830), 11–13
common brewers: England and Wales, 110–26; growth of, 66–75; *see also* country brewers; London brewers
companies, creation of, 123, 136, 226–66, 270, 305–6, 346–8, 383–7, 449–50
Companies Acts, 251, 257, 459
company law, 250, 255, 451, 459
compensation: for nationalisation, 327–9; for surrender of licences, 286–95, 415, 422
concentration, *see* brewing
Concordia case, 594
consumer goods, availability of, 37–9, 285, 339–40
consumption of beer per capita: (pre–1830), 1, 9; (1830–1914), 27–40, 265, 281, 285, 286, 293–5; (1914–90), 317, 336–41, 345, 350, 353, 368, 409, 451–5, 569, 581–2, 618–19, 630
continuous brewing, *see* brewing process
contraceptive machines, 578
Cook, Arthur, 538
Co-operative Wholesale Society, 414
coopers, 93, 128, 130, 199, 202, Pl. 9
coppers, 53, Pl. 72
Cork, 100, 116, 155 n 72, 156 n 74
Cork and Orrery, Earl of, 260
Corke, Martin, 496
Corn Laws, 9, 11
Cosbie, Arthur, 537
costs of brewing, *see* brewing
country brewers: difficulties of, 306–7; distribution of, 147–68; England and Wales, 110–26; hierarchy of, 116; labour force, 330–1; management, 237–49; private trade, 66; production, 79, 331; profits, 308–9; takeovers and mergers, 334, 349; tied estate, 277–86
Country Brewers' Gazette, 211 n 70, 251, 256
Country Brewers' Society, 6, 8, 12, 13, 14, 61, 115, 196, 209, 210, 211, 278, 296 n 90
Courage (Courage & Co., 1787–1955; Courage & Barclay, 1955–60; Courage, Barclay & Simonds, 1960–70; Courage, 1970–): advertising and market research, 565, 562, 567, 636; and alcohol abuse, 585 n 9; brewery closures, 587; capital, 380, 381; costs, 512 n 34; distribution and transport, 141, 303, 549, 556; diversification, 590; and games machines, 579; and Harp consortium, 458, 480, 495; and hops, 185; and imported beer, 586; management, 86, 236; market-position, 586; mergers and takeovers, 391, 395, 449, 450, 464, 469–71, 474, 475, 477–8, 482, 496, 524, 567, 587, 592, 593, 597; new and rebuilt breweries, 506, 515, 556, Pl. 69; production, 79, 80, 504, 507, 588; profits, 502, 588; public house improvements, 424, 426 n 52; and public house monopolies, 573; research, 538, 543; supplied with pale ale, 84; Tavern, 558; tied estate, 270, 279 n 33, 382 n 19, 439, 440 n 82, 444 n 98, 472, 501, 572, 573, 586, 588
Courage family, 218, 233
Courtaulds, 390
Coventry, 73
Cowling, Keith, 499, 503

Craigmillar (Edinburgh), 106 n 78
Crawshay, Charles, 313
Crawshay (Norwich), 149
credit for pub customers, 324
Crest Hotels, 590
Croft & Co., 500
Crook, John (Darwen), 239
Crossman, John, 97
Crossman, Peter, 529
Crossman, Robert, 134, 136, 237, 249
Cubitt, Jack, 494
Cullingham, Charles (Ipswich), 241

D'Abernon, Lord, 326, 329
Dale & Co. (Cambridge), 494
Daniell & Sons' Breweries (Colchester), 260 n 90, 264 n 98
Daresbury, Lord (Sir Gilbert Greenall, Bt.), 223, 293
Darlington, 166 n 104, 168
Dartford Brewery, 398
Davenport, James, 396
Davenport, Lord, 319
Davenport & Sons (Birmingham), 354, 355, 411, 418, 503, 549, 591, 592
'Davy Jones Brewery', 543
Dawnay, Hon. George, 241
Day, John, & Sons (St Neots), 148
De la Rue, 478
de Zoete & Bevan, 475 n 78
Deakin (Manchester), 125
Defence of the Realm Act (DORA) (1914), 328
Delafield, Edward, 234
Dell, William, 235
Dempsey, General Sir Miles, 387, 394, 494
Denmark, imports from 453, 454 n 17
Derby, 73, 80, 153, 219 n 85
Deuchar, Robert (Edinburgh), 106 n 78, Pl. 5
Devanha Brewery (Aberdeen), 104
Devenish, J. A. (Weymouth), 383 n 21, 488, 590 n 19, 592, 598
diastase, 51, 52
diet, beer in working-class, 28, 32, 37
Dingle, A. E., 36, 37, 38
discounts to publicans, 39, 45, 107, 144, 146, 147, 156, 200, 205, 208, 209, 210, 217, 255, 269, 273, 301, 303–4
Disher's Ten Guinea Ale, 106
Distillers' Company, 541, 587
distribution of beer, 127–78, 200–1, 205, 358, 512, 548–57
diversification, 500–3, 587–91
dividends, 331–4, 342–5, 369–70, 620–1, *see also* profits
Dixon, Bernard, 392, 491, 492, 494 n 139, 547
Doncaster, 166, 281
Donnachie, Ian, xix, 106, 158
Donnington (Stow-on-the-Wold), 590
Dorchester, 80
Down, T. J., 267 n 1
Doyle Dane Bernbach, 559
drays and draymen, 130, 140–3, 146, 152, 157, 159, 199
drinking and driving, 569, 584
drunkenness, 15, 17, 27, 32–3, 35, 129, 251, 254, 286, 288, 289, 324–6, 335–7, 358, 569, 617
Drybrough (Edinburgh), 463
Dublin, 100, 116, 126, 155, 159, 171
Duddingston Brewery (Edinburgh), 106 n 78, Pl. 5
Dudgeon (Dunbar), 107
Duncan, George, 475, 476
Duncan, W. W., 26–17, 259, 262, 386, 388
Duncombe, Hon. Cecil, 240
Dundee, 104, 106, 107
Durham (County), 33, 73, 108, 118
Durham, Earl of, 165 n 102, 241
Dutton's Blackburn Brewery, 395, 460, 473, 492
duty, *see* beer duties; taxation
Dymore Brown, J., & Son (Reading), 122–3
Dymore Brown, James, 122–3

Eadie, James (Burton upon Trent), 347, 404
Eadie, James A., 404
Eagles, J. S., 400
East Anglian Breweries (Ely), 496
East India Company, 90, 234
Eastleigh, 163
economic depressions: of the 1820s, 10–11; of 1873–96, 25, 97, 254, 255, 265; of the 1900s, 293, 295; of the 1930s, 337, 342–3
economies of scale, 505–8
Economist, The, 257, 264, 276, 342, 345, 357, 374, 406
Edinburgh: agencies in, 155 n 72, 156 n 74, 158; ales, 45, 46; beer sales in London, 119, 149; common brewers in, 72, 74, 99, 103–10, 116, 126, 158, 164, 241, 384–5, 467–8; exports from, 171, 173, 377; tied trade in, 283; water supply, 105
Edinburgh United Breweries, 260 n 90, 263 n 97
Editorial Services Ltd, 353
education and training: of brewers, 61–3,

241–5, 378, 389–90, 405, 536, 570–1; brewers' support for, 210
effluent disposal, 536
Elders IXL, 587, 592, 593, 597, 598
Eldridge Pope & Co (Dorchester), 162–3, Pl. 25; capital, 380; incorporated, 259, 261 n 91; independence preserved, 484, 487, 492; management, 312 n 126, 492; production, 589; profits, 215, 217, 589; share splitting, 485–6; tied estate, 115 n 101, 163, 436, 496, 589
Elgood & Sons (Wisbech), 507
Ellerman, Sir John, 224, 263, 264, 265, 307, 396 n 59
Elliot, Watney & Co. (London), 133, 134, 138, 233
Elliott, John, 234
Ellis, E., 267 n 1
Elveden estate, Suffolk, 220
Ely brewery (Cardiff), 464
Emerald & Phoenix (New York), 264 n 99
English Lager Beer Brewery (Batheaston), 177 n 129
Erroll Committee on Liquor Licensing (1972), 479, 570, 572, 574, 575
Escrick Hall, York, 67
Estcourt's Licensing Act (1828), 8, 252
European beers and breweries, 40, 44, 264–5, *see also by country*
European Commission, 593, 594
European Economic Community, 477, 555, 572–3, 583
Evans family, 89
Everard (Leicester), 96, 487, 550
Eversley, Viscount (Shaw-Lefevre), 228
Excess Profits Duty and Tax, 332, 356–7
excise districts, 26, 67, 73, 77, 129
excise duties, *see* beer duties; taxation of the industry
excursions for brewery employees, 168, 198–9, Pls. 27, 28
Exeter, 156 n 74
expenditure on beer, 27–36, 341, 569, 600–2
export trade, 25, 169–75, 338–9, 377, 400, 453, 607–9, 631; America, South, 169, 173–4; Australasia, 44, 109, 110, 169–75, 317; Baltic, 89–90, 95, 170; Belgium, 156, 177, 300, 317, 348, 454; Colonies, 44, 175; East Indies, 169, 172; Europe, 317; France, 171, 300; India, 90–1, 95, 109, 110, 150, 170–2, 175, 317; Ireland, 169, 170; Mediterranean, 169; South Africa, 172; USA, 44, 169, 171, 173, 175, 176, 317, 454; West Indies, 109, 169, 173
Faber, J. D. B. (David), 240, 307, 311, 312, 349, 384
Fair Trading Act (1973), 451 n 12
Falkirk, 107
Falmouth, Lord, 14
Farnell, J. & R. (Isleworth), 236, 237
Farnell, John, 14
Farnham, 289, 290
Farnham United Breweries, 264 n 98
Faversham, 80
Fellowship of Freedom and Reform, 419, 420 n 27
fermentation systems, 47, 55–60, 82, 640; bottom, 58, 59, 548; Burton union, 57, 58, 84, 91, 545, 639; Pl. 3; conical fermenters, 541–5; continuous, 538, 542–4, 639, Pl. 79; irregular, 49, 53, 55; protracted, 169; research on, 541–5; secondary, 56, 57, 58, 59; temperature, 106; top, 56; tower fermenter, 544; Yorkshire (stone) square, 56 n 85, 57, 545, 643
Fern Vale Brewery (Rhondda), 438 n 81
Field, Barclay, 236
Fielden, John, 65
Fielding, Daniel (Halifax), 549
filtered beers and filtering, *see* brewing process
filters for water, 49–50
Finch, Charles H., 374, 396 n 59
Finlays, 590
Firkin pubs, 591
Fisher, H. A. L., 330
Flower, Dennis, 491
Flower, Fordham, 491
Flower & Sons (Stratford-upon-Avon), 84, 392, 427, 491, 496
Flowers Breweries, 392, 458, 460, 470 n 64, 473, 490–2, 494–5, 620–1
Flowers Keg, 458, 491
Ford, John, 537
Forest Hill Brewery Co. (London), 348
Foster, M. B., & Sons, bottlers (London), 299
Fosters, 585, 587, 598
Fowler, John, & Co. (Prestonpans), 106, 468
Fox's (Farnborough), 50
France: brewers, 508; exports to, 171, 300
Fraser & Carmichael, 493
Fraser family, 493
Fraud Squad, 464 n 44
free trade in beer, 4, 7, 11, 13, 17, 18, 22, 92, 98, 102, 110, 119–23, 147, 149, 158, 164–6, 206–8, 255, 436–8, 557
Fremlins (Maidstone), 84, 301, 371, 473, 549, 620–2

French Wars (1793–1815), 206, 209, 227
Friary Holroyd & Healy (Guildford), 440 n 82, 444 n 98, 462, 470 n 64, 549
Friary Meux (Guildford), 473, 501, 568
friendly societies, 231
Fuller, Smith & Turner (London), 423, 426 n 52, 482, 484, 485, 486

Gainsborough, 190
Gainsborough, Thomas, R. A., 87
Gale, George (Horndean), 485, 547
Gallup, 565
gambling machines, 577–9
Gardner (Clerkenwell), 236, *see also* Cannon Brewery
Garrard, Frank, 403
Garton, Sir Richard, 311, 312 n 124, 393, 423
Garton & Co. (Bristol), 163
Gates, Percy, 285, 293
General Strike (1926), 516
gentlemen brewers, 239–41
Geoghegan family, 246
George, C. E. A., 280
George, Christopher, 391
George IV, 11, 13
George family, 223, 391
Georges, *see* Bristol Brewery Georges
Germany: brewing industry in, 53, 58, 61, 62, 172, 173, 175, 176, 514; German brewers in Britain, 177
gibberellic acid, 540, 638, 640
Gibbs Mew (Salisbury), 482, 563
Giffard, Edward, 295, 391, 393, 423
Gilbey, W. & A., 500
Gilchrist family, 485 n 111
Gladstone, Rt. Hon. W. E., 24, 46, 92–3, 184, 193, 195, 291
Glasgow, 103–10, 155, 158, 161, 241, 339
Glenquoich estate, 220
Godman family, 228, 386
goodwill, 264, 303, 304, 306, 309
Goole, 166 n 104
Gothenburg scheme, 287
'Government Ale', 321, 323
Gow, George, 232
Graham, C., 60
Grand Metropolitan Hotels (Grand Met), 450, 474, 475–9, 500, 529, 530, 562, 568, 592, 598, 636
Grantham, 190, 281
gravity, *see* specific gravity
Great Exhibition (1851), 94, 173
Great Yarmouth, 50, 74, 75, 79–81, 148, 149, 189–90
Green, Harold, 392
Green, J. W. (Luton): copper room, Pl. 72; distribution and transport, 549; free trade, 436; keg ales, 547; management, 378, 386, 392, 393; profit, 621; takeovers and mergers, 371, 392, 406, 458, 491; tied estate, 382 n 19, 436, 442
Green, J. W. (traveller), 167–8
Green, John William, 392
Green, Sidney, 392
Green, Winifred, 491
Greenall, Sir Gilbert, Bt., *see* Daresbury, Lord
Greenall Whitley & Co. (St Helens): advertising, 563; cessation of brewing, 598; incorporation, 251 n 65, 261 n 91, 262, 383 n 21; independence preserved, 483; market-share, 590; production, 507, 588; profits, 309, 502, 588; share splitting, 487; takeover, 591, 592; tied estate, 262, 279 n 33, 309, 382 n 19, 588; transport, 302
Greene, Edward, 121, 218, 242, 244, 245, 246, 248, 249, 262 n 92
Greene, Edward, & Son (Bury St Edmunds), 43, 197 n 39, 215, 247 n 54, 248
Greene, Sir Edward, Bt., 387, 388
Greene, Sir Walter, Bt., 222, 224, 242, 244, 245, 262 n 92, Pl. 31
Greene family, 223 n 105, 224, 242, 244, 387
Greene King (Bury St Edmunds): advertising, 563; agencies, 162; bottling, 300 n 100; capitalisation, 380; free trade, 121, 162, 436; gravities, 363; incorporated, 383 n 21; independence preserved, 484, 487, 494–5; management, 282, 309–11, 378, 387, 394, 395, 406; mergers and takeovers, 122, 248, 261, 334, 349, 376, 387, 469 n 61, 494; production, 38, 331, 507, 588; profits, 306, 308, 342, 344, 502, 503, 588, 620–1; stores, 162; tied estate, 121–2, 261, 268 n 3, 281–2, 285, 427, 436, 440, 588; trading agreements, 480, 483, 492; transport, 302, 549
Gretton, Frederick, 222, 224
Gretton, Hugh Frederic, 321 n 12
Gretton, John (Lord Gretton), 157, 218, 223, 224, 321, 329, 403, 404, 423 n 40
Gretton family, 95, 219 n 87, 403
Greville, Hon. Mrs, 221, 385
Grier's (Eltham), 177 n 129
Griess, Philip, 59
Grigg, Sir James, 404, 532
Grimsby, 166, 168, 281

Grimston, H. L., 391, 398
Grinstead, Stanley, 530, 532
Gripper Brothers (Tottenham), 271 n 11
Groves, J. G., 267 n 1
Groves, James, 235
Groves, W. P. G., 124
Groves & Whitnall (Salford), 123, 124, 159, 190, 238 n 19, 268, 306, 380
Grundy, Percival, 389
Guinness: advertising and market research, 102, 346, 350–1, 354, 355, 441, 480, 483, 559, 560, 562, 563, 565, 567, 636, Pl. 47; agency system, 92, 100, 101, 151, 157–8, 161, 258; and alcohol abuse, 585 nn 8 and 9; alcohol-free beer, 585; banking links, 396 n 59; bottled trade and bottling, 103, 171, 258, 299, 300, 438; cans, 586; capitalisation, 380, 381, 384; coopers, 202; difficulties of, 284 n 49; distribution and transport, 45, 127, 358, 549, 550, 554, Pls. 17, 18; diversification, 587; Draught, 454 n 17, 471, 480, 481, 482, 483, 495, 558; exports abroad, 171–4, 177, 339, 377; exports to England, 99–101, 119, 139–40, 337, 453; Extra Stout, 321 n 13, 331, 350–1, 438; fear of adulteration, 139–40; flotation, 136, 250, 255, 257–8; free trade, 121, 351, 438, 497, 586; growth of, 98–103; and Harp, *see* Harp Lager; hops, 185, 406; labour force, 197, 199, 203, 330; licence fees, 293 n 82; loans to companies, 482; management, 246, 377, 383, 386, 387, 389, 390; market preference for, 354–5; new pub at Hatfield, 571; Park Royal brewery, 338, 454 n 17, 507, 539, 544; Park Royal Transport, 554; production, 331, 371, 504, 507, 588; profits, 214, 216, 258, 264, 306, 332 n 59, 333, 334, 342, 344, 369, 370, 503, 588, 620, 622; research and technology, 59–61, 536, 538–9, 541, 543, 544, 547; sales, 101; specific gravity, 321, 331; success of, 146, 249, 449; survey of drinking habits, 417; tied estate, 472; trading agreements, 480–3, 495; water supply, 49
Guinness, Arthur Jr., 100
Guinness, Sir Benjamin, 218
Guinness, Edward Cecil: first Earl of Iveagh, 102, 218, 219, 220, 223, 224, 225, 250, 257, 258, 387, Pl. 13
Guinness, Rupert: second Earl of Iveagh, 387
Guinness Book of Records, 566
Guinness family, 223, 249, 386 n 31
Guinness Mahon, 475 n 78
Guinness Transport, 554
Gurdon-Rebow, Hector, 263
Gurney, J. J., 13
Gurney family, 227
Gutzke, David, 114, 221, 253
gypsum, 50, 83

Hadley, Arthur and Arthur Cecil, 391
Halifax, 72, 74, 281
Hall & Woodhouse (Blandford Forum): advertising, 563–4; capitalisation, 380, 485; distribution and transport, 549; free and tied trade, 115 n 101, 436, 437, 442, 496, 589; independence preserved, 484, 492–3; production, 589; profits, 589, 620–1; trading agreement, 482
Hall, Cutlack & Harlock (Ely), 440
Halliwell (Bolton), 238 n 19
Hall's (Alton), 84
Hall's (Oxford), 568
Halsbury, Lord, 252
Hammerton (London), 354, 355, 383 n 21, 461
Hammond's Bradford Brewery Co., 260 n 90, 342, 394
Hammonds United, 371, 394, 395, 440 n 82, 449, 460, 467, 469, 488, 493
Hanbury, Charles Addington, 88
Hanbury, George, 236
Hanbury, J. M., 48, 60, 62, 187
Hanbury, Osgood, 236
Hanbury, Robert, 88
Hanbury family, 218, 223, 227, 231, 232
Hancock, Sir Henry, 466
Hancock, William (Cardiff), 342, 440 n 82, 468, 474
Hansen, E. C., 55, 58–60, 63
Hanson Trust, 587, 593
Happy Eater, 590
Harcourt, Rt. Hon. Sir William, 65
Hardcastle, J. A., 218
Hardys & Hansons (Kimberley, Notts.), 238 n 19, 488
Hardy's Kimberley Brewery (Notts.), 66 n 6, 440 n 82, 488
Harman, C. L., 375–6, 486
Harp Lager, 458, 461, 471, 480–3, 495, 497, 504, 506, 515, 523, 567, Pl. 60
Harrison, Brian, 15, 16, 33
Harrison, G., 353
Hartley's (Ulverston), 592
Harvester, 590
Harvey & Son (Lewes), 568
Hattersley, Rt. Hon. Roy, 573, 575
Hawkins, K. H., xix, 253, 255, 262 n 93, 267, 274, 278, 346, 371, 397, 439, 440, 449, 467, 503

Head, Alfred, 12
head-brewers, 203–4, 232, 233, 239, 244, 246, 249, 388
Heavitree Brewery (Exeter), 306
Heilbron, Sir Ian, 538
Heineken Brewery, Netherlands, 478, 585 n 8
Henty & Constable (Chichester), 461
Hepworth (Ripon), 66 n 6
Heriot Watt College, Edinburgh, 536, 539
Hertfordshire Trust Houses, 419
Hewitt, W. T., 218
high-gravity brewing, *see* brewing process
Higson's Brewery (Liverpool), 125, 442, 592
Hindlip, Lord, 223
Hitchman & Co. (Chipping Norton), 375 n 6
Hoare & Co. (London), 79, 86, 141, 197, 233, 298, 347, 380 n 16, 538
Hobhouse, Sir Benjamin, Bt., 86, 227
Hobhouse family, 223 n 105, 228
Hobsbawm, E. J., 37
Hodgson's Kingston Brewery Co., 91
Holder family, 223 n 105
Holder's Brewery (Birmingham), 334
Holiday Inns, 590 n 18
Holland: breweries in, 172, 450, 478, 508, 525; imports from, 453, 454 n 17
Holmes, William, 15
Holsten, 563
Holt, Edward, 238
Holt, Joseph, 238
Holt, Joseph (Manchester), 238–9, 383 n 21, 484, 488, 507, 589
Holt family, 223 n 105, 238
Home Brewery (Nottingham), 592
home consumption and deliveries of beer, 66, 411, 418, 446, 457, 557, 566, 590
Hook Norton (Nr. Banbury), 381, 382, 484, 485, 507, 549, 589
Hoover, Herbert, 322
Hope & Anchor Breweries (Sheffield), 395, 438, 449, 466–7, 488
Hope-Stone, Hugh, 502
Hopkins, E. Threlfall, 423 n 40
hops: duty, 9, 194–6; English Hop Growers, 362; extracts, 541–2, 641; government control of, 320, 359, 362; growing, 93, 184–5, 193–4, 362, 541; hopping rates, 50, 53–4, 169, 185, 194, 362–3; imported, 185; 193, 362; marketing, 193, 312 n 124, 362; pellets, 541, 542; prices, 205, 207, 208, 212, 255, 294, 363, 614–16; research on, 536, 540–2; Select Committee (1890), 85; separators, 541; syndicate, 193 n 28, 312 n 124; transport of, 150
horse power, 52, 140
horse transport, *see* transport
Hotham, William, 165 n 102
Hotham & Co. (York), 164, 240
Hoyle, William, 35
Hudson's Cambridge & Pampisford Brewery, 163
Huggins & Co. Ltd (London), 333
Hughes, Arthur, 377
Hull, 73, 74, 89, 108, 149, 156 n 74, 166 n 104, 268
Hull Brewery Co., 217, 263 n 97, 264 n 98, 306, 308, 309
Hunt, Edmunds & Co. (Banbury), 375–6, 378, 473, 486
Huskisson, William, 6
Hutt, Christopher, 567
Hydes (Manchester), 484, 563

ice, 58, 82, 176
Imperial Group/Imperial Tobacco, 450, 474, 477–8, 500, 524, 529, 587, 593, 636
imports: of beer, 40, 176–8, 338, 453, 454 n 17, 607–9, 631; government restrictions on, 319, 322; of raw materials, 183–5, 188–9, 192–3, 361, 362
Improved Public House Co. (Whitbread), 424
Incorporated Brewers' Guild, 536
Ind Coope (Ind Coope & Allsopp, 1934–62): advertising, 562, 563, 636; agencies, 158, 161; banking links, 396 n 59; bottling, 141; in Burton upon Trent, 84, 96, 97, 303; capitalisation, 380, 381, 384; club trade, 413; country trade, 146; difficulties of, 285 n 49, 304, 305; discounts, 273; distribution and transport, 141, 549, 550, 554; diversification, 500; free trade, 436, 438; labour force, 197, 204; malt, 190; management, 394, 398, 528; mergers and takeovers, 346, 347, 449, 464, 466, 469–71, 483, 524, 527; private trade, 66; production, 371 n 164; profits, 217, 370, 620–1; public house improvements, 427; rationalisation, 346; Romford brewery, 346 n 96; tied estate, 275, 306, 382 n 19, 413, 436, 438, 440 n 82, 525; trading agreements, 401
Ind Coope (Scotland), 527, 528
Ind Coope Tetley Ansell (ICTA), 449, 458, 471, 489, 524–8
Independent Broadcasting Authority, 561
India, exports to, 90–1, 95, 109, 110, 150, 170–2, 175, 317

India Pale Ale (IPA), *see* ale
Industrial Publicity Service Ltd, 351
Industrial Reconstruction Corporation, 451
industrial relations, 321, 508, 514, 516, 551, 554–5, *see also* trade unions
Inn Leisure, 592
Institute of Brewing, 60–3, 536, 538
'Intermediate Beer' Act (1823), 7, 8
International Distillers & Vintners (IDV), 477, 500
investment, *see* brewing, capital structure
Ipswich, 75, 190
Ireland: agency system in, 108; brewing in, 99–103; exports, 99–101, 119, 139–40, 171–4, 177, 337, 339, 377, 453; gravities, 322; imports, 119–20, 169–70; *see also* Guinness
Irish Ale Breweries, 483
Italy, brewers in, 508
isinglass, 57, 196 n 33
Iveagh, Earls of, *see* Guinness

J. & B. Rare Scotch, 500
J. Walter Thompson, 567
Jasper, H., & Co., 464
Jeffrey, John (Edinburgh), 383 n 21, 438, 449, 467, Pl. 70
Jellicoe, Basil, 426
Jennings (Cockermouth), 381
Jennings (Windsor), 119
Jevons, W. W., 35
John Bull Censuses, 354, 355
John Smith's Tadcaster Brewery Co.: advertising, 567; agency, 158; capitalisation, 380, 487; free trade, 166, 168, 255, 436; incorporated, 238, 258, 259, 261, 279; labour force, 197, 198; maltings, 190 n 22; management, 124, 238, 386; mergers, 371, 474, 567; profits, 258, 259, 264, 620, 622; tied trade, 238, 259, 279, 436, 439, 440 n 82, 444 n 98; transport, 549
Jones, Leif, M.P., 239
Jones, Robert, 501, 502
Jones & Co. (Bromley), 271 n 11
Joseph, Maxwell, 474–6, 529, 530
Joule, John, & Sons Ltd (Stone), 45, 161, 162, 474, 567
Journal of the Institute of Brewers, 60–1
Jubilee Stout, 466–7
Jude, Hanbury & Co. (Kent), 348, 400
jug and bottle trade, 137
Justerini & Brooks, 500

Kaiser Lager Beer Co., 177 n 129
keg beers, 457–8, 539, 547, 557, 558, 560, 564, 566–8
Kenwood, Hampstead, 219
King, F. W., 262 n 92
King, F. W., & Sons (Bury St Edmunds), 122, 248, 261
King, George, 493, 494
King & Barnes (Horsham), 563
King family, 387
King's Lynn, 75, 149, 190
Kirkstall, 166 n 104
Kirkstall Brewery Co. (Leeds), 251 n 63
Knatchbull, Sir Edward, 13, 14
Knox, D. M., 268
Kumar, M. S., 499

La Touche, C. D., 390
Labatt (Canada), 469 n 61
laboratories, 59–61, 63, 124, 536, Pls. 4, 5
Laboratory Club, 60, 63
labour costs, 182, 196–9, 509–10, 512–13
labour force, 196–200, 330, 356, 362, 363, 513, 633
labour productivity, 197, 503, 512–15, 633
labour relations, *see* industrial relations
Lacon, Sir Edmund, & Co. (Great Yarmouth): accounts, 182; agencies, 117, 118, 161, 162, 200; brewery, Pl. 12; brewing costs, 182; capitalisation, 380; distribution and transport, 200–1, 549; duties, 196; incorporated, 261 n 91, 262; in London market, 79–82, 119; management, 117, 311, 313; production, 117–18; profits, 181, 214, 247 n 54; success of, 116–17; tied estate, 262, 279, 501
Lacon, Sir Edmund, Bt., 117
Lacon, W. Sterling, 117 n 107
Lacon family, 223 n 105, 242, 247
lager: advertising and market research, 560, 561, 564, 565, 567, 636; 'battle of the lagers', 471, 480–1; British production of, 176, 177, 192, 304, 339, 454, 548; demand for, 175, 176, 458, 539, 557, 558, 560, 561, 565, 590, 594; imports, 338, 453; lager-type beers, 44, 57, 58, 162; louts, 584; *see also* beer brands
Lake, Edward, 261, 262 n 92, 282, 285, 291, 310–12, 363, 394
Lake, Harold, 394, 403
Lake, Neville, 376
Lake family, 387
Lambrick, John, 276, 403
Lancashire, drunkenness statistics, 33
landowners, brewing families as, 219–21
Langenbach, 500

Latham, Thomas, 390
lauter tun, 545, 547, 641
Law, R. W. R., 391
Lawson, Sir Wilfred, 286
leaseholds, *see* public houses
Leeds: agencies in, 125, 155; beer houses in, 149; Burton beers in, 108; drunkenness in, 17; free and tied trade, 149, 159, 281, 283; Institute of Brewing, 61; maltings in, 190; public house improvements in, 422; publican brewers in, 73, 74, 108, 123
Leeds & Batley brewery, 306
Leeds & District Clubs, 411
Leeds & Wakefield Breweries, 263 n 97, 309, 468 n 60
Lees, J. W. (Middleton Junction), 159, 239
Leicester, 156 n 74, 281
leisure activities of the working classes, 29, 37, 39–40, 200, 285, 335
Leith Brewery, 158
Leney, Frederick, & Sons (Kent), 348, 400
Levi, Leone, 29, 34, 35, 183, 196, 267 n 2
Lewis & Ridley (Banbury), 162
Licensed Defence League of England and Wales, 137 n 18
licensed victuallers: beer output of, 67–73, 77; per head of population, 252; *see also* public houses
Licensed Victuallers' Association, 209 n 65
Licensed Victuallers' Gazette, 67 n 8, 84, 150, 153, 239, 240
Licensed Victuallers' Protection Society, 137 n 18
licences: to brew, 4–8, 13, 16, 17, 26, 65, 66, 294, 295, 328, 331, 349–50; duty on, 17, 26, 66, 294, 295; maltsters', 186 n 13; restricted, suppressed, surrendered and exchanged, 128, 135, 286–95, 317, 331, 411, 422, 434; to sell beer, 3–5, 8, 13, 14, 17, 107, 129, 135, 252, 288, 293–4, 328, 331, 350, 456, 569; to sell spirits, 3, 8, 129, 134; surrender schemes, 288–9; *see also* off-licences; public houses; Royal Commissions
Licensing Acts: (1828), 8; (1872), 252 n 67; (1902), 289; (1904), 289–91, 411, 415, 422; (1910), 293; (1919), 433 n 71; (1921), 323, 330; (1949), 442; (1961), 455–6, 569; (1964), 455; (1976), 572; (1988), 584
Licensing Bills: (1871), 286; (1907–8), 292–4, 422, Pl. 41; (1948), 365, 442
light ales, 48, 58, *see also* ale; 'running' ales
Limerick, 101
Lincoln, 94, 190, 191, 281
Lion Brewery (Ashford), 66 n 6, 163, 251 n 63, 298
Liquor (Disinterested Ownership and Management) Bill (1928), 429
Lister Institute of Preventive Medicine, 219
Liverpool: agencies in, 100, 125, 152, 154, 155, 158, 159, 161; beer houses in, 16; bottlers in, 171; Burton beers in, 150, 152; common brewers in, 72–4, 123, 241; drunkenness statistics, 33, 326; licences in, 288; market supplied by other breweries, 95, 101 n 67, 124; stores in, 155, 160; tied trade in, 268, 283
Livesey, Joseph, 31
Lloyd, Evadne, 491
Lloyd, Pen, 491
Lloyd George, David, 293, 318–21, 323, 327–9
Lloyds Bank, 463
loans to publicans, 75–6, 87, 88, 92, 102, 107, 108, 128–36, 144, 147, 156, 210, 217, 227, 228, 233, 236, 269, 271–80, 284, 296, 297; loan-tie, 128, 209, 229, 268–9, 278, 597
local brewers, 589, 590
Local Option on restricting licences, 287, 288, 292, 419
London: agencies in, 100, 108, 152, 155, 156, 158, 159; bottlers and bottling in, 171, 299–303; common brewers in, 72, 75–89, 126, 128–38; distribution in, 128–46; labouring life in, 36; market supplied by non-London breweries, 78–82, 106, 118–19, 133, 144, 149, 150; population, 129; porter brewers in, 41, 42, 78–80, 83, 84, 111, 128, 130, 134, 139, 144, 170, 227, 229; production in, 610–12; rationalisation in, 346; stores in, 155, 160; tied trade in, 128–31, 208, 227, 268–73; water supply, 42, 50, 79, 83
London Brewers' Association, 210, 211
London Central Board, 137 n 18
London County Council housing, 424–5
London Press Exchange, 352, 353, 356, 398
Long John whisky, 500, 590 n 18
'long pull', 39, 208, 209 n 65, 255, 324, 641
Lorimer & Clark (Edinburgh), 395
Lott, Frank, 62

Lovell, Percival, 392
Lovibond, John (London), 333
Lovibond, T. W., 267 n 1
low-alcohol beers, 585
Lubbock, Cecil, 389, 422
Lubbock, Edgar, 267 n 1, 299
Lucas (Hitchin), 283 n 48
Lucas, William, 241, 249
Lynch, Patrick, 98, 99, 100
Lyons, J., & Co., 450, 474, 479, 527, 528
  see also Allied

Maberly, W. L., 13
McColl, 587
McEwan, William, 218–20, 222, 249, 385
McEwan, William & Co. (Edinburgh): agencies, 164; capitalisation, 380, 384–5; distribution, 45, 158; exports, 109, 158, 174, 377; free trade, 436, 438; management, 386, 388, 389; mergers and takeovers, 103, 346 n 100, 384–5; profits, 306, 620, 622; success of, 249; tied estate, 436, 442
McEwan Hall, Edinburgh, 219
McKay, George, 310
Mackeson, 348, 381, 400, 401, 483, 488, 566
Maclay (Alloa): distribution and transport, 549; free trade, 438; independence preserved, 484, 487, 493–4; management, 493–4; production, 589; profits, 369, 370, 589, 620, 622; tied estate, 442, 589
McLean, Hugh, 110
McMaster, Charles, 103 n 79
McMullen, Lance, 543
McMullen, O. H., 218
McMullen (Hertford), 283 n 48, 380, 442, 482, 571
mail order sales, 496
maize, 45, 53, 184, 187, 189, 362
Majoribanks family, 223 n 104
Malmesbury, Lord, 14
malt and malting, 185–93; concentrates, 546; cost of, 10, 141; government restrictions on, 320, 322; high-roasted, 79; imported, 188; kilning, 192; licences, 186 n 13; pneumatic, 192; price of, 137, 185, 192, 205, 208, 212, 255, 273, 294, 613; process, 51, 186–77; produced by brewers, 75, 115, 117, 186–92; research on, 540, 542, 548; Select Committee on the Malt Tax (1867), 192; shortages of, 363; tax, 9, 10, 11, 13, 16, 23, 25, 26, 29, 30, 43, 65, 67, 77, 137, 184, 186 n 13, 194–6, 211; transport of, 143, 150, 187; unmalted grains in brewing, 53; varieties of, 48, 188
maltings, 94, 190, 191, Pl. 26
maltose, 51, 55, 59
management, *see* breweries
Manchester: agencies in, 125, 153, 155, 159, 161; College of Technology, 62, 536; common brewers in, 125, 126, 159; Institute of Brewing at, 61; population growth, 123; publican brewers in, 72–4; stores in, 160; tied trade in, 268
Manchester Breweries, 395
Manchester Brewery Co., 125, 264 n 98, 291, 306
Manders (Dublin), 102
Mann, Crossman & Paulin, 244; Albion Brewery, 97, 134, 236; in Burton upon Trent, 84, 96, 97, 303; capital, 380; distribution and transport, 138, 141, 302, 549; loans, 214; management, 237; market preference for beer of, 354, 355; mergers, 449, 461, 462; off-licence trade, 418; production, 20, 42, 79, 80, 85–6, 134, 237, 610–12; profits, 214, 237; public house improvements, 426; tied estate, 418
Mann, Edward, 141
Mann, James, 236
Mann, Robert, 134
Mann family, 220, 223 n 105
Manners, Arthur, 403, 404, 462 n 34
Manners, W. P., 96, 224, 225, 275, 305, 403
Mansfield Brewery, 248, 503, 590–2
Manual of British Brewery Companies, 386, 388
Mark, John, 511
market research, 346, 350–6, 441, 559–68
Marplan, 565
Marshall, James, 173–4
Marshall, R. D., 240
Marston, Thompson & Evershed (Burton upon Trent), 273, 395, 484, 488, 554, 563, 588, 590–2
Martineau family, 228, 386
Martins, newsagents, 587
Maryport Brewery, 324 n 23
mash tun, 'freeing' of, 187, 195
mash tuns, 51–2, 545, 641
Mason, Frank, 422
Mason & Co., 400, 485
Mass-Observation, 417, 565
Massey's (Burnley), 342, 473
Mathew, Father, 101
Mathias, Peter, xix, 75, 78, 112, 116, 128, 130, 140, 186, 194, 212

Matthews & Canning (Chelsea), 271 n 11
Mauldon, J. C., & Sons (Sudbury), 494
Mealing & Mills, maltsters (Coltishall), 188
medicinal benefit of beer drinking, 32, 38, 66, 92, 351
Meeks, G., 498–9
Meeson, 587
Meiklejohn (Alloa), 107
Melbourne Breweries (Leeds), 468
Melrose, James, 165 n 102
Members of Parliament, brewers as, 221
Menestheus, MV, 543
Merchant, W. W., 392
mergers, 112, 260–1, 272, 309, 345–9, 373, 392–400, 447–97, 591–3, 623–9: post-merger profits, 498–503; *see also* takeovers
Merrett Cyriax, 478 n 90, 571
Merthyr Tydfil, 16
Meux, Sir Henry, 218
Meux family, 48, 223, 298
Meux's Brewery Co. (Wandsworth): adulteration of beer, 139; banking links, 396 n 59; in difficulties, 285 n 49, 296, 298; free trade, 436; management, 227, 233, 388, 393; mergers and takeovers, 462, 470, 488; Nine Elms Brewery, 346 n 96; product, 85; profits, 333, 620–1; public house improvements, 426 n 52; rationalisation, 346; specific gravities, 47; tied estate, 436, 438
Middlesbrough, 422
Middleton, William, 96
Midland Brewery Co, 223 n 105, 334
Milner, Lord, 329
Milner, Sir Frederick, Bt., 164 n 100, 240–1
Milwaukee & Chicago Brewery, 265
mineral waters, 284, 300, 302, 444
Mistley, 190
Mitchell, Henry, 290
Mitchell, Henry, & Co., 159, 279
Mitchell, John, 139
Mitchell Bros. (Castleford), 166 n 105, 167, 168
Mitchell family, 386
Mitchells (Birmingham), 125
Mitchells (Lancaster), 238 n 19
Mitchells & Butlers (Birmingham): Cape Hill Brewery, 547; capitalisation, 380, 384; distribution and transport, 554, Pls. 20, 21; free trade, 436; Harp consortium, 480; industrial relations, 516; labour force, 331 n 52; management, 284 n 49, 311, 386, 440; market preference for beer of, 354, 355; mergers and takeovers, 305, 334, 405, 471; off-licence trade, 418; production, 371; profits, 33 n 59, 306, 333, 334, 369, 620–1; public house improvements, 286 n 52, 421, 422; tied estate, 325, 418, 436, 440 n 87, 441, 442, 444 n 98, 531; *see also* Bass
Molson's Brewery (Quebec), 465
Monck, J. B., 13
Monopolies and Mergers Commission, 451 n 12, 479, 572, 581, 590–3, 596, 597
Monopolies Commission, 437, 449, 451, 478, 479, 501, 509 n 27, 519, 526, 559, 571, 572, 574
Moors' & Robson's Breweries (Hull), 263 n 97
Morgan Grenfell, 475, 476
Morgan's (Norwich), 149, 312, 357, 496, 529
MORI, 565, 568
Morison, J. & J. (Edinburgh), 468
Moritz, E. R., 45, 55, 6), 61, 63, 326
Morland (Abingdon), 394, 395, 440 n 82, 488
Morris, G. H., 55
Morris, Joseph, 247
Morris, Robert, 247
Morris family, 247
Morse, Arthur, 374
Morse, George Henry, 242, 374, 383 n 21, 396 n 59
Morse family, 223
mortgages, 247, 310
Motion, Andrew, 210 n 68, 272, 274, 275 n 10, 290, 295
motor transport, *see* transport
munitions areas, government controls for, 322–4, 326
Munro, R. H., 164 n 99, 264 n 99
Murray, Sir George, 196
Murray, William, & Co. (Edinburgh), 468
Musman, E. B., 427

Nathan, L., 543
National Federation (Union) of Licensed Victuallers, 137 n 18, 578
National Trade Defence (Development) Association, 285 n 49, 293, 319, 423, 570, 571
National Trade Defence Fund, 210
nationalisation of brewing and retailing, 317, 323–30, 358, 368, 418, 429
National Economic Development Office, Brewing Sector Working Group, 518, 557

Nevile, Sir Sydney, 325, 326, 351, 353, 361 n 140, 386, 387, 393, 422, 423, 432, 433, 536, 570, 576, Pl. 44
Neville, Edith, 420
New Westminster Brewery (London), 251 n 63, 284 n 49, 285
New York, 171
Newark, 126, 190
Newbold, C. J., 361 n 140, 390, 538
Newbould, G. D., 498
Newcastle Breweries: capitalisation, 380, 395; and clubs, 288 n 61; in difficulties, 284 n 49, 292 n 74, 294, 307; free trade, 436; licences, 289; management, 388; mergers and takeovers, 260, 334, 468; profits, 333, 342, 344, 345 n 94, 620, 622; tied trade, 436, 440 n 82, 442, 444
Newcastle upon Tyne: agencies and travellers in, 125, 153, 155–8, 166, 168; beers produced in, 45; common brewers in, 74; free trade in, 122; Scottish beers in, 106, 107, 109; tied trade in, 281, 283, 441
Newton, H., & Co. (Penrith), Pl. 8
Nicholl's, H. & V. (Lewisham), 244, 271 n 11
Nicholson, Sir Frank, 361 n 140, 394, 423 n 40, 432, 441, 444
Nimmo, J. (Castle Eden), 483, 489 n 125
Nixey, Coleclough & Baxter (West Hartlepool), 263 n 97
Nock & Co., 549
Norman & Pring (Exeter), 383 n 21, 395, 473
North Country Breweries (Hull), 592
Northampton Brewery Co., 48, 162, 163, 239, 260 n 90, 440 n 82, 444 n 98, 548
Northern Breweries (Britain), 449, 460, 467, 468
Northern Breweries (Montreal), 465
Northern Clubs' Federation, 411, 413, 414, 482
Norwich: agencies in, 117, 161; common brewers in, 72–5, 114, 115, 148–9, 331, 334, 374–7; maltings in, 190; tied trade in, 283
Norwich Union Insurance, 152, 396
Notting Hill Brewery Co. (London), 348
Nottingham, 156, 281
Nottingham Brewery, 159, 260 n 90
Nunneley, Joseph (Burton upon Trent), 96
Nuttall & Co. (Blackburn), 378
Nutting, Ronald, 396

oats, used in brewing, 362
Odhams Press censuses, 354, 355
Office of Fair Trading, 573
off-licences, 14, 252, 285, 408–9, 412–13, 416, 456–7, 557; duty on, 17; free, 418; number of, 456, 569; proportion of sales through, 127, 285, 288, 296, 409, 557; tied, 408, 418
O'Hagan, H. Osborne, 263–5
Ohlsson's Cape Brewery, 265
Oldham brewery, 592
Oliver, Basil, 421, 427
Oliver family, 387
on-licences, *see* licences; public houses; tied houses
opening hours, *see* public houses
O'Sullivan, Cornelius, 59
Ottley, Richard, 406
output, *see* production
overcapacity, *see* brewing
Overend Gurney, 231

packaging of beers, 378, 457, 546–7, 557
Paget & Co. (Great Yarmouth), 114
Paine & Co. (St Neots), 381, 620–2
pale ales, *see* ale
Palmar, Sir Derek, 532
Palmer, Geoffrey, 540
Palmer (Bridport), 484
Panda Soft Drinks, 496
Panmure Gordon, 475 n 78
Parker, Hon. Reginald, 164 nn 99 and 100, 241, 264 n 99
Pass, C. L., xix, 255, 262 n 93, 267, 278, 346, 371, 449, 503
Pasteur, Louis, 55, 58–9, 60, 62
pasteurisation of beers, 299, 378, 457, 534, 537–8, 641
paternalism, 198–200, 219, 373, 407, 516
Patteson, Henry, 245
Patteson, John, 113–14
Paul, Hugh, 361, 362
Paulin, Thomas, 237
Paxton, Sir Joseph, 219
Payne, Peter, 380 n 16
Peacock, Hugh, 385 n 29
Pead, William, 246
Pearson, William, 149
Pease, Sandy, 475, 476
Peat Marwick Mitchell, 400 n 71, 478 n 90
Peel, Viscount, 289
Peel Commission, *see* Royal Commission on Liquor Licensing Laws
Penrose, Edith, 382, 460
People's Refreshment House Association, 419
Perkins, C. A. C., 387, 391 n 46
Perkins family, 227, 386
'perpendicular drinking', 421, 425, 434, Pl. 52

Peter Dominic, 500
Peterborough, 281
Phillips, C. J., 311, 312 n 124
Phillips, John, 247
Phillips, Thomas, 96 n 61, 280
Phillips & Sons (Newport), 96 n 61, 343
Phillips Brothers (Northampton), 96 n 61
Phillips family, 247
Phipps & Co. (Northampton), 259, 279, 306, 308, 380, 442, 463
Phoenix Brewery (Dover), 66 n 6, 163
Phoenix Brewery (Wakefield), 166 n 105
Pick, Martin, 350–1
Pidgeon system of brewing, 53
Pike, Frank, 492, 493
Pike, Spencer & Co. (Portsmouth), 66 n 6
pilferage, 94, 147, 150
Pizza Hut, 590
Plender, Sir William, 327
Plymouth, 73, 117, 118, 155, 161, 268
Plymouth Breweries, 259–61, 306, 440 n 82
pontos, 57
Pope, Alfred, 162
Pope, Edwin, 218, 312 n 126
Pope, George, 312 n 126
Pope, Philip, 486, 492
Pope, Rolph, 486
Pope family, 244, 486
population growth, 91, 129, 252, 454–5
population shift to suburbs, 296, 335, 422
porter, 642; country brewers of, 79; Irish, 99–103, 139–40; London brewers of, 41, 42 , 78–80, 83, 84, 111, 128, 130, 134, 139, 144, 170, 227, 229; prices, 137–8, 205, 209; production of, 50, 57, 58, Pl. 6; Scottish, 105
Porter-Lancastrian Ltd, 547
Portland Beer Stores, Sheffield, Pl. 39
Portman Group, 585
Portsmouth, 163, 326
potatoes, used in brewing, 362
Prais, Jon, 514
Pratt, E. A., 46, 47
Preece, Isaac, 548
Pressurised Beers Liaison Committee, 480
Prest, A. R., 34, 602
Price, H. Davenport, 396
Price Commission, 502, 509, 519–21, 528, 571, 572, 593
Price Waterhouse, 398, 399
prices, of beers: (1830–1914), 6, 8, 10, 12, 20, 21, 39, 92, 105, 137–8, 169, 170, 205–11, 255, 274, 301, 602–3; in World War I, 322–3; interwar period, 332, 335, 340–1, 352; in World War II, 356, 357, 366, 370; post-war, 373, 502, 519–21, 570, 583, 637; *see also* barley; brewing materials; hops; malt
Prices and Incomes Board, 437, 509–10, 512, 519, 570
Pringle, J. S., 374
Pritchard, Derek, 489, 490, 525
Pritchard, John, 19
private brewers, 25, 64, 65, 112, 126
production of beer: (1818–1914), 9, 20, 23–6, 254, 338, 366–8, 600–3; (1914–80), 317–23, 331, 337–9, 359, 360, 364–8, 409–11, 581–2, 588–9, 602, 618–19, 630
Production-Engineering, 526, 532
productivity, 192–4, 197–8, 503, 512–15, 632
profits: brewers', 9, 97, 180–2, 212–17, 227–48, 272, 281, 306, 308–9, 331–5, 342–5, 363, 365, 368–71, 579, 588–9, 620–1; Excess Profits Duty, 332, 356
prohibition, 33, 253, 320, 322–4, 327, 419
Prosser, Robert, 139
Pryor, A. V., 189 n 18
Pryor, Alfred, 242, 244, 247 n 51
Pryor, Arthur, 88, 233 n 7
Pryor, Frederick, 243
Pryor, John, 242, 247
Pryor, John Izzard, 233 n 7, 242, 243, 246
Pryor, Morris, 242, 243, 247 n 52
Pryor, Robert, 231, 233 n 7
Pryor (Baldock), 242–3, 246, 247
Pryor family, 231, 232, 242–3, 249
Pryor Reid (Hatfield), 283 n 48
Public Attitude Surveys, 567
public houses:
architecture of, 424–5; certificate of improvement, 420; closures, 324, 574, 598; construction of, 129–30; decline in numbers of, 411–13; decline in popularity of, 285–6, 566, 569; deterioration of, 365; 'fewer but better' policy, 421; first-class, 269–70, 272; food in, 418–22, 424, 426, 434, 570, 576–7; freehold, 255; games in, 577–9; improvement of, 135, 136, 254, 275, 284, 286, 313, 325, 346, 411, 417, 418–37, 570–9, 594, Pls. 34–8, 53–8; leasehold, 128, 133, 136, 148, 149, 255, 268–71, 275, 278, 279; licences, 4–5, 129, 135, 252, 293–4; London, 128–38, 268–73; managed, 422–3, 432–3, 436, 437, 439, 440–6, 574–5; management of, 378, 426, 570–9; music in, 576–7; non-alcoholic drink sales in, 418, 419; number of, 288, 328, 408, 412, 414–16, 456, 569, 597; opening hours, 17, 138, 287, 324, 330, 456, 572, 584; per capita, 252–3;

planning, 421; price of, 248, 251, 253–4, 270, 281; proportion of beer sold in, 408–9; purchase of, 250, 255, 266–309; rateable values of, 293, 294; recreational facilities in, 417, 421; relocation of, 433; as retail outlets, 408–46; staff, 426, 432, 570–1; supply of, 251; swops, 572, 573; tenanted, 164–5, 422–3, 433, 435, 436, 439, 440–6, 570, 574–5; theme pubs, 594; value of, 135–7, 299; women in, 325, 423, 435; *see also* beer houses; tied houses
public houses (named):
'Anchor', Somers Town, 426, 430, 433; 'Angel', Victoria, 276 n 25; 'Beaconsfield', Hammersmith, 269; 'Belle View', Clapham Common, 425 n 45; 'Berkeley Arms', Cranford, 427; 'Cherry Tree', Becontree, 425 n 46; 'Comet', Hatfield, 427; 'Crooked Billet', Newcastle upon Tyne, 281, Pl. 38; 'Crown', Cricklewood, Pls. 34, 35; 'Crown', Edgware Road, Pl. 64; 'Crown and Anchor', Finsbury Pavement, 275 n 22; 'Fellowship Inn', Bellingham, S.E. London, 425 n 46; 'Grapes', Hayes, 431; 'Gretna Tavern', Carlisle, 325; 'Holly Bush', Birmingham, Pls. 55, 56; 'King's Head', Cumberland Market, 425; 'Mitre', Holland Park, 425 n 45; 'Myllet Arms', Perivale, 427; 'Nag's Head', Covent Garden, Pl. 52; 'Ord Arms', Newcastle upon Tyne, 281; 'Princess Alice', Forest Gate, 270; 'Priory', Clapton, 275 n 22, 276; 'Queen's Arms', Peckham, Pl 36; 'Rest House', Kenton, 431; 'Robin Hood', Becontree, 425 n 46, 431, 432; 'Rockingham', London, 276; 'Roebuck', Chiswick, 270; 'Rose', Camberwell, 425; 'Rose and Crown', Tooting, 431, 433 n 71; 'Tavistock', Somers Town, 425–6; 'Terminus Hotel', Bristol, Pl. 58; 'Three Queens Hotel', Weston-super-mare, 434 n 72; 'Traveller's Rest', Birmingham, Pls. 53, 54; 'Valley Hotel', Caterham, 431, 432; 'Warrington Hotel', Maida Vale, 425 n 49; 'Welcome Inn', Eltham, 431, Pl. 83; 'White Hart', Tottenham, 431, 432; 'Windsor Castle', Victoria, 425 n 45, 430; 'Woolpack', Moorgate, 276
publican brewers, 25, 41, 64, 66, 69, 73–5, 108, 111, 112, 119, 123, 126, 173, 238, 281
pupillage, 243–5, 405
Pure Beer Bill (1901), 296 n 90
Purser family, 246

Quakers, 35

Raffety, John, 232
Raggett's, Jermyn Street, 276
railways, *see* transport
Rainbow, Cyril, 543
Rainnie, G. F., 505
Ramsden, John Taylor, 247
Rangemoor (Staffs), 156, 219–20
Rank Organisation, 477 n 84, 478
Ratcliff, Percy, 404
Ratcliff, Richard, 218
Ratcliff, Samuel, 157
Ratcliff family, 95, 219 n 87, 403
rates and rateable values, 135, 291, 294
rationalisation, *see* breweries
Rayment's Brewery (Furneux Pelham), 376
'real ale', *see* Campaign for Real Ale
Red Tower Lager Brewery (Manchester), 466, 467 n 52
Redfern, Harry, 421
refrigerators, 54–5, 58, 82, 547
Regent Brewery (Plymouth), 260
regional breweries, 379–81, 468, 483–4, 487, 490, 588, 590–1
regional variations in beer, 41–2, 45
Reid, George, 494
Reid, Neville (Windsor), 119, 244
Reid family, 115
Reid's (London): Clerkenwell brewery, 234; country and town trade, 143–4; distribution, 134; labour force, 204; loans, 132; management, 86, 87, 233, 234; prices, 602; production, 79, 80, 85, 610–12; rest books, 82 n 23; spending on colouring, 7; Stout, 481; tied estate, 131
Remnant, J. F., 304
Renny-Tailyour, H. W., 390
rents of public houses, 282, 296, 297, 439–41; 'dry' rent, 208, 437, 440, 443, 444, 571, 574, 575; 'wet' rent, 137, 208, 437, 440, 443, 444, 575, 642
resale price maintenance, 451, 457
rest books, 82
Restaurant Public Houses Association, 420, 425, 430–3
restrictive practices, 451
'Retail Brewing' Act (1824), 7, 8
retail sales, 92, 317, 408–46, 519–21, 557–68
Retford, 190, 191
rice, used in brewing, 45, 53, 184, 189
Richmond, Duke of, 14

Ridley, Rt. Hon. Nicholas, 571
Ridley (Essex), 442
Riley-Smith, F. and H. H., 258, 259, 279
Riley-Smith family, 238, 386
Ringwood (Hants), 591
Ritchie, Charles, 494
Roberts, Charles, M.P., 37
Robertson, J., 515
Robin (Brighton), 66 n 6, 163
Robinson, Frederick (Stockport), 590 n 19, 591, 592
Rogers (Bristol), 162
Rothschilds, 478 n 90
Rothwell, W. T., 63
Rowan, Sir Leslie, 466
Rowntree, Joseph, 27, 35, 281, 325 n 25
Rowntree, Seebohm, 36
Royal Brewery (Brentford), 398, 423
Royal Commission on Arsenical Poisoning (1901), 296 n 90
Royal Commission on Gambling, 578
Royal Commission on Licensing (England and Wales) (1931), 408, 413, 419, 420–1, 427–9, 432, 434, 441, 444
Royal Commission on Liquor Licensing Laws (1896–9), 267 n 1, 268, 269, 278, 283, 289, 291, 441
Royal Commission on Technical Instruction, 60
Rubinstein, W. D., 217, 218, 220
Ruddle, G. (Oakham), 395, 442, 482, 488, 507, 592
Runciman, Walter, 319
Russells & Wrangham (Malton), 342, 344, 436, 438, 468 n 60, 620, 622
Ryder, Charles, 158, 220

saccharometer, 48, 56
St Anne's Well Brewery (Exeter), 333, 381
St Leonard's Brewery (Edinburgh), 310
St Pancras Station, 151, 153, 155
salaries, 203–4, 232, 245–6, *see also* wages
Salisbury, 163
Salt, Thomas (Burton upon Trent), 90 n 44, 93, 96, 97, 273, 303, 304, 347
Samuel, Herbert, 327
Sandeman, David, 500
Sanderson, Thomas, 149
Savill (Stratford, E. London), 141, 236
Scarborough, 166 n 104
Schroders, 402
Schweppes, 495
Scotland: bottling in, 299; brewing industry in, 103–10, 158, 328 n 39, 339, 384–5, 467–8, 523–4, 572; exports, 107, 109–10, 173–4; free and tied trade in, 158, 161, 409; sales in England, 106–9, 166 n 103
Scott, Walter, 537
Scottish & Newcastle breweries: advertising, 562, 636; and alcohol abuse, 585 n 9; closure, 587; costs, 512 n 34; diversification, 590; formed, 103, 449, 468; Home Brewery, Nottingham, 507; market-position, 586; mergers and takeovers, 477, 523–5, 591–3, 597; new and rebuilt breweries, 506, 556; production, 504, 507, 588; profits, 588; research, 539; structure, 523; tied estate, 472, 523, 586, 588; trading agreements, 371 n 164, 458, 480
Scottish Brewers, 108, 346 n 100, 385, 467, 468, 620, 622
Scrivens family, 227
sea routes, *see* transport
Seagram, 585 n 9
Sears Holdings, 449, 462
Seaward, Alan, 559
Seckham, S. L., 96 n 61, 239
Seligman, Richard, 537, 538
Selley, Ernest, 421
Serocold, Oswald, 234, 423
'75' Club, 555
Shadwell, Arthur, 325 n 25
Shand, A. T., 174
shares, 231, 250–66, 284, 285, 290, 485–7
Sharp v. Wakefield (1891), 252, 265, 288
Shaw-Lefevre family, 228
Sheffield: agencies in, 156; common brewers in, 126, 159, 161; publican brewers in, 73, 74, 123; surrender scheme, 289 n 62
Sheldon, Arthur, 408
Shepherd family, 493–4
Shepherd Neame (Faversham), 185, 438 n 81
Sheppard, Sir Allen, 530, 532
Sherwell, A., 27, 35, 281, 325 n 25
Shipstone (Nottingham), 354
Shipstone & Stour, 162
Shorthose, John, 157, Pl. 23
Showell's (Birmingham), 305, 306, 309, 312
Showerings Vine Products & Whiteways, 478, 500, 525, 526
Sigsworth, Eric, 58, 73, 74
Silkin, Rt. Hon. John, 573
Simonds, Duncan, 559
Simonds, F. A., 361 n 140, Pl. 50
Simonds, H. & G. (Reading): agencies, 163; free trade, 436, 438; management, 245–6, 387, 394; mergers and takeovers, 349, 449, 492; profits, 215, 343; tied

estate, 280, 382 n 19, 436, 440 n 87, 444 n 98; transport, 119
Simonds family, 115, 247
Simonds-Gooding, Anthony, 567
Simpkiss (Brierley Hill), 592
Simpson (Baldock), 256, 387, 494
Singh, A., 498
Sir John Cass's Technical Institute (London), 62, 536
Sketchley family, 89
Sleaford maltings, 191, Pl. 26
small beers, *see* beers, 'table'
Smith, Andrew, 106
Smith, Edward and Frederick, 241–2
Smith, Frederick (Birmingham), 438 n 81
Smith, John, 124, 238–9, Pl. 14
Smith, Samuel (Tadcaster), 438, 485, 590
Smith, Sydney, 15, 29
Smith (Grimsby), 166 n 105
Smith's John, *see* John Smith's Tadcaster Brewery Co.
Snowden, Philip, Viscount, 33, 36, 326, 327, 329, 341
Soames (Spalding), 371, 385 n 29
Soames (Wrexham), 45, 238 n 19
Sotham, Louise, 420
South Africa, 172, 265
South Milford (Yorkshire), 190
South Wales & Monmouthshire Club Brewery, 414
Southampton, 156 n 74, 163
Southborough Committee on the Disinterested Management of Public Houses (1927), 408, 420, 424
Southby, E. R., 49–50, 52, 53, 180
specific gravity, 46, 47, 56, 195, 337, 367–8, 411, 594, 602, 641; government control of, 317, 318, 320–3, 326, 329, 332, 361, 364
spirits: consumption of, 10, 34, 35, 99, 138, 325, 359, 457, 500, 581; duty, 10, 293; licence to sell, 3, 8, 129, 134; municipalisation of, 287 n 55; prices, 340, 519; production, 192; tie, 136, 284, 437, 444; transport of, 302; whisky trade, 104
sponsorship, 566
sporting activities, 39, 40, 200, 335
Springwell Brewery (Heckmondwike), 263 n 97, 264 n 99, 309, 333
stables and stablemen, 141
Stag Brewery (Pimlico), 233, 461–3
standard barrelage, *see* production
Star (Eastbourne), 438 n 81
Star (Great Britain) Holdings, 463
starches, research on, 59
Starkey, Knight & Co. (Bridgwater), 282
Starkey, Knight & Ford (Bridgwater), 473
Statist, 263, 264, 295, 440, 446, 501
steam power, 51, 82, 93, 124, 141
steam yachts, 222
Steel, Coulson & Co. (Glasgow and Edinburgh), 306, 468
Steel's mashing machine, 53
Stella Artois, 558
Stephens, James H., 393
Steward, Donald, 245
Steward, Donald C., 376–7, 496
Steward, Walter, 245
Steward, William, 12, 13
Steward & Patteson (Steward, Patteson, Finch & Co., 1837–95) (Norwich): agencies, 163; bottling, 300 n 100; capitalisation, 381, 385; free trade, 436; incorporation, 261 n 91, 374, 383 n 21; maltings, 190; management, 245, 374, 376–7, 406; market preference for beer of, 354, 355; mergers and takeovers, 148, 371, 385 n 29, 463, 484, 496, 529; and Norwich Union, 396; Pockthorpe brewery, 114; production, 331; profits, 306, 308, 309, 333, 334, 369, 620–1; research, 547; sales in London, 118; tied estate, 113–15, 149 n 56, 261 n 91, 262, 279 n 33, 309, 436, 437, 442
Steward family, 223
Stewart, J., 305
stock market, 250–66, 270–3, 303–4, 383–4, 401–2, 450–1, 463–4, 469–70, 485–8, 490
Stocks (Halifax), 306
Stockton-on-Tees, 155, 166 n 104, 168
Stoke-on-Trent, 152, 155
Stone, Richard, 341
Stone Trough Brewery (Halifax), 247
Stones, William (Sheffield), 474
Stopes, A. O., 219
stores and store managers, 92, 101, 127, 144, 151–3, 155, 157, 158, 161, 162
stout, 32, 50, 57, 58, 642; double, 101, 147; extra, 101, 139, 321; Irish, 99–103, *see also* Guinness; London brewers', 80, 144; milk stout, 348, *see also* Mackeson
Stowmarket, 190
Stretton's Derby Brewery, 260 n 90, 263 n 97
Strong (Romsey): bottling, 311; capital, 384; free trade, 436; and licence restriction, 291; management, 240, 241, 307, 309, 311, 378; profits, 306; rationalisation, 349; takeovers and alliances, 334, 349, 395, 474; tied estate, 436, 438

Stroud Brewery, 395
Stuart, Rev. Wilson, 325 n 25
Style & Winch (Maidstone), 333, 334, 346 n 100, 387, 393, 398, 399, 620–2
sugar: duty, 195, 292; government control, 359, 364; used in brewing, 23, 45, 53, 59, 67, 184, 188, 193, 196 n 33, 546
Sully, J., 264
'summer' ales, *see* ale, 'running'; beer, summer brewed
Sunderland, 108, 117, 161
supermarket off-licences, 418, 456, 457, 460, 557
Sutton, C. E., 390
Swansea, 108, 162
Sykes (Batley), 264 n 99
Symonds, W. F., 485 n 113

Tabor, J. B. S., 392
Tadcaster, 50, 126, 238
Tadcaster Tower Brewery: agencies and travellers, 166; army trade, 122, 125, 168, 241; coopers, 202; in difficulties, 306; discounts, 201 n 46, 273; free trade, 122, 164–8; labour force, 198 n 39; management, 165–6, 240–1, 249; profits, 167, 181, 333; Snobs brewery, 240; takeovers, 264, 394; tied estate, 122, 159, 164–8, 180 n 1, 254, 282–3
takeovers, 264, 346–9, 371, 373, 392–406, 447–97, *see also* mergers
Tamplin & Sons (Brighton), 264 n 98, 334, 387, 461, 568, 620–1
Tanqueray, John, 234
Tattershall-Walker, G., 238 n 21
Taunton ales, 41, 169
taxation of the industry: (1830–1914), 291–5; (1914–80), 286, 291, 317–18, 356, 509–11; *see also* beer duties, cider duty, hop duty, licences, malt duty, sugar duty
Taylor (brewer), 133
Taylor, Edward Plunket (E. P.), 461, 465–74, 483, 484, 492, 495, 532, Pl. 65
Taylor, Timothy (Keighley), 438, 568
Taylor Walker (London), 301, 347, 354, 355, 383 n 21, 440 n 82, 464, 524, 549, 568
tea drinking, 39, 339
technology, *see* brewing
temperance movement, 17, 22, 27, 28, 31, 33, 38, 40, 101, 129, 183, 207, 251, 253–5, 318, 323, 325 n 25, 327, 352, 418, 419, 420; and licence restriction, 285, 286, 288, 289
Tennant, Anthony, 475, 532
Tennant, Robert, 240, 242
Tennant Brothers (Sheffield), 395, 440 n 82, 473, 488, 489 n 125, 492
Tennent, H. T., 220
Tennent, J. & R. (Glasgow): advertising, 567; exports, 109, 110, 173, 174, 177; Guinness intervention, 483; lager, 177, 339, 558, 565; profits, 216; takeovers, 103, 473; Wellpark brewery, 177 n 129
Tennent Caledonian, 103, 493, 566
Terry, Arthur, 391
Tetley, C. F., 244, 245
Tetley, Charles H., 388
Tetley, F. W., 158
Tetley, Henry, 390
Tetley, Joshua (Leeds): agencies, 158–9; capitalisation, 248; distribution and transport, 302, 550, Pl. 81; free trade, 147, 166, 168, 436; incorporated, 261 n 91; IPA, 158; labour force, 197, 330; malt, 190 n 22; management, 124, 220, 245, 386 n 32, 388, 528; market preference for beer of, 354, 355; mergers and takeovers, 371, 449, 468, 525, 527; production, 158–9; profits, 334–5, 369, 620, 622; stores, 160; tied estate, 121, 281, 436, 440 n 82, 444
Tetley family, 386
Tetley Walker, 449, 524, 528
TGI Friday, 590
Theakston, T. & R. (Masham), 592
thermometers, 48, 52, 56
Thirsk, 190 n 22
Thistle Hotels, 524, 590
Thompson, Edward, 464 n 43, 465–7, 469, 471, 484, 524, 526
Thompson, John, & Son (Burton upon Trent), 273
Thompson & Evershed (Burton upon Trent), 395, 488
Thornton, F. W., 136, 137
Threlfall's (Manchester), 125, 259, 306, 380, 440 n 82, 442
Threlfalls Chesters, 473
Thwaites & Co. (Blackburn), 279 n 33, 444 n 98, 482, 485, 487, 502, 590 n 19, 591, 592
Tidbury, Sir Charles, 531, 532
tied houses, 7, 13, 19, 20, 37, 40, 44, 207; acquisition of, 63, 122, 210, 266–313; brewers ranked by, 472; decline in, 569; importance of for common brewers, 72, 74–5, 113–16, 121, 161, 262, 381, 382 n 19; in London, 128–31, 208, 227, 268–73; and monopolies, 4, 6, 267, 281, 286, 292, 501, 570–4, 594–8; number of, 588–9; prices in, 570; proportion of public houses tied, 408–48; time

restriction on, 594; zoning scheme for, 357; in Scotland, 107, 108, 121, 278; *see also* discounts; loans; public houses
Tizard, W. L., 40–1, 48, 49, 52 n 75, 53–5, 101
tobacco, 39, 284
Tollemache, Lord, 241
Tollemache (Ipswich), 241, 418
Tollemache & Cobbold (Ipswich), 547, 590
Tollemache family, 241
Tottenham Brewery, 177
Tower Brewery (Grimsby), 218
trade marks, 173, 300
trade unions, 198–200, 516–19, 551, 554–5, *see also* industrial relations
training, *see* education and training
transport: costs, 140–3, 146, 147, 162, 508, 511; horse, 130, 140–3, 146, 152, 153, 157, 159, 179, 199, 302, 358, 549–50, Pls. 17, 20, 80; inland waterways, 74, 90, 94, 100, 116, 119, 120, 127, 147, 148, 150, 163, 550, Pl. 18; motor and road, 143, 157, 302–3, 307, 313, 346, 357, 358, 444, 518, 437, 549–57, Pls. 19–21; railways, 43, 92, 93, 95, 101, 106, 116, 127, 128, 144, 147, 149–51, 154, 159, 163, 173, 202, 358, 549–5, Pl. 16; sea routes, 74, 75, 81, 100, 106, 116–18, 120, 147, 169, 550
Transport Act (1968), 555
Transport and General Workers' Union (TGWU), 516–19, 554
travellers, 127, 152, 156, 158, 159, 168, 197, 203, 204, *see also* agents and agency system
Trent Valley Brewery Co., 240
Tripp, C. H., 164 n 99, 168, 204, 208 n 64, 283 n 47
Trouncer (Shrewsbury), 440 n 82
True Temperance Association, 419, 420 n 27
Truman, Hanbury & Buxton (London): agencies, 152; beer, 42; bottling, 141, 142, 301–2; Brick Lane brewery, 475; in Burton upon Trent, 84, 96; capitalisation, 229–32, 380, 395; casks and coopers, 202; coal consumption, 196 n 33; costs, 512 n 34, 613; difficult times, 298; distribution and transport, 140, 142–4, 152, 302, 549, Pls. 16, 80; exports, 172; family portraits, 87–8; free trade, 138, 206 n 61; labour force, 197–9, 232; loans, 132, 135, 269–71, 276; management, 86–8, 227–9, 232, 233, 236, 242–3, 247; mergers and takeovers, 96 n 61, 450, 474–7, 529; production, 20, 42, 79, 80, 85, 296, 610–12; profits, 213, 247 n 54; public house improvements, 424, 426 n 52, 434; quality, 139, 140; raw materials, 184, 187–9, 193, 194, 312 n 124; research, 536; rest books, 82 n 23, specific gravities, 47, 56; tied estate, 138, 206 n 61, 208, 210, 253–4, 269–71, 272, 275, 440 n 82, 444 n 98, 474, 572; trading agreements, 401; union room, Pl. 3; water supply, 49, 50
Truman, Sir Benjamin, 88
trust companies, 419, 420
Trust House Forte, 474, 479, 590 n 18
Trust Houses Ltd, 419
Tuborg, 586
Tweedmouth, Lord, 223, 298

Ulster Brewery (Belfast), 468 n 57
underbacks, 53
unemployment, 306–7, 582
Unilever, 474, 478–9, 525
union system, *see* fermentation systems
United Africa Company, 478
United Breweries, 449, 461, 468, 470–1, 473, 482, 565
United Breweries (Copenhagen), 586
United Caledonian, 468
United States of America: breweries in, 175, 176, 264–5, 299, 508, 514, 586; exports to, 44, 169, 171, 173, 175, 176, 317, 454; imports from 585–6; prohibition in, 33, 322
urbanisation, 32–4, 113, 123, 129
Ure, Andrew, 7
Urwick Orr, 531
Ushers (Trowbridge), 358 n 133, 440 n 82, 463, 492, 568
Utton, M. A., 498

Vaizey, J. E., xix, 98–100, 299, 408, 409
Vale Brewery (Darwin), 159
Valuation of the Metropolis Act (1869), 135
Value Added Tax (VAT), 510, 582, 632
Vandenheuvel-Ixelberg Brewery, Belgium, 530
vats, 84–5
Vaux (Sunderland): advertising, 563; costs, 512 n 34; growth of, 125, 159; independence preserved, 484; management, 394; market-share, 590; production, 588; profits, 502, 588; rents, 440 n 87; mergers, alliances and takeovers, 395, 468, 488; tied estate, 432, 588
Vaux & Associated Breweries, 394

Veasey, T. H., 387
Venning (Liskeard), 438 n 81
Victoria Wine, 500
Villebois, Henry, 86, 88
Villebois, J. T., 229–31
Villebois family, 232
Vincent, Sir Henry (Lord D'Abernon), 326 n 33
Vipan, Thomas (Thetford), 115

Wadworth (Devizes), 371, 482, 568, 589
wages: and beer consumption, 28–9, 37, 91, 105, 113, 285, 295, 600–3; of brewery employees, 142–3, 181, 196–200, 373, 517–19
Wakefield, 166
Walker, A. B. (Warrington), 96, 275
Walker, Sir Alan, 531, 532, Pl. 76
Walker, Sir Andrew, 219, 220, 223, 249, Pl. 15
Walker, Hiram, 593
Walker, Peter, 249
Walker, Peter, & Sons (Warrington): in Burton upon Trent, 96; capital, 380; management, 124, 218, 238 n 19; market preference for beer of, 354, 355; store, 159; takeover, 568; tied estate, 279 n 33, 286, 440 n 82, 444 n 98
Walker, William, 199
Walker & Homfrays (Salford), 380 n 16, 395, 543
Walker Art Gallery, Liverpool, 219
Walker Cain (Liverpool), 354, 355, 382 n 19, 427, 468, 525, 549
Walker family, 218, 223 n 105
Wandsworth Brewery, 218
Warburgs, 470, 475 n 78
Warrington, 283
Warwicks & Richardsons (Newark), 163, 281
water supply, 33, 42, 49–50, 83, 89, 91, 105, 106, 126
water transport, *see* transport
Watkins (Hereford), 162
Watney, Daniel, 233
Watney, James, 218, 233, 235
Watneys (Elliot, Watney & Co., 1849–58; Watney & Co., 1858–98; Watney Combe Reid, 1898–1958; Watney Mann, 1958–72): advertising, 351, 562–4, 636, Pl. 74; bottling, 301; capitalisation, 380–1; beer conditioning, 537; costs, 512 n 34; in difficulties, 284 n 49, 295–8; distribution and transport, 142–3, 358, 549; diversification, 500; fermentation system, 544; hops, 124, 193 n 28, 312; incorporation, 251 n 63; keg beers, 457–8; labour force, 330, 331 n 52; lagers, 454; management, 233–5, 311, 383; market-position, 586; market preference for beer of, 354, 355; mergers and takeovers, 204, 235, 272, 297, 347, 449, 450, 459, 461–4, 474–8, 484, 492, 496–7, 500, 529; off-licence trade, 418; production, 79, 504; public house building and improvements, 420, 424–7, 430, 435; Red, 529, 558, 563, 565, 566; Red Barrel, 458, 481, 529, 558, 563–5; 'Red Revolution', 566 Pl. 74; research, 536, 543; Starlight, 565; structure, 529–30; taxation, 294; tied estate, 279 n 33, 281, 382 n 19, 430, 439, 440 n 82, 444 n 98, 472, 501, 524, 572, 586, Pl. 64; welfare provision, 516
Watney Mann & Truman (Grand Met), 530, 544, 568; closures, 587; and games machines, 579; and imported beers, 585–6; monopoly, 573; new and rebuilt breweries, 506; production, 588; profits, 588; tied estate, 573, 588
Watson, Forbes, 60
Watson, Katherine, 262
Webb, Beatrice and Sidney, 8, 11, 12, 15
Webbs (Aberbeeg), 438 n 81, 468 n 57
Webster, Michael, 462 n 34, 476, 529, 530
Welcome Break, 590
Wells, Charles (Bedford), 484
Wells, Sir Richard, 361 n 140
Wells (Wallingford), 119
Wells & Winch (Biggleswade), 469 n 61, 494, 495
Welton Breweries, 334
Wenlock, Lady, 165 n 102
Wenlock, Lord, 66
Wenlock Brewery (London), 292, 403, 462 n 34
West Country Brewers, 473, 488
Westminster Wine, 500
Weston (Norwich), 149
Wethered, Thomas (Marlow), 119, 331 n 52, 380, 440 n 82, 444 n 98
Wexford, 116
Weymouth, 163
wheat, used in brewing, 546
Wheeler, Robert, 12
wheelwrights, 141
Whitbread: advertising and market research, 39, 300, 346, 350, 351, 354, 355, 483, 563–5, 636, Pl. 48; and alcohol abuse, 585 nn 8 and 9; banking links, 396 n 59; bottled beer, 141, 143, 146, 272, 299–300, 302, 348, 353, 400, 401; breweries, 326 n 32, 331, 506–8, 515, 556; brewery closures, 587;

capitalisation, 380, 384, 401–2; Central Catering Co., 422; club trade, 413; costs, 512 n 34; country trade, 143–4, 146; in difficulties, 298; distribution and transport, 46, 134, 141–3, 302, 358, 556; diversification, 500; exports, 172, 300, 339, 348, 377, 400; food in public houses, 422, 426, 433; Forest Brown, 401; free trade, 271, 348, 436, 438; hops, 185, 193; Improved Public House Co., 424, 432; incorporated, 271; industrial relations, 508; labour force, 330; lager brewing, 454; loans, 132–5, 269, 271; low-alcohol beer, 585; maltings, 187; management, 86, 87, 227, 228, 233, 386, 388, 389, 400–3, 530–1, Pl. 75; market-position, 586; mergers and takeovers, 347–8, 400, 450, 460, 464, 470, 473–5, 488–92, 494, 590 n 18; off-licence trade, 418; prices, 521; production, 20, 48, 79, 80, 85, 113, 172, 331, 347, 504, 507, 588, 610–12; profits, 212–14, 308, 332 n 59, 333, 342, 344, 345 n 94, 369, 370, 502, 521, 588, 620–1; public house building, 432; public house improvements, 420, 424, 426 n 52, 430, 431–3; rationalisation, 348; research, 536; rest books, 82 n 23; sales, 431; share splitting, 485; sponsorship, 566; Tankard, 558, 565; tied estate, 131–3, 271, 281, 348, 400, 413, 418, 433, 436, 439, 440 n 82, 444 n 98, 472, 474, 501, 524, 586, 588; town trade, 143–4; trading agreements, 401; Trophy Bitter, 565; 'umbrella', 395–6, 402–3, 449, 459, 473, 484, 488–92, 598, Pl. 51; water supply, 50; White Label, 585
Whitbread, Francis Pelham (Frank), 393, 422, 423, 536
Whitbread, S. C., 212
Whitbread, Colonel W. H. ('Bill'), 395, 400, 402, 403, 464–5, 489, 490, 531, Pl. 67
Whitbread family, 218, 223, 228, 386, 400
Whitbread Investment Co., 402, 488
Whitby, 73, 74
White, R., 500
Whiteways, 500, 525
Whittaker, Sir Thomas, 286
Wiener, Martin, 249
Wigglesworth, George, 567
Wigram, Sir Robert, 227
Wigram family, 223 n 105, 234
Williams, Ernest, 421
Willow Brewery (Kirkstall), 166 n 105
Wilshere, William, 227
Wilson, G. B., 23, 24, 28, 29, 31, 65
Wilson & Walker (Manchester), 395, 463, 469 n 61
Wilson family, 89
Wilson's (Manchester), 380 n 16, 394, 395, 403, 587
Winch, George B., 387, 398
Winchester, depot in, 163
wine: consumption of, 34, 35, 457, 500, 581, 583, 584; price of, 519; tie, 284, 437, 444
Wolverhampton, 155 n 71, 156 n 74
Wolverhampton & Dudley Breweries: flotation, 263 n 97; independence preserved, 483–4, 487; market-share, 590; production, 588; profits, 502, 503, 588; takeovers and agreements, 260, 480, 591, 592; tied estate, 501, 588
women as buyers and consumers, 35–6, 325, 423, 435, 455, 457, 565, 566
Wood, Alan, 567
Wood, Benjamin, 14
Wood, C. P., 309
Wood, Frank, 567
Wood, John, 16
Wood, T. McKinnon, 327 n 37
Woodbridge, Suffolk, 190
Woodforde, The Rev. James, 64
Woolton, Earl of, 358
Working Men's Clubs and Institute Union (CIU), 413, 415
World War I, 317–35, Pl. 42
World War II, 356–71, 413, 429, 430
Worsley family, 228
wort, 52–4, 548
Worthington: advertising, 351; agencies, 97, 153, 154, 305; bottled beers, 277, 305, 404; capital, 380; discounts, 273; distribution and transport, 45, 151, 553; free trade, 154, 155; laboratory, Pl. 4; labour force, 197, 198; loans, 273–4; management, 96, 98, 383; market preference for beer of, 354, 355; mergers and takeovers, 305, 347, 393; research, 59; stores, 153; tied estate, 154, 155, 275, 276, 305; Worthington E, 154, 558
Worthington, A. O., 218
Worthington family, 89
Wragg, R., 515
Wrexham, 50, 126, 339
Wrexham Brewery, 177
Wrexham Lager Beer Co., 177 n 129, 339, 438 n 81
Writtle Brewery (Chelmsford), 218
Wyper, William, 374

Yates & Jackson (Lancaster), 592

yeast waggons, 57
yeasts, 55–60, 63, 537, 539, 545, 643
York: agencies in, 159; Burton beers in, 108; common brewers in, 74, 241; labouring life in, 36; stores, 160; tied houses in, 122, 159, 164, 165, 166, 254–5
Yorke, Francis, 421
Young, C. F., 218
Young, James, 232
Young, John (Musselburgh), 549
Young (Norwich), 149
Young & Co. (Wandsworth), 484, 485, 486, 502, 548, 568, 589
Younger, Bernard and Robert, 109
Younger, George, Viscount Younger of Leckie, 222, 223, 328, 329
Younger, George (Alloa), 103, 105, 108–9, 174, 468
Younger, H. J., 109, 174, 220
Younger, Robert, 385
Younger, Robert (Alloa), 468
Younger, William, 385, 389
Younger, William, & Co., (Edinburgh): advertising, Pl. 45; agencies, 158; breweries, 104, 105, 123; capitalisation, 380; distribution, 45, 358; exports, 109, 173, 177, 377; free trade, 438; lager, 177; malt, 190; management, 106; market preference for beer of, 354, 355; mergers, 103, 384–5; profits, 306; research, 536; sales in London, 108, 119; salesmen, 107, 108; Tartan, 523, 558; tied estate, 278
Younger, William McEwan, 523
Younger family, 223 n 105
Youngs, Crawshay & Youngs (Norwich), 313
youth market, 455